AMERICAN GOVERNMENT
POWER AND PURPOSE

CORE SIXTEENTH EDITION

AMERICAN GOVERNMENT
POWER AND PURPOSE

Theodore J. Lowi
Late of Cornell University

Benjamin Ginsberg
Johns Hopkins University

Kenneth A. Shepsle
Harvard University

Stephen Ansolabehere
Harvard University

W. W. NORTON & COMPANY
Independent Publishers Since 1923

W. W. Norton & Company has been independent since its founding in 1923, when William Warder Norton and Mary D. Herter Norton first published lectures delivered at the People's Institute, the adult education division of New York City's Cooper Union. The firm soon expanded its program beyond the Institute, publishing books by celebrated academics from America and abroad. By mid-century, the two major pillars of Norton's publishing program—trade books and college texts—were firmly established. In the 1950s, the Norton family transferred control of the company to its employees, and today—with a staff of four hundred and a comparable number of trade, college, and professional titles published each year—W. W. Norton & Company stands as the largest and oldest publishing house owned wholly by its employees.

Editor: Laura Wilk
Editorial Assistant: Catherine Lillie
Project Editor: David Bradley
Managing Editor, College: Marian Johnson
Managing Editor, College Digital Media: Kim Yi
Production Manager: Eric Pier-Hocking
Media Editor: Spencer Richardson-Jones
Associate Media Editor: Michael Jaoui
Media Editorial Assistant: Lena Nowak-Laird
Marketing Manager: Ashley Sherwood
Design Director: Rubina Yeh
Book Designer: Kiss Me I'm Polish LLC, New York
Director of College Permissions: Megan Schindel
Composition: GraphicWorld
Manufacturing: LSC Crawfordsville

Permission to use copyrighted material is included in the credits section of this book, which begins on page C1.

The Library of Congress has cataloged another edition as follows:

Names: Lowi, Theodore J., author. | Ginsberg, Benjamin, author. | Shepsle, Kenneth A., author. | Ansolabehere, Stephen, author.
Title: American government : power and purpose / Theodore J. Lowi, Late of Cornell University, Benjamin Ginsberg, Johns Hopkins University, Kenneth A. Shepsle, Harvard University, Stephen Ansolabehere, Harvard University.
Description: Sixteenth Edition. | New York : W.W. Norton & Company, [2021] | Includes bibliographical references and index.
Identifiers: LCCN 2020051031 | **ISBN 9780393427691** (Paperback)
Subjects: LCSH: United States—Politics and government—Textbooks.
Classification: LCC JK276.L69 2021 | DDC 320.473—dc23
LC record available at https://lccn.loc.gov/2020051031

ISBN: 978-0-393-42770-7 (pbk.)

W. W. Norton & Company, Inc., 500 Fifth Avenue, New York, NY 10110
wwnorton.com

W. W. Norton & Company Ltd., 15 Carlisle Street, London W1D 3BS

1 2 3 4 5 6 7 8 9 0

For Our Families

Angele, Anna, and Jason Lowi
Sandy, Cindy, and Alex Ginsberg
Rise Shepsle, Seth Shepsle, and
    Nilsa Sweetser
Laurie Gould and Rebecca and
    Julia Ansolabehere

Contents

2 Constructing a Government: The Founding and the Constitution 30

PART 2   INSTITUTIONS

6   Congress: The First Branch   194

7   The Presidency as an Institution   256

9   The Federal Courts   344

PART 3　DEMOCRATIC POLITICS

10　Public Opinion　392

11   Elections   446

Appendix A1

Preface

This book was written for faculty and students who are looking for a little more than just "nuts and bolts" and who are drawn to an analytical perspective. No fact about American government is intrinsically difficult to grasp, and in an open society such as ours, facts abound. The philosophy of a free and open media in the United States makes information about the government that would be suppressed elsewhere readily available. The advent of the internet and other new communication technologies has further expanded the opportunity to learn about our government. The ubiquity of information in our society is a great virtue. Common knowledge about the government gives our society a vocabulary that is widely shared among its citizens and enables us to communicate effectively with each other about politics. But it is also important to reach beyond that common vocabulary and develop a more sophisticated understanding of politics and government. The sheer quantity of facts in our society can be overwhelming. In a 24/7 news cycle it can be hard to pick out what stories are important and to stay focused on them. Today, moreover, Americans may choose among a variety of news sources, including broadcast, print, and various digital formats, all clamoring for attention. The single most important task of the teacher of political science is to confront popular ideas and information and to choose from among them the small number of really significant concepts that help us make better sense of the world. This book aims to help instructors and students accomplish this task.

The analytical framework of this book is oriented around five principles that we use to help make sense of politics:

1. All political behavior has a purpose.

2. Institutions structure politics.

3. All politics is collective action.

4. Political outcomes are the products of individual preferences and institutional procedures.

5. How we got here matters.

This Sixteenth Edition continues our endeavor to make *American Government: Power and Purpose* the most authoritative and contemporary introductory text on the market. The approach of the book has not changed. Those who have used this book in the past are familiar with the narrative it presents about American government and politics—the storyline of how the U.S. government has evolved, how it operates, and the characters involved in the unfolding development of our polity. This book also presents an analytical approach to understanding American politics based on the five principles outlined above. We are guided by the belief that students of government need an analytical framework for understanding political phenomena—a framework rooted in some of the most important insights the discipline of political science has to offer and that encourages students to draw out the general lessons about collective action and collective decision making. With this goal in mind, we are pleased to launch InQuizitive, Norton's adaptive assessment program that will help students master these concepts, and more importantly, begin to apply the Five Principles framework to begin to make sense of politics on their own (see below).

The major changes in this Sixteenth Edition, including a thorough analysis of the 2020 elections and the Trump presidency, are intended to combine authoritative, concise coverage of the central topics in American politics with smart pedagogical features designed to get students thinking analytically about quantitative data and current issues. The most significant changes include the following:

- **New InQuizitive**, Norton's digital, adaptive system helps students understand and apply what they've learned. InQuizitive features a mix of questions that allow students to both check their understanding of foundational knowledge and analyze key concepts or processes by applying the Five Principles of Politics.

- **New analysis of the 2020 elections**, including data figures, walks students through what happened and why. This edition includes a section devoted to the 2020 elections in Chapter 11 as well as updated data, examples, and other information throughout the book.

- **A revised primer, "Making Sense of Charts and Graphs,"** by Jennifer Bachner (Johns Hopkins University) at the end of Chapter 1 sets students up to understand the political data they encounter in the news and in the course, including in many new Timeplots and Analyzing the Evidence infographics throughout the book.

- **New coverage of public policy** from contributing author Elizabeth Rigby (George Washington University) is integrated throughout the book, including current coverage of issues like health care, the new

2017 tax law, recent legislation to relieve the economic burden during the coronavirus pandemic, the government's role in higher education, and the "hidden welfare state." The economic and social policy chapters have been completely revised to reflect updated scholarship.

- **New Policy Principle boxes,** also authored by Elizabeth Rigby, highlight the various players and structures that shape current policy debates, including automatic voter registration (Chapter 11) and President Trump's border wall proposals (Chapter 7).

- **New and revised Timeplot features** use quantitative data to illuminate long-term trends in American politics. For example, the new Timeplot in Chapter 13 (Groups and Interests) compares liberal and conservative outside spending over time.

- **New Analyzing the Evidence units** written by expert researchers highlight the political science behind the information in the book; the remaining units have been updated with new data and analysis. Each unit poses an important question from political science and presents evidence that can be used to analyze the question. The new units are

  "How Representative Is Congress?" in Chapter 6, contributed by Leah Stokes (University of California, Santa Barbara)

  "What Motivates Political Engagement among Young People?" in Chapter 12, contributed by David E. Campbell and Christina Wolbrecht (University of Notre Dame)

  "Who's Funding Google's PAC?" in Chapter 13, contributed by Zhao Li (Princeton University)

This Sixteenth Edition of *American Government: Power and Purpose* is accompanied by an innovative package of teaching and learning resources to support online and face-to-face classes:

- **New Inquisitive,** an adaptive learning tool, offers a range of "nuts and bolts" as well as applied and conceptual questions, drawing upon features of the text like the Analyzing the Evidence infographics, to help ensure that students master the material and come to class prepared.

- The **new "Evaluating Sources" InQuizitive module** walks students through the key aspects of identifying and understanding what a source is, how it is used in an argument, and whether it is a valid source or not (such as fake news).

- **New and revised Timeplot exercises** connect quantitative data to the historical development of key aspects of American politics. Each Timeplot exercise offers assessment on the feature, cultivating students' data literacy as well as their understanding of important historical trends in American government.

- **New Weekly News Quizzes** offer students a current news article, video, or podcast plus an assessment, all easily reported into a grade-book. Each Weekly News Quiz promotes media literacy and engagement with an important story concerning American government. The Weekly News Quiz also includes a recommended class activity as well as suggested chapter and topic connections.

- A **comprehensive resource package** to support teaching and learning includes activities that can be assigned through your Learning Management System, a comprehensive test bank, and lecture PowerPoints.

For the Sixteenth Edition we have profited greatly from the guidance of many teachers who have used earlier editions and from the suggestions of numerous thoughtful reviewers. We thank them by name in the Acknowledgments. We recognize there is no single best way to craft an introductory text, and we are grateful for the advice we have received.

Benjamin Ginsberg
Kenneth A. Shepsle
Stephen Ansolabehere

Acknowledgments

We note with sadness the passing of Theodore J. Lowi. We miss Ted but continue to hear his voice and benefit from his wisdom in the pages of this book.

Our students at Cornell, Johns Hopkins, and Harvard have been an essential factor in the writing of this book. They have been our most immediate intellectual community, a hospitable one indeed. Another part of our community, perhaps a large suburb, is the discipline of political science itself. Our debt to the scholarship of our colleagues is scientifically measurable, probably to several decimal points, in the footnotes of each chapter. Despite many complaints that the field is too scientific or not scientific enough, political science is alive and well in the United States. Political science has never been at a loss for relevant literature, and without that literature, our job would have been impossible. For this edition, we are grateful for Elizabeth Rigby's significant revisions and updates to the policy discussions throughout the book as well as the new Policy Principle sections outlined in the preface.

In light of important recent and ongoing discussions, we wanted to note that consistent with our strong commitment to diversity and our belief that all should be treated with respect, we are capitalizing the names of all racial, religious, and ethnic groups.

We are pleased to acknowledge our debt to the many colleagues who had a direct and active role in criticism and preparation of the manuscript. The First Edition was read and reviewed by Gary Bryner, Brigham Young University; James F. Herndon, Virginia Polytechnic Institute and State University; James W. Riddlesperger Jr., Texas Christian University; John Schwarz, University of Arizona; Toni-Michelle Travis, George Mason University; and Lois Vietri, University of Maryland. We also want to reiterate our thanks to the four colleagues who allowed us the privilege of testing a trial edition of our book by using it as the major text in their introductory American Government courses: Gary Bryner, Brigham Young University; Allan J. Cigler, University of Kansas; Burnet V. Davis, Albion College; and Erwin A. Jaffe, California State University, Stanislaus.

For the Second through Seventh Editions, we relied heavily on the thoughtful manuscript reviews we received from J. Roger Baker, Wittenburg University; Timothy Boylan, Winthrop University; David Canon, University of Wisconsin; Victoria Farrar-Myers, University of Texas at Arlington; John Gilmour, College of William and Mary; Mark Graber, University of Maryland; Russell Hanson, Indiana University; Robert Huckfeldt, University of California, Davis; Mark Joslyn, University of Kansas; William Keech, Carnegie Mellon University; Donald Kettl, University of Wisconsin; Anne Khademian, University of Wisconsin; Beth Leech, Rutgers University; James Lennertz, Lafayette College; Allan McBride, Grambling State University; William McLauchlan, Purdue University; Grant Neeley, Texas Tech University; Charles Noble, California State University, Long Beach; and Joseph Peek Jr., Georgia State University.

For the Eighth Edition, we benefited from the comments of Scott Ainsworth, University of Georgia; Thomas Brunell, Northern Arizona University; Daniel Carpenter, Harvard University; Brad Gomez, University of South Carolina; Paul Gronke, Reed College; Marc Hetherington, Bowdoin College; Gregory Huber, Yale University; Robert Lowry, Iowa State University; Anthony Nownes, University of Tennessee; Scott Adler, University of Colorado Boulder; John Coleman, University of Wisconsin—Madison; Richard Conley, University of Florida; Keith Dougherty, University of Georgia; John Ferejohn, Stanford University; Douglas Harris, Loyola College; Brian Humes, University of Nebraska—Lincoln; Jeffrey Jenkins, Northwestern University; Paul Johnson, University of Kansas; Andrew Polsky, Hunter College CUNY; Mark Richards, Grand Valley State University; Charles Shipan, University of Iowa; Craig Volden, Ohio State University; and Garry Young, George Washington University.

For the Ninth Edition, we were guided by the comments of John Baughman; Lawrence Baum, Ohio State University; Chris Cooper, Western Carolina State University; Charles Finochiaro, University at Buffalo—SUNY; Lisa Garcia-Bellorda, University of California, Irvine; Sandy Gordon, New York University; Steven Greene, North Carolina State University; Richard Herrera, Arizona State University; Ben Highton, University of California, Davis; Trey Hood, University of Georgia; Andy Karch, University of Texas at Austin; Glen Krutz, University of Oklahoma; Paul Labedz, Valencia Community College; Brad Lockerbie, University of Georgia; Wendy Martinek, Binghamton University—SUNY; Nicholas Miller, University of Maryland—Baltimore County; Russell Renka, Southeast Missouri State University; Debbie Schildkraut, Tufts University; Charles Shipan, University of Iowa; Chris Shortell, California State University, Northridge; John Sides, University of Texas at Austin; Sean Theriault, University of Texas at Austin; and Lynn Vavreck, University of California, Los Angeles.

For the Tenth Edition, we were grateful for the detailed comments of Christian Grose, Vanderbilt University; Kevin Esterling, University of California, Riverside; Martin Johnson, University of California, Riverside; Scott Meinke, Bucknell University; Jason MacDonald, Kent State University; Alan Wiseman, Ohio State University; Michelle Swers, Georgetown University; William Hixon, Lawrence University; Gregory Koger, University of Miami; and Renan Levine, University of Toronto.

For their advice on the Eleventh Edition, we thank Scott Ainsworth, University of Georgia; Bethany Albertson, University of Washington; Brian Arbour,

John Jay College; James Battista, University at Buffalo—SUNY; Lawrence Becker, California State University, Northridge; Damon Cann, Utah State University; Jamie Carson, University of Georgia; Suzanne Chod, Pennsylvania State University; Michael Crespin, University of Georgia; Ryan Emenaker, College of the Redwoods; Kevin Esterling, University of California, Riverside; Richard Glenn, Millersville University; Brad Gomez, Florida State University; Sanford Gordon, New York University; Christian Grose, Vanderbilt University; James Hanley, Adrian College; Ryan Hurl, University of Toronto; Josh Kaplan, University of Notre Dame; Wendy Martinek, Binghamton University; Will Miller, Southeast Missouri State University; Evan Parker-Stephen, Texas A&M University; Melody Rose, Portland State University; Eric Schickler, University of California, Berkeley; John Sides, George Washington University; and Lynn Vavreck, University of California, Los Angeles.

For the Twelfth Edition we looked to comments from John M. Aughenbaugh, Virginia Commonwealth University; Christopher Banks, Kent State University; Michael Berkman, Pennsylvania State University; Cynthia Bowling, Auburn University; Matthew Cahn, California State University, Northridge; Damon Cann, Utah State University; Tom Cioppa, Brookdale Community College; David Damore, University of Nevada, Las Vegas; Kevin Esterling, University of California–Riverside; Jessica Feezell, University of California, Santa Barbara; Charle J. Finocchiaro, University of South Carolina; Rodd Freitag, University of Wisconsin, Eau Claire; Kevin Jefferies, Alvin Community College; Nancy Jimeno, California State University, Fullerton; Gregory Koger, University of Miami; David E. Lewis, Vanderbilt University; Allison M. Martens, University of Louisville; Thomas M. Martin, Eastern Kentucky University; Michael Andrew McLatchy, Clarendon College; Ken Mulligan, Southern Illinois University, Carbondale; Geoffrey D. Peterson, University of Wisconsin, Eau Claire; Jesse Richman, Old Dominion University; Mark C. Rom, Georgetown University; Laura Schneider, Grand Valley State University; Scot Schraufnagel, Northern Illinois University; Ronald P. Seyb, Skidmore College; Martin S. Sheffer, Tidewater Community College; Charles R. Shipan, University of Michigan; Howard A. Smith, Florida Gulf Coast University; Michele Swers, Georgetown University; Charles Tien, Hunter College; Elizabeth Trentanelli, Gulf Coast State College; and Kenneth C. Williams, Michigan State University.

For the Thirteenth Edition we are indebted to Michael M. Binder, University of North Florida; Stephen Borrelli, The University of Alabama; Dan Cassino, Fairleigh Dickinson University; Jangsup Choi, Texas A&M University—Commerce; Martin Cohen, James Madison University; Jeff Colbert, Elon University; Richard S. Conley, University of Florida; Mark Croatti, American University; David Dulio, Oakland University; Andrew M. Essig, DeSales University; Kathleen Ferraiolo, James Madison University; Emily R. Gill, Bradley University; Brad T. Gomez, Florida State University; Paul N. Goren, University of Minnesota; Thomas Halper, Baruch College; Audrey A. Haynes, University of Georgia; Diane J. Heith, St. John's University; Ronald J. Hrebenar, University of Utah; Ryan Hurl, University of Toronto Scarborough; Richard Jankowski, State University of New York at Fredonia; Kevin Jefferies, Alvin Community College; Timothy R. Johnson, University of Minnesota; Kenneth R. Mayer, University of Wisconsin—Madison; Mark McKenzie, Texas Tech University; Fiona Miller, University of Toronto Mississauga; Richard M. Pious, Barnard College; Tim Reynolds, Alvin Community College; Martin Saiz, California State University, Northridge; Dante Scala, University of New Hampshire; Sean M. Theriault, University of Texas at Austin; J. Alejandro Tirado, Texas Tech University; Terri Towner, Oakland University; Nicholas Valentino, University of Michigan; Harold M. Waller, McGill University; and Jeffrey S. Worsham, West Virginia University.

We also thank the reviewers who advised us on the Fourteenth Edition: Michael E. Aleprete, Westminster College, Community College of Allegheny County; James Binney, Pennsylvania State University; William Blake, Indiana University—Purdue University Indianapolis; Eric Boyer, Colby-Sawyer College; Chelsie L. M. Bright, Mills College; Scott Englund, University of California–Santa Barbara; Amanda Friesen, Indiana University—Purdue University Indianapolis; Frank Fuller, Lincoln University; Baogang Guo, Dalton State College; Eric Hanson, State University of New York at Fredonia; Jennifer Haydel, Montgomery College; Tseggai Isaac, Missouri University of Science and Technology; Vicki Jeffries-Bilton, Portland State University; Nicole Kalaf-Hughes, Bowling Green State University; Ervin Kallfa, Hostos Community College of CUNY; Samantha Majic, John Jay College of Criminal Justice; William McLauchlan, Purdue University; Hong Min Park, University of Wisconsin—Milwaukee; John Patty, Washington University in St. Louis; John W. Ray, Montana Tech of the University of Montana; Eric Sands, Berry College; and Kathleen Tipler, Wake Forest University.

We are grateful for the comments from the reviewers for the Fifteenth Edition: Jeffrey Crouch, American University; Curtis R. Berry, Shippensburg University; David Darmofal, University of South Carolina; Paul Djupe, Denison University; Charles J. Finocchiaro, University of Oklahoma; Chris Galdieri, Saint Anselm College; Ben Gaskins, Lewis & Clark College; Greg Goelzhauser, Utah State University; Jake Haselswerdt, University of Missouri; Michael Herron, Dartmouth College; Krista Jenkins, Fairleigh Dickinson University; Kristin Kanthak, University of Pittsburgh; Daniel Levin, University of Utah; Janet M. Martin, Bowdoin College; Robert J. McGrath, George Mason University; Scott Meinke, Bucknell University; Nina M. Moore, Colgate University; Stephen Nichols, California State University, San Marcos; David O'Connell, Dickinson College; Mark Carl Rom, Georgetown University; Stella Rouse, University of Maryland; Travis S. Smith, Brigham Young University; Jennifer Nicoll Victor, George Mason University; Amber Wichowsky, Marquette University. We would also like to thank Andie Herrig and Johnathan Romero, students at Washington University in St. Louis, for identifying two errors in the book. We appreciate your close read.

For their advice on this Sixteenth Edition, we thank George Agabango, Bloomsburg University; Ian G. Anson, University of Maryland—Baltimore County; Michael Bailey, Georgetown University; Josh Berkenpas, Minnesota State University; Nicholas Boushee, San Diego City College; Jonathan N. Brown, Sam Houston State University; Richard S. Conley, University of Florida; Tracy Cooper, University of North Carolina, Pembroke; Murniz A. Coson, California State Polytechnic University, Pomona; Paulina Cossette, Washington College; Evan Crawford, University of San Diego; Kathleen Donovan, St. John Fisher College; Richard Haesly, California State University, Long Beach; George

Hawley, University of Alabama; Matthew Dean Hindman, University of Tulsa; Jeneen Hobby, Cleveland State University; Natalie Johnson, Francis Marion University; David Lucander, Rockland Community College; Amber Lusvardi, Millikin University; Domenic Maffei, Caldwell University; Brad Mapes-Martins, University of Wisconsin—Stevens Point; Mary McGrath, Northwestern University; Taneisha N. Means, Vassar College; Rosemary Nossiff, Marymount Manhattan College; Yu Ouyang, Purdue University Northwest; Maxwell Palmer, Boston University; Joseph W. Robbins, Valdosta State University; Samuel VanSant Stoddard, Springfield College; Michael E. Thunberg, Norwich University; Peggy R. Wright, Arkansas State University—Jonesboro. We would also like to thank Alec Alameddine at Washington University in St. Louis for identifying errors in the book. We appreciate your close read.

An important contribution to recent editions was made by the authors of the Analyzing the Evidence units. We are grateful to the authors of the new Analyzing the Evidence units in the Sixteenth Edition, who are named in the Preface. In addition, Jennifer Bachner, Jenna Bednar, David E. Campbell, Edward G. Carmines, Jeremiah D. Castle, Rachael Vanessa Cobb, Patrick J. Egan, Robert S. Erikson, Peter D. Feaver, Sean Gailmard, Christopher Gelpi, Martin Gilens, Sanford Gordon, John C. Green, David Konisky, Geoffrey C. Layman, Beth L. Leech, David Lewis, Andrew D. Martin, Kenneth Mayer, Rasmus Kleis Nielsen, David M. Primo, Kevin M. Quinn, Jason Reifler, Jon Rogowski, Eric R. Schmidt, Matthew S. Shugart, Dara Z. Strolovitch, Steven L. Taylor, and David C. Wilson contributed to this feature in earlier editions, and much of their work is still reflected in this edition.

We would also like to thank our partners at W. W. Norton & Company, who have continued to apply their talents and energy to this textbook. The efforts of Laura Wilk, Catherine Lillie, David Bradley, Eric Pier-Hocking, Spencer Richardson-Jones, and Lena Nowak-Laird kept the production of the Sixteenth Edition and its accompanying resources coherent and in focus. We also thank Ann Shin, Roby Harrington, and Steve Dunn, whose contributions to previous editions remain invaluable.

We are more than happy, however, to absolve all these contributors from any flaws, errors, and misjudgments that this book contains. We wish it could be free of all production errors, grammatical errors, misspellings, misquotes, missed citations, etc. From that standpoint, a book ought to try to be perfect. But substantively we have not tried to write a flawless book; we have not tried to write a book to please everyone. We have again tried to write an effective book, a book that cannot be taken lightly. Our goal was not to make every reader a political scientist. Our goal was to restore politics as a subject of vigorous and enjoyable discourse, releasing it from the bondage of the 30-second sound bite and the 30-page technical briefing. Every person can be knowledgeable because everything about politics is accessible. One does not have to be a philosopher to argue about the requisites of democracy, a lawyer to dispute constitutional interpretations, an economist to debate public policy. We will be very proud if our book contributes in a small way to the restoration of the ancient art of political controversy.

Benjamin Ginsberg
Kenneth A. Shepsle
Stephen Ansolabehere

AMERICAN GOVERNMENT
POWER AND PURPOSE

1

Five Principles of Politics

American government and politics are extraordinarily complex. The United States has many levels of government: federal, state, county, city, and town—to say nothing of a host of special and regional authorities. Each of these governments operates according to its own rules, has the authority to make its own laws, and is related to the others in complex ways. In many nations, regional and local governments are appendages of the national government. This is not true in the United States, where state and local governments possess considerable independence and autonomy. Each level of government, moreover, consists of an array of departments, agencies, offices, and bureaus, each with its own policies, jurisdiction, and (sometimes overlapping) responsibilities.

At times this complexity gets in the way of effective governance, as is often the case when governments must respond to emergencies. The United States' federal, state, and local public safety agencies seldom share information and frequently use incompatible communications equipment, so they sometimes cannot even speak to one another. For example, on September 11, 2001, New York City's police and fire departments could not effectively coordinate their responses to the attack on the World Trade Center because their communications systems were not linked. While communication between different levels of government has improved in the last two decades, many security and policy agencies, ranging from the Central Intelligence Agency (CIA) to the Department of Homeland Security (DHS), still maintain separate computer operating systems and databases, which inhibits their ability to cooperate.

However, the complexity of the U.S. government is no accident. Complexity was one element of the Founders' grand constitutional design. The framers of the Constitution hoped that an elaborate system of power sharing among national institutions and between the states and the federal government would allow competing interests to have a voice in public affairs across a variety of decision-making arenas—while preventing any single group or coalition from monopolizing power. One set of interests might be active in some states, other forces could be influential in the national legislature, and still others might prevail in the federal executive branch. This dispersion of power and opportunity would allow many groups to achieve at least some of their political goals. In this way, America's political tradition associates complexity with liberty and political opportunity.

Although this arrangement creates many avenues for political action, it also places a burden on citizens who wish to achieve something through political participation. They may be unable to discern where particular policies are actually made, who the decision makers are, and what forms of political participation are most effective. This is one of the paradoxes of political life: as opportunities increase for citizens to influence the government's use of its power, it becomes less clear how to take advantage of these opportunities. Indeed, precisely because the United States' institutional and political arrangements are so complex, many Americans are mystified by government. As we will see in Chapter 10, many Americans have difficulty making sense of even the basic features of the Constitution.

If the U.S. government seems complex, its politics can be utterly bewildering. For most Americans, the focal point of politics is the electoral process. As we will see in Chapter 11, tens of millions of Americans participate in national, state, and local elections, during which they hear thousands of candidates debate a perplexing array of issues. Candidates inundate the media with promises, charges, and countercharges, while pundits and journalists (whom we will discuss in Chapters 10 and 14) and even political scientists like us add their own clamor to the din.

Politics, however, does not end on Election Day. Long after the voters have spoken, political struggles continue in Congress, the executive branch, and the courts; they embroil political parties, interest groups, and the mass media. In some instances, the participants and their goals seem fairly obvious. For example, it is no secret that businesses and upper-income wage earners strongly support tax reduction, farmers support agricultural subsidies, and labor unions oppose increasing the eligibility age for Social Security. Each of these forces has created or joined organized groups to advance its cause by influencing members of government. We will examine some of these groups in Chapter 13.

LEARNING OBJECTIVES

 Identify the main purposes of government and the major types of governments.

 Define *politics* and explain the different goals and forms it takes.

 Identify the Five Principles of Politics and explain how they help make sense of the apparent chaos and complexity of the political world.

In other instances, though, the participants and their goals are not so clear. Sometimes corporate groups hide behind ostensibly environmental causes to promote their own economic interests. Other times, groups claiming to want to help the poor and downtrodden seek only to help themselves. And worse, many government policies are made behind closed doors, away from the light of publicity. Ordinary citizens can hardly be blamed for failing to understand bureaucratic rule making and other obscure procedures of government.

MAKING SENSE OF GOVERNMENT AND POLITICS

Can we find order in the apparent chaos of politics? Yes. Doing so is precisely the job of political scientists and is in fact the purpose of this text. The discipline of political science, and especially the study of American politics, seeks to identify and explain patterns in all the noise and maneuvering of everyday political life. This inquiry is motivated by two fundamental questions: What do we observe? And why?

The first question makes clear that political science is an *empirical* enterprise: it aims to identify facts and patterns that are true in the world around us. What strategies do candidates use to capture votes? How do legislators decide how to vote on bills? What groups put pressure on the institutions of government? How do the media report on politics? How have courts regulated political life? These questions (and many others) have prompted political scientists to observe and ascertain what is true about the political world, and we will take them up in detail in later chapters.

The second question—Why?—is the fundamental concern of science. We not only want to know whether something is, in fact, true about the world. We also want to know *why* it is true, which requires us to create a theory of how the world works. And a theory is constructed from basic principles. The remainder of this chapter presents a set of such principles to help us navigate the apparent chaos of politics and make sense of what we observe. In this way we not only describe politics, we analyze it.

Political science also asks a third type of question that is *normative* rather than empirical or analytical. Normative questions focus on "should" issues: What should the responsibilities of citizenship be? How should judges judge and presidents lead? In this book we believe that answers to the empirical and analytical questions help us formulate answers to the normative questions.

One of the most important goals of this book is to help readers learn to analyze what they observe in American politics.[1] Such analysis requires thinking about politics in an abstract, as opposed to specific, way. For example, in political science, we are not much interested in an "analysis" that explains *only* why

---

[1] For an entire book devoted to the issue of political analysis, see Kenneth A. Shepsle, *Analyzing Politics: Rationality, Behavior, and Institutions,* 2nd ed. (New York: Norton, 2010).

the Democrats gained congressional seats in the 2018 elections, or why the 2016 and 2020 presidential contests were so close. Such explanations are the province of pundits, journalists, and other commentators. Rather, we seek a more general theory of voting choice that we can apply to many particular instances—not just the 2020 elections but the 2022 elections as well.

In this chapter, we first discuss what we mean by *government* and *politics*. Then we introduce our five principles of politics. These principles are intentionally somewhat abstract because we want them to apply to a wide range of circumstances. However, we provide concrete illustrations along the way, and in later chapters we will apply the principles intensively to specific features of politics and government in the United States. We conclude the chapter with a guide to analyzing evidence, something you will find useful as we examine empirical information throughout the rest of the book.

What Is Government?

Government is the term generally used to describe the formal political arrangements by which a land and its people are ruled. Government is composed of institutions and processes that rulers use to strengthen and perpetuate their power or control. A government may be as simple as a small council that meets occasionally to advise a leader or as complex as our own vast establishment, with elaborate procedures, laws, governmental bodies, and bureaucracies. This more complex kind of government is sometimes called the *state*, an abstract concept referring to the source of all public authority.

Forms of Government

Governments vary in institutional structure, size, and modes of operation. Two key questions help us determine how governments differ: Who governs? And how much government control is permitted?

In some nations political authority is vested in a single individual—a king or dictator, for example. This state of affairs is called an **autocracy**. When a small group of landowners, military officers, or wealthy merchants controls most of the governing decisions, the government is an **oligarchy**. If more people participate and the populace has some influence over decision making, the government is tending toward **democracy**.

Governments also vary in terms of how much they control. In the United States and some other nations, governments are severely limited in *what* they are permitted to control (they are restricted by substantive limits) as well as in *how* they exercise that control (they are restricted by procedural limits). These are called **constitutional** governments. In other nations, the law imposes few real limits on the government, but government is nevertheless kept in check by other political and social institutions that it does not control, such as autonomous territories or an organized church. Such governments are called **authoritarian**. In a third, very small group of nations, including the Soviet Union under Joseph

 government

The institutions through which a land and its people are ruled.

 autocracy

A form of government in which a single individual rules.

 oligarchy

A form of government in which a small group of landowners, military officers, or wealthy merchants controls most of the governing decisions.

 democracy

A system of rule that permits citizens to play a significant part in government, usually through the selection of key public officials.

constitutional government

A system of rule that establishes specific limits on the powers of the government.

 authoritarian government

A system of rule in which the government's power is not limited by law, though it may be restrained by other social institutions.

Stalin, Nazi Germany, and present-day North Korea, governments not only are free of legal limits but also seek to eliminate organized social groups that might challenge their authority. These governments attempt to dominate political, economic, and social life and, as a result, are called **totalitarian**.

Politics

The term *politics* broadly refers to conflicts over the character, membership, and policies of any organization to which people belong. As the political scientist Harold Lasswell once put it, politics is the struggle over "who gets what, when, how."[2] Although politics exists in any organization, in this book **politics** refers to conflicts over the leadership, structure, and policies of governments—that is, over who governs and who has power. But politics also involves collaboration and cooperation. The goal of politics, as we define it, is to influence the composition of the government's leadership, how the government is organized, or what its policies will be.

Politics takes many forms. Individuals may run for office, vote, join political parties and movements, contribute money to candidates, lobby public officials, participate in demonstrations, write letters, talk to their friends and neighbors, go to court, and engage in numerous other activities. Some forms of politics are aimed at gaining power, some at influencing those in power, and others at bringing new people to power and throwing the old leaders out. Those in power use myriad strategies to try to achieve their goals. Power, in short, is valued in politics, but not always for its own sake. Power is sought as a means to attaining certain ends—to elevate some people and remove others, to introduce policies, or to preserve old ones.[3]

totalitarian government

A system of rule in which the government's power is not limited by law and in which the government seeks to eliminate other social institutions that might challenge it.

politics

Conflict and cooperation over the leadership, structure, and policies of government.

FIVE PRINCIPLES OF POLITICS

Politics possesses an underlying logic that can be understood in terms of five simple principles:

1. All political behavior has a purpose (the rationality principle).

2. Institutions structure politics (the institution principle).

3. All politics is collective action (the collective action principle).

---

2   Harold D. Lasswell, *Politics: Who Gets What, When, How* (New York: Meridian, 1958).

3   We distinguish between *power* and *authority*. Power deals with who can, *in fact*, make decisions and influence outcomes, whereas authority deals with who has the right, *in principle*, to make decisions. The powerful may not always have the authority to do what they do, and those authorized to do things may not be very effective (that is, powerful) in accomplishing their goals.

4. Political outcomes are the products of individual preferences, institutional procedures, and collective action (the policy principle).

5. How we got here matters (the history principle).

Some of these principles may seem obvious or abstract. They are useful, however, because they each possess a distinct kernel of truth, on the one hand, and are sufficiently general to help us understand politics in a variety of settings, on the other hand. Armed with these principles, we can perceive order within the apparent chaos of political events and processes whenever and wherever they take place.

The Rationality Principle: All Political Behavior Has a Purpose

All people have goals, and these goals guide their political behavior. For many citizens, political behavior is as simple and familiar as reading news headlines on Twitter or discussing political controversies with a neighbor over the back fence. Beyond these basic acts, political behavior broadens to include explicitly political activities that require some forethought, such as watching a political debate on television, arguing about politics with a coworker, signing a petition, or attending a city council meeting. Political behavior requiring even more effort includes casting a vote in the November election (having first registered to vote in a timely manner), contacting legislative representatives about a political issue, contributing time or money to a political campaign, or even running for local office.

Some of these acts require time, effort, financial resources, and resolve, whereas others place small, even insignificant, demands on a person. Nevertheless, all of them are done for specific reasons. They are not random; they are not entirely automatic or mechanical, even the smallest of them. They are purposeful. Sometimes people engage in these activities for the sake of entertainment (reading the front page in the morning) or just to be sociable (chatting about politics with a neighbor, coworker, or family member). At other times, people engage in them explicitly *because* they are political—because someone cares about, and wants to influence, an issue, a candidate, a party, or a cause. We will treat all of this political activity as purposeful, as goal-oriented. Indeed, our attempts to identify the goals of various political activities will help us understand them better.

The political activities of ordinary citizens are hard to distinguish from conventional everyday behavior—reading newspapers, surfing the internet, watching television news, discussing politics, and so on. For the professional politician, on the other hand—the legislator, executive, judge, party leader, bureau chief, or agency head—nearly every act is explicitly political. The legislator's decision to introduce a particular piece of legislation, give a speech in the legislative chamber, move an amendment to a pending bill, vote for or against a bill, or accept a contribution from a particular group requires her careful attention. There are pitfalls and dangers, and the slightest miscalculation can have huge consequences. If the legislator introduces a bill that appears to be too pro-labor in the eyes of her constituents, for example, before she knows it, her opponent in the next election is charging her with being too cozy with the unions. If she gives a speech against job quotas for minorities, she risks alienating the minority communities in her state or district. If she accepts campaign contributions from industries known to pollute, environmentalists will think she is no friend of the earth. Because nearly every move is fraught with risks, legislators make their choices with fore-thought and calculation. Their actions are, in a word, **instrumental**. Politicians think through the benefits and costs of each decision, speculate about and weigh the probabilities of future effects, and consider the risks of the decision in order to determine the personal value of the potential outcomes.

instrumental →

Done with purpose, sometimes with forethought, and even with calculation.

As examples of instrumental behavior, consider elected officials more gener-ally. Most politicians want to keep their positions or move up to more important positions. They like their jobs for a variety of reasons—the salaries, privileges, prestige, and opportunities for accomplishment that accompany them, to name just a few. So we can understand why politicians do what they do by thinking of their behavior as instrumental, with the purpose of keeping their jobs. This equa-tion is quite straightforward with regard to elected politicians, who often see no further than the next election; they think mainly about how to prevail and who can help them win. "Retail" politics involves dealing directly with constituents, such as when a politician helps an individual navigate a federal agency or find a misplaced Social Security check. "Wholesale" politics involves appealing to col-lections of constituents, such as when a legislator introduces a bill that would benefit a group active in his state or district, secures money for a public building in his hometown, or intervenes in an official proceeding on behalf of an inter-est group that will, in turn, contribute to his next campaign. Politicians may do these things for ideological reasons; they may have policy and personal concerns of their own, after all. But ultimately, elections provide incentives for politicians to help their constituents; the more responsive politicians are to the people they represent, the more likely they are to win their next election. Elections and elec-toral politics are thus premised on instrumental behavior by politicians.

Political scientists explain the behavior of elected politicians by treating the "electoral connection" as their principal motivation.[4] Elected politicians, in this view, base their behavior on the goal of maximizing votes at the next election or maximizing their probability of winning. Of course, other things motivate them as well—public policy objectives, power within their institution, and ambition for higher office.[5] The fact is, however, that reelection is a necessary condition for pursuing any of the other objectives.[6]

4   The classic statement of this premise is David R. Mayhew, *Congress: The Electoral Connection* (New Haven, CT: Yale University Press, 1974). Although nearly five decades old, this book remains a source of insight and wisdom.

5   The classic statement of this premise is Richard F. Fenno, *Congressmen in Committees* (Boston: Little, Brown, 1973), another book that remains relevant decades after its publication.

6   As Vince Lombardi, the famous coach of the Green Bay Packers football team, once said, "Winning isn't everything; it's the only thing."

But what about political actors who are not elected? What do they want? Consider a few examples:

- *Agency heads and bureau chiefs*, motivated by policy preferences and power, seek to maximize their budgets.

- *Legislative committee chairs* (who are elected to Congress but appointed to committees) are "turf minded," intent on maximizing their committee's policy jurisdiction and thus its power.

- *Voters*, motivated by their personal welfare as well as their beliefs about "what's best for the country," cast ballots to elect officials who will shape government policy in ways that will benefit them.

- *Justices*, serving lifetime terms, seek to maximize the prospects for their interpretation of the Constitution to prevail.[7]

In each instance, we can postulate motivations that fit the political context. These goals often have a strong element of self-interest, but they may also incorporate "enlightened self-interest." That is, these political actors may include the welfare of others such as their families, the entire society, or even all of humanity among their motivations.

The Institution Principle: Institutions Structure Politics

In pursuing political goals, people—especially elected leaders and other government officials—confront certain recurring problems, and they develop standard ways of addressing them. Routinized, structured relations for pursuing goals and addressing recurring problems are what we call institutions. **Institutions** are the rules and procedures that provide incentives for political behavior, thereby shaping politics. Institutions may discourage conflict, encourage coordination, and enable bargaining, thus facilitating decision making, cooperation, and collective action.

Institutions are part script and part scorecard. As scripts, they choreograph political activity. As scorecards, they list the players, their positions, what they want, what they know, and what they can do. As a consequence, institutions matter. The U.S. Senate, for example, was one kind of legislative body when its members were elected to their positions by state legislatures; it has become quite

> **institutions**
>
> A set of formal rules and procedures, often administered by a bureaucracy, that shapes politics and governance.

---

7 Most political actors are motivated by self-interest. The motivations of judges and justices, however, have proved more difficult to ascertain because their lifetime appointments free them from looking ahead to the next election or occasion for "contract renewal." For an interesting discussion of judicial motivations by an eminent law professor and former judge, see Richard A. Posner, "What Do Judges and Justices Maximize? (The Same Thing Everybody Else Does)," *Supreme Court Economic Review* 3 (1993): 1-41.

a different kind of legislative body now that its members are popularly elected by voters in each state. To take another example of how institutions matter, consider how the institution of term limits affects the power of an executive such as a mayor, governor, or president in her last term: a prohibition against running for reelection weakens an executive by removing the leverage she might have had if there were the possibility of securing another term in office.

Although the Constitution sets the broad framework for American political institutions, much adaptation takes place as strategic political actors bend the institutions for their own various purposes. We focus here on four ways in which institutions provide politicians with the necessary authority to pursue public policies: jurisdiction, agenda and veto power, decisiveness, and delegation.

Jurisdiction. A critical feature of an institution is the domain over which its members have the authority to make decisions. Political institutions are full of specialized **jurisdictions** controlled by various individuals or subsets of members. One feature of the U.S. Congress, for example, is its standing committees, whose jurisdictions are carefully defined by official rules. Most members of Congress become specialists in all aspects of their committees' jurisdictions, and they often seek committee assignments based on the subjects in which they want to specialize. Committees are granted the authority to set the agenda of the larger parent chamber when it comes to issues falling under their jurisdiction. For example, proposed legislation related to the military must pass through the Armed Services Committee before the entire House or Senate can consider it. Thus the structure of Congress's jurisdiction-specific committees affects the politics of the institution as a whole. Similarly, a bureau or agency is established by law, and its jurisdiction is firmly fixed. For example, the Food and Drug Administration (FDA) possesses the authority to regulate the marketing of pharmaceuticals but is not permitted to regulate products falling outside its jurisdiction.[8]

Agenda Power and Veto Power. Agenda power describes who determines what will be taken up for consideration in an institution. Those who exercise some form of agenda power are said to engage in gatekeeping. They determine which items may pass through the gate onto the institution's agenda and which alternatives will have the gate slammed in their face. Gatekeeping, in other words, consists of the power to make proposals and the power to block proposals from being made. The ability to keep something off of an institution's agenda should not be confused with **veto power**, which is the ability to defeat something even if it does become part of the agenda. In the legislative process, for example, the president has no general gatekeeping authority—he has no agenda power and thus cannot force the legislature to take up a proposal or block it from considering something—but he does have (limited) veto power. Congress, in contrast, controls its own agenda; its

jurisdiction

The domain over which an institution or member of an institution has authority.

agenda power

The control over what a group will consider for discussion.

veto power

The ability to defeat something even if it has made it on to the agenda of an institution.

---

8 It was only in August 2016, for example, that the FDA acquired the authority to regulate tobacco products.

---

members can place matters on the legislative agenda. No other institutions can prevent Congress from passing a measure, but a presidential veto can prevent a measure, once passed, from becoming the law of the land. Thus, when it comes to legislation, agenda power is vested in the legislature. Both the legislature and the president possess veto power; the assent of each is required for a bill to become a law. We will examine these processes in more detail in Chapters 6 and 7.

Decisiveness. Another crucial feature of an institution is its body of rules for making decisions. Indeed, establishing the rules for decision making often requires many conditions and qualifications. The more an organization values participation by a broad range of its members, the more it needs those rules: the requirement of participation must be balanced with the need to bring input or debate to a close so that decisions can be made. This is why it is possible on the floor of a legislature to "move" the question under discussion, a motion to close the debate and move immediately to a vote.[9] In some legislatures, though, inaction seems to take precedence over action; in the U.S. House of Representatives, for example, a motion to adjourn (and thus not vote on a measure) takes precedence over a motion to move to a vote. In the U.S. Senate, to take another example, a supermajority (60 votes) is required to close debate. **Decisiveness rules** thus specify when votes may be taken, the sequence in which votes may occur, and—most important—how many individuals supporting a motion are sufficient for it to pass.

Delegation. A final aspect of institutional authority concerns delegation. Representative democracy is the quintessential instance of **delegation**. Citizens, through voting, delegate the authority to make decisions on their behalf to representatives—chiefly legislators and executives—rather than exercising political authority directly. We can think of our political representatives as our *agents*, just as we may think of professionals and craftspeople (doctors, accountants, plumbers, and so on) as agents whom we hire to act on our behalf. Why would those with authority, whom we will call *principals*, delegate some of their authority to agents? The answer is that both principals and agents benefit from it. Principals benefit because they are able to off-load to specialists tasks that they themselves are less capable of performing. Ordinary individuals, for example, aren't as versed in the tasks of governance as are professional politicians, just as they aren't as versed in the job of fixing a burst water pipe as is a plumber. Agents benefit from delegation as well, since it puts their services in demand, enables them to exercise authority, and compensates them for their efforts. Delegation and its division and specialization of labor is thus the rationale for representative democracy.

decisiveness rules

A specification of when a vote may be taken, the sequence in which votes on amendments occur, and how many supporters determine whether a motion passes or fails.

delegation

The transmission of authority to some other official or body (though often with the right of review and revision).

---

9   For a general discussion of motions to close debate and get on with the decision, see Henry M. Robert, *Robert's Rules of Order* (1876), items III. 21 and VI. 38. *Robert's Rules* has achieved icon status and now exists in an enormous variety of forms. For a more current version, the 1915 edition can be found here: www.bartleby.com/176/.

Examples of principals and agents abound in politics. Elected officials, as just noted, are agents for citizen principals. Leaders are agents for their followers. Government bureaus—called *agencies* after all—serve as agents for elected principals in the executive and legislative branches.[10] Law clerks are agents for the judges who employ them. Lobbyists are agents of special interests. In short, the political world is replete with links between principals and agents.

The relationship between a principal and an agent allows the former to delegate to the latter, with benefits for both. But there is a dark side to this **principal-agent relationship**. As the eighteenth-century economist Adam Smith noted in *The Wealth of Nations* (1776), economic agents are not motivated by the welfare of their customers to grow vegetables, make shoes, or weave cloth; rather, they do those things out of their own self-interest. Thus when delegating to agents, a principal must take care that those agents are properly motivated to serve the principal's interests, either by sharing those interests or by deriving something of value for acting to advance them. The principal will need instruments by which to monitor what her agents are doing and then reward or punish them accordingly. Nevertheless, a principal will never eliminate entirely the possibility that her agents could deviate from her interests because of the **transaction costs** that would be involved. The effort necessary to negotiate and then police every aspect of a principal-agent relationship becomes, at some point, more costly than it is worth.

In sum, the upside of delegation is that specific activities will be assigned to precisely those agents who possess a comparative advantage in performing them. The downside is the chance that the agents' goals will not align with the principals' goals, and thus the possibility of agents marching to the beat of their own drummers. Delegation is a double-edged sword.

Characterizing institutions in terms of jurisdiction, agenda power, veto power, decisiveness, and delegation covers an immense amount of ground. Our purpose here has been to introduce the many ways in which collectivities arrange and routinize their business, thereby enabling cooperation and facilitating political bargaining and decision making. A second purpose has been to highlight the potential diversity of institutional arrangements; there are so many ways to do things collectively. This diversity underscores the intelligence of the framers of the Constitution and the institutional choices they made more than two centuries ago. Finally, we want to make clear that institutions not only make rules for governing but also present strategic opportunities for various political interests, depending on how the institutions are designed. As George Washington Plunkitt, the savvy political boss of Tammany Hall, said of the institutional situations in which he found himself, "I seen my opportunities, and I took 'em."[11]

principal-agent relationship ➡

The relationship between a principal (such as a citizen) and an agent (such as an elected official), in which the agent is expected to act on the principal's behalf.

transaction costs ➡

The cost of clarifying each aspect of a principal-agent relationship and monitoring it to make sure both parties comply with all arrangements.

---

10 Thus elected officials are simultaneously agents of their constituents and principals for bureaucrats to whom they delegate the authority to implement policy. See Sean Gailmard and John W. Patty, *Learning while Governing: Expertise and Accountability in the Executive Branch* (Chicago: University of Chicago Press, 2013).

11 In the nineteenth century and well into the twentieth, the Tammany Hall political organization ran New York City's Democratic Party like a machine.

The Collective Action Principle: All Politics Is Collective Action

Political action is collective: it involves building, combining, mixing, and amalgamating people's individual goals. It sometimes occurs in highly institutionalized settings—a committee, legislature, or bureaucracy, for example. However, it also occurs in less institutionalized settings—a campaign rally, a get-out-the-vote drive, or a civil rights march. Moreover, collective action can be difficult to orchestrate because the individuals involved often have different goals, preferences, and motives for cooperation. Conflicting goals are inevitable; the question is how they can be accommodated. The most typical means of resolving collective dilemmas is bargaining among individuals. But when the number of parties involved is too large for face-to-face bargaining, there must be a shared incentive to motivate everyone to act collectively.

Informal Bargaining. Political bargaining may be highly formal or entirely informal. We engage in informal bargaining often in our everyday lives. One of this book's authors, for example, shares a hedge on his property line with one of his neighbors. First one takes responsibility for trimming the hedge and then the other, alternating from year to year. This arrangement (or bargain) is merely an understanding, not a legally binding agreement, and it was reached amicably and without much fuss or fanfare after a brief conversation. No organized effort—such as hiring lawyers; drafting an agreement; and having it signed, witnessed, notarized, and filed at the county courthouse—was required.

Bargaining in politics can be similarly informal. Whether called horse trading, back-scratching, logrolling, or wheeling and dealing, it has the same flavor as the casual negotiation between neighbors. Deals will be struck depending on the participants' preferences and beliefs. If preferences are incompatible or beliefs inconsistent with one another, then a deal among participants simply may not be possible. If the participants' preferences and beliefs are not too far out of line, then there will be a range of possible bargaining outcomes, some advantaging one party, others advantaging other parties. In short, there will be room for a compromise. In situations of repeated informal bargaining, regular practices—"ways of doing things around here"—often emerge as ways of coming to an agreement, such as taking turns, splitting the difference, or flipping coins.

In fact, much of politics *is* informal, unstructured bargaining. First, many disputes subject to bargaining are of sufficiently low impact that establishing formal machinery for dealing with them is not worth the effort. Rules of thumb (or *norms*) such as the shortcuts just mentioned often develop as benchmarks for dealing with certain types of conflicts. Second, repetition can contribute to successful cooperation. If a small group engages in bargaining today over one matter and tomorrow over another—as neighbors bargain over draining a swampy meadow one day, fixing a fence another, and trimming a hedge on yet another—then patterns develop. If one party constantly tries to extract maximal advantage, then the others will cease doing business with him. If, however, each party "gives a little to get a little," then a pattern of cooperation develops. It is the repetition of similar, mixed-motive occasions that allows this pattern to emerge without formal trappings. Many political circumstances are either amenable to informal rules or are repeated often enough to allow cooperative patterns to emerge.[12]

Formal Bargaining. Other bargaining situations are governed by rules. The rules describe such things as who gets to make the first offer, how long the other parties have to consider it, whether other parties can make counteroffers, the method by which parties convey assent or rejection, what happens when all (or some decisive subset) of the others accept an offer, and what happens next if the proposal is rejected. It may be hard to imagine two neighbors deciding how to trim their common hedge under procedures as explicit as these. It makes more sense, however, to imagine a bargaining session between labor and management over wages and working conditions at a large manufacturing plant proceeding in just this manner. The distinction suggests that some bargaining is more suited to formal proceedings, whereas other bargaining situations can be resolved well enough without them. The same may be said about personal situations that involve bargaining. A husband and wife are likely to divide household chores by informal bargaining, but this same couple would employ a formal procedure if they were dividing household assets in a divorce settlement.

Formal bargaining is often associated with events in official institutions—legislatures, courts, party conventions, administrative agencies, and regulatory agencies, for instance. In these settings, situations involving mixed motives arise repeatedly. Year in and year out, legislatures pass statutes, approve executive budgets, and oversee the administrative branch of government. Courts administer justice, determine guilt or innocence, resolve differences between disputants, and render interpretive opinions. Party conventions nominate candidates and approve their campaign platforms. Administrative and regulatory agencies implement policy and make rulings about its applicability. All of these are mixed-motive circumstances in which different parties have different goals; thus while gains from cooperation are possible, bargaining failures are also a definite possibility. In general, the formal bargaining that takes place within institutions is governed by rules that regularize proceedings, both to maximize the prospects of reaching agreement and to guarantee that procedural wheels are already in place each time a similar bargaining problem arises. This is our first application of the institution principle: institutions facilitate (but do not always succeed in producing) collective action.

Collective Dilemmas and Bargaining Failures. Even when gains are possible from collective action—when people share some common objective, for example—it still may not be feasible to arrive at a satisfactory conclusion. Consider two farmers, Farmer Jones and Farmer Smith, interested in mending

---

12 For a wonderful description of how ranchers in Shasta County, California, organized their social lives and collective interactions in just this fashion, see Robert C. Ellickson, *Order without Law: How Neighbors Settle Disputes* (Cambridge, MA: Harvard University Press, 1991).

a fence that separates their properties. Suppose that the farmers each value the mended fence at some positive amount, V. Suppose that the total cost (in terms of time or effort) to do this chore is c, a big enough cost to make the job not worth the effort if a farmer had to do it all by himself. For example, if each farmer values the mended fence at $700, but the cost of one of them to repair it on his own is $1,000, the net benefit to one farmer repairing it alone ($700 − $1,000) is less than zero—and thus not an attractive option. If they shared the cost equally, though, their net benefit each would be the value of the mended fence minus the total cost split by the two of them: $V − c/2$, in our example, $700 − $500—a positive net benefit of $200 to each. If one of the farmers, however, could off-load the entire project on his neighbor, then he would not have to bear any of the cost and would still enjoy the mended fence valued by him at V ($700). The situation is displayed in Figure 1.1. The two rows show the options available to Jones and the two columns show the options available to Smith. The lower-left entry in each cell is the payoff to Jones if he selects the row option and Smith selects the column option; the upper-right entry is Smith's payoff in each scenario. Thus, if both choose to mend the fence (the upper-left cell), then they each enjoy a positive net benefit of $V − c/2$. If, however, Jones takes on the job but Smith does not (the upper-right cell), then Jones pays the full price and receives $V − c$ (which is negative) and Smith gets the full value, V. The other two cells are filled in according to this logic.

Consider now how Jones might think about this problem. On the one hand, if Smith chooses to mend the fence (left column in the figure), then Jones gets $V − c/2$ if he helps Smith. But he does even better, getting the full value of V, if he lets Smith do the whole job. On the other hand, if Smith chooses not to mend the fence (right column in the figure), then Jones gets a *negative* value, $V − c$, if he does the job himself, but gets zero if he too does not take up the task. Putting these together, Jones realizes that *no matter what Smith does, Jones is better off not*

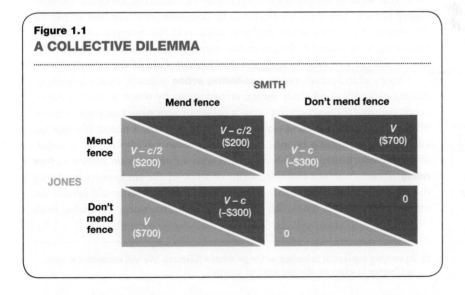

Figure 1.1
A COLLECTIVE DILEMMA

mending the fence. Following the same logic, Smith will arrive at the same conclusion. So each chooses "don't mend the fence," and each gets a payoff of zero, even though both would have been better off if both had chosen "mend the fence."

This is a famous dilemma in social science.[13] It is a dilemma because the two individuals share a common goal—a mended fence—but each person's individual rationality causes both of them to do worse than they would have done had they "suspended" their rationality and contributed to the common objective. Even if the two farmers tried to overcome this dilemma, the dilemma persists, as each has a rational temptation to defect from a bargain in which both agree to mend the fence. Moreover, each is likely nervous that the other will defect, given the incentives of the situation, and so feels compelled to defect himself.

The broad point of this example is that even common values and objectives do not guarantee that a positive outcome will result from bargaining. We encounter dilemmas and bargaining failures frequently in politics, but some methods exist that can partially mitigate these failures.

Collective Action, Free Riders, Public Goods, and the Commons. The idea of political bargaining suggests an intimate kind of politics, involving face-to-face relations, negotiation, compromise, give-and-take, and so on. Such bargaining results from the combination of mixed motives and small numbers. When the number of individuals or other actors involved becomes large, bargaining may no longer be practical. If 100 people own property bordering a swampy meadow, how does this community solve the swamp's mosquito problem? How does the community secure the benefits that arise from cooperation? In short, what happens if a simple face-to-face interaction, possibly amenable to bargaining, now requires coordination among a large number of people? How does a community become a *community* and not just a collection of individuals?

In the swampy meadow example, everyone shares some common value—eliminating the mosquito habitat—but they may disagree on other matters. Some may want to use pesticides; others may be concerned about the environmental impact. And there are bound to be disagreements over how to pay for the project. A collective action problem arises, as in this example, when there is something to be gained if the group can cooperate and assure one another that no one will get away with bearing less than her fair share of the effort.

Groups of individuals intent on **collective action** ordinarily establish decision-making procedures: relatively formal arrangements by which to resolve differences, coordinate the group to pursue a course of action, and sanction slackers. Workers in a manufacturing plant may attempt to form a union; like-minded citizens may organize a political party. Most groups will also require a leadership structure, which is necessary to deal with a phenomenon known as **free riding**. To return to our example, if one or a few of the landowners bordering the swamp were to clear the mosquitos alone, their actions would benefit the other owners as well. The other owners would be free riders, benefiting from

collective action

The pooling of resources and the coordination of effort and activity by a group of people (often a large one) to achieve common goals.

free riding

Enjoying the benefits of some good or action while letting others bear the costs.

---

13 In another context, it is known as the prisoner's dilemma. We will encounter it again in Chapter 13 when we discuss interest groups.

---

the efforts of a few without contributing themselves. (The same issue faced farmers Smith and Jones in the fence-mending problem described earlier.) It is this prospect of free riding that risks undermining collective action. Leadership structures are thus put in place to enforce punishments meant to discourage individuals from reneging on the individual contributions required to enable the group to pursue its common goals.

Another way to think about this is to describe a commonly shared goal— say, the mosquito-free meadow—as a public good. A **public good** is a benefit that others cannot be denied from enjoying once it has been provided. Once the meadow is mosquito free, it will constitute a benefit to *all* members of the group, even those who have not contributed to its provision. More generally, a public good is one that can be "consumed" by all individuals, with no exclusions, and that will not run out as people continue to use it. A classic example is a lighthouse. Once erected, it aids all ships, and there is no simple way to charge a ship for using it. Likewise, national defense protects taxpayers and tax avoiders alike. Another example is clean air. Once enough people restrict the pollutants they emit into the air, the cleaner air may be enjoyed even by those who have not restricted their own pollution. Because public goods have these properties, it is easy for some members of a group to free ride on others' efforts or sacrifices. And as a result, it may be difficult to get anyone to provide public goods in the first place. Collective action is required, and so leaders (or governments) with the capacity to induce all group members to contribute often need to get involved.

One of the most notorious collective action problems involves too much of a good thing. Known as the **tragedy of the commons**, this type of problem reveals how unbridled self-interest can have damaging collective consequences. A political party's reputation, for example, can be seen as something that benefits all politicians affiliated with the party. This collective reputation is not irreparably harmed if one legislator takes advantage of the party's reputation to secure a minor amendment helpful to a special interest in her district. But if lots of party members do it, the party comes to be known as the champion of special interests, and its reputation is tarnished. A pool of resources is not much depleted if someone takes a little of it, but it is if lots of people take from it—a forest is lost one pine tree at a time; the atmosphere is polluted one particle at a time. The party's reputation, the forest, and the atmosphere are all *commons*.[14] The problem to which they are vulnerable is *overgrazing*: when a common resource is irreparably depleted by individual actions.[15]

To summarize, individuals try to accomplish goals not only as individuals but also as members of larger collectivities (families, associations, political parties)

 public good

A good that (1) may be enjoyed by anyone if it is provided and (2) may not be denied to anyone once it has been provided. Also called *collective good*.

 tragedy of the commons

The idea that a common resource, available to everyone, will more likely than not be abused or overused.

---

14 The original meaning of *commons* is a shared pasture on which many people graze their cows, to the point of damaging the land. A most insightful discussion of "commons problems," of which these are examples, is Elinor Ostrom, *Governing the Commons: The Evolution of Institutions for Collective Action* (New York: Cambridge University Press, 1990).

15 The classic statement is Garrett Hardin, "The Tragedy of the Commons," *Science* 162, no. 3859 (1968): 1243-8.

---

and even larger categories (economic classes, ethnic groups, nationalities). The rationality principle (all political behavior has a purpose) accounts for individual initiative. The collective action principle describes the paradoxes encountered, the obstacles to be overcome, and the incentives necessary when individuals attempt to coordinate their energies, accomplish collective purposes, and secure the dividends of cooperation. Much of politics is about doing this or failing to do this. The institution principle provides a logical solution to these problems of collective action: collective activities that are both important and frequently occurring are regularized in the form of institutions. Institutions do the public's business while relieving communities of the need to reinvent collective action each time it is required. Thus we have a rationale for government.

The Policy Principle: Political Outcomes Are the Products of Individual Preferences, Institutional Procedures, and Collective Action

Ultimately, we are interested in the results of politics—the collective decisions that emerge from the political process. A Nebraska farmer, for example, cares about how public laws affect his welfare and that of his family, friends, and neighbors. He cares about how export policies affect the prices his crops can earn in international markets and how monetary policy influences the cost of seed and fertilizer; about the funding of research and development efforts in agriculture; and about the affordability of the state university where he hopes to educate his children. He also will care, eventually, about inheritance laws and their effect on his ability to pass his farm on to his kids without the government taking much of it in estate taxes. As students of American politics, we need to consider the links that individual goals, institutional arrangements, and collective action have with policy outcomes. How do all of these leave their marks on policy? What biases and tendencies manifest themselves in public decisions?

The linchpin connecting individuals and institutions with policy is the various motivations of political actors. As we saw in our discussion of the rationality principle, their ambitions—ideological, personal, electoral, and institutional—provide incentives to craft policies in particular ways. In fact, most policies make sense only as reflections of individual politicians' interests, goals, and beliefs. Examples include:

Personal interests: Congressman X is an enthusiastic supporter of government subsidies for home heating oil, but he opposes regulation to keep its price down because some of his friends own heating-oil distributorships.[16]

----

16 The congressman's friends may benefit from a government subsidy if it reduced the price point of the oil, making it accessible to more customers, but they would not want the price they can charge for the oil to be restricted.

Electoral ambitions:	Senator Y, a well-known political moderate, has lately been introducing very conservative amendments to bills dealing with the economy in an effort to appeal to conservatives who might donate to her budding presidential campaign.
Institutional ambitions:	Representative Z has given a rousing speech on the House floor in support of an amendment that is near and dear to her party leader. She hopes her support for the amendment will earn her his endorsement for an assignment to the prestigious Appropriations Committee.

These examples illustrate how policies are a product of both institutional procedures and individual aspirations. The procedures are essentially a series of chutes and ladders that shape, channel, filter, and prune the alternatives from which policy choices are ultimately made. The politicians who populate these institutions are driven both by private objectives and by public purposes, pursuing their private interests while working on behalf of the public interest, as they see it.

Because the institutional features of the American political system are complex, and policy change requires success at every step, change is often impossibly difficult. Thus, the status quo usually prevails. A long list of players must be satisfied with any given change, or it won't happen. Most of these politicians will need some form of "compensation" to provide their endorsement and support. For instance, in order to build majority support for a bill, the legislator who drafts the bill must include provisions that benefit other members of the legislature, thereby ensuring that a sufficient number of his colleagues will vote in support of it. Derisively, this is called pork-barrel legislation. In fact, most pork-barrel projects can be justified as valuable additions to the public good. What may be pork to the critic may be actual bridges, roads, and post offices for people living in the legislators' districts.

Elaborate institutional arrangements, complicated policy processes, and intricate political motivations make for a highly combustible mixture. The policies that emerge may be lacking in the neatness that citizens desire, but they are sloppy and slapdash for a reason: the tendency to spread benefits broadly results when political ambition comes up against a decentralized political system.

The History Principle: How We Got Here Matters

One final aspect of our analysis is important: we must ask how we have gotten where we are. How did we get the institutions and policies that are in place today? By what series of steps? When by choice and when by accident? Every question and problem we confront has a history. History will not tell the same story for every institution, but without it we have neither a sense of how institutions developed and evolved nor a full sense of how they are related to one another. In explaining why governments do what they do, we must turn to history to see what choices were available to political actors at a given time, what consequences resulted, and what consequences might have flowed had different paths been chosen.

Imagine a tree growing from the bottom of the page. Its trunk grows upward from a root ball at the bottom, dividing into branches that continue upward, further dividing into smaller branches. Imagine a path through this tree, from its bottommost roots to the tip of one of the highest branches at the top of the page. There are many such paths, from the one point at the bottom to any of the points at the top. If this were a time diagram, the root ball would represent some beginning point and all of the branch endings would represent the present. Each path is now a possible history. Alternative histories entail irreversibilities: once one starts down a historical path, one cannot always retrace one's steps.[17] Some futures are foreclosed by the choices people have already made or, if not literally foreclosed, then made extremely unlikely.

In this sense we can explain a current situation at least in part by describing the historical path that led to it. Certain scholars use the term **path dependency** to suggest that some possibilities are more or less likely because of earlier events and choices. Both the status quo and the paths that diverge from it significantly delimit future possibilities. For example, in the early 1990s, President Bill Clinton formulated the "Don't Ask, Don't Tell" policy for the treatment of gay men and women in the military: the military could not ask about a soldier's sexual orientation, and gay troops could serve so long as they did not reveal their sexual orientation. This move made it virtually impossible to return to the old status quo in which gay men and women could not serve at all. However, the policy chosen by the Clinton administration also made it difficult to progress to a more enlightened policy in which gay troops were not prevented from expressing their identity. This change did not happen for two decades because Don't Ask, Don't Tell dissuaded members of the military from advocating for a new policy in ways that might have exposed their sexual orientation. Acquiring half a loaf sometimes makes the full loaf more challenging to secure.

Three factors help explain why history often matters in political life: rules and procedures, loyalties and alliances, and historically conditioned points of view. As for rules and procedures, choices made during one point in time continue to have consequences for years, decades, or even centuries. For example, the United States' single-member-district, plurality voting rules, established in the eighteenth century, continue to shape the nation's party system today.[18] Those voting rules, as we will see in Chapter 12, help explain why the

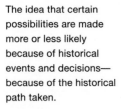

path dependency

The idea that certain possibilities are made more or less likely because of historical events and decisions—because of the historical path taken.

---

17 With tree climbing this is not literally true, or else once we started climbing a tree, we would never get down! The tree analogy is not perfect here.

18 In political systems with single-member districts, one legislator is selected to represent each district. (Other electoral systems may select multiple members from each district.) A plurality voting rule declares that the one legislator selected to represent a district is the one who earns the most votes (not necessarily a majority of the votes) in an election.

United States has a two-party system rather than a multiparty system, as is found in many other Western democracies. Thus a set of choices made more than 200 years ago affects party politics today.

History also often matters in terms of political loyalties and alliances. Many of the most important political alliances in the United States today are products of events from decades ago. For example, Jewish voters are among the Democratic Party's most loyal supporters, consistently giving 80 or 90 percent of their votes to Democratic presidential candidates. Yet on the basis of economic interest, Jewish people, a generally middle- and upper-middle-class social group, might be expected to vote for Republicans. Moreover, recently the GOP has been a strong supporter of Israel. Why, then, do Jewish voters overwhelmingly support Democrats? Part of the answer has to do with history. The Jewish community, historically, has suffered discrimination in the United States. In the 1930s, the Democratic Party under Franklin Delano Roosevelt became one vehicle through which Jewish people in America began to enjoy greater economic opportunity. This historical experience continues to shape Jewish political identity. Similar historical experiences underlie the political loyalties of African Americans to the Democrats and Cuban Americans to the Republicans.

A third factor explaining why history matters is that past events shape current perspectives. For example, many Americans in their late 60s and 70s viewed the wars in Iraq and Afghanistan through the lens of their experience with the Vietnam War, expecting U.S. military involvement in a third world country to lead to a quagmire of costs and casualties. But at the time of the Vietnam War, many older Americans viewed the events in Vietnam through the lens of the 1930s, when Western democracies were slow to resist Adolf Hitler's Germany. These people saw a failure to respond strongly to aggression as a form of appeasement that would only encourage hostile powers to use force against U.S. interests. Thus, at any given time, people's perspectives are shaped by what they have learned from their own histories.

CONCLUSION: PREPARING TO ANALYZE THE AMERICAN POLITICAL SYSTEM

This introductory chapter has set the stage for an analytical treatment of the phenomena that constitute American politics. This analytical approach requires attention to *argument* and *evidence*. To construct an argument about some facet of American politics—Why do incumbent legislators in the House and Senate have so much success in securing reelection? Why does the president dominate media attention?—we can draw on a set of five principles. The linchpin is the rationality principle, which emphasizes individual goal seeking as a key explanation for behavioral patterns. But politics is a collective undertaking, and it is often structured by political arrangements, so we also focus on collective action and the institutions in which such action occurs through the lens of the collective action principle and the institution principle. The combination of goal-seeking individuals engaging in collective activity in institutional contexts provides leverage for understanding why governments govern as they do—making laws, passing budgets, implementing policies, rendering judicial judgments—that is, the policy principle. But we could not make entire sense of these activities without an appreciation of the broader historical path: the history principle. These five principles, then, are tools of analysis. They are also tools of discovery, permitting the interested observer to uncover new ideas about why politics works as it does.

To know if an argument truly contributes to our understanding of the real world, we need to look at evidence. In the study of American politics, much of this evidence takes the form of quantitative data, and much of it is accessible online. Making sense of such evidence is what political scientists do. In Analyzing the Evidence, beginning on p. 24, we provide a brief glimpse of how to go about this task. We hope it helps you think analytically about political information as we move through the rest of the book.

Drawing on the lesson of the history principle, we will begin in the remaining chapters of Part 1 by setting the historical stage. Then, with analytical principles and strategies in hand, we can understand what influenced and inspired the founding generation to create a national government and a federal political system, while preserving individual rights and liberties.

For Further Reading

Bianco, William T. *American Politics: Strategy and Choice.* New York: Norton, 2001.

Crawford, Sue E. S., and Elinor Ostrom. "A Grammar of Institutions." *American Political Science Review* 89, no. 3 (1995): 582–600.

Downs, Anthony. *An Economic Theory of Democracy.* New York: Harper and Row, 1957.

Ellickson, Robert C. *Order without Law: How Neighbors Settle Disputes.* Cambridge, MA: Harvard University Press, 1991.

Gailmard, Sean, and John W. Patty. *Learning while Governing: Expertise and Accountability in the Executive Branch.* Chicago: University of Chicago Press, 2013.

Hardin, Garrett. "The Tragedy of the Commons." *Science* 162, no. 3859 (1968): 1243–8.

Kiewiet, D. Roderick, and Mathew D. McCubbins. *The Logic of Delegation: Congressional Parties and the Appropriations Process.* Chicago: University of Chicago Press, 1991.

Mayhew, David R. *Congress: The Electoral Connection*. New Haven, CT: Yale University Press, 1974.

Olson, Mancur, Jr. *The Logic of Collective Action: Public Goods and the Theory of Groups*. 1965. Second printing with a new preface and appendix. Cambridge, MA: Harvard University Press, 1971.

Shepsle, Kenneth A. *Analyzing Politics: Rationality, Behavior, and Institutions*. 2nd ed. New York: Norton, 2010.

Tuck, Richard. *Free Riding*. Cambridge, MA: Harvard University Press, 2008.

Making Sense of Charts and Graphs

CHAPTER 01

Contributed by
Jennifer Bachner
Johns Hopkins University

Throughout this book, you will encounter graphs and charts that show some of the quantitative data that political scientists use to study government and politics. This section provides three general steps to help you interpret and evaluate common ways data are presented—both in this text and beyond.

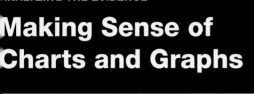

Step 1 ▸ Identify the Purpose of the Graph or Chart

When you come across a graph or chart, your first step should be to identify its purpose. The title will usually indicate whether the purpose of the graph or chart is to describe one or more variables or to show a relationship between variables. Note that a variable is a set of possible values. The variable "years of education completed," for example, can take on values such as "8," "12," or "16."

Descriptive Graphs and Charts. The title of the graph in Figure A, "Party Identification in the United States, 2020," tells us that the graph focuses on one variable, party identification, rather than showing a relationship between two or more variables. It is therefore a descriptive graph.

If a graph is descriptive, you should identify the variable being described and think about the main point the author is trying to make about that variable. In Figure A, we see that party identification can take on one of three values ("Republican," "Democrat," or "Independent") and that the author has plotted the percentage of survey respondents for each of these three values using vertical bars. The height of each bar indicates the percentage of people in each category, and comparing the bars to each other tells us that most Americans identified as Independents in 2020. This is one main takeaway from the graph.

Figure A: Party Identification in the United States, 2020

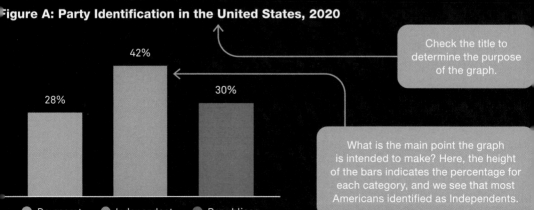

Check the title to determine the purpose of the graph.

What is the main point the graph is intended to make? Here, the height of the bars indicates the percentage for each category, and we see that most Americans identified as Independents.

Graphs and Charts That Show a Relationship. Let's turn to Table A, "Policy Priorities by Age Group." Notice that there are two variables—policy priorities and age—mentioned in the title, which indicates that the chart will compare them. We know, therefore, that the chart will illustrate the relationship between these two variables rather than simply describe them.

The first column in Table A displays the values for age group, which in this case are ranges. The other columns provide data about policy priorities; they display the percentage of survey respondents in each age group who said that Social Security (in the second column) and the environment (in the third column) should be among the government's top priorities. We can compare the columns to determine if there is a relationship between age and policy priorities. We see that a greater percentage of respondents in the higher age ranges said that Social Security should be a top priority; in the oldest age group, 74 percent of respondents would have the government prioritize Social Security compared to 46 percent in the youngest age group. In the lower age groups, more respondents said the environment should be a top priority. This is strong quantitative evidence of a relationship between age and policy priorities, which is the main point.

Table A: Policy Priorities by Age Group

Percent who say that . . . should be a top priority for the government.

AGE GROUP	SOCIAL SECURITY	THE ENVIRONMENT
18-29	46%	77%
30-49	61%	67%
50-64	70%	57%
65+	74%	55%

*Respondents were allowed to pick more than one option.

Does the title mention more than one variable? If so, that usually means the chart or graph is intended to show a relationship between the variables.

By comparing the values for each variable, we can see if there is a relationship between them. Here, we see that the lower age groups were more likely to choose the environment, while the higher age groups were more likely to choose Social Security.

Step 2 Evaluate the Argument

After you've identified the main point of a graph or chart, you should consider: Does the graph or chart make a compelling argument, or are there concerns with how the evidence is presented? Here are some of the questions you should ask when you see different types of graphs.

Is the Range of the y-Axis Appropriate? For a bar graph or line graph, identify the range of the y-axis and consider whether this range is appropriate for the data being presented. If the range of the y-axis is too large, readers may not be able to perceive important fluctuations in the data. If the range is too small, insignificant differences may appear to be huge.

Median Household Income over Time

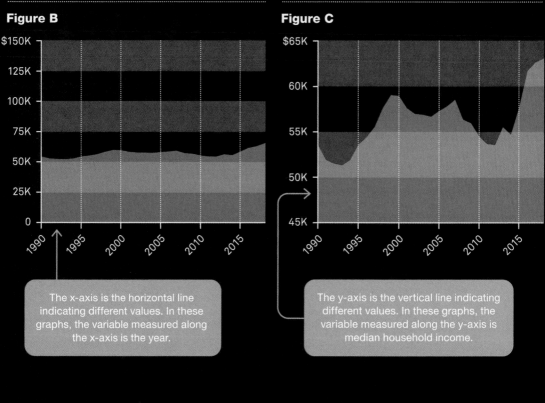

Figure B

The x-axis is the horizontal line indicating different values. In these graphs, the variable measured along the x-axis is the year.

Figure C

The y-axis is the vertical line indicating different values. In these graphs, the variable measured along the y-axis is median household income.

Figures B and C present exactly the same data but on graphs with very different y-axes. Both graphs plot median U.S. household income from 1990 to 2018. In the first graph, the range of the y-axis is so large that it looks like household income has barely changed over the past 28 years. In the second graph, the range is more appropriate. The second graph highlights meaningful changes in a household's purchasing power over this time period.

Is the Graph a Good Match for the Data? Different types of graphs are useful for different types of data. A single variable measured over a long period of time is often best visualized using a line graph, whereas data from a survey question where respondents can choose only one response option might best be displayed with a bar graph. Using the wrong type of graph for a data set can result in a misleading representation of the underlying data.

For example, in the months leading up to the 2018 midterm election, pollsters were interested in measuring the importance of various policy issues to voters. Some surveys asked respondents how important each of a series of policy issues would be to their vote decision (for example, "Now for each of those items, please tell me how important each will be in your vote for Congress this year.") Other surveys listed a set of policy issues and asked respondents to select which one of them would be the single most important factor in their vote decision. Both approaches captured the importance of different policy issues to vote choice, but they did so in different ways.

Top Policy Priorities, October 2018

Figure D: A Very Important Policy Issue

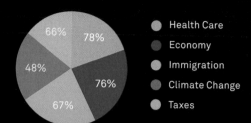

- Health Care
- Economy
- Immigration
- Climate Change
- Taxes

Figure E: The Most Important Policy Issue

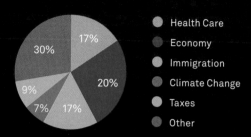

- Health Care
- Economy
- Immigration
- Climate Change
- Taxes
- Other

Figures D and E are pie charts that illustrate the data from the two surveys. The difference in how the graphs portray the importance of, say, health care to voters is striking. The first graph, based on the survey in which respondents selected all issues that were very important to them, implies that health care is the most important factor for voters, whereas the second graph indicates that, if respondents can only select one policy issue from the given options, the economy is the single most important issue. Note, however, that 30 percent of respondents in the second graph selected "other" policy issues (such as foreign policy, abortion, and opioid addiction).

This example demonstrates why a pie chart is a poor graph choice for a variable in which the response categories do not add up to 100 percent. In choosing what type of graph to use, researchers and authors have to make thoughtful decisions about how to present data so the takeaway is clear and accurate.

Does the Relationship Show Cause and Effect—or Just a Correlation? If a graph or chart conveys a relationship between two or more variables, it is important to determine whether the data are being used to make a causal argument or if they simply show a correlation. In a causal relationship, changes in one variable lead to changes in another. For example, it is well established that, on average, more education leads to higher earnings, more smoking leads to higher rates of lung cancer, and easier voter registration processes lead to higher voter turnout.

Other times, two variables might move together, but these movements are driven by a third variable. In these cases, the two variables are correlated, but changes in one variable do not cause changes in the other. A classic example is the relationship between ice cream consumption and the number of drowning deaths. As one of these variables increases, the other one does too, but not because one variable is causing a change in the other one—both variables are driven by a third variable. In this case, that third variable is temperature (or season). Both ice cream consumption and drowning deaths are driven by increases in the temperature because more people eat cold treats and go swimming on hot days.

There are many examples of data that are closely correlated but for which there is no causal relationship. Figure F displays a line graph of two variables: per capita consumption of mozzarella cheese and the number of civil engineering doctorates awarded in the United States. The two variables are strongly correlated (96 percent), but it would be wrong to conclude that they are causally related. A causal relationship requires theoretical reasoning—a chain of argument linking cause to effect. Distinguishing causal relationships from mere correlations is essential for policy makers. A government intervention to fix a problem will work only if that intervention is causally related to the desired outcome.

Figure F: Per Capita Consumption of Mozzarella Cheese Correlates with Civil Engineering Doctorates Awarded

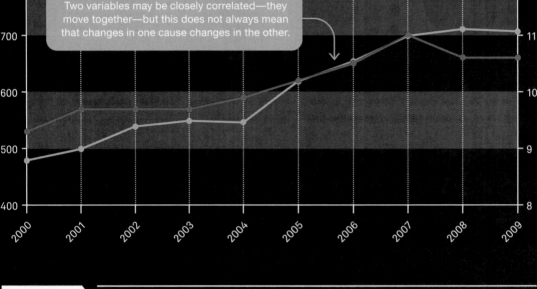

Two variables may be closely correlated—they move together—but this does not always mean that changes in one cause changes in the other.

Step 3 ▶ Consider the Source

In addition to making sure you understand what a data graphic says, it's important to consider where the data came from and how they were collected.

- **What is the source of the data?** Good graphs should have a note citing the source. In the United States, reliable sources include government agencies and mainstream news organizations, which generally gather data accurately and present it objectively. Data from individuals or organizations that have specific agendas, such as interest groups, should be more carefully scrutinized.

- **Is it clear what is being measured?** For example, in a poll showing "Support for Candidate A," do the results refer to the percentage of all Americans? The percentage of likely voters? The percentage of Democrats or Republicans? A good data figure should make this clear in the title, in the labels for the variables, and/or in a note.

- **Do the variables capture the concepts we care about?** There are many ways, for example, to measure whether a high school is successful (such as math scores, reading scores, graduation rate, or parent engagement). The decision about which variables to use depends on the specific question the researcher seeks to answer.

- **Are survey questions worded appropriately?** If the graph presents survey data, do the questions and the answer options seem likely to distort the results? Small changes in the wording of a survey question can drastically alter the results.

- **Are the data based on a carefully selected sample?** Some data sets include all individuals in a population; for example, the results of an election include the choices of all voters. Other data sets use a sample: a small group selected by researchers to represent an entire population. Most high-quality data sources will include information about how the data were collected, including the margin of error based on the sample size. ("Measuring Public Opinion" in Chapter 10 provides more information on sampling and other factors that affect the reliability of polls.)

Figure G: Voter Registration Rates by Age, 2018

Check to see where the data in the figure come from. The source note for this figure indicates that the data came from a U.S. Census Bureau survey. If we check the Census Bureau report, it includes "technical documentation" about how the survey was conducted, including the exact question wording, the sample size, and the margin of error.

SOURCE: U.S. Census Bureau, "Voting and Registration in the Election of November 2018," Table 2, All Races, www.census.gov/data/tables/time-series/demo/voting-and-registration/p20-583.html (accessed 5/6/20).

SOURCES FOR OTHER FIGURES IN THIS SECTION:

Figure A	Gallup, www.gallup.com/poll/15370/party-affiliation.aspx (accessed 3/3/20).
Table A	Pew Research Center, "As Economic Concerns Recede, Environmental Protection Rises on the Public's Policy Agenda," February 13, 2020, www.people-press.org/2020/02/13/as-economic-concerns-recede-environmental-protection-rises-on-the-publics-policy-agenda (accessed 3/5/20).
Figures B,C	U.S. Census Bureau (via Federal Reserve Bank of St. Louis), https://fred.stlouisfed.org/series/MEHOINUSA672N (accessed 3/3/20).
Figure D,E	PollingReport.com, "Problems and Priorities," www.pollingreport.com/prioriti.htm (accessed 3/3/20).
Figure F	Spurious Correlations, http://tylervigen.com/view_correlation?id=3890 (accessed 3/7/20).

2

Constructing a Government: The Founding and the Constitution

To understand the character of the American Founding and the meaning of the U.S. Constitution, we must look beyond myths and rhetoric. Our first principle of politics is that all political behavior has a purpose. The men and women who became revolutionaries were guided by numerous purposes. Most of the nation's founders, though highly educated, were not political theorists. Rather, they were hardheaded and pragmatic in their commitments and activities. Although their interests differed, they agreed that a relationship of political and economic dependence on a colonial power, one that did not treat them as full-fledged citizens of the empire, was intolerable. This state of affairs motivated the decision to break away from Britain in 1776 and the subsequent effort to fashion institutions of self-governance.

Many of those most active in the initial days of the Revolution felt backed into a corner, their decisions forced by Britain's changing relationship with the colonies. For years, the imperial center in London, preoccupied by wars with France spread across several continents, had left the colonists to their own devices. These were years of substantial local control and home rule—institutional arrangements that suited merchants, farmers, and planters in the separate colonies. Local control under the mild direction of colonial governors left colonists to tend to their own business for the most part. But suddenly, as war with France concluded in the 1760s, the British presence became more onerous. This incited collective action.

In reaction to British attempts to extract tax revenues to pay for troops—which were in fact being sent to defend the American colonial frontier—protests erupted throughout the colonies. The most notorious attempt to levy taxes was the infamous Stamp Act of 1765, which required that all printed and legal documents—including newspapers, pamphlets, advertisements, notes and bonds, leases, deeds, and licenses—be printed on official paper stamped and sold by British officials. To show their displeasure with the act, the colonists held mass meetings, participated in parades, and conducted other demonstrations throughout the spring and summer of 1765. In Boston, for example, a stamp agent was hanged and burned in effigy, which led to the actual agent's resignation. Later the home of the Massachusetts lieutenant governor was sacked because of a rumor that he supported the Stamp Act. By November 1765, business was proceeding and newspapers were being published without stamps; in March 1766, Parliament repealed the detested law. Through their protests, subsequent boycotts of imported British goods, and the Stamp Act Congress that met in October 1765, the colonists took the first steps down a path that ultimately would lead to war and the establishment of a new nation.

This is where we begin our story in the present chapter. We first assess the political backdrop of the American Revolution. The history principle can help us understand how nearly a century of light-handed colonial administration produced a set of expectations among the colonists that later British actions unmistakably violated. Then we examine the Constitution that ultimately emerged—after a bumpy experience in self-government just after the Revolution—as the basis for America's government. This document is the quintessential institutional arrangement that structures political relationships, facilitates collective action, and encourages peaceful conflict resolution. We conclude with a reflection on the Founding by emphasizing a lesson that resonates throughout American history: politics generally involves struggles among conflicting interests. In 1776, the main conflict was between pro-revolutionary and anti-revolutionary forces.

LEARNING OBJECTIVES

➡ Describe the major political and historical developments that led to the Constitutional Convention of 1787.

➡ Explain why the Articles of Confederation was not strong enough to provide effective governance.

➡ Outline the major provisions of the U.S. Constitution.

➡ Analyze how the framers attempted to balance representation with effective governance.

➡ Describe how the amendment process allows the Constitution to evolve over time.

In 1787, the major struggle was between the Federalists and the Antifederalists. Today the struggle is between the Democratic and Republican parties, which represent competing economic, social, and sectional interests. Often, political ideas are developed by competing interests as weapons to further their own causes. The New England merchants who cried "no taxation without representation" cared more about lower taxes than about expanded representation. Yet today, representation is one of the foundations of American democracy.

Institutions matter a good deal to our understanding of American politics. First, the institution principle tells us that institutions structure politics and affect the results of political conflicts—who wins and who loses. Second, the policy principle tells us that institutional procedures (coupled with individual preferences) help determine policy outcomes—what the government can and cannot do. In the United States, no set of institutions is more important than the Constitution. What are the basic rules embodied in the Constitution? What significance have constitutional precepts had for American life? This chapter addresses these key questions. Of course, the history principle suggests that the Constitution itself was affected by the events of the colonial and founding periods. So, let's first turn to the events that preceded and shaped America's most fundamental set of laws.

THE FIRST FOUNDING: INTERESTS AND CONFLICTS

Competing ideals often reflect competing interests, and so it was in Revolutionary America. Both the American Revolution and the Constitution were born from struggles among economic and political forces within the colonies. In colonial politics, five sectors of society had important interests: (1) the New England merchants; (2) the southern planters; (3) the "royalists," or holders of royal lands, offices, and patents (licenses to engage in a profession or business activity); (4) shopkeepers, artisans, and laborers; and (5) small farmers. Throughout the eighteenth century, these groups differed over issues of taxation, trade, and commerce. For the most part, however, the southern planters, the New England merchants, and the royal officeholders and patent holders—in other words, the colonial elite—maintained a political alliance that held in check the more radical shopkeepers, laborers, and small farmers. After 1750, however, by threatening the interests of New England merchants and southern planters, British tax and trade policies split the elite. This split permitted radical forces to expand their political influence and unfurled a chain of events that culminated in the American Revolution.[1]

---

1   The social makeup of colonial America and some of the social conflicts that divided colonial society are discussed in Jackson Turner Main, *The Social Structure of Revolutionary America* (Princeton, NJ: Princeton University Press, 1965).

British Taxes and Colonial Interests

Beginning in the 1750s, debts and other financial problems forced the British government to search for new revenue sources. This search led to the Crown's North American colonies, which paid remarkably little in taxes to the mother country—especially considering that they accounted for a sizable portion of Britain's debt, owing to (1) the Crown's defense of the colonies during the recent French and Indian War, (2) its continuing protection of the colonists from Native American attacks, and (3) the protection that the British navy provided for colonial shipping. Thus the British government thought it was quite reasonable to impose new taxes on the colonists particularly because, even with the new taxes, the colonists would still pay far less in taxes than residents of Britain itself.

Like most governments of the period, the British regime had only limited ways to collect revenue. The income tax (which in the twentieth century became the most important source of government revenue) had not yet been developed. In the mid-eighteenth century, governments generally relied on tariffs, duties, and other taxes on commerce, and it was to such taxes, including the Stamp Act, that the British turned during the 1760s. British interests (revenue) and institutions (Parliament and colonial administration) combined to produce a plausible solution to an existing problem, as suggested by the policy principle.[2]

The colonists, accustomed to managing their own affairs, resented this British meddling. Moreover, the Stamp Act and other taxes on commerce, such as the Sugar Act of 1764, mainly affected the two groups whose commercial interests were most extensive: the New England merchants and the southern planters. Because their interests coincided, these two groups engaged in collective action to organize opposition to the new taxes under the famous slogan "no taxation without representation." They broke with their royalist allies and turned to their former adversaries—the shopkeepers, small farmers, laborers, and artisans, all of whom had their own grievances against the established colonial government—for help in organizing demonstrations and boycotts of British goods. These actions ultimately forced the Crown to rescind most of its new taxes. For the merchants and planters, the British government's decision to eliminate most of the hated taxes meant a victorious end to their struggle with the mother country. The more radical groups, however, were not satisfied. It was in the context of this unrest that a confrontation arose between colonists

---

2   Parliament also enacted the Proclamation of 1763 as part of the British settlement with Native Americans at the end of the French and Indian War. The Proclamation withdrew the colonists' right to settle lands west of the Appalachian Mountains, preserving them for native populations. Among others, the families of George Washington and Benjamin Franklin had speculated on these lands and thus faced serious financial loss. See Norman Schofield, *Architects of Political Change: Constitutional Quandaries and Social Choice Theory* (New York: Cambridge University Press, 2006), chap. 3. A compact version is found in Norman Schofield, "Evolution of the Constitution," *British Journal of Political Science* 32, no. 1 (2002): 1-20.

and British soldiers in front of the Boston custom house on the night of March 5, 1770, resulting in what came to be known as the Boston Massacre. Nervous British soldiers opened fire on the mob surrounding them, killing five colonists and wounding eight others. News of the event quickly spread throughout the colonies and served to fan anti-British sentiment.

Eager to end the unrest they had helped arouse, the merchants and planters supported the British government's efforts to restore order. Indeed, most respectable Bostonians supported the actions of the British soldiers involved in the Boston Massacre. In their subsequent trial, the soldiers were defended by John Adams, a pillar of Boston society and a future president of the United States. Adams asserted that the soldiers' actions were entirely justified, provoked by a "motley rabble of saucy boys, negroes and mulattoes, Irish teagues and outlandish Jack tars." All but two of the soldiers were acquitted.[3]

Despite the efforts of the British government and the colonial elite, it proved difficult to end the political strife. The more radical forces continued to agitate for political and social change. Generally representing the middle classes, who often had some education and a respectable trade or skill but little political influence, the radicals believed that people like themselves were just as fit to govern as members of the colonial elite. Led by individuals such as Samuel Adams, a cousin of John Adams, the radicals asserted that British power supported an unjust political and social structure within the colonies, and they began to advocate an end to British rule.[4]

Britain's revenue-raising policies backfired so dramatically because British leadership greatly underestimated colonial resistance. Indeed, the Stamp Act cost more to enforce than it produced in revenue. The rationality principle, though, requires only that people do the best they can at the time they act. Unanticipated factors are bound to arise and necessitate subsequent adaptation. The revenue-raising policies seemed sensible to the British before they were issued, and when the policies later appeared mistaken, they were rescinded. So Britain's attempts to raise revenue and then adapt because of the resulting unrest were rational, but it proved difficult to undo the damage caused by issuing the taxes in the first place.

Organizing resistance to the British authorities required widespread support. Collective action, as noted, may emerge spontaneously in certain circumstances, but the colonists' campaign against Britain required strategic planning, coalition building, bargaining, persuading, compromising, and coordinating—all elements of the give-and-take of politics. Cooperation would thus need cultivation and encouragement, and leadership would be a necessary ingredient.

----

3   Quoted in David Emory Shi, *America: A Narrative History*, 11th ed. (New York: Norton, 2019), p. 186.

4   For a discussion of events leading up to the Revolution, see Charles M. Andrews, *The Colonial Background of the American Revolution: Four Essays in American Colonial History* (New Haven, CT: Yale University Press, 1924).

Political Strife and the Radicalizing of the Colonists

The political strife sparked by the Stamp Act provided the background for the events of 1773–74. With the Tea Act of 1773, the British government granted the politically powerful East India Company a monopoly on the export of tea from Britain, eliminating a lucrative trade for colonial merchants. Worse, the East India Company sought to sell the tea directly in the colonies instead of working through colonial merchants. Because tea was an important commodity in the 1770s, the act posed a mortal threat to the New England merchants—who once again called on their radical adversaries for support. The most dramatic result was the Boston Tea Party of 1773, led by Samuel Adams and carried out by protesters, mostly radicals, who hoped to undermine the British government's authority. (The modern "Tea Party" protesters were generally conservatives opposing taxes and regulation.)

The Boston Tea Party was decisive in American history. While the merchants had wanted to force the British government to rescind the Tea Act, they certainly did not seek independence from Britain. Samuel Adams and the other radicals, however, hoped to provoke the British government into taking actions that would alienate its colonial supporters and pave the way for a rebellion. By dumping the East India Company's tea into Boston Harbor, Adams and his followers goaded the British into enacting harsh reprisals: a series of acts that closed the port of Boston to commerce, took away the right of Massachusetts to govern itself, provided for the removal of accused persons to Britain for trial, and added new restrictions on western movement from the southern colonies—further alienating the southern planters who depended on access to new lands. These acts of retaliation helped radicalize Americans and move them toward collective resistance to British rule.[5]

This course of action by British politicians is puzzling in retrospect, but at the time a show of force appeared reasonable. Those who prevailed in Parliament felt that, if they tolerated lawlessness and made concessions, it would only prompt the more radical colonists to take additional liberties and demand further concessions. The British, in effect, drew a line in the sand. Their repressive response became a clear point around which dissatisfied colonists could rally. Radicals had been agitating for the use of more violent measures to deal with Britain, but ultimately, they needed Britain's political reprisals to create widespread support for independence.[6]

Thus the Boston Tea Party sparked a cycle of disputes that ultimately led to the First Continental Congress in 1774, with delegates attending from across the colonies. The Congress called for a total boycott of British goods and, under

---

5 For an intriguing take on the role of dense population networks in cities that promoted collective action against the British, see Edward L. Glaeser, "Revolution of Urban Rebels," *Boston Globe*, July 4, 2008, sec. A.

6 For an extensive discussion of how misunderstandings and incorrect beliefs caused the situation to spin out of control, see Jack N. Rakove, Andrew R. Rutten, and Barry R. Weingast, "Ideas, Interest, and Credible Commitments in the American Revolution," February 2000, https://papers.ssrn.com/sol3/papers.cfm?abstract_id=1153515 (accessed 11/13/19).

the radicals' prodding, began to consider independence from British rule. The eventual result was the Declaration of Independence.

The Declaration of Independence

In 1776, the Second Continental Congress appointed a committee consisting of Thomas Jefferson of Virginia, Benjamin Franklin of Pennsylvania, Roger Sherman of Connecticut, John Adams of Massachusetts, and Robert Livingston of New York to draft a statement of American independence from British rule. The Declaration of Independence was written by Jefferson, drawing on the ideas of British philosopher John Locke, whose work was widely read in the colonies. Adopted by the Second Continental Congress, the Declaration is an extraordinary document in both philosophical and political terms. Philosophically, the Declaration is remarkable for its assertion (derived from Locke) that certain "unalienable" rights—including life, liberty, and the pursuit of happiness—cannot be abridged by governments. In the world of 1776, in which some kings still claimed to rule by divine right, this was a dramatic statement. Politically, the Declaration is remarkable because, despite the colonists' widely differing interests, it focused on grievances, aspirations, and principles that might unify the various colonial groups. The Declaration attempted to articulate a history and a set of principles that might help forge national unity.[7]

The Declaration of Independence, however, was not a blueprint for governance. Often, scholars call the Declaration a more radical or even libertarian document and the Constitution a more conservative text. The two documents, however, share common philosophical underpinnings: both apply Locke's idea that the purpose of government is the protection of life, liberty, and property. The Declaration uses these ideas to justify overthrowing a tyrannical government. The Constitution, in contrast, seeks to create a government that will, in fact, defend these rights for its citizens. Thus America's founding documents share philosophical roots but apply them to different purposes.

The Revolutionary War

In 1775, even before formally declaring their independence, the colonies began to fight the British. The Revolutionary War commenced with the battles of Lexington and Concord, Massachusetts, where colonial militias acquitted themselves well against trained British soldiers. Nevertheless, the task of defeating Britain, then the world's premier military power, seemed impossible. To maintain their hold on the colonies, the British deployed a huge expeditionary force, comprising British regulars and German mercenaries along with artillery and equipment. To face this force, the colonists relied on inexperienced and lightly

---

7 A "biography" of the Declaration is found in Pauline Maier, *American Scripture: Making the Declaration of Independence* (New York: Knopf, 1997).

armed militias. To make matters worse, the colonists were hardly united in their opposition to British rule. Many colonists saw themselves as loyal British subjects and refused to take up arms against the king. Thousands, indeed, took up arms *for* the king and joined pro-British militia forces.

The war was brutal and bloody; the colonists, British troops, and Native Americans who fought on both sides suffered tens of thousands of casualties, in total. Eventually the Revolutionary armies prevailed, mainly because the cost of fighting a war thousands of miles from home became too great for Britain to bear. Colonial militias prevented British forces from acquiring enough food and supplies locally, so they had to be brought from Europe at enormous expense. The colonial forces did not have to defeat the British—they needed only to prevent the British from defeating them until Britain's will and ability to fight waned. Thus, with the eventual help of Britain's enemy, France, the colonists fought until Britain had enough. The war ended in 1783 with the signing of the Treaty of Paris, which officially granted the 13 American colonies their independence.

The Articles of Confederation

Having declared their independence, the colonies needed to establish a governmental structure—a set of institutions through which to govern. In November 1777, the Continental Congress adopted the **Articles of Confederation and Perpetual Union**—the United States' first written constitution. Although it was not ratified by all the states until 1781, it was the country's operative constitution for almost 12 years, until March 1789. When the Articles were drafted, each of the 13 original colonies was, in effect, an independent nation. While each saw the advantages of cooperating with the others, none of the 13 new governments—now calling themselves "states" to underscore their nationhood—gave much thought to the idea of surrendering their independence. Accordingly, the Articles of Confederation established a central government of defined and strictly limited power, with most actual governmental authority left in the hands of the individual states.

The central government, such as it was, was based entirely in the Congress of the Confederacy. Because the government was not intended to be powerful, it was given no executive branch or judiciary. Execution and interpretation of its laws were left to the individual states. The Congress, moreover, had little power. Its members were not much more than messengers from the state legislatures; they were chosen by the state legislatures, paid out of the state treasuries, and subject to immediate recall by state authorities. In addition, each state, regardless of size, had only a single vote. Furthermore, amendments to the Articles required the unanimous agreement of the 13 states.

Congress was given the power to declare war and make peace, to make treaties and alliances, to coin and borrow money, and to regulate trade with Native Americans. It could also appoint the senior officers of the United States Army. However, it could not levy taxes or regulate commerce among the states. Moreover, the army officers it appointed had no army to serve in because the

 Articles of Confederation and Perpetual Union

The United States' first written constitution. Adopted by the Continental Congress in 1777, the Articles were the formal basis for America's national government until 1789, when they were superseded by the Constitution.

nation's armed forces were composed of state militias. An especially dysfunctional aspect of the Articles of Confederation was that the central government could not regulate commerce between the individual states and foreign nations.

In brief, the relationship between Congress and the states under the Articles of Confederation was much like the contemporary relationship between the United Nations and its member states, a relationship in which the states retain virtually all governmental powers. It was properly called a confederation because, as provided under Article II, "each state retains its sovereignty, freedom, and independence, and every power, jurisdiction, and right, which is not by this Confederation expressly delegated to the United States, in Congress assembled." Not only was there no executive but there was also no judicial authority or other means of enforcing Congress's will. Any enforcement would be done by the states.[8] In essence, each state was an independent nation-state. All told, the Articles of Confederation was an inadequate institutional basis for collective action.

THE SECOND FOUNDING: FROM COMPROMISE TO CONSTITUTION

Institutional arrangements, devised to accomplish collective purposes by creating routines and processes, aren't always well suited to these tasks. The Declaration of Independence and the Articles of Confederation were insufficient to hold the nation together as an independent and effective nation-state. Almost from the moment war with the British ended in 1783, moves were afoot to reform and strengthen the Articles of Confederation.

International Standing, Economic Difficulties, and Balance of Power

Reform was, in part, motivated by a special concern for the country's international position. Competition among the states for foreign commerce allowed the European powers to play the states against one another, creating confusion on both sides of the Atlantic. At one point, John Adams, a leader in the struggle for independence, was sent to negotiate a new treaty with the British that would cover disputes left over from the war. The British government responded that, because the United States under the Articles of Confederation was unable to enforce existing treaties, it would negotiate with each of the 13 states separately. Moreover, absent the protection of the British navy, American shipping—on

---

8   See Merrill Jensen, *The Articles of Confederation: An Interpretation of the Social-Constitutional History of the American Revolution, 1774–1781* (Madison: University of Wisconsin Press, 1963).

which the New England states depended—was easy prey for pirates and predator nations. The government under the Articles could offer no help.

At the same time, well-to-do Americans—in particular the New England merchants and southern planters—were troubled by the influence of populist forces in the Congress of the Confederacy and in several state governments. The colonists' victory in the Revolutionary War not only had meant the end of British rule but also had significantly changed the balance of political power within the new states. As a result of the war, one key segment of the colonial elite—the royal land, office, and patent holders—was stripped of its economic and political privileges. In fact, many of these individuals, along with throngs of other colonists who considered themselves loyal British subjects, left for Canada after the British surrender. As the prerevolutionary elite became weaker, the prerevolutionary radicals became controlling forces in several states, where they pursued economic and political policies that struck terror into the political establishment. In Rhode Island, for example, a legislature dominated by representatives of small farmers, artisans, and shopkeepers instituted economic policies, including drastic currency inflation, that frightened businessmen and property owners throughout the country. Of course, the central government under the Articles of Confederation was powerless to intervene. Commerce within the states stagnated, and several states borrowed money just to finance their Revolutionary War debts. Americans were facing their first, but not last, debt crisis.

The Annapolis Convention

Continued international weakness and domestic economic turmoil led many Americans to consider whether their newly adopted form of government already required revision. After nearly a decade under the Articles, many state leaders accepted an invitation from the Virginia legislature to discuss this question at a conference of state representatives. Delegates from five states actually attended. This conference, held in Annapolis, Maryland, in the fall of 1786, was the first step toward the second founding. Representatives agreed to a resolution calling on Congress to send commissioners to Philadelphia at a later time "to devise such further provisions as shall appear to them necessary to render the Constitution of the Federal Government adequate to the exigencies of the Union."[9] This resolution was drafted by Alexander Hamilton, a New York lawyer who had served during the Revolution as George Washington's secretary and who would play a more significant role in framing the Constitution and forming the new government in the 1790s. At the time of the Annapolis Convention, however, the resolution did not necessarily imply any desire to do more than improve and reform the Articles of Confederation.

---

9 Quoted in Samuel Eliot Morison, Henry Steele Commager, and William E. Leuchtenburg, *The Growth of the American Republic,* 6th ed. (New York: Oxford University Press, 1969), vol. 1, p. 244.

Shays's Rebellion

It is possible that the Constitutional Convention of 1787 in Philadelphia would never have taken place if not for a single event that occurred soon after the Annapolis Convention: Shays's Rebellion. Like the Boston Tea Party, Shays's Rebellion was a turning point in the young country's history.

Daniel Shays, a former army captain, led a mob of farmers in a rebellion against the government of Massachusetts in 1787. The farmers' goal was to prevent the county courts from sitting so that the judges could not process foreclosures on the farmers' debt-ridden land. The state militia dispersed the mob, but for several days Shays and his followers attempted to capture the federal arsenal at Springfield, provoking the terrified state government to appeal to Congress to help restore order. Within a few days, the state government regained control and captured 14 of the rebels (all were eventually pardoned). Later that year, a newly elected Massachusetts legislature granted some of the farmers' demands. Although the incident ended peacefully, its effects lingered and spread.

Shays's Rebellion showed that the Congress of the Confederacy could not act decisively in a time of crisis. The mob concentrated attention, coordinated beliefs, produced widespread fear and apprehension among the people, and thus convinced waverers that something needed fixing. It prompted collective action by providing critics of the Articles of Confederation with the evidence they needed to convince the broader public that the Articles were insufficient and to push Hamilton's Annapolis resolution through the Congress.[10] Thus the states were asked to send representatives to Philadelphia to discuss constitutional revision. Every state except Rhode Island eventually sent delegates.

The Constitutional Convention

In May 1787, 29 of the 73 total delegates selected by the state governments convened in Philadelphia. Recognizing that political strife, international embarrassment, national weakness, and local rebellion were symptoms of fundamental flaws in the Articles of Confederation, the delegates soon abandoned plans for revising the document and undertook a second founding instead—an ultimately successful attempt to create a legitimate and effective national system from scratch. Americans had learned a good deal from the shortcomings of the Articles of Confederation: for example, that executive power was a necessary component of effective government, and that without an army or navy the government could not protect its citizens' interests. Demonstrating once again that history matters, Americans' experiences under the Articles helped shape the new Constitution.

---

10 For an easy-to-read argument that supports this view, see Keith L. Dougherty, *Collective Action under the Articles of Confederation* (New York: Cambridge University Press, 2001).

Interests or Ideals? For years, scholars have disagreed about the motives of the Founders in Philadelphia. Among the most controversial views is the "economic" interpretation put forward by the historian Charles Beard and his disciples.[11] According to Beard, America's founders were a collection of securities speculators and property owners whose only aim was personal enrichment. From this perspective, the Constitution's lofty principles are little more than sophisticated masks behind which the most venal representatives sought to enrich themselves. Although Beard's arguments are extreme, there is some foundation for them. Representatives with economic interests in the North feared debtor revolts, while southern planters feared a revolt led by enslaved people. Capital investment and its protection were weak under the Articles not only because of potential rebellions but also because of inflated currencies, limited credit markets, and outstanding public debt. Also, manufacturers needed protection from foreign competition, and exporters (primarily of southern cotton) needed the security of safe passage for their cargoes on the high seas.

Contrary to Beard's approach is the view that the Founders were in fact concerned with philosophical and ethical ideas—that indeed, the Founders sought to devise a system of government consistent with the dominant philosophical and moral values of the day.[12] Lurking in the background was a generalized suspicion of distant central government. As historian Joseph Ellis observed, this was the "core argument used to discredit the authority of Parliament and the British monarch."[13]

In fact, these two interpretations (interests and ideals) belong together: the Founders' interests were reinforced by their principles. The Constitutional Convention was chiefly organized by New England merchants and southern planters. Although the delegates did not all hope to profit personally from an increase in the value of their securities, as Beard would have it, they did hope to benefit by breaking the power of their radical foes and establishing a system of government more compatible with their long-term economic and political interests. Thus the framers—in line with the rationality principle—desired a new government capable of promoting commerce and protecting property from radical state legislatures. They also sought to liberate the national government from the power of individual states and sometimes corrupt local politicians. At the same time, they wanted a government that would be less susceptible than the existing state and national regimes were to hostile populist forces. The Constitutional Convention was thus a grand exercise in rationality and collective action.

The Great Compromise. The proponents of a new government fired their opening shot on May 29, 1787, when Edmund Randolph of Virginia offered a resolution that proposed corrections and enlargements to the Articles of Confederation. Not a simple motion, it provided for virtually every aspect of a

---

11 Charles A. Beard, *An Economic Interpretation of the Constitution of the United States* (New York: Macmillan, 1913).

12 For an analytical treatment, see Schofield, *Architects of Political Change*, chap. 4.

13 Joseph J. Ellis, *Founding Brothers: The Revolutionary Generation* (New York: Knopf, 2000), p. 7.

Representation in Congress: States' Ranks

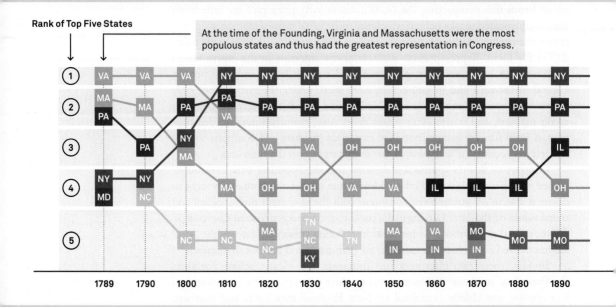

Rank of Top Five States

At the time of the Founding, Virginia and Massachusetts were the most populous states and thus had the greatest representation in Congress.

Rank	1789	1790	1800	1810	1820	1830	1840	1850	1860	1870	1880	1890
1	VA	VA	VA	NY	NY	NY	NY	NY	NY	NY	NY	NY
2	MA / PA	MA	PA	PA / VA	PA	PA	PA	PA	PA	PA	PA	PA
3		PA	NY	VA / MA	VA	VA	OH	OH	OH	OH	OH	IL
4	NY / MD	NY / NC		MA	OH	OH	VA	VA	IL	IL	IL	OH
5		NC	NC	MA / NC	TN / NC / KY	TN	MA / IN	VA / IN	MO / IN	MO	MO

TIMEPLOT SOURCE: U.S. Census Bureau, www.census. gov/dataviz/visualizations/ 023 (accessed 9/30/19).

new government—and it did in fact serve as the framework for what ultimately became the Constitution.[14]

This proposal, known as the Virginia Plan and authored by James Madison, provided for a system of representation in the national legislature based on the population of each state, the proportion of each state's contributions to overall national revenue, or both. (Randolph also proposed a second branch of the legislature, but it was to be elected by the members of the first branch.) Because the states varied enormously in size and wealth, the Virginia Plan appeared to be heavily biased in favor of larger states, which would have greater representation under the plan.

While the convention was debating the Virginia Plan, additional delegates arriving in Philadelphia began to mount opposition to it. Their resolution, introduced by William Paterson of New Jersey and known as the New Jersey Plan, did not oppose the Virginia Plan point for point. Instead, it concentrated on

14 There is no verbatim record of the debates, but Madison was present during virtually all of the deliberations and kept full notes on them. Madison's notes, along with the somewhat less complete records kept by several other participants in the convention, are available in a four-volume set. See Max Farrand, ed., *The Records of the Federal Convention of 1787*, rev. ed., 4 vols. (New Haven, CT: Yale University Press, 1966).

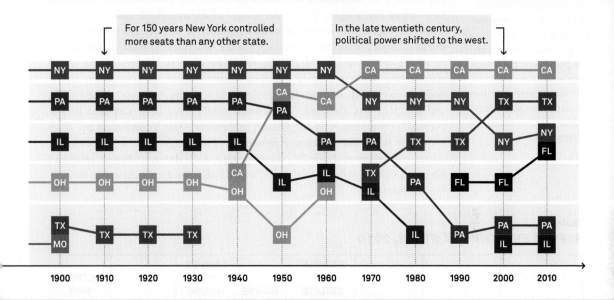

For 150 years New York controlled more seats than any other state.

In the late twentieth century, political power shifted to the west.

weaknesses in the Articles of Confederation, in the spirit of revision rather than radical replacement of that document. However, the plan's vision for representation was different enough from the Virginia Plan's scheme of representation that both documents were put before the committee to be reconciled into a common document. In particular, delegates from the less populous states, which included Delaware, New Jersey, and Connecticut, asserted that the more populous states, such as Virginia, Pennsylvania, North Carolina, and Massachusetts, would dominate the new government if representation were to be determined by population. The smaller states argued that each state should be equally represented regardless of its population.

The issue of representation threatened to wreck the entire constitutional enterprise. Delegates conferred, factions maneuvered, and tempers flared. James Wilson of Pennsylvania told the small-state delegates that if they wanted to disrupt the Union, they should go ahead. Gunning Bedford of Delaware declared that the small states might look elsewhere for friends, if they were forced. "The large states," he said, "dare not dissolve the confederation. If they do the small ones will find some foreign ally of more honor and good faith, who will take them by the hand and do them justice." These sentiments were widely shared. Convention delegates, acting as agents for the interests of their respective states, bargained and made attempts at persuasion in the rational pursuit of their preferred results.

Great Compromise ⬌

An agreement reached at the Constitutional Convention of 1787 that gave each state an equal number of senators regardless of the size of its population, but linked representation in the House of Representatives to population size. Also called the *Connecticut Compromise*.

The outcome of this debate was the **Great Compromise**, also known as the Connecticut Compromise. Under its terms, in the first chamber of Congress—the House of Representatives—members would be apportioned according to the number of inhabitants of each state. This was what delegates from the large states had sought. But in the second chamber—the Senate—each state would have an equal number of votes regardless of its size; this would address the small states' concerns. This compromise was not immediately satisfactory to all the delegates. Indeed, two of the most vocal supporters of the small-state faction were so incensed that they stormed out of the convention. In the end, however, both sides preferred compromise to the breakup of the Union, and the plan was accepted. The framers might have been surprised by the eventual consequences of the Great Compromise. The Timeplot on pp. 42–3 shows the states with the most representatives in Congress from 1789 to today. As we can see from Table 2.1, the two states with the most House seats and Electoral College delegates (electors) in 2010 did not even exist at the time of the Founding.

Table 2.1

REPRESENTATION BY STATE, 2010

STATE	POPULATION	SENATORS	PEOPLE PER SENATE SEAT	HOUSE SEATS	PEOPLE PER HOUSE SEAT	ELECTORS	PEOPLE PER ELECTOR
Alabama	4,802,982	2	2,401,491	7	686,140	9	533,665
Alaska	721,523	2	360,762	1	721,523	3	240,508
Arizona	6,412,700	2	3,206,350	9	712,522	11	582,973
Arkansas	2,926,229	2	1,463,115	4	731,557	6	487,705
California	37,341,989	2	18,670,995	53	704,566	55	678,945
Colorado	5,044,930	2	2,522,465	7	720,704	9	560,548
Connecticut	3,581,628	2	1,790,814	5	716,326	7	511,661
Delaware	900,877	2	450,439	1	900,877	3	300,292
Florida	18,900,773	2	9,450,387	27	700,029	29	651,751
Georgia	9,727,566	2	4,863,783	14	694,826	16	607,973
Hawaii	1,366,862	2	683,431	2	683,431	4	341,716
Idaho	1,573,499	2	786,750	2	786,750	4	393,375
Illinois	12,864,380	2	6,432,190	18	714,688	20	643,219
Indiana	6,501,582	2	3,250,791	9	722,398	11	591,053
Iowa	3,053,787	2	1,526,894	4	763,447	6	508,965
Kansas	2,863,813	2	1,431,907	4	715,953	6	477,302
Kentucky	4,350,606	2	2,175,303	6	725,101	8	543,826
Louisiana	4,553,962	2	2,276,981	6	758,994	8	569,245

Table 2.1
(Continued)

STATE	POPULATION	SENATORS	PEOPLE PER SENATE SEAT	HOUSE SEATS	PEOPLE PER HOUSE SEAT	ELECTORS	PEOPLE PER ELECTOR
Maine	1,333,074	2	666,537	2	666,537	4	333,269
Maryland	5,789,929	2	2,894,965	8	723,741	10	578,993
Massachusetts	6,559,644	2	3,279,822	9	728,849	11	596,331
Michigan	9,911,626	2	4,955,813	14	707,973	16	619,477
Minnesota	5,314,879	2	2,657,440	8	664,360	10	531,488
Mississippi	2,978,240	2	1,489,120	4	744,560	6	496,373
Missouri	6,011,478	2	3,005,739	8	751,435	10	601,148
Montana	994,416	2	497,208	1	994,416	3	331,472
Nebraska	1,831,825	2	915,913	3	610,608	5	366,365
Nevada	2,709,432	2	1,354,716	4	677,358	6	451,572
New Hampshire	1,321,445	2	660,723	2	660,723	4	330,361
New Jersey	8,807,501	2	4,403,751	12	733,958	14	629,107
New Mexico	2,067,273	2	1,033,637	3	689,091	5	413,455
New York	19,421,055	2	9,710,528	27	719,298	29	669,692
North Carolina	9,565,781	2	4,782,891	13	735,829	15	637,719
North Dakota	675,905	2	337,953	1	675,905	3	225,302
Ohio	11,568,495	2	5,784,248	16	723,031	18	642,694
Oklahoma	3,764,882	2	1,882,441	5	752,976	7	537,840
Oregon	3,848,606	2	1,924,303	5	769,721	7	549,801
Pennsylvania	12,734,905	2	6,367,453	18	707,495	20	636,745
Rhode Island	1,055,247	2	527,624	2	527,624	4	263,812
South Carolina	4,645,975	2	2,322,988	7	663,711	9	516,219
South Dakota	819,761	2	409,881	1	819,761	3	273,254
Tennessee	6,375,431	2	3,187,716	9	708,381	11	579,585
Texas	25,268,418	2	12,634,209	36	701,901	38	644,958
Utah	2,770,765	2	1,385,383	4	692,691	6	461,794
Vermont	630,337	2	315,169	1	630,337	3	210,112
Virginia	8,037,736	2	4,018,868	11	730,703	13	618,287
Washington	6,753,369	2	3,376,685	10	675,337	12	562,781
West Virginia	1,859,815	2	929,908	3	619,938	5	371,963
Wisconsin	5,698,230	2	2,849,115	8	712,279	10	569,823
Wyoming	568,300	2	284,150	1	568,300	3	189,433

SOURCE: The Green Papers, www.thegreenpapers.com/Census10/FedRep.phtml (accessed 6/21/19). These will be recalculated and apportioned after the 2020 Census.

The Question of Slavery: The Three-Fifths Compromise. Many of the conflicts facing the Constitutional Convention reflected the fundamental differences between slave and nonslave states, differences that pitted the southern planters and the New England merchants against each other. This was the first premonition of a conflict that would almost destroy the Republic in later years.

Over 90 percent of all enslaved persons resided in five states—Georgia, Maryland, North Carolina, South Carolina, and Virginia—where they accounted for 30 percent of the population. In some places, enslaved persons outnumbered non-slaves by as much as 10 to 1. Were they to be counted as part of a state's population even though they had no rights, thereby giving slave states increased representation in the House? If the Constitution were to embody any principle of national supremacy, some basic decisions would have to address the place of slavery in the general scheme.

Whatever they thought of the institution of slavery, most delegates from the northern states opposed counting enslaved persons when determining the distribution of congressional seats. Wilson of Pennsylvania, for example, argued that if enslaved persons were citizens, they should be treated and counted like other citizens. If, however, they were property, then why should not other forms of property count toward apportionment? But southern delegates asserted that if the northerners refused to give in, they would never agree to the new government. Virtually all southerners insisted on including enslaved persons in state population counts for the purposes of congressional seat allocation, even though some, such as James Madison and George Mason of Virginia, believed that slavery was immoral. This conflict was so divisive that many delegates came to question the possibility of creating and maintaining a union of the two sections of the nation.

Northerners and southerners eventually reached agreement through the **Three-Fifths Compromise**. The seats in the House of Representatives would be apportioned according to a "population" in which only three-fifths of enslaved persons would be counted. These people would not be allowed to vote, but the number of representatives would be apportioned accordingly. This compromise was accepted, albeit reluctantly, by both northerners and southerners.

The issue of slavery was the most difficult one the framers faced, and it nearly destroyed the Union. Although some delegates considered slavery morally wrong, an evil institution that made a mockery of the ideals and values espoused in the Constitution, expedience, not morality, was the main factor that caused the framers to support or oppose the Three-Fifths Compromise. Northerners even agreed to permit the transatlantic slave trade to continue to keep the South in the Union. Eventually, of course, a bloody war broke out when the two sides' disparate interests could no longer be reconciled.

Three-Fifths Compromise

An agreement reached at the Constitutional Convention of 1787, stating that for the purpose of distributing congressional seats on the basis of state populations, only three-fifths of enslaved persons would be counted.

THE CONSTITUTION

The political significance of the Great Compromise and the Three-Fifths Compromise was to restore the unity of the northern merchants and southern planters, paving the way for the creation of a new government. The Great Compromise reassured those of both groups who feared that their own local or regional influence would be threatened, and the Three-Fifths Compromise temporarily defused the rivalry between the groups over slavery. Their unity secured, members of the alliance moved to fashion a constitution for a new government consistent with their economic and political interests.

The framers of the Constitution understood that well-designed institutions make it easier to achieve collective goals. They also understood that the institutions they built could affect political outcomes for decades, if not centuries, to come. (The Policy Principle section on p. 48 examines the effects of the Great Compromise throughout American history.) Accordingly, the framers took great care to construct institutions that, over time, would help the nation accomplish certain important political purposes.

First, the framers wanted a government strong enough to promote commerce and protect property from radical state legislatures. This goal became the basis for the institution of national control over commerce and finance, the establishment of national judicial supremacy, and the effort to construct a strong presidency. Second, the framers sought to prevent the threat posed by the "excessive democracy" of the state and national governments under the Articles of Confederation. Here again the framers' historical experience mattered. This goal inspired such constitutional principles as a **bicameral legislature** (the division of Congress into two chambers), checks and balances, staggered terms of office, and indirect election (selection of the president by an Electoral College rather than directly by the voters). Third, lacking the power to force the states or the public at large to accept the new form of government, the framers sought to identify principles that would help secure support. This goal became the basis for the direct popular election of representatives and, later, the addition of the Bill of Rights. Finally, the framers wanted to ensure that the new government did not use its power to pose even more of a threat to citizens' liberties and property rights than did the radical state legislatures they feared and despised. To prevent the new government from abusing its power, they incorporated into the Constitution such principles as the separation of powers and federalism.

The framers provided us with a grand lesson in purposeful behavior. They came to Philadelphia united by a distaste for government under the Articles and animated by the agitation following Shays's Rebellion. They didn't always agree on what they disliked about the Articles or on how to proceed—hence the historic compromises. But they did believe that fostering commerce and protecting property could be served by a set of institutional arrangements better than the one provided by the Articles. They believed that both too much democracy, on the one hand, and too much governmental power, on the other, could threaten the common good, and they strove to find instruments and principles that balanced these forces. Let's assess the major provisions of the Constitution's seven articles to see how each one relates to these objectives.

 bicameral legislature

A legislative body composed of two chambers, or houses.

The Legislative Branch

The first seven sections of Article I of the Constitution provide for a Congress consisting of two chambers—a House of Representatives and a Senate. Members of the House of Representatives hold two-year terms of

The Constitution and Policy Outcomes

What if representation in the Senate was based on state population?

The policy principle tells us that political outcomes are the products of individual preferences and institutional procedures. One extension of this principle is the idea that individuals involved in politics try to create institutions that will help them achieve policy outcomes they favor and prevent policy outcomes they oppose. For any political actors, the right institutional arrangements can put them at an advantage—and their opponents at a disadvantage—in conflicts over policy for many years.

This idea is illustrated by the struggles at the Constitutional Convention. Delegates from the smaller states thought their states had much to gain by creating legislative institutions that gave each state an equal vote regardless of population. The larger states, however, especially Virginia, Massachusetts, New York, and Pennsylvania, were centers of commerce; their delegates believed that the new government's commercial policies would be more likely to serve those states' interests if its legislative institutions reflected their advantage in population. Nevertheless, representatives of both groups of states agreed that a new government was likely to produce better policies than those developed under the Articles of Confederation and so were willing to compromise. They eventually settled, in what is

known as the Great Compromise, on an institutional arrangement that gave the large states more weight in the House of Representatives and the small states equality of representation in the Senate.

This Great Compromise has affected policy outcomes throughout American history, giving less-populous states disproportionate influence in the legislative process. For instance, the late Yale political scientist Robert A. Dahl thought that slavery survived longer than it would have otherwise because the small-population southern states had disproportionate influence. The House of Representatives passed eight antislavery measures between 1800 and 1860, but all died in the Senate. Moreover, the civil rights movement of the mid-twentieth century was slowed by senators representing small-population states.

Today, the 37 million citizens of California, 25 million citizens of Texas, and 19 million citizens of New York are each represented by two senators, as are the 568,000 inhabitants of Wyoming, 630,000 Vermonters, and 676,000 North Dakotans. This disparity means that groups and interests in the latter three states exercise influence in the Senate far out of proportion to their states' populations. Overrepresentation in the Senate is one reason why the smaller states and their public agencies receive far more federal aid per capita than the larger states do. In a recent year, residents of Wyoming received $4,180 per capita while Texans and Californians each received a bit over $1,700. Also in recent years, bills designed to reform the immigration system, alter U.S. climate policy, and increase disclosure of campaign spending won the support of senators representing a majority of the population, but they failed to pass because those senators did not constitute a majority of votes in the Senate. After almost 250 years, the Great Compromise continues to affect public policy in the United States.

office and are elected directly by the people. Members of the Senate were originally appointed by the state legislatures (a provision changed in 1913 by the Seventeenth Amendment, which instituted direct election of senators) for six-year terms. These terms are staggered so that the appointments of one-third of the senators expire every two years. The Constitution assigns somewhat different tasks to the House and the Senate. Though the enactment of a law requires the approval of both chambers, the Senate alone can ratify treaties and approve presidential appointments. The House has the sole power to originate revenue bills.

The character of the legislative branch reflects the framers' major goals. The House of Representatives was designed to be directly responsible to the people, to encourage popular consent for the new Constitution, and to help enhance the power of the new government. At the same time, to guard against "excessive democracy," the power of the House is checked by the Senate, whose members were to be appointed, rather than directly elected by the people, to serve comparatively long terms. The purpose of this provision was to avoid "an unqualified complaisance to every sudden breeze of passion, or to every transient impulse which the people may receive."[15] Staggered terms of service in the Senate, moreover, would further insulate that body from popular pressure. Because only one-third of the senators would be selected at any given time, the institution would be protected from changes in popular preferences transmitted by state legislatures, thereby preventing what James Madison called "mutability in the public councils arising from a rapid succession of new members."[16]

The issues of power and consent are important throughout the Constitution. Article I, Section 8 lists the specific powers of Congress, which include the authority to collect taxes, borrow money, regulate commerce, declare war, and maintain an army and navy. By granting the legislature these powers, the framers ensured that the new government would be far more influential than its predecessor under the Articles. At the same time, by giving these important powers to Congress, the framers sought to promote popular acceptance of this critical change by reassuring citizens that their views would be fully represented whenever the government exercised its new powers.

As a further guarantee that the new government would pose no threat to the people, the Constitution implies that only those powers specifically expressed in its text are granted to the federal government; this is the doctrine of **expressed powers**. The national government cannot take on additional powers without a constitutional amendment. Any powers not listed are, in turn, "reserved" to the states (or the people).

Because the framers desired an active and powerful federal government, they also included the **necessary and proper clause**, sometimes known as the *elastic clause*, which grants Congress the power to make all laws that are "necessary and

 expressed powers

Powers that the Constitution explicitly grants to the federal government.

 necessary and proper clause

The last paragraph of Article I, Section 8, which gives Congress the power to make all laws needed to exercise the powers listed in Section 8. Also called the *elastic clause*.

15 Clinton L. Rossiter, ed., *The Federalist Papers; Alexander Hamilton, James Madison, and John Jay* (New York: New American Library, 1961), no. 71 (Alexander Hamilton), p. 464.

16 Rossiter, *Federalist Papers*, no. 62 (James Madison), p. 405.

proper" to exercise the powers listed in Section 8. This clause signifies that the expressed powers are meant to be a source of strength to the national government, not a limitation on it. As we will see, the question of what powers the federal government can or cannot exercise is still debated today. For example, opponents of the Affordable Care Act of 2010 (also known as Obamacare) claimed that the federal government lacked the power to require Americans to purchase health insurance. The Supreme Court, however, upheld major provisions of the law.[17]

The Executive Branch

The Constitution establishes the presidency in Article II. According to Alexander Hamilton, this article was intended to create "energy in the Executive" in an effort to overcome the stalemates built into both the bicameral legislature and the separation of powers among the legislative, executive, and judicial branches. The Constitution affords the president a measure of independence from the people and from the other branches of government, particularly Congress.

Some of the framers wanted to install a plural executive or executive council to avoid the evils associated with a monarch. However, Hamilton argued that "energy in the Executive" required a single executive with "competent powers" to direct the nation's business.[18] These would include the unconditional power to accept ambassadors from (essentially, to "recognize") other countries; the power to negotiate treaties subject to Senate approval; the right to grant reprieves and pardons, except in cases of impeachment; the power to appoint major departmental personnel; the power to convene Congress in a special session; and the power to veto congressional enactments. Checks and balances and other devices would be in place to guard against abuses of power. The veto power, for instance, is not absolute because Congress can override it by a two-thirds vote. (Analyzing the Evidence on pp. 52–3 explores the various points at which legislation can be halted in the United States as compared with other countries.)

A modern description of executive-legislative relations is: "The president proposes; the Congress disposes." That is, the president may propose certain items to the legislature as outlined in the Constitution, such as a treaty, a major departmental appointment, or a federal judge or justice, which are then subject to approval by the Senate. In these instances, the president is a legislative "agenda setter." When, however, the president proposes a law or budget, it is only a "suggestion" that the legislature may choose to dispose of altogether. Such proposals are said to be "dead on arrival" because Congress marches to the beat of its own drummer.

The framers hoped to create a presidency that would give the federal government, rather than the states, the energy to take timely and decisive action to

---

17 567 U.S. 519 (2012).

18 Rossiter, *Federalist Papers*, no. 70 (Alexander Hamilton).

---

deal with public issues and problems.[19] At the same time, however, the framers wanted the president to be able to withstand democratic pressures, and so designed the office to be subject to indirect election through the Electoral College. In Chapter 7 we will discuss the extent to which the framers' hopes were realized.

The Judicial Branch

Article III of the Constitution, which establishes the judicial branch, reflects the framers' preoccupations with enhancing the power of the national government, checking radical democratic impulses, and preventing the government from interfering with the liberty and property rights of its citizens.

The framers created a court that was to be literally a supreme court of the United States, not merely the highest court of the national government. In accordance with this intention, the Constitution gives the Supreme Court the power to resolve any conflicts that might emerge between federal and state laws. In particular, the Supreme Court has the right to determine whether a power is exclusive to the federal government, concurrent with the states, or exclusive to the states. Justice Oliver Wendell Holmes, Jr. noted the significance of this provision: "I do not think the United States would come to an end if we lost our power to declare an act of Congress void. I do think the union would be imperiled if we could not make that declaration as to the laws of the several states."[20]

In addition, the Constitution assigns the Supreme Court jurisdiction over controversies between citizens of different states. The long-term significance of this provision was that, as the country developed a national economy involving residents of all states, the federal judiciary, rather than the state courts, became the primary venue for the resolution of disputes.

The Constitution stipulates that federal judges must hold lifetime appointments, a provision that protects them from popular politics and interference from the other branches. To further safeguard judicial independence, Congress is prohibited from reducing the salary of any sitting judge. These provisions do not, however, mean that the judiciary remains totally impartial to political considerations or to the other branches; the president appoints the judges and the Senate approves the appointments. Congress also has the power to create inferior (lower) courts, change the federal courts' jurisdiction, add or subtract federal judges, and even change the size of the Supreme Court.

The Constitution makes no direct mention of **judicial review**—the power of the courts to determine whether the actions of the president, Congress, and the state legislatures are consistent with the Constitution. Scholars generally feel that judicial review is implicit in the existence of a written constitution and in the power given to the federal courts over "all Cases . . . arising under this

judicial review

The power of the courts to determine whether the actions of the president, the Congress, and the state legislatures are consistent with the Constitution.

---

19 Rossiter, *Federalist Papers*, no. 70.

20 Oliver Wendell Holmes, Jr., *Collected Legal Papers* (New York: Harcourt, Brace, 1920), pp. 295-6.

---

nstitutional Engineering: w Many Veto Gates?

Contributed by
Steven L. Taylor
Troy University
Matthew S. Shugart
University of California, Davis

ven constitution contains a number of individual elements that interact to produce a specific making environment. These parameters determine how policy decisions are made as well as which l actors can stop them from proceeding through the process. One area of comparative constitutiona involves how many *veto gates* a system contains. A veto gate is an institution that serves as a poin egislative process where the progress of a proposal can be halted. This notion conceives of the ive process as being made up of one or more such gates that have to be opened to allow an idea to past on its way to becoming law. Each gate, however, is locked and can be opened only b ional actors who hold the keys.

e simplest possible model of such a system would be an absolute dictator who has to consult only his own preferences before acting. Democratic governance, on the other hand, is a system that builds x (and often multiple) gates and then creates and empowers players to open those gates or not.

e exact mix of institutional elements in a given constitution has a profound impact not only on how s made but also on what kinds of policies are made. More veto gates and players in a given systen nerate more need for negotiation and compromise versus systems with fewer such actors. Wher ng veto gates, we can ask three questions:

Presidential veto: Is there an elected president who can veto legislation? In parliamentary systems ike the United Kingdom and India, there is no elected presidency at all. Other systems have electec presidents who may be important in some respects but who are not empowered with a veto (fo nstance, France). The strongest presidents are both elected and have a veto, such as the U.S president.

Number of legislative chambers: How many legislative chambers are there? Does the government have one chamber (unicameral) or two (bicameral)? If there is only one legislative chamber, as in Costa Rica and Denmark, then obviously there can be only one veto gate among egislative actors. We need, however, a final question to differentiate among forms of bicameralism.

Symmetry of chambers: If there is a second chamber, are the two symmetrical in their powers? Many second chambers are less powerful in their systems than the U.S. Senate, which is symmetrical in power with the House of Representatives. Some other bicameral legislatures are asymmetrical, meaning the second chamber has minimal powers beyond delaying power, as in Austria, or it has substantial powers in some areas but not others, as with the Canadian Senate and the United Kingdom's House of Lords.

n see from the table of 40 established democracies that there are multiple ways in which nationa utions can configure the lawmaking process in terms of the type and number of veto gates ver, the United States is not typical. Only 9 of these 40 democracies have three veto gates in the king process. Most other established democracies have fewer veto gates, although several have e veto players—such as frequent coalition governments where political parties have to compromise ne another. This combination of veto gates and veto players has a direct effect on policy and may

Countries				
ARGENTINA, BRAZIL, CHILE, COLOMBIA, DOMINICAN REPUBLIC, MEXICO,* PHILIPPINES, UNITED STATES, URUGUAY	Yes	●●	High	✕✕✕
COSTA RICA,† PANAMA, SOUTH KOREA	Yes	●	Unicameral	✕✕
POLAND	Yes	●●	Low 1 strong chamber 1 weak chamber	✕✕
AUSTRALIA, ITALY, **SWITZERLAND**	No	●●	High 2 strong chambers	✕✕
CANADA, GERMANY, INDIA, JAPAN, **NETHERLANDS,** SOUTH AFRICA, **UNITED KINGDOM**	No	●●	Medium 1 strong chamber 1 chamber with limitations	✕✕
AUSTRIA, BELGIUM, CZECH REPUBLIC, FRANCE, SPAIN	No	●●	Low	✕
BULGARIA, DENMARK, **FINLAND**, GREECE, HUNGARY, IRELAND, ISRAEL, **NEW ZEALAND,** NORWAY, PORTUGAL, SLOVAKIA, **SWEDEN**	No	●	Unicameral	✕

Beyond the legislative process, there are other constitutional factors that can create veto gates for policy implementation: a federal system may empower states to block the implementation of policy passed at the national level; Supreme Courts or constitutional tribunals may have the ability to declare laws unconstitutional, and therefore null and void. All of these factors derive from constitutional design.

SOURCES: Steven L. Taylor, Matthew S. Shugart, Arend Lijphart, and Bernard Grofman, *A Different Democracy: American Government in a Thirty-One-Country Perspective* (New Haven, CT: Yale University Press, 2014); and authors' classifications.
Mexico's second chamber has no power over spending bills.

Constitution, the Laws of the United States, and Treaties made, or which shall be made, under their Authority" (Article III, Section 2). The Supreme Court eventually assumed the power of judicial review, as we will see in Chapter 9, not on the basis of the Constitution itself but on the basis of the politics and membership of the Court in later decades.

National Unity and Power

Various provisions in the Constitution address the framers' concern with national unity and power, including Article IV's provisions for comity (reciprocity) among states and among the citizens of all states. Each state is prohibited from discriminating against the citizens of other states in favor of its own citizens, and the Supreme Court is charged with resolving associated disputes. The Constitution also restricts the power of the states in favor of ensuring that the federal government holds enough power to support a free-flowing national economy.

The framers' concern with national supremacy also surfaces in the **supremacy clause**, which provides that national laws and treaties "shall be the supreme Law of the Land" (Article VI). This means that all laws made under the "Authority of the United States" are superior to those of any state or other subdivision, and the states are expected to respect all treaties made under national authority. This provision keeps the states from dealing separately with foreign nations or businesses. The supremacy clause also binds the officials of all state, local, and federal governments to take an oath of office to support the Constitution.

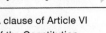

supremacy clause

A clause of Article VI of the Constitution, stating that all laws and treaties approved by the national government are the supreme laws of the United States and superior to all laws adopted by any state or local government.

Amending the Constitution

The Constitution establishes procedures for its own revision in Article V. The amendment process is so difficult that Americans have successfully used it only 17 times since 1791, when the first 10 amendments were adopted. Many other amendments have been proposed, but fewer than 40 have come close to fulfilling the Constitution's requirement of a two-thirds vote in Congress, and only a fraction have approached adoption by three-fourths of the states. The Constitution can also be amended by a constitutional convention, but no national convention has been called since the Philadelphia Convention of 1787; Congress has submitted all proposed amendments to the state legislatures for ratification.

Any body of rules, including a national constitution, must balance the need to respond flexibly to changes on the one hand with the caution not to be too flexible on the other. An inflexible body of rules that cannot accommodate major change risks being rebelled against—a circumstance in which those in power wipe the slate clean and design new rules—or ignored altogether. Too much flexibility, however, is disastrous. It invites those who lose in everyday politics to replay battles at the constitutional level. If institutional change is too easy to accomplish, the stability of the political system becomes threatened. As the institution principle suggests, a constitution should create institutional arrangements that provide a framework for politics, not ones that specify explicit political outcomes. To determine whether a constitutional document has the right degree of flexibility, it must pass the test of time. The fact that ours has survived for more than two centuries is a point in its favor.

Ratifying the Constitution

Article VII sets forth the rules for ratification of the Constitution of 1787. This provision actually violated the amendment provisions of the Articles of Confederation. For one thing, it adopts a nine-state rule in place of the unanimous approval required by the Articles. For another, it stipulates that ratification must occur in special state conventions rather than in state legislatures. All the states except Rhode Island eventually did set up state conventions to ratify the Constitution.

Constitutional Limits on the National Government's Power

As we have indicated, although the framers desired a powerful national government, they also wanted to guard against possible misuse of that power. Thus they incorporated two key principles into the Constitution: the **separation of powers** and **federalism** (see Chapter 3). A third set of limitations, in the form of the **Bill of Rights**, was ratified later as a series of amendments.

The Separation of Powers. No principle of politics was more widely shared at the time of the Founding than the idea that power must be used to balance power. The French political theorist Baron de Montesquieu (1689–1755) believed that this balance was an indispensable defense against tyranny. His writings "were taken as political gospel" at the Philadelphia Convention. Although the separation-of-powers principle was not explicitly stated in the Constitution, the national government was structured precisely according to Article I, the legislature; Article II, the executive; and Article III, the judiciary (Figure 2.1).

However, separation of powers is nothing but mere words on parchment without a method to maintain the separation. The method laid out in the Constitution became known as **checks and balances**. Each branch has not only its own powers but also some power over the other two branches. Among the most familiar checks and balances are the president's veto power over Congress and Congress's control over presidential appointments to high executive posts and the judiciary. Congress also has power over the president with its control of appropriations and the Senate's right to approve treaties. The judiciary has the assumed power of judicial review over the other two branches.

Another feature of the separation of powers is the principle of giving each branch a distinctly different constituency, what theorists such as Montesquieu called a "mixed regime." As such, the president is chosen indirectly by electors, the House by popular vote, the Senate (originally) by state legislatures, and the judiciary by presidential appointment. Because each branch is held accountable by a different group, the members of each branch would develop very different

 separation of powers

The division of governmental power among several institutions that must cooperate in decision making.

 federalism

The system of government in which a constitution divides power between a central government and regional governments.

 Bill of Rights

The first 10 amendments to the U.S. Constitution, adopted in 1791. The Bill of Rights ensures certain rights and liberties to the people.

 checks and balances

The ways in which each branch of government is able to influence the activities of the other branches.

Figure 2.1

THE SEPARATION OF POWERS

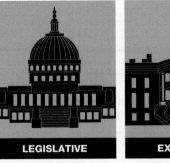

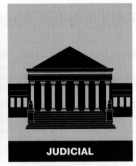

LEGISLATIVE	EXECUTIVE	JUDICIAL
Passes federal laws	Enforces laws	Reviews lower-court decisions
Controls federal appropriations	Serves as commander in chief of armed forces	Decides constitutionality of laws
Approves treaties and presidential appointments	Makes foreign treaties	Decides cases involving disputes between states
Regulates interstate commerce	Nominates Supreme Court justices and federal court judges	
Establishes lower-court system	May pardon those convicted in federal court	

outlooks on how to govern, definitions of the public interest, and alliances with private interests.

Federalism. Compared with the Articles of Confederation, federalism was a step toward greater centralization of power. Seeking to place more power at the national level without completely undermining the power of state governments, the framers devised a system of two sovereigns, or supreme powers—the states and the nation—with the hope that competition between the two would limit the power of both.

The Bill of Rights. Late in the Philadelphia Convention, a motion was made to include a bill of rights in the Constitution. After a brief debate, it was almost unanimously turned down. Most delegates felt that, because the federal government was already limited to the powers expressed in the Constitution, no further protection for citizens was necessary. These delegates argued that the states should adopt bills of rights instead because their greater powers needed greater limitations. But almost immediately after the Constitution was ratified, a movement to adopt a national bill of rights arose. This is why the Bill of Rights, adopted in 1791, makes up the first 10 amendments to the Constitution and is not incorporated into the body of it. We will further explore the Bill of Rights in Chapter 4.

THE FIGHT FOR RATIFICATION: FEDERALISTS VERSUS ANTIFEDERALISTS

The first hurdle the new Constitution faced was ratification by state conventions of delegates elected by the people of each state. This struggle for ratification thus encompassed 13 separate, state-level campaigns, each influenced by local as well as national considerations. Two major ideological groups faced off throughout the states, however, calling themselves Federalists and Antifederalists (Table 2.2).[21] The Federalists supported the Constitution and preferred a strong national government. The Antifederalists opposed the Constitution and preferred a decentralized federal government; they took their name in reaction to their better-organized opponents.

During the struggle over ratification, Americans argued about great political issues and ideals. How much power should the national government have? What safeguards were most likely to prevent the abuse of power? What institutional arrangements could best ensure adequate representation for all Americans? Which was worse: tyranny of the many or tyranny of the few?

In political life, of course, ideals—and values—are seldom completely divorced from interests. In 1787, divisions along economic, regional, and political lines influenced Americans' attitudes toward these political questions. Many well-to-do merchants and planters favored a stronger central government with the capacity to protect property, promote commerce, and keep the more radical state legislatures in check. At the same time, many powerful state leaders feared that strengthening the national government would reduce their own influence and status. Each of these interests justified its position with an appeal to basic values.

Ideas can be important weapons in political warfare, and seeing how, by whom, and for what interests they are wielded can illuminate their implications. Once an idea has been articulated, however, it can take on a life of its own and have implications that transcend the narrow interest it was initially meant to serve. For instance, some opponents of the Constitution criticized the absence of a bill of rights in the initial document simply in hopes of blocking the entire Constitution's ratification. Yet the Bill of Rights has proved for over two centuries to be a bulwark of civil liberty in the United States. As this example shows, truly great political ideas transcend the interests that initially set them forth.

The first step in evaluating a political value involves understanding who promotes it and why. The second step involves understanding the full implications of the idea itself—implications that may go far beyond the interests that

---

21 An excellent analysis of the ratification campaigns based on a quantitative assessment of the campaigners' own words—as found in campaign documents, pamphlets, tracts, public letters, and the eighteenth-century equivalent of op-ed pieces (such as the individual essays that make up the *Federalist Papers*)—is William H. Riker, *The Strategy of Rhetoric: Campaigning for the American Constitution*, ed. Randall L. Calvert, John Mueller, and Rick K. Wilson (New Haven, CT: Yale University Press, 1996).

Table 2.2

FEDERALISTS VERSUS ANTIFEDERALISTS

	FEDERALISTS	ANTIFEDERALISTS
Who were they?	Property owners, creditors, merchants	Small farmers, frontiersmen, debtors, shopkeepers
What did they believe?	Elites are best fit to govern and "excessive democracy" is dangerous	Government should be close to the people and the concentration of power in the hands of the elites is dangerous
What system of government did they favor?	Strong national government insulated from the whims of public opinion with the power to pursue national goals	Retention of power by state governments and protection of individual rights
Who were their leaders?	Alexander Hamilton, James Madison, George Washington	Patrick Henry, George Mason, Elbridge Gerry, George Clinton

launched it. Whatever clashing interests may have guided them, the Federalists and the Antifederalists presented important alternative visions of America.

During the ratification struggle, thousands of essays, speeches, pamphlets, and letters circulated in support of and in opposition to the proposed Constitution. The best-known pieces supporting ratification were the 85 essays written under the name "Publius" by Alexander Hamilton, James Madison, and John Jay in late 1787 and early 1788. The *Federalist Papers*, as they are known today, defended the principles of the Constitution and sought to dispel fears of a national authority. The Antifederalists published essays of their own, arguing that the new Constitution betrayed the Revolution and was a step toward monarchy. Among the best Antifederalist works were the essays written under the name "Brutus," sometimes attributed to New York Supreme Court justice Robert Yates, that were published in the *New York Journal* at the same time the *Federalist Papers* appeared. The Antifederalist view also appeared in pamphlets and letters that may have been written by a former delegate to the Continental Congress, Richard Henry Lee of Virginia, using the pen name "the Federal Farmer." These essays highlighted the major differences between Federalists and Antifederalists.

Federalists appealed to basic principles of government in support of their nationalist vision. Antifederalists cited equally fundamental precepts to support their vision of a looser confederacy of small republics. The two sides engaged in what was almost certainly the first nationwide political campaign in the history of the world.

Representation

One major area of contention was the question of representation. The Antifederalists asserted that representatives must be "a true picture of the people, . . . [possessing] the knowledge of their circumstances and their wants."[22] This could only be achieved, argued the Antifederalists, in small, relatively homogeneous republics such as the existing states. In their view, the size and extent of the entire nation precluded the construction of a truly representative form of government. Citizens without sufficient representation, in turn, would lack attachment to the national government and refuse to obey its laws. As a result, according to the Antifederalists, the remote federal government described by the Constitution would have to use force to secure popular compliance; the Federal Farmer asserted that its laws would be "in many cases disregarded, unless a multitude of officers and military force be continually kept in view, and employed to enforce the execution of the laws, and to make the government feared and respected."[23]

Federalists, for their part, saw no reason why representatives should be precisely like the people they represented. In their view, government must be representative *of* the people but must also have some autonomy *from* the people, capable of serving the long-term public interest even if doing so conflicted with public opinion. In more contemporary terms, Federalists sought representatives who were *trustees*, whereas Antifederalists sought *delegates*.

Federalists also dismissed the Antifederalists' claim that the distance between representatives and constituents would lead to popular disaffection and compel the government to use force to secure obedience. Federalists replied that the system of representation they proposed was more likely to produce effective government, which, in turn, should inspire popular trust and confidence more effectively than simple social proximity would.

The Threat of Tyranny

A second important issue dividing Federalists and Antifederalists was the threat of **tyranny**: unjust rule by the group in power. Both opponents and defenders of the Constitution frequently affirmed their fear of tyrannical rule. Each side, however, had a different view of the most likely source of tyranny and hence thought differently about how best to forestall it.

From the Antifederalist perspective, the great danger was the tendency of all governments—including republican governments—to become increasingly

 tyranny

Oppressive government that employs the cruel and unjust use of power and authority.

---

22 Melancton Smith, quoted in Herbert J. Storing, *What the Anti-Federalists Were For: The Political Thought of the Opponents of the Constitution* (Chicago: University of Chicago Press, 1981), p. 17.

23 Herbert J. Storing, ed., *The Anti-Federalist* (Chicago: University of Chicago Press, 1985), p. 258.

"aristocratic," with a few individuals in positions of authority gaining more and more power over the general citizenry. In essence, the few would use their power to tyrannize the many. For this reason, Antifederalists were sharply critical of features of the Constitution that divorced governmental institutions from direct responsibility to the people—institutions such as the Senate, the executive, and the federal judiciary.

The Federalists, too, recognized the threat of tyranny; they agreed that individuals could be opportunistic and self-interested. However, they believed that the danger associated with republican governments was not aristocracy but, instead, majority tyranny. The Federalists were concerned that a popular majority, "united and actuated by some common impulse of passion, or of interest, adverse to the rights of other citizens," would endeavor to "trample on the rules of justice."[24] From the Federalist perspective, it was precisely those features of the Constitution that the Antifederalists attacked as potential sources of tyranny that offered the best hope of averting oppression. The size and extent of the nation, for instance, were for the Federalists a bulwark against tyranny. In Madison's famous formulation, reflecting the logic of the collective action principle,

> The smaller the society, the fewer probably will be the distinct parties and interests . . . the more frequently will a majority be found of the same party; and the smaller the number of individuals composing a majority, and the smaller the compass within which they are placed, the more easily will they concert and execute their plans of oppression. Extend the sphere, and you take in a greater variety of parties and interests; you make it less probable that a majority of the whole will have a common motive to invade the rights of other citizens; or if such a common motive exists, it will be more difficult for all who feel it to discover their own strength, and to act in unison with each other.[25]

The Federalists understood that temporary majorities could abuse their power in a democracy, and the Constitution reflects their misgivings. The indirect election of senators, the indirect election of the president, the insulation of the judicial branch from the people, the separation of powers, the president's veto power, the bicameral design of Congress, and the system of federalism were all means to curb majority tyranny. These features suggest, following the institution principle, the framers' awareness of the problems of majority rule and the need for institutional safeguards. Except for the indirect election of senators (which was changed in 1913), these aspects of the constitutional structure remain in place today.[26] In essence, the Federalists sought to place limits

---

24 Rossiter, *Federalist Papers*, no. 10 (James Madison), p. 57.

25 Rossiter, *Federalist Papers*, no. 10 (James Madison), p. 60.

26 A classic development of this theme is found in James M. Buchanan and Gordon Tullock, *The Calculus of Consent: Logical Foundations of Constitutional Democracy* (Ann Arbor: University of Michigan Press, 1962). For a review of the voting paradox and a case study of how it applies today, see Kenneth A. Shepsle, *Analyzing Politics: Rationality, Behavior, and Institutions,* 2nd ed. (New York: Norton, 2010), pp. 53–89.

on collective action in order to protect liberty. We will return to this idea in Chapters 4 and 5.

To some extent, the Federalists and Antifederalists were influenced by different understandings of history. Federalists believed that colonial history, to say nothing of the history of Ancient Greece, showed that mob rule often endangered republican governments. For the Antifederalists, by contrast, history revealed the dangers of aristocratic conspiracies against popular liberties. History matters, but it is always subject to interpretation.

Governmental Power

A third major difference between Federalists and Antifederalists was the issue of governmental power. Both groups agreed on the principle of limited government, but they differed on how best to limit governmental action.

Antifederalists favored limiting and enumerating the powers granted to the national government in relation to both the states and the people at large. To them, the powers given to the national government ought to be "confined to certain defined national objects."[27] Otherwise, the national government would "swallow up all the power of the state governments."[28] Antifederalists bitterly attacked the supremacy clause and the necessary and proper clause of the Constitution as unlimited and dangerous grants of power.[29] They also demanded that a bill of rights be added to the Constitution to limit the government's ability to exercise power over the citizenry.

Federalists favored the construction of a government that could defend the nation against foreign foes, guard against domestic strife and insurrection, promote commerce, and expand the nation's economy. Hamilton pointed out that these goals could not be achieved without allowing the government to exercise broad powers. Federalists acknowledged, of course, that every power could be abused, but they argued that the way to prevent misuse of power was not by depriving government of the strength it needed to achieve national goals. Instead, they argued, abuses of power would be mitigated by the Constitution's system of internal checks. As Madison put it,

> The power surrendered by the people is first divided between two distinct governments, and then the portion allotted to each subdivided among distinct and separate departments. Hence a double security arises to the rights of the people. The different governments will control each other, at the same time that each will be controlled by itself.[30]

27 Herbert J. Storing, *The Complete Anti-Federalist* (Chicago: University of Chicago Press, 1981), vol. 1, pp. 145-50.

28 *The Complete Anti-Federalist*, pp. 145-50.

29 Storing, *What the Anti-Federalists Were For*, p. 28.

30 Rossiter, *Federalist Papers*, no. 51 (James Madison), p. 339.

Because the Federalists' wanted to avoid unwarranted limits on governmental power, they opposed a national bill of rights, which they saw as unnecessarily restrictive. For the Federalists, the issue was one of national versus state power, not substantive rights as such, and they feared that a bill of rights would weaken the federal government relative to the states.

The Federalists acknowledged that abuses of power remained possible, but they felt that the risk had to be taken because of the goals they wanted their government to achieve. "The very idea of power included a possibility of doing harm," said the Federalist John Rutledge during South Carolina's ratification debates. "If the gentleman would show the power that could do no harm," Rutledge continued, "he would at once discover it to be a power that could do no good."[31]

CHANGING THE INSTITUTIONAL FRAMEWORK: CONSTITUTIONAL AMENDMENT

The Constitution has endured for more than two centuries as the framework of government. But it has not endured without change. Without change, the Constitution might have become merely a sacred relic, stored under glass.

Amendments: Many Are Called, Few Are Chosen

The framers of the Constitution recognized the need for change, and they incorporated provisions for amending the document into Article V. Since 1791, when the first 10 amendments (the Bill of Rights) were added, only 17 amendments have been adopted. Two of them—Prohibition and its repeal—cancel each other out. Overall, therefore, only 15 amendments have been added since 1791, despite vast changes in American society and its economy.

Article V provides for four methods of amendment:

1. Passage in the House and Senate, each by two-thirds vote; then ratification by majority vote in the legislatures of three-fourths (now 38) of the states.

2. Passage in the House and Senate, each by two-thirds vote; then ratification by conventions called for that purpose in three-fourths of the states.

3. Passage in a national convention called by Congress in response to petitions by two-thirds (now 34) of the states; ratification by majority vote in the legislatures of three-fourths of the states.

---

31 Quoted in Storing. *What the Anti-Federalists Were For*, p. 30.

4. Passage in a national convention, as in method 3; then ratification by conventions called for that purpose in three-fourths of the states.

Figure 2.2 illustrates each of these methods. Because no amendment has ever been proposed by national convention, however, routes 3 and 4 have never been employed. And route 2 has been used only once (for the Twenty-First Amendment, which repealed the Eighteenth Amendment, or Prohibition). Thus route 1 has been used for all the others.

The Twenty-Seven Amendments

The Constitution and its 27 amendments are reproduced at the end of this book. All but two are concerned with the structure or composition of government. This is consistent with the definition of *constitution* in another sense, as the "makeup or composition of a thing." It is also consistent with the concept of a constitution as higher law, that is, a framework within which government and the process of making ordinary laws can take place. There is

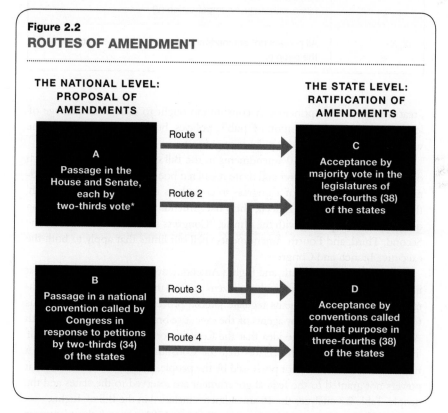

Figure 2.2
ROUTES OF AMENDMENT

THE NATIONAL LEVEL: PROPOSAL OF AMENDMENTS

THE STATE LEVEL: RATIFICATION OF AMENDMENTS

A
Passage in the House and Senate, each by two-thirds vote*

B
Passage in a national convention called by Congress in response to petitions by two-thirds (34) of the states

Route 1

Route 2

Route 3

Route 4

C
Acceptance by majority vote in the legislatures of three-fourths (38) of the states

D
Acceptance by conventions called for that purpose in three-fourths (38) of the states

*In each amendment proposal, Congress has the power to choose the method of ratification, the time limit for consideration by the states, and other conditions of ratification.

Table 2.3

THE BILL OF RIGHTS: ANALYSIS OF ITS PROVISIONS

AMENDMENT	PURPOSE
I	Congress may not make any law establishing a religion or abridging the freedom of speech, press, or assembly or the right to petition the government.
II, III, IV	No branch of government may infringe on the right of people to keep arms (II), force people arbitrarily to let soldiers live in their houses (III), or engage in the search or seizure of evidence or arrest people without a court warrant (IV).
V, VI, VII, VIII	The courts may not hold trials for serious offenses without provision for a grand jury (V), a petit (trial) jury (VII), a speedy trial (VI), the presentation of charges, and the confrontation of hostile witnesses (VI). Individuals may not be compelled to testify against themselves (V) and are immune from trial more than once for the same offense (V). Neither bail nor punishment can be excessive (VIII), and no property can be taken without just compensation (V).
IX, X	All powers not enumerated are reserved to the states or to the people.

great wisdom in this principle. A constitution ought to enable the passage of legislation and implementation of public policies, but it should not determine what that legislation or those policies ought to be.

The purpose of the 10 amendments in the Bill of Rights was to give each of the three branches clearer and more restricted boundaries. The First Amendment restricts the power of Congress to enact laws regulating religion, speech, the press, and assembly. Indeed, the First Amendment makes this limitation quite explicit by opening with the phrase, "Congress shall make no law . . ." The Second, Third, and Fourth Amendments spell out limits that apply to both the executive branch and Congress.

The Fifth, Sixth, Seventh, and Eighth Amendments contain some of the most important safeguards for individual citizens against the exercise of governmental power. These amendments regulate judicial proceedings and outlaw various forms of arbitrary action by agents of the executive branch. The Ninth and Tenth Amendments reinforce the idea that the Constitution creates a government of limited powers. The Ninth declares that the Constitution's failure to mention a right does not mean it is not possessed by the people, while the Tenth states that powers not granted to the federal government are reserved to the states and the people. Table 2.3 analyzes the 10 amendments included in the Bill of Rights.

Six of the 17 amendments adopted since 1791 expand the electorate (Table 2.4). The framers could not agree on uniform qualifications defining

Table 2.4

AMENDING THE CONSTITUTION TO EXPAND THE ELECTORATE

AMENDMENT	PURPOSE	YEAR PROPOSED	YEAR ADOPTED
XIV	Prohibits states from denying voting rights to any male citizen over the age of 21. Provides penalties for states that do so.	1866	1868
XV	Extended voting rights to men of all races	1869	1870
XIX	Extended voting rights to women	1919	1920
XXIII	Extended voting rights to residents of the District of Columbia	1960	1961
XXIV	Extended voting rights to all classes through the abolition of poll taxes	1962	1964
XXVI	Extended voting rights to citizens ages 18–21	1971	1971

the boundaries of the national electorate. Instead, in Article I, Section 2, they indicted that eligibility to vote in a national election would be the same as "the Qualifications requisite for Electors of the most numerous Branch of the State Legislature." Article I, Section 4, added that Congress could alter state regulations as to the "Times, Places and Manner of holding Elections for Senators and Representatives," but said nothing about voting qualifications. This meant that any important expansion of the American electorate would almost certainly require a constitutional amendment.

Six more amendments are also electoral in nature, though not concerned directly with voting rights (Table 2.5). These amendments deal with the elective offices themselves (the Twentieth, Twenty-Second, and Twenty-Fifth) or with the relationships between elective offices and the electorate (the Twelfth, Fourteenth, and Seventeenth).

Another five amendments have expanded or limited the powers of the national and state governments (Table 2.6).[32] The Eleventh Amendment

---

32 The Fourteenth Amendment is included in Table 2.6 as well as Table 2.4 because it not only defines citizenship but also seems to intend that this definition include, along with the right to vote, all rights conferred by the Bill of Rights, regardless of the states in which citizens reside. A great deal more will be said about this in Chapter 4.

Table 2.5

AMENDING THE CONSTITUTION TO CHANGE THE RELATIONSHIP BETWEEN THE ELECTED OFFICES AND THE ELECTORATE

AMENDMENT	PURPOSE	YEAR PROPOSED	YEAR ADOPTED
XII	Provided a separate ballot for the vice president in the Electoral College	1803	1804
XIV	Asserts the principle of national citizenship and prohibits the states from infringing on the rights of citizens of the nation	1866	1868
XVII	Provided for the direct election of senators. This diminished the power of the state legislatures and reinforced the idea of a direct relationship between Americans and the government of the United States.	1912	1913
XX	Shortened the time between elections and the inauguration of the new president and Congress	1932	1933
XXII	Limited the presidential term	1947	1951
XXV	Provided for presidential succession in case of disability	1965	1967

protects the states from suits by private individuals and denies the federal courts any power to hear suits by private individuals of one state (or a foreign country) against another state. Three other amendments presented in Table 2.6 reduce state power (the Thirteenth), reduce state power and expand national power (the Fourteenth), and expand national power (the Sixteenth). The Twenty-Seventh limits Congress's ability to raise its members' salary.

The two missing amendments underscore the meaning of the rest: the Eighteenth Amendment, or Prohibition, and the Twenty-First Amendment, its repeal. They represent the only instance in which the country tried to *legislate* by constitutional amendment. In other words, the Eighteenth is the only

Table 2.6

AMENDING THE CONSTITUTION TO EXPAND OR LIMIT THE POWER OF GOVERNMENT

AMENDMENT	PURPOSE	YEAR PROPOSED	YEAR ADOPTED
XI	Limited the jurisdiction of federal courts over suits involving the states	1794	1795
XIII	Eliminated slavery and the rights of states to allow property in the form of persons	1865*	1865
XIV	Established due process of law in state courts for all persons; later used to apply the entire Bill of Rights to the states	1866	1868
XVI	Established the national power to tax income	1909	1913
XXVII	Limited Congress's power to raise its own salary	1789	1992

* The Thirteenth Amendment was proposed on January 31, 1865, and adopted less than a year later, on December 6, 1865.

amendment that was designed to address a substantive social problem. It is also the only amendment ever to have been repealed. Two other amendments—the Thirteenth, which abolished slavery, and the Sixteenth, which established the federal government's power to levy an income tax—essentially had the effect of legislation. But the purpose of the Thirteenth Amendment was to restrict the states' power by forever forbidding them to treat any human being as property. As for the Sixteenth Amendment, it is certainly true that income tax legislation followed immediately; nevertheless, the amendment concerns itself strictly with establishing Congress's power to enact such legislation.

For those whose hopes for change center on the Constitution, it must be emphasized that the amendment route to social change is, and always will be, extremely limited. This is "path dependency," as captured in the history principle, with a vengeance. The status quo—the original Constitution—and the arduousness of its amendment process provide durability on the one hand and constrain the prospects for change on the other. Through a constitution it is possible to establish a working structure of government, and through a constitution it is possible to establish basic rights of citizens by placing limitations and obligations on that government's powers.

No written constitution can or should prevent political change. We see change every year: at the ballot box, in congressional rules, in the form of new legislation, and so forth. The purpose of a constitution is to maintain boundaries, to protect the rule of law, to ensure the stability without which no economy can function, and to assure citizens that change will not take away their rights and liberties.

CONCLUSION: REFLECTIONS ON THE FOUNDING—IDEALS OR INTERESTS?

At the start of this chapter, we stressed the need to look beyond the myths and rhetoric of the founding era to analyze the Founders' goals, their struggle to resolve their conflicts and reach their collective ambitions, and the institutions that resulted from their endeavor. The story of the Founding— the initial decision of Britain's American colonies to chart a separate course (the Declaration of Independence), a successful revolution and the creation of a confederation of states with a weak central government (the Articles of Confederation), and the creation of an entirely elaborated new body of institutional arrangements (the Constitution)—is a chronicle of purposeful collective action leading to the creation of a unique political scaffolding for governance.

The revolutionary generation, the politicians of the Articles years, and those who met in Philadelphia to create a new nation were rational actors with specific goals. Northern merchants and manufacturers wanted property protection and security; unfettered opportunities to trade in domestic and international markets; and the financial security of sound currency, low taxes, and limited public debt. Southern planters also wanted protection for their property and the slave trade; low tariffs to obtain manufactured goods cheaply; and access to international markets for their products. Small farmers, tradesmen, and artisans wanted easy credit, relief from onerous taxes, and permissive policies toward debt. Independence, loose federation, and finally a new nation with a central government capable of effective action were the goals, at different times, toward which many of these groups pointed.

To orchestrate a revolution, organize a confederation, or draft a constitution requires a large variety of collective actions. Behaviors must be coordinated, participation must be induced, efforts must be focused on common objectives, and free riding must be discouraged. During the founding period, political leaders facilitated this process. Jefferson and Adams brought the colonies to the point of separating from the motherland; George Washington was pivotal in the revolutionary phase; numerous politicians bargained over the directions to be taken by the Confederation; Madison, Hamilton, Washington, and ultimately Franklin presided over the drafting of the Constitution. In sum, collective action, coordinated by motivated leadership, paved the historical path from colony to new nation.

We've also seen that new institutions were needed to organize the new government successfully. Colonial institutions were satisfactory for 150 years, especially while the mother country was preoccupied with events elsewhere. Independence and self-governance became institutional objectives when the burdens of colonialism began to stifle the colonists' economic circumstances and political freedoms. From roughly 1775 to 1790, the Founders experimented with and ultimately crafted a political order that, in most aspects, has survived more than two centuries intact. The final product of the Constitutional Convention stands as an extraordinary victory for the groups that most forcefully wanted a new system of government to replace the Articles of Confederation. Antifederalist criticisms forced the Constitution's proponents to accept a bill of rights designed to limit the powers of the national government. In general, however, it was the Federalist vision of America that triumphed, leading eventually to a powerful national government able to defend the nation's interests, promote its commerce, and maintain national unity.

Though the Constitution was the product of a particular set of political forces, the form of government it established has had significance far beyond its authors' original interests. As we have observed, political ideals often take on lives of their own. The great political values incorporated into the Constitution continue to shape our lives in ways that the framers may not have anticipated. For example, when they empowered Congress to regulate commerce among the states, they could hardly have anticipated that this provision would become the basis for many federal regulatory activities in areas as diverse as the environment and civil rights.

We will discuss two great constitutional notions, federalism and civil liberties, in Chapters 3 and 4, respectively. As we close our discussion of the Founding, though, it is worth reflecting on the Antifederalists. Although they were defeated, they can help us imagine an America that might have been. Would we have been worse or better off if we had been governed by a confederacy of small republics linked by a national administration with limited powers? Were the Antifederalists correct in predicting that a government given great power in the hope that it might do good would, through "insensible progress," inevitably come to serve the interests of the few at the expense of the many? More than two centuries of government under the federal Constitution are not enough to definitively answer these questions. Even today, some argue for an increase in the power of states and local communities. The Antifederalists lost the debate, but only time will tell if they were right or wrong.

For Further Reading

Amar, Akhil Reed. *The Constitution Today: Timeless Lessons for the Issues of Our Era.* New York: Basic Books, 2016.

Atkinson, Rick. *The Revolution Trilogy.* Vol. 1, *The British Are Coming.* New York: Henry Holt, 2019.

Bailyn, Bernard. *The Ideological Origins of the American Revolution.* Cambridge, MA: Harvard University Press, 1967.

Beard, Charles A. *An Economic Interpretation of the Constitution of the United States.* New York: Macmillan, 1913.

Dahl, Robert. *How Democratic Is the American Constitution?* 2nd ed. New Haven, CT: Yale University Press, 2003.

Farrand, Max, ed. *The Records of the Federal Convention of 1787.* Rev. ed. 4 vols. New Haven, CT: Yale University Press, 1966.

Ferling, John. *Whirlwind: The American Revolution and the War That Won It.* New York: Bloomsbury Press, 2015.

Gerstle, Gary. *Liberty and Coercion: The Paradox of American Government from the Founding to the Present.* Princeton, NJ: Princeton University Press, 2015.

Gienapp, Jonathan. *The Second Creation: Fixing the American Constitution in the Founding Era.* Cambridge, MA: Belknap Press, 2018.

Glaeser, Edward L. "Revolution of Urban Rebels." *Boston Globe*, July 4, 2008, sec. A.

Jones, Martha S. *Birthright Citizens: A History of Race and Rights in Antebellum America.* New York: Cambridge University Press, 2018.

Paulson, Michael S., and Luke Paulson, *The Constitution: An Introduction.* New York: Basic Books, 2017.

Riker, William H. *The Strategy of Rhetoric: Campaigning for the American Constitution.* Edited by Randall L. Calvert, John Mueller, and Rick K. Wilson. New Haven, CT: Yale University Press, 1996.

Rossiter, Clinton L., ed. *The Federalist Papers; Alexander Hamilton, James Madison, and John Jay*, esp. nos. 10 and 51. New York: New American Library, 1961.

Stewart, David O. *Madison's Gift: Five Partnerships That Built America.* New York: Simon and Schuster, 2015.

Storing, Herbert J., ed. *The Complete Anti-Federalist.* 7 vols. Chicago: University of Chicago Press, 1981.

West, Thomas G. *The Political Theory of the American Founding: Natural Rights, Public Policy, and the Moral Conditions of Freedom.* New York: Cambridge University Press, 2017.

Wilentz, Sean. *No Property in Man: Slavery and Antislavery at the Nation's Founding.* Cambridge, MA: Harvard University Press, 2018.

3

Federalism and the Separation of Powers

Two of the United States' most important institutional features are federalism and the separation of powers. Federalism seeks to limit government by dividing it into two levels, national and state, each with sufficient independence to compete with the other, thereby restraining the power of both.[1] The separation of powers seeks to limit the national government's power by dividing government against itself—by giving the legislative, executive, and judicial branches separate functions, thus forcing them to share power. Both federalism and the separation of powers derive from James Madison's idea, developed in *Federalist 51*, that the best way to restrain governmental power is to divide it among several institutions that will work to keep one another in check. Setting "power against power," in Madison's words, would be a far more effective means of protecting citizens' liberties than merely guaranteeing liberties on paper.[2]

In Chapter 1 we observed that institutions organize political life. Institutions, however, take many forms and can choreograph collective action in a variety of ways. One important way in which political institutions vary is the manner in which they distribute decision, agenda, and veto powers. Institutions established by authoritarian regimes usually concentrate power in a small group of leaders who determine what laws and policies will be considered, make the

---

1   The notion that federalism requires separate spheres or jurisdictions in which lower and higher levels of government are uniquely decisive is developed fully in William H. Riker, *Federalism: Origin, Operation, Significance* (Boston: Little, Brown, 1964). The American version of federalism is applied to the federal arrangements emerging in the People's Republic of China during the 1990s in Barry R. Weingast, "The Economic Role of Political Institutions: Market-Preserving Federalism and Economic Development," *Journal of Law, Economics, and Organization* 11, no. 1 (1995): 1-31.

2   Clinton L. Rossiter, ed., *The Federalist Papers; Alexander Hamilton, James Madison, and John Jay* (New York: New American Library, 1961), no. 51 (James Madison), p. 337.

---

final decisions, and seek to block the actions of others. The political institutions of democratic states, in contrast, usually allow a variety of groups to participate in decision making and provide at least a measure of agenda and veto power to numerous actors.

In the United States, the framers of the Constitution created institutions that would widely disperse involvement in decision making. Federalism assigns agenda, decision, and veto powers to the federal government and to each of the 50 states. The separation of powers gives several federal institutions a degree of control over the agenda, the power to affect decisions, and the ability to block the actions of other institutions. The framers feared that concentrating power in a small number of hands would threaten citizens' liberties, and they were correct. Yet, although the dispersion of power among federal institutions and between the federal government and the states may well protect our liberties, it often makes collective action seem impossible. This lack of decisiveness sometimes appears to negate the most important reason for building institutions in the first place.

Since the adoption of the Constitution, politicians have developed various strategies for overcoming the barriers to policy change that inevitably arise in our federal system of separated powers. Often, those seeking to promote a new program will find ways of spreading the program's benefits so other politicians find it in their interest to go along. For example, if the executive branch hopes to win congressional support for a new weapons system, it may try to ensure that portions of the new system are subcontracted to firms in as many congressional districts as possible. In this way, dispersion of benefits can help overcome the separation of powers between the executive and legislative branches. Similarly, as we see later in this chapter, federal officials often secure state cooperation with national programs by offering the states funding, in the form of grants-in-aid, in exchange for their compliance. In this way, grants help overcome the limitations of federalism. Thus, consistent with our discussion of the five

LEARNING OBJECTIVES

 Define federalism and explain how it limits national power.

 Trace how federalism evolved in the United States from the Founding through the twentieth century.

 Describe the shift toward increased national power since 1937 and the major features of American federalism today.

 Identify the major checks and balances among the institutions of government.

principles of politics in Chapter 1, America's public policies are shaped by the institutions—in these examples, the separation of powers and federalism—through which individual efforts must flow.

However, institutions are not carved in stone. They are subject to modification as competing forces seek new decision-making powers that will give them an advantage, and as the leaders of institutions seek to strengthen their own power and expand their own jurisdictions at the expense of other institutions. In recent decades, for instance, the presidency has increased in power relative to Congress, and the jurisdiction of the federal government has grown relative to that of the states. Nevertheless, the core institutional features of federalism and the separation of powers remain at the heart of the American system of government. Let's examine them and assess their consequences for American government.

WHO DOES WHAT? FEDERALISM AND INSTITUTIONAL JURISDICTIONS

federalism

The system of government in which a constitution divides power between a central government and regional governments.

sovereignty

Independent political authority.

Federalism can be defined as the division of powers and functions between the national government and the state governments. By endowing these two levels of government with significant **sovereignty**, federalism effectively limits the power of both levels, as each has the ability to restrain the other. As we saw in Chapter 2, the states existed as individual colonies before independence, and for nearly 13 years they operated as virtually autonomous units under the Articles of Confederation. In effect, the Articles granted the states too much power relative to the national government, a problem that led directly to the Annapolis Convention in 1786 and to the Constitutional Convention in 1787. Disorder within states was beyond the reach of the national government during this time (see Shays's Rebellion, discussed in Chapter 2), and conflicts of interest between states were not manageable. For example, states were making their own trade agreements with foreign countries and companies, which then played the states against each other to win special advantages. Some states adopted barriers to foreign commerce that were contrary to the interests of other states.[3] States also erected tax and trade barriers among themselves.[4] But even after ratification of the Constitution, the states remained more important than the national government. For nearly a century and a half, virtually all of the fundamental policies governing Americans' lives were made by state legislatures, not by Congress.

3   For a good treatment of these conflicts of interest between states, see Forrest McDonald, *E Pluribus Unum: The Formation of the American Republic, 1776–1790* (Boston: Houghton Mifflin, 1965), chap. 7, esp. pp. 319–38.

4   See David M. O'Brien and Gordon Silverstein, *Constitutional Law and Politics*, 11th ed. (New York: Norton, 2020), vol. 1, pp. 601–3.

Why Keep the States: The Importance of History

Many of the Constitution's framers, particularly Alexander Hamilton, had hoped to create something close to a unitary national government that severely circumscribed the power of the individual states. The fact that the framers established a federal system in which the states retained significant powers illustrates the importance of history. Each state had well-established governmental institutions staffed by legislators, judges, and executive officials who had no desire to see their power and autonomy submerged in a new national government. At the same time, citizens identified with their own states. The people of the former colonies were not "Americans"; rather, they had already been identifying, for several generations, as Virginians, New Yorkers, Pennsylvanians, and so on. For this reason, even the most nationalistic framers had to accept that the states would continue as important entities. In a sense, the framers faced the same historical realities faced today by advocates of a stronger European Union (EU). The nations of Europe have historically distinct identities, well-entrenched governments, and loyal citizens. Given the force of history, uniting these nations is no easy matter and is never guaranteed to be successful, as the world saw when the United Kingdom voted to leave the EU in 2016. Britain's formal departure from the EU, known as Brexit, took place in 2020. Like America's founders, the architects of the EU, bowing to history, built the regime on federal foundations. A federal system also allows geographically concentrated groups to wield more power than they would be able to wield in a central system.

Federalism in the Constitution: Who Decides What

The Constitution reifies the principle of federalism by recognizing two sovereign powers: it grants a few expressed powers to the national government and reserves the rest to the states. Thus the Constitution defines the jurisdiction of each level of government.

The Powers of the National Government. As we saw in Chapter 2, the expressed powers granted to the national government are found in Article I, Section 8, of the Constitution. These 17 powers include the powers to collect taxes, coin money, declare war, and regulate commerce (which became a very important power for the national government). Article I, Section 8, also contains an important additional source of federal power: the **implied powers** that enable Congress "to make all Laws which shall be necessary and proper for carrying into Execution the foregoing Powers." Not until several decades after the Founding did the Supreme Court allow Congress to exercise these powers, but ultimately the necessary and proper clause allowed the national government to expand the scope of its authority. In addition to expressed and implied powers, the Constitution affirms the national government's power in the supremacy clause (Article VI), which distinguishes all national laws and treaties as "the supreme Law of the Land."

 implied powers

Powers derived from the necessary and proper clause (Article I, Section 8) of the Constitution. Such powers are not specifically expressed in the Constitution but are implied through the interpretation of delegated powers.

The Powers of State Governments. One way in which the framers preserved a strong role for the states was through the Tenth Amendment. This amendment presents a decision rule, or a general principle that governs decision making, stating that the powers the Constitution does not delegate to the national government or deny to the states are "reserved to the States respectively, or to the people." The Antifederalists, who feared that a strong central government would encroach on individual liberty, pressed for such an amendment as a way of limiting national power. Federalists agreed to the amendment because they did not think it would do much harm, given the powers the Constitution already granted to the national government. The Tenth Amendment is also called the **reserved powers** amendment because it aims to reserve powers to the states.

The most fundamental power retained by the states is that of coercion—the power to develop and enforce criminal codes, administer health and safety rules, and regulate the family via marriage and divorce laws. The states also have the power to regulate individuals' livelihoods: if you're a doctor, a lawyer, a plumber, or a barber, for instance, you must be licensed by the state. Even more fundamental, the states have the power to define private property; private property exists because state laws against trespassing define who is and who is not entitled to use a piece of property. If you own a car, your ownership isn't worth much unless the state is willing to enforce your right to possession by making it a crime for anyone else to drive your car without your permission. Similarly, your ownership of a house or piece of land means that the state will enforce your possession by prohibiting others from occupying the property against your will. At the same time, however, under its power of **eminent domain**, the state may seize your property for anything it deems to be a public purpose (though it is required by its own constitution and the federal Constitution to compensate you for your loss).

A state's authority to regulate these fundamental matters, commonly referred to as the **police power** of the state, includes the power to regulate the health, safety, welfare, and morals of its citizens. When you are issued a traffic ticket, the state is exercising its police power, often through the agency of a county or city police officer. Policing is what states do—they coerce you in the name of the community for the purpose of maintaining public order. This was exactly the type of power that the Founders intended the states to exercise.

In some policy areas, the states share **concurrent powers** with the national government. For example, they share some power to regulate commerce and affect the currency by chartering banks, granting or denying corporate charters, and regulating product quality or labor conditions.

The issue of concurrent versus exclusive power has come up at times in our history. Whenever federal and state laws directly conflict, the issue is generally resolved in favor of national supremacy. However, when the federal government does not set a strong policy in an area of concurrent powers, states can each decide their own policies. Analyzing the Evidence on pp. 78–9 explores the states' varying approaches to renewable energy policies in the absence of a strong national policy.

---

reserved powers

Powers that are not specifically delegated to the national government or denied to the states by the Constitution. Under the Tenth Amendment, these powers are reserved to the states.

---

eminent domain

The right of the government to take private property for public use, with reasonable compensation awarded to the owner.

---

police power

The power reserved to the state governments to regulate the health, safety, and morals of citizens.

---

concurrent powers

Authority possessed by *both* state and national governments, such as the power to levy taxes.

States' Obligations to One Another. The Constitution also creates obligations among the states. These obligations, spelled out in Article IV, were intended to promote national unity. By requiring the states to recognize actions taken in other states as legal and proper, the framers aimed to make the states less like independent countries and more like parts of a single nation. Article IV, Section 1, calls for "Full Faith and Credit" among states, meaning that each state is expected to honor the "public Acts, Records, and Proceedings" that take place in any other state. So, for example, if two people are married in Texas—marriage being regulated by state law—Missouri must recognize that marriage even though the couple was not married under Missouri state law.

This **full faith and credit clause** recently became an important factor in a case involving adoption. The 2016 case of *V.L. v. E.L.* involved a same-sex couple and their children, who were the biological children of one parent and legally adopted by the other parent in the state of Georgia. When the couple moved to Alabama and separated, the parent who had adopted the children was denied joint custody and visitation rights because the state of Alabama refused to recognize the legal validity of the adoption. However, the Supreme Court held that the full faith and credit clause required Alabama courts to recognize the Georgia adoption.[5]

Article IV, Section 2, known as the **comity clause**, also promotes national unity; it provides that citizens enjoying the "privileges and immunities" of one state should be entitled to similar treatment in other states. Essentially, a state cannot discriminate against someone from another state or give special privileges to its own residents. For example, in the 1970s, the Supreme Court struck down as unconstitutional an Alaska law that gave residents preference over non-residents in obtaining work on the state's oil and gas pipelines.[6] There are many exceptions to the comity clause. For example, states may charge out-of-state students a higher tuition rate at state colleges and universities.

The comity clause also regulates criminal justice among the states by requiring states to return fugitives to other states from which they have fled. For example, in 1952, when an Alabama inmate escaped and sought to avoid being returned on the grounds that he was being subjected to "cruel and unusual punishment" there, the Supreme Court ruled that he must be returned, according to Article IV, Section 2.[7] This case highlights the difference between the obligations among states and those among different countries. For example, despite the recent restoration of diplomatic relations between Cuba and the United States, Cuba refused in 2017 to return several American fugitives who had claimed asylum in the country, including convicted murderer Joanne Chesimard. The Constitution clearly forbids states from doing something similar.

 full faith and credit clause

The provision in Article IV, Section 1, of the Constitution requiring that each state normally honor the governmental actions and judicial decisions that take place in another state.

 comity clause

Article IV, Section 2 of the Constitution, which prohibits states from enacting laws that treat the citizens of other states in a discriminatory manner.

5   *V.L. v. E.L.*, 577 U.S. ____ (2016).

6   *Hicklin v. Orbeck*, 437 U.S. 518 (1978).

7   *Sweeney v. Woodall*, 344 U.S. 86 (1952).

State Policies on Renewable Energy

Contributed by
David Konisky
Indiana University

In a federal system like the United States, laws and policies may vary considerably from state to state. Over the past two decades, many state governments have put in place policies to stimulate the development and use of renewable energy sources such as wind and solar power. One of the key policies that states have employed is the renewable portfolio standard (RPS). An RPS is a mandate that a state's electricity providers generate a specific amount of their power from renewable sources by a particular date.

How do these renewable energy policies differ from state to state, and how does that variation affect outcomes across states? As the map below shows, as of early 2020, 30 states and the District of Columbia had binding RPS policies in place, and an additional 7 states had voluntary RPS goals. States with RPSs are located throughout the country, with the notable exception of the southeastern United States where only North Carolina has a mandatory standard.

State RPSs vary considerably with respect to the target percentage of renewable energy use and the date of expected achievement. States with ambitious targets include Oregon (50 percent by 2040), California (60 percent by 2030), New York (70 percent by 2030), Vermont (75 percent by 2032), and Hawaii (100 percent by 2045).

State Renewable Energy Policies

● Mandatory RPS ● Voluntary RPS goal ● None

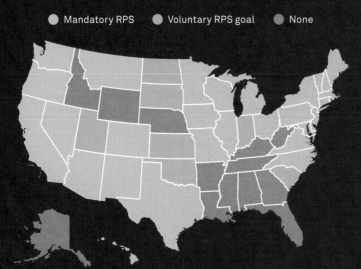

RPS TARGETS (SELECTED STATES)	
California	60% by 2030
Texas	5880 MW by 2015
New York	70% by 2030
Ohio	8.5% by 2026
Pennsylvania	18% by 2021
Illinois	25% by 2026
Colorado	30% by 2020
North Carolina	12.5% by 2021
Missouri	15% by 2021

SOURCE: NC Clean Technology Center, https://s3.amazonaws.com/ncsolarcen-prod/wp-content/uploads/2019/07/
RPS-CES-June2019.pdf (accessed 3/15/20); National Conference of State Legislatures, "State Renewable Portfolio Standards and Goals," April 17, 2020, https://www.ncsl.org/research/energy/renewable-portfolio-standards.aspx (accessed 4/27/20).

Another important way in which RPSs differ is in terms of what counts as renewable energy. Generally, all of the standards include wind and solar power, but some have broader definitions of renewable sources (for example, many include energy efficiency), and several require a portion of the electricity to come from specific sources. For example, the Illinois RPS specifies that 75 percent comes from wind power, and the Maryland RPS requires that 2.5 percent comes from solar power.

Do RPS policies work? The graph below shows how much electricity has been generated from renewable sources since 2000. In states that have mandatory RPSs, electricity generation from non-hydroelectric renewable sources increased by almost 1,500 percent between 2000 and 2018. The use of renewable energy has grown in other states as well, but to a much smaller degree. For this reason, RPSs are often promoted as an effective way to reduce emissions of air pollutants, such as sulfur dioxide, nitrogen oxides, and volatile organic compounds that cause smog, and greenhouse gases like carbon dioxide that contribute to climate change.

Particularly in the absence of a strong national policy on renewable energy, state-level RPS policies have helped start a transition in the U.S. electricity sector toward cleaner, less carbon-intensive sources of energy.

Renewable Energy Generation*

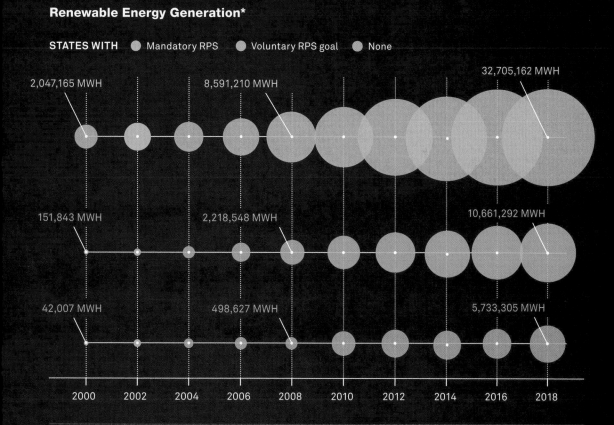

STATES WITH ● Mandatory RPS ● Voluntary RPS goal ● None

2,047,165 MWH   8,591,210 MWH   32,705,162 MWH

151,843 MWH   2,218,548 MWH   10,661,292 MWH

42,007 MWH   498,627 MWH   5,733,305 MWH

2000 2002 2004 2006 2008 2010 2012 2014 2016 2018

* Non-hydroelectric renewable energy measured in megawatt hours.

SOURCE: U.S. Energy Information Administration, https://www.eia.gov/electricity/data/state/ (accessed 3/15/20).

Limitations on the States. Although most of the truly coercive powers are reserved to the states, the Constitution does impose some significant limitations, including those placed on states by the full faith and credit and comity clauses. Another potential limit on states is in a clause in Article I, Section 10, which provides that "no State shall, without the Consent of Congress, ... enter into any Agreement or Compact with another State." Compacts are legally binding agreements that allow two or more states to solve a problem that crosses state lines. In the early years of the Republic, states turned to compacts primarily to settle border disputes. Today, subject to the approval of the federal government, compacts cover a wide range of issues but are especially important in regulating the distribution of river water, addressing environmental concerns, and operating transportation systems that cross state lines.[8] A well-known example is the Port of New York Authority (now the Port Authority of New York and New Jersey), an organization formed by a compact between New York and New Jersey in 1921. Without it, such public works as the enormous Verrazzano-Narrows Bridge connecting Brooklyn and Staten Island, the bridges connecting New Jersey and Staten Island, the Lincoln Tunnel, the George Washington Bridge, and the expansion and integration of the three major airports that serve New York City could not have been financed or completed.[9]

The federal government has occasionally blocked a proposed interstate compact, thus limiting state action in certain spheres.

Local Government and the Constitution. Local government, including the structures that govern counties, cities, and towns, occupies a peculiar but very important place in the American system. In fact, the status of American local government is probably unique among governments around the world. First, it must be pointed out that local government has no status in the American Constitution. *State* legislatures create (and can eliminate or redraw the boundaries of) local governments, and *state* constitutions and laws permit local governments to take on some of the state-level responsibilities. Most states amended their own constitutions to give their larger cities **home rule**—a guarantee of state noninterference in various areas of local affairs.[10]

Local governments became important early in the Republic because the states possessed little administrative capability; states relied on cities and counties

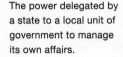

home rule

The power delegated by a state to a local unit of government to manage its own affairs.

---

8 Patricia S. Florestano, "Past and Present Utilization of Interstate Compacts in the United States," *Publius* 24, no. 4 (Fall 1994): 13-25.

9 A good discussion of the political status of the New York Port Authority is found in Wallace Sayre and Herbert Kaufman, *Governing New York City: Politics in the Metropolis* (New York: Russell Sage Foundation, 1960), chap. 9.

10 A good discussion of the constitutional position of local governments is in York Y. Willbern, *The Withering Away of the City* (Birmingham: University of Alabama Press, 1964). For more on the structure and theory of federalism, see Thomas R. Dye, *American Federalism: Competition among Governments* (Lexington, MA: Lexington Books, 1990), chap. 1; and Martha Derthick, "Up-to-Date in Kansas City: Reflections on American Federalism," *PS: Political Science and Politics* 25, no. 4 (December 1992): 671-5.

to implement their laws. Local government thus provided an alternative to a statewide bureaucracy. Today, local governments and state bureaucracies both compete and cooperate with one another. Take, for example, the relationship between state and county police forces, which usually involve a mix of collegiality and rivalry.

The Slow Growth of the National Government's Power

Before the 1930s, America's federal system was essentially one of **dual federalism**: a two-layered system—national and state—in which the states and their local principalities did most of the governing. That is, the jurisdiction of the states was broader than that of the federal government. We call this the "traditional" system because it remained relatively stable during two-thirds of America's history (with the exception of the Civil War years).

Under dual federalism, the state and federal tiers were functionally quite different from each other, and every generation since the Founding debated how to divide responsibilities between the two. As we have seen, the Constitution delegates specific powers to the national government and reserves the rest to the states. The final, "elastic" clause of Article I, Section 8, however, leaves room for interpretation; the three words *necessary and proper* have invited struggle over the distribution of powers between national and state governments throughout the nation's history. In the period of dual federalism, however, the national government remained steadfastly within the strict limits established by Article I, Section 8.

In the early years, the Supreme Court delivered several decisive rulings on the distribution of powers between national and state governments. At issue in the first such case, *McCulloch v. Maryland* (1819), was whether Congress could charter a bank—in particular, the Bank of the United States, which Congress had created in 1791 over Thomas Jefferson's opposition.[11] Although no express power to create banks exists in Article I, Section 8, Chief Justice John Marshall stated that such a power could be "implied" from the **commerce clause** by applying the necessary and proper clause. Essentially, Marshall ruled that if the Constitution permitted Congress to exercise a certain power, and it did not specifically prohibit the means by which Congress chose to exercise that power, then Congress's action would be permissible. Because the Constitution expressly granted Congress the power to regulate commerce, and chartering a bank was both reasonably related to commerce and not prohibited by the Constitution, Congress's action was constitutionally permissible.

With this decision, the Court significantly increased the potential scope of the national government's power: Congress could now exercise powers implied by the powers specifically mentioned in Article I, Section 8. The power to regulate commerce, in particular, has become the foundation of a vast array of

 dual federalism

The system of government that prevailed in the United States from 1789 to 1937, in which fundamental governmental powers were shared between the federal and state governments, with the states exercising the most important powers.

 commerce clause

The clause found in Article I, Section 8, of the Constitution that delegates to Congress the power "to regulate Commerce with foreign Nations, and among the several States, and with the Indian Tribes."

---

11 *McCulloch v. Maryland*, 17 U.S. 316 (1819).

governmental actions not mentioned in the Constitution. A network of communications satellites, for example, would have been beyond the wildest dreams of the framers, but Congress had no difficulty finding authority in the commerce clause for regulating this industry.

A second question of national versus state power arose in *McCulloch*: Could the state of Maryland tax the bank that Congress had created? Again, Marshall and the Supreme Court sided with the national government, arguing that a bank created by a legislature representing all the people (Congress) could not be taxed by a state legislature (Maryland) representing only a fraction of the American people. Here, the Supreme Court relied on the supremacy clause of Article VI: whenever a state law conflicts with a federal law, the state law is invalid because "the Laws of the United States . . . shall be the supreme Law of the Land." (For more on federal supremacy, see Chapters 2 and 9.)

The Court reinforced its nationalistic interpretation of the Constitution with its 1824 decision in *Gibbons v. Ogden*. At issue was whether the state of New York could grant a monopoly to a steamboat company to operate between New York and New Jersey. Aaron Ogden had secured his license from the state, whereas Thomas Gibbons, a former partner of Ogden's, had secured a competing license from the U.S. government. Chief Justice Marshall argued that Gibbons could not be kept from competing because the state of New York did not have the power to grant the monopoly in the first place, since it affected the commercial interests of other states. Marshall based his decision on the commerce clause, which delegates to Congress the power "to regulate Commerce with foreign nations, and *among the several States* and with Indian tribes" (emphasis added). Marshall insisted that the definition of "commerce" in this clause was "comprehensive" but added that the comprehensiveness was limited "to that commerce which concerns more states than one." This opinion gave rise to the legal concept that later came to be called interstate commerce.[12]

Despite the Court's expansive reading of national power in the Republic's early years, between the 1820s and the 1930s federal power grew slowly. However, efforts to expand the national government's power were bitterly contested. During the presidency of Andrew Jackson, a **states' rights** coalition developed in Congress. Among the most important members were state party leaders who often directed their state legislatures to appoint them to the Senate, where they jealously guarded the powers of the states they ruled. Of course, the representatives from the South had a particular reason to support states' rights: so long as the states were powerful and the federal government was weak, the institution of slavery could not be threatened.

Aside from the interruption of the Civil War, the states' rights coalition dominated the federal government until the 1930s: it controlled Congress, affected presidential nominations—a matter also controlled by state party leaders—and influenced judicial appointments. Indeed, the Supreme Court turned away from Chief Justice Marshall's nationalistic jurisprudence in favor of a states' rights interpretation of the Constitution, especially in cases concerning the commerce clause.

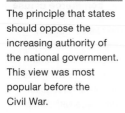

states' rights

The principle that states should oppose the increasing authority of the national government. This view was most popular before the Civil War.

---

12 *Gibbons v. Ogden*, 22 U.S. 1 (1824).

Despite the establishment of important federal agencies, such as the Interstate Commerce Commission (1887) and the Federal Trade Commission (1914), which were built to lay the groundwork for federal economic management, the Supreme Court generally ruled against federal intervention in commercial issues of fraud, the production of impure goods, the use of child labor, or the existence of dangerous working conditions or long hours. Regulation in these areas would mean that the federal government was entering the factory and the workplace—areas that the Court considered inherently local because the goods produced there had not yet been bought or sold across state lines. Rather, the Court held that regulation of these spaces fell under the realm of police power, a power reserved to the states. No one questioned the power of the national government to regulate certain kinds of businesses, such as railroads, gas pipelines, and waterway transportation, because they intrinsically involved interstate commerce.[13] But well into the twentieth century, most other efforts by Congress to regulate commerce were blocked by the Supreme Court's restrictive understanding of federalism.

After his election in 1932, President Franklin Delano Roosevelt was eager to expand the power of the national government; the success of his New Deal agenda depended on governmental power to regulate the economy and to intervene in every facet of American society. Roosevelt's efforts provoked sharp conflicts between the executive branch and the federal judiciary. After appointing a host of new judges and threatening to expand the size of the Supreme Court, Roosevelt managed to bend the judiciary to his will. Beginning in the late 1930s, the Court issued a series of decisions that would solidify the commerce clause as a great engine of national power.

One key case was *National Labor Relations Board v. Jones & Laughlin Steel Corporation* (1937).[14] At issue was the National Labor Relations Act, which prohibited corporations from interfering with employees' efforts to unionize, to bargain collectively over wages and working conditions, and to go on strike and engage in picketing. When the newly formed National Labor Relations Board (NLRB) ordered Jones & Laughlin to reinstate workers whom the company had fired because of their union activities, the steel company refused on the grounds that its manufacturing activities, being local, were constitutionally beyond the federal government's reach. The Court ruled in favor of the NLRB, however, arguing that a large corporation with subsidiaries and suppliers in many states was inherently involved in interstate commerce and hence subject to congressional regulation. In other important decisions that strengthened the power of the commerce clause, the Court upheld minimum wage laws, the Social Security Act, and federal rules controlling how much of any given commodity local farmers might grow.[15]

13 In *Wabash, St. Louis, and Pacific Railway Company v. Illinois,* 118 U.S. 557 (1886), the Supreme Court struck down a state-level railroad regulation as a violation of the commerce clause. In response, Congress passed the Interstate Commerce Act of 1887, creating the Interstate Commerce Commission, the first federal regulatory agency.

14 *National Labor Relations Board v. Jones & Laughlin Steel Corporation,* 301 U.S. 1 (1937).

15 *Wickard v. Filburn,* 317 U.S. 111 (1942).

Federal and State/Local Spending, 1930–2019

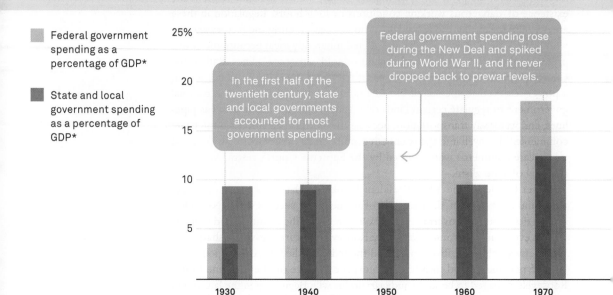

Federal government spending as a percentage of GDP*

State and local government spending as a percentage of GDP*

In the first half of the twentieth century, state and local governments accounted for most government spending.

Federal government spending rose during the New Deal and spiked during World War II, and it never dropped back to prewar levels.

Years shown: 1930, 1940, 1950, 1960, 1970

*TIMEPLOT NOTE: GDP, or gross domestic product, is a measure of the economy as a whole based on the total value of goods and services produced within the country.

TIMEPLOT SOURCE: Michael Shuyler, "A Short History of Government Taxing and Spending in the United States," https://taxfoundation.org/short-history-government-taxing-and-spending-united-states/; Federal Reserve Economic Data, "Federal Net Outlays as Percent of Gross Domestic Product," https://fred.stlouisfed.org/series/FYONGDA188S and "State and Local Government Current Expenditures," https://fred.stlouisfed.org/series/SLEXPND (accessed 5/6/20).

After 1937, the Court threw out the old distinction between interstate and intrastate commerce. The Court would not even review appeals that challenged congressional acts contributing to the "regulatory state" and the "welfare state," such as those that protected employees' rights to organize and engage in collective bargaining, regulated the amount of farmland in cultivation, extended low-interest credit to small businesses and farmers, and restricted corporate activities dealing in the stock market. These decisions and other New Deal programs signaled the beginning of a significant shift toward national government power. As the Timeplot shows, spending on federal programs surpassed spending by state and local governments after the 1940s and has increased over the past 80 years.

Cooperative Federalism and Grants-in-Aid: Institutions Shape Policies

Roosevelt was able to overcome judicial resistance to his expansive New Deal programs, but Congress forced him to recognize the continuing importance of the states. It carried out Roosevelt's policy agenda in a way that encouraged the

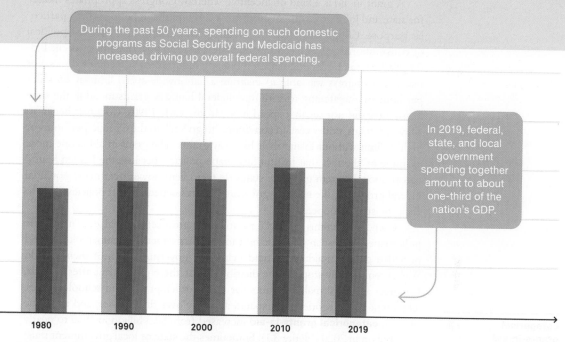

During the past 50 years, spending on such domestic programs as Social Security and Medicaid has increased, driving up overall federal spending.

In 2019, federal, state, and local government spending together amount to about one-third of the nation's GDP.

| 1980 | 1990 | 2000 | 2010 | 2019 |

states to pursue nationally set goals while leaving them some leeway to administer programs according to local needs.

If the traditional system of two sovereigns performing highly different functions can be called dual federalism, then the system that prevailed after the 1930s could be called **cooperative federalism**: a system of supportive relations, sometimes partnerships, between the national government and the state and local governments. Under this brand of federalism, the federal government subsidizes strategic state and local activities through **grants-in-aid**. Because many of these state and local programs would not exist without the grants-in-aid, the grants are an important form of federal influence. (We discuss another form of federal influence, the mandate, in the next section.)

Thus the shift from dual federalism to cooperative federalism was a subtle but important institutional change. Whereas dual federalism left decision, agenda, and veto powers with respect to domestic policy firmly in the hands of the states, cooperative federalism gave the federal government far greater control over the domestic political agenda. Under dual federalism, for example, corporations mainly concerned themselves with state-level regulation of their business. Most firms hardly even lobbied in Washington. With the emergence of cooperative federalism and a more prominent role for the federal

 cooperative federalism

The system of government that has prevailed in the United States since the New Deal era (beginning in the 1930s), in which grants-in-aid have been used strategically to encourage states and localities to pursue nationally defined goals.

 grants-in-aid

Funds given by Congress to state and local governments on the condition that they be used for a specific purpose.

government in the nation's economy, hardly any firm could afford not to lobby in Washington.

A grant-in-aid is a kind of incentive whereby Congress appropriates money for state and local governments with the condition that it be spent for a particular purpose. Congress uses grants-in-aid because it does not have the political or constitutional power to command state and local governments to do its bidding. When you can't command, a monetary inducement sometimes works. For instance, Congress was able to institute a nationwide speed limit of 55 miles per hour by threatening to withdraw federal highway grants-in-aid if the state legislatures did not set that speed limit. In the early 1990s, Congress began to allow the states, under certain conditions, to go back to the 65-mile-per-hour (or higher) limit without losing their highway grants. The grant-in-aid is one more example of the fact that institutions shape policies: because the United States' constitutional system gives the states de facto veto power over many potential federal programs, the national government has learned to craft policies likely to elicit the states' cooperation.

When applying this approach to cities, Congress set national goals in specific policy categories, such as public housing and assistance to the unemployed, and provided grants-in-aid that would help local governments meet them. World War II temporarily stopped the distribution of these grants. But after the war, Congress resumed making grants for urban development and school lunches. The range of categories has expanded greatly over the decades, and the value of such **categorical grants-in-aid** increased from $2.3 billion in 1950 to nearly $750 billion in 2020 (Figure 3.1). Sometimes the state or local government must match the national contribution, but for some programs the congressional grant-in-aid covers much of the cost. Recently, President Trump threatened to withdraw aid from states and cities that refuse to enforce immigration laws. Several states, including California, have declared themselves to be "sanctuary states" for undocumented immigrants. Within these states, some cities have defied the state government's resistance to federal policy. Bakersfield, California, for example, declared that it was a "law and order" city, not a sanctuary.[16]

For the most part, the categorical grants created before the 1960s simply helped the states perform their traditional functions, such as educating and policing.[17] In the 1960s, however, the role of categorical grants expanded. For example, during the 89th Congress (1965–66) alone, the number of categorical grant-in-aid programs grew from 221 to 379.[18] The grants authorized during this decade announced national purposes much more strongly than earlier grants did. Central to that national purpose was the need to provide opportunities to the poor.

categorical grants-in-aid

Funds given to state and local governments by Congress that are earmarked by law for specific policy categories, such as education or crime prevention.

---

16 Michael Greenberg, "California: The State of Resistance," *The New York Review of Books,* January 17, 2019, p. 50-2.

17 Kenneth T. Palmer, "The Evolution of Grant Policies," in *The Changing Politics of Federal Grants,* by Lawrence D. Brown, James W. Fossett, and Kenneth T. Palmer (Washington, DC: Brookings Institution, 1984), p. 15.

18 Palmer, "The Evolution of Grant Policies," p. 6.

Figure 3.1

THE HISTORICAL TREND OF CATEGORICAL GRANTS-IN-AID, 1950–2020

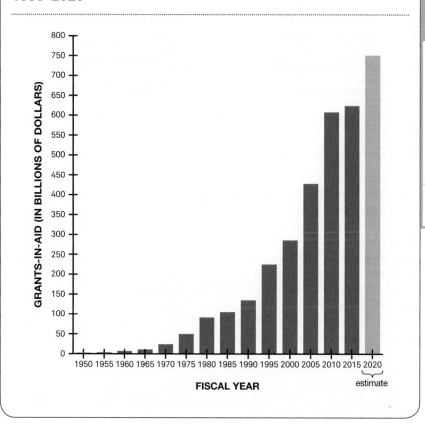

NOTE: Excludes outlays for national defense, international affairs, and net interest.
SOURCE: Office of Management and Budget, Table 12.1, https://www.whitehouse.gov/omb/historical
-tables/ (accessed 2/14/2020).

ANALYZING THE EVIDENCE

Federal grants-in-aid began to expand dramatically during the 1960s. What political trends might explain this expansion? What are the ramifications of this trend for individuals and for states?

Many of the categorical grants enacted during the 1960s were **project grants**, which require state and local governments to submit proposals to federal agencies. In contrast to the older **formula grants**, which used a formula (composed of such elements as need and state and local capacities) to distribute federal funds, the new project grants made funding available on a competitive basis—that is, federal agencies would award grants to the proposals they judged to be the best. Through these project grants, the national government acquired substantial control over which state and local governments got money, how much they got, and how they spent it. A well-known project grant program is the Department of Education's "Race to the Top," which was implemented during the Obama administration. Under this program, the federal government awarded grants to states able to show the highest levels of improvement in teacher quality and student achievement. In a similar vein, the Department of

 project grants

Grants-in-aid for which state and local governments submit proposals to federal agencies, which provide funding for them on a competitive basis.

formula grants

Grants-in-aid for which a formula is used to determine the amount of federal funds a state or local government will receive.

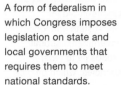

Figure 3.2

TWO HISTORIC VIEWS OF FEDERALISM

DUAL FEDERALISM	COOPERATIVE FEDERALISM

Cooperation on some policies

National Government

State Governments

Layer Cake

National Government

State Governments

Marble Cake

Transportation has made nearly $1 billion available to states that propose the most innovative ideas to repair and improve the nation's infrastructure.

Political scientist Morton Grodzins characterized the shift to post–New Deal cooperative federalism as a move from "layer cake federalism" to "marble cake federalism,"[19] in which it is difficult to say where the national government ends and the state and local governments begin. Figure 3.2 depicts the basis of the marble cake idea. In the late 1970s, federal aid constituted 25 to 30 percent of the operating budgets of all the nation's state and local governments (Figure 3.3). In 2010, federal aid accounted for more than 35 percent of these budgets. This increase was temporary, resulting from the Obama administration's $787 billion stimulus package designed to help state and local governments weather the 2007–9 recession. Briefly, however, federal aid became the single largest source of state revenue, exceeding sales and property tax revenues for the first time in U.S. history. Today, federal aid accounts for 31 percent of state and local budgets.

regulated federalism ⇨

A form of federalism in which Congress imposes legislation on state and local governments that requires them to meet national standards.

Regulated Federalism and National Standards

Developments from the 1960s to the present have pushed the U.S. federal system well beyond cooperative federalism to what might be called **regulated federalism**.[20] Regulated federalism is an important decision rule that has enhanced the national government's power. In some areas—especially civil

---

19 Morton Grodzins, "The Federal System," in *Goals for Americans: The President's Commission on National Goals* (Englewood Cliffs, NJ: Prentice Hall, 1960), p. 265. In a marble cake, the white cake is distinguishable from the chocolate cake, but the two are streaked rather than arranged in distinct layers.

20 The concept and the best discussion of this modern phenomenon can be found in Donald F. Kettl, *The Regulation of American Federalism* (Baltimore: Johns Hopkins University Press, 1987), esp. pp. 33-41.

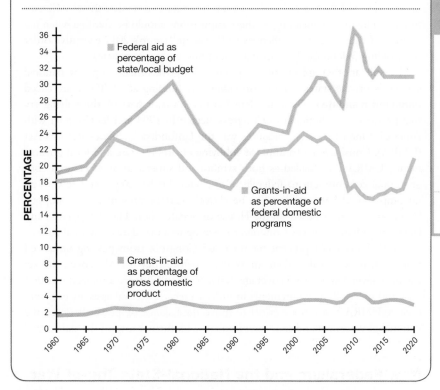

Figure 3.3

THE RISE, DECLINE, AND RECOVERY OF FEDERAL AID, 1960–2020

- Federal aid as percentage of state/local budget
- Grants-in-aid as percentage of federal domestic programs
- Grants-in-aid as percentage of gross domestic product

(y-axis: PERCENTAGE; x-axis years: 1960, 1965, 1970, 1975, 1980, 1985, 1990, 1995, 2000, 2005, 2010, 2015, 2020)

SOURCE: Robert J. Dilger, "Federal Grants to State and Local Governments," Congressional Research Service, 2017; Budget of the U.S. Government Fiscal Year 2020, www.whitehouse.gov/wp-content/uploads/2019/03/spec-fy2020.pdf (accessed 2/14/20).

ANALYZING THE EVIDENCE

The extent to which state and local governments rely on federal funding has varied a great deal over time. What difference does it make if the states depend fiscally on the federal government?

rights, poverty programs, and environmental protection—the national government actually regulates state and local governments by threatening to withhold grant money unless they conform to national standards. These standards are called federal mandates. This focus reflects a shift away from federal oversight of economic activities toward "social regulation," or intervention on behalf of individual rights and liberties, environmental protection, workplace safety, and so on. Here the national government provides grant-in-aid financing, but it sets conditions in the form of standards that the states must meet in order to keep the grants. Examples include the Asbestos Hazard Emergency Act of 1986, which requires school districts to inspect for asbestos hazards and remove them from school buildings when necessary, and the Americans with Disabilities Act of 1990, which requires all state and local governments to promote access for the disabled to all public and private places open to the general public. The net effect of these national standards is that state and local policies are more uniform from coast to coast. National regulations and standards provide coordination across states and localities and solve collective action problems.

A number of judicially developed rules govern federal mandates. In *South Dakota v. Dole* (1987), the Supreme Court held that mandates must be unambiguous, must not be "coercive," and must not force states to violate the U.S. Constitution.[21] The precise meaning of these stipulations should be clarified when the Supreme Court rules on challenges to President Trump's 2017 executive order withholding federal funds from states adopting sanctuary policies.

In still another group of programs, the government imposes national standards on the states without providing any funding at all. These are called **unfunded mandates**. These burdens became a major part of the rallying cry that produced the Republican Congress elected in 1994 and its Contract with America. One of its first measures was the Unfunded Mandates Reform Act (UMRA). Considered a triumph of lobbying efforts by state and local governments, UMRA was "hailed as both symbol and substance of a renewed congressional commitment to federalism."[22] Under this law, any mandate with an uncompensated cost estimated to be above a certain amount can be stopped by a point of order raised on the House or Senate floor. This "stop, look, and listen" requirement forces Congress to own up to a mandate's potential costs.

UMRA does not prevent members of Congress from passing unfunded mandates; it only makes them think twice before they do. Moreover, the act exempts several areas from coverage; states must still enforce antidiscrimination laws and meet other requirements in order to receive federal assistance. Nonetheless, UMRA is a serious effort to move the balance of power between the national government and state governments a bit further toward the state side.[23]

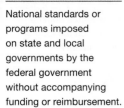

unfunded mandates

National standards or programs imposed on state and local governments by the federal government without accompanying funding or reimbursement.

New Federalism and the National-State Tug-of-War

Federalism in the United States is partly a tug-of-war between those seeking more uniform national standards and those seeking more variability from state to state. Even before UMRA, Presidents Richard Nixon and Ronald Reagan called their efforts to reverse the trend toward national standards "new federalism." They helped craft national policies that would return more discretion to the states. Examples include Nixon's revenue sharing and Reagan's **block grants**, which consolidated a number of categorical grants into one larger category, leaving the state (or local) governments that received them more discretion to decide how to use the money.

block grants

Federal funds given to state governments to pay for goods, services, or programs, with relatively few restrictions on how the funds may be spent.

---

21 *South Dakota v. Dole*, 483 U.S. 203 (1987); Brian T. Yeh, *The Federal Government's Authority to Impose Conditions on Grant Funds*, CRS Report for Congress no. R44797 (Washington, DC: Congressional Research Service, 2017).

22 Paul Posner, "Unfunded Mandate Reform: How Is It Working?" *Rockefeller Institute Bulletin* (1998): 35.

23 Robert Jay Dilger, *Unfunded Mandates Reform Act: History, Impact and Issues*, CRS Report for Congress no. R40957 (Washington, DC: Congressional Research Service, 2019).

President Barack Obama, in contrast, believed firmly in regulated federalism, with the national government using the states as administrative arms rather than independent laboratories. For example, under the Affordable Care Act, every state was encouraged to establish an insurance exchange where individuals in need of health insurance could shop for the best rate. Citizens purchasing insurance through these exchanges would receive federal tax subsidies. Some states did not establish exchanges, but the Supreme Court ruled that their citizens could receive tax benefits for the policies they purchased through the federal government's exchange.[24] The law also required states to expand their Medicaid programs, adding as many as 15 million Americans to the Medicaid rolls. Several states were concerned that the costs of the new program would fall on their strained budgets, and 12 state attorneys general brought suit, charging that the program's mandates violated the Tenth Amendment. Ultimately, the Supreme Court upheld major provisions of the legislation, although the Court ruled that the federal government could not require that Medicaid rolls be expanded.[25]

President Donald Trump, for his part, seems committed neither to new federalism nor to regulated federalism. Instead, Trump chooses whichever approach best serves his political goals. For example, in 2017, Trump issued an executive order reducing federal control over K-12 education, declaring, "For too long the government has imposed its will on state and local governments. . . . My administration has been working to reverse this power grab."[26] Trump has also given the states more flexibility in implementing the Affordable Care Act in an effort to water down provisions he was unable to convince Congress to repeal. At the same time, however, in the realm of immigration, Trump seems to be a champion of regulated federalism; he has endeavored to force states to comply with his policies by threatening to withhold funds from those that oppose them. Some states have responded by resisting federal directives, an action that pundits have dubbed "uncooperative federalism." Several state attorneys general have filed suit against Trump's immigration and energy directives, among other policies.

The Supreme Court as Referee

The courts establish the decision rules that determine the relationship between federal and state power. For much of the nineteenth century, federal power remained limited. The Tenth Amendment was used to bolster arguments for states' rights, which in their extreme version claimed that the states did not have to submit to national laws when they believed the national government

---

24 *King v. Burwell*, 576 U.S. 988 (2015).

25 *National Federation of Independent Business v. Sebelius*, 567 U.S. 519 (2012).

26 S.A. Miller, "Trump to Pull Feds out of K-12 Education," *Washington Times*, April 26, 2017, www.washingtontimes.com/news/2017/apr/26/donald-trump-pull-feds-out-k-12-education (accessed 11/14/19).

had exceeded its authority. States' rights arguments were voiced less often after the Civil War, but the Court continued to use the Tenth Amendment to strike down laws it thought exceeded national power, including the 1875 Civil Rights Act.

In the early twentieth century, however, the Tenth Amendment appeared to lose its force. Reformers began to press for national regulations to limit the power of large corporations and to preserve the health and welfare of citizens. The Supreme Court approved some of these laws but struck down others, including a law combating child labor. The Court stated that the law violated the Tenth Amendment because only states should have the power to regulate conditions of employment. By the late 1930s, however, as we discussed earlier in this chapter, the Court had approved such an expansion of federal power that the Tenth Amendment appeared irrelevant.

The 1990s saw a revival of interest in the Tenth Amendment, and during this decade the Supreme Court issued important decisions limiting federal power. Much of the interest stemmed from conservatives who believed that a strong federal government encroaches on individual liberties, so power should be returned to the states. One of the most important Court rulings in this realm came in *United States v. Lopez* (1995); the Court struck down a federal law that barred handguns near schools on the grounds that the law exceeded Congress's authority under the commerce clause. Another significant Tenth Amendment decision came in *Printz v. United States* (1997), in which the Court struck down a key provision of the Brady Handgun Violence Prevention Act (commonly known as the Brady Bill). Under the act, which was enacted in 1993 to regulate gun sales, state and local law enforcement officers were required to conduct background checks on prospective gun purchasers. The Court held that the federal government cannot require states to administer or enforce federal regulatory programs such as background checks.[27] Overall, rulings such as these signaled a move toward a somewhat more restricted federal government.

This trend continued with *Gonzales v. Oregon* (2006). *Gonzales* involved Oregon's assisted-suicide law, which permits doctors to prescribe lethal doses of medication to terminally ill patients who request help ending their lives. In 2001, the U.S. attorney general issued an order declaring that any physician involved in such a procedure would be prosecuted for violating the federal Controlled Substances Act. The state of Oregon joined several physicians and patients in a suit against the order. Eventually, the Supreme Court ruled that the federal government could not overrule state laws determining how drugs should be used so long as the drugs themselves were not prohibited by federal law.[28]

In 2012, the Court seemed to shift in favor of national power in the national-state tug-of-war. In addition to the decision cited earlier that largely upheld the federal Affordable Care Act (though declared state expansion of the Medicaid

---

27 *Printz v. United States*, 521 U.S. 898 (1997).

28 *Gonzales v. Oregon*, 546 U.S. 243 (2006).

rolls optional), the Court struck down portions of an Arizona immigration law, declaring that immigration was a federal, not a state, matter.[29] In a 2013 decision, it struck down an Arizona law that required individuals to show documentation of citizenship when registering to vote; the Court ruled that this state-level voting restriction was preempted by the federal National Voter Registration Act, which requires states to use the official federal voter registration form.[30] In two other cases, the Court ruled against state legislatures on questions involving congressional-district boundaries.[31]

The Court, however, shifted back toward support of state power in 2018. In the case of *Murphy v. NCAA*, the Court held that a federal law prohibiting the states from authorizing sports gambling violated previous Supreme Court edicts prohibiting the federal government from "commandeering" state executive or legislative authority.[32] And, in a widely discussed 2019 decision, the Supreme Court ruled that the federal courts cannot impose their own judgements on the states when it comes to the drawing of legislative district boundaries.[33] Thus, even if state legislatures appear to draw district boundaries to unfairly advantage one political party or the other, the federal courts do not have the constitutional authority to intervene.

Of course, shifting interpretations of the Constitution often reflect underlying struggles for political power, and the political forces controlling the national government generally advocate a jurisprudence that favors the federal government. Those uncertain of their ability to control Capitol Hill and the White House, but more sure of their hold on some states, support respect for state power.

Until recently, Republicans, who control a majority of the states, have expressed respect for states' rights, while Democrats have sought to increase the power of the federal government. Since Donald Trump's election, however, Democrats have manifested a newfound respect for the states, supporting, for example, the idea that states and even localities can refuse to enforce federal immigration policies and declare themselves to be "sanctuaries" for undocumented immigrants. Democrats also support the right of states like California to continue to abide by the Paris Agreement on climate change, even though President Trump pulled the federal government out of the agreement in 2017. This idea, in effect, supports the right of states to conduct their own foreign policies.

Similar debates continue over the legalization of marijuana (see the Policy Principle box on p. 94). How state and federal institutions will influence decision, agenda, and veto powers is a matter of political principle—and political interest.

---

29 *Arizona v. United States*, 567 U.S. 387 (2012).

30 *Arizona v. Inter Tribal Council of Arizona*, 570 U.S. 1 (2013).

31 *Alabama Legislative Black Caucus v. Alabama*, 575 U.S. ____ (2015) and *Arizona State Legislature v. Arizona Independent Redistricting Commission*, 576 U.S. ____ (2015).

32 *Murphy v. National Collegiate Athletic Association*, 584 U.S.____ (2018).

33 *Rucho v. Common Cause*, 588 U.S. ____ (2019).

Federal vs. State Marijuana Laws

A medical marijuana dispensary in Oregon.

In 2012, the citizens of Colorado and Washington voted to legalize the recreational use of marijuana. Similar ballot measures passed soon after in six other states—Alaska and Oregon later in 2012, and then California, Maine, Massachusetts, and Nevada in 2016. Yet, despite clear changes in these states' laws, any form of marijuana use and possession remains illegal under federal law. Specifically, marijuana is included as a Schedule I controlled substance (alongside cocaine, heroin, and other drugs) in the Controlled Substances Act enacted by Congress in 1970. As a result, the cultivation and distribution of marijuana remains a felony under federal law, regardless of state law, a position that was reinforced by the Supreme Court in 2005.

With federalism, the framers of the Constitution wanted to create an institutional arrangement that dispersed power across the national government and the states to avoid concentrating power in just a few hands. However, as the case of marijuana laws shows, this institutional arrangement complicates policy on some issues—particularly when federal and state law clearly conflict.

Conflicting state and federal laws regarding marijuana put many people who are following their state law at risk of being charged with a federal crime. Under federal law, individual users of marijuana (who are charged with possession with no intent to distribute) can be sentenced to up to a year in prison combined with fines of up to $1,000, and people involved in the marijuana business can face steeper fines up to $25,000 and up to five years in prison. It is not only growers and distributors who risk incurring penalties under federal law; any other business that provides goods and services to a marijuana dispensary can be charged with profiting from an illegal drug business. Landlords who rent to marijuana dispensaries risk both fines and federal asset forfeiture, in which the police are allowed to seize money and property simply based on a suspicion that the asset was used to commit a federal crime.

Despite the clear federal law, the federal government has not prioritized its enforcement in states that have legalized marijuana. One reason is that the federal government depends on cooperation from state and local law enforcement, who are unlikely to help federal agents raid dispensaries that are legal under their own state law. In fact, state legislatures in California and Washington have considered bills that would prohibit a state or local agency from assisting federal agencies in marijuana investigations or enforcement.

This hands-off approach by the federal government was made more explicit in 2013 when the Obama administration issued the Cole Memorandum. This memo—addressed to federal prosecutors—stated that the Justice Department would not enforce federal marijuana laws in states that have legalized use of marijuana, except in cases in which there is harm to the public (for example, cases involving gang operations or selling drugs to children). However, President Trump's former attorney general Jeff Sessions challenged this approach, emphasizing that the federal government retained the authority to enforce federal drug laws regardless of state law. Sessions rescinded the Cole Memorandum in early 2018, raising more questions about the appropriate balance of state and federal authority in this policy area.

THE SEPARATION OF POWERS

As we have noted, the separation of powers enables several different federal institutions to influence the nation's agenda, to affect decisions, and to prevent the other institutions from taking action—dividing agenda, decision, and veto power. The Constitution's framers saw this arrangement, although cumbersome, as an essential means of protecting liberty.

In his discussion of the separation of powers, James Madison quoted the originator of the idea, the French political thinker Baron de Montesquieu: "There can be no liberty where the legislative and executive powers are united in the same person . . . [or] if the power of judging be not separated from the legislative and executive powers."[34] Using the same reasoning, many of Madison's contemporaries argued that the Constitution did not create *enough* separation among the three branches, and Madison had to backtrack to insist that complete separation was not required:

> Unless these departments [branches] be so far connected and blended as to give to each a constitutional control over the others, the degree of separation which the maxim requires, as essential to a free government, can never in practice be duly maintained.[35]

This is the secret of how the United States has made the separation of powers effective: they have made it self-enforcing by giving each branch of government the means to participate in, and partially or temporarily obstruct, the workings of the other branches.

Checks and Balances: A System of Mutual Vetoes

The means by which the executive, legislative, and judicial branches of the federal government interact with each other is known informally as checks and balances. This arrangement gives each branch agenda and veto power and requires all the branches to agree on national policies (Figure 3.4). Examples include the presidential power to veto legislation passed by Congress; the power of Congress to override the veto by a two-thirds majority vote; the power of the Senate to approve presidential appointments; the power of the president to appoint Supreme Court justices and other federal judges with Senate approval; and the power of the Court to engage in judicial review (which we discuss later in this chapter). The framers sought to guarantee that the three branches would use the checks and balances as weapons against each other by giving each branch

---

34 Rossiter, *Federalist Papers*, no. 47 (James Madison), p. 302.

35 Rossiter, *Federalist Papers*, no. 48 (James Madison), p. 308.

Figure 3.4
CHECKS AND BALANCES

LEGISLATIVE

EXECUTIVE OVER LEGISLATIVE

President can veto acts of Congress

President can call a special session of Congress

President carries out, and thereby interprets, laws passed by Congress

Vice president casts tiebreaking vote in the Senate

JUDICIAL OVER LEGISLATIVE

Court can declare laws unconstitutional

Chief justice presides over Senate during hearing to impeach the president

LEGISLATIVE OVER EXECUTIVE

Congress can override presidential veto

Congress can impeach and remove president

Senate can reject president's appointments and refuse to ratify treaties

Congress can conduct investigations into president's actions

Congress can refuse to pass laws or provide funding that president requests

LEGISLATIVE OVER JUDICIAL

Congress can change size of federal court system and number of Supreme Court justices

Congress can propose constitutional amendments

Congress can reject Supreme Court nominees

Congress can impeach and remove federal judges

Congress can amend court jurisdictions

Congress controls appropriations

JUDICIAL OVER EXECUTIVE

Court can declare executive actions unconstitutional

Court has the power to issue warrants

Chief justice presides over impeachment of president

EXECUTIVE OVER JUDICIAL

President nominates Supreme Court justices

President nominates federal judges

President can pardon those convicted in federal court

President can refuse to enforce the courts' decisions

EXECUTIVE

JUDICIAL

a different political constituency: direct, popular election of the members of the House and indirect election of senators (until the Seventeenth Amendment, adopted in 1913); indirect election of the president (still in effect, at least formally); and appointment of federal judges for life. The best characterization of the separation-of-powers principle in action is "separated institutions sharing power."[36]

Legislative Supremacy

Within the system of separated powers, the framers provided for **legislative supremacy** by making Congress the preeminent branch. Legislative supremacy made the provision of checks and balances that the other branches could employ against Congress all the more important.

The framers' intention of legislative supremacy is evident in their decision to place the provisions for national powers in Article I, the legislative article, and to treat the powers of the national government as powers of Congress. In a system based on the rule of law, the power to make the laws is the supreme power. Article I, Section 8 provides in part that "*Congress* shall have Power To lay and collect Taxes . . . ; To borrow Money . . . ; To regulate Commerce" (emphasis added). The Founders also provided for legislative supremacy by giving Congress sole power over appropriations, stipulating that all revenue bills must originate in the House of Representatives. Madison recognized legislative supremacy as part and parcel of the separation of powers:

> It is not possible to give to each department an equal power of self-defense. In republican government, the legislative authority necessarily predominates. The remedy for this inconveniency is to divide the legislature into different branches; and to render them, by different modes of election and different principles of action, as little connected with each other as the nature of their common functions and their common dependence on the society will admit.[37]

Essentially, Congress was so likely to dominate the other branches that it would have to be divided against itself, into House and Senate. One could almost say that the Constitution provided for four branches of government, not three.

Although "presidential government" gradually supplanted legislative supremacy after 1937, the relative power position of the executive and legislative branches since that time has varied with the rise and fall of political parties. It has been especially tense during periods of **divided government**, when one party controls the White House and another controls Congress. For instance, in 2018 when President Trump (a Republican) declared a national emergency along the southern border of the United States and issued executive orders

 legislative supremacy

The preeminent position within the national government that the Constitution assigns to Congress.

 divided government

The condition in American government in which one party controls the presidency, while the opposing party controls one or both houses of Congress.

36 Richard E. Neustadt, *Presidential Power and the Modern Presidents: The Politics of Leadership from Roosevelt to Reagan* (New York: Free Press, 1990), p. 33.

37 Rossiter, *Federalist Papers*, no. 51 (James Madison), p. 322.

diverting funds from the Department of Defense's budget to start work on a border wall, Congress reacted sharply. The Democrat-controlled House of Representatives voted to block the president's emergency declaration, and even some GOP lawmakers sharply criticized the president's actions.

The Rationality Principle at Work

The framers' idea that the president and Congress would check and balance each other rests, in part, on an application of the rationality principle. The framers assumed that each branch would seek to maintain or expand its power and would resist "encroachments" by the other branch. This idea seems consistent with the actual behavior of presidents and congressional leaders who have battled over institutional prerogatives since at least the Nixon administration. For example, the Watergate scandal began when President Nixon sought a reorganization of the executive branch that would have increased presidential control and reduced congressional oversight powers.[38] After Nixon's resignation, Congress acted to delimit presidential power; but subsequently President Reagan undid Congress's efforts and bolstered the White House. During President George W. Bush's second term, Congress and the president battled constantly over the president's refusals to disclose information on the basis of **executive privilege** and his assertions that only the White House was competent to manage the nation's security. Bush famously stated, "I am the decider." President Obama faced divided government for the final six years of his administration. In the 2016 elections, Americans chose a Republican president and left the GOP in control of both houses of Congress. This development might have brought about closer cooperation between the executive and legislative branches, but ideological conflicts within the Republican coalition often undermined leaders' ability to enact major pieces of legislation.

In 2018, the Democrats won control of the House of Representatives and launched a number of investigations into the activities of President Trump and his aides. Trump responded by ordering White House staffers and other officials to refuse to testify before Congress and by asserting executive privilege to deny Congress access to information. This tactic touched off a series of legal battles between the president and Congress. In 2020, the Democratic House of Representatives impeached President Trump, charging him with abuse of power in an effort to coerce Ukraine to investigate Trump's political rival, former vice president Joseph Biden. After a brief trial, Trump was acquitted by the Republican-controlled Senate.

Over time, the president has generally possessed an advantage in this struggle between institutions. The president is a unitary actor, whereas Congress, as a collective decision maker, suffers from collective action problems (see Chapter 6). That is, each member may have individual interests that are inconsistent with the collective interests of Congress as a whole. For example, though Congress initially

executive privilege ➡

The claim that confidential communications between the president and close advisers should not be revealed without the president's consent.

---

38 Benjamin Ginsberg and Martin Shefter, *Politics by Other Means: Politicians, Prosecutors, and the Press from Watergate to Whitewater*, 3rd ed. (New York: Norton, 2002), chap. 1.

supported Bush's plan to use force in Iraq in 2003, members were uneasy about his assertion that he did not need congressional approval to do so. The president used the war to underline claims of institutional power, but few members of Congress thought it politically safe to express their concerns about presidential overreach when the public was clamoring for action. These considerations help explain why, over time, the powers of the presidency have grown and those of Congress have diminished.[39] We will return to this topic in Chapter 7.

The Role of the Supreme Court: Establishing Decision Rules

The role of the judicial branch in the separation of powers has depended on the power of judicial review (see Chapter 9), a power not provided for in the Constitution but asserted by Chief Justice Marshall in 1803:

> If a law be in opposition to the Constitution; if both the law and the Constitution apply to a particular case, so that the Court must either decide that case conformable to the law, disregarding the Constitution, or conformable to the Constitution, disregarding the law; the Court must determine which of these conflicting rules governs the case: This is of the very essence of judicial duty.[40]

Marshall's decision was an extremely important assertion of judicial power: in effect, he declared that whenever there was doubt or disagreement about which rule should apply in a particular case, the Court would decide. In this way, Marshall made the Court the arbiter of all future debates between Congress and the president and between the federal and state governments.

Judicial review of the constitutionality of acts of the president or Congress is relatively rare. For example, there were no Supreme Court reviews of congressional acts in the 50-plus years between *Marbury v. Madison* (1803) and *Dred Scott v. Sandford* (1857). In the century or so between the Civil War and 1970, 84 acts of Congress were held unconstitutional (in whole or in part), but there were long periods of complete Court deference to Congress, punctuated by flurries of judicial review during times of social upheaval. The most significant was in 1935–36, when the Court invalidated 12 acts of Congress, blocking virtually the entire New Deal program.[41] Thereafter the Court did not void any significant

---

39 Benjamin Ginsberg, *Presidential Government* (New Haven, CT: Yale University Press, 2016).

40 *Marbury v. Madison*, 5 U.S. 137 (1803).

41 The Supreme Court struck down 8 out of 10 New Deal statutes. For example, in *Panama Refining Company v. Ryan*, 293 U.S. 388 (1935), the Court ruled that a section of the National Industrial Recovery Act of 1933 was an invalid delegation of legislative power to the executive branch. And in *A. L. A. Schechter Poultry Corporation v. United States*, 295 U.S. 495 (1935), the Court found the National Industrial Recovery Act itself to be invalid for the same reason.

---

acts until 1983, when it declared unconstitutional the legislative veto, a practice in which Congress would authorize the president to take certain kinds of actions while reserving the right to override particular actions with which it disagreed.[42] The Court became much more activist (that is, less deferential to Congress) after the appointment of Chief Justice William H. Rehnquist in 1986.[43] Each of the cases in Table 3.1 altered some aspect of federalism by declaring unconstitutional all or an important portion of an act of Congress.

Since the New Deal period, the Court has been far more deferential toward the president, with only five significant confrontations. One was the so-called steel seizure case of 1952, in which the Court refused to permit President Harry Truman to use "emergency powers" to take control of the country's steel mills during the Korean War.[44] In a second case, the Court rejected President Nixon's claim that he was not required to turn over subpoenaed tape recordings relevant to the Watergate investigation. The Court argued that, although executive privilege protected the confidentiality of communications to and from the president, this protection did not extend to data in presidential files or tapes linked to criminal prosecutions.[45] In yet another instance, the Court struck down the Line Item Veto Act of 1996, which allowed the president to veto specific items in spending and tax bills without vetoing the entire bill. The Court held that any such change in the procedures of adopting laws would have to be made by amendment to the Constitution, not by legislation.[46]

Another important confrontation came a few years after the September 11, 2001, terrorist attacks. In 2004 the Court held that the estimated 650 "enemy combatants" detained without formal charges at the U.S. naval station at Guantánamo Bay, Cuba, had the right to seek release through a **writ of habeas corpus**.[47] Congress answered this decision with the Military Commissions Act (2006), which included a provision declaring that enemy combatants held at Guantánamo Bay could not avail themselves of the right of *habeas corpus*. Then, in 2008, the Supreme Court responded by striking down the offending provision and affirming that the Guantánamo detainees had the right to challenge their detentions in federal court.[48] The Court noted that *habeas corpus* was among the most fundamental of constitutional rights and was included in the Constitution even before the Bill of Rights was added.

During the Trump era, a number of federal district and circuit courts have ruled against the president, particularly on immigration issues. The Supreme

writs of *habeas corpus*

A court order demanding that an individual in custody be brought into court and shown the cause for detention; *habeas corpus* is guaranteed by the Constitution and can be suspended only in cases of rebellion or invasion.

---

42 *Immigration and Naturalization Service v. Chadha*, 462 U.S. 919 (1983).

43 Cass R. Sunstein, "Taking Over the Courts," *New York Times*, November 9, 2002, p. A19.

44 *Youngstown Sheet and Tube Company v. Sawyer*, 343 U.S. 579 (1952).

45 *United States v. Nixon*, 418 U.S. 683 (1974).

46 *Clinton v. City of New York*, 524 U.S. 417 (1998).

47 *Rasul v. Bush*, 542 U.S. 466 (2004).

48 *Boumediene v. Bush*, 553 U.S. 723 (2008).

Table 3.1

A NEW FEDERAL SYSTEM? THE CASE RECORD, 1995–2019

CASE	DATE	COURT HOLDING
United States v. Lopez, 514 U.S. 549	1995	Voids federal law barring handguns near schools: this law is beyond Congress's power to regulate commerce
Seminole Tribe of Florida v. Florida, 517 U.S. 44	1996	Voids federal law giving tribes the right to sue a state in federal court: "sovereign immunity" requires that a state grant permission to be sued
Printz v. United States, 521 U.S. 898	1997	Voids a key provision of the Brady Bill requiring states to make background checks on gun purchases: as an "unfunded mandate," it violated state sovereignty under the Tenth Amendment
City of Boerne v. Flores, 521 U.S. 507	1997	Restricts Congress's power under the Fourteenth Amendment to regulate city zoning and health and welfare policies to "remedy" rights: Congress may not expand those rights
Alden v. Maine, 527 U.S. 706	1999	Declares states "immune" from suits by their own employees for overtime pay under the Fair Labor Standards Act of 1938 (see also the Seminole case)
United States v. Morrison, 529 U.S. 598	2000	Extends the Seminole case by invalidating the Violence Against Women Act: states may not be sued by individuals for failing to enforce federal laws
Gonzales v. Oregon, 546 U.S. 243	2006	Upholds state assisted-suicide law over attorney general's objection: federal government cannot outlaw a medical practice authorized by a state's laws
National Federation of Independent Business v. Sebelius, 567 U.S. 519	2012	Upholds the Affordable Care Act and expansion of federal control over health care policy: requiring individuals to purchase health insurance was a permissible exercise of congressional power to levy taxes
Murphy v. NCAA, 584 U.S. ____	2018	Declares that the federal government cannot tell the states what laws to enact: states cannot be prohibited from allowing sports gambling
Rucho v. Common Cause, 588 U.S. ____	2019	Declares that the federal courts cannot overturn districting plans drawn up by state legislatures even if these served partisan purposes: let stand gerrymandering schemes in North Carolina and Maryland

Court, however, has thus far refrained from directly confronting the president. The closest it has come involved the matter of whether a question asking respondents about their citizenship status could be added to the 2020 census. Critics charged that the question was designed to reduce legislative representation for and federal funding to states with large numbers of undocumented immigrants. Lower federal courts ruled that the question should not be included in the census questionnaire, and the Supreme Court refused to make a final determination, instead sending the matter back to the lower courts for further adjudication.[49]

CONCLUSION: FEDERALISM AND THE SEPARATION OF POWERS—COLLECTIVE ACTION OR STALEMATE?

As asserted by the institution principle, institutions are designed to solve collective action problems. The solutions, however, can take many different forms. The framers believed that agenda, decision, and veto powers should be dispersed among many different federal institutions. And because the 13 existing states already possessed significant autonomy when the Constitution was drafted—and history matters—the framers had little choice but to relinquish considerable agenda, decision, and veto powers to them as well. The result was our federal system of separated powers.

Critics of the American constitutional framework have often pointed to this dispersion of governmental power as a source of weakness and incoherence in the United States' policy-making processes. Because of federalism, the United States' national government is often unable to accomplish what might be a matter of course in most other nations. As we saw in *United States v. Lopez*, for example, the Supreme Court invalidated a federal statute prohibiting the possession of firearms near schools on the grounds that it was an unconstitutional encroachment on the sovereignty of the states. In a country with a unitary system of government, this statute would not face such a hurdle.

Over the course of American history, as we have seen, the power of the states has waned relative to that of the national government. Nevertheless, the states still matter, and under the terms of "new federalism," the states can exert a good deal of power over nominally federal programs. Still, the United States began as a nation of semi-sovereign states and is now closer to being a unitary republic.

As for the separation of powers, the policy principle tells us that political outcomes are the products of individual preferences and institutional

---

49 *Department of Commerce v. New York*, 588 U.S. ____ (2019).

procedures. Because of the separation of powers, an institutional procedure, Congress is often stymied by the president—or the president by Congress—in its efforts to develop and implement policies. The president can veto congressional action; Congress can, by legislation, limit the powers of the executive. In 2011, for example, the newly elected Republican House of Representatives promised to repeal President Obama's recently enacted health care program, the Affordable Care Act (ACA). The Senate, still controlled by Democrats, disagreed, and the president promised to veto any bill that threatened what he viewed as the major achievement of his first term in office. In the meantime, legal challenges to the new law eventually led to a Supreme Court decision upholding the ACA's main provisions. The dispersion of power among different institutions of government ensures that collective action will be difficult, though not impossible.

At times, however, a stalemate between Congress and the president may become so severe that the government is paralyzed. In their continued fight against the ACA, in 2013 House Republicans refused to allow a vote on any continuing resolution (CR) to extend the government's spending authority that contained funding for the ACA. Senate Democrats and the president said they would not accept a CR that did not provide such funding. Without a CR, much of the government's spending authority lapsed, such that most federal agencies had to close in a "government shutdown." After a tense 16 days, Republicans and Democrats agreed to a spending bill and a temporary new debt ceiling.

The political importance of the separation of powers became even more clear after the 2018 elections gave Democrats control of the House of Representatives. Almost immediately, congressional investigators looked into every nook and cranny of the Trump administration and its policies. Many Democrats hoped to find evidence that would lead to the president's impeachment. The president, for his part, made no secret of his disdain for Congress and its leaders, often referring to House Speaker Nancy Pelosi as "Nervous Nancy," and tweeting that she was a "nasty, vindictive, horrible person."

Thus the separation of powers has real political consequences. The framers, though, did not want to make collective action too easy. They thought it was important to provide checks and balances that would protect the nation from the tyrannical actions of a small number of leaders, as well as from "majority tyranny," or precipitous actions on the part of larger groups. The framers believed that well-constructed institutions should diminish the likelihood of inappropriate and unwise collective action, even at the cost of an occasional stalemate. In recent years, the U.S. government has often been criticized more for what it *has* done, especially in regard to foreign military operations, than for what it *has not* done. Many Americans believe that Congress should have done more to thwart presidential war policies and hope the judiciary will do more to delimit presidential war powers in the future. The framers likely would have understood this desire to check the executive branch. Stalemate is not always the worst collective outcome.

For Further Reading

Chafetz, Josh. *Congress's Constitution: Legislative Authority and the Separation of Powers*. New Haven, CT: Yale University Press, 2017.

Council of State Governments. *The Book of the States*, Vol. 51. Lexington, KY: Council of State Governments, 2019.

Ferejohn, John A., and Barry R. Weingast, eds. *The New Federalism: Can the States Be Trusted?* Stanford, CA: Hoover Institution Press, 1997.

Fisher, Louis. *Supreme Court Expansion of Presidential Power: Unconstitutional Leanings*. Lawrence: University Press of Kansas, 2017.

Ginsberg, Benjamin. *Presidential Government*. New Haven, CT: Yale University Press, 2016.

Gray, Virginia, Russell L. Hanson and Thad Kousser, eds., *Politics in the American States: A Comparative Analysis*. 11th ed. Thousand Oaks, CA: CQ Press, 2018.

Gulasekaram, Pratheepan, and S. Karthick Ramakrishnan. *The New Immigration Federalism*. New York: Cambridge University Press, 2015.

Hopkins, Daniel J. *The Increasingly United States: How and Why American Political Behavior is Nationalized*. Chicago: University of Chicago Press, 2018.

LaCroix, Alison L. *The Ideological Origins of American Federalism*. Cambridge, MA: Harvard University Press, 2010.

Manheim, Lisa and Kathryn Watts. *The Limits of Presidential Power: A Citizen's Guide to the Law*. Self-published, 2018.

Moellers, Christoph. *The Three Branches: A Comparative Model of Separation of Powers*. New York: Oxford University Press, 2013.

Moncrief, Gary F. and Peverill Squire. *Why States Matter: An Introduction to State Politics*. 2nd ed. Lanham, MD: Rowman and Littlefield, 2017.

Nolette, Paul. *Federalism on Trial: State Attorneys General and National Policymaking in Contemporary America*. Lawrence: University Press of Kansas, 2015.

Riker, William H. *Federalism: Origin, Operation, Significance*. Boston: Little, Brown, 1964.

Robertson, David Brian. *Federalism and the Making of America*. 2nd ed. New York: Routledge, 2017.

Rossiter, Clinton L., ed. *The Federalist Papers; Alexander Hamilton, James Madison, and John Jay*, esp. no. 39. New York: New American Library, 1961.

Samuels, David J., and Matthew S. Shugart. *Presidents, Parties and Prime Ministers: How the Separation of Powers Affects Party Organization and Behavior*. New York: Cambridge University Press, 2010.

4

Civil Liberties

Institutions serve to solve collective action problems, and in the United States, constitutional protections for civil liberties and civil rights are among the most important instruments used to achieve this purpose. To solve such problems, however, does not mean simply to *facilitate* collective action. Instead, the principles of civil liberties and civil rights presented in the Bill of Rights also *regulate* collective action. Civil liberties limit or restrict the collective actions that government can take; in effect, they define certain spheres of activity, such as speech or worship, in which the government's authority to interfere with individual conduct is limited. Civil rights both determine who may participate or be represented in collective decision-making processes and regulate the ways in which government can treat its citizens. Thus, generally speaking, civil liberties limit collective action by restricting the government's jurisdiction. Civil rights, in contrast (as we will see in Chapter 5), regulate collective action by establishing decision rules for government's conduct.

From the perspective of the framers, the portions of the Constitution designed to limit action were just as important as those designed to promote action. As we will see in Chapter 6, for example, the framers knew that bicameralism—the separation of Congress into two houses—would sometimes interfere with the passage of legislation, but they saw this constraint as a necessary brake on poorly considered laws. They thought legislative efficiency was less important than legislative judgment.

So too in the realm of citizens' liberties: the framers believed it was essential to check the government's ability to pass laws that might infringe on citizens' freedoms. And to make certain that citizens' liberties would have solid institutional safeguards rather than protections only on paper, the framers designed a set of federal courts that could transcend day-to-day political squabbles. Jurisdiction over civil liberties and civil rights issues is primarily exercised by the courts, which have developed myriad decision rules and procedures to resolve controversies in these areas. The U.S. Supreme Court, in particular, asserts significant agenda and veto power in interpreting these constitutional principles, deriving its jurisdiction from Article III of the Constitution, from statutes, and from prior Court decisions. But consistent with the concept of checks and balances, other actors—particularly Congress—also claim agenda and veto power. Congress's jurisdiction stems from Article II of the Constitution, which gives it the power to make the laws, and from its role in the process of amending the Constitution as outlined in Article V.

In their rulings, the courts are heavily influenced by the history of prior decisions relating to the principles at hand; that is, they rely on *precedent*. When issuing decisions, courts constantly refer to the opinions of prior courts to justify their interpretations, logic, and ultimate findings. Seldom will a court depart from established precedent. Even the Supreme Court always justifies its decisions by citing precedents and seldom overturns established legal principles. Because the job of a court is to apply rather than to make the law, history in the form of precedent is an important factor limiting judicial discretion.

As we observed when discussing federalism and the separation of powers, institutional principles are not carved in stone. Over the past century, numerous civil liberties have been strengthened, thereby placing greater limits on collective action. In the realm of civil rights, as Chapter 5 will show, African Americans and others who were once excluded from participation in many collective processes have won the right to be included. In both areas, change resulted from public political struggles that ultimately inspired battles within and between Congress and the courts. With these considerations in mind, let's examine the character and evolution of civil liberties in America, to be followed in the next chapter by a discussion of civil rights.

LEARNING OBJECTIVES

 Describe the origins of the Bill of Rights and how they are meant to protect citizens from improper governmental actions.

 Summarize how the establishment of dual citizenship and the Fourteenth Amendment led to the nationalization of the Bill of Rights.

 Explain how precedent and interpretation continue to shape the Bill of Rights today.

 Outline the relationship between civil liberties and collective action.

ORIGINS OF THE BILL OF RIGHTS

The history principle tells us that choices made during one point in time can continue to have important consequences decades or even centuries later. When the first Congress met under the new Constitution in 1789, it made a choice—10 of them to be exact—that shapes our politics today. Its most important item of business was to consider a proposal to add a bill of rights to the Constitution. The framers had turned down such a proposal in the waning days of the 1787 Constitutional Convention because some Federalists, including Alexander Hamilton, argued that a bill of rights was irrelevant in a constitution that provided the national government with only delegated powers. How could the national government abuse powers not given to it in the first place? Hamilton pointed out that the Constitution's system of checks and balances was designed to prevent tyrannical conduct and stressed that other elements of the Constitution, such as the right of *habeas corpus* contained in Article I, Section 9, already guaranteed popular liberties. Hamilton worried that a bill of rights would weaken the new government by limiting its jurisdiction even before it had an opportunity to organize itself. But when the Constitution was submitted to the states for ratification, Antifederalists reiterated Thomas Jefferson's argument that the omission of a bill of rights was a major imperfection of the document. In response, Federalists in Massachusetts, South Carolina, New Hampshire, Virginia, and New York made an "unwritten but unequivocal pledge" to add a bill of rights, and they promised to confirm the understanding that all powers not delegated to the national government or explicitly prohibited to the states were reserved to the states or to the people.[1]

James Madison, who had been a delegate to the Philadelphia Convention and later became a member of Congress, may still have believed privately that a bill of rights was unnecessary. But in 1789, recognizing the urgency of obtaining the Antifederalists' support for the Constitution and the new government, he fought for a bill of rights, arguing that the ideals it embodied would acquire "the character of fundamental maxims of free Government, and as they become incorporated with the national sentiment, counteract the impulses of interest and passion."[2]

"After much discussion and manipulation . . . at the delicate prompting of Washington and under the masterful prodding of Madison," the House adopted 17 amendments, of which the Senate adopted 12. Ten were ratified by the necessary three-fourths of the states, making them part of the Constitution on December 15, 1791. From the start, these 10 were called the Bill of Rights.[3]

---

1   Clinton L. Rossiter, *1787: The Grand Convention* (New York: Norton, 1987), p. 302.

2   Quoted in Milton Konvitz, "The Bill of Rights: Amendments I–X," in *An American Primer*, ed. Daniel J. Boorstin (Chicago: University of Chicago Press, 1966), vol. 1, p. 159.

3   Rossiter, *1787*, p. 303, where the author also reports that "in 1941 the States of Connecticut, Massachusetts, and Georgia celebrated the sesquicentennial of the Bill of Rights by giving their hitherto withheld and unneeded assent."

Civil liberties can be defined as protections of citizens from improper governmental action. When adopted in 1791, the Bill of Rights was seen as guaranteeing a private sphere of personal liberty free from governmental restrictions. As Jefferson put it, a bill of rights "is what people are entitled to against every government on earth." In this sense, we could call the Bill of Rights a bill of liberties because the amendments focus on what government must *not* do. For example (with emphasis added):

← **civil liberties**

The protections of citizens from improper governmental action.

1. "Congress shall make *no* law . . ." (I)
2. "The right . . . to . . . bear Arms, shall *not* be infringed." (II)
3. "*No* Soldier shall . . . be quartered . . ." (III)
4. "*No* Warrants shall issue, but upon probable cause . . ." (IV)
5. "*No* person shall be held to answer . . . unless on a presentment or indictment of a Grand Jury . . ." (V)
6. "Excessive bail shall *not* be required . . . *nor* cruel and unusual punishments inflicted." (VIII)

Thus the Bill of Rights is a series of "thou shalt nots"—restraints addressed to government, limiting its jurisdiction. Some of these restraints are *substantive*, limiting *what* the government has the power to do. For instance, the Bill of Rights prohibits the government from establishing a state religion, quartering troops in private homes without consent, or seizing private property without just compensation. Other restraints are *procedural*, addressing how the government is supposed to act. For example, even though the government has the substantive power to declare certain acts to be crimes and to arrest and imprison persons who violate its criminal laws, it may not do so except by a fairly meticulous observance of procedures designed to protect the accused. The best-known procedural rule is that a person is presumed innocent until proven guilty. This rule does not restrict the government's power to punish someone for committing a crime; it restricts only the way the government determines who committed the crime.

Substantive and procedural restraints constitute the realm of civil liberties. While the distinction between civil liberties and civil rights seems clear in theory, in practice several provisions of the Bill of Rights assert both a liberty and right. Proponents of the Bill of Rights wished to ensure that their enumeration of rights and liberties would not be deemed exhaustive. The Ninth Amendment addresses this concern, declaring that the Constitution's enumeration of some rights "shall not be construed" to mean that the people do not retain other rights as well.

NATIONALIZING THE BILL OF RIGHTS

The First Amendment provides that "Congress shall make no law respecting an establishment of religion . . . or abridging the freedom of speech, or of the press; or the right of [assembly and petition]." This is the only amendment that exclusively addresses the national government. For example, the Second Amendment provides that "the right of the people to keep and bear Arms, shall not be infringed." The Fifth Amendment says, among other things, that *no person* "shall . . . be twice put in jeopardy of life or limb" for the same crime, that *no person* "shall be compelled in any criminal case to be a witness against himself," that *no person* shall "be deprived of life, liberty, or property, without due process of law," and that private property cannot be taken "without just compensation."[4] Because the First Amendment is the only part of the Bill of Rights that explicitly limits the national government, a fundamental question arises: Do the other amendments of the Bill of Rights put limits on state governments too, or do they put them only on the national government?

Dual Citizenship

The question of whether the Bill of Rights also limits the actions of state governments seemed to have been settled in the case of *Barron v. Baltimore* (1833). The facts were simple. In paving its streets, the city of Baltimore had disposed of so much sand and gravel in the water near John Barron's wharf that its value for commercial purposes was virtually destroyed. Barron sued the city on the grounds that it had, under the Fifth Amendment, unconstitutionally deprived him of his property.

Here Chief Justice John Marshall, in one of the most significant Supreme Court decisions ever handed down, wrote:

> The Constitution was ordained and established by the people of the United States for themselves, for their own government, and not for the government of individual States. Each State established a constitution for itself, and in that constitution provided such limitations and restrictions on the powers of its particular government as its judgment dictated. . . . If these propositions be correct, *the fifth amendment must be understood as restraining the power of the General Government, not as applicable to the States*.[5] (emphasis added)

In other words, if an agency of the *national* government had deprived Barron of his property, there would have been little doubt about Barron winning his case. But if the constitution of the state of Maryland contained no such provision protecting citizens of Maryland from such action, then Barron had no legal leg to stand on against Baltimore, an agency of the state of Maryland.

-----

4   It would be useful at this point to review all provisions of the Bill of Rights to confirm this distinction between the wording of the First Amendment and the wording of the rest (see the Appendix). The emphasis in these examples is not in the original. For an enlightening essay on the extent to which the entire Bill of Rights is about equality, see Martha Minow, "Equality and the Bill of Rights," in *The Constitution of Rights: Human Dignity and American Values*, ed. Michael J. Meyer and William A. Parent (Ithaca, NY: Cornell University Press, 1992), pp. 118–28.

5   *Barron v. Mayor and City of Baltimore*, 32 U.S. 243 (1833).

Barron v. Baltimore confirmed the principle of "dual citizenship"—that each American was both a citizen of the national government and separately a citizen of one of the states. This meant that the Bill of Rights did not apply to decisions or procedures of state (or local) governments. Even slavery could continue because the Bill of Rights could not protect anyone from state laws treating people as property. In fact, nearly another century would pass before the Bill of Rights would truly come into its own; it did not become a vital instrument for the extension of civil liberties until after a bloody civil war and the intervention of the revolutionary Fourteenth Amendment.

When it comes to the application of the Bill of Rights, America's history has truly mattered. Because America's states predated the creation of the federal government, and they retained many of their sovereign powers after joining the Union, nationalization of governmental powers has proceeded slowly, in fits and starts. By contrast, in many other nations, subnational governments were created by and for the administrative convenience of the central government.

The Fourteenth Amendment

From a constitutional standpoint, the defeat of the South in the Civil War settled one question and raised another. It probably settled forever the question of whether any state could secede from the Union. After 1865, the United States were meant to be more "united" than "states." But the question of just how much the states were obliged to obey the Constitution—in particular, the Bill of Rights— did not have an easy answer. The words of the Fourteenth Amendment suggest that it was almost perfectly designed to impose the Bill of Rights on the states and thereby reverse *Barron v. Baltimore*. Consider the amendment's first words:

> All persons born or naturalized in the United States, and subject to the jurisdiction thereof, are citizens of the United States and of the State wherein they reside.

This statement provides for a single national citizenship, which at a minimum means that civil liberties should not vary drastically from state to state. This seems to be the spirit of the Fourteenth Amendment: to nationalize the Bill of Rights by nationalizing the definition of citizenship.

This interpretation is reinforced by the next clause:

> No State shall make or enforce any law which shall abridge the privileges or immunities of citizens of the United States; nor shall any State deprive any person of life, liberty, or property, without due process of law.

All of this sounds like an effort to extend the entire Bill of Rights to citizens wherever they might reside, but the Supreme Court did not interpret the clause in this way for nearly a century. Within five years of the Fourteenth Amendment's ratification in 1868, the Court was making decisions as though the amendment had never been adopted. The shadow of *Barron* grew longer.

In an important 1873 decision known as the *Slaughter-House Cases*, the Supreme Court determined that the federal government was under no obligation to protect the "privileges and immunities" of citizens of a particular state against arbitrary actions by that state's government. The Court argued that the framers of the Fourteenth Amendment could not have intended to incorporate the entire Bill of Rights.[6] Yet when the Court was asked to consider the Civil Rights Act of 1875, which attempted to protect Black Americans from discriminatory treatment by proprietors of hotels, theaters, and other public accommodations, it disregarded its argument in the *Slaughter-House* case. This time the Court distinguished between state action and private action, and it declared that the Fourteenth Amendment did in fact apply to discriminatory actions by state officials "operating under cover of law." However, it did not apply to discrimination against Black Americans by private individuals, even though these private entities were companies offering services to the public.[7] Thus the Court held that the Civil Rights Act of 1875 was unconstitutional, and private individuals had the right to continue their discriminatory practices. The narrow interpretations in these two cases raised the question of whether the Fourteenth Amendment had incorporated any of the Bill of Rights. The amendment would remain in the shadows of *Barron v. Baltimore* and the Court's unwillingness to "nationalize" civil liberties—that is, to interpret the Bill of Rights as imposing limitations not only on the federal government but also on the states—until the mid-twentieth century.

It was not until the late nineteenth century that the Supreme Court began to nationalize the Bill of Rights by incorporating its civil liberties provisions into the Fourteenth Amendment. Incorporation can be seen as an expansion of the federal government's authority and an erosion of the individual states' autonomy. It is no accident that the major periods of incorporation were the 1930s and the 1960s, when Congress and the president sought to enhance federal power relative to the states and encouraged the courts to facilitate the effort. During the 1930s, several First Amendment limitations were imposed on states' actions; during the 1960s, the courts compelled the states to adhere to many of the remaining provisions of the Bill of Rights.

Table 4.1 outlines the major steps in the process of incorporation. The only expansion in civil liberties during the first 60 years after the adoption of the Fourteenth Amendment came in 1897, when the Supreme Court held that the amendment's due process clause did in fact prohibit states from taking property for a public use without just compensation.[8] This decision effectively overruled *Barron* because it henceforth protected citizens of any state from a "public taking" of property, even if the relevant state constitution did not provide such protection. In a broader sense, however, *Barron* still cast a shadow because the Court had "incorporated" into the Fourteenth Amendment only the property

---

6 *The Slaughter-House Cases*, 83 U.S. 36 (1873).

7 *The Civil Rights Cases*, 109 U.S. 3 (1883).

8 *Chicago, Burlington, and Quincy Railroad Company v. Chicago*, 166 U.S. 226 (1897).

Table 4.1

INCORPORATION OF THE BILL OF RIGHTS INTO THE FOURTEENTH AMENDMENT

SELECTED PROVISIONS AND AMENDMENTS	DATE INCORPORATED	KEY CASES
Eminent domain (V)	**1897**	*Chicago, Burlington, and Quincy Railroad Company v. Chicago,* 166 U.S. 226
Freedom of speech (I)	**1925**	*Gitlow v. New York,* 268 U.S. 652
Freedom of the press (I)	**1931**	*Near v. Minnesota ex rel. Olson,* 283 U.S. 697
Freedom of assembly (I)	**1937**	*De Jonge v. Oregon,* 299 U.S. 353
Free exercise of religion (I)	**1940**	*Cantwell v. Connecticut,* 310 U.S. 296
Nonestablishment of state religion (I)	**1947**	*Everson v. Board of Education of the Township of Ewing,* 330 U.S. 1
Freedom from warrantless search and seizure ("exclusionary rule") (IV)	**1961**	*Mapp v. Ohio,* 367 U.S. 643
Freedom from cruel and unusual punishment (VIII)	**1962**	*Robinson v. California,* 370 U.S. 660
Right to counsel in any criminal trial (VI)	**1963**	*Gideon v. Wainwright,* 372 U.S. 335
Right against self-incrimination and forced confessions (V)	**1964**	*Escobedo v. Illinois,* 378 U.S. 478
Right to privacy (III, IV, and V)	**1965**	*Griswold v. Connecticut,* 381 U.S. 479
Right to remain silent (V)	**1966**	*Miranda v. Arizona,* 384 U.S. 436
Right against double jeopardy (V)	**1969**	*Benton v. Maryland,* 395 U.S. 784
Right to bear arms (II)	**2010**	*McDonald v. Chicago,* 561 U.S. 742
Freedom from excessive fines (VIII)	**2019**	*Timbs v. Indiana,* 586 U.S. ____
Right to a unanimous verdict (VI)	**2020**	*Ramos v. Louisiana*

protection provision of the Fifth Amendment and no other clause, let alone the other amendments of the Bill of Rights. In other words, although the Fifth Amendment states that no person shall "be deprived of life, liberty, or property, without due process of law; nor shall private property be taken for public use, without just compensation," the Court's ruling did not speak to the "life" or "liberty" provisions of the amendment.

No further expansion of civil liberties through incorporation occurred until 1925, when the Supreme Court held that freedom of speech is "among the fundamental personal rights and 'liberties' protected by the due process clause of the Fourteenth Amendment from impairment by the states."[9] In 1931, the Court added freedom of the press to the short list of civil liberties protected from state action; in 1937, it added freedom of assembly; and in 1940 it added freedom of religion.[10] But that was as far as the Court would go. This one-by-one application of the provisions of the Bill of Rights is known as *selective incorporation.*

As late as 1937, the Court was still loath to nationalize civil liberties beyond the First Amendment. In fact, in that year it took an extreme turn backward toward *Barron v. Baltimore* when it considered the case of *Palko v. Connecticut.* The state of Connecticut had indicted a man named Frank Palko for first-degree murder, but a lower court found him guilty of the lesser charge of second-degree murder and sentenced him to life in prison. Unhappy with the verdict, the state of Connecticut appealed the conviction to its highest court and, in a retrial of the first-degree murder charge, ultimately succeeded in convicting Palko. Palko appealed to the Supreme Court on what seemed an open-and-shut case of *double jeopardy*—being tried twice for the same crime. While a majority of the Court agreed that Palko had been subjected to double jeopardy, the justices decided that the Fifth Amendment's prohibition of double jeopardy was *not* incorporated into the Fourteenth Amendment as a restriction on states' powers. Justice Benjamin Cardozo rejected the argument made by Palko's lawyer that "whatever is forbidden by the Fifth Amendment is forbidden by the Fourteenth also." Cardozo responded tersely, "There is no such general rule." Palko was eventually executed for the crime—all because he lived in Connecticut rather than in a state whose constitution included a guarantee against double jeopardy.

Cases like *Palko* extended the shadow of *Barron* into its second century, despite the adoption of the Fourteenth Amendment. The Constitution, as interpreted by the Supreme Court, justified a framework in which states had the power to determine their own laws on numerous fundamental issues. States would still have the power to pass laws segregating the races—a power that 13 states chose to exercise. States would still be able to engage in searches and seizures without a warrant, indict accused persons without benefit of a grand jury, deprive persons of trial by jury, force persons to testify against themselves, deprive accused persons of their right to confront adverse witnesses, and as we

---

9 *Gitlow v. New York,* 268 U.S. 652 (1925).

10 *Near v. Minnesota ex rel. Olson,* 283 U.S. 697 (1931); *De Jonge v. Oregon,* 299 U.S. 353 (1937); *Cantwell v. Connecticut,* 310 U.S. 296 (1940).

---

have seen, prosecute accused persons more than once for the same crime.[11] The provisions of the Bill of Rights that protected citizens from these practices were implicitly identified in *Palko* as "not incorporated" into the Fourteenth Amendment as limitations on the powers of the states.

Before we leave the topic, it is worth mentioning that, aside from its implications for the Bill of Rights, one specific part of the Fourteenth Amendment itself is being called into question today: the provision that all persons "born or naturalized" in the United States are citizens. Some politicians and public figures, most notably President Donald Trump, have argued that children born in the United States to undocumented immigrants should not be considered U.S. citizens and should be subject to deportation. Others say that the provision encourages foreigners to come to the United States specifically to have children here; with children born as American citizens, these immigrants hope to gain an advantage in securing their own American citizenship. Another issue is raised by the plight of the so-called Dreamers: undocumented individuals brought to the United States as children and raised here. Many of these people speak only English and identify as Americans, yet they are subject to deportation. Though the United States is a nation of immigrants, the grandchildren of yesterday's immigrants are not always eager to welcome the next group.

The Constitutional Revolution in Civil Liberties

Signs of impending change in the constitutional framework came with the Court's ruling in *Brown v. Board of Education* (1954), which found state-level school segregation laws unconstitutional.[12] Even though *Brown* was not a civil liberties case, it indicated rather clearly that the Supreme Court had an expansive view of civil liberties; with *Brown*, the Court effectively promised that it would actively subject the states and all congressional legislation or executive actions affecting civil rights and civil liberties to strict scrutiny. In retrospect, *Brown* jump-started a constitutional revolution, even though the results were not apparent until after 1961, when the number of incorporated civil liberties increased (see Table 4.1).

Just as the expansion of interstate commerce regulation affected the balance of power between the federal government and the states (as we discussed in Chapter 3), the constitutional revolution in civil liberties was a move toward nationalization. But the two revolutions required opposite motions on the part of the Supreme Court. In the area of commerce (the first revolution), the Court sat back as Congress expanded the meaning of Article I, Section 8's commerce clause through new legislation. This expansion has been so extensive that the national government can now constitutionally regulate a single farmer growing 20 acres of wheat or a small restaurant selling barbecue to local "Whites only"

---

11 *Palko v. Connecticut*, 302 U.S. 319 (1937), was reversed in *Benton v. Maryland*, 395 U.S. 784 (1969), in which the Court said that double jeopardy was in fact incorporated into the Fourteenth Amendment as a restriction on the states.

12 *Brown v. Board of Education of Topeka, Kansas*, 347 U.S. 483 (1954).

without the farmer or the restaurant being anywhere near interstate commerce routes. In the second revolution, involving the Bill of Rights and the Fourteenth Amendment, the Court assumed an active role; it closely reviewed the laws of state legislatures and the decisions of state courts to apply a single, national standard to the rights and liberties of all citizens.

Table 4.1 shows that until 1961, only the First Amendment had been more or less fully and clearly incorporated into the Fourteenth Amendment.[13] After 1961, the Court incorporated several other important provisions of the Bill of Rights through its rulings in cases such as *Gideon v. Wainwright*, which established the right to counsel in a criminal trial, and *Mapp v. Ohio*, which held that evidence obtained in violation of the Fourth Amendment's ban on unreasonable searches and seizures would be excluded from trial.[14] This "exclusionary rule" was particularly irksome to police and prosecutors because it meant that patently guilty defendants sometimes got to go free when evidence that clearly damned them could not be used. In *Miranda v. Arizona*, the Court ruled that arrested persons must be informed of their legal rights to remain silent and have counsel present during interrogation.[15] This is the basis of the **Miranda rule**, familiar to most Americans from police movies and TV shows. (See, too, the discussion of self-incrimination later in this chapter.) By 1969, the Supreme Court had come full circle regarding the rights of the criminally accused; its ruling in *Benton v. Maryland* reversed the *Palko* ruling and thereby incorporated double jeopardy.

Beginning in the mid-1950s, the Court expanded another important area of civil liberties: the right to privacy. In 1958, the Court recognized "privacy in one's association" in its decision to prevent the state of Alabama from using the membership lists of the National Association for the Advancement of Colored People (NAACP) to inform its investigations.[16] As we explore later in this chapter, legal questions about the right to privacy have come to the fore in more recent cases concerning birth control, abortion, homosexuality, and physician-assisted suicide.

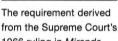

Miranda rule

The requirement derived from the Supreme Court's 1966 ruling in *Miranda v. Arizona* that persons under arrest must be informed of their legal rights, including the right to counsel, before undergoing police interrogation.

THE BILL OF RIGHTS TODAY

Because liberty requires restraining the power of government, the general status of civil liberties can never be considered fixed and permanent. Though the Supreme Court adheres to law and precedent, every provision in the Bill

---

13 The one exception was the right to a public trial (the Sixth Amendment), which was incorporated with *In re Oliver*, 333 U.S. 257 (1948). The Oliver case did not mention the right to a public trial as such, instead putting the issue more generally as "due process," but later opinions, such as *Duncan v. Louisiana*, 391 U.S. 145 (1968), cited the Oliver case as the precedent for incorporating public trials as part of the Fourteenth Amendment.

14 *Mapp v. Ohio*, 367 U.S. 643 (1961).

15 *Miranda v. Arizona*, 384 U.S. 436 (1966).

16 *NAACP v. Alabama*, 357 U.S. 449 (1958).

of Rights is subject to its interpretation, and interpretations always reflect the interpreter's interest in the outcome. As we have seen, the Court continuously reminds everyone that if it has the power to expand the Bill of Rights, it also has the power to contract it.[17]

One good way to examine the Bill of Rights today is to take the provisions one at a time. Some are settled areas of law; some are not. Any one of them could be reinterpreted by the Court at some point. The right of individuals to possess firearms, for example, was only incorporated in 2010. Many have argued that this was a judicial error and should be reconsidered in light of the numerous shootings that anger and terrify Americans each year.

The First Amendment and Freedom of Religion

> Congress shall make no law respecting an establishment of religion, or prohibiting the free exercise thereof; or abridging the freedom of speech, or of the press; or the right of the people peaceably to assemble, and to petition the Government for a redress of grievances.

The Bill of Rights begins by guaranteeing freedom of religion, and the First Amendment provides for that freedom in two distinct clauses: "Congress shall make no law [1] respecting an establishment of religion, or [2] prohibiting the free exercise thereof." The first clause is the *establishment clause*, and the second is the *free exercise clause*. Let's examine the meaning of each.

Separation between Church and State. The **establishment clause** and the idea of "no law" regarding an establishment of religion can be interpreted in several ways. One interpretation, which probably reflects the views of many of the First Amendment's authors, is that the clause only prohibits the government from establishing an official church. Official state churches, such as the Church of England, were common in the eighteenth century and seemed to many Americans to be inconsistent with a republican form of government. Indeed, many colonists had fled Europe to escape the persecution they faced for rejecting state-sponsored churches. A second possible interpretation, the "nonpreferentialist" or "accommodationist" view, holds that the government may not take sides among competing religions, but it is not prohibited from providing assistance to religious institutions or ideas so long as it shows no favoritism. Institutions of U.S. government accommodate religious beliefs in various ways, from the reference to God on U.S. currency to the prayer that begins every session of Congress. These expressions of religion have never been struck down by the courts.

The third view regarding religious establishment, and the most commonly held today, is the idea of a "wall of separation" between church and state

 establishment clause

The First Amendment clause that says, "Congress shall make no law respecting an establishment of religion."

---

17 For a lively and readable treatment of how the Court has restricted provisions of the Bill of Rights without reversing earlier decisions, see David G. Savage, *Turning Right: The Making of the Rehnquist Supreme Court* (New York: Wiley, 1992).

that the government cannot breach. The concept of a wall of separation was Jefferson's formulation, and it has figured in many Supreme Court cases invoking the establishment clause. For centuries, Jefferson's words have had a powerful impact on our understanding of the proper relationship between church and state in the United States. Analyzing the Evidence on pp. 120–1 explores Americans' attitudes toward the separation of church and state.

Despite the absolute sound of the phrase *wall of separation*, there is ample room to disagree on its nature. For example, the Court has been consistently strict in its rulings on prayer in public schools, striking down such practices as Bible reading,[18] nondenominational prayer,[19] a moment of silence for meditation or voluntary prayer, and pregame prayer at public sporting events.[20] In each case, the Court reasoned that religious observations in a school setting, even of an apparently nondenominational character, are highly suggestive of school sponsorship and therefore violate the prohibition against establishment of religion. Yet the Court has been more willing to allow other forms of officially sanctioned prayer. For example, in 2014 the Court decided that the town of Greece, New York, could permit volunteer chaplains to open its legislative sessions with a prayer.[21]

For decades, the Court has faced cases involving government funding for religious schools. In the 1971 case of *Lemon v. Kurtzman*, the Court established three criteria to guide its decisions and those of lower courts in these types of cases, indicating circumstances under which state financial assistance to religious schools is constitutionally permissible. Collectively, these criteria became known as the **Lemon test**. The Court held that government aid to religious schools would be accepted as constitutional if (1) it had a secular purpose, (2) its effect was neither to advance nor to inhibit religion, and (3) it did not entangle government and religious institutions in one another's affairs.[22]

Although these restrictions make it hard to pass the *Lemon* test, imaginative authorities have found ways to do so. The Supreme Court, for its part, has demonstrated a willingness to let them, perhaps signaling a move toward a more accommodationist view of the establishment clause. In 1995, for example, the Court narrowly ruled that a University of Virginia student group could not be denied funds from the school's budget for student activities merely because it was a religious group espousing a particular viewpoint about a deity. The Court called the denial "viewpoint discrimination" and declared that the University had violated the group's free speech rights.[23] Two years later, the Court

Lemon test

A rule, articulated in *Lemon v. Kurtzman*, that says governmental action with respect to religion is permissible if it is secular in purpose, does not lead to "excessive entanglement" of government with religion, and neither promotes nor inhibits the practice of religion. The *Lemon* test is generally used in relation to government aid to religious schools.

---

18 *School District of Abington Township, Pennsylvania v. Schempp*, 374 U.S. 203 (1963).

19 *Engel v. Vitale*, 370 U.S. 421 (1962).

20 *Wallace v. Jaffree*, 472 U.S. 38 (1985).

21 *Town of Greece v. Galloway*, 572 U.S. ____ (2014).

22 *Lemon v. Kurtzman*, 403 U.S. 602 (1971). The *Lemon* test is still good law, but as recently as the 1994 Court term, four justices urged that it be abandoned. Here is a settled area of law that may become unsettled.

23 *Rosenberger v. Rector and Visitors of the University of Virginia*, 515 U.S. 819 (1995).

again demonstrated a politically more conservative approach to the separation of church and state when it accepted the practice of sending public school teachers into parochial schools to provide remedial education to disadvantaged children.[24] And, in the 2002 case of *Zelman v. Simmons-Harris*, the Court upheld an Ohio program that provided tuition vouchers to impoverished students attending private schools, including those enrolled in religious schools.[25]

In 2004, the Court considered the question of whether the phrase "under God" in the Pledge of Allegiance violates the establishment clause. As originally written in 1892, the pledge did not include any religious references. But in 1954, in the midst of the Cold War, Congress voted to add "under God" to the pledge in response to the "godless Communism" of the Soviet Union. Ever since this change was made, there has been a constant murmur of discontent from those who object to a government-sanctioned profession of belief in a deity. In 2003, Michael Newdow, the atheist father of a California kindergartner, brought suit against his daughter's school district, arguing that the reference to God turned the daily recitation of the pledge into a religious exercise. The case was appealed to the Supreme Court, which ruled that Newdow lacked a sufficient personal stake in the case to bring the complaint.[26] This inconclusive decision left "under God" in the pledge while keeping the issue alive for possible resolution in a future case.

In two 2005 cases, the Court ruled, also inconclusively, on government-sponsored displays of religious symbols. Both cases involved displays of the Ten Commandments. In *Van Orden v. Perry*, the Court ruled that a display of the Ten Commandments in the Texas State Capitol did not violate the Constitution.[27] However, in *McCreary v. ACLU*, the Court determined that a display of the Ten Commandments inside two Kentucky court houses was unconstitutional.[28] Justice Stephen Breyer, the swing vote in both cases, intimated that the different rulings stemmed from the different purposes of the two displays. Most legal observers, though, could see little difference between them. This issue continues to be litigated without a clear conclusion.

In a 2019 case, the Court ruled that the "Bladensburg Peace Cross," a World War I memorial on state-owned land in Bladensburg, Maryland, could be left to stand on the grounds that it should be seen as a secular rather than religious symbol.[29] This interpretation seemed to satisfy no one; some were offended that a government-sponsored religious symbol was allowed to remain, while others were offended by the Court's claim that an important religious symbol was merely secular.

---

24 *Agostini v. Felton,* 521 U.S. 203 (1997). The case being overruled was *Aguilar v. Felton,* 473 U.S. 402 (1985).

25 *Zelman v. Simmons-Harris,* 536 U.S. 639 (2002).

26 *Elk Grove Unified School District v. Newdow,* 542 U.S. 1 (2004).

27 *Van Orden v. Perry,* 545 U.S. 677 (2005).

28 *McCreary County v. ACLU,* 545 U.S. 844 (2005).

29 *The American Legion v. American Humanist Association,* 588 U.S. ____ (2019).

Americans' Attitudes toward Church and State

CHAPTER 04

Contributed by
David E. Campbell
University of Notre Dame

Almost all Americans agree that their nation has a separation of church and state, but translating the abstract principle of church-state separation into practice is often contentious. The phrase "separation of church and state" does not actually appear in the Constitution, but religion is mentioned twice in the document.

The first mention of religion is in the First Amendment, which states that "Congress shall make no law respecting an establishment of religion, or prohibiting the free exercise thereof." These two phrases have come to be known as the establishment and free exercise clauses.

A national survey asked Americans about their attitudes toward two applications of the First Amendment: whether it is constitutional for the Ten Commandments to be displayed in a county courthouse (establishment) and whether a florist can refuse to provide flowers for a same-sex wedding on religion grounds (free exercise). The graphs compare the views of Republicans, Independents, and Democrats.

Should the Ten Commandments Be Displayed in a County Courthouse?

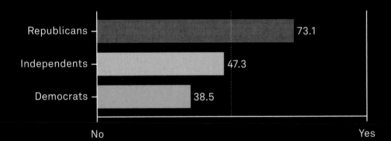

In this study, respondents placed their opinion on a 0–100 scale between "should not be allowed" and "should be allowed." We find that roughly half of all Americans agree that the Ten Commandments can be displayed in a county courthouse. Democrats are more likely to object than Republicans, with independents in between. In response to whether one agrees that a florist can refuse to provide flowers for a same-sex wedding on religious grounds, Republicans are the most likely to agree, and Democrats to disagree, with independents falling in the middle.

Can a Florist Refuse to Provide Flowers for a Same-Sex Wedding?

SOURCE: David E. Campbell, Geoffrey C. Layman, and John C. Green, "The Secular America Study" (2017).

The second place that the Constitution mentions religion is Article VI, which says that "no religious Test shall ever be required as a Qualification to any Office or public Trust under the United States." Yet while formal religious tests are expressly forbidden, historically some voters have been unwilling to vote for candidates with particular religious backgrounds—that is, they have imposed their own religious test.

The graph below displays historical trends in the percentage of Americans who say that they would vote for a presidential candidate (from their preferred party) who is Catholic, Jewish, Mormon, Muslim, or atheist.

Would You Vote for a _____ Candidate?

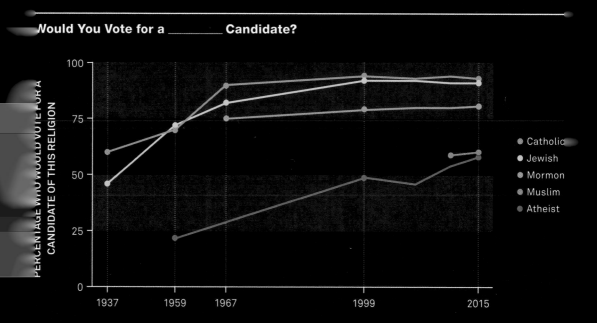

Over the decades, the percentage of Americans who say that they would vote for a Catholic or Jewish presidential candidate has risen steeply (and, of course, in 1960 Americans elected John F. Kennedy, a Catholic). The percentage saying that they would vote for a Mormon has risen only a little since the 1960s. Thus when Mitt Romney, a Mormon, ran for the presidency in 2012, he faced opposition to his religion that was comparable to the anti-Catholicism faced by Kennedy in 1960. While Americans are significantly more willing to vote for an atheist today than in the 1950s, in 2015 only 58 percent of Americans said they would be willing to vote for an atheist. This is comparable to the percentage willing to vote for a Muslim (60 percent). Antagonism toward atheist and Muslim candidates today is about the same as the opposition faced by Catholics and Jews in the 1930s.

SOURCES: Results through 2007: Jeffrey M. Jones, February 20, 2007, www.gallup.com/poll/26611/Some-Americans-Reluctant-Vote-Mormon-72Year%20Old-Presidential-Candidates.aspx; 2012 results: Jeffrey M. Jones, June 21, 2012, www.gallup.com/poll/155285/atheists-muslims-bias-presidential-candidates.aspx; 2015 results: Frank Newport, September 22, 2015, www.gallup.com/opinion/polling-matters/185813/six-americans-say-yes-muslim-president.aspx (accessed 2/26/2016).

free exercise
clause

The First Amendment
clause that protects the
right of citizens to believe
and practice whatever
religion they choose.

Free Exercise of Religion. The **free exercise clause** protects the right of citizens to believe and practice whatever religion they choose; it also protects the right to be a nonbeliever. Generally speaking, problems arise under this clause not because the government decides to interfere with religion, but because generally applicable secular laws intrude on the beliefs of one group or another. A Supreme Court precedent articulated in the 1879 case of *Reynolds v. United States* established that the government could intrude on religious practices if they constituted criminal acts.[30] In this case, Reynolds, a religious polygamist, had been charged with violating a federal anti-bigamy act.

Today, a variety of exceptions to the *Reynolds* principle are recognized. The precedent-setting case was *West Virginia State Board of Education v. Barnette* (1943), which involved the children of a family of Jehovah's Witnesses who refused to salute and pledge allegiance to the American flag, as required by state law, on the grounds that their religious faith did not permit it. Three years earlier, the Court had upheld a requirement that students must salute the flag and had permitted schools to expel students for refusing to do so. But the nation's recent entry into World War II in defense of democracy, coupled with the ugly treatment to which the children had been subjected, induced the Court to reverse itself and endorse the free exercise of religion, even when it may offend the beliefs of the majority.[31]

Although the Court has been fairly consistent in protecting the free exercise of religious belief, it has distinguished between religious beliefs and *actions* based on those beliefs. The 1940 case of *Cantwell v. Connecticut*, which concerned the efforts of two Jehovah's Witnesses to engage in door-to-door fund-raising, established the "time, place, and manner" rule: Americans are free to adhere to any religious beliefs, but the time, place, and manner of their exercise are subject to regulation in the public interest.[32]

In recent years, the principle of free exercise has been bolstered by statutes prohibiting religious discrimination by both public and private entities in a variety of realms, including hiring, land use, and the treatment of prison inmates. Three recent cases illustrate this point. In the first case, a Muslim inmate in an Arkansas jail asserted that the jail's policy against facial hair constrained his ability to exercise his religious beliefs, which required him to grow a beard.[33] The Court held that the prison's policy violated both the free exercise clause and a federal statute designed to protect the ability of prisoners to worship as they pleased. In the second case, the Equal Employment Opportunity Commission brought suit against Abercrombie & Fitch for refusing to hire a Muslim woman who wore a head scarf as part of her religious practice.[34] The Court held that the store's actions constituted religious discrimination in hiring, a violation of

---

30 *Reynolds v. United States*, 98 U.S. 145 (1879).

31 *West Virginia State Board of Education v. Barnette*, 319 U.S. 624 (1943). The case it reversed was *Minersville School District v. Gobitis*, 310 U.S. 586 (1940).

32 *Cantwell v. Connecticut* (1940).

33 *Holt v. Hobbs*, 574 U.S. ____ (2015).

34 *Equal Employment Opportunity Commission v. Abercrombie & Fitch Stores*, 575 U.S. ____ (2015).

Title VII of the 1964 Civil Rights Act, which prohibits private employers from discriminating based on race, color, religion, gender, and national origin.

The third case involved the owners of the Hobby Lobby chain of craft stores, who claimed that their religious beliefs were violated by the section of the Affordable Care Act that required employers to provide their female employees with health insurance coverage of contraception. They based their argument on the 1993 Religious Freedom Restoration Act (RFRA), which requires the government to prove that it has "compelling interest" for requiring individuals to obey a law that violates their religion. In 1997, the Supreme Court found that RFRA could not be applied to the states, but it allowed its application to the actions of the federal government. The 2014 Hobby Lobby case involved a federal statute, so the Court applied RFRA to rule in favor of Hobby Lobby.[35]

In light of the Court's 1997 ruling, a number of states have enacted their own versions of RFRA. These laws have fostered concerns that individuals will use claims of religious freedom to justify discrimination against members of the LGBTQ community. This concern came to the fore in 2018 when the Court ruled in favor of a Colorado baker who refused to create a wedding cake for a same-sex couple because same-sex marriage violated his religious beliefs.[36] In three decisions announced in 2020, the Supreme Court expanded the right of religious exercise and affirmed the special place of religious institutions in American life. Taken together, these decisions seemed to give the free exercise of religion a measure of priority over other political rights in America.

The First Amendment and Freedom of Speech and the Press

> Congress shall make no law . . . abridging the freedom of speech, or of the press.

Because democracy depends on an open political process and politics is basically talk, freedom of speech and freedom of the press are considered critical. For this reason, they hold a prominence in the Bill of Rights equal to that of freedom of religion. In 1938, freedom of speech (which in all important respects includes freedom of the press) was given extraordinary constitutional status when the Supreme Court declared that any legislation attempting to restrict these fundamental freedoms would "be subjected to a more exacting judicial scrutiny . . . than are most other types of legislation."[37] By establishing this principle, the Court in effect signaled that the democratic political process must be protected at almost any cost.

This higher standard of judicial review came to be called **strict scrutiny**. It implies that speech—at least some kinds of speech—will be protected almost

strict scrutiny

The strictest standard of judicial review of a government's actions, in which the government must show that the law serves a "compelling state interest."

---

35 *Burwell v. Hobby Lobby Stores*, 573 U.S. ____ (2014).

36 *Masterpiece Cakeshop v. Colorado Civil Rights Commission*, 584 U.S. ____ (2018).

37 *United States v. Carolene Products Company*, 304 U.S. 144 (1938), p. 384. This footnote is one of the Court's most important doctrines. See Alfred H. Kelly, Winfred A. Harbison, and Herman Belz, *The American Constitution: Its Origins and Development*, 7th ed. (New York: Norton, 1991), vol. 2, pp. 519–23.

absolutely. In 2011, for example, the Supreme Court ruled 8–1 that the West-boro Baptist Church, a tiny Kansas institution, had a First Amendment right to picket the funerals of American soldiers killed in action while displaying signs reading "Thank God for Dead Soldiers." Church members believe that these deaths represent divine punishment for America's tolerance of homosexual-ity and other matters. In his opinion, Chief Justice John Roberts wrote, "As a nation we have chosen to protect even hurtful speech on public issues to ensure that we do not stifle public debate."[38] But even though the Courts have ruled that the Constitution protects many types of controversial speech, only some are fully protected against restrictions. Many forms of speech are less than abso-lutely protected—even though they are entitled to a preferred position.

Political Speech. Political speech—speech commenting on the actions of the government and political leaders—was of the greatest concern to the framers, even though they found freedom of speech one of the more difficult liberties to observe. Within seven years of the ratification of the Bill of Rights, Congress adopted the infamous Alien and Sedition Acts (long since repealed), which, among other things, made it a crime to say or publish anything that might defame or bring into disrepute the U.S. government. The acts criminalized the very conduct given absolute protection by the First Amendment. Fifteen violators, including several newspaper editors, were indicted, and a few were convicted before the relevant portions of the acts were allowed to expire.

The first modern free speech case arose immediately after World War I. It involved persons who had been convicted under the federal Espionage Act of 1917 for opposing American involvement in the war. The Supreme Court upheld the act and refused to protect the defendants' speech rights on the grounds that their activities—appeals to draftees to resist the draft—constituted a **"clear and present danger"** to national security.[39] Although the courts no longer use it, the "clear and present danger" test is the first and most famous test of when government intervention or censorship can be permitted.

It was only after the 1920s that real progress was made toward a genuinely effective First Amendment. Since then, the courts have protected political speech even when it has been deemed "insulting" or "outrageous." In the 1969 case *Brandenburg v. Ohio,* the Supreme Court ruled that as long as speech falls short of actually "inciting or producing imminently lawless action," it cannot be pro-hibited, even if it is hostile to or subversive of the government and its policies.[40] In the *Brandenburg* case, a Ku Klux Klan leader named Charles Brandenburg had been convicted in Ohio courts of violating the state's Criminal Syndicalism Act when he advocated "revengent" action against the president, Congress, and the Supreme Court, among others, if they continued "to suppress the white, Cau-casian race." Although Brandenburg was not carrying a weapon, some members of his audience were. Upon its review of the case, the Supreme Court reversed

clear and present danger

The criterion formerly used to determine whether speech is protected or unprotected, based on its capacity to present a clear and present danger to society.

38 *Snyder v. Phelps,* 562 U.S. 443 (2011).

39 *Schenck v. United States,* 249 U.S. 47 (1919).

40 *Brandenburg v. Ohio,* 395 U.S. 444 (1969).

the state courts and declared Ohio's Criminal Syndicalism Act unconstitutional because it punished persons who "advocate, or teach the duty, necessity, or propriety [of violence] as a means of accomplishing industrial or political reform" or who publish materials or "voluntarily assemble . . . to teach or advocate the doctrines of criminal syndicalism." The Court argued that the statute did not distinguish "mere advocacy" from "incitement to imminent lawless action." It would be difficult to go much further in protecting freedom of speech.

Typically, federal courts strike down restrictions on speech if they are deemed to be "overbroad," "vague," or lacking "neutrality" in terms of the content of the speech—for example, if a statute prohibited the views of the political left but not the political right, or vice versa, or if a statute seemed to restrict speech broadly without specifying the type of speech or conditions for restrictions.

Additional expansion of political speech, particularly the loosening of limits on spending and donations to political campaigns, occurred in 1976 with the Supreme Court's decision in *Buckley v. Valeo*.[41] Campaign finance reform laws of the early 1970s had set severe limits on campaign spending in response to the Watergate scandal. In *Buckley*, the Court declared numerous important provisions of these laws unconstitutional on the basis of the idea that spending money by or on behalf of candidates is a form of speech protected by the First Amendment (as contrasted with contributions to campaigns, which Congress has more authority to regulate). The issue arose again after passage of a more severe campaign finance law, the Bipartisan Campaign Reform Act (BCRA), in 2002. In a 2003 ruling on several BCRA provisions, a Court majority seriously reduced the area of speech protected by *Buckley v. Valeo* by holding that Congress was within its power to limit the amount individuals could spend, the amount of "soft money" that corporations and their political action committees (PACs) could spend, and the amount interest groups could spend on issue advertising before Election Day. The Court argued that "the selling of access . . . has given rise to the appearance of undue influence [that justifies] regulations impinging on First Amendment rights . . . in order to curb corruption or the appearance of corruption."[42]

This decision proved to be an anomaly, however. In 2007, the Court struck down a key portion of BCRA, finding that the act's limitations on political advertising violated the First Amendment's guarantee of free speech.[43] In *Citizens United v. Federal Election Commission* in 2010, the Court ruled that corporate funding of independent election ads could not be limited under the First Amendment.[44] And in 2014, the Court struck down aggregate limits on an individual's contributions to candidates for federal office, political parties, and PACs. The decision stated that such limits do not further the government's

---

41 *Buckley v. Valeo*, 424 U.S. 1 (1976).

42 *McConnell v. Federal Election Commission*, 540 U.S. 93 (2003).

43 *Federal Election Commission v. Wisconsin Right to Life*, 551 U.S. 449 (2007).

44 *Citizens United v. Federal Election Commission*, 558 U.S. 310 (2010).

interest in preventing corruption and are thus invalid under the First Amendment.[45] As a result of this decision, several wealthy donors contributed more than $10 million each to presidential candidates in 2016. In all three of these decisions, the Court maintained that limits on political spending amounted to limits on free speech.

Symbolic Speech, Speech Plus Action, and the Rights of Assembly and Petition. The First Amendment treats the freedoms of assembly and petition as equal to the freedoms of religion and political speech. Freedom of assembly and freedom of petition are closely associated with speech but take speech a step further by associating it with action. Since at least 1931, the Supreme Court has protected actions that are designed to send a political message. (Usually the purpose of a symbolic act is not only to send a message but also to draw spectators and thus strengthen the message.) Generally speaking, state and federal governments may enact reasonable regulations governing the time, place, and manner of speech so long as they do not discriminate against particular messages or messengers. A limitation on political parades after 7 p.m., for example, must apply to *all* parades. Following this reasoning, the Court held unconstitutional a California statute making it a felony to display a red flag "as a sign, symbol or emblem of opposition to organized government" because the ordinance seemed to target one particular political view.[46]

Although today there are limits on how far one can go with actions that symbolically convey a message, protections for such actions are very broad. In the case of a man who was charged with a crime for burning his draft card in protest of the Vietnam War, the Court upheld the federal law criminalizing his act on the grounds that the government had a compelling interest in preserving draft cards.[47] In another case just a year later, however, the Court ruled in favor of students who wore black armbands to school to protest the war, concluding that their act was a protected form of assembly.[48] In such cases, a court will often use the standard articulated in the draft card case, *United States v. O'Brien*, now known as the *O'Brien* test. Under this test, a statute that restricts expressive or symbolic speech must be justified by a compelling governmental interest and be narrowly tailored toward achieving that interest.

Another example of symbolic speech is the burning of the American flag in protest. In 1984, at a rally during the Republican National Convention in Dallas, a political protester burned an American flag in violation of a Texas statute prohibiting the desecration of a venerated object. In a 5–4 decision, the Supreme Court declared the Texas law unconstitutional on the grounds that flag burning is expressive conduct protected by the First Amendment.[49] In an

---

45 *McCutcheon v. Federal Election Commission*, 572 U.S. ____ (2014).

46 *Stromberg v. California*, 283 U.S. 359 (1931).

47 *United States v. O'Brien*, 391 U.S. 367 (1968).

48 *Tinker v. Des Moines Independent Community School District*, 393 U.S. 503 (1969).

49 *Texas v. Johnson*, 491 U.S. 397 (1989).

attempt to overturn the Court's decision with legislation, Congress passed the Flag Protection Act of 1989. Protesters promptly violated this act and were brought to court. Federal district courts ruled in favor of the protesters and declared the new law unconstitutional, and the Supreme Court affirmed the lower courts' decision.[50]

In 2003, the Court struck down a Virginia statute against cross burning as too strict, ruling that states could make cross burning a crime only if the statute required prosecutors to prove that the burning was intended to intimidate rather than simply express an opinion. Justice Sandra Day O'Connor wrote that the First Amendment permits the government to forbid cross burning as a "particularly virulent form of intimidation," but not as "a form of symbolic expression."[51] This decision will likely become a more generalized First Amendment protection of any conduct that can be considered a form of symbolic expression.

Closer to the original intent of the First Amendment's assembly and petition clause is the category of **speech plus**—speech accompanied by physical activity such as picketing, distributing leaflets, or other forms of peaceful demonstration or assembly. Such assemblies are consistently protected by courts under the First Amendment; state and local laws regulating these activities in public spaces are frequently overturned. But the same kinds of assemblies on private property are quite another matter, and they can often be regulated. For example, the directors of a shopping center can lawfully prohibit an assembly protesting a war or supporting a ban on abortion. Assemblies in public areas can also be restricted under some circumstances, especially when the health, safety, or rights of others are jeopardized. This condition was the basis of the Supreme Court's decision to uphold a lower-court order restricting abortion protesters' access to the entrances of abortion clinics.[52]

 speech plus

Speech accompanied by activities such as sit-ins, picketing, and demonstrations.

Freedom of the Press. Freedom of speech includes freedom of the press. With the exception of electronic media, which are subject to federal regulation, the press is protected under the doctrine prohibiting **prior restraint**. Since 1931, the Supreme Court has held that, except under extraordinary circumstances, the First Amendment prohibits government agencies from seeking to prevent newspapers or magazines from publishing whatever they wish.[53] Indeed, in *New York Times v. United States* (1971), the so-called Pentagon Papers case, the Court ruled that the government could not even block publication of secret Defense Department documents furnished to the *New York Times* by a Vietnam War opponent who had obtained the documents illegally.[54] In 1990, however, the

 prior restraint

An effort by a government agency to block publication of material by a newspaper or magazine; censorship.

50 *United States v. Eichman,* 496 U.S. 310 (1990).

51 *Virginia v. Black,* 538 U.S. 343 (2003).

52 For a good general discussion of speech plus, see Louis Fisher, *American Constitutional Law* (New York: McGraw-Hill, 1990), pp. 544–6. The case upholding the buffer zone against the abortion protesters is *Madsen v. Women's Health Center,* 512 U.S. 753 (1994).

53 *Near v. Minnesota ex rel. Olson* (1931).

54 *New York Times Company v. United States,* 403 U.S. 713 (1971).

Court upheld a lower-court order restraining the Cable News Network (CNN) from broadcasting tapes of conversations between former Panamanian dictator Manuel Noriega and his lawyer that had supposedly been recorded by the American government. The Court held that CNN could be restrained from broadcasting the tapes until the trial court had heard the tapes and decided whether their broadcast would violate Noriega's right to a fair trial.[55]

The government may prosecute journalists for refusing to reveal their sources and may seek to prosecute individuals who leak information to the press. During the Obama presidency, seven individuals were charged with or prosecuted for disclosing classified information. They included Private First Class Chelsea (then known as Bradley) Manning, an army intelligence analyst sent to prison for providing classified documents to WikiLeaks, and Edward Snowden, an employee of the National Security Agency (NSA) who fled the country to escape arrest after revealing details of the agency's domestic spying operations.

Libel and Slander. Some speech is not protected at all. If a written statement is made in "reckless disregard of the truth" and is considered damaging to the victim because it is "malicious, scandalous, and defamatory," it can be punished as **libel**. An oral statement of such nature can be punished as **slander**.

Today most libel suits involve freedom of the press. Historically, newspapers were subject to the law of libel, which provided that newspapers printing false and malicious stories could be compelled to pay damages to those they defamed. Recently, however, American courts have narrowed the meaning of libel and made it extremely difficult, particularly for public figures, to win a libel case against a newspaper. In *New York Times v. Sullivan*, the Court held that, to be deemed libelous, a story about a public official not only has to be untrue but also has to result from "actual malice" or "reckless disregard" for the truth.[56] That is, the newspaper has to *deliberately* print false and malicious material. But this level of intent is nearly impossible to prove, so the print media essentially have been able to publish anything they want about public figures. The courts have been more sympathetic to libel and slander claims made by private individuals.

In at least one case, however, the Court has opened up the possibility for public officials to file libel suits against the press. In 1985, the Court held that the press is immune from libel charges only when the material in question is "a matter of public concern." In other words, in future cases a newspaper accused of libel would have to show that the public official was engaged in activities that were indeed *public*. This principle has made the press more vulnerable to libel suits, but it still leaves an enormous realm of freedom for the press. As a candidate, President Trump declared that he would push for tougher libel laws to protect public figures like himself from what he called the "lying media." As president, however, Trump has failed to act on the threat.

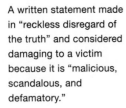

libel

A written statement made in "reckless disregard of the truth" and considered damaging to a victim because it is "malicious, scandalous, and defamatory."

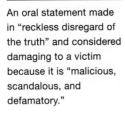

slander

An oral statement made in "reckless disregard of the truth" and considered damaging to a victim because it is "malicious, scandalous, and defamatory."

---

55 *Cable News Network v. Noriega,* 498 U.S. 976 (1990).

56 *New York Times Company v. Sullivan,* 376 U.S. 254 (1964).

Obscenity and Pornography. If libel and slander cases involve the difficult problem of determining the truth of statements and whether they are malicious and damaging, cases involving pornography and obscenity can be even stickier. It is easy to say that pornography and obscenity fall outside the realm of protected speech, but it is impossible to clearly define where protection ends and unprotected speech begins. The Supreme Court first confronted this problem in 1957 with a definition of obscenity that may have caused more confusion than it cleared up. Justice William Brennan, in writing the Court's opinion, defined obscenity as speech or writing that appeals to "prurient interest"—that is, books, magazines, films, and other material that "the average person, applying contemporary community standards," would judge as meant to excite lust. Even so, Brennan added, a work should be judged as obscene only when it is "utterly without redeeming social importance."[57] In 1964, Justice Potter Stewart confessed that although he found pornography impossible to define, "I know it when I see it."[58]

All attempts by the courts to define pornography and obscenity have proved impractical because each instance required courts to screen thousands of pages of print material or hours of film alleged to be pornographic. The vague standards meant ultimately that almost nothing could be banned on the grounds that it was conclusively pornographic and obscene. In 1973, the Supreme Court attempted to strengthen its definition of pornography: a work that as a whole is deemed prurient by the "average person" according to "community standards," depicts sexual conduct "in a patently offensive way," and lacks "serious literary, artistic, political, or scientific value." Pornography would thus be determined according to local rather than national standards. For instance, a local bookseller might be prosecuted for selling a volume that was a best seller nationally but was deemed pornographic locally.[59] The Court's new definition did not help much, and not long after 1973 the Court again began to review all such community antipornography laws, reversing most of them. This area of free speech is far from settled.

Lately the battle against obscene speech has focused on internet pornography, which opponents argue should be strictly regulated because of children's easy access to the internet. The first significant effort to regulate online content occurred in 1996 with the Telecommunications Act. Attached to the legislation was an amendment, the Communications Decency Act (CDA), that sought to regulate the online transmission of obscene material. A coalition of interests led by the American Civil Liberties Union (ACLU) immediately challenged the CDA's constitutionality. In the 1997 case of *Reno v. ACLU*, the Supreme Court struck down the CDA, ruling that it suppressed speech that "adults have a constitutional right to receive."[60] Congress again tried to limit children's access

---

57 *Roth v. United States*, 354 U.S. 476 (1957).

58 Concurring opinion in *Jacobellis v. Ohio*, 378 U.S. 184 (1964).

59 *Miller v. California*, 413 U.S. 15 (1973).

60 *Reno v. ACLU*, 521 U.S. 844 (1997).

with the 2001 Children's Internet Protection Act, which required public libraries to install antipornography filters on all library computers with internet access. In 2003 the Court upheld the law, asserting that its provisions did not violate library patrons' First Amendment rights.[61]

In 2000, the Court also extended First Amendment protection to cable (not broadcast) television. In *United States v. Playboy Entertainment Group*, the Court struck down a portion of the Telecommunications Act of 1996 that required cable TV companies to limit the broadcast of sexually explicit programming to late-night hours. In its decision, the Court noted that the law already provided parents with the means to restrict access to sexually explicit cable channels through blocking devices. Moreover, such programming could enter the home only if parents purchased these channels in the first place.[62]

Other conflicts have focused on the use of children in pornography rather than their access to it. In 2003, Congress enacted the Prosecutorial Remedies and Other Tools to end the Exploitation of Children Today (PROTECT) Act, which outlawed the sale of child pornography via the internet along with the creation and possession of child pornography. The Supreme Court upheld this act in 2008, ruling that criminalizing efforts to disseminate child pornography did not violate free speech guarantees.[63]

Student Speech. One category of conditionally protected speech is the free speech of students in public schools. The landmark case in this realm is *Tinker v. Des Moines Independent Community School District* (1969).[64] The case involved several students who, in violation of school policy, wore black armbands to school to protest the Vietnam War. The students were suspended, and the parents, together with the Iowa Civil Liberties Union, brought suit. Upon review of the case, the Supreme Court ruled in favor of the students and declared that the First Amendment applied to speech in public schools. To censor student speech, administrators would need to show that the speech in question threatened to substantially disrupt educational activities.

In 1986, however, the Court backed away from a broad protection of student free speech rights by upholding the punishment of a high school student for making a sexually suggestive speech. The Court held that such speech interfered with the school's goal of teaching students the limits of socially acceptable behavior.[65] Two years later, the Court further restricted students' speech and press rights, defining school-sponsored student communications as part of the educational process and not to be treated with the same standard as adult speech in a regular public forum.[66] A more recent case involving high school students

---

61 *United States v. American Library Association*, 539 U.S. 194 (2003).

62 *United States v. Playboy Entertainment Group*, 529 U.S. 803 (2000).

63 *United States v. Williams*, 553 U.S. 285 (2008).

64 *Tinker v. Des Moines Independent Community School District* (1969).

65 *Bethel School District No. 403 v. Fraser*, 478 U.S. 675 (1986).

66 *Hazelwood School District v. Kuhlmeier*, 484 U.S. 260 (1988).

arose from school policies in Juneau, Alaska.[67] In 2002, the Olympic torch relay passed through Juneau on its way to the Winter Olympics. As the torch passed Juneau-Douglas High, a senior, Joseph Frederick, unfurled a banner that read, "Bong Hits 4 Jesus." The school's principal promptly suspended Frederick, who then brought suit, alleging violation of his free speech rights. Like most public schools, Juneau-Douglas High prohibits expressions on school grounds that advocate illegal drug use. Civil libertarians see these policies as restricting students' rights to free speech. The Court ruled in favor of the principal, however, stating that the First Amendment does not require schools to permit student speech endorsing illegal drug use.

Free speech controversies often surface at the college level, as well. For instance, scores of universities have attempted to develop speech codes to suppress racial or ethnic slurs. The Department of Education's Office for Civil Rights encouraged universities to draft such codes to facilitate their compliance with Title IX of the Higher Education Act, which requires colleges to vigorously prosecute charges involving racial or sexual harassment. However, speech codes at public universities generally have been struck down by federal judges as unconstitutional infringements on speech. In 2018, Secretary of Education Betsy DeVos criticized college speech codes and said that she planned to issue new guidelines for colleges and universities. Putting speech codes aside, on a number of campuses protesters have forced the cancellation of speeches by controversial figures such as conservative firebrands Ann Coulter and Milo Yiannopoulos. Some students and professors argue that hateful speech has no place on college campuses, while others assert that colleges should be bastions of free speech even when the speech is offensive.

Large corporations have also made efforts to formalize speech guidelines in a realm where many successful complaints and lawsuits have alleged that employers' or supervisors' words create a "hostile or abusive working environment." The Supreme Court has held that "sexual harassment" that creates a "hostile working environment" includes "unwelcome sexual advances, requests for sexual favors, and other *verbal* or physical conduct of a sexual nature"[68] (emphasis added). These regulations of hostile behavior thus involve a fundamental free speech issue.

Hate Speech. Many jurisdictions have drafted ordinances banning forms of expression that assert hatred toward a specific group, be it African Americans, Jews, Muslims, or other people. Such laws seldom pass constitutional muster. The leading Supreme Court case in this realm is the 1992 decision in *R.A.V. v. City of St. Paul.*[69] Here, a White teenager was arrested for burning a cross on the lawn of a Black family in violation of a municipal ordinance that banned cross burning as well as the use of racist symbols designed to intimidate others.

---

67 *Morse v. Frederick*, 551 U.S. 393 (2007).

68 *Meritor Savings Bank v. Vinson*, 477 U.S. 57 (1986).

69 *R.A.V. v. City of St. Paul*, 505 U.S. 377 (1992).

The Court struck down the ordinance on the grounds that it was not *content neutral*—that is, it prohibited actions directed at some groups but not others. Cross burning, historically, has been used as an expression of hatred toward African Americans. Since an alternative statute banning all forms of hateful expression would be deemed overly broad, the *R.A.V.* standard may in practice protect virtually all hate speech.

In a 1993 case, however, the Court ruled that a state can consider whether a crime was motivated by bias against a minority group. So-called hate crimes can be more severely punished than similar acts committed for other reasons.[70] The Court distinguished this judgment from the *R.A.V.* decision by noting that *R.A.V.* was concerned with expression, whereas the ordinance in question in the 1993 case was aimed at violent action.

The question of what constitutes hate speech is often difficult to resolve. To some, a display of the Confederate flag is a symbol of racism and oppression. To others, such a display may constitute respect for regional traditions and heritage. The question is made even more complicated by the fact that hate speech can sometimes turn into violent action. For instance, in 2017, a plan by the city of Charlottesville, Virginia, to remove a number of Confederate monuments near the University of Virginia campus led to violence when groups protesting in support of and opposition to removal of the monuments clashed. One person was killed when a neo-Nazi who had come to Charlottesville to oppose the statues' removal drove his car into a crowd of anti-monument demonstrators.

Commercial Speech. Commercial speech, such as newspaper or television advertising, does not have full First Amendment protection because it cannot be considered political speech. Initially considered to be entirely outside the protection of the First Amendment, commercial speech made gains during the twentieth century. Some commercial speech is still unprotected and therefore regulated. For example, regulation of false and misleading advertising by the Federal Trade Commission is a well-established power of the federal government. The Supreme Court long ago approved the constitutionality of laws prohibiting the electronic media from carrying cigarette advertising.[71] It also has upheld city ordinances prohibiting the posting of all signs on public property (as long as the ban is total, with no hint of favoritism toward certain viewpoints)[72] as well as Puerto Rico's statute restricting gambling advertising aimed at residents of Puerto Rico.[73]

However, gains far outweigh losses in the effort to expand the protection commercial speech enjoys under the First Amendment. As the scholar Louis Fisher explains, "In part, this reflects the growing appreciation that commercial speech is part of the free flow of information necessary for informed choice

---

70 *Wisconsin v. Mitchell*, 508 U.S. 476 (1993).

71 *Capital Broadcasting Company v. Mitchell*, 333 FSupp 582 (D.C. Cir., 1971).

72 *City Council v. Taxpayers for Vincent*, 466 U.S. 789 (1984).

73 *Posadas de Puerto Rico Associates v. Tourism Company of Puerto Rico*, 478 U.S. 328 (1986).

and democratic participation."[74] For example, the Court in 1975 struck down a state statute making it a misdemeanor to sell or circulate advertisements encouraging abortions; the Court ruled that the statute infringed on constitutionally protected speech and the reader's right to make informed choices.[75] On a similar basis, the Court reversed its own earlier decisions upholding laws that prohibited lawyers, dentists, and other professionals from advertising their services. The Court determined medical and legal services to be matters of public interest that could be advanced by the free flow of information, including information disseminated through advertising.[76] In a 1983 case, the Court struck down a congressional statute prohibiting the unsolicited mailing of advertisements for contraceptives. In 1996, it struck down Rhode Island laws and regulations banning the advertisement of liquor prices.[77] And in a 2001 case, the Court ruled that a Massachusetts ban on all cigarette advertising violated the tobacco industry's First Amendment right to advertise its products to adult consumers.[78] These rulings on commercial speech are significant because they indicate the breadth and depth of the freedom that exists today to appeal broadly to a large public, whether to sell goods and services or to mobilize people for political purposes.

The Second Amendment and the Right to Bear Arms

A well regulated Militia, being necessary to the security of a free State, the right of the people to keep and bear Arms, shall not be infringed.

The purpose of the Second Amendment is to provide for militias to assist the government in the maintenance of local public order. Most of the framers viewed militias as military or police resources for state governments; they were thus distinct from armies and troops, which fell within the sole constitutional jurisdiction of Congress. Many individuals, though, have argued that the Second Amendment also establishes an individual right to bear arms.

The judicial record of Second Amendment cases is far sparser than the record of First Amendment cases, and for almost 60 years, the Court made no Second Amendment decisions. The United States has a higher gun ownership rate than any other developed country (see Figure 4.1 for a comparison with selected countries), but there are few national policies regulating firearms. Various states and localities have very different gun ownership standards. For instance, in Wyoming, there is no ban on owning any type of gun, there is no

---

74 Fisher, *American Constitutional Law*, p. 546.

75 *Bigelow v. Virginia*, 421 U.S. 809 (1975).

76 *Bates v. State Bar of Arizona*, 433 U.S. 350 (1977).

77 *44 Liquormart v. Rhode Island*, 517 U.S. 484 (1996).

78 *Lorillard Tobacco Company v. Reilly*, 533 U.S. 525 (2001).

Figure 4.1
GUN OWNERSHIP IN COMPARISON

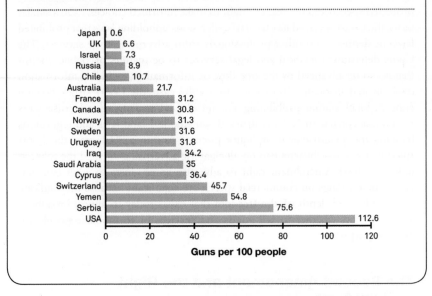

Country	Guns per 100 people
Japan	0.6
UK	6.6
Israel	7.3
Russia	8.9
Chile	10.7
Australia	21.7
France	31.2
Canada	30.8
Norway	31.3
Sweden	31.6
Uruguay	31.8
Iraq	34.2
Saudi Arabia	35
Cyprus	36.4
Switzerland	45.7
Yemen	54.8
Serbia	75.6
USA	112.6

Guns per 100 people

SOURCE: Hugh Morris, "Mapped: The Countries with the Most Guns," *Telegraph*, https://www
.telegraph.co.uk/travel/maps-and-graphics/mapped-the-countries-with-the-most-guns (accessed
5/15/20).

waiting period to purchase a firearm, and individuals are not required to obtain a permit to carry a concealed weapon. In California, by contrast, the possession of assault weapons is banned, there is a 10-day waiting period to purchase a firearm, and a permit is required to carry a concealed weapon. In Virginia, individuals may practice "open carry" of handguns without a permit, but a license is required to carry a concealed weapon.

In a 2008 decision, the Supreme Court ruled that the federal government could not prohibit individuals from owning guns and keeping them in their homes for self-defense. The case involved a District of Columbia ordinance that made it virtually impossible for residents to possess firearms legally. In the majority opinion, Justice Antonin Scalia stated that the decision was not intended to cast doubt on all laws limiting firearm possession, such as prohibitions on gun ownership by felons or the mentally ill.[79] In his dissenting opinion, Justice John Paul Stevens asserted that the Second Amendment protects only the rights of individuals to bear arms as part of a militia force, not in an individual capacity. Because the District of Columbia is an entity of the federal government, the Court's 2008 ruling applied only to federal laws concerning gun ownership; the Court did not indicate that its ruling extended to state firearms laws as well. However, in a 2010 case the Court struck down a Chicago

79 *District of Columbia v. Heller*, 554 U.S. 570 (2008).

firearms ordinance and, in doing so, applied the Second Amendment to the states.[80] The Chicago case concerned an ordinance that made it extremely difficult to own a gun within city limits, and the Court's ruling had the effect of overturning the law.

Despite these rulings, the debate over gun control continues to loom large in American politics today. A recent series of tragic shootings (including the killing of 20 elementary school students in Newtown, Connecticut; 50 people at a nightclub in Orlando, Florida; 58 people at a concert in Las Vegas, Nevada; 27 congregants at a church near San Antonio, Texas; and 14 students at a high school in Parkland, Florida) has kept the issue of gun laws firmly on the national agenda. In 2016, President Obama issued several executive orders designed to expand background checks for gun purchasers and licensure requirements for firearms dealers, but these did not end the debate; indeed, President Trump rescinded a portion of the Obama-era checks.

Rights of the Criminally Accused

Most of the battle to apply the Bill of Rights to the states was over the protections granted to individuals who are accused of a crime, who are suspected of committing a crime, or who are brought before court as witnesses to a crime. The Bill of Rights entitles every American to **due process** of law, which means that the government must respect all the legal rights to which every individual is entitled. The Fourth, Fifth, Sixth, and Eighth Amendments constitute the essence of due process, even though the words *due process* do not appear until the end of the Fifth Amendment. In the next sections, we consider cases that illuminate the dynamics of this important constitutional issue. The procedural safeguards that we discuss help define the limits of governmental action against the personal liberty of every citizen. Many Americans believe that "legal technicalities" are responsible for setting many criminals free. In many cases, that is true. In fact, setting defendants free is the very purpose of the requirements that constitute due process, though few convictions are actually lost because of excluded evidence. One of our nation's most strongly held juridical values is that "it is far worse to convict an innocent man than to let a guilty man go free."[81] In civil suits, verdicts rest on "the preponderance of the evidence"; in criminal cases, guilt must be proved "beyond a reasonable doubt"—a far higher standard. The provisions for due process in the Bill of Rights were added to improve the probability that the standard of reasonable doubt will be respected.

 due process

The requirement that citizens be treated according to the law and be provided adequate protection for individual rights.

---

80 *McDonald v. Chicago*, 561 U.S. 742 (2010).

81 *In re Winship*, 397 U.S. 358 (1970). An outstanding treatment of due process in issues involving the Fourth through Seventh Amendments is found in Fisher, *American Constitutional Law*, chap. 13.

The Fourth Amendment and Searches and Seizures

> The right of the people to be secure in their persons, houses, papers, and effects, against unreasonable searches and seizures, shall not be violated, and no Warrants shall issue, but upon probable cause, supported by Oath or affirmation, and particularly describing the place to be searched, and the persons or things to be seized.

The purpose of the Fourth Amendment is to guarantee the security of citizens against unreasonable (that is, improper) searches and seizures. In 1990, the Supreme Court summarized its understanding of this amendment: "A search compromises the individual interest in privacy; a seizure deprives the individual of dominion over his or her person or property."[82] Here the Court reaffirmed the so-called *Katz* test, named for the case of *Katz v. United States*, in which the Court declared that the Fourth Amendment protects areas where a person has "a reasonable expectation of privacy."[83] But how do we define what is reasonable and what is unreasonable?

The 1961 case of *Mapp v. Ohio* illustrates the beauty and the agony of one of the most important procedures to have grown out of the Fourth Amendment: the **exclusionary rule**, which prohibits evidence obtained during an illegal search from being introduced in a trial. Dollree (Dolly) Mapp was described by local newspapers as "a Cleveland woman of questionable reputation" (by some accounts), the ex-wife of one prominent boxer, and the fiancée of an even more famous one. Acting on a tip that Mapp was harboring a suspect in a bombing incident, policemen forcibly entered her house, claiming they had a warrant to look for the suspect. They did not find the suspect, but they did find what they viewed as obscene materials as well as illegal betting slips. Although the warrant was never produced, the evidence that the police had seized was admitted by a court, and Mapp was charged with and convicted of illegal possession of obscene materials. The question before the Court was whether any evidence produced under the circumstances of the search of Mapp's home was admissible. The Court's opinion affirmed the exclusionary rule: under the Fourth Amendment (applied to state law through the Fourteenth Amendment), "all evidence obtained by searches and seizures in violation of the Constitution . . . is inadmissible." Thus even people who are clearly guilty of the crime of which they are accused cannot be convicted if the only evidence supporting their conviction was obtained illegally.

The exclusionary rule is the most severe restraint imposed by the Constitution and the courts on police behavior. It is a dramatic restriction because it often rules out the evidence that produces a conviction; it frees those people who are *known* to have committed the crime of which they have been accused. Because it works so powerfully in favor of persons known to have committed

exclusionary rule ➡️

The requirement that courts exclude evidence obtained in violation of the Fourth Amendment.

---

82 *Horton v. California*, 496 U.S. 128 (1990).

83 *Katz v. United States*, 389 U.S. 347 (1967).

---

a crime, the Court has since softened the rule's application. Recently, federal courts have relied on a discretionary use of the exclusionary rule, whereby they make a judgment as to the "nature and quality of the intrusion." It is thus difficult to know ahead of time whether the courts will or will not acquit a defendant on the basis of the Fourth Amendment's protection from illegal searches.[84]

Another issue involving the Fourth Amendment is the controversy over mandatory drug testing. Such testing is widely used on public employees. In two important 1989 cases, the Supreme Court upheld the U.S. Customs Service's drug testing program for its employees[85] and approved drug and alcohol tests for railroad workers who had been involved in serious accidents.[86] After these decisions, more than 40 federal agencies initiated mandatory employee drug tests, reinforced by a presidential executive order touted as the "campaign for a drug-free federal workplace." These practices gave rise to public appeals against "suspicionless testing" of employees, which seemed to violate the Fourth Amendment. A 1995 case in which the Court upheld a public school district's policy requiring all student athletes to submit to random drug tests surely contributed to federal, state, and local agencies' efforts to initiate random drug and alcohol testing of their own.[87]

A 1997 case suggested, however, that the Court would consider limits on the "war" against drugs; in an 8–1 decision, the Court applied the Fourth Amendment as a shield against "state action that diminishes personal privacy" when the officials in question are not performing high-risk or safety-sensitive tasks.[88] Using random and suspicionless drug testing to symbolically fight drug use was, in the Court's opinion, carrying the exceptions to the Fourth Amendment too far. More recently, the Court found it unconstitutional for police to use trained dogs in roadblocks set up to look for drugs in cars. Unlike roadblocks intended to check for drunk drivers, where public safety is involved, narcotics roadblocks "cannot escape the Fourth Amendment's requirement that searches be based on suspicion of individual wrongdoing."[89]

As new technologies develop, the Court will continue to face the question of what constitutes a reasonable search. The Court has ruled that police may not use thermal-imaging devices to detect suspicious patterns of heat emerging from private homes without obtaining a search warrant.[90] In 2012, the Court held that GPS tracking (such as attaching a GPS device to a vehicle to track its

---

84 For a good discussion of the issue, see Fisher, *American Constitutional Law*, pp. 884–9.

85 *National Treasury Employees Union v. Von Raab*, 489 U.S. 656 (1989).

86 *Skinner v. Railway Labor Executives' Association*, 489 U.S. 602 (1989).

87 *Vernonia School District 47J v. Acton*, 515 U.S. 646 (1995).

88 *Chandler v. Miller*, 520 U.S. 305 (1997).

89 Linda Greenhouse, "In Year of Florida Vote, Supreme Court Also Did Much Other Work," *New York Times*, July 2, 2001, p. A12. The case in question is *City of Indianapolis v. Edmond*, 531 U.S. 32 (2000).

90 *Kyllo v. United States*, 533 U.S. 27 (2001).

movements) also constitutes a search under the Fourth Amendment and therefore requires a warrant.[91] In the 2014 case of *Riley v. California*, the Court held that the police are constitutionally prohibited from seizing and searching the digital contents of a cell phone during an arrest.[92]

In a high-profile controversy over Fourth Amendment protections in 2016, the FBI sought to compel the Apple Corporation to unlock the contents of the cell phone used by Syed Farook, an alleged terrorist who, along with his wife, Tashfeen Malik, killed 14 people in San Bernardino, California, in 2015. Apple refused, arguing that creating new software to enable the FBI to unlock the phone would allow the agency to invade the privacy of millions of iPhone users if it so desired. Civil libertarians applauded the position, but those concerned with the nation's security were aghast at Apple's refusal, believing that the FBI should have access to data that could aid in a terrorism investigation. The case became moot when the FBI was able to unlock the phone without Apple's help, so this issue did not appear before federal courts.

Fourth Amendment issues have also been raised by aggressive police tactics, particularly the "stop and frisk" approach to policing. This is a tactic in which the police confront an individual whom they believe to be acting "suspiciously," question the individual, and conduct a search for weapons. The practice was reviewed by the Supreme Court in the 1968 case of *Terry v. Ohio*, and the Court then held that if an officer had "probable cause" to believe the individual was armed, such a search was permitted.[93] In recent years, some police departments have made stop and frisk a routine practice, searching thousands of individuals whom they deem to look suspicious. In the case of New York City, who aggressively used the tactic for a number of years, the police maintained that the practice reduced crime rates. In August 2013 a federal judge, Shira Scheindlin, ruled that most police stops occurred in minority communities and amounted to a form of racial profiling. Her order ending the practice, however, was stayed by a federal appeals court that removed Judge Scheindlin from the case and accused her of improper bias. After his election in 2014, Mayor Bill de Blasio announced an end to aggressive stop and frisk tactics. Critics charged that the mayor's orders were responsible for a subsequent increase in New York crime rates.

Stop and frisk is intended to protect communities from violent crime, but opponents view it as invasion of privacy and unreasonable search without sufficient cause. Furthermore, detractors charge that such tactics damage the relationship between the police and the community.

Finally, the Fourth Amendment places limits on government surveillance of individuals, an ongoing and controversial issue in the United States today. For example, a federal judge in Washington, D.C., recently ruled that an NSA

---

91 *United States v. Jones*, 565 U.S. 400 (2012).

92 *Riley v. California*, 573 U.S. ____ (2014).

93 *Terry v. Ohio*, 392 U.S. 1 (1968).

program that collected millions of records of telephone calls was impermissible under the Fourth Amendment. The Policy Principle box on p. 140 examines government surveillance in the context of the Fourth Amendment.

The Fifth Amendment and Criminal Proceedings

No person shall be held to answer for a capital, or otherwise infamous crime, unless on a presentment or indictment of a Grand Jury, except in cases arising in the land or naval forces, or in the Militia, when in actual service in time of War or public danger; nor shall any person be subject for the same offense to be twice put in jeopardy of life or limb; nor shall be compelled in any criminal case to be a witness against himself, nor be deprived of life, liberty, or property, without due process of law; nor shall private property be taken for public use, without just compensation.

Grand Juries. The right to have a **grand jury** determine whether a trial is warranted is "the oldest institution known to the Constitution."[94] A grand jury is a body of citizens that must agree the prosecutor has sufficient evidence to bring criminal charges against a suspect. Grand juries play an important role in federal criminal cases. However, the provision for a grand jury is the one important civil liberties safeguard of the Bill of Rights that the Supreme Court has not incorporated into the Fourteenth Amendment and applied to state criminal prosecutions. Thus some states operate without grand juries; the prosecuting attorney simply files a "bill of information" affirming that there is sufficient evidence available to justify a trial. If the accused person is to be held in custody, the prosecutor must take the available information before a judge to determine whether the evidence shows probable cause.

 grand jury

A jury that determines whether sufficient evidence is available to justify a trial. Grand juries do not rule on the accused's guilt or innocence.

Double Jeopardy. "Nor shall any person be subject for the same offense to be twice put in jeopardy of life or limb" is the constitutional protection from **double jeopardy,** or being tried more than once for the same crime. This protection was at the heart of the *Palko* case in 1937, which, as we saw earlier in this chapter, also helped establish the principle of selective incorporation of the Bill of Rights. It took another 30 years after *Palko* for the Court to nationalize the constitutional protection against double jeopardy.

 double jeopardy

The Fifth Amendment right providing that a person cannot be tried twice for the same crime.

Self-Incrimination. Perhaps the most significant liberty found in the Fifth Amendment is the guarantee that no citizen "shall be compelled in any criminal case to be a witness against himself." The most famous case concerning self-incrimination is of such importance that Chief Justice Earl Warren assessed its results as going "to the very root of our concepts of American criminal jurisprudence." In 1966, Ernesto Miranda was charged with kidnapping and raping

---

94 Sue Davis, *Corwin and Peltason's Understanding the Constitution*, 17th ed. (Belmont, CA: Thomson Wadsworth, 2008), p. 286.

The Fourth Amendment and Government Surveillance

Surveillance at a traffic control center in Colorado.

Policies are usually a product of preferences and institutions, but occasionally immediate preferences clash with institutional constraints. Take the matter of government surveillance. Amid heightened fear of terrorism, government surveillance of communications, travel, and personal conduct has become a fact of American life. Such surveillance can occur through electronic interception of telephone calls, examination of email communications and social media postings, security cameras tied to crowd-scanning software, traffic monitoring, and airport searches. Modern analytic methods allow the government to process and analyze enormous quantities of data, looking for possible indications of illicit activity.[1]

Many Americans feel that they are the beneficiaries rather than the potential victims of government surveillance.[2] But the framers of the Constitution believed popular government requires citizen privacy and knowledge of government actions: citizens must know what the government is doing to exert influence over it, and they must be protected from the state's scrutiny and the possibility of retaliation and intimidation. For example, the efforts of the party not currently in power can be compromised if the government becomes privy to its plans. In one such case in 1972, the Republican Nixon administration attempted to use

surveillance activities to undermine Democratic campaign plans. Known political dissidents, moreover, may face some risk of official reprisal. Accordingly, some citizens may refrain from acting on their political beliefs for fear that they will draw attention to themselves and become targets of government efforts to find evidence of misconduct (for example, through tax audits) that can be used against them. Privacy for political activities is, like the secret ballot, an important element of political freedom.

This concept underlies the Constitution's Fourth Amendment prohibiting unreasonable searches. The framers worried that government intrusions into private homes were often aimed at identifying papers, manuscripts, and books that might point to efforts to foment political discontent.[3] While many people today see the Fourth Amendment as related to evidence in criminal cases, its original purpose was to serve as an instrument for protecting liberty of political expression.

Policy makers' preferences for surveillance and secrecy may threaten the institutional constraints established by the Fourth Amendment. Though some of the government's current policies seem inconsistent with these foundational ideas, the United States' institutional arrangements have begun to reshape policies. In recent years, the courts have ruled that the police cannot search cell phones or employ GPS trackers without search warrants, and Congress has sought to rein in the activities of intelligence agencies. Though immediate preferences can clash with institutional constraints, these constraints eventually tend to reassert themselves.

1 Jennifer Bachner, Benjamin Ginsberg, and Katherine Wagner, eds., *Analytics, Policy, and Governance* (New Haven, CT: Yale University Press, 2017).

2 Daniel J. Solove, *Nothing to Hide: The False Tradeoff between Privacy and Security* (New Haven, CT: Yale University Press, 2011).

3 Thomas P. Crocker, "The Political Fourth Amendment," *Washington University Law Review* 88, no. 2 (2010): 303–79.

an 18-year-old woman. She had identified him in a police lineup and, after two hours of questioning, Miranda confessed, subsequently signing a statement that his confession had been made voluntarily, without threats or promises of immunity. These confessions were admitted into evidence and served as the basis for Miranda's conviction. Miranda appealed this decision, arguing that his confession had not been truly voluntary because he had not been informed of his right to remain silent or his right to consult an attorney. The confession, therefore, should not have been admitted as evidence. The Supreme Court agreed and overturned the original conviction. In one of the most intensely criticized decisions ever handed down by the Court, Miranda's case produced the rules that police now must follow before questioning an arrested criminal suspect.

The reading of a person's "Miranda rights" has become a standard scene in every police station and in many dramatizations of police action on television and in the movies. *Miranda* advanced the civil liberties of accused persons not only by expanding the scope of the Fifth Amendment clause covering coerced confessions and self-incrimination but also by confirming the right to counsel. The Supreme Court under Chief Justices Warren Burger and William Rehnquist considerably softened the Miranda restrictions, making the job of the police a little easier, but the Miranda rule still stands as a protection against egregious police abuses of arrested persons.

Eminent Domain. Another fundamental clause of the Fifth Amendment is the "takings clause," which extends to each citizen a protection against the government taking private property "without just compensation." Although this clause is not specifically concerned with protecting persons accused of crimes, it does deal with an important instance in which the government and citizens are adversaries. As discussed earlier, the power of any government to take private property for a public use, such as highway construction, is called eminent domain. This power is essential to the very concept of sovereignty. The Fifth Amendment neither invented eminent domain nor took it away; its purpose was to limit that inherent power through procedures that require the government to demonstrate a public purpose and provide fair payment for the seizure of someone's property. This provision is now universally honored in all American principalities, but it has not always been meticulously observed.

The first modern case confronting the issue of public use involved a small variety store in a rundown neighborhood on the southwest side of the District of Columbia. In carrying out an urban redevelopment program in the 1950s, the city government of Washington, D.C., took the property as one of many privately owned lots to be cleared for new housing and business construction. The owner of the store and his successors, after his death, took the government to court on the grounds that taking property from one private owner and eventually turning that property back, in altered form, to another private owner was an unconstitutional use of eminent domain. The store owners lost their case, though they received cash compensation for their property. The Supreme Court's argument was that taking land in the "public interest" can mean virtually anything a legislature says it means. In other words, because the overall slum clearance and redevelopment project was in the public interest, according to the legislature, the eventual transfers of property that were going to take place as part of the project were justified.[95] In 1984 and again in 2005 the Supreme Court reaffirmed that decision.[96] In 2019, however, the Court reversed course; for the first time in its history, it ruled that property owners can file federal suits (without first pursuing litigation in state courts) challenging local land-use regulations they allege restrict their property rights to the point that they constitute an unjust government taking.[97]

The Sixth Amendment and the Right to Counsel

> In all criminal prosecutions, the accused shall enjoy the right to a speedy and public trial, by an impartial jury of the State and district wherein the crime shall have been committed, which district shall have been previously ascertained by law, and to be informed of the nature and cause of the accusation; to be confronted with the witnesses against him; to have compulsory process for obtaining witnesses in his favor, and to have the Assistance of Counsel for his defense.

Some provisions of the Sixth Amendment, such as the right to a speedy trial and the right to confront witnesses before an impartial jury, are not very controversial. The "right to counsel" provision, however, like the exclusionary rule of the Fourth Amendment and the self-incrimination clause of the Fifth Amendment, is notable because it is occasionally invoked to overturn cases and free defendants who seem to be guilty as charged.

Gideon v. Wainwright is the perfect case study because it involved a disreputable person who seemed patently guilty of the crime for which he was convicted. In and out of jails for most of his 51 years, Clarence Earl Gideon received a 5-year sentence for breaking into and entering a poolroom in Panama City, Florida, on the basis of a trial in which the state of Florida refused to appoint him an attorney. While serving time in jail, Gideon became a fairly well-qualified "jailhouse lawyer," made his own appeal on a handwritten petition, and eventually won the landmark ruling on the right to counsel in all felony cases.[98] *Gideon* was decided in 1963, and in the following year the Supreme Court ruled that suspects had a right to counsel during police interrogations, not just when their cases reached trial.[99]

---

95 *Berman v. Parker*, 348 U.S. 26 (1954). For a thorough analysis of the case, see Benjamin Ginsberg, "*Berman v. Parker*: Congress, the Court, and the Public Purpose," *Polity* 4, no. 1 (1971): 48–75.

96 *Hawaii Housing Authority v. Midkiff*, 467 U.S. 229 (1984); and *Kelo v. City of New London*, 545 U.S. 469 (2005).

97 *Knick v. Township of Scott, Pennsylvania*, 588 U.S. ____ (2019).

98 *Gideon v. Wainwright*, 372 U.S. 335 (1963). For a full account of the trial and release of Clarence Earl Gideon, see Anthony Lewis, *Gideon's Trumpet* (New York: Random House, 1964).

99 *Escobedo v. Illinois*, 378 U.S. 478 (1964).

The right to counsel has since been expanded further to encompass the quality of the counsel provided. For example, although state and federal court systems originally satisfied the right to counsel by assigning lawyers from the community to defendants who could not afford legal representation, most states and cities now employ public defense lawyers specifically for this purpose. And although these defendants cannot choose their public defense attorneys, they may have the right to appeal a conviction on the grounds that the counsel provided by the state was deficient. For example, in 2003 the Supreme Court overturned the death sentence of a Maryland death row inmate, holding that the defense lawyer had failed to fully inform the jury of the defendant's personal history of "horrendous childhood abuse."[100] Moreover, the right to counsel extends to any trial that holds the possibility of imprisonment.[101]

The Eighth Amendment and Cruel and Unusual Punishment

The Eighth Amendment prohibits "excessive bail," "excessive fines," and "cruel and unusual punishment." In 2019, in the case of *Timbs v. Indiana*, the Supreme Court ruled for the first time that the excessive fines clause applies to the states.[102] Virtually all debate over Eighth Amendment issues, though, focuses on the protection from cruel and unusual punishment. One of the greatest challenges in interpreting this provision consistently is that what is considered "cruel and unusual" varies from culture to culture and from generation to generation. Unfortunately, it also varies by class and race.

In recent years, federal courts have considered a number of Eighth Amendment questions. In the case of *Miller v. Alabama*,[103] for example, the Court ruled that mandatory sentences of life without the possibility of parole constitute cruel and unusual punishment for juvenile offenders. The most important questions concerning cruel and unusual punishment are raised by the use of the death penalty. While some Americans believe that execution is inherently cruel, in its consideration of the death penalty, the Supreme Court has generally avoided ruling on this specific question. In 1972, the Supreme Court overturned several state death penalty laws not because they were cruel and unusual, but because they were being applied in a capricious manner.[104] Shortly thereafter, a majority of states revised their capital punishment provisions to provide clearer standards.[105] Since 1976, the Court has consistently upheld state laws providing

---

100 *Wiggins v. Smith,* 539 U.S. 510 (2003).

101 For further discussion of these issues, see Davis, *Corwin and Peltason's Understanding the Constitution,* pp. 319–23.

102 *Timbs v. Indiana,* 586 U.S. ____ (2019).

103 *Miller v. Alabama,* 567 U.S. 460 (2012).

104 *Furman v. Georgia,* 408 U.S. 238 (1972).

105 *Gregg v. Georgia,* 428 U.S. 153 (1976).

for capital punishment, although it continues to review numerous death penalty appeals each year. In 2015, a Massachusetts jury voted to impose the death penalty on Dzhokhar Tsarnaev, who was found guilty for his role in the 2013 Boston Marathon bombings. This jury finding is currently still under appeal.

Between 1976 and March 2020, states executed 1,517 people. Texas led the way with 569 executions. As of 2020, 30 states authorized some form of capital punishment, a penalty approved of by about two-thirds of all Americans. Although all criminal conduct is regulated by the states, Congress has mandated capital punishment for more than 50 types of federal crimes.

Debate about the death penalty remains intense, and cases continue to come before the courts. In 1997, for example, the American Bar Association called for a halt to the death penalty until concerns about the fairness of both death penalty trials and the application of the punishment are addressed. In 2002, the Supreme Court banned all executions of mentally handicapped defendants;[106] in 2008, it declared that death was too harsh a penalty for a child rapist,[107] and it invalidated a death sentence for a Black defendant on the grounds that the prosecutor had improperly excluded African Americans from his jury.[108] But in recent years, the Court has also upheld lethal injection as a mode of execution multiple times, despite arguments that it is likely to cause considerable pain.

Many death penalty supporters praise its deterrent effects on other would-be criminals, claiming that preventing even one additional murder or other heinous crime is ample justification for the punishment. Although studies of capital crimes usually fail to demonstrate a direct deterrent effect, the punishment's "failure" in this regard may be due to the lengthy delays—typically years and even decades—between convictions and executions. Moreover, although constitutional objections to the death penalty often invoke the Eighth Amendment's protection against cruel and unusual punishments, supporters claim that the death penalty cannot be considered to violate this protection because it was commonly used in the eighteenth century and most early American leaders supported it.

Death penalty opponents point out that the death penalty has not been proved to deter crime. They also argue that executing criminals debases rather than elevates society by extolling vengeance and that, though most of the Founders supported the death penalty, they also countenanced slavery and lived at a time when society was both less informed about and more indifferent to the human condition. Furthermore, execution is expensive—more expensive than life imprisonment—because the government must make every effort to ensure that it is not executing an innocent person. Curtailing legal appeals would make the possibility of a mistake too great. And although most Americans support the death penalty, people also support life without the possibility of parole as an

---

106 *Atkins v. Virginia*, 536 U.S. 304 (2002).

107 *Kennedy v. Louisiana*, 554 U.S. 407 (2008).

108 *Snyder v. Louisiana*, 552 U.S. 472 (2008).

alternative.[109] According to opponents, a life sentence may be a worse punishment than the death penalty. Race, too, intrudes in death penalty cases: people of color are disproportionately more likely to be sentenced to death than are Whites charged with identical crimes.

The Right to Privacy and the Constitution

At times, almost all of us would like to be left alone, to have our own private domain into which no one—friends, family, government, church, or employer—has the right to enter without permission.

Many Jehovah's Witnesses felt that way in the 1940s. As we noted earlier in our discussion of the free exercise of religion, they risked serious punishment in 1940 by telling their children not to salute the flag or say the Pledge of Allegiance in school because of their understanding of the first commandment's prohibition of the worship of "graven images." These cases arose under the First Amendment's freedom of religion provisions, but they were also the first cases to consider the possibility of the right to be left alone. When the Court became more activist in the mid-1950s and 1960s, this idea of a **right to privacy** was revived. In 1958, the Court recognized "privacy in one's association" in its decision preventing the state of Alabama from using an NAACP membership list to inform its investigations.

Birth Control. The sphere of privacy was drawn in earnest in 1965, when the Court ruled that a Connecticut statute forbidding the use of contraceptives violated the right of marital privacy. Estelle Griswold, executive director of the Planned Parenthood League of Connecticut, was arrested by the state of Connecticut for providing information, instruction, and medical advice about contraception to married couples. She and her associates were found guilty as accessories to the crime of contraception use and fined $100 each. Ultimately, the Supreme Court reversed the lower court's decisions and declared the Connecticut law unconstitutional because it violated "a right of privacy older than the Bill of Rights—older than our political parties, older than our school system." Justice William O. Douglas's opinion in *Griswold v. Connecticut* argued that this right of privacy is grounded in the Constitution because it fits into a "zone of privacy" created by the Third, Fourth, and Fifth Amendments. Justice Arthur Goldberg's concurring opinion added that "the concept of liberty . . . embraces the right of marital privacy though that right is not mentioned explicitly in the Constitution [and] is supported by numerous decisions of this Court . . . and *by the language and history of the Ninth Amendment*"[110] (emphasis added).

right to privacy

The right to be left alone, which has been interpreted by the Supreme Court to entail individual access to birth control and abortions.

---

109 J. Baxter Oliphant, "Public Support for the Death Penalty Ticks Up," Pew Research Center, June 11, 2018, www.pewresearch.org/fact-tank/2018/06/11/us-support-for-death-penalty-ticks-up-2018 (accessed 12/4/19).

110 *Griswold v. Connecticut*, 381 U.S. 479 (1965); and *Griswold v. Connecticut*, concurring opinion. In *Eisenstadt v. Baird*, 405 U.S. 438 (1972), the Court extended the privacy right to unmarried women.

The Ninth Amendment provides that "the enumeration in the Constitution, of certain rights, shall not be construed to deny or disparage others retained by the people." According to Goldberg, this language means, in effect, that just because the Constitution does not specifically mention a particular right to privacy, it does not mean that the people do not retain that right. The language of the Ninth Amendment, when taken with the evidence provided by the First, Third, Fourth, and Fifth Amendments, was sufficient for the Court to find that the Bill of Rights implies a constitutional right to privacy. Other justices found a right to privacy implied by the language of the Fourteenth Amendment.

Abortion. The right to privacy was further defined in 1973 in one of the most important Supreme Court decisions in American history: *Roe v. Wade*. This decision established a woman's right to seek an abortion and prohibited states from making abortion a criminal act before the point at which the fetus becomes viable (in 1973, the 27th week of pregnancy).[111] The decision was of particular significance in terms of the historical context leading up to it. Most states did not regulate abortions in any fashion until the 1840s, at which time only six states had regulations governing it. In addition, many states had begun to ease their abortion restrictions well before the 1973 *Roe* decision. But none of these prior circumstances had specifically addressed the issue of privacy. In recent years a number of states have reinstated restrictions on abortion, including lowering the viability standard to 20 weeks (Texas), 12 weeks (Arkansas), and 6 weeks (North Dakota). However, Arkansas's ban was struck down by a federal appeals court, and North Dakota's ban was blocked by the Supreme Court. In 2018 and 2019, several states legislated new restrictions prohibiting abortions if a fetal heartbeat could be detected. This comes close to an outright ban on abortion, since many women might not even be aware of their pregnancy before modern technology is able to detect a heartbeat.

The *Roe* decision dramatically changed abortion practices in America. It also galvanized and nationalized the abortion debate. Groups opposing abortion, such as the National Right to Life Committee, organized to fight the liberal standard, while abortion rights groups have sought to maintain protection for the procedure. The legal standard has shifted against abortion rights in five key Supreme Court cases.

In 1989, in *Webster v. Reproductive Health Services*, the Court narrowly upheld (by a 5–4 majority) the constitutionality of restrictions on the use of public medical facilities for abortion.[112] And in the 1992 case of *Planned Parenthood v. Casey*, another 5–4 majority upheld *Roe* but narrowed its scope. The Court's

---

111   *Roe v. Wade*, 410 U.S. 113 (1973).

112   *Webster v. Reproductive Health Services*, 492 U.S. 490 (1989), upheld a Missouri law that restricted the use of public medical facilities for abortion. The decision opened the way for other states to limit the availability of abortion.

decision defined the right to an abortion as a "limited or qualified" right subject to regulation by the states as long as the regulations do not constitute an "undue burden."[113] More recently, the Court had another opportunity to rule on what constitutes an undue burden: in 2000, in *Stenberg v. Carhart*, the Court struck down Nebraska's ban on late-term abortions because the law had the "effect of placing a substantial obstacle in the path of a woman seeking an abortion."[114] In 2007, however, the Court upheld a federal ban on late-term abortions, essentially overturning the earlier decision.[115]

In June 2020, the Supreme Court struck down an effort by Louisiana to restrict abortion rights. A state law required that abortion providers have admitting privileges in a nearby hospital if they were to be allowed to perform abortions. In a 5-4 decision the Court ruled that this law, like a similar Texas statute that had been previously overturned, was an impermissible effort to restrict abortion rights.[116]

Sexual Orientation. In recent decades, the right to be left alone has come to encompass the privacy rights of gay men and women. The first key case in this arena was *Bowers v. Hardwick*. One morning in Atlanta in the mid-1980s, Michael Hardwick was arrested by a police officer who discovered him in bed with another man. The officer had come to serve a warrant for Hardwick's arrest for failure to appear in court to answer charges of drinking in public. When the officer found Hardwick and another man engaging in "consensual sexual behavior," he arrested Hardwick under Georgia's laws against heterosexual and homosexual sodomy. Hardwick filed a lawsuit against the state, challenging the constitutionality of the Georgia law, and won his case in the federal court of appeals. After the state of Georgia appealed the lower court's decision to the Supreme Court, the Court reversed it, with a majority holding against Hardwick on the grounds that "the federal Constitution confers [no] fundamental right upon homosexuals to engage in sodomy" and that there was therefore no basis to invalidate "the laws of the many states that still make such conduct illegal and have done so for a very long time."[117]

Seventeen years later, the Court overturned *Bowers v. Hardwick* with a dramatic pronouncement that gay men and women are "entitled to respect for their private lives" as a matter of constitutional due process. After the Court's ruling in *Lawrence v. Texas*, state legislatures no longer had the authority to make private sexual behavior a crime.[118] Drawing from the tradition of negative liberty, or freedom from governmental interference, the Court maintained, "In

---

113 *Planned Parenthood v. Casey*, 505 U.S. 833 (1992).

114 *Stenberg v. Carhart*, 530 U.S. 914 (2000).

115 *Gonzales v. Carhart*, 550 U.S. 124 (2007).

116 *June Medical Services v. Russo* 18-1323, 591 U.S. ____ (2020).

117 *Bowers v. Hardwick*, 478 U.S. 186 (1986).

118 *Lawrence v. Texas*, 539 U.S. 558 (2003).

our tradition the State is not omnipresent in the home. And there are other spheres of our lives and existence outside the home, where the State should not be a dominant presence." Explicitly encompassing gay men and women within the umbrella of privacy, the Court concluded that the "State cannot demean their existence or control their destiny by making their private sexual conduct a crime." This decision added substance to the idea that the Ninth Amendment allows for a "right to privacy."

In 2015, the Court took another important step in the protection of gay rights by declaring state bans on same-sex marriage unconstitutional.[119] The Court said that the refusal to issue marriage licenses to same-sex couples constituted a violation of the Fourteenth Amendment's equal protection and due process clauses.

The Right to Die. Another area ripe for further litigation and public discourse is the so-called right to die. A number of highly publicized physician-assisted suicides in the 1990s focused attention on whether people have a right to choose the circumstances of their own death and receive assistance in carrying it out. Will this become part of the privacy right or perhaps be accepted as a new kind of right? In the 2006 case of *Gonzales v. Oregon*, the Supreme Court upheld an Oregon law that allowed doctors to use drugs to facilitate the deaths of terminally ill patients who requested such assistance.[120] This decision is not a definitive ruling on the right-to-die question, but it does suggest that the Court is not hostile to the idea. In recent years a number of lower-court decisions have reaffirmed this principle. In 2014, for example, a Pennsylvania county judge threw out a case against a nurse who had been accused of homicide for making a bottle of morphine available to her ill 93-year-old father.[121]

Privacy and New Technologies. Technological change has confronted the courts with a number of privacy issues that could not have been foreseen when the Supreme Court wrote its *Griswold* decision a half-century ago. Does the right to privacy extend to information stored in a suspect's GPS tracking device?[122] Can the authorities collect DNA from suspects as part of a routine booking procedure?[123] It is certain that new technologies will present further questions about privacy for the courts to consider in the future.

---

119 *Obergefell v. Hodges*, 576 U.S. ____ (2015).

120 *Gonzales v. Oregon*, 546 U.S. 243 (2006).

121 Richard Knox, "Judge Dismisses Assisted Suicide Case against Pennsylvania Nurse," NPR, February 12, 2014, www.npr.org/sections/health-shots/2014/02/12/275913772/ judge-dismisses-assisted-suicide-case-against-pennsylvania-nurse?_r50 (accessed 12/4/19).

122 *United States v. Jones* (2012).

123 *Maryland v. King*, 569 U.S. 435 (2013).

CONCLUSION: CIVIL LIBERTIES AND COLLECTIVE ACTION

The Constitution, and especially its Bill of Rights, guarantees Americans a variety of liberties, including the freedoms of speech and religion, protection against having their homes arbitrarily searched, and a number of procedural rights, including trial by jury, protection against self-incrimination, and the right to counsel in criminal cases. The Bill of Rights initially applied only to the actions of the federal government, but in the twentieth century, under the doctrine of selective incorporation, the Supreme Court gradually applied most of the provisions of the Bill of Rights to the states. The most recent of such actions were incorporation of the Second Amendment's right to bear arms in the 2010 case of *McDonald v. Chicago* and the Eighth Amendment's prohibition of the imposition of excessive fines in the 2019 case of *Timbs v. Indiana*.

Constitutional guarantees of civil rights and civil liberties often seem clear in the abstract, but they inevitably produce thousands of complex questions and controversies every year when they are applied to concrete cases. Every government agency, for example, is constitutionally required to respect Americans' civil liberties. The government, though, is also obligated to protect the public's health and safety. This duty, sometimes called the "general police power," is exercised by the governments of the states. The federal government does not have a general police power since the Tenth Amendment limits it to the powers expressly granted by the Constitution. However, the Court has interpreted the Constitution's commerce clause broadly to enable the federal government to protect the public's health and safety by making policies in such realms as health care, education, and crime control.

Suppose that Congress enacts a law allowing national security agencies to sift through millions of phone calls searching for evidence of terrorist plots. Is such a law an unjustified intrusion on civil liberties or a necessary and legitimate effort to prevent bloodshed? In 2008, the Supreme Court declined to hear a case on a similar question brought by a civil liberties group that wanted to halt a large-scale federal wiretapping program aimed at identifying possible terrorist communications. This action let stand a lower-court ruling that had allowed the program to continue. These concerns surfaced again in 2013, when an NSA contract employee released details of an elaborate NSA eavesdropping effort that resulted in the agency accessing the phone and email records of millions of Americans. Civil libertarians charged that the NSA had violated the law and the Constitution. President Obama and NSA officials answered that some inadvertent violations of the relevant statutes might have occurred, but that the agency's actions were needed to protect American security. As these examples suggest, the precise character of constitutional limitations on collective action is always open to debate. As part of that debate, we examine our history to identify similar situations in the past and to determine whether the decisions made then still apply to the present. We call this the history principle; the courts call it precedent.

Civil liberties are also important examples of the collective action principle. All politics is collective action, but civil liberties are limitations on collective action. They identify spheres of individual autonomy into which the nation as a whole, acting through its government, is not permitted to intrude. The authors of the Bill of Rights agreed that collective action could go only so far; if it led to restrictions on speech, religion, assembly, the press, and so forth, it would not be allowed. Demonstrating the importance of the history principle, this decision, made more than two centuries ago, has continued to shape our nation. If not for the Bill of Rights, collective action could quickly become tyranny.

For Further Reading

Amar, Akhil Reed. *The Law of the Land: A Grand Tour of Our Constitutional Republic.* New York: Basic Books, 2015.

Ash, Timothy Garton. *Free Speech: Ten Principles for a Connected World.* New Haven, CT: Yale University Press, 2016.

Barbas, Samantha. *Newsworthy: The Supreme Court Battle over Privacy and Press Freedom.* Stanford, CA: Stanford University Press, 2017.

Blocher, Joseph and Darrell A. H. Miller. *The Positive Second Amendment: Rights, Regulation and the Future of* Heller. New York: Cambridge University Press, 2018.

Friendly, Fred W. *Minnesota Rag: The Dramatic Story of the Landmark Supreme Court Case That Gave New Meaning to Freedom of the Press.* New York: Random House, 1981.

Gray, David. *The Fourth Amendment in an Age of Surveillance.* New York: Cambridge University Press, 2017.

Lawler, Peter Augustine and Richard M. Reinsch II. *A Constitution in Full: Recovering the Unwritten Foundation of American Liberty.* Lawrence: University Press of Kansas, 2019.

Lewis, Anthony. *Freedom for the Thought That We Hate: A Biography of the First Amendment.* New York: Basic Books, 2008.

Lewis, Anthony. *Gideon's Trumpet.* New York: Random House, 1964.

Norton, Helen. *The Government's Speech and the Constitution.* New York: Cambridge University Press, 2019.

O'Brien, David M. and Gordon Silverstein. *Constitutional Law and Politics: Civil Rights and Civil Liberties.* 11th ed. Vol. 2. New York: Norton, 2020.

Ong Hing, Bill. *American Presidents, Deportations, and Human Rights Violations: From Carter to Trump.* New York: Cambridge University Press, 2018.

Richards, Neil. *Intellectual Privacy: Rethinking Civil Liberties in the Digital Age.* New York: Oxford University Press, 2015.

Smith, Steven D. *The Rise and Decline of American Religious Freedom.* Cambridge, MA: Harvard University Press, 2014.

Solove, Daniel J. *Nothing to Hide: The False Tradeoff between Privacy and Security.* New Haven, CT: Yale University Press, 2011.

Tebbe, Nelson. *Religious Freedom in an Egalitarian Age.* Cambridge, MA: Harvard University Press, 2017.

Waldron, Jeremy. *The Harm in Hate Speech.* Cambridge, MA: Harvard University Press, 2012.

Weinrib, Laura. *The Taming of Free Speech: America's Civil Liberties Compromise.* Cambridge, MA: Harvard University Press, 2016.

Winkler, Adam. *Gunfight: The Battle over the Right to Bear Arms in America.* New York: Norton, 2011.

5

Civil Rights

civil rights

The rules that government must follow in regard to the treatment of individuals, especially concerning participation in political and social life.

As we observed in Chapter 4, civil liberties are restrictions on government, and as such they restrain the collective decision making of the people as expressed through the decisions of governmental institutions. **Civil rights** also shape collective action and decision making but in a very different way. Civil rights regulate *who* can participate in the political process and civil society and *how* they can participate—for example, who can vote, who can serve in office, who can be granted a trial or serve on juries, and when and how citizens can petition the government. The vast scope of civil rights also encompasses how people are treated in employment, education, and other aspects of American society.

In some nations, citizens have few, if any, civil rights. They have no right to vote, no right to stand for office, and no right to be judged by their peers if accused of a crime. The United States, however, began life as a nation with numerous civil rights guaranteed in both the federal and state constitutions. The federal Constitution provided the right to be represented in Congress (Article I, Section 2), established who can serve in Congress and become president (Article I, Sections 2 and 3; and Article II, Section 1), and guaranteed the privilege of *habeas corpus* for all people (Article I, Section 9). The Bill of Rights defined civil rights further, especially the right of all persons to due process of law, as guaranteed in the Fifth Amendment.

The United States' early conception of civil rights was narrower than it is today. Originally, the Constitution did not guarantee a general right to vote; it left the provision of voting rights and many other civil rights to the states. The Founders' initial rules permitted widely disparate treatment of different categories of individuals, including women, racial and ethnic minorities, owners of property, and others. One way in which states limited civil rights was by linking them to property ownership and restricting who could own property. For instance, women were often not allowed to inherit property or could not own property in their own name if they were married. In addition, women were denied the right to vote and their access to education was limited. Members of minority racial and ethnic groups have also historically faced many forms of legally sanctioned discrimination that prevented them from voting, owning property, or securing employment.

Since the adoption of the Constitution, there has been a tremendous expansion of civil rights to different groups of people and to different spheres of civil life. The gradual extension of civil rights to previously excluded groups, African Americans in particular, is one of the most important transformations in American political history; it required collective action by excluded groups, often against entrenched, even violent opposition. Groups fighting for civil rights built organizations and leadership structures such as churches and community associations. They used a variety of political tools and techniques to advance their interests, including the ballot box when it was available to them as well as litigation, media campaigns, demonstrations, and disruption when the ballot was not available or not enough.

At the time the Constitution was written, 8 of the 13 original states permitted slavery. Enslaved persons, who came almost entirely from Africa or the Caribbean, possessed no civil rights. Though the Constitution banned the importation of enslaved people after 1808, it permitted slavery to continue. Immediately before the Civil War, roughly 4 million Africans were enslaved in the southern states, where their labor supported the region's agricultural economy. By then, slavery was prohibited in most of the northern states, and the issue of whether slavery should be allowed in America's western territories bitterly divided the nation. In the 1857 *Dred Scott v. Sandford* case, the Supreme Court ruled that enslaved people were not citizens, they could not bring suit in court, and they were the personal property of their masters; moreover, slavery could not be excluded from the territories.[1] This decision inflamed sectional divisions, infuriated antislavery groups in the North, and helped provoke the Civil War.

LEARNING OBJECTIVES

 Define civil rights and explain how they influence collective action in the United States.

 Outline the historical struggle for civil rights in the areas of voting, discrimination, and equal access to education in the United States.

 Explain how legislation led to an expansion of civil rights.

 Describe the compensatory actions taken to overcome the consequences of past discrimination and foster greater diversity.

 Outline how civil rights and civil liberties regulate collective action.

---

1 *Dred Scott v. Sandford*, 60 U.S. 393 (1857).

Following the Civil War, Congress adopted the Thirteenth, Fourteenth, and Fifteenth amendments to the Constitution to protect the civil rights that the practice of slavery had violated. The Thirteenth Amendment prohibited slavery and involuntary servitude in the United States. The Fifteenth extended the right to vote to Black Americans: "The right of citizens of the United States to vote shall not be denied or abridged by the United States or by any State on account of race, color, or previous condition of servitude." The Fourteenth Amendment asserted the idea of civil rights much more broadly for all citizens. Section 1 of the amendment states:

> All persons born or naturalized in the United States, and subject to the jurisdiction thereof, are citizens of the United States and of the State wherein they reside. No State shall make or enforce any law which shall abridge the privileges or immunities of citizens of the United States; nor shall any State deprive any person of life, liberty, or property, without due process of law; nor deny to any person within its jurisdiction the equal protection of the laws.

equal protection clause

The provision of the Fourteenth Amendment guaranteeing citizens "the equal protection of the laws." This clause has been the basis for the civil rights of African Americans, women, and other groups.

The last clause of this section, the **equal protection clause**, has transformed civil rights in the United States because it creates the foundation for asserting equal civil rights for all persons. Though this amendment was ratified in the context of the Civil War, it launched more than a century's worth of political movements and legal efforts to press for the expansion of civil rights to many groups in American society. African Americans' quest for civil rights inspired many other groups—including other racial and ethnic groups, women, people with disabilities, gay men and women, and transgender people—to seek new laws and constitutional guarantees of their civil rights. Their struggles were aided by the simplicity of the equal protection clause, which offers its guarantee to any person.

Under the Constitution today, no American may be excluded from participation or representation in collective decision-making processes or treated adversely by decision makers because of such factors as race, gender, or ethnic background. Legislative actions and legal decrees, however, have rarely been sufficient to guarantee civil rights. Activists and other citizens have fought for the establishment and consistent enforcement of civil rights protections, and debates persist over the extent of the government's responsibility to ensure equal protection. The reason is that civil rights are not defined only by laws or Constitutional interpretation; they are also highly contextual, and whether they are relevant in a given situation depends on the behavior of the people involved. Do social divisions between Whites and racial and ethnic minorities cause a majority of the White population to oppose the preferred candidates of a majority of the Black or Hispanic populations? Is there evidence of intentional discrimination in election administration, employment, and housing? Does the criminal justice system discriminate against Black Americans, as might be suggested by the disproportionately high rates at which Black men are incarcerated and are the victims of police shootings? Does America's history of denying civil rights to African Americans justify demands for the payment of reparations to America's Black citizens, as some have argued?[2] Questions like these remain unsettled.

WHAT ARE CIVIL RIGHTS?

Civil rights are the rules that government must follow in regard to the treatment of individuals when making collective decisions. Some civil rights concern who can be involved in collective decisions and how; others concern how people are treated in civil society, including who has access to public facilities such as schools and public hospitals. Increasingly, civil rights have extended to private spheres, such as the workplace, the home, and other private clubs and organizations. Even when no legal right to something currently exists, such a right may be asserted as a matter of justice or morality. When there is a demand for new civil rights, society must decide whether and how these rights should be extended.

Civil rights encompass three features: who, what, and how much. *Who* has a right and who does not? A right to *what*? And *how much* is any individual allowed to exercise that right? For example, consider the right to vote. The "what" is the vote. The "who" concerns which persons are allowed to vote. Today, all U.S. citizens 18 years of age and older are eligible to vote. States impose additional criteria that affect who is permitted to vote, such as requirements that voters show photo IDs or laws that prohibit voting by ex-felons. The "how much" concerns whether that right can be exercised equally—whether election laws create greater obstacles to voting for some people than they do for others, or whether some people's votes count more than others' votes do. For instance, until the mid-1960s, the California State Senate had one senator from Los Angeles County, with 6 million people, and one from Inyo County, with 14,000 people. The votes of the 14,000 people thus translated into the same amount of representation as the votes of the 6 million people. The U.S. Supreme Court ruled that such arrangements violated the equal protection clause and hence the civil rights of residents of the more populous counties.

Over the course of American history, two general principles have emerged that answer *who* enjoys civil rights and *how much*. First, civil rights ought to be universal: all persons should enjoy them. Second, civil rights ought to be equal: all people who enjoy a civil right ought to be allowed an equal ability or opportunity to practice that right.

Before these principles became widely accepted, however, profound debates and deep divisions in American society concerned *who* had civil rights. At the time of the Founding, most states granted voting rights exclusively to White male property owners. Many states' constitutions and laws also imposed religious

---

2   Ta-Nehisi Coates, "The Case for Reparations," *The Atlantic*, June 2014, www.theatlantic.com/magazine/archive/2014/06/the-case-for-reparations/361631 (accessed 12/9/19).

restrictions, forbidding Catholics or Jews from voting, running for office, and engaging in other public activities.

Today, civil rights are guaranteed to all U.S. citizens. Any person born in the United States is automatically a citizen; these people are called natural-born citizens. In addition, legal immigrants can become citizens through a process of naturalization. Generally speaking, naturalization requires that the immigrant has been a legal resident of the United States for at least five years; has demonstrated the ability to read, write, and speak English; has passed a basic U.S. civics and history test; and is of good moral standing.[3] Citizens can live in the country and travel to other countries with all the privileges and protections of the United States. In addition, citizens who are age 18 or older can vote. Only citizens can serve in Congress. Only a natural-born citizen can be president of the United States.

Age is also a criterion for some civil rights. Until 1971, the voting age in most states was 21, but in reaction to the draft during the Vietnam War, which subjected men 18 and older to military conscription, the Constitution was amended to set the voting age at 18. In terms of seeking office, individuals must be at least age 25 to serve in the U.S. House, age 30 to serve in the Senate, and age 35 to serve as president. Today, the largest groups of people not allowed to participate in American elections are those who are underage and those who are not citizens.

Citizenship has not always been a requirement for voting in the United States. Until the beginning of the nineteenth century, many states and cities allowed noncitizens to vote. In reaction to that era's influx of immigrants from Germany and other central European countries, states began to impose citizenship requirements. Even as late as the 1920s, however, there remained some municipalities in which noncitizens could vote in local elections.

The *what* of civil rights covers a wide range of fundamental rights. Perhaps the most basic civil right in any country is the right to be in the country to begin with. For much of our nation's first century, there were virtually no restrictions on who could enter the country. In 1875, Congress passed the Page Act, which prohibited specific groups of "undesirable" immigrants. The act was introduced by Senator Horace Page to "end the danger of cheap Chinese labor and immoral Chinese women."[4] Subsequent acts have further limited who may enter the country, how, and for how long, including country-specific quotas on immigrants that lasted from 1924 to 1966. Today, U.S. immigration law requires that persons wishing to reside permanently in the United States acquire "lawful permanent resident" status (commonly known as a "green card") through family- or employment-based sponsorship. The law limits the number of green cards that can be approved in a year. Problems arise, however, for people who

---

3   "Citizenship Through Naturalization," U.S. Citizenship and Immigration Services, April 17, 2019, www.uscis.gov/naturalization (accessed 12/9/19).

4   George Anthony Peffer, "Forbidden Families: Emigration Experiences of Chinese Women under the Page Law, 1875–1882," *Journal of American Ethnic History* 6, no. 1 (1986): 28–46.

have entered the country without documentation or who have stayed beyond the term allowed for temporary visitors. As we discuss later in the chapter, management of the right to be in the country remains one of the central debates over civil rights.

Political rights are also civil rights. These include the right to vote, the right to run for office, and the right to association. Indeed, much of the historical struggle over civil rights has concerned the expansion of political rights, which today nearly all adult citizens enjoy.

Legal rights are another class of civil rights. The right of *habeas corpus*—the right to be presented before a court if one is accused of a crime—dates back at least to the Magna Carta, the charter of liberties in England adopted in 1215. It is treated as a fundamental civil right granted to any person in the United States or its territories. Another legal right, one of the most powerful in the Constitution, is the right to due process of law. The Fifth Amendment states that "No person shall . . . be deprived of life, liberty, or property, without due process of law." That is, the federal government must respect the legal rights that are owed to a person; it cannot harm a person without following the exact course of the law. Later, the Fourteenth Amendment extended the requirement to respect due process to state governments as well. This right applies to all persons, not just certain types of people. Consequently, due process underlies the assertion of many types of rights and the expansion of rights to new groups.

Less obvious are rights in other aspects of society. Do you have a right to own property? Do you have a right to education? Do you have a right to a job, to a minimum standard of living, or to medical care? Do you have a right to serve in the military, or not to serve in the military in the case of a draft? Do you have a right to attend public school and receive various social services if you are an undocumented immigrant? A wide range of economic and civil activities are, in fact, governed by civil rights. You have a right to due compensation if the government takes your property. You have the right to access public schools, and public hospitals cannot turn you away at their emergency rooms. Answers vary as to whether you have a right to employment or to form a union with other workers to bargain for better wages and benefits. In some states, it is exceedingly hard to form a union, while in other states and in some industries, one must belong to a union in order to practice a trade. Medical practice today, for instance, raises complicated questions about the right to work. An immigrant who was trained and licensed in a foreign country as a medical doctor must go through American medical training and licensing procedures in order to practice in the United States. This is a restriction on the right of these people to work.

The question of *how much* individuals can exercise their civil rights is perhaps the subtlest of the three dimensions. To begin with, Americans adhere to a belief in equality even when it is difficult to achieve in practice. The Declaration of Independence begins with the proposition that "all men are created equal." The Constitution establishes the House of Representatives to represent all people (not just citizens, voters, or other subgroups). Perhaps most important, the Fourteenth Amendment establishes the right to equal protection of the laws for all persons. Like due process, equal protection applies regardless of one's race, gender, wealth, residency, or citizenship.

The Fourteenth Amendment's equal protection clause has been instrumental in asserting broad and equal rights in the United States; it applies to all persons and all laws. One of the first ordinances struck down by the U.S. Supreme Court under the Fourteenth Amendment pertained to requirements for construction permits and business licenses that discriminated against Chinese legal residents.[5] And in a series of decisions spanning 1962–68, the Court ruled that, under the equal protection clause, all people have equal voting rights: one person's vote cannot have a greater say in the country's collective decision making than another person's.

Decisions about which civil rights we enjoy and who is permitted to enjoy them are themselves political. The Constitution identifies a small number of civil rights. The Bill of Rights asserts a larger number of legal rights. But many of the civil rights we have now were left to Congress and the states to determine; they are the result of legislation, litigation, and administration that occurred after the country was founded. More often than not, these government actions came about as a result of collective action led by people who fought to expand their civil rights.

THE STRUGGLE FOR CIVIL RIGHTS

Who has what civil rights is a source of contention precisely because those who have civil rights, such as the right to vote, are often the ones who hold the power to extend those rights to those who do not have them. White male property owners had disproportionate political power in 1790 because they alone had voting rights. To expand voting rights to other groups, those in power had to decide to remove property qualifications, extend voting rights to women and non-White Americans, and loosen other restrictions, such as age and religious requirements. Needless to say, the expansion of voting rights has not always gone smoothly. Indeed, democracy can be a barrier to the creation of civil rights.

Consider noncitizens' voting rights. The first constitution of New York State, adopted in 1777, allowed all male inhabitants the right to vote. This meant that noncitizens and Black people could vote, a right they enjoyed for over 40 years. The state then experienced a backlash against the growing numbers of European immigrants and Black migrants settling in New York City; most of the people in the state of New York—who were White citizens—feared the increasing power of immigrants, Black people, and city dwellers. Rather than lose power, they decided to take away the rights of immigrant and Black populations. A popular vote authorized a convention to revise the state's constitution, which was subsequently rewritten to exclude these groups. The second constitution, adopted in 1821, restricted voting rights to male *citizens* only and

---

5   *Yick Wo v. Hopkins,* 118 U.S. 356 (1886).

removed property qualifications for White citizens, but not for Black citizens.[6] This situation exemplifies what James Madison feared during the debate over the Constitution—that a tyranny of the majority would take away the rights of the minority.[7]

American history has many stories akin to the 1821 revision of New York's constitution. Since the Founding, legislatures have restricted voting rights via poll taxes, literacy tests, registration, and redistricting. Even today, courts, legislatures, and executive branch departments have determined that some states' new election laws have the effect of disenfranchising poorer people, minorities, seniors, and students. Although we might find such voting restrictions objectionable, they are acceptable to those in power, who seek to safeguard their own interests by limiting the size of the group that can participate in collective decision making.

More amazing, then, is the fact that Americans have chosen to expand civil rights more often than they have chosen to restrict them. Civil rights in legal, political, and civil society have expanded steadily over time, and not always through the ballot or legislation. Often it is the courts that insist on the creation or expansion of civil rights. But, as we will learn in Chapter 9, the courts cannot act alone. They need the concurrence of the people as well as legislative and executive support to define and protect civil rights. Often, as with property qualifications and women's suffrage, a public consensus emerges that our Constitution and our laws must be changed to expand our conception of civil rights. At other times, legal decisions precede a broader change in the consensus, as when the courts rule in support of certain rights even when the public's instinct runs to the contrary. However, it can take decades, even centuries, to change political cultures and to give political power and civil rights to those who are powerless.

The Right to Vote

Voting is one of the most basic civic acts in American society; it is the backbone of our representative democracy. But the right to vote (indeed, like most civil rights) is not guaranteed in our Constitution. When it comes to the act of voting, the Constitution left the power to run elections up to the states, and initially, the states carried over the suffrage rules from their colonial charters. Thus in most states only White men with property had the right to vote, and in some, only Protestants had that right. Ever since the Founding, voting restrictions have been a source of political conflict; legislatures and courts have defined and redefined who does and does not have this basic right.

---

6 For the text of the first constitution, see "The Constitution of New York: April 20, 1777," The Avalon Project, https://avalon.law.yale.edu/18th_century/ny01.asp; for the text of the second constitution, see "The Second Constitution of New York, 1821," New York State Unified Court System, www.nycourts.gov/history/legal-history-new-york/documents/Publications_1821-NY-Constitution.pdf (accessed 7/3/19).

7 Clinton L. Rossiter, ed., *The Federalist Papers; Alexander Hamilton, James Madison, and John Jay* (New York: New American Library, 1961), no. 10 (James Madison).

The right to suffrage and other civil rights cut to the core of what democracy means. Is America a democracy of all people? Can a democracy be legitimate if participation is restricted to less than half of the population? Excluded groups have struggled to gain the right to vote, and those who benefit from restrictions on the franchise have tried to maintain those boundaries. This willingness to fight over the right to vote demonstrates how significant a right it is.

Property qualifications for voters were the first restrictions to be lifted by the various states. At the time of the Founding, most states required some form of property ownership as a criterion for voting or running for office. They inherited this practice from Britain, where land conferred social title, status, and wealth upon those who possessed it, and where democracy was still a practice of the landed elite.[8] Throughout the first half of the nineteenth century, the states began to shed the requirement that people hold property in order to vote or stand for office. This political change was partly motivated by economic change; as the economy became more industrial and less agricultural, many people moved to cities for work and thus were less likely to own property. By 1850, property qualifications were eliminated across all states as a requirement for voting and seeking office. Even still, many states (for example, Wisconsin and Texas) levied poll taxes well into the twentieth century. Voters were required to pay a nominal amount, such as two dollars, every time they voted. Poll taxes abridged poor people's civil rights and often served to discriminate against Black voters. The Twenty-Fourth Amendment eliminated poll taxes in 1964.

While property-based restrictions on the right to vote were removed with relatively little protest, the struggle to extend this right to women and to racial and ethnic minorities proved much more contentious, fueling two of the greatest political movements in American history. Protection of voting rights and other civil rights for African Americans and other minorities remains a struggle today. The legal guarantee of those rights came relatively recently, with the Civil Rights Act (1964) and the Voting Rights Act (1965). The conflict over race runs so deep in U.S. politics that we will discuss that matter separately. Suffice it to say here that the Voting Rights Act remains an important, yet controversial, tool in fighting discrimination against Black, Hispanic, and Asian voters in the administration of elections.

Women's Suffrage. Early in the 1800s, few municipalities granted women the right to vote. It took an entire century of agitation and activism, of protest and political maneuvering, to guarantee women's voting rights. In the decades before the Civil War, attitudes about women's civil rights began to change, in part because of the practical problems of maintaining property, inheritance,

---

8   Throughout the nineteenth century and into the twentieth century, the United Kingdom changed the voting requirements in England, Scotland, and Wales, most significantly dropping property requirements in the 1832 and 1867 Reform Acts. For an excellent history of the politics of electoral reform in nineteenth-century England, see Charles Seymour, *Electoral Reform in England and Wales: The Development and Operation of the Parliamentary Franchise, 1832–1885* (New Haven, CT: Yale University Press, 1915).

and settlement in new states and territories. The United States had adopted laws of inheritance and property from Britain, which granted men control over all property, and those laws proved problematic in a country of settlers rather than established families and classes. It is no coincidence that many of the newer states, such as Indiana and Kentucky, were the first to give women economic rights, such as the rights to settle and own property. Around that time, American women began to engage in collective action to advance their political and social rights, including the right to vote. In 1848, women and men attending the Seneca Falls Convention issued the "Declaration of Sentiments and Resolutions," which asserted that women were entitled to rights in every way equal to those of men. Present at the meeting were individuals who would later lead the movement for women's civil rights—Elizabeth Cady Stanton, Lucretia Mott, Mary Ann McClintock, and the abolitionist leader Frederick Douglass.

In 1869, the National Woman Suffrage Association (NWSA) was formed in New York, and it immediately began to advocate for amending the U.S. Constitution to allow women to vote. By the 1880s, the issue of voting rights for women was the subject of mass meetings, parades, and protests, and as of 1917, NWSA had 2 million members. Laws to extend suffrage to women first appeared in the western states and territories. In 1869, Wyoming (still a territory then) was the first to extend women the right to vote, followed by Colorado in 1893 and Utah in 1895. In 1916, Montana became the first state to elect a woman to the U.S. Congress. And in 1917, New York, the home of the women's suffrage movement, at last granted suffrage to women. By 1918, all of the western states and territories plus Michigan and New York had granted women full suffrage. Soon it was only a matter of time before Congress changed federal law. In 1919, Congress passed the Nineteenth Amendment granting women the right to vote in federal elections.[9] Two months later, the states ratified the amendment, and women nationwide voted in the presidential election of 1920.

The Right to Vote for Black Americans. The struggle to extend full voting rights to racial minorities, especially Black Americans, reflects even deeper divisions in American society. It took a full century after the Civil War for Congress to guarantee minorities' voting rights with the Voting Rights Act of 1965, and the battle to protect those rights continues today.

The Fifteenth Amendment gives African Americans voting rights, and during Reconstruction the federal government enforced those rights. Following the withdrawal of federal troops from the South, however, state legislatures and local governments there (and elsewhere) enacted practices that excluded Black voters from elections or weakened their political power. In many states, they were excluded from voting in primary elections—a practice called the White primary. Poll taxes, literacy tests, registration list purges, and other tactics served

---

9 "Woman Suffrage," *Collier's New Encyclopedia*, vol. 10 (New York: Collier, 1921), pp. 403–5, http://en.wikisource.org/wiki/Collier%27s_New_Encyclopedia_%281921%29/Woman_ suffrage (accessed 7/3/19).

to keep Black people from voting.[10] District and municipal boundaries were drawn to place them in jurisdictions where they had little or no impact on the election of representatives or the approval of public expenditures.[11]

Black southerners had little hope of changing their states' laws because the laws worked in favor of state legislators who were not sympathetic to their cause. Congress was also reluctant to pass federal legislation to enforce the Fifteenth Amendment. At last the Supreme Court took action; it struck down the White primary in *Smith v. Allwright* in 1944, asserting the federal government's power to intervene in the states' conduct of elections in order to protect the voting rights of Black Americans.[12] The Court acted again in 1960, ruling that state and local governments could not draw election district boundaries in ways that discriminated against Blacks.[13] Finally Congress codified protections for African Americans' right to vote with the Voting Rights Act, sweeping aside many discriminatory state laws and practices. The 1965 act has been amended several times to expand who is covered, including Hispanics (1975) and language groups (1982), and what sorts of activities are prohibited, most notably racially discriminatory districting.

The fight to protect minority voting rights, however, continues. Voter ID laws and the redrawing of legislative district maps every 10 years, including after the 2020 census, have been subject to intense debate. More recently, the fight has extended to the restoration of voting rights to ex-felons who have served their time. Detractors of these policies frequently allege that they adversely affect minorities' voting rights and even embody intentional discrimination. Disputes over these laws often end up in front of federal judges, who must not only assess the circumstances in which the laws were passed but also examine the electoral behavior in the area in question. Since the 1982 amendments to the Voting Rights Act, adjudicating these conflicts has required consultation with social scientists to develop measures of how Black, Hispanic, and White people usually vote and estimates of the laws' likely effect on minorities' ability to elect their preferred candidates. We discuss how political scientists address these concerns in Chapters 10 and 11. Since the 1960s, the courts—not the legislatures—have become the arena in which minorities, poor people, city dwellers, and many others seek protection of their voting rights.

The Supreme Court's 2013 ruling in *Shelby County v. Holder* declared unconstitutional an important section of the Voting Rights Act. This section—Section 4(b)—obligated jurisdictions in Alabama, Alaska, Arizona, Georgia, Louisiana, Mississippi, South Carolina, and Texas, as well as municipalities and counties in other states, to obtain approval of any change to their election administration procedures from the Department of Justice or the Federal District Court in the District of Columbia—a procedure called *pre-clearance*. In writing the original 1965 law, Congress had determined which states needed to obtain pre-clearance by using a

10 V. O. Key, *Southern Politics in State and Nation* (New York: Knopf, 1949).

11 Bernard Taper, Gomillion versus Lightfoot: *The Tuskegee Gerrymander Case* (New York: McGraw-Hill, 1962).

12 *Smith v. Allwright*, 321 U.S. 649 (1944).

13 *Gomillion v. Lightfoot*, 364 U.S. 339 (1960).

formula that compared the turnout of minorities with the turnout of White people. The Supreme Court ruled that the states singled out in the act were no longer justified by the formula, as the ratio of minority turnout to White turnout in Alabama was similar to that in Massachusetts. Other parts of the Voting Rights Act still hold, however, and the *Shelby County* decision has shifted the legal battles to those other sections.[14] It has also put the question of pre-clearance back on Congress's agenda.

Racial Discrimination from the Nineteenth Century until Today

The Supreme Court was initially no more ready to enforce the civil rights aspects of the Fourteenth Amendment than it was to enforce the civil liberties provisions. This became evident when the Court considered the Civil Rights Act of 1875, a key piece of Reconstruction legislation that guaranteed Black Americans equal treatment in public accommodations, such as public transportation, and prohibited states and local governments from excluding Black people from jury service. The Court declared this act unconstitutional on the grounds that it sought to protect Blacks from discrimination by *private* businesses; according to the Court, the Fourteenth Amendment was intended to protect individuals from discrimination only in the case of actions by *public* officials of state and local governments. This decision gutted much of the legislation needed to make the provisions in the Thirteenth, Fourteenth, and Fifteenth Amendments a reality.

***Plessy v. Ferguson*: "Separate but Equal."** In 1896, the Court went further in the infamous *Plessy v. Ferguson* case, upholding a Louisiana statute that required racial segregation on trolleys and other public carriers (and, by implication, in all public facilities, including schools). Homer Plessy, a man defined as "one-eighth black," had violated a Louisiana law that provided for "equal but separate accommodations" on trains and imposed a $25 fine on any White passenger who sat in a car reserved for Blacks or any Black passenger who sat in a car reserved for Whites. The Supreme Court held that laws drawing racial distinctions did not violate the Fourteenth Amendment's "equal protection of the laws" as long as they applied to both races equally. Many people generally pretended that Black people were treated equally to White people as long as some accommodation for them existed. The Court said that although

> the object of the [Fourteenth] Amendment was undoubtedly to enforce the absolute equality of the two races before the law, . . . it could not have intended to abolish distinctions based on color, or to enforce social, as distinguished from political, equality, or a commingling of the two races upon terms unsatisfactory to either.[15]

---

14 *Shelby County v. Holder*, 570 U.S. 529 (2013).

15 *Plessy v. Ferguson*, 163 U.S. 537 (1896). The sole dissent to this decision came from Justice John Marshall Harlan, who wrote, "Our constitution is colorblind, and neither knows nor tolerates classes among citizens."

In effect, the Court thus argued that the use of race as a criterion of exclusion in public matters was not unreasonable. This was the origin of the **"separate but equal" rule**, which would not be reversed until 1954.

Challenging "Separate but Equal."

"separate but equal" rule

The legal principle that public accommodations could be segregated by race and still be equal.

The Supreme Court began to change its position on racial discrimination before World War II by defining more strictly what counted as "equal facilities" under the "separate but equal" rule. Notably, in 1938, the Court rejected Missouri's policy of funding out-of-state law school tuition for Black applicants who could not be admitted to the all-White University of Missouri Law School.[16]

After the war, modest progress resumed. In 1950, the Court rejected Texas's claim that its new "law school for Negroes" afforded an education equal to that of the all-White University of Texas Law School. Without confronting the "separate but equal" principle, the Court's decision anticipated *Brown v. Board of Education* by opening the question of whether any segregated facility could be truly equal.[17] The same was true in 1944, when the Court struck down White primaries. Here the Court's decision categorized political parties as "an agency of the State," so any discrimination against Blacks was therefore "state action within the meaning of the Fifteenth Amendment."[18] The most important pre-1954 decision was probably *Shelley v. Kraemer*, in which the Court ruled against the widespread practice of racially restrictive covenants, clauses in an agreement between the seller of a property and the buyer prohibiting the buyer from selling the property to any racial or religious minorities in the future.[19] The Court ruled that such restrictive covenants could not be judicially enforced because the Fourteenth Amendment prohibits any organ of the state, including the courts, from denying the equal protection of its laws.

However, none of these pre-1954 cases directly confronted the "separate but equal" rule and its legal and constitutional support for racial discrimination. Each victory by the Legal Defense Fund of the National Association for the Advancement of Colored People (NAACP) was another step toward the ultimate victory of eliminating the doctrine altogether. The southern states' massive effort to resist direct desegregation and to avoid legal action by making a show of the equality of White and Black schools suggested to the NAACP that the Supreme Court was not ready for a full confrontation with the constitutional principle sustaining segregation. That said, because Congress, dominated by southern Democrats during this period, refused to address racial segregation in the South, the NAACP's leadership saw the court system as its only hope. In 1952, the NAACP brought cases in South Carolina, Virginia, Kansas, Delaware, and the District of Columbia, arguing that the principle of segregation itself was unconstitutional. The strategy was to file suits simultaneously in different

---

16 *Missouri ex rel. Gaines v. Canada,* 305 U.S. 337 (1938).

17 *Sweatt v. Painter,* 339 U.S. 629 (1950).

18 *Smith v. Allwright* (1944).

19 *Shelley v. Kraemer,* 334 U.S. 1 (1948).

federal districts so that inconsistent results between any two states would more quickly lead to Supreme Court acceptance of at least one appeal.[20] The Kansas case ultimately became the focal point. It was further along in the adjudicatory process in its district court, and it had the special advantage of being located in a state outside the South, which would lessen local resistance to a decision outlawing segregation.[21]

Brown v. Board of Education.

Brown v. Board of Education. Oliver Brown, the father of three girls, lived in a low-income, racially mixed Topeka neighborhood. Every school-day morning, his daughter Linda took a school bus to the all-Black Monroe School about a mile away. In September 1950 Brown took Linda to the all-White Sumner School, which was closer to home, to enter her in the third grade, in defiance of state law and local segregation rules. When they were refused, Brown took his case to the NAACP, and soon thereafter *Brown v. Board of Education* was born. In mid-1953, the Court announced that the several cases related to racial segregation then wending their way through the courts would be reargued within the context of questions involving the intent of the Fourteenth Amendment. A year later, the Court responded with one of the most important decisions in its history.

In deciding the case, the Court, to the surprise of many, rejected as inconclusive all the widely accepted scholarly arguments about the intent and the history of the Fourteenth Amendment and committed itself to considering only the *consequences* of segregation:

> Does segregation of children in public schools solely on the basis of race, even though the physical facilities and other "tangible" factors may be equal, deprive the children of the minority group of equal educational opportunities? We believe that it does. . . . We conclude that, in the field of public education, the doctrine of "separate but equal" has no place. Separate educational facilities are inherently unequal.[22]

The *Brown* decision altered the constitutional framework protecting civil rights in two fundamental respects. First, after *Brown*, the states no longer had the power to use race as a criterion of discrimination in law. Second, the national

20 The best reviews of these strategies, tactics, and goals can be found in John Hope Franklin, *From Slavery to Freedom: A History of Negro Americans,* 4th ed. (New York: Knopf, 1974), chap. 22; and Richard Kluger, *Simple Justice: The History of* Brown v. Board of Education *and Black America's Struggle for Equality* (New York: Knopf, 1975), chaps. 21 and 22.

21 The District of Columbia case came up too, but because the District of Columbia is not a state, the case did not directly involve the Fourteenth Amendment and its equal protection clause. It confronted the Court on the same grounds, however: that segregation is inherently unequal. Its victory in effect was incorporation in reverse, with equal protection moving from the Fourteenth Amendment to become applicable to federal law. See *Bolling v. Sharpe,* 347 U.S. 497 (1954).

22 *Brown v. Board of Education,* 347 U.S. 483 (1954).

government from then on had a constitutional basis for extending its authority to intervene against discriminatory actions of state or local governments, school boards, employers, and many others in the private sector.

Civil Rights after *Brown v. Board of Education*. Although *Brown v. Board of Education* withdrew all constitutional authority to use race as a criterion of exclusion in the realm of education, this historic decision was merely a small first step in establishing equal civil rights for Black Americans. First, most states refused to cooperate with the Court's decision until sued, and many ingenious schemes served to delay their obedience (such as paying White students' tuition at newly created "private" academies). Second, even as southern school boards began to eliminate their legally enforced **de jure segregation**, extensive **de facto segregation** remained in the North and the South as a consequence of racially segregated housing, which the *Brown* decision did not affect. Third, *Brown* did not directly touch discrimination in employment, public accommodations, juries, voting, and other areas of social and economic activity.

A decade of frustration following *Brown* indicated that adjudication alone would not succeed in desegregating American society. The goal of equal protection required positive, or affirmative, action by Congress and administrative agencies. And given massive resistance in the South and the generally negative national public opinion toward racial integration, progress would not be made through the courts, Congress, or federal agencies without well-organized support.

Organized demonstrations for equal voting rights and public accommodations increased slowly but surely in the first 14 years after *Brown*.[23] In an impressive demonstration of collective political action, hundreds of thousands of Americans, both Black and White, exercised their right to peaceably assemble and petition the government for a redress of grievances, demanding that the civil rights guaranteed to White Americans now be recognized and protected for Black Americans too. By the 1960s, the many organizations constituting the civil rights movement had accumulated experience and built networks capable of launching massive direct-action campaigns against southern segregationists. The Southern Christian Leadership Conference, the Student Nonviolent Coordinating Committee, and many other organizations built a movement across the South that used the media to attract nationwide attention and support. In the massive March on Washington in 1963, Reverend Martin Luther King, Jr. staked out the movement's moral claims in his "I Have a Dream" speech. Widely circulated images of protesters being beaten, attacked by police dogs, and set on with fire hoses won broad sympathy for the Black civil rights cause and discredited state and local governments in the South. In this way, the movement created intense pressure for a reluctant federal government to take more assertive steps to defend the civil rights of African Americans.

In the realm of civil rights, institutions mattered. On the one hand, the rules of the Senate allowed southern conservatives, a minority in the Senate, to use filibusters and other Senate procedures to slow or even stymie civil rights legislation. On the other hand, a different institution, the federal courts, generally

---

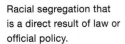

de jure segregation

Racial segregation that is a direct result of law or official policy.

de facto segregation

Racial segregation that is not a direct result of law or governmental policy but a reflection of residential patterns, income distributions, or other social factors.

---

23 Jonathan D. Casper, *The Politics of Civil Liberties* (New York: Harper & Row, 1972), p. 90.

supported the cause of civil rights and proved able to overturn rules and procedures that stood in the way of the civil rights movement.

The Black Lives Matter Movement. In recent years, the politics of
African American civil rights has shifted from voting and employment to far
more difficult and contentious arenas. Beginning in 2014, a variety of protests
have coalesced under the banner of the Black Lives Matter movement to focus
attention on allegations of police misconduct directed at African Americans,
especially police shootings (see Figure 5.1). The movement took off in Ferguson,

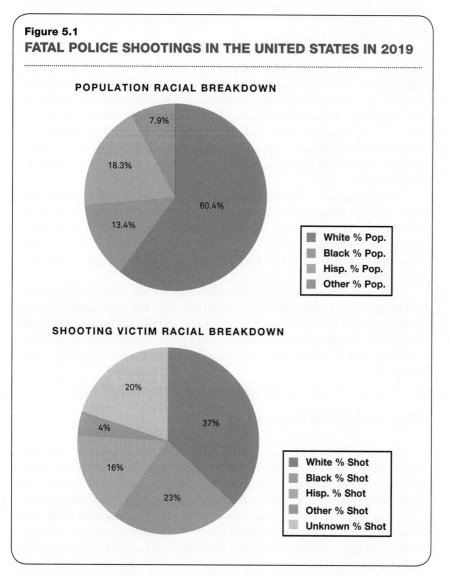

Figure 5.1
FATAL POLICE SHOOTINGS IN THE UNITED STATES IN 2019

POPULATION RACIAL BREAKDOWN

7.9%
18.3%
13.4%
60.4%

White % Pop.
Black % Pop.
Hisp. % Pop.
Other % Pop.

SHOOTING VICTIM RACIAL BREAKDOWN

20%
4%
16%
23%
37%

White % Shot
Black % Shot
Hisp. % Shot
Other % Shot
Unknown % Shot

SOURCE: *Washington Post*, https://www.washingtonpost.com/graphics/2019/national/police-
shootings-2019/ (accessed 12/2/2019) and 2018 U.S. Census Bureau data.

Missouri, after the 2014 shooting of Michael Brown, an unarmed Black teenager, by a White police officer. It spread across the nation as the media carried reports, photos, and videos of police violence against Black people in Chicago, South Carolina, Baltimore, New York, and other parts of the country. African Americans had long asserted that they were often victims of racial profiling and more likely than Whites to be harassed, physically harmed, or arrested by the police. Police departments often responded to these accusations by charging that Black people were more likely than White people to be engaged in criminal activity. In July 2016, widely publicized deaths of two Black men at the hands of police within one day of each other again spurred nationwide protests. While most of these protests were peaceful, a sniper killed five police officers at one demonstration in Dallas, Texas.

The Black Lives Matter movement lays bare the racial fissures that continue to lie at the heart of American society. Since its inception, the movement has expanded to focus more broadly on issues of freedom, protesting mass incarceration and advocating for the restoration of full voting rights to ex-felons. To supporters, the movement highlights the continuing injustices suffered by Blacks at the hands of White authorities—the fact that Black lives seem not to matter. However, some critics have embraced a competing slogan, "all lives matter," which many Black Lives Matter supporters see as an effort to denigrate their concerns.

In 2020, protests erupted when a white Minneapolis police officer was seen on video killing a Black man who had been taken into custody. A video showed another Black man killed by Atlanta, Georgia police who were apparently attempting to arrest him. These killings sparked calls under the banner, "defund the police," for the imposition of major police reforms throughout America.

The 2020 protests led to renewed demands for the removal of Confederate statues and other reminders of slavery. Are the Confederate statues benign or racist? Is the effort to remove them an effort to rewrite history or an attempt to eliminate racist imagery from public spaces? History matters, and America's history of slavery and segregation continues to shape politics to this day.

Opportunity in Education

Education has been the focus of some of the most important battles over civil rights, largely because Americans believe that everyone should have an equal chance to succeed. That commitment to equality is underscored by the centrality of public education in our country. Since the early nineteenth century, American communities and states have provided public education to all persons. The education system has been essential in helping immigrants join our society—it helps them learn English, American values, and the skills necessary for employment. Universal access to public education has also helped forge one of the world's most productive workforces. Leaving large segments of the population uneducated is potentially bad for the economy, and it is certainly bad for the people who do not receive an education. Grossly unequal opportunities for children to receive an education will likely mean grossly unequal opportunities later in life to have a good job, participate in politics, and realize their potential.

Inequities in educational opportunities were painfully obvious in the 1950s. Equal access to quality education, it was thought, would reduce and perhaps eliminate disparities in other areas over the course of a generation.

School Desegregation, Phase One. Although the District of Columbia and some school districts in the border states responded almost immediately to court-ordered desegregation, states in the Deep South responded with a delaying tactic known as *massive resistance*. Southern politicians stood shoulder to shoulder to declare that the Supreme Court's decisions and orders would not change their segregationist policies. These states' legislatures enacted statutes ordering school districts to maintain segregated schools and directing state superintendents to terminate state funding wherever there was racial integration in the classroom.

Most of these plans were tested in the federal courts and struck down as unconstitutional.[24] But southern resistance went beyond legislation. Perhaps the most serious incident occurred in 1957, in Arkansas. On the first day of school, a mob assembled at Little Rock Central High School to protest integration. Governor Orval Faubus mobilized the Arkansas National Guard to prevent Black students from entering the school, in defiance of a federal court order. Following a three-week standoff between the Arkansas governor and the federal courts, President Eisenhower was forced to deploy U.S. troops and place the city under martial law in order to integrate the school.

The end of massive resistance marked the beginning of other strategies, such as pupil placement laws.[25] Ten years after *Brown,* fewer than 1 percent of Black school-age children in the Deep South were attending schools with White children. The federal courts could not do the job alone.

At last, Congress passed the Civil Rights Act of 1964, which outlawed discrimination against racial, ethnic, and religious minorities and against women; it also allowed federal agencies to withhold federal grants, contracts, and loans from states and municipalities found to discriminate or obstruct the Civil Rights

---

24 The two most important cases were *Cooper v. Aaron,* 358 U.S. 1 (1958), which required Little Rock, Arkansas, to desegregate, and *Griffin v. School Board of Prince Edward County,* 377 U.S. 218 (1964), which forced all the schools of that Virginia county to reopen after they had been closed for five years to avoid desegregation.

25 *Shuttlesworth v. Birmingham Board of Education,* 358 U.S. 101 (1958), upheld a pupil placement plan purporting to assign students to different schools on various bases, with no mention of race. This case interpreted *Brown* to mean that school districts must stop explicit racial discrimination but were under no obligation to take positive steps to desegregate. For a while, Black parents were doomed to wait for slow case-by-case approaches in the federal courts.

Cause and Effect in the Civil Rights Movement

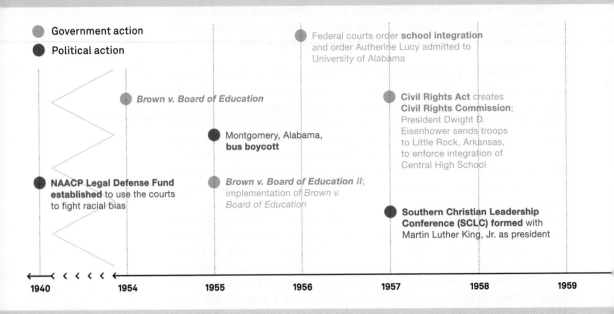

- ● Government action
- ● Political action

Federal courts order **school integration** and order Autherine Lucy admitted to University of Alabama

Brown v. Board of Education

Civil Rights Act creates **Civil Rights Commission**; President Dwight D. Eisenhower sends troops to Little Rock, Arkansas, to enforce integration of Central High School

Montgomery, Alabama, **bus boycott**

NAACP Legal Defense Fund established to use the courts to fight racial bias

Brown v. Board of Education II; implementation of *Brown v. Board of Education*

Southern Christian Leadership Conference (SCLC) formed with Martin Luther King, Jr. as president

| 1940 | 1954 | 1955 | 1956 | 1957 | 1958 | 1959 |

TIMEPLOT SOURCE: Data compiled by author.

Act's implementation. Also extremely important was the 1965 Elementary and Secondary Education Act, which promised funding to school districts that met a number of criteria, including conformance with federal desegregation policies. Many school districts made sure to develop desegregation plans in order to qualify for federal dollars.

It is important to note the mutual dependence of the courts and Congress. Not only did Congress need constitutional authority to act but the courts also needed legislative and political assistance—through the power of the purse, the power to organize administrative agencies to implement court orders, and the ability to focus political support—to ensure that their decisions could be enforced. And even as Congress finally addressed school desegregation (and other areas of equal protection) through legislation, the courts continued to exercise their powers by issuing orders against recalcitrant school districts and by extending and reinterpreting aspects of the equal protection clause to support legislative and administrative actions (see the Timeplot above).

School Desegregation: Busing and Beyond. One of the most important judicial extensions of civil rights in education after 1954 was the *Swann v. Charlotte-Mecklenburg Board of Education* decision of 1971, which held

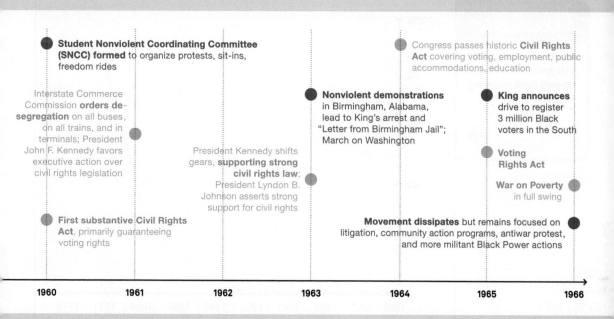

Student Nonviolent Coordinating Committee (SNCC) formed to organize protests, sit-ins, freedom rides

Interstate Commerce Commission orders de-segregation on all buses, on all trains, and in terminals; President John F. Kennedy favors executive action over civil rights legislation

President Kennedy shifts gears, supporting strong civil rights law; President Lyndon B. Johnson asserts strong support for civil rights

First substantive Civil Rights Act, primarily guaranteeing voting rights

Congress passes historic Civil Rights Act covering voting, employment, public accommodations, education

Nonviolent demonstrations in Birmingham, Alabama, lead to King's arrest and "Letter from Birmingham Jail"; March on Washington

King announces drive to register 3 million Black voters in the South

Voting Rights Act

War on Poverty in full swing

Movement dissipates but remains focused on litigation, community action programs, antiwar protest, and more militant Black Power actions

1960   1961   1962   1963   1964   1965   1966

that state-imposed desegregation could be brought about by busing children to different school districts, even across relatively long distances. The decision also added that under certain circumstances even racial quotas could serve as the "starting point in shaping a remedy to correct past constitutional violations" and that the pairing or grouping of schools and the reorganizing of school attendance zones would also be acceptable (Figure 5.2).[26]

Three years later, however, *Swann* was severely restricted when the Supreme Court determined that only cities found guilty of deliberate, de jure racial segregation (segregation in law) would have to desegregate their schools. This decision was handed down in the 1974 case of *Milliken v. Bradley*, which involved the city of Detroit and its suburbs.[27] The *Milliken* ruling had the effect of exempting most northern states and cities from busing because school segregation in northern cities is generally de facto (segregation in fact), resulting from segregated housing patterns and thousands of acts of private discrimination against Black people and other minorities.

---

26 *Swann v. Charlotte-Mecklenburg Board of Education*, 402 U.S. 1 (1971).

27 *Milliken v. Bradley*, 418 U.S. 717 (1974).

Figure 5.2

PERCENTAGE OF SOUTHERN BLACK CHILDREN ATTENDING SCHOOL WITH WHITES, 1955–1973

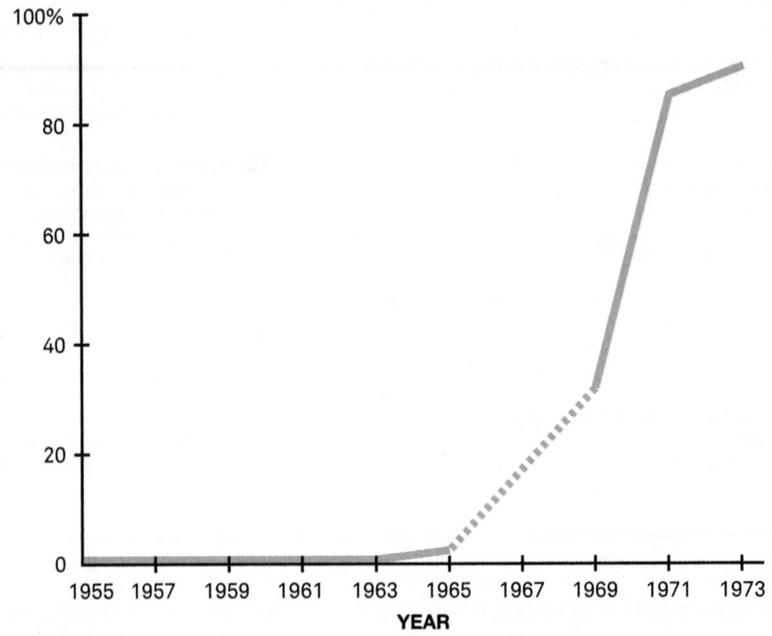

ANALYZING THE EVIDENCE

What happened in 1964 that accounts for the upward trend beginning in 1965?

NOTE: Dashed line indicates missing data.
SOURCE: Gerald N. Rosenberg, *The Hollow Hope: Can Courts Bring About Social Change?* (Chicago: University of Chicago Press, 1991), pp. 50–51.

Additional progress in school desegregation will likely be extremely slow unless the Supreme Court permits federal action against de facto segregation and the various kinds of private schools and academies that have sprung up for the purpose of avoiding integration. Prospects for further school integration diminished with several Court decisions handed down in the 1990s. In 1995, for example, the Court signaled to the lower courts that they should "disengage from desegregation efforts"[28] —a direct threat to the main basis of the holding in the original 1954 *Brown v. Board of Education* decision. In 2007, the Court went further, declaring that Louisville and Seattle school district programs that attempted to achieve racial diversity by using race as a determining factor in admissions were unconstitutional. Provocatively, Chief Justice John Roberts

---

28 *Missouri v. Jenkins*, 515 U.S. 70 (1995). The quotation is from David M. O'Brien, *Supreme Court Watch 1996* (New York: Norton, 1996), p. 220.

quoted the counsel for Oliver Brown in his majority decision, writing, "We have one fundamental contention which we will seek to develop in the course of this argument, and that contention is that no state has any authority under the equal protection clause of the Fourteenth Amendment to use race as a factor in affording educational opportunities among its citizens."[29] This judicial retrenchment is one reason that America's schools have gradually become resegregated. A recent study by the Government Accountability Office shows that the number of American schools that are "intensively segregated"—that is, those with student bodies composed primarily of low-income students and students of color—has more than doubled since 2001.[30]

In recent years, the idea that race should not be used as a factor in the realm of educational opportunities has also become important in the area of college admissions. For example, in the 2013 case of *Fisher v. University of Texas*,[31] the Supreme Court indicated that an affirmative action college admissions program that seems to discriminate *in favor of* Black students must be subjected to the same "strict scrutiny" as a program that seems to discriminate *against* Black students. After sending the case back to the lower courts for further consideration, the Court ruled on the University of Texas's plan in 2016, declaring that some intrusion on equal protection was warranted by the importance of creating a diverse student body.[32] Strict scrutiny (see Chapter 4) is the most stringent standard of judicial review; it requires the government to show that a law furthers a compelling governmental interest and is narrowly tailored to achieve that interest.

Women and Education. Women have also suffered from unequal access to education. Throughout the nineteenth century, relatively few colleges and professional schools admitted women. (Oberlin College was the first to do so.) Even as late as the 1960s, elite universities such as Princeton and Yale did not admit women, and colleges that did admit women offered them fewer opportunities to participate in programs, clubs, and athletics. Congress began to remedy these inequities with the Civil Rights Act of 1964, but the most significant federal legislation to guarantee women equal access to education is the 1972 Education Act. Title IX of this act forbids gender discrimination in education. By the mid-1970s, most universities had become fully coed. Enforcing equality, however, would prove to be more difficult.

Although the Education Act did not include strong enforcement provisions, it has proven effective in litigation. A significant step came in 1992, when the Court ruled that violations of the act's Title IX could be remedied with monetary

---

29 *Parents Involved in Community Schools v. Seattle School District No. 1*, 551 U.S. 701 (2007).

30 Emma Brown, "On the Anniversary of *Brown v. Board*, New Evidence That U.S. Schools Are Resegregating," *Washington Post*, May 17, 2016, www.washingtonpost.com/news/education/wp/2016/05/17/on-the-anniversary-of-brown-v-board-new-evidence-that-u-s-schools-are-resegregating/?utm_term=.4fdcc7cbba13 (accessed 12/9/19).

31 *Fisher v. University of Texas*, 570 U.S. 297 (2013).

32 *Fisher v. University of Texas*, 579 U.S. ____ (2016).

damages.[33] This ruling opened the door for further legal action in the area of education and led to stronger enforcement of the act's provisions against sexual harassment, gender inequities in resources (such as lab space, research support for faculty, and athletics), and gender inequities in compensation. In the two years after the 1992 ruling, complaints to the Education Department's Office for Civil Rights about unequal treatment of women's athletic programs nearly tripled. Subsequently, some prominent universities have been ordered to create more women's sports programs; many other colleges and universities have added more women's programs to avoid potential litigation.[34]

In 1996, the Supreme Court put an end to all-male schools supported by public funds when it ruled that the Virginia Military Institute's policy of not admitting women was unconstitutional.[35] Along with the Citadel, an all-male military college in South Carolina, Virginia Military Institute (VMI) had never admitted women. VMI argued that its unique educational experience, including intense physical training and the harsh treatment of freshmen, would be destroyed if women were admitted. The Court, however, ruled that the male-only policy denied "substantial equality" to women. Two days after the Court's ruling, the Citadel announced that it would begin to accept women. VMI considered becoming a private institution in order to remain all-male, but ultimately its board voted to change the school's admissions policy to admit women.

Title IX has also played an important role in the area of sexual harassment. During the Obama administration, the Department of Education issued a letter to all of America's colleges and universities declaring that sexual harassment and sexual violence were forms of discrimination outlawed by Title IX. The letter set forward guidelines to be followed when dealing with charges of sexual harassment on campus. Critics asserted that the guidelines offered no protection to men accused of sexual harassment and encouraged women to make false charges. President Trump's secretary of education, Betsy DeVos, rescinded the Obama-era guidelines and issued new instructions designed to enhance legal safeguards for those accused of an offense. Critics of the new guidelines warned that they would discourage victims from bringing charges.

THE POLITICS OF RIGHTS

The Nineteenth Amendment, *Brown v. Board of Education*, the Civil Rights Acts, and the Voting Rights Act were the signal achievements of the civil rights movements of women and Black Americans. The movements helped redefine civil rights in America not just for those groups but for all people. They became

33 *Franklin v. Gwinnett County Public Schools*, 503 U.S. 60 (1992).

34 Jennifer Halperin, "Women Step Up to Bat," *Illinois Issues*, September 1995, pp. 10–14.

35 *United States v. Virginia*, 518 U.S. 515 (1996).

models for other groups to press civil rights claims, and the NWSA and NAACP strategies have been widely mimicked. The principles behind equality in voting and in education have since been applied to other areas, including employment, housing, immigration, access to public facilities, and athletics. With the push for rights in these spheres, there has also been a push back. Just how far do civil rights extend?

Outlawing Discrimination in Employment

The federal courts and the Justice Department entered the arena of discrimination in employment with Title VII of the Civil Rights Act of 1964, which outlaws job discrimination on the basis of race, color, religion, sex, or national origin by all private and public employers, including government agencies (such as fire and police departments), that employ more than 15 workers. In Chapter 4, we saw that the Supreme Court interpreted "interstate commerce" in a way that was broad enough to give Congress the constitutional authority to ban discrimination by virtually any employers.[36]

A potential difficulty with Title VII is that the complaining party must show evidence of deliberate discrimination that prevented them from getting a job or a training opportunity. Of course, employers rarely admit discrimination on the basis of race, sex, or any other illegal factor. Recognizing this reality, the courts have allowed aggrieved parties to make their case if they can show that hiring practices had the *effect* of exclusion. This idea is known as *disparate* or *adverse impact*. A leading case in 1971 involved a class action by several Black employees of the Duke Power Company in North Carolina, who attempted to show with statistical evidence that Black employees had been relegated to one undesirable department of the company. The employees also argued that they had been kept out of contention for better jobs because the employer had added high school education and passing grades on special aptitude tests as qualifications for advancement. The Supreme Court held that, although the statistical evidence did not prove intentional discrimination and the employer's requirements were race neutral in appearance, their effects were sufficient to shift the burden of justification to the employer to show that the requirements were a "business necessity" that bore "a demonstrable relationship to successful performance."[37] The Court's ruling was subsequently applied to other hiring, promotion, and training programs.[38]

Recently, the Court has placed some limits on employment discrimination suits. In 2007, for example, it ruled that complaints of gender discrimination

---

36 See especially *Katzenbach v. McClung*, 379 U.S. 294 (1964).

37 *Griggs v. Duke Power Company*, 401 U.S. 424 (1971). See also Allan P. Sindler, *Bakke, DeFunis, and Minority Admissions: The Quest for Equal Opportunity* (New York: Longman, 1978), pp. 180–9.

38 For a good treatment of these issues, see Charles O. Gregory and Harold A. Katz, *Labor and the Law*, 3rd ed. (New York: Norton, 1979), chap. 17.

must be brought within 180 days of the time the alleged discrimination occurred, in effect blocking suits based on events that might have taken place in the past.[39] In 2009, Congress overturned the Court's decision with the Ledbetter Fair Pay Act, which gives workers more time to file pay discrimination claims. In two important 2008 decisions, the Court helped individuals seeking to bring employment discrimination complaints by declaring that employers are barred from retaliating against them.[40] Today, several federal statutes enforced by the Equal Employment Opportunity Commission (EEOC) prohibit employer retaliation against workers who file discrimination complaints.

Women and Gender Discrimination

Although women gained voting and property rights long ago, they continue to suffer discrimination in various forms. In the realm of employment discrimination, women benefited from the civil rights movement and, especially, from Title VII, which in many ways fostered the growth of the women's movement. The National Organization for Women's first major campaign involved picketing the EEOC for its refusal to ban sex-segregated employment advertisements.

Building on these victories and the growth of the women's movement, women's rights activists sought an equal rights amendment (ERA) to the Constitution. The proposed amendment's substantive passage stated that "equality of rights under the law shall not be denied or abridged by the United States or by any State on account of sex." Supporters believed that such a sweeping guarantee of equal rights was necessary to end all discrimination against women and make gender roles more equal. Opponents charged that the amendment would be socially disruptive and would introduce changes—such as coed restrooms—that many Americans did not want. The amendment easily passed Congress in 1972 and won quick approval in many state legislatures, but it fell three states short of the 38 needed for ratification by the 1982 deadline.[41]

intermediate scrutiny

The test used by the Supreme Court in gender discrimination cases, which places the burden of justifying a law or policy's use mainly on the government.

Despite the ERA's failure to pass, gender discrimination expanded dramatically as an area of civil rights law, in part thanks to the conservative Burger Court of the 1970s. Although the Court refused to treat gender discrimination as equivalent to racial discrimination,[42] it made it easier for plaintiffs to file and win suits on the basis of gender discrimination by applying an "intermediate" level of review to these cases.[43] **Intermediate scrutiny** places the burden of justifying a law or policy's use of gender on the government.

---

39 Ledbetter v. Goodyear Tire and Rubber Company, 550 U.S. 618 (2007).

40 CBOCS West v. Humphries, 553 U.S. 442 (2008); Gómez-Pérez v. Potter, 553 U.S. 474 (2008).

41 See Jane J. Mansbridge, Why We Lost the ERA (Chicago: University of Chicago Press, 1986) and Gilbert Y. Steiner, Constitutional Inequality: The Political Fortunes of the Equal Rights Amendment (Washington, DC: Brookings Institution, 1985).

42 Frontiero v. Richardson, 411 U.S. 677 (1973).

43 Craig v. Boren, 429 U.S. 190 (1976).

Elevated awareness of sexual harassment as a form of gender discrimination has also advanced the cause of women's civil rights. In a 1986 case, the Supreme Court recognized two forms of sexual harassment: the quid pro quo type, which involves sexual extortion, and the hostile environment type, which involves sexual intimidation.[44] In its decision the Court said that sexual harassment may be legally actionable even if the employee did not suffer tangible economic or job-related losses in relation to it. In a subsequent case, the Court ruled that sexual harassment may be legally actionable even if the employee did not suffer tangible psychological costs as a result.[45] In two 1998 cases, the Court further strengthened the law when it ruled that, whether or not sexual harassment results in economic harm to the employee, an employer is liable for the harassment if it was committed by someone with authority over the employee—by a supervisor, for example. The Court also said, however, that an employer may defend itself against these charges by showing that it had a sexual harassment prevention and grievance policy in effect.[46]

The development of gender discrimination as an important part of the civil rights struggle has coincided with the rise of women's politics as a discrete movement in American politics. As with the struggle for racial equality, changes in government policies have to a great degree produced political action. Today the existence of a powerful women's movement derives largely from Title VII of the Civil Rights Act of 1964 and from the Burger Court's application of the law to the protection of women. In 2018, cases of sexual harassment involving prominent media and political figures led more and more women to come forward and name those who had victimized them. What came to be called the #MeToo movement revealed the extent to which sexual harassment still pervades American society. #MeToo was founded by New York civil rights activist Tarana Burke, but it is less an organized movement than a loosely organized expression of concern and outrage directed against sexual violence. #MeToo encourages victims of sexual violence to come forward, share their stories, name their attackers, and thereby give notice that sexual harassment will not be tolerated.

Many of the victories won in the realm of gender discrimination have, in recent years, been applied to discrimination against transgender individuals. In 2015, President Barack Obama issued an executive order prohibiting federal contractors from discriminating against workers based on their sexual orientation or gender identity. Two months later, the EEOC filed its first-ever lawsuits to protect transgender workers under Title VII of the Civil Rights Act. In late December of that year, Attorney General Eric Holder announced that, going forward, the Justice Department would consider discrimination against transgender people as covered by the Civil Rights Act's prohibition of sex discrimination.[47]

---

44 *Meritor Savings Bank v. Vinson*, 477 U.S. 57 (1986).

45 *Harris v. Forklift Systems*, 510 U.S. 17 (1993).

46 *Burlington Industries v. Ellerth*, 524 U.S. 742 (1998); *Faragher v. City of Boca Raton*, 524 U.S. 775 (1998).

47 Claire Zillman, "Barnes & Noble Is Latest Retailer to Face Transgender Discrimination Lawsuit," *Fortune*, May 7, 2015, www.fortune.com/2015/05/07/barnes-noble-transgender-lawsuit (accessed 7/3/19).

In 2016, gay rights advocates brought a federal suit against North Carolina over the state's new law prohibiting local governments from adopting special protections for members of the LGBTQ community. The law was enacted in response to a Charlotte, North Carolina, ordinance allowing transgender people to use public restrooms aligned with their gender identity. The state opposed the law on the grounds that, supposedly, it would allow sexual predators to enter women's bathrooms. Gay rights groups called the state's argument false and simply a pretext for discriminatory action. When the Department of Justice warned North Carolina that the law violated the Civil Rights Act, the state sued the federal government in order to defend its new law. In 2019, the state agreed to allow transgender individuals to use restrooms that match their gender identities in the state's public buildings.

In the midst of the battle over North Carolina's law, in June 2016, the U.S. military dropped its ban against openly transgender people serving in the armed forces, though in 2017, President Trump declared that he would reinstate the ban. Trump's move met with opposition from within the military hierarchy, which feared disruption and litigation, and it was not clear what effect the president's new edict would have. The Policy Principle box on p. 179 looks at changing policy around the movement for transgender rights.

Latinos and Latinas

The labels *Latino* and *Hispanic* encompass a wide range of groups with diverse national origins, cultural identities, and particular experiences. The early political experiences of Mexican Americans were shaped by race and region. In 1898, Mexican Americans gained formal political rights, including the right to vote. In many places, however, especially in Texas, Mexican Americans were segregated and prevented from voting by such means as the White primary and the poll tax.[48] In addition, before World War II segregated schools along with housing and employment restrictions were common in Texas and California. In 1947, the League of United Latin American Citizens (LULAC) won a key victory in *Mendez v. Westminster*, which overturned an Orange County, California, policy of school segregation aimed at Mexican Americans.[49] *Mendez*, an important precedent for *Brown v. Board of Education*, is a landmark case in the civil rights struggle.

Following World War II, LULAC and the American GI Forum worked to stem discrimination against Mexican Americans. By the late 1950s, the first

---

48 New Mexico has a different history because not many non-Hispanic Whites of European descent settled there initially. Mexican Americans had considerable power in territorial legislatures between 1865 and 1912. See Lawrence H. Fuchs, *The American Kaleidoscope: Race, Ethnicity, and the Civic Culture* (Hanover, NH: University Press of New England, 1990), pp. 239–40.

49 *Mendez v. Westminster*, 161 F2d 744 (Ninth Cir., 1947).

Transgender Rights and Policy

The campaign for transgender equality seeks to end discrimination against transgender people in employment, housing, health care, and public accommodations. Roughly 700,000 Americans openly identify as transgender or gender nonconforming, meaning that they do not necessarily identify with the sex they were assigned at birth. The United States' history of rights advocacy on the part of African Americans, women, and other groups blazed a trail for transgender people to follow, demonstrating tactics and offering potential allies to their cause. Illustrating the history principle, earlier victories by these groups established legal principles, laws, and political institutions that transgender advocates could use to develop and implement policies for their own purposes.

For example, in recent years transgender advocates lobbied effectively to achieve court decisions and executive orders that applied laws originally crafted to protect African Americans and women from workplace discrimination to members of the transgender community. The federal courts, the Justice Department, and the EEOC have all agreed that Title VII of the 1964 Civil Rights Act, which prohibits sex discrimination in employment, prohibits discrimination against transgender and gender nonconforming individuals as well. Two executive orders, the first by President Clinton in 1998 and the second by President Obama in 2014, prohibit discrimination in federal employment and in hiring by federal contractors, respectively, based on sexual orientation or gender identity. Thus favorable federal policies emerged because transgender individuals could channel their policy preferences through an already-existing set of institutions.

The effort to end gender identity–based discrimination in public accommodations has taken a somewhat different path. Discrimination by hotels, restaurants, theaters, and so forth was not a focus for the women's movement, and thus federal antidiscrimination law for public accommodations covers race, religion, national origin, and disability but not gender. As a

An inclusive restroom that people of any gender identity may use.

result, the transgender movement did not inherit an existing legal framework or set of institutions through which to pursue its policy goals. While continuing to work for federal legislation in this area, advocates have made strides at other levels of government: as of 2020, 20 states and at least 400 localities have expressly prohibited discrimination based on gender identity in public accommodations. In this case, preferences channeled through sympathetic state and local institutions rather than federal ones have produced the movement's desired policy outcomes.

These successes have sometimes proved only temporary, however. In 2015, an antidiscrimination ordinance in Houston was repealed in a referendum. And in 2016, a similar measure in Charlotte, North Carolina, was reversed by the state's legislature, which enacted a bill prohibiting transgender individuals from using bathrooms that correspond to their gender identity in schools and other government buildings. After the federal Department of Justice warned the state that the law violated the Civil Rights Act, the state and the department filed opposing lawsuits over the issue. In 2017, President Trump declared that the U.S. military would no longer accept transgender troops. However, two federal courts ruled against such a ban and the military leadership was reluctant to implement Trump's order.

Mexican American was elected to Congress; four others followed in the 1960s. In the late 1960s, a new kind of Mexican American political movement arose, inspired by the Black civil rights movement. Mexican American students boycotted high school classes in Los Angeles, Denver, and San Antonio; students in colleges and universities across California joined in as well. Among their demands were bilingual education, an end to discrimination, and greater cultural recognition. In Crystal City, Texas, which non-Hispanic White politicians had dominated despite an overwhelmingly Mexican American population, the newly formed La Raza Unida Party took over the city government.[50]

In recent years, Latino political strategy has developed along two tracks. One path focuses on voter registration to increase Latino voter turnout. This path capitalizes on the enormous growth of the Latino population, which has resulted in part from immigration. The second track is a legal strategy using civil rights laws designed to ensure fair access to the political system. The Mexican American Legal Defense and Educational Fund (MALDEF) has played a key role in designing and pursuing the latter strategy.

During the Trump presidency, Latino immigration has been a major political issue. President Trump has declared that immigrants from Central American countries who enter the United States without documentation or seek to claim asylum represent a serious threat to American safety and security. As a result of Trump's actions, many Latinos have stepped up their level of political activity, mainly in support of Democratic politicians. Trump's perceived hostility toward Latinos will probably have political repercussions for years to come as America's most rapidly growing population group will see the GOP as a party hostile to its interests.

Asian Americans

The early Asian experience in the United States was shaped by naturalization laws dating back to 1790, the first of which declared that only White immigrants were eligible for citizenship. In the 1850s, Chinese immigrants drawn to California by the gold rush faced hostility and virulent antagonism, which led Congress in 1870 to declare them ineligible for citizenship. In 1882, the first Chinese Exclusion Act suspended the entry of Chinese laborers.

At the time of the Exclusion Act, the Chinese community predominantly comprised single male laborers, with few women and children. The few Chinese children in San Francisco were denied entry to public schools. Only after parents of American-born Chinese children pressed legal action were the children allowed to attend, and even then they had to attend a separate Chinese school. In 1898 the Supreme Court confirmed that American-born Chinese children

---

50 On the La Raza Unida Party, see Carlos Muñoz Jr. and Mario Barrera, "La Raza Unida Party and the Chicano Student Movement in California," in *Latinos and the Political System*, ed. F. Chris Garcia (Notre Dame, IN: University of Notre Dame Press, 1988), pp. 213–35.

could not be denied citizenship, ruling that anyone born in the United States was entitled to full citizenship.[51] Still, new Chinese immigrants were barred from the United States until 1943; China by then had become a wartime ally, and Congress repealed the Chinese Exclusion Act and permitted Chinese immigrants to become citizens. While Chinese immigrants were welcomed during the war, President Franklin Delano Roosevelt issued executive orders sending most Japanese Americans on the West Coast to internment camps for the duration of the war. Families lost their jobs and property and were forced to live in squalid conditions because they were suspected of sympathizing with Japan after the Japanese empire launched its December 1941 attack against the United States at Pearl Harbor.

Overall levels of immigration climbed rapidly after the 1965 Immigration and Nationality Act, which lifted discriminatory quotas. Nevertheless, limited English proficiency prevented many Asian Americans and Latinos from participating fully in American life. Two developments in the 1970s, however, established rights for language minorities. The 1970 amendments to the Voting Rights Act of 1965 permanently outlawed literacy tests as a prerequisite for registering to vote and mandated bilingual ballots or oral assistance for voters who speak Spanish, Chinese, Japanese, Korean, or Native American languages. And in 1974, the Supreme Court ruled in a suit filed on behalf of Chinese students in San Francisco that school districts must provide education for students whose English is limited.[52] The Court did not mandate bilingual education, but it established a duty to provide instruction that students could understand.

Immigration and Rights

The United States has always struggled to define the rights of immigrants and the notion of citizenship. Approximately one in eight persons in the United States today was born in another country. Such a high level of immigration has led to efforts to stem the influx. Waves of immigration have inspired legislation restricting who can come to the United States legally. These regulations have included quotas, visas, and other controls on how long people can reside in the United States and what privileges they may enjoy while here. Immigration has also raised questions as to whether immigrants should enjoy the same civil rights as citizens, such as the right to vote and the right to access education, or a narrower set of rights. Advocates for immigrants' rights have supported legislation such as the proposed DREAM Act, which would open a path to citizenship for undocumented immigrants; the Deferred Action for Childhood Arrivals program (DACA), which granted quasi-legal status to nearly 1 million individuals who had entered the United States illegally as children; and President Obama's controversial attempt in 2014 to expand DACA via executive order to

---

51 *United States v. Wong Kim Ark*, 169 U.S. 649 (1898).

52 *Lau v. Nichols*, 414 U.S. 563 (1974).

make more people eligible for the program. Opponents of increased immigration disputed the executive order, leading to a Supreme Court case in 2016. In the wake of the death of Justice Antonin Scalia, the eight-member Supreme Court split 4–4, which let stand a lower-court decision striking down Obama's order. Opponents of increased immigration have also proposed banning Syrian refugees from entering the country and reducing the flow of Latinos into the country. During the 2016 presidential election, Donald Trump promised to build a wall along the U.S.-Mexican border and to put in place a temporary ban on Muslim immigration to the United States.

After his election, Trump instructed U.S. immigration authorities to step up their enforcement of immigration laws and speed deportations. A number of cities and several states declared themselves to be "sanctuaries" for undocumented immigrants, saying that they would not cooperate with federal immigration agents. The White House, in turn, threatened these sanctuaries with a loss of federal aid. In the meantime, Trump issued executive orders banning travelers from several predominantly Muslim countries. These orders were struck down by lower federal court decisions, but the Supreme Court temporarily upheld Trump's orders, with certain limitations, pending a full dress review to come later in the year.[53] President Trump also issued executive orders ending the DACA program, but said that no deportation proceedings would begin before Congress had an opportunity to act on the issue.

In 2020, the Supreme Court ruled that the Trump administration had made a number of procedural errors when it ended the program. This decision, authored by Chief Justice Roberts, gave the 700,000 DACA recipients a reprieve while the administration considered its next steps. Immigration rights advocates suffered a major defeat in 2020, however, when the U.S. Court of Appeals for the District of Columbia ruled that the Department of Homeland Security had acted properly when it expanded its "expedited removal" program to apply to all individuals without documentation who have lived in the U.S. for less than two years.

Asian Americans, Latinos, and other groups have been concerned about the impact of immigration laws on their civil rights. Many Asian American and Latino organizations opposed the Immigration Reform and Control Act of 1986 because it imposed sanctions on employers who hire undocumented workers. Such sanctions, they feared, would lead employers to discriminate against Latinos and Asian Americans. Indeed, a 1990 report by the General Accounting Office found that employer sanctions had created a "widespread pattern of discrimination" against Latinos and others who appear foreign.[54] Organizations such as MALDEF and the Asian Law Caucus monitor and challenge such discrimination; they also work to maintain the rights of legal and undocumented immigrants in the face of growing anti-immigrant sentiment.

---

53 *Trump v. International Refugee Assistance Project*, 582 U.S. ____ (2017).

54 Dick Kirschten, "Not Black-and-White," *National Journal*, March 2, 1991, p. 497.

The Supreme Court has ruled that undocumented immigrants are eligible for education and medical care but can be denied other social benefits. In 2017, for example, a federal appeals court held that a pregnant young woman in federal custody who had entered the United States illegally did not have the right to an abortion.[55] Legal immigrants, for their part, are entitled to be treated much the same as citizens and to become eligible for actual citizenship through a process of naturalization after living in the United States for five years. But growing numbers of immigrants and mounting economic insecurity have undermined these practices. Groups of voters nationwide now strongly support drawing a sharper line between immigrants and citizens. The movement to deny benefits to noncitizens began in California, which experienced sharp economic distress in the early 1990s and has the highest levels of immigration of any state. In 1994, Californians voted to deny illegal immigrants all services except emergency medical care. Supporters hoped to discourage illegal immigration and pressure undocumented immigrants already in the country to leave. Opponents contended that denying basic services to undocumented immigrants risked creating a subclass whose lack of education and poor health would threaten all Americans. Generally, federal courts have held that undocumented immigrants are entitled to public education, and many immigrants are able to find basic health care at some 1,400 federally funded health care centers. Of course, those lacking documentation are often reluctant to request services, afraid to alert the authorities to their presence.

The Constitution begins with the phrase "We the People of the United States"; likewise, the Bill of Rights refers to the rights of *people*, not the rights of citizens. Undocumented immigrants are certainly people, though not citizens. Americans continue to be divided on the question of the rights to which these particular people are entitled.

Americans with Disabilities

The concept of rights for people with disabilities emerged in the 1970s as the civil rights model spread to other groups. The seed was planted in a little-noticed provision of the 1973 Rehabilitation Act that outlawed discrimination against individuals on the basis of disabilities. As in many other cases, the law itself helped spark the movement for rights.[56] Mimicking the NAACP's Legal Defense Fund, the disability movement founded the Disability Rights Education and Defense Fund to press its legal claims. The movement's greatest success has been the passage of the Americans with Disabilities Act (ADA) of 1990, which guarantees people with disabilities equal employment rights and access to public businesses. Claims of discrimination in violation of this act are considered by the EEOC. The law's impact has been far-reaching as businesses and public

---

55 *Garza v. Hargan*, 874 F3d 735 (D.C. Cir., 2017).

56 See the discussion in Robert A. Katzmann, *Institutional Disability: The Saga of Transportation Policy for the Disabled* (Washington, DC: Brookings Institution, 1986).

facilities have installed ramps, elevators, and other accommodations to meet its requirements.[57]

The LGBTQ Community

The gay rights movement has become one of the largest civil rights movements in contemporary America. Beginning with street protests in the 1960s, it is now a well-financed, sophisticated lobby. The Human Rights Campaign is the primary national organization that raises and distributes campaign money to further gay rights interests. It provides campaign financing and volunteers to work for candidates endorsed by the group. The movement has also formed legal rights organizations, including the Lambda Legal Defense and Education Fund, now commonly referred to as Lambda Legal.

The 1990s witnessed the first national anti-gay laws and the first Supreme Court declaration protecting the civil rights of gay men and women. In 1993, President Clinton confronted the question of whether to lift the ban on gay people serving in the military. As a candidate, he had favored repealing the ban; but after much controversy and nearly a year of deliberation, his administration enunciated a compromise: its "Don't Ask, Don't Tell" policy, which allowed gay men and women to serve in the military as long as they did not openly proclaim their sexual orientation or engage in homosexual activity. Two years later, in another setback for the movement, Clinton signed the Defense of Marriage Act (DOMA), which defined marriage as the union of one man and one woman for the purposes of the application of federal laws, such as taxes and benefits.

As with other civil rights movements, it was the Supreme Court that took a major step in protecting gay men and women from discrimination. This marked an important departure from its earlier jurisprudence; the first case involving gay rights that the Court decided, *Bowers v. Hardwick* (1986), ruled against a right to privacy that would protect consensual homosexual activity. After the *Bowers* decision, the gay rights movement sought suitable legal cases to test the constitutionality of discrimination against gay men and lesbians, much as the civil rights movement had done in the late 1940s and 1950s.[58] Cases were brought challenging local ordinances restricting gay rights (including the right to marry), job discrimination, and family law issues such as adoption and parental rights. In 1996, the Court explicitly extended fundamental civil rights protections to gay men and women by declaring unconstitutional a 1992 amendment to the Colorado state constitution that prohibited local governments from passing ordinances to protect gay rights.[59] The decision's forceful language highlighted

---

57 For example, after pressure from the Justice Department, one of the nation's largest car rental companies agreed to make special hand controls available to any customer requesting them. See "Avis Agrees to Equip Cars for Disabled," *Los Angeles Times*, September 2, 1994, p. D1.

58 *Bowers v. Hardwick*, 478 U.S. 186 (1986).

59 *Romer v. Evans*, 517 U.S. 620 (1996).

the connection between gay rights and civil rights as it declared discrimination against gay people unconstitutional.

Finally, in 2003, the Court overturned *Bowers* and struck down a Texas statute criminalizing certain intimate sexual conduct between consenting partners of the same sex.[60] The 2003 decision extended at least one aspect of civil liberties to sexual minorities: the right to privacy. However, it did not undo other significant exclusions that deprived gay men and women of full civil rights.

Another important victory occurred in 2010, when Congress finally repealed Don't Ask, Don't Tell. Because Barack Obama had promised to repeal the act during his campaign for election in 2008, gay rights activists criticized him for not doing so early in his administration. After a lengthy study by the Defense Department of the possible consequences of allowing openly gay men and women to serve, Congress voted to repeal Don't Ask, Don't Tell.

Gay Marriage. The focal point of the gay rights movement soon turned to the right to marry. Unlike women and Black people, who fought for equal treatment in education, employment, and voting, gay rights activists targeted marital rights. In part this was symbolic, as same-sex couples sought social and legal recognition of their relationships equal to the recognition afforded to opposite-sex couples. And in part it was economic, as federal and state laws treat married couples differently with respect to such economic policies as taxes, inheritance, and employment benefits.

The first changes to the right to marry occurred at the state level. In 2004, the Supreme Judicial Court of Massachusetts ruled that under the state's constitution, same-sex couples were entitled to marry. The state senate then requested the court to rule on whether a civil union statute (avoiding the word *marriage*) would, as it did in Vermont, satisfy the court's ruling; in response, the court ruled negatively, asserting that drawing a distinction between civil unions and marriage would be too much like the "separate but equal" doctrine that maintained legalized racial segregation from 1896 to 1954. Between 2004 and 2014, same-sex marriage became legal in 35 states through a process of court orders, voter initiatives, and legislative enactments. However, as with the women's suffrage movement a century earlier, these changes faced pushback. In many states, voters and state legislatures had supported constitutional amendments banning same-sex marriage. By June 2015, same-sex marriage remained illegal in 13 states.

The discrepancy between some state laws, which recognized same-sex marriage, and the federal law under DOMA, which did not, was ultimately DOMA's undoing. The nation's laws extend to everyone equally; that is the meaning of equal protection under the Fifth and Fourteenth Amendments. In 2013 the Supreme Court ruled DOMA unconstitutional "as a deprivation of the equal liberty of persons that is protected by the Fifth Amendment."[61]

---

60 *Lawrence v. Texas*, 539 U.S. 558 (2003).

61 *United States v. Windsor*, 570 U.S. 744 (2013). That same day the Court also cleared the way for legalization of gay marriage in California in *Hollingsworth v. Perry*, 570 U.S. 693 (2013).

In 2015, the Supreme Court ruled definitively on the issue of same-sex marriage. In the case of *Obergefell v. Hodges* the Court ruled that the right to marry is guaranteed to same-sex couples by the due process clause of the Constitution and the equal protection clause of the Fourteenth Amendment.[62] The decision required states to issue marriage licenses to same-sex couples and to recognize same-sex marriages performed in other jurisdictions. In 2020, LGBTQ and transgender individuals won a significant victory in the Supreme Court. In a 6-3 decision written by Justice Neil Gorsuch, the Court ruled that the 1964 Civil Rights Act prohibited employment discrimination based upon sexual orientation just as it prohibited employment discrimination based upon race and gender.

AFFIRMATIVE ACTION

affirmative action

A policy or program designed to correct historical injustices committed against specific groups by making special efforts to provide members of these groups with access to educational and employment opportunities.

Over the past half century or so, the relatively narrow goal of equalizing opportunity by eliminating discriminatory barriers evolved into the broader goal of **affirmative action**—compensatory action to overcome the consequences of past discrimination and encourage greater diversity. In 1965, President Lyndon Johnson issued executive orders promoting minority employment in the federal civil service and in companies doing business with the national government. However, affirmative action did not become a prominent goal until the 1970s.

The Supreme Court and the Standard of Review

As the affirmative action movement spread, it divided civil rights activists and their supporters. The issue of qualification versus minority preference was addressed in the case of Allan Bakke, a White man with no minority affiliation. He brought suit against the University of California Medical School at Davis on the grounds that, in denying him admission, the school had discriminated against him on the basis of his race. (That year the school had reserved 16 of 100 available slots for minority applicants.) He argued that his grades and test scores ranked him well above many students who were accepted and that he had been rejected because the others were Black or Hispanic and he was White. In 1978, Bakke won his case before the Supreme Court and was admitted to the medical school, but he did not succeed in getting affirmative action declared unconstitutional altogether. The Court rejected the procedures at the University of California because its medical school had used both a quota and a separate admissions system for minorities. The Court agreed with Bakke that racial categorizations are suspect categories that place a severe burden of proof on those using them to show that they serve "compelling public

---

62 *Obergefell v. Hodges*, 576 U.S. ____ (2015).

purpose." It went on to say that achieving "a diverse student body" was such a public purpose, but the method of a rigid quota of student slots assigned on the basis of race was incompatible with the equal protection clause. Thus the Court permitted universities (and other schools, training programs, and hiring authorities) to continue to consider minority status, but it limited the use of quotas to situations in which discrimination had previously been a problem and the quotas served more as a guideline for social diversity than as a mathematically defined ratio.[63]

For nearly a decade after *Bakke*, the Court was tentative and permissive in considering efforts by corporations and governments to experiment with affirmative action programs in employment.[64] But in 1989, it returned to the *Bakke* position, ruling that any "rigid numerical quota" is suspect and holding that the burden of proof of unlawful discrimination should be shifted from the defendant (the employer) to the plaintiff (the person claiming to be the victim of discrimination).[65] This decision virtually overruled the Court's prior holding.[66] That same year, the Court ruled that any affirmative action program already approved by federal courts could be challenged by individuals (who usually ended up being White men) alleging that the program had discriminated against them.[67]

In 1995, another Supreme Court ruling further weakened affirmative action. This decision stated that race-based policies imposed by governments, such as preferences given by the government to minority contractors, must survive strict scrutiny, placing the burden on the government to show that such affirmative action programs serve a compelling government interest and address identifiable past discrimination.[68]

Other developments in the courts and the states worked to restrict affirmative action. One of the most significant was *Hopwood v. State of Texas*, in which White students charged that the University of Texas Law School's affirmative action program for admissions discriminated against White applicants. Critics of affirmative action have asserted that the practice amounts to "reverse discrimination," in which the rights of the majority are curtailed through race-conscious policies.

In 2003, affirmative action was challenged in two cases arising from the University of Michigan. The first suit alleged that by automatically awarding 20 points (out of 150 possible, with 100 needed to be admitted) to African American, Latino, and Native American applicants, the university's undergraduate

---

63 *Regents of the University of California v. Bakke*, 438 U.S. 265 (1978).

64 *United Steelworkers of America v. Weber*, 443 U.S. 193 (1979); *Fullilove v. Klutznick*, 448 U.S. 448 (1980).

65 *Wards Cove Packing Company v. Atonio*, 490 U.S. 642 (1989).

66 *Griggs v. Duke Power Company* (1971).

67 *Martin v. Wilks*, 490 U.S. 755 (1989).

68 *Adarand Constructors v. Peña*, 515 U.S. 200 (1995).

admissions policy discriminated unconstitutionally against White students with otherwise equal or superior academic qualifications. The Supreme Court agreed, arguing that something tantamount to a quota was involved because undergraduate admissions lacked the necessary "individualized consideration" of applicants, employing instead a "mechanical one" that was based too much on the favorable minority points.[69]

The second case broke new ground. Barbara Grutter sued the University of Michigan Law School on the grounds that it had discriminated in a race-conscious way against White applicants with grades and law boards equal or superior to those of minority applicants. A 5–4 vote aligned the majority of the Supreme Court with Justice Lewis Powell's opinion in *Bakke* for the first time. Powell had argued that diversity in education is a compelling state interest and that constitutionally, race could be considered a positive factor in admissions decisions. In *Grutter v. Bollinger*, the Court reiterated Powell's holding and, applying strict scrutiny to the law school's policy, found that its admissions process was tailored to the school's compelling state interest in diversity because it gave a "highly individualized, holistic review of each applicant's file," in which race counted but was not used in a "mechanical way."[70]

Today, the subject of affirmative action has not yet been fully settled. In 2009, the Supreme Court ruled that New Haven, Connecticut, officials had discriminated against White firefighters when they threw out a promotions exam just because no non-White candidate received a high enough score for promotion.[71] The Court said that this was not enough to show that the city had engaged in racially discriminatory action. Most recently, in the *Fisher* case discussed earlier in the chapter, the Court upheld the principles stated in *Grutter* and *Bakke*, ruling that universities, municipalities, and other agencies can engage affirmative action but that those programs are subject to strict scrutiny by the courts.[72] It seems that race can be one factor in the admissions process but may not be the single or defining criterion for college admission. Public opinion on affirmative action remains somewhat divided, with lower support for programs that help racial minorities than for those that help women. (See Analyzing the Evidence on pp. 190–1).

Because of America's troubled history of slavery and segregation, we automatically tend to associate discrimination with efforts to exclude African Americans from full participation in American society. Yet, as we have seen, other groups have also faced discrimination in employment and housing. Even today, women face job and salary discrimination and Latinos face severe barriers in winning acceptance and citizenship in the United States. America's practices often do not live up to American ideals.

69 *Gratz v. Bollinger*, 539 U.S. 244 (2003).

70 *Grutter v. Bollinger*, 539 U.S. 306 (2003).

71 *Ricci v. DeStefano*, 557 U.S. 557 (2009).

72 *Fisher v. University of Texas* (2016).

CONCLUSION: CIVIL LIBERTIES AND CIVIL RIGHTS—REGULATING COLLECTIVE ACTION

Over the past century, America has strengthened its citizens' liberties and expanded their rights. Both civil liberties and civil rights are solutions to collective action problems. Strengthening the former means imposing more restrictions on some forms of collective action. Expanding the later means allowing more individuals to take part in collective decision making and imposing restrictions on the sorts of decisions that can be reached.

Institutions help solve collective action problems, but no solution is carved in stone. Contending political forces continually seek to change institutional rules to serve their particular purposes. In the United States today, some groups seek additional rights for gay men and women, immigrants, and others who have faced political, social, and economic discrimination. Opponents assert that the expansion of civil rights to include, for instance, such matters as social and educational benefits for illegal immigrants is inappropriate. The Black Lives Matter movement contends that current police practices violate the rights and endanger the lives of African Americans. Opponents argue that absent aggressive policing, America's streets would be less safe. The outcomes of such struggles over liberties and rights are never certain. Institutions matter, but exactly how they will matter in the years to come is always subject to change.

The case of civil rights also illustrates the history principle in action. The African American civil rights movement learned tactics from the women's suffrage movement of the nineteenth century. Court victories later won by African Americans helped inspire the contemporary women's movement and provided legal principles that the federal courts could later apply to gender discrimination, particularly in the realm of employment. Women took advantage of Title VII of the 1964 Civil Rights Act, written to prohibit racial discrimination in employment, to demand enforcement against gender discrimination. In a similar vein, other groups facing discrimination relied on the victories of the civil rights and the women's movements to advance their own causes. It was a logical step from the prohibition of gender discrimination to banning transgender discrimination. The history principle tells us that history creates paths, rules, alliances, and points of view. American history certainly created legal paths that successive groups could follow and led to alliances among groups suffering discrimination. The acronym LGBTQ stands for one such alliance among groups with a variety of sexual and gender identities (lesbian, gay, bisexual, transgender, queer, and other identities).

But what about points of view? Has our history made us more tolerant of the rights of individuals with whom we disagree or whom we view as different from ourselves? Has the history of the past century made America more inclusive or more prone to building walls? The history principle cannot provide us with a conclusive answer to this question.

Is the Public Principled or Prejudiced When It Comes to Affirmative Action?

Contributed by
David C. Wilson
University of Delaware

Are opinions about affirmative action based on principled policy positions or prejudices toward beneficiaries? Supporters argue that affirmative action helps redress centuries of prejudice and discrimination that denied certain citizens the opportunity to prosper. They argue that without affirmative action, institutions and employers would be able to discriminate without penalty. Opponents argue that it's a matter of principle: they believe affirmative action grants unfair advantage to racial minorities and other groups at the expense of nonminorities. They claim some people are benefiting from their demographics rather than qualification merits. That is, race and gender unfairly privilege some citizens over others.

In reviewing decades of public opinion research on affirmative action, my colleagues and I discovered that few, if any, studies examined how people's views concerning one targeted beneficiary group (for example, racial minorities) were affected by views concerning another group (such as women). This question bears on the extent to which opinion on affirmative action is based on racial prejudice versus principled reasoning. A principled position would propose that affirmative action is detrimental regardless of what group it benefits, because "special consideration" based on any characteristic is unfair to other individuals who don't receive such consideration. A prejudiced position would mean that people favor some groups over others and the less favored groups are less deserving of the benefits of affirmative action. In theory, principled positions should be consistent across groups, and prejudiced positions should prefer some groups over others.

Using a public opinion experiment embedded in a 2003 Gallup Poll, we assessed whether people's group biases led them to support or oppose affirmative action because of racial or gender cues. In the poll half the respondents were asked an initial question about affirmative action programs for women and then were asked a follow-up question about affirmative action for racial minorities. The other half were asked the questions in reverse order. The experiment allowed us to determine people's support for each type of affirmative action program when considered in isolation from the other (based on how they responded to whichever question they were asked first), and when considered in the context of the other (based on how they responded to whichever question they were asked second). If context affects opinion, that would mean the public is prejudiced toward one group relative to the other, but if context has no effect on opinion then the public is principled in their policy positions.

Overall, our results showed that public opinion toward affirmative action is biased by positive beliefs about women and negative beliefs about racial minorities.

SOURCE: David Wilson, David W. Moore, Patrick F. McKay, and Derek R. Avery, "Affirmative Action Programs for Women and Minorities: Support Affected by Question Order," *Public Opinion Quarterly* 73 (2008): 514–22.

The Effect of Context on Opinion toward Affirmative Action

FIRST QUESTION	SECOND QUESTION	SUPPORT FOR AFFIRMATIVE ACTION FOR WOMEN

Affirmative action for women? → 63%

Affirmative action for racial minorities? → Affirmative action for women? → 57%

SUPPORT FOR AFFIRMATIVE ACTION FOR RACIAL MINORITIES

Affirmative action for racial minorities? → 50%

Affirmative action for women? → Affirmative action for racial minorities? → 57%

We found that the public decreases its support for affirmative action for women (–6 percent) when considered in the context of affirmative action for racial minorities but increases its support for affirmative action for racial minorities (+7 percent) in the context of affirmative action for women.

Support for Affirmative Action for Women

QUESTION ORDER → ● Women → Minorities   ▨ Minorities → Women

RESPONDENTS ↓
- White males
- White females
- Black males
- Black females

0%   25%   50%   75%   100%

Separating opinions based on a respondent's race and gender helps us understand where the principles and prejudices lie. Whites, both male and female, decrease their support for affirmative action for women when it is considered in the context of race; however, Blacks are consistent regardless of the beneficiary.

Support for Affirmative Action for Racial Minorities

QUESTION ORDER → ● Women → Minorities   ▨ Minorities → Women

RESPONDENTS ↓
- White males
- White females
- Black males
- Black females

0%   25%   50%   75%   100%

White respondents, both male and female, increase their support for affirmative action for racial minorities when it is considered in the context of gender. Once again, Black respondents remain consistent regardless of the beneficiary.

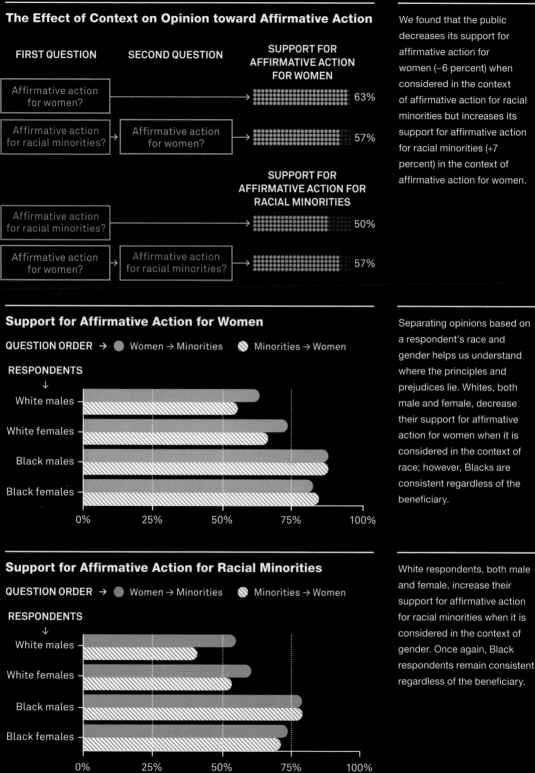

For Further Reading

Baer, Judith A., and Leslie Friedman Goldstein. *The Constitutional and Legal Rights of Women: Cases in Law and Social Change*. 3rd ed. Los Angeles: Roxbury, 2006.

Berrey, Ellen, Robert L. Nelson, and Laura Beth Nielson, *Rights on Trial: How Workplace Discrimination Law Perpetuates Inequality*. Chicago: University of Chicago Press, 2017.

Chavez, Leo R. *The Latino Threat: Constructing Immigrants, Citizens, and the Nation*. 2nd ed. Palo Alto, CA: Stanford University Press, 2013.

Davis, Lennard J. *Enabling Acts: The Hidden Story of How the Americans with Disabilities Act Gave the Largest US Minority Its Rights*. Boston: Beacon Press, 2015.

Dawson, Michael C. *Not in Our Lifetimes: The Future of Black Politics*. Chicago: University of Chicago Press, 2011.

Fallon, Richard. *The Nature of Constitutional Rights: The Invention and Logic of Strict Judicial Scrutiny*. New York: Cambridge University Press, 2019.

Fileborn, Blanca and Rachel Loney-Howes, eds. *#MeToo and the Politics of Social Change*. New York: Palgrave Macmillan, 2019.

Garrow, David J. *Bearing the Cross: Martin Luther King, Jr., and the Southern Christian Leadership Conference*. New York: Morrow, 1986.

Gerstmann, Evan. *Same-Sex Marriage and the Constitution*. New York: Cambridge University Press, 2004.

Glendon, Mary Ann. *Rights Talk: The Impoverishment of Political Discourse*. New York: Free Press, 1991.

Lewis, Anthony. *Gideon's Trumpet*. New York: Random House, 1964.

Mukhopadhyay, Samhita and Kate Harding, eds. *Nasty Women: Feminism, Resistance, and Revolution in Trump's America*. New York: Picador, 2017.

Nicholls, Walter J. *The Immigrant Rights Movement: The Battle Over National Citizenship*. Stanford, CA: Stanford University Press, 2019.

Norton, Helen. *The Government's Speech and the Constitution*. New York: Cambridge University Press, 2019.

O'Brien, David and Gordon Silverstein. *Constitutional Law and Politics, Volume 2: Civil Rights and Civil Liberties*. 11th ed. New York: Norton, 2020.

Olivas, Michael, ed. *"Colored Men" and "Hombres Aquí":* Hernandez v. Texas *and the Emergence of Mexican-American Lawyering.* Houston, TX: Arte Público Press, 2006.

Regan, Margaret. *Detained and Deported: Stories of Immigrant Families Under Fire.* Boston: Beacon Press, 2015.

Riemer, Matthew and Leighton Brown. *We Are Everywhere: Protest, Power and Pride in the History of Queer Liberation.* New York: Ten Speed Press, 2019.

Rosenberg, Gerald N. *The Hollow Hope: Can Courts Bring About Social Change?* 2nd ed. Chicago: University of Chicago Press, 2008.

Shird, Kevin and Nelson Malden. *The Colored Waiting Room: Empowering the Original and the New Civil Rights Movements; Conversations Between an MLK Jr. Confidant and a Modern-Day Activist.* New York: Apollo Publishers, 2018.

Taylor, Jami K., and Donald P. Haider-Markel, eds. *Transgender Rights and Politics: Groups, Issue Framing, and Policy Adoption.* Ann Arbor: University of Michigan Press, 2014.

Waldman, Michael. *The Fight to Vote.* New York: Simon and Schuster, 2016.

6

Congress:
The First Branch

The U.S. Congress is the "first branch" of government under Article I of our Constitution and is also among the world's most important representative bodies. Most of the world's representative bodies only represent—that is, their governmental functions consist mainly of affirming and legitimating the national leadership's decisions. The U.S. Congress is one of the few that actually possesses powers of governance. For example, the U.S. Congress never accedes to the president's budget proposals without making major changes, whereas both the British House of Commons and the Japanese Diet always accept the budget exactly as proposed by the government.

This unique status of the American Congress illustrates the institution principle. In the separation-of-powers regime institutionalized by the U.S. Constitution, the American executive cannot govern alone: the legislature actively participates. In political scientist Richard Neustadt's memorable phrase, the executive and the legislature in the United States are "separated institutions sharing power."[1] In parliamentary regimes, such as those of Britain and Japan, by contrast, the executive controls its majority in Parliament. These different institutional arrangements give different powers to different players. In the American case, the institutional arrangements were intended to give Congress a great deal of power relative to the president.

Congress controls a formidable battery of powers that it uses to shape policies and, when necessary, defend its prerogatives against the executive branch. Congress has vast authority over the two most important powers

---

1   Richard E. Neustadt, *Presidential Power: The Politics of Leadership* (New York: Wiley, 1960), p. 42.

given to any government: the power of force (control over the nation's military forces) and the power over money. Specifically, according to Article I, Section 8, Congress can "lay and collect Taxes," deal with indebtedness and bankruptcy, impose duties, borrow and coin money, and generally control the nation's purse strings. It also may "provide for the common Defence and general Welfare," regulate interstate commerce, undertake public works, acquire and control federal lands, promote science and "useful Arts" (pertaining mostly to patents and copyrights), and regulate the militia.

In the realm of force and foreign policy, Congress has the power to declare war, deal with piracy, regulate foreign commerce, and raise and regulate the armed forces and military installations. These powers over war and the military are supreme; even the president, as commander in chief of the military, must obey the laws and orders of Congress *if* Congress chooses to assert its constitutional authority. (In the past century, Congress has usually ceded this authority to the president.) Further, the Senate has the power to approve treaties (by a two-thirds vote) and the appointment of ambassadors. Capping these powers, Congress is charged with making laws "which shall be necessary and proper for carrying into Execution the foregoing Powers, and all other Powers vested by this Constitution in the Government of the United States, or in any Department or Officer thereof."

If it seems to you that many of these powers, especially those having to do with war and spending, belong to the president, that is because modern presidents do exercise great authority in these areas. The modern presidency is a more powerful institution than it was two centuries ago, and much of that power has come from Congress, either because Congress has delegated power to the

LEARNING OBJECTIVES

→ Identify the diverse views and interests members of Congress balance as they represent their districts.

→ Describe the organization of the United States Congress and identify some of the challenges that arise for legislators as a result of this organization.

→ Identify the congressional procedures for how a bill becomes a law.

→ Outline the factors that inform the legislative agenda of Congress.

→ Describe the Congressional powers beyond lawmaking.

president by law or because Congress has allowed, or even urged, presidents to be more active.[2]

Still, the constitutional powers of Congress remain intact in the document and, as we will see, congressional power cannot be separated from congressional representation. Without its array of powers, Congress could do little to represent the views and interests of its constituents effectively. At the same time, without its capacity to represent important groups and forces in American society, the powers of Congress would be undermined. As we will see throughout this chapter, not only is representation key, but all five principles of politics from Chapter 1 are important to our understanding of the institutional structure of the contemporary Congress.

We begin our discussion with a brief consideration of representation. Then we examine the institutional structure of Congress today and the manner in which congressional powers are organized and employed. Throughout, we point out the connections between these two aspects—the ways in which representation affects congressional operations (especially through "the electoral connection") and the ways in which congressional institutions, particularly the committee system, enhance or diminish representation.

REPRESENTATION

constituency

The citizens who reside in the district from which an official is elected.

delegates

Legislators who vote according to the preferences of their constituents.

trustees

Legislators who vote according to what they think is best for their constituents.

Congress is the most important representative institution in American government. Each member's primary responsibility is to the **constituency** of his or her district, not to the congressional leadership, their political party, or even Congress itself. Yet the task of representation is not simple. Views about what constitutes fair and effective representation differ, and constituents can make very different demands of their representatives. Members of Congress must consider these diverse views and demands as they represent their districts (Figure 6.1).

Legislators vary in the weight they give to personal priorities as opposed to the desires of their campaign contributors and supporters. Some see themselves as having been elected to do the bidding of their constituents who sent them to the legislature, and they act as **delegates**. Others see themselves as having been selected by their constituents to do what they think is "right," and they act as **trustees**. Most legislators are a mix of these two types. And all need to survive the next election to pursue their chosen role. Rational agents must focus on survival.

---

2 On the issue of congressional delegation of powers to the executive, two valuable sources are D. Roderick Kiewiet and Mathew D. McCubbins, *The Logic of Delegation: Congressional Parties and the Appropriations Process* (Chicago: University of Chicago Press, 1991); and David Epstein and Sharyn O'Halloran, *Delegating Powers: A Transaction Cost Politics Approach to Policy Making under Separate Powers* (New York: Cambridge University Press, 1999).

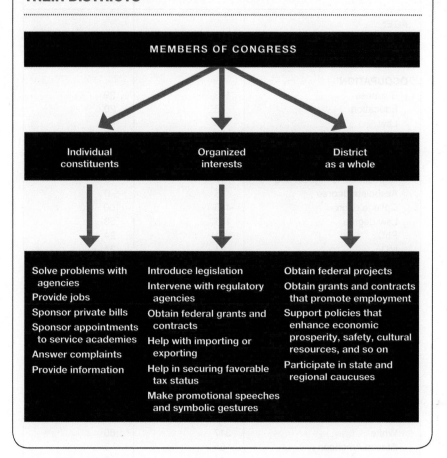

Figure 6.1

HOW MEMBERS OF CONGRESS REPRESENT THEIR DISTRICTS

MEMBERS OF CONGRESS

Individual constituents	Organized interests	District as a whole
Solve problems with agencies	Introduce legislation	Obtain federal projects
Provide jobs	Intervene with regulatory agencies	Obtain grants and contracts that promote employment
Sponsor private bills	Obtain federal grants and contracts	Support policies that enhance economic prosperity, safety, cultural resources, and so on
Sponsor appointments to service academies	Help with importing or exporting	Participate in state and regional caucuses
Answer complaints	Help in securing favorable tax status	
Provide information	Make promotional speeches and symbolic gestures	

Legislators not only represent others; they may be representative *of* others as well. The latter point is especially salient for gender and racial minorities, for whom descriptive representation is symbolically significant at the very least. Female and minority representatives serve and draw support from those with whom they share an identity, both within their formal constituency and in the nation at large. (See Table 6.1 for a summary of the demographic characteristics of members of Congress.) Descriptive representation for African American and Hispanic minorities has been facilitated during the process of drawing new congressional-district boundaries after each decennial census, thus creating some districts with these groups in the majority—so-called majority-minority districts.

As we discussed in Chapter 1, one person might be trusted to speak for another if the two are formally bound together in such a way that the representative is accountable to those he purports to represent. If representatives can

Table 6.1

DEMOGRAPHICS OF MEMBERS OF THE 116TH CONGRESS

	HOUSE	SENATE
AGE*		
Average	58 years	63 years
Range	32–87 years	39–83 years
OCCUPATION†		
Business	183	29
Education	73	20
Law	145	47
Public service/politics	184	47
EDUCATION‡		
High school is highest degree	17	0
Associate degree	6	0
College degree	415	100
Law degree	161	53
PhD	21	24
MD	21	34
RELIGION**		
Protestant	233	60
Catholic	141	22
Jewish	26	8
Mormon	6	4
GENDER		
Women	106	25
Men	332	75
RACE/ETHNICITY††		
White	317	80
African American	55	3
Hispanic/Latino	45	5
Asian/Pacific Islander	17	3
American Indian	4	0
CONGRESSIONAL SERVICE		
Number serving in first term	90	9
Average length of service	4.3 terms (8.6 years)	1.7 terms (10.1 years)

*Age at beginning of 116th Congress.

†Most members list more than one occupation.

‡Education categories are not exclusive (for example, a representative with a law degree might also be counted as having a college degree).

**About 98 percent of members cite a specific religious affiliation. Other affiliations not listed here include Buddhist, Muslim, Hindu, Greek Orthodox, Unitarian, and Christian Science.

††Some members are in two race categories. Includes Delegates and Resident Commissioners.

SOURCE: Jennifer E. Manning, *Membership of the 116th Congress: A Profile*, CRS Report for Congress no. R45583 (Washington, DC: Congressional Research Service, 2019).

somehow be held to account for failing to speak properly for their constituents, then we know they have an incentive to provide good representation even if their own backgrounds, views, and interests differ from those of the people they represent. This is **agency representation**—the sort of representation that occurs when constituents have the power to hire and fire their representatives (who act as their agents). Frequent competitive elections are an important means by which constituents select their representatives, hold them to account, and keep them responsive to their own views and preferences. The idea of a representative as the agent for constituents is like the relationship between lawyer and client. True, the relationship between a member of the House and as many as 700,000 "bosses" in his district or that between the senator and possibly millions of bosses in her state is very different from that of the lawyer and client, but the criteria of performance are comparable.

We would expect at the very least that representatives will constantly seek to understand the interests of their constituencies and will speak for those interests in Congress and other centers of government.[3] We expect this because we believe that members of Congress, like politicians everywhere, are ambitious. For many, this ambition is satisfied by maintaining a hold on their present congressional office and advancing up the rungs of power within that body. Some, however, may be looking ahead to the next level—as when a legislator desires to move from a House seat to a Senate seat, runs for her state's governorship, or even seeks the presidency.[4] This means that members of Congress may not only be concerned with their present *geographic* constituency; they may also want to appeal to a different geographic constituency, for instance, or seek support from a gender, ethnic, or racial community. We return to this topic shortly when we discuss congressional elections. But we can say here that in each of these cases, legislators are eager to serve the interests of constituents, either to enhance their prospects of contract renewal at the next election or to improve their chances of moving to another elected office. In short, the agency conception of representation works in proportion to the ambition of politicians (as "agents") and the capacity of constituents (as "principals") to reward or punish on the basis of each legislator's performance and reputation.[5]

 agency representation

The type of representation in which representatives are held accountable to their constituents if they fail to represent them properly. That is, constituents have the power to hire and fire their representatives.

---

3   The classic description of interactions between politicians and "the folks back home" is given by Richard F. Fenno Jr., *Home Style: House Members in Their Districts* (Boston: Little, Brown, 1978). Essays elaborating on Fenno are found in Morris P. Fiorina and David W. Rohde, eds., *Home Style and Washington Work: Studies of Congressional Politics* (Ann Arbor: University of Michigan Press, 1989).

4   For more on political careers generally, see John R. Hibbing, "Legislative Careers: Why and How We Should Study Them," *Legislative Studies Quarterly* 24, no 2 (May 1999): 149–71. See also Cherie D. Maestas, Sarah Fulton, L. Sandy Maisel, and Walter J. Stone, "When to Risk It? Institutions, Ambitions, and the Decision to Run for the U.S. House," *American Political Science Review* 100, no. 2 (May 2006): 195–208.

5   Constituents aren't a legislative agent's only principals. A legislator may also be beholden to party leaders and special interests as well as to members and committees in the chamber. See Forrest Maltzman, *Competing Principals: Committees, Parties, and the Organization of Congress* (Ann Arbor: University of Michigan Press, 1997).

House and Senate: Differences in Representation

bicameral legislature

A legislative body composed of two chambers, or houses.

money bill

A bill concerned solely with taxation or government spending.

The framers of the Constitution provided for a **bicameral legislature**: a legislative body composed of two chambers. As we saw in Chapter 2, the framers intended each chamber to represent a different constituency. Members of the House of Representatives, elected by popular vote every two years, were meant to be "close to the people." Because they saw the House as the institution most directly representative of the people, the framers gave it a special power. All **money bills**—that is, bills authorizing new taxes or authorizing the government to spend money for any purpose—are required to originate in the House. Until the Seventeenth Amendment (1913) provided for the direct popular election of senators, members of the Senate were appointed by state legislatures. The framers intended for senators to represent the elite members of society and to be attuned more to the interests of property than to those of the population. Today members of both the House and the Senate are elected directly by the people. The 435 members of the House are elected from districts apportioned according to population; the 100 members of the Senate are elected by state, with two senators from each. Senators have longer terms in office and usually represent much larger and more diverse constituencies than do their counterparts in the House of Representatives (Table 6.2).

The House and the Senate play different roles in the legislative process. The Senate is the more deliberative body: it is the forum in which all ideas can receive a thorough public airing. The House is the more centralized and more organized body: it is better equipped to facilitate governmental processes. In part, this difference stems from the different rules governing the two bodies. These rules give House leaders more control over the legislative process and provide for House members to specialize in certain legislative areas. The rules of the much smaller, more freewheeling Senate give its leadership relatively

Table 6.2

DIFFERENCES BETWEEN THE HOUSE AND THE SENATE

	HOUSE	SENATE
Minimum age of member	25 years	30 years
Length of U.S. citizenship	At least 7 years	At least 9 years
Length of term	2 years	6 years (staggered)
Number per state	Depends on population: approx. 1 per 30,000 in 1789; approx. 1 per 700,000 today	2 per state
Constituency	Tends to be local	Is both local and national

little power and discourage specialization.[6] This is the institution principle at work. The differences in the organization of the two legislative chambers reflect not only their differences in size but also their differences in electoral rhythm, constituencies, and roles. House members specialize in certain policy areas, their specialized activities take place mainly in committees, and deliberations by the full House occur mainly in response to committee proposals. The institution is thus organized to facilitate expeditious consideration of committee bills. The Senate does many of the same things, but senators are less specialized, partly because of their more heterogeneous constituencies, and therefore address many more areas of policy. Senate proceedings permit wider participation and more open-ended deliberation.

Formal and informal factors also contribute to the differences between the two chambers of Congress. Differences in term lengths and the require-ments for holding office generate differences in how the members of each body develop their constituencies and exercise their powers. As a result, mem-bers of the House more effectively and more frequently serve as the agents of well-organized local interests with specific legislative agendas, such as used-car dealers seeking relief from regulation, labor unions seeking more favorable legislation, or farmers looking for higher subsidies. The small size and rela-tive homogeneity of their constituencies and the frequency with which they must seek reelection make House members more attuned than senators to the legislative needs of local interest groups. This is what the Constitution's framers intended—namely, that the House of Representatives would be "the people's house" and that its members would reflect and represent public opinion in a timely manner.

Senators, in contrast, serve larger and more heterogeneous constituen-cies. As a result, they are better able than members of the House to serve as the agents of groups and interests organized on a statewide or national basis. Moreover, with longer terms in office, senators have the luxury of consider-ing "new ideas" or seeking to bring together new coalitions of interests, rather than simply serving existing ones because they are focused on getting reelected. This, too, was the framers' intent—that the Senate should provide a balance to the more responsive House. The Senate was said to be the saucer that cools the tea, bringing deliberation, debate, inclusiveness, calm, and caution to policy formulation.

For much of the late twentieth century, the House exhibited more intense partisanship and ideological division than the Senate. Because of the diverse interests within their constituencies, senators were inclined to seek compromise positions, whereas members of the House, representing homogenous districts usually dominated by one party, were more willing to stick to their partisan and

---

6 This, however, has changed in the last decade; the Senate majority leader has demonstrated a growing ability to control the chamber's agenda. Both Democratic leader Harry Reid (D-Nev.) and Republican leader Mitch McConnell (R-Ky.) have exerted firm control when their party was in the majority. Today Senate and House leaders alike, whether in the majority or the minority, find themselves "herding cats" as they attempt to coordinate the activities of their respective party caucuses.

ideological guns. For instance, the House divided almost exactly along partisan lines on the 1998 vote to impeach President Bill Clinton. In the Senate, by contrast, 10 Republicans joined Democrats to acquit Clinton of obstruction of justice charges, and in a separate vote five Republicans joined Democrats to acquit Clinton of perjury.[7] The evidence from the impeachment of President Donald Trump in 2020 suggests that things are now different. Both the House in its impeachment vote and the Senate in its acquittal vote followed straight party lines (with only one crossover vote in the Senate).

However, beginning with the presidency of George W. Bush, even the Senate grew more partisan and polarized. During Barack Obama's presidency, many of the president's initiatives dealing with the economic crisis, health care, financial rescues, and most other areas received virtually no Republican support. The Trump presidency looks like a carbon copy of the Obama era in terms of obstructionist partisanship. During Trump's first two years, a firmly Republican House and a bare majority Republican Senate sought legislative accomplishments without Democratic participation. The Democrats played an exclusively oppositional role, exemplified by their almost unanimous disapproval of Trump's nominees to the Supreme Court, Neil Gorsuch in 2017 and Brett Kavanaugh in 2018. The 2018 elections flipped the House to Democratic control while slightly increasing the Republican majority in the Senate. Democrats in both chambers continue to oppose presidential initiatives, and the Republican Senate has been a graveyard for initiatives put forth by the Democratic House. This extreme partisanship came to the fore in 2019 and 2020 during the impeachment proceedings against President Trump. As noted above, the House with its Democratic majority voted along party lines to impeach the president on charges of obstruction of Congress and abuse of power for withholding congressionally approved defense funds for Ukraine. When the proceedings moved to the majority Republican Senate, the case was ultimately dismissed along the same party lines.

The Electoral System

Considering their role as agents of various constituencies in their states and districts and the importance of elections as a mechanism by which principals (constituents) reward and punish their agents, representatives are significantly influenced by electoral considerations. Three factors related to the American electoral system affect who gets elected and what the winners do once in office. The first factor concerns who decides to run for office and which candidates have an edge over others. The second factor is the advantage incumbents have in winning reelection. The third and final factor is the way that congressional-district lines are drawn. Let's examine the impact of each of these considerations on who serves in Congress.

---

7 Eric Pianin and Guy Gugliotta, "The Bipartisan Challenge: Senate's Search for Accord Marks Contrast to House," *Washington Post*, January 8, 1999, p. 1.

Running for Office. Voters' choices are restricted from the start by who decides to run for office. In the past, local party officials decided who would run for an elected office: they might nominate someone who had a record of service to the party, who was owed a favor, or whose turn had come up.[8] Today few party organizations have the power to slate candidates in that way. Instead, the decision to run for Congress is a more personal choice. One of the most important factors is a person's ambition.[9] A potential candidate may also assess whether he can attract enough money to mount a credible campaign through connections to other politicians, interest groups, and the national party organization. Wealthy individuals may finance their own races, although the spiraling cost of campaigns is making the self-financed campaign increasingly a relic of the past. In 2020, the most expensive Senate races—in Maine, South Carolina, Georgia, and Kentucky—witnessed massive fund-raising efforts by both candidates and their respective party organizations.

Features distinctive to each congressional district also affect the field of candidates. Among them is the range of other political opportunities that may lure potential candidates away. In addition, the way congressional districts overlap with state legislative boundaries may affect a candidate's decision to run. A state-level representative or senator who is considering a run for the U.S. Congress is more likely to assess her prospects favorably if her state district largely coincides with the congressional district that she's hoping to win because the voters will already know her. For similar reasons, U.S. House representatives from small states, whose districts cover a large portion of the state, are far more likely to run for statewide office than are representatives from large states. For example, John Thune was elected as the lone representative from South Dakota in 1996. His constituency thus completely overlapped those of the state's two senators, and in 2004, he ran for and won a seat in the U.S. Senate.

For any candidate, decisions about running must be made early because once money has been committed to declared candidates, it is harder for new

---

8   In the nineteenth century, it was often considered an obligation, not an honor, to serve in Congress. The real political action was back home in the state capital or a big city, not in Washington. So, the practice of "rotation" was devised, according to which a promising local politician would do a tour of duty in Washington before being slated for an important local office. This is not to say that electoral incentives—the so-called electoral connection, in which a legislator's behavior is motivated by the desire to retain the seat for himself or his party—was absent in nineteenth-century America. See, for example, Jamie L. Carson and Erik J. Engstrom, "Assessing the Electoral Connection: Evidence from the Early United States," *American Journal of Political Science* 49, no. 4 (2005): 746–57. See also William T. Bianco, David B. Spence, and John D. Wilkerson, "The Electoral Connection in the Early Congress: The Case of the Compensation Act of 1816," *American Journal of Political Science* 40, no. 1 (Feb. 1996): 145–71.

9   See Linda L. Fowler and Robert D. McClure, *Political Ambition: Who Decides to Run for Congress* (New Haven, CT: Yale University Press, 1989); Alan Ehrenhalt, *The United States of Ambition: Politicians, Power, and the Pursuit of Office* (New York: Times Books, 1991); Jennifer L. Lawless, *Becoming a Candidate: Political Ambition and the Decision to Run for Office* (New York: Cambridge University Press, 2012); and Andrew B. Hall, *Who Wants to Run?: How the Devaluing of Political Office Drives Polarization* (Chicago: University of Chicago Press, 2019).

candidates to break into a race. Thus, the outcome of a November election is partially determined many months earlier when decisions to run are finalized.[10]

Incumbency. Incumbency plays a key role in the American electoral system and in the kind of representation citizens get in Washington. Over the twentieth century, Congress developed into a professional legislature, one whose members serve full time for multiple terms and are typically eager to make a career out of politics (Figure 6.2).[11] And **incumbent** legislators have created an array of tools

incumbent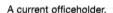

A current officeholder.

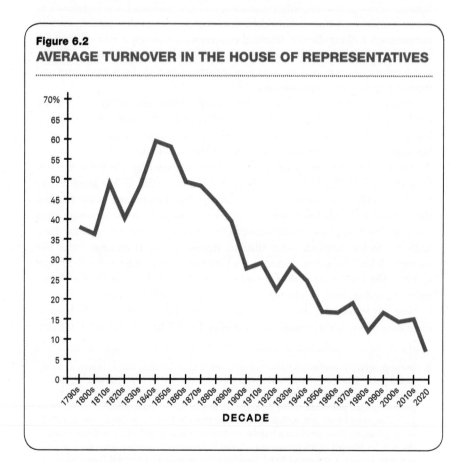

Figure 6.2
AVERAGE TURNOVER IN THE HOUSE OF REPRESENTATIVES

DECADE

NOTE: Average turnover is the percent of new members in the House averaged over five House elections in a decade. In the period 1790–2012, the mean turnover was 30.7.
SOURCE: Based on John Swain, Stephen A. Borelli, Brian C. Reed, and Sean F. Evans, "A New Look at Turnover in the U.S. House of Representatives, 1789–1998," *American Politics Quarterly* 28, no. 4 (2000): 435–57, plus author updates.

10 On the thesis of "strategic candidacy," see Gary C. Jacobson and Jamie L. Carson, *The Politics of Congressional Elections*, 10th ed. (New York: Rowman and Littlefield, 2015).

11 Nelson W. Polsby, "The Institutionalization of the U.S. House of Representatives," *American Political Science Review* 62, no. 1 (March 1968): 144–68.

that stack the deck in favor of their reelection—the rationality principle at work once again. Through effective use of this arsenal of weapons, an incumbent establishes a reputation for competence, imagination, and responsiveness, which are the attributes most principals look for in an agent.

Perhaps the most important advantage of incumbency is the opportunity to serve on legislative committees. Doing so enables legislators to burnish their policy credentials, develop expertise, and help constituents, either by affecting the legislative agenda or by interceding with the bureaucracy on their constituents' behalf. Committee work allows incumbents to establish a track record of accomplishments—an especially strategic advantage when a legislator's committees address issues of great concern to his constituents. (Party leaders in Congress are adept at matching their members to the "right" committees—another example of the rationality principle at work.) Finally, continuous service or seniority on a committee positions a legislator for committee leadership posts. This seniority principle is another means by which incumbents make themselves so valuable to their constituents that the latter are loath to replace them.[12]

The opportunity to help constituents, and thereby gain support in the district, goes beyond the committees on which a member serves. A considerable amount of each member's (and their staff's) time is devoted to **casework**. Not merely a matter of writing and mailing letters, casework includes talking to constituents, providing them with minor services, introducing special bills for them, working with local officials, and attempting to influence decisions by bureaucratic agencies and regulatory commissions on their behalf.

One significant way in which incumbent members of Congress serve as the agents of their constituencies on a larger scale is through **patronage**. Patronage refers to a variety of direct services and benefits that members provide for their districts. One of the most important forms of patronage is **pork-barrel legislation**, through which representatives seek to capture federal projects and federal funds for their home districts or states and thus "bring home the bacon."

A common form of pork barreling is the earmark, the practice through which members of Congress insert provisions into otherwise pork-free bills for projects that benefit their own constituents.[13] For example, among

casework

Efforts by members of Congress to gain the trust and support of constituents by providing personal services. One important type of casework is helping constituents to obtain favorable treatment from the federal bureaucracy.

patronage

Direct services and benefits that members of Congress provide to their constituents, especially making partisan appointments to offices and conferring grants, licenses, or special favors to supporters.

pork-barrel legislation

Appropriations that members of Congress use to provide government funds for projects benefiting their home district or state.

---

12 If an incumbent is replaced, his or her junior replacement lacks seniority and therefore is automatically lower on the pecking order of influence and less entitled to leadership posts. See Jon X. Eguia and Kenneth A. Shepsle, "Legislative Bargaining with Endogenous Rules," *Journal of Politics* 77, no. 4 (Oct. 2015): 1076–88.

13 For a study of academic earmarking, see James D. Savage, *Funding Science in America: Congress, Universities, and the Politics of the Academic Pork Barrel* (New York: Cambridge University Press, 1999). For a general study of pork-barrel activity, see the excellent book by Diana Evans, *Greasing the Wheels: Using Pork Barrel Projects to Build Majority Coalitions in Congress* (New York: Cambridge University Press, 2004). For a more recent assessment of earmarking, see Scott A. Frisch and Sean Q Kelly, *Cheese Factories on the Moon: Why Earmarks Are Good for American Democracy* (Boulder, CO: Paradigm Publishers, 2011).

the more outrageous projects earmarked in a 2005 transportation bill was a bridge in Alaska that would have cost more than $223 million and would have connected the mainland to an island with only 50 residents (the so-called bridge to nowhere). This earmark inspired so much adverse publicity and proved so embarrassing to the Republicans that they rescinded the appropriation. Congressional rules now require that any earmark be explicitly associated with its requesting member, who must list it on his official website and certify that neither he nor his family members benefit financially from it.

Pork-barrel legislation brings several of our principles from Chapter 1 into play. Incumbent legislators engage in the practice because it furthers their electoral objectives (the rationality principle). They succeed to the degree that they exchange support with fellow legislators for one another's projects (the collective action principle). These efforts are facilitated by institutional procedures: amendments to appropriations bills, omnibus legislation, and opportunities to insert special provisions into bills (the institution principle). And they influence the mix and location of spending by the federal government (the policy principle). From time to time the practice becomes so egregious, as with the "bridge to nowhere," that Congress establishes procedures to restrict the activity, thereby constraining legislators' future actions (the history principle). In 2010 the newly elected Republican majority in the House banned the practice of earmarking, and the ban has since remained in place.

All these benefits of incumbency are publicized through another advantage that incumbents enjoy—the franking privilege. Under a law enacted by the 1st Congress in 1789, members of Congress may send mail to their constituents free of charge to keep them informed of governmental business and public affairs. Under current law, members receive an average of about $100,000 in free postage for mailings to their constituents. Although there are restrictions on how members use these funds, especially around election time, the franking privilege helps incumbents publicize their activities and make themselves visible to voters.

An additional incumbency advantage is in fund-raising: incumbents are able to raise campaign funds throughout their term, often in such quantities as to overwhelm prospective challengers. Members of Congress almost always can outspend their opponents (Figure 6.3).[14] Over the past quarter-century, and despite campaign finance regulations that have aimed to level the playing field, the gap between incumbent and challenger spending has grown. Members of the majority party in the House and Senate are particularly attractive to donors who want access to those in power.[15]

---

14 Stephen Ansolabehere and James M. Snyder, "Campaign War Chests in Congressional Elections," *Business and Politics* 2, no. 1 (April 2000): 9–33. Also see Alexander Fouirnaies and Andrew B. Hall, "The Financial Incumbency Advantage: Causes and Consequences," *Journal of Politics* 76, no. 3 (May 2014): 711–24.

15 Gary W. Cox and Eric Magar, "How Much Is Majority Status in the U.S. Congress Worth?" *American Political Science Review* 93, no. 2 (June 1999): 299–309.

Figure 6.3
HOUSE AND SENATE CAMPAIGN EXPENDITURES

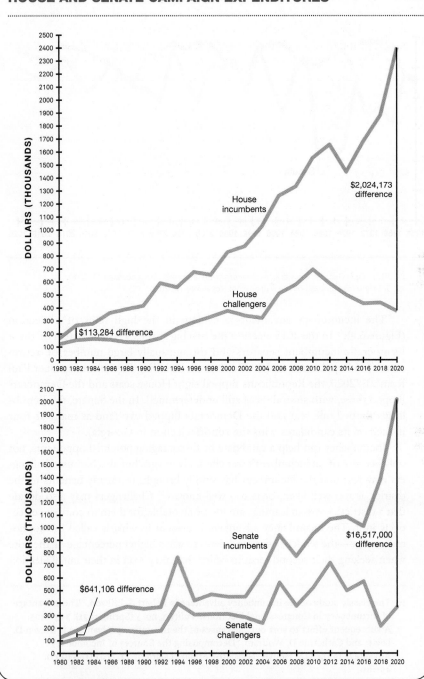

NOTE: Costs in nominal dollars.

SOURCES: 1980-2018: The Campaign Finance Institute, http://www.cfinst.org/data.aspx;
2020: OpenSecrets, "Incumbent Advantage," https://www.opensecrets.org/elections-overview
/incumbent-advantage (accessed 11/17/20).

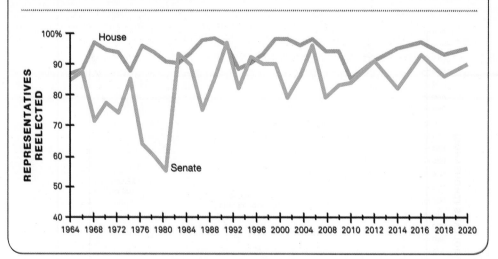

Figure 6.4
THE POWER OF INCUMBENCY

SOURCE: OpenSecrets, www.opensecrets.org/overview/reelct.php (accessed 11/8/18);
2020: Estimates compiled by the author as of November 10, 2020.

The incumbency advantage is evident in the high rates of reelection (Figure 6.4).[16] In the 2018 election the two big stories were the defeat of three Democratic incumbent senators and the unusually large number of retirements (40 Republicans and 20 Democrats, including Republican speaker Paul Ryan). In 2020, the Republicans flipped eight House seats and the Democrats flipped three, with several races still undetermined. In the Senate, the Republicans flipped one seat and the Democrats flipped two (and as many as four if each of its candidates wins the runoff election in Georgia).

Incumbency can help a candidate by discouraging potential opponents, not only because of an incumbent's war chest advantages but also because challengers may fear that the incumbent has simply brought too many benefits to the district, is too well liked, or is too well-known.[17] Challengers may also decide that a district's partisan leanings are too unfavorable for them to compete effectively in it. The incumbency advantage is evident in what is called the sophomore surge—the tendency for candidates to win a higher percentage of the vote when seeking their second term in office than they won in their initial election

16 The classic study of the incumbency advantage is Robert S. Erikson, "The Advantage of Incumbency in Congressional Elections," *Polity* 3, no. 3 (Spring 1971): 395–405. A subsequent effort to sort out the causes of the incumbency advantage is Steven D. Levitt and Catherine D. Wolfram, "Decomposing the Sources of Incumbency Advantage in the U.S. House," *Legislative Studies Quarterly* 22, no. 1 (Feb 1997): 45–60.

17 Kenneth N. Bickers and Robert M. Stein, "The Electoral Dynamics of the Federal Pork Barrel," *American Journal of Political Science* 40, no. 4 (Nov 1996): 1300–26.

victory. The advantage of incumbency tends to preserve the status quo in Congress by discouraging potentially strong challengers from running.

When faced by strong challengers, however, incumbents are often defeated.[18] Strong challengers throw their hat into the ring when they believe the incumbent is weak, out of touch, too preoccupied with national affairs, or plagued by scandal or declining capabilities. Indeed, incumbents afflicted in any of these ways may choose to retire voluntarily (strategic retirement) instead of subjecting themselves to a high probability of defeat. Incumbents may also become vulnerable when their party is unpopular. The Democrats mounted very strong challenges against vulnerable Republicans in both the House and the Senate in 2020 and attracted record amounts of campaign contributions. But in most cases, Republican candidates survived, despite the unpopularity of the candidate heading the ticket. This is the result of split-ticket voting—moderate Republicans voting against Trump but supporting their fellow legislative partisans. The extreme case is Maine, where Democrats won both congressional seats and Joe Biden carried the state with a 53–44 margin, but incumbent Republican senator Susan Collins was reelected with a 51–44 margin.

The role of incumbency also has implications for the social composition of Congress. For example, the incumbency advantage makes it harder for women to increase their numbers in Congress because most incumbents are men. Female candidates who run for open seats (for which there are no incumbents in the race) are just as likely to win as male candidates, but seats rarely open up.[19] Supporters of term limits argue that the incumbency advantage and the tendency of many legislators to view politics as a career will stifle turnover unless limits are imposed on the number of terms a legislator can serve.

But the tendency toward the status quo is not absolute. In 2018, the Democrats picked up more than forty seats, thereby capturing a House majority, but lost seats in the Senate, allowing the Republicans to increase their control—partial retention of the status quo. The 2020 election was a surprise, defying most polls that suggested the potential for a Democratic landslide. Instead, the Democrats lost seats in the House and barely increased their minority representation in the Senate—in effect, a reversion to the status quo despite turning out the incumbent president. As these elections suggest, the advantages of incumbency, always considerable, are not necessarily decisive.

Congressional Districts. The final factor that affects who wins a seat in Congress is the way congressional districts are drawn. Every 10 years, the seats in the House of Representatives are reapportioned among the states to reflect population changes. In 1929, Congress enacted a law fixing the total number of congressional seats at 435. As a result, when states with fast-growing populations

---

18 Jacobson and Carson, *The Politics of Congressional Elections.*

19 See Barbara C. Burrell, *A Woman's Place Is in the House: Campaigning for Congress in the Feminist Era* (Ann Arbor: University of Michigan Press, 1994). An excellent study is Sarah F. Anzia and Christopher R. Berry, "The Jackie (and Jill) Robinson Effect: Why Do Congresswomen Outperform Congressmen?" *American Journal of Political Science* 55, no. 3 (July 2011): 478–93.

gain districts, they do so at the expense of states with slower population growth. In recent decades, this has meant that states in the South and West have gained congressional seats, while states in the Northeast and the Midwest have lost them (Figure 6.5). Once the new number of districts is determined for each state, state legislatures must redraw their congressional districts accordingly.

Redrawing congressional districts is a highly complex, political process: in most states, districts are shaped to create an advantage for the party that commands a majority in the state legislature, which controls the process. (The new district plan is subject to a possible veto by the governor, who may be of a different party.) Those charged with drawing districts use sophisticated programs to generate the most favorable district boundaries. Redistricting can create open seats and may pit incumbents of the same party against each other, ensuring that one of them will lose. Redistricting can also give an advantage to one party by clustering voters with some ideological or demographic characteristics in a single district or by separating those voters into two or more districts.

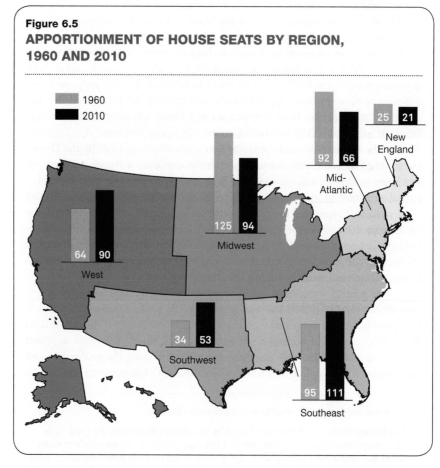

Figure 6.5

APPORTIONMENT OF HOUSE SEATS BY REGION, 1960 AND 2010

1960
2010

New England 25 / 21

Mid-Atlantic 92 / 66

Midwest 125 / 94

West 64 / 90

Southwest 34 / 53

Southeast 95 / 111

SOURCE: U.S. Census Bureau, www.census.gov/prod/cen2010/briefs/c2010br-08.pdf (accessed 5/23/20).

Redistricting will take place after the 2020 election and the completion of the census (which will determine apportionment of congressional seats among the states). Governors and state legislatures in most states oversee this process. The 2018 elections were kind to the Democrats—they picked up a handful of governors; 2020 was not—they lost several state legislatures.

Gerrymandering can have a major effect on the outcome of congressional elections. It took an especially dramatic form in the state of Texas after the 2000 census. Texas, as elsewhere, drew new congressional districts based on the census, and the 2002 congressional election was the first one to be held under the new district plan. In 2003, the Texas legislature, controlled by the Republicans for the first time in 130 years, set to work drawing up a *new* set of congressional districts. Ordinarily this exercise is performed only once per decade, after the constitutionally required census. Texas Republicans argued, however, that nothing prohibits a state from doing it more frequently. Democrats in the Texas state legislature were furious about the Repubicans' ploy to redraw the districts in their favor and twice staged walkouts, even fleeing across the border to Oklahoma to avoid a posse of Texas Rangers sent to retrieve them. These walkouts delayed proceedings by making it difficult to assemble enough legislators to meet the minimum required to do legislative business. Finally, the Republicans prevailed in redrawing the congressional districts in a way that heavily favored their party. In the next election in 2004, the Republicans gained five House seats in Texas, defeating four Democratic incumbents, in part as a result of their redistricting maneuver.[20] Examples such as this explain why the two national parties invest substantial resources in state legislative and gubernatorial contests during the electoral cycle preceding the year in which congressional-district boundaries will be redrawn. The 2020 elections set the stage for the next round of redistricting, which will apply to the 2022 elections.

As we will see in Chapter 11, since the passage of the 1982 amendments to the 1965 Voting Rights Act, race has become a major—and controversial—consideration in drawing congressional districts. These amendments, which encouraged the creation of districts in which racial minorities have decisive majorities, have greatly increased the number of minority representatives in Congress.[21]

 gerrymandering

The drawing of electoral districts in such a way as to give advantage to one political party.

20 In late 2004, the U.S. Supreme Court ordered a lower federal court to reconsider the "extra" Texas redistricting plan, and the case eventually worked its way back to the Supreme Court. In June 2006, the Court ruled that the Texas legislature was within its rights to redistrict more than once per decade; however, it also ruled that some of the particular decisions about district boundaries violated the rights of Latino voters. In its 2019 term, the Court, in a 5–4 decision, ruled that redistricting involving even extreme partisan gerrymandering cannot be reversed through judicial remediation (unless racial bias is evident). The Court thus left it to state legislatures, and ultimately to voters, to oversee the redistricting process.

21 Among the most fervent supporters of the new minority districts were White Republicans, who used the opportunity to create more districts dominated by White Republican voters. See David Lublin, *The Paradox of Representation: Racial Gerrymandering and Minority Interests in Congress* (Princeton, NJ: Princeton University Press, 1997).

Yet these developments raise thorny questions about representation. Some analysts argue that, although this system may grant minorities greater descriptive representation (also called sociological representation), it has made it more difficult for them to win substantive policy goals.[22] There is no doubt that descriptive representation has grown. After the 2016, 2018, and 2020 elections, the House now has more female and minority members than ever in its history.[23] However, the growing number of majority-minority districts has meant that minority voter proportions in other districts have become diluted, opening up the possibility that representatives from those districts will be less responsive to minorities' policy concerns.

PROBLEMS OF LEGISLATIVE ORGANIZATION

The U.S. Congress is not only a representative assembly. It is also a legislative body. For Americans, representation and legislation go hand in hand. Yet governing is a challenge. It is extraordinarily difficult for a large, representative assembly to formulate, enact, and implement laws. Just the internal complexities of conducting business within Congress—the legislative process itself—are daunting. In addition, many individuals and institutions have the capacity to influence the legislative process. Because successful legislation requires the confluence of so many factors, it is little wonder that most of the thousands of bills considered by Congress each year are defeated long before they reach the president.

The supporters of legislative proposals often feel that the formal rules of the congressional process are designed to prevent their own deserving proposals from ever seeing the light of day. But these rules allow Congress to play an important role in lawmaking. If it wants to be more than a rubber stamp for the executive branch, which many other representative assemblies around the world are, a national legislature such as Congress must develop a division of labor, set an agenda, maintain order through rules and procedures, and place limits on discussion. If it wants to accomplish these tasks in a representative setting made up of diverse political preferences, then it must find the ways and means to facilitate cooperation and to make compromises. We will first take up the general issues that face any legislature or decision-making group composed of members with disparate viewpoints and goals: the problems of cooperation, coalitions, and compromises.

22 Lani Guinier, *The Tyranny of the Majority: Fundamental Fairness in Representative Democracy* (New York: Free Press, 1994). See also David Epstein and Sharyn O'Halloran, "Measuring the Electoral and Policy Impact of Majority-Minority Voting Districts," *American Journal of Political Science* 43, no. 2 (Apr. 1999): 367–95.

23 See Table 6.1 for data on race and gender in the 116th Congress (2019–20).

Cooperation in Congress

As the collective action principle suggests, a number of factors make cooperation difficult in Congress. A popularly elected legislative assembly—whether the
Boston City Council, the Kansas state legislature, the U.S. Congress, the French
National Assembly, or the European Parliament—consists of politicians who harbor a variety of political objectives. Because they got where they are by winning an
election, and many hope to stay where they are or possibly advance their political
careers, these politicians are intimately aware of whom they must please to do so:

- Because campaigns are expensive propositions, most politicians are eager
  to please those who can supply resources for the next campaign: campaign
  donors, political action committees (PACs), important endorsers, party
  officials, and volunteer activists.

- The most recent campaign—the one that the politicians won—provides
  information about what categories of voters supported them and may
  support them again if their performance in office is adequate.

- Many politicians not only aim to please others (campaign contributors
  and voters) but also have an agenda of their own. Whether for private
  gain or public good, politicians come to the legislature with policy goals
  of personal importance. They need to please themselves.

Congress consists of a heterogeneous group of legislators who seek to
pursue public policies that are many and varied. They may be considered from
two perspectives. First, owing to their different constituencies, legislators will
give priority to different realms of public policy. A Cape Cod congressman
will be interested in shipping, fishing, coastal preservation, harbor development,
tourism, and shipbuilding. A Philadelphia congresswoman may focus instead on
welfare reform, civil rights policy, aid to public school systems, and job-training
programs. And Montana's sole member of Congress is probably most interested in ranching, agriculture, mining, and public land use. Evidently, Congress
encompasses a mélange of legislative priorities.

Second, members' opinions on any given issue are diverse. Although interest
in environmental protection, for example, may vary in terms of degree (ranging
from high interest among members who count many Sierra Club supporters
among their constituents to low interest among members who have other
priorities), once environmental protection is on the agenda, there is a broad
range of possible preferences for specific initiatives. Some want pollution
discharges to be monitored and regulated by watchdog agencies; others prefer more decentralized and less intrusive means, such as marketable pollution
permits—so-called cap-and-trade policies. Still others think the entire issue
is overblown and that the country would be best served by leaving well
enough alone. (See Analyzing the Evidence on pp. 214–5 for a discussion of
congressional recognition of and response to these priorities.)

Diversity in priorities and preferences means that no single view predominates among legislators. Legislative consensus must be built: support must be

How Representative Is Congress?

Contributed by
Leah Stokes
University of California, Santa Barbara

Significant evidence suggests that the public supports action on climate change.[1] Yet the federal government has done little to enact policies aimed at reducing carbon emissions. How can we explain this gap between public support for action and the absence of climate policy?

One hypothesis is that firms that profit from carbon pollution, including fossil fuel companies and electric utilities, have blocked such policies from passing. There are a number of theories for how these companies influence the policy process. Firms can lobby to change the content of bills and their likelihood of passing. Researchers have also found that campaign contributions can facilitate access to politicians. But just because an individual or group has access, does that mean they will be able to influence public policy?

To try to assess this, I undertook research with Alexander Hertel-Fernandez and Matto Mildenberger. We surveyed the most senior staffers working in Congress and asked them whether they had advised the Congress members for whom they work to change their vote on a bill after meeting with campaign contributors. Knowing that staff were unlikely to admit to being swayed by campaign contributions, we used a questionnaire designed to ensure that respondents didn't just tell us what they thought we wanted to hear.

First, we asked congressional staff to prioritize the opinions that shaped their stance on an issue. As you can see in the figure below, they overwhelmingly reported that constituent opinions and communications from constituents were the most influential factors in how they advised their member of Congress.

Considerations Staffers Reported as Extremely or Very Important in Shaping Their Advice to Their Members, by Staffer Party

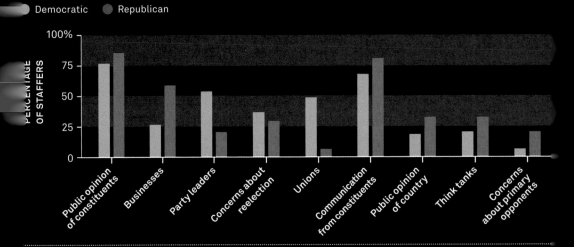

○ Democratic ○ Republican

SOURCE: Alexander Hertel-Fernandez, Matto Mildenberger, and Leah C. Stokes, "Legislative Staff and Representation

Staffer Perceptions of Constituent Preferences

🔘 Republican ⚪ Democratic

AVERAGE CONSTITUENT'S VIEW

◀ UNDERESTIMATED SUPPORT   ▼   OVERESTIMATED SUPPORT ▶

Support background checks for gun sales	-11 (Democratic)	-49 (Republican)
Regulate carbon emissions as pollutants	-5 (Democratic)	-31 (Republican)
Support infrastructure spending package	-9 (Democratic)	-28 (Republican)
Raise minimum wage to $12	-11 (Democratic)	-22 (Republican)
Repeal the Affordable Care Act	-24 (Democratic)	+10 (Republican)

-60   0   +60

Next, we asked them what they thought their constituents' preferences were on regulating carbon emissions, among other issues. You can see the results in the above figure. Each row represents the staffers' perceived constituent opinions on an issue. Interestingly, both Republicans and Democrats consistently underestimated their constituents' support for various issues. For regulating carbon emissions, Republicans underestimated support by 31 percent and Democrats by 5 percent.

What accounts for this gap between what constituents want and what congressional staffers think they want? In order to understand this, we examined the role of interest group contact using the questionnaire. We found that 45 percent of staff had changed their minds about a policy after meeting with a campaign contributor. So, the more an office meets with or takes campaign contributions from fossil fuel companies as compared to grassroots environmental groups, the more the office underestimates its constituents' support for climate policy.

Taken together, these studies suggest that fossil fuel companies have been able to block public policy on climate change. Returning to the larger question of representation, one can conclude that the access that comes with campaign contributions has a troubling influence on how attentive representatives are to constituent interests on environmental legislation, as well as other issues.

SOURCE: Alexander Hertel-Fernandez, Matto Mildenberger, and Leah C. Stokes, "Legislative Staff and Representation in Congress," *American Political Science Review* 113, no. 1 (2019): 1–18.

1 Peter D. Howe, Matto Mildenberger, Jennifer R. Marlon, and Anthony Leiserowitz, "Geographic Variation in Opinions on Climate Change at State and Local Scales in the USA," *Nature Climate Change* 5 (2015): 596–603.

2 Joshua L. Kalla and David E. Broockman, "Campaign Contributions Facilitate Access to Congressional Officials: A Randomized Field Experiment," *American Journal of Political Science* 60, no. 3 (2016): 545–58.

3 Alexander Hertel-Fernandez, Matto Mildenberger, and Leah C. Stokes, "Legislative Staff and Representation in Congress," *American Political Science Review* 113, no. 1 (2019): 1–18.

assembled, deals consummated, and promises and threats used. In short, legislators intent on achieving their objectives must cooperate, coalesce, and compromise. And these activities are facilitated, as indicated by the institution principle,
by rules and procedures. This system leads to the division and specialization
of legislative work, the regularization of procedures, and the creation of agenda
power. All of these organizational features of Congress arise as part of a governance structure to promote cooperation and coalition building—activities
that yield compromise policies.

Underlying Problems and Challenges

Before we can understand why Congress selects particular ways to institution-
alize its practices, we need a finer appreciation of other underlying problems
with which legislators must grapple. Then we can consider how Congress deals
with these problems.

Matching Influence and Interest. Legislatures are highly egalitarian
institutions. Each legislator has one vote on any issue that comes before the
body. Whereas a consumer has a cash budget that she may allocate in any
way she wishes, a legislator is not given a vote budget in quite the same sense.
Instead, his budget of votes is "dedicated"—one vote for each motion before
the assembly. He cannot aggregate the votes in his possession and cast all
or some large fraction of them for a motion on a subject near and dear to
his heart (or the hearts of his constituents). This is a source of frustration
because the premise of instrumental behavior dictates that legislators would, if
they could, concentrate whatever resources they command on the subjects of
highest priority to them. The egalitarian arrangement thus forces legislators to
make deals with one another: "I'll support you on this motion if you support
me on a future motion."

Information. Legislators do not vote for outcomes directly but, rather, for
instruments (or policies) that produce outcomes. Thus, legislators must know
the connection between the instruments they vote for and the effects they
desire. In short, they must have information and knowledge about how the
world works.

Few legislators—indeed, few people in general—know beyond a superficial
level how the world works in very many policy domains. Nearly everyone in the
legislature would benefit from the production of valuable information—at the
very least, information that would enable them to eliminate ineffectual policy
instruments. Producing such information, however, is not a trivial matter. Simply
digesting the knowledge that is produced outside the legislature by academics,
scientists, journalists, and interest groups is a taxing task. Clearly, institutional
arrangements that provide incentives to some legislators to produce, evaluate,
and disseminate this knowledge for the benefit of other legislators will permit a
more effective use of public resources. Because legislatures are in competition
with other branches of government—particularly the executive—legislators

need to meet certain informational requirements just to keep up with their competition.

Compliance. The legislature is not the only game in town. The promulgation of public policies is a joint undertaking in which judges, executives, bureaucrats, and others participate alongside legislators. If the legislature has no means to monitor what happens after a bill becomes law, then it risks seeing public policies implemented in ways that it did not intend. But it is just not practical for all 435 representatives and all 100 senators to scrutinize the executive branch agencies in downtown Washington to ensure appropriate implementation. Like the production and dissemination of reliable information at the policy-formulation stage, the need for oversight of the bureaucracy is but an extension of the need for cooperation to produce legislation in the first place. It, too, must be institutionalized.

We have suggested in this discussion about legislative institutions and practices that the diversity of beliefs and preferences in Congress requires cooperation, coalitions, and compromise to achieve successful policy goals. In addition, there is a mismatch of influence and interest (owing to one person, one vote); information about the effectiveness of alternative policies is in short supply; and the legislature must worry about how the other branches of government treat its product—our public laws. Solving or mitigating these problems requires devising sound institutional arrangements. This is where the rationality principle and the institution principle join forces.

THE ORGANIZATION OF CONGRESS

We now examine the basic building blocks of congressional organization: political parties, the committee system, congressional staff, the caucuses, and the parliamentary rules of the House and Senate. Each of these factors plays a key role in the organization of Congress and in the process through which it formulates and enacts laws. We also look at the powers Congress has in addition to lawmaking and explore the future role of Congress in relation to the powers of the executive.

Party Leadership and Organization in the House and the Senate

One significant aspect of legislative life is not even part of the *official* organization of Congress: political parties. The legislative parties—primarily Democratic and Republican in modern times, but numerous others over the course of American history—are organizations that foster cooperation, coalitions, and compromise. In short, political parties in Congress are vehicles of collective action, the fundamental building blocks from which policy coalitions are fashioned to pass

**party caucus
or party
conference**

A nominally closed meeting to select candidates or leaders, plan strategy, or make decisions regarding legislative matters. Termed a *caucus* in the Democratic Party and a *conference* in the Republican Party.

**Speaker of
the House**

The chief presiding officer of the House of Representatives; elected at the beginning of every Congress on a straight party vote, he or she is the most important party and House leader.

majority leader

The elected leader of the party holding a majority of the seats in the House of Representatives or in the Senate. In the House, the majority leader is subordinate in the party hierarchy to the Speaker.

minority leader

The elected leader of the party holding less than a majority of the seats in the House or Senate.

legislation and monitor its implementation, thereby providing a track record on which members build electoral support.[24]

Every two years at the start of a new Congress, the parties in each chamber choose leaders. In the House, the members gather into partisan groups—called the **party caucus** by the Democrats and the **party conference** by the Republicans—to elect leaders and decide other matters of party policy. The elected leader of the majority party is later proposed to the whole House and automatically elected to the position of **Speaker of the House**, with voting along straight party lines. The Speaker of the 116th Congress is Nancy Pelosi (D-Calif.). The House majority caucus (or conference) also elects a **majority leader**, a title given to Steny Hoyer of Maryland in the 116th Congress. The minority party goes through the same process and selects the **minority leader**: for the 116th Congress, Republicans elected Kevin McCarthy of California. Both parties also elect "whips" who line up party members on important votes and relay voting intentions to the party leaders: for the 116th Congress, these are Republican Steve Scalise of Louisiana and Democrat James Clyburn of South Carolina.

At one time, party leaders in the House strictly controlled committee assignments and used them to enforce party discipline. Today representatives often expect to receive the assignments they want and resent leadership efforts to control assignments. The leadership's best opportunities to use committee assignments as rewards and punishments come when more than one member seeks the same seat on a committee.

Generally, representatives seek assignments that will allow them to influence decisions of special importance to their districts. Representatives from farm districts, for example, may request seats on the Agriculture Committee.[25] This is one method by which members of the House can overcome the egalitarian allocation of power in the legislature: even though each legislator has just one vote on each issue in the full chamber, by serving on the right committees they can acquire extra influence in areas important to their constituents. Seats on powerful committees such as Ways and Means, which is responsible for tax legislation, and Energy and Commerce, responsible for health, energy, and regulatory policy, are especially popular.

---

24 For a historically grounded analysis of the development of political parties as well as a treatment of their general contemporary significance, see John H. Aldrich, *Why Parties?: A Second Look* (Chicago: University of Chicago Press, 2011). For an analysis of the parties in the legislative process, see Gary W. Cox and Mathew D. McCubbins, *Legislative Leviathan: Party Government in the House*, 2nd ed. (New York: Cambridge University Press, 2007). See also their *Setting the Agenda: Responsible Party Government in the U.S. House of Representatives* (New York: Cambridge University Press, 2005). A provocative essay questioning the role of parties is Keith Krehbiel, "Where's the Party?" *British Journal of Political Science* 23, no. 2 (Apr. 1993): 235–66.

25 For an extensive discussion of the committee assignment process in the U.S. House, see Kenneth A. Shepsle, *The Giant Jigsaw Puzzle: Democratic Committee Assignments in the Modern House* (Chicago: University of Chicago Press, 1978); and Scott A. Frisch and Sean Q Kelly, *Committee Assignment Politics in the U.S. House of Representatives* (Norman: University of Oklahoma Press, 2006). See also E. Scott Adler, *Why Congressional Reforms Fail: Reelection and the House Committee System* (Chicago: University of Chicago Press, 2002).

In the Senate, the president pro tempore, a position designated in the Constitution, exercises mainly ceremonial leadership; usually the majority party awards this position to the member with the greatest seniority. Real power is in the hands of the majority and minority leaders, each elected by their respective party caucus or conference. Together they control the Senate's legislative calendar, or agenda. In addition, the senators from each party elect a whip. The Senate majority leader in the 116th Congress is Mitch McConnell of Kentucky, the Senate minority leader is Chuck Schumer of New York, and the majority and minority whips are John Thune of South Dakota and Richard Durbin of Illinois, respectively.

Party leaders often reach outside their respective chambers to augment their power and enhance prospects for their party programs. One important external strategy involves fund-raising. In recent years, congressional leaders have established their own PACs. Interest groups are usually eager to contribute to these "leadership PACs" to curry favor with powerful members of Congress. The leaders, in turn, use the funds to support the various campaigns of their party's candidates and thereby create a sense of obligation and loyalty among the candidates they help.[26]

In addition to organizing committees, congressional party leaders set the legislative agenda and regulate deliberation over specific items on the agenda. This aspect of agenda setting is multifaceted. In the House, for example, a bill is initially filed with the clerk as a legislative proposal. The Speaker then determines which committee has jurisdiction over it. Indeed, since the mid-1970s, the Speaker has been given additional bill-assignment powers, permitting him or her to assign different parts of a bill to different committees or the same parts sequentially or simultaneously to several committees.[27] This steering and agenda setting process works, however, within an institutional framework consisting of structures and procedures.

Why do members allow themselves to be governed by powerful party leaders? Leaders, after all, are elected by their rank-and-file members, and in their respective party caucuses or conferences the rank and file determine how powerful they will permit their leaders to be. Indeed, the power of party leaders

26 Rank-and-file members, especially those from safe districts who face limited electoral challenges, have also created their own PACs, which enable them to contribute to their party and its candidates. See Eric S. Heberlig, "Congressional Parties, Fundraising, and Committee Ambition," *Political Research Quarterly* 56, no. 2 (2003): 151–61.

27 For a historical look, see David W. Rohde and Kenneth A. Shepsle, "Leaders and Followers in the House of Representatives: Reflections on Woodrow Wilson's *Congressional Government*," *Congress and the Presidency* 14, no. 2 (1987): 111–33. An analysis of the House leadership is Eric Schickler and Kathryn Pearson, "The House Leadership in an Era of Partisan Warfare," in *Congress Reconsidered*, ed. Lawrence C. Dodd and Bruce I. Oppenheimer, 8th ed. (Washington, DC: CQ Press, 2005), pp. 207–26. A companion piece on the Senate is C. Lawrence Evans and Daniel Lipinski, "Obstruction and Leadership in the U.S. Senate," in *Congress Reconsidered*, ed. Dodd and Oppenheimer, 8th ed., pp. 227–48. An update is Kathryn Pearson and Eric Schickler, "The Transition to Democratic Leadership in a Polarized House," in *Congress Reconsidered*, ed. Lawrence C. Dodd and Bruce I. Oppenheimer, 9th ed. (Washington, DC: CQ Press, 2008), pp. 165–89.

has ebbed and flowed over time. Political scientists John Aldrich and David Rohde have sought to understand these ebbs and flows in the power of a party over its members, what they call "conditional party government." They suggest that the institutional strength of party leaders is conditional: it depends on circumstances, chief among them being the degree to which party members share policy goals. If the rank and file are relatively homogeneous in this respect, they will endow their leaders with considerable power to prosecute their shared agenda. If, however, party members are heterogeneous in their goals, they will be less disposed to empower a leader. Thus, the Democratic Party of the 1940s and 1950s, with its northern liberal wing and its southern conservative wing, was heterogeneous in the extreme and provided its leaders with few power resources. The party started to become ideologically more homogenous in the 1970s, in part thanks to the 1965 Voting Rights Act. After the passage of the act, formerly Democratic constituencies in the South started electing Republicans, thereby reducing the diversity in the Democratic ranks. Under these changed circumstances, Democratic Party legislators, who were more focused than before on moderate and liberal goals, were prepared to empower their leaders.[28]

Ideological changes like the ones experienced by House Democrats in the 1970s have also occurred in the ranks of House Republicans and both parties in the Senate. A half-century after the Voting Rights Act, each of the four legislative parties is ideologically more homogeneous than it was in an earlier era, and there is very little ideological overlap in either chamber between the parties. Through this sorting, the parties have become polarized, with Democrats skewed toward the liberal side of the political spectrum and Republicans skewed toward the conservative side. With homogeneity within the party ranks, but vast disagreement between the parties, there is very strong pressure for the majority to push its consensus and very little pressure to compromise with the party in the minority. Polarization has thus undermined interparty cooperation and compromise.

Polarization was apparent in the attempt to replace Justice Antonin Scalia on the Supreme Court in 2016. After his death in February of that year, Senate Majority Leader Mitch McConnell made it very clear that the majority Republicans would refuse to consider any nominee put forth by President Obama; they argued that Obama should leave the nomination to the next president, who would be determined in the upcoming November election. When

---

28 A now-classic treatment of the ebbs and flows of parties and their leaders in the modern era is David W. Rohde, *Parties and Leaders in the Postreform House* (Chicago: University of Chicago Press, 1991). For a historical perspective, see David W. Rohde, John H. Aldrich, and Mark M. Berger, "The Historical Variability in Conditional Party Government, 1877–1986," in *Party, Process, and Political Change in Congress: New Perspectives on the History of Congress*, ed. David W. Brady and Mathew D. McCubbins (Palo Alto, CA: Stanford University Press, 2002), pp. 17–35. For a development of the analytical argument, see David W. Rohde and John H. Aldrich, "The Logic of Conditional Party Government: Revisiting the Electoral Connection," in *Congress Reconsidered*, ed. Lawrence C. Dodd and Bruce I. Oppenheimer, 7th ed. (Washington, DC: CQ Press, 2001), pp. 265–92. A complementary theoretical perspective is offered by the political scientists Gary Cox and Mathew McCubbins in both *Legislative Leviathan* and *Setting the Agenda*.

Obama nominated a moderate Democrat, Merrick Garland of the D.C. Circuit Court of Appeals, to replace Scalia, Republicans refused to hold hearings on the nomination in the hopes that a Republican president would be elected and could appoint another conservative to the Court. Indeed, after the election of Republican Donald Trump to the presidency, the Senate acted quickly on the new president's first nominee. Neil Gorsuch, also a U.S. Court of Appeals judge, was confirmed to the Supreme Court in the spring of 2017. The polarization in the Senate remained extreme, with Republicans having to resort to unusual legislative tactics to secure his place on the Court; only three Democrats voted in support of his nomination. Brett Kavanaugh, Trump's 2018 nominee to the Court, faced similar opposition, with only one Democrat in support (see Chapter 9).

The Committee System: The Core of Congress

If the system of leadership in each party and chamber constitutes the first set of organizational arrangements in the U.S. Congress, then the committee system provides a second set of organizational structures. Committees are a division- and specialization-of-labor system, while party leadership arrangements constitute a hierarchy-of-power system.

Congress began as a relatively unspecialized assembly, with each legislator participating equally in every step of the legislative process in all realms of policy. By the time of the War of 1812, if not earlier, Congress had begun employing a system of specialists—the committee system—because members with different interests and talents wished to play disproportionate roles in certain areas of policy making while ceding influence in areas in which they were less interested.[29] If, Rip Van Winkle–like, a congressman had fallen asleep in 1805 and woke up in 1825, he would have found a transformed legislative world. The legislative chambers in the beginning of that period consisted of bodies of generalists; by 1825, the legislative agenda was dominated by groups of specialists serving on standing committees. If, in contrast, our legislator had fallen asleep in 1825 and awoke a *century* later, the legislature would not seem so different. In short, organizational decisions in the first quarter of the nineteenth century affected legislative activity far into the future. This is the history principle at work.

The congressional committee system consists of a set of **standing committees** that are given a permanent status by the official rules. Each standing committee has a fixed membership, officers, rules, a staff, offices, and above all, a jurisdiction that is recognized by all other committees and, usually, the leadership as well (Table 6.3). The jurisdiction of each standing committee is defined by the subject matter of the legislation it considers. With important exceptions, the different committee jurisdictions parallel those of the major departments or agencies of the executive branch. Except for the Rules Committee in the House and the Rules

standing committee

A permanent legislative committee that considers legislation within its designated subject area.

29 The story of the early nineteenth-century evolution of the standing-committee system in the House and the Senate is told in Gerald Gamm and Kenneth A. Shepsle, "Emergence of Legislative Institutions: Standing Committees in the House and Senate, 1810–1825," *Legislative Studies Quarterly* 14, no. 1 (Feb. 1989): 39–66.

Table 6.3
STANDING COMMITTEES OF CONGRESS, 2020*

HOUSE COMMITTEES	
Agriculture	Intelligence
Appropriations	Judiciary
Armed Services	Natural Resources
Budget	Oversight and Government Reform
Education and Labor	Rules
Energy and Commerce	Science, Space, and Technology
Ethics	Small Business
Financial Services	Transportation and Infrastructure
Foreign Affairs	Veterans' Affairs
Homeland Security	Ways and Means
House Administration	

SENATE COMMITTEES	
Agriculture, Nutrition, and Forestry	Finance
Appropriations	Foreign Relations
Armed Services	Health, Education, Labor, and Pensions
Banking, Housing, and Urban Affairs	Homeland Security and Governmental Affairs
Budget	Judiciary
Commerce, Science, and Transportation	Rules and Administration
Energy and Natural Resources	Small Business and Entrepreneurship
Environment and Public Works	Veterans' Affairs

*These were the committees in the 116th Congress (2019–20). Committee names and jurisdictions change over time, as does the number of committees.

and Administration Committee in the Senate, all the important committees receive proposals for legislation and process them into official bills. The House Rules Committee decides the order in which bills come up for a vote and determines the rules that govern the length of debate and opportunity for amendments. The Senate Rules and Administration Committee focuses more on administrative matters—managing Senate buildings, the Government Printing Office, the Senate library, and other services—but also on substantive matters, including the regulation of corrupt practices, presidential succession, and federal elections.

Jurisdiction. The world of policy is partitioned into policy jurisdictions, which become the responsibility of specific committees. The members of the Armed Services Committees in the House and Senate, for example, become specialists in all aspects of military affairs. Legislators tend to have disproportionate influence over bills within their respective committee jurisdictions, not only because they are the most knowledgeable members in those policy areas but also because they exercise various forms of agenda power, a subject we develop further in the next section.

Dividing up institutional activities among jurisdictions, thereby encouraging participants to specialize, has advantages. But it has costs, too. If the House Armed Services Committee had no restraints, its members would undoubtedly shower their own districts with military facilities and contracts. In short, the delegation of authority and resources to specialized subunits exploits the advantages of the division and specialization of labor but risks jeopardizing the collective objectives of the group as a whole. The monitoring of committee activities thus goes hand in hand with delegation.

Sometimes new issues arise that do not fit neatly into any jurisdiction. Some, such as the energy crisis of the 1970s, are so multifaceted that bits and pieces of them are spread across many committee jurisdictions. Other issues, such as the regulation of tobacco products, fall into a gray area claimed by several committees. In this case, the House Energy and Commerce Committee, with its traditional claim on health-related issues, fought with the Agriculture Committee, whose traditional domain includes crops such as tobacco, for jurisdiction. Sometimes new committees, such as the Homeland Security committees, arise at a time of crisis and overlap with the jurisdictions of other existing committees. In these situations, it takes time to sort out turf responsibilities. Indeed, turf battles between committees of Congress are notorious.[30]

Authority. Committees may be thought of as agents of the House or Senate to which the parent body delegates provisional, jurisdiction-specific authority. In this section, we describe committee authority in terms of gatekeeping and after-the-fact authority.

---

30 An outstanding description and analysis of these battles is found in David C. King, "The Nature of Congressional Committee Jurisdictions," *American Political Science Review* 88, no. 1 (March 1994): 48–62. See also King's *Turf Wars: How Congressional Committees Claim Jurisdiction* (Chicago: University of Chicago Press, 1997).

gatekeeping authority ➡

The right and power to decide if a change in policy will be considered.

proposal power ➡

The capacity to bring a proposal before the full legislature.

after-the-fact authority ➡

The authority to follow up on the fate of a proposal once it has been approved by the full chamber.

conference committee ➡

A joint committee created to work out a compromise between House and Senate versions of a bill.

oversight ➡

The effort by Congress, through hearings, investigations, and other techniques, to exercise control over the activities of executive agencies.

Normally any member of the legislature can submit a bill calling for changes in some policy area. Almost automatically this bill is assigned to the committee with jurisdiction, and nearly always, there it languishes. In a typical session in the House of Representatives, about 8,000 bills are submitted, fewer than 1,000 of which see any action by the appropriate committee. In effect, then, although any member is entitled to make proposals, committees get to decide whether to give bills any serious attention and whether to release them to the full chamber for a vote—they can open the gates or not. Related to this **gatekeeping authority** is a committee's **proposal power**. After a bill is referred to a committee, the committee may take no further action on it, amend the legislation in any way, or even write its own additional legislation before bringing the bill to the floor for a vote. Committees, then, are lords of their jurisdictional domains, setting the table, so to speak, for their parent chamber.[31]

In addition to their before-the-fact gatekeeping and proposal powers, committees are also responsible for bargaining with the other chamber and for conducting oversight, in what is known as **after-the-fact authority**. Because Congress is bicameral, once one chamber passes a bill, the other chamber must consider it. If the other chamber passes a bill different from the one passed in the first chamber, and the first chamber refuses to accept the changes, then the two chambers must resolve the differences. Often they meet in a **conference committee**, in which representatives from each chamber hammer out a compromise. In the great majority of cases, conferees are drawn from the committees that had original jurisdiction over the bill.[32] Committees' effective authority to represent their chambers in conference-committee proceedings constitutes the first manifestation of after-the-fact power.[33]

A second manifestation of after-the-fact committee authority consists of committees' primacy in legislative **oversight** of policy implementation by the executive bureaucracy. Even after a bill becomes a law, career bureaucrats in the civil service, commissioners in regulatory agencies, and political appointees in the executive branch may not do precisely what the law requires, especially

---

31 This setup gives committee members extraordinary power in their respective jurisdictions, allowing them to push policy into line with their own preferences—but only up to a point. If the abuse of their agenda power becomes excessive, the parent body has structural and procedural remedies available to counteract the committee's actions, such as stacking the committee with more compliant members, deposing a particularly obstreperous committee chair, or removing policies from a committee's jurisdiction. These measures are rarely employed; their mere presence keeps committees from the more outrageous forms of advantage taking.

32 See Kenneth A. Shepsle and Barry R. Weingast, "The Institutional Foundations of Committee Power," *American Political Science Review* 81, no. 1 (March 1987): 85–104. For a more recent description, see Elizabeth Rybicki, *Conference Committees and Related Procedures: An Introduction*, CRS Report for Congress no. 96-708 (Washington, DC: Congressional Research Service, 2013).

33 In recent years the conference procedure has fallen into relative disuse. Instead, majority-party leaders in each chamber orchestrate back-and-forth negotiations in order to resolve differences between different versions of a bill. This represents a decline in committee power, with party leaders filling the power vacuum.

because statutes are often vague and ambiguous. Congressional committees are thus continuously watchful of the way legislation is implemented and administered. They play this after-the-fact role by allocating staff and resources to track what the executive branch is doing and, from time to time, holding oversight hearings in which policies and programs undergo intense scrutiny. In an extraordinary instance of oversight, former secretary of state Hillary Clinton was intensively grilled by a House committee in 2016 for actions taken, and not taken, by the Obama administration in the wake of the 2012 attack on the U.S. consulate in Benghazi, Libya. In 2018, former FBI director James Comey testified in a House Judiciary Committee oversight hearing regarding his investigation of Hillary Clinton's handling of classified email traffic while she was secretary of state.

The power of oversight, in turn, gives congressional committees an additional source of leverage over policy in their jurisdictions. With unified control of the House, the Senate, and the presidency during the first two years of the Trump administration, Republicans were not inclined to engage in legislative oversight. But since the Democrats won control of the House in the 2018 elections, they have been actively engaging in oversight of Trump and his appointees. We will discuss oversight further in Chapter 8 on the bureaucracy.

Subcommittees. The standing committees of the U.S. House are further divided into about 100 specialized subcommittees. These subcommittees serve their full committees in precisely the same manner as the full committees serve the parent chamber. Thus, in their narrow jurisdictions they have gatekeeping, proposal, interchamber bargaining, and oversight powers. A bill on wheat to be taken up by the full Agriculture Committee, for example, must first clear the subcommittee on General Farm Commodities. All the issues involving assignments, jurisdictions, and authority that apply to full committees apply at the subcommittee level as well.

Hierarchy. At the committee level, the mantle of leadership falls on the committee chair. The chair, together with the party leaders, determines the committee's agenda and then coordinates the committee's staff, investigatory resources, and subcommittee structure.[34] This coordination involves scheduling hearings, "marking up" bills—that is, transforming legislative drafts into final versions— and scripting the process by which a bill goes from committee to floor proceedings to final passage. For many years, Congress followed a rigid **seniority** rule for the selection of committee chairs. The benefits of this rule were twofold. First, it ensured that the chair would be occupied by someone knowledgeable in the committee's jurisdiction, familiar with interest group and executive branch players, and politically experienced. Second, it spared the larger institution divisive leadership contests that reduced the legislative process to efforts in vote

seniority

The priority or status ranking given on the basis of how long an individual has served on a congressional committee.

---

34 Because subcommittee chairs do essentially the same things in their narrower jurisdictions, we won't provide a separate discussion of them.

grubbing. There were costs, however, as senior individuals may be unenergetic, out of touch, even senile. Since the mid-1970s, committee chairs have been elected by the majority-party members of the full legislature, though there remains a presumption (which may be rebutted) that the most senior committee member will normally assume the chair.[35]

Decisiveness on Committees. When a committee goes about its business, its chair exercises agenda power, as noted. But she is not a dictator. Any proposal made by the chair must ultimately secure the support of a majority of committee members. In this setting, who is *decisive*? That is, whose vote is necessary and sufficient for a motion to pass? The answer is provided by the *median voter theorem*. This theorem can be stated as follows: (1) if the alternatives under consideration can be represented as points on a line, (2) if individuals have a most-preferred point, and (3) if their preferences decrease steadily for points farther away, then the most-preferred point of the median (middle) voter can defeat any other point in a majority contest.

In Figure 6.6 we have a five-person committee that must choose a point on the line ranging from 0 to 100. Each member has a favorite point, represented by the peak of his curve, and his preferences decline steadily as points farther and farther away are considered. The median voter theorem asserts that the favorite point of member 3 can beat any other point in a majority contest. A majority comprising members 3, 4, and 5 prefers 3's favorite to any point to its left; a majority comprising members 1, 2, and 3 prefers 3's favorite to any point to its right; therefore 3's favorite can prevail against *any* point. We will discuss the median voter theorem again in Chapter 11 in the context of elections.

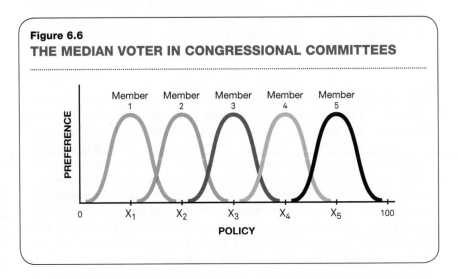

Figure 6.6
THE MEDIAN VOTER IN CONGRESSIONAL COMMITTEES

35 Beginning with the Republican takeover of the House in 1995, committee chairs have been term limited. After three terms, a chair must step down. Today, it appears that party leaders exert more authority in the appointment of new chairs.

Monitoring Committees. If unchecked, committees might take advantage of their authority. Indeed, what prevents committees from exploiting their before-the-fact gatekeeping and proposal power and their after-the-fact bargaining and oversight authority? As we saw in Chapter 1, in our discussion of the principal-agent problem, principals must be certain that agents are properly motivated to serve the principal's interests, either by sharing the principal's interests themselves or by deriving something of value (reputation, compensation, and so on) for acting to advance those interests. Alternatively, principals will need to have some instruments by which to monitor and validate what their agents are doing and to reward or punish them accordingly.

Consider again the example of congressional committees. The House or Senate delegates responsibility to its Committee on Agriculture to recommend legislative policy in the field of agriculture. Legislators from farm districts are most eager to get onto this committee, and for the most part their wishes are accommodated. The Committee on Agriculture, consequently, comprises mainly these farm legislators. And other legislators are relieved at not having to spend their time on issues of little interest to them or their constituents. By constructing the delegation in this way, however, the parent legislature is putting itself in the hands of its farm colleagues, benefiting from their expertise on farm-related matters, to be sure, but laying itself open to the danger of planting the fox squarely in the henhouse. The Committee on Agriculture becomes not only a collection of specialists but also a collection of advocates for farm interests. How can the parent body be certain, therefore, that a recommendation from that committee is not more a reflection of its advocacy than of its expertise? This is the risk inherent in delegation in principal-agent relationships.

For this very reason, the parent legislature maintains a variety of tools and instruments that it uses to protect itself from being exploited by its agents. First, it does not allow committees to make final decisions on policy; it allows only recommendations, which the parent legislature retains the authority to accept, amend, or reject. A committee has agenda power, but it is not by itself decisive. Second, the parent body relies on the committee's concern for its own reputation. Making a recommendation on a piece of legislation is not a one-shot action; the committee will return to the parent body time and time again with legislative recommendations, and it will not want to tarnish its reputation for expertise with too much advocacy. Third, the parent body relies on competing agents—interest groups, expert members not on the committee, specialists in the other chamber of the legislature, executive branch specialists, and even academics—to keep its own agents honest. Fourth, party leaders, through their control of time on the floor, monitor committee products to make sure they are compatible with party goals. Finally, in the House there is an institutional "club behind the door"—the discharge petition. A committee that sits on a bill, denying the full chamber the chance to take it up, can be discharged of responsibility for the bill if a majority of the chamber signs a petition to that effect.

Nevertheless, a principal will not bother to eliminate *entirely* the possibility that agents who have interests of their own will deviate from the principal's interests. A principal will suffer some **agency loss** from having delegated authority to a "hired hand"; therefore, nearly all principal-agent relationships

 agency loss

The difference between what a principal would like an agent to do and the agent's performance.

will be imperfect in some respects from the principal's perspective. The Committee on Agriculture, for example, cannot get away with spending huge proportions of the federal budget on agricultural subsidies to farmers. But it can insert small items into agriculture bills from time to time—an experimental grain-to-fuel conversion project in an important legislator's state or district, for example, or special funds to the U.S. trade representative to prioritize agriculture-related trade issues. The parent body will keep an eye on the Agriculture Committee, but it won't be worth its while to act on every instance of the committee's indulgence. The transaction cost of monitoring and overseeing committee performance gets excessive if perfection is the objective.

Thus, we see the institution principle providing some guidance on how a group of legislators organizes itself for business. The group takes advantage of the division and specialization of labor, dividing its members into specialized subgroups (committees and subcommittees) and benefiting from these subunits' expertise. But the group also guards against the subunits' excessive pursuit of their own narrower interests. The parent legislature in effect uses institutional arrangements to regulate and oversee its subunits' activities.

Committee Reform. Over the years, Congress has reformed its organizational structure and operating procedures. Most changes have served to make Congress more efficient, but some reforms have also come in response to political considerations. In the 1970s, a series of reforms substantially altered the organization of power in Congress; a number of important new rules provided for the election of committee chairs, increased the number of subcommittees, gave greater autonomy to subcommittee chairs, opened most committee deliberations to the public, and created a system of multiple referral that allowed several committees to consider one bill at the same time. One of the driving impulses behind these reforms was an effort to reduce the power of committee chairs.

As a consequence of these reforms, power became more fragmented, making it harder for members of Congress to reach agreement on legislation. To remedy this problem, in 1995, the Republican leadership of the 104th Congress sought to concentrate more authority in the party leadership (something that Democratic leadership had initiated in the 1970s). One of the ways the Republicans achieved this was by continuing the practice of bypassing seniority in the selection of committee chairs, weighing party loyalty heavily instead. This move tied committee chairs more closely to the leadership. In addition, the Republican leadership eliminated 25 of the House's 115 subcommittees and gave committee chairs more power over their subcommittees. The result was an unusually cohesive congressional majority, which pushed forward a common agenda. House Republicans also imposed a three-term limit on committee and subcommittee heads. As a result, all the chairs were replaced in 2001, with a net result of a redistribution of power in the House of Representatives. Since 2001, however, some of the earlier practices have slowly begun to reassert themselves. For example, House Speaker Nancy Pelosi and the Democratic majority in 2007 observed seniority in the appointment of nearly all committee chairs. But appointment is not automatic, and committee chairs are on notice that significant deviations from the majority party's policy consensus will not be tolerated.

The role of committees in the legislative process was evident during President Obama's first term. During the financial crisis, taxing and spending committees played major roles in shepherding a stimulus package and a rescue of the auto industry through both chambers. These committees also monitored the implementation of the earlier rescue of banks and other financial players. During this period, the banking committees produced major regulatory reforms for their industry. At the same time, the health committees produced what ultimately became Obama's health care policy. House Speaker Pelosi and Senate Majority Leader Harry Reid conducted and choreographed these activities. The legislative record of the 111th Congress was thus testimony both to an efficient division- and specialization-of-labor committee system *and* to authoritative and strong party leadership.

The role of committees and strong party leadership was also evident in Obama's second term. But in this case, it was the committees and party leaders of the Republican House majority in the 113th Congress and of the Republican majorities in both the House and Senate in the 114th Congress that thwarted Obama's policy efforts. President Trump had Republican majorities in both legislative chambers in the 115th Congress (2017–18). Though not as legislatively ambitious, this Congress was more like the unified Democratic Congress of Obama's first two years, characterized by specialized committees strictly directed by party leaders. With the House and Senate controlled by different partisan majorities in the 116th Congress, party discipline resulted in Democratic legislative activism in the House being blocked by a cohesive Republican majority in the Senate.

Finally, we should reiterate that the strengthening of party leaders in each chamber—one of the effects of the homogenization of ideology within the parties and the consequent polarization between them—has in turn affected the committee system. It may no longer be assumed that senior committee leaders are the movers and shakers in each chamber. Party leaders have accrued powers that once were enjoyed by these senior committee members. The position of committee chair is still consequential, make no mistake about that, but increasingly the committee chairs serve party leaders and their objectives, whereas in the past it was the reverse.[36]

The Staff System: Staffers and Agencies

A congressional institution ranking just below committees and parties in importance is the staff system. Every member of Congress employs a large number of staff members, whose tasks include handling constituency requests and, to a

---

36 See Andrew B. Hall and Kenneth A. Shepsle, "The Changing Value of Seniority in the U.S. House: Conditional Party Government Revised," *Journal of Politics* 76, no. 1 (Oct 2014): 98–113.

growing extent, dealing with legislative details and the activities of administrative agencies. Increasingly, staffers bear the primary responsibility for drafting proposals, organizing hearings, interfacing with the bureaucracy, and negotiating with lobbyists. Indeed, legislators typically communicate through staff members rather than through direct, personal contact. Representatives and senators together employ nearly 11,000 staffers in their Washington and district (state) offices. In addition, Congress employs roughly 2,000 permanent committee staffers. These individuals, who often keep their positions regardless of turnover in Congress, are responsible for administering each committee's work, doing research, scheduling, organizing hearings, and drafting legislation.

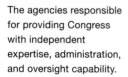

staff agencies

The agencies responsible for providing Congress with independent expertise, administration, and oversight capability.

Congress has also established three **staff agencies** that provide resources and expertise independent of the executive branch. These agencies enhance Congress's capacity to oversee administrative agencies and evaluate presidential programs and proposals. They are the Congressional Research Service, which researches facts and competing arguments relevant to policy proposals or other legislative business; the Government Accountability Office, through which Congress can investigate the financial and administrative affairs of any government agency or program; and the Congressional Budget Office, which assesses the economic implications and likely costs of proposed federal programs.

Informal Organization: The Caucuses

congressional caucus

An association of members of Congress based on party, interest, or social characteristics such as gender or race.

In addition to the official organization of Congress, an unofficial organizational structure also exists: the caucuses, or congressional member organizations (CMOs). A **congressional caucus** is an association of senators or representatives who share certain opinions, interests, or social characteristics. There are ideological caucuses such as the conservative Freedom Caucus. There are also many caucuses representing particular economic or policy interests, such as the Travel and Tourism Caucus, the Steel Caucus, and the Concerned Senators for the Arts. Legislators who share common backgrounds or social characteristics have organized such caucuses as the Congressional Black Caucus, the Women's Caucus, and the Congressional Hispanic Caucus. All these caucuses advance the interests of specific groups by promoting legislation, encouraging Congress to hold hearings, and pressing administrative agencies for favorable treatment.

RULES OF LAWMAKING: HOW A BILL BECOMES A LAW

The institutional structure of Congress, as we have seen, is one key factor that shapes the legislative process. Equally important are the rules that govern congressional procedures, from introducing a bill through submitting it to the president for signing. Not only do these regulations influence the fate of every bill, but they also help determine the distribution of power in Congress.[37]

Committee Deliberation

Even if a member of Congress, the White House, or a federal agency has spent months developing a piece of legislation, it does not become a bill until a representative or a senator officially submits it to the clerk of the House or Senate and it is referred to the appropriate committee for deliberation. No floor action on any bill can occur until the committee with jurisdiction over it has taken all the time it needs to deliberate.[38] During its deliberations, the committee typically refers the bill to a subcommittee, which may hold hearings, listen to expert testimony, and amend the proposed legislation before referring it back to the full committee for consideration. The full committee may accept the recommendation of the subcommittee or hold its own hearings and prepare its own amendments. Even more frequently, the committee and subcommittee may do little or nothing with a bill and simply allow it to die.

Once a bill's assigned committee or committees in the House of Representatives have acted affirmatively, the whole bill or various parts of it are transmitted to the Rules Committee, which determines the rules under which the legislation will be considered by the full House. Together with the Speaker, it influences when debate will be scheduled, for how long, what amendments will be in order, and the order in which they will be considered. The Speaker also rules on all procedural points of order and points of information raised during the debate. A bill's supporters generally prefer a **closed rule**, which puts severe limits on floor debate and prohibits amendments. Opponents of a bill usually prefer an **open rule**, which permits potentially damaging floor debate and makes it easier to add amendments that may cripple the bill or weaken its chances of passing.

closed rule

The provision by the House Rules Committee that restricts the introduction of amendments during debate.

Debate

A bill that passes in committee and clears the Rules Committee is then scheduled for debate by the full House. Majority-party control of the agenda is reinforced by the rule that gives the Speaker of the House and the majority leader of the Senate the power of recognition during debate on a bill. Usually the Speaker or Senate majority leader knows the purpose for which a member intends to

open rule

The provision by the House Rules Committee that permits floor debate and the addition of amendments to a bill.

---

37 We should emphasize that a legislature suspends its rules as often as it follows them. There are unorthodox ways to avoid procedural logjams, and the House and, especially, the Senate frequently resort to them. See Barbara Sinclair, *Unorthodox Lawmaking: New Legislative Processes in the U.S. Congress*, 3rd ed. (Washington, DC: CQ Press, 2007).

38 A bill can be pulled from a committee by a discharge petition, but this extreme measure is resorted to only rarely. Other parliamentary tricks may also be attempted, but most of the time it is the committee of jurisdiction that influences the course of a bill.

speak well in advance of the occasion. Spontaneous efforts to gain recognition are often foiled. For example, the Speaker may ask, "For what purpose does the member rise?" before deciding whether to grant recognition. In general, the party leadership in the House has total control over debate. In the Senate, each member has substantial power to block the close of debate. A simple majority in the House can override a member's opposition to ending debate, whereas it takes an extraordinary majority (60 votes) to close debate in the Senate. In recent years, with partisanship in both chambers on the rise, prolonging debate, using procedural delays, and generally dragging one's feet have been potent tools for the minority to frustrate the majority.

In the House, the bill's sponsor and its leading opponent control virtually all the time allotted by the Rules Committee for debate on a given bill. These two participants have the power to allocate most of the debate time in small amounts to members who seek to speak for or against the measure, though all members must still be recognized by the Speaker.

In the Senate, other than the power of recognition, the leadership has much less control over floor debate. Indeed, the Senate is unique among the world's legislative bodies for its commitment to unlimited debate. Once given the floor, a senator may speak for as long as she wishes unless an extraordinary majority (three-fifths of the members, or 60 senators) votes to set a time limit on debate, a procedure called **cloture**. On a number of memorable occasions, senators have used the right to continue speaking to prevent action on legislation they opposed. Through this tactic, called the **filibuster**, small minorities or even one individual in the Senate can force the majority to give in to their demands. During the 1950s and 1960s, for example, opponents of civil rights legislation often sought to block its passage by filibustering. The filibuster remains potent today, though Senate rules have reduced its value for blocking the confirmation of executive and judicial appointments.

Although it is the best known, the filibuster is not the only technique used to block Senate action. Under Senate rules, members have a virtually unlimited ability to propose amendments to a pending bill. Each amendment must be voted on before the bill can come to a final vote. The introduction of new amendments can be stopped only by unanimous consent. This strategy can permit a determined minority to filibuster by amendment, indefinitely delaying the passage of a bill. Senators can also place anonymous "holds," or stalling devices, on bills to delay debate. Senators do this when they fear that openly opposing the bills will be unpopular. Because holds are kept secret, the senators placing the holds do not have to take public responsibility for their actions.[39]

Once a bill is debated on the floor of the House and the Senate, the leaders schedule it for a vote on the floor of each chamber. Leaders do not bring legislation to the floor unless they are fairly certain it is going to pass. On rare occasions, however, the last moments of the floor vote can be dramatic, as each

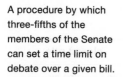

cloture

A procedure by which three-fifths of the members of the Senate can set a time limit on debate over a given bill.

filibuster

A tactic in which members of the Senate prevent action on legislation they oppose by continuously holding the floor and speaking until the majority abandons the legislation. Once given the floor, senators have unlimited time to speak, and a cloture vote by three-fifths of the Senate is required to end a filibuster.

---

39 This and other features of the Senate rules came under intense scrutiny in the 112th Congress (2011–12) and remain on the reform agenda today. The ability to maintain the anonymity of the senator placing a hold has been reduced.

---

party's leadership puts its whip organization into action to make sure wavering members vote with the party.

Conference Committee: Reconciling House and Senate Versions of a Bill

Getting a bill out of committee and through both houses of Congress is no guarantee that it will be enacted. Frequently bills that began with similar provisions in both chambers emerge at odds with one another. For example, a bill may be passed unchanged by one chamber but undergo substantial revision in the other. If the differences cannot be worked out by passing the revised version back to the first chamber and having it accept any changes, a conference committee composed of the senior members of the committees or subcommittees that initiated the bills may be assembled to iron out differences. Sometimes members or leaders will let objectionable provisions pass on the floor with the idea that they will be eliminated in conference. Conference agreement requires majority support from both the House delegation and the Senate delegation. Legislation that emerges successfully from a conference committee is more often a compromise than a clear victory of one set of forces over another.

When a bill comes out of conference, it faces one more hurdle. Before it can be sent to the president for signing, the House-Senate conference report must be approved on the floor of each chamber. It must be voted up or down; no amendments are in order. Usually such approval comes quickly. Occasionally, however, a bill's opponents use the report as one last opportunity to defeat a piece of legislation.[40]

Presidential Action

Once adopted by the House and the Senate, a bill goes to the president, who may choose to sign the bill into law or **veto** it (Figure 6.7). The veto is the president's constitutional power to reject acts of Congress. To veto a bill, the president returns it within 10 days to the house of Congress in which it originated, along with his objections to it. If Congress adjourns during the 10-day period and the president has taken no action, the bill is considered to have been vetoed by means of the **pocket veto**. The possibility of a presidential veto affects legislators' willingness to push for different pieces of legislation at different times. If they think a proposal is likely to be vetoed, they might shelve it for a later time. Alternatively, the sponsors of a popular bill that is opposed by the president might push for passage to force the president to pay the political costs of vetoing it.[41] In President Obama's first term, he vetoed only two bills. This low

 veto

The president's constitutional power to reject acts of Congress.

 pocket veto

A veto that occurs automatically when Congress adjourns during the 10 days a president has to approve a bill and the president has taken no action on it.

40 In recent years party leaders have replaced the conference procedure. Instead, they negotiate a compromise between House and Senate versions of a measure themselves and bring their version to their respective chambers for a final passage vote.

41 John B. Gilmour, *Strategic Disagreement: Stalemate in American Politics* (Pittsburgh: University of Pittsburgh Press, 1995).

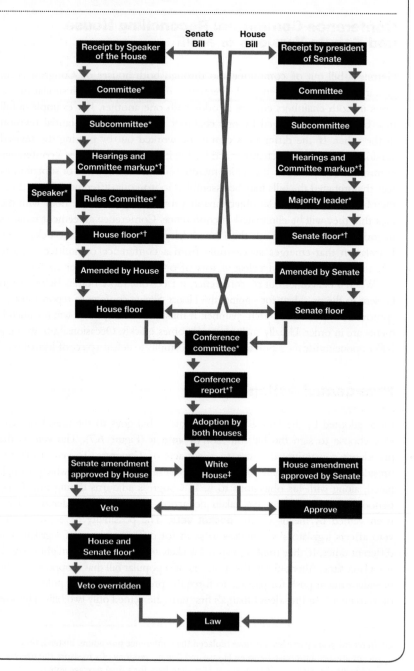

Figure 6.7
HOW A BILL BECOMES A LAW

ANALYZING THE EVIDENCE

A bill must pass through many stages and succeed at all of them to become a law. To prevent a bill from becoming a law, opponents need prevail at only one stage. What effects do the complications in the process have on policy outcomes?

Senate Bill

House Bill

Receipt by Speaker of the House

Receipt by president of Senate

Committee*

Committee

Subcommittee*

Subcommittee

Hearings and Committee markup*†

Hearings and Committee markup*†

Speaker*

Rules Committee*

Majority leader*

House floor*†

Senate floor*†

Amended by House

Amended by Senate

House floor

Senate floor

Conference committee*

Conference report*†

Adoption by both houses

Senate amendment approved by House

White House‡

House amendment approved by Senate

Veto

Approve

House and Senate floor*

Veto overridden

Law

*Points at which the bill can be amended.
†Points at which the bill can die.
‡If the president neither signs nor vetoes the bill within 10 days, it automatically becomes law.

veto rate reflected the fact that Obama's party controlled at least one chamber of Congress during his first term. By contrast, in his last two years in office, when the Republican Party controlled both chambers of Congress, Obama vetoed 10 bills. Similarly, in President Trump's first two years in office, with his party holding a majority in each chamber, the president did not have to use his veto pen. Once Trump lost his majority in the House after the 2018 midterm election, his veto activity increased (but only slightly, since many bills initiated by the Democratic House were either defeated or not taken up at all by the Republican Senate).

A presidential veto may be overridden by a two-thirds vote in both the House and the Senate. A veto override says much about the support that a president can expect from Congress, and it can deliver a stinging blow to the executive branch. For example, in 2007 when President George W. Bush vetoed a popular pork-barrel bill, the Water Resources Development Act, both houses overwhelmingly overrode Bush's veto. Near the end of Obama's second term in September 2016, to take another example, both houses decisively overrode his veto of the Justice Against Sponsors of Terrorism Act, which permits families of the victims of September 11 to sue the Saudi Arabian government for damages. In fact, presidents will often back down from their threat to veto a bill if they believe Congress will override the veto. However, congressional proponents will often modify or withdraw entirely a bill that the president threatens to veto. We will take up these strategic interactions between the legislature and the executive branch in the next chapter.

Procedures in Congress: Regular and Unorthodox

As it has become more difficult to pass legislation through regular processes, the total number of acts passed by Congress has declined (see the Timeplot on pp. 238-9). Unorthodox procedures are often seen as necessary to pass legislation, especially as party polarization has increased in recent decades.[42] The final passage of President Obama's health care bill in 2010 provides an excellent example. The House initially passed a health care bill in November 2009 with no Republican support and much grumbling from some Democrats who were unhappy with various aspects of the legislation. But the Senate was the real battleground. A Senate version of the health care bill passed on Christmas Eve, 2009. Upon their return from the holiday recess, Democratic leaders in the House and Senate plotted how to combine the two versions. But a shock disrupted their plans: on January 19, 2010, Scott Brown, a Republican, won the Senate seat for Massachusetts that had been temporarily held by a Democrat after the death of Senator Ted Kennedy, a Democrat and a strong supporter of health care reform. Until Brown's election, which put the number of Republican senators at 41, the Senate had been filibuster-proof with 60 Democrats in the majority. Now the Republican minority could block any further vote in the Senate to approve changes to the health care bill. What was to be done?

---

42 See James M. Curry, *Legislating in the Dark: Information and Power in the House of Representatives* (Chicago: University of Chicago Press, 2015).

The Democrats took an unusual route. Speaker Pelosi and the Democratic leadership convinced Democrats in the House to support the Senate version of the bill, passing it by a vote of 219 to 212. The identical bill was thus passed by both chambers, and no further vote was needed in the Senate. House Democrats were not happy with the Senate version, but they were placated by the promise of a second bill in which their concerns would be addressed. The second bill employed the so-called reconciliation procedure, a mechanism normally reserved for spending and budgeting subjects (so somewhat novel in this context), which requires only a simple majority in each chamber. Thus, a filibuster was avoided in the Senate. On March 21, the House passed this second bill, 220 to 211; four days later the Senate passed it, 56 to 43; and the way was clear for Obama to sign health care reform into law.

Before leaving this topic, it is worth noting that normal and abnormal procedures involve either the conventional or the creative application of existing rules. However, the Constitution grants each chamber the privilege of formulating its own rules of procedure. So, from time to time, the House or the Senate will change its rules. At other times, a dominant coalition in a chamber will threaten to do so unless it is allowed its way under the existing rules. Here we see the confluence of the rationality principle and the institution principle, as rational legislators seek to (re)arrange their chamber's institutional procedures to accomplish purposes or realize goals.

This phenomenon was dramatically illustrated in May 2005, when President Bush's nominations to the federal judiciary were put before the Senate for approval. Even though Republicans held a majority, Democratic senators threatened to filibuster Bush's nominations. In the face of a potential blocking action by the minority party, the Senate majority leader unveiled the *nuclear option*—a clever parliamentary maneuver in which debate could be ended not by securing the 60 votes normally required (which the Republicans did not control) but by a simple majority. To execute the nuclear option, Republicans would request the Senate president to end debate without a cloture vote because the issue was the constitutional one of "advising and consenting" on a presidential judicial nomination. It was expected that Democrats would then appeal any ruling by the Senate president to end debate. But that ruling required only a majority vote to be sustained. In this manner, the Republicans could end-run the practice of unlimited debate that normally prevails in the Senate.

The nuclear option was not implemented at that time, however. The very threat of it induced some moderate senators to support a motion to end debate (thereby producing the 60 needed votes) and bring a presidential nominee forward for a final vote. These senators agreed to accommodate future votes so long as the president and the Republican majority did not abuse their concession by bringing forward "extremist" nominees.[43]

This compromise sufficed for a few years, but during the Obama presidency, the same issue arose: now a Democratic president was prevented from

---

43 For a model of the judicial confirmation process, see David W. Rohde and Kenneth A. Shepsle, "Advising and Consenting in the 60-Vote Senate: Strategic Appointments to the Supreme Court," *Journal of Politics* 69, no. 3 (Aug. 2007): 664–77.

---

appointing judges and senior executive branch officials by a determined Republican minority. Senate Majority Leader Harry Reid invoked the nuclear option. As a result of Reid's maneuver, presidential executive appointments and all judicial nominations except those to the Supreme Court required only a simple majority to end debate and proceed to a vote on confirmation. In 2017, one of President Trump's nominees to the Supreme Court was blocked by minority Democratic obstruction, forcing Majority Leader Mitch McConnell to expand the nuclear option to include Supreme Court nominations. This enabled the 52-member Republican majority to end debate and confirm Neil Gorsuch to the Court. Likewise, by simple majority votes, the Republican Senate confirmed Brett Kavanaugh in 2018 and Amy Coney Barrett in 2020.

The Distributive Tendency in Congress

To pass a policy, Congress must provide statutory authority to a government agency to implement the legislation and then appropriate funds for the policy's implementation. The list of politicians whose consent is required in these processes is extraordinarily long. At a minimum, it includes majorities of the relevant committees and subcommittees of each chamber (almost certainly including their chairs), the Appropriations Committees and relevant appropriations subcommittees in each chamber (including their chairs), the House Rules Committee, chamber majorities (including leaders of the majority party), and the president. Some legislators may go along with this process without requiring much for their states or districts in return, on the assumption that their turn will come on another bill. But most of these politicians negotiate some form of compensation for providing their support.

With so many hurdles to clear before a legislative initiative can become a law, the benefits must be spread broadly. It is as though bills travel on a toll road past a number of tollbooths, each one housing a collector with her hand out for payment. On some occasions, the toll takes the form of a personal bribe—a contract to a firm run by a congressman's brother, a job for a senator's daughter, a "military inspection" trip to a Pacific isle for a legislator and his companion. Occasionally there is a wink-and-a-nod understanding, usually given by the majority leader or committee chair, that support from a legislator today will ensure reciprocal support for legislation of interest to her down the road.

More frequently, however, a bill becomes widely attractive by making its provisions more inclusive, spreading the benefits among a broad set of beneficiaries. This is the **distributive tendency**. The distributive tendency is part of the American system of representative democracy. In advocating their constituents' interests, legislators are eager to advertise their ability to deliver for their state or district. They maneuver to put themselves in a position to claim credit for good things and duck blame for bad things. This is the way they earn trust back home, deter strong challengers in upcoming elections, and defeat those who run against them. It means that legislators must take advantage of every opportunity to secure funding that presents itself. In some instances, the results may seem bizarre. In April 2003, for example, a senator from Mississippi

 distributive tendency

The tendency of Congress to spread the benefits of a policy over a wide range of members' districts.

Acts Passed by Congress, 1789–2019

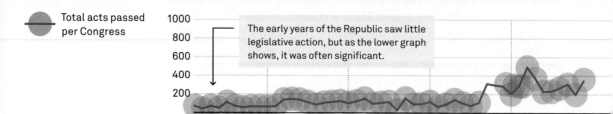

Total acts passed
per Congress

1000
800
600
400
200

The early years of the Republic saw little
legislative action, but as the lower graph
shows, it was often significant.

1789   1807   1827   1847   1867

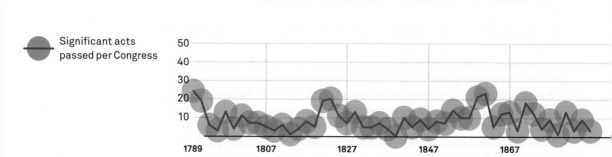

Significant acts
passed per Congress

50
40
30
20
10

1789   1807   1827   1847   1867

TIMEPLOT SOURCE:
George B. Galloway,
*History of the United States
House of Representatives*,
revised by Sidney Wise,
2nd ed. (New York:
Thomas Y. Crowell, 1976);
and Library of Congress,
www.congress.gov/
legislation?q=%7B%22-
bill-status%22%3A%
22law%22%7D
(accessed 9/10/20).

inserted language into the bill funding the war in Iraq providing $250 million for "disaster relief" for southern catfish farmers.[44] Most Americans would never have guessed that driving Saddam Hussein from power would have an effect on catfish farming in Mississippi.

This system, which is practiced in Washington and most state capitals, means that political pork gets spread around; it is not controlled by a small clique of politicians. But it also means that public authority and appropriations do not go where they are most needed. The most impoverished cities do not get as much money as they need because some of the available money gets diverted to buy political support. The neediest individuals often do not get tax relief, health care, or occupational subsidies for reasons unrelated to philosophy or policy grounds. It is the distributive tendency at work. And it is one of the unintended consequences of the separation of powers and multiple veto

44 Interest groups from a legislator's home state or district (which we discuss later) can provide useful information concerning the significance of particular issues for various constituency groups. See Ken Kollman, *Outside Lobbying: Public Opinion and Interest Group Strategies* (Princeton, NJ: Princeton University Press, 1998).

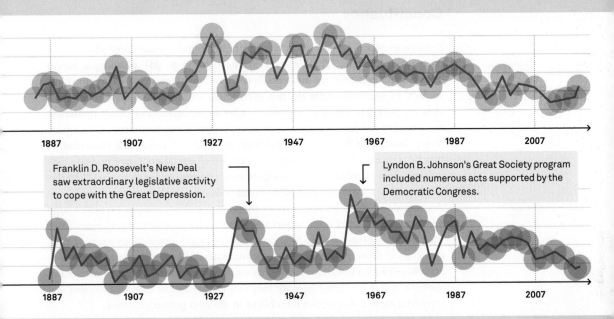

1887   1907   1927   1947   1967   1987   2007

Franklin D. Roosevelt's New Deal saw extraordinary legislative activity to cope with the Great Depression.

Lyndon B. Johnson's Great Society program included numerous acts supported by the Democratic Congress.

1887   1907   1927   1947   1967   1987   2007

points.[45] As the policy principle suggests, legislators, in accordance with the rationality principle, take advantage of institutional practices to leave their marks on the shape of policy.

HOW CONGRESS DECIDES

What determines the kinds of legislation that Congress ultimately produces? The process of creating a legislative agenda, drawing up a list of possible measures, and deciding among them is very complex. In this process, a variety of influences from inside and outside government play important roles. External influences include legislators' constituents and various interest groups.

45 See George Tsebelis, *Veto Players: How Political Institutions Work* (Princeton, NJ: Princeton University Press, 2002).

Influences from inside government include party leadership, congressional colleagues, and the president. Let's examine each of these influences individually and then consider how they interact to produce congressional policy decisions.[46]

Constituency

Because members of Congress want to be reelected, constituents' views influence their decisions. The Policy Principle box on p. 241 provides a recent example. Yet constituency influence is not so straightforward as we might think. In fact, most constituents do not even know what policies their representatives support. The number of citizens who *do* pay attention to such matters— the attentive public—is usually very small. Nonetheless, members of Congress worry about what their constituents think because they realize that their choices may be scrutinized in future elections and used as ammunition by opposing candidates. Thus members try to anticipate their constituents' policy views.[47] In this way, constituents may affect congressional policy choices even when there is little direct evidence that they are aware of those choices. For example, because a large number of voters will not support a candidate who supports cuts to mandatory spending programs such as Medicare, legislators are unwilling to support such cuts even as those programs approach unsustainable levels. Similarly, even moderate Republicans in Congress support very conservative positions on issues like abortion and gun control because they fear the possibility that angry voters will support a more conservative Republican in the next primary election.

Interest Groups

Interest groups are another important external influence on the policies that Congress produces. When members are deciding how to vote, interest groups that have some connection to the members' constituents or districts are most likely to be influential. For this reason, interest groups with the ability to mobilize followers in many congressional districts may be especially influential. The small business lobby, for example, played an important role in defeating President Clinton's proposal for comprehensive health care reform in 1993–94. The mobilization of networks of small businesses across the country meant that virtually every member of Congress had to take their views into account. In 2009, the Obama administration brought small business groups and the insurance industry

---

46 There are, of course, many other factors, including differences between the chambers, the different electoral cycles for representatives and senators, and the agenda inherited from the unfinished business of earlier legislative sessions.

47 See John W. Kingdon, *Congressmen's Voting Decisions* (New York: Harper and Row, 1973), chap. 3; and R. Douglas Arnold, *The Logic of Congressional Action* (New Haven, CT: Yale University Press, 1990). See also Joshua D. Clinton, "Representation in Congress: Constituents and Roll Calls in the 106th House," *Journal of Politics* 68, no. 2 (May 2006): 397–409.

Congress and the Opioid Epidemic

More than 70,000 people died of drug overdoses in 2017, and the majority of those deaths involved opioid drugs such as heroin, prescription painkillers, and fentanyl (a synthetic opioid). An estimated 2 million Americans suffer from an opioid use disorder.[1] The Centers for Disease Control and Prevention calculated the economic burden of prescription drug misuse (just one part of the opioid epidemic) at nearly $80 billion a year. Among Americans, 43 percent view the use of prescription pain drugs as a very serious or extremely serious problem in their communities, and 37 percent say the same about heroin.[2]

Awareness of this growing opioid epidemic has also reached Capitol Hill. During the 115th Congress (2017–18), members introduced more than 200 separate bills mentioning opioids, and during the 114th (2015–16), 153 such bills were introduced—a very significant increase from the previous two Congresses. In the 113th, only 24 bills even mentioned the word "opioid," and in the 112th there were only four.[3]

One reason for this proliferation of bills addressing the same policy issue is that members of Congress, who want to be reelected, seek to demonstrate their interest in addressing their constituents' concerns. The institutional rules of Congress, specifically the fragmentation of authority between chambers and across numerous committees, have contributed to the fragmented approach.

One concern about Congress's approach to the problem is the use of discretionary spending (common practice in federal policy making), which requires yearly action by the appropriation process to actually allocate any funding to the program. Significant funding to address the opioid crisis was included in the Bipartisan Budget Act of 2018—with $4.6 billion budgeted for law enforcement, prevention, and treatment programs. But because the new funds are discretionary spending rather than mandatory spending, it is uncertain whether Congress will continue to fund these efforts at this level in future years.

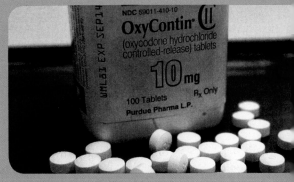

Congress's piecemeal approach to the opioid epidemic has disappointed advocates.

This congressional response to the opioid epidemic reflects a common pattern described by political scientists Timothy Conlan, Paul Posner, and David Beam, who identify four common pathways by which policies are enacted.[4] One of their pathways is the "symbolic pathway," which is characterized by the following sequence of events: the public becomes aware of a problem that must be solved, and Congress takes action to respond. However, members of Congress have a greater incentive to respond quickly than to craft comprehensive and substantive legislative solutions. As a result, policies that take shape via the symbolic pathway are often underfunded or poorly coordinated, and therefore less effective on the ground.

[1] U.S. Department of Health and Human Services, "The Opioid Epidemic by the Numbers," www.hhs.gov/opioids/sites/default/files/2018-01/opioids-infographic.pdf (accessed 7/17/18).
[2] Associated Press-NORC Center for Public Affairs Research, "Americans Recognize the Growing Problem of Opioid Addiction," Issue Brief, April 2018, www.apnorc.org/PDFs/Opioids%202018/APNORC_Opioids_Report_2018.pdf.
[3] Congress.gov, www.congress.gov (accessed 7/17/18).
[4] Timothy J. Conlan, Paul L. Posner, and David R. Beam, Pathways of Power: The Dynamics of National Policymaking (Washington, DC: Georgetown University Press, 2014).

into their planning for health care reform early in the process precisely for this reason. Today many Republican legislators who are committed to replacing the Affordable Care Act feel pressure from citizen groups, the insurance industry, and others dependent on features of the act to "amend it, don't end it," causing great complications for President Trump and Republican legislative leaders.

In addition to mobilizing voters, interest groups contribute money. In the 2018 and 2020 electoral cycles, interest groups and PACs gave many millions of dollars in campaign contributions to both incumbent legislators and challengers. What does this money buy? A popular conception is that campaign contributions buy legislative votes—that they are, in effect, bribes. In this view, legislators vote for whichever proposal favors the bulk of their contributors. Although the vote-buying hypothesis makes for good campaign rhetoric, it has little factual support. Empirical studies by political scientists show little evidence that contributions from large PACs influence legislative voting patterns.[48]

If contributions don't buy votes, what do they buy? Campaign contributions influence legislative behavior in ways that are difficult for the public to observe and political scientists to measure. The institutional structure of Congress provides opportunities for interest groups to influence legislation outside the public eye, which legislators and contributors prefer.

Committee proposal power enables legislators on the relevant committees to introduce legislation that favors contributing groups. Gatekeeping power enables committee members to block legislation that would harm contributing groups. The fact that certain provisions are *excluded* from a bill is just as much an indicator of PAC influence as the fact that certain provisions are *included*. The difference is that it is hard to measure what you don't see. Committee oversight powers enable members to intervene in bureaucratic decision making on behalf of contributing groups.

The point here is that voting on the floor, the alleged object of campaign contributions according to the vote-buying hypothesis, is a highly visible, highly public act, one that could get a legislator in trouble with his broader electoral constituency. The committee system, in contrast, provides numerous opportunities for legislators to deliver "services" to PAC contributors and other donors that are better hidden from public view. Thus, the most appropriate places to look for traces of donor and interest group influence are in the manner in which committees deliberate, mark up proposals, and block legislation from the floor.[49]

Interest groups mobilize voters and contribute campaign funds, but they also convey information. While it is true that legislators become specialists, acquire expertise, and hire expert staff to assist them, for much specialized knowledge,

---

48 See Jacobson and Carson, *The Politics of Congressional Elections*. For a view that interest groups spend too little, not too much, money, see Stephen Ansolabehere, John M. de Figueiredo, and James M. Snyder Jr., "Why Is There So Little Money in U.S. Politics?" *Journal of Economic Perspectives* 17, no. 1 (Winter 2003): 105–30.

49 A complementary effect of campaign contributions is not to buy the votes of legislators who are unlikely to vote in favor of a donor's cause. It is, rather, to increase the likelihood that legislators *already sympathetic* to the cause will be reelected. Interest groups thus primarily support their friends, rather than their opponents, with contributions.

Figure 6.8
PARTY UNITY SCORES BY CHAMBER

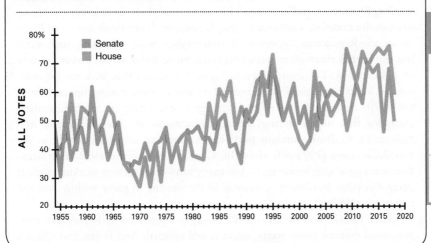

NOTE: The scores represent the percentage of recorded votes on which the majority of one party voted against the majority of the other party.
SOURCE: Roll Call, www.rollcall.com/news/congress/party-unity-congressional-votes (accessed 12/17/19).

ANALYZING THE EVIDENCE

Party voting increased in the 1970s and has remained fairly high since then. What contributes to party voting?

especially about how policies will affect local constituencies, they depend on lobbyists. Informational lobbying is a very important inside-the-beltway activity. Interest group expenditures on lobbying dwarf the money that they give in campaign contributions.[50]

Party Discipline

In both the House and the Senate, party leaders have substantial influence over their party members' behavior. This influence, sometimes called party discipline, was once so powerful that it dominated the lawmaking process. Let's define as a **party vote** a roll-call vote in the House or Senate in which at least 50 percent of the members of one party take a particular position and are opposed by at least 50 percent of the members of the other party. At the beginning of the twentieth century, most **roll-call votes** in both chambers were party votes. The frequency of party votes declined through most of the twentieth century as the legislative parties grew more ideologically diverse. Democrats included liberals from the big cities and conservatives from the South. Republicans included conservatives from the Midwest and West and moderates from the Northeast. The tail end of this decline in party voting, evident in Figure 6.8, is roughly between 1970 and 1975.

 party vote

A roll-call vote in the House or Senate in which at least 50 percent of the members of one party take a particular position and are opposed by at least 50 percent of the members of the other party.

roll-call votes

Voting in which each legislator's yes or no vote is recorded.

50 See Morten Bennedsen and Sven E. Feldmann, "Informational Lobbying and Political Contributions," *Journal of Public Economics* 90 (May 2006): 631–56.

Beginning in the 1970s, however, the legislative parties in the House grew more homogeneous and more polarized. Conservative southern districts began electing Republicans, and liberal northeastern districts began sending Democrats to Congress. This meant that there were fewer conservatives in the ranks of Democratic legislators, and fewer moderates and liberals among Republican legislators. Party members were becoming more alike, but the parties themselves were becoming more different—the very essence of polarization. The data shown in Figure 6.8 reflect this, with the percentage of votes that could be classified as party votes ticking upward from the 1970s onward. Some of this change is the result of intense partisan struggles that began during the administrations of Ronald Reagan and George H. W. Bush. Straight party-line voting was also seen briefly in the 103rd Congress (1993–94) after Bill Clinton's election in 1992. The situation soon gave way, however, to the many long-term factors working against party discipline in Congress, as seen in the decline in party voting over the rest of the 1990s.[51]

Since the election of George W. Bush, accompanied by Republican congressional control, party voting again ticked upward. And in the first Obama administration, party voting in both chambers was strong; Republican votes supporting Obama initiatives were quite rare.[52] Obama's second term showed little improvement and, in the midterm election of 2014, the Republicans increased their House majority and won control of the Senate. With the Republicans now in complete control of Congress, they had to assume some responsibility for governing; a degree of bargaining between them and the minority Democrats emerged as a consequence. The Trump years witnessed little bargaining between the parties and a return to earlier form—namely, high levels of partisan voting with members rarely crossing the aisle to vote with the other party.

To some extent, party divisions are based on ideology and background. Republican members of Congress are more likely than Democrats to be drawn from rural or suburban areas. Democrats are likely to be more liberal on economic and social questions than their Republican colleagues. This ideological gap has been especially pronounced since 1980 (Figure 6.9).[53] Differences in ideology and background certainly help explain roll-call

---

51 There were fluctuations during George W. Bush's presidency; party voting declined following September 11 and then surged and declined in subsequent years (see Figure 6.8).

52 One of the hidden consequences of party polarization is what is *not* voted on. In the Senate, especially, the majority leader often pulls from the floor bills that would be sunk by unified minority opposition.

53 Figure 6.9 is slightly misleading in its depiction of southern Democrats. This group is becoming more liberal, but for a nonobvious reason: there are fewer and fewer southern Democrats, with the ones remaining most likely to be minority legislators or to represent urban districts.

Figure 6.9

THE WIDENING IDEOLOGICAL GAP BETWEEN THE PARTIES

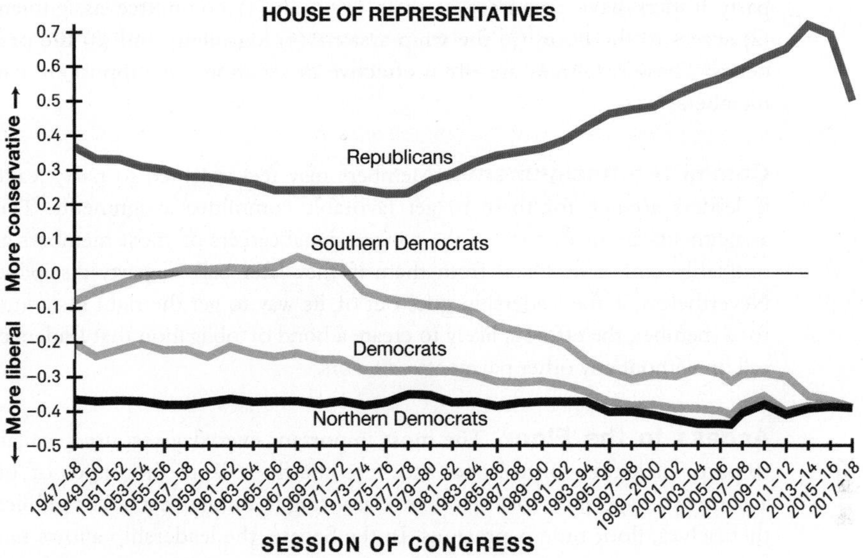

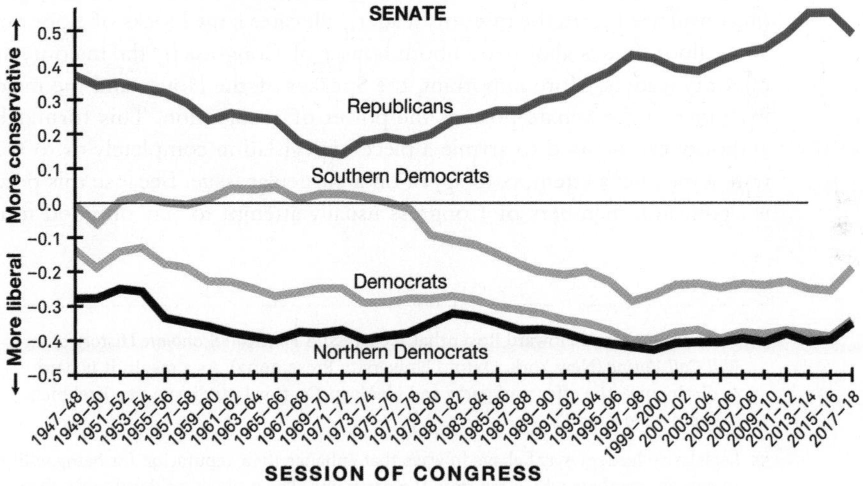

SOURCE: Voteview, http://voteview.org/political_polarization_2015.htm (accessed 5/24/20).

divisions between the two parties, but they are only part of the explanation.[54] The other part has to do with party organization and leadership. Although legislative party organization weakened throughout most of the twentieth century, there was an uptick in the late 1970s and early 1980s. Today's party leaders have resources at their disposal: (1) committee assignments, (2) access to the floor, (3) the whip system, (4) logrolling, and (5) the presidency. These resources are often effective in securing the support of party members.[55]

Committee Assignments. Members may feel indebted to party leaders if leaders arrange for them to get favorable committee assignments. These assignments are made early in the congressional careers of most members and ordinarily cannot be taken from them if they later balk at party discipline.[56] Nevertheless, if the leadership goes out of its way to get the right assignment for a member, the effort is likely to create a bond of obligation that leaders can call on without any other payments or favors.

Access to the Floor. The most important everyday resource available to party leaders is control over access to the floor. With thousands of bills awaiting passage and most members clamoring to influence a bill or publicize themselves, floor time is precious. In the Senate, the leadership allows ranking committee members to influence the allocation of floor time—who will speak for how long. In the House, the Speaker, as head of the majority party (in consultation with the minority leader), allocates large blocks of floor time. Thus, floor time is allocated in both houses of Congress by the majority and minority leaders. More important, the Speaker of the House and the majority leader in the Senate possess the power of recognition. This formidable authority can be used to stymie a piece of legislation completely or to frustrate a member's attempts to speak on a particular issue. Because this power is significant, members of Congress usually attempt to stay on good terms

54 Keith T. Poole and Howard Rosenthal, *Congress: A Political-Economic History of Roll Call Voting* (New York: Oxford University Press, 1997). As a result, it is hard to distinguish the effects of party and ideology. On this latter issue, see Krehbiel, "Where's the Party?"

55 Legislative leaders may behave in ways that enhance their reputation for being willing to punish members who stray from the party line. The problem of developing such a credible reputation is analyzed in Randall L. Calvert, "Reputation and Legislative Leadership," *Public Choice* 55 (Sep. 1987): 81–119, and is summarized in Kenneth A. Shepsle, *Analyzing Politics: Rationality, Behavior, and Institutions,* 2nd ed. (New York: Norton, 2010), pp. 460–8.

56 There have been occasions in which members have lost their committee posts because of their failure to support the leadership. In a bold move at the end of the 112th Congress, for example, as the nation approached an end-of-year set of tax and spending deadlines, Speaker John Boehner removed several recalcitrant Republicans from the Budget Committee.

with the Speaker and the Senate majority leader to ensure they will continue to be recognized.[57]

The Whip System. Some influence accrues to party leaders through the **whip system**, which is primarily a communications network. Between 12 and 20 assistant and regional whips are selected by geographic zones to operate at the direction of the majority or minority leader and the majority or minority whip. They poll all the members of Congress to learn their intentions on specific bills. This information lets the leaders know if they have enough support to allow a vote or if the vote is so close that they need to put pressure on a few swing votes. Leaders also use the whip system to convey their wishes and plans to the members.[58]

Logrolling. An agreement between two or more members of Congress who have nothing in common except the need for mutual support is called **logrolling**. The agreement states, in effect, "You support me on bill X, and I'll support you on a bill of your choice." Because party leaders are the center of the communications networks in the two chambers, they can help members create large logrolling coalitions. Hundreds of logrolling deals are made each year, and although there are no official records, it would be a poor party leader whose whips did not know who owed what to whom.[59]

In some instances, logrolling produces strange alliances. A seemingly unlikely alliance emerged in Congress in 1994, when 119 mainly conservative senators and representatives from oil-producing states met with President Clinton to suggest they might be willing to support the president's health care proposals in exchange for his support for certain tax breaks for the oil industry. Another strange alliance came together in favor of the Trans-Pacific Partnership (TPP), a trade deal sought by Democratic President Obama in 2015 and supported mainly by *Republicans*. The logroll would open up Asian markets to U.S. exports, something favored by Republicans and their friends

whip system

A party communications network in each house of Congress. Whips poll their party's members to learn their intentions on specific bills and also convey the leadership's views and plans to members.

logrolling

Agreements among members of Congress to vote for one another's bills.

---

57 An analysis of how floor time is allocated is found in Cox and McCubbins, *Setting the Agenda.*

58 Needless to say, the structure of the whip system varies over time, between chambers, and between parties.

59 For an analysis of the formal problems that logrolling (or vote trading) both solves and creates, see Shepsle, *Analyzing Politics,* pp. 374–6. It is argued there that logrolling cannot be the entire solution to the problem of assembling majority coalitions from the diverse preferences found in any political party. The reason is that, although party leaders can try to keep track of who owes what to whom, the bookkeeping is imperfect and highly complex at best. Nevertheless, if anyone is positioned to orchestrate a system of logrolling, it is the party leaders. And of all those who have tried to facilitate such "cooperation," Robert Byrd (D-W.Va.), who served as both majority whip and majority leader in the Senate during the late twentieth century, was the acknowledged master. For an insightful analysis of the ways party leaders build majority coalitions through the strategic use of pork-barrel projects, see Evans, *Greasing the Wheels.*

in the business community, in exchange for the imposition of environmental restrictions and labor market liberalization in Asian economies, reforms favored by the president and some of his Democratic allies. Many Democrats and their union supporters, however, opposed the deal because they feared that it would adversely affect manufacturing employment in the United States. Good logrolling, it would seem, is not hampered by minor ideological concerns. Nevertheless, soon after taking office in 2017, President Trump withdrew from the TPP, stealing a tune from the Democratic songbook: he justified withdrawal because the TPP would, he claimed, harm American industry and cost workers (many of whom had voted for him) their manufacturing jobs.

Logrolling, to sum up, works when members are willing to support a policy that they do not like in exchange for reciprocal support for a policy that they care passionately about (the rationality principle), and when separation-of-powers institutional arrangements allow the president, party leaders, and legislators to cut deals (the institution principle).

The Presidency. Of all the influences that maintain the clarity of party lines in Congress, the influence of the presidency is probably the most important. Indeed, it is a touchstone of party discipline in Congress. Since the late 1940s, under President Harry Truman, presidents each year have identified bills to be considered part of their administration's program. By the mid-1950s, both parties in Congress began to look to the president for these proposals, which became the most significant part of Congress's agenda. Some major presidential initiatives, like Dwight D. Eisenhower's program to build a national highway system in the mid-1950s, persuaded leaders of *both* parties to push their followers to support the program. In recent years, however, support for and opposition to presidential initiatives has come to define party loyalty; fellow partisans are expected to support their president's initiatives while the other party's members oppose them. The Affordable Care Act of 2010 (commonly called Obamacare) was the classic instance of a presidential initiative that plainly and unmistakably drew party lines and defined party loyalty. With Trump in the White House and Republican majorities in both legislative chambers during his first two years, legislators' intent to repeal Obamacare also clearly drew party lines. But Republicans found it difficult to unite around a viable replacement. They did, however, unite effectively in support of a major tax bill in 2018, and again in 2020 during the coronovirus pandemic to support legislation to mitigate economic pain from extensive job losses, among other issues.

Weighing Diverse Influences

Clearly many factors affect congressional decisions. But at various points in the decision-making process, some factors are more influential than others. For example, interest groups may be more effective at the committee stage, when their expertise is especially valued and their visibility is less obvious. Because committees play a key role in deciding what legislation reaches the floor of the House or the Senate, interest groups can often put a halt to bills they dislike, or they can ensure that options that do reach the floor are those that the group's members support. To take another example, once legislation reaches the floor and members of Congress are deciding among alternatives in visible roll-call votes, constituents' opinions will become more important.

The influence of the external and internal forces that we have so far described also varies according to the kind of issue under consideration. On policies of great importance to powerful interest groups—farm subsidies, for example—those groups are likely to have considerable influence. On other issues, members of Congress may be less attentive to narrow interest groups and more willing to consider what they see as the general interest.

Finally, the mix of influences varies according to the historical moment. Democrats had hoped 2020 would be another historically significant election. And it was: the successful Biden-Harris ticket meant that Kamala Harris is the first woman, the first person of color, the first American of South Asian descent, and the first child of immigrants to be chosen as vice president. But in another sense it was significant in a way not wished for by the Democrats: for the first time in history a president was elected along with losses for his party in the House of Representatives.

BEYOND LEGISLATION: ADDITIONAL CONGRESSIONAL POWERS

In addition to its power to make the law, Congress has at its disposal an array of other instruments through which it can influence the process of government. These include advice and consent in several areas as well as the extreme step of impeachment.

Advice and Consent: Special Senate Powers

The Constitution has given the Senate a special power, one that is not based on lawmaking: the president has the power to make treaties and appoint top executive officers, ambassadors, and federal judges, but only "with the Advice and Consent of the Senate" (Article II, Section 2). For treaties, two-thirds of those senators present for a vote must concur; for appointments, a majority is required.

The Senate only occasionally exercises its power to reject treaties and appointments. More common than Senate rejection of presidential appointees is a senatorial "hold" on an appointment. Any member may place an indefinite hold on the confirmation of a mid- or lower-level presidential appointment. The hold may be a signal of a senator's willingness to filibuster a nomination, but it typically aims to wring concessions from the White House on matters unrelated to the appointment in question. Regarding judicial appointments, Senate Democrats actively scrutinized the nominations of President George W. Bush and prevented final confirmation votes on a dozen especially conservative nominees. Of course, Republicans had done the same thing to many judicial nominations in the preceding Clinton administration and continued the practice in the Obama administration. President Trump, on the other hand, was slow to fill either judicial or middle- and lower-level administrative positions requiring Senate confirmation in his first year, thus denying the Democrats many opportunities for obstruction. In 2018, however, the Trump administration was very active in filling judgeships in lower federal courts. Because of a Senate rule change making it no longer possible to filibuster these appointments, the Republican majority has prevailed in confirming them.

Senatorial advice and consent is also required on treaties. For example, at the end of the first Congress of Obama's presidency—one featuring frequent obstruction from Republicans—it was surprising that Senate Republicans joined Democrats in consenting to the New Strategic Arms Reduction Treaty with Russia to reduce nuclear arsenals. Most presidents make every effort to take potential Senate opposition into account when they negotiate treaties and frequently resort to **executive agreements** with foreign powers instead of treaties when they find the prospects of Senate advice and consent unlikely. The Supreme Court has held that such agreements are equivalent to treaties, but they do not need Senate approval.[60]

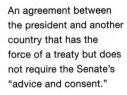

executive agreement

An agreement between the president and another country that has the force of a treaty but does not require the Senate's "advice and consent."

In the past, presidents sometimes concluded secret agreements without informing Congress. In 1972, Congress passed the Case Act, which requires the president to inform Congress of any executive agreement within 60 days of its having been reached. Congress then has the opportunity to cancel agreements that it opposes. In addition, Congress can limit the president's ability to conduct foreign policy through executive agreement by refusing to appropriate the funds needed to implement an agreement. In this way, for example, Congress can modify or even cancel executive agreements to provide economic or military assistance to foreign governments.

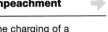

impeachment

The charging of a government official (president or other) with "Treason, Bribery, or other high Crimes and Misdemeanors" and bringing him or her before Congress to determine guilt.

Impeachment

The Constitution, in Article II, Section 4, also grants Congress the power of **impeachment** over the president, vice president, and other executive officials; that is, Congress can charge a government official (president or otherwise) with "Treason, Bribery, or other high Crimes and Misdemeanors" and bring him or her before Congress to determine guilt. Impeachment is thus like a criminal indictment in which the House of Representatives acts like a

---

60 *United States v. Pink*, 315 U.S. 203 (1942). For a good discussion of the problem, see William G. Howell, *Power without Persuasion: The Politics of Direct Presidential Action* (Princeton, NJ: Princeton University Press, 2003).

grand jury, voting (by simple majority) on whether the accused ought to be impeached. If a majority of the House votes to impeach, the impeachment trial is held in the Senate, which acts like a trial jury by voting whether to convict and forcibly remove the person from office. (This vote requires a two-thirds majority.)

Controversy has arisen over what can constitute grounds for impeachment, especially the meaning of "high Crimes and Misdemeanors." A strict reading of the Constitution suggests that the only impeachable offense is an actual crime. But a more commonly accepted definition is that "an impeachable offense is whatever the majority of the House of Representatives considers it to be at a given moment in history."[61] In other words, impeachment, especially impeachment of a president, is a political decision.

The United States came closest to impeaching and convicting a president in 1867. Andrew Johnson, a southern Democrat who had battled a congressional Republican majority over Reconstruction, was impeached by the House but saved from conviction by one vote in the Senate. At the height of the Watergate scandal in 1974, the House started impeachment proceedings against President Richard Nixon, but Nixon resigned before the House could proceed. The possibility of impeachment arose again in 1998, when President Clinton was accused of lying under oath and obstructing justice in the investigation into his sexual affair with White House intern Monica Lewinsky. In October 1998, the House voted to impeach the president. At the conclusion of the Senate trial in 1999, Democrats, joined by a handful of Republicans, acquitted Clinton of both charges. In December 2019 the House began an impeachment inquiry against President Trump, concluding with straight party-line votes on two articles of impeachment: abuse of power and obstruction of Congress. A month-long delay followed these votes, in which Speaker Pelosi would not transmit the articles of impeachment to the Senate until Senate Majority Leader McConnell provided procedural assurances. The Senate then took up the articles in a two-week trial, following which the president was acquitted of both charges in a nearly straight party-line vote. (One Republican senator, Mitt Romney of Utah, voted to convict on one of the articles.)

CONCLUSION: POWER AND REPRESENTATION

Because they feared both executive and legislative tyranny, the framers of the Constitution pitted Congress and the president against each other. And as the history principle suggests, this has yielded a legacy of interbranch competition.

61 Carroll J. Doherty, "Impeachment: How It Would Work," *CQ Weekly Report*, January 31, 1998, p. 222.

During the first century of American government, Congress was the dominant institution. American foreign and domestic policy was formulated and implemented by Congress, and generally the most powerful figures in American government were the Speaker of the House and the leaders of the Senate—not the president. During the nineteenth century, the War of 1812 was planned and fought by Congress.[62] The great sectional compromises before the Civil War were formulated in Congress without much intervention from the executive; and even during the Civil War—a period of extraordinary presidential leadership—a joint congressional committee played a role in formulating war plans and campaign tactics and even in promoting officers. After the Civil War, when President Andrew Johnson sought to interfere with congressional plans for Reconstruction, he was summarily impeached, saved from conviction by only one vote.

Congressional preeminence began to diminish in the twentieth century, so that by the 1960s the executive had become the dominant branch of American government. The major domestic policy initiatives of the twentieth century—Franklin Delano Roosevelt's New Deal, Harry Truman's Fair Deal, John F. Kennedy's New Frontier, and Lyndon B. Johnson's Great Society—were essentially developed, introduced, and implemented by the executive. In foreign policy, although Congress continued to be influential, the focus of decision-making power clearly moved into the executive branch. The United States' involvement in World War I, World War II, Korea, Vietnam, Iraq, Afghanistan, and numerous lesser conflicts was initiated essentially by presidential—not congressional—action.

The relationship between the two branches is one of ebb and flow. In the last 40 years, there has been a resurgence of congressional power vis-à-vis the executive. This has occurred in part because Congress has represented many important political forces, specifically the civil rights, women's, environmental, consumer, and peace movements in the 1970s and 1980s, conservative movements of the social and religious right in the last quarter-century, and movements centered on the LGBTQ and immigrant communities most recently. These groups, in turn, have become constituencies for congressional power. The resurgence of congressional power has also been helped by the creation of congressional agencies to provide informational support independent of the executive branch

As we have seen, the U.S. Congress is a bicameral legislature with the authority to develop and pass legislation (with the concurrence of the president) on the one hand, and the power to oversee policy implementation by the president and the executive bureaucracy on the other hand. It is present at the creation of laws, and its responsibility continues after laws are crafted. Each chamber keeps an eye on the other chamber, and the two chambers ultimately must come to terms with each other on joint legislative products that

---

62 President James Madison's resolve against the war dissolved under relentless pressure from congressional war hawks led by Speaker of the House Henry Clay.

are sent to the president for signature. But each chamber has a life of its own as well. Each is organized by its majority party and possesses an organizational structure of leaders and followers. In addition to pursuing substantive policy objectives through legislation by authorizing new programs and reauthorizing existing ones, the two chambers play a special role in the financial realm—raising revenue from taxes and appropriating monies to fund authorized programs. In addition, the Senate's further responsibilities include the approval of treaties and the confirmation of federal judges, Supreme Court justices, and high administrative officers.

In analytical terms, the U.S. Congress is an institutional arrangement. In light of the rationality principle, it arranges itself in accordance with the policy and career ambitions of its members. Politicians are ambitious for themselves, their party, and their constituencies. To accomplish at least some of the personal objectives of the 435 individuals in the House and the 100 in the Senate, politicians engage in bargaining, coordination, and cooperation that are orchestrated by institutional rules, structures, and procedures. Given the size of the majorities required in each chamber to produce results, policy benefits must be distributed widely according to the distributive tendency. The resulting product isn't always pretty; there are occasional "bridges to nowhere" and other undesirable pork-barrel projects. But this is what it takes to accomplish goals in a diverse, multiperson, elected body. For more than two centuries, each chamber has created ways of doing business, reformed them, and sometimes engineered entirely new ways of conducting its affairs. The history of what has gone before channels this institutional engineering.

The two chambers of the American legislature do not operate in a vacuum. In front of them are the president, the executive bureaucracy, and the courts, which jointly participate in lawmaking and its implementation. Behind them are public opinion and organized interests, which ultimately render judgment on their efforts by rewarding or punishing individuals and parties through elections. In the next three chapters we take up the presidency, the executive branch, and the court system. In Part 3 we explore public opinion, organized interests, parties, and elections.

For Further Reading

Adler, E. Scott. *Why Congressional Reforms Fail: Reelection and the House Committee System*. Chicago: University of Chicago Press, 2002.

Adler, E. Scott, Jeffery A. Jenkins, and Charles R. Shipan. *The United States Congress*. New York: W. W. Norton & Company, 2019.

Aldrich, John H., and David W. Rohde. "The Republican Revolution and the House Appropriations Committee." *Journal of Politics* 62, no. 1 (Feb. 2000): 1–33.

Berry, Christopher R., and Anthony Fowler. "Cardinals or Clerics: Congressional Committees and the Distribution of Pork." *American Journal of Political Science* 60, no. 3 (July 2016): 692–708.

Binder, Sarah A. *Stalemate: Causes and Consequences of Legislative Gridlock.* Washington, DC: Brookings Institution, 2003.

Brady, David W., and Mathew D. McCubbins, eds. *Party, Process, and Political Change in Congress: New Perspectives on the History of Congress.* Palo Alto, CA: Stanford University Press, 2002 (vol. 1); 2007 (vol. 2).

Broockman, David E. "Black Politicians Are More Intrinsically Motivated to Advance Blacks' Interests: A Field Experiment Manipulating Political Incentives." *American Journal of Political Science* 57, no. 3 (July 2013): 521–36.

Carson, Jamie L., ed. *New Directions in Congressional Politics.* New York: Routledge, 2012.

Cox, Gary W., and Jonathan N. Katz. *Elbridge Gerry's Salamander: The Electoral Consequences of the Reapportionment Revolution.* Cambridge: Cambridge University Press, 2002.

Cox, Gary W., and Mathew D. McCubbins. *Legislative Leviathan: Party Government in the House.* 2nd ed. New York: Cambridge University Press, 2007.

Cox, Gary W., and Mathew D. McCubbins. *Setting the Agenda: Responsible Party Government in the U.S. House of Representatives.* New York: Cambridge University Press, 2005.

Frisch, Scott A., and Sean Q Kelly. *Committee Assignment Politics in the U.S. House of Representatives.* Norman: University of Oklahoma Press, 2006.

Harbridge, Laurel, and Neil Malhotra. "Electoral Incentives and Partisan Conflict in Congress: Evidence from Survey Experiments." *American Journal of Political Science* 55, no. 3 (2011): 494–510.

Jacobson, Gary C. and Jamie L. Carson. *The Politics of Congressional Elections.* 10th ed. New York: Rowman and Littlefield, 2015.

Jenkins, Jeffery A. and Eric M. Patashnik, eds. *Congress and Policy Making in the 21st Century.* New York: Cambridge University Press, 2016.

Krehbiel, Keith. *Pivotal Politics: A Theory of U.S. Lawmaking.* Chicago: University of Chicago Press, 1998.

Lee, Frances E. *Insecure Majorities: Congress and the Perpetual Campaign.* Chicago: University of Chicago Press, 2016.

Rohde, David W. *Parties and Leaders in the Postreform House.* Chicago: University of Chicago Press, 1991.

Stewart III, Charles. *Analyzing Congress.* 2nd ed. New York: Norton, 2012.

Theriault, Sean M. *Party Polarization in Congress.* New York: Cambridge University Press, 2008.

Wawro, Gregory J., and Eric Schickler. *Filibuster: Obstruction and Lawmaking in the U.S. Senate.* Princeton, NJ: Princeton University Press, 2006.

The Presidency as an Institution

Nine of the last ten American presidents have left office under political clouds and, in six cases, sooner than they wanted. Lyndon Johnson did not run for reelection in 1968 after the Vietnam War turned much of his own party against him. As the Watergate scandal unfolded and the House prepared to vote on impeachment, Richard Nixon chose to resign in 1974 to avoid almost certain conviction. Nixon's appointed successor, Gerald Ford, was defeated in his campaign for election to a full term in 1976. Jimmy Carter, who ousted Ford, was denied reelection by Ronald Reagan, who himself left office with a reputation damaged by the Iran-Contra scandal. Reagan's successor, George H. W. Bush, was defeated for reelection by Bill Clinton, who served two full terms but faced impeachment and numerous scandals. Clinton's successor, George W. Bush, will be remembered as one of the least popular presidents in the history of opinion polling, having left office with historically low approval ratings despite enjoying very high ones earlier in his presidency. Barack Obama, elected in 2008 as a popular successor to Bush, won reelection in a bruising campaign in 2012, despite presiding over four years of economic sluggishness and indifferent international performance in his first term. Although Obama, too, suffered relatively low popularity during the early part of his second term, he left office as the exception to this pattern, enjoying high approval ratings at the time of his departure. Finally, in 2020, after a single term and a popularity rating that never exceeded 45 percent during his entire term, Donald J. Trump was turned out of office (by the slimmest of margins).

Yet even as many presidents have limped out of the White House or struggled to remain there, the presidency as an institution has grown in power and prominence. Indeed, over the past century the presidency has become the United States' most powerful institution in the realms of foreign and military policy and, arguably, domestic policy as well. One reason why is that the presidency is the country's only political institution characterized by unitary rather than collective decision making. Members of Congress and the judiciary must deliberate, compromise, and vote before reaching decisions. Presidents may wish to seek advice from many sources but, in the end, they either exercise the powers of the office directly, on their own authority, or these powers are exercised by those to whom the president has delegated authority. As former president George W. Bush once said, "I am the decider."

In contrast to collective decision-making bodies that are burdened by coordination problems and the need to compromise (as the collective action principle suggests), the unitary decider is not so burdened and usually sees a direct relationship between the power of the institution and the ability to achieve political goals. Presidents Reagan and Clinton worked diligently to expand the president's power of regulatory review (which we discuss later in this chapter) precisely so that they could use this process to achieve their policy goals without the need for congressional approval. For example, in 2008 Congress responded to enormous political pressure for quick action on the nation's financial crisis by giving the executive branch unprecedented new economic powers. President Obama used these new powers to promote new rules to refinance federally guaranteed mortgages and to ease repayment schedules for federal student loans in 2008. In his second term he relied on executive orders in the face of a gridlocked Congress. President Trump has followed Obama's example, also relying heavily on executive orders to enact his preferred policies.

At the same time, collective decision makers often feel pressure to cede power to unitary deciders when expeditious action seems of paramount importance. During times of crisis, when a quick response is needed and the public is impatient with constitutional limitations on collective action, Congress and the judiciary typically accede to presidential demands for new executive powers to deal with the emergency.[1]

LEARNING OBJECTIVES

 Identify the constitutional origins and the powers of the presidency.

 Outline key historical events and actions that gave rise to presidential government.

 Describe the president's formal and informal resources and how they affect the president's capacity to govern.

 Assess the common myths and realities of presidential power.

1   See William G. Howell and Stephane Wolton, "The Politician's Province," *Quarterly Journal of Political Science* 13, no. 2 (2018): 119–46; William G. Howell, Kenneth Shepsle, and Stephane Wolton, "Executive Absolutism: A Model," 2019, https://ssrn .com/abstract=3440604 (accessed 1/21/20).

Hence the character of the presidency as an institution—the fact that the president is a unitary decider—helps explain why the position has gained in power at the expense of other institutions, particularly Congress. However, as presidents gain power in more policy spheres, they also have opportunities to make more mistakes and generate more opposition. Thus, ironically, the growing power of the presidency is one reason so many of our recent chief executives have become unpopular after a few years in office. President Obama, for instance, entered office in January 2009 with over 60 percent approval, a rating that dropped to just 38 percent by October 2011. Approval hovered near 50 percent at the start of Obama's second term but fell to the low 40s by 2014. By the end of his presidency, his approval had rebounded to 55 percent. President Trump's approval rating followed a similar trend. Leading up to the 2018 midterm elections, his approval rating was in the high 30s, down from 45 percent at the beginning of his administration. In the months before the 2020 presidential election, after a temporary spike in approval during the coronavirus pandemic earlier that year, his approval rating was in the low 40s.

Our focus in this chapter is on the development of the institutional character of the presidency, the power of the presidency, and the relationship between the two. First, we review the constitutional origins and powers of the presidency. Second, we review the history of the American presidency to see how the office has evolved since it was first established by the Constitution. Third, we assess the means by which presidents can enhance their own ability to govern.

THE CONSTITUTIONAL ORIGINS AND POWERS OF THE PRESIDENCY

The presidency as an institution was established by Article II of the Constitution, which asserts, "The executive Power shall be vested in a President of the United States of America." The article goes on to describe the manner in which the president is to be chosen, qualifications for the office (one must be a natural-born citizen, 35 years of age or older, and a resident of the United States for at least 14 years), and the basic powers of the presidency. By vesting the executive power in a single president, the framers were emphatically rejecting proposals for collective leadership, most of which sought to avoid undue concentration of power in the hands of one individual. While some of the framers favored a multiheaded executive, most hoped the president would be capable of taking quick and decisive action; they thought a unitary executive would be more energetic than some form of collective leadership. They believed that a powerful executive would help protect the nation's interests vis-à-vis other nations and promote the federal government's interests relative to the states. In other words, the framers opted for a decider rather than a deliberative body.

Immediately following the first clause of Article II, Section 1, the Constitution defines the manner in which the president is to be chosen. This odd sequence says something about the difficulty the delegates to the Constitutional Convention had over how to provide great power of action to the executive and at the same time balance that power with limitations. This tension reflected the twin struggles deeply etched in the memories of the founding generation: a fight against the powerful executive authority of King George III, on the one hand, and the challenges posed by the dismal, low energy of the government under the Articles of Confederation, on the other. Some delegates wanted the president to be selected by, and thus responsible to, Congress; others preferred that the president be elected directly by the people. Direct popular election would create a more independent and more powerful presidency. But by adopting a scheme of indirect election through the Electoral College, in which electors would be selected by the state legislatures (and close elections would be resolved in the House of Representatives), the framers hoped to achieve a "republican" solution: a strong president responsible to state and national legislators rather than directly responsible to the electorate. This indirect method of electing the president dampened the power of most presidents in the nineteenth century by denying them a broad political base of popular support and legitimacy.

The presidency was strengthened somewhat in the 1830s with the introduction of the national convention system of nominating presidential candidates. Until then, candidates had been nominated by their party's congressional delegates. The convention system was seen as a victory for democracy over the congressional elite, giving the presidency a base of power independent of Congress. This additional independence did not immediately transform the presidency into the office we recognize today, but the national convention did begin to open the presidency to larger social forces and newly organized interests in society.

Article II, Sections 2 and 3, outline the powers and duties of the president. The scope of presidential power can be derived from two places within these sections. One source is the specific language of the Constitution. For example, the Constitution specifically authorizes the president to make treaties, grant pardons, and nominate judges and other public officials. These clearly defined powers, called the **expressed powers** of the office, cannot be revoked by Congress or any other agency without an amendment to the Constitution. Other expressed powers include the power to receive ambassadors and to command the nation's military forces.

The second source of presidential power lies in the declaration that the president "shall take Care that the Laws be faithfully executed." Because the laws are enacted by Congress, this language implies that Congress is to delegate to the president the power to implement or execute its will. Powers given to the president by Congress are called **delegated powers**. In principle, Congress delegates to the president only the power to identify or develop the means through which to carry out its decisions. So, for example, if Congress determines that air quality should be improved, it might delegate to an agency in the executive branch the power to identify and implement the best means of bringing about such an improvement. In practice, of course, decisions about how to clean the air are likely to have an enormous effect on businesses, organizations, and individuals throughout the nation. As it delegates power to the executive branch, therefore, Congress substantially enhances the importance of the presidency. In most cases, Congress delegates power to bureaucratic agencies in the executive

 expressed powers

Powers that the Constitution explicitly grants to the federal government.

 delegated powers

Constitutional powers that are assigned to one branch of the government but exercised by another branch with the permission of the first.

branch rather than directly to the president. Congress does this in part because it has continuing influence over those agencies (through its power of the purse, for example). As we will see, however, contemporary presidents have found ways to capture a good deal of this delegated power for themselves.

Presidents have claimed a third source of institutional power beyond expressed and delegated powers. These **inherent powers** are not specified in the Constitution or the law but are said to stem from "the rights, duties and obligations of the presidency."[2] They are most often asserted by presidents in times of war or national emergency. For example, after the fall of Fort Sumter and the outbreak of the Civil War, President Abraham Lincoln issued a series of executive orders, although he had no clear legal basis for doing so. Without even calling Congress into session, Lincoln combined the state militias into a 90-day national volunteer force, called for 40,000 new volunteers, enlarged the regular army and navy, diverted $2 million in unspent appropriations to military needs, instituted censorship of the U.S. mail, ordered a blockade of southern ports, suspended the writ of habeas corpus in the border states, and ordered military police to arrest individuals whom he deemed to be guilty of engaging in or even contemplating treasonous actions.[3] Lincoln asserted that these extraordinary measures were justified by the president's inherent power to protect the nation.[4]

inherent powers

Powers claimed by a president that are not expressed in the Constitution but are said to stem from "the rights, duties, and obligations of the presidency."

Expressed Powers

The president's expressed powers, as defined by Article II, Sections 2 and 3, fall into several categories:

1. *Military.* Article II, Section 2, provides for the power as "Commander in Chief of the Army and Navy of the United States, and of the Militia of the several States, when called into the actual Service of the United States."

2. *Judicial.* Article II, Section 2, provides the "Power to grant Reprieves and Pardons for Offences against the United States, except in Cases of Impeachment."

3. *Diplomatic.* Article II, Section 2, provides the "Power, by and with the Advice and Consent of the Senate, to make Treaties." Article II, Section 3, provides the power to "receive Ambassadors and other public Ministers."

....

2   In the case of *In re Neagle*, 135 U.S. 1 (1890), David Neagle, a deputy U.S. marshal, had been authorized by the president to protect a Supreme Court justice whose life had been threatened by an angry litigant. When the litigant attempted to carry out his threat, Neagle shot and killed him. Neagle was then arrested by local authorities and tried for murder. His defense was that his act was "done in pursuance of a law of the United States." The Supreme Court declared that Nagle's actions were appropriate because, even though the directive he followed was not an act of Congress, he was following an executive order of the president and the protection of a federal judge was a reasonable extension of the president's power to "take Care that the Laws be faithfully executed."

3   James G. Randall, *Constitutional Problems under Lincoln* (New York: Appleton, 1926), chap. 1.

4   Edward S. Corwin, *The President: Office and Powers*, 4th ed. (New York: New York University Press, 1957), p. 229.

4. *Executive.* Article II, Section 3, authorizes the president to see to it that all the laws are faithfully executed. Section 2 gives the chief executive power to appoint, remove, and supervise all executive officers and appoint all federal judges.

5. *Legislative.* Article I, Section 7, and Article II, Section 3, give the president the power to participate authoritatively in the legislative process.

Military Power. The president's military powers are among the most important of the powers exercised by the chief executive.[5] The position of **commander in chief** gives the president control over the entire defense establishment, making the president the highest military authority in the United States. The president is also head of the nation's intelligence network, which includes not only the Central Intelligence Agency (CIA) but also the National Security Council (NSC), the National Security Agency (NSA), the FBI, and a host of less well-known but very powerful international and domestic security agencies.

Domestic Defense Power. The president's military powers extend into the domestic sphere. Article IV, Section 4, provides that "the United States shall . . . protect [every state] against Invasion . . . and . . . domestic Violence." Congress has made this an explicit presidential power through statutes directing the president as commander in chief to discharge these obligations.[6] The Constitution restrains the president's use of domestic force by providing that a state legislature (or governor when the legislature is not in session) must request federal troops before the president can send them into the state to provide public order. Yet this proviso is not absolute. First, presidents are not obligated to deploy national troops merely because a state legislature or governor requests them. And more important, the president may deploy troops in a state or city without such a request if the president considers it necessary in order to maintain an essential national service during an emergency, enforce a federal judicial order, or protect federally guaranteed civil rights.

One historic example was the decision by President Dwight Eisenhower in 1957 to send troops into Little Rock, Arkansas, to enforce court orders to integrate Little Rock Central High School; he did so only after failed negotiations with the state's governor, who had posted the Arkansas National Guard at the entrance of the school to prevent the admission of nine Black students. This case makes quite clear that the president does not have to wait for an invitation from a state legislature or a governor before acting as domestic commander in chief. More recently, President George W. Bush sent various military units to the Gulf Coast in response to Hurricanes Katrina and Rita in 2005, and in 2010 President Obama sent the Coast Guard and teams from other agencies to participate in rescue and cleanup efforts following the *Deepwater Horizon* explosion and oil spill in the Gulf of Mexico. In 2018 President Trump sent troops to the U.S.-Mexican border in response to what he felt was an immigration crisis.

 commander in chief

The president's role as commander of the national military and of the state National Guard units (when they are called into service).

---

5   On war powers, see William G. Howell, Saul P. Jackman, and Jon C. Rogowski, *The Wartime President: Executive Influence and the Nationalizing Politics of Threat* (Chicago: University of Chicago Press, 2013).

6   These statutes are contained mainly in Title 10 of the U. S. Code, Sections 331, 332, and 333.

In most instances of domestic disorder—whether a result of human or natural events—presidents tend to exercise unilateral power by declaring a state of emergency, thereby making available federal grants, insurance, and direct assistance. President Trump, for example, declared a national emergency in order to reallocate funds from the Department of Defense budget (which had been authorized and appropriated for other purposes) to be used to begin construction of a border wall between Mexico and the United States. In 2020, he declared a state of emergency to contain and combat the coronavirus pandemic.

Military emergencies have also prompted expansions in the domestic powers of the executive branch. This was true during World Wars I and II and has been the case during the ongoing war on terrorism as well. Within a month of the September 11 attacks, the White House had drafted, and Congress had enacted, the USA PATRIOT Act, expanding the power of government executive agencies to engage in domestic surveillance, including electronic surveillance, and restricting judicial review of such efforts. In the following year Congress created the Department of Homeland Security, combining the offices of 22 federal agencies into one huge new cabinet department that would be responsible for protecting the nation from attack. President Obama signed a four-year extension of the Patriot Act in 2011. In 2015, Congress passed and Obama signed the USA Freedom Act, which renewed expiring sections of the Patriot Act but scaled back the domestic surveillance authority of the NSA.

reprieve

Cancellation or postponement of a punishment.

pardon

Forgiveness of a crime and cancellation of relevant penalty.

amnesty

A pardon extended to a group of persons.

Judicial Power. The presidential power to grant **reprieves**, **pardons**, and **amnesties** involves the power of life and death over all individuals who may be a threat to the nation's security. Presidents may use this power on behalf of a particular individual, as Gerald Ford did when he pardoned Richard Nixon in 1974 "for all offenses against the United States which he . . . has committed or may have committed."[7] Or they may use it on a large scale, as Jimmy Carter did in 1977 when he extended amnesty to all Vietnam War draft evaders.

Diplomatic Power. The president is the United States' chief representative in dealings with other nations. As head of state, the president has the power to make treaties for the United States (with the advice and consent of the Senate). When President George Washington received Edmond Genêt ("Citizen Genêt") as the formal emissary of the revolutionary government of France in 1793 and directed his cabinet officers and Congress to back his decision, he established a greatly expanded interpretation of the power to "receive Ambassadors and other public Ministers," extending it to the power to "recognize" other countries. This power gives the president the almost unconditional authority to review the claims of any new ruling group to determine whether it indeed controls the territory and population of its country and therefore can, in the president's opinion, legitimately commit to treaties and other agreements.

---

7 Proclamation No. 4311, 39 Fed. Reg. 32601 (Sept. 10, 1974).

In recent years, presidents have expanded the practice of using executive agreements instead of treaties to establish relations with other countries.[8] An **executive agreement** is like a treaty because it is a contract between two countries, but it does not require approval by the Senate. (A treaty requires a two-thirds vote of approval by the Senate.) Ordinarily executive agreements are used to carry out commitments already made in treaties or to arrange for matters well below the level of policy. But when presidents have found it expedient to use executive agreements in place of treaties, Congress has typically acquiesced.

Executive Power. The most important basis for the president's power as chief executive is found in Article II, Section 3, which stipulates that the president must see that all laws are faithfully executed, and Section 2, which provides that the president will appoint and supervise all executive officers and appoint all federal judges (with Senate approval). The power to appoint the principal executive officers and to require each of them to report to the president on matters under their jurisdiction makes the president the true chief executive officer of the nation. In this manner, the Constitution focuses executive power and legal responsibility on the president. The famous sign on President Harry S. Truman's desk, "The buck stops here," was not merely an assertion of his personal sense of responsibility but was in fact a recognition of his legal and constitutional responsibilities as president.

The president's executive power is not absolute, however, as many presidential appointments—including nominees to ambassadorships, cabinet offices, federal district and circuit courts, the Supreme Court, and other high-level administrative positions—are subject to majority approval by the Senate. And in fact, the Senate has often refused to confirm presidential nominees or has held them hostage by failing even to hold an up-or-down vote. This pattern is evident in the confirmation process for federal judges. Table 7.1 shows, for the Clinton, Bush, and Obama presidencies, as well as the first two years of Trump's presidency, the presidential success rate for federal circuit and district court nominations.

The George W. Bush administration, supported by conservative scholars, argued that Article II of the Constitution vests all executive power in the president, who, by implication, is in full control of the executive branch. This idea is called the theory of the unitary executive. It is controversial in part because it denies Congress a significant role in managing the bureaucracy, concentrating this authority instead in the hands of the executive. This undermines the idea that the executive and legislature are two branches "sharing powers" within the American separation-of-powers system.[9]

Another component of the president's power as chief executive is **executive privilege**—the claim that confidential communications between a president and close advisers should not be revealed without the president's consent. Presidents

executive agreement

An agreement between the president and another country that has the force of a treaty but does not require the Senate's "advice and consent."

executive privilege

The claim that confidential communications between a president and close advisers should not be revealed without the president's consent.

---

8 In *United States v. Pink*, 315 U.S. 203 (1942), the Supreme Court confirmed that an executive agreement is the legal equivalent of a treaty despite the absence of Senate approval.

9 For a famous statement of this, see Richard E. Neustadt, *Presidential Power and the Modern Presidents: The Politics of Leadership from Roosevelt to Reagan*, rev. ed. (New York: Wiley, 1960; repr., New York: Free Press, 1990).

Table 7.1

NOMINATIONS TO FEDERAL DISTRICT AND CIRCUIT COURTS, 1993–2018

PRESIDENT	U.S. CIRCUIT COURT NOMINEES	SUCCESS RATE	U.S. DISTRICT NOMINEES	SUCCESS RATE
Bill Clinton (1993–2000)	90	72.2%	350	87.1%
George W. Bush (2001–08)	85	71.8%	286	91.3%
Barack Obama (2009–16)	68	80.9%	322	83.2%
Donald Trump* (2017–18)	43	69.8%	112	47.3%

*The statistics for the Trump presidency are for the first two years of his presidency, not for his entire term in office. Consequently, the statistics presented for the Trump presidency may not be directly comparable to the statistics provided for the other presidents listed in the table. SOURCE: Congressional Research Service, "Judicial Nominations Statistics and Analysis: U.S. District and Circuit Courts, 1977–2018," Table 2: U.S. Circuit and District Court Nominees of Seven Most Recent Presidents: Number Nominated, Number Confirmed, Percent Confirmed, March 21, 2019, https://fas.org/sgp/crs/misc/R45622.pdf (accessed 6/3/20).

have made this claim ever since George Washington declined a request from the House of Representatives to deliver documents concerning negotiations of an important treaty. Washington refused (successfully) on the grounds that, first, the House was not constitutionally part of the treaty-making process and, second, that diplomatic negotiations required secrecy.

Executive privilege became a part of the network of checks and balances between the president and Congress, and presidents have usually had the upper hand when invoking it. Although many presidents have claimed executive privilege, the concept was not tested in the courts until the Watergate affair of the early 1970s, during which President Nixon refused congressional demands that he turn over secret White House tapes that congressional investigators thought would establish Nixon's complicity in illegal activities. In *United States v. Nixon*, the Supreme Court ordered Nixon to turn over the tapes.[10] The president complied with the order and resigned from office to avoid impeachment and conviction. *United States v. Nixon* is often seen as a blow to presidential power, but the Court's ruling recognized for the first time the validity of a claim of executive privilege (though it held that it did not apply in this instance).

Subsequent presidents have cited *United States v. Nixon* in support of their claims of executive privilege. In 2012 the Obama administration appealed to executive privilege in refusing to comply with a subpoena from the House of Representatives for documents related to "Operation Fast and Furious," a Justice Department program to combat drug trafficking. And more recently, President Trump invoked these privileges to justify his refusal to allow members of his cabinet and close advisers to testify in Congress regarding Russian interference

---

10 *United States v. Nixon*, 418 U.S. 683 (1974).

---

during the 2016 election, his businesses and personal finances, and various investigations of his alleged abuses of power. Although Trump did not explicitly appeal to executive privilege during his impeachment trial, he refused to cooperate with the House, withholding documents and ordering subordinates not to testify.

Legislative Power. The president's power in the legislative arena comes primarily from two constitutional provisions. Article II, Section 3, states that the president "shall from time to time give to the Congress Information of the State of the Union, and recommend to their Consideration such Measures as he shall judge necessary and expedient." The second of the president's legislative powers is the veto power assigned by Article I, Section 7.[11]

Delivering a State of the Union address might not appear to be of any great import. It is a mere obligation on the part of the president to make recommendations for Congress's consideration. But as political and social conditions have come to favor an increasingly prominent role for presidents, each president has relied on legislative powers to become (1) the primary initiator of proposals for legislative action in Congress, (2) the principal source for public awareness of national issues, and (3) the most important individual participant in legislative decisions. Few today doubt that the president, together with the executive branch as a whole, is the primary source of many important congressional actions.

The **veto** is the president's constitutional power to turn down acts of Congress (Figure 7.1). It alone makes the president the most important single legislative actor.[12] No bill vetoed by the president can become law unless both the House and the Senate override the veto by a two-thirds vote. In the case of a **pocket veto**, Congress does not have the option of overriding the veto. A pocket veto can occur when the president is presented with a bill during the last 10 days of a legislative session. Usually if a president does not sign a bill within 10 days, it automatically becomes law. But this is true only while Congress is in session. If a president chooses not to sign a bill presented within the last 10 days that Congress is in session, then the 10-day limit expires while Congress is out of session, and instead of becoming law, the bill is considered vetoed. However, Congress may reintroduce the bill in the next session.

In 1996, Congress added a new power to the president's lineup, the **line-item veto**, which gave the president the power to strike specific spending items from appropriations bills passed by Congress. Congress then would have the opportunity to reenact these provisions by a two-thirds vote of both the House and the Senate. In 1997, President Clinton used this power 11 times to strike

veto

The president's constitutional power to reject acts of Congress.

pocket veto

A veto that occurs when Congress adjourns during the 10 days a president has to approve a bill and the president takes no action on it.

line-item veto

The power of the president to veto specific provisions (lines) of a bill passed by the legislature (declared unconstitutional by the Supreme Court in 1998).

---

11   There is a third source of presidential power implied in the provision for faithful execution of the laws: the president's power to impound funds—that is, to refuse to spend money Congress has appropriated for certain purposes. One author referred to this as a "retroactive veto power"; see Robert E. Goostree, "The Power of the President to Impound Appropriated Funds," *American University Law Review* 11 (1962): 32–47.

12   For more on the veto, see Chapter 6. Also see Robert J. Spitzer, *The Presidential Veto: Touchstone of the American Presidency* (Albany: State University of New York Press, 1988); and Charles M. Cameron, *Veto Bargaining: Presidents and the Politics of Negative Power* (New York: Cambridge University Press, 2000).

Figure 7.1
THE VETO PROCESS

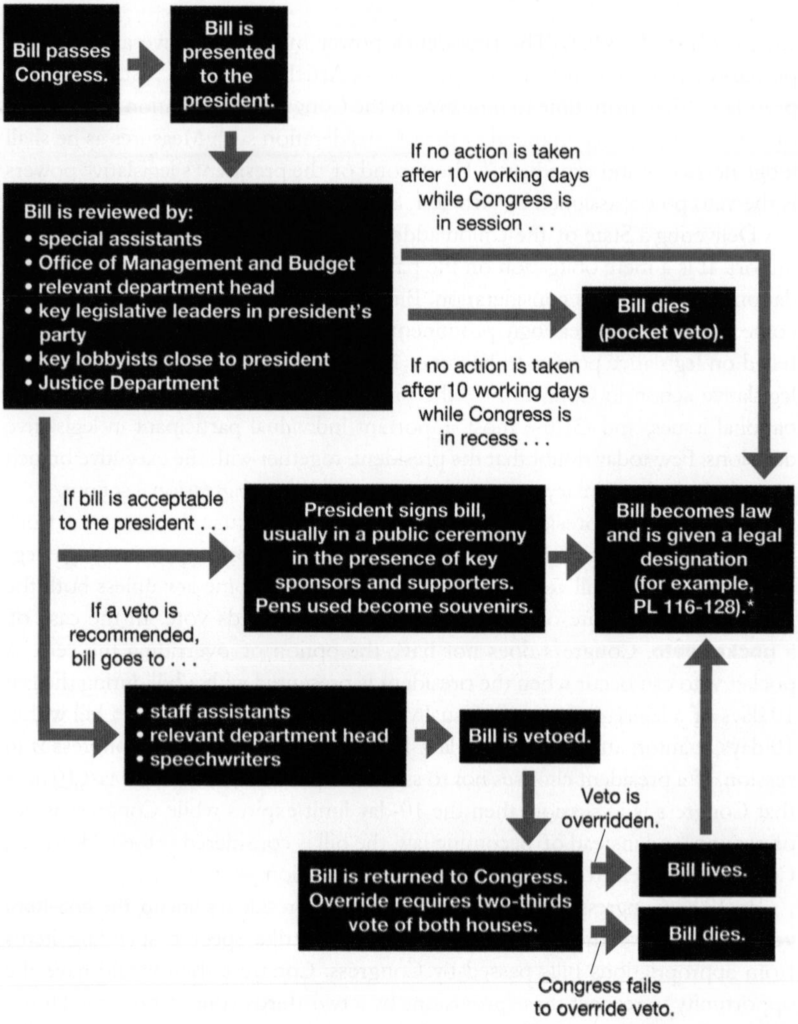

Bill passes Congress. → **Bill is presented to the president.**

↓

Bill is reviewed by:
- special assistants
- Office of Management and Budget
- relevant department head
- key legislative leaders in president's party
- key lobbyists close to president
- Justice Department

If no action is taken after 10 working days while Congress is in session . . . → **Bill dies (pocket veto).**

If no action is taken after 10 working days while Congress is in recess . . . → **Bill becomes law and is given a legal designation (for example, PL 116-128).***

If bill is acceptable to the president . . . → **President signs bill, usually in a public ceremony in the presence of key sponsors and supporters. Pens used become souvenirs.** → **Bill becomes law and is given a legal designation (for example, PL 116-128).***

If a veto is recommended, bill goes to . . .
- staff assistants
- relevant department head
- speechwriters

→ **Bill is vetoed.**

↓

Bill is returned to Congress. Override requires two-thirds vote of both houses.

Veto is overridden. → **Bill lives.**

Congress fails to override veto. → **Bill dies.**

*PL stands for "public law." 116 is the Congress (the 116th Congress was in session in 2019–20), and 128 is the number of the law.

82 items from the federal budget. But in 1998 the Supreme Court ruled that the Constitution does not authorize the line-item veto.[13] Only a constitutional amendment would give this power to the president.

13 *Clinton v. City of New York*, 524 U.S. 417 (1998).

The Games Presidents Play: The Veto. Use of the veto varies according to the political situation that each president confronts. In President Obama's first term, during which he enjoyed Democratic control of the Senate and, for the first two years, the House, he vetoed only two bills. In his second term, during which his party did not control the House and controlled the Senate for only one Congress, Republicans pursued the strategy of obstruction, and very little legislation was produced. Obama's vetoes nevertheless increased to the low double digits.[14] In general, presidents have used the veto to equalize or upset their balance of power with Congress. The politics surrounding the veto is complicated, and vetoes are usually part of an intricate bargaining process between the president and Congress, involving threats of vetoes, the repassage of legislation, and second vetoes.[15] As the Timeplot on pp. 268–9 shows, divided government does not necessarily result in more vetoes.

President Trump did not exercise his veto authority during his first two years. In 2019, he vetoed bills or resolutions on five occasions, and in 2020 he vetoed six bills or resolutions. Nevertheless, his occasional threats to veto legislation have deterred Congress from moving ahead on some bills. In particular, during the 2019–20 legislative session, Senate Majority Leader Mitch McConnell often refused to schedule bills passed by the Democratic House for consideration in the Senate because he believed Trump would veto the bills even if the Senate passed them.

The fact that presidents vetoed only several hundred of the more than 20,000 public bills that Congress sent to them between 1945 and 2015 belies the centrality of the veto to presidential power. Many of these bills were insignificant and not worth the veto effort. Thus it is important to separate "significant" legislation, which is more frequently vetoed, from insignificant legislation.[16] Vetoes can also be effective because of the rationality principle: individuals will condition their actions on the basis of how they think others will respond.[17] With respect to vetoes, this means that members of Congress will alter the content of a bill to make it more to a president's liking to discourage a veto. Thus, the veto power can be influential even when the veto pen remains in its inkwell. It is a club behind the door, its use only rarely required.[18]

Rhetoric and reputation take on particular importance when vetoes become part of a bargaining process. In fact, bargaining between Congress and the president is strategic and an example of the rationality principle in action. The key to veto bargaining is uncertainty: legislators are often unsure about the fine grain

---

14 For the complete list of presidential vetoes, see U.S. Senate, "Summary of Bills Vetoed, 1789-Present," www.senate.gov/reference/Legislation/Vetoes/vetoCounts.htm (accessed 7/9/19).

15 Cameron, *Veto Bargaining*; see also David W. Rohde and Dennis M. Simon, "Presidential Vetoes and Congressional Response: A Study of Institutional Conflict," *American Journal of Political Science* 29, no. 3 (1985): 397–427.

16 David R. Mayhew, *Divided We Govern: Party Control, Lawmaking, and Investigations, 1946–1990* (New Haven, CT: Yale University Press, 1991).

17 Jack H. Nagel, *The Descriptive Analysis of Power* (New Haven, CT: Yale University Press, 1975).

18 Rohde and Simon, "Presidential Vetoes and Congressional Response."

Presidential Vetoes, 1789–2020

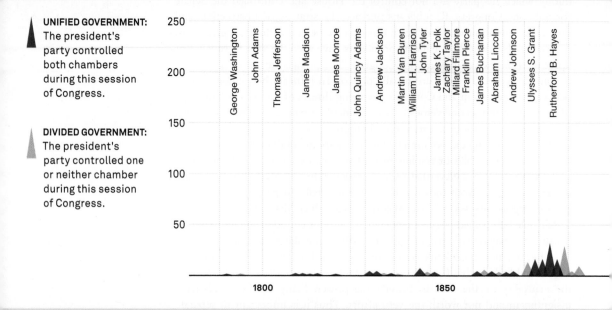

UNIFIED GOVERNMENT: The president's party controlled both chambers during this session of Congress.

DIVIDED GOVERNMENT: The president's party controlled one or neither chamber during this session of Congress.

of presidents' policy preferences and therefore don't know which bills they are willing to sign. When the policy preferences of the president and Congress diverge, as they typically do in a divided government, presidents try to convince Congress that their preferences are more extreme than they really are to get Congress to enact legislation that is closer to what they actually want. Thus, through the strategic use of veto threats, presidents try to shape Congress's beliefs about their policy preferences so that legislators are more likely to offer some concessions in order to avoid a veto. Reputation is central to presidential effectiveness in this process.[19] By influencing congressional beliefs, the president is building a policy reputation that will affect future congressional behavior.

In 2018, President Trump threatened to veto a $1.3 trillion spending bill passed by Congress that would raise the debt ceiling and prevent a federal government shutdown because it didn't include provisions for a border wall with Mexico, which was one of his campaign promises. He ultimately agreed to sign it, acknowledging the boost in national defense spending it would provide.

19 Neustadt, *Presidential Power and the Modern Presidents.*

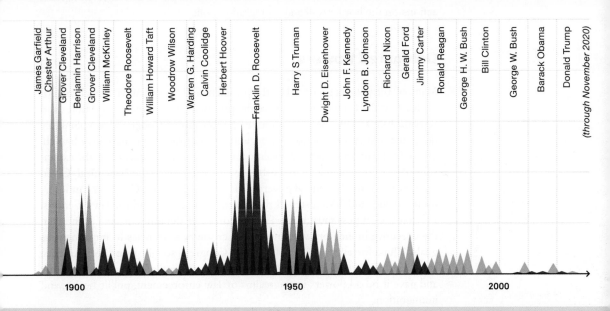

CHAPTER 07

James Garfield
Chester Arthur
Grover Cleveland
Benjamin Harrison
Grover Cleveland
William McKinley
Theodore Roosevelt
William Howard Taft
Woodrow Wilson
Warren G. Harding
Calvin Coolidge
Herbert Hoover
Franklin D. Roosevelt
Harry S Truman
Dwight D. Eisenhower
John F. Kennedy
Lyndon B. Johnson
Richard Nixon
Gerald Ford
Jimmy Carter
Ronald Reagan
George H. W. Bush
Bill Clinton
George W. Bush
Barack Obama
Donald Trump
(through November 2020)

1900   1950   2000

During the first year of his presidency, Barack Obama threatened to veto a defense spending bill that contained $1.75 billion in funding to produce F-22 fighter jets. After receiving the backing of key defense personnel, the funds were stripped so the bill could move forward.

What about the relationship between mass public support for the president and the use of the veto? At least for the modern presidency, a crucial resource for the president in negotiating with Congress has been public approval as measured by opinion polls.[20] In some situations, members of Congress will pass a bill that the president disagrees with not because they want to change policy but because they want to force the president to veto a popular bill.[21] As a result, vetoes may come at a price to the president. According to the rationality principle, presidents must weigh the advantages of using or threatening to use the veto—a move intended to gain concessions from Congress—against the hit

20 Theodore J. Lowi, *The Personal President: Power Invested, Promise Unfulfilled* (Ithaca, NY: Cornell University Press, 1985).

21 Timothy Groseclose and Nolan McCarty, "The Politics of Blame: Bargaining before an Audience," *American Journal of Political Science* 45, no. 1 (2001): 100–119.

they might take in popularity. Presidents may be reluctant to use the veto or the threat of a veto if it will hurt them in the polls, but in some cases, they may be willing to sacrifice their approval ratings for the sake of vetoing a bill that is drastically inconsistent with their policies.[22] The Policy Principle box on p. 271 describes how President Trump used the veto threat to influence Congress's actions on the border wall and immigration policy.

Delegated Powers

Many of the powers exercised by the president and the executive branch are not set forth in the Constitution but are the products of congressional statutes and resolutions. Over the past three-quarters of a century, Congress has voluntarily delegated a great deal of its own legislative authority to the executive branch. To some extent, this has been an almost inescapable consequence of the expansion of governmental activity in the United States since the New Deal. Given the vast range of the federal government's responsibilities, Congress cannot by itself execute and administer all the programs it creates and the laws it enacts. Inevitably Congress must turn to the hundreds of departments and agencies in the executive branch or, when necessary, create new agencies to implement its goals. Thus, for example, in 2002, when Congress sought to protect America from terrorist attacks, it established the Department of Homeland Security and gave it broad powers in the realms of law enforcement, public health, and immigration.

As they implement congressional legislation, federal agencies interpret Congress's intent; promulgate thousands of rules aimed at fulfilling that intent; and issue thousands of orders to individuals, firms, and organizations nationwide to impel them to conform to the law. Congress sometimes grants agencies only limited discretionary authority, providing very specific guidelines and standards that the administrators charged with program implementation must follow. Consider the Internal Revenue Service (IRS). Most Americans view the IRS as a powerful agency whose dictates can have an immediate and sometimes unpleasant effect on their lives, yet congressional tax legislation is so specific and detailed that it leaves little to the discretion of IRS administrators.[23] The agency certainly develops rules and procedures to streamline the process of tax collection, but it is Congress that establishes the structure of the tax liabilities, exemptions, and deductions that determine each taxpayer's burdens and responsibilities.

---

22 For a study of the ways presidents mobilize mass public opinion on behalf of policies they pursue, see Brandice Canes-Wrone, *Who Leads Whom? Presidents, Policy, and the Public* (Chicago: University of Chicago Press, 2006). Also see Lawrence R. Jacobs and Robert Y. Shapiro, *Politicians Don't Pander: Political Manipulation and the Loss of Democratic Responsiveness* (Chicago: University of Chicago Press, 2000).

23 Kenneth F. Warren, *Administrative Law in the Political System*, 5th ed. (New York: Routledge, 2018).

President Trump's Border Wall

During the 2016 election campaign, one of then-candidate Trump's major promises was to build a wall along the entire U.S.-Mexican border. A common chant at his campaign rallies was "Build the Wall." Once elected, President Trump maintained this as a key policy priority—and used a wide range of presidential powers to try to make good on his promise. Yet, with a very high price tag (some estimates are $45 billion) and very little cooperation from Congress, his efforts have not produced the promised wall.

In January 2017, during his first month in office, President Trump issued Executive Order No. 13767 directing the federal government to begin wall construction.[1] However, since a president is not able to appropriate new funding in an executive order, it instructed the government to use existing federal funding. Without identifying the specific federal funding to divert to this expensive project, no construction occurred as a result of the executive order.

In January 2018, the administration released a budget proposal to provide $18 billion in new money to fund a part of the wall. However, this was only a proposal; it was Congress who needed to pass the law and appropriate funding. To put pressure on Congress, the president threatened to veto any spending bill that did not include funding for his wall. The result was a standoff between the president and Congress, resulting in a partial government shutdown that lasted for 35 days. The shutdown ended with Congress providing $1.4 billion in funding for the wall—far less than the president's request.

The president used his other presidential powers to keep his campaign promise. For example, in February 2019, he signed a declaration of national emergency establishing the border situation as a national crisis. President Trump called for a reallocation of federal funding to address the crisis—by building the wall. Then, when Congress voted to overturn this declaration, the president used his veto power to strike back.

President Trump has continued to look for ways to fund the wall. Secretary of Defense Mark Esper (who was appointed by the president and confirmed by the Senate) announced a plan to use $3.6 billion in

President Trump's actions concerning the border wall raised questions about the use of executive orders and presidential power to drive policy priorities.

funds that Congress had allocated to military construction for building part of the wall. Yet, stalled by legal challenges, the Trump administration instead diverted $3.8 billion in funding that had been designated for the military's antidrug and antiterrorism efforts. Legal challenges to this reallocation of funds continue.

Despite these challenges, the Trump administration has been able to invest $15 billion in wall construction through Customs and Border Protection and the Department of Defense. During the summer of 2020, the Trump administration held a press conference in Yuma, Arizona, to celebrate the completion of nearly 300 miles of the wall.[2] Yet his critics note that this represents a small segment of the nearly 2,000-mile border and that all but 30 miles of this work are constituted of replacement fencing rather than new wall construction.[3]

1 Donald J. Trump, "Executive Order: Border Security and Immigration Enforcement Improvements," January 25, 2017, https://www .whitehouse.gov/presidential-actions/executive-order-border-security -immigration-enforcement-improvements/ (accessed 9/18/20).

2 Donald J. Trump, "Remarks by President Trump During Border Wall Construction and Operational Update," August 18, 2020, https://www .whitehouse.gov/briefings-statements/remarks-president-trump-border -wall-construction-operational-update-yuma-az/ (accessed 9/18/20).

3 Mark Niquette, "The Border Wall That the U.S., Not Mexico, Is Paying For," Bloomberg, September 1, 2020, https://www.bloomberg.com/ news/articles/2020-09-01/the-border-wall-that-u-s-not-mexico-is -paying-for-quicktake (accessed 9/18/20).

In many instances, however, congressional legislation is not very detailed. Often Congress defines a broad goal or objective and delegates enormous discretionary power to administrators to determine how that goal is to be achieved. For example, the 1970 act creating the Occupational Safety and Health Administration (OSHA) states that the purpose of the legislation is "to assure so far as is possible every working man and woman in the nation safe and healthful working conditions." The act, however, neither defines such conditions nor suggests how they might be achieved.[24] The result is that agency administrators have enormous discretionary power to draft rules and regulations that have the effect of law. Indeed, the courts treat these administrative rules like congressional statutes. Essentially, when Congress creates an agency such as OSHA and gives it a broad mandate to achieve some purpose, it transfers its own legislative power to the executive branch.

In the nineteenth and early twentieth centuries, Congress typically wrote laws that provided clear principles and standards to guide executive implementation. For example, the 1922 Fordney-McCumber Tariff Act empowered the president to increase or decrease duties on certain manufactured goods to reduce the difference in cost between products produced domestically and those manufactured abroad. The act authorized the president to make the final determination, but his discretionary authority was quite constrained. At least since the New Deal, however, Congress has tended to give executive agencies broad mandates through legislation that offers few clear standards or guidelines for implementation. The 1972 Consumer Product Safety Act, for example, authorized the Consumer Product Safety Commission to reduce unreasonable risks of injury from household products, but it offered no suggestions to guide the commission's determination of what constituted reasonable and unreasonable risks or ideas about how to reduce them.[25]

This shift from issuing relatively well-defined congressional guidelines for administrators to broadly delegating congressional power to the executive branch is partially a consequence of the great scope and complexity of the tasks that the contemporary government of the United States has undertaken. During much of the nineteenth century, the federal government had relatively few domestic responsibilities, and Congress could pay close attention to details. Today the operation of an enormous executive establishment and thousands of programs under varied and changing circumstances requires that administrators be allowed considerable discretion to carry out their jobs. Nevertheless, the result is to shift power from Congress to the executive branch.[26]

---

24 Theodore J. Lowi, *The End of Liberalism: The Second Republic of the United States*, 2nd ed. (New York: Norton, 1979), pp. 117–18.

25 Lowi, *The End of Liberalism*, p. 117.

26 To some extent, though, the shift in power is illusory. Whatever authority Congress delegates, it can recover. The wise president or executive branch administrator is eminently aware of this and conditions her discretionary decisions with one eye cast over her shoulder at a watchful Congress (as the rationality principle would suggest).

Inherent Powers

Some presidential powers are neither expressed explicitly in the Constitution nor delegated by congressional statute or resolution. They are said to be "inherent" powers of a sovereign nation exercised by its chief executive. One inherent power of sovereign nations is self-protection. Today, this power is mainly exercised by the White House.

War and Inherent Presidential Power. The Constitution gives Congress the power to declare war. Presidents, however, have gone a long way toward capturing this power for themselves. Congress has not declared war since December 1941, and yet since then American military forces have engaged in numerous campaigns throughout the world under orders of the president. When North Korean forces invaded South Korea in June 1950, Congress was prepared to declare war, but President Truman decided not to ask for congressional action. Instead, Truman asserted the principle that the president, and not Congress, could decide when and where to deploy America's military might. Truman dispatched U.S. forces to Korea without a congressional declaration, and in the face of the emergency Congress felt it had to acquiesce. It passed a resolution approving the president's actions, and this sequence of events became the pattern for future congressional-presidential relations in the military realm. The wars in Vietnam, Bosnia, Afghanistan, and Iraq, as well as a host of lesser conflicts, were all fought without declarations of war.

In 1973, Congress responded to presidential unilateralism by passing the **War Powers Resolution**—over President Richard Nixon's veto. This resolution reasserted Congress's power to declare war, required the president to inform Congress of any planned military campaign, and stipulated that forces must be withdrawn within 60 days in the absence of a specific congressional authorization for their continued deployment. Presidents have generally ignored the War Powers Resolution, however, claiming that the mobilization of troops falls under their inherent executive power to defend the nation. For example, President George W. Bush responded to the 2001 attacks by Islamist terrorists by organizing a major military campaign to overthrow the Taliban regime in Afghanistan, which had sheltered the terrorists. In 2003, Bush ordered a major U.S. campaign against Iraq, which he accused of posing a threat to the United States. Although Congress passed resolutions approving the president's actions in both cases, the War Powers Resolution was barely mentioned on Capitol Hill and was ignored by the White House.[27]

However, the fact that presidents since 1974 have ignored the War Powers Resolution, with virtually no objections from Congress, does not mean that tensions stemming from the separation of powers between the president and Congress have ceased. The powers of the purse and of investigation give

War Powers Resolution

A 1973 resolution by Congress declaring that the president can send troops into action abroad only if Congress authorizes the action or if U.S. troops are already under attack or seriously threatened.

---

27 These were, in fact, joint resolutions authorizing the use of military force—Public Law 107-40 for Afghanistan and Public Law 107-243 for Iraq—thus protecting some role for Congress in the deployment of military forces.

Congress levers with which to constrain even the most freewheeling executive. For all these reasons, presidents restrain themselves, often self-censoring to minimize adverse political consequences.[28] In 2017 and 2018, President Trump authorized U.S. strikes against Syria in response to Syrian president Bashar al-Assad's alleged use of chemical weapons against civilians. After the attack he notified Congress that he would authorize additional attacks if he thought it necessary for national security. Lawmakers from both parties called on Trump to request permission from Congress before authorizing any future attacks. In 2018 and 2019, U.S. troops were sent to Syria on Trump's command, without congressional approval. A firestorm of congressional protest arose in 2019 when Trump peremptorily withdrew those troops, deserting America's Kurdish allies in the region.

legislative initiative

The president's inherent power to bring a policy agenda before Congress.

Legislative Initiative. Although not explicitly stated, the Constitution provides the president with the power of **legislative initiative**, or the ability to formulate proposals for important policies. To initiate means to originate, and in government to originate can mean power. The president, as an individual with a great deal of staff assistance, can initiate decisive action more frequently than Congress, whose large assemblies have to deliberate before taking action and thus are subject to the hurdles inherent in collective action. Though the framers of the Constitution clearly saw legislative initative as one of the keys to executive power, it should be emphasized that Congress is under no constitutional obligation to take up policy proposals from the president. The president can, according to Article II, Section 3, only "recommend to their Consideration such Measures as he shall judge necessary and expedient." That said, with some important exceptions, Congress banks on the president to set the agenda of public policy. And there is power in being able to set the terms of discourse in the making of public policy.

For example, in 2009, soon after taking office, President Obama presented Congress with a record-breaking $3 trillion budget proposal that included a host of new programs in such areas as health and human services, transportation, housing, and education. Obama told Congress that he would soon be requesting several hundred billion dollars more for a financial bailout to rescue banks and revive the nation's credit markets. Not only did Congress respond to the president's initiatives but lawmakers also *expected* the president to take the lead in responding to the financial emergency and other problems.

During his term, President Trump produced some legislative priorities—a major tax bill reducing corporate and individual tax rates stands as a crowning achievement. Newly elected President Biden's legislative ambitions had been expected to be bold. But the loss of seats in the House and the addition of too few seats in the Senate will likely force Democrats to trim their sails, restricting them to an agenda that can secure the blessing of Senate Republicans.

As a general matter, the Budget and Accounting Act of 1921 empowered the president to submit an annual budget, a responsibility that has given all subsequent presidents enormous agenda power in the formulation of tax and spending policy. As just noted, however, Congress expects presidential leadership but does not

28 On this point, see William G. Howell and Jon C. Pevehouse, *While Dangers Gather: Congressional Checks on Presidential War Powers* (Princeton, NJ: Princeton University Press, 2007).

always feel compelled to follow. It takes the president's budget recommendations as suggestions, not mandates, and in the world of divided government, many presidential budget proposals are said to be "dead on arrival" on Capitol Hill.

For example, Obama worked with the Democratic 111th Congress to achieve important legislative results in his first two years: the Ledbetter Fair Pay Act, the Children's Health Insurance Program Reauthorization Act, the American Recovery and Reinvestment Act, financial reform legislation, and of course, health care reform legislation. In working strategically to get these bills passed, Obama's team was mindful of the institutional rules and practices that would affect the outcomes. Despite Obama's efforts to assemble bipartisan support, Republicans, with some exceptions, mainly opposed the legislation. After Republicans won control of the House in 2010, the president had fewer major legislative successes. And after the 2012 and 2014 elections, which increased the number of Republicans in Congress and enabled them to capture the Senate in 2014, Obama's legislative successes slowed to a trickle.

There were also legislative disappointments. Obama took on enormous political risks when he staked his presidency on legislative accomplishments. The overarching risk was that he would fail to accomplish what he had set out to do. More specifically, the messy and often ugly process of creating and passing legislation can frustrate presidents' efforts to meet their legislative goals. There is a reason German statesman Otto von Bismarck said, "Laws are like sausages. It's better not to see them being made." Compromise is at the heart of politics in a democracy. When presidents give special favors to those whose votes might help their legislation pass or when a majority leader tries to pass amendments that favor a particular senator or representative, the seamy side of politics is rearing its head. During the attempt to pass health care reform, for example, Nebraska was given a Medicare exemption that no other state received solely to secure the vote of the pivotal Nebraska senator—something Obama's opponents took great pains to point out. The Republicans called out the inconsistencies between Democratic pledges for open, honest government and the closed-door negotiations, proposals, and counterproposals that were taking place. Even worse, elements of the coalitions that supported Obama saw their objectives sacrificed or ignored in the quest to get *something* done. In short, the messiness of the political process negatively affected the Democrats and left the Republicans largely unscathed.

The 2016 elections were a Republican sweep, with Donald Trump winning the presidency and the Republicans maintaining their hold on both the House and Senate. Between Democratic threats to filibuster in the Senate and Republican factionalism in the House, Congress was not all that productive despite two years of unified government. In the second two years of Trump's term, with the Democrats holding a majority in the House and the president distracted by impeachment battles, the legislative spigot—and the president's lead in legislative agenda setting—was all but shut off. The economic and health impact of the coronavirus pandemic in 2020, however, provided an occasion for some bipartisan legislative efforts to mitigate these effects.

Presidential initiative does not end with the president's ability to direct and participate in the congressional lawmaking process. The president has still another legislative role (in all but name) within the executive branch: the power

executive order

A rule or regulation issued by the president that has the effect of law.

to issue **executive orders**. The executive order is first and foremost a normal tool of management, a power virtually any CEO possesses to make company policy. Most presidential executive orders provide for the reorganization of executive branch structures and procedures; they may be applied in some cases to all agencies and in other cases to a single agency or department. In modern times, executive orders have not been "merely administrative" but rather have had the broader effects of legislation—rules with actual policy content—despite avoiding the formal legislative process.

The power to issue executive orders illustrates that, although reputation and persuasion are typically required in presidential policy making, the practice of issuing executive orders, within limits, allows a president to govern without needing to persuade.[29] We take a closer look at how modern presidents have used executive orders later in the chapter.

THE RISE OF PRESIDENTIAL GOVERNMENT

Most of the real influence of the modern presidency derives from the powers granted by the Constitution and the laws made by Congress. Presidential power is institutional. Thus, any person properly elected and sworn in as president will possess almost all the power held by the strongest presidents in American history. What variables account for a president's success in exercising these powers? Why are some presidents considered great successes, others colossal failures, and most somewhere in between? These questions relate broadly to the very concept of presidential power. Is the president's power a reflection of the person who holds the office, or is it more a characteristic of the political situations that a president encounters? The personal view of presidential power dominated political scientists' thinking for several decades,[30] but recently scholars have argued that presidential power should be analyzed in terms of the strategic interactions that a president has with other political actors.[31] With the occasional exception, it took more than a century before presidents came to be seen as consequential players in these encounters. A bit of historical review will clarify how the presidency has risen to its current level of influence.

---

29 This point is developed in both Kenneth R. Mayer, *With the Stroke of a Pen: Executive Orders and Presidential Power* (Princeton, NJ: Princeton University Press, 2001); and William G. Howell, *Power without Persuasion: The Politics of Direct Presidential Action* (Princeton, NJ: Princeton University Press, 2003).

30 Neustadt, *Presidential Power and the Modern Presidents.*

31 Charles M. Cameron, "Bargaining and Presidential Power," in *Presidential Power: Forging the Presidency for the Twenty-First Century*, ed. Robert Y. Shapiro, Martha Joynt Kumar, and Lawrence R. Jacobs (New York: Columbia University Press, 2000); see also Samuel Kernell, *Going Public: New Strategies of Presidential Leadership*, 4th ed. (Washington, DC: CQ Press, 2007).

The Legislative Epoch, 1800–1933

In 1885, a then-obscure political science professor named Woodrow Wilson titled his general textbook *Congressional Government* because American government was just that—congressional government. There is ample evidence that Wilson's description of the national government was consistent not only with nineteenth-century reality but also with the intentions of the framers. Within the system of three separate and competing powers, the clear intent of the Constitution was legislative supremacy. In the early nineteenth century, some observers saw the president as little more than America's chief clerk. Indeed, most historians agree that after Thomas Jefferson and until the beginning of the twentieth century, presidents Andrew Jackson and Abraham Lincoln were the only exceptions to a succession of weak presidents. Both Jackson and Lincoln are considered great presidents because they used their power in momentous ways. But it is important in the history of the presidency that neither of them left his powers as an institutional legacy to his successors. Once Jackson and Lincoln left office, the presidency reverted to the subordinate role that it played throughout the nineteenth century.

One of the reasons so few great men became president in the nineteenth century is that there was rarely room for greatness.[32] As we observed in Chapter 3, the national government of that period was not a particularly powerful entity. The presidency was also weak at this time because it was not closely linked to major national political and social forces. Federalism had fragmented political interests and diverted the energies of interest groups toward the state and local levels of government, where most key decisions were being made.

As we discussed earlier in the chapter, the presidency was strengthened in the 1830s by the introduction of national nominating conventions for presidential candidates. However, this additional independence did not change the presidency into the office we see today because once the national election was over, the parties disappeared, returning to the states and Congress. In addition, as the national government grew, Congress kept a tight rein on the president's power. For example, when the national government began to exercise authority over the country's expanding industrial economy (beginning with the Interstate Commerce Act of 1887 and the Sherman Antitrust Act of 1890), Congress sought to keep this regulatory power away from the president and the executive branch by placing the new policies in "independent regulatory commissions" responsible to Congress rather than to the president (see also Chapter 8).

---

32 For related appraisals, see Jeffrey K. Tulis, *The Rhetorical Presidency* (Princeton, NJ: Princeton University Press, 1987); Stephen Skowronek, *The Politics Presidents Make: Leadership from John Adams to Bill Clinton* (Cambridge, MA: Belknap Press, 1997); and Robert J. Spitzer, *President and Congress: Executive Hegemony at the Crossroads of American Government* (Philadelphia: Temple University Press, 1993).

The New Deal and the Presidency

The key moment in the history of American national government came during President Franklin Delano Roosevelt's administration. The 100 days at the outset of Roosevelt's presidency in 1933 had no parallel in U.S. history—but they were only the beginning. The policies proposed by Roosevelt and adopted by Congress during this short time so changed the size and character of the national government that they constitute a moment in American history equivalent to the Founding or the Civil War. The president's constitutional obligation to see "that the laws be faithfully executed" became, during Roosevelt's presidency, virtually a responsibility to shape the laws before executing them.

Many of the New Deal programs were extensions of the traditional national government approach, which we described in Chapter 3. But the New Deal also championed types of policies never tried on a large scale; the federal government began intervening in economic life in ways that had hitherto been reserved to the states. For example, during the Great Depression the Roosevelt administration created the Works Progress Administration, seeking to put able-bodied Americans back to work. The federal government became the nation's largest employer at this time. The Social Security Act, to give another example, sought to improve the economic conditions of the most impoverished segment of the population: the elderly. In other words, the national government began to directly regulate individuals as well as provide roads and other services.

The new programs were such dramatic departures from the traditional policies of the national government that their constitutionality was in doubt. The Supreme Court in fact declared several of them unconstitutional, mainly on the grounds that in regulating the conduct of individuals or their employers, the national government was reaching beyond "*inter*state" and involving itself in "*intra*state"—essentially local—matters. Most of the New Deal remained in constitutional limbo until 1937, five years after Roosevelt was first elected and one year after his landslide 1936 reelection.

The turning point came with *National Labor Relations Board v. Jones & Laughlin Steel Corporation*, a Supreme Court case challenging the federal government's authority to regulate labor relations. With its decision, the Court affirmed that the federal government had a right to be involved in regulation of the national economy.[33] Since the end of the New Deal, the Court has never again seriously questioned the legitimacy of interventions of the national government in the economy or society.[34]

---

33 *National Labor Relations Board v. Jones & Laughlin Steel Corporation*, 301 U.S. 1 (1937).

34 Some will argue that there are exceptions to this statement. One was *National League of Cities v. Usery*, 426 U.S. 833 (1976), which declared unconstitutional Congress's effort to apply national minimum wage standards to state and local government employees. However, the Court reversed itself on this nine years later in *Garcia v. San Antonio Metropolitan Transit Authority*, 469 U.S. 528 (1985). Cases such as these are few and far between, and they touch on only part of a law, not the constitutionality of an entire program.

The most important constitutional effect of Congress's New Deal–era actions and the Supreme Court's approval of those actions was the enhancement of presidential power. Most major acts of Congress in this period involved significant exercises of control over the economy, but few programs specified the actual mechanisms of control to be used. Instead, Congress authorized the president or new agencies to determine what the controls would be. Although some of the new agencies were independent commissions responsible to Congress, most of the new agencies and programs were placed in the executive branch, directly under presidential authority. The institutional power of the presidency was thus greatly increased.

Technically this form of congressional act rests on the delegation of power. In theory, the delegation of power works as follows: (1) Congress recognizes a problem, (2) Congress acknowledges that it has neither the time nor the expertise to deal with the problem, and (3) Congress therefore sets the basic policies and then delegates the power to fill in the details to an executive agency. But in practice, Congress was delegating to the executive branch not merely the power to fill in the details but also real policy-making powers—that is, real legislative powers. This level of delegation produced a fundamental shift in the American constitutional framework.[35]

Of course, Congress can rescind these delegations of power, restrict them with subsequent amendments, and oversee the exercise of delegated power through congressional hearings, oversight agencies, budget controls, and other administrative tools. Thus, while it is fair to say that presidential government has become an administrative fact of life as government by delegation has expanded over the past century, it is important to remember that Congress still has many clubs behind the door with which to influence and contain the executive branch.[36]

PRESIDENTIAL GOVERNMENT

The locus of policy decision making shifted to the executive branch over time as Congress delegated authority to the president for instrumental reasons, much as a principal delegates to an agent. An expanded agenda of political demands,

---

35 The Supreme Court did in fact *disapprove* broad delegations of legislative power by declaring the National Industrial Recovery Act of 1933 unconstitutional on the grounds that Congress did not accompany the delegations with sufficient standards or guidelines for presidential discretion (*Panama Refining Company v. Ryan,* 293 U.S. 388 [1935]; and *A. L. A. Schechter Poultry Corporation v. United States,* 295 U.S. 495 [1935]). The Supreme Court has never reversed those two decisions, but neither has it really followed them. Thus, broad delegations of legislative power from Congress to the executive branch can be presumed to be constitutional. See Sotirios A. Barber, *The Constitution and the Delegation of Congressional Power* (Chicago: University of Chicago Press, 1975).

36 David Epstein and Sharyn O'Halloran, *Delegating Powers: A Transaction Cost Politics Approach to Policy Making under Separate Powers* (New York: Cambridge University Press, 1999).

necessitated not just by economic crisis—the Great Depression—but also by the effects of nearly a century's worth of industrialization, urbanization, and greater integration into the world economy compelled Congress to off-load some of its responsibilities. When World War II confronted the national government with management of the war effort, the legislature, given its limited capacity to undertake these growing responsibilities, was forced to delegate. These acts of delegation gave a far greater role to the president, empowering this "agent" to initiate in his own right.

Despite this trend toward presidential government, Congress retains many tools with which to threaten, cajole, encourage, and persuade its executive agent to do its bidding. What's more, presidents are not *only* agents of Congress and not *only* dependent on Congress for resources and authority. They are also agents of national constituencies with their own policy agendas, and they are eager to demonstrate leadership in executing constituents' goals.[37]

Likewise, congressional delegations of power are not the only resources available to presidents; they have at their disposal other formal and informal resources that have important implications for their ability to govern. Indeed, without these other resources, presidents would lack the ability—the tools of management and public mobilization—to make much use of the power and responsibility given to them by Congress. Let's first consider the president's formal, or official, resources and then turn to the more informal resources that affect a president's capacity to govern.

The Formal Resources of Presidential Power

Cabinet

The heads of the major departments of the federal government.

The Cabinet. In the American system of government, the **Cabinet** is the traditional but informal designation for the heads of the major departments of the executive branch (Figure 7.2). The Cabinet has only a limited constitutional status.[38] In contrast to the United Kingdom and many other parliamentary countries, where the cabinet *is* the government, the American Cabinet is not a collective body. It meets but makes no decisions as a group. Each appointment must be approved by the Senate, but cabinet members are not responsible to the Senate or to Congress at large. Cabinet appointments help build party and popular support, but the Cabinet is not a party organ. It is made up of directors but is not a true *board* of directors. Because cabinet appointees generally have not shared political careers with the president or with one another and because they may meet each other for the first time after their selection, the formation of an effective governing group out of this disparate collection of appointments is unlikely. Although the Cabinet is not always powerful, it does serve an

---

37 See Terry M. Moe, "Presidents, Institutions, and Theory," in *Researching the Presidency: Vital Questions, New Approaches,* ed. George C. Edwards III, John H. Kessel, and Bert A. Rockman (Pittsburgh, PA: University of Pittsburgh Press, 1993), p. 367.

38 The Twenty-Fifth Amendment gives the Cabinet a formal role in the process of removing the president from office in case of disability.

Figure 7.2
THE INSTITUTIONAL PRESIDENCY, 2020

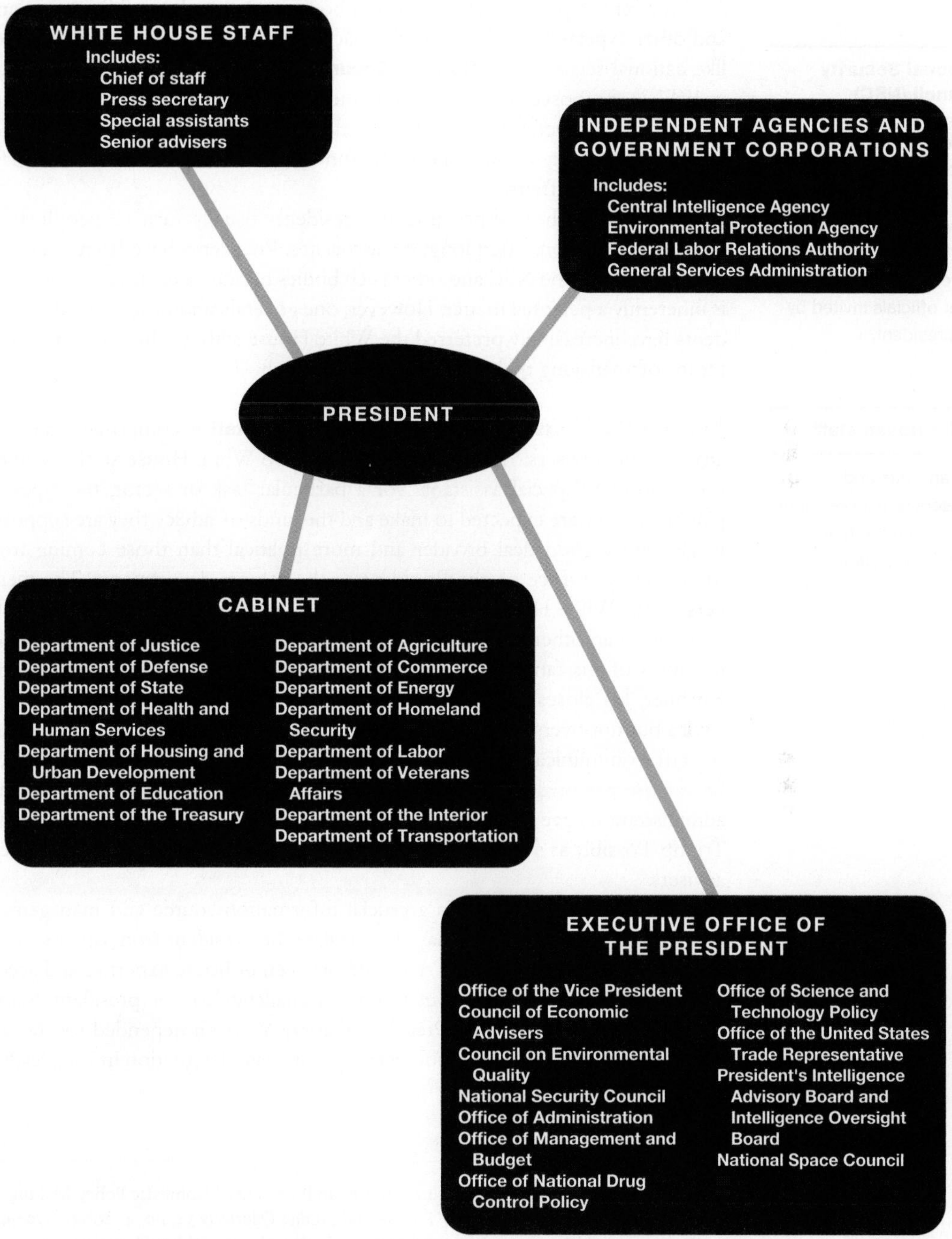

WHITE HOUSE STAFF
Includes:
  Chief of staff
  Press secretary
  Special assistants
  Senior advisers

INDEPENDENT AGENCIES AND GOVERNMENT CORPORATIONS
Includes:
  Central Intelligence Agency
  Environmental Protection Agency
  Federal Labor Relations Authority
  General Services Administration

PRESIDENT

CABINET

Department of Justice
Department of Defense
Department of State
Department of Health and
  Human Services
Department of Housing and
  Urban Development
Department of Education
Department of the Treasury

Department of Agriculture
Department of Commerce
Department of Energy
Department of Homeland
  Security
Department of Labor
Department of Veterans
  Affairs
Department of the Interior
Department of Transportation

EXECUTIVE OFFICE OF THE PRESIDENT

Office of the Vice President
Council of Economic
  Advisers
Council on Environmental
  Quality
National Security Council
Office of Administration
Office of Management and
  Budget
Office of National Drug
  Control Policy

Office of Science and
  Technology Policy
Office of the United States
  Trade Representative
President's Intelligence
  Advisory Board and
  Intelligence Oversight
  Board
National Space Council

important role in managing policy for the president and his political associates. For instance, members of the Cabinet travel on the president's behalf, make policy speeches, and negotiate with other political leaders, both at home and abroad.

Presidents typically rely on specialist bodies composed of cabinet personnel and other experts to advise them in policy areas of great national significance, like national security. The **National Security Council (NSC)**, established by law in 1947, is composed of the president, the vice president, the secretary of state, the secretary of defense, and other officials invited by the president. It has its own staff of foreign policy specialists run by the assistant to the president for national security affairs.

For these highest appointments, presidents usually turn to people from outside Washington, often longtime associates. Presidents have been uneven in their reliance on the NSC and other such bodies because executive management is inherently a personal matter. However, one generalization can be made: presidents have increasingly preferred the White House staff to the Cabinet as their means of managing the gigantic executive branch.

The White House Staff. The **White House staff** is composed mainly of analysts and advisers. Although many of the top White House staff members carry the title "special assistant" for a particular task or sector, the types of judgments they are expected to make and the kinds of advice they are supposed to give are a good deal broader and more political than those coming from the Executive Office of the President or the cabinet departments. The members of the White House staff also tend to be more closely associated with the president than other executive branch officials. President Trump, in fact, made members of his family, including his daughter Ivanka and her husband, Jared Kushner, his closest political advisers. Other staff members are expected to advise but not overshadow the president. While many of these staffers—chief of staff, communications director, and so on—have in previous administrations been close personal associates of the president, staff members in the Trump administration have typically not had intimate prior relationships with President Trump. Possibly as a result, there has been much flux and turnover among these advisers.

The White House staff is a crucial information source and management tool for the president, but it may also insulate the president from other sources of information. Managing this trade-off between in-house expertise and access to independent outside opinions is a major challenge for the president. Sometimes it is botched, as when President George W. Bush depended too heavily on his staff for information about weapons of mass destruction in Iraq, leading him to erroneous conclusions.[39]

National Security Council (NSC)

A presidential foreign policy advisory council made up of the president, the vice president, the secretary of state, the secretary of defense, and other officials invited by the president.

White House staff

The analysts and advisers to the president, often given the title "special assistant."

---

39 See George A. Krause, "The Secular Decline in Presidential Domestic Policy Making: An Organizational Perspective," *Presidential Studies Quarterly* 34, no. 4 (2004): 779–92. On the general issue, see James P. Pfiffner, ed., *The Managerial Presidency*, 2nd ed. (College Station: Texas A&M University Press, 1999).

The Executive Office of the President. The development of the White House staff can be appreciated only in its relation to the larger **Executive Office of the President (EOP)**. Created in 1939, the EOP is a major part of what is often called the institutional presidency—the permanent agencies that perform defined management tasks for the president. The most important and the largest EOP agency is the Office of Management and Budget (OMB). Its roles in preparing the national budget, reporting on agency activities, and overseeing regulatory proposals make OMB personnel part of virtually every presidential responsibility. The status and power of the OMB have grown in importance with each successive president. The process of budgeting was at one time a bottom-up procedure, with expenditure and program requests passing from the lowest bureaus through the departments to "clearance" in the OMB and from there to Congress, where each agency could be called in to reveal what its original request had been before it was revised by the OMB. Now the budgeting process is top-down: the OMB establishes the processes and proceedures for administering the president's budget across the executive branch and in Congress. The director of the OMB is now one of the most powerful officials in Washington.

The staff of the Council of Economic Advisers constantly analyzes economic trends and attempts to help the president anticipate events, being proactive rather than reactive. The Council on Environmental Quality functions in a similar manner for environmental issues. Members of the NSC meet regularly with the president to give advice on the large national security picture. The staff of the NSC assimilates and analyzes data from all intelligence-gathering agencies (such as the CIA). Other EOP agencies perform more specialized tasks.

Somewhere between 1,500 and 2,000 highly specialized staffers work for EOP agencies.[40] The importance of each agency in the EOP varies according to the personal orientation of the president. For example, the NSC staff was of immense importance under President Nixon, especially because it served essentially as the personal staff of presidential assistant Henry Kissinger before his elevation to the office of secretary of state. But it was of less importance to President George H. W. Bush, who looked outside the EOP on military policy matters, turning much more to the Joint Chiefs of Staff and its chair at the time, General Colin Powell.

The Vice Presidency. The vice presidency is a constitutional anomaly. According to the Constitution, the vice president exists for two purposes only: to succeed the president in case of death, resignation, or incapacitation and to preside over the Senate, casting a tiebreaking vote when necessary.[41]

The main value of the vice presidency is as an electoral resource for the president. Traditionally a presidential candidate's most important rule for the

Executive Office of the President (EOP)

The permanent agencies that perform defined management tasks for the president; created in 1939, it is made up of the Office of Management and Budget, the Council of Economic Advisers, the National Security Council, and other agencies.

---

40 The actual number is difficult to estimate because, as with White House staff, some EOP personnel, especially those in national security work, are detailed to the office from outside agencies.

41 Article I, Section 3, provides that "the Vice President . . . shall be President of the Senate, but shall have no Vote, unless they be equally divided." This is the only vote the vice president is allowed.

---

choice of a running mate is that he should bring the support of at least one state (preferably a large one) not otherwise likely to support the ticket or he should provide some regional, ideological, or ethnic balance. It is very doubtful that John F. Kennedy would have won in 1960 without his vice presidential candidate, Lyndon B. Johnson, and the contribution Johnson made to winning in Texas. In 2016, Donald Trump chose Governor Mike Pence of Indiana as his running mate for several reasons. Before serving as governor, Pence had served in Congress for 12 years. He worked to reassure skeptical party leaders that Trump was a qualified candidate. Most important, as a devout Christian Pence increased Trump's electoral appeal among social conservatives, and as a Midwesterner he aided Trump's successful campaign forays into Michigan, Wisconsin, Ohio, and Pennsylvania. With the Democratic victory in 2020, we still don't know the effect of Kamala Harris as vice presidential candidate. The first woman of color on a presidential ticket, she may well be credited with affecting the very large turnout of African Americans in the large cities of battleground states; while plausible, this contention will be the subject of ongoing serious analysis.

As the institutional presidency has grown in size and complexity, most presidents of the past 35 years have sought to use their vice presidents as management resources after the election. The presidency of George W. Bush resulted in unprecedented power and responsibility for his vice president, Dick Cheney, who was active in cabinet meetings and policy formation as well as in organizing the war on terrorism and launching the Iraq War. Cheney is widely viewed as one of the most—if not the most—influential vice presidents in American history. In the Obama administration, Vice President Joe Biden wielded considerable influence as a liaison to Congress and as a sounding board on matters involving foreign affairs. Likewise, Vice President Mike Pence has served a similar liaison role with Congress and the conservative establishment in the Trump administration.

The President and Policy. The president's powers and institutional resources, taken together, give the chief executive a substantial voice in the nation's policy-making processes. Strictly speaking, presidents cannot introduce legislation; only members of Congress can formally propose new programs and policies. However, presidents often do send proposals to Congress, which in turn refers them to the committee with relevant jurisdiction. Sometimes these proposals are said to be dead on arrival, an indication that presidential preferences are at loggerheads with those in the House or Senate. This is especially common during periods of divided government. In such circumstances, presidents and legislators engage in bargaining, although in the end the status quo may prevail—a situation sometimes termed *gridlock*. Presidents are typically in a weak position under these conditions, especially if they have grand plans to change the status quo.[42] During periods of unified government, when presidents have fellow partisans in charge of each chamber, they may indeed seize the

---

42 D. Roderick Kiewiet and Mathew D. McCubbins, *The Logic of Delegation: Congressional Parties and the Appropriations Process* (Chicago: University of Chicago Press, 1991).

initiative and work to coordinate policy from the White House. Political scientist Charles Cameron suggests that the distinction between unified and divided government is quite consequential for presidential "style": when the government is unified, it makes the chief executive coordinator in chief; when divided, the president is the bargainer in chief.[43]

As noted earlier, Congress has come to expect the president to propose the government's budget since the Budget and Accounting Act of 1921, and the nation has come to expect presidential initiatives to deal with major problems. Some of these initiatives have encompassed multiple programs, such as Franklin Delano Roosevelt's New Deal. Sometimes presidents craft a single program in the hope that it will have a significant effect on both the nation and their political fortunes. In 2009 President Obama launched a major health care policy reform as his signature policy initiative. The Patient Protection and Affordable Care Act (ACA), known colloquially as Obamacare, was adopted during Obama's first term and remained a contentious issue, both in Congress and in the courts, throughout his second term. In 2012 and 2015, the Supreme Court ruled against challenges to Obamacare and upheld the major provisions of the law.[44] However, in 2014 the Court affirmed in *Burwell v. Hobby Lobby* a broader interpretation of the "religious exemption" clause of the ACA; by a 5-to-4 vote this decision allowed employers to decline to provide no-cost contraceptive coverage for female employees.[45] In 2017, President Trump made the replacement of Obama's signature policy one of his main priorities. The House passed a measure to "repeal and replace" Obamacare, but the Senate failed to do so.

There have been no further legislative attempts to repeal Obamacare. The Trump White House instead made extensive use of administrative tools—executive orders and agency decisions—to whittle away at the ACA, as well as regulatory arrangements in other economic and social areas.

The Contemporary Bases of Presidential Power

In the nineteenth century, when Congress was the United States' dominant institution of government, its members sometimes treated the president with disdain. Today, however, no one would assert that the presidency is an unimportant institution. This strength is not so much a function of personal charisma or political savvy as it is a reflection of the increasing power of the position. Presidents seek to dominate the policy-making process and claim the inherent power to lead the nation in times of war. The expansion of presidential power over the past century has come about not by accident but as the result of an ongoing

---

43 Cameron, "Bargaining and Presidential Power."

44 *National Federation of Independent Businesses v. Sebelius,* 567 U.S. 519 (2012); *King v. Burwell,* 576 U.S. 988 (2015).

45 *Burwell v. Hobby Lobby Stores,* 573 U.S. 682 (2014).

effort by successive presidents to enlarge the powers of the office. As the framers of the Constitution predicted, presidential ambition has been a powerful and unrelenting force in American politics.

Generally, presidents can expand their power through three means: their party, popular mobilization, and administration. In the first instance, presidents may construct or strengthen national partisan institutions that they can use to influence the legislative process and implement their programs. Alternatively, or in addition, presidents may use popular appeals to create a mass base of support that enables them to subordinate their political foes. This tactic has sometimes been called the strategy of going public or the "rhetorical" presidency.[46] In the third instance, presidents may seek to bolster their control of executive agencies or create new administrative institutions and procedures that will reduce their dependence on Congress and give them a more independent governing and policy-making capability. The use of executive orders in lieu of seeking to persuade Congress to enact legislation is, perhaps, the most obvious example.

Party as a Source of Power. All presidents have relied on the members and leaders of their own party to implement their legislative agendas. But presidents do not control their party; party members have considerable autonomy. President Obama made immigration reform one of his first-term priorities, but he failed to induce the Democratic-controlled Congress to take up the issue. In his second term, he had even more difficulty with his own party on the issue of trade, a matter on which the president had hoped for a signature accomplishment. The Trans-Pacific Partnership, an effort to cement trade agreements with the United States' Asian partners, was initially defeated in the House because too few Democrats would support it. It ultimately succeeded because of an unusual coalition between Obama and Republican majorities in the two legislative chambers. (However, Trump reversed this agreement in one of his first acts after his inauguration.)

When Obama was first elected, he declared his intention to seek bipartisan support for all his programs. Congressional Republicans, however, seeing little to gain from supporting Obama and much to lose if his administration were successful, opposed the president's domestic and foreign policy initiatives. With overwhelming Democratic majorities in both houses of Congress in 2009–11, Obama had no difficulty turning to the Democratic leadership for support. After Republicans captured the House in the 2010 election, and even more so after they won the Senate in 2014, neither Democrat-only coalitions nor bipartisan overtures from the president were sufficient to produce major policy victories.

After the 2016 election, Republicans controlled the presidency and both chambers of Congress, constituting a unified government that usually bodes well for the party in control. This was not the case in the early days of the Trump administration. In each chamber, sufficient heterogeneity within the Republican ranks made it difficult at best to pass legislation relying only on fellow partisans. The 2018 midterm elections, in which the Democrats captured the House, complicated life further for the Trump administration. With bipartisan legislative

---

46 Kernell, *Going Public*; see also Tulis, *The Rhetorical Presidency*.

Figure 7.3

THE PRESIDENTIAL BATTING AVERAGE,* 1953–2019

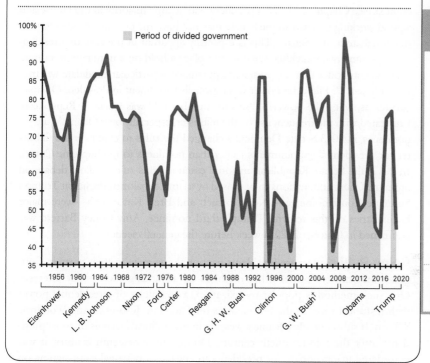

*Percentage of congressional votes in which the president took the position supported by Congress.
†In 2001, the government was divided for only part of the year.
NOTE: Percentages are based on votes on which presidents took a position.
SOURCES: *Congressional Quarterly Weekly Report*, January 3, 2011, pp. 18–24; CQ Almanac, https://library.cqpress.com/cqalmanac/toc.php?mode=cqalmanac-appendix&level=2&values=Presidential+Support+Tables (accessed 3/8/18); and authors' update.

solutions beyond his reach, Trump relied less on Congress and turned instead to purely executive actions.

As Obama's final six years and Trump's last two years have illustrated, in the U.S. system of separated powers, the president's party may be in the minority in Congress and unable to do much for the chief executive's programs (Figure 7.3). This is because the majority party in a legislative chamber may control not only votes on the floor but also *what* is voted on. When the president's party is the minority, it lacks agenda control. Consequently, although party colleagues can be valuable to chief executives, the president's party is not a fully reliable tool. The more unified the president's party is in supporting the president's legislative requests, the more unified the opposition party is likely to be. The president often professes to be above partisanship to win bipartisan support in Congress. But to the extent that presidents pursue a bipartisan strategy, they cannot throw themselves fully into building the party loyalty and discipline that would maximize the value of their own party's support in Congress. This is a dilemma for every president, and it is particularly acute with an opposition-controlled Congress.

The role of the filibuster in the Senate should not be underestimated in this context (see Chapter 6). Even a president with a large majority in the House and a good working majority in the Senate may not have the 60 votes needed to shut down debate in the Senate. This is especially apparent in the case of presidential appointments; individual senators can place a hold on a nomination, putting everyone on notice that the president's pursuit of a particular candidate will trigger a filibuster.[47] Filibuster power was especially prominent in President Obama's two terms, when the powerful "senator number 60" was usually a Republican. Frustrated with the frequent use of the filibuster, especially over Obama's judicial nominees, in 2013 Senate Democrats changed the rules to eliminate the filibuster for presidential appointments (other than nominees to the Supreme Court). In 2017, the Senate Republican majority extended this rule to allow debate on Supreme Court nominations to be closed by a simple majority. President Trump's Supreme Court nominees—Neil Gorsuch and Brett Kavanaugh—were major beneficiaries of this reform. Trump's third nominee, Amy Coney Barrett, was confirmed in October 2020, a week before the general election.

Going Public. Because presidents cannot always rely on their party in Congress, they must consider other methods of advancing their policy interests. One such method is popular mobilization, a technique of presidential power with historical roots in the presidencies of Theodore Roosevelt and Woodrow Wilson. It subsequently became a weapon in the political arsenals of most presidents after the mid-twentieth century. During the nineteenth century, it was considered inappropriate for presidents to engage in personal campaigning on their own behalf or in support of programs and policies. When Andrew Johnson broke this unwritten rule and made a series of speeches vehemently seeking public support for his Reconstruction program, even some of his most ardent supporters were shocked at what was seen as a lack of decorum and dignity.[48]

The president who used public appeals perhaps most effectively was Franklin Delano Roosevelt. Political scientist Sidney Milkis observes that Roosevelt was "firmly persuaded of the need to form a direct link between the executive office and the public."[49] Roosevelt developed a number of tactics aimed at forging such a link. Like his predecessors, he often embarked on speaking trips around the nation to promote his programs. On one such tour, he told a crowd, "I regain strength just by meeting the American people."[50] In addition, Roosevelt made limited but important use of the new electronic medium, radio, to reach millions of Americans. In his famous "fireside chats," the president, or

---

47 A powerful argument that invokes this logic is that of Keith Krehbiel in *Pivotal Politics: A Theory of U.S. Lawmaking* (Chicago: University of Chicago Press, 1998).

48 Tulis, *The Rhetorical Presidency*, p. 91.

49 Quoted in Sidney M. Milkis, *The President and the Parties: The Transformation of the American Party System since the New Deal* (New York: Oxford University Press, 1993), p. 97.

50 Quoted in James MacGregor Burns, *Roosevelt: The Lion and the Fox (1882–1940)* (New York: Harcourt, Brace, 1956), p. 317.

at least his voice, came into living rooms across the country to discuss programs and policies and to assure Americans that he was aware of their difficulties and working diligently toward solutions.[51]

Roosevelt was also an innovator in the realm of what now might be called press relations. When he entered the White House, he faced a mainly hostile press largely controlled by conservative members of the business establishment. As the president wrote, "All the fat-cat newspapers—85 percent of the whole—have been utterly opposed to everything the Administration is seeking."[52] Roosevelt hoped to use the press to mold public opinion, but to do so he needed to circumvent the editors and publishers who were generally unsympathetic to his goals. To this end, the president worked to cultivate the reporters who covered the White House: he held twice-weekly press conferences at which he offered candid answers to reporters' questions and made important policy announcements that would provide the reporters with significant stories to file with their papers.[53] Roosevelt had the good sense to designate the role of press secretary, who organized the press conferences and made certain that reporters distinguished presidential comments that were off the record from those that could be attributed directly to the president.

All presidents since Roosevelt have sought to craft a public relations strategy that emphasizes their strengths and maximizes their popular appeal. The White House Communications Office became an important institution within the EOP beginning with the Clinton administration.[54] Since then the Communications Office has been responsible not only for responding to reporters' queries but also for developing a coordinated communications strategy: promoting the president's policy goals, developing responses to unflattering news stories, and ensuring that a favorable image of the president dominates the news, insofar as it's possible. Consistent with President Obama's successful use of social media in his 2008 election campaign, the Obama administration's Communications Office emphasized social networking techniques to reach newsmakers and the American people directly. President Trump, like candidate Trump, has extensively used Twitter as part of an innovative going public strategy. Going over the heads not only of his own party but also of the traditional media, Trump communicates directly with his followers, maintaining an almost personal relationship with his political base, and attacks his opponents, especially the press. His rocky relationship with the mainstream media has been exacerbated by turnover among his press secretaries, on the one hand, and their inclination to limit press briefings, on the other.

---

51 The distribution of radio ownership in the 1930s was quite uneven, however. Roosevelt reinforced his "going public" radio addresses with a similarly uneven distribution of relief funds during the Great Depression. Counties with a high concentration of radio ownership received more relief funds, even after controlling for income and unemployment. Popular mobilization and public policy worked hand in hand to burnish the president's reputation. See David Strömberg, "Radio's Impact on Public Spending," *Quarterly Journal of Economics* 119, no. 1 (2004): 189–221.

52 Burns, *Roosevelt*, p. 317.

53 Kernell, *Going Public*, p. 79.

54 The office had been established in the Nixon administration and was also used very effectively by President Reagan.

Figure 7.4
PUBLIC APPEARANCES BY PRESIDENTS

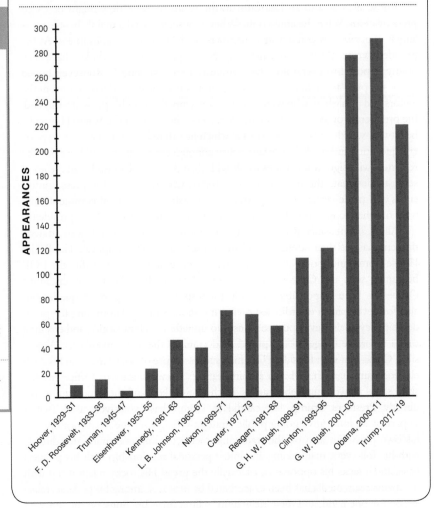

ANALYZING THE EVIDENCE

In the nineteenth century, presidents seldom made public speeches or other public appearances. By the end of the twentieth century, the number of times presidents went public had increased dramatically. What accounts for the growth in public appearances? What do presidents hope to accomplish through speeches and other public events? What risks do presidents take when they seek to develop and use popular support as a political tool?

NOTE: Only the first two years of each term are included, because the last two years include many purely political appearances for the president's reelection campaign.

SOURCES: Samuel Kernell, *Going Public: New Strategies of Presidential Leadership*, 4th ed. (Washington, DC: CQ Press, 2007), p. 118; Lyn Ragsdale, *Vital Statistics on the Presidency*, 3rd ed. (Washington, DC: CQ Press, 2009), pp. 202–3; *Washington Post*, http://projects.washingtonpost.com/potus-tracker (accessed 8/8/11); and authors' updates.

In addition to using the media, recent presidents have reached out directly to the American public to gain its approval (Figure 7.4). During his first full month in office, for example, Obama addressed Congress and the American people on numerous occasions. President Trump has relied less on formal speeches from the Oval Office or to Congress and more on campaign-style rallies around the country. And, of course, his flurry of tweets is a daily occurrence.

Figure 7.5
PRESIDENTIAL PERFORMANCE RATINGS

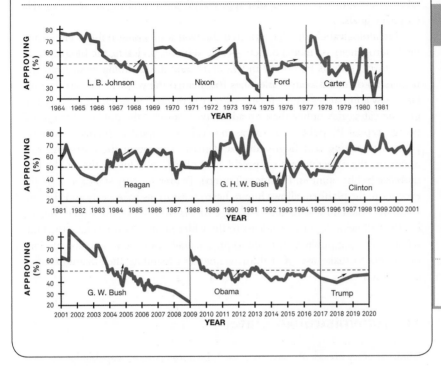

ANALYZING THE EVIDENCE

In the presidential performance-rating poll, respondents are asked, "Do you approve of the way the president is handling his job?" The graphs show the percentage of positive responses. What factors help explain changes in presidential approval ratings? Does popular approval really affect presidential power?

NOTE: Arrows indicate preelection upswings.
SOURCE: Gallup, https://news.gallup.com/interactives/185273/presidential-job-approval-center.aspx (accessed 10/6/20).

The Limits of Going Public. Although some presidents have made effective use of popular appeals to overcome congressional opposition, popular support has not been a firm foundation for presidential power. To begin with, it is notoriously fickle. President George W. Bush maintained an approval rating of over 70 percent for more than a year after the September 11 terrorist attacks. By 2003, however, his rating had fallen nearly 20 points as American casualties in Iraq mounted, and his popularity steadily declined through the remainder of his presidency. Obama began his presidency with a very high approval rating, but after 2010 it hovered in the 40s and 50s. By the time he left office in 2017, however, it had rebounded dramatically to nearly 60 percent approval. Trump began his presidency with low popular approval; throughout his term it remained low, hovering in the high 30s to low 40s. Such declines in popular approval during a president's term in office are nearly inevitable and follow a predictable pattern (Figure 7.5). New presidents generate popular support by promising to undertake important programs that will contribute directly to the well-being of large numbers of Americans, but presidential performance almost always falls short of those promises, leading to a sharp decline in public support and an ensuing collapse of presidential influence. Reagan and Clinton are the exceptions among modern presidents—they both left office at least as popular as when they arrived. Trump is an exception of a different sort, having taken office with very low popular approval despite promising an active agenda of policy goals.

Technological change has affected the tactics of going public. The growing heterogeneity of media outlets—cable stations, podcasts, the blogosphere, social media such as Facebook and Twitter—and the declining viewership and readership of mainstream outlets has fragmented the public. This has necessitated new approaches with a focus on "narrowcasting" to reach targeted demographic categories rather than broadcasting to reach "the public." Instead of going "capital P" public, narrowcasting seeks to appeal to myriad "small p" publics. Shrinking and fragmented audiences have raised the costs and cast doubt on the effectiveness of presidential efforts to educate the public and mobilize public opinion. President Trump's Twitter strategy stands as a partial exception; the platform allows him to narrowcast to his base easily and cheaply, while the conventional media's coverage of his tweets magnifies their impact, in effect allowing him to broadcast to the wider public. Nevertheless, the limitations of going public as a route to presidential power have also led modern presidents to make use of a third technique: expanding their administrative capabilities.

The Administrative State

Contemporary presidents have increased the administrative capabilities of their office in two important ways. First, they have sought to increase White House control over the federal bureaucracy. Second, they have expanded the role of executive orders and other instruments of direct presidential governance. Taken together, these components of administrative strategy have given presidents the capacity to achieve their programmatic and policy goals even when they are unable to secure congressional approval, which is often the case under divided government. Indeed, some recent presidents have been able to accomplish quite a bit without much congressional, partisan, or even public support.

regulatory review

The Office of Management and Budget's function of reviewing all agency regulations and other rule making before they become official policy.

Appointments and Regulatory Review. Presidents have sought to increase their influence through bureaucratic appointments and **regulatory review**. By appointing loyal supporters to top jobs in the bureaucracy, presidents increase the likelihood that agencies will follow the president's wishes. As Analyzing the Evidence on pp. 294–5 shows, recent presidents have increased the number of political appointees in the bureaucracy.

Through regulatory review, presidents have tried to control rule making by the agencies of the executive branch. Whenever Congress enacts a statute, its implementation requires the promulgation of hundreds of rules by the agency charged with administering the law. Some congressional statutes are quite detailed and leave agencies with relatively little discretion. Typically, however, Congress enacts a broad statement of legislative intent and delegates to the appropriate agency the power to fill in many important details.[55] In other words, Congress often says to an administrative agency: "Here is the problem. Deal with it."[56]

The discretion Congress delegates to administrative agencies has provided recent presidents with an important avenue for expanding their power. For example, President Clinton believed the president had full authority to order agencies of the executive branch to adopt such rules as the president thought appropriate, and he issued 107 directives ordering administrators to propose specific rules and regulations. Presidential rule-making directives have covered a wide variety of topics. For example, after Clinton ordered the Food and Drug Administration (FDA) to develop rules restricting the marketing of tobacco products to children, White House and FDA staffers prepared nearly a thousand pages of new regulations affecting tobacco manufacturers and vendors.[57] Although Republicans denounced Clinton's actions as a usurpation of power,[58] President George W. Bush continued the practice of issuing presidential directives to agencies to spur them to issue new rules and regulations. When he assumed office, President Obama appointed the Harvard law professor Cass Sunstein to head his regulatory review effort; under Sunstein, regulatory review became an even more important arrow in the president's quiver. In each of these cases, presidents, often frustrated by partisan opposition in the legislature, have drawn on tools enabling them to bypass Congress altogether.

The Trump administration did not face a partisan disadvantage in the legislature when its term began. The growing dysfunction within the Republican majorities in each chamber, however, has frustrated Trump's efforts nonetheless, leading Trump along the same path as his predecessors in seeking new modes of governance—in his case, rule by executive order.

Governing by Decree: Executive Orders. Contemporary presidents have enhanced their power to govern unilaterally through the use of executive orders and other forms of presidential decrees, including executive agreements, national security findings and directives, proclamations, reorganization plans, signing statements, and others.[59] Executive orders have a long history in the United States and have served as the vehicles for a number of important government policies. These include the purchase of Louisiana, the annexation of

---

55 The classic critique of this process is Lowi, *The End of Liberalism*.

56 Kenneth Culp Davis, *Administrative Law Treatise* (St. Paul, MN: West, 1958), p. 9.

57 Elena Kagan, "Presidential Administration," *Harvard Law Review* 114 (2001): 2265.

58 For example, Douglas W. Kmiec, "Expanding Executive Power," in *The Rule of Law in the Wake of Clinton,* ed. Roger Pilon (Washington, DC: Cato Institute, 2000), pp. 47–68.

59 A complete inventory is provided in Harold C. Relyea, *Presidential Directives: Background and Review,* CRS Report for Congress no. 98–611 (Washington, DC: Congressional Research Service, 2001).

Unilateral Action and Presidential Power

Contributed by
Jon Rogowski
Harvard University

As we've seen in this chapter, Article II of the U.S. Constitution grants the president a limited number of expressed powers, but modern presidents have claimed additional powers and have sometimes used them to act unilaterally on controversial issues. Critics of these unilateral actions express concern that they represent an overreach of presidential power, by allowing presidents to circumvent the legislative process.

But what does research tell us about how and when presidents exercise unilateral powers? Executive orders are perhaps the most prominent examples of unilateral action. Franklin Roosevelt used executive orders to implement parts of the New Deal and to intern Japanese Americans during World War II. More recent presidents have used them to allow warrantless wiretapping by the National Security Administration, to suspend deportation proceedings for some undocumented immigrants, and to deny entry to the United States for people from countries suspected of terrorist connections. However, executive orders are not the only means through which presidents can exercise unilateral powers. Presidents can also use memoranda, proclamations, and other tools to change policies through the executive branch without involving Congress.

The figure below shows how presidents have used these various tools between 1933 and 2016. As the red line illustrates, executive orders have accounted for a relatively small percentage of unilateral actions issued by recent presidents. Since Presidents Kennedy and Johnson issued 510 executive orders in 1963, the most in any year since the conclusion of World War II, the number of executive orders has generally declined.

Types of Unilateral Action, 1933–2016

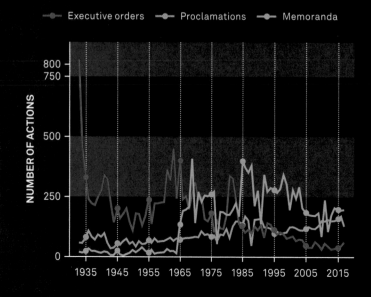

Presidents' declining uses of executive orders, however, should not be taken as evidence that presidents have shied away from unilateral action. We see that presidents have generally made greater use of memoranda, proclamations, and other forms of unilateral action when they issued fewer executive orders. For instance, relatively few memoranda were issued in the 1950s, 1960s, and early 1980s, when the annual number of executive orders was fairly high, but in the 1970s, late 1980s, and 1990s, memoranda generally outnumbered executive orders. Presidents have also made greater use of proclamations, as their number has increased rather steadily from 52 in 1945 to 168 in 2016.

Presidential Unilateral Action, 1933–2016

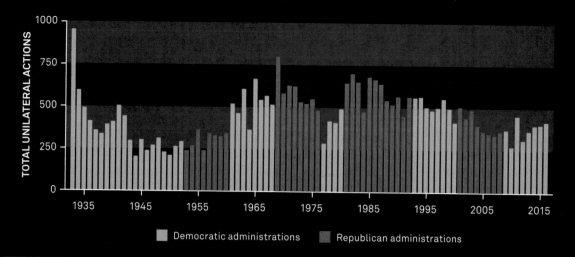

Democratic administrations ■   Republican administrations ■

But has the overall use of unilateral action increased in recent years? Combining the various tools of unilateral power, the figure above displays the total number of unilateral actions issued by presidents between 1933 and 2016. Overall, presidents' use of unilateral powers has remained relatively stable over the last seven decades. The red and blue regions of the plot indicate Republican and Democratic presidents, respectively. These data show some partisan differences in how presidents use unilateral powers, with an annual average of 475 for Republicans and 419 for Democrats.

Unilateral Action and Divided Government

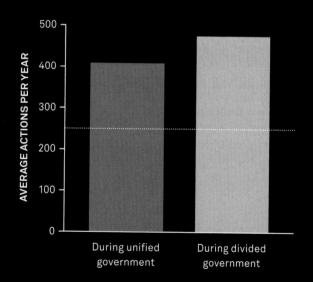

Every president from Nixon to Obama, however, confronted divided government for at least part of their term. During periods of divided government, presidents issued significantly greater numbers of unilateral actions, with an average of 409 per year during unified government compared with 475 during divided government. This finding suggests that contemporary presidents make increased use of unilateral powers when the opposite party controls Congress and presents challenges for a president's legislative agenda.

While the data presented here do not tell us about the content or the policy significance of presidents' unilateral actions, the patterns suggest that unilateral powers may allow presidents to sidestep policy disagreements between the White House and Capitol Hill. The implications of this development merit careful contemplation.

SOURCE: Aaron R. Kaufman and Jon C. Rogowski, "The Unilateral Presidency, 1953–2017," presented at the Annual Meeting of the American Political Science Association, San Francisco, CA, August 31–September 3, 2017.

**ANALYZING
THE EVIDENCE**

During the twentieth
century, presidents
made increasingly
frequent use of
executive orders
to accomplish their
policy goals. What
factors explain this
development? How
have Congress and the
courts responded to
increased presidential
assertiveness?

Figure 7.6
EXECUTIVE ORDERS, 1789–2020

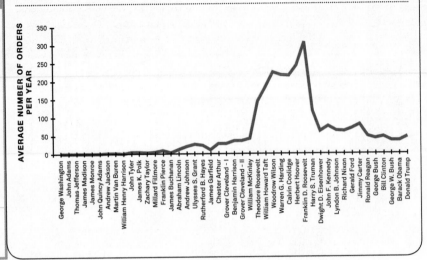

SOURCE: American Presidency Project, www.presidency.ucsb.edu/data/orders.php (accessed
11/1/20).

Texas, the emancipation of the enslaved people, the internment of the Japanese
in World War II, the desegregation of the military, the initiation of affirmative action, and the creation of important federal agencies, among them the
Environmental Protection Agency, the FDA, and the Peace Corps.[60]

In the realm of foreign policy, unilateral presidential actions in the form
of executive agreements have virtually replaced treaties as the nation's chief
foreign policy instruments.[61] Although wars and national emergencies produce
the highest volume of executive orders, such presidential actions also occur
frequently in peacetime (Figure 7.6). For example, President Obama took the
United States into the Paris Agreement on climate change, and President Trump
withdrew from it, each entirely on their own authority and without congressional participation. Of course, presidents may not use executive orders to issue
whatever commands they please. If presidents issue an executive order, proclamation, directive, or the like, in principle they do so pursuant to the powers
granted to them by the Constitution or delegated to them by Congress, usually
through a statute. When presidents issue such orders, they generally state the
constitutional or statutory basis for their actions. For example, when President
Truman ordered the desegregation of the armed services, he did so pursuant

60 Terry M. Moe and William G. Howell, "The Presidential Power of Unilateral Action,"
Journal of Law, Economics, and Organization 15, no. 1 (1999): 132–79. Also see Howell,
Power without Persuasion.

61 Moe and Howell, "The Presidential Power of Unilateral Action," p. 164.

to his constitutional powers as commander in chief. In a similar vein, when President Johnson issued an executive order establishing equal employment opportunity and barring hiring discrimination for federal contract positions, he asserted that the order was designed to implement the 1964 Civil Rights Act, which prohibited employment discrimination. When an executive order has no statutory or constitutional basis, the courts have held it to be void. The most important case illustrating this point is *Youngstown Sheet and Tube Company v. Sawyer*, the so-called steel seizure case of 1952.[62] Here the Supreme Court ruled that President Truman's seizure of the nation's steel mills during the Korean War had no statutory or constitutional basis and was thus invalid.

A number of court decisions, though, have established broad boundaries that leave considerable room for presidential action. By illustration, the courts have held that Congress may approve a presidential action after the fact or through "acquiescence"—for example, by not objecting for long periods or by continuing to fund programs established by executive orders. In addition, the courts have indicated that some areas, most notably military policy, are presidential in character, and they have allowed presidents wide latitude to make policy in these realms by executive decree. Thus, within the very broad limits established by the courts, presidential orders can be important policy tools.

Although all presidents have used the executive order as a policy tool, government by executive order has become an especially common practice since the Clinton presidency, reflecting the growing difficulty of making policy through the legislative process. Divided government and increasing interparty policy differences have raised these costs. Clinton's frequent use of this strategy showed that an activist president could develop and implement a significant policy agenda without legislation—a lesson that was not lost on his successors. One of President George W. Bush's most important orders was a directive authorizing the creation of military tribunals to try noncitizens accused of involvement in acts of terrorism.[63] By the end of his second term alone, President Obama had issued more than 250 executive orders, including a significant and controversial one that would protect some four million undocumented immigrants from the threat of deportation. That order spurred a variety of legal challenges and one federal court ruling blocking its implementation. In June 2016, in a major blow to Obama's immigration policy, the Supreme Court upheld the lower-court decision. President Trump issued 33 executive orders in the first 100 days of his administration, more than any of his predecessors issued over this period. Many of these directives were aimed at reversing policies of the Obama years.[64]

---

62 *Youngstown Sheet and Tube Company v. Sawyer*, 343 U.S. 579 (1952).

63 *Hamdan v. Rumsfeld*, 548 U.S. 557 (2006). In 2006, the Supreme Court determined that the military tribunals established by Bush's executive order to try detainees at the U.S. naval base at Guantánamo Bay, Cuba, violated both the Uniform Code of Military Justice and the Geneva Conventions.

64 National Archives and Records Administration, "2017 Donald Trump Executive Orders," www.federalregister.gov/presidential-documents/executive-orders/donald-trump/2017 (accessed 1/21/20).

Signing Statements. Recent presidents have made frequent use of presidential signing statements to negate congressional actions with which they disagree.[65] A **signing statement** is an announcement made by the president when signing a bill into law. Sometimes these statements present the president's interpretation of the law or predict the benefits the new law will bring to the nation. Occasionally, presidents have used signing statements to point to sections of the law they deem improper or unconstitutional and to instruct executive branch agencies on how to execute the law.[66]

An announcement made by the president when signing a bill into law, sometimes presenting the president's interpretation of the law, as well as remarks predicting the benefits it will bring to the nation.

Presidents have made signing statements throughout American history, though many were not recorded and so did not become part of the official legislative record. Ronald Reagan's attorney general, Edwin Meese, is generally credited with transforming the signing statement into a routine tool of presidential direct action.[67] Meese believed that carefully crafted signing statements would provide a basis for action by executive agencies and, perhaps even more important, would become part of the historical context of a piece of legislation if judicial interpretation ever became necessary. Indeed, to make certain that signing statements became part of the legislative history, Meese reached an agreement with the West Publishing Company to include them in its authoritative texts.[68] Reagan then proceeded to use detailed and artfully designed signing statements—prepared by the Department of Justice—to attempt to reinterpret certain congressional acts.

Despite subsequent court rulings decrying the notion that the president has the power to declare acts of Congress unconstitutional[69] and stating that the president does not have the authority to "excise or sever provisions of a bill with which he disagrees,"[70] George H. W. Bush[71] and George W. Bush continued the same tactic of reinterpreting and nullifying congressional enactments. The latter challenged more than 800 legislative provisions with his signing statements, including important domestic and security matters such as a congressional effort to ban the use of torture by American interrogators. Though Democrats denounced George W. Bush's use of signing statements, President Obama occasionally used the same tactic. By the end of his presidency in November 2016, Obama had issued 36 signing statements in which he offered his own interpretations of portions of the bills he signed into law. Through 2019, President Trump issued 51 signing statements.

65 Mark R. Killenbeck, "A Matter of Mere Approval? The Role of the President in the Creation of Legislative History," *University of Arkansas Law Review* 48 (1995): 239.

66 Philip J. Cooper, *By Order of the President: The Use and Abuse of Executive Direct Action* (Lawrence: University Press of Kansas, 2002), p. 201.

67 Cooper, *By Order of the President*, p. 201.

68 Cooper, *By Order of the President*, p. 203.

69 *Ameron v. U.S. Army Corps of Engineers*, 610 FSupp 750 (D.N.J., 1985).

70 *Lear Siegler v. Lehman*, 842 F2d 1102 (Ninth Cir., 1988).

71 Cooper, *By Order of the President*, p. 207.

Meese's contrivance has become a full-blown instrument of presidential power. Adding to the importance of this power in recent years, as Meese had hoped, courts have begun giving weight to presidential signing statements when interpreting the meaning of statutes.[72] Still, the legal status of signing statements has not been fully resolved.

The Advantages of the Administrative Strategy. Through the course of American history, party leadership and popular appeals have played important roles in presidential efforts to overcome political opposition, and both continue to be instruments of presidential power. Reagan's tax cuts and Clinton's budget victories were achieved with strong partisan support. George W. Bush, lacking the oratorical skills of a Reagan or a Roosevelt, nevertheless made good use of sophisticated communications strategies to promote his agenda. Yet in the modern era, parties have waned in institutional strength, and the effects of popular appeals have often proved evanescent. The limitations of the alternatives have increasingly impelled presidents to expand the administrative capabilities of the office and their own capacity for unilateral action as means of achieving their policy goals. Recent efforts such as the expansion of the EOP; the development of regulatory review; and the use of executive orders, signing statements, and the like have enabled presidents to achieve significant policy results despite congressional opposition.

To be sure, the administrative strategy does not always succeed. In some instances, the federal courts have struck down unilateral actions by the president. And occasionally Congress acts to reverse presidential orders. For example, in 1999, Congress enacted legislation prohibiting the Department of Education from carrying out a presidential directive to administer national tests of reading and mathematics.[73] And before that, in 1996, in an attempt to strengthen its capacity to block President Clinton's aggressive regulatory review program, the Republican-controlled Congress enacted the Congressional Review Act (CRA). This legislation requires federal agencies to send all proposed regulations to Congress for review 60 days before they take effect. It also allows the House and Senate to enact a joint resolution of disapproval that would not only void the regulation but also prohibit the relevant agencies from subsequently issuing any substantially similar rule.[74]

In principle, perhaps, Congress could respond even more vigorously to unilateral policy making by the president. Certainly, a Congress willing to impeach

72 Kristy L. Carroll, "Whose Statute Is It Anyway?: Why and How Courts Should Use Presidential Signing Statements When Interpreting Federal Statutes," *Catholic University Law Review* 46, no. 2 (1997): 475–521.

73 Kagan, "Presidential Administration," p. 2351.

74 Terry M. Moe, "The Presidency and the Bureaucracy: The Presidential Advantage," in *The Presidency and the Political System*, ed. Michael Nelson, 7th ed. (Washington, DC: CQ Press, 2003), pp. 425–57. As it has turned out, Congress used this procedure only once, in 2001, until 2017. During the first 100 days of the Trump administration, the Republican Congress passed 14 resolutions objecting to administrative rules issued during the Obama years.

presidents should have the mettle to overturn their administrative directives. But the president has significant advantages in such struggles with Congress. In battles over presidential directives and orders, Congress is on the defensive, reacting to presidential initiatives. The framers of the Constitution saw "energy," or the ability to take initiative, as a key feature of executive power.[75] While the president can take action quickly and decisively, in order to respond, Congress must initiate the cumbersome and time-consuming lawmaking process, overcome internal divisions, and enact legislation that the president may ultimately veto. Moreover, in such battles Congress faces a significant collective action problem insofar as members are likely to be more sensitive to the substance of a president's action and its immediate effects on their constituents than to the more general implications of presidential administration for the long-term vitality of Congress.

The Limits of Presidential Power

Presidents are powerful political actors and have become increasingly so during the past century. This is the take-home point of this chapter. But there are limits to presidential power. Indeed, presidents have had to resort to institutional and behavioral invention—signing statements, executive orders, public appeals—precisely because their official powers are limited. As the framers intended, the separation of powers is a mighty constraint. As the popular Washington adage goes, "the president proposes; the Congress disposes." Presidents cannot always bend Congress to their will, though it is an easier task when their party controls the two chambers. And yet, even the most powerful congressional players must obtain the president's consent to pursue their agendas, as the presentment clause of the Constitution requires. Through veto power the president can defeat—but more important, can influence in advance—congressional aspirations. Presidential power is real, but it is tempered by the necessity of bargaining with the legislature and managing the bureaucracy, along with the constraints imposed by rulings of the federal judiciary. The growth in presidential power over the last hundred years has required the acquiescence if not the outright support of all the other players in the game.

CONCLUSION: PRESIDENTIAL POWER—MYTHS AND REALITIES

We began this chapter by observing that presidents have a distinct institutional advantage vis-à-vis other governmental actors. Presidents are unitary "deciders," whereas other political actors must contend with institutions whose

---

75 Clinton L. Rossiter, ed., *The Federalist Papers; Alexander Hamilton, James Madison, and John Jay* (New York: New American Library, 1961), no. 70 (Alexander Hamilton) pp. 423–30.

decision-making processes are collective, requiring deliberation, debate, compromise, and voting. Unitary actors have an advantage in pursuing their self-interest (rationality principle); actors in collective institutions have to overcome the infirmities of and barriers to collective action (collective action principle). The institutional differences between executives and legislatures determine their relative capacities to initiate and execute policy in a complex modern world (institution principle) and have contributed to the steady growth of presidential power. This has occasioned an ongoing debate between the advocates of a strong presidency and those who favor the United States' traditional separation of powers system. We conclude this chapter with an assessment of this debate in terms of some myths and realities of presidential power.

Myth 1: Executive Superiority in National Emergencies. Advocates of presidential power have typically advanced three arguments for deferring to the White House. The first, which echoes themes articulated by Alexander Hamilton and others among the nation's Founders, is that executive power is needed to deal with emergencies and to ensure the nation's security.[76] Although no one could argue with this position in the abstract, particularly in an age of global terrorism, presidents can sometimes be too anxious to act forcefully in response to what they perceive as security threats. The framers of the Constitution gave Congress, and not the president, the power to make war precisely because they feared that presidents might be too quick to commit the nation to armed conflicts. "The strongest passions and most dangerous weaknesses of the human breast," wrote James Madison, "ambition, avarice, vanity, the honorable or venial love of fame, are all in a conspiracy [within the executive branch] against the desire and duty of peace. Hence it has grown into an axiom that the executive is the department of power most distinguished by its propensity to war."[77]

But if the president is too anxious to go to war, is Congress too reluctant to respond to emergencies? The short answer is no. It would be difficult to identify an instance in the past half-century in which the nation's security was compromised because Congress refused to act, though in some cases, including perhaps the Iraq War, the president was too quick to take vigorous action. When the nation has faced actual emergencies, Congress has seldom refused to grant appropriate powers to the president.

Thus, support of presidential power on the grounds of the executive's superior capacity to respond to emergencies is a false basis on two counts: the

---

76 A contemporary statement of this position is Harvey C. Mansfield Jr., *Taming the Prince: The Ambivalence of Modern Executive Power* (New York: Free Press, 1989), chap. 1.

77 Richard Loss, ed., *The Letters of Pacificus and Helvidius* (Delmar, NY: Scholars Facsimiles and Reprints, 1976), pp. 91–2. It may be noted that the context in which the framers met was one in which European kings had displayed this same propensity to wage war and pursue foreign adventures, a tendency checked in England by a more activist Parliament only after centuries of disputation with the monarch.

---

legislature is not an obstacle to expeditious responses to emergency, and presidents all too frequently use executive power for purposes other than responding to emergencies. Executive superiority in national emergencies is Myth 1.

Myth 2: Superior Presidential Responsiveness to the Public Interest.

A second argument in favor of expanded presidential power is that the president champions the national interest as opposed to the particularistic interests defended by members of Congress, party politicians, bureaucrats, and most other political actors. This notion that the president is above party politics seems reminiscent of the premodern yearning for a wise and beneficent king who would brush aside the selfish claims of manipulative courtiers and rule in the best interests of all his subjects. Perhaps such kings have existed, but the behavior of the kingly stratum as a whole does not inspire much confidence in the notion that powerful executives are a good antidote to factional selfishness and the entreaties of special interests.

Presidents, to be sure, are unitary actors. As such they may find it more difficult than members of Congress to escape responsibility for their conduct or, through inaction, to become free riders on the efforts of others. And presidents are indeed accountable to a larger, more heterogeneous constituency than most House members or senators. To this extent, proponents of Myth 2 might have some merit. Empirically, however, presidents do not appear much more likely than senators or representatives to set aside personal concerns in favor of some abstract public good. Presidents often enough promote programs designed mainly to reward important political backers and contributors rather than to serve the larger public interest. In such instances, personal or political calculations appear to outweigh presidential concern for the public interest. Hence Myth 2, with some qualifications, is superior presidential responsiveness to the public interest.[78]

Myth 3: The Presidency as More Democratic Than Congress.

A third argument in support of enhanced presidential power is the contention that the presidency is a more democratic institution than Congress.[79] This argument has a certain surface plausibility. The president is, of course, the nation's only elected official who can claim to represent all the people. As a decision-making institution, however, the presidency is perhaps America's least democratic entity.

Presidential decision making generally takes place in private and is often shrouded in secrecy. Recent presidents have asserted that the processes leading up to their decisions are shielded by executive privilege. The Obama administration, for example, resisted requests for transparency in many of its foreign

---

78 A detailed presentation of this argument with supporting evidence may be found in Douglas L. Kriner and Andrew Reeves, *The Particularistic President: Executive Branch Politics and Political Inequality* (New York: Cambridge University Press, 2015).

79 Grant McConnell, *The Modern Presidency* (New York: St. Martin's Press, 1976). See also Steven Calabresi, "Some Normative Arguments for the Unitary Executive," *Arkansas Law Review* 48 (1995): 23–104.

---

policy pursuits, including the Trans-Pacific Partnership trade deal and negotiations with Iran on ending its nuclear program in 2015. A number of Trump administration immigration policies have been formulated inside the White House without much external scrutiny. Indeed, sometimes presidential decisions themselves are not revealed to the public or even to Congress. Many so-called national security directives issued by recent presidents have been used to initiate secret missions by intelligence and defense agencies.[80] For many years, too, presidents have signed secret executive agreements with other governments obligating the United States to various forms of action without congressional knowledge, much less approval.

Arguably, Congress is inherently a more democratic decision-making institution than the presidency. To exert influence, competing factions in Congress must maintain active relationships with important groups and forces in civil society. Journalists may cluck their tongues at the "senator from Goldman Sachs" or the "congressman from Boeing." But ties to the financial sector, the aerospace industry, or other key constituencies help members of Congress exercise influence on Capitol Hill and strengthen the collective body vis-à-vis the executive branch. Today, indeed, Congress must sometimes mobilize constituency pressure just to compel the president to implement its decisions—for as we have seen, it depends on the executive to carry out and enforce most of its dictates. As we saw when we discussed presidential signing statements, presidents are increasingly likely to claim they are not required to implement decisions with which they disagree.

Presidents, of course, can also mobilize supporters and interests in order to overwhelm their political opponents at the polls and in the national legislature. When it comes to the routines of governance, however, presidents usually prefer processes that limit political debate and social mobilization. In an open political struggle among many competing forces, presidents may win or they may lose. But when decisions are made discreetly or covertly, in the corridors and offices of the White House with minimal external intervention, then surely the president will prevail. And unlike Congress, presidents do not have to rely on agencies outside their sphere of control to implement their decisions. To a far greater extent, presidents control bureaucrats and soldiers and contractors and mercenaries. They view the involvement of other political actors as more likely to hinder their plans than to help them govern. For these reasons, presidents seek to develop institutions and procedures that restrict the number of participants in decision making and limit the scope of political debate. These observations would seem entirely inconsistent with the idea that the presidency is somehow a more democratic institution than the Congress. Institutions matter a great deal, and the claim that the presidency is the more democratic branch is Myth 3.

Our discussion of the presidency, its historical development (history principle), its institutionalization (institution principle), and its capacity for independent and proactive execution relative to institutions like legislatures (collective

---

80 Christopher Simpson, *National Security Directives of the Reagan and Bush Administrations: The Declassified History of U.S. Political and Military Policy, 1981–1991* (Boulder, CO: Westview Press, 1995).

---

action principle) suggests that the office has evolved into a sleek, efficient, political machine. But it would be a mistake to attribute too much efficiency to the presidency. While it may have many of the features of a unitary actor, it is more than its occupant; it is an interconnected complex of separate pieces. Though these moving parts are often coordinated by the singular aspirations of the incumbent in office (rationality principle), the presidency is nevertheless an organization rather than an individual. This is no more apparent than when we extend our attention to the full-blown executive branch over which the president presides. This is the topic of the next chapter.

For Further Reading

Cameron, Charles M. *Veto Bargaining: Presidents and the Politics of Negative Power.* New York: Cambridge University Press, 2000.

Canes-Wrone, Brandice. *Who Leads Whom? Presidents, Policy, and the Public.* Chicago: University of Chicago Press, 2006.

Cotlar, Seth, and Richard J. Ellis, eds. *Historian in Chief: How Presidents Interpret the Past to Shape the Future.* Charlottesville: University of Virginia Press, 2019.

Crenson, Matthew, and Benjamin Ginsberg. *Presidential Power: Unchecked and Unbalanced.* New York: Norton, 2007.

Deering, Christopher J., and Forrest Maltzman. "The Politics of Executive Orders: Legislative Constraints on Presidential Power." *Political Research Quarterly* 52, no. 4 (1999): 767–83.

Gailmard, Sean, and John W. Patty. *Learning While Governing: Expertise and Accountability in the Executive Branch.* Chicago: University of Chicago Press, 2013.

Howell, William G. *Power without Persuasion: The Politics of Direct Presidential Action.* Princeton, NJ: Princeton University Press, 2003.

James, Scott C. *Presidents, Parties, and the State: A Party System Perspective on Democratic Regulatory Choice, 1884–1936.* New York: Cambridge University Press, 2000.

Kriner, Douglas L., and Andrew Reeves. *The Particularistic President: Executive Branch Politics and Political Inequality.* New York: Cambridge University Press, 2015.

Krutz, Glen S., and Jeffrey S. Peake. *Treaty Politics and the Rise of Executive Agreements.* Ann Arbor: University of Michigan Press, 2009.

Lowi, Theodore J. *The Personal President: Power Invested, Promise Unfulfilled.* Ithaca, NY: Cornell University Press, 1985.

McGrath, Robert J., Jon C. Rogowski, and Josh M. Ryan. "Veto Override Requirements and Executive Success." *Political Science Research and Methods* 6, no. 1 (2018): 153–79.

Milkis, Sidney M. *The President and the Parties: The Transformation of the American Party System since the New Deal.* New York: Oxford University Press, 1993.

Nelson, Michael, ed. *The Presidency and the Political System.* 11th ed. Washington, DC: CQ Press, 2018.

Neustadt, Richard E. *Presidential Power and the Modern Presidents: The Politics of Leadership from Roosevelt to Reagan.* New York: Wiley, 1960. Rev. ed. New York: Free Press, 1990.

Pfiffner, James P. *The Modern Presidency.* 6th ed. Boston, MA: Wadsworth, 2011.

Reeves, Andrew, and Jon C. Rogowski. "Public Opinion toward Presidential Power." *Presidential Studies Quarterly* 45, no. 4 (2015): 742–59.

Rogowski, Jon C. "Presidential Influence in an Era of Congressional Dominance." *American Political Science Review* 110, no. 2 (2016): 325–41.

Skowronek, Stephen. *The Politics Presidents Make: Leadership from John Adams to Bill Clinton.* Cambridge, MA: Belknap Press, 1997.

8

The Executive Branch

The bureaucracy is the administrative heart and soul of government. It is where the policies formulated and passed into law by elected officials are interpreted, implemented, and ultimately delivered to a nation's citizens. Government touches the lives of ordinary citizens most directly in their interactions with bureaucratic agents—at the Department of Motor Vehicles when obtaining a driver's license, in filing an income tax return with the Internal Revenue Service (IRS), at a recruiting center when enlisting in one of the armed services, at the Board of Elections when registering to vote. We examine the federal bureaucracy in this chapter both as an organizational setting within which policies are interpreted and implemented and as a venue in which politicians pursue their own (and sometimes the public's) interests.

As an organizational setting, a bureaucracy is a set of agencies created by elected politicians. These politicians seek to coordinate governmental efforts in order to accomplish public purposes (and private objectives) as well as to solve collective action problems. Sometimes bureaucracies are created in the face of a pressing need or crisis. A good example is the Department of Homeland Security (DHS). In 2003, the federal government combined 22 agencies involved in the prevention of international terrorism to create the DHS (Table 8.1)—the most dramatic reform of the federal bureaucracy since the establishment of the Department of Defense in 1947. Following the catastrophic events of September 11, 2001, both Republicans and Democrats realized that the public was going to demand an ongoing response to the terrorist threat beyond the immediate military response in Afghanistan.[1] A congressional investigation revealed serious security lapses and a lack of coordination among the agencies responsible for domestic and foreign intelligence during the Bill Clinton and George W. Bush administrations. Both political parties might be blamed if the government did not respond

---

1   John W. Kingdon calls events that limit and focus our political options "windows of political opportunity." See his *Agendas, Alternatives, and Public Policies* (Boston: Little, Brown, 1984).

aggressively to the terrorist threat. Furthermore, the major alternative solution—creation of a homeland security "czar"—proved inadequate. In the end, Congress created a new cabinet-level department responsible for coordinating efforts to protect domestic security.[2]

Whatever the impetus might be for creating a new bureaucracy, new agencies are shaped by politicians who represent a variety of perspectives and must hammer out agreements (often involving bargaining and compromise) about the agencies' size, scope, and authority. The DHS amalgam of 22 major units previously housed in seven cabinet departments and several other independent entities was stitched together through intense negotiations between President Bush's White House and legislators on Capitol Hill. Bureaucracies thus are administrative in purpose but are born through a political process. Their features are designed by politicians who appreciate, as suggested by our institution principle, that the institutional powers with which they endow a bureaucracy have consequences for the kinds of decisions bureaucratic agents subsequently make.

LEARNING OBJECTIVES

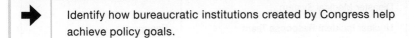 Identify how bureaucratic institutions created by Congress help achieve policy goals.

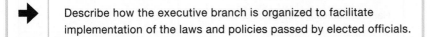 Describe how the executive branch is organized to facilitate implementation of the laws and policies passed by elected officials.

 Explain the challenge of keeping the government bureaucracy accountable to elected political authorities.

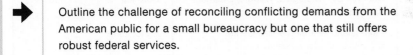 Outline the challenge of reconciling conflicting demands from the American public for a small bureaucracy but one that still offers robust federal services.

➡ Analyze the relationship between public bureaucracies and politics.

---

2   It also provided an opportunity for substantive policy change unrelated to national security. The Bush administration included some responsibilities unrelated to security within the purview of the DHS—such as coastal environmental enforcement by the U.S. Coast Guard—knowing that these programs would be at a disadvantage in the battle for resources within the department. Their impact would thus be reduced (in this case, the Coast Guard would not have the funds to effectively enforce environmental regulations). See Dara Kay Cohen, Mariano-Florentino Cuéllar, and Barry R. Weingast, "Crisis Bureaucracy: Homeland Security and the Political Design of Legal Mandates," *Stanford Law Review* 59, no. 3 (2006): 673–760.

Table 8.1

THE SHAPE OF A DOMESTIC SECURITY DEPARTMENT

DEPARTMENT OF HOMELAND SECURITY	AGENCIES AND DEPARTMENTS NOW PART OF THE MAIN DIVISIONS OF THE DHS	PREVIOUSLY RESPONSIBLE AGENCY OR DEPARTMENT
Border and Transportation Security Directorate	U.S. Customs and Border Protection	Treasury
	U.S. Citizenship and Immigration Services	Justice
	U.S. Immigration and Customs Enforcement	Treasury/Justice
	Federal Protective Service	General Service Administration
	Transportation Security Administration	Transportation
	Federal Law Enforcement Training Center	Treasury
	Animal and Plant Health Inspection Service*	Agriculture
	Office for Domestic Preparedness	Justice
Emergency Preparedness and Response Directorate	Federal Emergency Management Agency†	Health and Human Services
	Strategic National Stockpile and the National Disaster Medical System	Health and Human Services
	Nuclear Incident Response Team	Energy
	Domestic Emergency Support Teams	Justice
	National Domestic Preparedness Office	FBI
Science and Technology Directorate	CBRN (Chemical, Biological, Radiological and Nuclear) Countermeasures Programs	Energy
	Environmental Measurements Laboratory	Energy
	National BW (Biological Warfare) Defense Analysis Center	Defense
	Plum Island Animal Disease Center	Agriculture
Information Analysis and Infrastructure Protection Directorate**	Federal Computer Incident Response Center	General Services Administration
	National Communications System	Defense
	National Infrastructure Protection Center	FBI
	Energy Security and Assurance Program	Energy
Secret Service		Treasury
Coast Guard		Transportation

*Only partially under the aegis of DHS; some functions remain elsewhere.
†Previously independent.
**Established to analyze information provided by the CIA, the FBI, the Defense Intelligence Agency, the NSA, and other agencies.
SOURCE: Department of Homeland Security, www.dhs.gov/who-joined-dhs (accessed 1/30/20).

Bureaucracies are also venues in which bureaucratic actors pursue public and private purposes. Bureaucrats are politicians who make decisions, form coalitions, and engage in bargaining; they bring private preferences to the table as they engage in various administrative processes—just as the rationality principle suggests. The hopes and aspirations they bring to this setting interact with the institutional features of their bureaucracy to produce policies, outcomes, and decisions. And these, as the policy principle tells us, will reflect both the private interests of bureaucrats and the institutional ways in which they conduct their business.

In our focus on the federal bureaucracy—the administrative structure that on a day-to-day basis runs the American government—we first describe bureaucracy as a social and political phenomenon. Second, we explore American bureaucracy in action by examining the government's major administrative agencies, their role in the governmental process, and their political behaviors.

WHY BUREAUCRACY?

Government bureaucracies touch nearly every aspect of daily life as they implement decisions generated by the political process. Bureaucracies are characterized by routine because routine ensures that services are delivered regularly and that agencies fulfill their mandates. For this reason, students often conclude—mistakenly—that bureaucracy is mechanical and cumbersome. But bureaucracy is not just about collecting garbage or mailing Social Security checks; it involves much more. Mainly, it reflects political deals consummated by elected politicians, turf wars among government agents and private-sector suppliers and contractors, successes and failures in delivering policy, and responses by the same officials who cut the deals in the first place. Bureaucracy, thus, is politics through and through; politics and administration are not separate spheres, they are intertwined.

Public bureaucracies are powerful because legislatures and chief executives—and, indeed, the people—delegate to them vast power to make sure a particular job is done, leaving the rest of us free to pursue our own private ends.[3] The public sentiments that emerged after September 11 revealed this underlying appreciation for public bureaucracies. When faced with the challenge of ensuring the safety of air travel, the public strongly supported giving the federal government responsibility for airport security, even though this meant expanding the bureaucracy by making the security screeners federal employees. A fearful public believed that a public bureaucracy would provide more effective protection than the cost-conscious private companies that had handled airport security in the past.

---

3   Private bureaucracies at the heart of modern corporations and nonprofit organizations are also powerful, as students who must deal with college and university bureaucracies well know. In this chapter we focus on government bureaucracies.

We can shed light on public attitudes toward government bureaucracy by examining one of the standard questions posed in election years by the American National Election Studies (ANES). In surveying the American public, the ANES asks a range of questions, including "Do you think that people in the government waste a lot of the money we pay in taxes, waste some of it, or don't waste very much of it?" Although framing the issue in terms of "waste" may affect responses and, in any case, doesn't allow for much nuance, the question allows respondents to register a blunt evaluation of bureaucratic performance. Results from the past several decades appear in Figure 8.1. The percentage of the public who perceived the bureaucracy as inefficient grew during the 1960s and 1970s; peaked in 1980, when nearly 80 percent of respondents believed government "wastes a lot"; and held steady near the low 60 percent range between 1984 and 2000. There was a signifi-cant downward tick in 2002, just after September 11. But despite whatever honeymoon there might have been after the terrorist attacks, the public is once again increasingly cynical about bureaucratic performance. The poor response of the Federal Emergency Management Agency (FEMA)—part of the DHS—to Hurricane Katrina in 2005, domestic terrorist incidents later in the decade that seem to have evaded early detection, wars in Iraq and

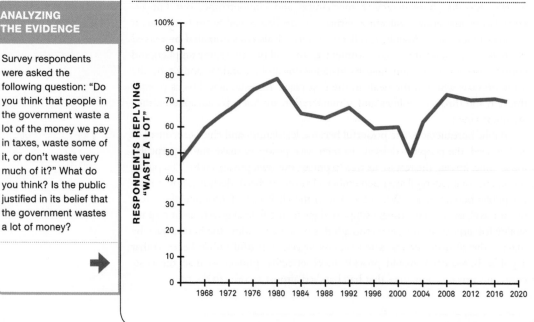

Figure 8.1

PUBLIC OPINION ON WASTE IN GOVERNMENT, 1964–2018

ANALYZING THE EVIDENCE

Survey respondents were asked the following question: "Do you think that people in the government waste a lot of the money we pay in taxes, waste some of it, or don't waste very much of it?" What do you think? Is the public justified in its belief that the government wastes a lot of money?

SOURCES: American National Election Studies, https://electionstudies.org/wp-content/uploads/2018/03/anes_timeseries_2016_qnaire_pre.pdf (accessed 6/6/20).

Afghanistan that dragged on and on, and yearly deficit spending contributed to further cynicism.

Bureaucratic Organization Enhances the Efficient Operation of Government

Despite their tendency to criticize bureaucracy, most Americans recognize that maintaining order in a large society is impossible without a large governmental apparatus staffed by professionals with expertise in public administration. **Bureaucracy** refers to the complex structure of offices, tasks, rules, and principles of organization that large institutions use to coordinate their work. The key to bureaucratic effectiveness is the strategic division of labor among experts performing complex tasks. If each job is specialized to gain efficiencies, then each worker must depend on other workers' output, and that requires careful allocation of jobs and resources. Inevitably bureaucracies become hierarchical, often pyramidal. At the base of the organization are workers with the fewest skills and specializations; one supervisor can oversee many workers. At the next level of the organization, which involves more highly specialized workers, each supervisor oversees fewer workers. Toward the top, a handful of high-level executives manage the organization, meaning that they organize and reorganize all of its tasks and functions. They also oversee the allocation of supplies and the distribution of the organization's output to the market (if it is a private-sector organization) or to the public.

By dividing up tasks, matching tasks to employees that develop appropriately specialized skills, routinizing procedure, and providing the incentive structure and oversight arrangements to get large numbers of people to operate in a coordinated fashion, bureaucracies accomplish tasks and missions in a manner that would otherwise be unimaginable. The provision of an array of "government goods"—as broad as the defense of people, property, and national borders or as narrow as a subsidy to a wheat farmer—requires organization, routines, standards, and ultimately, the authority for someone to cut a check and put it in the mail. And, of course, delivering the mail is as old as the Republic itself! Bureaucracies are created to do these tasks. Although bureaucracies sometimes make mistakes, a bureaucracy reflects instrumental thinking about how to accomplish particular undertakings; it is the rationality principle at work.

Bureaucracy also consolidates complementary programs and insulates them from opposing political forces. By working for the benefit of specific clienteles—in the legislature, in the world of interest groups, and among the public—a bureaucracy establishes a coalition of supporters, some of whom will fight to keep it in place. Clienteles, after all, value consistency, predictability, and durability. It is well-known that everyone in the political world cares deeply about certain policies and agencies and opposes others, yet their feelings of opposition are not nearly as strong as their feelings of support. To reverse a policy once it is in place, opponents must clear many hurdles; to maintain a policy, proponents must marshal their forces only at a few veto points. Opponents typically make

bureaucracy

The complex structure of offices, tasks, rules, and principles of organization that large institutions use to coordinate the work of their personnel.

the easier decision to give up and concentrate instead on protecting what they care most deeply about. Politicians appreciate this fact of life. Consequently, both opponents and proponents of governmental activities wage the fiercest battles at the time programs are enacted and a bureaucracy is created. Once created, these policies and the organizations that implement them assume a status of relative permanence; future developments are shaped, as the history principle suggests, by these "initial conditions."[4]

This raises an interesting dilemma, which we will develop in the next section. In principle, bureaucratic agents are "servants" of elected politicians in the White House and on Capitol Hill. They are charged with implementing statutes and policies produced by these "masters." But the bureaucracy's relative permanence is a form of insulation—servants have discretion, and masters have limited ability to control them. Elected officials who might want to steer bureaucracy in a different direction often find substantial obstacles. Only those with intense concern for the jurisdiction of a bureaucracy are likely to persist in efforts to guide it; others have more important objectives in different bureaucratic jurisdictions. Thus, bureaucratic agents are most affected by legislators with extraordinary interest in their mission. Those in opposition succumb to the obstacles and move their attention elsewhere.

So, in terms of how bureaucracy makes government possible, efficiency and credibility both play a role. Bureaus are created both to deliver government goods efficiently and to signal a credible commitment to the long-term existence of a policy (because once a bureaucracy is in place, it is very hard to change).

Bureaucrats Fulfill Important Roles

Bureaucracy often conveys a picture of hundreds of office workers shuffling millions of pieces of paper. There is truth in that image, but we must look more closely at what papers are being shuffled and why.

Implementing Laws. Bureaucrats, whether in public or in private organizations, communicate with one another to coordinate the specialized tasks for which their organization is responsible. This coordination is necessary to carry out the primary task of bureaucracy, which is **implementation**—that is, implementing the organization's objectives as laid down by its board of directors (if a private company) or by law (if a public agency). In government, the bosses are ultimately the legislature and the chief executive. As we saw in Chapter 1, in a principal-agent relationship it is the principal who stipulates what he wants done, relying on incentives and other control mechanisms to secure the agent's compliance. Thus, we can argue that legislative principals establish bureaucratic agents—in the form of departments, bureaus, agencies, institutes, and

implementation

The development of rules, regulations, and bureaucratic procedures to translate laws into action.

---

4 For a nuanced discussion of agency creation and persistence, see David E. Lewis, *Presidents and the Politics of Agency Design: Political Insulation in the United States Government Bureaucracy, 1946–1997* (Stanford, CA: Stanford University Press, 2003).

commissions of the federal government—to implement the policies promulgated by Congress and the president.

Making and Enforcing Rules. When the bosses—Congress, in particular—are clear in their instructions to bureaucrats, implementation is straightforward. Bureaucrats translate the instructions—that is, the law—into specific routines for each employee of an agency. But what happens to routine implementation when there are several bosses who disagree over what the instructions ought to be? The agent of multiple, disagreeing principals often gets caught in a bind. She must chart a delicate course, doing the best she can and trying not to offend any of the bosses too much. This requires yet another job for the bureaucrats: interpretation. Interpretation is a form of implementation in that the bureaucrats must carry out what they see as the intentions of their superiors. But when bureaucrats have to interpret a law before implementing it, they are in effect engaging in lawmaking.[5] Congress often deliberately delegates the responsibility of lawmaking to an administrative agency. When members of Congress conclude, for instance, that some area of industry needs regulating or some area of the environment needs protection, but they are unwilling or unable to specify just how that should be done, they use the procedures of **rule making** and administrative adjudication to delegate to the appropriate agency a broad authority within which to make law.

 rule making

A quasi-legislative administrative process that produces regulations by government agencies.

Rule making is similar to the legislative process; in fact, it is often called a "quasi-legislative" process. The rules issued by government agencies provide more detailed indications of what a policy will mean. For example, the Forest Service is charged with making policies that govern the use of national forests. Just before President Clinton left office in 2000, the agency issued rules that banned new road building and development in the forests, a goal that had long been sought by environmentalists and conservationists. In 2005, under President Bush, the Forest Service relaxed the rules, allowing states to make proposals for the construction of new roads within the national forests. Just as the timber industry opposed the Clinton rule banning road building, environmentalists challenged these Bush administration rulings and sued the Forest Service in federal court for violating clean-water and endangered-species legislation. Both the courts and the Democratic Obama administration tended to side with the Clinton rules. But further litigation and Trump administration reviews of the policy mean that these rules—like bureaucratic rules more generally—are in constant flux.

New rules proposed by an agency take effect only after a period of public comment. Reactions from the people or businesses that would be affected by

---

5   When bureaucrats engage in interpretation, the result is what political scientists call bureaucratic drift. This occurs because the bosses (in Congress) and the agents (within the bureaucracy) don't always share the same objectives. Bureaucrats pursue their own agendas, which may drift from those of their principals. A vast body of political science literature focuses on the relationship between Congress and the bureaucracy. For a review, see Kenneth A. Shepsle, *Analyzing Politics: Rationality, Behavior, and Institutions*, 2nd ed. (New York: Norton, 2010), pp. 420–40.

the rules may cause an agency to modify them. Public participation involves filing statements and giving testimony in public forums. This occurs after a draft rule or regulation is announced but before it becomes official, giving the agency time to revise its draft. The rule-making process is thus highly political. Once rules are approved, they are published in the *Federal Register* and have the force of law.[6]

administrative adjudication

The application of rules and precedents to specific cases to settle disputes with regulated parties.

Settling Disputes. **Administrative adjudication** is very similar to what the judiciary ordinarily does: it involves applying rules and precedents to specific cases to settle disputes with regulated parties. In administrative adjudication, an agency charges a person or business suspected of violating the law, and the eventual ruling applies only to the case being considered. Many regulatory agencies use administrative adjudication to make decisions about specific products or practices. For example, the National Labor Relations Board (NLRB) uses administrative adjudication to decide whether or not to certify unions. In these kinds of cases, groups of workers seek the right to vote on forming a union or the right to affiliate with an existing union as their bargaining agent. They may be opposed by their employers, who assert that relevant provisions of labor law do not apply. The NLRB takes testimony case by case and makes determinations for one side or the other, acting essentially like a court.

In sum, bureaucrats in government do essentially the same things that bureaucrats in large private organizations do. But because of the coercive nature of government, far more constraints are imposed on public bureaucrats than on private bureaucrats. Public bureaucrats are required to maintain a thorough paper trail and are subject to more access by members of the public, including newspaper reporters. In addition, the Freedom of Information Act (FOIA), adopted in 1966, has vastly facilitated public access to the bureaucracy: this act gives ordinary citizens the right to access agency files and data so they can learn what the agency is up to (and, in some cases, determine whether agency materials contain derogatory information about them).

Bureaucracies Serve Politicians

We have so far provided two main answers to the question, Why bureaucracy? (1) Bureaucracies enhance efficiency, and (2) they are the instruments of policy implementation. But there is a third important answer: the legislature finds it valuable to delegate to bureaucracies.

In principle, the legislature could make all bureaucratic decisions itself by writing very detailed legislation. In some jurisdictions—tax policy, for example—this in fact happens. Tax policy is promulgated in significant detail by the House Ways and Means Committee, the Senate Finance Committee, and the

---

6   The *Federal Register* is the daily journal of the executive branch. It is published every day by the Government Printing Office and contains publications and notices related to government agencies.

Joint Committee on Taxation. The IRS, the agency charged with implementation, engages in relatively less discretionary activity than many other regulatory and administrative agencies. But it is the exception.

The norm is for statutory authority to be delegated to the bureaucracy, often in vague terms, with the bureaucracy expected to fill in the gaps. This does not mean, however, that the legislature gives the bureaucracy a blank check for unconstrained discretion. The bureaucracy will be held to account by the legislature's oversight of bureaucratic performance. The latter is monitored by the staffs of relevant legislative committees, which also serve as repositories for complaints from affected parties.[7] Poor performance or the exercise of discretion inconsistent with important legislative preferences invites sanctions, ranging from the browbeating of senior bureaucrats to the trimming of budgets and the clipping of authority.

HOW IS THE EXECUTIVE BRANCH ORGANIZED?

Cabinet departments, agencies, and bureaus are the operating parts of the bureaucratic whole. They can be separated into four general types: (1) cabinet departments, (2) independent agencies, (3) government corporations, and (4) independent regulatory commissions.

Figure 8.2 is an organizational chart of the Department of Agriculture, though any other department could serve as an illustration. At the top is the department head, called the secretary of the department. Below him and his deputy are several top administrators, such as the general counsel and the chief economist, whose responsibilities span the various departmental functions and enable the secretary to manage the entire organization. Working alongside these officials are the undersecretaries, each with management responsibilities for a group of operating agencies, which are arranged vertically below the undersecretaries.

This tier of agencies, generally called the bureau level, is the highest level of responsibility for specialized programs. These bureau-level agencies are often very well known to the public: the Forest Service and the Food Safety and Inspection Service are examples. Sometimes they are officially called bureaus, as in the Federal *Bureau* of Investigation (FBI), which is a bureau in the Department of Justice. Within the bureaus are divisions, offices, services, and units.

A second type of agency, the independent agency, is established by Congress outside the departmental structure altogether, even though the president appoints and directs these agencies' heads. Independent agencies usually have

---

7   See Mathew D. McCubbins and Thomas Schwartz, "Congressional Oversight Overlooked: Police Patrols versus Fire Alarms," *American Journal of Political Science* 28, no. 1 (1984): 165–79.

Figure 8.2

ORGANIZATIONAL CHART OF THE DEPARTMENT OF AGRICULTURE

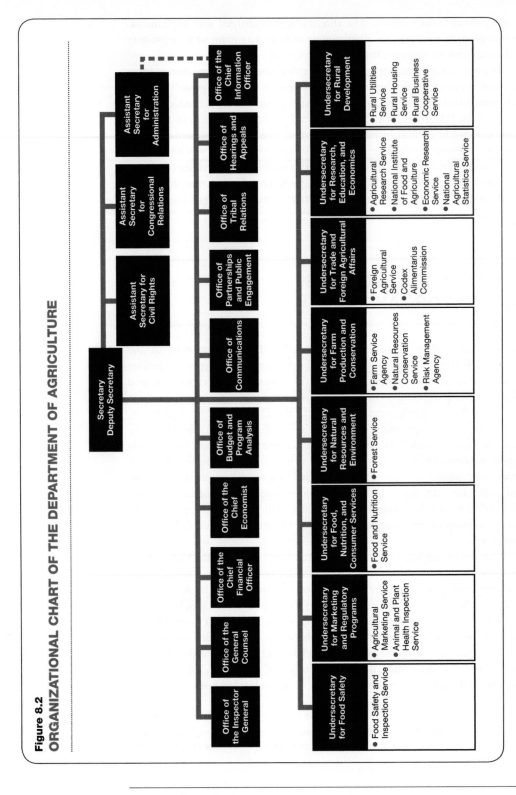

SOURCE: U.S. Department of Agriculture, www.usda.gov/sites/default/files/documents/usda-organization-chart.pdf (accessed 1/9/2020).

broad powers to provide public services that are either too expensive or too important to be left to private initiatives. Examples are the National Aeronautics and Space Administration (NASA), the Central Intelligence Agency (CIA), and the Environmental Protection Agency (EPA). Government corporations are a third type of agency but are more like private businesses performing and charging for a market service, such as transporting railroad passengers (Amtrak).

Yet a fourth type of agency is the independent regulatory commission, which has broad discretion to make rules. The first regulatory agencies established by Congress, beginning with the Interstate Commerce Commission in 1887, were set up as independent regulatory commissions because Congress recognized that regulatory agencies are mini-legislatures, whose rules and rulings are the same as legislation and legislative interpretation but require the kind of expertise and full-time attention that is beyond the capacity of Congress. Until the 1960s, most of the regulatory agencies set up by Congress, such as the Federal Communications Commission (1934), were independent regulatory commissions. But beginning in the late 1960s and early 1970s, all new regulatory programs, with a few exceptions (such as the Federal Election Commission), were placed within existing departments and made directly responsible to the president. Since then, no new major regulatory programs were established until the financial crisis of 2007–09, when Congress and the president formulated new arrangements involving the Federal Reserve System, the Federal Deposit Insurance Corporation, the Treasury, and related agencies. The Dodd-Frank Wall Street Reform and Consumer Protection Act of 2010 brought major changes to the regulation of banks and other financial institutions; it created several new regulatory bodies, including the Financial Stability Oversight Council, the Office of Financial Research, and the Bureau of Consumer Financial Protection.

There are too many agencies in the executive branch to identify them all here, so a simple set of categories will be helpful. The classification that follows organizes each agency by its mission, as defined by its jurisdiction: clientele agencies, agencies for maintenance of the Union, regulatory agencies, and redistributive agencies.

Clientele Agencies

The entire Department of Agriculture is an example of a **clientele agency**. So are the departments of the Interior, Labor, and Commerce. Although all administrative agencies have clienteles, certain agencies are directed by law to promote the interests of their clientele. For example, the Department of Commerce and Labor was founded in 1903 as a single department "to foster, promote, and develop the foreign and domestic commerce, the mining, the manufacturing, the shipping, and fishing industries, and the transportation facilities of the United States."[8] It

clientele agency

A department or bureau of government whose mission is to promote, serve, or represent a particular interest.

---

8   An Act To establish the Department of Commerce and Labor, Public Law 57-87, U.S. Statutes at Large 32 (1903): 825–30; 15 U.S. Code 1501.

remained a single department until 1913, when legislation created the separate departments of Commerce and Labor, with each statute providing for the same obligation: to support and foster each agency's respective clientele.[9] The Department of Agriculture serves the many farming interests that, taken together, form one of the largest economic sectors of the United States.

Most clientele agencies locate many of their personnel in field offices dealing directly with their clientele. A familiar example is the Extension Service of the Department of Agriculture, with its local "extension agents" who consult with farmers on farm productivity. The same agencies also provide "functional representation"—that is, they learn what their clients' interests and needs are and then operate almost as a lobby in Washington on their behalf. In addition to the departments of Agriculture, Interior, Labor, and Commerce, five of the newest cabinet departments are clientele agencies: Housing and Urban Development (HUD, created in 1965), Transportation (DOT, 1966), Energy (DOE, 1977), Education (ED, 1979), and Health and Human Services (HHS, 1979).[10]

Agencies for the Maintenance of the Union

The Constitution entrusts many critical functions of public order, such as the maintenance of a police force, to state and local governments. But some agencies vital to maintaining the stability of the country do exist at the federal level, and they can be grouped into three categories: (1) agencies for managing the sources of government revenue, (2) agencies for controlling conduct defined as an internal threat to national security, and (3) agencies for defending American security from external threats. The most powerful departments in these areas are the Treasury, Justice, Defense, State, and Homeland Security Departments.

Revenue Agencies. The Treasury Department's IRS is the most important revenue agency and one of the federal government's largest bureaucracies. Over 100,000 employees across four regions work in hundreds of district service centers and local offices. In 2019, the IRS collected nearly $3.5 trillion, processed more than 250 million tax returns and other forms, and issued almost $464 billion in tax refunds.

Agencies for Internal Security. The United States is fortunate to enjoy national unity maintained by civil law rather than imposed by military force. If the country is not in a state of insurrection, most of the task of maintaining

---

9 For a detailed account of the creation of the Department of Commerce and Labor and its division into separate departments, see Theodore J. Lowi, *The End of Liberalism: The Second Republic of the United States*, 2nd ed. (New York: Norton, 1979), pp. 78–84.

10 Until 1979, the Department of Education and the Department of Health and Human Services were joined in a single department, Health, Education, and Welfare (HEW), which was established by Congress in 1953.

the Union involves legal work, and the main responsibility for that lies with the Department of Justice. The most important agency in the Justice Department is the Criminal Division, which enforces all federal criminal laws except a few assigned to other divisions. Criminal litigation is conducted by the U.S. attorneys; a presidentially appointed U.S. attorney is assigned to each federal judicial district, and he or she supervises the work of assistant U.S. attorneys. The work or jurisdictions of the Antitrust and Civil Rights Divisions are described by their official names. The FBI, another bureau of the Justice Department, serves as the information-gathering agency for all the other divisions.

As noted earlier, in 2002, Congress created the Department of Homeland Security to coordinate the nation's defense against the threat of terrorism. This department's responsibilities include protecting commercial airlines from would-be hijackers. Most visible to the traveling public are the employees of the Transportation Security Administration (TSA). Consisting of 47,000 security officers and employees who protect airports and rail and bus depots and staff security screening operations, the TSA is the largest unit of the DHS.

Agencies for External National Security. Two departments occupy center stage for national security: State and Defense. A few key agencies outside State and Defense also have external national security functions.

Although diplomacy is generally considered the State Department's primary task, that is only one of its organizational dimensions. The State Department also comprises geographic, or regional, bureaus concerned with all problems within that region of the world; "functional" bureaus, which handle such things as economic and business affairs, intelligence, and research; and relationships with international organizations and bureaus of internal affairs, which handle such areas as security, finance, management, and legal issues.

Despite the State Department's importance in foreign affairs, fewer than 20 percent of all U.S. government employees working abroad are directly under its authority. By far the largest number of career government professionals working abroad are under the authority of the Defense Department.

The creation of the Department of Defense between 1947 and 1949 was an effort to unify the two historic military departments, the War Department and the Navy Department, and integrate them with a new department, the Air Force Department. Real unification did not occur, however. Instead, the Defense Department added more pluralism to national security.

The United States' political problems with its military have been relatively mundane compared to the experiences of many other countries, which have struggled to keep their militaries out of the politics of governing. Rather, Americans' primary military problem involves pork-barrel politics: defense contracts are often highly lucrative for local districts, so military spending becomes a matter not just of military need but also of narrow interests. For instance, proposed military base closings, always a major part of budget cutting, inevitably cause a firestorm of opposition from affected members in both parties and even from some members of Congress who otherwise favor slashing the Pentagon's budget. Emphasis on jobs rather than strategy and policy means that the military is often invoked in pork-barrel projects for political purposes. This is a classic way for a bureaucracy to defend itself politically in a democracy. It illustrates the distributive tendency, in which the bureaucracy ensures political support among elected officials by distributing things—military bases, contracts, facilities, and jobs—to the states and districts that elected the legislators.

Regulatory Agencies

Federal regulation of economic and social affairs did not begin until the late nineteenth century. Until then, regulation was strictly a state and local affair.[11] The federal **regulatory agencies** are, as a result, relatively new (most date from the 1930s), but they have become extensive and important. In this section, we consider them as an administrative phenomenon, with its attendant politics.

The United States has many regulatory agencies. Some are bureaus within departments, such as the Food and Drug Administration in the Department of Health and Human Services and the Occupational Safety and Health Administration in the Department of Labor. Others are independent regulatory commissions—for example, the Federal Trade Commission. But whether departmental or independent, an agency or commission is considered regulatory if Congress delegates to it broad powers over a sector of the economy or a type of commercial activity and authorizes it to make rules governing the conduct of people and businesses within that jurisdiction. Rules made by regulatory agencies have the force of legislation; indeed, such rules are referred to as **administrative legislation**. And when these agencies make decisions or orders settling disputes between parties or between the government and a party, they are acting like courts.

Because regulatory agencies exercise so much influence and because their rules are a form of legislation, Congress was at first loath to turn them over to the executive branch as ordinary agencies under the president's control. Consequently, most of the important regulatory programs were delegated to independent commissions with direct responsibility to Congress rather than to the White House. Thus, some in the 1930s called them the "headless fourth branch."[12] With the rise of presidential government, most recent presidents have supported more regulatory programs but have successfully opposed the expansion of regulatory independence. The 1960s and 1970s witnessed the adoption of an unprecedented number of new regulatory programs within the purview of the executive branch but only a few new independent commissions.

regulatory agency

A department, bureau, or independent agency whose primary mission is to make rules governing a particular type of activity.

administrative legislation

Rules made by regulatory agencies that have the force of law.

---

11 A comprehensive historical survey is found in Jonathan R. T. Hughes, *The Governmental Habit Redux: Economic Controls from Colonial Times to the Present* (Princeton, NJ: Princeton University Press, 1991).

12 *Final Report of the President's Committee on Administrative Management* (Washington, DC: Government Printing Office, 1937). The term *headless fourth branch* was invented by a member of the committee staff, Cornell University government professor Robert Cushman.

Agencies of Redistribution

Welfare, fiscal, and monetary agencies transfer hundreds of billions of dollars annually between the public and the private spheres, and through such transfers these agencies influence how people and corporations spend and invest trillions of dollars annually. We call them agencies of redistribution because they influence the amount of money in the economy, who has it, who has credit, and whether people will invest or save their money rather than spend it.

Fiscal and Monetary Policy Agencies. Governmental activity relating to money constitutes fiscal and monetary policy. **Fiscal policy** includes taxing and spending activities. **Monetary policy** focuses on banks, credit, and currency.

The administration of fiscal policy is primarily a Treasury Department responsibility. It is no contradiction to include the Treasury both here and with the agencies that work to maintain the Union. This duplication indicates that (1) the Treasury performs more than one function of government and (2) traditional controls over the government's financial activities have been adapted to modern economic conditions and new technologies.

Today, in addition to administering and policing income tax and other tax collections, the Treasury manages the enormous federal debt. The Treasury also prints currency, but that currency is only a tiny portion of the entire money economy. Most of the trillions of dollars exchanged in the nation's private and public sectors are done so electronically, not in currency.

Another important fiscal and monetary policy agency is the **Federal Reserve System (the Fed)**, headed by the Federal Reserve Board. Established by Congress in 1913, the Fed has authority over the credit rates and lending activities of the nation's most important banks, and it is responsible for adjusting the supply of money to satisfy both the needs of banks in the different regions and the commerce and industry in each. It also ensures that banks do not overextend themselves by adopting overly permissive lending policies. The basis for this responsibility is the fear of a sudden economic scare that would make dubious loans uncollectible and thus destabilize the health of the banking system. At its worst, such a shock to the economy could cause another terrible crash like the one in 1929 that ushered in the Great Depression. The Federal Reserve Board sits at the top of a pyramid of 12 district Federal Reserve banks, which are "bankers' banks," serving the hundreds of member banks in the national bank system. The subprime mortgage crisis of 2007–09, caused by banks and other lenders providing risky home mortgages that led to foreclosures, reflected gaps in the regulation of the banking sector. In the midst of the resulting recession, the Fed played a major role by reducing interest rates to lower the price of borrowing and by overseeing support to struggling banks. In the subsequent decade of recovery from the crisis, as employment and economic activity has improved, the Fed slowly and modestly raised interest rates to keep inflation in check, and then proceeded to lower them as the economy slowed down during the Trump years. In 2020, public health measures to fight the coronavirus pandemic shut down the economy and again required stimulus from the Fed.

 fiscal policy

Regulation of the economy through taxing and spending powers.

 monetary policy

Regulation of the economy through manipulation of the supply of money, the price of money (interest rates), and the availability of credit.

 Federal Reserve System (Fed)

The system of 12 Federal Reserve banks that facilitates exchanges of cash, checks, and credit; regulates member banks; and uses monetary policy to fight inflation and deflation in the United States.

Information about and coordination of the nation's finances are provided by the Office of Management and Budget (OMB) in the White House and the Congressional Budget Office (CBO), an arm of the two legislative chambers. The OMB organizes the president's budget and plays a coordinating role in clearing spending and regulatory decisions. The CBO plays primarily an informational role, providing the legislative chambers and their committees with assessments of budgetary proposals and conducting long-range forecasts of budget, spending, and tax policies. In 2017, it played a significant role in the attempts by the Trump administration and the Republican-controlled Congress to forge a new health care policy. The CBO "scored" various legislative and administration proposals on the number of people who would lose insurance coverage if that proposal were enacted, thereby affecting the views of pivotal legislators and leading Congress to reject even modest revisions of Obamacare.

Welfare Agencies. No single agency is responsible for all the programs that make up the "welfare state." The largest agency in the field is the Social Security Administration (SSA), which manages the social insurance aspects of Social Security and Supplemental Security Income (SSI). These include massive expenditures that finance monthly Social Security checks for retirees as well as payments to the disabled, the unemployed, and individuals that meet other specific criteria. These programs are funded by taxes levied on employees and employers. As the baby boom generation ages, a growing bloc of voters (and their children) worry that without some adjustments in benefit schedules, taxes, or retirement age, the present population will begin drawing down funds in the Social Security trust fund in two decades and will exhaust it in 40 years.

Agencies in the Department of Health and Human Services administer Temporary Assistance to Needy Families (TANF) and Medicaid, and the Department of Agriculture is responsible for the food stamp program. With the exception of Social Security, these are *means-tested* programs, requiring applicants to demonstrate that their annual cash earnings fall below an officially defined poverty line. These public-assistance programs carry a large administrative burden. In 1996, Congress abolished virtually all national means-tested public-assistance programs as federal programs, devolving power over them to the state governments.

THE PROBLEM OF BUREAUCRATIC CONTROL

Two centuries, millions of employees, and trillions of dollars after the Founding, we must return to James Madison's observation that "you must first enable the government to control the governed; and in the next place oblige it to control itself."[13]

---

13 Clinton L. Rossiter, ed., *The Federalist Papers: Alexander Hamilton, James Madison, and John Jay* (New York: New American Library, 1961), no. 51 (James Madison).

Today the problem is the same, but the form has changed; the challenge the government faces today is keeping the bureaucracy accountable to elected political authorities.

Motivational Considerations of Bureaucrats

Economist William Niskanen proposed that a bureau or department of government is analogous to a division of a private firm and that a bureaucrat is like the manager who runs that division.[14] In particular, Niskanen argued that the behavior of a bureau chief or department head should be thought of as following the rationality principle. In his view the bureaucrat is a rational maximizer of her budget (just as the private-sector counterpart is a maximizer of his division's profits).

There are many motivational bases on which bureaucratic budget maximizing might be justified. A cynical (though some would say realistic) explanation is that the bureaucrat's own compensation is often tied to the size of her budget. Not only might bureaus with large budgets have higher-salaried executives with more elaborate fringe benefits, but there also may be enhanced opportunities for career advancement, travel, a posh office, possibly even a chauffeured car.

A second, related motivation for seeking large budgets is nonmaterial personal gratification. An individual enjoys the prestige that comes from running a major enterprise. Her self-esteem and stature are surely buoyed by the conspicuous fact that her bureau or division has a large budget. Overseeing a large number of subordinates, made possible by a large bureau budget, is another aspect of this ego gratification.

But personal salary, on-the-job consumption, and power tripping are not the only forces motivating a bureaucrat to gain as large a budget as possible. Some bureaucrats, perhaps most, actually *care* about their mission and believe in the importance of helping people in their community.[15] As they rise through the ranks and assume management responsibilities, this mission orientation still drives them. Thus, whether we're talking about a chief of detectives in a big-city police department, a head of procurement in the air force, a supervisor of the social work division in a county welfare department, or an assistant superintendent of a town school system, individuals try to secure as large a budget as possible to succeed in the mission to which they have devoted their professional lives.

---

14 William A. Niskanen Jr., *Bureaucracy and Representative Government* (Chicago: Aldine, 1971).

15 John Brehm and Scott Gates, *Working, Shirking, and Sabotage: Bureaucratic Response to a Democratic Public* (Ann Arbor: University of Michigan Press, 1997). For detailed insight about how government service can be motivated by a combination of personal and patriotic interests, consider the case of Henry Paulson, a Wall Street financier who became George W. Bush's secretary of the treasury. Paulson's story is described well in Andrew Ross Sorkin, *Too Big to Fail: The Inside Story of How Wall Street and Washington Fought to Save the Financial System—And Themselves* (New York: Viking, 2009), chap. 2.

Whether for self-serving motives or for noble public purposes (doing "well" or doing "good," respectively), it is plausible that individual bureaucrats seek to persuade others (typically legislators or taxpayers) to provide them with as many resources as possible. Indeed, it is sometimes difficult to distinguish the saint from the sinner because each sincerely argues that he needs more to do more. This is one nice feature of the rationality principle in general and Niskanen's assumption of budget maximizing in particular: it doesn't matter *why* a bureaucrat is interested in a big budget; what matters is simply that she prefers more resources to fewer.

This does not mean that the legislature has to fork over whatever the bureau requests.[16] To budget allocations, Congress will evaluate a bureau's performance. Legislative committees hold hearings, request documentation, assign investigatory staff to research tasks, and query bureau personnel on the veracity of their data and their use of the lowest-cost technologies. After the fact, the committees engage in oversight, making sure that what the bureau told the legislature during the allocation stage actually holds in practice.

Reinforcing the budget-maximizing objective of bureaus is the fact that they are intimately associated with interest groups (their clienteles) and legislative committees and subcommittees whose members count those interest groups as major supporters. These close connections among agency, interest group, and legislative committee are known as "cozy little triangles," "policy whirlpools," "unholy trinities," and "policy subgovernments." Interest groups, who provide electoral support, lobby legislators to advocate for large bureau budgets; legislators deliver in providing authority and appropriations for bureaus; and bureaus, in turn, deliver by implementing favorable policies for interest groups. Interest groups express their appreciation by starting the cycle all over again. Because there are few incentives to oppose this system, it remains and repeats itself. Indeed, legislators appalled by this arrangement in one policy area are often embedded in similar arrangements in other areas. Presidents may try to trim the more outrageous manifestations of this practice, but they are not always willing to go to the mat to eliminate it entirely.

Before leaving motivational considerations, we should remark that budget maximizing is not the only objective that bureaucrats pursue. We must reemphasize that career civil servants and high-level political appointees are *politicians*. They spend their professional lives pursuing political goals, bargaining, forming alliances and coalitions, solving cooperation and collective action problems, making policy decisions, operating within and interfacing with political institutions— in short, doing what other politicians do. Although they do not have to win elections themselves, elections do affect their conditions of employment by determining the composition of the legislature and the partisan and ideological complexion of the chief executive. Bureaucrats are politicians beholden to other politicians for authority and resources. They are servants of many masters.

---

16 This and other related points are drawn from Gary J. Miller and Terry M. Moe, "Bureaucrats, Legislators, and the Size of Government," *American Political Science Review* 77, no. 2 (June 1983): 297–323.

Because they are subject to the oversight and authority of others, bureaucrats must be strategic and forward thinking. Whichever party wins control of the House, Senate, and presidency, whoever chairs the legislative committee with authorization or appropriation responsibility over their agency, bureau chiefs have to adjust to the prevailing political winds. To protect and expand their authority and resources, bureaucratic politicians seek, in the form of autonomy and discretion, insurance against political change. They don't always succeed, but they do try to insulate themselves from changes in the broader political world.[17] So their motivations include budget-maximizing behavior, to be sure, but they also seek the autonomy to weather changes in the political atmosphere and the discretion and flexibility to achieve their goals.

Bureaucracy and the Principal-Agent Problem

As we mentioned earlier in this chapter, bureaucrats can be understood as the agents of elected officials (the principals). In any principal-agent relationship, two broad categories of control mechanisms enable a principal to guard against opportunistic or incompetent behavior by an agent. Consider a homeowner (the principal) who seeks out a contractor (the agent) to remodel a kitchen. The first category of control operates before any work is delegated and depends on the agent's reputation. The homeowner guards against selecting an incompetent or corrupt agent (contractor) by relying on various methods for authenticating the agent's promises. These include advice from trustworthy people (neighbors who just had their kitchen remodeled), certification by various official boards (an association of kitchen contractors), credentials (specialized training programs), and interviews. Before-the-fact protection assumes that an agent's reputation is a valuable asset that she does not want to depreciate.

The second category of control mechanisms operates after the fact. Payment may be made contingent on completion of various tasks by specific dates, so that it may be withheld for nonperformance. Alternatively, financial incentives (for example, bonuses) for early or on-time completion may be part of the arrangement. An inspection process, after the work is completed, may lead to financial penalties, bonuses, or legal action. Of course, the principal can always seek legal relief for breach of contract if the agent does not complete the work or completes it poorly, either through an injunction stipulating that the agent comply or through an order demanding that the agent pay damages.

How does the principal-agent problem apply to the president's and Congress's control of the bureaucracy? Let's consider a hypothetical Land Management Bureau (LMB) whose existence Congress must renew every 10 years by passing new legislation. The issue facing the House, the Senate, and the president

---

17 For an expanded view of bureaucratic autonomy and insulation with historical application to the U.S. Department of Agriculture and the Postal Service, see Daniel P. Carpenter, *The Forging of Bureaucratic Autonomy: Reputations, Networks, and Policy Innovation in Executive Agencies, 1862–1928* (Princeton, NJ: Princeton University Press, 2001).

in considering renewal involves how much authority to give this bureau and how much money to permit it to spend. Suppose the House is conservative on land management issues and prefers to give the LMB limited authority and a limited budget. The Senate wants the agency to have wide-ranging authority but is prepared to give it only slightly more resources than the House (because of its concern with the government's overall budget deficit). The president agrees to split the difference between the House and Senate on the matter of authority but feels beholden to land management interests and is thus prepared to shower the LMB with resources. Bureaucrats in the LMB want more authority than the Senate is prepared to grant and more resources than the House is willing to grant. Eventually relevant majorities in the House and the Senate (including the support of relevant committees) and the president agree on a policy reflecting a compromise among their various points of view.

The LMB bureaucrats are not pleased with this compromise because it gives them considerably less authority and funding than they had hoped for. If they flout their principals' wishes and implement a policy exactly to their liking, they risk the unified wrath of the House, the Senate, and the president. Undoubtedly the politicians would react with new legislation (and might also replace the current LMB leadership). If, however, the LMB leadership implements some policy partway between its own preferences and those of its principals—conceding its own preferences only a little bit—it might get away with it. That is, at the margin, the bureau tilts policy toward its own preferences and away from the political compromise reached by the executive and legislature, but the tilt is subtle enough that it does not stimulate a political response.

Thus, we have a principal-agent relationship in which a political principal—a collective principal consisting of the president and coalitions in the House and Senate—formulates policy and creates an implementation agent to execute its details. The agent, however, has policy preferences of its own and, unless subjected to further controls, will inevitably implement a policy that drifts toward its ideal. (The Policy Principle box on the next page looks at a real case in which the EPA and President Obama worked together against a Republican-controlled Congress to expand the agency's authority. In this case, the shift toward the policy preferences of the bureaucratic agents and the president *did* provoke an outcry from legislators in Congress.)

Various controls might conceivably restrict this **bureaucratic drift**. Indeed, legislative scholars often point to congressional hearings in which bureaucrats may be publicly humiliated; annual appropriations decisions that may serve to punish out-of-control bureaus; and watchdog agents, such as the Government Accountability Office (GAO), that may be used to scrutinize the bureau's performance. But these all come after the fact and may be only partially credible threats to the agency.[18]

bureaucratic drift

The tendency of bureaucracies to implement laws in ways that tilt toward the bureaucrats' policy preferences and possibly away from the intentions of the elected officials who created the laws.

---

18 For the classic statement that despite before-the-fact and after-the-fact tools available to the political principals, the bureau agent will "drift" in policy implementation toward its own preferences, see Mathew D. McCubbins, Roger G. Noll, and Barry R. Weingast, "Structure and Process, Politics and Policy: Administrative Arrangements and the Political Control of Agencies," *Virginia Law Review* 75, no. 2 (1989): 431–82.

The EPA: Regulating Clean Air

In 1970, Congress passed the Clean Air Act to provide a platform for policy initiatives focused on reducing air pollution. It was closely aligned with the National Environmental Policy Act, passed earlier that year, which created the Environmental Protection Agency (EPA). Congress delegated authority to the EPA to regulate substances deemed harmful to air quality. Originally the list of such substances was limited, including only carbon monoxide, nitrogen oxide, sulfur dioxide, and lead. Over time, as preferences about environmental regulation changed from one presidential administration to another, several institutions shaped (and reshaped) new policies.

A coal-burning power plant in Ohio.

On September 20, 2013, more than 40 years after the passage of the Clean Air Act, President Obama announced his intention to extend the EPA's authority to require polluters to cut their emissions of harmful substances, and in particular to begin regulating emissions of carbon dioxide (CO_2). Obama's objective was to reduce CO_2 emissions by 30 percent by 2030. In 2014, the EPA published its proposed plan to achieve this goal and invited commentary from the general public. By December 1, 2014, the end of a 165-day comment period during which the agency received over 2 million responses, the EPA began writing its regulations. In addition, President Obama announced plans for his administration to issue other rules governing CO_2 emissions, such as restricting coal-burning power plants directly. This is an example of how the powers delegated to the president and a regulatory agency by statute can change in response to a change in an administration's goals.

Continued pressure to combat greenhouse gases associated with climate change pitted bureaucratic agents in the Obama White House and the EPA against legislators in Congress. Obama sought to leave a legacy of environmental protection, and the EPA wished to interpret its regulatory mandate broadly, but many in Congress were anxious to protect carbon-based fuel industries in their states and districts. The majority leader in the Senate, Mitch McConnell, from coal-rich Kentucky, was eager to prevent the EPA's expanded interpretation of its authority to regulate CO_2. McConnell took advantage of the institutional powers available to him to shape the EPA's CO_2 policy. For example, in 2015 he introduced a bill that would block new EPA regulations on carbon emissions from going into effect unless a review by the Labor Department found they would not reduce jobs or the reliability of the electricity supply. Thus, as in many struggles involving the federal bureaucracy, executive, regulatory, and legislative agents all have pressed forward with their respective preferences, producing policy that is never truly settled.

Indeed, beginning in 2017, President Trump, who had campaigned on saving jobs in the coal industry, and his first EPA administrator, Scott Pruitt from oil-rich Oklahoma, began systematically to undo many of the Obama-era clean-air regulations.

A second powerful before-the-fact weapon, following from the institution principle, is procedural controls. The general rules and regulations that direct the way federal agencies operate are specified in the Administrative Procedure Act. This act is almost always the boilerplate of legislation creating and renewing federal agencies. Sometimes, however, an agency's procedures are tailored to suit particular circumstances.

Before-the-Fact Controls. The most powerful before-the-fact political weapon is the appointment process. The adroit control of a bureau's political stance by the president and Congress, through their joint powers of nomination and confirmation (especially if they can arrange for appointees who share their political consensus on policy), is a mechanism for ensuring reliable agent performance.

Coalitional Drift as a Collective Action Problem. Not only do politicians want the legislative deals that they strike to be faithfully implemented by the bureaucracy, but they also want those deals to endure. This is especially problematic in American political life, considering its shifting alignments. Today's coalition transforms itself overnight. Opponents one day are partners the next, and vice versa. A victory today, even one implemented in a favorable manner by the bureaucracy, may unravel tomorrow. What is to be done? To some extent, legislators are disinclined to undo legislation. If a coalition votes for handsome subsidies to grain farmers, say, it is very hard to reverse this policy without the gatekeeping and agenda-setting assistance of members on the House and Senate Agriculture Committees; these same committee members, however, undoubtedly participated in the initial deal and are unlikely to turn against it. But even these structural units are unstable; old politicians depart, and new ones are enlisted. For example, for most of this decade Republicans have been eager to reverse the 2010 Affordable Care Act, informally known as Obamacare. By 2017 the stars seemed to be aligned when Republicans captured the presidency and majorities in both chambers of Congress.[19] Try as they might, however, congressional Republicans could not agree on any version of either repealing or replacing Obamacare.

Clearly (but not always, as the current status of Obamacare suggests) legislatively formulated and bureaucratically implemented output is subject to **coalitional drift.**[20] To prevent shifting coalitional patterns from endangering carefully fashioned policies, the legislature might insulate the bureaucracy and its implementation activities from legislative interventions. If an enacting coalition makes it difficult for its *own* members to intervene in implementation, then it also stymies opponents from disrupting the flow of bureaucratic output. This political insulation can be achieved by giving bureaucratic agencies long lives, their heads long terms of office and wide-ranging administrative authority, and

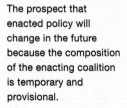

coalitional drift

The prospect that enacted policy will change in the future because the composition of the enacting coalition is temporary and provisional.

---

19 Earlier, in 2015, the Supreme Court validated portions of the health care legislation, making it clear to Republicans that they would get no help in reversing Obamacare through legal challenges. New cases are percolating through the courts. At least one of these will be heard by the Supreme Court—with two new justices appointed by President Trump—in its 2020 session, providing another opportunity for the Court to rule on the constitutionality of Obamacare.

20 This idea, offered as a supplement to the analysis of bureaucratic drift, is found in Murray J. Horn and Kenneth A. Shepsle, "Administrative Process and Organizational Form as Legislative Responses to Agency Costs," *Virginia Law Review* 75, no. 2 (1989): 499–508. It is further elaborated in Kenneth A. Shepsle, "Bureaucratic Drift, Coalitional Drift, and Time Consistency," *Journal of Law, Economics, and Organization* 8, no. 1 (1992): 111–18.

other political appointees overlapping terms of office and secure sources of revenue. Such insulation comes at a price, however. The civil servants and political appointees of these bureaus are thereby empowered to pursue independent courses of action, meaning an increased potential for bureaucratic drift. This is one of the great trade-offs in intergovernmental relations.

The President as Manager-in-Chief

In 1937, President Franklin Delano Roosevelt's Committee on Administrative Management gave official sanction to an idea that had been growing increasingly urgent: "The president needs help." The national government had grown rapidly during the preceding 25 years, but structures and procedures necessary to manage the burgeoning executive branch had not yet been established. The response to this call for help initially took the form of three management policies: (1) all communications and decisions related to executive policy must pass through the White House; (2) to cope with such a flow, the White House must have an adequate staff of specialists in research, analysis, legislative and legal writing, and public affairs; and (3) the White House must have additional staff to follow through on presidential decisions—to ensure that those decisions are made, communicated to Congress, and carried out by the appropriate agency.

The story of the modern presidency can be told largely as a series of responses to the plea for managerial help. Indeed, each expansion of the national government into new policies and programs in the twentieth century was accompanied by a parallel expansion of the president's management authority. This pattern began even before Roosevelt's presidency with the policy innovations of President Woodrow Wilson between 1913 and 1920. In response to Wilson's policies, Congress granted the president agenda-setting power over budgeting with the 1921 Budget and Accounting Act. Presidents now transmit comprehensive budgetary recommendations to Congress in their annual budget messages. Because Congress retains ultimate legislative authority, a president's proposals are sometimes said to be dead on arrival on Capitol Hill. Nevertheless, the power to frame deliberations constitutes an important management tool. Each successive president has continued this pattern of setting the congressional agenda, creating what we now know as the managerial presidency.

Along with the managerial presidency came expectations of administrative competence. (See Analyzing the Evidence on pp. 330–1.) Presidents are now *expected* to be CEOs and are roundly criticized for ineptitude. George W. Bush, the first president with a graduate degree in business, followed a standard business school dictum: select skilled subordinates and delegate responsibility to them. Although Bush followed this model in appointing highly experienced officials to cabinet positions, it did not guarantee policy success, as doubts emerged about the conduct of the Iraq War and the administration's mishandling of relief after Hurricane Katrina. Barack Obama's administrative style received high marks for the quality of his appointees but was heavily dependent on personal staff inexperienced in dealing with Congress and the bureaucracy. The Trump administration has constituted something of an experiment in transferring Trump's

Explaining Vacancies in Presidential Appointments

Contributed by
Sanford Gordon
New York University

The president is the chief executive of a vast bureaucratic apparatus consisting of more than 2 million men and women. With this in mind, incoming administrations devote considerable resources and attention toward staffing the roughly 1,500 key positions reserved for presidential political appointees.

A surprising number of these appointed positions, however, remain unfilled well into a president's term. While some appointee vacancies reflect a failure of the Senate to act on a nomination submitted by the president, others occur because the president neglects to nominate someone in the first place. Legal scholar Anne Joseph O'Connell describes three negative consequences of appointee vacancies: agency inaction, agency confusion, and a reduction in agency accountability. At the same time, presidents may tolerate vacancies in order to buy time to select the right person for the job, to foster innovation (through high turnover), or to deliberately hobble an agency in the face of uncertainty or political disagreement.[1]

When we look at how presidents negotiate these complicated trade-offs, we would expect to see variation across different administrations as well as variation across agencies within administrations in the tolerance for vacancies. To study these patterns, I gathered data on the total number of available political appointee positions for cabinet-level executive departments and the number of those positions filled in the first seven months of the George W. Bush, Obama, and Trump administrations.

The graph below plots the number of available political appointee positions against the total size of each agency (in terms of full-time civil service employment). The dashed line is one that best fits the data; the fact that it is flat suggests little to no relationship between these two quantities. To the extent that political appointments are seen as a response to the difficulty of controlling a vast civil service, that difficulty is not reducible to the size of the workforce itself.

Agency Size and Appointed Positions, 2016

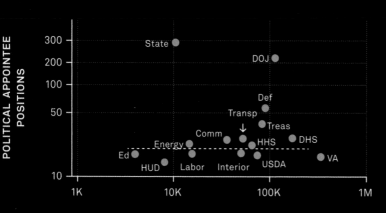

SOURCE: Political appointee data are from United States Government Policy and Supporting Positions (Plum Book), 2016, https://www.govinfo.gov/ content/pkg/ GPO-PLUMBOOK-2016/html/ GPO-PLUMBOOK-2016.htm (accessed 6/6/20). Full-time civilian employment data are available from the Office of Personnel Management.

The graph below plots, for each of the three presidents, the percentage of filled appointee position by department, with the departments ordered according to their reputations for ideological liberalism conservatism. The data do not show Republican presidents (Bush and Trump) rushing to fill positions stereotypically left-leaning agencies (as you might expect if they were motivated by mistrust), or Democratic president (Obama) rushing to fill those in right-leaning ones. In fact, the Bush and Obam ines look fairly similar across the departments. Of greater note is the fact that the line for Preside Trump lies nearly uniformly below the other two.

Appointed Positions Filled in First 7 Months

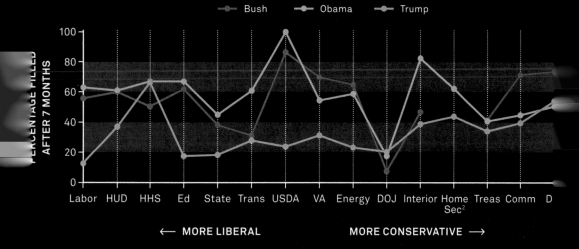

Trump's lower rate of filling appointed positions may reflect his lack of government experience alternatively, his lack of political debts to would-be officeholders. The two exceptions to the pattern Trump's case are the higher percentages of positions filled in the Department of Health and Human Service HHS) and the Department of Justice (DOJ)—perhaps not surprising, given his priorities related to heal care reform and law and order. More surprising is the relatively low percentage of filled appointments for th Department of Homeland Security, given Trump's focus on immigration enforcement (the U.S. Immigratio and Customs Enforcement agency is housed in Homeland Security).

Anne Joseph O'Connell, "Vacant Offices: Delays in Staffing Top Agency Positions," *Southern California Law Review* 82 (2007): 913–1000.

2 The Department of Homeland Security did not exist during this period of Bush's presidency.

SOURCE: Agency ideological reputation from Joshua D. Clinton and David E. Lewis, "Expert Opinion, Agency Characteristics, and Agency Preferences," Political Analysis 16, no. 1 (2008): 3–20. Number of filled positions by agency and administration numerator of fraction filled) from Jan Diehm, Sergio Hernandez, Aaron Kessler, et al., CNN, www.cnn.com/interactive/2017/politics/trump-nominations (accessed 6/6/20). Total number of political appointments (denominator of fraction filled) from United States Government Policy and Supporting Positions (Plum Book), 2016, https://www.govinfo.gov/content/pkg/GPO-PLUMBOOK-2016/html/GPO-PLUMBOOK-2016.htm (accessed 6/6/20).

business style to Washington. The president has relied heavily on friends and family with little public sector experience, on generals used to giving commands but unused to the give and take of Washington politics, and on unconventional personal interventions by the president himself, resulting in more disorder than is the norm. Throughout Trump's administration, senior posts remained unfilled, and those that were filled experienced high turnover. Indeed, in order to avoid fraught confirmation battles in the Senate, Trump relied heavily on "acting" senior administrators whose authority was weaker than that of fully confirmed officials.

Congressional Oversight and Incentives

Congress is constitutionally essential to responsible bureaucracy because legislation is key to governmental responsibility. When a law is passed and its intent is clear, then the president knows what to "faithfully execute," and the responsible agency understands what is expected of it. Today, legislatures rarely make laws directly for citizens; most laws are really instructions to bureaucrats and their agencies. But when Congress enacts vague legislation, agencies must rely on their own interpretations. The president and the federal courts step in to tell them what the legislation intended. So do interest groups. But when so many players get involved in interpreting legislative intent, to whom is the agency responsible?

oversight ➡️

The effort by Congress, through hearings, investigations, and other techniques, to exercise control over the activities of executive agencies.

The answer lies in the process of **oversight**. The more legislative power Congress has delegated to the bureaucracy, the more it has sought to get back into the game through committee and subcommittee oversight of executive agencies. The standing committee system in Congress is well suited to provide this oversight, as most of the congressional committees and subcommittees are organized according to jurisdictions roughly parallel to one or more executive departments or agencies. Appropriations committees and authorization committees have oversight powers, as do their subcommittees. In addition, there are committees responsible for monitoring government operations in both the House and the Senate, each with oversight powers not limited by departmental jurisdiction.

The best, most visible example of Congress's oversight efforts is the holding of public hearings at which bureaucrats and other witnesses are required to defend agency budgets and decisions. Committee or subcommittee hearings in 2014, for example, focused on a wide range of topics, including the 2012 attack on the U.S. consulate in Benghazi, Libya; the handling of the Ebola crisis; and IRS abuses. In 2015, there were continuing hearings on Benghazi along with hearings on the Export-Import Bank, on job growth, and on Hillary Clinton's use of a personal email server for official State Department business. During the Trump years, the congressional hearings apparatus has been much more muted; hearings have been held on Russian intervention in the American electoral system, possible executive branch collusion with these activities, other matters of cybersecurity, ensuring the safety of workers after the coronavirus pandemic, and questions of obstruction of justice related to President Trump's impeachment.

However, often the most effective control over bureaucratic accountability is the power of the purse—the ability of congressional committees and subcommittees on appropriations to scrutinize agency performance through the microscope of the annual appropriations process. The process makes bureaucrats attentive to Congress, especially members of the relevant authorizing committee and appropriations subcommittee, because they know that Congress has a chance each year to reduce their authority or funding.[21] This might be another explanation for why there may be some downsizing but almost no terminations of federal agencies.

Oversight can also be carried out by individual members of Congress on standard "casework" missions for their constituents. Inquiries addressed to bureaucratic agencies on behalf of individual constituents can sometimes turn up significant questions of public responsibility. Oversight also often occurs through communication between congressional staff and agency staff. Congressional staff has grown tremendously since the Legislative Reorganization Act of 1946, and staffers, especially committee staff, are just as specialized as executive agency staff. In addition, Congress has created for itself three large agencies that conduct constant research on problems in the executive branch: the Government Accountability Office, the Congressional Research Service, and the Congressional Budget Office. Each gives Congress information independent of what it learns through hearings and other communications directly with the executive branch.[22]

Congressional Oversight: Abdication or Strategic Delegation?

Congress often grants the executive branch bureaucracies discretion in determining certain features of a policy during the implementation phase. Although the complexities of governing a modern industrialized democracy make the granting of discretion necessary, some argue that Congress delegates too much policy-making authority to the unelected bureaucrats. Congress, in this view, has created a "runaway bureaucracy" in which unelected officials accountable neither to the electorate nor to Congress make important policy decisions.[23] By enacting vague statutes that give bureaucrats broad discretion, so the argument goes, members of Congress abdicate their constitutionally designated roles and remove themselves from the policy-making process. These critics say that ultimately this extreme degree of delegation has left the legislative branch ineffectual, with dire consequences for our democracy.

---

21 See Aaron Wildavsky, *The New Politics of the Budgetary Process*, 2nd ed. (New York: HarperCollins, 1992), pp. 15–16.

22 On the congressional staff more generally, see Robert H. Salisbury and Kenneth A. Shepsle, "U.S. Congressman as Enterprise," *Legislative Studies Quarterly* 6, no. 4 (1981): 559–76. On the role and activities of the Government Accountability Office, see Anne Joseph O'Connell, "Auditing Politics or Political Auditing?" (February 21, 2007), UC Berkeley Public Law Research Paper No. 964656, https://papers.ssrn.com/sol3/papers.cfm?abstract_id=964656 (accessed 6/5/20).

23 Lowi, *The End of Liberalism*; and Lawrence C. Dodd and Richard L. Schott, *Congress and the Administrative State* (New York: Wiley, 1979).

Others claim that Congress fails to use its tools to engage in effective oversight, as we do not see Congress carrying out much oversight activity.[24] However, political scientists Mathew McCubbins and Thomas Schwartz argue that these critics have missed a type of oversight that benefits members of Congress in their bids for reelection (in accord with the rationality principle).[25] McCubbins and Schwartz distinguish between two types of oversight: police patrol and fire alarm. Under police-patrol oversight, Congress systematically initiates investigations into the activity of agencies. Under fire-alarm oversight, Congress waits for adversely affected citizens or interest groups to bring bureaucratic perversions of legislative intent to their attention. To ensure that individuals and groups publicize these violations—to set off the fire alarm, so to speak—Congress helps them make claims against the bureaucracy, both granting them legal standing before administrative agencies and federal courts and giving them access to government-held information through FOIA.

McCubbins and Schwartz argue that fire-alarm oversight is more efficient than the police-patrol variety, given the costs involved and the electoral incentives of members of Congress. Why should members spend their scarce resources (mainly time) to initiate investigations without having any evidence that they will reap electoral rewards? Police-patrol oversight can waste taxpayers' dollars too, because many investigations will not turn up evidence of violations of legislative intent. It is much more cost effective for members to conserve their resources and then claim credit for fixing the problem after the fire alarms have been sounded.

In contrast, bureaucratic drift might be contained if Congress spent more time clarifying its legislative intent and less time on oversight activity. If its original intent in its laws were clearer, Congress could afford to defer to presidential management to maintain bureaucratic responsibility. Bureaucrats are more responsive to clear legislative guidance than to anything else. But when Congress and the president (or coalitions within Congress) are at odds, bureaucrats can evade responsibility by playing one side against the other.

Policy Implications. Because the bureaucracy is squarely in the middle of the separation of powers between the legislature and the executive, it often eludes systematic oversight. The institution principle suggests as much. Rational political actors in both branches will pay some attention to the bureaucracy, but their own goals may not be well served by obsessive attention. The result is a bureaucracy that retains some discretion—partly because the specialization of bureaucrats' jobs warrants it but also because political arrangements permit oversight to fall between the institutional cracks. Bureaus, in turn, perform their missions in ways that maintain this kind of independence. They produce rulings,

---

24 Morris S. Ogul, *Congress Oversees the Bureaucracy: Studies in Legislative Supervision* (Pittsburgh, PA: University of Pittsburgh Press, 1976); and Peter Woll, *American Bureaucracy*, 2nd ed. (New York: Norton, 1977).

25 McCubbins and Schwartz, "Congressional Oversight Overlooked."

interpretations, and implementations of policy that deter after-the-fact oversight, allowing sleeping dogs (potential overseers) to lie.

Rational political adaptations to these institutional arrangements have policy consequences. In particular, bureaucrats will be extraordinarily attentive to the policy needs of those legislators who are in a position to help or harm them. Thus states and districts represented on the House and Senate authorizing committees, as well as on the relevant appropriations subcommittees, can expect government largesse to be steered their way. Legislative lore cites instances in which, for example, a major weapons system is sustained politically by an implicit agreement between Defense Department agents and private-sector contractors to ensure that subcontracts are distributed geographically to politically significant locations.

A repeated pattern of deals among agency officials, powerful legislators, and private-sector special interests over many projects in many policy areas yields a "distributive tendency" in which legislators and bureaucrats must distribute spending widely to play the political game successfully. Efficiency takes a back seat to ensuring that the "right" states and districts are taken care of. One classic example is President Lyndon B. Johnson's attempt in the mid-1960s to focus federal assistance on 10 central cities in direst need of economic stimulus. But 10 was too small a number in a political system with 50 states and 435 legislative districts. By the time Johnson's proposal had worked its way through the legislative process, the relevant bureaucratic entities had won the discretion to spread funds to *hundreds* of distressed cities and even to tackle rural poverty as well. The policy principle suggests that institutional arrangements (bicameralism and the separation of powers, in this instance) combined with rational political behavior (reelection motivations of legislators and programmatic survival instincts of bureaucrats) produce policy distortions (wide distribution of funds to sustain programs and to avoid the risk of critical oversight).

REFORMING THE BUREAUCRACY

Americans don't like big government because it means big bureaucracy, and bureaucracy means the federal service—about 2.8 million civilian and 1.4 million military employees.[26] Promises to cut the bureaucracy are popular campaign appeals; "cutting out the fat" by reducing the number of federal employees is touted as a surefire way of cutting the deficit.

Yet the federal service has hardly grown at all during the past 30 years; it reached its peak post–World War II level in 1968 with 2.9 million civilian employees plus an additional 3.6 million military personnel (a figure swollen by the war in Vietnam). The number of civilian employees has not changed much since that time. Growth of the federal service is even less imposing when placed

---

26 "Federal Employees by State," *Governing*, www.governing.com/gov-data/federal-employees-workforce-numbers-by-state.html (accessed 11/11/19).

Figure 8.3

EMPLOYEES IN THE FEDERAL SERVICE: TOTAL NUMBER AS A PERCENTAGE OF THE WORKFORCE, 1950–2021

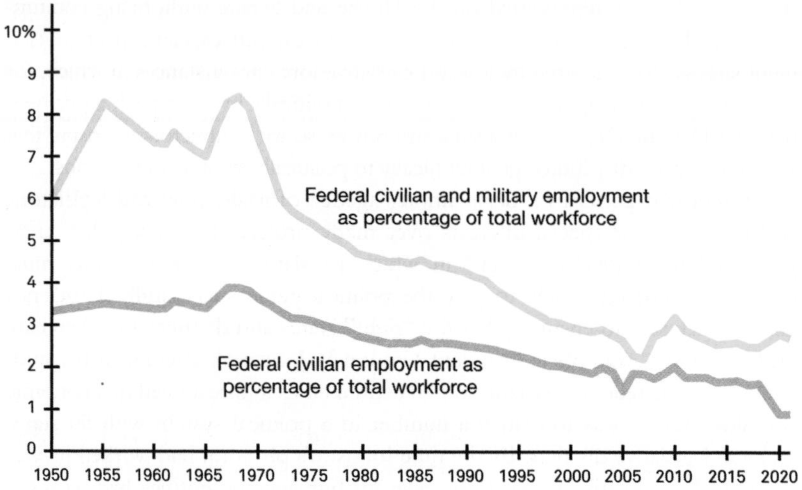

NOTE: Workforce includes unemployed persons; 2020 and 2021 numbers reflect OMB estimates.
SOURCES: Tax Foundation, *Facts and Figures on Government Finance* (Baltimore, MD: Johns Hopkins University Press, 1990), pp. 22, 44; Office of Management and Budget, https://www.whitehouse.gov/sites/whitehouse.gov/files/omb/assets/OMB/budget/fy2009/ (accessed 6/6/20); U.S. Office of Personnel Management, https://www.opm.gov/policy-data-oversight/data-analysis-documentation/federal-employment-reports/ (accessed 6/6/20); U.S. Bureau of Labor Statistics; https://stats.bls.gov/webapps/legacy/cpsatab1.htm; Congressional Research Service, "Federal Workforce Statistics Sources: OPM and OMB," March 25, 2020, https://crsreports.congress.gov/product/pdf/R/R43590 (accessed 6/17/20).

in the context of the total workforce and compared to state and local public employment, which comprised 14.8 million full-time and 4.8 million part-time employees in 2018.[27] Figure 8.3 indicates that, since 1950, the ratio of federal service employment to the total workforce has been fairly steady, declining only slightly in the past 50 years. Figure 8.4 offers another useful comparison: although the dollar increase in federal spending shown by the bars looks substantial, the orange line indicates that even here the national government has simply kept pace with the growth of the economy.

In sum, the federal service has not been growing any faster than the economy or the rest of society. The same is roughly true of state and local public personnel. Our bureaucracy keeps pace with our society, despite our seeming dislike for it, because we cannot operate the air traffic control towers, the Social Security

27 U.S. Census Bureau, "2018 Government Employment and Payroll Tables," www.census.gov/data/tables/2018/econ/apes/annual-apes.html (11/11/19).

Figure 8.4
ANNUAL FEDERAL OUTLAYS, 1960–2025

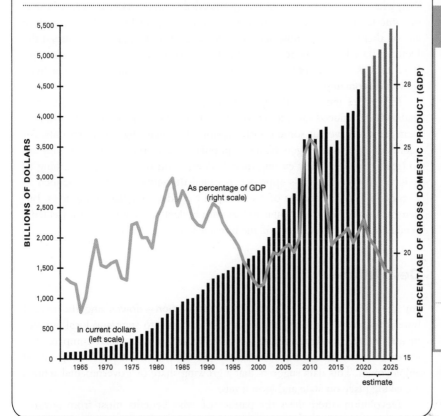

NOTE: Data for 2020–25 are estimated.
SOURCE: Office of Management and Budget, Historical Tables, Table 1.3: "Summary of Receipts, Outlays, and Surpluses or Deficits In Current Dollars, Constant Dollars, and Percentage of GDP: 1940–2025," https://www.whitehouse.gov/omb/historical-tables/ (accessed 6/6/20).

system, and other essential elements of the state without it. And we could not conduct wars in Iraq and Afghanistan without a gigantic military bureaucracy.

Termination

The only *certain* way to reduce the size of the bureaucracy is to eliminate programs. But most agencies have a supportive constituency—people and groups that benefit from the programs—that will fight to reinstate any cuts. Termination is the only way to ensure an agency's reduction, and it is a rare occurrence.

The overall lack of success in terminating bureaucracy is a reflection of Americans' love/hate relationship with the national government. As antagonistic as Americans may be toward bureaucracy in general, they grow attached to the services and protections offered by particular agencies. A good example was the agonizing problem of closing military bases following the end of the Cold War, when the United States no longer needed so many. Because every base is in some Congress member's district, Congress was unable to decide to close any of them. Consequently, between 1988 and 1990, Congress established the Defense Base Realignment and Closure Commission to decide on base closings. Even though the matter is now out of Congress's hands, the process has been slow and agonizing.

In a more incremental approach to downsizing the bureaucracy, elected leaders have reduced the budgets of all agencies across the board by small percentages and have cut some poorly supported agencies by larger amounts. An additional approach targets highly unpopular regulatory agencies, but they are so (relatively) small that cutting their budgets contributes virtually nothing to reducing the deficit. This approach is called **deregulation**, simply defined as a reduction in the number of rules issued by federal regulatory agencies. But deregulation is still incremental and, as with budget reduction, has not yielded a genuine reduction in the size of the bureaucracy.

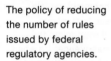

deregulation

The policy of reducing the number of rules issued by federal regulatory agencies.

Devolution

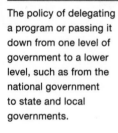

devolution

The policy of delegating a program or passing it down from one level of government to a lower level, such as from the national government to state and local governments.

An alternative to genuine reduction is **devolution**—downsizing the federal bureaucracy by delegating program implementation to state and local governments. Indirect evidence for this appears in Figure 8.5, which compares the increase in state and local government employment with flat or declining federal employment. This data suggests that a growing share of governmental actions are taking place on state and local levels.

Devolution often alters the pattern of who benefits most from government programs. In the early 1990s, a major devolution in transportation policy sought to open up decisions in this realm to a new set of interests. Since the 1920s, transportation policy had been dominated by road-building interests in the federal and state governments. Many advocates for cities and many environmentalists believed that the emphasis on road building hurt cities and harmed the environment. A 1992 transportation policy reform, initiated by environmentalists, gave more power to metropolitan planning organizations and lifted many federal restrictions on how federal transportation grants could be spent. Reformers hoped that, through these changes, those advocating alternatives to road building, such as mass transit, bike paths, and walkways, would be able to assert more influence. Although change has been slow, devolution has indeed brought new voices to decisions about transportation spending, and alternatives to highways have received increasing attention.

More recently, Republicans in Congress failed in their efforts to devolve more control over Medicaid to the states as part of their 2017 attempt to replace Obamacare. Republicans had hoped to place a total dollar cap on Medicaid spending (mainly health care for low-income citizens), ration this amount among the states according to a formula, and allow the states to devise and allocate money across

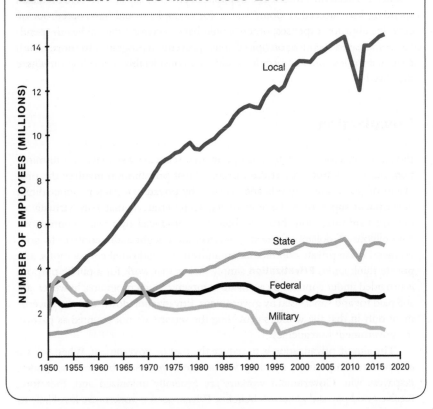

Figure 8.5
GOVERNMENT EMPLOYMENT 1950–2017

NOTE: Federal government employment figures include only civilians. Military employment figures include only active-duty personnel; 2013 data not available.

SOURCE: U.S. Census Bureau, *Statistical Abstract of the United States,* 2011 and 2012 (Washington, DC: U.S. Government Printing Office, 2011); 2013–2017 state, federal, and local employment: Governing, "State and Local Government Employment: Monthly Data," https://www.governing.com/gov-data/public-workforce-salaries/monthly-government-employment-changes-totals.html (accessed 6/17/20); 2013–2017 military employment: Department of Defense, DoD Personnel, "Military and Civilian Personnel by Service/Agency by State/Country," https://www.dmdc.osd.mil/appj/dwp/dwp_reports.jsp (accessed 6/17/20).

their own spending categories. In response to these legislative failures, the Trump administration has taken administrative actions to trim Medicaid availability—for example, limiting spending on those who do not meet work requirements and allowing states to deny coverage to those who otherwise had been eligible.[28]

Often devolution seeks to provide more efficient and more flexible government services, yet it entails variation across the states. In some states, government

28 Center on Budget and Policy Priorities, "Trump Administration's Harmful Changes to Medicaid," June 12, 2019, www.cbpp.org/research/health/trump-administrations-harmful-changes-to-medicaid (accessed 11/11/19).

services may improve as a consequence of devolution. In other states, services may deteriorate as devolution leads to spending cuts and reduced services. This would have been the effect if the Republican effort to cap and devolve Medicaid spending had succeeded. Some states, for example, would have opted out of covering abortion expenses; others would have decreased mental health spending or increased spending on opioid abuse prevention programs. In short, health coverage for low-income people would vary considerably depending on where they lived.

Privatization

Privatization, another downsizing option, may seem like a synonym for termination, but that is true only at the extreme. Most privatization involves the provision of government goods and services by private contractors under direct government supervision. Except for top-secret strategic materials, virtually all military hardware, from boats to bullets, is produced by private contractors. And billions of dollars of research services are bought under contract by government; these private contractors are universities, industrial corporations, and private think tanks. **Privatization** simply means that work for a public purpose is provided under contract by a private company.[29] Such programs, however, are still paid for and supervised by government. Privatization downsizes the government only in that the workers providing the service are not counted as part of the government bureaucracy.

privatization

The act of moving all or part of a program from the public sector to the private sector.

The aim of privatization is to reduce the cost of government. When private contractors can perform a task as well as the government but for less money, taxpayers win. Government workers are generally unionized and, therefore, receive good pay and generous benefits. Private-sector workers are less likely to be unionized, and private firms often provide lower pay and fewer benefits. For this reason, public-sector unions have been one of the strongest voices against privatization. Other critics observe that private firms may not be more efficient or less costly than government, especially when there is little competition among private firms and when public bureaucracies cannot bid in the contracting competition. When private firms have a monopoly on service provision, they may be more expensive than the government. There are, in addition, important questions about how private contractors can be held accountable.

Indeed, the new demands of domestic security have altered the thrust of bureaucratic reform. Despite strong agreement on the goal of fighting terrorism, the effort to streamline the bureaucracy by focusing on this single purpose is likely to face considerable obstacles. Strong constituencies may attempt to block changes that they believe will harm them, and initiatives for improved

---

29 A more general term is *outsourcing*. Privatization is outsourcing to the private sector. Devolution is outsourcing to a lower level of government. A third example of outsourcing is the opposite of devolution, as when a small community contracts with a county for, say, police services.

coordination among agencies may provoke political disputes if the proposed changes threaten to alter groups' access to the bureaucracy. Groups that oppose bureaucratic changes may appeal to Congress to intervene on their behalf.

CONCLUSION: PUBLIC BUREAUCRACIES AND POLITICS

Bureaucracy is one of humanity's most significant inventions. It is an institutional arrangement that allows for division and specialization of labor; harnesses expertise; and coordinates collective action for social, political, and economic purposes. It enables governments to exist and perform. In this chapter, we have focused on what public bureaucracies do, how they are organized at the national level in the United States, and how they are controlled (or not) by elected politicians.

At a theoretical level, public bureaucracy is the concrete expression of rational, purposeful, political action (rationality principle). Elected politicians have goals—as broad as defending the realm, maintaining public health and safety, or promoting economic growth; as narrow as securing a post office for Possum Hollow, Pennsylvania, or an exit off the interstate highway for Springfield, Massachusetts. Bureaucracy is the instrument by which political objectives, established by elected legislators and executives, are transformed from ideas and intentions into the actual "bricks and mortar" of implemented policies (policy principle).

At a practical level, this transformation depends on the motivations of bureaucratic agents and the institutional machinery that develops around every bureaucratic entity. Elected politicians engage in institutional design in creating agencies. They have their greatest impact at this point. Once an agency is operating, elected officials can only imperfectly control their bureaucratic agents. Institutional arrangements (institution principle) and individual motivations (rationality principle) provide agencies with a degree of insulation, determining the precise mix of bureaucratic "free agency" and political control that guide an agency's actions. That is, bureaucrats can march to their own drummers some of the time, but they are not entirely free agents.

The policy principle suggests that the combination of bureaucratic arrangements and individual motivations produces evident patterns in policy. Because of its insulation, an agency's policies, once under way, are difficult to reverse. Insulation thwarts all but the most intensely motivated interventions in an agency's affairs. This has the benefit of commitment—interested parties are reassured about the continued provision of a bureaucratic product or service. The farmer can rely on his subsidy check, the senior citizen can count on receiving her monthly Social Security stipend; truckers and other motorists can be confident that the interstate highways will be there for them.

But these commitments have distributive costs. Bureaucrats will be most attentive to the most interested parties. Thus policies will be skewed in particular ways. The efficiency gains arising from the expertise and coordinating services of bureaucracy are thus diminished by these political pressures. For example, highway funds will find their way disproportionately to the states and districts of legislators who sit on the public works authorizing and appropriating committees.

In describing the federal bureaucracy in this chapter, we have sought to make clear the ways in which rationality, institutional processes, and the resulting policy outputs are a consequence of the way in which agencies straddle the divide produced by the separation of powers. Attuned partly to the executive and partly to the legislature, bureaucratic agents tread a careful line between their several masters, somewhat insulated but vulnerable to intense political pressure. Politics is at the very heart of these organizations and the policies they produce.

For Further Reading

Besley, Timothy. *Principled Agents? The Political Economy of Good Government.* New York: Oxford University Press, 2007.

Brehm, John, and Scott Gates. *Working, Shirking, and Sabotage: Bureaucratic Response to a Democratic Public.* Ann Arbor: University of Michigan Press, 1997.

Carpenter, Daniel P. *The Forging of Bureaucratic Autonomy: Reputation, Networks, and Policy Innovation in Executive Agencies, 1862–1928.* Princeton, NJ: Princeton University Press, 2001.

Gailmard, Sean, and John W. Patty. "Slackers and Zealots: Civil Service, Policy Discretion, and Bureaucratic Expertise." *American Journal of Political Science* 51, no. 4 (2007): 873–89.

Gailmard, Sean, and John W. Patty. *Learning While Governing: Expertise and Accountability in the Executive Branch.* Chicago: University of Chicago Press, 2013.

Goodsell, Charles T. *The Case for Bureaucracy: A Public Administration Polemic.* 4th ed. Washington, DC: CQ Press, 2003.

Heclo, Hugh. *On Thinking Institutionally.* Boulder, CO: Paradigm, 2007.

Huber, John D., and Charles R. Shipan. *Deliberate Discretion? The Institutional Foundations of Bureaucratic Autonomy.* New York: Cambridge University Press, 2002.

Kerwin, Cornelius M., and Scott R. Furlong. *Rulemaking.* 5th ed. Washington, DC: CQ Press, 2018.

Kettl, Donald F. *Politics of the Administrative Process.* 7th ed. Washington, DC: CQ Press, 2017.

Light, Paul C. *The True Size of Government.* Washington, DC: Brookings Institution, 1999.

Lipsky, Michael. *Street-Level Bureaucracy: Dilemmas of the Individual in Public Services.* 30th Anniversary Expanded Edition. New York: Russell Sage, 2010.

McCubbins, Mathew D., Roger G. Noll, and Barry R. Weingast. "Structure and Process, Politics and Policy: Administrative Arrangements and the Political Control of Agencies." *Virginia Law Review* 75, no. 2 (1989): 431–82.

McCubbins, Mathew D., and Thomas Schwartz. "Congressional Oversight Overlooked: Police Patrols Versus Fire Alarms." *American Journal of Political Science* 28, no. 1 (1984): 165–79.

Meier, Kenneth J., and John Bohte. *Politics and the Bureaucracy.* 5th ed. Belmont, CA: Wadsworth, 2006.

Wilson, James Q. *Bureaucracy: What Government Agencies Do and Why They Do It.* New York: Basic Books, 1989.

9

The Federal Courts

Courts serve an essential function. When disputes arise, a neutral arbiter is needed to help settle them. When laws must be enforced, justice requires an impartial judge to determine guilt and innocence and, if the accused is found guilty, the appropriate punishment. And when questions arise about the meaning of those laws, we rely on the wisdom of judges to interpret what Congress intended the laws to mean and how that meaning applies in given circumstances. It is not possible, or even wise, to pass a law to cover every contingency. Thus nearly every nation today has established a system of courts to satisfy the need for an arbiter and interpreter.

Perhaps the most distinctive feature of the American judiciary is its independence. As we will see, four institutional features of the American judiciary ensure a powerful, independent court system. First, the Constitution establishes the federal courts as a separate branch of government from Congress and the president. Second, authority among the courts is hierarchical; federal courts are able to overturn state courts, and the U.S. Supreme Court is the ultimate authority. Third, the Supreme Court and other federal courts of appeals can strike down actions of Congress, the president, or the states if judges deem those acts to be violations of the Constitution. This authority is the power of *judicial review*. And fourth, federal judges are appointed for life. They are not subject to the pressures of running for reelection and need not be highly responsive to changes in public opinion.[1]

An independent judiciary has been one of our government's most successful institutions. It has settled constitutional crises when Congress and the president have been at odds. It has guaranteed that no person is above the law, even members of Congress and the president. It has helped ensure that all people, even noncitizens, enjoy equal protection of the laws. It has enabled small businesses, large corporations, and workers to engage in economic activities and agreements, knowing that their rights will be protected. It has ensured that the

---

1   However, judges in many state and local courts are elected.

branches of government operate in a democratic manner and that every citizen's vote counts equally in electing representatives. The independent judiciary has ensured a stable, successful democracy and economy.[2]

Although granting judges lifetime appointments and the power to strike down acts of Congress might seem to permit tyrannical rule, the federal courts lack Congress's power of the purse, the president's ability to move troops or order other entities of the executive branch to act, and the bureaucracy's power to police. Courts are also passive in that they must wait for people to file lawsuits in order to make decisions or issue decrees. The nature and sources of judicial power in American government are subtle and democratic.

The real power of the courts emanates from society's trust in their ability to interpret laws fairly. Courts are powerful to the extent that the people and groups involved accept judges' decrees. If people ignored the rulings of judges in local courts or if Congress routinely passed legislation contradicting the Supreme Court, the judicial function in our society would vanish. Herein lies the judiciary's ability not just to interpret but also to make law. Indeed, each court decision or settlement is an act of lawmaking, a function as important as the

LEARNING OBJECTIVES

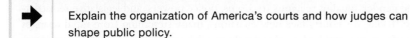 Explain the organization of America's courts and how judges can shape public policy.

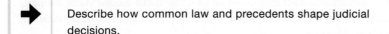 Describe how common law and precedents shape judicial decisions.

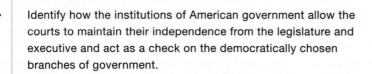 Identify how the institutions of American government allow the courts to maintain their independence from the legislature and executive and act as a check on the democratically chosen branches of government.

 Explain the significance of judicial review.

Analyze the institutions of the court and how they influence decision making.

---

2   The administration of President Donald Trump, possibly more than any other in the history of the Republic, has pushed the envelope on judicial independence both by interfering with the work of the U.S. Department of Justice and by insulating the president and others in the administration from legal probes by the federal courts.

passage of a statute by the legislature. Any decision may serve as a precedent for deciding a future case, and the accumulation of many such decisions, accepted by common practice, eventually becomes the norm.

Common law consists of all past agreements that ordinary people accept when reaching any legally binding decision. A contract for a real estate sale, for example, comprises many pages of language pertaining to contingencies that might arise, what would happen in each case, and who would bear responsibility. Each clause has been developed through past legal decisions accumulated over centuries, even dating back in some instances to ancient Rome. The Supreme Court is similarly constrained by past decisions. When a majority of justices issues an opinion interpreting the law in a particular way, that opinion has the standing of precedent and constrains future courts. The history principle matters more fundamentally for the judiciary than for the other branches of government. If judges themselves were to ignore precedent, they would undercut the power of the courts and their own authority.[3]

Usually, the courts' influence on American politics is incremental. At times, however, courts have made sweeping changes in the country's law and politics. With industrialization in the late nineteenth century came new ideas about the enforcement of contracts that dominated the courts' thinking. The New Deal eventually won the support of the Supreme Court and ushered in a new acceptance of a broader role for the federal government in the economy and society. During the 1950s and 1960s, the Supreme Court confronted conflicts over racial and gender equality, religious freedoms, police powers, and legislative redistricting. Today, the courts face new questions, many stemming from rapid changes in information and biological technologies: Who owns your DNA? Do you have a right to privacy when sending an email or using social media? As in the past, the courts will settle cases that address such questions and shape the meaning of the law in doing so.

The judiciary's role in our system of government points to a basic lesson about courts worldwide: they are fundamentally political. Just like presidents and legislators, judges have preferences about what government should do, and they use their powers to interpret, apply, and review laws to shape public policy. Judges are also constrained by the institutional setting within which they operate. They know that others in the political process may try to alter or undo their court's rulings.

In this chapter, we first examine the judicial process and the structure of the federal court system. Second, we analyze courts as political institutions and consider their roles in the political system. Third, we consider judicial review and how it makes the Supreme Court a lawmaking body. Fourth, we examine the

----

3　Precedent provides the Supreme Court the means to control lower courts; Supreme Court rulings in effect set the standard with which subsequent lower-court decisions must comply. However, precedent also constrains the Court's own future decisions. See Ethan Bueno de Mesquita and Matthew Stephenson, "Informative Precedent and Intrajudicial Communication," *American Political Science Review* 96, no. 4 (December 2002): 755–66.

flow of cases through the courts and various influences on Supreme Court decisions. Finally, we analyze the process of judicial decision making and the power of the federal courts in the American political process, looking in particular at the growth of judicial power in our nation.

THE JUDICIAL PROCESS

Many centuries ago a court was the place where a king and his entourage governed. Judging—settling disputes between citizens—was part of governing. Over time the function of settling disputes was slowly separated from the king and his court and became a separate institution of government. Courts have taken over the power to settle controversies by hearing the facts on both sides and deciding which side possesses greater merit. But because judges are not kings, they must have a basis for their authority. That basis in the United States is the Constitution and the law. Courts decide cases by applying the relevant law or principle to the facts. This approach lends authority derived from past law and past social compacts. It also provides a basis for continuing judicial independence, as common law and the record of cases that can serve as precedents evolve on their own, often separate from legislation passed by Congress and the executive. What are these systems of rules that guide the judiciary? What are the organizations and institutions of the judiciary, and how do they help judges administer and interpret the law?

Court cases in the United States proceed under two broad categories of law: criminal and civil. One form of civil law, public law, is so important that we consider it as a separate category (Table 9.1).

In cases of **criminal law** the government charges an individual with violating a statute that has been enacted to protect public health, safety, morals, or welfare. In criminal cases, the government is always the plaintiff (the party that brings charges) and alleges that a named defendant has committed a criminal violation. Most criminal cases arise in state and municipal courts and involve matters ranging from traffic offenses to robbery and murder. Although much of criminal law is administered at the state level, a growing body of federal criminal law addresses such matters as tax evasion, mail fraud, and the sale of narcotics. Defendants found guilty of criminal violations may be fined or sent to prison.

Cases of **civil law** involve disputes between individuals or between individuals and the government where no criminal violation is charged. Unlike criminal cases, the losers in civil cases cannot be fined or sent to prison, although they may be required to pay monetary damages. In a civil case, the one who brings a complaint is the plaintiff and the one against whom the complaint is brought is the defendant. The two most common types of civil cases involve contracts and torts, and both are often handled by state courts. In a typical contract case, an individual or corporation charges that it has suffered because of another's violation of an agreement between the two parties. For example, Smith Manufacturing Corporation may charge that Jones Distributors failed to honor an

criminal law

Cases arising out of actions that allegedly violate laws protecting the health, safety, morals, and welfare of the community.

civil law

Cases involving disputes among individuals or between the government and individuals that do not involve criminal penalties.

Table 9.1

TYPES OF LAWS AND DISPUTES

TYPE OF LAW	TYPE OF CASE OR DISPUTE	FORM OF CITATION
Criminal law	Cases arising out of actions that violate laws protecting the health, safety, morals, and welfare of the community. The government is always the plaintiff.	*United States (or state) v. Jones, Jones v. United States (or state)* if Jones lost and is appealing
Civil law	Law involving disputes between individuals or between a government and an individual when no crime is alleged. Two general types are contract law and tort law. Contract cases are disputes that arise over voluntary actions. Tort cases are disputes that arise out of obligations inherent in social life. Negligence and slander are examples of torts.	*Smith v. Jones, New York v. Jones, United States v. Jones, Jones v. New York*
Public law	All cases in which the powers of government or the rights of citizens are involved. The government is the defendant. Constitutional law involves judicial review of the basis of a government's action in relation to specific clauses of the Constitution as the judiciary interprets it. Administrative law involves disputes over the statutory authority, jurisdiction, or procedures of administrative agencies.	*Jones v. United States (or state), In re Jones, Smith v. Jones* if a license or statute is at issue in their private dispute

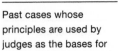

precedents

Past cases whose principles are used by judges as the bases for their decisions in present cases.

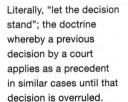

stare decisis

Literally, "let the decision stand"; the doctrine whereby a previous decision by a court applies as a precedent in similar cases until that decision is overruled.

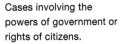

public law

Cases involving the powers of government or rights of citizens.

agreement to deliver raw materials at a specified time, causing Smith to lose business. Smith asks the court to order Jones to compensate it for the damage allegedly suffered. In a typical tort case, one individual charges that she has been injured by another's negligence or malfeasance. Medical malpractice suits are one example of tort cases.

In deciding cases, courts apply statutes (laws) and legal **precedents** (prior decisions). State and federal statutes often govern the conditions under which contracts are and are not legally binding. The court might decide that Jones Distributors was not obliged to fulfill its contract with Smith Manufacturing because actions by Smith—the failure to make promised payments—constituted fraud under state law. A court might acquit a physician of malpractice based on prior instances in which courts ruled that actions similar to the doctor's did not constitute negligence. Such precedents are applied under the doctrine of **stare decisis**, a Latin phrase meaning "let the decision stand."

A case becomes a matter of **public law** when a plaintiff or defendant in a civil or criminal case seeks to show that his case involves the powers of government or the rights of citizens as defined by the Constitution or by statute. One major form of public law is constitutional law, under which a court will determine whether the government's actions conform to the Constitution as the judiciary interprets it. Thus what began as an ordinary criminal case may enter the realm of public law if, for example, a defendant claims that the police violated her constitutional rights. Another arena of public law is administrative law, which involves disputes over the jurisdiction, procedures, or authority of administrative agencies. Under this type of law, civil litigation between an individual and the government may become a matter of public law if the individual asserts that the government is violating a statute or abusing its constitutional power. For example, landowners have asserted that some federal and state regulations on land use violate the Fifth Amendment's restrictions on the government's ability to confiscate private property. Recently the Supreme Court has been very sympathetic to such claims, which effectively transform an ordinary civil dispute into a major issue of public law.

Most of the Supreme Court cases we examine in this chapter concern the constitutional or statutory basis of the actions of government agencies. In this arena of public law, Court decisions can have significant consequences for American politics and society.

THE ORGANIZATION OF THE COURT SYSTEM

Types of Courts

In the United States, court systems have been established both by the federal government and by individual state governments. Both systems have several levels (Figure 9.1), though it should be acknowledged that the one federal system and the 50 state systems are all distinctive in a number of ways. Nearly 99 percent of all court cases in the United States are heard in state courts. The majority of criminal cases, for example, involve violations of state laws prohibiting such actions as murder, robbery, fraud, theft, and assault. If such a case is brought to trial, it will be heard in a state **trial court** in front of a judge and sometimes a jury, who will determine whether the defendant violated state law. If the defendant is convicted, he may appeal the conviction to a higher court, such as a state **court of appeals,** and from there to a state's **supreme court**. Similarly, most civil litigation is brought in state courts. For example, a patient bringing suit against a physician for malpractice would file the suit in the appropriate court in the state where the alleged malpractice occurred. The judge hearing the case would apply state law and state precedent to the matter. (However, in both criminal and civil matters, most cases are settled before trial through negotiated agreements between the parties. In criminal cases, these agreements are called plea bargains. Such bargains may affect the severity of the charge and/or the severity of the sentence.)

In addition, the U.S. military operates its own court system under the Uniform Code of Military Justice, which governs the behavior of men and women in the armed services. On rare occasions, the government has constituted special military tribunals to hear cases deemed inappropriate for the civil courts. Such tribunals tried Nazi saboteurs apprehended in the United States during World War II and individuals suspected of acts of terrorism against the United States

trial court

The first court to hear a criminal or civil case.

court of appeals

A court that hears the appeals of lower-court decisions. Also called *appellate court.*

supreme court

The highest court in a particular state or in the country.

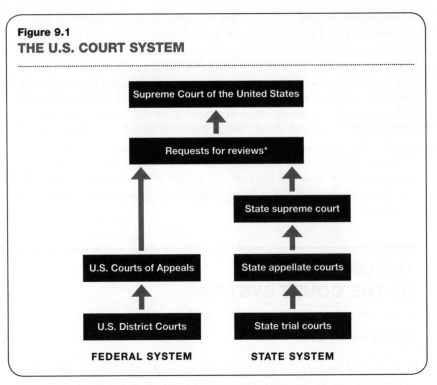

Figure 9.1

THE U.S. COURT SYSTEM

Supreme Court of the United States

Requests for reviews*

State supreme court

U.S. Courts of Appeals

State appellate courts

U.S. District Courts

State trial courts

FEDERAL SYSTEM

STATE SYSTEM

*The U.S. Supreme Court is not obligated to accept appeals. This is also true of some state supreme courts.

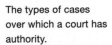

jurisdiction

The types of cases over which a court has authority.

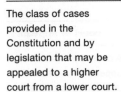

appellate jurisdiction

The class of cases provided in the Constitution and by legislation that may be appealed to a higher court from a lower court.

original jurisdiction

The class of cases provided in the Constitution (Article III) that may be taken directly to a federal court.

after September 11. More recently, special courts have been created, sometimes in conjunction with the Department of Veterans Affairs, to hear criminal cases involving veterans of the recent wars in Iraq and Afghanistan.

Federal Jurisdiction

Cases are heard in the federal courts if they involve federal laws, treaties with other nations, or the U.S. Constitution; these areas constitute the federal courts' official **jurisdiction**. In addition, any case in which the U.S. government is a party is heard in the federal courts. If, for example, an individual is charged with violating a federal criminal statute—such as evading the payment of federal income taxes—charges would be brought before a federal judge by a federal prosecutor. Civil cases involving the citizens of more than one state in which more than $75,000 is at stake may be heard in either the federal or the state courts.

But even if a matter belongs in federal court, how do we know which federal court should exercise jurisdiction? The answer is complex. Each federal court's jurisdiction is derived from the Constitution and federal statutes. Article III of the Constitution gives the Supreme Court **appellate jurisdiction** in all federal cases and **original jurisdiction** in cases involving foreign ambassadors and issues in which a state is a party. That is, the Supreme Court may hear cases appealed to it by a party to a case first heard in a lower federal court or a state court (appellate jurisdiction); it may also be the initial destination of cases involving a state or an ambassador (original jurisdiction). Article III assigns original jurisdiction in all other federal cases to the lower courts. Over the years, as Congress enacted statutes creating the federal judicial system, it also specified the jurisdiction of each type of court it established. Congress generally has assigned jurisdictions on the basis of geography. The nation is currently, by statute, divided into 94 judicial districts, including one court for each of three U.S. territories: Guam, the U.S. Virgin Islands, and the Northern Mariana Islands. Each of the 94 U.S. district courts exercises jurisdiction over federal cases arising within its territorial domain. The judicial districts are, in turn, organized into 11 regional circuits and the District of Columbia circuit. Each circuit court exercises appellate jurisdiction over cases heard by the district courts within its region.

Geography is not the only basis for federal court jurisdiction. Congress has also established specialized courts with nationwide original jurisdiction in certain types of cases. These include the U.S. Court of International Trade, which addresses trade and customs issues, and the U.S. Court of Federal Claims, which handles damage suits against the United States. Other federal courts with specialized jurisdictions are the U.S. Court of Appeals for Veterans Claims, which exercises exclusive jurisdiction over cases involving veterans' claims, and the U.S. Court of Appeals for the Armed Forces, which addresses questions of law arising from trials by court martial. In addition, Congress has established a court with nationwide appellate jurisdiction: the U.S. Court of Appeals for the Federal Circuit, which hears appeals involving patent law and appeals arising from the decisions of the trade and claims courts.

With the exception of the claims court and the Court of Appeals for the Federal Circuit, these specialized courts were created by Congress on the basis of the powers granted to it by Article I of the Constitution. Article III was designed to protect judges from political pressure by granting them life tenure and prohibiting reduction of their salaries while they serve. The judges of Article I courts, by contrast, are appointed by the president for fixed terms of 15 years and are not protected from salary reduction. As a result, these so-called legislative courts are generally viewed as less independent than the courts established under Article III. The three territorial courts were also established under Article I, and their judges are appointed for 10-year terms.

The federal courts' appellate jurisdiction also extends to cases originating in the state courts. In both civil and criminal cases, a decision of the highest state court can be appealed to the U.S. Supreme Court by raising a federal issue. Appellants might assert, for example, that they were denied the right to counsel or otherwise deprived of the **due process** guaranteed by the federal Constitution, or they might assert that important issues of federal law were at stake in their case. The Supreme Court will accept such an appeal only if it believes that the matter has considerable national significance. (We return to this topic later in the chapter.)

In addition, defendants who have been convicted of a criminal charge in a state court may request a **writ of habeas corpus** from a federal district court.

 due process

The requirement that citizens be treated according to the law and be provided adequate protection for individual rights.

 writ of habeas corpus

A court order demanding that an individual in custody be brought into court and shown the cause for detention; *habeas corpus* is guaranteed by the Constitution and can be suspended only in cases of rebellion or invasion.

Habeas corpus is a court order to the authorities to show cause for the incarceration of a prisoner. In 1867, Congress's distrust of southern state courts led it to authorize federal district judges to issue such writs on behalf of prisoners who they believed had been deprived of their constitutional rights in state trials. Generally speaking, state defendants seeking a federal writ of *habeas corpus* must have exhausted all available state remedies and raise issues not previously raised in their state appeals. Federal courts of appeals and, ultimately, the U.S. Supreme Court have appellate jurisdiction over federal district court *habeas* decisions.

Over recent decades, the federal courts' caseload has more than quadrupled to 450,000 cases annually, in large part because Congress has greatly expanded the number of federal crimes (particularly those involving drug possession and sale). Behavior that was once a state criminal matter has, to some extent, come within the reach of federal law. In 1999, Chief Justice William Rehnquist criticized Congress for federalizing too many offenses and intruding into areas that the states should handle.[4] About 85 percent of federal cases end in the district courts; the remainder are appealed to the circuit courts. Of these circuit court decisions, thousands annually are appealed to the Supreme Court. Most cases filed with the Supreme Court are dismissed. The Court has broad latitude to decide what cases it will hear and generally listens only to those cases it deems to raise the most important issues. Thus in recent years, fewer than 100 cases annually have been given full-dress Supreme Court review (with the nine justices actually sitting *en banc*—in full court—to hear lawyers argue the case), and 80 or so written opinions have been issued per year.[5]

Although the federal courts hear only a fraction of all civil and criminal cases decided each year, their decisions are extremely important (Table 9.2). It is in the federal courts that the Constitution and federal laws governing all Americans are interpreted and their meaning and significance established. Moreover, it is in the federal courts that the powers and limitations of the increasingly powerful national government are tested. Finally, through their power to review the state courts' decisions, it is ultimately the federal courts that dominate the American judicial system.

Federal Trial Courts

Federal district courts are trial courts of general jurisdiction, and their cases are, in form, indistinguishable from cases in state trial courts.

There are 89 district courts in the 50 states, one each in the District of Columbia and Puerto Rico, and one in each of three U.S. territories—94 in all. There are 678 district judgeships. District judges are appointed by the president and confirmed by the Senate. The number of judgeships on a district court

---

4   Roberto Suro, "Rehnquist: Too Many Offenses Are Becoming Federal Crimes," *Washington Post*, January 1, 1999, p. A2.

5   U.S. Courts, "Judicial Business 2015," www.uscourts.gov/statistics-reports/judicial-business-2015 (accessed 3/25/20).

Table 9.2

LANDMARK SUPREME COURT CASES

Not all cases and decisions are equally important. Landmark cases are decisions that revolutionize an area of law and announce new legal standards or have far-reaching political consequences.

Marbury v. Madison (1803). The Court declared part of the Judiciary Act unconstitutional, establishing the Court's power of judicial review.

McCulloch v. Maryland (1819). The Court justified the "implied powers" of the government under the Constitution, enabling Congress and the president to assert their authority beyond those activities explicitly mentioned in the Constitution.

Gibbons v. Ogden (1824). This decision established the supremacy of the federal government over the states in the regulation of commerce so as to create uniform business law.

Dred Scott v. Sandford (1857). The Court declared that people of African origin brought to the United States as part of the slave trade were not given the rights of citizenship under the Constitution and could, therefore, claim none of the rights and privileges that the Constitution provides.

Wabash v. Illinois (1886). The Court allowed that Congress may make laws and reasonable regulations as may be required for interstate commerce.

Plessy v. Ferguson (1896). The Court interpreted the post–Civil War amendments to the Constitution in such a way as to allow segregation, so long as facilities were "separate but equal."

Lochner v. New York (1905). The Court established a general right to enter freely into contracts as part of business, including the right to purchase and sell labor. The decision made it more difficult for unions to form.

Schenck v. United States (1919). The Court declared that the right to free speech does not extend to words that are "used in such circumstances and are of such a nature as to create a clear and present danger."

Korematsu v. United States (1944). The Court allowed the U.S. government to intern Japanese Americans in concentration camps during World War II as a safeguard against insurrection or spying.

Brown v. Board of Education (1954). The Court ruled that separate educational facilities could not be equal, overturning *Plessy*, and ordered an end to segregation "with all deliberate speed."

Mapp v. Ohio (1961). The Court ruled that all evidence obtained by searches and seizures in violation of the federal Constitution is inadmissible in a court of law.

Baker v. Carr (1962). The justices established that the Court has the authority to hear cases involving legislative districting, even though it is a "political matter," ultimately guaranteeing equal representation in the state legislatures and the U.S. House of Representatives.

Griswold v. Connecticut (1965). The Court struck down a Connecticut law prohibiting counseling on the use of contraceptives and declared that the Bill of Rights implied a right to privacy.

Continued

Table 9.2
(Continued)

Brandenburg v. Ohio (1969). The Court ruled that inflammatory speech may not be punished by government unless it is likely to incite imminent lawless action.

Roe v. Wade (1973). The Court held that a woman may abort her baby for any reason up to the point that the fetus becomes "viable" and that any law passed by a state or Congress inconsistent with this holding violates the right to privacy and the right to enter freely into contracts.

Grutter v. Bollinger (2003). The Court held that colleges and universities have a legitimate interest in promoting diversity.

Roper v. Simmons (2005). The Court held that it is cruel and unusual punishment to execute persons for crimes they committed before the age of 18.

Kelo v. City of New London (2005). The Court upheld the power of local governments to seize property for economic development.

Boumediene v. Bush (2008). The Court declared that foreign terrorism suspects have the constitutional right to challenge their detention (using the writ of *habeas corpus*) at the Guantánamo Bay naval base in U.S. courts, even though the detainees are not citizens.

Obergefell v. Hodges (2015). The Court held that states must both allow same-sex couples to marry and recognize same-sex marriages from other states.

depends in part on workload; the busiest court may have as many as 28 judges. Only one judge is assigned to each case, except where statutes provide for three-judge courts to deal with special issues. The procedures of the federal district courts are essentially the same as those of the lower state courts, except federal procedural requirements tend to be stricter. States, for example, do not have to provide a grand jury or a 12-member trial jury. Federal courts must provide both of these. As mentioned earlier, in addition to district courts, cases are handled by several specialized courts, including the U.S. Tax Court, the Court of Federal Claims, and the Court of International Trade.

Federal Appellate Courts

Roughly 20 percent of all federal lower-court cases, along with appeals of some federal agency decisions, are subsequently reviewed by a federal appeals court. As noted earlier, the country is divided into 12 judicial circuits, each with a U.S. Court of Appeals (see Figure 9.2). An additional appellate court, the U.S. Court of Appeals for the Federal Circuit, is defined by subject matter (patent law and decisions of trade and claims courts) rather than geographic jurisdiction.

Except for cases selected for Supreme Court review, decisions made by the appeals courts are final. Because of this finality, certain safeguards have

Figure 9.2
GEOGRAPHIC BOUNDARIES OF U.S. COURTS OF APPEALS

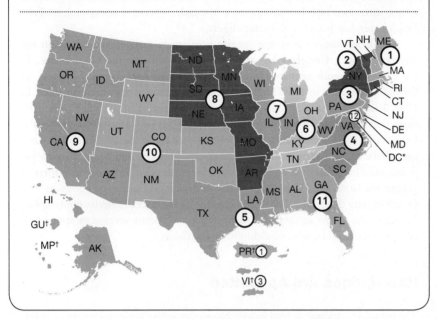

* The District of Columbia has its own circuit, called the D.C. Circuit.
† U.S. Postal Service abbreviations for Guam (GU), Northern Mariana Islands (MP), Puerto Rico (PR), and the U.S. Virgin Islands (VI).
SOURCE: Administrative Office of the U.S. Courts, www.uscourts.gov/uscourts/images/CircuitMap.pdf (accessed 3/17/20).

been built into the system. Most important is the provision of more than one judge for every appeals case. Each court of appeals has from 3 to 28 permanent judgeships. Although normally three judges hear appealed cases, in some instances a larger number sit *en banc*. Another safeguard involves the assignment of a Supreme Court justice as the circuit justice for each of the 12 circuits. The circuit justice addresses requests for special action by the Supreme Court. Circuit justices most frequently review requests for stays of execution when the full Court cannot—mainly during its summer recess.

The Supreme Court

Article III of the Constitution vests "the judicial Power of the United States" in the Supreme Court, which is supreme in fact as well as form. The Supreme Court comprises a chief justice and eight associate justices. The **chief justice** presides over the Court's public sessions and conferences. In the Court's actual deliberations and decisions, however, the chief justice has no more authority than his colleagues. Each justice casts one vote. The chief justice, though, always speaks first when the justices deliberate. In addition, if the chief justice has

 chief justice

The justice on the Supreme Court who presides over the Court's public sessions.

voted with the majority, he decides which justice will write the formal Court opinion. To some extent, the chief justice's influence is a function of his leadership ability. Some chief justices, such as Earl Warren, have led the Court in a new direction; in other instances, a forceful associate justice, such as Felix Frankfurter, has been the dominant figure.

The Constitution does not specify how many justices should sit on the Supreme Court; Congress has the authority to change the Court's size. In the early nineteenth century, there were six justices; later, seven. Congress set the number at nine in 1869, and the Court has remained that size ever since. In 1937, President Franklin Delano Roosevelt, infuriated by several Court decisions that struck down his New Deal programs, asked Congress to enlarge the Court so that he could add sympathetic justices to the bench. Although Congress balked, the Court yielded to Roosevelt's pressure and began to view his policy initiatives more favorably. The president, in turn, dropped his efforts to enlarge the Court. The Court's surrender to Roosevelt came to be known as "the switch in time that saved nine."[6] Today, some in Democratic circles contemplate enlarging the Court in response to Republicans' recent success in appointing conservative justices, who now dominate the Court.

How Judges Are Appointed

The president appoints federal judges. Nominees are typically prominent or politically active members of the legal profession—former state court judges or state or local prosecutors, prominent attorneys or elected officials, or highly regarded law professors.[7] Prior experience as a judge is not necessary, either for appointment or, ultimately, success. Many of the greatest Supreme Court justices, including John Marshall, Louis Brandeis, and Earl Warren had no prior experience as judges; they were political and intellectual leaders. Marshall was John Adams's secretary of state. Brandeis was a prominent Boston lawyer and policy advocate. Warren was governor of California and the Republican vice presidential candidate in 1948.

In general, presidents endeavor to appoint judges who possess legal experience and good character and whose partisan and ideological views are similar to their own. During the presidencies of Richard Nixon, Ronald Reagan, George H. W. Bush, and George W. Bush, most federal judicial appointees were conservatives. Bill Clinton's and Barack Obama's appointees, in contrast, tended to be liberals. George W. Bush made a strong effort to appoint Hispanic judges. Bill Clinton and Barack Obama also strove to appoint women and African Americans. (See Figure 9.7 on p. 384 for more information on the diversity of court

---

6   The view that the Court "surrendered" to pressure from the elective branches is disputed. For an alternative view, see David R. Mayhew, "Supermajority Rule in the Senate," PS: Political Science and Politics 36, no. 1 (2003): 31–6.

7   Supreme Court justice Thurgood Marshall was the chief counsel for the NAACP and argued Brown v. Board of Education before the Court. Felix Frankfurter was a prominent law professor at Harvard University and adviser to Franklin Delano Roosevelt. Hugo Black was an important U.S. Senator.

---

appointees.) Donald Trump's 2017 appointee to the Supreme Court, Neil Gorsuch, was a deeply conservative circuit court judge. Brett Kavanaugh, Trump's 2018 appointee, was likewise a deeply conservative judge on the U.S. Court of Appeals for the District of Columbia Circuit. Finally, Amy Coney Barrett, Trump's 2020 appointee, was another very conservative judge; she served on the Seventh Circuit Court of Appeals.

The Constitution requires the Senate to "advise and consent" to federal judicial nominations, thus imposing an important check on the president's influence over the judiciary. Before the president formally nominates a candidate for a federal district judgeship, senators from the nominee's state must indicate that they support her. This practice is called **senatorial courtesy**. If one or both senators from a prospective nominee's home state belong to the president's political party, the nomination will almost invariably receive their blessing. Because the president's party in the Senate will rarely support a nominee opposed by a home-state senator from their ranks, these senators hold virtual veto power over appointments to the federal bench in their own states. Senators often see this power as a way to reward important allies and contributors in their states. If the state has no senator from the president's party, the governor or members of the state's House delegation may make suggestions. Senatorial courtesy is less consequential for appellate court appointments and plays no role in Supreme Court nominations.

Once the president has formally nominated an individual, the appointment must be considered by the Senate Judiciary Committee and confirmed by a majority vote in the full Senate. The politics and rules of the Senate determine the fate of judicial nominees and influence the types of people the president selects for judicial positions. As with any legislation, a nomination must originate in the relevant committee, be brought to the Senate floor, and receive a majority of votes to be approved. There once was the risk of a filibuster, in which closure of debate required a three-fifths affirmative vote (see Chapter 6 for discussion of these procedures). This possibility was eliminated from the Senate rules in 2013 for lower federal judges and in 2017 for Supreme Court justices. The composition of the Senate Judiciary Committee, as well as the Senate as a whole, then, is critical in determining whether a particular nominee will succeed. Moreover, in recent years the most important judicial nominations are given intense scrutiny by the media, thus engaging the broader public in the process.

Before the 1950s, the Senate Judiciary Committee rarely questioned nominees on their judicial views, focusing instead on qualifications. This changed in 1954, however, when President Dwight D. Eisenhower nominated John Marshall Harlan II to succeed Robert Jackson on the Supreme Court. The Senate did not act on his nomination, and Eisenhower had to nominate Jackson a second time. The chairman of the Senate Judiciary Committee (a southerner) and several other southern Democratic senators delayed any hearings, fearing that Harlan would support school integration and further strengthen the Court's efforts to desegregate the South. When the committee finally did hold hearings, the senators grilled Harlan about his views on *Plessy v. Ferguson* and other judicial opinions. All Supreme Court nominees since Harlan have faced questions about their views from the Judiciary Committee.

Since the mid-1950s, judicial appointments have become increasingly partisan and, ultimately, ideological. Today, the Senate Judiciary Committee subjects

 senatorial courtesy

The practice whereby the president, before formally nominating a person for a federal district judgeship, finds out whether the senators from the candidate's state support the nomination.

nominees to lengthy questioning about issues ranging from gun rights to abortion to federal power under the commerce clause. Senators' support or opposition turns on the individual's ideological and judicial views as much as on the nominee's qualifications.

Trends in Presidential Appointments. Presidents nominate individuals who share their own political philosophy. Reagan and George H. W. Bush, for example, sought appointees who believed in reducing government intervention in the economy and supported the moral positions taken by the Republican Party in recent years, particularly opposition to abortion. However, not all Reagan and Bush appointees fulfilled their sponsors' expectations. David Souter, for example, appointed by President George H. W. Bush, was attacked by conservatives as a turncoat for his decisions on school prayer and abortion rights. Nevertheless, through their appointments, Reagan and George H. W. Bush created a strongly conservative Supreme Court. Hoping to counteract the influence of their appointees, President Clinton endeavored to appoint liberal justices, naming Ruth Bader Ginsburg and Stephen Breyer to the Court.

In 2005, President George W. Bush had an opportunity to put his own stamp on the Supreme Court after Justice Sandra Day O'Connor decided to retire and Chief Justice William Rehnquist died. Bush quickly nominated the federal appeals court judge John Roberts, initially to replace O'Connor and then as chief justice after Rehnquist's death. Roberts, a moderate conservative, was confirmed with minimal Democratic opposition. When Bush named White House counsel Harriet Miers to replace O'Connor, though, he sparked an intense battle within his own party. Opposition among Republicans, many of whom felt she lacked judicial qualifications and was insufficiently conservative, was so intense that she ultimately withdrew from consideration. Bush then turned to a more conventional nominee, the federal appeals court judge Samuel Alito, who pleased conservative Republicans.

Barack Obama's nominations of Sonia Sotomayor and Elena Kagan to the Court were easily approved, despite Republican criticisms, thanks to a strong Democratic majority in the Senate. Because Sotomayor and Kagan replaced liberal justices, they did not affect the balance of power on the Court. In 2016, however, the death of conservative justice Antonin Scalia gave President Obama an opportunity to replace Scalia with a more liberal jurist, and Obama nominated federal circuit court judge Merrick Garland. The Senate's Republican leadership, however, refused to take action on the Garland nomination, hoping that the 2016 presidential election would bring a Republican president and a chance to replace Scalia with another conservative.[8] With only eight justices for most of

---

8   It is important to underscore that a nomination is assessed not only in terms of the nominee's character, experience, and judicial philosophy but also in terms of how his or her presence will affect (if at all) the ideological balance on the Supreme Court. This requires considering whom a nominee replaces (and explains why the attempt to replace conservative Scalia with moderate Garland was so fraught). See Charles M. Cameron and Jonathan Kastellec, "Are Supreme Court Nominations a Move-the-Median Game?" *American Political Science Review* 110, no. 4 (November 2016): 778–97.

Table 9.3

SUPREME COURT JUSTICES, 2020

NAME	YEAR OF BIRTH	PRIOR EXPERIENCE	APPOINTED BY	YEAR OF APPOINTMENT
John G. Roberts Jr., *chief justice*	1955	Federal judge	G. W. Bush	2005
Clarence Thomas	1948	Federal judge	G. H. W. Bush	1991
Stephen G. Breyer	1938	Federal judge	Clinton	1994
Samuel A. Alito Jr.	1950	Federal judge	G. W. Bush	2006
Sonia Sotomayor	1954	Federal judge	Obama	2009
Elena Kagan	1960	Solicitor general	Obama	2010
Neil Gorsuch	1967	Federal judge	Trump	2017
Brett Kavanaugh	1965	Federal judge	Trump	2018
Amy Coney Barrett	1972	Federal judge	Trump	2020

2016, several important Supreme Court cases ended in 4–4 ties (a tie lets the lower-court decision stand). The Republicans' strategy paid off when Donald Trump was elected president; he nominated conservative jurist Neil Gorsuch in 2017 (Table 9.3). Brett Kavanaugh, Trump's second nomination, came under intense scrutiny from both sides when multiple women accused him of sexual assault. After an intense Senate hearing in which Kavanaugh and Dr. Christine Blasey Ford, one of his accusers, both testified, his nomination ultimately moved forward, but not without bitter accusations from Democrats that Republicans were willing to push through their candidate no matter what. Republicans, in turn, claimed that Democrats were purposefully trying to sabotage Kavanaugh's appointment by uncovering wrongdoing from his youth. These struggles over judicial appointments reflect the growing intensity of partisanship today. They were manifested again in the intense partisan struggle to confirm Amy Coney Barrett following the death of Justice Ruth Bader Ginsburg.

The increasing role of partisanship or ideology in the nomination process creates a potential danger for the court system. After all, courts derive considerable authority from their position of political independence as nonpartisan arbiters. Fortunately, the individuals appointed to the federal judiciary tend to have a strong independent sense of themselves and their mission.

HOW COURTS WORK AS POLITICAL INSTITUTIONS

Judges are central players in important political institutions, and this role makes them politicians. To understand what animates judicial behavior, we need to consider the role of the courts in the political system more generally. In doing so, we emphasize the courts' role as dispute resolvers, coordinators, and interpreters of rules.

Dispute Resolution

Much productive activity occurs in a modern society because its members need not devote substantial resources to protecting themselves and their property or monitoring compliance with agreements. For any potential violation of person or property or defection from an agreement, all parties know that an aggrieved party may take an alleged violator to court. The court, in turn, is a venue in which the facts of a case are established, punishment is meted out to violators, and compensation is awarded to victims. An employee, for example, may sue his employer for allegedly violating the terms of a privately negotiated employment contract. Or a consumer may sue a producer for violating the terms of a product warranty. The court, then, is an institution that engages in fact finding, judgment, and dispute resolution. In criminal cases, the "aggrieved party" is not only the victim of the crime but also the entire society whose laws have been violated.

Coordination

Dispute resolution occurs after the fact—that is, after a dispute has occurred. We may also think of courts and judges as before-the-fact coordination mechanisms: the anticipation of legal consequences allows private parties to form rational expectations and thereby coordinate their actions in advance of possible disputes. Legal rules and precedents thus provide both positive and negative behavioral incentives for various parties. On the negative side, a prospective embezzler, estimating the odds of getting caught, prosecuted, and punished, may think twice about going through with the crime. Conversely, on the positive side, two acquaintances may confidently consider going into business together, knowing that the sword of justice hangs over their collaboration.

In this sense, the court system is just as important for what it does indirectly as for what it does directly. Courts and law coordinate private behavior by providing incentives and disincentives for specific actions, which can result in avoiding the use of the courts altogether. Many cases, for example, are settled out of court, before a judge or court has any role to play. Indeed, the very prospect of litigation discourages disputes and violations of the law, and thus obviates the need for dispute resolution.

Rule Interpretation

In handing down decisions, judges are not entirely free agents. In matching the facts of a specific case to judicial principles and statutory guidelines, judges must interpret existing law and precedent: they must determine what particular statutes or judicial principles mean, establish which ones fit the facts of a given case, and then ascertain the case's disposition. Does the statute of 1927 regulating the electronic transmission of radio waves apply to television, cell phones, ship-to-shore radios, fax machines, or email? Does the 1937 law governing the transportation of dangerous substances across state lines apply to nuclear fuels, infected animals, or artificially created biological hazards? Often the enacting legislative body does not make the scope of legislation clear.

Interpreting the rules is probably the most important activity in which higher courts engage. This is because the court system is hierarchical; higher courts' judgments constrain the discretion of judges in lower courts.[9] If the Supreme Court rules that the 1937 dangerous-substances law does cover nuclear fuels, then lower courts must render subsequent judgments in a manner consistent with this ruling.

As the following section explains, courts and judges engage not only in statutory interpretation but in constitutional interpretation as well. In determining, for example, whether the dangerous-substances law is constitutional, Supreme Court justices might invoke the commerce clause of the Constitution (which allows the federal government to regulate interstate commerce) to justify the act's constitutionality. In contrast, the Court might also rule that a shipment of spent fuel rods from a nuclear reactor in Kansas City to a nuclear-waste facility outside St. Louis is not covered by this clause because the shipment occurred within the boundaries of a single state and thus did not constitute interstate commerce.

In short, judges and justices continually elaborate, embellish, and even rewrite the rules by which private and public life are organized. However, judicial interpretation of statutes, even if conducted by the nation's highest court, is subject to review by Congress. If Congress disagrees with a specific statutory interpretation, it may amend the legislation in question to overcome the Court's objection. In 2005, for example, in *United States v. Booker*, the Supreme Court struck down mandatory sentencing rules that had been enacted in 1984.[10] The rules severely limited judicial discretion in sentencing and had long been resented by the bench. The Court found that mandatory minimum sentences violated the Sixth Amendment, because the latter required that only evidence provided at trial, together with the defendant's previous criminal record, could be used in determining a sentence. In response, members of Congress vowed to reinstate the guidelines through new legislation. Since the *Booker* decision,

---

9 See Clifford J. Carrubba and Tom S. Clark, "Rule Creation in a Political Hierarchy," *American Political Science Review* 106, no. 3 (August 2012): 622–43.

10 *United States v. Booker*, 543 U.S. 220 (2005).

mandatory sentencing guidelines, at both state and federal levels, remain in flux. Of course, if the Court makes a constitutional ruling, Congress cannot abrogate that ruling through new legislation. Congress would need to commence the constitutional amendment process to overturn an interpretation with which it disagrees.

THE POWER OF JUDICIAL REVIEW

The phrase **judicial review** refers to the power of the judiciary to examine and, if necessary, invalidate actions by the legislative and executive branches. The phrase sometimes also describes the scrutiny that appellate courts give to the actions of trial courts, but strictly speaking, that is an improper usage.

Judicial review, which is not explicitly mentioned in the Constitution, is one of the most powerful expressions of the independent judiciary. In countries without an independent judiciary and without judicial review, the parliament or the executive is the ultimate authority in determining what is or is not constitutional. In British law, for example, Parliament is sovereign. Judicial review exists only in scrutinizing administration of the laws. An individual cannot challenge an act of Parliament and ask that the courts void that law as a violation of the constitution. In the U.S. system of government, by contrast, judicial review is an essential means by which the judiciary checks the legislature and the executive.

Judicial Review of Acts of Congress

Because the Constitution does not give the Supreme Court the authority to declare acts of Congress unconstitutional, the Court's exercise of judicial review may be considered a usurpation of power. Among the proposals debated at the Constitutional Convention was one to create a council composed of the president and the judiciary that would share veto power over legislation. Another proposal was to route all legislation through both the Court and the president; overruling a veto by either one would have required a two-thirds vote of the House and the Senate. Those and other proposals were rejected, and no further effort was made to give the Supreme Court review power over the other branches. This does not prove that the framers opposed judicial review, but it does indicate that "if they intended to provide for it in the Constitution, they did so in a most obscure fashion."[11]

Disputes over the framers' intentions were settled in 1803 in *Marbury v. Madison*.[12] In that case, William Marbury sued Secretary of State James Madison for Madison's failure to complete Marbury's appointment to a lower judgeship, which had been initiated by the outgoing administration of President

11 C. Herman Pritchett, *The American Constitution* (New York: McGraw-Hill, 1959), p. 138.

12 *Marbury v. Madison*, 5 U.S. 137 (1803).

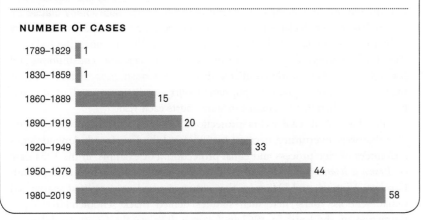

Figure 9.3

SUPREME COURT RULINGS INVALIDATING ACTS OF CONGRESS

NUMBER OF CASES

1789–1829	1
1830–1859	1
1860–1889	15
1890–1919	20
1920–1949	33
1950–1979	44
1980–2019	58

SOURCE: U.S. Government Printing Office, www.congress.gov/constitution-annotated (accessed 3/17/20).

John Adams. Apart from the details of the suit, Chief Justice John Marshall used the case to declare a portion of a law unconstitutional. In effect, he stated that although the substance of Marbury's request was not unreasonable, the Court could not redress Marbury's situation because its jurisdiction in hearing the matter was in fact invalid—it was based on a section of the Judiciary Act of 1789 that the Court deemed to be unconstitutional.

Although Congress and the president have often been at odds with the Court, the Court's legal power to review acts of Congress has not been seriously questioned since 1803. One reason is that judicial power has come to be accepted as natural, if not intended. Another reason is that during the early years of the Republic, the Supreme Court used its power sparingly, striking down only two pieces of legislation during the first 75 years of its history. One of these decisions was the 1857 ruling in *Dred Scott v. Sandford*. Chief Justice Roger Taney wrote in the majority opinion that the fact that an enslaved person, Dred Scott, had been transported to a free state (Illinois) and a free territory (Wisconsin) before returning to the slave state of Missouri did not alter the fact that he was property.[13] This ruling invalidated a portion of the Missouri Compromise and thus permitted slavery in all the country's territories, which ultimately helped precipitate the Civil War. More recently, with the power of judicial review now widely accepted, the Court has been more willing to use it. Between 1980 and 2019, the Supreme Court struck down 58 acts of Congress in whole or in part (Figure 9.3).[14]

---

13 *Dred Scott v. Sandford*, 60 U.S. 393 (1857).

14 For an analysis of the Court's use of judicial review to nullify acts of Congress, see Ryan Emenaker, "Constitutional Interpretation and Congressional Overrides: Changing Trends in Court-Congress Relations," *Journal of Legal Metrics* 2 (2013): 197–223.

Judicial Review of State Actions

supremacy clause

A clause of Article VI of the Constitution stating that all laws and treaties approved by the national government are the supreme laws of the United States and superior to all laws adopted by any state or other subdivision.

The power of the Supreme Court to review and determine the constitutionality of state legislation or other state actions is neither granted by the Constitution nor inherent in the federal system. But the logic of the **supremacy clause** of Article VI—which declares the Constitution and laws made under its authority to be the supreme law of the land—is very strong. Furthermore, the Judiciary Act of 1789 conferred on the Court the power to reverse state constitutions and laws whenever they clearly conflict with the U.S. Constitution, federal laws, or treaties.[15] This power gives the Supreme Court jurisdiction over all of the millions of cases handled by American state courts each year.

The history of civil rights protections abounds with examples of state laws that were overturned because they violated the Fourteenth Amendment's guarantees of due process and equal protection. For example, in the 1954 case of *Brown v. Board of Education*, the Court overturned statutes in Kansas, South Carolina, Virginia, and Delaware that either required or permitted segregated public schools, ruling that such statutes denied Black schoolchildren equal protection of the law.[16] In 1967 in *Loving v. Virginia*, the Court invalidated a Virginia statute prohibiting interracial marriages.[17] In 2015 in *Obergefell v. Hodges*, the Court held that "the Fourteenth Amendment requires a state to license a marriage between two people of the same sex and to recognize a marriage between two people of the same sex when their marriage was lawfully licensed and performed out-of-state," thus invalidating a Michigan law prohibiting same-sex unions.[18] State statutes in areas other than civil rights are equally subject to challenge. The Court has overturned a number of state laws that conflict with federal law; in 2012 in *Arizona v. United States,* for instance, the Court struck down parts of an Arizona law regulating immigration on the grounds that they were preempted by federal law.[19]

Judicial Review of Federal Agency Actions

Although Congress makes the law, it delegates power to the president and to a huge bureaucracy to administer the thousands of programs it has enacted. For example, if Congress wishes to improve air quality, it cannot possibly anticipate all the circumstances that may arise with respect to this general goal. Inevitably, it will delegate to the appropriate executive branch agency substantial

15 This review power was affirmed by the Supreme Court in *Martin v. Hunter's Lessee*, 14 U.S. 304 (1816).

16 *Brown v. Board of Education*, 347 U.S. 483 (1954).

17 *Loving v. Virginia*, 388 U.S. 1 (1967).

18 *Obergefell v. Hodges*, 576 U.S. 644 (2015). Quotation from SCOTUSblog, "Obergefell v. Hodges," www.scotusblog.com/case-files/cases/obergefell-v-hodges (accessed 3/25/20).

19 *Arizona v. United States*, 567 U.S. 387 (2012).

discretionary power to determine the best ways to achieve improved air quality in the face of changing circumstances. Thus, over time, almost any congressional program will result in thousands and thousands of pages of administrative regulations developed by executive agencies.

The issue of delegation of power has led to a number of court decisions over the past two centuries, generally involving the question of the appropriate scope of the delegation. Courts have also been called on to decide whether the rules and regulations adopted by federal agencies are consistent with Congress's express or implied intent.

As presidential power expanded during the New Deal era, Congress increasingly enacted laws that contained few if any principles limiting executive discretion. Congress enacted legislation, often at the president's behest, that gave the president and executive agencies virtually unfettered authority to address a particular concern. For example, the Emergency Price Control Act of 1942 authorized the executive branch to set "fair and equitable" prices without indicating what those terms might mean. Although the Court initially challenged such delegations of power, a confrontation with President Franklin Delano Roosevelt caused the Court to retreat from its position. Perhaps as a result, no congressional delegation of power to the president has been struck down as impermissibly broad since then. In the last two decades in particular, the Supreme Court has generally let federal rules and regulations stand as long as they are "based upon a permissible construction" or "reasonable interpretation" of Congress's statutes. Generally the courts defer to administrative agencies as long as those agencies have undertaken the appropriate rule-making process as governed by statute. These statutes include the 1946 Administrative Procedure Act, which requires agencies to notify parties affected by proposed rules and to allow them time to comment before the rules go into effect.

Judicial Review and Presidential Power

The federal courts may also review the actions of the president. As we saw in Chapter 7, presidents have increasingly made use of unilateral executive powers rather than relying on congressional legislation to achieve their objectives. Often, presidential orders and actions have been challenged in the federal courts by members of Congress and by individuals and groups opposing the president's policies. In recent years, the federal bench has generally upheld assertions of presidential power in such realms as foreign policy, war and emergency powers, legislative power, and administrative authority. Indeed, the federal judiciary has sometimes rationalized extraordinary presidential claims made for temporary purposes—that is, the Court has converted them into permanent instruments of presidential government.

Consider Richard Nixon's sweeping claims of executive privilege. In *United States v. Nixon*, although the Court rejected the president's refusal to turn over tape recordings to congressional investigators, for the first time the justices recognized the validity of the principle of executive privilege and discussed situations in which such claims might be appropriate.[20] This judicial recognition encouraged presidents Bill Clinton and George W. Bush to claim executive privilege on many occasions, and Donald Trump to threaten to use it.[21] Executive privilege has even been invoked to protect the deliberations of the vice president from congressional scrutiny.

This pattern of judicial deference to presidential authority was also manifest in the Supreme Court's decisions regarding President George W. Bush's war on terrorism. Perhaps the most important of these cases was *Hamdi v. Rumsfeld*.[22] In 2004, the Court ruled that U.S. citizen and alleged terrorist Yaser Esam Hamdi was entitled to a lawyer and "a fair opportunity to rebut the government's factual assertions." However, the Court affirmed that the president possessed the authority to declare a U.S. citizen an enemy combatant and order that such an individual be held in federal detention. Several justices intimated that once designated an enemy combatant, a U.S. citizen might be tried before a military tribunal, with the normal presumption of innocence suspended. Although the Court later ruled that the military commissions established to try enemy combatants and other detainees violated both the Uniform Code of Military Justice and the Geneva Conventions, it affirmed the president's unilateral power to declare individuals, including U.S. citizens, enemy combatants whom federal authorities could detain under adverse legal circumstances.[23]

In recent years, the Court's decisions regarding the exercise of presidential power have been mixed. In June 2016 the Supreme Court sustained a federal appeals court decision blocking President Barack Obama's ambitious program to prevent millions of undocumented immigrants from being deported. At issue was whether Obama had abused his office by using an executive order instead of the legislative and administrative processes to formulate immigration policy. The eight-member Court (in the wake of the death of Justice Antonin Scalia) split 4–4, thereby letting stand the lower-court decision.[24] The Court thus thwarted Obama's attempt to create new policy through executive action alone. During its 2019–20 term, the Court has been inundated with suits related to the Trump administration's immigration policy; its conservative majority has been generally inclined to favor executive authority in these cases.[25]

---

20 *United States v. Nixon*, 418 U.S. 683 (1974).

21 On Clinton, see Jonathan Turley, "Paradise Lost: The Clinton Administration and the Erosion of Executive Privilege," *Maryland Law Review* 60, no. 1 (2001): 205–48. On Bush, see Jeffrey P. Carlin, "*Walker v. Cheney*: Politics, Posturing, and Executive Privilege," *Southern California Law Review* 76 (November 2002): 235–76.

22 *Hamdi v. Rumsfeld*, 542 U.S. 507 (2004).

23 *Hamdan v. Rumsfeld*, 548 U.S. 557 (2006).

24 *United States v. Texas*, 579 U.S. ____ (2016).

25 See Richard Wolf, "President Trump's Immigration Crackdown Inundates Supreme Court," *USA Today*, February 20, 2020, www.usatoday.com/story/news/politics/2020/02/27/immigration-donald-trump-crackdown-floods-supreme-court/4794704002 (accessed 3/17/20).

Judicial Review and Lawmaking

Much of the courts' work involves applying statutes to particular cases. Over the centuries, however, judges have developed a body of rules and principles of interpretation that are not grounded in specific statutes. This body of judge-made law is called common law.

The federal appellate courts are in another realm; their rulings can be considered laws that govern only the behavior of the judiciary. They influence citizens' conduct only because, in the words of Justice Oliver Wendell Holmes, Jr. (who served on the Supreme Court from 1902 to 1932), lawyers make "prophecies of what the courts will do in fact."[26]

Appellate courts' written opinions are about halfway between common law and statutory law. Like common law, the opinions are judge made and draw heavily on the precedents of previous cases. In that the opinions try to articulate the rule of law controlling the case in question and future cases like it, they are like statutes. But both common law and statutes address the future conduct of citizens, whereas written opinions mainly address the willingness or ability of future courts to take cases and render favorable opinions.

An example may clarify the distinction. In *Gideon v. Wainwright*, the Supreme Court ordered a new trial for Clarence Earl Gideon, an indigent defendant, because he had been denied the right to legal counsel. This ruling signaled to all trial judges and prosecutors that henceforth they would be wasting their time if they cut corners in the trials of indigent defendants.[27] The Court was thereby predicting what it would and would not do in future cases of this sort. It also invited thousands of prisoners to appeal their convictions.

Many areas of civil law have been constructed in the same way—by judicial messages to other judges, some of which are codified eventually in legislative enactments. It has become "the law," for example, that employers are liable for injuries in the workplace without regard to employee negligence. But the law in this instance is simply a series of messages to lawyers that they should advise their corporate clients not to appeal injury decisions.

In the realm of criminal law, almost all dramatic changes in the treatment of criminals and persons accused of crimes have been made by the appellate courts, especially the Supreme Court. Indeed, the Supreme Court ignited a veritable revolution in the criminal process with three cases over less than five years, beginning with *Gideon v. Wainwright* in 1963. The second case, *Escobedo v. Illinois*, in 1964, gave suspects the right to remain silent and the right to have counsel present during questioning.[28] But the decision left confusion that allowed lower courts to make differing decisions. In the third case, *Miranda v. Arizona*, in 1966, the Court cleared up the confusion by setting forth what is known as the Miranda rule: arrested people have

---

26 Oliver Wendell Holmes, Jr., "The Path of the Law," *Harvard Law Review* 10 (1897): 457.

27 *Gideon v. Wainwright*, 372 U.S. 335 (1963).

28 *Escobedo v. Illinois*, 378 U.S. 478 (1964).

the right to remain silent, the right to be informed that anything they say can be held against them, and the right to counsel before and during police interrogation.[29]

One of the most significant changes wrought by the Supreme Court was the revolution in legislative representation unleashed by the 1962 landmark case of *Baker v. Carr*.[30] Here, the Court held that it could no longer avoid reviewing complaints about the apportionment of seats in state legislatures. Following that decision, the federal courts went on to force reapportionment of all state, county, and local legislatures nationwide.

As these cases illustrate, the appellate courts are intimately involved in creating and interpreting laws. Many experts on court history and constitutional law criticize the federal appellate courts for being too willing to introduce radical change. Often these experts are troubled by the courts' willingness (especially the Supreme Court) to jump into cases that deal with controversial issues prematurely—before the constitutional issues have been fully clarified by decisions of district and appeals courts in other related cases in various parts of the country.[31] But from the perspective of the appellate judiciary, and especially the Supreme Court, the situation is one of choosing between the lesser of two evils: they must take the cases as they come and then weigh the risks of opening new options against the risks of embracing the status quo.

THE SUPREME COURT IN ACTION

The Supreme Court sits at the pinnacle of the U.S. judiciary. It is the only court mentioned in the Constitution, and it is one of the most distinctive political bodies in the American political system. The Court is often the focal point for understanding the judiciary because it has special constitutional status and because it embodies many principles of the American court system—its independence, its durability, the collective nature of court decision making, and the delicate balance that judges strike between historical precedent and new interpretation. The Court plays a vital role in government, as it is part of the structure of checks and balances that prevents the legislative and executive branches from abusing their power. The Court also operates as an institution unto itself, with its own internal rules for decision making. The policy principle, which we discussed in Chapter 1, thus applies to the Court in a unique way.

29 *Miranda v. Arizona*, 384 U.S. 436 (1966).

30 *Baker v. Carr*, 369 U.S. 186 (1962).

31 See Philip B. Kurland, *Politics, the Constitution, and the Warren Court* (Chicago: University of Chicago Press, 1970).

How Cases Reach the Supreme Court

Given the millions of disputes that arise every year, the Supreme Court's job would be impossible if it were not able to control the flow of cases and its own caseload. The Court has original jurisdiction in a limited variety of cases defined by the Constitution, including (1) cases between the United States and one of the states, (2) cases between two or more states, (3) cases involving foreign ambassadors or other ministers, and (4) cases brought by one state against citizens of another state or against a foreign country. The most common of these are disputes between states over land, water, or old debts. Generally the Court deals with these cases by appointing a "special master," usually a retired judge, to hear the case and present a report. The Court then allows the disputing states to present arguments for or against the master's opinion.[32]

Rules of Access. Over the years, the federal courts have developed rules governing which cases within their jurisdiction they will and will not hear. Thus the court system is an institution very much in control of its own agenda, which, according to the institution principle, gives it considerable independence to follow its members' preferences.[33] To have access to the courts, cases must meet certain criteria that are initially applied by the trial court but may be reconsidered by appellate courts (including the Supreme Court). These rules of access fall into three major categories: case or controversy, standing, and mootness.

Both Article III of the Constitution and past Supreme Court decisions define judicial power as extending only to "cases and controversies." That is, a case before a court must involve an actual controversy, not a hypothetical one, with two truly adversarial parties. These criteria together are called "**ripeness**." The courts have interpreted this language to mean they do not have the power to render advisory opinions to legislatures or agencies about the constitutionality of proposed laws or regulations. Furthermore, even after a law is enacted, the courts generally refuse to consider its constitutionality until it is actually applied.

Those seeking to bring a case must also have **standing**—they must show a substantial stake in the case's outcome. The traditional requirement for standing has been that one must show injury to oneself; the injury can be personal, economic, or even aesthetic, for example. For a group or class of people to have standing (as in **class-action suits**), each member must show specific injury. This means that a general interest in the environment, for instance, does not provide a group with sufficient standing.

The third criterion in determining whether the courts will hear a case is **mootness**. In theory, this requirement disqualifies cases that are brought too late—after the relevant facts have changed or the problem has been resolved

ripeness

The requirement that a case must involve an actual controversy between two parties, not a hypothetical one.

standing

The requirement that anyone initiating a court case must show a substantial stake in the outcome.

class-action suit

A lawsuit in which a large number of persons with common interests join together under a representative party to bring or defend a lawsuit.

moot

No longer requiring resolution by the courts, typically because the facts of the case have changed or been resolved by other means.

---

32 Walter F. Murphy, "The Supreme Court of the United States," in *Encyclopedia of the American Judicial System: Studies of the Principal Institutions and Processes of Law*, ed. Robert J. Janosik (New York: Scribner, 1987).

33 The appellate jurisdiction of the courts is determined by Congress. Currently, this jurisdiction is quite expansive, but Congress may restrict this at any time.

by other means. However, the courts have begun to relax the rules pertaining to mootness, particularly in cases in which a situation that has been resolved is likely to recur. In the abortion case of *Roe v. Wade*, for example, the Court rejected the lower court's argument that because the pregnancy had already come to term, the case was moot. The Court agreed to hear *Roe* because no pregnancy would be likely to outlast the lengthy appeals process in any subsequent cases concerning abortion.

Putting aside the formal criteria, the Supreme Court is most likely to accept cases that involve conflicting decisions by federal circuit courts, cases that present important questions of civil rights or civil liberties, and cases in which the federal government is the appellant.[34] Ultimately, however, the question of which cases are accepted can come down to the justices' preferences and priorities. If several justices believe that the Court should intervene in a particular area of policy or politics, they are likely to look for a case or cases that will be vehicles for judicial intervention. For several decades, for example, the Court was not interested in considering challenges to affirmative action or other programs designed to provide particular benefits to minorities. Eventually, however, several of the more conservative justices sought to scale back these kinds of programs and therefore accepted cases that allowed them to do so. In 1995, the Court's decisions in three cases placed new restrictions on federal affirmative action programs, school desegregation efforts, and attempts to increase minority representation in Congress through the creation of "minority districts" (see Chapter 11).[35]

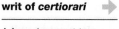

writ of *certiorari*

A formal request to have the Supreme Court review a decision of a lower court.

Most cases reach the Supreme Court through a **writ of *certiorari***, a formal request to have the Court review a lower-court decision (Figure 9.4). *Certiorari* is an order to a lower court to deliver the records of a particular case to a higher court to be reviewed for legal errors. The term is sometimes shortened to *cert*, and cases deemed to merit *certiorari* are referred to as *cert* worthy. An individual who loses in a lower federal court or state court and wants the Supreme Court to review the decision has 90 days to file a petition for a writ of *certiorari* with the clerk of the Supreme Court. There are two types of petitions: paid petitions and petitions *in forma pauperis* ("in the form of a pauper"). The former requires payment of filing fees, submission of a certain number of copies, and compliance with numerous other rules. For *in forma pauperis* petitions, usually filed by prison inmates, the Court waives the fees and most other requirements.

Since 1972, most of the justices have participated in a "*certiorari* pool" in which their law clerks evaluate the petitions. Each petition is first reviewed by one clerk, who writes a memo summarizing the facts and issues and making a recommendation for all the justices participating in the pool. Clerks for the other justices add their comments. After the justices have reviewed the memos,

34 Gregory A. Caldeira and John R. Wright, "Organized Interests and Agenda Setting in the U.S. Supreme Court," *American Political Science Review* 82, no. 4 (December 1988): 1109–27.

35 *Adarand Constructors v. Peña*, 515 U.S. 200 (1995); *Missouri v. Jenkins*, 515 U.S. 70 (1995); and *Miller v. Johnson*, 515 U.S. 900 (1995).

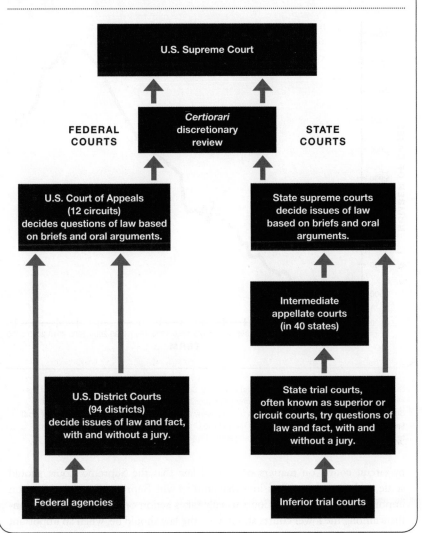

Figure 9.4

REACHING THE SUPREME COURT THROUGH *CERTIORARI*

U.S. Supreme Court

FEDERAL COURTS

Certiorari discretionary review

STATE COURTS

U.S. Court of Appeals (12 circuits) decides questions of law based on briefs and oral arguments.

State supreme courts decide issues of law based on briefs and oral arguments.

Intermediate appellate courts (in 40 states)

U.S. District Courts (94 districts) decide issues of law and fact, with and without a jury.

State trial courts, often known as superior or circuit courts, try questions of law and fact, with and without a jury.

Federal agencies

Inferior trial courts

any one of them may place any case on the discuss list, which is circulated by the chief justice. If a case is not placed on the list, it is automatically denied *certiorari*. Cases placed on the list are considered and voted on during the justices' closed-door conference. According to the **rule of four**, *certiorari* is granted if at least four judges are convinced that the case satisfies Rule 10 of the Rules of the U.S. Supreme Court, which stipulates that *certiorari* is not a matter of right but is to be granted only when there are special and compelling reasons. These include conflicting decisions by two or more circuit courts or state courts of last resort, conflicts between circuit courts and state courts of last resort, decisions

 rule of four

The rule that *certiorari* will be granted for petitions to the Supreme Court only if at least four justices vote in favor of the petition.

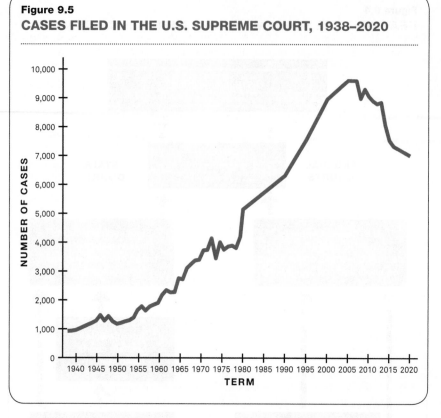

Figure 9.5

CASES FILED IN THE U.S. SUPREME COURT, 1938–2020

SOURCES: Years 1938–69: successive volumes of U.S. Census Bureau, *Statistical Abstract of the United States* (Washington, DC: Government Printing Office); 1970–79: Office of the Clerk of the Supreme Court; 1980–2010: U.S. Census Bureau, www.census.gov/prod/2011pubs/12statab/law.pdf (accessed 6/11/13); 2010–20: Supreme Court of the United States, www.uscourts.gov/statistics-reports/caseload-statistics-data-tables (accessed 11/1/20).

by circuit courts on matters of federal law that the Supreme Court should settle, and circuit court decisions that conflict with Supreme Court decisions on important questions. The Court usually takes action only when there are conflicts among the lower courts about what the law should be, when an important legal question raised in the lower courts has not been definitively answered, or when a lower court deviates from the principles and precedents established by the high court. Few cases satisfy these requirements. In recent sessions, although thousands of petitions have been filed (Figure 9.5), the Court has granted *certiorari* to fewer than 90 petitioners each year—about 1 percent of those seeking a Supreme Court review.

A handful of cases reach the Supreme Court through avenues other than *certiorari*. One is the writ of certification, which can be used when a court of appeals asks the Supreme Court for instructions on a point of law that has never been decided. Another avenue is the writ of appeal, which serves to appeal the decision of a three-judge district court.

Controlling the Flow of Cases

In addition to the judges, two other actors are key in shaping the flow of cases through the federal courts: the solicitor general and the federal law clerks.

The Solicitor General. If any person has greater influence than the individual justices over the work of the Supreme Court, it is the solicitor general of the United States. This person is third in status in the Justice Department (below the attorney general and the deputy attorney general) but is the top government lawyer in virtually all cases before the appellate courts in which the government is a party. Although others can regulate the flow of cases, the solicitor general has the greatest control, with no review of his actions by any higher authority in the executive branch. More than half the Supreme Court's total workload consists of cases under the charge of the solicitor general.

The solicitor general exercises especially strong influence by screening cases involving the federal government long before they approach the Supreme Court; indeed, the justices rely on the solicitor general to do so. Typically, the solicitor general rejects more requests for appeals than he accepts. Agency heads may lobby the president or otherwise try to circumvent the solicitor general, and a few of the independent agencies have a statutory right to make direct appeals, but without the solicitor general's support these cases are seldom reviewed by the Court.

By writing an **amicus curiae** ("friend of the court") brief, the solicitor general can enter a case even when the federal government is not a direct litigant. A friend of the court is not a direct party to a case but has a vital interest in its outcome. Thus when the government has such an interest, the solicitor general can file an *amicus curiae* or the Court can invite such a brief because it wants an opinion in writing. Other interested parties may file briefs as well.

amicus curiae

"Friend of the court," an individual or group that is not a party to a lawsuit but has a strong interest in influencing the outcome.

In addition to influencing the flow of cases, the solicitor general wields influence in the way he shapes his arguments and characterizes the issues before the Court. This individual is the person appearing most frequently before the Court and, theoretically, is the most disinterested. The solicitor general's credibility is not hurt when several times each year he withdraws a case with the admission that the government has made an error.[36]

Law Clerks. Every federal judge employs law clerks to research legal issues and assist in preparing opinions. Each justice is assigned four clerks, almost always honors graduates of the nation's most prestigious law schools. A clerkship with a Supreme Court justice generally indicates that the fortunate individual is likely to reach the very top of the legal profession. One of the clerks' most

---

36 On the strategic and informational role played by the solicitor general, see Kevin T. McGuire, "Explaining Executive Success in the U.S. Supreme Court," *Political Research Quarterly* 51, no. 2 (1998): 505–26. Also see Michael A. Bailey, Brian Kamoie, and Forrest Maltzman, "Signals from the Tenth Justice: The Political Role of the Solicitor General in Supreme Court Decision Making," *American Journal of Political Science* 49, no. 1 (January 2005): 72–85.

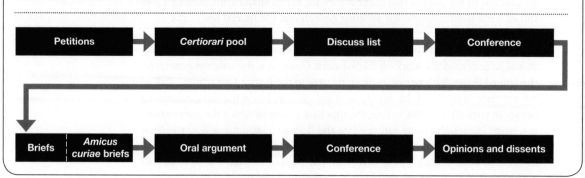

Figure 9.6

THE SUPREME COURT'S DECISION-MAKING PROCESS

Petitions → *Certiorari* pool → Discuss list → Conference →

Briefs | *Amicus curiae* briefs → Oral argument → Conference → Opinions and dissents

important roles is screening the thousands of petitions for writs of *certiorari* that come before the Court.[37] Some justices rely heavily on their clerks for advice in writing opinions and deciding whether individual cases ought to be heard. It is often rumored that certain opinions were actually written by clerks rather than justices.[38] Indeed, at the end of long judicial careers, justices such as William O. Douglas and Thurgood Marshall had become so infirm that they had to rely on the judgments of their law clerks.

The Supreme Court's Procedures

The Preparation. The Court's decision to accept a case is the beginning of a lengthy and complex process (Figure 9.6). First, attorneys on both sides must prepare **briefs**—written documents explaining why the Court should rule in favor of their client. The document filed by the individual bringing the case, called the petitioner's brief, summarizes the facts of the case and presents the legal basis on which the Court is being asked to overturn the lower court's decision. The document filed by the side that prevailed in the lower court, called the respondent's brief, explains why the Court should affirm the lower court's verdict. The petitioners then file a brief answering and attempting to refute the points made in the respondent's brief. This document is called the petitioner's reply brief. Briefs contain many references to precedents showing that other courts have frequently ruled in the same way that the petitioner or respondent is asking the Supreme Court to rule.

As the attorneys prepare their briefs, they often ask sympathetic interest groups for help by means of *amicus curiae* briefs. In a case involving separation

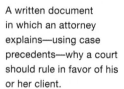

brief ➡

A written document in which an attorney explains—using case precedents—why a court should rule in favor of his or her client.

---

37 H. W. Perry Jr., *Deciding to Decide: Agenda Setting in the United States Supreme Court* (Cambridge, MA: Harvard University Press, 1991).

38 Edward Lazarus, *Closed Chambers: The First Eyewitness Account of the Epic Struggles inside the Supreme Court* (New York: Times Books, 1998).

of church and state, for example, liberal groups such as the American Civil Liberties Union and People for the American Way are likely to file *amicus* briefs in support of strict separation, whereas conservative religious groups—the Family Research Council or Focus on the Family, for example—are likely to file *amicus* briefs advocating increased public support for religious ideas. Often dozens of briefs are filed on each side of a major case.

Oral Argument. During the next stage, **oral argument**, attorneys for both sides present their positions before the Court and answer the justices' questions. Each attorney has only a half hour to present her case, including interruptions for questions. Oral argument can be very important to the outcome, for it allows justices to better understand the heart of a case and raise questions that the opposing sides' briefs do not address. Sometimes justices go beyond the strictly legal issues and ask opposing counsel to discuss the case's implications for the Court and the nation at large.[39] In oral arguments on the constitutionality of the Defense of Marriage Act in 2013, for example, Justice Kennedy frequently questioned whether the definition of marriage resided with the states rather than with the federal government.

The Conference. After oral argument, the Court discusses the case in its Wednesday or Friday conference. The chief justice presides and speaks first; the others follow in order of seniority. No outsiders are permitted to attend. The justices reach a decision on the basis of a majority vote. As the case is discussed, justices may try to influence one another's opinions. At times, this may result in compromise decisions.

Opinion Writing. After a decision has been reached, one of the justices in the majority is assigned to write the **opinion**. This assignment is made by either the chief justice or the most senior justice in the majority if the chief justice is on the losing side. The wording and emphasis of the opinion can have important implications for future litigation, so the justices must carefully weigh the choice of who writes it; they must consider the impression the case will make on lawyers and the public, as well as the probability that one justice's opinion will be more widely accepted than another's.[40]

This tactical consideration occurred dramatically in 1944, when Chief Justice Harlan F. Stone chose Justice Felix Frankfurter to write the opinion in the "White primary" case *Smith v. Allwright*, which overturned the southern practice of prohibiting Black voters' participation in primary elections. The day after Stone made the assignment, Justice Robert H. Jackson wrote a letter to

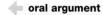

oral argument

The stage in Supreme Court proceedings in which attorneys for both sides appear before the Court to present their positions and answer questions posed by the justices.

opinion

The written explanation of the Supreme Court's decision in a particular case.

---

39 On the consequences of oral arguments for decision making, see Timothy R. Johnson, Paul J. Wahlbeck, and James F. Spriggs II, "The Influence of Oral Arguments on the U.S. Supreme Court," *American Political Science Review* 100, no. 1 (February 2006): 99–113.

40 For this and other strategic aspects of the Court's process, see Forrest Maltzman, James F. Spriggs II, and Paul J. Wahlbeck, *Crafting Law on the Supreme Court: The Collegial Game* (New York: Cambridge University Press, 2001).

Stone arguing that Frankfurter, a foreign-born Jew from New England, would not win over the South with his opinion, regardless of his brilliance. Stone accepted Jackson's advice and reassigned the opinion to Justice Stanley Reed, an American-born Protestant from Kentucky and a southern Democrat in good standing.[41]

Once the majority opinion is drafted, it is circulated to the other justices. Some members of the majority may agree with both the outcome and the rationale but wish to highlight a particular point and so draft a concurring opinion, called a regular **concurrence**. Alternatively, one or more justices may agree with the majority's decision but disagree with the rationale. Those justices may draft a special concurrence, explaining their disagreements with the majority. The pattern of opinions that emerge on a case ultimately depends on bargaining among the justices, as suggested by the collective action principle.

Dissent. Justices who disagree with the majority decision may publicize the character of their disagreement in the form of a **dissenting opinion**, which is generally assigned by the senior justice among the dissenters. Dissents can signal to defeated political forces that some members of the Court support their position. Ironically, the most dependable way an individual justice can exercise a direct influence on the Court is to write a dissent. Because there is no need to please a majority, dissenting opinions can be more eloquent and less guarded than majority opinions. The current Supreme Court often produces 5–4 decisions, with dissenters writing long and detailed opinions that, they hope, will convince a swing justice to join their side on the next round of cases addressing a similar topic. Thus, for example, Justice David Souter wrote a 34-page dissent in a 2002 case upholding the use of government-funded school vouchers to pay for parochial school tuition. Souter called the decision "a dramatic departure from basic Establishment Clause principle" and went on to say that he hoped it would be reconsidered by a future court.[42]

Dissents play a special role in the work and impact of the Court because they amount to appeals to lawyers nationwide to keep bringing cases of the sort at issue. Therefore, an effective dissent influences the flow of cases through the Court as well as the arguments that lawyers will make in later cases.

These rules of collective decision making shape how the Supreme Court addresses cases. But they are just the structure within which judges operate. The rules indicate that judicial authority is restrained and cautious, incremental and rational. But ultimately the rules reveal little about how judges will deal with the great political and social questions of the day. How the courts ultimately decide matters of law depends on the views of those in the judiciary, the nature of the

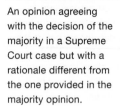

concurrence

An opinion agreeing with the decision of the majority in a Supreme Court case but with a rationale different from the one provided in the majority opinion.

dissenting opinion

A decision written by a justice who voted with the minority opinion in a particular case, in which the justice fully explains the reasoning behind his or her opinion.

---

41 *Smith v. Allwright*, 321 U.S. 649 (1944).

42 Warren Richey, "Dissenting Opinions as a Window on Future Rulings," *Christian Science Monitor*, July 1, 2002, p. 1.

problems they address, and the relationship of the courts to the other branches of government.

JUDICIAL DECISION MAKING

The judiciary is conservative in its procedures, but its effect on society can be radical.[43] The extent of its effect depends on numerous factors, two of which stand out above the rest. The first is the individual members of the Supreme Court, their attitudes and goals, and their relationships with one another. The second is the other branches of government, particularly Congress.

The Supreme Court Justices

The Supreme Court explains its decisions in terms of law and precedent. But ultimately the members of Court itself decide what laws mean and what importance precedents will have. Throughout its history, the Court has shaped and reshaped the law. If any individual judges in the country influence the federal judiciary, the Supreme Court justices are the ones who do.

From the 1950s to the 1980s, the Court was active in such areas as civil rights, civil liberties, abortion, voting rights, and police procedures. It was more responsible than any other governmental institution for breaking down America's system of racial segregation. It virtually prohibited states from interfering with a woman's right to seek an abortion, sharply curtailed state restrictions on voting rights, and placed restrictions on the behavior of local police and prosecutors in criminal cases. But since the early 1980s, resignations, deaths, and new appointments have brought many shifts in the mix of ideologies represented on the Court. In a series of decisions between 1989 and 2001, conservative justices appointed by presidents Ronald Reagan and George H. W. Bush were able to swing the Court to a more conservative position on civil rights, affirmative action, abortion rights, property rights, criminal procedure, voting rights, desegregation, and the power of the national government.

The importance of ideology was very clear during the Court's 2000–01 term. In key decisions, the most conservative justices—Scalia, Rehnquist, and Clarence Thomas, usually joined by Kennedy—generally voted as a bloc.[44] Indeed, Scalia and Thomas voted together in 99 percent of all cases. At the same

---

43 A broad consideration of various approaches to judicial decision making may be found in Lee Epstein and Jack Knight, *The Choices Justices Make* (Washington, DC: CQ Press, 1998).

44 Linda Greenhouse, "In Year of Florida Vote, Supreme Court Also Did Much Other Work," *New York Times*, July 2, 2001, p. A12.

time, the most liberal justices—Breyer, Ginsburg, Souter, and John Paul Stevens—also generally formed a voting bloc.[45] Justice O'Connor, a moderate conservative, was often the swing vote.[46] This ideological division led to a number of important 5–4 decisions. In the case *Bush v. Gore*, which concerned the recounting of ballots in Florida in the 2000 presidential election, O'Connor joined with the conservative bloc to give Bush a 5–4 victory. Indeed, more than 33 percent of all cases heard by the Court in its 2000–01 term were decided by a 5–4 vote.

However, precisely because the Court was so evenly split during this period, the conservative bloc did not always prevail. In the 2003 case of *Missouri v. Seibert*, for example, Kennedy joined a 5–4 majority to strengthen Miranda rights.[47] On abortion, women's rights, and affirmative action, Justice O'Connor often joined the liberal bloc. With the departure of O'Connor and her replacement by Alito in 2006, many anticipated a series of new 5–4 decisions favoring the conservatives under new chief justice John Roberts.[48] In 2007, for example, the Court upheld the Partial-Birth Abortion Ban Act—a law favored by conservatives—by a 5–4 majority. O'Connor's departure shifted the center of the Court (the pivotal vote in formulating opinions) to Justice Kennedy, whose jurisprudence did not significantly differ from O'Connor's. Thus the Court's conservative drift since then has been slight and certainly not as dramatic as the replacement of O'Connor with Alito might have suggested to the untutored eye.[49]

We should note that the liberal-conservative bloc structure on the Court is not always predictive, even in important cases. In *National Federation of Independent Business v. Sebelius*, the 2012 case on the constitutionality of President Obama's Affordable Care Act, it was Chief Justice Roberts, a firm member of the conservative bloc, who joined the four liberals to uphold the law.[50] Roberts again sided with the four liberals in *King v. Burwell* (2015) to uphold the constitutionality of Obamacare. Writing for the Court majority, Roberts supported the lower court's opinion that millions of Americans were entitled to public subsidies that keep insurance affordable, no matter whether the subsidies were established by individual states or the federal government.[51]

45 Charles Lane, "Laying Down the Law," *Washington Post*, July 1, 2001, p. A6.

46 For an insightful discussion about identifying the swing justice on the Court, see Andrew D. Martin, Kevin M. Quinn, and Lee Epstein, "The Median Justice on the U.S. Supreme Court," *North Carolina Law Review* 83, no. 5 (2005): 1275–322.

47 *Missouri v. Seibert*, 542 U.S. 600 (2004).

48 Adam Liptak, "Entrances and Exits: The New 5-to-4 Supreme Court," *New York Times*, April 22, 2007.

49 For a development of this argument, see David W. Rohde and Kenneth A. Shepsle, "Advising and Consenting in the 60-Vote Senate: Strategic Appointments to the Supreme Court," *Journal of Politics* 69, no. 3 (August 2007): 664–77.

50 Adam Liptak, "Supreme Court Upholds Health Care Law, 5–4 in Victory for Obama," *New York Times*, June 28, 2012, www.nytimes.com/2012/06/29/us/supreme-court-lets-health-law-largely-stand.html (accessed 3/25/20).

51 *King v. Burwell*, 576 U.S. 988 (2015).

Finally, the Court's policy influence comes not from the "horse race" vote results often trumpeted by the media but from the written opinions providing the constitutional or statutory rationale for policy in the future. These opinions establish the guidelines that govern how federal courts must decide similar cases in the future.

Activism and Restraint. One element of judicial philosophy is the issue of activism versus restraint. Over the years, some justices have believed that courts should interpret the Constitution according to the framers' stated intentions and defer to the views of Congress when interpreting federal statutes. Justice Felix Frankfurter, for example, advocated judicial deference to legislative bodies and avoidance of the "political thicket" that arises when the courts consider questions that are essentially political rather than legal. Advocates of **judicial restraint** are sometimes called strict constructionists because they look strictly to the words of the Constitution in interpreting its meaning. (Of course, it should be emphasized that there are *degrees* of restraint, ranging from a literal interpretation of the words of the Constitution to a more nuanced stance in which the "spirit" rather than the words per se are the source of restraint.)

The alternative to restraint is **judicial activism**, which involves going beyond the words of the Constitution or a statute to consider the broader societal implications of the Court's decisions. Activist judges sometimes strike out in new directions, promulgating new interpretations or inventing new legal and constitutional concepts when they deem them socially desirable. For example, Justice Harry Blackmun's opinion in *Roe v. Wade* was based on a constitutional right to privacy that is not directly found in the words of the Constitution but was, rather, based on the Court's prior decision in *Griswold v. Connecticut*. Blackmun and the other members of the majority in *Roe* argued that certain constitutional provisions imply the right to privacy. In this instance of judicial activism, the Court knew the result it wanted to achieve and was not afraid to make the law conform to the desired outcome.

It is sometimes difficult to discern a difference between restraint and different flavors of activism. The Court's conservative bloc sometimes does try to rein in the more expansive posture of previous activist majorities. In other cases, however, it seeks to move "boldly" and "actively" in areas previously regarded as settled law. In *Citizens United v. Federal Election Commission* in 2010, for example, the Court held that corporations and unions could not be restricted from financial participation in elections.[52] It did not reverse previous prohibitions on corporate donations directly to candidates, but it did allow independent expenditures—for example, advertising during a campaign—so long as they were not coordinated with any individual campaign. This seems to fit uncomfortably with a philosophy of restraint.

Political Ideology. The second component of judicial philosophy is political ideology. The liberal or conservative attitudes of justices play an important

 judicial restraint

The judicial philosophy whose adherents refuse to go beyond the text of the Constitution in interpreting its meaning.

 judicial activism

The judicial philosophy that the Court should see beyond the text of the Constitution or a statute to consider the broader societal implications of its decisions.

---

52 *Citizens United v. Federal Election Commission*, 558 U.S. 310 (2010).

role in their decisions.[53] The philosophy of activism versus restraint is sometimes a smoke screen for political ideology. In the past, liberal judges have been activists, willing to use the law to achieve social and political change, whereas conservatives have been associated with judicial restraint. It is interesting, however, that in recent years some conservative justices have become activists in seeking to undo part of the work of liberal jurists over the past three decades. The Rehnquist Court, dominated by conservatives, was among the most activist Supreme Courts in American history, striking out in new directions in areas such as federalism and election law.

Our discussion of congressional politics in Chapter 6 described legislators as policy oriented. If one were to conceive of judges as "legislators in robes," then it is not all that far-fetched to claim that judges, like other politicians, have policy preferences that they seek to implement. Analyzing the Evidence on pp. 382–3 looks at ideology on the Court.

Other Institutions of Government

Congress. At both the national and the state level, courts and judges are players in the policy game because of the separation of powers. Essentially, the legislative branch formulates policy (defined constitutionally and institutionally by a legislative process), the executive branch implements policy (according to well-defined administrative procedures), and the courts, when asked, rule on the faithfulness of the legislated and executed policy, either to the substance of the statute or to the Constitution itself. The courts may strike down an administrative action either because it exceeds the authority granted in the relevant statute (statutory rationale) or because the statute itself exceeds the authority granted to the legislature or executive by the Constitution (constitutional rationale).

If the Court declares that the action in question is outside permissible bounds, the majority opinion can declare whatever policy it wishes. If the legislature is unhappy with this judicial action, it may either recraft the legislation (if the rationale for striking it down was statutory) or initiate a constitutional amendment that would enable the policy to pass constitutional muster (if the rationale for originally striking it down was constitutional).[54]

In reaching their decisions, Supreme Court justices must anticipate Congress's response. As a result, judges do not always vote according to their true preferences because doing so may provoke Congress to enact legislation that moves the policy further from what the judges prefer. By voting for a lesser preference, the justices can get something they prefer to the status quo without provoking congressional action to overturn their decision. In

---

53 C. Herman Pritchett, *The Roosevelt Court: A Study in Judicial Politics and Values, 1937–1947* (New York: Macmillan, 1948); Jeffrey A. Segal and Harold J. Spaeth, *The Supreme Court and the Attitudinal Model* (New York: Cambridge University Press, 1993); Segal and Spaeth, *The Supreme Court and the Attitudinal Model Revisited* (New York: Cambridge University Press, 2002).

54 William N. Eskridge Jr., "Overriding Supreme Court Statutory Interpretation Decisions," *Yale Law Journal* 101 (1991): 331–55.

short, the interactions between the Court and Congress are part of a complex strategic game.[55]

The President. The president's most direct influence on the federal courts is the power to nominate justices. Presidents typically nominate individuals whose policy preferences seem close to their own and to those of a majority of senators, who must confirm the nomination. In addition to ideological congruence, a president may also consider race, gender, and ethnicity. As displayed in Figure 9.7 on p. 384, the most recent presidents have appointed a number of judges from underrepresented groups, with Trump being a notable exception.

The president must also confront Congress in shaping the judiciary. By using the filibuster (see Chapter 6), both parties have blocked judicial nominees: the Democrats repeatedly blocked nominees when George W. Bush was president, and the Republicans did so when Obama was president. Acrimony over judicial nominees prompted both parties to threaten to change Senate rules so that their preferred nominees could be approved more easily. In 2013, Senate Democrats carried through with the threat, eliminating the filibuster for most presidential nominees (although allowing filibusters for Supreme Court nominees); in 2017 the filibuster was removed by the Senate Republican majority for Supreme Court nominees as well. Of course, opponents of a nomination may block it in other ways. The judiciary committee may refuse to consider the nominee, as in the case of Judge Merrick Garland, President Obama's Supreme Court nominee in 2016.

The Implementation of Supreme Court Decisions

The president and the rest of the executive branch, along with Congress, the states, the lower courts, and a variety of private organizations and individuals, play key roles in the implementation of Supreme Court decisions. Once the high court has made a decision, numerous other government agencies must put it into effect. The lower courts must apply the principles asserted by the Court to new cases. The executive branch must enforce the Court's decision. State legislators and governors must implement the decision in their own jurisdictions. And often individuals and organizations must take action in the courts and in the political arena to demand that the Supreme Court's verdicts be fully implemented. At each of these stages, opposition by relevant actors may delay full national implementation of a decision, sometimes for years.

For example, if lower-court judges strongly disagree with a Supreme Court decision, they may use a variety of tactics to avoid fully implementing it. They may, for example, avoid applying the case by disposing of similar cases on

---

55 A full strategic analysis of the maneuvering among legislative, executive, and judicial branches in the separation-of-powers arrangement choreographed by the U.S. Constitution may be found in William N. Eskridge Jr. and John Ferejohn, "The Article I, Section 7 Game," *Georgetown Law Review* 80 (1992): 523–64. The entire issue of this journal is devoted to the theme of strategic behavior in American institutional politics. A more recent treatment is Tom S. Clark, *The Limits of Judicial Independence* (New York: Cambridge University Press, 2011).

Ideological Voting on the Supreme Court

Contributed by
Andrew D. Martin
Washington University in St. Louis
Kevin M. Quinn
University of Michigan

Do the political preferences of Supreme Court justices influence their behavior? The starting point for the analysis of the behavior of Supreme Court justices is to look at their votes.[1] For non-unanimous decisions, we can compute agreement scores—the fraction of cases in which a pair of justices vote the same way. We display these agreement scores for the Court's 2018–19 term in the first figure below. If you examine this figure, you will see that two groups of justices emerge. Within each group, the justices agree with one another a lot; in many cases, over 80 percent of the time for justices on both the left and the right. Voting is more structured than we would expect by chance.

One way to represent that structure is by arranging the justices on a line as in the diagram below to the right.[2] Justices who agree a lot should be close to one another; justices who disagree a lot should be far apart.

Does the fact that there are patterns of agreement mean that the justices are deciding based on political ideology? Not necessarily. These patterns are consistent with ideological decision making, but other things might explain the patterns as well. However, when we evaluate the content of particular cases and see who wins or loses, there is a great deal of support for the idea that political ideology influences how justices vote.[3]

Agreement Scores for the 2018–19 Term

	Sotomayor	Ginsburg	Breyer	Kagan	Roberts	Kavanaugh	Gorsuch	Alito	Thomas
Sotomayor	1	.89	.75	.80	.45	.38	.34	.30	.18
Ginsburg	.89	1	.73	.82	.43	.41	.36	.32	.20
Breyer	.75	.73	1	.81	.52	.51	.27	.41	.20
Kagan	.80	.82	.77	1	.52	.51	.45	.41	.34
Roberts	.45	.43	.52	.52	1	.87	.48	.80	.59
Kavanaugh	.38	.41	.51	.51	.87	1	.54	.85	.67
Gorsuch	.34	.36	.27	.45	.48	.54	1	.59	.70
Alito	.30	.32	.41	.41	.80	.85	.59	1	.75
Thomas	.18	.20	.20	.34	.59	.67	.70	.75	1

- < 0.35
- 0.35–0.44
- 0.45–0.54
- 0.55–0.64
- 0.65–0.74
- 0.75–0.99

POSITION

Sotomayor
Ginsburg
Breyer
Kagan
Roberts
Kavanaugh
Gorsuch
Alito

Thomas

The figure to the left contains the agreement scores for the 2018–19 term of the U.S. Supreme Court for all non-unanimous cases. These scores indicate the proportion of cases when each justice agreed with every other justice. Two justices that always disagreed with each other would get a zero; two justices who always agreed would get a one. Red indicates low agreement scores; green indicates high agreement scores. The policy dimension to the right of the figure is one that best represents the patterns in the agreement scores.

0 = Justices always disagreed
1 = Justices always agreed

This type of analysis can be done for any court, but it becomes more difficult if we are interested in comparing justices across time instead of during just one term. What if we are interested in whether the Supreme Court is becoming more ideologically polarized over time? Or whether individual justices have become more liberal or conservative? Martin-Quinn scores based on a statistical model of voting on the Court help solve this problem.[4]

A number of interesting patterns emerge. Consider the case of Justice Harry Blackmun, who often claimed, "I haven't changed; it's the Court that changed under me."[5] The figure below shows that Justice Blackmun's position did in fact change ideologically over the course of his career. This evidence is consistent with some clear changes in Justice Blackmun's voting behavior, especially in the area of the death penalty.

We can also look at patterns in the positions of chief justices. While the chief's vote counts just the same as the votes of the other justices, he or she plays an important role in organizing the court. Justice William H. Rehnquist was the most conservative justice on the court when he arrived in 1971, but as the figure below shows, after he was elevated to chief justice in 1986, he too drifted more toward the middle. This is what we would expect to see of a justice who was working strategically to build coalitions, as any good chief would.

Ideological Trajectories of Selected Justices

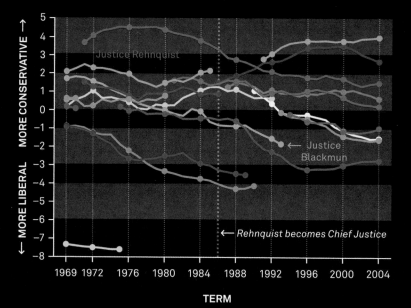

JUSTICES

- Black
- Blackmun
- Brennan
- Breyer
- Burger
- Douglas
- Ginsburg
- Harlan
- Kennedy
- Marshall
- O'Connor
- Powell
- Rehnquist
- Scalia
- Souter
- Stevens
- Stewart
- Thomas
- White

This figure shows the Martin-Quinn scores for selected justices serving in the Burger (1969–86) and Rehnquist Courts (1986–2004). Each line represents the trajectory of each justice on the ideological dimension.

1 C. Herman Pritchett, *The Roosevelt Court: A Study in Judicial Politics and Values, 1937–1947* (New York: Macmillan, 1948).
2 Glendon A. Schubert, *The Judicial Mind: The Attitudes and Ideologies of Supreme Court Justices, 1946–1963* (Evanston, IL: Northwestern University Press, 1965).
3 Jeffrey A. Segal and Harold J. Spaeth, *The Supreme Court and the Attitudinal Model* (New York: Cambridge University Press, 1993).
4 Andrew D. Martin and Kevin M. Quinn, "Dynamic Ideal Point Estimation via Markov Chain Monte Carlo for the U.S. Supreme Court, 1953–1999," *Political Analysis* 10, no. 2 (2002): 134–53, http://mqscores.lsa.umich.edu (accessed 3/27/20).
5 Linda Greenhouse, *Becoming Justice Blackmun: Harry Blackmun's Supreme Court Journey* (New York: Times Books, 2005).

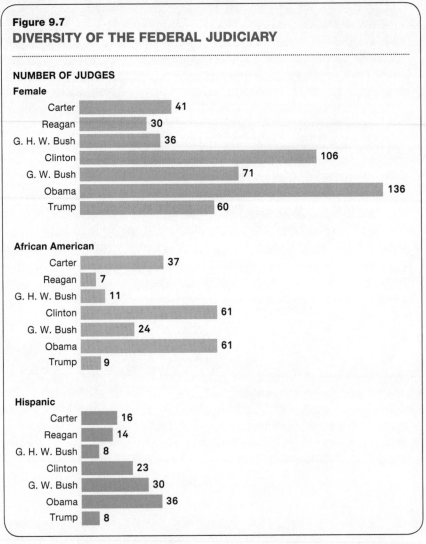

Figure 9.7

DIVERSITY OF THE FEDERAL JUDICIARY

NUMBER OF JUDGES

Female

President	Number
Carter	41
Reagan	30
G. H. W. Bush	36
Clinton	106
G. W. Bush	71
Obama	136
Trump	60

African American

Carter	37
Reagan	7
G. H. W. Bush	11
Clinton	61
G. W. Bush	24
Obama	61
Trump	9

Hispanic

Carter	16
Reagan	14
G. H. W. Bush	8
Clinton	23
G. W. Bush	30
Obama	36
Trump	8

NOTE: Jimmy Carter appointed 261 federal judges; Ronald Reagan, 364; George H. W. Bush, 188; Bill Clinton, 372; George W. Bush, 321; and Barack Obama, 329. As of July 2020, the U.S. Senate has confirmed 189 judges nominated by Donald Trump.

SOURCES: Federal Judicial Center, www.fjc.gov/history/home.nsf/page/judges_diversity.html; Pew Research Center, www.pewresearch.org/fact-tank/2018/10/02/trump-has-appointed-a-larger-share-of-female-judges-than-other-gop-presidents-but-lags-obama (accessed 3/27/20); Renee Klahr, "Federal Judge Appointments Tracker (2009–PresentPresident)," NPR Politics, https://docs.google.com/spreadsheets/d/1O0ZUPKogqk1PMoJn50_gdbdBwyj54i-RqHUDFQ7Z5E8/edit#gid=1242775320 (accessed 6/7/20).

technical or procedural grounds. Similarly, they may apply the case as narrowly as possible or declare that some portion of the Court's opinion was merely "dicta"—useful as guidance but not binding.

Most Supreme Court decisions must be implemented by federal, state, and local agencies. If these agencies are unsympathetic to a decision, they may obstruct, delay, or even refuse to accept it. In the nineteenth century, President Andrew

Jackson famously refused to obey a Supreme Court decision, declaring, "John Marshall has made his decision. Now let him enforce it." In 2015 Kim Davis, clerk of Rowan County, Kentucky, refused to issue marriage licenses to same-sex couples, despite the recent Court ruling in *Obergefell v. Hodges* requiring her to do so (see the Policy Principle on p. 386). She spent five days in jail for contempt of court before being released in exchange for agreeing to allow her office to issue licenses (though she refused to issue them herself). Although few officials or agencies have been so defiant, many have quietly ignored or sought to circumvent the Court. For example, many local school boards have searched for years for ways to sidestep the Court's rulings prohibiting religious observance in public schools.

Strategic Behavior in the Supreme Court

In describing the role and effect of the Supreme Court, we have occasionally referred to the strategic opportunities the Court provides. We can divide this strategic behavior into three stages. Stage 1 begins with a period of "normal" politics at the national or local level—these include everyday interactions in legislatures, executive and regulatory agencies, political processes like elections, and among public and private entities. Conflict arises, and interested parties must decide what to do: live with the results, attempt to resolve the conflict through normal political channels using legislatures and agencies, or move the conflict into the courts. Stage 2 involves a court's response, with judges both reacting to demands from the outside and fashioning their own behavioral strategies within the legal process. Stage 3 involves what happens once a court renders a decision, how the actors in stages 1 and 2 anticipate the decision, and how they adjust their behavior to the court's expectations. Although our discussion could be developed for all courts, we will primarily address the Supreme Court and its internal strategic environment at stage 2, when it both reacts to developments that preceded its involvement in a conflict (stage 1) and anticipates what will happen if it responds in a particular manner (stage 3).

Stage 1. Assume that a conflict has arisen and appeals have been made through normal channels. Administrative and regulatory agencies, for example, often have well-defined procedures for appealing a ruling within the agency, with the opportunity of a subsequent appeal to a court always available. Dissatisfied with the outcome, one of the parties moves the dispute to the courts, and at some point in the process the option of appeal to the Supreme Court is available. The aggrieved party has a decision to make. It is a calculated, strategic decision in two respects.

First, an appeal will consume resources that might otherwise serve different purposes. A prospective appellant must weigh an appeal against this "opportunity cost." The Sierra Club, for example, might use resources to appeal a lower-court decision on environmental protection to the Supreme Court or, alternatively, devote some of the same resources to lobbying Congress on other issues.

Second, all options are uncertain propositions whose resolutions stretch out over time. Regarding uncertainty, a prospective appellant must recognize that the probability of successfully getting to the Court is slim, and even if it obtains *certiorari*, the Court may not rule in its favor. Regarding the time dimension, even if the

Changing Judicial Direction: Gay Marriage

Gay rights advocates celebrate the Court's 2015 decision.

In 1970, Richard Baker and James McConnell applied for a marriage license in Hennepin County, Minnesota. The county clerk, Gerald Nelson, refused to give them a license because they were both men. The couple sued Nelson, claiming that the Minnesota statute barring them from receiving a marriage license was unconstitutional. They appealed the case all the way to the Minnesota Supreme Court, which held in *Baker v. Nelson* (1971) that "The institution of marriage as a union of man and woman, uniquely involving the procreation and rearing of children within a family, is as old as the book of Genesis." In 1972, the U.S. Supreme Court issued a brief affirmation of the Minnesota ruling.

In the years and decades following this setback, the gay rights movement proceeded down other litigation avenues, bringing a series of lawsuits aimed at changing policies that discriminated against gay men and lesbians. Their collective effort to use the institution of the courts to change policy gradually saw results. A quarter of a century after *Baker v. Nelson,* the U.S. Supreme Court struck down a provision of Colorado state law that denied gay and lesbian residents a variety of privileges that the law

labeled "special rights." Justice Anthony Kennedy, writing for the 6–3 majority in *Romer v. Evans* (1996), states "We find nothing special in the protections [being withheld]. These protections . . . constitute ordinary civil life in a free society."

The *Romer* opinion, written in the same year Congress passed the Defense of Marriage Act (DOMA) limiting marriage to one man and one woman, shows how the Court can turn away from both its own precedents and congressional policy to actively chart a new direction. As the policy principle suggests, collective action directed toward the courts, combined with new political preferences in the courts, generated a change in policy.

Justice Kennedy went on to author opinions decriminalizing sodomy in *Lawrence v. Texas* (2003), declaring DOMA unconstitutional in *United States v. Windsor* (2013), and eventually establishing a right for same-sex couples to marry across the United States in *Obergefell v. Hodges* (2015). Though by the time of *Obergefell* many states had already legalized same-sex marriage, the Court was consistently on the front line of the debate in one of its most consistent shows of judicial activism in recent times. Kennedy's *Obergefell* opinion was aimed at history, not merely at setting a legal precedent. It showed clearly his intention to shape a policy and enshrine a right, rather than argue over semantics or precedent.

Though public opinion on same-sex marriage has been changing rapidly in its favor, the *Obergefell* decision did not silence dissent. In August 2015, post-*Obergefell,* another county clerk (this time in Kentucky) refused to issue a marriage license to a gay couple. Yet, rather than affirming her action, as had happened in Minnesota four decades earlier, a court held her in contempt and jailed her.

appellant wins, the legal process may take years, making the delayed victory bittersweet. Ultimately these strategic calculations revolve around what an appellant can expect in pursuing an appeal—that is, what might happen in stages 2 and 3.[56]

Stage 2. Thousands of cases are appealed to the Supreme Court. The nine justices (or, more accurately, their clerks) must sort through these petitions and, according to the rule of four, build their docket each session. The Court, in short, has the power to create its own agenda.

In building their docket for the current session, how do justices think about the available options? They support some cases out of a strong belief that an area is ripe for constitutional clarification. They support others out of an interest in the development of legal principles in a particular area—criminal rights, privacy, the First Amendment, abortion, affirmative action, federal-state relations, and so on—or in the belief that contradictory decisions in lower courts need to be sorted out. The justices may oppose certain appeals because they believe a particular case will not provide a sufficiently clear-cut basis for clarifying a legal issue. That is, even though a case might attract a justice's interest on substantive grounds or might be perceived by a justice as containing procedural errors that could lead to a reversal, she might not support *certiorari* because of a strategic calculation that the case is not a particularly good vehicle for achieving a certain policy goal or that a better vehicle might come up through the appeals process in a subsequent session.[57]

Once a case is included on the docket, oral arguments have been delivered by the litigants' attorneys, and *amicus curiae* briefs have been filed by other interested parties, the case becomes the subject of two decisions.[58] The first takes place after the justices discuss it in one of their regularly scheduled conferences during the Court's term. When discussion has concluded and all attempts at persuasion have ended, there is a vote in favor of the appeal or against it. In principle, this vote affects only the parties to the case, either affirming or reversing the lower-court decision.

The second decision has a wider bearing. Having decided one way or the other, the justices must determine whether they agree on the reasons for their decision. This calculation is highly strategic because the Court's impact over and above its effect on the contesting parties depends on the reasons it gives for the decision at hand. A Court majority's reasons set legal precedent for similar cases in the future, thus influencing litigation in lower courts. If the majority cannot agree on why they decided as they did, there is no binding effect on

---

56 There are subtleties to the strategies of appellants. They may seek an appeal to the Supreme Court, for example, as a bluff to induce the winner in the lower court to accommodate some of their preferences—in effect, to settle out of court. Why might the lower-court winners be induced to accommodate the losers? There are at least two reasons: first, to avoid the exorbitant costs of fighting an appeal to the Supreme Court and, second, to avoid the prospect that their victory in the lower court may be reversed.

57 An excellent discussion of this facet of Supreme Court decision making is found in Perry, *Deciding to Decide*.

58 On the strategic decisions of *amicus* groups, see Thomas G. Hansford, "Information Provision, Organizational Constraints, and the Decision to Submit an *Amicus Curiae* Brief in a U.S. Supreme Court Case," *Political Research Quarterly* 57, no. 2 (2004): 219–30.

other comparable cases. Drafting an opinion that can attract the signatures of at least five justices is therefore of pivotal significance. A justice on the winning side who stakes out an extreme position relative to the others is unlikely to be able to draft such an opinion, so moderate justices usually do the heavy lifting of opinion drafting for especially controversial cases. In cases where a majority does not reach consensus on the reasons, there will be no majority opinion, though each justice is free to write his or her own opinion (possibly cosigned by others). These opinions have no binding effect on future lower-court cases but may still serve a strategic signaling role, conveying to the lower courts and the legal community where a justice stands on the issues involved.[59]

Stage 3. The Supreme Court is the top rung of one branch in a separation-of-powers system. Its decisions are not automatically implemented; it must depend on executive agencies for implementation and on lower courts for enforcement of its dicta. In fact, it ultimately depends on the willingness of others, especially ordinary citizens, to conform to its rulings. In some instances, the Court may worry about resistance. Throughout the 1940s and 1950s, for example, there were concerns that issues relating to integration would meet with popular disapproval and defiance in the South. Indeed, when writing the majority opinion in the 1954 *Brown* decision desegregating public schools, Chief Justice Earl Warren strategically softened some of its language in order to attract the signatures of all nine justices. The 9–0 decision and opinion signaled to a potentially defiant South that the Court was united and that it would take a very long time (the time needed to replace at least five justices) before there would be any prospect of reversal.

In addition to compliance, enforcement, and resistance, the Court considers the possibility of reversal. A Court decision on a statutory issue—for example, whether an existing law covers a particular situation—may be overturned if majorities in both houses of Congress and the president pass a new statute revising the law in question. If, for example, the Court rules that the Radio Act of 1927 does not cover transmissions by cell phones, but Congress and the president think otherwise, then Congress may pass legislation, and the president may sign it into law, amending the act so that its provisions definitively govern the regulation of cell phones.[60] Members of the Court may have no particular stake in being reversed—that is, they may not care whether the "political" branches decide, for example, that cell phones should be covered by the Radio Act. Indeed, they may feel a certain satisfaction that the act, as originally written, had a narrow scope that only subsequent statutory activity could broaden. Then again, to affect politics generally, the Court would not want their decisions questioned, reversed, or defied routinely.

For decisions made on constitutional (as opposed to statutory) grounds, no mere revision of existing law is sufficient to reverse the Court; a constitutional

59 For an insightful discussion of the strategic elements influencing how the senior justice in the winning coalition assigns opinion writing, see David W. Rohde, "Policy Goals, Strategic Choice and Majority Opinion Assignments in the U.S. Supreme Court," *Midwest Journal of Political Science* 16, no. 4 (November 1972): 652–82.

60 On the strategic interaction among the Court, Congress, and the president, see Eskridge and Ferejohn, "The Article I, Section 7 Game."

amendment is required. President George W. Bush, for example, gave his blessing to efforts to amend the Constitution to reverse the *Roe v. Wade* decision.

In the long run, the Supreme Court is the final legal authority on whether governmental and interpersonal practices satisfy statutory or constitutional scrutiny. But the justices are not free agents; the other branches of government must be taken into account as justices vote on cases and write legal opinions. Hence strategic calculation can never be far from their thinking.

CONCLUSION: THE EXPANDING POWER OF THE JUDICIARY

Since the end of World War II, the place of the judiciary in American politics and society has changed dramatically. Demand for legal solutions has increased, and the judiciary's reach has expanded. Some now call for reining in the power of the courts and discretion of judges in areas ranging from criminal law and sentencing to property rights to liability and torts. How our society deals with these issues will shape the judiciary's future independence and effectiveness. Even the most conservative justices now seem reluctant to relinquish their newfound power, authority that has become accepted and thus established.

Let's summarize what we have learned so far. Judges enjoy great latitude because they are not subject to electoral pressures. Judges and justices, more than other politicians in America, can pursue their own goals, preferences, and ideologies (rationality principle). They are, however, constrained by institutional rules governing access to the courts, by other courts, by Congress and the president, by their lack of enforcement powers, and most important, by the past in the form of precedent and common law (institution principle). For much of its history, the federal judiciary acted very cautiously. The Supreme Court rarely challenged Congress or the president. The justices instead tended to legitimate laws passed by Congress and actions of the president. The scope of the Court's decisions was limited only to those individuals whose cases the Court agreed to hear.

Three judicial revolutions have expanded the power and reach of the federal judiciary since World War II. The first revolution brought about the liberalization of a wide range of public policies in the United States. As we saw in Chapters 4 and 5, in certain policy areas—such as school desegregation, legislative apportionment, criminal procedure, obscenity, abortion, and voting rights—the Supreme Court was at the forefront of sweeping changes in the role of the U.S. government and, ultimately, the character of American society (policy principle). The Court put many of these issues before the public long before Congress or the president was prepared to act.

At the same time that the courts forged these policy innovations, they were bringing about a second, less visible revolution. During the 1960s and 1970s, the Supreme Court and other federal courts liberalized the concept of standing to permit almost any group seeking to challenge an administrative agency's actions to bring its case before the federal bench. It thus encouraged groups to come to the judiciary, rather than to Congress or the executive branch, to resolve disputes. Complementing this, the federal courts also broadened the scope of relief to permit themselves to act on behalf of broad categories of persons in class-action cases, rather than just on behalf of individuals.[61] The possibility of class-action cases facilitated collective action by allowing legal entrepreneurs to organize entire groups of petitioners who would otherwise face potentially insurmountable coordination and free-rider obstacles (collective action principle).

In a third revolution, the federal courts began to employ so-called structural remedies, in effect retaining jurisdiction over cases until their rulings had been implemented to their satisfaction.[62]

Through these three mechanisms, the federal courts paved the way for an unprecedented expansion of national judicial power. In essence, liberalization of the rules of standing and expansion of the scope of judicial relief drew the federal courts to connect with important social interests and classes. The introduction of structural remedies likewise enhanced the courts' ability to serve these constituencies. Thus during the 1960s and 1970s the power of the federal courts expanded through links with groups—including those advocating civil rights, consumers' rights, gay rights, women's rights, and environmental issues—who staunchly defended the Supreme Court in its battles with Congress, the executive, and other interest groups.

During the 1980s and 1990s, the Reagan and Bush administrations sought to end the relationship between the Court and liberal political forces. Conservative judges appointed by these Republican presidents modified the Court's positions in areas such as abortion, affirmative action, and judicial procedure, though not so completely as some conservative writers and politicians had hoped. Within one week in 2003, for example, the Supreme Court affirmed the validity of affirmative action, reaffirmed abortion rights, strengthened gay rights, offered new protections to individuals facing the death penalty, and issued a ruling in favor of a congressional apportionment plan that dispersed minority voters across several districts—a practice that appeared to favor the Democrats.[63] The Court made these decisions based on the justices' interpretations of precedent and law, not simply personal beliefs. Nevertheless, in the last decade the Court has chipped away at aspects of the earlier more liberal consensus. The right to choose to have an abortion, for example, though not rejected outright—*Roe v. Wade* remains the law of the land—has been hedged and qualified, with the Court appearing more permissive in cases in which states restrict access, require parental permission for juveniles, and allow abortion clinic closings.

Despite its increasingly conservative composition, the current Court has not been conservative in one important sense: it has not been eager to surrender the expanded powers carved out by earlier Courts, especially in areas that assert

---

61 See "Developments in the Law: Class Actions," *Harvard Law Review* 89, no. 7 (May 1976): 1318–644.

62 See Donald L. Horowitz, *The Courts and Social Policy* (Washington, DC: Brookings Institution, 1977).

63 David Von Drehle, "Court That Liberals Savage Proves to Be Less of a Target," *Washington Post*, June 29, 2003, p. A18.

the power of the national government over the states. Indeed, the opponents to the U.S. Constitution (the Antifederalists in Chapter 2) feared the assertion of the national interest over the states through the independent judiciary. Over two centuries of U.S. history, the reach and authority of the federal judiciary has expanded greatly, and the judiciary has emerged as a powerful arm of our national politics (history principle). Whatever their policy beliefs or partisan orientations, judges and justices understand the newfound importance of the courts among the three branches of American government and act not just to interpret and apply the law but also to maintain the power of the courts.

For Further Reading

Abraham, Henry J. *The Judicial Process: An Introductory Analysis of the Courts of the United States, England, and France.* 7th ed. New York: Oxford University Press, 1998.

Bailey, Michael A., and Forrest Maltzman. *The Constrained Court: Law, Politics, and the Decisions Justices Make.* Princeton, NJ: Princeton University Press, 2011.

Baum, Lawrence. *The Puzzle of Judicial Behavior.* Ann Arbor: University of Michigan Press, 1997.

Casillas, Christopher J., Peter K. Enns, and Patrick C. Wohlfarth. "How Public Opinion Constrains the U.S. Supreme Court." *American Journal of Political Science* 55, no. 1 (January 2011): 74–88.

Clark, Tom S. *The Limits of Judicial Independence.* New York: Cambridge University Press, 2011.

Krehbiel, Keith. "Supreme Court Appointments as a Move-the-Median Game." *American Journal of Political Science* 51, no. 2 (April 2007): 231–40.

O'Brien, David M. *Storm Center: The Supreme Court in American Politics.* 12th ed. New York: Norton, 2020.

Rosenberg, Gerald N. *The Hollow Hope: Can Courts Bring About Social Change?* 2nd ed. Chicago: University of Chicago Press, 2008.

Segal, Jeffrey A., and Harold J. Spaeth. *The Supreme Court and the Attitudinal Model Revisited.* New York: Cambridge University Press, 2002.

Toobin, Jeffrey. *The Nine: Inside the Secret World of the Supreme Court.* New York: Doubleday, 2007.

Whittington, Keith E. *Political Foundations of Judicial Supremacy: The Presidency, the Supreme Court, and Constitutional Leadership in U.S. History.* Princeton, NJ: Princeton University Press, 2007.

10

Public Opinion

Public support is the coin of the realm in Washington politics. Popular presidents succeed; unpopular presidents struggle. A president who has the backing of a large majority of the public gains leverage in dealing with Congress and the bureaucracy, but a president who lacks public support often meets resistance from members of Congress, even those in his own party. Popularity is the president's political capital, an asset that must be spent wisely on a few well-chosen issues.[1]

Members of Congress are perhaps even more attuned than the president to the ups and downs of public opinion. Representatives in the U.S. House must run for reelection every two years, a very short election cycle. They cannot afford to make many unpopular decisions lest their constituents punish them in the next election. Members of Congress and party leaders pay close attention to indicators of public sentiment, including polls; visits to their districts or home states; and letters, phone calls, and emails from constituents. A saying among members of Congress goes, "It's okay to be on the losing side of a vote, but you don't want to be on the wrong side."

Even the courts are not immune to the influence of public opinion. Courts lack the power to enforce their decisions; they depend on the compliance of those affected and the cooperation of Congress, the president, and political leaders in the states. That cooperation is not always forthcoming. As we saw in Chapter 5, *Brown v. Board of Education*—perhaps the most important court decision of the twentieth century—met with immediate opposition in the southern states that hampered desegregation efforts. Only after public opinion turned in support of equal rights for all races did Congress and the president act, accelerating the pace of desegregation.[2]

---

1   Chris Suellentrop, "America's New Political Capital," *Slate*, November 30, 2004, www.slate.com/id/2110256 (accessed 3/2/20). Also see Richard Neustadt, *Presidential Power and the Modern Presidents: The Politics of Leadership from Roosevelt to Reagan*, rev. ed. (New York: Wiley, 1960; repr., New York: Free Press, 1990); and Brandice Canes-Wrone, *Who Leads Whom? Presidents, Policy, and the Public* (Chicago: University of Chicago Press, 2006).

2   Gerald N. Rosenberg, *The Hollow Hope: Can Courts Bring About Social Change?* (Chicago: University of Chicago Press, 1991).

Public opinion is also the standard by which we judge democracy. Ideally, representative democracy approximates what the nation as a whole would choose to do were all 330 million Americans to consider a given matter. Congress and the president are supposed to act as the public's agents, enacting laws that a clear majority of the public wants and rejecting laws that fail to achieve widespread support. If the norms of society shift strongly in one direction for a period of time, so too should the laws of the land. The nature and origins of public opinion are central concerns of modern political science precisely because democratic government is supposed to reflect the will of the people.

Public opinion is, ultimately, the rationale behind democratic government. The public provides democratic government the will to act. The rationality principle applied to the public holds that average people have preferences about what government should and shouldn't do. At stake in many government decisions are individuals' interests and values, and people undertake political actions, such as voting, in an attempt to influence the government to their benefit. Democratic politics in its various forms aggregates people's preferences and beliefs into an expression of what a majority of people want. How individuals' preferences are transformed into electoral decisions and public policies depends on institutions, problems of collective action, and history. These factors will be emphasized in later chapters on elections, interest groups, political parties, and the media. Public opinion operates through these institutions to determine who serves in government, what problems government must address, and the principles and values that shape public policy. This chapter concerns what

LEARNING OBJECTIVES

➡️ Define public opinion and explain how it can be understood at the aggregate and individual levels.

➡️ Explain the ways in which institutional and personal preferences and beliefs can shape individuals' opinions.

➡️ Describe the relationship between public opinion and political knowledge.

➡️ Identify how politicians, interest groups, the media, and others try to shape public opinion.

➡️ Compare the different ways in which public opinion can be measured.

➡️ Analyze the ways in which public opinion influences government policy.

people want their government to do and how people understand the political choices that they confront.

While individuals pursue their own interests and values when making decisions about politics, they do not necessarily understand fully the choices they face. People look for information—facts, labels, cues—that can help simplify their decision making. This notion of the electorate is quite different from what is commonly found in civics books, which generally present an idealized citizenry who closely follow important issues; who are well-informed about their representatives' decisions; who understand the consequences of their own actions; and who participate in public debate, elections, and public decision making. Were we all that attentive, we would have little time for our education, our jobs, our families, and other aspects of daily life. In fact, researchers have long found that most Americans are not highly attentive to the issues before their representatives in their state's capital or in Washington, D.C. Lack of attention to public affairs is a necessary feature of representative democracy, but it also creates a potential problem.

Does public opinion adequately reflect the true preferences of the people? If citizens do not fully know what their choices are, then there is the possibility that elites might manipulate public decisions or that people may simply make the wrong choices. American history contains numerous examples of politicians, newspaper editors, and other elites misleading the public and manipulating public opinion for their own gain.[3] The prospect that elites can readily manipulate the public presents a lingering and difficult problem. The United States continually grapples with this challenge, especially in ongoing struggles to reform electoral rules such as those that regulate campaign finance. Interestingly enough, the solution to the weaknesses of democracy seems to be more democracy. Most of the legal decisions and electoral laws governing the United States embrace the notion that participation ought to be universal but voluntary and that public discourse ought to be unfettered and wide open. That, so the theory goes, is the best guarantee that government does what society wants.

WHAT IS PUBLIC OPINION?

public opinion

Citizens' attitudes about political issues, personalities, institutions, and events.

Public opinion may be understood on both aggregate and individual levels. The term *public opinion* itself refers to an aggregate—the public. It is, however, the accumulation of millions of individuals' expressions of their opinions, attitudes, and choices.

There are many different procedures for aggregating individual opinion, including voting, town meetings, protests, and other forms of political participation as well as public-opinion polls. The aggregate expression of people's

3   William Riker, *The Art of Political Manipulation* (New Haven, CT: Yale University Press, 1986).

choices or opinions is rarely unanimous; instead, the term *public opinion* is usually shorthand for what most people want or think—in other words, majority rule.

Aggregate opinion may not always appear rational, but there is power in numbers. The basic idea behind democracy holds that the sum of many millions of votes is a better outcome than the decision of a small number of people. This idea is brilliantly expressed in Condorcet's jury theorem. The Marquis de Condorcet, a French political philosopher of the eighteenth century, argued that the majority of a jury would more likely reach the right decision in a trial than would a single individual who heard the same evidence. Every person would like to make the right decision, but there is some chance that an individual will make a mistake. Adding up the judgments of many separate individuals, however, reduces the probability of a mistake. A majority of a 12-person jury, then, is less likely to reach the wrong decision than a single individual. And millions of voters are even more likely to produce the right verdict.[4] Democracy works, then, because voting is an efficient way of collecting the knowledge widely held in society.

This idea was rediscovered at the beginning of the twenty-first century, as new information technology expanded the opportunities for millions of people to express their opinions on virtually any matter. Firms such as Amazon aggregate the millions of decisions made by consumers to figure out who is likely to buy particular products. There is wisdom in masses, a lesson borne out in markets and democracy.[5]

Public opinion can also be understood at the level of individuals. For example, votes cast during elections, answers to surveys, and letters and emails to members of Congress reflect how individuals think and behave politically. Aggregate public opinion, after all, is the collection of these many expressions. An individual's political opinion depends on three factors: (1) the individual's basic preferences (what he wants), (2) his beliefs about the current circumstances and the consequences of different courses of action, and (3) the choices presented. A person will make a choice among the options presented, say, in an election or on a survey, because she wants a certain outcome (such as higher income or better education) and because she believes that a given option is the best among the alternatives. The choices offered in any situation are usually few—Democrat or Republican, a proposed bill versus the status quo, vote yes or vote no, get involved or stay at home. The significance of the individual's actions stems from *why* he chooses one of the alternatives.

---

4 Marquis de Condorcet, "Essai sur l'application de l'analyse à la probabilité des décisions rendues à la pluralité des voix," http://gallica.bnf.fr/ark:/12148/bpt6k417181 (accessed 8/7/19). Condorcet also argued that democracy has a weakness in that it need not always produce a definite majority-rule winner and may be manipulated by a clever agenda setter. This idea was rediscovered in the middle of the twentieth century by the Nobel Prize–winning economist Kenneth J. Arrow in *Social Choice and Individual Values* (New York: Wiley, 1951).

5 See Cass R. Sunstein, *Infotopia: How Many Minds Produce Knowledge* (Oxford: Oxford University Press, 2006).

Preferences and Beliefs

Preferences and beliefs are complex. Preferences reflect what people want, such as material goods and money, as well as people's values, such as justice and morality. Income is often taken as the basis for political preferences. People want to have higher income: other things being equal, they want lower taxes and more government spending on programs that benefit them directly. However, moral values, which are shaped by religion, family, and social conscience, also influence the way Americans behave.[6] These two factors—economic self-interest and social or moral values—are viewed as the basis for people's preferences in the political or public arena.

Preferences also are characterized by intensity: *how much* individuals want a certain outcome or care about a given issue. It is impossible to compare intensity of preferences directly—for instance, to say that one person wants something twice as much as someone else. But some people do have more intense preferences than others. Those who have strong opinions are more likely to express their views and take political action than those who do not. Also, public-opinion polls reveal that some people care more about some issues, such as taxes, while others care more about other issues, such as abortion.

Beliefs reflect what people know and how they understand the world and the consequences of their actions. An individual who has developed expertise about a topic usually will have more certainty about the choices involved and the consequences of different actions. However, strong beliefs about politics are not necessarily based only on fact. Often in politics, people have strong convictions about specific issues that are based on the intensity of their general political views. They may ignore facts that don't fit their theories. Thus Democrats and Republicans may observe the same event, such as a political debate, and come to opposite conclusions about who won. And public figures may, in the face of strong scientific evidence, reject the science if it does not favor their own political position. As in other aspects of life, people often find it easier to stick to their political beliefs than to change their minds.

Choices

Whether and how individuals' preferences and beliefs are expressed depends, ultimately, on a third component of opinion: the choice offered. We never really observe an individual's preferences and beliefs. Rather, we observe how she responds to the alternatives presented by a given situation or issue. In a public-opinion survey, respondents answer the questions put to them, which usually reflect important issues at a given time. In elections, we choose among the candidates or parties. Those candidates have taken stands on many different issues—taxes, spending, national defense, welfare, abortion, and so on. However, we

---

6   Ben J. Wattenberg, *Values Matter Most: How Republicans or Democrats or a Third Party Can Win and Renew the American Way of Life* (New York: Simon & Schuster, 1995).

cannot mix and match the different positions. If one candidate favors low taxes and anti-abortion policies and another favors high taxes and pro-choice policies, then the only choices are between those two clusters of policies. If a voter wants low taxes and is pro-choice, there is no candidate who reflects the cluster of policies (or perhaps ideology) that the voter prefers.

Moreover, some issues may not even be on the political agenda. An issue that is potentially of broad concern but has not yet reached the public arena is called *latent*. Because the issue is not on the agenda, there is no opportunity for people to express their preferences on it. Consider the following example. Throughout the 1930s and 1940s, the national Democratic leadership strove to keep race relations out of the Democratic Party platform in order to keep southern Democrats in the party. Yet race in the 1930s and 1940s was an issue on which most people had well-formed opinions. In 1948, when Minneapolis mayor Hubert Humphrey proposed a plank to the Democratic Party's national platform calling for desegregation, certain key southern politicians left the party to form a separate one (the Dixiecrats) espousing states' rights and segregation. These actions moved race from a latent issue to one at the forefront of the national agenda.

In contrast, some issues are so removed from public debate that many people would have difficulty formulating clear opinions about them because they have never thought about them. The process through which issues are vetted and debated publicly, then, is also key to the formulation and expression of public opinion. Americans had debated the question of race relations for centuries before the 1948 election, and they continue to debate the matter today, as seen most recently in 2020 during the national protests against racism and police brutality in the wake of the killing of George Floyd, a Black man, by a White police officer. Other potentially contentious issues receive little public debate. For example, in 1860 the Southern states decided to secede, or separate, from the United States. A similar independence movement seems unthinkable in the United States today and has not been actively discussed. But dissolution of the United States is not impossible. In fact, other developed countries are struggling with this issue currently: Scotland has threatened to leave the United Kingdom, and Catalonia has voted to leave Spain. One might imagine similar independence movements in the United States, but there has been little serious discussion on the topic. Were separatism to be put on a public-opinion poll today, many people likely would decline to give an opinion. But if there were extensive debate on the matter, people would eventually discover where their preferences lie.

The choices offered to people in elections, polls, town meetings, and other venues shape how preferences and beliefs are expressed in democratic politics. Public opinion, then, is never the pure expression of preferences but rather revealed preference—the choices among a given set of issues and alternatives.

Variety of Opinion

The term *public opinion* might suggest that all people are of the same mind. As we've noted, that is rarely the case. The term is really a shorthand description of the variety of opinions in society on a given question. One segment of the population supports the president, a second segment opposes him, and a third is unsure. A percentage of people are for a given bill in Congress, and a percentage are against it.

In some cases, Americans do hold common views on questions vital to governance and society. For example, there is consensus on the legitimacy of the U.S. Constitution, on the principle that no one is above the law, and on the idea that the outcomes of elections determine who governs. These commonly held opinions and values ensure peaceful transitions of government after each election and respect for laws produced by a legitimately chosen government.

There is also wide agreement on fundamental political values, such as equality of opportunity, liberty, and democracy.[7] Nearly all Americans agree that all people should have equal rights, regardless of race, gender, or social standing. Americans hold a common commitment to freedom. People who live in the United States are free to reside where they want, travel where they want, work where they want, say what they want, and practice whatever religion they wish, including no religion at all. And Americans have an undying belief in democracy—that whenever possible, public officials should be chosen by majority vote.[8]

On most matters that come before the government, however, the public does not hold a single view. Opinions are usually divided between those who support the government or a proposed action and those who do not. Politicians are still attuned to public opinion when it is divided, but what matters most are the balance and direction of opinion. What do the majority of their constituents want? Which way is opinion trending? Is it possible to find a popular middle ground?

People express their views in a variety of ways. Constituents contact their members of Congress through letters, phone calls, emails, and even personal visits to the members' offices. Most questions before Congress elicit little reaction from the public, but some issues start a maelstrom of objections. During the week of January 30, 2017, Congress set a new record for phone calls received in one day: 1.5 million. Most of the calls concerned President Trump's nominations to cabinet positions, such as Betsy DeVos for secretary of education.[9] People may also express their opinions more publicly through blogs, letters to newspapers, and op-ed pieces; in conversations with others; with lawn signs and bumper stickers; by working on campaigns; by giving money to candidates, groups, and party organizations; and most simply, by voting.

Such expressions of opinion are not always easy to interpret. If a constituent votes against a member of Congress, is it because she disagrees with a controversial bill that the legislator supported, because she decided to vote against all politicians from the legislator's party, or for some other reason?

---

7   See Louis Hartz, *The Liberal Tradition in America: An Interpretation of American Political Thought since the Revolution* (New York: Harcourt, Brace, 1955).

8   For a discussion of political beliefs of Americans, see Everett Carll Ladd, *The American Ideology: An Exploration of the Origins, Meaning, and Role of American Political Ideas* (Storrs, CT: Roper Center, 1994).

9   Kathryn Schulz, "What Calling Congress Achieves," *New Yorker*, March 6, 2017, www.newyorker.com/magazine/2017/03/06/what-calling-congress-achieves (accessed 3/2/20).

Political scientists and political consultants try to provide more refined and structured descriptions of public opinion using surveys. Public opinion on a given issue can be thought of as the distribution of opinion across the different options that government might pursue. Likewise, public opinion may represent the division of support for a leader or party. Survey results help us gauge where majority support lies and how intensely citizens across the spectrum hold their views. Increasingly, politicians rely on opinion polls to anticipate the effects of their decisions, to identify issues and policies on which they have opportunities to gain political support at the expense of the opposing party, and to develop ways to blunt any objections to controversial decisions. Answering a survey, then, can be a form of political action because it may influence political decisions.

A set of exclusive options that capture the range of opinions on a given issue is called a *variable*. For example, one might want to know whether people support the president. A survey can count how many people support the president, but support alone does not summarize all attitudes; it is only half of the variable. We can reformulate the question by counting the number of people who *support* the president, the number of people who *do not support* the president, and the number of people who *have no opinion* or *neither support nor oppose* the president. Such a dichotomy is perhaps the simplest variable, but also the most common: support or oppose, favor or not, yes or no.

Often, however, people think about politics in more subtle terms. Consider the debate over the legality of abortion. In the immediate aftermath of the *Roe v. Wade* decision, survey researchers sorted people into two polar positions—pro-life and pro-choice—and measured the percentage of respondents identifying as pro-life or as pro-choice or as having no opinion. As social scientists continued to study the politics of abortion, it became clear that people had more nuanced opinions and saw a much wider range of possible government policies. As a result, survey researchers developed more refined questions to ascertain the conditions under which people would and would not allow abortion. Would a respondent allow abortion for teenagers if their parents did not consent? What about cases of rape or incest? What if the pregnancy endangered the mother's life? Such refinements have allowed the public to express its preferences more precisely on this issue.

Opinions take a variety of forms, depending on the issue. It is helpful to keep in mind a few common examples in thinking about this subject.

- *Evaluations of those in government and other institutions.* Survey researchers use a variety of questions to gauge support for or opposition to the government. They ask about approval of the job that the president is doing, the job that Congress and its individual members are doing, and the job the Supreme Court is doing. At elections, voters express their support for and opposition to members of government directly through their votes. In political science as well as other disciplines, similar questions target social and economic institutions and leaders.

- *Assessments of public policies.* Do you support or oppose a given policy? Do you think a problem is important or not? What is the most important problem that government should address? How people answer such questions depends on the choices that are presented and the immediate circumstances. The distribution of respondents' views on specific issues may break along lines of political orientation if the issues directly affect partisan groups or derive from political debates between parties or ideological groups. For instance, a bill that would alter wages for public employees affects unions directly and thus touches a core constituency of the Democratic Party. So, we might find that Democrats are more likely to view this issue in a certain way.

- *Assessments of current circumstances.* Is the economy performing well or poorly? Is crime high or low? Is the country headed in the right direction? Such questions might seem to have clear-cut, objective answers, but opinions will differ depending on each individual's experiences and what she has read or heard through the media.

- *Political orientations.* The two most important indicators of individuals' general political orientations are party identification and ideology. Do you consider yourself a Democrat, a Republican, of another party, or of no party in particular? Do you consider yourself liberal, moderate, or conservative? These concepts capture general political orientations that are usually quite stable. Researchers have shown that party identification predicts voting preferences very well and correlates strongly with evaluations of those in office. Party identification often acts as a filter, a tinted lens that colors the way people view the world and interpret information. Immediately after an election, supporters of the winning party express greater optimism about the economy, about global affairs, and even about their own personal finances. And as we mentioned earlier, often a Democrat and a Republican will view a presidential debate differently, with the Democrat concluding that the Democratic candidate clearly won and the Republican concluding the opposite.

We can characterize the variation in public opinion by measuring the percentage of people who choose each option of a variable. A bar chart provides one way to display the distribution of public opinion: the height of each bar represents the percentage of people choosing each outcome of a variable, and the sum of these percentages equals 100 percent. Typically, we care about which option receives the most support (a plurality) or the support of a majority. In the 2020 presidential election, Joe Biden won 51 percent of all votes cast, while Donald Trump won 47 percent of all votes cast. Third-party candidates received 2 percent of the vote. Unlike the 2016 election, when Clinton won 48 percent of all votes and Trump 46 percent, Biden captured an outright majority of ballots of those voting. Political observers often view the size of the winner's vote margin as an indication of support for his or her policies and ideologies.

Survey data can provide more subtle and varied measures of public attitudes and political orientations than voting data can. Consider ideology (which we discuss in more detail later in this chapter). According to a Gallup poll in January 2020, 37 percent of Americans described themselves as conservative, 35 percent as moderate, and 24 percent as liberal. Another 5 percent do not think of themselves in these terms.[10] For an indicator such as ideology, then, no single camp has a clear majority, but we can say that self-described conservatives outnumber self-described liberals.

Polarization. One particularly important debate about public opinion today concerns ideological polarization. Observers have often argued that the public is deeply divided into very conservative and very liberal groups, with relatively few people in the middle, and that this view of "two Americas" holds true for questions about ideology and across a wide range of issues, such as taxation, health care, education, and foreign affairs. Political scientists Morris Fiorina, Jeremy Pope, and Samuel Abrams tackled this alleged polarization in their 2010 book *Culture War? The Myth of a Polarized America*. The co-authors made simple bar charts to describe the distribution of public opinion in the United States. Rather than a deep divide, they found that on most issues Americans are centrists—either moderate or leaning somewhat to the right or left. This finding has important implications for the ability to reach consensus in public debate. It also raises an even more elusive puzzle: although most Americans are centrists, most representatives in Congress vote either on the very liberal or on the very conservative end of the spectrum. The public, then, is not polarized, but Congress is. (See Analyzing the Evidence on pp. 402–3.) Why is this the case? Political scientists have suggested that polarization in government owes to (1) the nature of the debate in Washington and the choices put before Congress; (2) institutional factors, such as the organization of parties in Congress; or (3) the election process, including who votes and who doesn't, primary elections, and campaign contributors. The debate over this question has yet to reach a definitive resolution.[11]

Just as we do not think of public opinion as a consensus, we do not think of the public as monolithic. American society is a hodgepodge of different ethnic and racial groups; Americans differ greatly in educational attainment, income, and religion. The U.S. census, conducted every 10 years, measures variations in housing, family, employment, and other demographic characteristics. The Census Bureau also conducts monthly surveys measuring such activities as communication, employment, and voting. These data provide a rich picture of the diversity and complexity of American society. For example, 18 percent of Americans claim Hispanic ethnicity, 13 percent are Black or African

10 Lydia Saad, "The U.S. Remained Center-Right, Ideologically, in 2019," Gallup, January 9, 2020, https://news.gallup.com/poll/275792/remained-center-right-ideologically-2019.aspx (accessed 3/2/20).

11 For five different views, see Morris P. Fiorina, Samuel J. Abrams, and Jeremy C. Pope, *Culture War? The Myth of a Polarized America*, 3rd ed. (New York: Longman, 2010); Nolan McCarty, Keith T. Poole, and Howard Rosenthal, *Polarized America: The Dance of Ideology and Unequal Riches* (Cambridge, MA: MIT Press, 2006); Gary C. Jacobson, *A Divider, Not a Uniter: George W. Bush, the American People, the 2006 Election, and Beyond* (New York: Longman, 2007); Alan Abramowitz, "Constraint, Ideology, and Polarization in the American Electorate" (paper, Annual Meeting of the American Political Science Association, Chicago, IL, August 30–September 2, 2007); and Stephen Ansolabehere, Jonathan Rodden, and James M. Snyder Jr., "Purple America," *Journal of Economic Perspectives* 20, no. 2 (Spring 2006): 97–118.

Is the Public as Polarized as Congress?

Contributed by
**Edward G. Carmines and
Eric R. Schmidt**
Indiana University

Among Republican and Democratic elected officials, polarization has grown sharply in recent years, and compromise has been increasingly rare on Capitol Hill. Data on roll-call votes in Congress since 1789 suggest that the parties in Congress have become dramatically more polarized in recent decades, drawing comparisons to earlier, more contentious periods of American history.[1]

Some observers wonder if these trends imply that Americans are on the brink of a "second civil war."[2] However, there is debate over whether the *public* is as polarized as Congress. Some analysts argue that voters are far more moderate than their members of Congress. If that were true, we would expect the public to prefer that the parties compromise more often than they actually do.

Over the past 13 years, researchers at Indiana University have repeatedly surveyed eligible voters on whether members of Congress should "stand up for their principles no matter what" or "compromise to get things done."[3] The figure below shows the percentages of the public, from 2007 to 2019, that advocated compromise over principles. It appears that the public as a whole remains evenly divided on principled versus bipartisan lawmaking.

Americans Preferring "Compromise" over "Principles" in Congress

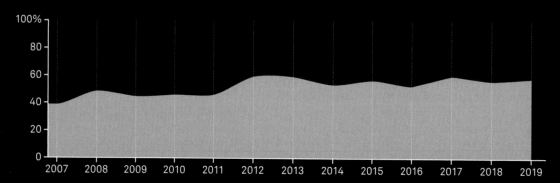

However, when we look at Republican and Democratic voters separately, the results are much more interesting. The figure below shows the percentage of voters from each party who support compromise lawmaking. We see a few trends.

1 Nolan McCarty, Keith T. Poole, and Howard Rosenthal, *Polarized America: The Dance of Ideology and Unequal Riches* (Cambridge, MA: MIT Press, 2006).

2 Ronald Brownstein, *The Second Civil War: How Extreme Partisanship Has Paralyzed Washington and Polarized America* (New York: Penguin, 2007).

3 In 2007, 2009–11, and 2013–19, this question was asked as part of the Cooperative Congressional Election Study (CCES). In 2008 and 2012, it appeared as part of the Cooperative Campaign Analysis Project (CCAP).

Eligible Voters Preferring "Compromise" over "Principles" in Congress, by Party and Political Attentiveness

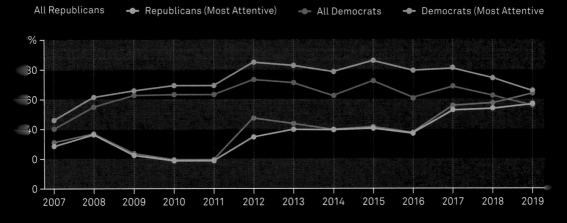

First, until 2019, Democratic voters were consistently more supportive of compromise than Republican voters. This was the case when the Democrats controlled both chambers of Congress from 2007 to 2011, when the Republicans gained control of the House (but not the Senate) from 2011 to 2015, and when the Republicans took control of both chambers in 2015. However, the gap has closed since President Trump's election in 2016.

Second, since Trump's election Republican voters have become more—not less—supportive of compromise. Trump's presidency marks the first years in our analysis where more than 50 percent of Republican voters preferred compromise. Especially remarkable is that this pattern persisted in 2019, when the Democrats retook control of the House. As our 2019 data were being collected, House Democrats were pursuing impeachment against President Trump, and on December 18, 2019, the House passed two articles of impeachment. However, this did not attenuate Republicans' newfound support for compromise.

While Republicans and Democrats *currently* support compromise at similar rates, this was not true for most of our series. Rather, responses have tended to fluctuate based on which party controls Congress. For example, Republican voters were most reluctant to compromise when the Democrats controlled both chambers of Congress (2007–11). This would seem to be the moment when refusing to compromise guaranteed that Republicans would receive their least-preferred outcomes. Had more Republican elected officials (and their voters) supported compromise, the public might have enjoyed more moderate policies with stronger bipartisan support.

You might ask whether Republican and Democratic voters who care about political outcomes reject compromise at similar rates. After all, if you follow current events most of the time, it is probably because your party's positions matter to you. Perhaps where Republicans and Democrats have similarly high levels of political interest, they are equally suspicious of compromise.

This is not what we find. The graph above also isolates partisans who are especially attentive to current affairs (see the light blue and orange lines). Remarkably, the gap in support for compromise has been even more extreme for the most attentive partisans. Since 2010, more than 65 percent of highly attentive Democrats have reported a preference for compromise over principles. Meanwhile, highly

American, 6 percent are Asian, 2 percent are Native American, Native Hawaiian or other Pacific Islander, and 60 percent identify themselves as non-Hispanic White. Among people under 18, only 52 percent identify themselves as non-Hispanic White. One person of every eight living in the United States today was not born here. However, among people under 18, only 1 in 20 was born elsewhere. Although the large majority of Americans identify as Christians and most with some form of Protestantism, the single largest sect is Roman Catholicism. Almost 31 percent of adults in the United States have a college degree;[12] 14 percent did not complete high school. The United States is one of the richest nations on earth, but approximately 1 in 8 Americans lives in poverty. The most populous region of the country is the South, home to about 35 percent of the population.[13] In describing and understanding the attitudes, opinions, needs, and wants of the American public, we must remember that the public itself is fractured into many subgroups and interests.[14]

ORIGINS AND NATURE OF OPINION

To understand the meaning and origins of the public's opinions, we must have some sense of the basis for individuals' preferences and beliefs. Opinions are the products of one's personality, social characteristics, and interests. They mirror who a person is, what she wants, and her relationship to family and community as well as to the broader economy and society. But opinions are also shaped by institutional, political, and governmental forces that make it more likely that an individual will hold some beliefs and less likely that he will hold others.

Foundations of Preferences

Self-Interest. Individuals' preferences about politics and public policy are usually rooted in self-interest. Laws and other governmental actions directly affect people's interests—their disposable income, the quality of public services

---

12 U.S. Census Bureau, QuickFacts, www.census.gov/quickfacts/fact/table/US/PST045218 (accessed 2/12/20).

13 Sandra L. Colby and Jennifer M. Ortman, "Projections of the Size and Composition of the U.S. Population: 2014 to 2060," *Current Population Reports*, P25-1143, U.S. Census Bureau, March 2015, www.census.gov/content/dam/Census/library/publications/2015 /demo/p25-1143.pdf (accessed 8/8/19).

14 As an exercise, we recommend consulting the *Statistical Abstract of the United States* and constructing bar charts (distributions) for the following demographic variables: (1) household incomes, (2) residency (urban, suburban, and rural), (3) region, (4) race, and (5) religion. Note the largest category for each variable. For income, calculate the level of income such that half of the people have income below that level and half have income above it (the median).

they receive, the goods they buy, and personal safety, to give just a few examples. Thus when people express their political opinions, they react to the effects that government actions have on them personally.

Economic interests are perhaps the most salient preferences. Government policies, ranging from export and import rules to regulations to spending and tax policies, directly affect individual Americans' personal well-being. Taxes, for example, reduce disposable income. The average American family has an income of $105,000 (including wages and salaries, income from businesses, investment income, and retirement income) before taxes and $81,000 after taxes.[15] Those taxes, of course, pay for government programs like Social Security, Medicare, Supplemental Nutrition Assistance (SNAP), Medicaid, national defense, and other public goods. But not all families and individuals are taxed equally, nor do all benefit equally from government programs. The people at the high end of the income distribution—those with incomes above $120,000—made 55 percent of all income, but after taxes and government transfers of income that was reduced to 48 percent of all income. The households with incomes below $45,000 made 12 percent of all income, but after taxes and transfers that rose to 18 percent of all income.

Government regulations also affect people's economic self-interests. Such rules protect people from potentially harmful pollutants, protect consumers from potential harm, and create the property rights necessary to maintain a well-functioning market economy. But they also limit how people use their property and may raise the cost of operating a business.

The government is also directly involved in the labor market. Approximately 22 million people, 12 percent of the U.S. civilian labor force, work for federal, state, or local governments; another 1.4 million people are in the armed services.[16] Government spending constitutes a substantial share of the national economy; federal expenditures alone account for about 20 percent of gross domestic product (GDP).[17] Virtually every American has an interest in the government's role in the nation's economy and strong preferences about tax rates and spending priorities. Given the enormous influence of the federal government in the economy, assessments of the president and the party in power often correspond to how well the nation's economy performs.

Individuals' attitudes toward government also reflect their interests in their families, their civic and religious organizations, and their communities. Zoning laws and urban redevelopment programs shape the nature of neighborhoods, including the mix of commercial and residential housing and the density of

---

15 Congressional Budget Office, "The Distribution of Household Income, 2016," July 9, 2019, www.cbo.gov/publication/55413 (accessed 8/8/19).

16 Federal Reserve of Saint Louis, Economic Research, "All Employees: Government: Federal," https://fred.stlouisfed.org/series/CES9091000001 (accessed 8/8/19); and World Bank, "Armed Forces Personnel, Total," http://data.worldbank.org/indicator /MS.MIL.TOTL.P1 (accessed 8/8/19).

17 The GDP consists of the value of all goods and services produced in the United States. It is one measure of the nation's income.

low-income housing in any given area. Tax laws treat nonprofits, such as universities, religious organizations, and social clubs, differently from for-profit companies, making it easier for nonprofit organizations to exist. Family law affects how easy it is for families to stay together, what happens when they break down, and what rights and responsibilities parents have. Proposed changes in such laws bring immediate reactions from those affected.

Values. Much of what individuals want from their government is also rooted in values concerning what is right or wrong—our philosophies about morality, justice, and ethics. Our value systems originate in many places—from families, religion, education, social groups, and so forth—and often determine our preferences in particular circumstances. For example, values may shape beliefs about economic justice and preferences about how government and society should distribute or redistribute income. Americans generally believe in equal opportunity, an idea that has driven our society to try to root out discrimination in employment, housing, and education and to create a universal public education system. In some states, such as New Hampshire, Ohio, and California, courts have invoked this principle of equality to insist that the states equalize expenditures per pupil across public school districts.

Values also shape our notions of what is a crime and what is a suitable punishment. One of the most morally laden debates in American history focuses on capital punishment. Does the government have the right to take an individual's life, even if that individual has taken the life of someone else? An ancient sense of justice seems to call for exactly that: an eye for an eye. Other ideas of morality speak against capital punishment. And our values about the appropriate powers of government say that people must be protected against arbitrary and capricious acts of government. The possibility that the government could make an irreversible error has led some to claim that it should never have the power to take the life of an individual.[18]

Our values also reflect established social norms, analogous to common law. What, for example, is marriage? One might consider it an economic convenience, as defined by laws that tie taxes and inheritance to marital status. Most people, however, express more complex ideas of marriage, including whether same-sex marriages ought to be allowed. Such norms change over time. For example, a century ago interracial marriages were deemed unacceptable by most in American society, and most states adopted laws to prevent interracial marriage. It took a Supreme Court decision in 1967, *Loving v. Virginia*, to eliminate the last of these laws.[19] Gay rights advocates drew similar parallels in their struggle to legalize same-sex marriage, and they too made their arguments in the courts. In the 2015 case of *Obergefell v. Hodges*, the Supreme Court declared same-sex marriage—previously a state-level policy—a fundamental right nationwide.[20]

---

18 *Furman v. Georgia*, 408 U.S. 238 (1972).

19 *Loving v. Virginia*, 388 U.S. 1 (1967).

20 *Obergefell v. Hodges*, 576 U.S. ____ (2015).

Values often conflict with one another, as when a law or policy touches on different values in conflicting ways. An issue like capital punishment evokes our notions of how much power government ought to have over individuals, even criminals, and our fundamental ideas of justice and vengeance. A person might support capital punishment as a just response to a heinous crime but also think that government should not have the power to kill its citizens. At a societal level, conflicting values are particularly difficult to resolve—especially when the differences strike at fundamental principles of right and wrong.

By the same token, there are many values that unite us. If Americans had few common values or perspectives, it would be very difficult to reach agreement on particular issues. Over the past half-century, political philosophers and political scientists have reflected on what those values are and have settled on three important precepts. Americans almost universally agree with (1) the democracy principle (that majority rule is a good decision rule), (2) the importance of equal opportunity, and (3) the idea that the government is best which governs least.

Social Groups. Individuals' preferences about politics and government are rooted in a third source—social groups. We are connected to one another through social characteristics and groups that include family, neighborhood, language, race, and religion. People often describe themselves using such characteristics. These descriptors tap fundamental psychological attachments that go beyond self-interest and values, though they are often reinforced by our interests and values.

Social groups affect political preferences in two ways. First, people prefer political decisions that benefit their groups and, indirectly, themselves. Social groups affect our preferences simply because we are members of those groups. A group or organization, such as a union or a church, helps overcome the collective action problem. Each of us usually joins a group for some private benefit, but the group helps us attain a common benefit through collective action that we could not achieve acting alone. Our preferences, then, shift to maintain the group because of the benefits it gains for us.

Second, social groups can change our values and even our view of ourselves. Consider someone who finishes college and takes a job at a corporation as an employee to earn wages. Upon doing so, the person begins to take on the perspective of that organization. On one level, this is a matter of self-interest: as goes the corporation, so go the person's wages. But on a deeper level, people often internalize the collective value as well: when the corporation does well, we feel proud of our contribution and are motivated to work harder. We identify in this way with our churches, schools, towns and cities, ethnicities, and other groups.

The process through which social interactions and social groups affect our perspectives and preferences is called **socialization**. Most 18-year-olds already have definite political attitudes that they have learned from parents and grandparents, friends, teachers, religious leaders, and others in their social groups and networks. Of course, socialization does not end after leaving home. We continue to learn about politics and what we should think about complex political questions from our family members, coworkers, and others we see and speak with daily.

socialization

A process in which individuals take on their communities' perspectives and preferences through social interactions.

Socialization works in many ways. First, through socialization we learn what is going on in the community and even in national politics. Socialization also takes the form of education or instruction. Parents teach their children how to think about a problem, what is a right or wrong choice or action, and how to participate in politics. This is how we as humans have learned to survive and adapt. But it means that by the time we are adults, we have learned much about what we want government to do, what sorts of people we want in government, and even whether it is worth our while to participate. Sometimes, socialization takes the form of outright pressure to think or behave in a certain way. If an employer asks her employees to vote a certain way or to work for a certain candidate, that employer is using a position of power to influence how others in her social group behave. In these and other ways, social groups shape the way people think and how they behave in politics.

Political Ideology

Political decisions, especially those about public policies, are complex. It can be difficult to figure out how to translate one's interests and values into votes. Political discourse and debate, however, are often simplified as a conflict between different ideologies. An ideology is a comprehensive way of understanding political or cultural situations; it is a set of assumptions about the way society works that helps us organize our beliefs, information, and reactions to new situations. It ascribes values to different alternatives and helps us balance competing values. Political decisions usually involve trade-offs between values or interests, and belief systems such as conservatism and liberalism help us think through these trade-offs. As such, understanding different political ideologies can help us make decisions in political, social, or cultural settings. Ideologies are very handy simplifications of an otherwise complex world.

In the United States today, people often describe themselves as liberals or conservatives. Liberalism and conservatism are political ideologies that include beliefs about the appropriate role of government, ideas about public policies, and notions about which groups in society should properly exercise power. In earlier times, these terms were defined differently. Before the New Deal in the 1930s, the terms "liberal" and "conservative" were used infrequently in the United States. To the extent that they were used, they referred to their European counterparts—where a liberal was someone who favored freedom from government power and laissez-faire economic policy, and a conservative was someone who supported the use of governmental power and favored continued influence by the state and aristocracy in national life.

Today in the United States, the term **liberal** implies support for political and social reform; government intervention in the economy; expansion of federal social services; more vigorous efforts on behalf of the poor, minorities, and women; and greater concern for consumers and the environment. In social and cultural areas, liberals generally support abortion rights and oppose state involvement with religious institutions and religious expression. In international affairs, liberals usually support arms control, oppose the development

liberal

A person who generally believes that the government should play an active role in supporting social and political change and generally supports a strong role for the government in the economy, the provision of social services, and the protection of civil rights.

and testing of nuclear weapons, support aid to poor nations, oppose the use of American troops to influence the domestic affairs of developing nations, and support international organizations such as the United Nations. Of course, liberalism is not monolithic. For example, among individuals who view themselves as liberal, many support American military intervention when it is tied to a humanitarian purpose or comes in response to a significant threat to the security of the United States, such as the terrorist attacks of September 11, 2001.

By contrast, the term **conservative** describes those who generally support the social and economic status quo, wish to maintain existing social hierarchies and orders, favor markets as solutions to social problems, and are suspicious of government involvement in the economy. Conservatives believe that a large and powerful government poses a threat to citizens' freedoms. Thus in the domestic arena conservatives generally assert that solutions to social and economic problems can be developed in the private sector. Conservatives claim that government regulation of business is frequently economically inefficient and costly and can ultimately lower the nation's standard of living. As for social and cultural positions, many conservatives oppose abortion and support school prayer. In international affairs, conservatism has come to mean support for the maintenance of American military power. Like liberalism, though, conservatism is far from monolithic. Some conservatives support many government social programs. President George W. Bush, a Republican, called himself a "compassionate conservative" to indicate that he favored programs to assist the poor and the needy. Other conservatives oppose efforts to outlaw abortion, arguing that government intrusion in this area is as misguided as government intervention in the economy. An important strain of conservatism has its roots in populism, which generally is isolationist in international affairs, favors limited powers of government, and advocates social nativism. The real political world is far too complex to interpret in terms of a simple struggle between liberals and conservatives.

There are many other ideologies besides liberalism and conservatism. Libertarians, for example, seek to expand liberty above all other principles and wish to minimize government intervention in the economy and society. Other ideologies seek a particular outcome, such as environmental protection, or may emphasize certain issues, such as economic growth, while de-emphasizing other issues, such as abortion. Communism and fascism are ideologies that support government control of all aspects of the economy and society; these ideologies dominated politics in many European countries from the 1920s through the 1940s. Political discourse in the United States, however, has revolved around the division between liberals and conservatives for most of the last century.

Liberal and conservative differences manifest themselves in a variety of contexts. For example, the liberal approach to chronically low test scores and high dropout rates at a public high school might be to increase funding for teachers and reduce class sizes. The conservative approach might be to remove the school's administrators or fire its teachers, or even to close the school. To some extent, contemporary liberalism and conservatism can be seen as different blends of the fundamental American political values of liberty and equality. For liberals, equality is often the most important core value; they tolerate government intervention in such areas as college admissions and business decisions to help remedy

 conservative

A person who generally believes that social institutions (such as churches and corporations) and the free market solve problems better than governments do, that a large and powerful government poses a threat to citizens' freedom, and that the appropriate role of government is to uphold traditional values.

race, class, or gender inequalities. For conservatives, in contrast, liberty is the core value; they oppose most efforts by government, however well intentioned, to intrude into private life or the marketplace. This simple formula for distinguishing liberalism and conservatism is of course not always accurate. Conservatives, for example, sometimes seek more government intervention in social policy realms involving family, marriage, same-sex relationships, and abortion, whereas liberals tend to resist government regulation of such social relations.

Political scientists often think of liberal and conservative ideologies as anchors on a spectrum of possible belief systems. The Pew Research Center offers just such a classification in its American Values Survey, conducted annually since 1987.[21] The Pew survey asks respondents about a wide range of political, social, and cultural preferences, behaviors, and beliefs. Many of these beliefs cluster: for instance, people who believe in the literal truth of the Bible tend to be pro-life, favor cuts in taxes, and call themselves conservative. However, the more questions one asks, the more finely one may sort the respondents. Classifying people this way, the Pew center finds that a large plurality of Americans have just as many conservative views as liberal views. As discussed earlier, that is essentially what Morris Fiorina and his colleagues concluded about the degree of polarization in the United States—most people are quite moderate. The Pew surveys also document that the number of Americans who choose more liberal than conservative policy positions is greater than the number of Americans who choose more conservative policy positions than liberal ones. This is true even though those who choose the conservative label outnumber those who choose the liberal label. Why this is the case is an interesting puzzle.

Identity Politics

Ideology offers one lens through which people can discern where their political interests and values lie. Identity provides an alternative simplification of the political world. Political identities are distinctive characteristics or group associations that individuals carry, reflecting their social connections or common values and interests with others in that group. A harm or benefit to any individual with a given identity is viewed as a harm or benefit to all people with that identity. Common identities in politics include race and ethnicity, religion, and gender.

Identities are both psychological and sociological. At the psychological level, identities are attachments felt by individuals, and at the sociological level, identities function as collectives, such as racial groups, genders, or language groups. Unlike ideological politics, identities are absolutes. A person either is or is not of a certain group. And identity politics are often zero-sum: if one group gains, another group loses. The term *identity politics* is sometimes used today to refer to the politics of groups that have been oppressed and that seek to assert their rights. But the concept is much broader. *Political identity* does not simply describe the situation

---

21 The American Values Survey is available at www.people-press.org/values-questions (accessed 7/3/20).

of groups that have suffered some harm; it applies to any collective identity. In fact, political identity often has a very positive side as the glue that holds society together and as another way to overcome problems of collective action.[22]

Identity politics are quite obvious in the United States today. All citizens and many noncitizens identify themselves as Americans. During international sporting competitions, we root for athletes representing the United States because we identify with that country; and when those athletes win, as Americans we feel happy and proud. We may feel similarly when an American wins a Nobel Prize or makes a significant scientific discovery. The same is true for any country: people feel pride in the accomplishments of others from their own country.

One of the most salient political identities in the United States is identification with a political party. The authors of *The American Voter* (1960), a classic work of political science research on the social and psychological foundations of electoral behavior in the United States, characterize party identification as a stable psychological attachment usually developed in childhood and carried throughout one's adult life. Party identifications are, of course, shaped by interests and values as well as by current events, but partisanship also has deep roots in family, local culture, and other factors. Moreover, people commonly rely on their partisan identities in filtering information—for instance, when they decide who won a presidential debate. Party also has a unique hold on voting behavior. Even after taking into account self-interest, moral values, and other identities, partisanship remains one of the best predictors of how someone will vote.[23] (See the discussion of party voting in Chapters 11 and 12.)

In 2006, political scientists Alan Gerber and Gregory Huber of Yale University conducted an ingenious study showing how identity matters to people's preferences. By tracking the consumption behavior of people after elections, the researchers found that individuals who identified strongly with a particular party and whose party won the election spent much more money on durable consumer goods, such as washing machines and other appliances, than did individuals whose candidates lost or who did not identify strongly with any party. Behavioral economists and social psychologists have documented other such phenomena, such as the effect of sports teams' victories on feelings of happiness.[24]

This is not to say that party does not reflect ideological choices or self-interest: it does. But it is certainly also the case that party functions as a social identity. People who hold a specific identity often express a strong affinity for others of the same identity—for example, someone may vote for a candidate of the same ethnicity apart from, or in spite of, the sorts of laws she promises to enact. Political scientists call this preference for people of the same identity

22 Rawi Abdelal, Yoshiko M. Herrera, Alastair Iain Johnston, and Rose McDermott, "Identity as a Variable," *Perspectives on Politics* 4, no. 4 (2006): 695–711.

23 Angus Campbell, Philip E. Converse, Warren E. Miller, and Donald E. Stokes, *The American Voter* (New York: John Wiley, 1960).

24 Alan S. Gerber and Gregory A. Huber, "Partisanship and Economic Behavior: Do Partisan Differences in Economic Forecasts Predict Real Economic Behavior?" *American Political Science Review* 103, no. 3 (2009): 407–26.

Immigration by Continent of Origin

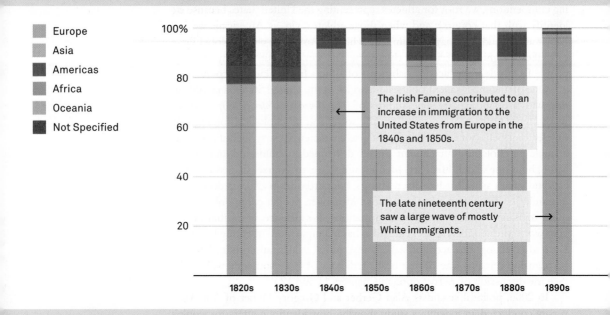

- Europe
- Asia
- Americas
- Africa
- Oceania
- Not Specified

The Irish Famine contributed to an increase in immigration to the United States from Europe in the 1840s and 1850s.

The late nineteenth century saw a large wave of mostly White immigrants.

1820s 1830s 1840s 1850s 1860s 1870s 1880s 1890s

TIMEPLOT SOURCE: Department of Homeland Security, "Yearbook of Immigration Statistics 2018," https://www.dhs.gov/immigration-statistics/yearbook/2018 (accessed 7/3/20).

descriptive representation, and it is an important subject in the area of race and elections. In fact, the Voting Rights Act tries to protect African Americans, Hispanics, and other racial and ethnic groups against discriminatory electoral practices that prevent those voters from electing their preferred candidates. Since the act was passed in 1965, the percentage of members of Congress who are African American and Hispanic has increased from 1 percent (6 in 1965) to 19 percent (101 in 2019).[25]

Race, gender, and social class all create strong identities that shape voting behavior. So do religion, region of the country, sexual orientation, occupation, and many other distinctive characteristics. In a provocative essay in the *Atlantic* following the 2000 election, commentator David Brooks wrote that Americans are divided not so much along ideological lines as they are divided along cultural lines.[26] His assessment gave rise to the argument that there are red (Republican)

25 Jennifer E. Manning, *Membership of the 116th Congress: A Profile*, CRS Report for Congress no. R45583 (Washington, DC: Congressional Research Service, 2020).

26 David Brooks, "One Nation, Slightly Divisible," *Atlantic*, December 2001, www.theatlantic.com/past/docs/issues/2001/12/brooks.htm (accessed 8/8/19).

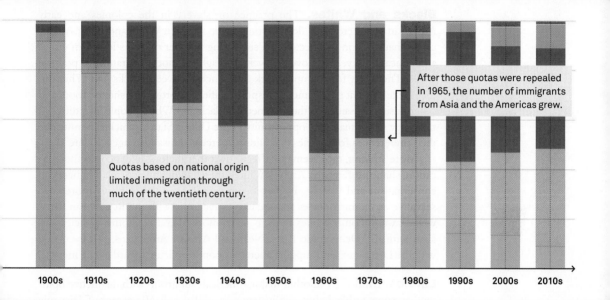

After those quotas were repealed in 1965, the number of immigrants from Asia and the Americas grew.

Quotas based on national origin limited immigration through much of the twentieth century.

| 1900s | 1910s | 1920s | 1930s | 1940s | 1950s | 1960s | 1970s | 1980s | 1990s | 2000s | 2010s |

and blue (Democratic) areas of the nation, with divisions based less on ideologies, interests, or economic considerations and more on who the voters are, where they live, and how they live. Brooks's characterization of red and blue America has proved enduring. Other differences occur across religious groups, between men and women, and between young and old. Some of these differences may be traced to self-interest, but most cannot. The explanations for differences in opinions and voting behaviors among social groups surely relates to the position of such groups in American society.

In this section, we first consider how racial and ethnic identity influences political attitudes. The United States is a racially and ethnically diverse country (as the Timeplot shows). Approximately 60 percent of people in the United States are native-born Whites. Within this population, people have a large variety of ethnic identities, usually tied to a country or culture in Europe from which their ancestors emigrated—Irish Americans, Italian Americans, Polish Americans, Jewish Americans, and so on. The remaining 40 percent of people in the United States consist of immigrants or of people who identify themselves as non-White or not of European origin. One in eight people in the United States were born in another country, and half of them are naturalized citizens (meaning that they fulfilled certain legal requirements that made them eligible for citizenship). As we mentioned in the previous section, according to Census data, 60 percent of people in the United States identify themselves as White non-Hispanic, 18 percent identify themselves as Hispanic; 13 percent identify themselves as Black or African American; 6 percent identify themselves as Asian. The strength of these identities and the relationships among these groups shape political attitudes.

Blacks and Whites. The practice of slavery in the colonies and early American states created a deep, lasting divide between White and Black Americans. That division is reflected in a staggering number of statistics, from wages and education levels to poverty levels to neighborhood integration to political ideals. There are, for example, stark differences between Blacks and Whites in their beliefs about government's responsibilities for providing shelter, food, and other basic necessities to those in need.[27] Black and White people also differ in their views of equality of opportunity in the United States, which can influence their preferences for policies that address perceived disadvantages (Figure 10.1).

More striking, race seems to affect how other factors, like income and education, shape preferences. Among Whites, there is a definite correlation between conservatism and income. Higher-income Whites tend to support more conservative economic policies and are likely to identify with the Republican Party, while lower-income Whites tend to favor more liberal economic policies and align with the Democratic Party. Nearly all African Americans, however, side with the Democrats and support liberal economic policies, regardless of income.

Latinos. Latinos are another major American subgroup with distinctive opinions on some public issues. For instance, in a 2014 poll, 60 percent of Hispanic voters approved of the Affordable Care Act, while 61 percent of non-Hispanic Whites disapproved—a significant disparity.[28]

Hispanic and Latino identities are often rooted in particular communities, such as Mexican American, Puerto Rican, and Cuban American groups.[29] Hispanic and Latino political identities are also strongly tied to particular issues of immigration.[30] These differences have led to heterogeneity in opinion on certain issues. Among Latinos, Cuban Americans have long been disproportionately

27 Pew Research Center, "The Black and White of Public Opinion," October 31, 2005, www.people-press.org/2005/10/31/the-black-and-white-of-public-opinion (accessed 8/8/19). See also Juliana Menasce Horowitz, Anna Brown, and Kiana Cox, "The Role of Race and Ethnicity in Americans' Personal Lives," Pew Research Center, April 9, 2019, https://www.pewsocialtrends.org/2019/04/09/the-role-of-race-and-ethnicity-in-americans-personal-lives/ (accessed 7/3/20).

28 Pew Research Center, "Wide Partisan Differences over the Issues That Matter in 2014," September 12, 2014, www.people-press.org/2014/09/12/wide-partisan-differences-over-the-issues-that-matter-in-2014 (accessed 8/8/19).

29 Gabriel R. Sanchez, "The Role of Group Consciousness in Latino Public Opinion," *Political Research Quarterly* 59, no. 3 (2006): 435–46; and Pamela Johnston Conover, "The Influence of Group Identifications on Political Perception and Evaluation," *Journal of Politics* 46, no. 3 (1984): 760–85.

30 Taeku Lee, "Race, Immigration, and the Identity-to-Politics Link," *Annual Review of Political Science* 11 (2008): 457–78.

Figure 10.1
DISAGREEMENT AMONG BLACKS AND WHITES

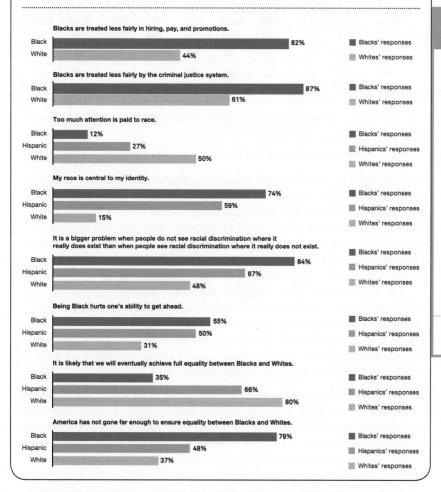

Blacks are treated less fairly in hiring, pay, and promotions.

Black	82%
White	44%

■ Blacks' responses
▨ Whites' responses

Blacks are treated less fairly by the criminal justice system.

Black	87%
White	61%

■ Blacks' responses
▨ Whites' responses

Too much attention is paid to race.

Black	12%
Hispanic	27%
White	50%

■ Blacks' responses
▨ Hispanics' responses
▨ Whites' responses

My race is central to my identity.

Black	74%
Hispanic	59%
White	15%

■ Blacks' responses
▨ Hispanics' responses
▨ Whites' responses

It is a bigger problem when people do not see racial discrimination where it really does exist than when people see racial discrimination where it really does not exist.

Black	84%
Hispanic	67%
White	48%

■ Blacks' responses
▨ Hispanics' responses
▨ Whites' responses

Being Black hurts one's ability to get ahead.

Black	55%
Hispanic	50%
White	31%

■ Blacks' responses
▨ Hispanics' responses
▨ Whites' responses

It is likely that we will eventually achieve full equality between Blacks and Whites.

Black	35%
Hispanic	66%
White	80%

■ Blacks' responses
▨ Hispanics' responses
▨ Whites' responses

America has not gone far enough to ensure equality between Blacks and Whites.

Black	78%
Hispanic	48%
White	37%

■ Blacks' responses
▨ Hispanics' responses
▨ Whites' responses

ANALYZING THE EVIDENCE

Although America's system of legally mandated racial segregation ended nearly half a century ago, its effects continue to linger. In contemporary America, Blacks and Whites have different perspectives on race relations. Do you think that Black-White differences have increased or decreased in the past few decades? Are these differences of opinion important?

SOURCES: Juliana Menasce Horowitz, Anna Brown, and Kiana Cox, "The Role of Race and Ethnicity in Americans' Personal Lives," Pew Research Center, April 9, 2019, https://www.pewsocialtrends.org/2019/04/09/the-role-of-race-and-ethnicity-in-americans-personal-lives/ (accessed 7/3/20).

Republican, while those of Mexican, Puerto Rican, and Central American descent identify more often as Democrats (Table 10.1). That difference reflects Cuban Americans' relationship with their homeland—many of them left Cuba because of the communist takeover there beginning in 1961—and the long-standing policy differences between Republicans and Democrats over U.S. relations with Cuba. It is interesting that the difference had largely vanished by 2008 but reemerged in 2015 and 2016, after the Obama administration announced that it would seek to normalize relations with Cuba. In the 2016 election, according to data from the Cooperative Congressional Election Study, Hillary Clinton won 52 percent of the Cuban vote nationwide (and just 48 percent of the Cuban vote in Florida, which

Table 10.1

CHANGING PARTY AFFILIATION IN THE LATINO COMMUNITY

BACKGROUND	2004 DEM. (%)	2004 REP. (%)	2008 DEM. (%)	2008 REP. (%)	2012 DEM. (%)	2012 REP. (%)	2016 DEM. (%)	2016 REP. (%)	2020 DEM. (%)	2020 REP. (%)
Cuban	17	52	53	20	35	37	51	37	36	29
Mexican	47	18	50	18	43	14	64	18	48	18
Puerto Rican	50	17	61	11	53	11	74	10	52	17

SOURCES: 2004–12: Jens Manuel Krogstad, "After decades of GOP support, Cubans shifting toward the Democratic Party," Pew Research Center, June 24, 2014, https://www.pewresearch.org/fact-tank/2014/06/24/after-decades-of-gop-support-cubans-shifting-toward-the-democratic-party/ (accessed 11/16/20); Pew Hispanic Center, https://www.pewresearch.org/hispanic/dataset/2018-national-survey-of-latinos/ (accessed 10/7/20); 2016, 2020: Cooperative Congressional Election Study, 2016, 2018, and Cooperative Election Study 2020.

has two-thirds of the Cuban Americans in the United States). However, she won 62 percent of other Latinos and Hispanics nationwide.[31] In the 2020 election, according to data from the Cooperative Congressional Election Study, Joe Biden won 62 percent of the Hispanic and Latino vote nationwide, and 65 percent of the Cuban vote nationwide, but just 48 percent of the Cuban vote in Florida. Looking across election years it is evident that the political alignment of Hispanics in the United States is quite fluid and varies by country of origin.[32]

As with Black identity, Hispanic and Latino identity tempers the way other demographic characteristics translate into political identities and values. Although higher-income Hispanics and Latinos identify more as Republican than lower-income Hispanics and Latinos do, the differences are not as stark as among Whites, and low-income Hispanics and Latinos are much more likely to identify as Democrats than low-income Whites.

Asians. The fastest growing racial or ethnic group in the United States is Asian Americans. Over the past two decades the total number of Asian Americans has more than doubled, and since 1980 they have risen from 1 percent of the population to 6 percent of the population today. Asian Americans are even more diverse than Hispanics; they come from vastly different cultures and countries—from China to Indonesia, from Japan to Vietnam to India, from Pakistan to the Philippines. These groups are often treated as having a common Asian identity, when in fact they are rooted in many different cultures. They have become part of American culture in their own, distinctive ways. As their numbers grow, Asian Americans are becoming a new political identity and voice in U.S. politics.

Gender. Men and women express differing political opinions as well. Women tend to be less militaristic than men on issues of war and peace, are more likely

31 Computed by the authors from the 2016 Cooperative Congressional Election Study. Stephen Ansolabehere and Brian F. Schaffner, 2017, "CCES Common Content, 2016," https://dataverse.harvard.edu/dataset.xhtml?persistentId=doi%3A10.7910/DVN/GDF6Z0 (accessed 7/3/20).

32 Computed by the authors from the 2018 Cooperative Congressional Election Study. Stephen Ansolabehere, Samantha Luks, and Brian Schaffner, 2019, "CCES Common Content, 2018," https://dataverse.harvard.edu/dataset.xhtml?persistentId=doi%3A10.7910/DVN/ZSBZ7K (accessed 7/3/20).

Table 10.2

DISAGREEMENTS AMONG MEN AND WOMEN ON ISSUES OF WAR AND PEACE

GOVERNMENT ACTION	APPROVE OF ACTION (%)	
	MEN	WOMEN
Killing of Iranian Major General Qasem Soleimani (2020)	63	43
Sending U.S. ground troops to fight Islamist militants in Iraq and Syria (2015)	52	41
U.S. missile strikes against Syria (2013)	43	30
Use of U.S. troops to attack a terrorist camp (2012)	71	55
Withdrawal of troops from Iraq (2008)	70	52
Use of U.S. troops to intervene in a genocide or civil war (2008)	53	42
Going to war against Iraq (2003)	66	50
Going to war against Iraq (1991)	72	53

SOURCES: Gallup, 1991, www.gallup.com/home.aspx; *Washington Post*, 2003, www.washingtonpost.com/politics/polling; Cooperative Congressional Election Study, 2008 and 2012, projects.iq.harvard.edu/cces/home; Langer Research, 2013, www.langerresearch.com; Pew Research Center, 2015, www.people-press.org; ABC News/Washington Post, 2020, www.langerresearch.com/wp-content/uploads/1210a4-Iran.pdf (accessed 3/6/20).

to favor measures to protect the environment, and are more supportive of government social and health care programs (Table 10.2). Perhaps because of these differences, women are more likely than men to vote for Democratic candidates, whereas men have become increasingly supportive of Republicans.[33] This tendency for men's and women's opinions to differ is called the **gender gap**. The gender gap in voting first became evident in the 1980 presidential election, where issues of war, peace, and women's equality dominated the political debate, resulting in an 8 percent gap between men and women who supported Ronald Reagan, the Republican candidate. While 55 percent of men supported him, just 47 percent of women did. This gap has persisted ever since, averaging about 8 percentage points. In the 2016 presidential election, Hillary Clinton was the first female major-party candidate, and the gender gap was the widest in history: Clinton won 54 percent of the votes of women, but only 41 percent of the votes of men. Four years later, the gender gap returned to 9 percentage points.

Why the gender gap emerged 40 years ago and persists today is a puzzle. Many scholars speculate that reproductive rights and abortion politics lie at the root of this division; yet a Pew Research Center poll from 2019 indicates little or no opinion gap between men and women on the abortion issue.[34] Rather,

 gender gap

A distinctive pattern of voting behavior reflecting the differences in views between women and men.

33 See Center for American Women and Politics, Eagleton Institute of Politics, Rutgers, State University of New Jersey, www.cawp.rutgers.edu/facts (accessed 8/8/19).

34 Pew Research Center, "Public Opinion on Abortion," August 29, 2019, www.pewforum.org/fact-sheet/public-opinion-on-abortion (accessed 9/29/19).

the gender gap appears to be more attributable to wages, to other differences between the ways men and women are treated in the economy and society, and to women's shared objective of ensuring equal treatment for all women.[35]

Religion. Religion shapes peoples' values and beliefs and, thus, their political ideologies, but it also serves as a strong identity quite apart from whatever specific values are at play. One of the clearest examples was the decades-long attachment of Catholics to the Democratic Party. This began in 1924 with the Democratic Party's nomination of Al Smith, a Catholic, for president of the United States. When Democrat John F. Kennedy became the country's first Catholic president in 1961, that bond was strengthened.[36] The lesson of Kennedy's election is clear: people are much more likely to vote for candidates of the same religion, even after controlling for ideology, party, and other measures of value. This pattern held true for born-again Christians and Jimmy Carter in 1976 and for Mormons and Mitt Romney in 2012.

Geography. Where we live also molds our sense of identity, affecting the ways we talk and dress. People from different regions of the country, even from specific states, often strongly identify with others from the same region or state and thus are more likely to trust them and to vote for someone from that background. We hold identities as westerners or southerners, or identify ourselves in terms of the economic characteristics of our place: the Pacific Coast states, the Breadbasket states (such as Nebraska, Kansas, and Iowa) or the Rust Belt (for example, Ohio, Pennsylvania, and Michigan). Some people hold negative stereotypes about those from other regions. An unfortunate consequence of the Civil War is a lasting discomfort that many people from the North and South still feel around one another—and that conflict was more than 150 years ago. We see these tensions expressed today in the debate over the place of symbols of that conflict, including the Confederate battle flag and Confederate monuments, in contemporary society.

Other geographic identities are tied to the type of community one lives in. The divisions between those in urban and rural areas often reflect self-interest—for instance, people from states with predominantly agricultural economies express stronger support for government farm subsidies. But geography also reflects different ways of living, and we tend to identify with people who live like us. Such differences are cultural. Where we shop, which restaurants we frequent, what we do in our spare time, and so forth—all are aspects of local culture that shape our identification with others of similar backgrounds and ways of living.

Residential segregation can also strengthen other aspects of identity politics. Because of disparities in housing costs across the country, people naturally segregate according to income based on what they can afford, which might strengthen social class identities. Income inequality also contributes to segregation by racial and ethnic identities. Those who live in highly segregated

---

35 An outstanding research paper along these lines is Ebonya L. Washington, "Female Socialization: How Daughters Affect Their Legislator Fathers' Voting on Women's Issues," *American Economic Review* 98, no. 1 (2008): 311–32.

36 See Campbell et al., *The American Voter*.

neighborhoods have much stronger identities with their own racial groups, and they also express much stronger prejudices against other groups.[37]

Outgroups. Some groups are defined not by who they are, but by who they are not: they are the outgroups in society. Discrimination is one manifestation of the treatment of an outgroup. Some industries, for example, will not employ workers who are not members of a union. Such "closed shop" rules benefit union members at the cost of non-union members. Often an outgroup is clearly identifiable and ostracized, leading to systematic discrimination or persecution. When the discrimination is intense, systematic, and long-held, the outgroup can itself develop a particular psychology. Social psychologist James Sidanius expresses this as a social dominance relationship in which more-numerous groups systematically discriminate against less-numerous groups, whose members develop a common identity and see their own situation in the treatment of others of their group. Writing about the particular psychology of African Americans in the United States, political scientist Michael Dawson calls this the "linked fate" of African Americans. It has been found in many other societies as well, such as Albanians in Italy.[38]

Discrimination, then, is the collective "bad" against which all in an outgroup must act. Even higher-income African Americans will thus be led by the collective needs and identities of their group to support policies that are likely to help large numbers of lower-income or underemployed African Americans. Groups that have experienced severe discrimination over very long periods are most likely to feel a sense of linked fate, which helps account for the persistence of a strong sense of common identity in some groups.[39]

Political, social, and economic discrimination is not limited to race and ethnicity. As we discussed in Chapter 5, the United States has witnessed struggles for equity for many different groups, including women, Catholics, Jews, the LGBTQ community, divorced fathers, and even urban residents. In all cases, members of these groups had to assert themselves politically to establish or protect their rights to property, to vote, or to equal protection of the laws. Because it is difficult for those with diminished political rights to work inside the legislative process, these people often had to pursue outsider strategies, including protests, propaganda, and litigation. Their rights were abrogated because they were treated as a class or group, and their identity was the target of discrimination.

37 Rene R. Rocha and Rodolfo Espino, "Racial Threat, Residential Segregation, and the Policy Attitudes of Anglos," *Political Research Quarterly* 62, no. 2 (2009): 415–26.

38 Being a numerical majority is not necessary. For over a century, Black in South Africa were oppressed by Afrikaners, even though the White population accounted for only about 10 percent of all people in the country. See also Felicia Pratto, Jim Sidanius, and Shana Levin, "Social Dominance Theory and the Dynamics of Intergroup Relations: Taking Stock and Looking Forward," *European Review of Social Psychology* 17 (2006): 271–320. See also Michael C. Dawson, *Behind the Mule: Race and Class in African-American Politics* (Princeton, NJ: Princeton University Press, 1995).

39 Paula D. McClain, Jessica D. Johnson Carew, Eugene Walton Jr., and Candis S. Watts, "Group Membership, Group Identity, and Group Consciousness: Measures of Racial Identity in American Politics?" *Annual Review of Political Science* 12 (2009): 471–85.

That same identity, however, also served as a source of power, leading these groups to organize and defend their political rights and identities.

PUBLIC OPINION AND POLITICAL KNOWLEDGE

When survey researchers poll the public, they seek to measure what government action the majority of Americans support, or which political party or faction enjoys the support of most people. But what do those responses really mean? At one level, they might mean that every respondent has weighed all sides of an issue and has made a reasoned judgment about which side is more consistent with his interests, values, or identity. Yet, from the advent of public-opinion research, observers have noted that most respondents have a stunning lack of knowledge about specific issues, even about the major political parties. Learned Hand, one of the most distinguished jurists in American history, described the problem of political knowledge as a collective action problem: people have so many other problems to worry about, and most issues are so complex, that simply studying the issues would leave us with little time to do anything else. It is far easier to rely on the wisdom of others.[40] Walter Lippmann, a great American journalist, wrote in the 1920s that this situation creates the opportunity for a learned class of elites to govern—not by winning elections, but by shaping how others think.[41]

One of the most troubling questions about American democracy is this: How is democracy possible when people seem to know so little? Here we present different perspectives on this matter.

Political Knowledge and Preference Stability

People constantly learn of new political events, issues, and personalities as they watch television, surf the web, talk to friends and family, or read the news. In our democracy we expect every citizen to have views about current issues and about who should be entrusted with the nation's leadership, and we expect people to cast informed votes about what government ought to do. Issues, however, come and go, and people are continually learning about new ones.

Some Americans know quite a bit about politics and many hold opinions on several issues. Few Americans, though, devote sufficient time, energy, or

---

40 Learned Hand, "Democracy: Its Presumptions and Realities" in *The Spirit of Liberty: Papers and Addresses of Learned Hand*, ed. Irving Dilliard (New York: Knopf, 1932).

41 Walter Lippmann, *Public Opinion* (New York: Harcourt, Brace, 1922).

attention to politics to really understand or evaluate the myriad issues that face us on a regular basis. Since the advent of polling in the 1930s, studies have repeatedly found that the average American appears to know little about current events or the basic facts of American government.[42]

Low levels of information lead to instability and incoherence in survey responses. Political scientist Philip Converse, in one of the most widely cited pieces of social science research, noted that most people do not seem to have clear opinions on important issues. Answers they gave to a question one year correlated poorly to answers they gave to the same question two years later, and the answers across issues did not seem to form a consistent pattern or system of belief. The incoherence of respondents' opinions was traceable to their level of education. Better-educated people gave more coherent answers and more stable answers over time. This research led social scientists to argue that most people are in fact not capable of expressing meaningful opinions on issues because of their low levels of information or cognitive ability.

Converse's views have represented an important pole in the debate over public knowledge and democracy. More recent research, including new analyses of Converse's data, has shown a markedly different picture: it is not that people are incapable of reasoning, but that surveys are imperfect instruments for measuring what people know and how they think. Vague or difficult questions, it turns out, explain much of the apparent incoherence that Converse's respondents expressed. When the data were reanalyzed and further studies were conducted, researchers found much more stability in people's preferences from year to year and much more coherence from issue to issue. Even respondents who had less than a high school education or did not know many common facts about government still expressed fairly coherent and stable preferences.[43] It was the survey, not the people, that failed the test.

Even so, there is something compelling about Converse's account. Why do people seem to know so little? What might be the consequences of low levels of information about current events and political institutions for the health of democracy in the long run?

---

42 How much the public knows and needs to know are two of the most important and hotly debated questions about American public opinion. The most important piece of research and expression of concern about the lack of knowledge of the American public is Philip E. Converse, "The Nature of Belief Systems in Mass Publics," in *Ideology and Discontent*, ed. David E. Apter (New York: Free Press, 1964). Converse argues that most people are not knowledgeable about and have little structure to their thinking about politics. For a contrary view, see Stephen Ansolabehere, Jonathan Rodden, and James Snyder, "The Strength of Issues: Using Multiple Measures to Gauge Preference Stability, Ideological Constraint, and Issue Voting," *American Political Science Review* 102, no. 2 (2008): 215–32.

43 See Christopher H. Achen, "Mass Political Attitudes and the Survey Response," *American Political Science Review* 69, no. 4 (1975): 1218–31; and Ansolabehere et al., "The Strength of Issues." Surveys may also ask about issues that are not of the highest concern to voters. See Vesla Weaver, Gwen Prowse, and Spencer Piston, "Too Much Knowledge, Too Little Power: An Assessment of Political Knowledge in Highly Policed Communities," *Journal of Politics* 81, no. 3 (2019): 1153–66.

Attending to the daily goings-on in Washington, the state capital, or the city council is costly; it means spending time, and often money as well, to collect, organize, and digest political information.[44] Because individuals anticipate that any informed actions they might take are not likely to make much difference and because the costs of informing oneself are rarely trivial, it may be rational to remain ignorant. Thus the rationality principle suggests that people can and will more profitably devote their personal resources—particularly their time—to more narrow personal matters. This idea is in turn suggested by the collective action principle, in which the bearing of burdens—such as the cost of becoming informed—is not likely to have much impact in a mass political setting. A more moderate version of "rational" ignorance recognizes that some kinds of information take little time or money to acquire, such as sound bites from television news shows or tweets from politicians. In such cases, an individual may become partially informed, but usually not in detail.

Precisely because becoming truly knowledgeable about politics requires a substantial investment of time and energy, many Americans seek to acquire political information and to make political decisions by using shortcuts, labels, and stereotypes, rather than by following current events closely. One "inexpensive" way to become informed is to take cues from trusted others—the local minister, the television commentator or newspaper editorialist, an interest group leader, friends, or relatives.[45] A common shortcut for political evaluation and decision making involves assessing new issues and events through the lenses of one's general beliefs and orientation. Thus if a conservative learns of a plan to expand federal social programs, she might express opposition to the endeavor without bothering to pore over the proposal's details.

These shortcuts are handy, but not perfect. Taking cues from others may lead individuals to accept positions that they would reject if they had more information. And general ideological orientations can be coarse guides to decision making on concrete issues. For example, what position should a liberal take on immigration? Should he favor keeping America's borders open to poor people from all over the world, or should he be concerned that open borders might create a pool of surplus labor that would permit giant corporations to drive down the wages of impoverished American workers? Many other issues defy easy ideological characterization.

Although it is understandable and perhaps inevitable, widespread inattentiveness to politics weakens American democracy in two ways. First, those who lack political information often do not understand where their political interests lie and thus do not effectively defend them. Second, the large number of politically inattentive or ignorant individuals means that public opinion and the political process can be more easily manipulated by the institutions and forces that seek to do so.

---

44 Anthony Downs, *An Economic Theory of Democracy* (New York: Harper and Row, 1957).

45 For a discussion of the role of information in democratic politics, see Arthur Lupia and Mathew D. McCubbins, *The Democratic Dilemma: Can Citizens Learn What They Need to Know?* (New York: Cambridge University Press, 1998).

As to the first of these problems, in our democracy millions of ordinary citizens take part in political life, at least to the extent of voting in national elections. But those with little knowledge of the issues, candidates, or voting procedures can find themselves acting against their own preferences and interests. One example is U.S. tax policy. Over the past several decades, the United States has substantially reduced the rate of taxation for its wealthiest citizens.[46] Tax cuts signed into law by President Bush in 2001 and mostly maintained throughout the decade provided a tax break mainly for the top 1 percent of the nation's wage earners, and further tax cuts by President Trump offered additional benefits to this privileged stratum. Polling data showed that millions of middle-class and lower-middle-class Americans who did not stand to benefit from the president's tax cuts seemed to favor them nonetheless.

These Americans' support for the tax cuts might have been based on principle. As political scientist Andrea Campbell argues in her work on the history of public attitudes toward taxes, public opinion toward taxation changed in the 1960s, and since then there has been a consistent ideological resistance to taxation among political conservatives and most moderates.[47] Support for the 2001 tax cuts among middle- and lower-income people might also have arisen out of ignorance or from following the wrong cue givers. Political scientists Larry Bartels, Paul Pierson, and Jacob Hacker, among others, attribute this state of affairs to a lack of political knowledge.[48] Millions of individuals who were unlikely to derive much advantage from President Bush's tax policy thought they would. Bartels has called this phenomenon "misplaced self-interest."[49] Knowledge may not always translate into political power, but lack of knowledge is almost certain to translate into political weakness. And according to the policy principle, a lack of knowledge and the concomitant political weakness often mean policy disappointment.

Campaigns and other forums for public discourse can change public attitudes on issues by altering the nature of the choices or by informing the public about the effects of certain policies. Continued debates around the tax issue throughout the 2008 and 2012 presidential campaigns brought about changes in public attitudes toward taxes, especially taxes on the wealthiest segment of the

46 One of the most detailed analyses of the distribution of the tax burden in advanced industrial democracies in the past half-century is Thomas Piketty and Emmanuel Saez, "How Progressive Is the U.S. Federal Tax System? Historical and International Perspectives" (NBER Working Paper 12404, National Bureau of Economic Research, August 2006), www.nber.org/papers/w12404 (accessed 7/3/20).

47 Andrea Campbell, How Americans Think about Taxes (Princeton, NJ: Princeton University Press, forthcoming).

48 Jacob S. Hacker and Paul Pierson, Winner-Take-All Politics: How Washington Made the Rich Richer—And Turned Its Back on the Middle Class (New York: Simon and Schuster, 2010).

49 Larry M. Bartels, "Homer Gets a Tax Cut: Inequality and Public Policy in the American Mind," Perspectives on Politics 3, no. 1 (2005): 15–31.

population. During the 2008 campaign, Barack Obama seized on the tax issue at a time when the economy was worsening and most voters' economic prospects looked bleak. He returned to that theme during the 2012 campaign, promising to raise taxes on the top 2 percent of income earners—those who make at least $250,000 a year. That promise was instrumental in both of Obama's successful election campaigns. In January 2013, confronting the possibility of potential automatic tax increases on all Americans, he was able to outmaneuver the Republican leadership in Congress and increase taxes on those with incomes over $400,000 per year—an increase that affected only 1 percent of the population, yet nearly failed to make it through Congress.

In his 2016 bid for the presidency, Donald Trump promised to simplify the U.S. tax code by reducing the number of tax brackets to three and cutting tax rates across the board. Once in office, Trump and the Republican majority in Congress successfully negotiated sweeping cuts in income taxes, a reduction in corporate income taxes, and cut the mortgage interest and state and local tax deduction. During the 2020 election, Democratic nominee Joe Biden attacked the Republican tax law and promised to raise taxes on those making over $400,000 a year and on corporate income.

Stability and the Meaning of Public Opinion

There is a great stability to public opinion in the United States. What people want government to do on specific issues and who people want to have in charge usually changes little from election to election. Political scientists Benjamin Page and Robert Shapiro's *The Rational Public* (1992) traces public attitudes since the 1950s and finds that, on most issues and political attitudes, aggregate public opinion is quite stable. For example, party identification for a large portion of the American public remains stable for life, as do notions of what is right and wrong, racial and ethnic identities, gender identities, and other cultural identities that are formed in childhood. Our occupations and educational achievement also shape our economic interests, which tend to be constant throughout our adult lives. Interests, identities, and values, in turn, influence attitudes about when and how government should act.[50]

One of the most important factors generating stability in public opinion is a fundamental truth about democracy: there is power (and stability) in numbers. Democratic theorists have long understood that aggregation counteracts the effects of political ignorance. When people do not fully know their interests,

---

50 Robert S. Erikson, Michael B. MacKuen, and James A. Stimson develop a similar view in their work *The Macro Polity* (New York: Cambridge University Press, 2001). A contrary line of thinking is expressed by authors such as John R. Zaller, *The Nature and Origins of Mass Opinion* (New York: Cambridge University Press 1992); and Scott L. Althaus, *Collective Preferences in Democratic Politics: Opinion Surveys and the Will of the People* (New York: Cambridge University Press, 2003). They argue that those with knowledge are influential in the aggregation of public opinions and that knowledge and information are not widely or evenly distributed in society. As a result, the electorate speaks with a decided accent.

they will make mistakes. Fortunately, when individuals' opinions and choices are aggregated, as they are in surveys or elections, those errors seem to average out. People may, for example, vote on the basis of how they are doing on a given day, without knowing the macroeconomic indicators such as unemployment and inflation rates. Some people are doing well economically; others are doing poorly. Adding up all those personal experiences, though, will lead to a collective sense of how society is doing. A wisdom of the masses thus emerges in public-opinion polls, election results, and other aggregates of people's preferences. More important, these aggregates are much more stable and more meaningful than individuals' opinions.

But public opinion is not static. At times in American history, the majority of Americans' opinions have changed dramatically and rapidly. Between 1945 and 1965, public opinion toward federal action to promote racial equality swung from majority opposition to majority support. This support translated into the passage of the Civil Rights Act and the Voting Rights Act as well as the integration of schools and other public places. And since the mid-1990s there has been a near about-face in public attitudes toward same-sex marriage. In 1996, Congress passed the Defense of Marriage Act, which defined marriage as a union between one man and one woman for the purpose of federal benefits. A CNN/USA Today/Gallup poll in 1996 showed that 68 percent of Americans opposed same-sex marriage and only 27 percent supported it. By 2019, though, a Pew poll found that 61 percent of Americans supported same-sex marriage and 31 percent opposed it.[51]

In both cases, public attitudes changed within the span of one or two decades. How and why does public opinion change? In part, the answer lies in the evolving positions of the candidates and parties and elite discourse. As party leaders, celebrities, and other elites debate an issue, the public often follows their cues and shifts sides. The answer also surely lies with public learning. As the public learns about an issue, the implications of government action and inaction become clearer, as does the right thing to do.

In turn, such evolutions in public opinion influence public policy. Political scientist James Stimson has provided a comprehensive assessment of the link between aggregate public opinion and public policy. His research tracks public opinion on a wide variety of issues from the 1950s to the present. When aggregate public opinion has shifted to the left, as it did in the 1960s, or to the right, as it did in the 1980s, public policy has generally followed suit. The high level of responsiveness of policy outcomes to changes in aggregate opinion suggests that the political system follows the general sense of aggregate opinion, or what Stimson calls the policy mood. This result, he argues, strongly suggests that "the magic of aggregation" provides a corrective for the typical citizen's low levels of knowledge.[52]

---

51 Pew Research Center, "Attitudes on Same Sex Marriage," May 14, 2019, www .pewforum.org/fact-sheet/changing-attitudes-on-gay-marriage (accessed 8/8/19).

52 Erikson et al., *The Macro Polity*.

SHAPING OPINION: POLITICAL LEADERS, PRIVATE GROUPS, AND THE MEDIA

The fact that many Americans are inattentive to politics and lack even basic political information means that there is a place for public debate and political discourse. Controversy educates us. Through debate, the average person comes to learn what is important and the information needed to make sensible decisions. Americans' general lack of information also creates opportunities for certain groups of elites to influence how the public thinks. Although direct efforts to manipulate opinion often don't succeed, three forces play especially important roles in shaping opinion. These are the government, private groups, and the news media.

Government and the Shaping of Public Opinion

All governments attempt, to a greater or lesser extent, to influence their citizens' beliefs. But the degree to which public opinion is affected by government public relations efforts is probably limited. The government—despite its size and power—is only one source of information in the United States. Very often, government claims are disputed by the media, interest groups, and at times by opposing forces within the government itself. Often, too, governmental efforts to manipulate public opinion backfire when the public is made aware of the government's tactics. Thus in 1971 the government's attempts to build popular support for the Vietnam War were hurt when CBS News aired its documentary *The Selling of the Pentagon*, which purported to reveal the extent of the government's efforts to sway popular sentiment—including planted news stories and faked film footage that had misrepresented the government's activities in Vietnam. These revelations undermined popular trust in the government's claims.

A hallmark of the administration of President Bill Clinton was the steady use of campaign-style techniques to bolster popular enthusiasm for White House initiatives. The president established a political "war room" similar to the one that operated in his campaign headquarters. In the presidential version, representatives from all cabinet departments met daily to discuss and coordinate the president's public-relations efforts. Many of the same consultants and pollsters who directed the successful Clinton campaign were also employed in selling the president's programs.[53]

After he assumed office in 2001, President Bush asserted that political leaders should base their programs on their own conception of the public interest, not on the polls. However, Bush still relied on a pollster to conduct a low-key operation, sufficiently removed from the limelight to allow the president to renounce polling while continuing to make use of survey data.[54] At the same

---

53 Gerald F. Seib and Michael K. Frisby, "Selling Sacrifice," *Wall Street Journal*, February 5, 1993, p. 1.

54 Joshua Green, "The Other War Room," *Washington Monthly*, April 2002.

---

time, the Bush White House developed an extensive public-relations program to bolster popular support for the president's policies, and even sought to sway opinion in foreign countries.

President Barack Obama, striving to maintain the political momentum from his 2008 election campaign, attempted to use social media to keep up the same enthusiasm for his legislative agenda. The Obama White House maintained a newsy website, a blog, a YouTube channel, a Facebook page, and a Twitter account, but many criticized the accounts' low level of actual engagement with the people. Each of these new media was being used like the old media—to talk at people rather than with them. Indeed, many White House reporters felt that the Obama press office was less accessible than its predecessors.[55]

President Donald Trump took media relations in a wholly new direction, relying heavily on social media, especially Twitter, to speak directly with the public. In the 2016 presidential primary elections, social media proved to be one of Trump's most distinctive campaign advantages over his Republican opponents. By the end of the primary season, Trump had 10.7 million Twitter followers, while Senators Marco Rubio and Ted Cruz each had 1.5 million followers, and Governor John Kasich had only 400,000.[56] Once in office, President Trump continued to rely on Twitter as a means of shaping public discourse. The strategy allowed him to talk around the mainstream media and put his own stamp on the news. President Trump rarely gave press briefings, and instead relied on his press secretaries to speak directly with the media. Sean Spicer, Trump's first press secretary, held daily press briefings. Press briefings became less frequent under his second press secretary, Sarah Huckabee Sanders, and his third press secretary, Stephanie Grisham, did not hold a press briefing for six months.[57] Instead of speaking with the press, President Trump relied on Twitter to get his message out. The president tweeted, on average, 300 times a month,[58] and the press frequently recirculated his tweets uncritically.[59]

55 Susan Milligan, "The President and the Press," *Columbia Journalism Review*, March/April 2015, www.cjr.org/analysis/the_president_and_the_press.php (accessed 3/3/20).

56 Statista, "2012 election: Twitter followers of Obama and Romney as of November 21," November 21, 2012, www.statista.com/statistics/243305/number-of-twitter-followers-of-barack-obama-and-mitt-romney (accessed 8/8/19).

57 Jordyn Phelps, "Trump White House hasn't held a traditional press briefing in 6 months," ABC News, September 11, 2019, https://abcnews.go.com/Politics/trump-white-house-held-traditional-press-briefing-months/story?id=65509975 (accessed 2/12/20).

58 Niall McCarthy, "Trump Has Never Been This Active On Twitter," Statista, October 7, 2019, www.statista.com/chart/19561/total-number-of-tweets-from-donald-trump (accessed 2/12/20).

59 Alexandria Neason, "On Twitter, News Outlets Amplify Trump's False Statements: Study," *Columbia Journalism Review*, May 3, 2019, www.cjr.org/politics/twitter-media-trump.php (accessed 2/12/20).

Private Groups and the Shaping of Public Opinion

The ideas that become prominent in political life are also developed and spread by important economic and political groups seeking to advance their causes. Rational political entrepreneurs pursue strategies that—in an application of the collective action principle—give the groups they lead a decided advantage in the political arena in comparison with latent, unorganized groups. In some instances, in the hope of bringing others over to their side, private groups espouse values they truly believe in. For example, this has been the case with anti-abortion activists who have campaigned against so-called partial-birth abortion, which led to the Partial-Birth Abortion Ban Act of 2003; proposed federal legislation that would ban all abortions after 20 weeks of pregnancy; and continued efforts at the state level to pass restrictions on abortions.[60] Proponents believed that prohibiting abortions under certain conditions would be a first step toward eliminating all abortions, something they view as a moral imperative.[61]

In other cases, groups promote certain issues in the service of furthering hidden agendas. One famous example is the campaign against cheap imported handguns—dubbed "Saturday night specials"—that was covertly financed by the domestic manufacturers of more expensive firearms. The campaign's organizers claimed that cheap handguns pose a grave risk to the public and should be outlawed. The real goal, though, was to protect the economic well-being of the domestic gun industry. A more recent example is the campaign against the alleged sweatshop practices of some American companies manufacturing their products in developing countries. This campaign is mainly financed by U.S. labor unions seeking to protect their members' jobs by discouraging American firms from manufacturing their products abroad.[62]

Typically, ideas are marketed most effectively by groups that have access to financial resources and sufficient skill to promote agendas that will win support. Thus the development and promotion of conservative ideas in recent years have been greatly facilitated by the millions of dollars that conservative corporations and business organizations (such as the U.S. Chamber of Commerce and the Public Affairs Council) spend each year on public information and "issues management." In addition, conservative business leaders have contributed millions of dollars to such conservative institutions as the Heritage Foundation, the Hoover Institution, and the American Enterprise Institute.[63] Many of the ideas that helped the right influence political debates were first articulated by scholars associated with institutions such as these. The Policy Principle box on p. 429 looks at

60 "An Overview of Abortion Laws," Guttmacher Institute, February 1, 2020, www .guttmacher.org/state-policy/explore/overview-abortion-laws (accessed 2/12/20).

61 Cynthia Gorney, "Gambling with Abortion," *Harper's Magazine*, November 2004, pp. 33–46.

62 David P. Baron and Daniel Diermeier, "Strategic Activism and Nonmarket Strategy," *Journal of Economics and Management Strategy* 16, no. 3 (2007): 599–634.

63 See David Vogel, "The Power of Business in America: A Re-appraisal," *British Journal of Political Science* 13, no. 1 (1983): 19–43.

Public Opinion on Climate Change

The federal government's role in environmental conservation stretches back to the early 1900s, with the creation of the National Park Service and other efforts to preserve natural beauty. In the 1970s, environmental policy became a major component of federal action, with new laws enacted under both Democratic and Republican administrations. Yet in the years since, as new scientific research has provided clearer evidence related to environmental hazards, conflicts have emerged over the government's proper role in protecting the environment.

Protest against the decision to withdraw from the Paris Agreement on climate change in 2018.

As scientists have learned more about the effects of human activity on the climate, the issue of climate change has risen on the national agenda with a correlated impact on public opinion. According to Gallup polls, in 1997 only 48 percent of Americans agreed that global warming was already occurring, but by 2017, 62 percent of respondents agreed with this statement.[1]

However, this shift may seem modest given the growing scientific consensus on this question. Sociologists Riley E. Dunlap, Aaron McCright, and Jerrod Yarosh emphasize that these changes in the aggregate do not tell the whole story. Instead, they call attention to what they refer to as "the political divide on climate change."[2] In 2017, 77 percent of Democrats agreed that climate change was already occurring, compared to only 41 percent of Republicans—a gap of 36 percentage points. In 1997, the gap between Democrats and Republicans on this question was only 4 percentage points. What happened?

Policy makers and researchers have undertaken efforts over the past two decades to inform the public about climate change. While skepticism of these messages has grown on the political right, Democrats are more likely to trust this news than they were in the past. Part of the explanation for this pattern appears to be that polarization on climate change is not really about climate change, but simply reflects the broader trend of party polarization in American politics.

This partisan gap in public opinion reached its height following the active involvement of the Obama administration in the 2016 Paris Agreement on climate change, a comprehensive international agreement signed by all 193 United Nations member countries and ratified by 178 as of June 2018. Many Democratic politicians heralded the agreement as a historic achievement, while many Republican elected officials expressed skepticism about the existence of climate change and argued that the treaty imposed unfair burdens on American companies. The issue is no less controversial today. The Trump administration undertook the complicated multiyear process of withdrawing the United States from the Paris Agreement.

The case of climate change illustrates some of the limits of public opinion in shaping policy. The collective action principle warns us that the playing field is not always level when it comes to which groups are able to organize effectively and further their policy goals. In fact, the preferences of the American public are often at odds with those of the organized interests that will bear the burdens of governmental regulations.

1. Lydia Saad, "Global Warming Concern at Three-Decade High in U.S.," Gallup, March 14, 2017, http://news.gallup.com/poll/206030/global-warming-concern-three-decade-high.aspx (accessed 3/6/20).
2. Riley E. Dunlap, Aaron M. McCright, and Jerrod H. Yarosh, "The Political Divide on Climate Change: Partisan Polarization Widens in the U.S.," *Environment: Science and Policy for Sustainable Development* 58, no. 5 (2016): 4–23.

how elites in government and private groups have influenced public opinion on climate change.

Although they usually lack access to financial assets that match those available to their conservative opponents, liberal intellectuals and professionals have ample organizational skills, access to the media, and practice in communicating and using ideas. During the past four decades, the chief vehicle through which liberal intellectuals and professionals have advanced their ideas has been the public interest group, a type of institution that relies heavily on voluntary contributions of time and effort from its members. Such groups include Common Cause, the National Organization for Women, the Sierra Club, Friends of the Earth, Union of Concerned Scientists, and Physicians for Social Responsibility.[64] In addition, research conducted at universities and liberal think tanks such as the Brookings Institution often provides the ideas on which liberal politicians rely.

The Media and Public Opinion

The communications media are among the most powerful forces operating in the marketplace of ideas. Most Americans say that their primary source of information about public affairs is news media—newspapers, broadcast and cable news, radio, and internet news providers. Alternatively, people may get their information from direct contact with politics, social groups, and family members or coworkers. Certainly, few people actually go to Washington to find out what's going on in American politics, and the number of people who have access to media outlets dwarfs the number of households that receive direct mail from organizations and elected officials. Personal conversation is also an important source of information, but people generally avoid controversial political topics in casual conversation.

The mass media, as the term suggests, can be thought of as mediators. They are the conduits through which much information flows. Through newspapers, radio, television, magazines, and the internet we can learn about what's going on in the world and in our government. Providing this opportunity to learn about the world and politics is the most important way the media contribute to public opinion.

Media outlets also are ubiquitous. Nearly every household in the United States (97.4 percent) has a television.[65] Nearly every county (94.5 percent) has at least one local newspaper.[66] The number of news programs has also expanded tremendously in recent decades. In the 1960s there were only three television

---

64 See David Vogel, "The Public-Interest Movement and the American Reform Tradition," *Political Science Quarterly* 95, no. 4 (Winter 1980): 607–27.

65 "Average number of televisions in U.S. homes declining," U.S. Energy Information Administration, February 28, 2017, www.eia.gov/todayinenergy/detail.php?id=30132 (accessed 3/3/20).

66 The University of North Carolina Hussman School of Journalism and Media tracks the presence of local newspapers in their online resource www.usnewsdeserts.com.

news outlets—CBS, NBC, and ABC. They aired evening and nightly news programs and allowed a half-hour slot for news from local affiliates. The rise of cable television in the 1980s brought a 24-hour news station, CNN; expanded news programming through PBS; and a network devoted exclusively to broadcasting the proceedings of Congress and government agencies, C-SPAN. Important competitors to the big three networks emerged, including Fox and the Spanish-language networks Univision and Telemundo. Today there is no shortage of televised news programming available at all hours.[67]

Technological innovations continue to push changes in political communication in the United States. As of 2018, almost 85 percent of American households have access to the internet at home, and 92 percent of households have a computer.[68] Conventional media—from the United States and around the world—have moved much of their content online, and they often provide it for free. The internet has also spawned new forms of communication, most notably blogs and Twitter, which provide platforms for anyone to have their say. Several websites, such as Google News and RealClearPolitics, are clearinghouses for traditional media, newswire stories, and blogs. This highly competitive media environment has radically changed the flow and nature of communication in the United States and the availability of information to the public. In Chapter 14, we discuss the media as a democratic institution at greater length. Our concern here is the media's role in how people learn about politics and public affairs.

Learning through mass media occurs both actively and passively. Active learning occurs when people search for a particular type of program or particular information: you turn on the nightly news to find out what has happened in national and international affairs or you search the web for information about your member of Congress. Passive learning may be just as important. Many entertainment programs discuss current affairs such as social issues or elections: you watch the program primarily for entertainment but gain information about politics at the same time. One study found that people learned as much from Oprah Winfrey as from the evening news.[69] Political advertising is perhaps the most common form of passive information. During the last month of national political campaigns, three or four political advertisements often air during one commercial break in a prime-time television program.

Mass media are our primary source for information about current affairs. They influence Americans' understanding of politics not just through the volume of information they provide but also through the choice of information they present and how they present it. Editors, reporters, and others involved in preparing the content of the news must ultimately decide what topics to cover, what facts to include, and whom to interview. Journalists usually try to present

67 See Stephen Ansolabehere, Roy L. Behr, and Shanto Iyengar, *The Media Game: American Politics in the Television Age* (New York: Macmillan, 1993).

68 U.S. Census Bureau, 2018 American Community Survey, Table S2801, https://data .census.gov/cedsci/table?q=S2801&tid=ACSST1Y2018.S2801 (accessed 3/3/20).

69 See Matthew Baum, *Soft News Goes to War: Public Opinion and American Foreign Policy in the New Media Age* (Princeton, NJ: Princeton University Press, 2003).

agenda-setting effect

The power of the media to focus public attention on particular issues.

priming

The use of media coverage to make the public take a particular view of an event or a public figure.

framing

The influence of the media over how events and issues are interpreted.

issues fairly, but it is difficult, perhaps impossible, to be perfectly objective. In fact, psychologists have identified two potential pathways through which media coverage shapes what people think. First, the news sets the public's agenda. Through this **agenda-setting effect**, the media cues people to think about some issues rather than others; it makes some considerations more salient than others. Suppose, for example, that the local news covers crime to the exclusion of all else. When someone who watches the local news regularly thinks about the mayoral election, crime is more likely to be his or her primary consideration, compared with someone who does not watch the local news. Psychologists call this **priming**.

Second, news coverage of an issue frames the way the issue is defined. Coverage of crime, to continue the example, may report on every murder that happens in a large city. Such coverage would likely make it seem that murder occurs much more often than it actually does. This in turn might heighten viewers' sense of insecurity or threat, leading to an exaggerated sense of risk of violent crime and increased support for tough police practices.[70] **Framing** refers to the media's power to influence how events and issues are interpreted.

Priming and framing are often viewed as twin evils. One can distract us from other important problems, and the other can make us think about an issue or a politician in a biased way. The cumulative effects of the media on public opinion depend ultimately on the variety of issues covered and the diversity of perspectives represented. That, after all, is the idea behind the guarantee of a free press in the First Amendment to the Constitution. Free and open media allow the greatest likelihood that people will learn about important issues, that they will gain the information they need to distinguish good ideas from bad ones, and that they will learn which political leaders and parties can best represent their interests.

In this regard, the most significant framing effects concern the balance in the information available to people. Those in politics—elected officials, candidates, leaders of organized groups—work hard to influence what the news covers. A competitive political environment usually translates into a robust flow of information. However, in some political environments only one view gets expressed and is reflected in the media. Congressional elections are a case in point. Incumbent politicians today raise about three times more money than their challengers. As a result, House elections often have a gross imbalance in the amount of advertising and news coverage between the two campaigns—that of the incumbent and that of the challenger. This will likely affect public opinion because voters hear the incumbent's views and message more often than the challenger's.

A further example of an imbalance in news coverage arises with the president and Congress. Presidential press conferences and events receive much more coverage than the press events of the leaders of the House or Senate. This gives the president the upper hand in setting the public agenda through the

---

70 The seminal work on priming and framing in public policy and politics is Shanto Iyengar and Donald R. Kinder, *News That Matters: Television and American Opinion* (Chicago: University of Chicago Press, 1987).

---

media because the public is more likely to hear the president's arguments for a particular policy. Of course, a president who pursues an ill-advised policy can easily squander this advantage. If the policy fails, the president's media advantage can be short-lived. The power of the president is the power to persuade, but control of information for political aims must be used with caution.

It is often difficult to measure bias in the media. Ultimately, judgment about media bias rests with the consumers. Do they get the coverage they demand? Do they get too much coverage of some issues or candidates, and too little of others? During the 2016 primary elections, the Pew Research Center conducted a public-opinion survey to ascertain whether some candidates received too much attention from the media and others too little. Seventy-five percent of respondents said that news organizations gave Donald Trump "too much coverage" and only 19 percent said news coverage of Trump was "just about right."[71]

Today, it is easy to learn about public affairs and to hear different opinions—even when we don't want to. Furthermore, the wide variety of media available today likely have facilitated learning and muted some of the biases that may emerge through priming and framing, especially when compared with prior generations who relied on a much more limited range of information sources. No one voice or perspective dominates our multifaceted media environment and competitive political system. Biases that do exist in the media often reflect not restrictive editorial control or a lack of outlets but, rather, failures of political competition.

MEASURING PUBLIC OPINION

A century ago, American political leaders gauged public opinion by people's applause and the size of crowds at meetings. This did not necessarily produce accurate knowledge of public opinion. It did, however, give political leaders confidence in their public support—and therefore confidence in their ability to govern by consent.

Abraham Lincoln and Stephen Douglas debated each other seven times in the summer and autumn of 1858, two years before they became presidential nominees. Their debates took place before audiences in parched cornfields and courthouse squares. More than a century and a half later, most presidential debates take place before a few hundred people, usually in auditoriums at university campuses, but they are really staged for national television audiences numbering in the millions. Candidates cannot experience the public's response firsthand. This distance between leaders and followers is one of the agonizing problems of modern democracy. The media provide information to millions

---

71 Pew Research Center, "Campaign Exposes Fissures over Issues, Values and How Life Has Changed in the U.S.," March 31, 2016, www.people-press.org/2016/03/31/1-views-of-the-primaries-press-coverage-of-candidates-attitudes-about-government-and-the-country (accessed 8/8/19).

of people, but they are not so efficient at providing leaders with feedback from the public. Is government by consent possible when the scale of communication is so large and impersonal? To compensate for the decline in their ability to experience public opinion for themselves, leaders have turned to science—in particular, the science of opinion polling.

It is no secret that politicians and public officials make extensive use of **public-opinion polls** to help them decide whether to run for office, what policies to support, how to vote on important legislation, and what types of appeals to make in their campaigns. President Lyndon B. Johnson was famous for carrying the latest Gallup and Roper poll results in his pocket, and it is widely believed that he began to withdraw from politics because the polls reported losses in public support. All recent presidents and other major political figures work closely with pollsters and consultants who themselves are steeped in the polls.

Constructing Public Opinion from Surveys

The population that we are interested in studying is usually quite large, such as all adults or all voters in the United States. To conduct their polls, survey researchers first identify the relevant population and choose a **sample** of the total. The selection of this sample is important. Above all, it must be representative: the views of those in the sample must accurately and proportionately reflect the views of the whole population. To a large extent, the validity of the poll's results depends on the sampling procedure used.

Sampling Techniques and Selection Bias. The most common techniques for choosing such a sample are probability sampling and random-digit dialing. In the case of **probability sampling**, the pollster begins with a list of the population to be surveyed. This list is called the sampling frame. After each member of the population has been assigned a number, a table of random numbers or a computerized random selection process is used to pick those members of the population to be surveyed.

It is important to emphasize, first, that a sample selected in this manner produces a subset of the population that is representative of the population. Whatever is learned about this representative sample can, thus, be attributed to the larger population with a high level of assurance. Random sampling helps ensure that the way in which people are chosen for the study is not related to the individuals' characteristics, such as their level of education.

This technique for constructing a sample is appropriate when the entire population can be identified. For example, all students registered at Texas colleges and universities can be identified from college records, and a sample of them can easily be drawn. For a national sample of Americans, however, this technique is not feasible because no complete list of Americans exists.[72]

public-opinion poll

A scientific instrument for measuring public opinion.

sample

A small group selected by researchers to represent the most important characteristics of an entire population.

probability sampling

A method used by pollsters to select a representative sample in which every individual in the population has an equal probability of being selected as a respondent.

---

72 Herb Asher, *Polling and the Public: What Every Citizen Should Know* (Washington, DC: CQ Press, 2001), p. 64.

Exit polls conducted during national elections use areas to construct their sample. The polling organization randomly selects a set of precincts (voting stations) within each state throughout the nation—usually between 50 and 150 such locations. The polling organization trains individuals to conduct the exit poll on Election Day at the voting stations. The pollster approaches people as they leave the voting area and persuades them to fill out the exit poll questionnaire. To guard against biases, the pollster is instructed on how many people to choose and which people to approach, such as every seventh person. As the day progresses, the pollsters tally the results of the exit poll and report them to the organization, which tallies those figures and distributes them to the media outlets that use them on election night.

The typical public-opinion poll today is conducted either over the internet or on the phone. Internet samples are recruited through a variety of means, including sampling from lists of people or soliciting people to do a survey using pop-up ads. People who agree to do a poll on the internet complete the questionnaire on their computer or mobile device. Phone polls usually draw samples using **random-digit dialing**, in which a computerized random-number generator produces a list of as many 10-digit numbers as the pollster deems necessary. Randomization—of which household is chosen and of which person is interviewed in each household—helps guard against potential biases. An ongoing debate concerns the best ways to guard against potential biases when using internet surveys, where random selection is very difficult or not used at all. Survey researchers using the internet construct representative samples that reflect the characteristics of the population they wish to study.

Recently, however, with the growth in cell phone use and the enactment of "do-not-call" legislation to discourage telemarketers, random-digit dialing has become less reliable. Computerized methods of random-digit dialing have difficulty reaching households that are registered on the do-not-call list or that have only cell phones. In addition, some people are simply more willing than others to talk to pollsters. If pollsters could be certain that those who respond to their surveys simply reflect the views of those who refuse to respond, there would be no problem. Some studies suggest, however, that the views of respondents and nonrespondents can differ, especially along social-class lines. Middle- and upper-middle-class individuals are more likely to respond to surveys than their working-class counterparts.[73] These considerations point to the fact that the ways in which people communicate in today's society can have an effect on public-opinion research.

Innovations in technology and the spread of online modes of communication are creating problems for establishing research methods, but they are also creating opportunities. Online methods often offer much cheaper ways to contact people and conduct research, but not everyone uses online platforms equally. The challenge inherent in harnessing the potential of online platforms is to figure out how to reach an acceptably broad segment of the population using these methods and how to ensure the representativeness of the resulting samples.

◄ **random-digit dialing**

A method used by pollsters in which respondents are selected at random from a list of 10-digit telephone numbers, with every effort made to avoid bias in the construction of the sample.

---

73 John Goyder, Keith Warriner, and Susan Miller, "Evaluating Socio-Economic Status (SES) Bias in Survey Nonresponse," *Journal of Official Statistics* 18, no. 1 (2002): 1–11.

Although these technical aspects of how surveys are constructed may seem obscure, the importance of sampling was brought home early in the history of political polling. A 1936 *Literary Digest* poll predicted that the Republican presidential candidate, Alf Landon, would defeat the Democrat, Franklin Delano Roosevelt, in that year's election. But the election ended in a Roosevelt landslide. The main problem with the survey was **selection bias** in drawing the sample: pollsters had relied on telephone directories and automobile registration rosters to produce a sampling frame. During the Great Depression, however, only wealthy Americans owned telephones and automobiles. Thus the millions of working-class Americans who constituted Roosevelt's principal base of support were excluded from the sample.

selection bias

A polling error in which the sample is not representative of the population being studied, so that some opinions are over- or underrepresented.

A more recent instance of polling error caused by selection bias occurred during the 1998 Minnesota gubernatorial election. A poll conducted by the *Minneapolis Star Tribune* just six weeks before the election showed the former professional wrestler Jesse Ventura running a distant third to the Democratic candidate, Hubert Humphrey III (who seemed to have the support of 49 percent of the electorate), and the Republican, Norm Coleman (whose support stood at 29 percent). Only 10 percent of those polled said they were planning to vote for Ventura. But on Election Day, Ventura outperformed both Humphrey and Coleman. Why had the preelection poll been so wrong? It was conducted only among individuals who had voted in the previous election in an effort to take account of the likelihood that respondents would actually vote. Ventura, however, brought to the polls not only individuals who had not voted in the last election but also many people who had never voted before in their lives.[74]

Selection bias may also have contributed to inaccurate electoral predictions in 2016 and 2020. Preelection polls painted an overly rosy projection for the Democrats in 2016 and 2020. In 2016, preelection polls suggested a clear victory for Hillary Clinton, and a blue wave in 2020 that would not only bring Biden to power but would sweep many Republicans in Congress out of power. While Biden did win the popular vote and the Electoral College in 2020, those other predictions did not come true, and Biden's victory was far narrower than the polls suggested. Specifically, the polls underestimated the turnout of key demographic groups that supported Donald Trump and the Republican party (see Figure 10.2). The errors in the polls were not universal but were concentrated in specific states. Most notably, the 2016 polls completely missed the surge of support for Donald Trump in the upper Midwest, especially Wisconsin, Michigan, and Pennsylvania—the key states that gave him his electoral college win. In 2020, the state surveys in Iowa, Maine, and North Carolina showed sizable leads for the Democratic senatorial challengers, but the incumbents in each state easily won their reelection. Polling organizations are ever mindful of these fateful stories. Their business depends on producing accurate representations of the American public's opinions and behavior. The challenges are to keep pace with the ever-changing ways that people communicate and to anticipate the sometimes surprising nature of the American electorate.

---

74 Carl Cannon, "A Pox on Both Our Parties," in *The Enduring Debate: Classic and Contemporary Readings in American Politics*, David T. Canon, Anne Khademian, and Kenneth R. Mayer, eds., 2nd ed. (New York: Norton, 2000), p. 389.

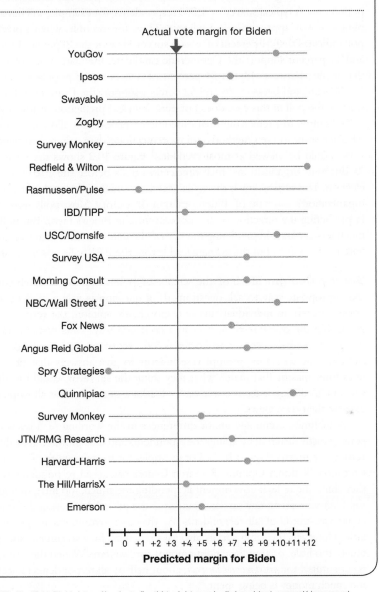

Figure 10.2
ACCURACY OF FINAL PREELECTION POLLS, 2020

Actual vote margin for Biden

Poll
YouGov
Ipsos
Swayable
Zogby
Survey Monkey
Redfield & Wilton
Rasmussen/Pulse
IBD/TIPP
USC/Dornsife
Survey USA
Morning Consult
NBC/Wall Street J
Fox News
Angus Reid Global
Spry Strategies
Quinnipiac
Survey Monkey
JTN/RMG Research
Harvard-Harris
The Hill/HarrisX
Emerson

−1 0 +1 +2 +3 +4 +5 +6 +7 +8 +9 +10 +11 +12

Predicted margin for Biden

SOURCES: FiveThirtyEight, https://projects.fivethirtyeight.com/polls/president-general/ (accessed 11/16/20).

Sample Size. The degree of reliability in polling is also a function of sample size. In U.S. polls, a typical sample ranges from 450 to 1,500 respondents. This number reflects a trade-off between cost and the degree of precision desired. A larger and hence more costly sample size is associated with greater precision in making generalizations to the full population than is a smaller sample size.

sampling error

A polling error that arises on account of the small size of the sample.

The chance that the sample does not accurately represent the population from which it is drawn is the **sampling error**, or *margin of error*. The margin of error acknowledges that any given sample may not perfectly represent the full population. A typical survey of 1,500 respondents, for example, will have a sampling error of approximately 3 percent. Thus, for example, when a preelection poll indicates that 51 percent of voters surveyed favor the Republican candidate and 49 percent support the Democratic candidate, the margin of error tells us that in fact between 48 and 54 percent of voters in the population favor the Republican, and between 46 and 52 percent support the Democrat. The precision of the poll in this case does not permit a clear prediction of a winner.

Attempts to predict the final outcome of an election allow us to examine whether some survey methods are more accurate than others and which surveys should be viewed as most credible.[75] Figure 10.2 shows the results from 21 different organizations' final preelection polls before the 2020 presidential election. The vertical line is the actual election outcome, and each dot is a survey organization's estimate of Biden's margin of victory. Most polls were correct in predicting the direction of the popular vote in Biden's favor. But polls were much less accurate in predicting the size of the vote margin. Biden won the final vote by 3.5 points, but the average lead across these 21 polls was 6.9 points.

Survey Design. Much of the science of public-opinion research concerns the appropriate way to ask questions. If a question is vague or confusing or doesn't match an individual survey respondent's opinion, the respondent will likely skip the question or answer in a confused way. Thus researchers frame questions in a balanced way and offer as full a set of options as possible. Moreover, leading questions prompt respondents to give answers that fit with the questions' bias or that match what they think the surveyor would like them to say. The challenge is to discover ways of asking questions that allow people to express their own views.

Sometimes, seemingly minor differences in the wording of a question can convey vastly different meanings to respondents and thus produce quite different response patterns (Figure 10.3). For example, for many years the University of Chicago's National Opinion Research Center has asked respondents whether they think the federal government is spending too much, too little, or about the right amount of money on "assistance for the poor." Answering this question, about two-thirds of all respondents say that the government is spending too little. However, the same survey also asks whether the government spends too much, too little, or about the right amount for "welfare." When the word *welfare* is substituted for *assistance for the poor*, about half of all respondents indicate that too much money is being spent.[76]

75 For a discussion of the difficulties with polls, especially in trying to assess the preferences of specific subgroups in the population, see David Leal, Matt Barreto, Jongho Lee, and Rodolfo O. de la Garza, "The Latino Vote in the 2004 Election," *PS: Political Science and Politics* 38, no. 1 (January 2005): 41–9.

76 Michael R. Kagay and Janet Elder, "Numbers Are No Problem for Pollsters, Words Are," *New York Times*, August 9, 1992, p. E6.

Figure 10.3
IT DEPENDS ON HOW YOU ASK

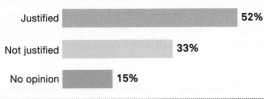

Variation 1:
The AP reported classified information about U.S. antiterrorism efforts and prosecutors have obtained AP's phone records through a court order. Do you think this action by federal prosecutors is or is not justified?

Justified — 52%

Not justified — 33%

No opinion — 15%

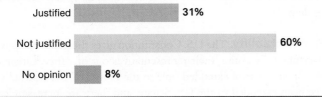

Variation 2:
As you may have heard, the U.S. Justice Department secretly seized extensive telephone records of calls on both work and personal phones for reporters and editors working for the Associated Press in the spring of 2012. At the time, the news organization, using government leaks, had broken a story about an international terrorist plot. The government obtained the phone records without giving the news organization prior notice, as is customary. Do you think the government was probably justified in taking these actions or does this sound more like the government went too far?

Justified — 31%

Not justified — 60%

No opinion — 8%

ANALYZING THE EVIDENCE

In 2012, the federal government subpoenaed the phone records of Associated Press (AP) journalists after the AP reported classified information related to U.S. antiterrorism efforts. Pollsters asking whether the government's actions were justified got different results, depending on the specifics of the question. What differences in the two versions of the question do you think account for the different answers?

SOURCE: Michael Dimock, "Polling When Public Attention is Limited: Different Questions, Different Results," Pew Research Center, May 22, 2013, https://www.pewresearch.org/fact-tank/2013/05/22/polling-when-public-attention-is-limited-different-questions-different-results/ (accessed 7/3/20).

Vague or poorly worded questions create **measurement error**, which can skew data analyses away from the true results. Suppose that 75 percent of people support a given piece of legislation and 25 percent oppose it. In a poorly designed survey question about the legislation, the wording is so confusing that 1 in 5 respondents misinterprets the meaning. In this case, then, one-fifth of the 75 percent (or 15 percent of all respondents) who support the bill will say they oppose it, and one-fifth of the 25 percent who oppose the bill (or 5 percent) will say they support it. As a result, only 65 percent of those surveyed will say that they support the bill and 35 percent will say that they do not.[77] In this way, measurement error can bias survey results.

measurement error

The failure to identify the true distribution of opinion within a population because of errors such as ambiguous or poorly worded questions.

---

77 The calculation is that the percentage who say they support it is four-fifths of the 75 percent who really support it (60 percent of all people in the survey) plus one-fifth of the 25 percent (5 percent of all people in the survey) who do not support it but mistakenly say that they do. The total percentage who say they support the bill is 60 percent plus 5 percent.

You, as a savvy consumer of political data, should be mindful of what surveys ask of respondents and of possible confusion or slant in any question. As our discussion has shown, the challenge is to ask questions that allow people to express their preferences and that capture what people really think about important issues. It is a good exercise to try writing a survey. The typical public-opinion survey over the phone lasts 5 to 10 minutes, and each question takes about 15 seconds to ask and answer. The typical survey consists of 20 to 40 questions that not only cover a broad set of current issues but also take into account respondents' demographic characteristics. Each question, then, must summarize the issue at stake in a few words and capture the full range of possible or likely answers in a reasonably small set of options.

HOW DOES PUBLIC OPINION INFLUENCE GOVERNMENT POLICY?

In democratic nations, leaders should pay heed to public opinion, and most evidence suggests that they do. Although public policy and public opinion do not always coincide, in general the government's actions are consistent with citizens' preferences. There are three important ways in which public opinion influences government policy.

Electoral Accountability. The U.S. Constitution gives the public the power to change government by voting their representatives out of office. Originally this means of popular control extended only to the House of Representatives, but it has since been extended to the U.S. Senate, and there are increasing calls to eliminate the last vestige of indirect representation, the Electoral College. We discussed the power that constituents have over their members of Congress in Chapter 6. Today, political scientists see members of Congress as single-mindedly focused on reelection. Legislators who are out of step with the majority in their constituency quickly find themselves out of office. We will discuss how elections work in the next chapter.

Building Coalitions. Legislative politics, however, goes beyond a member's own constituency. In order for legislation to pass, any bill must have public support (or at least no intense public opposition) in a majority of House districts, in a majority of states (the Senate's constituencies), and among a majority of people in the nation (the president's constituency). It is not enough, then, for a legislator to be attentive to her own constituency; she must be attuned to public opinion nationwide. Likewise, no president can push an agenda in Congress without having the support of the public, at least in a majority of states and districts. Some presidents have managed to pass major legislation even in the face of public opposition, but the consequences have usually been disastrous for the president's party. In January 2010, for example, in the face of stiff public opposition, President Obama pushed through the Affordable Care Act (ACA). Ten months later, the Democratic Party suffered a stunning defeat in the House and nearly lost its nine-seat majority in the Senate. As Republicans continued to campaign against the act, in 2014 the Democrats lost their majority in the Senate as well as additional seats in the House. With a Republican president in 2017 and 2018, the Republican-controlled Congress failed to muster the votes to repeal and replace the ACA and instead voted to repeal its mandate that individuals must buy health insurance. By 2018, a majority of Americans had come to support the Affordable Care Act and opposed its repeal.

Input in Rule Making and Legal Decisions. Some laws explicitly rely on public opinion or social science evidence concerning political behavior. The federal and state governments have various open meeting and sunshine laws that allow for public commentary on new rules and new laws. Federal advisory committees consist of experts and stakeholders—such as scientists, industry representatives, public interest group advocates, and people who are very interested in a subject—who advise federal agencies on the likely impact of particular rules or laws. These committees cover an enormous range of subjects and agencies, from approval of drugs by the Food and Drug Administration to space exploration by NASA to licensing of telecommunications under the Federal Communications Commission. Such committees operate in an open manner; they post public notices of meetings, hearings, or proposed rules and collect public commentary.

As a somewhat different example, under the Voting Rights Act (discussed in Chapters 5 and 11) federal courts rely heavily on information about the political preferences of ethnic and racial groups, including electoral and survey data, and on historical patterns of discrimination. Historians and political scientists have been vitally important in conveying what is known about how different racial groups vote in a given state or county and how members of these groups are viewed and treated in politics and other settings. This information is crucial in deciding whether states have discriminated against racial minorities in the administration of election laws.[78]

Public opinion and public policy, however, are not always in alignment. The institutions of American government were meant to be influenced and held accountable by the public, but they were also designed to work slowly and deliberately, to protect individual rights and property. The complex institutions of the American government, then, often create disparities between what the public wants and what the government does (or does not do).

Inconsistencies between opinion and policy might be reduced if the federal government used ballot initiatives nationwide, as many states do. This procedure allows propositions to be voted into law by the electorate, bypassing most of the normal machinery of representative government. Ballot measures in the

---

78 David L. Epstein, Richard H. Pildes, Rodolfo O. de la Garza, and Sharyn O'Halloran, eds., *The Future of the Voting Rights Act* (New York: Russell Sage Foundation, 2006).

states have been used to restrict property tax increases; ban the use of racial or gender preferences in government employment, contracting, and university admissions; enact environmental regulations; legalize marijuana; limit campaign spending; regulate auto insurance; change the rules governing redistricting; and raise the minimum wage.[79] Some states even use initiatives to pass budget agreements when the legislature does not want to be held responsible for casting unpopular votes.[80]

However, government by initiative offers little opportunity for reflection and compromise. Voters are presented with a proposition, usually sponsored by a special interest group, and must take it or leave it. Perhaps the true will of the people lies somewhere between the positions held by various interest groups. In a representative assembly, as opposed to a referendum campaign, a compromise position might be more satisfactory to all voters. This capacity for compromise is one reason the Founders strongly favored representative government rather than direct democracy.

CONCLUSION: GOVERNMENT AND THE WILL OF THE PEOPLE

Representative democracy was a novel form of government when the framers created the Constitution. Behind this radical system lies one central idea—that the government reflects the will of the people. The Constitution gives people the opportunity to express their preferences through elections, public meetings and organizations, and free expression and debate. Public deliberations and public choices, it is conjectured, aggregate individuals' preferences and opinions to form the collective "will of the people" that would guide those in office. This chapter has explored the meaning of this idea today.

We no longer speak of the people of the United States as an organic whole with a coherent will. Rather, we characterize the "people" as the aggregation of individuals' preferences about the choices presented to them—in a phrase, *public opinion*. The individual is the foundation of public opinion. Politicians assume that individuals will pursue their own preferences, will protect and expand their own property and wealth, will express their own ideologies about what is right, and will pursue their own happiness above the interests of the state or the community. The aggregation of all those actions constitutes the expression of public opinion.

Politicians take risks when attempting to convince the public to follow them, for they cannot anticipate which way the public will break on any given issue;

---

79 David Broder, *Democracy Derailed: Initiative Campaigns and the Power of Money* (New York: Harcourt, 2000).

80 Robert Tomsho, "Liberals Take a Cue from Conservatives: This Election, the Left Tries to Make Policy with Ballot Initiatives," *Wall Street Journal*, November 6, 2000, p. A12.

they must hope they have chosen issues that people care about and have framed policies in ways that seem consistent with the interests and values of a majority of voters. Politicians do this through speeches and op-eds, political advertising, social media, and working with the media to present issues in a certain way. Of course, their opponents also try to influence how people think. The public benefits from competition among politicians, as it brings out the best arguments for and against a given policy or government action. This is the real testament to the power of public opinion.

Public opinion and public policy are not always in agreement, and several factors contribute to this lack of consistency. First, the nominal majority on a particular issue may not be as committed as the intensely committed minority, which may be more willing to commit time, energy, and resources to the affirmation of its opinions. In the case of gun control, although proponents are in the majority by a wide margin, most do not regard the issue as critically, personally important and are unwilling to commit much effort to advancing their cause. Opponents, by contrast, are intensely committed, well organized, and well financed; as a result, they usually carry the day. In accordance with the institution principle, the collective action principle, and the policy principle, intense commitment, organization, and financial resources are potent assets in the legislature, the executive bureaucracy, and the courts.

Second, the framers of the Constitution, as we saw in Chapter 2, sought to create a system of government that was based on popular consent but did not invariably and automatically translate shifting popular sentiments into public policies. As a result, the American governmental process includes arrangements such as an appointed judiciary that can produce policy decisions that may run contrary to prevailing popular sentiment—at least for a time.

The succeeding chapters will consider how public opinion manifests itself through different institutions of democracy. As we discuss these institutions, it will be useful to keep in mind how we have described public opinion in this chapter. Most people in the United States hold fairly centrist or moderate views on most questions. Neither right nor left nor center commands an outright majority of public support on any issue of importance. Anyone adhering to one of these views must reach out beyond her particular ideological slant in order to find a coalition large enough to capture the support of a majority.

Democracy is complicated further by the heterogeneity of American society. The nation's political institutions tolerate all manner of religious and political beliefs and all manner of social and economic relations, and the United States has long been a refuge for immigrants seeking asylum or a better way of life. As a result, ours is one of the most diverse societies in the world, with freedom to practice every major religion, with a wide spectrum of political and social organizations, and with great concentrations of wealth and poverty. This would seem to be a recipe not for consensus but for disagreement and conflict, even civil conflict.

The open society in the United States, however, has worked for over two centuries because its members have a strong commitment to democracy itself. Americans, in essence, agree to disagree. We agree that it is best to tolerate many different opinions. We value liberty and restrain the government from imposing itself on how people think or express themselves politically. We further agree to allow the institutions of democracy to help us reach collective decisions about who should govern and how they should govern. The next four chapters examine in detail those institutions—the institutions of elections, political parties, interest groups, and media and communications technologies.

For Further Reading

Althaus, Scott. *Collective Preferences in Democratic Politics: Opinion Surveys and the Will of the People*. New York: Cambridge University Press, 2003.

Ansolabehere, Stephen, Jonathan Rodden, and James M. Snyder, Jr. "Purple America." *Journal of Economic Perspectives* 20, no. 2 (Spring 2006): 97–118.

Bartels, Larry M. *Unequal Democracy: The Political Economy of the New Gilded Age*. Princeton, NJ: Princeton University Press, 2008.

Berinsky, Adam J. *In Time of War: Understanding American Public Opinion from World War II to Iraq*. Chicago: University of Chicago Press, 2009.

Carter, Niambi M. "A Sanctuary for Whom? Race, Immigration, and the Black Public Sphere." In *Black Politics in Transition: Immigration, Suburbanization, and Gentrification*, edited by Candis Watts Smith and Christina M. Greer. New York: Routledge, 2019.

Erikson, Robert S., and Kent L. Tedin. *American Public Opinion: Its Origins, Content, and Impact*. 10th ed. New York: Routledge, 2019.

Fiorina, Morris P., Samuel J. Abrams, and Jeremy C. Pope. *Culture War? The Myth of a Polarized America*. 3rd ed. New York: Longman, 2010.

Iyengar, Shanto, and Sean J. Westwood. "Fear and Loathing across Party Lines: New Evidence on Group Polarization." *American Journal of Political Science* 59, no. 3 (2015): 690–707.

Kinder, Donald R., and Cindy D. Kam. *Us against Them: Ethnocentric Foundations of American Opinion*. Chicago: University of Chicago Press, 2010.

Lee, Taeku. *Mobilizing Public Opinion: Black Insurgency and Racial Attitudes in the Civil Rights Era*. Chicago: University of Chicago Press, 2002.

Levendusky, Matthew. *The Partisan Sort: How Liberals Became Democrats and Conservatives Became Republicans*. Chicago: University of Chicago Press, 2009.

Lupia, Arthur, and Mathew D. McCubbins. *The Democratic Dilemma: Can Citizens Learn What They Need to Know?* New York: Cambridge University Press, 1998.

McCarty, Nolan, Keith T. Poole, and Howard Rosenthal. *Polarized America: The Dance of Ideology and Unequal Riches*. Cambridge, MA: MIT Press, 2006.

Mummolo, Jonathan, and Clayton Nall. 2016. "Why Partisans Do Not Sort: The Constraints on Political Segregation." *Journal of Politics* 79, no. 1 (2016): 45–59.

Page, Benjamin I., and Robert Y. Shapiro. *The Rational Public: Fifty Years of Trends in Americans' Policy Preferences*. Chicago: University of Chicago Press, 1992.

Penn, Mark J., and E. Kinney Zalesne. *Microtrends: The Small Forces Behind Tomorrow's Big Changes*. New York: Hachette, 2007.

Stimson, James A. *Public Opinion in America: Moods, Cycles, and Swings*. 2nd ed. New York: Routledge, 2018.

Zaller, John R. *The Nature and Origins of Mass Opinion*. New York: Cambridge University Press, 1992.

11

Elections

The most profound expression of an individual's political preferences is the vote. It is a blunt but effective instrument for controlling the government. Though citizens usually cannot decide directly what laws are enacted, what the tax or interest rates will be, or whether to declare war, they can affirm a commitment to stay the course or to change their government when they think a new direction is needed. Voting is the people's way of reining in government and ensuring that elected officials remain attentive to public preferences. Elections have proved remarkably successful at ensuring continual renewal of government through peaceful means.

Frequent, regular elections are the hallmark of democracy. The United States embraces this idea more intensely than any other democracy. The United States has elections very frequently, with great regularity, and for all manner of governments. Voters elect the president, governors, and other executive officers every four years;[1] federal and state legislators every two years; and thousands of local mayors, councilors, and commissioners with similar frequency. All told there are more than 89,000 governments at the federal, state, and local levels in the United States, nearly all of them run by elected bodies.[2] A typical election involves choosing among candidates as well as deciding bond issues and other local questions, and in any given year a typical voter has the opportunity to vote three or four times.

How is it that elections create a government that reflects and responds to the preferences of the public? The simple idea behind democracy is that there is power, and perhaps even wisdom, in numbers. Voting allows each of us to express our preferences, and election procedures aggregate those votes into a legitimate collective choice. Election laws determine how votes are counted and translate into a government—who wins seats in the legislature, who is elected to the executive, and, in many states, who will serve as judges.

---

1   Vermont and New Hampshire elect their governors every two years.

2   One federal government, 50 state governments, about 3,000 county governments, about 36,000 municipal and town governments, about 13,000 school districts, and more than 37,000 special districts (for example, water or utility districts). U.S. Census Bureau, "Census of Governments," www.census.gov/programs-surveys/cog.html (accessed 8/21/19).

Elections in the United States choose who will govern, not what government should do or what the laws should be. We do not have direct democracy in federal elections, although many states and municipalities allow voting on bonds and a small number of laws. For the most part, elections are occasions when multiple principals—the citizens—choose political agents to act on their behalf.

Two problems immediately arise for the principals (the citizens). First, how can we be sure we are selecting the best people for the job? This problem of **adverse selection** stems from hidden information. We want to choose people who have the competence to write smart legislation or who have constituents' interests at heart, but we may not have the information to judge which candidate possesses those characteristics. Second, once elected, will politicians do their jobs as we want them to? This problem of **moral hazard** stems from hidden actions. Once selected, representatives cannot easily be monitored. When political leaders engage in acts that do not attract public attention, such as making deals with colleagues to build a winning coalition for a particular bill, we need to ensure that the politicians' decisions are the ones we want them to make. However, voters cannot know everything about the candidates for office or about politicians' actions once they are elected. In fact, the incentives to be highly knowledgeable are minimal. In a nation of 170 million registered voters or even a district of 700,000 voters, surely one's own ballot is unlikely to make a difference in the outcome, and the cost of making a mistake is nil. Why, then, bother to find out the details of the candidates' backgrounds and personalities or to learn about the goings-on in Congress?

In the face of these problems of incomplete information, voters use simple rules to guide their choices at the ballot box. They usually vote out of office any politicians who are caught in scandals or who can be held responsible for economic downturns, as occurred in 2008, 2010, and 2014. They also reward the party in power for economic good times and express their desire to continue with current economic policies, as occurred in 2004. In other years, when economic signals are mixed, such as 2016, elections are quite close. And in 2020,

 adverse selection

The problem of incomplete information—of choosing alternatives without fully knowing the details of available options.

 moral hazard

The problem of not knowing all aspects of the actions taken by an agent (nominally on behalf of the principal but potentially at the principal's expense).

LEARNING OBJECTIVES

 Describe how elections in the United States function as formal institutions for making collective decisions.

 Identify how voters make decisions during elections.

 Explain the role of money, media, and grassroots campaigns in elections.

 Analyze the results of the 2020 elections and the implications they will have moving forward.

in response to dramatic economic declines, job loses, and general uncertainly during the coronavirus pandemic, voters chose a new administration for the national government, electing Joe Biden the 46th president of the United States. The public, however, did not wholly embrace Biden's party. The election left control of the Senate in the hands of the Republicans, and it narrowed the size of the Democratic majority in the House of Representatives. The public in 2020 had decided to hold the Trump administration accountable for its handling of COVID, but they were not prepared to embrace a wholesale shift to the left in the policies the government pursues.

Ultimately, elections work through competition. The public relies on competition among politicians, the parties, interest groups, and the media to inform them. This chapter focuses on the politicians; later chapters address parties, interest groups, and the media. In the United States politicians are central. Rival politicians or teams of politicians (parties) seek to hold elective office—we consider that their primary motivation—and the competition inherent in elections creates strong incentives for those vying for office to reveal information to the electorate. They formulate positions on important policies that appeal to the greatest number of voters; they develop personal appeals; they advertise their ability to do the job at hand, their strength of character, and their fidelity to the public. Likewise, politicians draw attention to their rivals' failings. Candidates and parties use advertisements, press conferences, speeches, and other modes of reaching the public to highlight their opponents' policy decisions as being out of step with most voters' wishes, and they expose scandalous behavior and play up political gaffes. Politicians themselves bear much of the cost of informing the public about their own performance and ideas as well as those of their opponents.

Competition alone does not cure all. Proponents of electoral reform criticize many features of U.S. election laws, including the campaign finance system, redistricting procedures, the lack of third parties, and the relatively low levels of voter turnout. In this chapter, we consider how the institutional features of American elections shape the way that citizens' goals and preferences are reflected in their government and the decisions voters make among the candidates and questions put before them on the ballot. Democracy is a work in progress. Americans constantly tinker with the rules to make it a better system.

INSTITUTIONS OF ELECTIONS

Elections are formal institutions for making collective decisions. As in Congress, the executive branch, and the courts, rules (institutions) determine who is allowed to vote, how votes are cast and counted, and how we determine who wins office. Election rules consist of a mix of state and federal laws, legal decisions, and local administrative practices. Federal laws regulate the time of congressional and presidential elections, the qualifications for office, the allocation of seats in Congress, the structure of electoral districts, and the qualifications and rights of voters. State laws determine a wider range of factors, including how votes are cast and counted, the procedures for registering voters, candidate qualifications for most elected offices, the procedures for nominating candidates and getting on the ballot, the operations of the parties, and the conduct of all state and local elections. The responsibility for making all of this go smoothly falls on the roughly 5,000 local election offices in counties and municipalities across the country. These workers manage the registration lists, prepare the ballots and voting machinery, set up polling places, recruit and train poll workers, and tally and certify the votes. And at the nation's polling places on Election Day, roughly 1 million volunteer poll workers administer the election. The Policy Principle box on p. 450 shows how the decisions made by local officials can affect election outcomes, including increasing access to the ballot through automatic voter registration.

The laws and procedures governing elections have important consequences. They can skew the electorate toward one interest or another; they can impede certain political organizations; and they can create a legislature that either reflects the population's diversity or allows one segment of society to dominate.

Election laws, as the rules under which a given election is conducted, manifest the institution principle. Viewed over the long arc of history, however, election laws are also a product of the political system and exemplify the policy and rationality principles. Like any law, an election law is the product of bargaining and negotiation among elected officials and thus reflects the politics inside the legislature. The rationality principle is at work in that it is interests and values that motivate elected officials and voters. Finally, election laws also exhibit a great deal of stickiness: they typically change slowly, and laws passed decades, even centuries, ago continue to shape the way American democracy operates.

Four features of U.S. election laws deserve particular emphasis:

- First, *who*. The United States provides for universal adult suffrage—all citizens over the age of 18 have the right to vote.[3]

- Second, *how*. Americans vote in secret and choose among candidates for particular office using a form of the ballot called the "Australian ballot."

- Third, *where*. The United States selects almost all elected offices through single-member districts that serve equal populations—following the principle of one person, one vote.

- Fourth, *what* it takes to win. For most offices in the United States, the candidate who wins the most votes among all of those competing for a given seat wins the election.

We will see that these rules create a two-party system that broadly encompasses the entire adult population but that exaggerates the political power of the majority. Other features of election laws and procedures, including rules

---

3 However, adults currently serving sentences for felonies cannot vote; in addition, some states impose residency requirements and prohibit ex-felons from voting.

Election Administration and Automatic Voter Registration

Automatic voter registration initiatives ease obstacles to the ballot.

Efforts to increase voter turnout often point out the two-step process of voting in the United States as a particular problem. Citizens must first register to vote, and only then can they cast a ballot. In most states, there is a waiting period between those two steps that makes registration a significant barrier to voting.

At the time of the 2020 election, 17 states and the District of Columbia had enacted Election Day registration (sometimes called same-day registration) to make it easier for people who arrived at the polls to register and vote. However, potential voters often do not know that they have that option. In an effort to improve voter turnout, in the last five years, many states have taken a more aggressive step to knock down the registration barrier: automatic voter registration (AVR).

AVR is an automated process in which data on state residents, generally from the Department of Motor Vehicles (DMV), is electronically transferred to state voter registration systems without requiring individuals to fill out paper voter registration forms. These data also allow for regular updates to existing voter rolls as individuals update their addresses with the DMV or other state agencies.

A 2019 study showed that enactment of these policies significantly increases the number of people registered to vote and that a substantial portion of these newly registered individuals actually do vote, although usually at a rate lower than the overall (already registered) population.[1] It is unclear whether this increase in turnout is due to registration itself, or whether the cleaner and more up-to-date voter files allow candidates and parties to do a better job of reaching out to and mobilizing potential voters.

Although AVR is a new electoral reform, it is gaining attention and support; in fact, AVR is often able to secure bipartisan support given its potential to improve both access to voting (a priority among Democrats) and the integrity of the voting system (a priority among Republicans). Opponents of AVR question whether the opt-out mailing is enough to ensure that an individual has a true choice to register and, thus, whether AVR infringes on citizens' First Amendment rights. Many states have addressed this concern by providing the notification and method of opting out directly to individuals while they are at the DMV. Others express concerns about voter fraud and the privacy needs of particular groups of people who may not want their home addresses to be publicly available on a voter roll (such as victims of domestic violence). And implementation problems in California, among other states, have illustrated the capacity and planning needed to enact any sweeping electoral reform.

With the rapid move to voting by mail in light of the 2020 COVID-19 pandemic, Americans may become more comfortable with significant changes to how we vote. AVR is a reform that would help as many citizens as possible have access to the voting booth.

1   Kevin Morris and Peter Dunphy, "AVR Impact on State Voter Registration," Brennan Center for Justice, 2019, https://www.brennancenter.org/sites/default/files/2019-08/Report_AVR_Impact_State_Voter_Registration.pdf (accessed 9/17/20).

governing campaign expenditures and fund-raising, party nominations, and ballot access, further shape political competition in the United States.

Also notable are rules that the United States does not have. Federal and state laws do not limit the amount of television and other forms of advertising that campaigns can employ, total campaign spending, the activities of groups and parties on behalf of candidates, or how the media cover the campaigns. Most other countries limit the use of television or forbid it altogether, restrict how candidates can campaign and how much they can spend, and tightly regulate the activities of organized interest groups. Compared with other countries, then, the United States has a relatively unregulated electoral system that allows candidates to run on their own, separate from the parties, and to spend quite freely on media and other aspects of their campaigns. We turn to these activities in the next section, especially as they bear on the important question of what voters learn through campaigns.

The rules governing elections are not static, having evolved over time through legislation, court decisions, administrative rulings of agencies, and public agitation for electoral reform. The nation has gradually converged on our present system of universal suffrage with secret voting and the use of single-member districts with plurality rule. The future will likely bring further innovations. With waves of immigration, new communication technologies, and other changes reshaping society, the institutions of democracy must change as well. Perhaps the most dramatic changes under way involve the rise of "convenience voting"—voting by mail or voting early at a polling center or town hall. In 1972, approximately 5 percent of all votes nationwide were cast in absentia; in 2018, almost 41 percent of all votes were absentee or early ballots. In 2020, over 60 percent of ballots nationwide were cast absentee by mail or early in-person. The coronavirus pandemic caused people to find ways of voting that did not involve standing in lines or interacting with pollworkers. Oregon and Washington have long conducted elections entirely by mail. In 2020, Colorado, Hawaii, and Utah joined them. In addition, many other states relaxed absentee voting rules to facilitate voting during the pandemic. Eight states and the District of Columbia allow voters to download a ballot online and then scan it and submit it via email or through an online portal.[4]

Who Can Vote: Defining the Electorate

Over the course of American history the electorate has expanded greatly. At the beginning of the Republic, voting rights in most states were restricted to White men over 21 years of age, and many states further required that those people own property. Today, all citizens over 18 years of age are allowed to vote (with few exceptions), and the courts, Department of Justice, and activist organizations actively ferret out discrimination in elections.

---

4   https://www.ncsl.org/research/elections-and-campaigns/vopp-table-6-states-with-web-based-and-online-absentee-ballot-applications.aspx

The Growth of the U.S. Electorate, 1790–2018

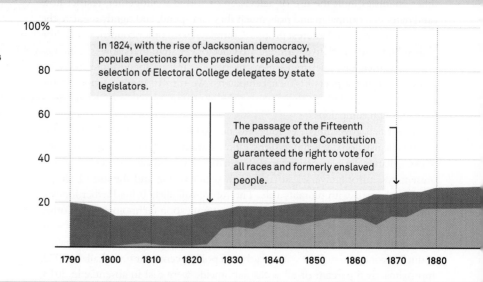

- ■ % of population eligible to vote in national elections
- ▨ % of population that voted in national election

In 1824, with the rise of Jacksonian democracy, popular elections for the president replaced the selection of Electoral College delegates by state legislators.

The passage of the Fifteenth Amendment to the Constitution guaranteed the right to vote for all races and formerly enslaved people.

TIMEPLOT SOURCE: Statistical Abstract of the United States (various years), Bureau of the Census, www.census.gov/library/publications/time-series/statistical_abstracts.html; United States Election Project, "2018 November General Election Turnout Rates," http://www.electproject.org/home/voter-turnout/voter-turnout-data (accessed 5/6/20).

While the right to vote is universal, the exercise of this right is not. In a typical U.S. presidential election, approximately 60 percent of those eligible to vote in fact do so; in midterm elections for Congress, around 45 percent of the electorate votes. And in local elections the percentage of people who vote can be quite low: in some locales, city elections attract only 10 to 20 percent of the electorate.[5] The Timeplot above compares the percentage of the American population eligible to vote with the percentage of the population that actually voted in national elections throughout U.S. history. Some of the most basic questions about the functioning and health of our democracy concern the exercise of the franchise. Who votes and why? How does nonparticipation affect election outcomes, and would election outcomes be different if everyone voted? Does low voter turnout threaten the legitimacy of government?

It is also important to point out that voting in the United States is a right, not a requirement. If we do not feel strongly about the outcome, we do not have to

5 Drew Desilver, "U.S. Trails Most Developed Countries in Voter Turnout," Pew Research Center, May 21, 2018, www.pewresearch.org/fact-tank/2018/05/21/u-s-voter-turnout-trails-most-developed-countries (accessed 3/22/20).

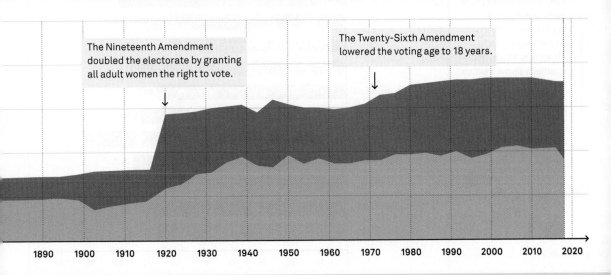

The Nineteenth Amendment doubled the electorate by granting all adult women the right to vote.

The Twenty-Sixth Amendment lowered the voting age to 18 years.

1890 1900 1910 1920 1930 1940 1950 1960 1970 1980 1990 2000 2010 2020

participate. If we want to express dissatisfaction with government, one way to do so is to not vote. Of course, if no one voted, it would be a disaster for American democracy, signaling the end of Americans' commitment to their form of government.

Participation Rates. Not all nations take the same view of democracy. While most democracies view voting as a right and a voluntary act, some also treat it as a responsibility of citizenship. In Mexico and Australia, for example, adult citizens are required to vote in national elections; those who fail to vote must either receive a medical exemption or pay a fine. These rules guarantee turnout rates in the range of 90 percent and make election results a reflection of the preferences of all citizens. Universal voting in the United States, however, is not viewed favorably: nonvoters don't want to face a potential fine, and those who do vote may not want the nonvoters diluting their power. Moreover, most Americans simply do not like the notion that the government can compel them to do something. Even without compelling participation, the United States is one of the world's most participatory democracies. For example, citizens can participate in electoral politics by blogging or posting on social media, speaking with others, joining organizations, giving money, and, of course, voting. When participation is measured in terms of these activities,

Figure 11.1
VOTER TURNOUT AROUND THE WORLD

Country	Percentage
Australia	75.5
Brazil	79.8
Canada	67.7
France	48.7
Italy	72.9
South Africa	66.1
Spain	71.8
Sweden	87.2
Thailand	74.7
Turkey	86.2
United Kingdom	67.6
United States	66.4

PERCENTAGE

NOTE: Turnout as a percentage of voting-age population in the most recent national presidential or parliamentary election as of November 2020.
SOURCE: International Institute for Democracy and Electoral Assistance, www.idea.int/data-tools /data/voter-turnout (accessed 3/20/20); The United States Election Project, http://www.electproject .org/2020g (11/16/20).

Americans participate in politics at much higher rates than people in nearly every other country.[6]

That said, levels of U.S. voter participation in the latter half of the twentieth century were quite low as compared with voter participation in other democracies (Figure 11.1)[7] and as compared with earlier eras of American history, especially the late nineteenth century (Figure 11.2).[8] The five decades after

6 Sidney Verba, Kay Lehman Schlozman, and Henry E. Brady, *Voice and Equality: Civic Voluntarism in American Politics* (Cambridge, MA: Harvard University Press, 1995).

7 See Walter Dean Burnham, "The Changing Shape of the American Political Universe," *American Political Science Review* 59, no. 1 (March 1965): 7–28. It should be noted that other democracies, such as India and Switzerland, have even lower turnout rates, as do some of the newer democracies in eastern Europe.

8 See statistics of the U.S. Census Bureau and the Federal Election Commission. For voting statistics for 2000 to 2018, see "United States Elections Project," www .electproject.org/home/voter-turnout/voter-turnout-data (accessed 3/22/20).

Figure 11.2
VOTER TURNOUT IN U.S. PRESIDENTIAL ELECTIONS

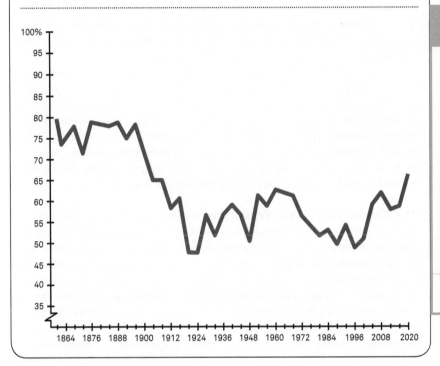

NOTE: Data reflect the population of eligible voters; the percentage of the voting-age population that voted in each election would be smaller.
SOURCES: 1860–2016: U.S. Census Bureau data; 2020: The United States Election Project, http://www.electproject.org/2020g (11/16/20).

ANALYZING THE EVIDENCE

Voter turnout for American presidential elections was significantly higher in the nineteenth century than in the twentieth. What institutional change caused the sharp decline in turnout between 1890 and 1910? Why did this change have such a dramatic effect? Did it have any positive outcomes?

World War II saw a steady erosion of voter turnout in the United States, with voter participation in presidential elections falling below 50 percent in 1996. That decline stirred Congress to reform voter registration rules in the mid-1990s. Turnout rates have grown since then, in response both to legal changes and to the observation by political parties and candidates that there was an opportunity to influence elections by bringing people back to the polls. During the 2016 presidential election, 59 percent of adult citizens in the United States voted. Similarly, during the 2020 presidential election, 66 percent of adult citizens voted. Midterm elections have much lower turnout than presidential elections. The 2018 midterm had unusually high participation rate of 48.5 percent of adult citizens casting votes.

Who Votes and Why? The answers to the questions of who votes and why lie partly in the motivations and behavior of individuals and partly with the laws of democracy, which are the institutions that shape elections. Later in this chapter we discuss the correlates of voting to understand who chooses to vote. We discuss here the legal institutions that define and constrain voting behavior.

First we must explain one term—the *turnout rate*. It is simple to define, but some of the subtleties of the definition are important to understand, especially when making comparisons over time or across countries. The turnout rate is the number of people who vote in a given election divided by the number of people who are allowed to vote. The first part of this ratio is relatively uncontroversial—the number of individuals who cast ballots.[9] The appropriate baseline in the turnout ratio is more difficult to define. Most commonly, the turnout rate presented for the United States (and other countries) is turnout as a percentage of the voting-age population (all adults). This understates the true turnout rate, because it includes noncitizens and people who are incarcerated or not allowed to vote in some states because they are ex-felons. It is possible to estimate from census reports the numbers of noncitizens and incarcerated populations, though getting reliable figures is difficult. Following the usual conventions, we focus here on the voting-age population. However, the eligible electorate is somewhat smaller owing to other restrictions on the franchise.[10]

The Electorate and the Franchise. How big is the U.S. electorate? There are approximately 330 million people in the United States today. But not all of them are allowed to vote. These include children under age 18, noncitizens, and people currently serving prison sentences. In addition, previously incarcerated people are not allowed to vote in most states. The biggest restriction on the size of the electorate is age. There are approximately 74 million people under age 18 in the United States. Noncitizenship reduces the electorate by another 13 million adults.[11] Finally, the total ineligible prison and felon population is estimated to be between 3 and 6 million persons.[12] Hence the electorate is approximately

---

9 Not all states report such figures in their certified tally of the vote. In fact, 11 states do not report the number of ballots cast, and researchers must substitute the total votes for all candidates for the presidency or another office on the top of the ballot. So, for example, if an individual voter in one of these states does not cast a vote for president but does vote on other questions on the ballot, this voter might not be counted in the total. However, because nearly all voters who turn out do vote on the races at the top of the ticket, counting those totals is a reasonably accurate substitute for official turnout records.

10 Michael P. McDonald and Samuel L. Popkin, "The Myth of the Vanishing Voter," *American Political Science Review* 95, no. 4 (December 2001): 963–74.

11 This figure excludes the 12 million undocumented persons who are estimated to reside in the United States. See Elaine Kamarck and Christine Stenglein, "How Many Undocumented Immigrants Are in the United States and Who Are They?" Brookings, November 12, 2019, www.brookings.edu/policy2020/votervital/how-many-undocumented-immigrants-are-in-the-united-states-and-who-are-they (accessed 3/22/20).

12 The United States Elections Project estimates the number of disenfranchised felons in the United States to be 3.1 million people. See United States Elections Project, "2018 November General Election Turnout Rates," December 14, 2018, www.electproject.org/2018g (accessed 3/20/20). The Sentencing Project puts that figure at 6.1 million people. See Christopher Uggen, Ryan Larson, and Sarah Shannon, "6 Million Lost Voters: State-Level Estimates of Felony Disenfranchisement, 2016," The Sentencing Project, October 6, 2016, www.sentencingproject.org/publications/6-million-lost-voters-state-level-estimates-felony-disenfranchisement-2016 (accessed 3/20/20).

235 million persons, or about three-fourths of the people living in the United States. Of course, throughout the nineteenth and much of the twentieth centuries there were even more limits on the franchise, including gender, race, and property restrictions. Perhaps the most significant changes in electoral institutions over the nation's nearly 250-year history have been those that have broken down historical barriers to voting.

To put the changes in election laws in perspective, suppose that the nineteenth century's restrictive rules applied today—that only White, male citizens over 21 were allowed to vote. If that had been the case in 2020, the eligible electorate would have totaled only about 76 million—about one in four people. Those restrictions would have made for a very different electorate in terms of interests, values, and preferences; they would have altered the political parties' strategies; and they would have yielded very different election outcomes.

Other restrictions on the franchise relate to how local officials run elections. As Figure 11.2 indicates, voter turnout declined markedly in the United States between 1890 and 1910. These years coincided with two changes in the institutions of elections. Many states (1) imposed rules such as literacy tests to keep immigrants, Black Americans, and other groups out of the electorate and (2) began to create registration systems and lists, so people had to be on a formal list of eligible voters in order to establish that they were allowed to vote on Election Day. Personal registration was one of several "progressive" reforms initiated early in the twentieth century, ostensibly to discourage fraud and "corruption." Among the organizations ostensibly in need of reform were political machines in large cities, which political parties had used to organize immigrant and ethnic populations. Election reforms not only tried to rein in corruption but also sought to weaken the urban factions' power and keep immigrants and Black people from voting.

Voter Registration. Over the years, voter registration restrictions have been modified somewhat to make registration easier. In 1993, for example, Congress approved and President Bill Clinton signed the National Voter Registration Act, commonly known as the "motor voter" law, which allows individuals to register to vote when applying for driver's licenses as well as in public assistance and military recruitment offices.[13] In many jurisdictions, casting a vote automatically registers the voter for the next election. In Europe, by contrast, the government automatically handles voter registration. This is one reason voter turnout rates there are higher than those in the United States.

The mere requirement that people register in order to vote affects turnout rates. Today, we can get reliable counts of the number of persons who are registered as well as the percentage of registered persons who vote. Studies of contemporary voter registration lists find that almost 90 percent of registered voters in fact vote, but only about 70 percent of eligible voters are currently registered to vote. In other words, the electorate is really only about 160 million

---

13 Helen Dewar, "'Motor Voter' Agreement Is Reached," *Washington Post*, April 28, 1993, p. A6.

people—those who are actually registered to vote.[14] There are approximately 50 million eligible voters who have not yet registered—disproportionately those ages 18–29 (Figure 11.3). Getting those people into the registration system, and keeping them on the rolls, is an important way to increase the turnout rate. If you are not registered to vote, you cannot vote.[15]

Why, then, have a registration system? Such systems contain a fairly reliable list of all people who are interested in voting. Local election offices and campaigns use the lists to communicate with voters about when, where, and how to vote. Campaigns use them to prepare grassroots organizing efforts and direct-mail campaigns.

Today, registration lists are the basis for administering elections. Local election offices rely on their registration databases to format ballots, set up precincts, determine which voters should vote in which places, and communicate with people. Any given area contains many overlapping election jurisdictions, creating many different, unique combinations of offices. For example, one voter might reside in Congressional District 1, State Senate District 7, State Representative District 3, City Council District 1, and so forth. Variations in district boundaries may mean that voters a few blocks apart live in entirely different districts. Although they live in the same city, these voters must vote on different ballots. The first voter is not supposed to vote in Congressional District 2, for instance. Registration lists have become vitally important in sorting out where people should vote. Using district boundaries, local election offices determine how many distinct ballots they must prepare. Each distinct ballot is assigned to a precinct, with only one ballot constellation per precinct. The local election office then uses the registration list to assign people to precincts and to communicate to individual voters exactly where they are supposed to vote. Without this means of assigning voters to precincts and communicating with voters, there would be considerable confusion on Election Day. Efforts to eliminate or reform registration requirements must confront this very practical problem.

Currently, 22 states (Alaska, California, Colorado, Connecticut, Hawaii, Idaho, Illinois, Iowa, Maine, Maryland, Michigan, Minnesota, Montana, Nevada, New Hampshire, New Mexico, North Carolina, Utah, Vermont, Washington, Wisconsin, and Wyoming) and the District of Columbia have same-day registration. Nineteen states automatically register people to vote when they have a transaction with the state government, such as the department of motor vehicles. People are allowed to opt out, but almost all choose to be registered to vote. Electronic voting equipment now makes it possible to program many different ballots on a single machine, so that each voter can key in his or her address to get the appropriate ballot and vote. Such machines enable people to vote anywhere

---

14 U.S. Census Bureau, "Voting and Registration in the Election of November 2018," April 23, 2019, www.census.gov/data/tables/time-series/demo/voting-and-registration/p20-583.html (accessed 3/31/20).

15 Stephen Ansolabehere and Eitan Hersh, "Validation: What Big Data Reveal about Survey Misreporting and the Real Electorate," *Political Analysis* 20, no. 4 (Autumn 2012): 437–59.

Figure 11.3
VOTER REGISTRATION RATES BY DEMOGRAPHIC

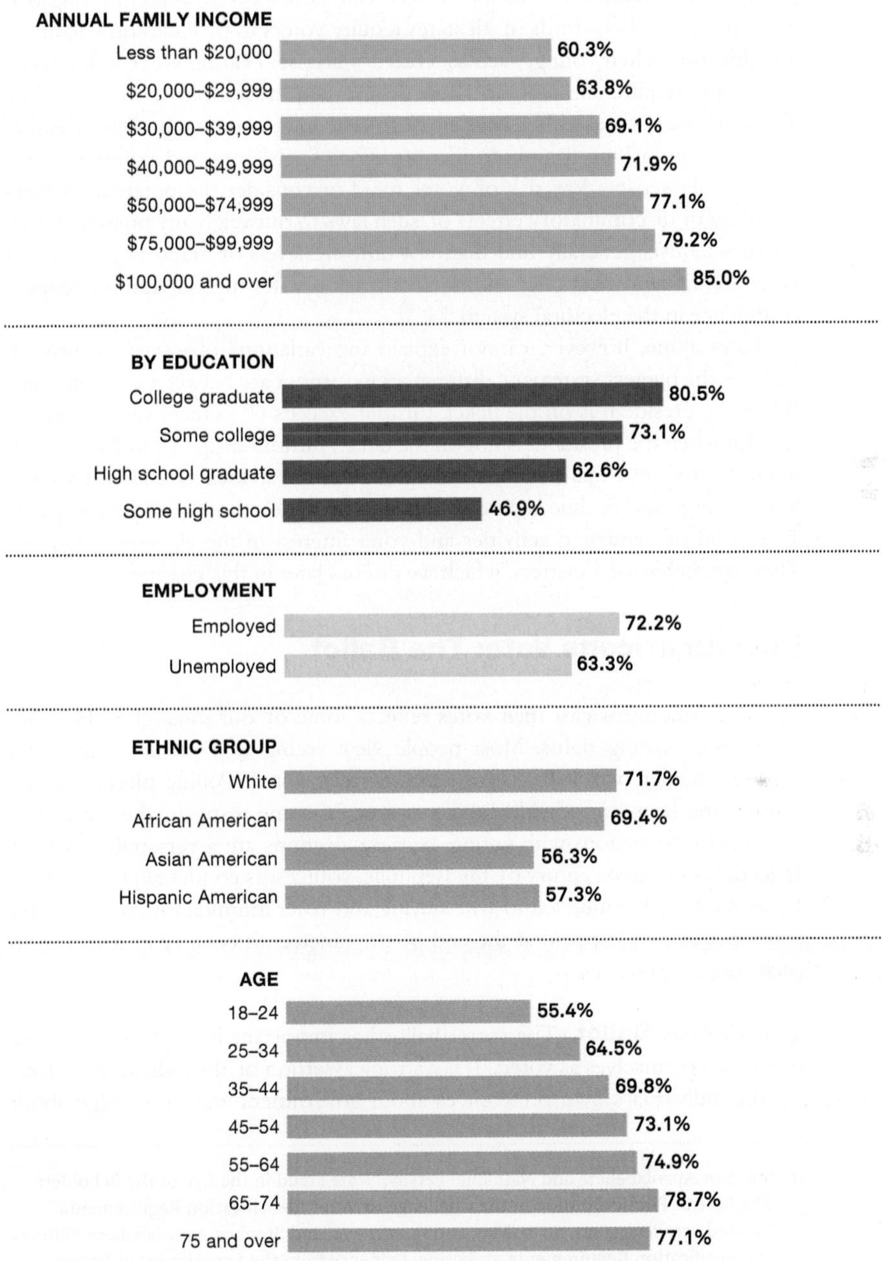

ANNUAL FAMILY INCOME

Less than $20,000	60.3%
$20,000–$29,999	63.8%
$30,000–$39,999	69.1%
$40,000–$49,999	71.9%
$50,000–$74,999	77.1%
$75,000–$99,999	79.2%
$100,000 and over	85.0%

BY EDUCATION

College graduate	80.5%
Some college	73.1%
High school graduate	62.6%
Some high school	46.9%

EMPLOYMENT

Employed	72.2%
Unemployed	63.3%

ETHNIC GROUP

White	71.7%
African American	69.4%
Asian American	56.3%
Hispanic American	57.3%

AGE

18–24	55.4%
25–34	64.5%
35–44	69.8%
45–54	73.1%
55–64	74.9%
65–74	78.7%
75 and over	77.1%

SOURCE: U.S. Census Bureau, www.census.gov/data/tables/time-series/demo/voting-and
-registration/p20-583.html (accessed 3/20/20).

and lessen the need for lists to assign voters to precincts. These innovations may lead ultimately to an election system that does not require or rely heavily on registration before Election Day, but even these mechanisms still require the voter to register.

The past decade has seen a push to create new ways of authenticating voters at the polls. Two-thirds of all states require voters to provide some form of identification when voting, such as a driver's license. Fearing voter fraud, some states now require all voters to show government-issued photo identification. The remaining states either have no formal requirements or prohibit election officials from asking for photo identification. Legislators and voters in these states either sense a low risk of voter fraud or consider the potential barriers to voting or discriminatory effects of such laws to outweigh any possible fraud. Social scientists generally find that, not only are levels of fraud negligible, but voter identification laws have minimal effects on voter turnout and on people's confidence in the electoral system.[16]

Laws alone, however, cannot explain the variations observed in turnout. Perhaps the biggest systematic differences in turnout are between election years. When the president is on the ticket, turnout exceeds 60 percent of the electorate. But when the president is not on the ticket, turnout drops 15 to 20 points in midterm congressional elections and up to 50 points in local elections. This pattern of surge and decline is partly a function of the election calendar and partly a function of campaign activities and voter interest in the election outcomes. These are behavioral matters, which we discuss later in this chapter.

How Americans Vote: The Ballot

The way Americans cast their votes reflects some of our most cherished precepts about voting rights. Most people view voting as a private matter and choose whether or not to tell others how they voted. Polling places provide privacy and keep an individual's vote secret. In some respects, the secret ballot seems incongruous with voting, because elections are a very public matter. Indeed, for the first century of the Republic, voting was conducted in the open. However, public voting led to vote buying and voter intimidation, so the secret ballot became widespread at the end of the nineteenth century in response to such corrupt practices.

The Secret Ballot. The secret ballot has important implications for how people see themselves as voters. It is a strong assertion of the individual, reflecting the individual's own preferences about government and knowledge about

---

16 Stephen Ansolabehere and Nathaniel Persily, "Vote Fraud in the Eye of the Beholder: The Role of Public Opinion in the Challenge to Voter Identification Requirements," *Harvard Law Review* 121, no. 7 (May 2008): 1737–74; and Stephen Ansolabehere, "Effects of Identification Requirements on Voting: Evidence from the Experiences of Voters on Election Day," *PS: Political Science and Politics* 42, no. 1 (January 2009): 127–30. For additional insights, see The National Conference of State Legislatures, https://www.ncsl.org/research/elections-and-campaigns/voter-id.aspx.

the choices—not the influences of others. In contrast, when voting is public, the choices individuals make reflect the group as well as their own thinking. Vestiges of public voting can be seen in town meetings in New England states and at party nominating caucuses such as those in Iowa, Nevada, and Minnesota.

Attend a caucus or town hall meeting and you will appreciate the difference between these events and voting in the seclusion of a voting booth. Town meetings and caucuses often exhibit the tendency of groups to follow particular individuals or to reflect a public conversation rather than each person's private opinion. Public voting also demands more of the individual—more time, more attention to the decision-making process—and thus draws in a much smaller and more committed electorate. These two methods can lead to very different results. During the 2020 Democratic primaries, Joe Biden won almost all of the states that held primary elections, and Bernie Sanders, whose campaign relied heavily on grassroots organizing, won most of the states that held caucuses.

The Australian Ballot. With the secret ballot came another innovation, the **Australian ballot**, which lists the names of all candidates running for a given office and allows the voter to select any candidate for any office. This procedure was introduced in Australia in 1851, and in the United States today it is universal. Before the 1880s some Americans voted in public meetings; others voted on paper ballots printed by the political parties or by slates of candidates. Voters chose which ballot they wished to submit—a Republican ballot, a Democratic ballot, a Populist ballot, a Greenback ballot, and so forth. The ballots were often printed on different colors of paper so that voters could easily distinguish them—and so that local party workers could observe who cast which ballots. With these party ballots, voters could not choose candidates from different parties for different offices; they had to vote the party line.

 Australian ballot

An electoral format that presents the names of all the candidates for any given office on the same ballot.

In the 10-year period from 1885 to 1895, nearly every state adopted the Australian ballot and, with it, the secret ballot. This new form of voting took hold in an era of administrative reform in government throughout the United States. County governments took on the job of formatting and printing ballots, and conducting elections became an administrative task of government rather than a political activity of the parties. The change also reflected state governments' efforts to break the hold of local political organizations. Because all ballots are identical under the Australian form, it became difficult to observe who voted for which party. More important, voters could choose any candidate for any office, breaking the parties' control over the vote. The introduction of the Australian ballot gave rise to the phenomenon of split-ticket voting, in which some voters select candidates from different parties for different offices.[17]

The secret and Australian ballot enabled voters to choose candidates as well as parties and facilitated the rise of the personal vote and the incumbency advantage in American electoral politics. (See the discussion of the incumbency advantage in Congress in Chapter 6.) In contrast, under the party ballot,

---

17 Jerrold G. Rusk, "The Effect of the Australian Ballot Reform on Split Ticket Voting, 1876–1908," *American Political Science Review* 64, no. 4 (December 1970): 1220–38.

voters could not choose particular candidates without voting for all candidates of the same party or slate. Voters could not choose, say, one party's nominee for president and another party's nominee for the House of Representatives. In the absence of a real possibility of split-ticket voting, a desire for change could manifest only as a vote against all candidates of the party in power. When the electorate voted to oust those in power at the national level, the opposing party or slate at state and local levels would sweep into office as well. As a result, elections in the United States before 1896 were highly partisan, often producing wholesale changes in control of government at all levels. Today, the Australian ballot allows voters to judge the performance both of individual officeholders and of the political parties as a whole. And the possibility of split-ticket voting has led to increasingly divided control of government as well as the rise of personal voting.

single-member district

An electoral district that elects only one representative—the typical method of representation in the United States.

Electoral College

An institution established by the Constitution for the election of the president and vice president of the United States. Every four years, voters in each state and the District of Columbia elect electors who, in turn, cast votes for the president and vice president. The candidate receiving a majority of the electoral vote for president or vice president is elected.

Where Americans Vote: Electoral Districts

Elected officials in the United States represent places as well as people. Today, the president, representatives, senators, governors, and many other state and local officials are elected through geographic areas called electoral districts. Generally speaking, the United States employs **single-member districts** with equal populations. This means that the U.S. House of Representatives, almost all state legislatures, and almost all local governments correspond to their own set of districts in which each district elects one representative, and all of the districts for a given legislative body must have equal populations.[18]

Representation in the Electoral College. Elections for the U.S. Senate and the presidency are the odd cases. In the Senate, the states are the districts. Senate districts, then, have multiple members and unequal populations. In presidential elections, every state is allocated votes in the **Electoral College** equal to its number of U.S. senators (two) plus its number of House members. The District of Columbia is assigned three electors. The states are the districts, and each state chooses all of its electors in a statewide vote. The electors commit to casting their votes for a certain candidate in the Electoral College.[19] Within the political parties, the nomination process in most states allocates delegates to the parties' national conventions on the basis of House districts, and thus population. However, some states choose delegates on a statewide basis, with all districts selecting multiple delegates to the party conventions.

The system of single-member districts with equal populations was not part of the Founders' original design. Rather, it evolved over nearly two centuries,

18 The exceptions in the state legislatures are Arizona, Idaho, Maryland, New Hampshire, New Jersey, North Dakota, South Dakota, Vermont, Washington, and West Virginia. These states use multimember districts in either their state house of representatives or their state senate.

19 The exceptions are Maine and Nebraska, which choose the House electors in individual House districts and the Senate electors in a statewide vote.

from 1790 to 1970. Article II of the Constitution designed the House to represent the people, with the number of seats elected by each state allocated on the basis of population following each decennial census, and designed the Senate to represent the states. The Constitution originally specified that state legislatures would choose the U.S. senators, with each state choosing two senators to serve staggered six-year terms. That system was jettisoned in 1913 with the adoption of the Seventeenth Amendment, providing for the direct election of senators.

The Constitution said nothing about the election of individual House members or electors to the Electoral College. That task fell to the states, and in early times the states used many different electoral systems for choosing their House delegations. Most of the early state laws adopted single-member districts: the states divided their territory into as many districts as they had House seats, and each district elected one member. Some states created multimember districts, in which a district would elect more than one legislator. This was common in urban counties and cities, where the population exceeded the number required for two or more districts, but the legislature did not want to draw district boundaries. And some states elected all their House members in a single, statewide election (an at-large election). An even greater hodgepodge of election procedures applied to the state legislatures and local councils.[20]

Congress tried to bring order to the election of House members with the 1842 Apportionment Act. Thanks to an amendment from Representative John Campbell of South Carolina, the act included an additional requirement for districts:

[I]n every case where a State is entitled to more than one Representative, the number to which each State shall be entitled under this apportionment shall be elected by districts, composed of contiguous territory, equal in number to the number of Representatives to which said State may be entitled; no one district electing more than one Representative.[21]

Most states complied with this provision, even though it made them responsible for creating appropriate districts, especially around urban areas. Some states, however, insisted on using at-large and multimember districts up to the 1960s. Finally, in the Uniform Congressional District Act of 1967, Congress forbade the use of anything but single-member districts.

Another important change in the nature of U.S. political districts occurred around the same time. In a series of decisions beginning with *Baker v. Carr* in 1962, the Supreme Court ruled that all federal and state legislative districts must have equal populations: one person, one vote. That simple aphorism today rings as the very definition of democracy, but before 1962 state legislative districts often had highly unequal populations, which meant that some votes in effect

20 For a history of districting politics, see Stephen Ansolabehere and James M. Snyder Jr., *The End of Inequality: One Person, One Vote and the Transformation of American Politics* (New York: Norton, 2008).

21 Congressional Globe, 27th Cong., 2nd Sess., 11, Part 1: 471, 348 (1842).

counted more than others. In the California State Senate, Los Angeles County elected as many seats as Alpine County, even though Los Angeles had almost 500 times as many people. As a result, voters in Alpine County had greater representation (500 times greater) relative to their population than did voters in Los Angeles County. Similar inequities reigned in every state legislature, producing a pattern of overrepresentation of rural areas and underrepresentation of most urban areas and, especially, suburban counties.

In most states these inequalities arose from neglect. Most state constitutions require redistricting to keep district populations equal, but as urban populations grew, especially in the first half of the twentieth century, those in power realized that redistricting might jeopardize their own reelection. As a result, the legislatures chose to do nothing. With each successive decade, representation in the United States became more unequal, and there seemed to be no way to force the state legislatures to act. Finally, the Court ruled in a series of important cases that unequal representation violated the Fourteenth Amendment's guarantee of equal protection under the law. By 1971, nearly every legislative district in the United States elected one representative, and the populations of the districts for each legislative chamber were equal. By now, single-member districts with equal populations have become the rule in the United States, from city councils and school districts to the House of Representatives.[22]

The U.S. Senate and the Electoral College remain the two great exceptions to the requirements of single-member districts with equal populations. The apportionment of Senate seats to states makes that chamber inherently unequal. California's 40 million people have the same number of senators as Wyoming's 600,000 people. The allocation of Electoral College votes thus creates an inequity in presidential elections whereby larger states select fewer electors per capita than smaller states do. In the 1960s, the Supreme Court let stand the unequal district populations in the Senate and the Electoral College because the representation of states in the Senate is specified in the Constitution. The Senate's scheme of representation can be traced back to the politics of the Constitutional Convention (see Chapter 2), at which delegates sought to craft a new federal legislature that would adequately represent their states' interests. The large states, which favored a legislature with representation for each state based on population, had to strike a deal with the small states, who stood to lose representation under such a plan. The resulting deal, the Connecticut Compromise, created the Senate—a chamber that balanced representation of people with representation of places—and led to a clause in Article V of the Constitution that guarantees equal representation for the states in the Senate.

Nonetheless, the Senate and the Electoral College share the salient feature of elections for the House and for state and local offices: the use of districts to select representatives. All elections in the United States and all elected officials are tied to geographically based constituencies rather than to the national electorate as a whole. This is certainly true for the House and Senate. It applies also

---

22 The story of this transformation is told in Ansolabehere and Snyder, *The End of Inequality*.

to presidential elections, in which candidates focus on winning key states in the Electoral College rather than on winning a majority of the popular vote.

Electoral Districts and Majority Rule.

Electoral districts have a particularly important political consequence: the use of districts tends to magnify the power of the majority. In a system like the one in the United States, with two parties and single-member districts, the party that wins a majority of the vote nationwide tends to win a disproportionate share of the seats. For example, in the 2018 elections for the House of Representatives, Democrats won 51 percent of the two-party vote but 53 percent of the seats nationwide. As an empirical matter, when the election is a tie, the parties win equal shares of the vote, and for every 1 percent of the vote above 50 percent, a party gains an additional 2 percent of the seats. This pattern has been observed in data on House elections over the last 60 years. In 2012, however, Democrats and Republicans finished in a virtual tie for popular votes cast in House races, but the GOP won 54 percent of the seats. This anomaly was partly the result of the Republican advantage at the time in redrawing district boundaries and partly the result of candidate recruitment, retirements, and reapportionment. The Electoral College tends to magnify the votes even more dramatically and can even turn the popular vote on its head. In 2016, Donald Trump won 46 percent of the popular vote, but captured 57 percent of the electoral votes. Electoral districts, then, create a very strong tendency toward majority rule.[23] In 2020, Joe Biden won 51.9 percent of the two-party vote for president, but won 56.9 percent of the delegates to the Electoral College.

This magnifying effect has caused problems for smaller parties and minority groups. Just as districts magnify the number of seats won by the majority party, they shrink the representation of small parties. If a party wins 5 percent of the vote nationwide, it has difficulty winning any seats or Electoral College delegates unless the support for that party is concentrated in a particular geographic area. The most successful third party in recent U.S. history was the Reform Party, started by Ross Perot in 1992. Perot won 19 percent of the presidential vote nationwide that year, but no Electoral College delegates.

The majoritarian tendency of districts also makes it very difficult for racial minorities to gain representation. Black and Latino Americans constitute more than a quarter of the population. Districts crafted without regard to race would spread the minority vote across many districts, making it unlikely that sufficiently large minority populations would exist in enough districts to elect proportionate numbers of Blacks or Latinos to the legislature. This problem, compounded by historic discrimination against Blacks and Latinos, led Congress to amend the Voting Rights Act in 1982 to provide for the creation of legislative districts with enough minority voters to elect House members representative of those groups. This law has been interpreted and implemented to mean that the

---

23 It should be kept in mind that plurality-rule systems such as the U.S. system can also produce unmajoritarian outcomes. Five times in U.S. history, the presidential candidate who has won a plurality of votes nationwide has not won a majority of delegates in the Electoral College. The tendency, however, is to magnify the majority, rather than to distort or subvert it.

---

state legislatures must draw majority-minority House districts whenever possible. As we discuss later, that provision has proved highly controversial in each subsequent round of districting, but the Voting Rights Act has been renewed repeatedly and withstood legal challenges.[24] Even with this rule, Blacks and Latinos made up only 19 percent of the members of the 116th Congress, though 29 percent of people in the United States identify with one of these two groups.

Periodic Redistricting. House districts and state legislative districts are not static. To ensure equal population representation, they must be remade every decade. Responsibility for drawing new district boundaries rests, in most states, with the state legislatures and the governors, with the supervision of the courts and sometimes with the consultation of commissions (Figure 11.4). Every 10 years, the U.S. census updates the states' official population figures and population counts to a fine level of geographic detail. The politicians and others with a stake in the outcome use the census data to craft a new district map; ultimately, the legislatures must pass and the governors must sign a law defining new U.S. House and state legislative districts. Elections to the state legislatures in the year immediately before redistricting, then, become very important, as those elections determine who will draw the maps for congressional and state legislative districts for the coming decade.

Periodic redistricting, although it corrects one problem, invites another. Those in charge may manipulate the new map to increase the likelihood of a particular outcome, such as the election of a majority of seats for one party or interest group. This problem arose with some of the earliest congressional district maps. A particularly egregious map of the 1812 Massachusetts House districts, drawn with the imprimatur of Governor Elbridge Gerry, prompted a *Boston Gazette* editorial writer to dub a very strangely shaped district the "Gerry-Mander." The term stuck, and **gerrymandering** refers broadly to any attempt to create electoral districts for political advantage.

It is easy to intentionally draw an unfair electoral map, especially with the sophisticated software and data on local voting patterns and demographics that are available today. To facilitate districting, the Census Bureau divides the nation into very small geographic areas, called census blocks, which typically contain a few dozen people. U.S. House districts contain over 700,000 people. Political mapmakers combine various local areas, down to census blocks, to construct legislative districts. Those seeking political advantage try to maximize the number of districts that contain a majority of their own voters. There are constraints on political cartography: the district populations must be equal, and all parts of the district must touch (be contiguous). Even with those constraints, the

gerrymandering

The drawing of electoral districts in such a way as to give advantage to one political party.

---

24 In 2013, the Supreme Court struck down Section 4 of the Voting Rights Act, which determined which states were automatically subject to pre-clearance (that is, which states were prohibited from implementing changes to voting without preapproval from the U.S. attorney general). The remaining sections, including the provision for mandatory majority-minority districts and the prohibition against intentional discrimination (Section 2), were not affected. See *Shelby County v. Holder*, 570 U.S. 529 (2013).

Figure 11.4
CONGRESSIONAL REDISTRICTING

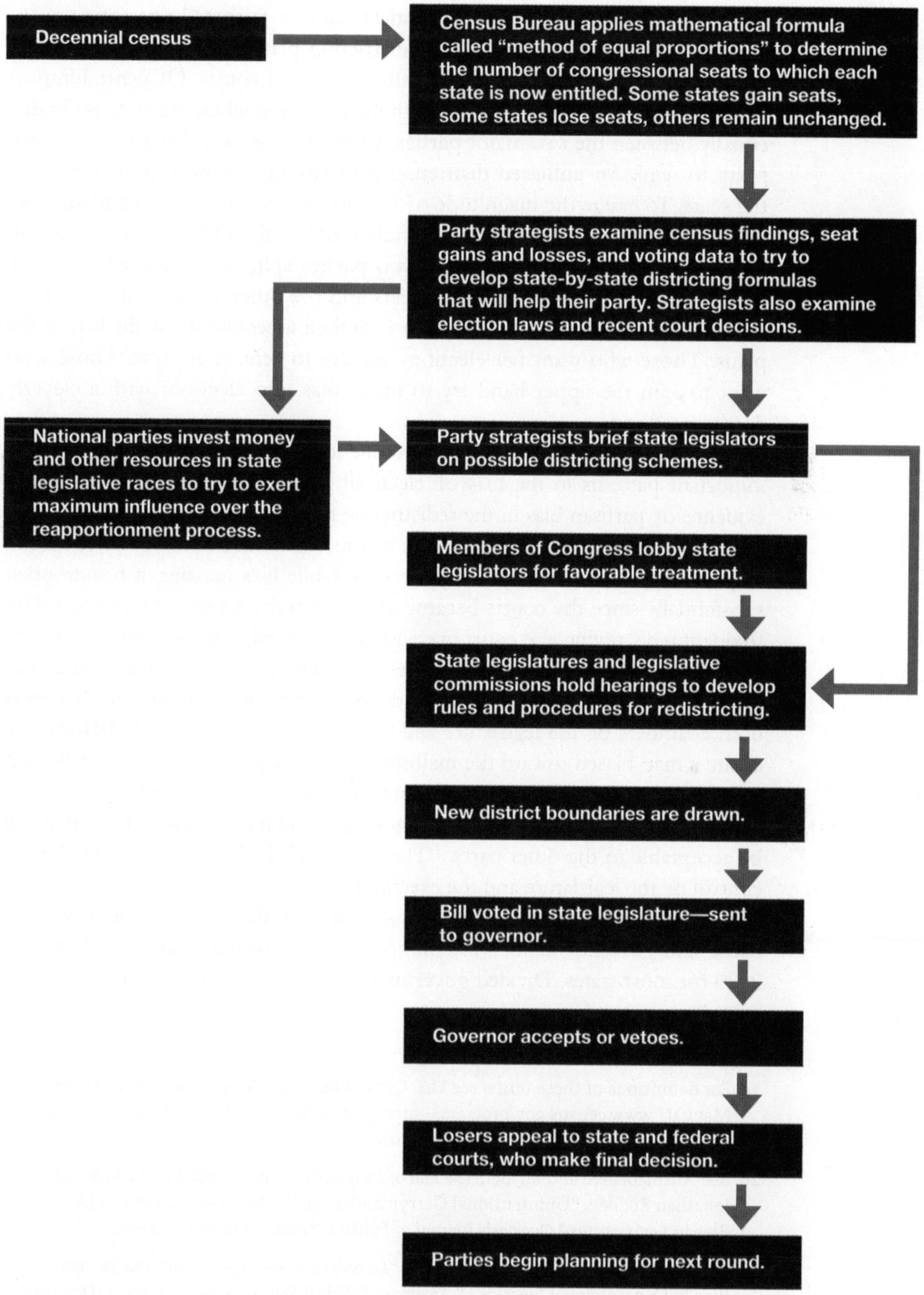

Decennial census → Census Bureau applies mathematical formula called "method of equal proportions" to determine the number of congressional seats to which each state is now entitled. Some states gain seats, some states lose seats, others remain unchanged.

↓

Party strategists examine census findings, seat gains and losses, and voting data to try to develop state-by-state districting formulas that will help their party. Strategists also examine election laws and recent court decisions.

↓

National parties invest money and other resources in state legislative races to try to exert maximum influence over the reapportionment process. → Party strategists brief state legislators on possible districting schemes.

↓

Members of Congress lobby state legislators for favorable treatment.

↓

State legislatures and legislative commissions hold hearings to develop rules and procedures for redistricting.

↓

New district boundaries are drawn.

↓

Bill voted in state legislature—sent to governor.

↓

Governor accepts or vetoes.

↓

Losers appeal to state and federal courts, who make final decision.

↓

Parties begin planning for next round.

number of possible maps that could be drawn for any one state's legislative districts is extremely large.[25] Gerrymandering exemplifies the policy principle at work in the area of elections.

Fairness and Bias. Political scientists examine fairness by assessing quantitatively the features of any given districting plan. Such measures are also widely used by state legislatures, commissions, and courts. Of central importance is the notion of bias. In a hypothetical election where the vote is divided equally between the two major parties, what share of seats do we expect each party to win? An unbiased districting plan would give both parties half of the seats. To gauge the magnitude of the bias in a given districting plan, then, political scientists use the plan to simulate an evenly split election. A bias of, say, 5 points means that when the two parties split the vote evenly, one of the parties wins 55 percent of the seats and the other 45 percent. With each round of districting, experts weigh in with their assessments of the bias in the plans. Those who want fair elections will try to achieve no bias. Those who want to gain the upper hand try to inject bias into elections with a cleverly constructed map.

Empirical study of U.S. House and state legislative elections has documented important patterns in the bias of electoral districts. First, there is significant evidence of partisan bias in the redistricting maps used today. In the 1990s and the first two decades of the 2000s, the bias in the average state legislative district map was approximately 5 points.[26] Second, while bias remains, it has dropped substantially since the courts became involved in the process. Since the 1960s, frequent redistricting and court oversight have forced state legislatures to create districting plans that treat both parties more fairly. Third, the bias is the largest in states where the legislature conducts redistricting and one party controls both chambers of the legislature and the governor's office: the legislature can create a map biased toward the majority party, and the governor will likely sign it. However, when different parties control the legislature and the executive, the legislature might face a veto from the governor and must create districts that will be acceptable to the other party.[27] This is one of the benefits of divided party control of the legislature and the executive.

These patterns underscore the importance of the elections for state legislature and governor in the year immediately before redistricting—which was 2020 for most states. Divided government or unified control of the legislature

25 For definitions of these units, see U.S. Census Bureau, "Geographic Areas Reference Manual," www.census.gov/programs-surveys/geography/guidance/geographic-areas-reference-manual.html (accessed 3/31/20).

26 See Ansolabehere and Snyder, *The End of Inequality,* chap. 11; and Jowei Chen and Jonathan Rodden, "Unintentional Gerrymandering: Political Geography and Electoral Bias in Legislatures," *Quarterly Journal of Political Science* 8 (2013): 239–69.

27 See Gary King and Robert X. Browning, "Democratic Representation and Partisan Bias in Congressional Elections," *American Political Science Review* 81, no. 4 (December 1987): 1251–73.

and governorship can determine the fairness of the boundaries drawn to elect members of Congress and the state legislatures throughout the coming decade. An unbiased map can make for fair representation of the public's preferences, but a biased map can distort the voice of the majority.

Politicians can use gerrymandering to dilute the strength not only of a party but also of a group. Consider racial minorities. One common strategy has involved redrawing congressional district boundaries so as to disperse a Black population that would otherwise constitute a majority within the original district. This form of gerrymandering was used in Mississippi during the 1960s and 1970s to prevent the election of Black candidates to Congress. Historically, the state's Black population was clustered along the Mississippi River Delta. From 1882 until 1966, the Delta constituted one congressional district in which Black voters had a clear majority; discrimination in voter registration and at the polls, however, guaranteed the continual election of White congressmen. With passage of the Voting Rights Act in 1965, this district would almost surely have gone to a Black candidate or one favored by the Black majority. To prevent that, the Mississippi legislature drew new House districts that split the Black population across three districts so that it constituted a majority in none. This gerrymandering scheme helped prevent the election of any Black representative until 1987, when Mike Espy became the first African American since Reconstruction to represent Mississippi in Congress.

Continuing controversies about the state legislatures' involvement in drawing their own districts have raised deep concerns about the fairness of the process. Even with some states creating commissions, appointing "special masters" to draw the maps, or even using independent commissions, it has proved difficult to find a satisfactory reform for redistricting.

Now, new developments in geographic information systems (GIS) software and the provision of census data enable anyone to draw credible district maps. Opening up the process, it is hoped, will lessen the extent and effect of gerrymandering.

What It Takes to Win: Plurality Rule

The fourth prominent feature of U.S. electoral law is the criterion for winning. Although Americans often embrace majority rule as a defining characteristic of democracy, the real standard is **plurality rule**. The candidate who receives the most votes in the relevant district or constituency wins the election, even if that candidate doesn't receive a majority of votes. Suppose three parties nominate candidates for a seat and divide the vote such that one wins 34 percent and the other two each receive 33 percent of the vote. Under plurality rule, the candidate with 34 percent wins the seat, even though he did not win a majority of votes (more than 50 percent). There are different types of plurality systems. The system most widely used in the United States combines plurality rule with single-member districts and is called "first past the post." In choosing delegates for the Electoral College, most states use a "winner take all" plurality system in which

 plurality rule

A type of electoral system in which victory goes to the individual who gets the most votes, but not necessarily a majority of the votes cast.

majority rule

A type of electoral system in which, to win an office, a candidate must receive a majority (50 percent plus one) of all the votes cast in the relevant district.

the candidate who receives the most votes wins all of the delegates.[28] In state-wide elections, two states, Louisiana and Georgia, require a candidate to receive at least 50 percent of all votes to win. This is **majority rule**. If no candidate receives a majority, a runoff election is held about one month later between the two candidates who received the most votes in the first round. Other systems also use plurality- and majority-rule criteria. For instance, some city councils still have multimember districts. The top vote-getters win the seats. If there are, say, seven seats to fill, the seven candidates who win the most votes each win a seat.

Plurality rule is often criticized for yielding electoral results that do not reflect the public's preferences. Votes for the losing candidates seem wasted because they do not translate into representation. Indeed, as the example of the three-candidate race suggests, it is possible that a majority of voters wanted someone other than the winner. In the aggregate, plurality rule with single-member districts tends to inflate the share of seats won by the largest party and deflate the others' shares. A striking example comes from Great Britain. In 2015, the British Conservative Party won 37 percent of the vote and 51 percent of seats, while the Labour Party placed second with 30 percent of the vote and 36 percent of seats. The remainder of the votes and seats were distributed very unevenly among three other parties. For example, the UK Independence Party came in third with 13 percent of the vote, but won only 1 seat in the 650-seat House of Commons. Nevertheless, single-member districts with plurality rule offer certain advantages. The system enables voters to choose individuals to represent them personally, not just political parties, and it picks a definite winner without the need for runoff elections.

Proportional Representation. Among the world's democracies, the main alternative to single-member districts with plurality rule is **proportional representation**. Under proportional representation, competing parties win legislative seats in proportion to their share of the popular vote. For example, if three parties running for seats in the legislature divide the vote such that one wins 34 percent and the other two receive 33 percent of the vote, the first party receives 34 percent of the seats and the other two receive 33 percent of the seats.

Proportional representation is used rarely in the United States. The most substantial elections in which it is employed are the Democratic presidential primary elections. During the 1988 primary season, Jesse Jackson routinely won 20 percent of the vote in the primaries but garnered only about 5 percent of the delegates. To make the Democratic National Convention and the party more representative of its disparate voting groups, Jackson negotiated with other party leaders to change the delegate allocation rules so that delegates within congressional districts would be assigned on a proportional basis. If a district elects five delegates, a candidate wins a delegate if the candidate receives at least

proportional representation

A multimember district system that awards seats to political parties in proportion to the percentage of the vote each party won.

---

28 Over the centuries, many systems for voting and determining electoral outcomes have been devised. For an excellent analysis of voting systems and a complete classification, see Gary W. Cox, *Making Votes Count: Strategic Coordination in the World's Electoral Systems* (New York: Cambridge University Press, 1997).

20 percent of the vote in the district, two delegates if the candidate wins at least 40 percent of the vote, and so forth. Before this rule change, the Democratic Party awarded all delegates from a given congressional district to the candidate who won a plurality of the vote. Like any districted system with plurality rule, this created a strong majoritarian tendency.

Plurality rule in single-member districts has a very important consequence. It is the reason for two-party politics in the United States. Worldwide, countries with plurality rule in single-member districts have far fewer political parties than other nations. Typically, elections under plurality rule boil down to just two major parties that routinely compete for power, with one of them winning a majority of legislative seats outright. Proportional representation systems, in contrast, tend to have many more than two parties. Rarely does a single party win a majority of seats. Governments form as coalitions of many different parties. Political scientist Maurice Duverger described that pattern in a path-breaking book, *Party Politics* (1951). Duverger formalized his law of politics quite simply: plurality rule creates two-party politics; proportional representation encourages more than two parties.

The rationale behind **Duverger's Law** has two components: the strategic behavior of politicians and the behavior of voters. Consider, first, how politicians would think about the prospects of forming a new party. Suppose that there already are two parties, a center-right party and a center-left party. For a politician from the far right, for example, the parties do not represent the ideals she espouses. She wants a far-right policy most, a center-right policy less, and least of all a center-left policy. One solution is for her to leave the center-right party and form a far-right party. But doing that helps the center-left party by splitting the vote of those on the right without affecting the vote for the center-left party. Under plurality rule, the center-left party would almost certainly win, an outcome that the far-right politician doesn't want at all. Thus politicians on the extremes cannot gain by forming a new party. A politician with a centrist orientation also cannot win the election if the center-right and center-left parties are not too extreme. The center-right party would win all votes of voters on the right and on the center right. The same is true for the center-left party. That would leave only a small segment of true centrists for a potential centrist party. Hence, if the current parties are not too extreme, there is no incentive for a third party to enter a two-party system when plurality rule is the criterion for winning.

Voters follow a similar logic. They do not want to waste their votes. If voters understand that the extremist party or candidate cannot win, they will vote for the more moderate alternative. Although second best for extremist voters, the moderate has a better chance of winning. This logic leads the extremist voters to choose the moderate party or candidate in order to have a better chance of selecting a candidate more to their liking. Extremist parties and candidates, then, have little incentive to enter a race, and when they do they usually attract few votes.

Such sophisticated voting occurs often in U.S. primary elections. For example, Mitt Romney was significantly more moderate than the typical Republican primary voter in 2012, and he was more moderate than the other Republican

 Duverger's Law

Law of politics, formalized by Maurice Duverger, stating that plurality-rule electoral systems will tend to have two political parties.

candidates. Romney won the nomination easily because many Republicans understood that he represented their best chance in the general election and because he was the strongest of the moderate candidates. Having many moderate candidates, as was the case in the 2016 Republican primaries, can make it difficult to coordinate around any one candidate.

Proportional representation, in contrast, creates an incentive for more parties and candidates to enter because they will win seats in proportion to their support among the national electorate. Proportional systems often have a multitude of parties, none of which represents a decisive majority. Elections in such systems often lead to coalition governments, because no one party wins enough seats to govern. In the Democratic Party, proportional representation has the further effect of stretching out the presidential nominating season. If a candidate wins a plurality of 40 percent of the vote in a state's Democratic primary, he or she wins roughly 40 percent of the delegates. As a result, it usually takes many more victories in the Democratic primaries to accumulate sufficient delegates to lock the nomination. In 2016 Hillary Clinton and Bernie Sanders split the vote and delegates relatively evenly. The election contest was not decided until the final day of the primaries. By contrast, plurality rule and winner take all contests in the Republican primaries mean that, even when there are many candidates, the primary elections are usually decided more quickly. By the end of the primary season, Donald Trump had won less than 47 percent of popularly cast votes, but 62 percent of delegates. At the beginning of May, with more than a month to go in the primaries, CNN declared Trump the GOP's presumptive nominee.

How votes are cast and counted and what it takes to win a seat, then, have substantial consequences for American politics. Plurality rule with single-member districts creates strong pressures toward two-party politics and majority rule in the legislature.

Direct Democracy: The Referendum and the Recall

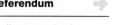

referendum

A direct vote by the electorate on a proposed law that has been passed by the legislature or on a specific governmental action.

Twenty-four states also provide for referendum voting. The **referendum** process allows citizens to vote directly on proposed laws or other governmental actions. Referendums may come about in two ways. First, some state constitutions and laws require that certain types of legislation (such as bonds or property tax increases) be approved by popular vote. Second, people may get a measure put on the ballot by obtaining enough signatures of registered voters to sign a petition. Recently, voters in several states have voted to set limits on tax rates, block state and local spending proposals, define marriage, and prohibit social services for undocumented immigrants. Although it involves voting, a referendum is not an election. The election is an institution of representative government through which voters choose officials to act for them. The referendum process, by contrast, is an institution of direct democracy; it allows voters to govern directly without intervention by government officials. Referendum results, however, are subject to judicial action. If a court finds that a referendum outcome violates the state or national constitution, it can overturn the result. For example, in 2008

California voters passed Proposition 8, which stated, "Only marriage between a man and a woman is valid or recognized in California." A federal district court ruled Proposition 8 unconstitutional in 2010. The Supreme Court let the district court's ruling stand and in 2015 ruled in *Obergefell v. Hodges* that marriage is a fundamental right guaranteed to all people.[29]

There are other means to place issues on the ballot besides the referendum. Twenty-four states also permit various forms of the initiative. Whereas the referendum process enables citizens to affirm or reject a policy already produced by legislative action, the **initiative** provides citizens with a way forward when no legislative action has been taken. They can place a policy proposal (legislation or a state constitutional amendment) on the ballot to be approved or rejected by the electorate. To gain a place on the ballot, a petition must be accompanied by a minimum number of voters' signatures—a requirement that varies from state to state—that have been certified by the state's secretary of state.

initiative

A process by which citizens may petition to place a policy proposal on the ballot for public vote.

The initiative process has both potential advantages and disadvantages. Ballot propositions generally involve policies that the state legislature cannot (or does not want to) resolve. Like referendum issues, they are often highly emotional and, consequently, not well suited to resolution via popular voting. However, one of the "virtues" of the initiative is that it may force action: legislative leaders may induce recalcitrant colleagues to move on controversial issues by raising the possibility that a worse outcome will result from inaction.[30]

Legal provisions for **recall** elections exist in 18 states. The recall is an electoral device that allows voters to remove governors and other state officials from office before the expiration of their term. Federal officials such as the president and members of Congress are not subject to recall. Generally speaking, a recall effort begins with a petition campaign. For example, in California, if 12 percent of the people who voted in the last general election sign petitions demanding a special recall election, the state board of elections must schedule one. Such petition campaigns are relatively common, but most fail to garner enough signatures to bring the matter to a statewide vote. In Colorado, a handful of legislative candidates were recalled in 2013 for their votes on gun control. Labor unions campaigned to recall Wisconsin governor Scott Walker following cuts in state employee benefits and the collective bargaining rights of unions, and they forced Walker to stand for a special election in June 2012. Governor Walker managed to fend off the challenge from Milwaukee mayor Tom Barrett.

recall

The removal of a public official by popular vote.

Direct democracy can change legislative, executive, and even judicial decision making. The referendum, initiative, and recall all entail shifts in agenda-setting power. The referendum gives an impassioned electoral majority the opportunity to reverse legislation that displeases it, thus affecting the initial strategic calculations of institutional agenda setters (who want to get as much of

29 *Hollingsworth v. Perry*, 570 U.S. 693 (2013); and *Obergefell v. Hodges*, U.S. 576 _____ (2015).

30 This point is developed in Morten Bennedsen and Sven E. Feldmann, "Lobbying Legislatures," *Journal of Political Economy* 110, no. 4 (August 2002): 919–46.

what they want without the electorate subsequently reversing it). The initiative has a similar effect, but here it motivates institutional agenda setters toward action rather than inaction. Combining the two, an institutional agenda setter faces a dilemma: Do I act, risking a reversal via referendum, or do I maintain the status quo, risking an overturn via initiative? The recall complements both of these choices, keeping institutional agenda setters on their toes to avoid being ousted. As the institution principle implies, these arrangements do not just provide citizens with governance tools. They also affect the strategic calculations of institutional politicians—legislators and governors.

While initiatives and referendums are often touted as a means of ensuring that the legislature represents the public's preferences, they are also criticized for being expensive, for slowing down government action, and for making bad laws. The issues brought before the public are often emotional matters, which require deliberation and reflection, and many more complicated questions, such as public spending, might be better addressed in a legislative setting where trade-offs can serve to maintain balance in the overall policy area (such as the budget). Many critics of direct democracy point to the fiscal problems that confront California, where a long history of ballot measures restrict how California can raise revenue and how it must distribute expenditures. This leaves the legislature and governor little flexibility when facing an economic downturn.

HOW VOTERS DECIDE

While rules and laws—the institutional side of elections—impose order on the electoral process, elections ultimately reflect the political preferences of millions of individuals. The rationality principle comes into play in understanding what voters want and how they think. The policy principle reflects how they behave in the presence of electoral institutions. Do voters choose to change government or to keep the present government in place? To change the direction of public-policy making, broadly speaking, or stay the course?

The voter's decision can be understood as two linked decisions: *whether* to vote and *for whom* to vote. Social scientists have examined both factors by studying election returns, survey data, and laboratory experiments as well as conducting field experiments during elections. Generations of research into these questions has yielded a broad picture of how voters decide. First, the decision to vote or not correlates strongly with individuals' social characteristics, especially age and education, but it also depends on the electoral choices and context. An individual who knows nothing about the candidates or dislikes all of the choices is unlikely to vote. Second, which candidates or party the voters choose depends primarily on partisan loyalties, issues, and candidate characteristics. Partisan loyalties appear to be the strongest predictor of the vote, though party attachments also reflect issues and individuals' experience with candidates. Party, issues, and candidates act together to shape vote choice.

Voters and Nonvoters

According to the Census Bureau's Current Population Survey, 61 percent of adults reported that they were registered voters in 2018, and 49 percent of adults reported that they voted that year. Excluding noncitizens, who are ineligible to vote in federal elections, 67 percent of the adult citizen population is registered, and 53 percent of citizens of voting age turned out in 2018. Thus almost 50 percent of those who could have voted did not. Why do so many people not vote?

A general explanation is elusive, but social scientists find that a few demographic characteristics are strong predictors of who votes. Most important are age, education, and residential mobility. Other factors, such as gender, income, and race, also matter, but to a much smaller degree. According to the 2018 Current Population Survey, only 36 percent of those under age 29 voted that year; by comparison, 66 percent of those over age 65 years voted—a difference in turnout between the groups of 30 percentage points. The effect of age on voting surely translated into an electoral difference. The interests of retirees are much more likely to receive attention from the government than are the interests of those in college or just entering the labor force.

Grouping voters by level of education shows similarly large differences. More than 65 percent of people with a college education voted, and the rate was 74 percent among those with a professional degree. In contrast, just 27 percent of those without a high school diploma voted, and 42 percent of those with only a high school degree voted.[31] Finally, consider residency and mobility. Only 55 percent of people who had lived in their current residence for less than a year reported voting, compared with 76 percent of people who had lived in their residence for at least five years. Those who own their home or apartment vote at a 63 percent rate, but only 41 percent of renters vote.[32] Politicians listen to those who vote, and they are disproportionately older, better educated, and more rooted in their communities.

As discussed earlier, election laws have historically had a large effect on the size and character of the electorate. The decision to vote itself consists of two steps: registration and turnout. Minimizing registration requirements may increase participation, as the option of Election Day registration has shown. As of 2019, 21 states plus the District of Columbia allow people to register on Election Day at the polls or at a government office.[33] The three states with

---

31 Jordan Misra, "Behind the Midterm Election Turnout," U. S. Census Bureau, April 23, 2019, www.census.gov/library/stories/2019/04/behind-2018-united-states-midterm-election-turnout.html (accessed 3/20/20).

32 The most reliable source of information about the demographics of voting is the Current Population Survey, conducted by the U.S. Census Bureau. For these and other statistics see U.S. Census Bureau, "Voting and Registration in the Election of November 2018."

33 "Same Day Voter Registration," National Conference of State Legislatures, June 28, 2019, www.ncsl.org/research/elections-and-campaigns/same-day-registration.aspx (accessed 3/20/20).

the longest experience with same-day registration—Minnesota, Wisconsin, and Maine—do have higher turnout than most other states, and most studies suggest that in a typical state adopting such a law would increase turnout by 3 to 5 percent.[34]

Demographics and laws are only part of what accounts for voting and nonvoting. The choices presented to voters are also important. The problem is that many people do not feel engaged by current elections or dislike politics altogether. People who are disinterested, are "too busy to vote," or do not like the candidates tend not to vote. The Census Bureau survey asks registered nonvoters why they did not vote. The top four reasons are: "too busy," "sick or disabled," "not interested," and "did not like the choices."

Not voting may also stem partly from a sense that the election does not hinge on how any individual votes. As advanced by economist Anthony Downs in *An Economic Theory of Democracy*, rational citizens may decide whether to vote based on a calculation of the potential benefits and costs of voting plus their personal sense of civic duty or psychological compunction to vote. There are, however, strong differences in voting rates across demographic groups, and these might have political consequences. What if everyone voted? In some domains, universal voting would certainly alter government policy. Increasing the voting rate of younger cohorts would probably affect government policy on Social Security, for instance. But 100 percent turnout would not likely lead to electing a different person for president or putting a different party in control of Congress. Voters and nonvoters, for all of their demographic and political differences, hold fairly similar partisan views, ideological orientations, and preferences about the candidates.[35] Voters are somewhat more conservative and more Republican than nonvoters, as a result of the higher income levels and higher home ownership incidence of voters, but the median voter would be only slightly more liberal if everyone voted.

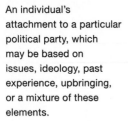

party identification

An individual's attachment to a particular political party, which may be based on issues, ideology, past experience, upbringing, or a mixture of these elements.

Partisan Loyalty

The strongest predictor of how a person will vote is that individual's attachment to a political party. The American National Election Studies, exit polls, and media polls have found that even in times of great political change, the overwhelming majority of Americans identify with one of the two major political parties and vote almost entirely in accordance with that identity. Survey researchers ascertain **party identification** with simple questions along the following

34 The classic study in this area is Raymond E. Wolfinger and Steven J. Rosenstone, *Who Votes?* (New Haven, CT: Yale University Press, 1980). See also Steven J. Rosenstone and John Mark Hansen, *Mobilization, Participation, and Democracy in America* (New York: Macmillan, 1993); and Barry C. Burden, David T. Canon, Kenneth R. Mayer, and Donald P. Moynihan, "Election Laws, Mobilization, and Turnout: The Unanticipated Consequences of Election Reform," *American Journal of Political Science* 58, no. 1 (January 2014): 95–109.

35 See, for instance, Verba, Schlozman, and Brady, *Voice and Equality*.

lines: "Generally speaking, do you consider yourself to be a Democrat, a Republican, an Independent, or what?"[36] Survey researchers further classify respondents by asking of those who choose a party whether they identify strongly or weakly with that party, and by asking independents whether they lean toward one party or another.

Over the past three decades, party identifications have broken evenly between Democrats and Republicans. Figure 12.2 on p. 532 shows the historical fluctuations in party identification. From the 1930s to the 1970s, those who identified as Democrats outnumbered those who identified as Republicans; but from the 1980s through 2000, the balance was stable. From 2002 through mid-2009, Democrats gained in overall party identification and Republicans lost ground, largely because of generational changes and the backlash against the Iraq War.[37] In President Barack Obama's first term, however, partisan battles over health care and other legislative initiatives, continuing wars in Iraq and Afghanistan, and high unemployment rates eroded public support for the Democrats. Today, public support for the parties is fairly evenly split, with a 6 to 9 point edge for the Democrats.[38] Over the decade since the American public turned against the Iraq War, the percentage of independents has crept steadily upward and is now the largest group in the electorate. Over 40 percent of Americans identify as independents, while 25 percent call themselves Republican and 28 percent call themselves Democrats. The parties have struggled to gain traction among an electorate that has become skeptical of the government's ability to protect and create jobs and to conduct clear, strong foreign policy. Although they don't identify with one party or the other, many independents lean toward one of the two parties.[39] As of July 2020, Gallup reported that 25 percent of Americans are Republicans or lean Republican, 31 percent are Democrats or lean Democratic, and 40 percent are independents.[40]

Party identifications capture voters' predispositions toward their party's candidates. Many of these predispositions reflect voters' public policy preferences,

36 This is the wording used by the Gallup Poll. Others ask, "In politics today . . ." or offer "or another party" instead of "or what."

37 Jeffrey M. Jones, "More Independents Lean GOP; Smallest Gap since '05," September 30, 2009, www.gallup.com/poll/123362/independents-lean-gop-party-gap-smallest-since-05.aspx (accessed 8/26/19).

38 Surveys differ in their estimates of the percentages in each of the party groups depending on how the question is asked. Courtney Kennedy and Scott Keeter, "Why Public Opinion Polls Don't Include the Same Number of Republicans and Democrats," Pew Research Center, October 25, 2019, www.pewresearch.org/fact-tank/2019/10/25/why-public-opinion-polls-dont-include-the-same-number-of-republicans-and-democrats (accessed 3/31/20).

39 Marc Hetherington, "Resurgent Mass Partisanship: The Role of Elite Polarization," *American Political Science Review* 95, no. 3 (September 2001): 619–31; and Pew Research Center, "Party Identification," www.pewresearch.org/topics/political-party-affiliation (accessed 4/22/20).

40 Gallup, "Party Affiliation," https://news.gallup.com/poll/15370/party-affiliation.aspx (accessed 7/4/20).

such as those on taxes, abortion, or civil rights. These long-standing policy positions lead to divisions in party identification and voting patterns among different demographic groups. Large majorities of African Americans and Latinos, for example, identify and vote with the Democratic Party. Since 1980 there has also been a gender gap in voting. Women identify and vote more with the Democrats than men do. That gap has persisted, averaging 7 percentage points over the past three decades.[41] The 2016 presidential election saw the widest gender gap in history, with the first female major-party candidate, Democrat Hillary Clinton, in the running: Clinton received 54 percent of women's votes but only 41 percent of the vote among men, a difference of 13 points. That difference is also significant because women now make up a majority (53 percent) of voters. Clinton was particularly popular among Black women and Latinas, among whom she won 82 percent of the vote. Her support among these women was 8 points higher than her support among Black and Latino men. Clinton fared far less well among White voters, losing a majority of the vote of White men and—surprisingly, considering the campaign's themes—White women. But the highest gender gap in history was driven primarily by White men, who voted more strongly for Trump than they had for any other Republican since polling began.[42]

It is a subject of considerable debate as to why the gender gap arose in the late 1970s and early 1980s and why it has persisted. The timing of its emergence is consistent with the two parties' alignment on a range of civil rights issues that affect women. On issues such as pay equity, divorce law, abortion, and women's health, Democratic administrations and Congress have pursued policies much more favorable to the interests of women. In 2020, Joe Biden asserted that it is a woman's right to choose to have an abortion, and he stressed his support for Planned Parenthood as a provider of many different women's health services. Donald Trump promised to end federal funding for Planned Parenthood and argued that abortion is acceptable only when a pregnancy threatens the life of the mother or is due to rape or incest. These views alienated many women voters and likely contributed to the increase in the gender gap in the 2020 election. It is, however, hard to pin down the exact causes of the initial shift because so many of the relevant issues emerged at the same time (the 1970s), and shifts in party attachments tend to be subtle and complex.[43] Issues played some part in the rise of the gender gap, but cultural, racial, and regional differences might also explain some of this phenomenon.

Although specific features of the choices and context in a particular election matter, party identifications express how a voter would likely vote in a "neutral" election. Party identifications are extremely good predictors of voting behavior

41 See Pew Research Center, "Wide Gender Gap, Growing Educational Divide in Voters' Party Identification," March 20, 2018, www.people-press.org/2018/03/20/wide-gender-gap-growing-educational-divide-in-voters-party-identification (accessed 4/22/20).

42 Danielle Paquette, "The Unexpected Voters behind the Highest Gender Gap in Recorded Election History," *Washington Post*, November 9, 2016, www.washingtonpost.com/news/wonk/wp/2016/11/09/men-handed-trump-the-election (accessed 3/31/20).

43 Christina Wolbrecht, *The Politics of Women's Rights: Parties, Positions, and Change* (Princeton, NJ: Princeton University Press, 2000).

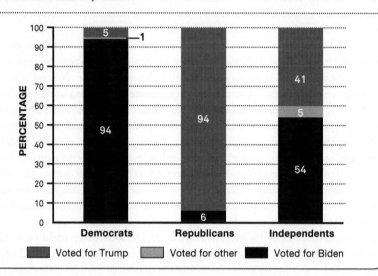

Figure 11.5

THE EFFECT OF PARTY IDENTIFICATION ON THE VOTE FOR PRESIDENT, 2020

Democrats: Voted for Biden 94, Voted for other 1, Voted for Trump 5
Republicans: Voted for Biden 6, Voted for Trump 94
Independents: Voted for Biden 54, Voted for other 5, Voted for Trump 41

Legend: Voted for Trump | Voted for other | Voted for Biden

SOURCE: CNN, "Exit Polls," https://www.cnn.com/election/2020/exit-polls/president/national-results (accessed 11/11/20).

in less prominent elections, such as those for state legislatures or lower-level statewide offices, about which voters may know relatively little. Even in presidential elections, with their extensive advertising and thorough news coverage, party predispositions predict individual voting behavior. Figure 11.5 displays the percentages of self-identified Democrats, Republicans, and independents who voted for Biden, Trump, or someone else in 2020. The 2020 election showed even higher partisan loyalties that past elections. Almost 95 percent of partisans, either Democrat or Republican, chose their party's standard bearer. Independents were pivotal, and they broke 54 percent for Biden and 41 percent for Trump with the remaining 5 percent choosing third-party candidates. Biden's popular vote victory owed to very high levels of loyalty among Democrats and the support of a majority of Independents. We will take a closer look at party identification in Chapter 12. But party is not the only factor in voting. We consider next how issues and candidates shape voting behavior.

Issues

Voting on issues and policies cuts to the core of our understanding of democratic accountability and electoral control over government. A simple, idealized account of **issue voting** goes as follows: Governments make policies and laws on a variety of issues that affect the public. Voters who disagree with those policies and laws on principle or who think those policies have failed will vote against the elected officials who made the decisions. Voters who support the

 issue voting

An individual's tendency to base the decision of which candidate or party to vote for on the extent to which he or she agrees with the candidate or party on specific issues.

policies or like the outcomes will support the incumbent legislators or party. It is important to note that politicians' choices of what laws to enact and what administrative actions to take are made with the express aim of attracting electoral support. Voters choose the candidates and parties that stand for the policies and laws most in line with their own preferences. Even long-term factors like party identification are related to voters' preferences.

The issues that voters decide to pay attention to in a given election stem from their judgments about the past behavior of competing parties and candidates and their hopes and fears about candidates' future behavior. Political scientists call choices that focus on future behavior **prospective voting** and those based on past performance **retrospective voting**. To some extent, whether prospective or retrospective evaluation is more important in a particular election depends on the strategies of the competing candidates. Candidates always endeavor to define election issues in terms that will serve their interests. Incumbents running during a period of prosperity will seek to take credit for the strong economy and define the election as revolving around their record of success. This strategy encourages voters to make retrospective judgments. By contrast, an insurgent running during a period of economic uncertainty will tell voters it is time for a change and ask them to make prospective judgments. In 2020, Donald Trump had a very mixed record to run on. The economy grew steadily for his first three years, and unemployment hit an all-time low in 2019. But the pandemic took 300,000 Americans lives and cost tens of millions of people their jobs as the economy shut down to slow the spread of coronavirus. The election was very much a referendum on Donald Trump's handling of the economy and the coronavirus epidemic.

Not all issues, however, are alike. Politics involves different sorts of issues, such as economic concerns, moral questions, and foreign affairs. Some voters might favor low taxes and no government restrictions on abortion (a libertarian perspective), while others want low taxes and a prohibition on abortion; still others may prefer high taxes and no restrictions on abortion, and so on. Moreover, some voters weigh economics more heavily while others give the greatest weight to social issues, and still others are national security voters. In 2020, the national exit polls presented voters with five issues and asked which was most important to their votes. The issues were the economy, racial inequality, coronavirus, crime and safety, and health care. The economy was the number one issue, chosen by 35 percent of respondents, and Trump won those voters 83 percent to 17 percent. Racial inequality was number two, chosen by 20 percent of respondents, and Biden won those voters 92 percent to 7 percent. Coronavirus was a close third (17 percent), and Biden won 81 percent of voters who identified the coronavirus as the most important issue in their votes. Of the 11 percent who selected crime and safety, Trump won 71 percent to 27 percent. And, of the 11 percent who identified health care as most important, Biden won 62 percent to 37 percent for Trump. These figures are quite a reversal from 2016, when Clinton won 52 percent of those most concerned about the economy.[44]

---

44 CNN Politics, "Exit Polls," https://www.cnn.com/election/2020/exit-polls/president/national-results (accessed 11/16/20).

Broadly speaking, issues may be distinguished as spatial issues or valence issues. **Spatial issues** are those on which voters have preferences about what particular policy is pursued; they have beliefs about which policies will lead to the best outcomes, or they have moral convictions that lead them to value the means of the policy, not just the ends. Valence issues are those on which voters do not care about the means (the policy), only the ends (the outcome). When it comes to valence issues, voters care about having peaceful and prosperous lives, quite apart from how they are achieved.

Spatial Issues. When issues elicit conflicting preferences over policies and outcomes, we call these spatial preferences because the choices can be mapped along a continuum or line. Tax rates or the appropriate size of government are good examples of spatial issues. Consider, for example, income taxes. Each taxpayer must pay income taxes at a certain rate, as determined by the government. Currently, the effective federal tax rate is progressive—that is, people with higher incomes pay a higher percentage of their income in taxes. An alternative proposal is for a flat tax rate of 20 percent, which would raise approximately the same amount of revenue for the government overall. That proposal would raise the rates on low- and middle-income households and lower the rate on higher-income households. People in higher-income households tend to like flat taxes, and people in low-income households do not like flat taxes.

Politicians compete for votes by pursuing policies they think will attract the most voters. In the 2020 presidential election, Donald Trump promised to "Keep America Great," and to continue his economic and foreign policies. He promised to keep a tough line in his relations with China and to withdraw further from commitments to Europe. And, he promised to deliver a coronavirus vaccine by Election Day. Joe Biden countered with the theme of "A Presidency for All Americans." He promised to put in place a group of leading scientists and experts to implement a COVID action plan immediately upon his inauguration. He promised to protect Obamacare, to codify Roe v. Wade in legislation, and to pass a climate plan based on infrastructure development for new energy technologies. And, he promised to increase taxes on corporations and on individuals making more than $400,000 a year while keeping low tax rates on those making less than that amount.

Spatial voting is one way that voters can deal with the two problems inherent in voting that we discussed at the beginning of this chapter: the problem of adverse selection and the moral hazard problem. Adverse selection arises if, due to a lack of information about the candidates, we choose people for office who do not fit with our interests. Party identities might lead us to this situation, for a "one size fits all" party label may not correctly reflect how an individual candidate will vote on legislation. If, instead, voters choose on the basis of what policies the candidates represent or promise to support, then they can choose the right people to represent their interests and values. Spatial voting also helps correct for moral hazard, which arises when politicians, once elected, act in ways that voters can't control. However, politicians must run for reelection. People who are attentive to what laws elected officials support and oppose during their time in office can vote against politicians with whom they disagree. Recent research on congressional roll-call voting suggests that this is

 spatial issue

An issue for which a range of possible options or policies can be ordered, say, from liberal to conservative or from most expensive to least expensive.

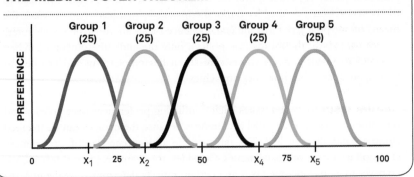

Figure 11.6
THE MEDIAN VOTER THEOREM

When voters engage in issue voting, competition between two candidates
pushes the candidates' issue positions toward the middle of the distribution of
voters' preferences. This is known as the **median voter theorem**.[46] (Chapter 6
discussed the median voter theorem in the context of congressional committees.)
To see the logic of this claim in the context of elections, imagine a series of
possible stances on a policy issue as points along a line, stretching from 0 to 100
(Figure 11.6). Voters are represented by an "ideal" policy and preferences, which
decline as policy moves away from this ideal. Thus voters in group 1 prefer
policy X_1 most, and their preference declines as the policy moves to the left or
right of X_1. Voters whose ideal policy lies between, say, 0 and 25 are said to be
liberal on this policy (groups 1 and 2), those whose ideal lies between 75 and
100 are conservative (groups 4 and 5), and those whose favorite policy is
between 25 and 75 are moderate (group 3). An issue voter cares about only
issue positions, not partisan loyalty or candidates' characteristics, and would,
therefore, vote for the candidate whose announced policy is closest to his or her
own most preferred policy.

Consider now an electorate of 125 voters evenly distributed among the five
groups shown in Figure 11.6.[47] The middle group contains the median voter
because half or more of this electorate has an ideal policy at or to the left of X_3
(groups 1, 2, and 3), and half or more has an ideal policy at or to the right of

a strong factor in U.S. House elections and accounts for a significant portion of
party identification.[45]

**median voter
theorem**

A proposition predicting
that, when policy options
can be arrayed along
a single dimension,
majority rule will pick the
policy most preferred by
the voter whose ideal
policy is to the left of half
of the voters and to the
right of exactly half of the
voters (see Chapter 6 for
further discussion).

---

45 See Stephen Ansolabehere and Philip Edward Jones, "Constituents' Responses to Congressional
Roll-Call Voting," *American Journal of Political Science* 54, no. 3 (July 2010): 583–97.

46 See Duncan Black, *The Theory of Committees and Elections*, 2nd ed. (Boston: Kluwer,
1998); and Downs, *An Economic Theory of Democracy*. A general, accessible treatment of
this subject is found in Kenneth A. Shepsle, *Analyzing Politics: Rationality, Behavior, and
Institutions*, 2nd ed. (New York: Norton, 2010), chap. 5.

47 For the sake of this illustration, 25 voters have been included in each group. This argument
holds true with any distribution of voters among the groups.

X_3 (groups 3, 4, and 5). Group 3 is in the driver's seat, as the following reasoning suggests. If a candidate announces X_3 as her policy—the median voter's most preferred alternative—and if her opponent picks any point to the right, then the median voter and all those with ideal policies to the left of the median voter's (groups 1–3) will support the first candidate. They constitute a majority, by definition of the median, so this candidate will win. Suppose instead that the opponent chose as his policy some point to the left of the median ideal policy. Then the median voter and all those with ideal policies to the right of the median voter's (groups 3–5) will support the first candidate—and she wins, again. In short, the median voter theorem says that the candidate whose policy position is closest to the ideal policy of the median voter will defeat the other candidate in a majority contest. We can conclude from this brief analysis that issue voting encourages candidate convergence (in which both candidates cozy up to the position of the median voter). Even when voters are not exclusively issue voters, two-candidate competition still encourages a tendency toward convergence, although it may not fully run its course.[48]

Valence Issues.

Valence Issues. Some issues lack conflict: all people want the same outcome. All people want less crime, more prosperity, less poverty, less inflation, better health, peace, and security. They may have different beliefs about how to attain those objectives, but they don't really care about the means; they care about the outcome.

In the context of elections, economic conditions are the most important **valence issue**. If voters are satisfied with their economic prospects, they tend to support the party in power, while voters' unease about the economy tends to favor the opposition. Presidents Richard Nixon, Ronald Reagan, Bill Clinton, and George W. Bush won reelection easily in the midst of favorable economies. Jimmy Carter in 1980, George H. W. Bush in 1992, and Donald Trump in 2020 ran for reelection amidst economic downturns, and all lost. Analyzing the Evidence on pp. 484–5 explores voters' perceptions of the economy in relation to their support for the incumbent party.

How bad must the economy be for the incumbent to get turned out of office? Social scientists have developed several rules of thumb based on historical correlations between economic performance and the vote. A common sort of empirical analysis uses economic growth (annual percentage changes in gross domestic product [GDP]) to predict the vote. The idea is that large numbers of individuals vote against the incumbent party in bad times and for the incumbent party in good times. Adding up the 100 million or so votes will aggregate every individual's experiences and reflect the state of the economy as it affects vote choice. The correlation between economic growth and votes for the incumbent party is sufficient to allow statistically minded political scientists to make forecasts.

 valence issue

An issue or aspect of a choice for which all voters prefer a higher value, in contrast to a spatial issue—for example, voters prefer their politicians to be honest, and honesty is a valence issue.

---

48 This convergence will also be a moderating force as candidates move toward what they believe will appeal to voters in the middle. But if the middle of the voter distribution of preferences tilts toward the right or the left, it may not be very moderate. If X_3, for example, were barely to the left of X_4, then the median voter would be fairly right wing rather than in the middle of the issue dimension.

Economic Influence on Presidential Elections

Contributed by
Robert S. Erikson
Columbia University

The state of the economy is a key factor in presidential elections. When the United States prospers, the presidential party performs much better than when economic conditions are poor. The economic influence on presidential elections can be seen by predicting the vote based on objective indicators such as GDP growth leading up to the election. The simplest measure, however, is a subjective one—voters' responses when asked in polls whether the economy has been performing well or badly. When survey respondents are asked early in the election year how they plan to vote, candidate and party preferences show little relationship to economic perceptions at that time. By Election Day, however, the national vote falls surprisingly in line with the voters' perceptions of economic performance. In short, the election campaign increases the importance of the economy to voters.

The precise indicator of economic perceptions used here is the average response to the following question, asked regularly by the Survey of Consumers at the University of Michigan in April and November of the election year: "Would you say that at the current time business conditions are better or worse than they were a year ago?"

April Poll Results

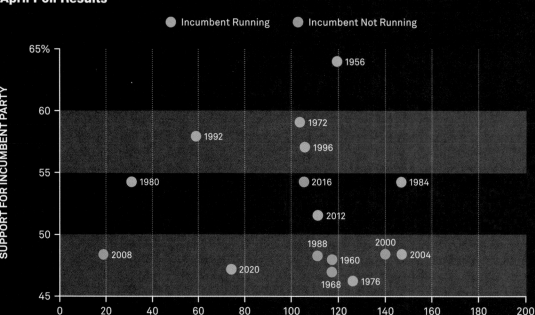

The lack of any consistent pattern in the first graph (at left) shows that what voters think about the economy in April of an election year has little bearing on their vote intentions at that time—as if voters had not yet thought about the November election sufficiently to factor in the economy. Especially noteworthy examples are 1980 and 1992 when incumbents Jimmy Carter and George H. W. Bush, respectively, were favored in the early polls, despite being seen as presiding over poor economies. Both lost the general election. John McCain (representing the incumbent Republican Party) was only slightly behind Barack Obama in early 2008, despite an economy that already was almost universally seen as worsening.

The clear pattern in the second graph (below) shows that by November, the vote falls into rough alignment with economic perceptions: the better the average perception of business conditions, the greater the support for the incumbent party. The three weakest economies in terms of perceptions (1980, 1992, 2008) all saw the incumbent party lose. How does this pattern help us make sense of the 2020 presidential election results?

November Poll Results

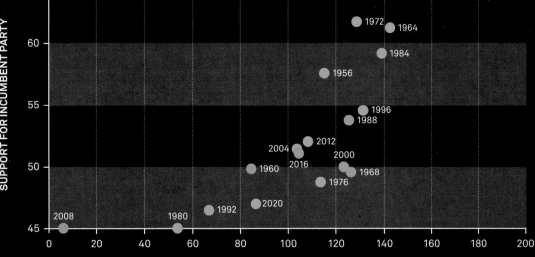

SOURCE: Surveys of Consumers, www.sca.isr.umich.edu/tables.html (accessed 12/15/2017); and author's compilation.

Roughly speaking, every additional 1 percent growth in the GDP corresponds to a 1 percentage point increase in the vote for the incumbent president's party.[49]

Another approach relies on the Consumer Confidence Index, which is calculated by the Conference Board, a business research group. The Consumer Confidence Index is based on a public opinion survey that measures people's sense of the economy in their region of the country and their expectations over the coming months. A score above 100 means that most respondents are optimistic about the economy and that job growth is strong. A score below 100 means that most respondents are pessimistic about the economy and job growth is weak. It has proven a fairly accurate predictor of presidential outcomes. A generally rosy view, indicated by a score greater than 100, augurs well for the party in power. An index score of less than 100, on the other hand, suggests that incumbents should worry about their job prospects. In October 2020, the Consumer Confidence Index stood at 100.9. The results of the election were mixed. Democrats won the Presidential vote by 3 percent, and Republicans retained control of the Senate and gained seats in the Democrat-controlled House. A middling economic circumstance returned divided government.

Economic voting is one way voters solve the moral hazard problems inherent in representative democracy. They cannot monitor every policy the government initiates. They do, however, have a rudimentary way to hold the government accountable—staying the course when times are good, and voting for change when the economy sours.

Candidate Characteristics

Candidates' personal attributes always influence voters' decisions. The more important characteristics are race, ethnicity, religion, gender, geography, and social background. In general, voters presume that candidates with whom they share these attributes will likely have views close to their own. Moreover, they may be proud to see someone of their ethnic, religious, or geographic background in a position of leadership. This is why, for many years, politicians sought to "balance the ticket," making certain their party's ticket included members of as many important groups as possible.

Just as a candidate's personal characteristics may attract some voters, so too may they repel others. Many voters are prejudiced against candidates of certain ethnic, racial, or religious groups. In 2008 and 2016, many people embraced the opportunity to vote for the first Black candidate (Barack Obama) and the first woman (Hillary Clinton) nominated by a major party to be president of the United States. Others voted against Obama and Clinton because they were uncomfortable with having a Black or woman president or because they felt the candidates' race or gender was being used as a campaign gimmick.[50]

49 Perhaps the most comprehensive study of the responsiveness of elections to fluctuations in the U.S. economy is Robert S. Erikson, Michael B. MacKuen, and James A. Stimson, *The Macro Polity* (New York: Cambridge University Press, 2002).

50 See Michael Tesler and David O. Sears, *Obama's Race: The 2008 Election and the Dream of a Post-Racial America* (Chicago: University of Chicago Press, 2010); and John Sides and Lynn Vavreck, *The Gamble: Choice and Chance in the 2012 Presidential Election* (Princeton, NJ: Princeton University Press, 2013).

Voters also consider candidates' personality characteristics, such as their competence, honesty, and vigor, because they figure that politicians with these attributes are likely to produce good outcomes—such as laws that work, fair and honest administration of government, and effective crisis management.[51] Campaigns may also stress the weakness or absence of certain desirable traits in their opponents. In 2016, the Trump campaign repeatedly questioned Clinton's honesty; the Clinton campaign repeatedly characterized Trump as not having a presidential temperament. In 2020, Trump questioned Biden's age and vigor, referring to him as "Sleepy Joe." The highly negative campaigns on both sides chose traits that all voters value and proceeded to drive home the message that the opposition lacked the temperament, honesty, health, acumen, and sensibility to be president.

Incumbency is another important candidate characteristic; as discussed in Chapter 6, the incumbency advantage is one of the most distinctive features of American politics. Why this advantage has emerged and grown remains a puzzle. Redistricting is almost certainly not the explanation: incumbency effects are as large in gubernatorial elections, where there are no districts, as they are in House elections. It is thought that about half of the incumbency advantage reflects the activities of the legislator in office; it is the result of voters rewarding incumbents for their performance. The other half evidently can be attributed to the incumbents' opponents.[52] The average challenger may not have the personal appeal of the typical incumbent, who, after all, has already won office once. Moreover, challengers usually lack the experience and resources that the incumbent has for running a campaign. This is a critical disadvantage, as the ability to communicate with the voters can give a politician the edge in close elections.

Although party, issues, and candidate characteristics are perhaps the three most important factors shaping voting decisions, political scientists debate the relative importance of each. Problems of measurement and the limitations of research methods complicate the assessment. Recent scholarship suggests that the three factors have roughly equal weight in explaining the division of the vote in national elections.[53] Part of the difficulty in understanding their importance is that the extent to which these factors matter depends on the electorate's information levels. In the absence of much information, most voters rely almost

51 Walter J. Stone and Elizabeth N. Simas, "Candidate Valence and Ideological Positions in U.S. House Elections," *American Journal of Political Science* 54, no. 2 (April 2010): 371–88.

52 The partitioning of the incumbency effect into officeholder advantages and challenger qualities begins with the important work of Gary C. Jacobson. See, for example, his *The Politics of Congressional Elections*, 10th ed. (New York: Rowman and Littlefield, 2015). Estimating exactly what fraction of the incumbency effect is due to officeholder benefits is tricky. See Stephen Ansolabehere, James M. Snyder Jr., and Charles Stewart III, "Old Voters, New Voters, and the Personal Vote: Using Redistricting to Measure the Incumbency Advantage," *American Journal of Political Science* 44, no. 1 (January 2000): 17–34.

53 See Stephen Ansolabehere, Jonathan Rodden, and James M. Snyder Jr., "The Strength of Issues: Using Multiple Measures to Gauge Preference Stability, Ideological Constraint, and Issue Voting," *American Political Science Review* 102, no. 2 (May 2008): 215–32. See also D. Sunshine Hillygus and Todd G. Shields, *The Persuadable Voter: Wedge Issues in Presidential Campaigns* (Princeton, NJ: Princeton University Press, 2008).

exclusively on party cues. A highly informed electorate relies more heavily on issues and candidate characteristics.[54]

CAMPAIGNS: MONEY, MEDIA, AND GRASS ROOTS

American political campaigns are freewheeling events with few restrictions on what candidates may say or do. Candidates in hotly contested House and Senate races spend millions of dollars to advertise on television, radio, and the internet as well as via direct mail and door-to-door canvassing. Those seeking office are in a race to become as well known and as well liked as possible and to get more of their supporters to vote. Federal laws limit how much an individual or organization may give to a candidate but, with the exception of presidential campaigns, place no restrictions on how much a candidate or party committee may spend.

Adding to the freewheeling nature of campaigns is their organizational structure. Most political campaigns are temporary organizations, formed for the sole purpose of winning the coming elections and disbanding shortly afterward. To be sure, political parties in the United States have permanent, professional campaign organizations that raise money, strategize, recruit candidates, and distribute resources. These are, on the Republican side, the Republican National Committee, the National Republican Senatorial Committee, and the National Republican Congressional Committee. On the Democratic side are the Democratic National Committee, the Democratic Senatorial Campaign Committee, and the Democratic Congressional Campaign Committee. They account for roughly one-third of the money in politics and have considerable expertise. But most campaigns are formed by and around individual candidates, who often put up the initial cash to get the campaign rolling and rely heavily on family and friends as volunteers. During an election thousands of such organizations are at work, with relatively little coordination among them. The two presidential campaigns operate 50 different state-level operations, with other campaigns competing for 33 or 34 Senate seats, 435 House seats, dozens of gubernatorial and other statewide offices, and thousands of state legislative seats. All simultaneously seek to persuade as many people as possible to vote for their candidate on Election Day.

What It Takes to Win

All campaigns face similar challenges—how to mobilize volunteers, how to raise money, how to coordinate activities, what messages to run, how to communicate with the public, and so on. There is no single best way to run a campaign. There are many tried-and-true approaches, including building up a campaign from local

---

54 The classic study showing this is Philip Converse, "The Nature of Belief Systems in Mass Publics," in *Ideology and Discontent*, ed. David E. Apter (New York: Free Press, 1964).

connections, or the "grass roots." Candidates have to meet as many people as possible and persuade their friends and their friends' friends to support them. In-person campaigning becomes increasingly difficult in larger constituencies. Candidates continually experiment with new ways of reaching large segments of the electorate: in the 1920s, radio advertising eclipsed handbills and door-to-door canvassing; in the 1960s, television began to eclipse radio; in the 1980s and 1990s, cable television, phone polling, and focus groups allowed campaigns to target specific demographic groups. The great innovation of the Obama campaign was to meld internet networking tools with old-style organizing methods to develop a massive communications and fund-raising network, what came to be called a "netroots" campaign. The Clinton campaign in 2016 capitalized on the infrastructure built by Obama and developed extensive get-out-the-vote activities throughout the United States. The Trump campaign, by contrast, relied heavily on Twitter and other social media, and brought back an older American campaign tradition: rallies. In 2020, COVID completely disrupted these intensely personal ways of campaigning. Campaigning door-to-door, canvassing neighborhoods for support, and holding large rallies and conventions risked spreading coronavirus further. The president did hold a few such rallies, but not on the same scale or frequency as 2016. Instead, the Republican campaign relied even more heavily than before on social media, and the Biden campaign took to having virtual town halls. And, both campaigns upped their television advertising.

Campaigns play an essential role in American democracy. They enable politicians to present themselves to the public to explain who they are, what they have accomplished, and what they will do in office. Television advertisements, get-out-the-vote activities, and direct mail provide voters with factual information about the candidates' personal characteristics and ideologies, about the meaning of the party labels, and about the issues that distinguish the politicians.

Campaigns are also a time when the foibles and failures of those in office may be revealed. Challengers will claim that a new direction is needed, arguing that the incumbent is the wrong person to represent the constituency (a case of adverse selection) or has failed to do the job as constituents wanted (a case of moral hazard). Incumbents, for their part, appeal to voters on the basis of their ideological fit with their constituents and their performance in office. It has become an assumption of American elections and election law that candidates and parties will mount competitive campaigns to win office. They will spend millions, even billions, of dollars to persuade people to vote and how to vote. And because of those efforts, voters will better understand the choices they face. In short, campaigns inform voters through competition.

In addition to being costly, American political campaigns are long. Presidential campaigns officially launch a year and a half to two years in advance of Election Day. Serious campaigns for the House of Representatives and the Senate begin at least a year ahead of the general election date and often span the better part of two years. To use the term of the Federal Election Commission, an election is a two-year *cycle*, not a single day or even the period between Labor Day and Election Day loosely referred to as "the general election."

Long campaigns are due largely to the effort required to mount them. There are roughly 330 million people in the United States, and the voting-age population exceeds 245 million people. Communicating with all of those individuals is expensive and time-consuming. In the 2020 election cycle, the Biden campaign and allied committees spent $1.7 billion; the Trump campaign and allied committees spent $1.1 billion—a combined total of $2.8 billion.[55] Approximately half of that sum purchased airtime for television advertising. The money was raised through personal and political networks that the campaigns and candidates built up over months, even years, of effort.

The campaign season is further extended by the election calendar. American national, state, and local elections proceed in two steps: the party primary elections and the general election. General elections for federal offices are set by the U.S. Constitution to take place on the first Tuesday after the first Monday in November. The first presidential caucuses and primaries come early in January and last through the beginning of June. State and congressional primaries do not follow the same calendar; most occur in the spring and early summer, with some states waiting to hold their nominating elections until September of the election year. The result of this calendar of elections is to stretch the campaigns over the entire election year.

American electoral campaigns contrast starkly with those in other democracies, such as Germany, France, Japan, and the United Kingdom. Parliamentary systems have short campaigns: once the government calls for an election, the campaign proceeds for a few months, and an election is held. The years-long gestation of an American election is considered unseemly in most other democracies, which also limit candidates' campaign expenditures and fund-raising activities. Money and resources in other democracies flow through party organizations, often with little government oversight. Most democracies also regulate how candidates and parties campaign; while posters, billboards, and public campaign forums are common in other countries, very few permit television advertising, phone banks, or door-to-door canvassing. These restrictions make the campaigns themselves less important and make media coverage of the parties, the candidates, and the government more prominent.

Campaign Finance

The expense, duration, and chaos of American campaigns have prompted many efforts at reform, including attempts to limit campaign spending, shorten the campaign season, and restrict what candidates and organizations can say in advertisements. The most sweeping campaign reforms came in 1971, when Congress passed the Federal Election Campaign Act (FECA). It limited the amounts that a single individual could contribute to a candidate or party to $1,000 per election for individuals and $5,000 for organizations (these limits have since been increased, as Table 11.1 indicates). It further regulated how business firms, unions, and other organizations could give money, prohibiting donations directly from an organization's treasury and requiring the establishment of a separate, segregated fund—a **political action committee (PAC)**. And

political action committee (PAC)

A private group that raises and distributes funds for use in election campaigns.

---

55 Karl Evers-Hillstrom, "Donors, Big and Small, Propel Biden to Victory," OpenSecrets, November 7, 2020, https://www.opensecrets.org/news/2020/11/biden-wins/ (accessed 11/16/20).

Table 11.1

FEDERAL CAMPAIGN FINANCE CONTRIBUTION LIMITS

	TO EACH CANDIDATE OR CANDIDATE COMMITTEE PER ELECTION	TO NATIONAL PARTY COMMITTEE PER CALENDAR YEAR	TO STATE, DISTRICT, AND LOCAL PARTY COMMITTEE PER CALENDAR YEAR	TO EACH PAC (SSF AND NONCONNECTED) PER CALENDAR YEAR*
Individual may give	$2,800†	$35,500†	$10,000 (combined limit)	$5,000
National party committee may give	$5,000	No limit	No limit	$5,000
State, district, and local party committee may give	$5,000 (combined limit)	No limit	No limit	$5,000 (combined limit)
PAC* (multicandidate) may give‡	$5,000	$15,000	$5,000 (combined limit)	$5,000
PAC (not multicandidate) may give	$2,800†	$35,500†	$10,000 (combined limit)	$5,000
Candidate committee may give	$2,000	No limit	No limit	$5,000

*PAC refers to a committee that makes contributions to other federal political committees. Super PACs may accept unlimited contributions. SSF refers to separate segregated funds.
† Indexed for inflation in odd-numbered years.
‡ A multicandidate committee is a political committee with more than 50 contributors that has been registered for at least six months and, with the exception of state party committees, has made contributions to five or more candidates for federal office.
SOURCE: Federal Election Commission, www.fec.gov/help-candidates-and-committees/candidate-taking-receipts/contribution-limits (accessed 3/20/20).

it set up the Federal Election Commission (FEC) to oversee public disclosure of information and to enforce the laws.[56]

Congress has amended the FECA several times, most importantly in the Bipartisan Campaign Reform Act (BCRA) of 2002 (also called the McCain-Feingold Act, after senators John McCain and Russell Feingold, its primary

---

56 The FEC's website (www.fec.gov) is an excellent resource for those interested in U.S. campaign finance.

sponsors). The McCain-Feingold Act prohibited unlimited party spending (called soft money) and banned certain sorts of political attack advertisements from interest groups in the last weeks of a campaign. Table 11.1 presents a summary of some of the rules governing campaign finance in federal elections.

The FECA also established public funding for presidential campaigns. If candidates agree to abide by spending limits, their campaigns are eligible for matching funds in primary elections and full public funding in the general election. The general election amount was set at $20 million in 1974 and allowed to increase with inflation. Until 2000, nearly all candidates bought into the system. But George W. Bush chose to fund his 2000 primary election campaign outside this system and spent $500 million to win the Republican nomination. Barack Obama and Hillary Clinton ignored the public financing system in their 2008 primary contest, and Obama opted out of the public system in the general election as well, allowing him to spend several hundred million more dollars than the Republican nominee, John McCain. In 2020, the only general election candidate to receive public funds was Green Party candidate Howie Hawkins.

The FECA originally went much further than the law that survives today. Congress originally passed mandatory caps on spending by House and Senate candidates; the law also prohibited organizations from running independent campaigns (that is, campaigns not coordinated with any candidate) on behalf of or in opposition to a candidate. James Buckley, a candidate for U.S. Senate in New York, challenged the law, arguing that the restrictions on spending and contributions limited his right to free speech and that the FEC had excessive administrative power. In the 1976 landmark case *Buckley v. Valeo*, the Supreme Court agreed in part.[57] It ruled that "money is speech," but at the same time it held that the government has a compelling interest in protecting elections from corrupt practices, such as bribery through large campaign donations. The justices declared the limits on candidate spending unconstitutional because they violated the free speech rights of candidates and groups. However, the need to protect the integrity of the electoral process led the justices to leave contribution limits in place. The Court also validated the presidential public-funding system because it is voluntary: candidates are not required to opt into the system, hence there is no violation of free speech. What survived *Buckley* is a system in which candidates, groups, and parties may spend as much as they like to win office, but donations must come in small amounts. This is a more democratic process of campaign finance, but it increases the effort and time needed to construct a campaign.

The Supreme Court's decision in *Buckley* rests on an essential truth of American democracy and elections. The First Amendment right to free speech amounts to a "profound national commitment to the principle that debate on public issues should be uninhibited, robust, and wide-open."[58] Furthermore, in

----

57 *Buckley v. Valeo*, 424 U.S. 1 (1976).

58 The majority opinion in Buckley quotes an earlier landmark case, *New York Times Company v. Sullivan*, 376 U.S. 254 (1964).

2010 the Court reinforced its reasoning in *Buckley* in the case of *Citizens United v. Federal Election Commission*.[59] Here the justices ruled that the BCRA of 2002 had erred in imposing restrictions on independent spending by corporations. It overturned key components of the law and reversed its ruling in a previous case that had upheld BCRA.[60] The majority opinion struck down limits on independent expenditures from corporate treasuries but kept in place limits on direct contributions from corporations and other organizations to candidates; it also solidified corporations' right to free political speech, on par with the right to free speech of individuals. Following this decision, two sorts of organizations formed—501c(4) organizations, which derive their title from the section of the tax code that allows such entities, and super PACs. Each can raise and spend unlimited amounts of money on campaigns, though super PACs are subject to more disclosure laws. Super PACs spent approximately $1.2 billion in 2016 and $1.8 billion in 2020. Conservative and liberal super PACs spent about equal amounts.

Congressional Campaigns

Congressional campaigns share a number of important features with presidential campaigns, but they are also distinctive—especially in terms of the incumbency advantage. Incumbency advantage is more important for congressional representatives, who have no term limits. Beginning around 1970, political scientists noted that congressional incumbents were winning reelection at higher rates than in previous generations and by wider margins, and that this phenomenon appeared due to incumbency itself. As a simple experiment, political scientist Robert Erikson compared a series of elections that involved politicians running first as nonincumbents and then, in subsequent elections, as incumbents. In the first sort of election, the politicians ran for seats left vacant by an incumbent's retirement or against an incumbent and won. In the second sort of election, the politicians had just won the previous election and had to defend their seats as "sophomores." Erikson called the increase in each politician's vote share from the first election to the second the "sophomore surge"— attributable solely to the fact that the politician ran as an incumbent rather than as a nonincumbent. Erikson found an incumbency effect of approximately 5 percentage points around 1970. If the party division of the vote in a congressional district without an incumbent is, say, 50–50, then in a race where one candidate is the incumbent, the same district would vote for the incumbent 55 percent to 45 percent.

The incumbency advantage has increased in both magnitude and importance in U.S. elections. Incumbency advantages in House elections grew from 1 or 2 percentage points in the mid-1950s to 5 or 6 points by the late 1960s. Today,

---

59 *Citizens United v. Federal Election Commission*, 558 U.S. 310 (2010).

60 *McConnell v. Federal Election Commission*, 540 U.S. 93 (2003).

---

almost every elective office at the state and federal level exhibits an incumbency advantage. Those advantages have ranged from about 5 percent in state legislative elections to 10 percent for U.S. House, U.S. Senate, and governor. A 10 percent incumbency advantage is a massive electoral edge. It turns a competitive race into a blowout for the incumbent.[61]

Congressional incumbents' advantages arise in campaign spending as well as votes. Like presidential campaigns, congressional campaigns have witnessed increased spending over time. The average U.S. House incumbent in 2020 raised $2.5 million, while the average House challenger raised $377,000.[62] A successful campaign builds on early successes, often starting small by holding meetings with various groups, then bringing in more supporters and volunteers, and culminating with intensive advertising campaigns in the final months or weeks before Election Day. The personal style of political campaigning that Americans have come to appreciate reflects an enormous investment of time and resources that takes the better part of a year to grow. Incumbent members of Congress have particular advantages in campaign fund-raising: they have already been tested, they have campaign organizations in place, and they have connections in their constituencies as well as in Washington, D.C.

Effectiveness of Campaigns

Campaigns address the information problems discussed at the beginning of this chapter. Candidates and parties bear much of the responsibility for disseminating electoral information and for creating an informed electorate. Indeed, voters would otherwise have little incentive or opportunity to find information about the many candidates and ballot measures at issue. Through advertising and other campaign efforts, politicians try to shape the electorate and the election outcome. Parties and candidates spend money in order to present voters with the information they need to make a decision come Election Day—what the candidates and parties have done and what they promise to do, who they are, and which person is right for the job and the challenges the country faces.

Political scientists have long wondered how much money matters, given the high rates of party loyalty among most people. Research on the effectiveness of campaign spending and advertising began in earnest in the 1970s with the pathbreaking studies of political scientist Gary Jacobson. He found that challengers did better in races in which they spent more money, holding constant the underlying partisan division of the district, but that incumbents who spent higher amounts did no better. Part of the explanation, Jacobson reasoned, was that vulnerable incumbents would have to raise and spend more money, so the observation of high spending reflected the eventual outcome as much as it

---

61 See Stephen Ansolabehere and James M. Snyder Jr., "The Incumbency Advantage in U.S. Elections: An Analysis of State and Federal Offices, 1942–2000," *Election Law Journal* 1, no. 3 (September 2002): 315–38.

62 OpenSecrets, "Incumbent Advantage," Center for Responsive Politics, https://www.opensecrets.org/elections-overview/incumbent-advantage (accessed 11/16/20).

influenced it. It was impossible to tell how much money influenced votes and how much votes influenced money.[63] A decades-long debate over how to measure the effectiveness of campaign spending has ensued, most of it focusing on the same sort of aggregate data that Jacobson used.

In the 1990s, political scientists turned to experiments. Rather than look at the correlation between votes received and money spent, they could manipulate who sees TV commercials or receives mailers and then measure respondents' attitudes toward the candidates, whether they vote, and how they vote. The first such study was conducted by Stephen Ansolabehere and Shanto Iyengar, who found that seeing a single TV commercial from a candidate in the context of a news program increased support for that candidate by, on average, 7 percentage points. That holds constant how much the other candidate spends and other important features of the electoral context. It is interesting that the effect of advertising was found to vary across people. Those who were ideologically hostile to a candidate could not be persuaded to change their opinions and cross party lines. Rather, the ads affected independent voters and people of the same party or ideological orientation as the candidate who appeared in the ad. This finding echoes a much older argument owing to the social psychologist Paul Lazarsfeld, who found in the 1940s that political messages and conversations tended not to *convert* people but to *reinforce* their beliefs. Such is the case today. TV ads strengthen support for a candidate among that candidate's partisans and among independents.[64]

Following on this project, political scientists Alan Gerber and Donald Green undertook a measure of the effectiveness of canvassing, direct mail, and other means of voter mobilization. Working with political campaigns, they conducted dozens of field experiments in which some households and precincts received get-out-the-vote messages and some did not. They then measured the participation rates and vote shares of those households and precincts. Although the effects on rates of participation and candidates' vote shares were somewhat smaller than the TV advertising studies, they were still significant.[65] These research projects provide strong evidence of the effectiveness of campaigns, a conclusion masked by studies of aggregate election patterns.

Elections, of course, fail to serve the important function of informing the electorate when competition is weak or lacking all together. Today, some observers fear that the incumbency advantage stifles electoral competition. As noted earlier, incumbents enjoy a sizable electoral advantage—some of which reflects the voters' reward of the incumbents' performance in office and some of which reflects an imbalance in campaign politics. That imbalance is most obvious in campaign funds. In 2020, the 407 House incumbents who ran for reelection raised a little over $1 billion. The 1,136 candidates who challenged them in

63 Gary C. Jacobson, *Money in Congressional Elections* (New Haven, CT: Yale University Press, 1980).

64 Stephen Ansolabehere and Shanto Iyengar, Going Negative: *How Political Advertisements Shrink and Polarize the Electorate* (New York: Free Press, 1995).

65 Donald P. Green and Alan S. Gerber, *Get Out the Vote: How to Increase Voter Turnout*, 4th ed. (Washington, DC: Brookings Institution, 2019).

primary or general elections raised less than half that amount, $427 million. Incumbents raised $2.37 for every $1 raised by candidates who opposed them. Incumbents' funding advantages allow them to communicate more extensively with constituents than their opponents.

THE 2020 ELECTIONS

2020: A Dynamic Year

The outbreak of the novel coronavirus in February abruptly and radically altered the course of the 2020 election. Early in the year, Donald Trump looked assured to win reelection to the presidency, and Republicans appeared almost certain to hold their Senate majority. The country was prosperous and at peace. During Trump's first three years in office, the number of unemployed persons who were actively seeking work had declined from 8 million, or 5 percent of the workforce, to 6 million, just 3.5 percent of the workforce; the economy was robust and expanding, spurred by Trump's 2017 tax cut and administrative decisions that reduced economic, environmental, and financial regulations. Forecasters predicted continued economic growth throughout 2020.

If anything, it was the Democrats who appeared to be in the more vulnerable political position. Coming into the 2020 election year, they held a 16-seat majority in the House of Representatives following a sweeping electoral victory in the 2018 midterm elections. Thirty-one House Democrats held seats in swing districts where Trump had won a majority of the vote for president in 2016. The Republican Party and allied interest groups planned to capitalize on the good economic times in targeting those 31 Democrats, as well as 24 vulnerable others, in what looked to be a promising year for the Republicans.

Compounding the Democrats' problems was the fact that the Republicans had resisted congressional Democrats' efforts to impeach the president, or at least drag down his popularity with a scandal, in his first term. In 2019, House Democrats wrapped up a three-year investigation into Russian interference in the 2016 election. Those inquiries resulted in convictions for several of Trump's political associates, including his personal lawyer. On December 13, 2019, the Democratic-controlled House of Representatives voted to levy two articles of impeachment against the president. Within two weeks, the Republican-controlled Senate had rejected those articles. Much to the Democrats' chagrin, public support for the president remained unchanged throughout the investigation; the party's failed gambit thus appeared more likely to hurt them. As with the attempt to remove President Bill Clinton in 1998 following the Monica Lewinsky scandal, the context of a good economy seemed to make the president impervious to attack. By the beginning of February 2020, the dust had settled on the Russia probe and the Democratic primary season was underway. The oddsmakers heavily favored Trump. The headline in one prominent international newspaper read: "Markets have made their prediction: Trump will win the next election."[66]

Coronavirus Pandemic. Then, COVID-19 hit. As the pandemic worsened throughout March and April, Republicans' poll numbers at all levels began to plummet. The president's job approval rating slid, reaching the mid-30s by early summer. Fear of getting the virus and efforts to contain it kept people indoors. Americans began wearing masks and maintaining physical distance in public. They started working from home; they stopped traveling, eating out, going to movies and bars; they canceled vacations. The economy shrank quickly, and millions lost their jobs. Of the 160 million Americans in the workforce, 23 million were out of work by April 2020, an unemployment rate of 15 percent. While employment rose slightly over the course of the summer, the unemployment rate was at 8 percent by the beginning of September.[67]

The Trump administration's response to the COVID-19 pandemic was to downplay the virus and even deny that it was a problem, and administration officials expressed the hope that the disease would go away quickly. Simple actions reinforced by both governments and individual citizens, such as maintaining safe physical distance, wearing masks, and avoiding crowded places, such as bars, buses, and theaters, had helped stem the spread in Asian countries, including South Korea and China. President Trump, however, refused to wear a mask, arguing that it was a sign of weakness. And conflicts in several states, such as Michigan and Minnesota, emerged when Democratic governors recommended or required their residents to wear masks. People protested that mask mandates were violations of their individual civil liberties, not simply safety guidelines meant to protect everyone.

By the end of October 2020, as the public was preparing to vote for its next government, at least 9 million people had contracted the virus[68] and the country had suffered 300,000 deaths above what would normally be expected.[69]

----

66 Ian McGugan, "Markets Have Made Their Verdict: Donald Trump Will Win the Next Election," *Globe and Mail*, February 6, 2020, www.theglobeandmail.com/investing /markets/inside-the-market/article-wall-street-bullish-on-trumps-growing-re -election-momentum (accessed 11/17/20); see also Adam Goodman, "Don't Watch Opinion Polls to Predict Trump's Fate. Watch the Stock Market," *Tampa Bay Times*, August 9, 2019, www.tampabay.com/opinion/2019/08/09/dont-watch-opinion-polls -to-predict-trumps-fate-watch-the-stock-market-adam-goodman (accessed 11/17/20).

67 U.S. Bureau of Labor Statistics, "Unemployment Rate Rises to Record High 14.7 Percent in April 2020," May 13, 2020, www.bls.gov/opub/ted/2020/unemployment-rate-rises -to-record-high-14-point-7-percent-in-april-2020.htm (accessed 11/17/20).

68 Centers for Disease Control and Prevention, "United States COVID-19 Cases and Deaths by State," https://covid.cdc.gov/covid-data-tracker/#cases_casesinlast7days (accessed 10/30/20).

69 Centers for Disease Control and Prevention, "Excess Deaths Associated with COVID-19," www.cdc.gov/nchs/nvss/vsrr/covid19/excess_deaths.htm (accessed 11/17/20).

Social Justice and Black Lives Matter Movements. As summer began, a restless America confronted yet another crisis: several high-profile incidents of police brutality against African Americans thrust simmering issues of criminal and racial justice into the national consciousness, spurring nationwide protests. On March 13, police in Louisville raided the home of Breonna Taylor, a medical worker, under a "no-knock warrant." In the melee that ensued, police shot and killed Taylor, who was unarmed.[70] Two months later, George Floyd died after being handcuffed and pinned to the ground by a White officer of the Minneapolis Police Department. A video recorded by a bystander captured the incident, including Floyd's pleas of "I can't breathe."[71] The Taylor and Floyd killings were just the latest in a string of police brutality charges and investigations that had gained national attention in recent years. Against the background of the desperation accompanying the COVID-19 outbreak and economic shutdown, these two tragedies for the Black community in the United States felt like the last straw. Floyd's death sparked nationwide protests against police brutality and calls for criminal justice reform. In Minneapolis, rage boiled over into violence. The Minneapolis Police Department's Third Precinct was burned along with dozens of businesses along the Lake Street corridor in the city.[72]

The killings and ensuing protests polarized the 2020 candidates. President Trump tweeted that the protesters were "thugs" who must be stopped and that the violence following the protests required a strong "law and order" response.[73] He also claimed to have done more for the Black community in his three years as president than Joe Biden had done in 43 years in Washington.[74] The Democrats hit back with calls for police and criminal justice reform. As the summer carried on, the Floyd and Taylor cases remained in the public eye.

Regional Shifts. The events of 2020 emerged against a backdrop of economic and demographic shifts in three regions of the country that would turn

---

70 Richard A. Oppel Jr., Derrick Bryson Taylor, and Nicholas Bogel-Burroughs, "What to Know About Breonna Taylor's Death," *New York Times*, October 30, 2020, www .nytimes.com/article/breonna-taylor-police.html (accessed 11/17/20).

71 "What We Know About the Death of George Floyd in Minneapolis," *New York Times*, November 5, 2020, www.nytimes.com/article/george-floyd.html (accessed 11/17/20).

72 "Unrest After George Floyd's Death: Violence Spans Twin Cities, 3rd Precinct Overtaken & Burned, CNN Reporter Arrested," CBS Minnesota, May 29, 2020, https:// minnesota.cbslocal.com/2020/05/29/protesters-take-minneapolis-police-3rd-precinct-building-during-3rd-night-of-george-floyd-protests (accessed 11/17/20).

73 Donald J. Trump, "These THUGS are dishonoring the memory of George Floyd, and I won't let that happen. Just spoke to Governor Tim Walz and told him that the Military is with him all the way. Any difficulty and we will assume control but, when the looting starts, the shooting starts. Thank you!," Twitter, May 29, 2020, 12:53 a.m., https:// twitter.com/realDonaldTrump/status/1266231100780744704 (accessed 11/18/20).

74 Katelyn Burns, "Trump's Latest Tweets Are from an Alternate Reality Where the Protests Are out of Control," Vox, June 3, 2020, www.vox.com/policy-and-politics/ 2020/6/3/21279088/trump-tweets-alternate-reality-george-floyd-protests (accessed 11/17/20).

out to shape the election results. First, the states of the Midwest—Minnesota, Wisconsin, Michigan, and Pennsylvania—had been among the most reliable for the Democratic Party since the election of Bill Clinton in 1992; Hillary Clinton had called them the "Blue Wall." These states are home to more traditional, heavily unionized manufacturing industries, especially automotive and food processing, that have hemorrhaged jobs in the face of foreign competition, especially from China. The region also faced demographic challenges. These states were settled by European immigrants during the last big immigration boom at the end of the nineteenth and beginning of the twentieth centuries, and their population is older and Whiter than much of the rest of the nation. The Republican Party had gradually gained strength in the Midwest, and President Trump's aggressive foreign policies toward China and Mexico proved very popular in the region. These states gave Trump his Electoral College majority in 2016.

Second, the Southwest—Arizona, California, Colorado, Nevada, New Mexico, and Texas—had been moving in the opposite direction, inching away from the Republican Party. The main driver here was the rapid influx of immigrants from Central and South America, especially from Mexico. Latino voters in the region have been trending toward the Democratic Party since the early 1990s, when the Republican Party began to back policies unpopular among Latinos, such as English-only initiatives. Donald Trump's policy focus on building a border wall to limit illegal immigration and his efforts to expel undocumented immigrants pushed many Southwest voters away from the Republicans. Most of the Democratic gains in the 2018 U.S. House elections came in this region.

Third, less obvious than the changes in the Midwest and the Southwest, were shifts occurring in the Southeast, especially Florida, Georgia, North Carolina, South Carolina, and Virginia. These states' populations have grown faster than the rest of the nation, and they have increasingly attracted new industries, such as tech, media, and aerospace. Baby-boomer retirees from the Northeast and Midwest have likewise flocked to these states. These new populations tend to have a more centrist or liberal political orientation, and the combination of these "new southerners" with the strongly Democratic minority populations in the region have made these states less reliably Republican. Florida has long been, and remains, a highly competitive state, but the other four have shifted noticeably away from the Republicans. Republicans virtually conceded the presidential election in Virginia to the Democrats before the race even started. Georgia, North Carolina, and South Carolina joined Florida on the list of the nation's electoral battleground states, setting the stage for a hotly contested race in 2020.

The Presidential Primaries

The 2020 presidential campaign was as strange as the year. The Democratic field boasted an impressive and diverse set of candidates from a wide range of backgrounds. Two very well-known and prominent candidates in the race, former vice president Joe Biden and Senator Bernie Sanders, had run for the presidential nomination of their party in the past and once again set out to become the Democrats' standard bearer. There were 10 U.S. senators or former senators in the race; in addition to Biden and Sanders, Senators Elizabeth Warren (Massachusetts), Kamala Harris (California), Cory Booker (New Jersey), Amy Klobuchar (Minnesota), Michael Bennet (Colorado), and Kirsten Gillibrand (New York) also ran. The race attracted four governors;[75] five current and former members of the U.S. House of Representatives;[76] five mayors and former mayors;[77] a state senator;[78] an entrepreneur, Andrew Yang; and a self-help author and new age lecturer, Marianne Williamson.

The Democrats spent the better part of 2019 raising funds and developing field organizations in the early primary and caucus states. From June 2019 to February 2020, the Democrats held eight debates, often struggling to find a format that would allow up to 29 contestants on the stage at once. The caucuses and early primaries quickly narrowed the field. In the Iowa caucus on February 3, Bernie Sanders narrowly defeated the surprise candidate of the season, Pete Buttigieg, a little-known but charismatic mayor from South Bend, Indiana. Elizabeth Warren trailed the two leaders, and Joe Biden posted a distant fourth-place showing. Biden's New Hampshire effort was no better, and his candidacy looked to be on the ropes. The election increasingly seemed to be a two-way race between Warren and Sanders. Biden made his comeback bid in the third primary of the season, in South Carolina. South Carolina's primary electorate is predominantly African American, and Kamala Harris was banking on a win here to keep her candidacy alive. But, on February 29, Biden scored a huge victory in South Carolina, and the race suddenly was Biden versus Sanders and Warren, who were splitting the vote on the left wing of the party.

On the Republican side, President Trump faced opposition from former governor William Weld of Massachusetts, former governor Mark Sanford of South Carolina, and radio talk show host Joe Walsh. But none of these challengers garnered more than small percentages in the polls when put up against President Trump. As a result, many states decided simply to cancel the Republican primary elections rather than spend the cost of running them.

The campaign for the Democratic nomination looked to be following the same pattern as 2016: an insider, establishment candidate (Biden in 2020 and Clinton in 2016) would face off against a candidate representing the left (Sanders in 2016 and Sanders or Warren in 2020). Unlike 2016, President Trump faced no real opposition and he was positioned to use the primary to begin touring the United States with a rousing set of rallies and other events of the sort that had proved incredibly successful four years earlier.

---

75 Deval Patrick (Massachusetts), Steve Bullock (Montana), Jay Inslee (Washington), and John Hickenlooper (Colorado).

76 Tulsi Gabbard (Hawaii), John Delaney (Maryland), Seth Moulton (Massachusetts), Beto O'Rourke (Texas), and Eric Swalwell (California).

77 Pete Buttigieg (South Bend, Indiana), Julián Castro (San Antonio), Bill de Blasio (New York City), Michael Bloomberg (New York City), and Wayne Messam (Miramar, Florida).

78 Richard Ojeda (West Virginia).

During the week from February 29 to March 3, COVID-19 erupted into the national consciousness. The virus had been spreading throughout the month of February, but serious super-spreader events in Washington State and Boston, Massachusetts, set off alarms among public health officials, and the pandemic began to rule the nightly news. Suddenly, the issues that had dominated the Democratic primaries—health insurance, income inequality, race relations—became secondary concerns. People felt vulnerable, and they wanted experienced leadership to manage the crisis. The shift of the issues away from the economy and equality and to questions of experience and leadership gave Biden a huge boost among the public. It also became impossible to hold campaign events and rallies; even the simple act of voting appeared to be a threat to one's health. Democratic campaigns were forced to take to the airwaves, and that helped Joe Biden secure the nomination, as his campaign emphasized advertising more than events.

The General Election

The events of the spring, however, hinted at the chaos that awaited the election come fall. States that had March and April primaries struggled to conduct voting. They had difficulty recruiting people to be poll workers and finding places to hold in-person voting. Many local election offices were unprepared for the surge in absentee balloting, complicating vote counting and creating concerns. Most states were sued to remove barriers to absentee voting in order to accommodate the COVID-19 crisis. States that had late-summer primaries had fewer problems. By fall, it was evident that a significant percentage of the ballots cast in the 2020 election would be absentee by mail or early votes. Several states adopted universal voting by mail, while others relaxed absentee balloting provisions to make it easier for people to cast ballots by mail or early. These seismic changes to the conduct of the election raised the prospect of legal challenges to the counting of ballots, especially absentee ballots received after Election Day, in the event of a close election on November 3.

The polls the week before the election showed a wide lead for Biden overall but tight races in the dozen states essential to winning the Electoral College. Biden held a 7 to 10 percentage point lead in almost every national poll, and most surveys showed that he would win an outright majority of all votes cast. The Electoral College, however, was another matter. In 2016, Trump had nearly completely dismantled Clinton's Midwestern Blue Wall: Michigan, Minnesota, Pennsylvania, and Wisconsin. Those very same states were up for grabs again in 2020. In the Southwest, the rising tide of Latino voters gave the Biden campaign hopes of picking up Arizona and possibly Texas, but the Trump campaign also made a strong bid to move Nevada into the Republican column. In the Southeast, polls showed the candidates to be tied in Florida, Georgia, and North Carolina. Biden appeared to have more scenarios under which he could put together a majority of the electoral votes needed to win. The near-consensus in January that Trump would win reelection had completely vanished.

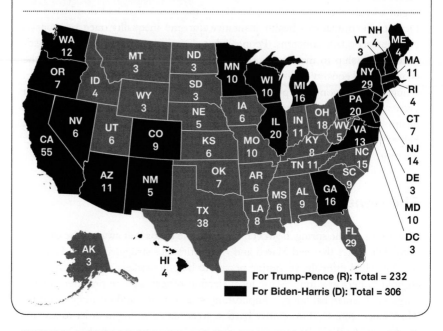

Figure 11.7

DISTRIBUTION OF ELECTORAL VOTES IN THE 2020 PRESIDENTIAL ELECTION

For Trump-Pence (R): Total = 232
For Biden-Harris (D): Total = 306

NOTE: Maine and Nebraska allocate Electoral College votes by congressional district.
SOURCE: Compiled by author. Results reflect projections as of November 11, 2020; *New York Times*, "Presidential Election Results," https://www.nytimes.com/interactive/2020/11/03/us/elections/results-president.html (11/11/2020).

Election night was tense. Early returns indicated that Joe Biden captured an outright majority of the vote, but the vote totals for the two candidates were quite close in the dozen states that held the key to the Electoral College (See Figure 11.7). The Democrats won Minnesota and took back Michigan and Wisconsin. Trump held onto Florida, Iowa, Ohio, and Texas. In the days following the election, the returns revealed extremely close contests in Arizona, Georgia, Nevada, and Pennsylvania; all four states went to Biden, giving him the Electoral College win.

Ultimately, the American electorate was energized by the events of 2020 rather than dispirited. Approximately 155 million people voted. Almost two out of every three eligible adults in the United States cast a ballot, far exceeding the high-water mark for turnout over the past 100 years, set in the 2008 election.[79]

---

79 The modern era for measuring turnout began with the expansion of the franchise to women in 1920.

The Congressional Elections

Coming into 2020, the Democrats hoped that their fierce challenge of Trump would spread down the ballot to races for the U.S. Senate, U.S. House, and state legislative elections.

At the beginning of the year, the U.S. Senate seemed out of reach for the Democrats. Although there were more Republican seats than Democratic seats on the ballot, almost all of the Republican senators up for reelection came from states that had been reliably Republican in recent years, such as Arizona, Georgia, South Carolina, and Texas, or where there were long-standing Republican incumbents who were relatively popular in their states, such as Susan Collins in Maine. As Trump's electoral fortunes waned, so too did support for Republicans running for the Senate. Eight Republican incumbents—Susan Collins in Maine, David Perdue in Georgia, Kelly Loeffler in Georgia, Thom Tillis in North Carolina, Lindsey Graham in South Carolina, Steve Daines in Montana, Cory Gardner in Colorado, and Martha McSally in Arizona—started the year favored to win reelection. But as the year wore on, they found themselves in increasingly competitive races. By the fall, the Cook Political Report listed all as vulnerable or likely to lose. The Democrats seemed likely to lose only one Senate seat, the one held by Doug Jones in Alabama.[80] Democrats needed to net four seats to win a majority, and by Election Day, that looked more likely than not.

Based on estimates in late November—with two runoffs in Georgia to happen in January 2021—the Democrats look to have come up short. John Hickenlooper defeated Cory Gardner in Colorado and Mark Kelly defeated Martha McSally in Arizona, but the Democrats were unable to tip any of the other seats, leaving Republicans to hold onto their majority (see Table 11.2A).

The election for the House of Representatives followed a similar course. At the beginning of the year, it looked likely that the Democrats would lose seats in the November election— possibly even their majority. As 2020 rolled on, the tables gradually turned. On the eve of the election, the Cook Political Report showed no Democratic seats to be leaning or likely to be won by Republicans, but five Republican seats leaned toward or were likely pickups for the Democrats. Another 17 Republican seats and nine Democratic seats were toss ups.[81]

As with the Senate, neither party was able to expand its majority. Based on late-November estimates the Republicans look to ultimately pick up a net of five seats, leaving the House more narrowly split between the two parties (see Table 11.2B).

---

80 "Ratings," Cook Political Report, https://cookpolitical.com/ratings (accessed 11/17/20).

81 "Ratings," Cook Political Report, https://cookpolitical.com/ratings (accessed 11/17/20).

Table 11.2A

SENATE ELECTION RESULTS, 2000–2020

YEAR	TURNOUT (%)	PARTY RATIO	SEAT SHIFT	DEMOCRATS REELECTED (%)	REPUBLICANS REELECTED (%)
2000	54.2	50 D, 50 R	+5 D	93.3	64.3
2002	39.5	48 D, 51 R	+1 R	83.3	93.3
2004	60.3	44 D, 55 R	+4 R	92.9	100.0
2006	40.2	50 D, 49 R	+6 D	100.0	57.1
2008	61.0	59 D, 41 R	+8 D	100.0	66.7
2010	37.8	53 D, 47 R	+6 R	76.9	100.0
2012	54.0	55 D*, 45 R	+2 D	100.0	71.0
2014	36.4	44 D*, 54 R	+9 R	64.7	100.0
2016	58.0	48 D*, 52 R	+2 D	100.0	90.9
2018	48.5	47 D*, 53 R	+2 R	84.6	87.6
2020	66.4	48 D, 50 R	+1 D	91.7	90.0

*Includes two independents who caucus with the Democrats.
NOTE: Data are based on election results as of 11/19/20. Senate races in several states remained undecided pending recounts and runoff elections.
SOURCE: 2000-2018: United States Elections Project, http://www.electproject.org/home (accessed 11/19/20); 2020 results reflect authors' calculations as of 11/19/20.

The State Elections

The year 2020 also saw the election of 11 state governors and more than 5,800 state legislators in 86 state legislative chambers across 44 states. Little change was expected in the gubernatorial elections, as the states holding these elections were solidly Republican or solidly Democratic—with the exception of Montana, where the incumbent Democratic governor was term limited. The state legislatures would be a better indicator of the changing political fortunes of 2020.

Coming into the election, Republicans controlled 58 state legislative chambers (upper or lower house) and Democrats controlled 40. Of those 98 chambers, 19 were in danger of changing from one party's control to the other's. Louis Jacobson of the Cook Political Report wrote two weeks before the election that, "ominously for Republicans, the GOP holds 14 of the 19 vulnerable

Table 11.2B

HOUSE ELECTION RESULTS, 2000–2020

YEAR	TURNOUT (%)	PARTY RATIO	SEAT SHIFT	DEMOCRATS REELECTED (%)	REPUBLICANS REELECTED (%)
2000	54.2	212 D, 222 R	+1 D	98.0	97.5
2002	39.5	205 D, 229 R	+8 R	97.4	97.5
2004	60.3	201 D, 232 R	+3 R	97.4	99.0
2006	40.2	233 D, 202 R	+30 D	100.0	89.6
2008	61.0	257 D, 178 R	+24 D	97.9	92.1
2010	37.8	193 D, 242 R	+64 R	78.8	98.7
2012	54.0	201 D, 234 R	+8 D	89.0	90.0
2014	36.4	188 D, 247 R	+13 R	94.0	98.9
2016	58.0	194 D, 241 R	+6 D	97.0	95.1
2018	48.5	231 D, 204 R	+37 D	100.0	88.3
2020	66.4	223 D, 212 R	+10 R	93.7	99.5

NOTE: Data are based on election results as of 11/19/2020. House races in several states remained undecided pending recounts and runoff elections.
SOURCE: 2000-2018: United States Elections Project, http://www.electproject.org/home (accessed 11/19/20); 2020 results reflect authors' calculations as of 11/19/20.

chambers on our list. This suggests that the Democrats are well-positioned to net up to a half-dozen new chambers this fall, and more if it's a genuine blue wave."[82]

The biggest implication of the state legislative elections was the extent to which the state legislative and executive branches would end up under the control of a single party or divided between the parties. Divided control forces the parties to negotiate budgets and laws across a wider set of interests than just those represented by any one party, but divided government can also lead to gridlock and ineffectiveness. The state governments are essential in dealing with public health and economic development, two challenges facing all states in

82 Louis Jacobson, "October Overview: Handicapping the 2020 State Legislature Races," Cook Political Report, October 21, 2020, https://cookpolitical.com/october-overview -handicapping-2020-state-legislature-races (accessed 11/17/20).

2020, as they manage much of the planning and policy making in these domains, including funding for infrastructure, hospitals, and other vital services. Leading up to the election, Republicans had complete control of the legislature and executive in 21 states, Democrats had complete control in 15 states, and control was divided in 14 states. The situation in 11 states seemed likely to change with the election. In nearly all cases, the shift was toward divided government.[83]

But the blue wave could not gain much strength. As with the U.S. House and Senate elections, the 2020 results in the state legislatures returned more of the same. Nearly all of the legislatures remained controlled by the party that had controlled them before the election. Tim Storey of the National Conference of State Legislatures observed that this was the least change in any set of state legislative elections since 1944.[84]

Looking to the Future

The 2020 election was transformed by the extraordinary events surrounding the COVID-19 pandemic. Over 300,000 Americans died as a result of the epidemic between March and November 2020, and the economy experienced the deepest short-term reduction in employment since the Great Depression. The public was concerned first and foremost about the economy and restarting businesses across the United States; they wanted the government to address problems of racial equity; and they wanted the new leadership to get a handle on the pandemic. According to national exit polls, 34 percent of voters said that the economy was their first concern, 21 percent were most concerned about racial equality, and 18 percent prioritized the coronavirus. These top concerns were followed by issues of crime and safety (11 percent) and health care (11 percent). As a sign of just how much things had changed, in 2018, just two years earlier, health care was the public's number-one concern. Immigration, which was the public's second-highest concern in 2018, did not even make the top-five list in 2020.

The new national and state governments had their work cut out for them. They had to address a pandemic that was again sweeping across the country with a second wave of infections and they had to address the economic dislocations and social unrest sparked by the virus. In addition, difficult questions of racial equity and police reform were now front and center. President-elect Biden wasted no time. The week following the 2020 general election, he established a team of public health experts to begin to address the pandemic.

83 Nathaniel Rakich, "Could Democrats Win Full Control of More State Governments Than Republicans?" FiveThirtyEight, October 20, 2020, https://fivethirtyeight.com /features/could-democrats-win-full-control-of-more-state-governments-than -republicans (accessed 11/17/20).

84 Tim Storey and Wendy Underhill, "2020 Legislative Election Results: It's Status Quo in the States," National Conference of State Legislatures, November 5, 2020, www.ncsl .org/blog/2020/11/05/2020-legislative-election-results-its-status-quo-in-the-states .aspx (accessed 11/17/20).

State governments will also shape the 2021 redistricting process. Following the 2020 census, the United States will reapportion its congressional seats among the states and every congressional district and state legislative district in the country will be redrawn. In nearly every state, the state legislature passes a redistricting law, and the governor may sign the law or veto it. Whoever controls the state legislatures and governorships in 2021, then, will determine the contours of representation in the states and U.S. Congress for the next decade. Following the 2020 election, Republicans controlled the legislature and the governor's office in 23 states; Democrats controlled the legislature and the governor's office in 15 states; and government was divided in 12 states.

The focal point of the 2020 election was surely the presidency. Joe Biden promised to depart from the Trump administration's policies on immigration, climate, energy, health care, racial equity, and, most important, the response to the pandemic. He promised a unity government that would reach out to all constituencies, rather than focusing just on the Democratic Party's base. That promise was more than a posture; it was a political necessity. With Republicans controlling a majority of the Senate and roughly half of all state governments, the Democratic administration would have to reach across the aisle and find common ground in order to deal with the challenges facing the country.

CONCLUSION: ELECTIONS AND ACCOUNTABILITY

Elections should stir wonder in even the most jaded person. In an election, no one person matters much, and each person acts in apparent isolation, indeed secrecy. Each individual voter's decisions reflect diverse experiences, opinions, and preferences about government and public policy. Yet the millions of votes cumulate into an expression of whom the majority wants to have as its representatives in state government, in Congress, and in the presidency. Through the institutions of elections, hundreds of millions of Americans collectively choose their government. That choice shapes all manner of subsequent public-policy making. It indicates whether people want to stay the present course or whether they want government to go in a new direction.

The Founders designed the institutions of American elections to facilitate majority rule. Single-member districts and plurality rule create strong pressures toward a two-party system and majoritarianism. Even in elections in which one party wins a plurality but not a majority, that party typically wins an outright majority of legislative seats. The election itself, then, determines the government. Other systems often produce multiparty outcomes, resulting in a period of negotiation and coalition formation among the parties to determine who will govern.

The significance of elections derives not so much from the laws as from the voters' expression of their preferences. Voting behavior depends in no small part on the tendency to vote for a given party as a matter of ingrained personal identity. If that were all there is to voting behavior, then elections might not provide a meaningful way of governing. However, voters' preferences are as strongly rooted in the issues at hand as in the choices themselves: the candidates. Voting decisions reflect individuals' assessments about whether it makes sense to keep public policies on the same track or to change direction; whether those in office have done a good job and deserve to be reelected, or whether they have failed and it is time for new representation. The aggregation of all voters' preferences responds collectively to fluctuations in the economy, to differences in the ideological and policy orientations of the parties, and to the personal attributes of the candidates.

For Further Reading

Ansolabehere, Stephen, and James M. Snyder Jr. *The End of Inequality: One Person, One Vote and the Transformation of American Politics.* New York: Norton, 2008.

Carmines, Edward G., and James A. Stimson. *Issue Evolution: Race and the Transformation of American Politics.* Princeton, NJ: Princeton University Press, 1989.

Gelman, Andrew. *Red State, Blue State, Rich State, Poor State: Why Americans Vote the Way They Do.* Princeton, NJ: Princeton University Press, 2008.

Ginsberg, Benjamin, and Martin Shefter. *Politics by Other Means: Politicians, Prosecutors, and the Press from Watergate to Whitewater.* 3rd ed. New York: Norton, 2002.

Green, Donald P., and Alan S. Gerber. *Get Out the Vote: How to Increase Voter Turnout.* 4th ed. Washington, DC: Brookings Institution, 2019.

Hayes, Danny, and Jennifer L. Lawless. *Women on the Run: Gender, Media, and Political Campaigns in a Polarized Era.* New York: Cambridge University Press, 2016.

Jacobson, Gary C., and Jamie L. Carson. *The Politics of Congressional Elections.* 10th ed. New York: Rowman and Littlefield, 2015.

McCarty, Nolan, Keith T. Poole, and Howard Rosenthal. *Polarized America: The Dance of Ideology and Unequal Riches.* Cambridge, MA: MIT Press, 2006.

Rosenstone, Steven J., and John Mark Hansen. *Mobilization, Participation, and Democracy in America*. New York: Macmillan, 1993.

Sides, John, and Lynn Vavreck. *The Gamble: Choice and Chance in the 2012 Presidential Election*. Princeton, NJ: Princeton University Press, 2013.

12

Political Parties

Political parties are teams of politicians, activists, and voters whose goal is to win control of government. They pursue this goal by recruiting and nominating candidates to run for office; by accumulating the resources needed to run political campaigns, especially manpower and money; and by pursuing a policy agenda that can appeal to large numbers of voters and secure electoral majorities. Once in office, parties attempt to put their stamp on the laws passed by Congress and the president. Their potential political power is immense.

The prospect of "party rule" has long made Americans suspicious of these organizations. Indeed, the separation of powers into different branches was meant to blunt any attempts by a "faction" or party to gain control of government, as might more readily occur in a parliamentary system.[1] Divided government, in which one party controls the presidency (or governorship) and the other has a majority in at least one chamber of the legislature, has been the norm in American national and state politics. In some elections, one party wins the presidency in a landslide but still fails to capture control of Congress. And in some midterm elections, voters give control of Congress to the party opposing the president in order to rein in the executive. The American political system intentionally makes it difficult for any party or organized interest to gain complete control of government, and when one does, unified government is often short-lived. Separation of powers and divided government have not, however, put the parties out of business.

The Democratic and Republican parties remain essential to the day-to-day operation of legislatures and the conduct of elections. It is difficult to imagine how candidates would emerge and how individuals would vote without political parties to organize the electoral system. Our inability to conceive of democracy without parties reflects a law of democratic politics: parties form to solve

---

1 James Madison famously made this argument in *Federalist* no. 51 during the campaign to ratify the U.S. Constitution. Clinton L. Rossiter, ed., *The Federalist Papers; Alexander Hamilton, James Madison, and John Jay* (New York: New American Library, 1961), no. 51 (James Madison), p. 219.

key problems of rationality and collective action in a democracy. They offer clear choices to voters, lowering the costs of collecting information about the candidates and making it easier for voters to hold government accountable. Parties also ease the transition from elections to governing. They bear the costs of bringing together representatives of disparate constituencies into coherent coalitions that can act collectively in government. In this chapter we highlight some of the general functions of parties in any democracy, but we are especially attentive to party politics in the United States.

The simplest observation about American parties is also perhaps the most important: the United States has just two major parties, the Democrats and the Republicans. The American two-party system is impressive in its durability and flexibility. Sustained third parties have not been able to compete with the Democrats and Republicans since the 1850s. The Democratic and Republican parties have, for the past 150 years, elected every president and nearly every member of Congress, governor, and state legislator in the country. Occasionally, governors or legislators run as third-party candidates, but those bids usually fail unless the candidates attach themselves to one of the major parties.

The Democratic and Republican parties themselves frequently experience divisions and challenges of the establishment politicians from within their ranks. In the 2016 presidential election, two anti-establishment outsider candidates—reality TV star and businessman Donald Trump and self-described democratic socialist Bernie Sanders—attached themselves to the Republican Party and Democratic Party, respectively, and gained widespread support. Sanders posed a serious challenge to Hillary Clinton in the Democratic primaries. Trump, though hardly a traditional Republican, won the GOP nomination, defeating a field of established Republican politicians and eventually won the presidency.

LEARNING OBJECTIVES

➡ Define what political parties are and identify the problems they solve in the U.S. political system.

➡ Describe how political parties solve problems of collective action.

➡ Identify the ways in which political parties influence the institutions of government and the policy-making process.

➡ Explain the relationship between political parties and the electorate.

➡ Outline how political parties are organized in the United States.

➡ Analyze the evolution of political parties in the United States and how it led to our current two-party system.

Many mainstream Republican leaders and politicians, including the party's 2012 nominee Mitt Romney, refused to endorse Trump and had uneasy relations with Trump throughout his term.[2] In 2020, Bernie Sanders ran again for the Democratic nomination, and after victories in the Iowa caucus and New Hampshire primaries, looked poised to win. But Joe Biden, the establishment candidate, rallied following victories in South Carolina and on Super Tuesday, and quickly wrapped up the nomination. The successes of Trump and Sanders exposed many Americans' frustrations with and lack of trust in the establishment. Neither candidate, however, would likely have been as successful if they had not affiliated with one of the two major parties.

When a faction does break from one of the parties, it generally returns to the fold eventually or moves into the other party. The parties have not remained static over time, however. For instance, the Democrats have shifted from a southern base of support to a northern one, and the Republicans' base has moved increasingly from the Northeast and Midwest to the South. The two parties have also adapted to radical changes in the ideologies and social structure of American society.

The institutions of a two-party system, combined with majority rule, mean that the choice between the parties directly translates into the choice of government. Whichever party wins a majority of seats in House or Senate elections wins control of that chamber. Whichever party wins a majority of electoral votes wins the presidency. Thus, voters choose the party in power if they want to maintain the status quo, and they choose the opposing party if they want to change the government.

In contrast, most parliamentary systems, especially those that allocate seats to parties based on the proportion of votes won nationwide, have more than two parties. In such systems, no party regularly wins a majority of seats in parliament, and governments consist of coalitions of several parties. It is difficult to anticipate which coalitions might form, and it is hard to assign blame to any one party in a coalition government. Comparatively, two-party systems are much simpler.

The Democratic and Republican parties have proved adept at accommodating diverse sets of interests while still presenting distinct visions for governing. They each capture a range of ideological views while keeping successful third parties at bay. This situation largely reflects the electoral and governmental institutions of the United States and the strategic skills of party leaders. Third parties have very limited opportunities to enter, much less win, races for congressional seats or the presidency.

The French political scientist Maurice Duverger laid out the reason for this state of affairs in his classic book *Political Parties*, relying on both the institution principle and the rationality principle. As we discussed in Chapter 11, any third-party movement that attempts to enter the American party system would likely fail to win, or worse, would improve the electoral fortunes of the party it most opposes. Also, voters generally don't want to waste a vote on a losing cause. Hence, the number of successful parties is inevitably two.

---

2   David A. Graham, "Which Republicans Oppose Donald Trump? A Cheat Sheet," *Atlantic*, August 18, 2016, www.theatlantic.com/politics/archive/2016/08/where-republicans-stand-on-donald-trump-a-cheat-sheet/481449 (accessed 4/10/20).

U.S. governmental institutions and electoral rules also create strong pressures to maintain just two parties. The two-party system simplifies politics inside governing institutions because it ensures that one party will have a majority and, consequently, control over decision making. It also simplifies vote choice: voters can identify with one of the two major parties or use the party labels to figure out the most effective way to vote.

Parties, however, are not benevolent. They don't solve the rationality and collective action problems simply for democracy's sake. Rather, these problems represent opportunities for individuals to secure elected office, to influence public policy, even to make a profit. For politicians, the parties create a clear path to office through the nominating system and to power through the party organization. For activists, the parties provide a way to pull governmental policies in more favorable directions. For interest groups, party ties offer the potential benefits of being closer to power and affecting what government does. At times, the influence of activists, party leaders, organized interests, and local bosses becomes too great. Regulations on campaign contributions and government contracting, sunshine laws, federal advisory rules, and even civil service reforms have all come about through efforts to prevent party bosses and interest groups from abusing their power. These reforms have weakened party organizations, but the parties have invariably found new resources to draw on. As a result of these actions and reactions, American history has witnessed eras of very strong party organization and periods of relative party weakness.

Today, American politics is characterized by relatively strong party organizations and disciplined legislative parties. The parties offer the American voter meaningful electoral choices and a simple strategy for changing the direction of government.

WHY DO POLITICAL PARTIES FORM?

Political parties, like interest groups, are organizations seeking influence over government. Ordinarily, they can be distinguished from interest groups by the means they use to achieve that goal. A party seeks to control the government by electing its members to office. Interest groups are also concerned with electing politicians—in particular, those who are inclined in their policy direction. But interest groups ordinarily do not sponsor candidates directly; instead they provide support through campaign contributions and other types of assistance. Between elections, they try to influence governmental policies no matter which politicians are in office.

Political parties form to solve three problems. The first is the problem of facilitating collective action in the electoral process. Parties help candidates overcome several hurdles that hinge on collective action: candidates must attract campaign funds, assemble a group of activists and workers, mobilize prospective voters, and persuade them to vote. The second problem is the challenging

political party

An organized group that attempts to control the government by electing its members to office.

nature of collective policy making.[3] The give-and-take within a legislature and between the legislature and the executive can make or break policy success and politicians' subsequent electoral success. The third problem is one of political ambition and competition. Like members of any organization, politicians seek success simultaneously for the organization and for themselves. In furthering their own ambitions, politicians may inadvertently undermine the collective aspirations of fellow partisans unless their actions are astutely managed. We briefly examine each of these problems in the following sections.

Ultimately, each is a problem faced by politicians, especially those already in office. This fact reveals an important reason that parties form—to serve politicians' interests. Ultimately, the political parties in the United States were formed by politicians to simplify the basic tasks of political life—running for office, organizing one's supporters, and forming a government.

To Facilitate Collective Action in the Electoral Process

Political parties as we know them today developed along with the expansion of suffrage and can be understood only in the context of elections. Parties and elections are so intertwined that American parties actually take their structure from the electoral process. Party organization in the United States follows a simple rule: for every district where an election is held, there should be some kind of party unit. These units provide local candidates the "brand name," the resources (human and financial), the buzz, and the link to the larger national organization, which all help arouse interest in the party's candidates and stimulate commitment by voters. These services in turn facilitate collective action, as they enable voters to better understand the choice of candidates and ultimately overcome the free riding that diminishes turnout in general elections.

Party organization also enables groups with similar interests to engage in electoral competition as a collective. The Republican Party has long been the party of business interests (among other groups), especially small businesses and peak associations (organizations of organizations) such as the Chamber of Commerce and the National Association of Manufacturers. Since the 1930s, the Democratic Party has been aligned with labor unions and reformers who want to regulate the economy. Often, large groups that lack substantial economic and institutional resources find their voice in the party system.

---

3 A slight variation on this theme is emphasized by Gary W. Cox and Mathew D. McCubbins in *Legislative Leviathan: Party Government in the House,* 2nd ed. (New York: Cambridge University Press, 2007). They suggest that parties in the legislature are electoral machines that serve to preserve and enhance party reputation, thereby giving meaning to the party labels when elections are contested. By keeping order within their ranks, parties ensure that individual actions by members do not discredit the party label. This is an especially challenging task for party leaders when there is diversity within each party, as has often been the case in American political history.

For example, women's organizations worked closely with the Progressive faction inside the Republican Party in the 1900s and 1910s in the struggle to gain suffrage for women. By the 1970s, changing social issues and party strategies led many newer women's groups, such as the National Organization for Women, to align with the Democratic Party. Throughout American history, immigrant groups have also aligned with the parties. Irish immigrants attached themselves to the Democrats, whose urban political organizations helped them find jobs and negotiate the immigration system. Italian immigrants, on the other hand, tended toward Republicans. Most Latino groups have gravitated to the Democrats because of the party's immigration policies, though Cubans have historically aligned with the Republicans because that party took a harder line against the Castro regime. In recent years, however, younger Cubans have been shifting to the Democratic Party because of their alignment on issues such as education and health care. In the 1970s disaffection with liberal policies concerning school prayer, funding of religious schools, abortion, and other social issues led fundamentalist Christians to align with the Republican Party.

The relationship between collective action by groups and party electoral strategy is clearly a two-way street. Groups that align with a party provide essential electoral resources, including a reliable voting bloc, money, personnel, and even candidates. When their party wins, these groups gain influence over public policy. Of course, there are risks as well: an organized interest may suffer if the party it supports loses the election.

To Resolve Problems of Collective Choice in Government

Political parties are also essential in the process of making policy. Within government, parties are coalitions of individuals with shared or overlapping interests who generally support one another's programs and initiatives. Even though there may be disagreement within each party, a common party label gives members a reason to cooperate. Because they are permanent coalitions, parties greatly facilitate the policy-making process. If alliances had to be formed from scratch for each legislative proposal, the business of government would slow to a crawl or halt altogether. Parties create a basis for coalition and thus sharply reduce the time and effort needed to advance legislation. Presidents work closely with the leaders of their party in the House and Senate, even if the party is in the minority, to ensure that the executive's agenda will be introduced into Congress and supported. Without party support, the president would have to undertake the probably impossible task of forming a completely new coalition for every policy proposal.

Party cohesion, however, sometimes breaks down over the need for action on a crucial issue. For instance, in 2008, facing a collapse of the financial industry, Republican president George W. Bush proposed a $700 billion intervention to unlock frozen credit markets. While Democratic leaders in the House produced a majority of Democratic votes in favor of the plan,

Republican leadership, faced with the opposition of an extreme conservative faction, failed to produce enough votes to pass the measure. Bush's failure to clear the plan with House Republican leadership in advance doomed the proposal.[4] In more recent years, with Republican majorities in both chambers shrinking, small defections have been costly. In the Senate, for example, four Republican senators broke with their party in March 2019 to end a partial shutdown of the federal government triggered when President Trump insisted that Congress appropriate $5.7 billion to build a wall along the U.S.-Mexican border.[5] Even when party coalitions appear to agree on an issue, the road to enacting actual policy can be complex (see the Policy Principle box on p. 517).

To Deal with the Problem of Ambition

Parties enable individual politicians to achieve their ambitions. The very brand names that parties provide are often a significant electoral asset. Moreover, once their candidates are elected, parties provide these politicians—who share principles, causes, and constituencies—with a basis for coordination, common cause, cooperation, and joint enterprise. But individual ambition constantly threatens to undermine any bases for cooperation. Political parties, by regulating career advancement, providing for the orderly resolution of competition, and attending to the post-career care of party officials, do much to rescue coordination and cooperation and permit fellow partisans to pursue common causes where feasible. Simple devices such as primary elections, for example, provide contexts in which to resolve clashing electoral ambitions. Representative partisan bodies, such as the Republican and Democratic committees in the House and Senate that distribute committee assignments to party members, resolve competing claims for power positions. And centralized fund-raising by national party organizations provides incentives for politicians to conduct their campaigns and vote in the legislature in line with their party. In short, politics consists not of foot soldiers walking in lockstep but, rather, of ambitious and autonomous individuals seeking power. The unchecked burnishing of individual careers is a formula for destructive competition in which the dividends of cooperation are rarely reaped. Political parties constitute organizations of relatively kindred spirits who try to capture some of those dividends by providing a structure in which ambition is not suppressed altogether but is not so destructive either.

---

4   Carl Hulse and David M. Herszenhorn, "Defiant House Rejects Huge Bailout; Next Step Is Uncertain," *New York Times*, September 29, 2008, www.nytimes.com/2008/09/30 /business/30cong.html (accessed 4/22/20).

5   Reuters, "Democrats May Have Votes to Block Trump's Border Emergency in U.S. Senate," March 3, 2019, www.reuters.com/article/us-usa-trump-congress /democrats-may-have-votes-to-block-trumps-border-emergency-in-us-senate -idUSKCN1QK0OP (accessed 4/10/20).

Party Coalitions and Abortion Policy

Political action involves merging people's individual preferences in order to pursue some collective purpose. For interest groups, collective action is relatively straightforward: people who share a common policy goal work together to achieve that goal. For political parties, however, collective action is more complicated. Parties hope not only to achieve policy goals but also to capture public offices. In some instances, party leaders find that they must compromise on policy goals in order to enhance the party's overall electoral chances.

An anti-abortion protest in Washington, D.C.

To complicate matters, the two major American political parties, the Republican Party and the Democratic Party, are coalitions of various forces and individuals who agree on some things but not on others. The Republican Party, for example, includes economic conservatives who favor lower taxes, social and religious conservatives who oppose abortion and same-sex marriage, libertarians who seek a smaller government, populists who oppose free-trade policies, and a number of other factions.

Every four years the parties write platforms summarizing their core principles and policy positions. Platforms are declarations of collective policy preferences, but the road from collective policy statement to policy action can be complex. Take the case of abortion. In 1973 the Supreme Court affirmed, in the case of Roe v. Wade, that women have the right to seek an abortion under the Fourteenth Amendment. Until that time, neither party had mentioned abortion in its platform, but in 1976 the first presidential election following the Court's decision, both parties issued broad statements on the issue. Republicans opposed abortion but called it "a moral and personal issue," on which people might disagree.

Over time, the Republican position hardened. By 1980 the Republican platform stated that the party supported a constitutional amendment protecting "the right to life for unborn children." The 2012 and 2016 Republican Party platforms called

for a constitutional amendment to overturn *Roe v. Wade*, opposed the use of public funds for abortion, demanded the prohibition of "partial birth abortion," called on the president to appoint judges who oppose abortion, and demanded an end to federal funding of embryonic-stem-cell research.

On the one hand, Republicans' increasingly staunch opposition to abortion reflected the growing importance of social conservatives in the electorate and the recognition that the party needed their support in many districts. On the other hand, despite electing three presidents since 1980 and frequently controlling the House, the Senate, or both, Republicans in government have enacted few policies to actually bring an end to abortion.

The explanation for this apparent contradiction between principles and practices is rooted in the nature of the American party system. Anti-abortion rhetoric energizes one faction of the party, but anti-abortion action runs counter to the views of many other Republicans and might offend moderate and independent voters whom the party also needs at the polls. This example illustrates how parties' efforts to appeal to various groups in the electorate may, in fact, make action in the policy arena more difficult.

WHAT FUNCTIONS DO PARTIES PERFORM?

Parties are mainly involved in nominations and elections: recruiting candidates for office, getting out the vote, and making it easier for citizens to choose their leaders. That is, they help solve the problems of collective action and ambition. They also influence the institutions of government, providing mechanisms of leadership and organization for the various congressional committees and activities on the floor in each chamber. In other words, they help solve the problems of collective choice that arise concerning institutional arrangements and policy formulation.

Recruiting Candidates

One of the most important party activities is the recruitment of candidates for office. Each election year, candidates must be found for thousands of federal, state, and local offices. When an incumbent is not seeking reelection or when an incumbent in the opposing party appears vulnerable, party leaders identify strong candidates and try to interest them in entering the campaign. The recruiting season begins early because, in some states, candidates must file as early as January of an election year to appear on November ballots. Candidate recruitment in the spring shapes the parties' messages and fortunes in the general election.

Over the past decade, the Republicans have done a much better job than Democrats have of recruiting and electing candidates to city councils and state legislative seats. Following the 2018 elections, Republicans held 3,846 (52 percent) and Democrats held 3,444 of 7,383 state legislative seats (93 state legislators aligned with neither party). State legislators are prime candidates to run for U.S. House and Senate and for statewide offices such as governor and attorney general.[6] The parties also use their recruitment efforts to target segments of the electorate in which they want to strengthen their appeal. The Republican Party, for example, established project GROW (Growing Republican Opportunities for Women) in 2013 to improve recruitment of women candidates for state legislatures and Congress.[7]

An ideal candidate will be charismatic, organized, knowledgeable, and an excellent debater; have an unblemished record; and possess the ability to raise enough money to mount a serious campaign. Party leaders usually will

---

6   Andrea Dew Steele, "DNC Chair Candidates: Recruitment and Training Works," *The Hill*, January 19, 2017, https://thehill.com/blogs/congress-blog/politics/315098-dnc-chair-candidates-recruitment-and-training-works (accessed 7/5/20).

7   Nicole Puglise, "GOP Women's Recruitment Effort Adapts for 2016," *Roll Call*, July 6, 2015, www.rollcall.com/2015/07/06/gop-womens-recruitment-effort-adapts-for-2016 (accessed 4/22/20).

not provide financial backing for candidates who cannot raise substantial funds on their own. For a House seat, this can mean candidates are expected to raise around $1 million; for a Senate seat, several million dollars; and upward of $1 billion for the presidency.[8] Often party leaders have difficulty finding attractive candidates and persuading them to run. In recent years, many potential congressional candidates have declined to run, saying they were reluctant to leave their homes and families for the hectic life of a member of Congress. Candidate recruitment has become particularly difficult in an era when political campaigns often involve mudslinging and the candidates' personal lives are scrutinized in the press.[9]

Nominating Candidates

Article I, Section 4, of the Constitution makes only a few provisions for elections. It delegates to the states the power to set the "Times, Places and Manner of holding Elections," even for U.S. senators and representatives. It does, however, reserve to Congress the power to make laws concerning elections if it so chooses. The Constitution has been amended at times to expand the right to participate in elections, and Congress has occasionally passed laws regulating elections, congressional districting, and campaign practices. But the Constitution and the laws are almost completely silent on nominations, setting only citizenship and age requirements for candidates. The president must be at least 35 years of age, a natural-born citizen, and a resident of the United States for 14 years. A senator must be at least age 30, a U.S. citizen for at least nine years, and a resident of the state he or she represents. A member of the House must be at least age 25, a U.S. citizen for seven years, and a resident of the state he or she represents.

Nomination is the process by which parties select their candidates for election to public office. Nomination is the parties' most serious and difficult business. The nominating process can precede the election by many months (Figure 12.1), as it does when presidential candidates are whittled down through a grueling series of debates and state primaries, caucuses, and conventions until there is only one survivor in each party.

 nomination

The process by which political parties select their candidates for election to public office.

Nomination by Convention. A nominating convention is a formal meeting of party members that is bound by rules governing participation and nominating procedures. Delegates to these conventions are elected by party members from the relevant county (a county convention) or state (a state convention).

---

8 Figures based on average amounts spent by winners in 2016, 2018, and 2020 according to the Federal Election Commission reports available at https://www.fec.gov/data /browse-data/?tab=spending. See also Kenneth P. Vogel, Dave Levinthal, and Tarini Parti, "Barack Obama, Mitt Romney Both Topped $1B," *Politico*, December 7, 2012, www.politico.com/story/2012/12/barack-obama-mitt-romney-both-topped-1-billion -in-2012-84737.html (accessed 4/22/20).

9 For an excellent analysis of the parties' role in recruitment, see Paul S. Herrnson, *Congressional Elections: Campaigning at Home and in Washington*, 7th ed. (Washington, DC: CQ Press, 2015).

Figure 12.1
TYPES OF NOMINATION PROCESSES

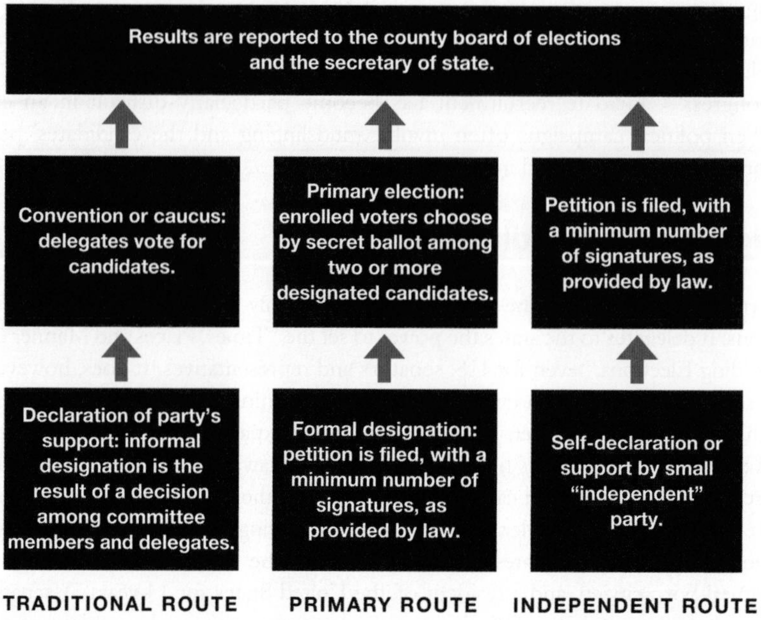

Results are reported to the county board of elections and the secretary of state.

| Convention or caucus: delegates vote for candidates. | Primary election: enrolled voters choose by secret ballot among two or more designated candidates. | Petition is filed, with a minimum number of signatures, as provided by law. |

| Declaration of party's support: informal designation is the result of a decision among committee members and delegates. | Formal designation: petition is filed, with a minimum number of signatures, as provided by law. | Self-declaration or support by small "independent" party. |

TRADITIONAL ROUTE   **PRIMARY ROUTE**   **INDEPENDENT ROUTE**

closed primary

A primary election in which only those voters who have registered their affiliation with the party by a specified time before the election can participate.

open primary

A primary election in which voters can choose on the day of the primary which party's primary to vote in.

Delegates to each party's national convention (which nominates the party's presidential candidate) are chosen by party members on a state-by-state basis; there is no single national delegate selection process.

Nomination by Primary Election. In primary elections, party members select the party's nominees directly, rather than selecting convention delegates who then select the nominees. Primaries are imperfect replacements for conventions because rarely do more than 25 percent of registered voters participate.[10] Nevertheless, primaries have replaced conventions as the dominant method of nomination.[11]

Primary elections fall mainly into two categories—closed and open. In a **closed primary**, participation is limited to individuals who have previously declared their affiliation by registering with the party. In an **open primary**, individuals declare their affiliation on the day of the primary election. To do so,

10 Anthony King, *Running Scared: Why America's Politicians Campaign Too Much and Govern Too Little* (New York: Martin Kessler Books, 1997).

11 At the present time, only a small number of states, including Connecticut, Delaware, and Utah, provide for state conventions to nominate candidates for statewide offices, and even those states follow their conventions with primaries whenever a substantial minority of delegates to the convention has voted for one of the defeated aspirants.

they simply go to the polling place and ask for the ballot of a particular party. The open primary allows each voter to consider candidates and issues before deciding whether and in which party's contest to participate. Open primaries, therefore, are less conducive to strong political parties. But in either case, primaries are more open than conventions or caucuses to new issues and new types of candidates.

Nomination by Caucus. In several states, including Iowa and Nevada, the presidential nominating process begins with meetings called caucuses. All registered voters are eligible to participate in the caucuses, but because the nomination process consists of extensive discussions and can last for several hours, only the most motivated voters attend. At the local caucuses, those present select delegates to county-level conventions, and, in turn, the county conventions select delegates to the state party convention. It is at the state party convention where caucus states elect delegates to the party's national convention.

The shift from party conventions to primary elections and caucuses creates an additional level of screening; candidates must now win both the primary and the general elections in order to hold office. As a result, the introduction of primary elections may have contributed to the rise of candidate-centered politics by advantaging politicians who are particularly strong campaigners but who may be less effective at governing.[12] Thus a selection effect results from the particular institutional arrangement a state employs. Institutions matter in this case because they encourage or discourage particular types of candidates, as the institution principle suggests.

Getting Out the Vote

The election period begins immediately after the nominations. Historically, this has been a time of glory for the political parties, whose popular base of support is on full display. All the paraphernalia of party committees and all the committee members are activated in the form of local party workforces.

The first step in the electoral process is voter registration, which takes place all year round. At one time party workers were responsible for this activity, but they have since been supplemented (and in many states displaced) by civic groups such as the League of Women Voters, unions, and chambers of commerce.

Those who have registered must decide on Election Day whether to go to the polling place, stand in line, and vote for the various candidates and referenda on the ballot. Political parties, candidates, and campaigning can make a big difference in persuading eligible voters to vote. Because it is costly for voters to participate in elections (they have to take time off work or spend the time to learn about the issues and candidates in a campaign), and because many of the

---

12 Matthew Crenson and Benjamin Ginsberg, *Presidential Power: Unchecked and Unbalanced* (New York: Norton, 2007).

benefits that winning parties bestow are public goods (that is, parties cannot exclude any individual from enjoying them), people often free ride by enjoying the benefits without incurring the costs of voting. Parties help overcome this free-rider problem (see Chapter 1) by mobilizing voters to support their candidates.

In recent years, nonprofit groups have mobilized large numbers of people to vote and raised millions of dollars for election organizing and advertising. Legions of workers and volunteers for "netroots" organizations have used new technologies to build and communicate with networks of supporters. To comply with federal election and tax law, these groups must maintain independence from the political parties, even though they have the same objectives as the parties and strive to elect politicians from a particular party.[13] Such organizations act as shadow appendages of the two parties, mobilizing supporters for one or the other. The netroots have become integral to campaign organizations, and these new forms of direct campaigning have produced a noticeable uptick in voter turnout.

Facilitating Electoral Choice

Parties make the electoral choice much easier for voters. It is often argued that people should vote for the best candidate regardless of party affiliation. But on any general-election ballot, voters likely know only a handful of candidates—namely, certain candidates for president, U.S. Senate, U.S. House, and governor. As one moves down the ballot, voters' familiarity with the candidates declines. Without party labels, voters would constantly confront a bewildering array of new choices and might have difficulty making informed decisions. Without a doubt, candidates' party affiliations help voters make reasonable choices.

Parties lower the information costs of participating in elections by providing a recognizable brand name. Without knowing much about a given candidate, voters can infer from party labels how the candidate will likely behave once elected. In the United States, the Democratic Party is associated with greater governmental regulation of the economy and a larger public sector; the Republican Party favors a limited governmental role in the economy and reduced government spending paired with tax reductions. The Democrats favor aggressive protection of civil rights for women and for sexual and racial minorities and a secular approach to religion in public life. The Republicans generally support banning abortion and favor governmental participation in expanding the role of religious organizations in civil society. The parties' positions on the economy were cemented in the 1930s, and their division on social issues emerged during the 1960s and 1970s. The Democratic positions are loosely labeled liberal and those of the Republicans loosely conservative.

---

13 If a group coordinates its activities with a political party, it is subject to additional reporting requirements and contribution limits, and such political action can violate the conditions for tax exempt status of nonprofits.

Most Americans identify with one of the two parties and are likely to vote with that party, but even those who do not can derive value from the party labels. Nonpartisan voters may be more conflicted about which party or candidate best represents their interests, but if they tried to learn about every politician running for every office, they would spend an enormous amount of time tracking down information. Party labels, then, help simplify the voter's choice to an evaluation of the parties' competing policy positions or the performance of those in office. The independent voter may ask, "Which of the two parties will better represent my ideals and interests?" and then choose the party that offers the best option today. Or the voter may ask, "Am I better off now than four years ago?" If not, she will vote against the president's party up and down the ballot. If yes, she will vote to keep the president and his party in power. Whichever strategy the independent voter uses, parties are essential for simplifying an otherwise bewildering choice.

For all voters, partisans and independents alike, the parties make it easier to hold government accountable. People can vote against the party in power in bad times and for the party in power in good times. They can vote against the party in power if it enacts unpopular legislation. Thus political parties solve one of the most important collective action problems facing American democracy: the problem of collective responsibility. If every politician ran independently, without regard to other candidates, districts, or the nation at large, each race for legislator or executive would become an isolated event. In such a setting it would be exceedingly difficult for voters to send a message that they want government to go in a different direction. Parties, then, lend coherence to government and meaning to elections.[14]

Party labels also benefit the politicians. The recognizable labels of "Democrat" and "Republican" spare candidates in most districts and states the great expense of educating voters about what they stand for. The policy positions and ideologies associated with these labels are largely consistent because like-minded people identify with the respective organizations. People who broadly share the principles espoused by a party and who wish to participate on a high level will attend party meetings, run for leadership positions in local and state party organizations, attend state and national conventions, and even run for elected office.[15] Each party, then, draws on a distinct pool of activists and candidates. Each successive election reinforces the division between the parties.

Influencing National Government

The two major parties are often called "big tents" because they position themselves as broad coalitions: they seek to attract as many groups and ideas as possible. This strategy prevents effective national third parties from emerging and

---

14 Morris P. Fiorina, "The Decline of Collective Responsibility in American Politics," *Daedalus* 109, no. 3 (Summer 1980): 25–45.

15 Comprehensive studies of delegates were conducted by Walter J. Stone and Ronald B. Rapoport from 1980 through 1996. See their *Three's a Crowd: The Dynamic of Third Parties, Ross Perot, and Republican Resurgence* (Ann Arbor: University of Michigan Press, 2005). Surveys of candidates find similar sorting.

guarantees that the Democrats and Republicans alone will vie for control of government. The coalitions that come together in the Democratic and Republican parties determine which interests and social groups align with the parties and what sorts of issues emerge, thus shaping the parties' platforms.

Many European observers regard the American parties as odd amalgams of contradictory ideas. Liberalism, as it developed as a political philosophy in Europe, naturally pairs laissez-faire economics with liberal views on civil rights. Conservatism, which maintains a respect for social and political order, prefers a stronger role for social organizations, especially religions; a greater respect for social hierarchies, most notably social classes and highly educated elites; and governmental power in the economy. The American parties, partly because of their histories, have scrambled these traditional views. In the Republican Party today, laissez-faire economics goes hand in hand with conservative views on civil rights and religion in society. In the Democratic Party today, liberal views on civil rights are tied to an expansive view of government in the economy. The American parties have mixed and matched different ideas in response to evolving issues and party leadership. For example, the coalition that President Franklin Delano Roosevelt assembled in the 1930s consisted of progressive Republicans, who favored greater economic regulation; old-line Democrats, especially in the South; and urban political machines in northern and midwestern cities. This peculiar coalition gave rise to the political philosophy and public policies pursued under the New Deal. It also constrained what Roosevelt could do on some issues. Most important, he could not push for expanding civil rights for Black Americans without losing the support of southerners. The meaning of Democratic liberalism in the United States, then, was very much a function of the history of the parties.

Even though American liberalism and conservatism do not coincide neatly with their European counterparts, they still represent distinct views about how government ought to act, and they appeal to different constituencies. The Democratic Party at the national level seeks to unite organized labor, the poor, racial minorities, and liberal upper-middle-class professionals. The Republicans, by contrast, appeal to business, upper-middle-class and upper-class groups in the private sector, social conservatives, and working-class conservatives. In 2020, for example, Joe Biden won a majority of votes of people with advanced degrees (such as law degrees or medical doctorates), while Donald Trump won a majority of votes of lower-middle-class Americans with high school degrees. Often party leaders seek to develop issues they hope will add new groups to their constituent base. During the 1980s, for example, under President Reagan, the Republicans devised a series of "social issues," including support for school prayer, opposition to abortion, and opposition to affirmative action, designed to cultivate the support of White southerners. This effort was extremely successful in increasing Republican strength in the once solidly Democratic South. In the 1990s, under President Bill Clinton, the Democratic Party developed social programs designed to solidify the party's base among working-class and poor voters and somewhat conservative economic programs aimed at attracting middle-class and upper-middle-class voters. As these examples suggest, party leaders can act as policy entrepreneurs, using new ideas and programs to expand their party's base of support while eroding that of the opposition.

Both parties translate their general goals into concrete policies through the members they elect to office. Republicans, for example, have cut taxes, increased defense spending, cut social spending, and enacted restrictions on abortion. Democrats have expanded social programs, increased social spending, and increased regulations on business, such as environmental protections, financial regulations, and fair employment rules. A good example of this is the Affordable Care Act (ACA). In 2009, President Obama and the Democratic-controlled Congress passed the ACA, a national health insurance system that guarantees all people access to health care. Such a program had been a key priority of the Democratic Party's platform since the 1940s. Beginning in 2010, the Republican Party made repeal of the ACA one of its central messages and policy promises, while the Democratic Party doubled down on its support for the act. In 2017, the House of Representatives, with the support of President Trump, passed a bill to repeal large portions of the ACA. Even still, the American parties are not unified teams that work in unison, and the repeal effort stalled in the U.S. Senate; conservative Republican senators refused to support it because it did not go far enough, and Republican senators from more moderate states, such as Dean Heller of Nevada and Susan Collins of Maine, balked at the bill because it went too far.

PARTIES IN GOVERNMENT

Parties operate in three spheres: elections, political institutions, and government. The ultimate test of a political party is its influence on the institutions of government and the policy-making process. We begin there.

Most parties originate inside the government. Political parties form to organize those who support the government's actions and those who do not; in the United Kingdom, these groups are called "Government" and "Opposition."[16] In the American context, at the federal level, parties vie to control both Congress and the presidency.

The Parties and Congress. The two major American political parties have a profound influence on the organization and day-to-day operation of Congress. The Speaker of the House, perhaps the most powerful person in Congress, is essentially a party officer. All House members participate in electing the Speaker, but the actual selection is made by the **majority party**. When the majority party caucus presents a nominee to the entire House, its choice is invariably ratified in a straight party-line vote.

The parties also organize the committee systems of both houses of Congress. Although the whole membership adopts the rules organizing and defining the jurisdictions of each committee, all other committee features are shaped by the

 majority party

The party that holds the majority of seats in a legislative chamber, such as the U.S. House or Senate.

---

16 Maurice Duverger, *Political Parties: Their Organization and Activity in the Modern State,* trans. Barbara North and Robert North (New York: Wiley, 1954).

party leadership and caucuses. For example, each party is assigned a quota of members for each committee that corresponds to the percentage of total seats it holds in the chamber. On the rare occasions when an independent or third-party candidate is elected, the leaders of the two parties must agree on whether to count the congressperson as a Democrat or a Republican for the purposes of committee allocation. Presumably, the member will not be able to serve on any committee until the quota question is settled.[17] As we saw in Chapter 6, the assignment of individual members to congressional committees is a party decision, and the chairperson of each committee is always a member of the majority party. Since the late nineteenth century, the most senior majority-party member of each committee has generally assumed the role of chair. This seniority system has survived only because the two parties support it, and each party can depart from it by a simple vote. During the 1970s, both parties reinstituted the practice of reviewing each chairmanship every two years. In 2001, Republicans limited House committee chairs to three terms. Existing chairs are forced to step down but are generally replaced by the next most senior Republican member of each committee.[18]

President and Party. The president carries the mantle of party leader, and the electoral fortunes of the parties rise and fall with the success of the president. During midterm congressional elections, when the president is not on the ballot, voters hold the president's party accountable for current problems. When the economy does poorly, Americans punish the president's party, even when the opposing party controls Congress.

The president also relies heavily on fellow party members in organizing the executive branch and passing legislation. Unlike in parliamentary governments, such as in the United Kingdom, the heads of executive departments are not sitting members of the legislature. With few exceptions, cabinet members and other key presidential appointments are people loyal to the president and his party; most have served as state governors or members of Congress or are close advisers who worked with the president in previous offices or campaigns.

The president and White House staff also work closely with congressional party leaders to shepherd legislation through Congress. The president cannot introduce legislation and must rely on members of Congress to do so. (There are a few exceptions such as nominations and treaties.) Nearly all of the president's legislative initiatives begin as bills introduced by fellow party members in the House and Senate. The party leadership of the president's party also negotiates with individual members of Congress to construct majority support for White House–sponsored bills. Sometimes even the president will try to persuade individual legislators to support a particular bill.

17 Scott A. Frisch and Sean Q. Kelly, *Committee Assignment Politics in the U.S. House of Representatives* (Norman: University of Oklahoma Press, 2006).

18 Daniel Newhauser, "Brain Drain: Self-Imposed Term Limits Shuffle Committees, House GOP Leadership," *Roll Call*, April 22, 2014, www.rollcall.com/2014/04/22/brain-drain-self-imposed-term-limits-shuffle-committees-house-gop-leadership-2 (accessed 4/10/20).

The president's ability to prevail in Congress depends on which party controls the House and Senate. When the president's party enjoys majorities in both chambers, president-backed bills succeed over 80 percent of the time. Presidents Obama and Trump set records for presidential support. During Obama's first two years, a majority of the Democratic-controlled Congress supported his position 96 percent of the time, the highest rate since World War II (when *Congressional Quarterly* began computing presidential support scores). Trump enjoyed even higher support during his first two years, with a majority of the Republican-controlled Congress supporting his position a record 98 percent of the time.[19]

When the opposing party controls at least one chamber, however, the president has a much more difficult time passing legislation. In the 113th Congress (2013–14), Democrats controlled the Senate and Republicans controlled the House. Bills supported by Democratic president Obama were passed in the Senate 93 percent of the time and in the House only 15 percent of the time.[20]

PARTIES IN THE ELECTORATE

Political parties are more than just political leaders; they comprise millions of people and organizations, such as labor unions, corporations, and other interest groups. Individuals align with the parties when they volunteer for campaigns, give money, register as partisans, or vote in a party's primary. Many groups have close connections to political parties, often providing money and organizing people for campaigns.

Party Identification

As we saw in Chapter 11, individual voters tend to develop **party identifications** with one of the political parties. There are three distinct views about what party identification is, and they point to very different understandings of the nature of party identification and its effect on elections.[21] Party identification may be based on the psychological attachments people form through their

party identification

An individual's attachment to a particular political party, which may be based on a psychological attachment formed through upbringing, on ideology and policy positions, on past experiences with politicians, or on a mixture of these elements.

19 John T. Bennett, "Trump's Winning Pattern with Legislation Might Become a Thing of the Past," *Roll Call*, February 28, 2019, www.rollcall.com/2019/02/28/trumps-winning -pattern-with-legislation-might-become-a-thing-of-the-past-cq-vote-studies (accessed 4/22/20).

20 Shawn Zeller, "Running on Empty: Few Bills, but Many Nominees, Approved Last Year," *CQ Weekly*, March 16, 2015, http://library.cqpress.com/cqweekly/file.php?path=/files /wr20150316-2014_Presidential.pdf (accessed 4/22/20).

21 For an excellent treatment of the meanings of party identification and analysis of the implications of different theories, see Donald Green, Bradley Palmquist, and Eric Schickler, *Partisan Hearts and Minds: Political Parties and the Social Identities of Voters* (New Haven, CT: Yale University Press, 2002).

upbringing, on their ideology and policy positions, or on their past experiences with politicians.

Party Identification as Psychological Attachment.
First, party identification is a psychological attachment that individuals hold, often throughout adulthood, to one of the parties. Voters generally form attachments to parties that reflect their views and interests, but people's attachments are also shaped by the loyalties of their parents and other family members, their friends, and their local communities, quite apart from issues and ideologies. Once those attachments are formed, they are likely to persist and even be handed down to children, unless certain very strong factors convince individuals to disavow their party. In some sense, party identification is similar to brand loyalty in the marketplace: consumers choose a brand of automobile for its appearance or mechanical characteristics and stick with it out of loyalty, habit, and unwillingness to reexamine their choices, but they may eventually switch if the old brand no longer serves their interests.

The first few presidential elections that an individual experiences as an adult are also thought to have a particularly profound influence on that voter's understanding of the parties and politics. And as different cohorts come into politics, their experiences carry forward throughout their lives. Those who were 18 to 24 years old in 1984, for example, identify overwhelmingly with the Republican Party, because those elections marked the triumph of Ronald Reagan's presidency and political philosophy, the rise of a revitalized Republican Party, and the beginning of the end of the Cold War. Those who were 18 to 24 years old in 2008, in contrast, identify disproportionately with the Democratic Party, because the Obama campaign galvanized young voters around a new vision for the future. We will have to wait to see the full effects of Donald Trump's 2016 victory on young people, but Analyzing the Evidence on pp. 530–1 provides some early insights. However it develops, an individual's psychological affinity for a party makes that person want to support it, even when she disagrees with the party on important policies or disapproves of its nominees for office.

Party Identification as Ideological Affinity.
Of course, the Democratic and Republican parties are quite different entities today than they were 40 or 80 years ago. On matters of race relations, for example, the Democratic Party has moved over the past century from supporting segregation to spearheading civil rights. The Republican Party was a bastion of economic protectionism before the 1940s, but from the 1950s to 2016, the party championed free trade. On this issue, change appears to be under way once again for the Republican Party: President Trump has questioned the basic principles of free trade, withdrew the United States from the Trans-Pacific Partnership, and has championed other policies that restrict imports and exports in order to protect U.S. jobs. However strong generational transmission of party identifications may be, the dissonance between identities and issues must surely weaken the pull of party, which suggests a second theory: that party identification reflects voters' underlying ideologies and parties' policy positions.

Parties in government are meaningful organizations for producing public policies. The relatively high degree of party loyalty in Congress and other branches of government means that voters can reasonably anticipate how politicians will act in office. Citizens identify with parties that pursue public policies more to their liking. For example, a union worker will feel a stronger attachment to the Democratic Party because the Democrats have historically protected union interests. A high-income earner may feel a strong pull toward the Republican Party because that party pushes for lower taxes overall, whereas the Democrats promote higher tax rates for higher-income households. In part, people who identify with a particular party feel that it represents their interests better than others; hence they are highly likely to vote for that party without even knowing a candidate's voting record or campaign promises.[22]

However, not all people fit neatly into one ideological camp or another. Some people do not think about politics in ideological or policy terms, and others are indifferent to the parties ideologically. A significant portion of Americans consider themselves centrists and feel that the Democrats are somewhat too liberal and the Republicans somewhat too conservative. They do not have a strong affinity for either party. Other people feel pulled in different directions by different issues and concerns. A union member who strongly opposes abortion, for example, is drawn to the Democrats' labor policies and the Republicans' abortion policies. Campaigns target such cross-pressured voters, who are often pivotal in elections.[23]

Party Identification as Tally of Experiences. A third explanation is that party identification reflects individuals' past experiences with political leaders and representatives, especially presidents. Americans hold their presidents, and to a lesser extent Congress, accountable for the country's economic performance and success in foreign affairs. A bad economy or a disastrous military intervention will lead voters to disapprove of the president and to lower their assessment of the president's party. Parties are, by this account, teams seeking to run the government: they consist of policy experts, managers, and leaders who will conduct foreign policy, economic policy, and domestic policies (such as environmental protection and health care). When things go well, voters infer that the incumbent party has a good approach to running national affairs; but when things go badly, they learn that the party lacks the people needed to run the government competently or the approach needed to produce economic prosperity, international peace, and other desirable outcomes. With each successive presidency and their experience of it, individuals update their beliefs about which party is better able to govern.

....

22 For a detailed assessment of the political use of information-economizing devices such as party labels, see Arthur Lupia and Mathew D. McCubbins, *The Democratic Dilemma: Can Citizens Learn What They Need to Know?* (New York: Cambridge University Press, 1998).

23 For a more in-depth discussion of independent voters, policy indifference, and cross pressure, see D. Sunshine Hillygus and Todd G. Shields, *The Persuadable Voter: Wedge Issues in Presidential Campaigns* (Princeton, NJ: Princeton University Press, 2008).

What Motivates Political Engagement among Young People?

Contributed by
David E. Campbell
and **Christina Wolbrecht**
University of Notre Dame

Donald Trump's 2016 victory over Hillary Clinton struck many as a blow against gender equality. Many described Clinton as a role model, but would her defeat discourage the very young women she had hoped to inspire?

To find out, we analyzed a nationally representative survey of 997 adolescents ages 15–18 and their parents, conducted online. Both teens and parents responded to two waves of this survey, the first during the fall 2016 campaign and a follow-up roughly one year later, in the fall of 2017. We asked about their views of American democracy and political engagement. By interviewing the same people both before and after the election, we were able to see whether their attitudes changed.

Here's what we found. First, disillusionment with the political system rose dramatically—but only among girls who identify as Democrats. In the fall of 2016, about a third of Democratic girls said that the political system in America "does not help people with their genuine needs," more or less the same proportion as Democratic boys and Republican girls and boys.[1] One year later, 53 percent of Democratic girls said that U.S. democracy does not help people with their needs—a significant jump, especially compared to the fact that the opinions of the other groups barely budged. (Both Republican boys and girls became slightly less pessimistic, presumably because their candidate won.)

Democratic Girls Become More Disillusioned with U.S. Politics after 2016 Election

Percent saying that the political system DOES NOT help people with their genuine needs

● 2016 ● 2017

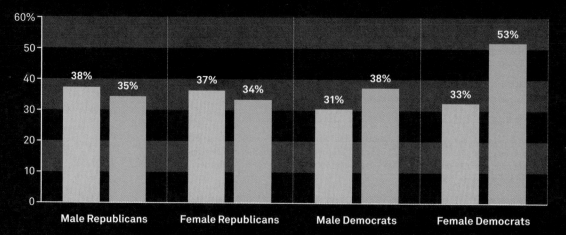

When people are disillusioned with democracy, they often disengage. Why bother getting involved if all is for naught? But Democratic girls who came to doubt American democracy responded quite differently.

After 2016, Democratic girls say they became more politically active—and particularly, they were more likely to say that they are or plan to be engaged in lawful political protest.[2] The biggest spike came among those Democratic girls who became disillusioned. Instead of dampening their enthusiasm for political engagement, their doubts about the state of U.S. politics seem to have increased their desire to be heard.

Democratic Girls Become More Interested in Protesting after 2016 Election

Percent saying that they have or will engage in political protest

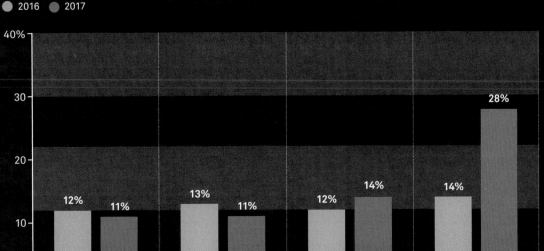

Why might Democratic girls in particular become interested in protesting after the 2016 election? We suspect that they're following role models—but not that of just one woman politician. The January 2017 Women's March on Washington, the largest single-day demonstration in U.S. history, protested Trump's inauguration as president and launched a wave of activism. Across the nation, the majority of activists have been women, many of whom use gendered rhetoric and symbols, such as the famous pink hats.

These protesters provided visible role models to Democratic girls for how to channel their post-2016 political frustration. Many have come to see protest as an important part of their own political repertoire. "The Resistance" is the role model.

1   David E. Campbell and Christina Wolbrecht, "The Resistance as Role Model: Disillusionment and Protest Among American Adolescents After 2016," Political Behavior 42 (2020): 1143–1168.

Figure 12.2

AMERICANS' PARTY IDENTIFICATION, 1940–2020

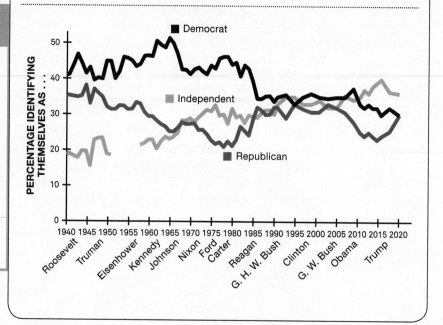

NOTE: Independent data not available for 1951–56.

SOURCES: Pew Research Center, www.people-press.org/interactives/party-id-trend; and Gallup, https://news.gallup.com/poll/15370/party-affiliation.aspx (accessed 4/10/20).

party activist

A partisan who
contributes time and
energy beyond voting to
support a party and its
candidates.

Most Americans identify with one of the two major political parties. Historically, approximately 7 in 10 Americans have considered themselves to be Republicans or Democrats, and those who do not choose those labels usually say that they lean toward one of the two parties. Over the past two decades, however, more and more people have chosen to call themselves independents, and that category is now consistently the single largest group of identifiers (Figure 12.2). Party identification gives citizens a stake in election outcomes that goes beyond the race at hand. This is why people who identify strongly with one party are more likely than other Americans to go to the polls and, of course, to support their party. **Party activists** are those who not only vote but also volunteer their time and energy to party affairs. Activists ring doorbells, stuff envelopes, attend meetings, and contribute money to the party cause—essential work that keeps the organization going. It is worth noting that someone's attachment to a party does not guarantee that they will vote for that party's candidates, though it does reflect a tendency. In general, however, strong identifiers vote for their party's candidate almost always, and weak identifiers do so most of the time. For example, according to the 2020 exit polls, 94 percent of those who called themselves Republicans voted for

Donald Trump, the Republican Party's nominee, and 94 percent of people who called themselves Democrats voted for Joe Biden, the Democratic Party's nominee.[24]

Group Basis of Parties

The Democratic and Republican parties are America's only national parties, drawing support from most regions of the country and from Americans of every racial, economic, religious, and ethnic group. The two parties do not draw equal support from members of every social stratum, however. When we refer to the Democratic or Republican coalition, we mean the groups that generally support one party or the other.

A pluralist view of political parties suggests that they consist of coalitions of many organized groups. The leaders of organizations such as the American Federation of Labor (AFL-CIO) and the Christian Coalition of America may choose to side with a party in an effort to affect what government does by influencing the party's policy orientation. A group can offer resources such as campaign workers, contributions, and votes; the party, in exchange, can pursue policies in line with what the groups want. The more disciplined the group and the more resources it can offer, the more power it will have in the party. Party leaders try to build coalitions consisting of many different groups that each hope to advance a distinct policy or political benefit. The Reagan coalition, for instance, consisted of corporate political leaders who wanted to minimize taxes, the Christian Coalition and other fundamental Christian groups that wanted changes in various social policies, and activists in western states who wanted open access to land. The challenge for political parties is to build coalitions that can win majorities in elections but not create too many conflicting demands.[25]

Broader social groups are equally important. Parties can appeal to different types of voters through distinct policy promises. A person with a particularly strong social group attachment might find one of the parties appealing because it aligns well on the social group's pet issue. For instance, the Republican Party's hard line toward Cuba and communism means that most Cuban Americans identify as Republican, even while other Latino groups line up with Democrats over issues such as immigration and education. In the United States today, a variety of group characteristics are associated with party identification. These include race and ethnicity, gender, religion, class, region, and age.

---

24 CNN Politics, "Exit Polls," https://www.cnn.com/election/2020/exit-polls/president /national-results (accessed 11/17/20).

25 A formulation of the pluralist model of parties is Kathleen Bawn, Martin Cohen, David Karol, Seth Masket, Hans Noel, and John Zaller, "A Theory of Political Parties: Groups, Policy Demands, and Nominations in American Politics," *Perspectives on Politics* 10, no. 3 (2012): 571–97.

Race and Ethnicity. Since the 1960s, when Democratic support played an important role in the civil rights movement, African Americans have been overwhelmingly Democratic in party identification. Approximately 90 percent of African Americans describe themselves as Democrats and support Democratic candidates in national, state, and local elections. Approximately 25 percent of the Democratic Party's support in presidential races comes from African American voters.[26]

Republicans, on the other hand, depend heavily on the support of White voters. Roughly 55 percent of the White electorate has supported the GOP in recent years. In 2020, Donald Trump appealed heavily to White working-class voters, promising to be tough on criminals, immigrants, and China. He won 58 percent of the White vote overall, but he did particularly well among Whites without college degrees, winning 67 percent of this group.[27]

Latino and Hispanic voters comprise people with disparate political orientations whose ancestors came from many different countries. Mexican Americans, the largest group, have traditionally aligned with the Democratic Party, as have Puerto Ricans and Central Americans. Historically, as we mentioned earlier, Cuban Americans have voted heavily for and identified as Republicans. Recently, however, Cubans have shifted toward the Democratic Party. This trend appears to reflect generational differences, as younger Cuban Americans tend to be as Democratic as other Hispanic and Latino groups.

Asian Americans tend to be divided as well, though more support the Democrats than the Republicans. Japanese, Chinese, Filipino, and Korean communities have long been established in the United States and have influential business communities. Higher-income Asians tend to be as Republican as higher-income Whites. It is unclear whether newer Asian immigrant groups, such as the Hmong, Vietnamese, Thais, and Indians, will follow the same trajectory as the Japanese and Chinese communities.

Gender. Women are somewhat more likely to support Democrats, and men to support Republicans. This difference, known as the **gender gap**, is fairly new in American politics. Early studies of the women's vote in the 1920s, shortly after the extension of the franchise, found little difference in voting behavior between men and women. If anything, women tended to be slightly more Republican, and they more strongly favored the prohibition of alcohol than men did. The modern gender gap emerged in the 1980 presidential election and has ranged from a difference of 4 percentage points in 1992 to 11 percentage points in 1996.[28] The 2016 election saw the first female presidential candidate for a major party—Democrat Hillary Clinton—which contributed to the especially large gender gap that year. Exit polls showed that Clinton won 54 percent

gender gap ➡

A distinctive pattern of voting behavior reflecting the differences in views between women and men.

---

26 For example, in 2016, 89 percent of Blacks voted for Clinton, and Black voters made up 23 percent of the votes she won overall. CNN Politics, "Exit Polls," updated November 23, 2016, www.cnn.com/election/2016/results/exit-polls (accessed 4/10/20).

27 CNN Politics, "Exit Polls," https://www.cnn.com/election/2020/exit-polls/president/national-results (accessed 11/17/20).

28 Susan J. Carroll, ed., *Women and American Politics: New Questions, New Directions* (Oxford: Oxford University Press, 2003).

of women's votes and 41 percent of men's votes, a 13-point gap. Although Clinton lost the vote of White women, the gender gap among Whites was particularly large. Trump won White women by 9 percentage points (52 to 43), but he won White men by 31 points (62 to 32).

Religion. Religion also maps on to partisanship. While Protestants are the single largest religious group in the United States, they are hardly the majority. Protestants comprise 38 percent of the public; Catholics are 20 percent; 19 percent are "nothing in particular;" atheists and agnostics are 11 percent; and the rest of the population is spread across many different religions, such as Judaism, Islam, Buddhism, and Hinduism. According to the 2018 Cooperative Congressional Election Study, 41 percent of Protestants identified as Republicans and 28 percent of Protestants identified as Democrats. More religiously conservative Protestant denominations tend to identify with the Republicans, while Protestants who are religiously liberal, such as Unitarians and Episcopalians, tend to identify as Democrats. Evangelical Protestants, in particular, have been drawn to the Republicans' conservative stands on social issues, such as gay marriage and abortion.

Among Catholics, 37 percent identified as Democrats and 31 percent as Republicans. Jews, Muslims, Buddhists, Hindus, atheists, and agnostics were all strongly Democratic. Jews and Muslims are among the most Democratic religions: 55 percent of Jews identified as Democrats, while just 21 percent identified as Republicans. Fifty-five percent of Muslims identified as Democrats, and only 8 percent identified as Republicans. Mormons, on the other hand, tend equally strongly toward the Republicans: 49 percent of Mormons identify as Republicans and 16 percent as Democrats.

Although religion is generally thought of as a traditional feature of society, there is nothing about religion in America that leads people to align with the Republican Party. Of people who identify with a denomination (as opposed to atheists, agnostics or "nothing in particular" respondents), 32 percent identify as Democrats, 35 percent identify as Republicans, and 33 percent are independents. That said, people who have no affiliation or who are atheists or agnostics are overwhelmingly Democrats: 42 percent identify as Democrats, 14 percent are Republicans, and 44 percent are independents.[29]

Class. Upper-income Americans are likely to affiliate with the Republicans, whereas very low-income Americans are likely to identify with the Democrats. Middle-class voters split evenly between Democrats and Republicans. This divide reflects the parties' differences on economic issues. In general, Republicans support cutting taxes and social spending—positions that reflect the interests of the wealthy. Democrats, however, favor increased social spending, even if this requires increasing taxes—a position consistent with the interests of less-affluent Americans. One important exception is that relatively wealthy

29 Stephen Ansolabehere, Samantha Luks, and Brian Schaffner, Cooperative Congressional Election Study, 2019, "CCES Common Content, 2018," https://dataverse.harvard.edu /dataset.xhtml?persistentId=doi:10.7910/DVN/ZSBZ7K (accessed 7/5/20).

individuals who work in the public sector or for foundations and universities also tend to affiliate with the Democrats. Such individuals are likely to appreciate the Democratic Party's support for an expanded role of government and high levels of public spending. White voters with less than a college education (a measure of class) have become less strongly affiliated with the Democrats over time. Indeed, in the 2020 presidential election, White voters without college degrees voted 67 percent for Republican Donald Trump, while only 32 percent voted for Democrat Joe Biden.[30]

Region. Between the time of the Civil War and the 1960s, the "Solid South" was a Democratic bastion. Today much of the South has become solidly Republican in national elections, although it is more divided in state elections. The areas of greatest Democratic Party strength are the Northeast and the West Coast (such as California, Washington, Oregon, and Hawaii). The Midwest is a battleground, more or less evenly divided between the two parties.

The explanations for these regional variations are complex. The parties' legislative agendas certainly play differently in the regions, with the Republican agenda of social conservatism, low taxes, and high military spending appealing more to voters in the South and Mountain West and the Democratic agenda of social liberalism and high domestic spending (especially on Medicare and Social Security) appealing more to residents of urban areas, the Northeast, and the far West. Republican strength in the South and Mountain West is related to the weakness of organized labor in these regions, as well as to the regions' dependence on military programs supported by the Republicans. Democratic strength in the Northeast reflects the continuing influence of organized labor in the region's large cities, as well as its large population of minority and elderly voters who benefit from Democratic social programs.

Age. Age is also associated with partisanship, mainly because individuals from the same age cohort all likely experienced a similar set of events during the period when their party loyalties were forming. Thus Americans in their 60s and 70s, who came of political age (that is, became aware of political issues and ideas) during the Cold War, the Vietnam War, and the civil rights movement, have generally responded more favorably to the role played by the Democrats than to the actions of Republicans. This trend is thought to reflect the strong effects of a person's first experiences voting and their first impressions of politics. It is fitting that most young Americans in their 20s and 30s, who came of age during an era of political scandals that tainted both parties, describe themselves as independents.

Figure 12.3 indicates the relationship between party identification and various social identities. Race, religion, income, and ideology seem to have the greatest influence on Americans' party affiliations. None of these characteristics is inevitably linked to partisan identification, however. There are, for example, union Republicans and business Democrats. The general party identifications just discussed are broad tendencies that both reflect and reinforce the issue and policy positions the two

---

30 *New York Times,* "National Exit Polls: How Different Groups Voted," https://www.nytimes.com/interactive/2020/11/03/us/elections/exit-polls-president.html (accessed 11/17/20).

Figure 12.3
PARTY IDENTIFICATION BY SOCIAL GROUP

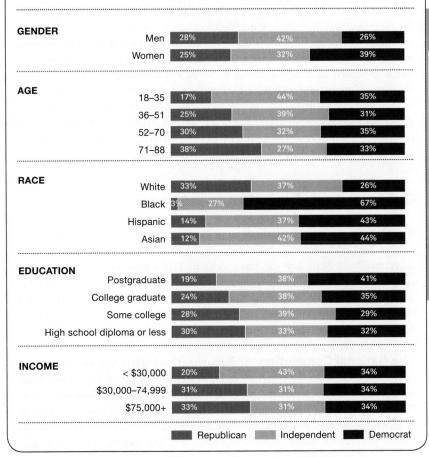

GENDER

	Republican	Independent	Democrat
Men	28%	42%	26%
Women	25%	32%	39%

AGE

	Republican	Independent	Democrat
18–35	17%	44%	35%
36–51	25%	39%	31%
52–70	30%	32%	35%
71–88	38%	27%	33%

RACE

	Republican	Independent	Democrat
White	33%	37%	26%
Black	3%	27%	67%
Hispanic	14%	37%	43%
Asian	12%	42%	44%

EDUCATION

	Republican	Independent	Democrat
Postgraduate	19%	38%	41%
College graduate	24%	38%	35%
Some college	28%	39%	29%
High school diploma or less	30%	33%	32%

INCOME

	Republican	Independent	Democrat
< $30,000	20%	43%	34%
$30,000–74,999	31%	31%	34%
$75,000+	33%	31%	34%

■ Republican ■ Independent ■ Democrat

ANALYZING THE EVIDENCE

The political parties do not draw equal support from members of each social stratum. What patterns in party identification do you see? How might these patterns influence which people are selected as candidates by political parties and which policies the parties support?

NOTE: Percentages do not add to 100 because the category "Other/don't know" is omitted.
SOURCE: Pew Research Center, "Trends in Party Affiliation Among Demographic Groups," https://www.pewresearch.org/politics/2018/03/20/1-trends-in-party-affiliation-among-demographic-groups/ (accessed 7/5/20).

parties take in national and local political arenas. They reflect the general tendency of groups—both organized and unorganized—to sort into partisan camps.

PARTIES AS INSTITUTIONS

Political parties in the United States today are not tightly disciplined, hierarchical organizations. Indeed, they never have been. Rather, they comprise extensive networks of politicians, interest groups, activists, donors, consultants, and, ultimately, voters. Some elements of the parties, such as the party caucuses in Congress, seem to have more influence than others over the policies and strategies pursued by the parties, but each political player can affect the party's ability to influence what government does. Party campaign finance committees may, for example, work with the congressional caucus to maximize the party's appeal to donors (campaign finance is discussed in more detail in Chapter 11). National party leaders must work with state and local party officials and activists to coordinate the many campaign activities involved in presidential and congressional elections. If parties are such wide-flung networks, how do they make their most momentous decisions, such as nominating candidates for office and choosing a policy platform? Such decisions happen at every level of government, in party committees, conventions, and primary elections, and it is through these institutions that the parties truly come together to make collective decisions.

Contemporary Party Organizations

The United States has party organizations at virtually every level of government (Figure 12.4). These are usually committees made up of a number of active party members. State law and party rules prescribe how such committees are constituted. Usually, committee members are elected at a local party meeting (a political **caucus**) or as part of the regular primary election. The best-known examples of these committees are the Democratic National Committee (DNC) and the Republican National Committee (RNC).

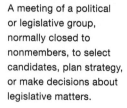

caucus

A meeting of a political or legislative group, normally closed to nonmembers, to select candidates, plan strategy, or make decisions about legislative matters.

The National Convention. At the national level, the party's most important institution is the national convention. Delegates from each of the states attend; as a group, they nominate the party's presidential and vice presidential candidates, draft the party's campaign platform for the presidential race, and approve changes in the rules and regulations governing party procedures. Before World War II, presidential nominations occupied most of the convention's time, requiring days of negotiation and compromise among state party leaders and many ballots before a nominee was selected. In recent years, however, presidential candidates have essentially nominated themselves by garnering enough delegate support in primary elections to win the official nomination on the first ballot. The convention itself has played little or no role in selecting the candidates.

The convention's other two tasks, establishing the party's rules and establishing its platform, remain important. Party rules can determine the relative influence of competing factions within the party as well as the party's chances for electoral success. In the 1970s, for example, the Democratic National Convention adopted new rules favored by the party's liberal wing, which required state delegations to the convention to include women and minority group members in rough proportion to those groups' representation among the state's party membership. The convention also approves the party platform. Platforms are often dismissed as platitude-laden documents that voters seldom bother to read. Furthermore, the parties' presidential candidates make little use of the platforms in their campaigns; usually they promote their own themes. Nonetheless,

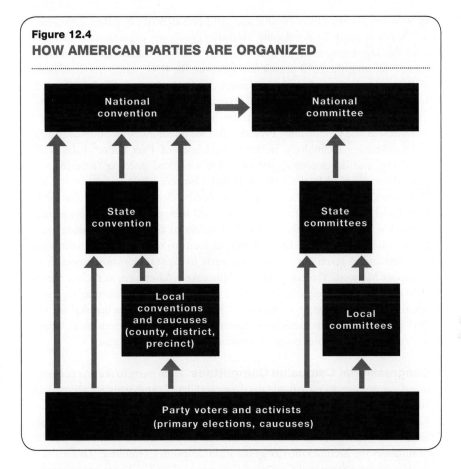

Figure 12.4

HOW AMERICAN PARTIES ARE ORGANIZED

National convention → National committee

State convention

State committees

Local conventions and caucuses (county, district, precinct)

Local committees

Party voters and activists (primary elections, caucuses)

the platform should be understood as a "treaty" in which the various party factions state their terms for supporting the ticket.

The National Committee. Between conventions, each national party is technically headed by its national committee: the Democratic National Committee (DNC) and the Republican National Committee (RNC). These committees raise campaign funds, head off factional disputes within the party, and endeavor to enhance the party's media image. Since 1972, both committees have grown substantially in terms of their numbers of staff and the amounts of money they raise. The actual work of each committee is overseen by its chairperson. Other committee members are generally major party contributors or fund-raisers.

Presidents appoint the national committee chairperson for their own party. Under a first-term president, the committee for the president's party focuses on the reelection campaign. The national committee for the party out of power selects its own chairperson; this person usually raises money and performs other activities on behalf of the party's members in Congress and the state legislatures. In 2006, the DNC was headed by former presidential contender Howard Dean, who crafted a midterm-election strategy to recruit quality candidates in all 50 states. Barack Obama's 2008 and 2012 presidential campaigns capitalized on Dean's strategy by developing extensive grassroots organizations in every state and registering many new Democratic voters in traditionally Republican areas. Following the 2012 presidential election, the RNC, under the leadership of Reince Priebus, conducted an extensive election "autopsy" called the Growth and Opportunity Project. Out of that comprehensive postelection review came a road map for retaining the House and regaining the Senate and the presidency. The Growth and Opportunity Project called for major investments in campaign and fund-raising technology, including the launch of Para Bellum Labs, a lab for testing and developing digital campaign tools and building "a permanent ground campaign."[31] In the wake of Hillary Clinton's surprising defeat and the Democrats' disappointing showing in the Senate elections in 2016, the DNC immediately launched an effort to evaluate what went wrong, with an eye toward improving the party's chances in the 2018 midterms and 2020 presidential race. In the run up to 2020, the DNC shifted its focus to rebuild confidence among its voters and to reach out to voters the party had lost touch with, especially in the upper Midwest. The party selected Milwaukee, Wisconsin, as the site for its 2020 convention. It reduced the number of superdelegates, signaling a greater openness to grassroots; it increased the number of debates scheduled for fall 2019 in order to give its candidates greater exposure; and it undertook an extensive organizing and voter protection initiative in battleground states.

Congressional Campaign Committees. Each party maintains congressional committees to raise funds for their candidates' campaigns for House and Senate. The Republicans call their House and Senate committees the National Republican Congressional Committee (NRCC) and the National Republican Senatorial Committee (NRSC). The Democrats call their House and Senate committees the Democratic Congressional Campaign Committee (DCCC) and the Democratic Senatorial Campaign Committee (DSCC). These organizations also have professional staff devoted to raising and distributing funds, developing strategies, recruiting candidates, and conducting on-the-ground campaigns. The committees, however, are accountable to the caucuses inside the House and Senate. The committee chairs come from within their respective chambers and rank high in the party leadership hierarchy. The national committees and the congressional committees are sometimes rivals. Both groups seek donations from the same pool of people but for different candidates: the national committee seeks funds primarily for the presidential race, whereas the congressional campaign committees focus on House and Senate seats.

State and Local Party Organizations. Each major party has a central committee in each state. The parties traditionally also have county committees and, in some instances, state senate district committees, judicial district committees, and in larger cities, citywide party committees and local assembly district

---

31 Jason Linkins, "RNC Touts Past Year's Progress from Grim 'Autopsy' in 2012," *Huffington Post*, March 18, 2014, www.huffpost.com/entry/rnc-autopsy-video_n_4986508 (accessed 7/5/20).

"ward" committees. Congressional districts may also have party committees. Some cities also have precinct committees.[32]

These organizations are very active in recruiting candidates, conducting voter registration drives, and providing financial assistance to candidates. Federal election law permits them to spend unlimited amounts of money on "party-building" activities such as voter registration and get-out-the-vote drives—with the result that the national party organizations, which are limited in the amount they can spend on candidates, transfer millions of dollars each year to state and local organizations. The state and local parties, in turn, spend these funds, sometimes called soft money, to promote national, state, and local candidates. As local organizations have become linked financially to the national parties, American political parties have grown more integrated and nationalized than ever before. At the same time, the state and local party organizations have come to control large financial resources and play important roles in elections despite the collapse of the old patronage machines.

The Contemporary Party as Service Provider to Candidates

Party leaders have adapted to the modern age. Parties as organizations are more professional, better financed, and better organized than ever before.[33] Political parties have evolved into "service organizations," without which it would be extremely difficult for candidates to win and hold office. For example, the national party organizations collect information, ranging from lists of likely supporters and donors in local areas to public opinion polls in states and legislative districts, and they distribute it directly to their candidates for state and federal offices. They also have teams of experienced campaign organizers and managers who provide assistance to understaffed local candidates.

Parties provide assistance to candidates in tight races. The national parties' campaign committees today target the closest 50 or so House races and the closest 5 to 10 Senate races, spending large sums on advertising and other campaign activities as well as providing tactical support. Consultants from the DCCC, NRCC, NRSC, and DSCC are often deployed to specific campaigns to assist with get-out-the-vote efforts, direct mail, and the like. The party organizations also maintain voter contact lists for the entire nation and can provide candidates with access to such information. Occasionally the party organizations put an entire campaign operation in place if there is the prospect of pulling off an upset.

The rise of party campaign organizations is fairly new. In the 1970s, the organizations (at least nationally) were extremely weak and underfunded, and

---

32 Well-organized political parties—especially the famous old machines of New York, Chicago, and Boston—provided for "precinct captains" and a fairly tight group of party members around them. Precinct captains were usually long-standing members of neighborhood party clubhouses.

33 John Aldrich, *Why Parties?: A Second Look* (Chicago: University of Chicago Press, 1995).

they were incapable of providing candidates with large-scale support. Congressional campaigns in the 1970s and 1980s were built entirely from the ground up by each candidate. Those who were unusually good at raising money, organizing volunteers, and attracting media attention prevailed. In the late 1980s, however, party leaders in Congress and in their national organizations saw that they could do better in national elections if they could somehow redistribute campaign resources to close races and away from safe seats.

The rise of party campaign organizations over the past three decades has altered the politics of swing districts. In the 1970s and 1980s, incumbents in the swing districts built up personal electoral advantages based on prior elections and their prowess as fund-raisers. This allowed these incumbents to vote in Congress less with their party and more with their districts.[34] The independence of these legislators frustrated party leaders in Congress, as conservative Democrats and liberal Republicans regularly crossed party lines on important votes. Since the early 1990s, the parties have poured resources into the most competitive seats in order to improve their chances of winning control of the legislature. The winners have since become more beholden to their party, as their electoral fortunes now depend more heavily on support from the national party organizations and congressional leadership.

PARTY SYSTEMS

Our understanding of political parties would be incomplete if we considered only their composition and roles. America's political parties compete with each other for offices, policies, and power. The struggle for control of government shapes the policies the parties put forth, the coalitions of interests they represent, and the ability of the parties, indeed the government, to respond to the demands of the time. In short, the fate of each party is inextricably linked to that of its major rival.

Political scientists often call the constellation of parties that are important at any given moment a nation's party system. The most obvious feature of a party system is the number of major parties competing for power. Usually the United States has had a two-party system, meaning that only two parties have ever had a serious chance to win national elections.

There are both institutional and psychological reasons why the United States has just two parties. The American electoral system is winner take all: whoever gets the most votes wins the congressional seat, and whoever gets

---

34 This argument is developed in great detail in David W. Rohde, *Parties and Leaders in the Postreform House* (Chicago: University of Chicago Press, 1991); and in the two books by Gary W. Cox and Mathew D. McCubbins: *Setting the Agenda: Responsible Party Government in the U.S. House of Representatives* (New York: Cambridge University Press, 2005) and *Legislative Leviathan*.

---

the most electoral votes wins the presidency. The Democratic and Republican parties have positioned themselves as center-left and center-right, respectively, neither extremely liberal nor extremely conservative. Their ideological positions maintain their policy distinctiveness and still divide the electorate about equally. If, for example, a far-left party (such as the Green Party) decided to pursue the presidency, it would divide the left-leaning voters between the Democrats and the Greens without decreasing Republican votes, effectively guaranteeing a Republican victory. A third party that entered in the middle, however, would be squeezed between the two parties with no hope of gaining sufficient support to win. Understanding this situation, most third parties stay out. Voters also appear to understand this situation. Those who would normally want to vote for the third party see that by doing so, they end up boosting the electoral prospects of the major party that they favor less. Getting on the ballot, recruiting candidates, building an organization—all carry tremendous costs. The best that the party could do would be to come in a distant third.

The same forces are less likely to influence elections in parliamentary systems that allocate legislative seats to parties in proportion to their share of the national vote. In parliaments, if no single party wins a majority, the smaller parties can join with larger parties in a coalition that together constitutes a governing majority. That creates an incentive for small parties to fracture off from larger parties or to form on their own.

The term *party system* refers to more than just the number of parties competing for power. It also connotes the balance of power between and within party coalitions that endure over many years, the social and institutional bases of the parties, and the issues and policies around which party competition is organized. The idea of a party system implies a sense of stability, of equilibrium. Voters can reliably expect that the Democrats and Republicans will be the main parties in the next election, that Democrats will generally be ideologically liberal and Republicans ideologically conservative, that Democrats will align with unions and urban interests while Republicans will align more with corporations and rural areas. The stability of the alignment between the parties is itself rooted in history. The party system of the past replicates itself as voters and candidates and groups align with one party or the other based on their past experiences with the party. This pattern is itself an outcome of the political system, reflecting the policies and coalitions of interest that those in office choose to champion.

The stability of the U.S. party system, however, does not mean that the system is static. Within each party there exists a tension between moderate and extreme factions. Conflicts among the factions are worked out in state and national conventions, in the caucuses inside Congress and the state legislatures, and in primary elections. The 2020 Democratic primary election field, for example, was divided between traditional liberals, such as Joe Biden, progressives, most prominently Senator Elizabeth Warren, and democratic socialists, given voice by Bernie Sanders. In addition, there were several prominent minority candidates, including Senators Cory Booker and Kamala Harris, former secretary of housing and urban development Julián Castro, and Hawaii representative Tulsi Gabbard. The ultimate goal of those involved in these intraparty political struggles is always to control government, to gain the upper hand.

The party system thus reflects the balance of the political struggles both within and between parties. Within this balance, from year to year, the alignment between parties changes, but only a little. Those who have the greatest influence over party policy making are already in office—the president and members of Congress—and they hesitate to embrace new principles or fundamentally alter the party coalitions, lest such radical changes harm their own position.

The character of a nation's party system changes as the parties realign their electoral coalitions and alter their public philosophies. Such realignment sometimes comes subtly and sometimes suddenly. Today's American party system is very different from the party system of 1950, even though the Democrats and the Republicans continue to be the major competing forces (Figure 12.5). Over seventy years ago, the Democrats' political strength lay in the South and the Republicans' in the North. Democrats favored racial segregation in the South, and Republicans wanted protectionist trade policies and the dismantling of Social Security. Gradual social and economic changes from the 1950s to today forced a shift in the parties' policy orientations and political coalitions. Political scientists have referred to this gradual change as a creeping realignment. One key issue driving the most recent realignment was race. Democratic leaders of the 1940s, such as Harry Truman and Hubert Humphrey, pulled their party to embrace a new platform to end racial segregation. That change in policy redefined the Democratic Party and took the better part of a generation.[35]

Change has also come abruptly to the American party system. Three such cataclysmic changes have occurred: first in the 1860s, as the nation was torn in half during the American Civil War; next in the 1890s, when the country sank into an economic crisis and depression; and again in the 1930s, with the onset of the Great Depression. These events brought lasting changes to the balance of power between the parties and to the policies they represented. How the parties in power responded to these historical circumstances redefined their image among the electorate.

Over the course of American history, changes in political forces and alignments have produced six party systems, each with distinctive political institutions, issues, and patterns of political power and participation. Of course, some political phenomena persist across party systems—such as conflicts over the distribution of wealth, an enduring feature of American political life. But even such phenomena manifest themselves in different ways during different political eras.

The First Party System: Federalists and Democratic-Republicans

Although George Washington and, in fact, many other leaders of the time deplored partisan politics, the two-party system emerged early in the history of the new Republic. Competition in Congress between northeastern mercantile

---

35 Edward G. Carmines and James A. Stimson, *Issue Evolution: Race and the Transformation of American Politics* (Princeton, NJ: Princeton University Press, 1989).

Figure 12.5
HOW THE PARTY SYSTEM EVOLVED

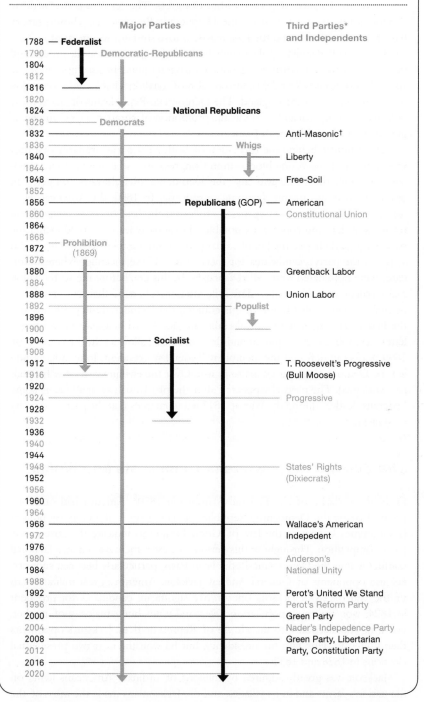

*In some cases, there was even a fourth party. Most of the parties listed here existed for only one term.
† The Anti-Masonics not only had the distinction of being the first third party but also were the first party to hold a national nominating convention and the first to announce a party platform.

and southern agrarian factions led Alexander Hamilton and the northeasterners to form a voting bloc within Congress. The southerners, led by Thomas Jefferson and James Madison, responded by cultivating a popular following to change the balance of power within Congress. The result was the birth of America's first national parties—the Democratic-Republicans, whose primary base was in the South, and the Federalists, whose strength was greatest in New England. The Federalists spoke mainly for New England mercantile groups and supported protective tariffs to encourage manufacturers, the assumption of the states' Revolutionary War debts, the creation of a national bank, and resumption of commercial ties with England. The Democratic-Republicans opposed these policies, favoring instead free trade, the promotion of agrarian over commercial interests, and friendship with France.

The rationale behind the formation of both parties was primarily that they would create stable voting blocs within Congress around cohesive policy agendas. Although the Federalists and the Democratic-Republicans competed in elections, their ties to the electorate were loose. In 1800, the American electorate was small, and voters generally followed the lead of local political and religious leaders and community notables. Local party leaders would gather the party elites and choose the people, usually from among themselves, who would stand as the party's candidates for local office. These meetings where candidates were nominated were called caucuses. In this era, before the secret ballot, many voters were reluctant to defy influential members of their community by publicly voting against them. In this context, the Democratic-Republicans and the Federalists organized political clubs and developed newspapers and newsletters to mobilize elite opinion and draw in more followers. In the election of 1800, Jefferson defeated the incumbent Federalist president, John Adams, and led the Democratic-Republicans to power. Over the ensuing years, the Federalists weakened. The party disappeared after the pro-British sympathies of some Federalist leaders during the War of 1812 led to charges that the party was guilty of treason.

The Second Party System: Democrats and Whigs

From the collapse of the Federalists until the 1830s, America had only one political party: the Democratic-Republicans. This period of one-party politics is sometimes known as the Era of Good Feeling to indicate the absence of party competition. Throughout this period, however, there was intense factional conflict within the Democratic-Republican Party, particularly between supporters and opponents of General Andrew Jackson, America's great military hero of the War of 1812. Jackson, one of five significant candidates for president in 1824, won the most popular and electoral votes but a majority of neither, throwing the election into the House of Representatives. Jackson's opponents then united to deny him the presidency, but he won the next two presidential elections in 1828 and 1832.

Jackson was greatly admired by millions of ordinary Americans living on the nation's farms and in its villages, and the Jacksonians made the most of the general's appeal to the common people via a program of suffrage expansion that would give Jackson's impecunious but numerous supporters the right to vote. To bring more voters to the polls, the Jacksonians built political clubs and held mass rallies and parades, laying the groundwork for a more popular politics. Jackson's vice president and eventual successor, Martin Van Buren, was the organizational genius behind the Jacksonian movement, establishing a central party committee, state party organizations, and party newspapers. In response to complaints about cliques of party leaders dominating the nominations at party caucuses, the Jacksonians also established state and national party conventions as the forums for nominating presidential candidates. The conventions gave control of the nominating process to the new state party organizations that the Jacksonians had created and expected to control. Unlike any political leader before him, Van Buren appreciated the possibilities of mass mobilization and the necessity of a well-oiled national organization to overcome free riding and other collective action problems.[36] He produced institutional solutions to these problems, leaving as a historical legacy the blueprint for the modern mass-based political party.

The Jacksonians, whose party became known as the Democratic Party, were not without opponents, especially in the New England states. During the 1830s, groups opposing Jackson for both political and personal reasons united to form the Whig Party—thus giving rise to the second American party system. During the 1830s and 1840s, the Democrats and the Whigs built party organizations throughout the nation and eliminated property restrictions and other barriers to voting in an effort to increase their bases of support (although voting was still restricted to White men). Support for the Whigs was strongest in the Northeast and among mercantile groups, hence to some extent the Whigs were the successors of the Federalists. Many Whigs favored a national bank, a protective tariff, and federally sponsored internal improvements. The Jacksonians opposed all three policies.

Yet conflict between the parties revolved around personalities as much as policies. The Whigs were a diverse group, united more by opposition to the Democrats than by agreement on programs. In 1840, the Whigs won their first presidential election under the leadership of General William Henry Harrison, a military hero. The election marked the first time in American history that two parties competed for the presidency in every state in the Union. The Whig campaign avoided taking a stand on any issues—because different party factions disagreed on most matters—and instead emphasized Harrison's personal qualities and heroism. The Whigs also invested heavily in campaign rallies and entertainment to win voters. The 1840 campaign came to be called the "hard cider campaign" to denote the practice of using food and, especially, drink to elicit electoral favor.

In the late 1840s and early 1850s, conflicts over slavery produced sharp divisions within both parties despite party leaders' efforts to develop sectional compromises that would bridge the widening gulf between North and South.

---

36 See Aldrich, *Why Parties?*, chap. 4.

By 1856, the Whig Party had all but disintegrated under the strain. The 1854 Kansas-Nebraska Act overturned the Missouri Compromise of 1820 and the Compromise of 1850, which together had hindered the expansion of slavery into the American territories. The Kansas-Nebraska Act gave each territory the right to decide for itself whether to permit slavery. Opposition to this policy led to the formation of a number of antislavery parties, with the Republicans emerging as the strongest.[37] They drew their membership from existing political groups—former Whigs, Know-Nothings of the American Party, Free-Soilers, and antislavery Democrats. In 1856, the party's first presidential candidate won one-third of the popular vote and carried 11 states.

The early Republican platforms appealed to commercial as well as anti-slavery interests. The Republicans favored homesteading, internal improvements, construction of a transcontinental railroad, and protective tariffs as well as the containment of slavery. In 1858, the Republican Party won control of the House of Representatives; in 1860, the Republican presidential candidate, Abraham Lincoln, was victorious. Lincoln's victory strengthened southern calls for secession from the Union and led, soon thereafter, to all-out civil war.

The Third Party System: Republicans and Democrats, 1860–1896

During the Civil War, President Lincoln depended heavily on Republican governors and state legislatures to raise troops, provide funding, and maintain popular support for a long and bloody military conflict. Although the South's secession had stripped the Democratic Party of many of its leaders and supporters, it nevertheless remained politically competitive and nearly won the 1864 presidential election due to war weariness on the part of the northern public. With the defeat of the Confederacy in 1865, some congressional Republicans sought to convert the South into a Republican bastion through Reconstruction, a program that enfranchised formerly enslaved people while disenfranchising many White voters and disqualifying many White politicians from seeking office. The enfranchisement of Black voters, it was believed, would create a sizable pro-Republican voting bloc in the South, and federal reconstruction funds, it was hoped, would bring many White southerners to the GOP. Reconstruction collapsed in the 1870s as a result of divisions within the Republican Party in Congress and violent resistance by southern Whites.

With the end of Reconstruction, the former Confederate states regained full membership in the Union and full control of their internal affairs. Throughout the South, African Americans were deprived of political rights, including the right to vote, despite post–Civil War constitutional guarantees to the contrary. The post–Civil War South was solidly Democratic, enabling the national Democratic Party to confront the Republicans on a more or less equal basis. From the end of the Civil War to the 1890s, the Republican Party remained the party of

---

37 See William E. Gienapp, *The Origins of the Republican Party, 1852–1856* (New York: Oxford University Press, 1987).

---

the North, with strong business and middle-class support, while the Democratic Party was the party of the South, with support from working-class and immigrant groups in the North.

Party Machines as a Strategic Innovation. It was during the third party system that party organizations became well-oiled machines. In the nineteenth and early twentieth centuries, many cities and counties, and even a few states, had such well-organized parties that they were called **party machines** and their leaders were called bosses. Party machines depended on the patronage of the spoils system, the party's power to control government jobs. Patronage worked as a selective benefit for anyone the party wished to attract to its side. With thousands of jobs to dispense to the party faithful, party bosses were able to recruit armies of political workers, who in turn mobilized millions of voters. During the height of the party machines, party and government were virtually interchangeable. Just as the creation of mass parties by Van Buren and other political entrepreneurs of the second party system solved a collective action problem, the well-oiled machines applied the selective incentives of patronage and nomination to maintain their organizations and diminish free riding. Many organizational aspects of party politics, in short, involve the ingenuity of rational politicians and leaders grappling with problems of coordination and collective action, as the rationality principle and the collective action principle suggest.

 party machine

In the late nineteenth and early twentieth centuries, the local party organization that controlled local politics through patronage and the nomination process.

Many critics condemned party machines as antidemocratic and corrupt. They argued that machines served the interests of powerful businesses and did not help the working people who voted for them. But one of the most notorious machine leaders in American political history, George Washington Plunkitt of New York City's Tammany Hall, considered machine politics and the spoils system to be "patriotic." Plunkitt grasped a central fact about purposeful behavior and overcoming the collective action problem: to create and retain political influence and power, "you must study human nature and act accordin'." He argued that the country was built by political parties, that the parties needed such patronage to operate and thrive, and that if patronage was withdrawn, the parties would "go to pieces." As we see shortly, this observation was prescient.

Institutional Reforms of the Progressives. As the nineteenth century gave way to the twentieth, the excessive powers and abuses of party machines and their bosses led to one of the great reform movements in American history, the so-called Progressive Era. Many Progressive reformers undoubtedly desired to rid politics of corruption and improve the quality and efficiency of government. But simultaneously, from the perspective of middle- and upper-class Progressives and the financial, commercial, and industrial elites with whom they were often associated, the weakening or elimination of party organization would also mean that power could more readily be acquired and retained by the "best men"—that is, those with wealth, position, and education.

The list of anti-party reforms of the Progressive Era is a familiar one. As we saw in Chapter 11, the introduction of voter registration laws required eligible voters to register in person well before an election. The Australian-ballot reform took away the parties' privilege of printing and distributing ballots and thus introduced the possibility of split-ticket voting. The introduction of nonpartisan local elections eroded grassroots party organizations. The instatement of "merit systems" for administrative appointments stripped party organizations of their access to patronage, thus reducing party leaders' capacity to control the nomination of candidates. These reforms substantially weakened party organizations in the United States. Early in the twentieth century, the strength of American political parties gradually diminished, and voter turnout declined precipitously. Between the two world wars, organization remained the major tool available to contending electoral forces, but in most regions the "reformed" state and local parties gradually lost their organizational vitality and became less effective campaign tools. Although most areas of the nation continued to boast Democratic and Republican party groups, reform did mean the elimination of the permanent mass organizations that had been the parties' principal campaign weapons.

The Fourth Party System, 1892–1932

During the 1890s, profound social and economic changes led to the emergence of a variety of protest parties, including the Populist Party, which won the support of hundreds of thousands of voters in the South and the West. The Populists appealed mainly to small farmers but also attracted western miners and urban workers. In the 1892 presidential election, the Populist Party carried four states and elected governors in eight states. In 1896, the Democrats in effect adopted the Populist Party platform and nominated William Jennings Bryan, a Democratic senator with Populist sympathies, for the presidency. The Republicans nominated the conservative senator William McKinley. In the ensuing campaign, northern and midwestern business interests made an all-out effort to defeat what they saw as a radical threat from the Democratic-Populist alliance. When the dust settled, the Republicans had won a resounding victory. In the nation's metropolitan regions, especially in the Northeast and upper Midwest, workers became convinced that the Democratic-Populist alliance threatened the industries that provided their jobs, while immigrants feared the nativist rhetoric of some Populist orators and writers. The Republicans carried the northeastern and midwestern states and confined the Democrats to their bastions in the South and the far West. For the next 36 years, the Republicans were the nation's majority party—very much the party of American business, advocating low taxes, high tariffs, and minimal governmental regulation. The Democrats were too weak to offer much opposition. Southern Democrats, moreover, were more concerned with maintaining the region's autonomy on issues of race than with challenging the Republicans on other fronts.

The Fifth Party System: The New Deal Coalition, 1932–1968

Soon after the Republican candidate Herbert Hoover won the 1928 presidential election, the nation's economy collapsed. The Great Depression, which produced unprecedented economic hardship, had a variety of causes, but millions of Americans blamed the Republican Party for not having done enough to promote economic recovery. In 1932, Americans elected Franklin Delano Roosevelt and a solidly Democratic Congress. Roosevelt's program for economic recovery, the New Deal, led to substantial increases in the size and reach of the national government. The federal government took responsibility for economic management and social welfare to an extent that was unprecedented in American history. Designing many of his programs specifically to expand the Democratic Party's political base, Roosevelt rebuilt the party around a nucleus of unionized workers, upper-middle-class intellectuals and professionals, southern farmers, Jews, Catholics, and northern African Americans (few Black people in the South could vote), which made the Democrats the nation's majority party for 36 years. Republicans struggled to respond to the New Deal, and they often wound up supporting its popular programs such as Social Security in what was sometimes derided as "me-too" Republicanism.

The New Deal coalition was severely strained during the 1960s by conflicts over President Lyndon Johnson's Great Society initiative, the African American civil rights movement, and the Vietnam War. A number of Johnson's Great Society programs, which targeted poverty and racial discrimination, involved the empowerment of local groups that were often at odds with city and county governments. These programs sparked battles between local Democratic political machines and the national administration that split the Democratic coalition. For its part, the struggle over civil rights initially divided northern Democrats, who supported the civil rights cause, and White southern Democrats, who defended racial segregation. Subsequently, as the civil rights movement launched a northern campaign seeking access to jobs and education and an end to discrimination in such realms as housing, blue-collar workers split away from the northern Democrats to vote Republican. The struggle over the Vietnam War further divided the Democrats, with upper-income liberal Democrats opposing the Johnson administration's decision to involve U.S. forces in Southeast Asia. These schisms within the Democratic Party provided an opportunity for the Republican Party to return to power, which it did in 1968 under President Richard Nixon.

The Sixth Party System, 1968–Present

In the 1960s, conservative Republicans argued that me-tooism was a recipe for continual failure and sought to reposition the party as a genuine alternative to the Democrats. In 1964, for example, the Republican presidential candidate, Barry Goldwater, author of a book titled *The Conscience of a Conservative*, argued in favor of substantially reduced levels of taxation and spending, less governmental regulation of the economy, and the elimination of many federal social programs. Although Goldwater was defeated by Lyndon Johnson, the ideas he espoused continue to be major themes of the Republican Party.

Goldwater's message, however, was not enough to lead Republicans to victory. It took Richard Nixon's "southern strategy" to end Democratic dominance of the political process. Beginning with his successful 1968 presidential campaign, Nixon appealed to disaffected White southerners, promising to reduce federal support for school integration and voting rights. With the help of the independent candidate and former Alabama governor George Wallace, Nixon's strategy sparked the voter shift that eventually gave the once-hated "party of Lincoln" a strong position in all the states of the former Confederacy. In the 1980s, under Ronald Reagan, Republicans added another important group to their coalition: religious conservatives who were offended by Democratic support for abortion rights as well as Democrats' alleged disdain for traditional cultural and religious values.

While Republicans built a political base with economic and social conservatives and White southerners, the Democratic Party maintained support among unionized workers and upper-middle-class intellectuals and professionals. Democrats also appealed strongly to racial minorities. The 1965 Voting Rights Act had greatly increased the participation of Black voters in the South and helped the Democratic Party retain some House and Senate seats there. And while the GOP appealed to social conservatives, the Democrats appealed to voters concerned about abortion rights, gay rights, feminism, environmentalism, and other progressive causes. Democrats have won 6 out of the 14 elections since the passage of the Voting Rights Act and have held at least one chamber of Congress for most of that time. Interestingly, this equilibrium has masked dramatic changes in the parties' regional bases. Republicans surged in the South but lost ground in the Northeast. The South, once solidly Democratic, had become the Republican base. New England, once the bedrock of the Republican Party, elected no members to the U.S. House of Representatives in 2020.

The electoral realignment that began in 1968 laid the foundations for the political polarization that has come to characterize contemporary politics. As southern Democrats and northeastern Republicans faded, the two parties lost their moderate wings. Southern White Democrats tended to come from rural areas; they were socially conservative but strongly aligned with the New Deal. As the rural population in the South declined and the suburbs rose in the 1970s, the southern Democrats were replaced by suburban Republicans that were much more economically conservative than their predecessors. The opposite dynamic was at work in the North. Republicans in places like New York and New England tended to be socially moderate and fiscally conservative. Social and political shifts in the northeastern states marginalized the Republican Party and led to the emergence of a strong liberal faction within the Democratic Party.[38] As a result, the moderate wings of both parties were substantially reduced, leaving Congress with a void among its moderate ranks and with a more polarized political alignment. There is a deep tension in the current political system, as both national parties have become more ideologically distinct and have catered more to their respective bases than to the center of the electorate. More and more people are seeking an alternative to the traditional Democratic and Republican formulas.

------

38 Matthew Levendusky, *The Partisan Sort: How Liberals Became Democrats and Conservatives Became Republicans* (Chicago: University of Chicago Press, 2009).

This is reflected in rising numbers of independent voters and in the appeal of unconventional candidates such as Bernie Sanders and Donald Trump.

Ideology and Parties. The shift of much of the South from the Democratic to the Republican camp, along with the other developments mentioned earlier, meant that each political party became ideologically more homogeneous after the 1980s. Today there are few liberal Republicans or conservative Democrats. Consequently, party loyalty in Congress has become a more potent force, leading to a dramatic resurgence of party-line voting. A simple measure of party developed by political scientist Stuart Rice in the 1920s and tracked by *Congressional Quarterly* since the 1950s is the party unity score. This is the percentage of bills on which a majority of one party votes against a majority of the other party. Between the 1950s and the 1970s, unity hovered around 70 percent. Since the 1980s, it has regularly exceeded 90 percent.[39] However, in 2018 and 2019, party unity plummeted to 59 percent in the House and 69 percent in the Senate as members of Congress from swing districts and swing states sought to position themselves closer to their constituencies.[40]

To some extent, ideology has replaced organization as the glue holding together each party's coalition. But in the long run, ideology is often an unreliable basis for party unity. Although party activists are united by some beliefs, ideological divisions also plague both parties. Within the Republican coalition, social conservatives are often at odds with economic conservatives, whereas among Democrats, proponents of regulatory reform and economic internationalism are frequently at odds with traditional liberals, who favor big government and protecting American workers from foreign competition. While the party workers of yesteryear supported the leadership almost no matter what, today's more ideologically motivated party activists withhold support if they disagree with the leadership's goals and plans. Because of internal divisions in the Republican Party, for example, Republican congressional leaders have adopted a strategy of avoiding votes on the many issues that might split the party, following an informal rule set by Speaker Dennis Hastert.[41] But the Hastert Rule has often allowed the extremists within the parties to block legislation that would appeal to moderates in both parties. For instance, President Trump's agenda foundered in 2017 as he attempted to create legislation that could appeal both to the conservative Freedom Caucus and to moderate Republicans. Close advisers to the

---

39 The classic statement of the connection between cohesive legislative parties and ideological homogeneity within party ranks is found in Rohde, *Parties and Leaders in the Postreform House.* An elaboration of this argument is presented in Cox and McCubbins, *Setting the Agenda.* See also Nolan McCarty, Keith T. Poole, and Howard Rosenthal, *Polarized America: The Dance of Inequality and Unequal Riches* (Cambridge, MA: MIT Press, 2006).

40 Jonathan Miller, "Party Unity on Congressional Votes Takes a Dive: CQ Vote Studies," *Roll Call*, February 28, 2019, www.rollcall.com/2019/02/28/party-unity-on-congressional-votes-takes-a-dive-cq-vote-studies (accessed 4/22/20).

41 Isaiah J. Poole, "Votes Echo Electoral Themes," *Congressional Quarterly Weekly Report*, December 11, 2004, pp. 2906–8.

Parties' Share of Electoral Votes, 1789–2020

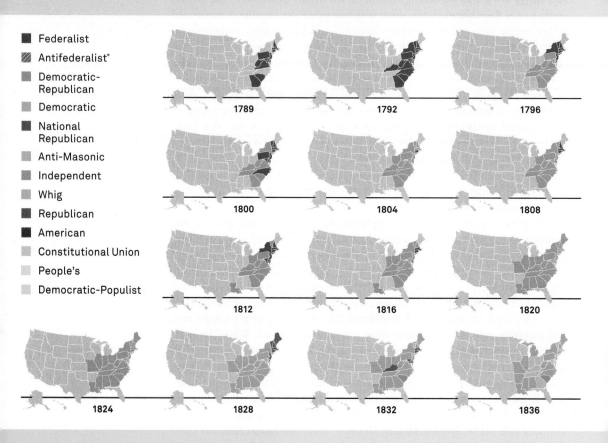

Federalist
Antifederalist*
Democratic-Republican
Democratic
National Republican
Anti-Masonic
Independent
Whig
Republican
American
Constitutional Union
People's
Democratic-Populist

1789 1792 1796
1800 1804 1808
1812 1816 1820
1824 1828 1832 1836

*TIMEPLOT NOTE: In the 1792 election, the Antifederalist candidates, who ran against Federalists George Washington and John Adams, did not win any states.

president called on Speaker Paul Ryan to abandon the Hastert Rule in order to move forward on important issues such as health care and taxes.[42] The price of unity based on ideology can be the inability to act.

The ideological gap between the two parties has been exacerbated by two other factors: each party's dependence on ideologically motivated activists and the changes in the presidential nominating system that were introduced during the 1970s. Regarding the first factor, Democratic political candidates depend heavily on the support of liberal activists—such as feminists, environmentalists,

42 Robert Wasinger, "Trump Needs GOP to Dump 'Hastert Rule' to Move Agenda," *The Hill*, March 31, 2017, https://thehill.com/blogs/pundits-blog/the-administration/326760-trump-needs-gop-to-dump-hastert-rule-to-move-agenda (accessed 4/10/20).

(continued on next page)

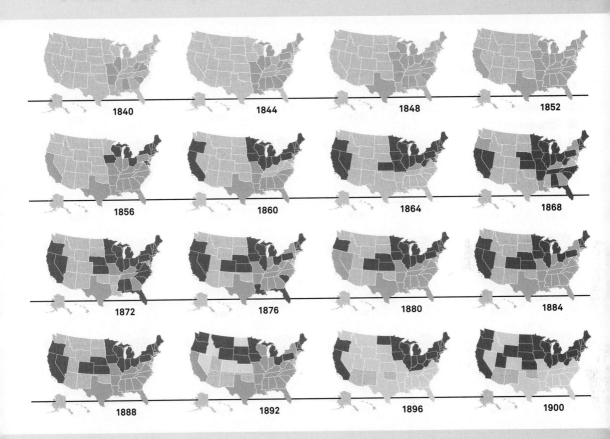

1840   1844   1848   1852

1856   1860   1864   1868

1872   1876   1880   1884

1888   1892   1896   1900

and civil libertarians—to organize and finance their campaigns, while Republican candidates depend equally on the support of conservative activists, including religious fundamentalists. In the nineteenth century, political activists were motivated more by party loyalty and political patronage than by programmatic concerns. Today's issue-oriented activists, by contrast, demand that politicians demonstrate strong commitments to moral principles and political causes in exchange for their support. Such demands have pushed Democrats further to the political left and Republicans further to the political right. Often, party activists attack as "sellouts" any politicians who make an effort to compromise on key issues, leading to stalemates on such matters as the budget and judicial appointments.

The second factor exacerbating the parties' ideological split—the changes in the presidential nominating system—took place in response to the Democratic Party's defeat in the 1968 presidential election. Liberal forces succeeded

TIMEPLOT SOURCE: 270 to Win, www.270towin. com/historical-presidential-elections (accessed 11/17/20).

Parties' Share of Electoral Votes, 1789–2020

(continued from previous page)

- Democratic-Populist
- Republican
- Democratic
- Progressive
- States' Rights Democratic
- American Independent

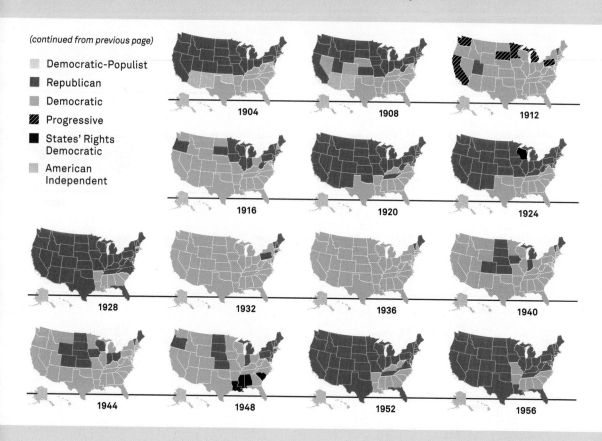

1904 1908 1912

1916 1920 1924

1928 1932 1936 1940

1944 1948 1952 1956

in changing the rules governing Democratic presidential nominations to reduce the power of party officials and party professionals while increasing the role of issue-oriented activists. Among other changes, the new rules required national convention delegates to be chosen in primaries and caucuses rather than by each state party's central committee. Subsequently, Republican activists pushed for similar changes, so that today both parties' presidential nominating processes are strongly influenced by precisely the sorts of grassroots activists who oppose centrist or pragmatic politicians in favor of those who show ideological purity. As a result, elections have generally pitted liberal Democrats against conservative Republicans. The two parties today differ sharply on social, economic, and foreign policy issues and are deeply divided over questions of taxation and government spending.

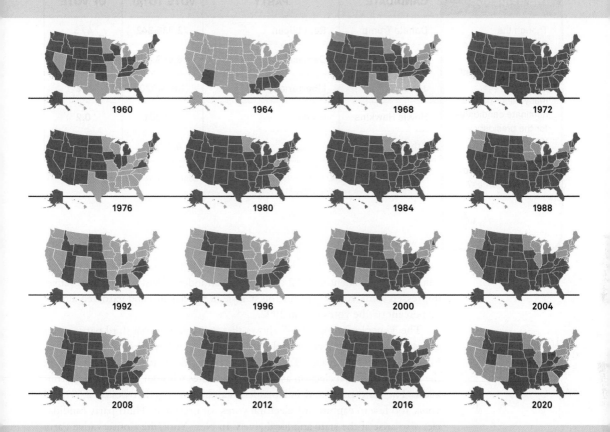

American Third Parties

Although the United States is said to possess a two-party system, we have always had more than two parties. Typically, **third parties** have served as vehicles for social and economic protest against the platforms of the two major parties.[43] Third parties have undeniably influenced ideas and elections. The Populists, centered in rural areas of the West and the Midwest during the late nineteenth century, and the Progressives, spokesmen for urban middle classes in the late nineteenth and early twentieth centuries, are important examples. Ross Perot,

 third party

A party that organizes to compete against the two major American political parties.

---

43 For a discussion of third parties in the United States, see Daniel A. Mazmanian, *Third Parties in Presidential Elections* (Washington, DC: Brookings Institution, 1974).

Table 12.1

PARTIES AND PRESIDENTIAL CANDIDATES, 2020

CANDIDATE	PARTY	VOTE TOTAL	PERCENT OF VOTE
Donald Trump	Republican	72,936,342	47.3
Joe Biden	Democrat	78,662,167	51.00
Jo Jorgensen	Libertarian	1,824,020	1.2
Howie Hawkins	Green	381,201	0.2
Others		425,972	0.3

SOURCE: 2020 U.S. Election Results, https://www.google.com/search?client=firefox-b-1-e&q=2020+presidential+election+results (accessed 11/17/20).

who ran for president in 1992 and 1996 as an independent fiscal conservative, impressed some voters with his folksy style in the debates and garnered almost 19 percent of the votes cast in 1992.

The Timeplot on pp. 554–7 shows that, while in the past third parties won entire states, the Democratic and Republican parties have dominated the electoral map in recent decades. Table 12.1 lists the parties that offered candidates in the 2020 presidential election as well as candidates who ran with no party affiliation. The third-party and independent candidates together polled 2,631,193 votes, too few to capture any electoral votes for president. Third-party candidacies also arise at the state and local levels. In New York, the Conservative Party has been on the ballot for decades, though it generally endorses the Republican candidates. Vermont senator Bernie Sanders is an independent who caucuses with the Democratic Party in the Senate. In 2016 and 2020, Sanders campaigned for the Democratic presidential nomination.

Although it is difficult for third parties to survive, it is worth noting that today's two major parties themselves started as third parties. As we have seen, the Democrats emerged as an alternative to the Federalists and their opponents, loosely, the Antifederalists. The Federalist Party gave way to the Whig Party, which was replaced by the Republicans. In some sense, then, the two major parties today started as alternative parties, and they have reinvented themselves ideologically to change with the times and to co-opt supporters of emerging parties. The Democratic Party, for example, became more liberal when it adopted most of the Progressive program early in the twentieth century. Similarly, the Democratic Party subsumed many Socialists when it adopted much of the Socialist Party's program as part of the New Deal, including old-age pensions, unemployment compensation, an agricultural marketing program, and laws guaranteeing workers the right to organize into unions.

The major parties' ability to evolve is one explanation for the short lives of third parties. Their causes are usually eliminated as the major parties absorb their programs and draw their supporters into the mainstream. There are, of course, additional reasons for the short duration of most third parties. One is the typical limitation of their electoral support to one or two regions—Populist support, for example, was primarily midwestern; the 1948 Progressive Party drew nearly half its votes from the state of New York; the American Independent Party, despite garnering the most electoral votes ever for a third-party candidate (George Wallace in 1968), primarily represented the Deep South. Moreover, voters usually assume that only the candidates nominated by the two major parties have any chance of winning. Thus a vote for a third-party or an independent candidate is often considered wasted. For instance, there is evidence that Ralph Nader, the third-party candidate in the 2000 presidential race between Democrat Al Gore and Republican George W. Bush, performed better in states where either Bush or Gore was nearly certain of winning than he did in more closely contested states. Third-party candidates must struggle—usually without success—to overcome the perception that they cannot win.

As many scholars have asserted, America's single-member-district plurality election system also hampers third-party prospects. In many other nations, several individuals are elected to represent each legislative district. With this system of multimember districts, weaker parties' candidates have a better chance of winning at least some seats. For their part, voters are less concerned about wasting ballots and usually more willing to support minor-party candidates.

Reinforcing the effects of single-member districts (as noted in Chapter 11), plurality voting rules generally have the effect of setting a high threshold for victory. To win a plurality race, candidates usually must secure many more votes than they would need to win a seat in most European systems of proportional representation. For example, to win an American plurality election in a single-member district with only two candidates, a politician must win more than 50 percent of the votes cast. To win a seat in a European multimember district under proportional-representation rules, a candidate may need only 15 or 20 percent of the votes cast. This high threshold in American elections discourages minor parties and encourages the various political factions that might otherwise form minor parties to minimize their differences and remain within the major-party coalitions.[44]

It would nevertheless be incorrect to assert (as some scholars have maintained) that America's single-member plurality election system guarantees that only two parties will compete for power in all regions of the country. All one can say is that American election law depresses the number of parties likely to survive over long periods of time. There is nothing magical about the number two.

---

44 See Duverger, *Political Parties*.

CONCLUSION: PARTIES AND DEMOCRACY

Political parties help make democracy work. Americans value a broadly participatory democracy and an effective government, but these are often at odds with each other. Effective government implies decisive action and the creation of well-thought-out policies and programs. Democracy, however, implies an opportunity for all citizens to participate fully in the governmental process. And full participation by everyone is usually inconsistent with getting things done in an efficient and timely manner. Strong political parties help the United States balance the ideals of democracy and efficiency in government. Parties can both encourage popular involvement and convert participation into effective government. However, as we have seen, the parties' struggle for political advantage can also lead to intense partisanship that cripples the government's ability to operate efficiently and in the nation's best interest.

As we've seen, parties simplify the electoral process. In essence, political parties function as informal political institutions in elections and in government. They set the electoral agenda via party platforms, recruit candidates, accumulate and distribute campaign resources, and register and mobilize people to vote. Party control of the nominating process and the pressures toward two-party politics in the United States mean that most voters must decide between just two choices in any election—two competing candidates, two ideas about what public policy should be. Parties both structure electoral choices and, as we saw in Chapter 6, manage the legislative agenda. In that way, parties serve as a bridge between elections and government.

Political parties also facilitate voters' decision making. Voters can reasonably predict what sorts of policies a party-endorsed candidate will represent if elected. Even before a candidate has received a party's nomination, most voters have already determined themselves to be Democratic or Republican and know for whom they will vote. This may seem like a gross simplification of politics. It reduces our society's many complex interests to just two competing teams whose platforms must accommodate the many subtle differences or ideological nuances among groups inside the party. It further reduces politics into warring factions that have little hope of finding common ground. However, the two-party system does give meaning to the vote. It empowers the voter to say, "I want to stay the course with the party in power" or "I want to go in a new direction."

But there is a downside. Simplification of the choices leaves some voters without an effective voice and without a party that approximates what they would like government to do. Parties also try to monopolize politics, seeking to control government for their own purposes and not necessarily the interests of the whole. And the competition for control between just two parties in a system with separation of powers can lead to gridlock and stalemate. George Washington, James Madison, John Adams, Alexander Hamilton and Thomas Jefferson all viewed parties with disdain. Washington's farewell address warned "against the baneful effects of the spirit of party." Jefferson wrote, "If I could not go to Heaven but with a party, I would not go there at all." Nonetheless, all of the

Founding Fathers ended up in one way or another involved with the creation of the political parties: Washington, Adams, and Hamilton, the Federalists; Jefferson and Madison, the Democratic-Republicans. They could not help but fall into parties because of the nature of politics and the need for organizations to solve the problems of selecting candidates, organizing elections, and simplifying electoral choice.

For Further Reading

Alberta, Tim. *American Carnage: On the Front Lines of the Republican Civil War and the Rise of President Trump*. New York: HarperCollins, 2019.

Aldrich, John H. *Why Parties?: A Second Look*. Chicago: University of Chicago Press, 2011.

Campbell, Angus, Philip E. Converse, Warren E. Miller, and Donald E. Stokes. *The American Voter*. New York: John Wiley, 1960.

Cohen, Marty, David Karol, Hans Noel, and John Zaller. *The Party Decides: Presidential Nominations before and after Reform*. Chicago: University of Chicago Press, 2008.

Coleman, John J. *Party Decline in America: Policy, Politics, and the Fiscal State*. Princeton, NJ: Princeton University Press, 1996.

Cox, Gary W., and Mathew D. McCubbins. *Setting the Agenda: Responsible Party Government in the U.S. House of Representatives*. New York: Cambridge University Press, 2005.

Hershey, Marjorie Randon. *Party Politics in America*. 17th ed. New York: Routledge, 2017.

Hofstadter, Richard. *The Idea of a Party System: The Rise of Legitimate Opposition in the United States, 1780–1840*. Berkeley: University of California Press, 1969.

Klein, Ezra. *Why We're Polarized*. New York: Simon and Schuster, 2020.

Levendusky, Matthew. *The Partisan Sort: How Liberals Became Democrats and Conservatives Became Republicans*. Chicago: University of Chicago Press, 2009.

Rohde, David W. *Parties and Leaders in the Postreform House*. Chicago: University of Chicago Press, 1991.

Skocpol, Theda, and Vanessa Williamson. *The Tea Party and the Remaking of Republican Conservatism*. New York: Oxford University Press, 2012.

13

Groups and Interests

Democratic politics in the United States does not end with elections. Federal, state, and local governments provide many additional avenues through which individuals and organizations can express their preferences. People may, for example, contact elected officials, their staff, and bureaucrats directly about a particular decision or problem. They may participate in public meetings about legislation or administrative rulings; some private citizens are even selected to serve on special government commissions because of their expertise or particular concerns. People may file lawsuits to request that a government agency take a particular action or to prevent it from doing so. They may express their opinions in newspapers, on television, on the internet, or through public protests, all without fear of persecution. Individuals, organizations, and even governments make frequent use of these many points of access. Many such encounters are episodic, as when an individual contacts an agency to solve a particular problem. But much political activity in the United States occurs through enduring, organized efforts that bring together many individuals into collective action in pursuit of a common goal.

Both a pull and a push drive organized political activity in the United States. The pull comes from the government's need to collect information about the impacts of decisions on various constituencies. A responsive government needs refined information about how a decision will affect society or about the best way to implement a law. Legislators, judges, and bureaucrats typically do not have the time or resources to study all potential problems. Instead they rely on information from outside individuals and organizations, many of whom represent competing viewpoints, to gauge the importance of a given problem and to learn about the consequences of particular decisions.

The push comes from people's willingness to contact government. Individuals and organizations express their concerns with some purpose in mind, to gain some benefit. One such benefit might simply be a better understanding of governmental regulations and actions. When a commission or department issues a new regulation, firms that are potentially affected must determine whether the regulation applies to them, how to comply, and how to interpret it. Firms frequently hire representation in Washington or state capitals just to stay on top of such matters. But many of those involved in direct political action want more than information; they want to change laws and policies to favor their particular interests. They want targeted appropriations or favorable regulatory rulings, potentially worth millions, even billions, of dollars.

Take, for example, the American Automobile Association (AAA). It is, by most accounts, the largest membership organization in the United States. Tens of millions of people belong to AAA because it provides them with roadside assistance, discounts, and other benefits. But AAA started, and continues to this day, as an advocacy group representing the interests of drivers and others in the transportation industry who are concerned with the construction and maintenance of federal, state, and local roads and highways. AAA is perhaps the largest lobbying organization in the United States, pursuing its policy goals at all levels of government. AAA advocates on behalf of its millions of members, even if they are not aware of it or did not join the organization for that reason. As you read this chapter, it is worth keeping AAA in mind as a major example (but certainly not the only example) of an organized interest.

Interest group politics in the United States involves thousands of organizations, like AAA, competing for the attention of elected representatives and government officials. Once they have gained that attention, these groups then compete with other groups and individuals to influence particular governmental decisions. There are roughly 12,000 registered lobbyists in Washington, D.C., and many more in state capitals and city governments. In the din of day-to-day politics, it can be hard to get a particular concern before Congress or the bureaucracy, and one group's "special interest" may not seem so special in comparison with others. The institutions of American government further shape the political outcomes that interest groups can achieve. Groups strategically seek out institutional venues that they think will be most hospitable to their interests, but our system of

LEARNING OBJECTIVES

 Explain what interest groups are and how they endeavor to influence government.

 Identify who creates interest groups, and explain how this influences whose needs are represented at all levels of government.

 Analyze the insider and outsider strategies employed by interest groups in their efforts to influence policy.

 Describe how interest groups solve collective action problems in the United States.

government often means that one must win in many different domains in order to change public policy. A group may succeed in a House committee, for example, only to be blocked in the analogous Senate committee. In fact, interest group politics commonly involves competition among groups, who try to block each other's efforts in many different parts of the government. As a result, interest group politics can make legislation and rule making slower and more complicated.

This is pluralism at work. It is messy and often unpopular, but it is an essential feature of American government. The U.S. Constitution embraces this idea fully. The more competition there is among many interests, the less likely it is that any one will triumph and the more likely it is that representatives and government officials will learn what they need to know.[1] There is always a risk, however, that organized interests will gain excessive influence over the government. Regulation of lobbying and campaign contributions, as well as governmental ethics rules, aim to prevent government from serving particular interests to the detriment of the common good.

One of the most difficult questions about the U.S. system of government is whether the separation of powers and free and open political competition provide sufficient safeguards against excessive influence by certain groups. How much should American governments limit what individuals and organizations can say and do in order to prevent certain interests from having too much influence? In short, how should we manage the trade-off between free speech and the potential corrupting influence of groups? These questions are continually debated in American government, from city councils to the Supreme Court.

In this chapter we analyze the social basis of organizations, the problems inherent in collective action, and some solutions to these problems. We discuss the character and balance of the interests promoted through our nation's pluralistic political system. We further examine the tremendous growth of interest groups in number, resources, and activity in recent decades. Finally, we examine the strategies that groups use to influence politics and consider whether their influence has become excessive.

WHAT ARE THE CHARACTERISTICS OF INTEREST GROUPS?

interest group

An organized group of people that attempts to influence governmental policies. Also called *lobby*.

An **interest group** is an organized group of individuals or organizations that makes policy-related appeals to government. Individuals form groups and engage in collective action to increase the chances that their views will be heard and their interests treated favorably by government. Interest groups are organized to influence governmental decisions; they are sometimes called *lobbies*.

1   This sentiment is expressed most eloquently in Clinton L. Rossiter, ed., *The Federalist Papers; Alexander Hamilton, James Madison, and John Jay* (New York: New American Library, 1961), no. 10 (James Madison), p. 143.

Interest group politics, however, is much broader than lobbying or campaign activity. It involves any organized effort by private interests in society to influence legislative, executive, and judicial actions. Interest groups also are not political parties. Political parties, as we explained in Chapter 12, can be viewed as teams seeking to gain control of the government. They are concerned with who is in office, and they may take positions on a wide range of policies for the sake of winning elections. Interest groups concern themselves primarily with their members' interests and governmental policies that affect these interests. For example, trade associations such as the Dairy Farmers of America or Associated Builders and Contractors are concerned with governmental policies that affect the dairy industry or the construction industry.

Interest Groups Not Only Enhance Democracy . . .

There are an enormous number of interest groups in the United States, involved in every aspect and level of American government. Millions of Americans are members of one or more groups, paying dues or attending an occasional meeting.[2] By representing such large numbers of people and encouraging political participation, organized groups enhance American democracy. They educate their members about relevant issues, lobby members of Congress and the executive branch, engage in litigation, and generally represent their members' interests in the political arena. Groups mobilize their members for elections and grassroots lobbying efforts. Interest groups also monitor governmental programs to ensure they do not adversely affect their members. In all these ways, organized interests promote democratic politics.

. . . But Also Represent the Evils of Faction

The framers of the U.S. Constitution feared the power that organized interests could wield. James Madison wrote:

> The public good is disregarded in the conflict of rival [factions], . . . citizens . . . who are united and actuated by some common impulse of passion, or of interest, adverse to the rights of other citizens, or to the permanent and aggregate interests of the community.[3]

2   There are no reliable estimates of the number of groups in the United States at all levels of government. Jeffrey M. Berry and Clyde Wilcox's *The Interest Group Society*, 5th ed. (New York: Routledge, 2016) provides a picture of the tens of thousands of groups at the state and federal levels. Indeed, every one of the 50 states has its own interest group ecosystem. See Virginia Gray and David Lowery, *The Population Ecology of Interest Representation: Lobbying Communities in the American States* (Ann Arbor: University of Michigan Press, 1996); and Alan Rosenthal, *The Third House: Lobbyists and Lobbying in the States*, 2nd ed. (Washington, DC: CQ Press, 2001). Interest group activity at the local level, including cities and towns, counties, and special districts, is potentially as extensive as the activity at state and federal levels, but is largely unmapped.

3   Rossiter, *Federalist Papers*, no. 10, p. 78.

Yet the Founders believed that interest groups would thrive because of the freedom, enjoyed by all Americans, to organize and express their views. To the framers, this problem presented a dilemma. If government had the power to regulate or forbid efforts by organized interests to interfere in the political process, it would in effect have the power to suppress freedom. Madison presented the solution to this dilemma:

> Take in a greater variety of parties and interests [and] you make it less probable that a majority of the whole will have a common motive to invade the rights of other citizens. . . . [Hence the advantage] enjoyed by a large over a small republic.[4]

According to Madison's theory, a good constitution encourages multitudes of interests so that no single interest can ever tyrannize the others. The assumption is that competition will produce balance and compromise, with all the interests regulating one another.[5] Today this principle of regulation is called **pluralism**. According to pluralist theory, all interests are and should be free to compete for influence in the government. Moreover, the outcome of this competition will necessarily be compromise and moderation, because no group is likely to achieve any of its goals without accommodating some of the views of its many competitors.[6]

pluralism

The theory that all interests are and should be free to compete for influence in the government.

There are tens of thousands of organized groups in the United States today competing to be heard and to influence government, but not all interests are fully and equally represented in the political process. The political deck is heavily stacked in favor of those that wield substantial economic, social, and institutional resources on behalf of their causes. Thus, within the universe of interest group politics, it is political power—not some abstract conception of the public good—that is likely to prevail. Moreover, this means that interest group politics, as a whole, works more to the advantage of some types of interests than to others. In general, a politics in which interest groups predominate is a politics with a distinctly upper-class bias.

Organized Interests Are Predominantly Economic

Most people think of interest groups as having a direct and private economic interest in governmental actions; and indeed, economic interest is one reason individuals and groups engage in political action. Interest groups are generally supported by groups of producers or manufacturers in a particular economic sector. Examples include the American Fuel & Petrochemical Manufacturers,

---

4   Rossiter, *Federalist Papers*, no. 10, p. 83.

5   Rossiter, *Federalist Papers*, no. 10.

6   The best statement of the pluralist view is in David B. Truman, *The Governmental Process: Political Interests and Public Opinion* (New York: Knopf, 1951), chap. 2.

the American Farm Bureau Federation, and the National Federation of Independent Business, which represents small business owners. At the same time that broadly representative groups such as these are active in Washington, specific companies—such as Disney, Shell, Microsoft, and General Motors—may be active on other issues.

Labor organizations, although fewer in number and more limited in financial resources, are extremely active lobbyists. The AFL-CIO, the United Mine Workers, and the International Brotherhood of Teamsters are examples of groups that lobby on behalf of organized labor. Recently, lobbies have arisen to further the interests of public employees, the most significant being the American Federation of State, County, and Municipal Employees. Other public-sector lobbies, such as the National League of Cities, represent state and local governments at the federal level.

Professional lobbies such as the American Bar Association and the American Medical Association have been particularly successful in furthering their interests in state and federal legislatures. The gun lobby, made up of representatives of firearms manufacturers and dealers as well as gun owners, is represented by the National Rifle Association (NRA). Financial institutions, represented by organizations such as the American Bankers Association and Independent Community Bankers of America, also are important in shaping legislative policy.

Recent decades have witnessed the growth of a powerful "public interest" lobby purporting to represent interests not addressed by traditional lobbies. These groups have been most visible in the consumer protection and environmental policy areas, although public interest groups cover a broad range of issues, from nuclear disarmament to civil rights to abortion. The Natural Resources Defense Council, the Union of Concerned Scientists, the National Association for the Advancement of Colored People (NAACP), the Christian Coalition of America, and Common Cause are all examples.

The perceived need for representation on Capitol Hill has also generated a "research" lobby comprising universities and think tanks—such as Harvard University, the Brookings Institution, and the American Enterprise Institute—that desire government funds for research and support. Indeed, universities have expanded their lobbying efforts even as they have reduced faculty positions and course offerings and increased tuition.[7] Even with the greater number of interests, most organizations involved in politics in Washington, D.C., and in the state capitals represent economic interests. The Policy Principle box on p. 568 gives an example of how the real estate industry has successfully opposed any changes to the mortgage interest tax deduction, a policy that is in their own economic interests even though it is not in the interest of most homeowners.

---

7   Betsy Wagner and David Bowermaster, "B.S. Economics," *Washington Monthly*, November 1992, 19–21; and Benjamin Ginsberg, "Administrators Ate My Tuition," *Washington Monthly*, September–October 2011, https://washingtonmonthly.com /magazine/septoct-2011/administrators-ate-my-tuition (accessed 4/22/20).

The Mortgage Interest Tax Deduction

A home for sale in Durham, North Carolina

When individuals and groups form coalitions to engage in collective action, players may not have equal access to information and other resources they need to act effectively. Take the case of the mortgage tax credit. This tax credit benefits the real estate and finance industries and wealthy households. These interests are politically very active, well-organized, well-informed, and have the resources to bring pressure through lobbying.

Under current law, individuals who file itemized personal income tax returns may deduct the interest on as much as $750,000 in mortgage indebtedness from their taxable income. Though the average deduction is only about $1,680 for homeowners who itemize, this law can result in thousands of dollars in savings for an upper-bracket taxpayer with a large mortgage.

Prior to 2017, the mortgage deduction was higher still. Homeowners could deduct the interest on mortgages of up to $1 million, and they could deduct their property taxes entirely. In 2017, Congress reduced the maximum mortgage deduction and capped the amount of state and local property taxes that could be deducted at $10,000. These changes were highly controversial but far less extreme than initial proposals, which would have eliminated the deduction for state and local property taxes entirely and set the mortgage deduction at $500,000.[1]

Proponents of the mortgage interest tax deduction, such as the real estate industry, argue that it benefits the middle class and encourages home ownership, in turn giving people a stake in the community and the nation and making them better neighbors and citizens. The mortgage interest deduction does in fact result in a direct savings to many Americans, but it also drives up home prices by allowing purchasers to assume larger mortgages. And, the benefits are not universal. Nearly 80 percent of the benefits provided by the mortgage interest deduction and other housing tax credits accrue to the wealthiest 20 percent of Americans. About half of all families with residential mortgages receive no tax benefit at all.

Even still, the mortgage interest deduction has long been viewed as politically untouchable—as evidenced by the controversy surrounding the 2017 changes. Wealthy homeowners and the real estate industry fought to keep the policy in place, and organized groups representing the real estate and lending industries vehemently oppose changing it. The availability of a tax deduction encourages wealthier Americans to purchase second homes, to purchase more expensive homes, and to borrow against the value of their homes. From the perspective of the real estate and lending industries, cuts in the mortgage interest deduction would shrink these lucrative markets.

So why did the Trump administration and the Republican leadership in Congress shrink the mortgage deduction in 2017, over objections from industry? To pay for other tax cuts as part of the larger Tax Cuts and Jobs Act, especially lowering the marginal tax rates of the wealthiest households. The net effect of the 2017 tax law was to cut the taxes of families with incomes over $730,000 by roughly $50,000. One interest won out at the expense of the other.

1 Reuben Fischer-Baum, Kim Soffen, Heather Long, and Kevin Uhrmacher, "Republicans Say It's a Tax Cut for the Middle Class. The Biggest Winners Are the Rich," *Washington Post*, January 30, 2018, www .washingtonpost.com/graphics/2017/business/what-republican-tax -plans-could-mean-for-you/?utm_term=.3f9ade7874b0 (accessed 6/5/18).

Most Groups Require Members, Money, and Leadership

Although there are many kinds of interest groups, most share certain key organizational components. First, most groups must attract and keep members. Usually, groups appeal to members not only by promoting certain political goals but also by providing direct economic or social benefits. Thus, for example, AARP (formerly the American Association for Retired Persons), which promotes senior citizens' interests, also offers insurance benefits and commercial discounts. Similarly, many groups with primarily economic or political goals also seek to attract members through social interaction and good fellowship. Thus the local chapters of many national groups provide a congenial social environment while collecting dues that finance the national office's efforts.

Second, every group must build a financial structure capable of sustaining an organization and funding its activities. Most interest groups rely on yearly dues and voluntary contributions. Many also sell ancillary services, such as insurance and vacation tours. Third, every group must have a leadership and decision-making structure. For some organizations, this structure is very simple. For others, it can involve hundreds of local chapters that are melded into a national apparatus. Finally, most groups include an agency that actually carries out the group's tasks. This may be a research organization, a public relations office, or a lobbying office in Washington or a state capital.

Group Membership Has an Upper-Class Bias

Membership in interest groups is not randomly distributed among the population. People with higher incomes, higher levels of education, and managerial or professional occupations are much more likely to join interest groups than are those on the lower rungs of the socioeconomic ladder.[8] Well-educated upper-income professionals are more likely to have the time, money, and skills needed to play a role in a group or association. Moreover, for business and professional people, group membership may provide personal contacts and access to information that can help advance their careers. At the same time, corporate entities—businesses and trade associations—usually have ample resources to form or participate in groups that seek to advance their causes.

The result is that interest group politics in the United States has a pronounced upper-class bias. Although many groups and political associations have a working-class or lower-class membership—labor organizations or welfare-rights organizations, for example—the great majority of interest group members are middle and upper-middle class. In general, interest groups serve the

8 Kay Lehman Schlozman, Sidney Verba, and Henry E. Brady, *The Unheavenly Chorus: Unequal Political Voice and the Broken Promise of American Democracy* (Princeton, NJ: Princeton University Press, 2012); and Martin Gilens, *Affluence and Influence: Economic Inequality and Political Power in America* (Princeton, NJ: Princeton University Press, 2012).

interests of society's "haves." Even when groups take opposing positions on issues, they usually reflect divisions among upper-income strata rather than conflicts between upper and lower classes.

Even groups associated with a progressive political agenda tend, in their own membership, to reflect middle- and upper-middle-class interests. Consider the NAACP and the National Organization for Women (NOW). Both groups advocate for historically marginalized groups, but they focus on issues that are mainly relevant to the middle-class and upper-middle-class segments of these groups—reflecting the socioeconomic status of their members. The politics *inside* the groups—the need to raise money and the interests of activists and leaders—make it difficult to stay focused on the needs of the disadvantaged in society. The NAACP is concerned with minority access to universities and the professions, a topic primarily of concern to its middle-class supporters. NOW seeks gender equality in education and access to positions in business and the professions—again, matters mainly of interest to its largely middle- and upper-middle-class membership.[9]

In general, to obtain adequate political representation, forces low on the socio-economic ladder must be organized on the massive scale associated with political parties. Indeed, parties can mobilize the collective energies of large numbers of people who, as individuals, may have very limited resources. Interest groups, in contrast, generally organize smaller numbers of the better-to-do. Thus the relative importance of political parties and interest groups has far-ranging implications for the distribution of political power. To use the language that became prevalent in the 2012 campaign, active interest groups generally empower the "1 percent." Strong political parties give the "99 percent" a chance as well.

Groups Reflect Changes in the Political Environment

As long as there is government, as long as government makes policies that add value or impose costs, and as long as there is liberty to organize, interest groups will abound. And if government expands, so will the number of interest groups. For example, a spurt of growth in the national government occurred during the 1880s and 1890s, arising largely from governmental efforts to fight large monopolies and regulate some aspects of interstate commerce. In the latter decade, a parallel spurt occurred in national interest groups, including the founding of the National Association of Manufacturers and other trade associations. Many groups organized around agricultural commodities as well, and trade unions as interest groups also began to expand. Later, in the 1930s, interest groups with headquarters and representation in Washington began to grow significantly, concurrent with that decade's expansion of the national government.

The past 50 years has seen an enormous increase both in the number of interest groups and in the extent of their opportunity to influence the political

---

9   Dara Z. Strolovitch, *Affirmative Advocacy: Race, Class, and Gender in Interest Group Politics* (Chicago: University of Chicago Press, 2007).

process. The total number of interest groups in the United States today is not known. There are certainly tens of thousands of groups at the national, state, and local levels. One indication of the proliferation of their activity is the growing number of political action committees (PACs), the vehicle through which most interest group money is spent to influence elections. Four times as many PACs operated in 2020 as did 40 years ago, increasing from 2,000 to almost 8,000.[10] The rise of PACs exhibits one of the most common features of business political activity: businesses are reactive. They are usually drawn into politics in response to regulations, rather than to create new programs.[11]

Similarly, federal social programs have occasionally sparked political organization and action on the part of groups seeking to influence the distribution of benefits in their favor. In turn, groups have organized in opposition to the programs or their cost. AARP, one of the nation's largest membership organizations, owes its emergence to the creation and expansion of Social Security and Medicare. Once older Americans had guaranteed retirement income and health insurance, they had a clear stake in protecting and expanding these benefits. AARP developed in response to attempts to pare back the program.[12]

Another factor accelerating the recent explosion of interest group activity has been the emergence of new social and political movements. The civil rights and antiwar movements of the 1960s, and the reactions against them, created a generation of upper-middle-class professionals and intellectuals who have seen themselves as a political force opposing the public policies and politicians associated with the nation's postwar regime. Following these movements came the decade-long debate over the equal rights amendment, the Sagebrush Rebellion (concerning land use in the West), the nuclear disarmament movement, and the anti-abortion movement. More recent social movements include the anti-tax Tea Party movement and the Black Lives Matter movement protesting racial discrimination and the social condition of African Americans. Such groups sought to make changes in social behavior and public policy, usually through civil disobedience.

Members of these movements during the late 1960s and early 1970s—collectively known as the New Politics movement—constructed or strengthened public interest groups such as Common Cause, the Sierra Club, the Environmental Defense Fund, Physicians for Social Responsibility, NOW, and the various organizations formed by consumer activist Ralph Nader. These groups influenced the media, Congress, and even the judiciary and successfully pushed for the enactment of many policies in their favor. Activist groups also

---

10 Federal Election Commission, "Campaign Finance Statistics," https://transition.fec.gov/press/campaign_finance_statistics.shtml (accessed 4/10/20).

11 The earlier expansions in interest groups—in the 1880s and 1930s—involved changes in the interest group universe that were as big or perhaps bigger than the changes in the 1960s and 1970s. See Daniel J. Tichenor and Richard A. Harris, "Organized Interests and American Political Development," *Political Science Quarterly* 117, no. 4 (Winter 2002-03): 587–612.

12 Andrea Louise Campbell, *How Policies Make Citizens: Senior Political Activism and the American Welfare State* (Princeton, NJ: Princeton University Press, 2003).

played a major role in promoting the passage of environmental, consumer, and occupational health and safety legislation.

Among the factors contributing to the rise and success of public interest groups is technology. Computerized direct-mail campaigns in the 1980s were perhaps the first innovation that allowed organizations to reach out to potential members. Today, email, Facebook, Twitter, and other social media enable public interest groups to reach hundreds of thousands of potential sympathizers and contributors. Relatively small groups can now efficiently identify and mobilize supporters nationwide. Individuals with perspectives in a small, anonymous minority can connect and mobilize for national political action through social networking tools that were unthinkable even 30 years ago.

Latent Groups

Of course, many individuals who share common interests do not form interest groups. For example, although college students share an interest in the cost and quality of education, they have not organized to demand lower tuition, better facilities, or more effective faculty. Students could be called a "latent group," of which there are many in American society. Often, the failure of a latent group to organize reflects individuals' abilities to achieve their goals without joining an organized effort. Individual students, for example, are free to choose among colleges that, in turn, compete for their patronage. Where the market or other mechanisms allow individuals to achieve their goals without joining groups, they are less likely to do so.

HOW AND WHY DO INTEREST GROUPS FORM?

Pluralist theory argues that because individuals in the United States are free to join or form groups that reflect their common interests, interest groups should readily form whenever a change in the political environment warrants it. If this argument is correct, groups should form roughly in proportion to people's interests. We should find a greater number of organizations around interests shared by a greater number of people. Evidence for this hypothesis is weak, however. In the 1980s, political scientists Kay Schlozman and John Tierney examined interest groups representing people's occupations and economic roles.[13] Using census data and lists of interest groups, they compared the number of people in particular economic roles with the number of organizations representing those roles in Washington. For example, they found that in the mid-1980s 4 percent of the population was looking for work, but only a handful of organizations

---

13 Kay Lehman Schlozman and John T. Tierney, *Organized Interests and American Democracy* (New York: Harper and Row, 1986).

Table 13.1

WHO IS REPRESENTED BY ORGANIZED INTERESTS?

WORKFORCE STATUS OF THE INDIVIDUAL	U.S. ADULTS (%)	ORGS. (%)	TYPE OF ORG. IN WASHINGTON	RATIO: % OF ORGS. TO % OF ADULTS
Executives	8.5	70.3	Business association	8.27
Professionals	13.0	23.7	Professional association	1.82
White-collar workers	14.0	1.1	White-collar union	0.08
Blue-collar workers	22.2	0.4	Blue-collar union	0.02
Farm workers	0.9	1.6	Agricultural workers' organization	1.78
Unemployed	6.2	1.7	Unemployment organization	0.27
Not in workforce	35.3	1.2	Senior citizens organization, organization for the handicapped, educational organization	0.03

SOURCE: Kay Lehman Schlozman, Sidney Verba, and Henry E. Brady, *The Unheavenly Chorus: Unequal Political Voice and the Broken Promise of American Democracy* (Princeton, NJ: Princeton University Press, 2012), p. 329. Updated data supplied by Schlozman, Verba, and Brady.

ANALYZING THE EVIDENCE

What types of interests are most likely to be represented by interest groups? If interest group politics is biased in favor of the wealthy and the powerful, should we curb group politics? What was James Madison's answer? Do you agree with Madison?

represented the unemployed in Washington, making up 0.1 percent of total organizations.[14]

There was a considerable disparity in representation across categories of people. Schlozman and Tierney noted, for example, at least a dozen groups representing senior citizens but none for the middle-aged. Their original study was repeated using data from the 2012 Statistical Abstract of the U.S. Census Bureau and the 2011 Washington Representatives Study (see Table 13.1).

14 Of course, the number of organizations is at best only a rough measure of the extent to which various categories of citizens are represented in the interest group world of Washington.

The observation that groups form only around some interests creates a problem for the pluralist notion of democracy. If there is a bias in the sorts of groups that form, such as a disproportionate number of wealthy groups, then political decisions may reflect the bias in who is organized and who is not. Economist Mancur Olson's work, discussed later in this chapter, is the best-known challenge to pluralist theory. It is in Olson's insights that we find the basis for interest group formation.

Interest Groups Facilitate Cooperation

Groups that pursue a common interest or shared objective—maintenance of a hunting and fishing habitat, creation of a network for sharing computer software, lobbying for favorable legislation, and so on—consist of individuals who bear some cost on behalf of the joint goal. Each member of the Possum Hollow Rod and Gun Club may, for example, pay annual dues and devote one weekend a year to cleaning up the rivers and forests of the club-owned game preserve.

We can think of this as an instance of two-person cooperation writ large. Accordingly, each one of a large number of individuals has, in the simplest situation, two options: "contribute" or "don't contribute" to achieving the shared objective. If the number of contributors to the group enterprise is sufficiently large, a group goal is achieved. However, there is a twist. If the group goal is realized, then all members enjoy the benefits, whether or not they contributed to its achievement.

The Prisoner's Dilemma and Free Riding. Researchers often rely on the metaphor of the prisoner's dilemma when theorizing about social situations of collective action. The prisoner's dilemma, a famous hypothetical problem from game theory, is used to discuss why people rationally take actions that may not be optimal or in the best interests of all. This is similar to the fence-mending example in Chapter 1's discussion of bargaining failure.

In the prisoner's dilemma, two prisoners are accused of jointly committing a crime. They are kept in separate interview rooms. The police have only minimal evidence, however, so they want (at least) one prisoner to snitch on the other so that the prosecutor's case becomes a slam dunk. Each prisoner is offered the same plea bargain: "Testify against the other prisoner in exchange for your freedom, provided that your accomplice does not also testify against you. Remain silent, and you will possibly get the maximum sentence if your accomplice testifies against you." Figure 13.1 displays Prisoner A's options along the rows and Prisoner B's along the columns; in each cell are the sentences (incentives) that each prisoner receives for each combination of actions. If neither snitches, each gets one year; if both snitch, each gets three years; and so on. The outcome of the plea bargain depends on what the other person does. Before reading on, study the table and think about what you would do if you were Prisoner A.

The prisoners face an unpleasant choice. They are self-interested, rational actors who will choose the alternative that offers the best deal. They prefer less jail time to more, and the police, understanding their motivations, have structured the choice so that each prisoner will rat on the other. Notice that in

Figure 13.1
THE PRISONER'S DILEMMA

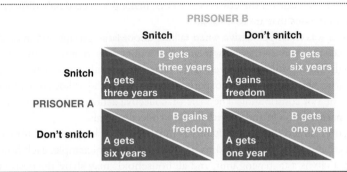

ANALYZING THE EVIDENCE

Given these incentives, what should Prisoner A do? Can you think of other scenarios with a similar pattern of incentives?

Figure 13.1, Prisoner A is better off choosing to snitch no matter what Prisoner B does. If B chooses to snitch, then A's choice to snitch gets A a three-year jail term, but a choice to remain silent by A results in six years for A—clearly a worse outcome. In contrast, if B chooses not to snitch, then A gets no jail time if he snitches instead of one year if he also chooses not to snitch. In short, A is always better off snitching. But this situation is symmetrical, so it follows that B is better off snitching, too. If both prisoners snitch, the prosecutor can convict both of them, and each serves three years. If they had both kept silent, they would have gotten only one year each. In terms of game theory, each player has a dominant strategy—snitching is best no matter what the other player does—and this leads paradoxically to an outcome in which each player is worse off.

The prisoner's dilemma provides the insight that rational individual behavior does not always lead to the best collective results. The logic is compelling: if A appreciates the dilemma and realizes that B also appreciates the dilemma, then A will still be drawn to the choice of snitching. The reasons for this are the temptation to get off scot free (if he testifies and his accomplice doesn't) and the fear of being suckered (if his accomplice testifies and he doesn't). The prisoner's dilemma carries a brilliant yet troubling insight about collective decision making: people often have difficulty achieving objectives that are in the collective good because the incentive to shirk, to defect, to free ride is just too strong.

Consider the collective action example described in Chapter 1, in which each person benefits from a local improvement project (such as a clearing a disease-carrying mosquito habitat or building a sewage treatment facility) even if she does not provide the required effort. As long as enough other people contribute, any individual can ride free on the others' efforts. This is a multiperson prisoner's dilemma because not providing effort, like snitching, is a dominant strategy; yet if everyone chooses not to contribute, an unwanted outcome results: spread of disease. The prospect of free riding, as we see next, is the bane of collective action.

The Logic of Collective Action. Economist Mancur Olson, writing in 1965, essentially took on the political science establishment by noting that the pluralist assumption—that individuals' common interests automatically transform into group organization and collective action—was problematic. Individuals wishing to engage in collective action face the prisoner's dilemma. They are tempted to free ride on the efforts of others, making it exceedingly difficult to achieve outcomes that are best for all.

Olson was most persuasive when talking about large groups and mass collective action, such as the antiwar and civil rights movements of the 1960s. Although these groups mobilized large rallies, most individuals who sympathized with the causes failed to participate; they instead followed a rational strategy of not contributing. The logic of collective action makes it difficult to induce participation in and contribution to collective goals.

Olson claimed that this difficulty is most severe in large groups for three reasons. First, such groups tend to be anonymous. For example, each household in a city is a taxpaying unit, and all households may share the desire for lower property taxes, but it is difficult to forge a group identity or a group effort toward lowering taxes on such a basis. Second, in the anonymity of the large-group context, it is especially plausible to claim that no single individual's contribution makes much difference. Should an individual citizen kill the better part of a morning writing a letter to his city council member in support of lower property taxes? If hardly anyone else writes, the council member is unlikely to pay much heed to this one letter; then again, if the council member is inundated with letters, would one more have a significant additional effect? Third, there is the problem of enforcement. In a large group, other members cannot prevent a slacker from receiving the benefits of collective action, should they materialize. (Every property owner's taxes will be lowered.) Moreover, in a large, anonymous group it is hard to know who has and who has not contributed, and because there is such limited group identity, it is hard to identify, much less take action against, slackers. As a consequence, many large groups that share common interests fail to mobilize at all—they remain latent.

The same problem plagues small groups, too. But Olson argued that small groups manage to overcome the problem of collective action more frequently and to a greater extent than their larger counterparts. Because small groups are more personal, their members are more vulnerable to interpersonal persuasion. Individual contributions may make a more noticeable difference, so individuals feel that their contributions are more essential. Contributors in small groups, moreover, often know who the slackers are. Thus punishment, ranging from subtle judgmental pressure to social ostracism, is easier to effect.

Contrasting large groups, which often remain latent, with smaller groups, Olson called the small groups privileged because of their advantages in overcoming the free-rider, coordination, and conflict-of-interest problems of collective action. It is for these perhaps counterintuitive reasons that small groups often prevail over, or enjoy greater privileges relative to, larger groups. These reasons help explain why we so often see producers win out over consumers, owners of capital win out over labor, and a party's elite win out over its mass members.

Selective Benefits: A Solution to the Collective Action Problem

Despite the free-rider problem, interest groups offer numerous incentives to join. Most important, as Olson noted, they make various **selective benefits** available only to their members. This means that individuals cannot free ride and still receive certain benefits, which makes participation more attractive. The benefits may be informational, material, solidary, or purposive. Table 13.2 gives examples in each category.

Informational benefits are the most important category of selective benefits offered to group members. Information is provided through conferences, training programs, and printed materials sent automatically to those who have paid dues. Material benefits include anything that can be measured monetarily, such as discount purchasing, shared advertising, and—perhaps most valuable—health and retirement insurance. For example, AARP, one of the largest groups in the United States, offers insurance packages to its members.

selective benefits

Benefits that do not go to everyone but, rather, are distributed selectively—to only those who contribute to the group enterprise.

Table 13.2
SELECTIVE BENEFITS OF INTEREST GROUP MEMBERSHIP

CATEGORY	BENEFITS
Informational benefits	Conferences and publications Professional contacts Training programs Coordination among organizations Research Legal help Professional codes Collective bargaining
Material benefits	Travel packages Insurance Discounts on consumer goods
Solidary benefits	Friendship Networking opportunities
Purposive benefits	Advocacy Representation before government Participation in public affairs

SOURCE: Adapted from Jack L. Walker, Jr., *Mobilizing Interest Groups in America: Patrons, Professions, and Social Movements* (Ann Arbor: University of Michigan Press, 1991), p. 86.

Among solidary benefits, most notable are the friendship and networking opportunities that membership provides. Another benefit in this category that has been important to nonprofit and citizens' groups is consciousness-raising. For example, many women's organizations claim that active participation conveys to each member an enhanced sense of her own value and a stronger ability to advance individual as well as collective civil rights.

Purposive benefits involve the appeal of the interest group's purpose. Religious interest groups provide good examples of such benefits. The Christian right is a powerful movement made up of numerous interest groups that offer virtually no material benefits to their members. Instead, the growth and success of these groups depend on their members' religious identification and affirmation. Many such religiously based interest groups have arisen, especially at state and local levels, throughout American history. For example, both the abolition and the Prohibition movements were driven by religious interest groups whose main attractions for members were their nonmaterial benefits. The sharing of a common ideology is another important nonmaterial benefit. In fact, many of the most successful citizens' or public interest groups of the past 20 years have coalesced around shared ideological goals, including government reform, election and campaign reform, civil rights, economic equality, "family values," even opposition to government itself. All are examples of purposive benefits.[15]

Of course, some groups use coercion in addition to selective benefits to address the collective action problem. Labor unions, for example, call workers who refuse to join a strike "scabs." At one time, unions employed violence and intimidation against scabs and some firms hired their own "security forces" to break strikes. Politics isn't as physical today, but inside a firm or organization there can be enormous pressure on members of management to contribute to a PAC or on employees to vote for (or against) unionizing. See Analyzing the Evidence on pp. 580–1, which explores Google as an example.

Political Entrepreneurs Organize and Maintain Groups

In a 1966 review of Olson's book, the economist Richard Wagner observed that Olson's arguments about groups and politics in general, and his theory of selective incentives in particular, said little about the internal workings of groups.[16] In Wagner's experience, groups often formed and then were maintained not only because of selective incentives but also because of the extraordinary efforts of specific individuals—leaders, or "political entrepreneurs," in Wagner's more colorful terminology.

15 Terry M. Moe, *The Organization of Interests: Incentives and the Internal Dynamics of Political Interest Groups* (Chicago: University of Chicago Press, 1980).

16 Richard Wagner, "Pressure Groups and Political Entrepreneurs: A Review Article," *Papers on Non-Market Decision Making* 1 (1966): 161–70. See also Robert H. Salisbury, "An Exchange Theory of Interest Groups," *Midwest Journal of Political Science* 13, no. 1 (1969): 1–32.

Wagner raised the issue of leaders because, in his view, Olson's theory was too pessimistic. Mass organizations in the real world—labor unions, consumer associations, senior citizens' groups, environmental organizations—all exist, some persisting over long periods. Contrary to Olson's suggestions, they seem somehow to get jump-started in the real world. Therefore, Wagner suggested a special kind of theory of selective incentives based on leadership: he argued that certain selective benefits may accrue to those who organize and maintain otherwise latent groups.

Most commonly, political entrepreneurs are people who are deeply passionate about a particular cause. Elizabeth Cady Stanton, one of the leading activists for women's rights in the United States in the nineteenth century, was a political entrepreneur, as was the abolitionist Harriet Tubman. They created organizations that became central to the push for women's rights and the emancipation of enslaved people. Today, the people central to organizing the #MeToo and Black Lives Matter movements are the leaders who are bearing the greatest cost of creating and maintaining these organizations.

Sometimes politicians can be interest group entrepreneurs. Senator Robert Wagner (no relation) in the 1930s and Congressman Claude Pepper in the 1970s each had private reasons—electoral incentives—to organize laborers and the elderly, respectively. Wagner, a Democrat from New York, had a large constituency of working men and women who would reelect him if he bore the cost of organizing workers (or at least of facilitating their organization). And this he did. The law that bears his name, the Wagner Act of 1935, made it much easier for unions to organize in the industrial North.[17]

In general, a political entrepreneur is someone who sees a prospective dividend from facilitating cooperation. In other words, he or she recognizes that if a latent group were to become manifest, it would enjoy the fruits of collective action. For an expected reward, whether in votes (as with Wagner), a percentage of the dividend, nonmaterial glory, or other perks, the entrepreneur bears the costs of organizing, expends effort to monitor for slacker behavior, and sometimes even imposes punishment on slackers (such as expelling them from the group and denying them its selective benefits).

Thus political entrepreneurs may be thought of as complements to Olsonian selective incentives in that both motivate groups to accomplish collective objectives. Indeed, if selective incentives resolve the paradox of collective action, then political entrepreneurs dissolve the paradox. Both are helpful—and sometimes necessary—to initiate and maintain collective action. Groups that manage, perhaps on their own, to organize with a low level of activity often take the next step of creating leaders and leadership institutions to increase the activity level and the resulting cooperation dividends. Richard Wagner, in other words, took Olson's theory of selective incentives and suggested an alternative explanation, one that made room for institutional solutions to the problem of collective action.

---

17 The Wagner Act made it possible for unions to organize by legalizing so-called closed shops, in which all shop workers must be dues-paying union members. Workers could no longer free ride on the efforts made by others to improve wages and working conditions.

Who's Funding Google's PAC?

Contributed by
Zhao Li
Princeton University

Many major companies in the United States set up political action committees (PACs) in order to make campaign contributions to politicians and influence policy making. An underappreciated fact about business PACs is that they are forbidden by law from using their parent companies' treasury accounts to finance their campaign contributions. Instead, business PACs rely entirely on voluntary and limited donations from employees (and other eligible individuals affiliated with the parent companies) for fund-raising.

How do employees' political identities impact business PAC fund-raising and, in turn, PAC spending in the United States more generally? This has become a particularly salient question for tech companies in Silicon Valley, where a company's best interests are often at odds with its employees' own political preferences. When we look at Google, we see an example of the impact—in terms of both PAC fund-raising and spending—that may provide answers to the enduring puzzle of why levels of PAC contributions aren't higher given what's at stake.[1]

Google, as a company, would benefit from supporting Republican legislators who are potential allies of Google's key policy concerns, including antitrust regulations. But, if we look at Google employees' personal campaign donation records (see chart below), we see that Google's workforce is predominantly liberal. As a result, even though giving to Republican lawmakers may generate better "bang for the buck" on PAC contributions, Google's PAC cannot do so without sacrificing fund-raising by alienating its Democratic-leaning donor base. Employees who support the Democratic Party are less willing to donate

Google PAC Donors' Inferred Partisan Leanings, 2016

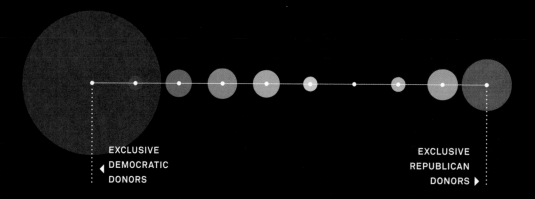

EXCLUSIVE ◀ DEMOCRATIC DONORS

EXCLUSIVE REPUBLICAN DONORS ▶

1 Stephen Ansolabehere, John M. de Figueiredo, and James M. Snyder Jr., "Why Is There So Little Money in U.S. Politics?" *Journal of Economic Perspectives* 17, no. 1 (2003): 105–30.

to their company's PAC when PAC contributions primarily go to Republican candidates, and similarly, Republican-leaning employees are less willing to donate to their company's PAC when PAC contributions primarily end up in the campaign accounts of Democratic candidates.

During the 2016 election cycle, roughly 55.7 percent of Google's PAC contributions went to Republican (as opposed to Democratic) candidates. At the same time, Google's PAC raised $1,778,775 in itemized donations from their employees and other eligible donors. Based on estimates derived from my analysis, had Google given all of its PAC contributions to Democratic recipients, it would have raised $2,594,931, representing a 45.9 percent increase relative to the observed fund-raising outcome. Alternatively, if Google had contributed every dollar to Republican politicians, it would have raised $1,140,520, which is a 35.9 percent reduction from the observed fund-raising outcome.

Observed vs. Counterfactual Fund-raising by Google's PAC, 2016

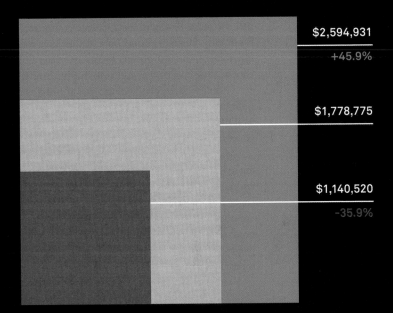

Observed PAC fund-raising

Counterfactual PAC fund-raising if 100% donations to Democratic recipients

Counterfactual PAC fund-raising if 100% donations to Republican recipients

$2,594,931

+45.9%

$1,778,775

$1,140,520

-35.9%

How does this type of behavior affect the overall strategic success of business PACs? Since donations to business PACs are required by law to be both voluntary and limited to no more than $5,000 per person per year (this contribution limit applies to all eligible donors, including, for example, corporate executives), business PACs will suffer substantial funding losses if they alienate employees and other eligible donors. As a result, in cases where the legislators that business PACs want to target the most are opposed by employees on partisan grounds, business PACs will be unable to concentrate their campaign contributions on these candidates without sacrificing fund-raising.

This would help us understand why, given what's at stake, these companies contribute much less to campaigns than is legally allowed.

SOURCE: Center for Responsive Politics, https://www.opensecrets.org/bulk-data (accessed 7/8/20).

HOW DO INTEREST GROUPS INFLUENCE POLICY?

By being organized, interest groups improve the probability that all levels of government will hear their policy concerns and treat them favorably. The quest for influence takes many forms, which we can roughly divide into "insider strategies" and "outsider strategies."

Insider strategies include gaining access to key decision makers and using the courts. Of course, influencing policy through traditional political institutions requires understanding how those institutions work. A lobbyist who wishes to address a problem with legislation will seek a sympathetic member of Congress, preferably on a committee with jurisdiction over the problem area, and will work directly with the member's staff. Likewise, an organization that decides to bring suit in the courts will sue in a jurisdiction where it has a good chance of getting a sympathetic judge or where the appellate courts are likely to support it. Gaining access is not easy. Legislators and bureaucrats have many requests to juggle; courts have full dockets. Interest groups themselves have limited budgets and staff. They must choose their battles well and map out the insider strategy most likely to succeed.

Outsider strategies include going public and using electoral tactics. Just as politicians can gain an electoral edge by informing voters, so can groups. A well-planned public information campaign, or targeted campaign activities and contributions, can have as much influence as working the corridors of Congress.

Many groups employ a mix of insider and outsider strategies. For example, environmental groups such as the Sierra Club lobby members of Congress and key congressional staff, participate in bureaucratic rule making by offering suggestions to agencies on new environmental rules, and bring lawsuits under various environmental acts, such as the Endangered Species Act. At the same time, the Sierra Club attempts to influence public opinion through media campaigns and to influence electoral politics by supporting candidates who share their views and opposing those who do not.

Direct Lobbying

lobbying

An attempt by a group to influence the policy process through persuasion of government officials.

Lobbying is an attempt by a group to influence the policy process through persuasion of government officials. Most Americans believe that interest groups exert their influence through direct contact with members of Congress, but lobbying encompasses a broad range of activities directed toward all sorts of government officials and the public as a whole.

Organized advocacy of political interests, known as lobbying, is a multibillion-dollar-a-year industry in Washington, D.C., alone, involving almost 12,000 individuals, firms, and other organizations.[18] Who is a lobbyist? The 1946 Federal Regulation of Lobbying Act defined a lobbyist as "any person who shall engage himself for pay or any consideration for the purpose of attempting to influence the passage or defeat of any legislation of the Congress of the United States."

According to the 1995 Lobbying Disclosure Act, any person who makes at least one lobbying contact with either the legislative or the executive branch in a year, any individual who spends 20 percent of his time in support of such activities, or any firm that devotes 10 percent of its budget to such activities must register as a lobbyist. They must report what topics they discussed with the government, though not which individuals or offices they contacted. Total federal lobbying expenditures have topped $3 billion every year since 2008. The industry that has spent the most over the past two decades (from 1999 to 2020) is the pharmaceutical and health products industry, with total expenditures of $4.2 billion. Pharmaceutical companies were not alone: over this same time period, insurance companies spent $2.9 billion, electric utilities spent $2.5 billion, electronics manufacturing and equipment companies spent $2.4 billion, the oil and gas industry spent $2.2 billion, and education organizations spent $1.7 billion.[19] Table 13.3 shows the top spenders on lobbying the federal government in 2019.

The amount spent to influence state legislatures is also substantial. For example, in 2019, lobbyists spent $296 million to influence California lawmakers,[20] $262 million in New York,[21] $36.4 million in Colorado,[22] and $40 million in Michigan.[23]

Lobbying involves significant activity on the part of individual lobbyists who work on behalf of interest groups: they pepper legislators, administrators, and committee staff members with facts about pertinent issues and with facts or claims about the degree to which the public supports them.[24] Indeed, lobbyists serve a useful purpose in the legislative and administrative processes by providing information that is relevant to the policy in question. Lobbying is a good way to express the intensity of the effects of a policy on an industry. If a proposed

----

18 According to the Center for Responsive Politics, there were 11,890 registered lobbyists in 2019 and 11,265 in 2020. See OpenSecrets, "Lobbying Database," Center for Responsive Politics, www.opensecrets.org/lobby (accessed 11/5/20).

19 OpenSecrets, "Industries," Center for Responsive Politics, www.opensecrets.org/lobby /top.php?showYear=a&indexType=i (accessed 9/20/19).

20 "Newsletter: Sacramento Lobbying Cost $296 Million this Year," *The Los Angeles Times*, November 4, 2019, https://www.latimes.com/politics/story/2019-11-04/essential-politics-newsletter-california-interest-groups-300-million-dollars-lobbying-sacramento (accessed 7/11/20).

21 New York Public Interest Research Group, "Lobbying Spending in New York Hits a Record," April 15, 2019, https://www.nypirg.org/capitolperspective/lobbying-spending-in-new-york-hits-a-record/ (accessed 7/11/20).

22 Sandra Fish, "Lobbying Spending Sets New Record in Colorado, As Interest Shift to Influence Democratic-Controlled Capitol," *The Colorado Sun*, August 20, 2019, https://coloradosun.com/2019/08/20/lobbying-spending-sets-new-record-colorado/ (accessed 7/11/20).

23 Carol Thompson, "Lobbyist Spending Topped the Charts in Michigan Last Year, Reports Show," *Lansing State Journal*, February 25, 2019, https://www.lansingstatejournal.com/story/news/local/2019/02/25/lobbyist-spending-michigan-2018/2884242002/ (accessed 7/11/20).

24 For discussions of lobbying, see Jeffrey M. Berry, *Lobbying for the People: The Political Behavior of Public Interest Groups* (Princeton, NJ: Princeton University Press, 1977); and John R. Wright, *Interest Groups and Congress: Lobbying, Contributions, and Influence* (Boston: Allyn and Bacon, 1996).

Table 13.3

TOP SPENDERS ON LOBBYING, 2019

ANALYZING THE EVIDENCE

Some groups spend more on lobbying than others. What patterns are there in this list of top spenders? Why are some groups willing to spend millions of dollars on lobbying? What groups are absent from the list?

LOBBYING CLIENT	TOTAL
U.S. Chamber of Commerce	$77,245,000
Open Society Policy Center	$48,470,000
National Association of Realtors	$41,241,006
Pharmaceutical Research and Manufacturers of America	$29,301,000
American Hospital Association	$26,232,680
Blue Cross/Blue Shield	$25,236,590
American Medical Association	$20,910,000
Business Roundtable	$19,990,000
Amazon.com	$16,790,000
Facebook Inc.	$16,710,000
National Association of Manufacturers	$14,610,000
NCTA — The Internet and Television Association	$14,220,000
Boeing Co.	$13,810,000
Northrop Grumman	$13,620,000
Comcast Corp.	$13,360,000
Lockheed Martin	$13,026,608
AT&T Inc.	$12,820,000
United Technologies	$12,790,000
National Association of Broadcasters	$12,720,000
Alphabet Inc.	$12,660,000

SOURCE: OpenSecrets, www.opensecrets.org/federal-lobbying/top-spenders?cycle=2019 (accessed 4/10/20).

policy will cause an entire industry to vanish and the jobs in that industry to move overseas, then the firms affected by that policy will take their concerns to Congress and the relevant executive agencies. In this way, our government learns whether a law will have a particularly intense effect on one segment of the public and can better evaluate whether those concentrated costs are justified.

Political organizing and lobbying can also inform policy makers about the range of opinions within a given industry or sector of the economy. Within each industry, any individual firm may have one interest—say, making the most money. But as a group, all firms in an industry might have another interest, such as protecting the industry from foreign competition, that aligns imperfectly (or not at all) with the goals of individual firms. A trade or industry association usually tries to represent the common interests of the entire industry. At the same time, individual firms may advocate for their own interests, often in conflict with other firms in the same industry. Thus the industry association may advocate for a policy that benefits all firms but may be undercut by the lobbying activities of individual firms. For example, the Entertainment Software Association, which spent roughly $5.2 million on lobbying on behalf of the video game industry in 2019, likely seeks a different set of regulations than Microsoft or Disney.[25]

Lobbying Members of Congress. Interest groups have substantial influence in setting the legislative agenda and helping craft the language of legislation (Figure 13.2). Today, sophisticated lobbyists win influence by providing information about policies to busy members of Congress, who actually may refuse to see the lobbyists unless they have useful information to offer. But this is only one of the many services lobbyists perform. They may also testify on their clients' behalf at congressional committee and agency hearings, help their clients identify potential allies with whom to construct coalitions, draft proposed legislation or regulations to be introduced by friendly lawmakers, and talk to reporters and organize media campaigns. Lobbyists also are important in fund-raising and directing clients' contributions to members of Congress and presidential candidates. Seeing an opportunity to harness the enthusiasm of political amateurs, lobbyists now organize comprehensive campaigns that combine simulated grassroots activity with information distribution and campaign funding for members of Congress.[26]

Some interest groups go still further. They develop strong ties to individual politicians or policy communities within Congress by hiring former staffers,

---

25 Ian Maitland, "Interest Groups and Economic Growth Rates," *Journal of Politics* 47, no. 1 (1985): 44–58, was the first to observe this tension between trade or industry associations and their member firms. See also Jeffrey M. Drope and Wendy L. Hansen, "New Evidence for the Theory of Groups: Trade Association Lobbying in Washington D.C.," *Political Research Quarterly* 62, no. 2 (2009): 303–16.

26 An excellent example is the mobilization of corporate executives in mid-1980s tax reform efforts. See Jeffrey H. Birnbaum and Alan S. Murray, *Showdown at Gucci Gulch: Lawmakers, Lobbyists, and the Unlikely Triumph of Tax Reform* (New York: Random House, 1987); and Marie Hojnacki and David C. Kimball, "Organized Interests and the Decision of Whom to Lobby in Congress," *American Political Science Review* 92, no. 4 (1998): 775–90.

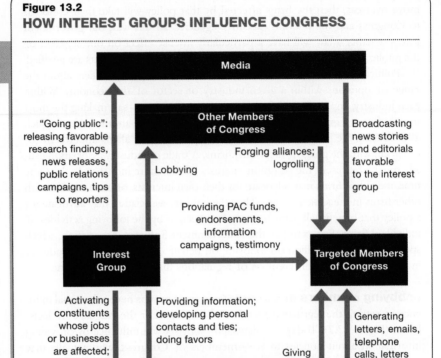

Figure 13.2

HOW INTEREST GROUPS INFLUENCE CONGRESS

former members of Congress, or even relatives of sitting members of Congress. The frequent rotation of former lawmakers and government employees into lobbying jobs, a practice known as revolving-door politics, is driven by the continual turnover of staff, lobbyists, and even the political parties in Washington. Because lobbying firms must stay current and connected to Congress to offer the best service to their clients, most large lobbying firms in Washington have strong ties to both the Democrats and the Republicans on the Hill. This revolving door has been cause for concern, and a number of states have restricted how quickly former lawmakers can return as lobbyists: 26 states have one-year restrictions, and 12 have two-year bans.[27]

27 "Revolving Door Prohibitions," National Conference of State Legislatures, February 24, 2020, www.ncsl.org/research/ethics/50-state-table-revolving-door-prohibitions.aspx (accessed 4/10/20).

Lobbying the President. All these efforts and more are needed when the target of a lobbying campaign is the president of the United States. So many individuals and groups clamor for the president's time and attention that only the most skilled and well connected can hope to influence presidential decisions. When running for president, Barack Obama made a bold promise to "free the executive branch from special-interest influence." No political appointee, the Obama team promised, "will be permitted to work on regulations or contracts directly and substantially related to their prior employer for two years." That promise proved exceedingly difficult to keep, as many in the Obama transition team had close ties to lobbyists or had worked for lobbying firms.[28] One of President Obama's first executive orders created an ethics standard and pledge for all executive branch appointments.[29] President Donald Trump similarly stated that appointees to his administration could not work as lobbyists after serving in government. Trump signed an executive order mandating that his appointees sign a pledge not to later work as lobbyists; however, at least eight prominent former Trump appointees have found ways around their pledges.

Lobbying the Executive Branch. Even when an interest group succeeds at getting its bill passed by Congress and signed by the president, full and faithful implementation of that law is not guaranteed. Often a group and its allies do not go home as soon as the president turns their lobbied-for law over to the appropriate agency. Instead, on average, 40 percent of interest group representatives continue to regularly contact legislative and executive branch organizations.[30]

In some respects, federal law actually promotes interest group access to the executive branch. The Administrative Procedure Act, enacted in 1946 and frequently amended, requires most federal agencies to provide notice and an opportunity for public comment before implementing proposed rules and regulations. This practice of notice-and-comment rule making gives interests an opportunity to make their views known and allows them to participate in the implementation of federal legislation that affects them. In 1990, Congress enacted the Negotiated Rulemaking Act to encourage administrative agencies to engage in direct and open negotiations with affected interests when developing new regulations. These two pieces of legislation, strongly enforced by the federal courts, have been important in opening the bureaucratic process up to interest group influence. Today, few federal agencies would consider implementing a new rule without consulting affected interests, or stakeholders.[31]

---

28 Chris Frates, "Daschle Lobby Ties Bump Obama Vow," *Politico*, November 30, 2008, www.politico.com/story/2008/11/daschle-lobby-ties-bump-obama-vow-016015 (accessed 4/22/20); and David Kirkpatrick, "In Transition, Ties to Lobbying," *New York Times*, November 14, 2008, www.nytimes.com/2008/11/15/us/politics/15transition.html (accessed 4/22/20).

29 Jacob R. Straus, *Lobbying the Executive Branch: Current Practices and Options for Change*, CRS Report for Congress no. 7-5700 (Washington, DC: Congressional Research Service: 2011), pp. 3–4.

30 John P. Heinz, Edward O. Laumann, Robert L. Nelson, and Robert H. Salisbury, *The Hollow Core: Private Interests in National Policy Making* (Cambridge, MA: Harvard University Press, 1993).

31 For an excellent discussion of the political origins of the Administrative Procedure Act, see Martin Shapiro, "APA: Past, Present, Future," *Virginia Law Review* 72, no. 2 (1986): 447–92.

Regulation of Lobbying. Because lobbyists seek constant access to important decision makers, stricter guidelines regulating lobbyists' actions have been adopted in recent decades. For example, as of 1993, businesses may no longer deduct the costs of lobbying from their taxes. Trade associations must report to their member businesses the proportion of their dues that goes to lobbying, and the members may not report that amount as a business expense. Most important, the 1995 Lobbying Disclosure Act (amended in 2007) significantly broadened the definition of individuals and organizations that must register as lobbyists. According to the filings under this act, almost 12,000 lobbyists were working the halls of Congress in 2019.

Congress also restricted interest group influence by passing legislation in 1996 that limited gifts to any government employee from a single source to $100 annually, with no single gift over $50 in value. It also banned the practice of compensating lawmakers for speaking engagements and other work on behalf of a lobby, a perk that many special interests had offered to supplement congressional salaries. But Congress did not limit the travel of representatives, senators, their spouses, or congressional staff members. Interest groups could pay for congressional travel as long as a trip was related to legislative business and was disclosed on congressional reports within 30 days. On these trips, meals and entertainment expenses were not subject to the $100 annual or $50-per-gift limits. Congressional rules also allowed members to travel on corporate jets as long as they paid an amount equal to first-class airfare.

In 2007, congressional Democrats secured the enactment of ethics rules prohibiting lobbyists from paying for most meals, trips, parties, and gifts for members of Congress. Lobbyists are also required to disclose the amounts and sources of small campaign contributions "bundled" into large contributions. And interest groups are required to disclose the funds they use to rally voters for or against legislative proposals. As soon as these rules were enacted, however, lobbyists and politicians found ways to circumvent them, and the reforms have had little impact. Executive rulings and memoranda issued by President Obama in 2009, including the revolving-door rules noted earlier, made it much more difficult for lobbying firms to influence executive decision making either through direct lobbying or by hiring people with direct access to decision makers.

Using the Courts

Interest groups sometimes turn to the courts to augment other avenues of access. They can use the courts to affect public policy in at least three ways: (1) by bringing suit directly on behalf of the interest group, (2) by financing suits brought by individuals, and (3) by filing an *amicus curiae* (literally, "friend of the court") brief to an existing court case.

Several cases key to the sexual revolution of the 1960s and the emergence of the movement for women's rights illustrate how groups can use court cases to effect political change. Beginning in the mid-1960s, a series of cases forced the federal courts to define a right to privacy in sexual matters. The effort began in *Griswold v. Connecticut* with a challenge to state restrictions on obtaining contraceptives; here the Supreme Court held that states could neither prohibit the dissemination of information about nor prohibit the actual use of contraceptives by married couples. In a subsequent case, the Court held that states could not prohibit the use of contraceptives by single persons any more than they could prohibit their use by married couples. One year later, in the 1973 case of *Roe v. Wade*, the Court held that states could not impose an absolute ban on voluntary abortions. These cases, along with several others, were part of the Court's enunciation of a constitutional doctrine of privacy.[32]

Roe v. Wade sparked a controversy that brought conservatives to the fore on a national level and inspired conservative groups to use the courts to whittle away the scope of the privacy doctrine. They obtained rulings, for example, that upheld legislation banning the use of federal funds to pay for voluntary abortions. And in 1989, right-to-life groups employed a strategy of litigation that significantly undermined the *Roe v. Wade* decision—particularly in the case of *Webster v. Reproductive Health Services*, which restored the right of states to place restrictions on abortion.[33]

The NAACP has also historically used the courts as a strategy for achieving political influence. The most important of its cases was *Brown v. Board of Education* in 1954, in which the Supreme Court held that school segregation was unconstitutional.[34]

Business groups, too, are frequent users of the courts because so many governmental programs apply to them, primarily in such areas as taxation, antitrust issues, interstate transportation, patents, and product quality and standardization. Often, a business comes to court when it is sued by other businesses or by government agencies. But many major corporations and their trade associations bring suit themselves to influence policy, paying huge fees each year to prestigious Washington law firms. Some of this money is expended in gaining access to influential members of Congress and the government who might further their cause, but most of it serves to keep the most experienced lawyers prepared to represent the corporations in court or before administrative agencies.

The forces of the New Politics movement made significant use of the courts during the 1970s and 1980s, and judicial decisions were instrumental in advancing their goals. Facilitated by changes in the rules governing access to the courts (the rules of standing are discussed in Chapter 9), the New Politics agenda was visible in decisions handed down in several key policy areas. In environmental policy, New Politics groups forced federal agencies to pay attention to environmental issues even when the agencies' activities were not directly related to environmental quality. By the 2000s, the courts often were the battleground on which the New Political movements waged their fights. Perhaps most dramatic were a string of lawsuits spanning 30 years (1986–2016) in which pro- and

32 *Griswold v. Connecticut*, 381 U.S. 479 (1965); *Eisenstadt v. Baird*, 405 U.S. 438 (1972); and *Roe v. Wade*, 410 U.S. 113 (1973).

33 *Webster v. Reproductive Health Services*, 492 U.S. 490 (1989).

34 *Brown v. Board of Education*, 347 U.S. 483 (1954).

anti-abortion organizations, such as the Pro-Life Action Network, Operation Rescue, and NOW, repeatedly sued state and local governments, and sometimes each other, to establish the rules governing protests near abortion clinics. Ultimately, the U.S. Supreme Court sided with the anti-abortion organizations, but not before deciding three separate cases on the matter at extremely high cost to both sides.[35]

Mobilizing Public Opinion

going public

Trying to influence public opinion for or against some proposed action by the government.

Organizations try to pressure politicians by mobilizing public opinion. This strategy is known as **going public**. When groups go public, they use their resources to try to persuade large numbers of people to pay attention to their concerns. They hope that greater visibility and public support will underscore the importance of their interests to those in power. Advertising campaigns, protests, and grassroots lobbying efforts are examples of going public. Increased use of this strategy can be traced to the rise of modern advertising at the beginning of the twentieth century. As early as the 1930s, political analysts distinguished between the "old lobby" of direct group representation before Congress and the "new lobby" of public-relations professionals addressing the public at large in order to reach Congress indirectly.[36] Going public, then, differs from other interest group strategies to influence public policy. The new lobby techniques seek to change the way people think, rather than changing the actions of insiders.

Advertising. One way of going public is through conventional advertising. For example, a casual scan of major newspapers, magazines, and websites will often reveal expensive, well-designed ads for major companies and industry associations, such as oil and gas, automobile, and health and pharmaceutical companies. Such ads frequently highlight what the firms do for the country, not merely the products they develop. Their purpose is to create and maintain a positive association between the organization and the community at large in hopes that the firm will be able to draw on the community's favorable feelings in later political controversies.

Sometimes groups advertise expressly to shift public opinion on a question. One of the most famous such advertising campaigns was run by the Health Insurance Association of America in 1993 and 1994 in opposition to President Bill Clinton's proposed national health insurance plan. These ads featured a middle-class couple, Harry and Louise, sitting at their kitchen table disparaging the excessive bureaucratic problems they would face under Clinton's plan. These ads are widely credited with turning public opinion against the plan, which never got off the ground in Congress. A decade later, when President Barack

---

35 *Scheidler v. National Organization for Women*, 547 U.S. 9 (2006).

36 E. Pendleton Herring, *Group Representation before Congress* (1928; repr., New York: Russell and Russell, 1967). See also Ken Kollman, *Outside Lobbying: Public Opinion and Interest Group Strategies* (Princeton, NJ: Princeton University Press, 1998).

Obama proposed an extensive overhaul of the health insurance industry, a trade group representing drug makers brought the same actors back and remade the Harry and Louise spot—but this time fully supporting the administration's plan. Louise concludes the new ad by saying, "A little more cooperation, a little less politics, and we can get the job done this time."[37]

Grassroots Lobbying. Grassroots lobbyists use many of the same organizing methods we see in political campaigns; they develop lists of supporters, urge them to voice their concern with an issue, and encourage them to recruit others to do so as well. It is common practice today for organizations to send direct mail that includes draft letters for recipients to adapt and send to their representatives in Congress. Groups also send mass emails urging people to contact their members of Congress regarding a particular bill or controversy. A grassroots campaign can cost anywhere from $40,000 to sway the votes of one or two crucial members of a committee or subcommittee to millions of dollars to mount a national effort aimed at Congress as a whole. Such grassroots campaigns are often organized around controversial, prominent legislation or appointments, such as nominees to the U.S. Supreme Court.

Grassroots lobbying has become more prevalent in Washington in recent decades because congressional rules limiting gifts to members have made traditional lobbying more difficult. But has grassroots campaigning gone too far? One case in particular illustrates the extremes of what has come to be known as "Astroturf" lobbying (a play on the brand name of an artificial grass). In 1992, 10 giant companies in the financial services, manufacturing, and high-tech industries began a grassroots campaign and spent millions of dollars in support of legislation that would limit investors' ability to sue for fraud. Retaining an expensive consulting firm, these corporations paid for the use of specialized software to persuade Congress that there was "an outpouring of popular support for the proposal." Thousands of letters from individuals flooded Capitol Hill. Many came from people who sincerely believed that investor lawsuits are often frivolous and should be curtailed, but much of the mail was phony, generated by the Washington-based campaign consultants. Such campaigns have increased in frequency as members of Congress grow more skeptical of Washington lobbyists and far more concerned about demonstrations of support from their constituents. It is interesting that, after the consulting firms generated thousands of letters attempting to influence the sue-for-fraud legislation, they came to the somber conclusion that "it's more effective to have 100 letters from your district where constituents took the time to write and understand the issue," because "Congress is sophisticated enough to know the difference."[38]

37 Natasha Singer, "Harry and Louise Return, with a New Message." *New York Times*, July 16, 2009, www.nytimes.com/2009/07/17/business/media/17adco.html (accessed 4/22/20).

38 Jane Fritsch, "The Grass Roots, Just a Free Phone Call Away," *New York Times*, June 23, 1995, pp. A1 and A22.

Protest. Protests are the oldest means of going public. Those who lack money, contacts, and expertise can always resort to protest as a means of making their concerns known. Indeed, the right to assembly is protected in the First Amendment. Protests may have many different consequences, depending on how they are managed. One basic consequence of a well-run protest is that it attracts attention. Peaceful demonstrations at city hall, the state legislature, Congress, the Supreme Court, or some other location typically involve people holding signs and chanting slogans. Passersby notice, and occasionally news outlets cover the event; the larger the protest, the more likely it is to attract attention. By getting on the news, the protesters hope to draw attention to their issue, raise the sympathies of others, and bring them into the movement.

Organized protests also create a sense of community among those involved and raise the consciousness of people outside the protest. Civil rights protests during the 1960s brought hundreds of thousands of people to march in the nation's capital. Newspapers and television news programs nationwide carried images of Martin Luther King, Jr. and other civil rights leaders speaking to an audience that stretched from the Lincoln Memorial across the National Mall, surrounding the Reflecting Pool. That image wrapped the civil rights movement in the symbolism of the nation; it was not a violent confrontation between protesters and police but a peaceful plea for equal voting and civil rights. Forty years later, similar marches mobilized protesters for immigrants' rights. In the spring of 2006, hundreds of thousands of people organized by Hispanic and Latino groups, as well as members of unions and local churches, marched in Washington, D.C., and in several state capitals to protest anti-immigration policies. That movement drew attention to immigrants' concerns in an increasingly hostile political environment, and it influenced the political debate over the issue. One in four Hispanics in the United States participated in these protests.[39] More recently, the encampments organized by Occupy Wall Street beginning in 2011 and the Women's Marches of 2017 promoted solidarity and community among protestors and drew attention to their concerns and causes.

The nature of organized protest has changed with the development of new communication and social media platforms. In July 2013, activist and organizer Alicia Garza wrote a Facebook post called "a love letter to Black people." The post expressed her disgust at the acquittal of George Zimmerman, a neighborhood watch volunteer who shot and killed Trayvon Martin, a Black teenager, but Garza also expressed her love of her community and her wish for strength and healing. "I continue to be surprised how little Black lives matter," she wrote, ending her post with, "Black people. I love you. I love us. Our lives matter." Her friend and fellow organizer Patrisse Cullors added the hashtag #BlackLivesMatter.[40] That social media post became a rallying point for a movement, slowly at first. The next summer, following the shooting of another Black

---

39 Pew Research Center, "Changing Faiths: Latinos and the Transformation of American Religion," April 25, 2007, www.pewforum.org/2007/04/25/changing-faiths-latinos-and-the-transformation-of-american-religion-2 (accessed 4/22/20).

40 Jelani Cobb, "The Matter of Black Lives," *New Yorker*, March 7, 2016, www.newyorker.com/magazine/2016/03/14/where-is-black-lives-matter-headed (accessed 4/22/20).

teenager, Michael Brown, by a police officer in Ferguson, Missouri, Black Lives Matter grew into a national movement raising awareness of structural racism. Similar incidents involving the deaths of Black men and women around the country have resulted in both peaceful protest and civil unrest. In 2020, after another police killing of an unarmed Black man, George Floyd, massive protests against police brutality and for criminal justice reform and racial equality spread across the country and globe.

Finally, protests often attempt to impose costs on others by disrupting traffic or commerce, thereby forcing people to bargain with the protesters. Labor strikes are one such form of political action against companies, industries, or the government. Striking workers refuse to work, costing the company the revenue it would have gained from services rendered. In the automotive industry, companies may have enough existing stock of cars and parts to continue for weeks or months of negotiations without disrupting sales. However, in an industry such as education or the airlines, once the teachers or pilots go on strike, all service stops. On rare occasions, labor organizations can instigate a general strike—all workers in an entire industry, city, or nation stay home from work, bringing all commerce to a stop. Such strikes have a significant effect on businesses and the larger economy; they remind government and industry leaders of labor's political pull.

But unions aren't the only groups that organize protests. One impressive demonstration occurred during the winter of 1977–78, when American farmers, frustrated with federal agricultural policies and increasing failures of family farms, organized a peaceful but highly disruptive convoy of 600 tractors and other farm vehicles to Washington, D.C. Snarling traffic for weeks and tearing up the grassy mall between the Lincoln Memorial and the Capitol, the protest generated compelling news photographs and garnered extensive coverage in national media. The farmers did not get a revision of the 1977 Farm Bill, but they did get a promise that the Federal Housing Administration (FHA) would temporarily cease seizures of land and equipment of farmers who could not repay their loans.[41] Farmers' protests, teachers' strikes, and other activities disrupt governmental and business activity in order to force negotiation of a better deal.

Of course, protests may become riots or civil conflicts, or they may spur counterprotests. Companies affected by protests, as well as the government, have an interest in containing or breaking up demonstrations and strikes. However, the First Amendment is generally interpreted as protecting free expression through protests and strikes as long as the demonstrations do not erupt into open rioting. For example, during George W. Bush's second inauguration in January 2005, 250 to 300 people protested the war in Iraq by marching through the streets of the Adams Morgan neighborhood in Washington, D.C. Police broke up the march with mass arrests. Some of the protesters sued to overturn their convictions and complained of alleged damages from police actions. The

---

41 "Furious Farmers," *Time*, December 19, 1977, http://content.time.com/time/magazine /article/0,9171,945836,00.html (accessed 4/22/20); and Marty Strange, *Family Farming: A New Economic Vision* (Lincoln: University of Nebraska Press, 1988).

district court sided with the protesters, reasoning that they had been engaged in peaceful demonstration, but noted that police actions may have been justified had the protestors been involved in riotous behavior.[42]

Using Electoral Politics

In addition to attempting to influence members of Congress and other government officials, interest groups use the electoral process to elect the "right" legislators in the first place and ensure that those elected will owe them a debt of gratitude for their support. To put matters into perspective, groups invest far more resources in lobbying than in electoral politics. Nevertheless, financial support and campaign activism can be important tools for organized interests.

Political Action Committees. By far, the most common electoral strategy employed by interest groups is that of giving financial support to the parties or to particular candidates. But such support can easily cross the threshold into outright bribery. In the 1920s and 1930s, Congress made it illegal for corporations and unions to contribute funds directly from their treasuries to political candidates, parties, and other organizations engaged in campaigns. Over time, unions, professional associations, and corporations found ways around these rules.

In the 1970s Congress laid out a different regulatory approach, which continues today and has been the model for the way most states regulate campaign finance in their elections. The Federal Election Campaign Act of 1971 (FECA; amended in 1974 and 1976) took a new approach to campaign finance. Since the 1970s, Congress has allowed corporations, unions, and other groups to make contributions but only through "separate and segregated funds" called political action committees (PACs). PACs are regulated under section 527 of the federal tax code, and they are subject to oversight by the IRS and the Federal Election Commission. PACs must disclose the sources of their money, their contributions, and their expenditures, and their direct contributions to political candidates and parties are subject to limits. Federal law also imposes restrictions on individuals' direct contributions. Individuals may now contribute no more than $2,800 to any candidate for federal office in any primary or general election.[43] Beyond this, the laws permit corporations, unions, and other interest groups to form PACs and pay the costs of soliciting funds from private citizens for the PACs.

Electoral spending by interest groups has increased steadily despite campaign finance reforms: total PAC contributions increased from nearly $260 million in 2000 to $1.8 billion in the 2020 election cycle. Interest groups focus their

---

42 *Carr et al. v. District of Columbia*, 565 F. Supp. 2d 94 (D.C. Cir., 2008).

43 Federal Election Commission, "Contribution Limits 2019–20," www.fec.gov/pages /brochures/contriblimits.shtml (accessed 9/20/19).

direct contributions on Congress, especially the House. (See the Timeplot on pp. 596–7 for a comparison of liberal and conservative spending over time.) After all, given the enormous cost of running modern political campaigns (see Chapter 11), most politicians are eager to receive PAC contributions. Typical House incumbents receive half of their campaign funds from interest groups. There is little evidence that interest groups buy roll-call votes or other favors from members of Congress with their donations; rather, group donations help keep those who are sympathetic to groups' interests in office.[44]

The potential influence of interest group campaign donations over the legislature has prompted frequent calls to abolish PACs or limit their activities. The challenge is how to regulate groups' participation without violating their members' rights to free speech and free association. In 1976, the Supreme Court weighed in on this matter in terms of the constitutionality of the FECA.[45] In its decision to let the act stand, a Court majority ruled that donors' rights of expression are at stake, but that these must be weighed against the government's interest in limiting corruption, or the perception of corruption. The Court has repeatedly upheld the key tenets of the decision: (1) that money is a form of speech but (2) that speech rights must be weighed against concerns about corruption. The balance between free speech and protection against corruption lies at the heart of not just campaign finance law but how Americans think about the representation of interests in our government. We value both the right of people and organizations to say freely what they want government to do and the quality and integrity of representation provided through the electoral and legislative processes.

Independent Expenditures. As we saw in Chapter 11, Congress in 2002 imposed significant limits on independent campaign expenditures via the Bipartisan Campaign Reform Act. BCRA restricted donations to nonfederal (for example, state party) accounts to limit corruption, and it imposed limits on the types of campaign commercials that groups could air within 60 days of an election. It also raised the limits on direct campaign contributions to compensate for inflation.

In 2010, the Supreme Court struck down the act's restrictions on independent advertising.[46] The case involved a political movie created by an organization called Citizens United that was critical of then-senator and presidential candidate Hillary Clinton. The movie aired on cable television inside the blackout date for independent political advertising as stipulated by BCRA. A 5–4 majority on the Court ruled that such blackout dates restricted the rights to free speech of corporations and other associations. This decision firmly established the right of business corporations and labor unions to engage in political advocacy and opened the gates to a flood of money in the political arena.

44 See Stephen Ansolabehere, John M. de Figueiredo, and James M. Snyder, Jr., "Why Is There So Little Money in U.S. Politics?" *Journal of Economic Perspectives* 17, no. 1 (2003): 105–30.

45 *Buckley v. Valeo*, 424 U.S. 1 (1976).

46 *Citizens United v. Federal Election Commission*, 558 U.S. 310 (2010).

Total Outside Spending, Liberal vs. Conservative 1990–2020

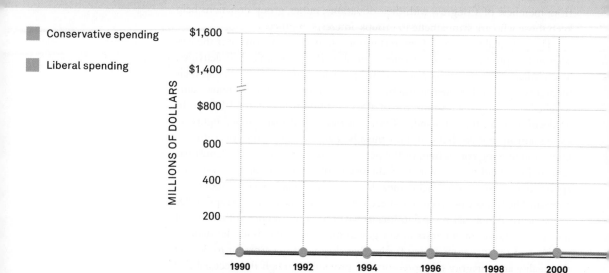

Conservative spending

Liberal spending

MILLIONS OF DOLLARS

$1,600

$1,400

$800

600

400

200

1990   1992   1994   1996   1998   2000

TIMEPLOT SOURCE: Center for Responsive Politics, "Total Outside Spending by Election Cycle, Excluding Party Committees," https://www.opensecrets.org/outsidespending/cycle_tots.php (accessed 11/5/20).

This flood was evident during the 2016 national elections, in which independent expenditures amounted to some $1.7 billion (Figure 13.3), and $2.6 billion in the 2020 elections. A significant portion of this money was raised by independent expenditure committees that the media dubbed "super PACs," which are allowed to raise unlimited amounts of money from any source—individuals, businesses, or other associations. There are some restrictions, however: super PACs must report donors to the Federal Election Commission, and they must not directly coordinate their activities with political candidates, though they are allowed to advertise for and against candidates. Super PACs differ in their tax status, as well; they are treated as nonprofit entities under section 501(c)4 of the federal tax code. In the 2020 election campaign, most super PAC money was spent on negative advertising, but a substantial amount also went to get-out-the-vote activities.

Campaign Activism. Financial support is not the only way in which organized groups seek influence through the electoral process. Sometimes activism can be even more important than campaign contributions.

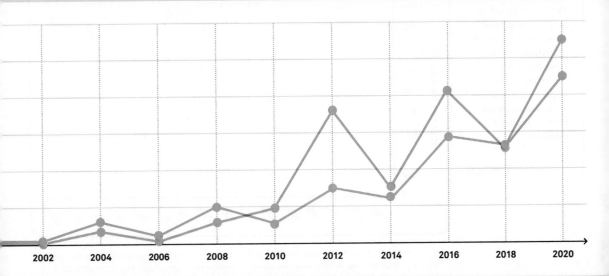

2002   2004   2006   2008   2010   2012   2014   2016   2018   2020

Perhaps the most notable instance of such activism occurs on behalf of Democratic Party candidates through labor unions, which regularly hold massive get-out-the-vote drives. The largest such activities come from the Service Employees International Union (SEIU), which represents workers ranging from hotel and restaurant workers to clerical staff, and the United Auto Workers (UAW). Other sorts of groups routinely line up behind the Democratic and Republican campaigns. The NRA, for example, spent $23 million in the 2020 election cycle, and all of that money was either in support of Republicans or against Democrats.

The cumulative effect of such independent campaign activism is difficult to judge. One important research initiative seeks to measure the marginal effectiveness of campaign contact. Political scientists Alan Gerber and Donald Green have developed a program of field experiments in which campaigns agree to randomly assign direct campaign activity to some neighborhoods but not others. The researchers have been able to measure the effect of an additional piece of mail, canvasser, or phone call on the likelihood that someone will vote, and they estimate that, in a typical election context, it costs about $40 to get an additional

ANALYZING
THE EVIDENCE

Independent campaign
expenditures on ads
advocating for the
election or defeat of
political candidates
increased significantly
in 2016 and 2020.
What might explain
this increase? What
might be the impact
of such an increase on
future campaigns and
elections?

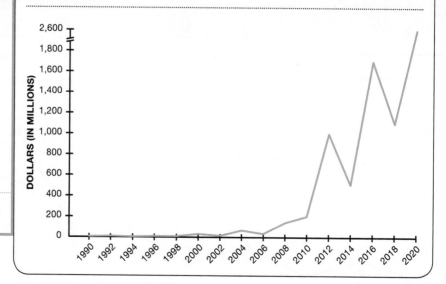

Figure 13.3

INDEPENDENT EXPENDITURES PER ELECTION CYCLE, 1990–2020

NOTE: The years 1992, 1996, 2000, 2004, 2008, 2012, 2016, and 2020 were presidential election years.
SOURCE: OpenSecrets, https://www.opensecrets.org/outsidespending/cycle_tots.php?cycle=2020 &view=Y&chart=A#viewpt (accessed 11/5/20).

voter to the polls. Gerber and Green further find that campaign activism initially can have a large impact, but after six or so attempted contacts the effects of campaign contact diminish dramatically. This research has given campaigns and reformers some sense of the effectiveness of campaign activism in stimulating turnout and possibly influencing elections. Especially in low-turnout elections, such as those for city council or state legislature, interest groups' get-out-the-vote activities can significantly affect the outcome. As other money enters the scene, especially candidates' own campaign expenditures, the effects of interest groups' direct campaign activities become muted.[47]

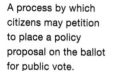

initiative

A process by which citizens may petition to place a policy proposal on the ballot for public vote.

The Initiative. Another political tactic sometimes used by interest groups is sponsorship of ballot initiatives at the state level. The **initiative** allows proposed laws to be placed on the general election ballot and submitted directly to voters, thus bypassing the state legislature and governor. Perhaps the most famous initiative was Proposition 13 in California, which placed a limit on property tax increases and forever changed the way that the state finances education.

47 Donald P. Green and Alan S. Gerber, *Get Out the Vote: How to Increase Voter Turnout,* 4th ed. (Washington DC: Brookings Institution Press, 2019).

Ironically, most initiative campaigns today are sponsored by interest groups seeking to circumvent legislative opposition to their goals. In recent years, for example, the insurance industry, trial lawyers' associations, and tobacco companies have sponsored initiative campaigns. The role of interest groups in initiative campaigns is no surprise because such campaigns can cost millions of dollars.

Are Interest Groups Effective?

Do interest groups have an effect on government and policy? A clear answer is difficult to find among the mountains of research on this question. A survey of dozens of studies of campaign contributions and legislative decision making found that in only about 1 in 10 cases was there evidence of a correlation between contributors' interests and legislators' roll-call votes.[48]

Earmarks are a good case in point. Earmarks are expenditures on particular projects in specific districts or states, and they are usually added to bills late in the legislative process to help secure enough votes for passage. Millions of dollars in earmarks are written into law every year. In a study of lobbyists' effectiveness in obtaining earmarks for college and university clients, lobbying was found to have a limited impact.[49] The more money schools spent on lobbying activities, the more earmarked funds they received; however, the magnitude of the effect depended greatly on institutional factors. A few cases showed exceedingly high returns. Schools in states with a senator on the Senate Committee on Appropriations received $18 to $29 in earmarks for every $1 spent on lobbying. Schools in congressional districts whose representative served on the House Committee on Appropriations received between $49 and $55 for every $1 spent on lobbying. Having a legislator on the relevant committee, then, explains most of the observed influence.[50]

These results suggest that institutions and politics are profoundly related. Schools without access to influential members of Congress cannot gain much from lobbying. Schools with such access still need to lobby to maximize the potential that representation on appropriations committees can give them. But if they do lobby their legislators, the potential return is substantial.

Perhaps the largest challenge to the claim that interest group politics drives American democracy arises when we consider how much political advocacy occurs on the whole. The usual argument about the influence of lobbyists and campaign contributions suggests that any dollar an organization puts toward political activity is a dollar well spent. One can turn that thinking on its head. If it is a dollar well spent, then groups should spend as much as possible on politics, and total spending should reflect the value of political action to those

---

48 Ansolabehere et al., "Why Is There So Little Money in U.S. Politics?"

49 John M. de Figueiredo and Brian S. Silverman, "Academic Earmarks and the Returns to Lobbying," *Journal of Law and Economics* 49, no. 2 (October 2006): 597–625.

50 De Figueiredo and Silverman, "Academic Earmarks and the Returns to Lobbying."

groups relative to their other investments. In other words, think of the political actions of any firm—and most organizations involved in politics are firms—as a business decision. What insight comes from that perspective?

Those engaged in lobbying provide a valued service for the firms they represent by helping shape legislation, influencing administrative decisions, and advocating in court. There are, however, other possible investments a firm can make: they may buy new machines, purchase another company, hire additional employees. How do lobbying expenditures and campaign contributions compare with those sorts of bottom-line decisions?

As a business and economic matter, the amount of money spent on political activity by firms is small. The value of goods purchased in a market is approximately equal to the amount of money someone is willing to pay for them. The total U.S. economy is valued at $21.4 trillion; government expenditures are about $4.2 trillion; corporate profits alone exceed $1.9 trillion. As a fraction of total government expenditures, total lobbying expenditures equal less than one-tenth of 1 percent, and lobbying is only a trace amount of firms' total expenses. This simple calculation suggests that the total influence of groups cannot be substantial.[51] If the returns on political investment were high, then we ought to see large firms like Microsoft, General Electric, and Walmart spending much more on politics.

Why isn't there more money in politics? Mancur Olson suggests that many groups are simply free riding on the efforts of those who do engage in lobbying. If this were true, however, those groups who did lobby would still have the opportunity to maximize their returns by spending even more money. The pluralist line of thinking suggests a more compelling answer. The United States has a wide-open political system with many points of access and influence, meaning that no one group can have much influence. There is not much money in politics because the separation of powers and other features of our political system make it exceedingly difficult to have much immediate influence over the legislative and executive branches. The pluralist argument is wrong in asserting that all interests will find expression through political organization, but it is perhaps right that a system of divided political authority, such as in the United States, still allows for the expression of many different interests and makes it very hard for particular groups to dominate the political process or even to pass a law.

CONCLUSION: INTEREST GROUP INFLUENCE IN U.S. POLITICS

The institutions of American government embrace an open and democratic process to ensure that government is responsive to the public's preferences and needs. The Bill of Rights provides for the rights of free speech, freedom of the

---

51 See Ansolabehere et al., "Why Is There So Little Money in U.S. Politics?"

press, and freedom of assembly. The nation's laws have further cemented this commitment, providing for open meetings, citizen advisory commissions, lobbying, direct contact from constituents, contributions from interested individuals and groups, an open legal system, protests, and many other routes through which individuals and groups may advocate for their interests. These institutions allow people to express intensely held preferences or interests that they can't communicate through simply voting. Through these many points of access, representatives and government officials learn how their decisions affect the public. Politics, then, becomes the arena in which many interests compete for the attention and support of government. Indeed, tens of thousands of organizations compete in the political sphere in the United States, and countless other movements and coordinated efforts of citizens rise and fall as issues come into the public arena. This is pluralism at work, and it aligns closely with the sort of politics the Founders envisioned.

But this system of government is hardly perfect. The American interest group system creates opportunities for organized, resource-rich groups to represent their interests before the government, and the policies and laws that government enacts, in turn, are often thought to favor those interests. People and organizations that can muster the financial resources or the manpower can best make their case before the legislature, before the administrative agencies of the executive, before the courts, and even before the electorate. This puts groups with latent interests at a disadvantage; they are often hampered by problems of collective action and free riding that prevent them from developing permanent organizations capable of pressuring the government. On the other hand, economic organizations, such as firms, unions, and the professional and industry organizations that represent them, usually have the least difficulty amassing such resources, and they do not face as many obstacles to organization and group maintenance as volunteer organizations do. Interest group politics in Washington, D.C., and state governments, consequently, can often reflect the interests of and conflicts among those engaged in economic activity.

Although firms, unions, and other organizations can solve the collective action problem, they do not necessarily succeed in the political arena. Unlike economic activity, politics involves power derived from the ability to vote on measures, introduce legislation or rules, or block actions from happening. Interest groups are outsiders that can do none of these things directly. Nonetheless, these organizations seek support in the appropriate institutions, such as a court with a sympathetic judge or a congressional subcommittee with a sympathetic chair. Often, groups succeed not by bringing pressure but by providing expertise to the government and by learning from those in office about the impact of new rules and regulations.

Interest group politics today does not fit stereotypical notions of political power and influence. There are as many lobbyists as ever, but the backroom dealings of the "old lobby" are an anachronism. Interest group politics spans all branches of government and involves myriad interests vying for attention in an increasingly crowded field. Competing interests may very well cancel out each other's efforts. Further, the activities of all groups constitute just one facet of legislators', judges', and executives' deliberations. Those who must ultimately make political decisions and be held accountable consider other voices as well, especially those of their constituents. Perhaps a better contemporary characterization is that the organized and disorganized interests participating in politics today are really contributing to a much broader sphere of political debate. That debate takes place inside the institutions of government—Congress, courts, executives, and elections. It also takes place in the media. That forum is the final leg of our discussion of democracy in America, and to that subject we turn in the next chapter.

For Further Reading

Alexander, Robert, ed. *The Classics of Interest Group Behavior*. New York: Wadsworth, 2005.

Ansolabehere, Stephen, John M. de Figueiredo, and James M. Snyder, Jr. "Why Is There So Little Money in U.S. Politics?" *Journal of Economic Perspectives* 17, no. 1 (2003): 105–30.

Baumgartner, Frank R., Jeffrey M. Berry, Marie Hojnacki, David C. Kimball, and Beth L. Leech. *Lobbying and Policy Change: Who Wins, Who Loses, and Why*. Chicago: University of Chicago Press, 2009.

Birnbaum, Jeffrey H. *The Lobbyists: How Influence Peddlers Work Their Way in Washington*. New York: Random House, 1993.

Esterling, Kevin M. *The Political Economy of Expertise: Information and Efficiency in American National Politics*. Ann Arbor: University of Michigan Press, 2004.

Galanter, Marc. "Why the 'Haves' Come Out Ahead: Speculations on the Limits of Legal Change." *Law and Society Review* 9, no. 1 (1974): 95–160.

Gilens, Martin. *Affluence and Influence: Economic Inequality and Political Power in America*. Princeton, NJ: Princeton University Press, 2012.

Hacker, Jacob S., and Paul Pierson. *Winner-Take-All Politics: How Washington Made the Rich Richer—And Turned Its Back on the Middle Class*. New York: Simon and Schuster, 2010.

Herrnson, Paul S., Christopher J. Deering, and Clyde Wilcox, eds. *Interest Groups Unleashed*. Washington, DC: CQ Press, 2013.

Hersh, Eitan. *Politics Is for Power: How to Move Beyond Political Hobbyism, Take Action, and Make Real Change*. New York: Simon and Schuster, 2020.

Lowi, Theodore J. *The End of Liberalism: The Second Republic of the United States*. 2nd ed. New York: Norton, 1979.

Nownes, Anthony. *Total Lobbying: What Lobbyists Want (and How They Try to Get It)*. New York: Cambridge University Press, 2006.

Olson, Mancur, Jr. *The Logic of Collective Action: Public Goods and the Theory of Groups*. 1965. Second printing with a new preface and appendix. Cambridge, MA: Harvard University Press, 1971.

Schlozman, Kay Lehman, Sidney Verba, and Henry E. Brady. *The Unheavenly Chorus: Unequal Political Voice and the Broken Promise of American Democracy*. Princeton, NJ: Princeton University Press, 2012.

Sides, John, Daron Shaw, Matt Grossmann, and Keena Lipsitz. *Campaigns and Elections*. 4th ed. New York: Norton, 2021.

Strolovitch, Dara Z. *Affirmative Advocacy: Race, Class, and Gender in Interest Group Politics*. Chicago: University of Chicago Press, 2007.

14

The Media

News first broke about mysterious cases of pneumonia in Wuhan, China, on New Year's Eve, 2019. Within days, researchers in China had identified the cause: a new, previously unidentified type of coronavirus. Within two weeks, Chinese media officially reported the country's first death from the virus. Within three weeks, the Chinese government closed Wuhan, a city of 11 million people, and Japan, South Korea, Taiwan, Thailand, and the United States reported their first cases. Although this rapid succession of events followed the trajectory of viral outbreaks in recent memory—including SARS in 2003 and H1N1 in 2009—the coronavirus pandemic coming into focus would be far worse than those pandemics. By the end of January 2020, the World Health Organization had declared a global health emergency. Just two months later, at least one million people worldwide were infected, 100,000 people had died, and the world was still in the early phase of the spread of the disease.[1] Public health officials warned of the potential loss of millions of lives within the year if the disease went unchecked.

As the pandemic unfolded early in 2020, people throughout the world took extraordinary actions to slow the spread of the virus. Though the United States and Europe ultimately shut down their economies to reduce interactions between people, individuals and organizations such as firms and churches began to change their behavior to stave off the virus long before governments took official action. They frequently washed their hands, wore face masks outside, and began social distancing, feeling that going to parties, traveling, and even voting exposed them to unacceptable health risks.[2] How did people become aware of a disease that only a small number of people had, and how did they know what to do to prevent its spread?

---

1 Derrick Bryson Taylor, "How the Coronavirus Pandemic Unfolded: A Timeline," *New York Times,* May 12, 2020, www.nytimes.com/article/coronavirus-timeline.html (accessed 5/17/20).

2 Pew Research Center, "Most Americans Say Coronavirus Outbreak Has Impacted Their Lives," March 30, 2020, www.pewsocialtrends.org/2020/03/30/most-americans-say-coronavirus-outbreak-has-impacted-their-lives (accessed 5/17/20).

Simply put, it was the media. Once the coronavirus pandemic took hold, people were hungry for information about the disease and what they could do to protect themselves. On March 10, 2020, mentions of coronavirus across all media reached almost 20 million—five times more than mentions of the president of the United States on the same day.[3] Broadcast TV news viewing almost doubled.[4] People turned to the internet to search for helpful websites. One YouTube video showing mathematical simulations of epidemics gained 3 million views in just 10 days. And people turned to social media to see what their friends had learned and to watch communications directly from public officials and other influential people.

The media are, collectively, the organizations and people who generate publicly valuable information and manage the distribution networks through which this information flows. The media consist of the reporters and journalists who investigate events and present the information we consume. They are the editors who make decisions about which stories are worth sharing and which do not merit the space or effort. They are the private firms, nonprofit organizations, and governments that maintain the channels of communication and distribution.

Crises such as the coronavirus pandemic reveal the vital importance of the media to the health of every society. The information systems and networks that bind us together are the conduits through which we learn what is happening in our world and how we can prepare for the future, not just in times of crisis but also in our day-to-day lives. So important are the media in modern politics that

LEARNING OBJECTIVES

 Describe the different types of American media and their primary objectives.

 Explain the ways in which the media inform the American electorate.

 Analyze the ways politicians, bureaucrats, organized interests, and private citizens can shape how the media portray public issues.

 Summarize the U.S. government's relationship with the media.

3   Rani Molla, "How Coronavirus Took Over Social Media," Vox, March 12, 2020, www .vox.com/recode/2020/3/12/21175570/coronavirus-covid-19-social-media-twitter-facebook-google (accessed 5/17/20).

4   Brian Steinberg, "Evening News Audiences Surge Amid Coronavirus. Can the Networks Keep Them?," Variety, April 15, 2020, https://variety.com/2020/tv/features/coronavirus-evening-news-david-muir-lester-holt-norah-odonnell-1234580594 (accessed 5/17/20).

they are often described as the "fourth branch of government," serving as a check on the powers of the legislature, the executive, and the judiciary and as a venue through which the public vets its leaders and issues facing the country.[5]

The media are a political institution, but they are not a singular institution designed to represent and govern, such as Congress or the presidency. Rather, the media are an industry that exists primarily to make money from communication and entertainment. The main business model is simple enough: using communication technologies such as the printing press and the internet, media firms develop and distribute content— news articles, TV shows, websites, and the like—to attract an audience. The audience pays for access to content by purchasing subscriptions; paying cover prices and access charges; and buying computers, televisions, and radios. More significant, other businesses, organizations, and individuals who want access to that audience will pay media firms to advertise their messages. Most media revenue derives from such advertising.[6] And the audiences are huge. Nearly every household in the United States has at least one television, and 90 percent of households have internet access or a smartphone. Television still dominates America's media consumption; the typical American adult watches five hours of television a day.[7] But, rather than replace TV, newspapers, and radio with new media, we consume more media overall and consume traditional content—including television—over new distribution networks. Today, typical American adults spend a total of 11 hours each day—most of their waking hours—interacting with media across TV, TV-connected devices, radio, computers, and mobile devices.[8]

Political coverage is an important component of media content. People are willing to pay for information about politics and public affairs, and politicians and organized interests are willing to pay to reach media audiences through advertisements or events that attract coverage. Most major media outlets offer political news coverage and analysis as a way to attract readers and listeners. The major television networks—ABC, CBS, NBC, and Fox—offer approximately six hours of news programming every day, and some media organizations are devoted exclusively to politics and public affairs. The cost of news programs to consumers is minimal, sometimes free, and the content is presented in a widely accessible manner. Thus the media offer an easy—sometimes

---

5   European cultures have long referred to the press as the Fourth Estate, after the clergy, the nobility, and the commoners. See Walter H. Annenberg, "The Fourth Branch of Government" in *Impact of Mass Media: Current Issues*, ed. Ray Eldon Hiebert and Carol Reuss (New York: Longman, 1985); Kristine A. Oswald, "Mass Media and the Transformation of American Politics," *Marquette Law Review* 77, no. 2 (1993): 385–414.

6   Pew Research Center, "State of the News Media," www.pewresearch.org/topics/state-of-the-news-media (accessed 4/20/2020).

7   Alexis C. Madrigal, "When Did TV Watching Peak?," *Atlantic*, May 30, 2018, www.theatlantic.com/technology/archive/2018/05/when-did-tv-watching-peak/561464 (accessed 5/17/20).

8   Tom Butts, "Nielsen: U.S. Adults Spend Majority of Waking Hours Interacting with Media," TV Technology, July 1, 2019, www.tvtechnology.com/news/nielsen-u-s-adults-spend-majority-of-waking-hours-interacting-with-media (accessed 5/17/20).

even entertaining—way to learn about the important actions of government, the state of the nation, and the choices in an election.

The media, then, address one of the most important problems of democracy—how to create an informed electorate. As we discussed in Chapters 10 and 11, democratic politics assumes some awareness among the electorate about who is in power, what problems the nation faces, and what actions and policies the government has taken. Most Americans learn about government and politics not through firsthand experience but from media sources, through the lenses of those who report the news or comment on issues and events. However, there is often a tension between the objectives of those in an industry that must make money and the public's interest in maintaining a healthy media.

The challenge for every democracy is how to foster the development of media that will allow for robust discourse and dissent. The United States, from its inception, has embraced the principle that a free press allows people to speak freely and to make reasoned electoral decisions. The First Amendment to the Constitution states that "Congress shall make no law . . . abridging the freedom of speech, or the press." Over time, the Supreme Court has expanded that idea to cover all forms of communication and has interpreted that restraint to apply to all levels and branches of government, not just Congress.

A free, open, and largely unregulated media environment is the engine of American democracy. It is the great marketplace of ideas. Collectively the media present a vast range of ideas, opinions, and information that any consumer may choose to watch, listen to, or read. Media outlets that do not attract consumers fail; those that offer what people want succeed. This system may not always provide the ideal outcome, but it is considered the best way to guarantee an adequately informed public.[9] The First Amendment, wrote Judge Learned Hand at the height of World War II, "presupposes that right conclusions are more likely to be gathered out of a multitude of tongues, than through any kind of authoritative selection. To many this is, and always will be, folly; but we have staked upon it our all."[10]

An alternative view holds that journalists and owners of media firms hold a privileged position in any society, and with that privilege comes responsibilities that can be ensured only through regulation. Most countries regulate political speech by limiting advertising, requiring a minimum amount of public affairs programming, and regulating what reporters may and may not say. Slander and libel laws apply to American journalists, as do restrictions owing to national security, but reporting is far less regulated in the United States than it is in just about every other country. Most other countries underwrite or own their main broadcast media outlets, such as the Canadian or British Broadcasting Corporations. In the United States, media firms succeed or fail as businesses based on their ability to attract audiences and revenue, not on whether they provide a public service or good.

---

9 This idea is most elegantly expressed in the majority opinion in the Supreme Court case *New York Times Company v. Sullivan*, 376 U.S. 254 (1964).

10 *United States v. Associated Press*, 52 F. Supp. 362, 372 (Southern Dist., N.Y., 1943).

How and how well does the marketplace of ideas work? Is there enough competition? Today, for example, very few cities are served by more than one local newspaper. Local news monopolies may give owners, editors, and journalists excessive political power in their markets. Or, perhaps there is too much competition. The internet has cut into the profit margins of traditional media, forcing newspapers as well as television and radio companies to lay off their more expensive staff—often the very reporters who produce news content. Media firms, Congress, and executive agencies (especially the Federal Communications Commission) must deal with these and other questions as new communications technologies transform the nation's media industry and the ways in which people become informed about and engage in politics.

THE MEDIA AS A POLITICAL INSTITUTION

Perhaps the most salient feature of the American media, as an industry and as a political institution, is the diversity of sources, firms, and technologies. There are thousands of newspapers, magazines, and journals. Countless websites deliver news from sources worldwide. These media reach every community in the United States and provide information in every language.

Types of Media

However, there is some order to the apparent chaos. American media are organized into three categories: print, broadcast, and digital. There is intense competition among these media for audience and advertising revenue. Newspapers were the main sources of information in the late nineteenth and early twentieth centuries, and the advent of radio in the 1920s and then television in the 1950s gave audiences new ways to access news. The internet and digital media have created entirely new information platforms that compete with newspapers, radio, and television for the same advertising dollars. Today, Americans get their news from a mix of all of these media (Figure 14.1). The Digital News Report published by the Reuters Institute for the Study of Journalism tracks news innovations and audiences throughout the world. When Americans surveyed for the report were asked to identify the first way they typically come across news in the morning, a third said television, but almost 40 percent now report that they encounter news first through social media. Only 6 percent rely on a traditional newspaper as their first source of news, and 10 percent turn to radio first.[11]

---

11 Nic Newman, Richard Fletcher, Antonis Kalogeropoulos, and Rasmus Kleis Nielsen, "Reuters Institute Digital News Report 2019," University of Oxford, Reuters Institute for the Study of Journalism, 2019, https://reutersinstitute.politics.ox.ac.uk/sites/default/files/2019-06/DNR_2019_FINAL_0.pdf (accessed 5/17/20).

Figure 14.1
AMERICANS' MAIN SOURCES FOR NEWS, 2019

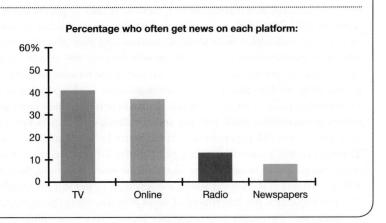

Percentage who often get news on each platform:

SOURCE: Pew Research Center, www.pewresearch.org/fact-tank/2017/09/07/americans-online-news-use-vs-tv-news-use; www.journalism.org/2019/03/26/nearly-as-many-americans-prefer-to-get-their-local-news-online-as-prefer-the-tv-set (accessed 5/20/20).

There are also synergies among media. Digital platforms, for example, have opened up new distribution networks for traditional newspapers. Because newspapers used to rely on sales of printed copies, the reach of a newspaper was limited to the city in which it was published and to its physical distribution networks—trucks, newsstands, house-to-house paper routes, and the "news boys" who would hawk papers on street corners. Today, half of all people who read newspapers use the print versions, and half are either primarily online readers or read a mix of content online and in print.[12] One of the most important innovations in the digital space has been the creation of news apps, messaging apps, and aggregators, which collect news items from across traditional media outlets and facilitate sharing stories on social media. Of those who rely primarily on their smartphones for news, 20 percent use news websites or apps, 11 percent use aggregators, and 43 percent receive news through social media. Much of the content on aggregator sites is high-quality reporting generated by traditional sources of news, such as newspapers, wire services (such as the Associated Press), and broadcast sources—not just clickbait. In fact, recent studies show that aggregators drive readership to higher-quality journalism.[13]

12 American Press Institute, "Print vs. Digital Subscribers: Demographic Differences and Paths to Subscription," May 2, 2017, www.americanpressinstitute.org/publications/reports/survey-research/print-vs-digital (accessed 5/17/20).

13 Chris Fleisher, "Is Google Hurting Quality Online Journalism?," American Economic Association, November 11, 2016, www.aeaweb.org/research/newspaper-aggregator-quality-impact (accessed 5/17/20).

Print Media. The Bill of Rights guarantees freedom of the press. At the time the U.S. constitution was written, "the press" consisted only of printed pamphlets and weekly papers. The circulation of these early newspapers was not nearly as universal as it is today; in fact, there were only 96 papers in the United States in 1792. Nonetheless, the papers were the primary means of circulating news at the time—apart from word of mouth—and were generally much more reliable than other sources.[14] The early press in America was essential to political discourse in the young nation. Over the course of the nineteenth century, newspapers came to dominate political communication as the population became more literate, political engagement and demand for information grew, and technological innovations made printing and circulating newspapers very inexpensive. There were 861 papers in the United States by 1828 and 1,800 by 1945.[15] Throughout the twentieth century, print media lost their central position in American society as broadcast and digital media emerged. Today, there are only 400 newspapers in the United States, and less than 10 percent of Americans say that a newspaper is the first source of news they consult in the morning.

Even so, newspapers and magazines remain important sources of news. As we see later in this chapter, the broadcast and digital media rely on leading print outlets to set their news agendas. Though national newspapers, such as the *New York Times*, the *Wall Street Journal,* and the *Washington Post*, and magazines, such as the *Economist* and *Time,* have relatively small circulations, they have large staffs of investigative journalists and are read by politically influential Americans who count on them for news and analysis. Periodicals based in Washington, D.C., such as *Congressional Quarterly*, *National Journal*, the *Hill*, and *Roll Call*, are important sources of political news for Washington insiders, including members of Congress, congressional staffers, and lobbyists. The print media may have a smaller audience than their cousins in broadcasting, but they have an audience that matters.

The broadcast media do very little actual reporting; they primarily cover stories that have been initially reported by the print media. One can almost say that if an event is not covered in the *New York Times*, it is unlikely to appear on the *CBS Evening News*. An important exception is breaking news; broadcast media can carry live coverage as news unfolds or soon after, whereas print media must catch up later. Increasingly, though, because news can be distributed more or less immediately over the internet, the print media are becoming just as effective as broadcasters at breaking news.

Today, however, the newspaper industry is in serious economic trouble. Online competition has dramatically reduced newspapers' revenues from traditional advertising, such as retail, help wanted, and personal ads. Newspaper advertising revenue declined from $50 billion in 2006 to less than $20 billion in

---

14 Ronald P. Formisano, *For the People: American Populist Movements from the Revolution to the 1850s* (Chapel Hill: University of North Carolina Press, 2008), p. 211.

15 Elaine C. Kamarck and Ashley Gabriele, "The News Today: 7 Trends in Old and New Media," Center for Effective Management at Brookings, November 2015, www.brookings.edu/wp-content/uploads/2016/07/new-media.pdf (accessed 5/17/20).

2017—a drop of over 50 percent.[16] Facing serious financial difficulties, some papers have closed (such as the *Rocky Mountain News* in Denver) or have discontinued their print editions (such as the *Seattle Post-Intelligencer*). Closures of major newspapers have left many large cities and metropolitan areas with only one or possibly no daily print newspapers. And in 2013, the Graham family, which had owned the *Washington Post* for three generations, surprised the industry by announcing the sale of the paper to Jeffrey Bezos, founder and CEO of Amazon.com.

All of these changes signal a wider shift in the structure of print media, but how this transformation will resolve itself is still unknown. For decades, print media have been laying off reporters and losing money and readers. If that trend continues, the country will have few or no print newspapers—the traditional "press"—in the future. It's not certain whether newspapers can somehow reverse course and whether online outlets, such as social media, blogs, or mobile news apps, can adequately replace print newspapers, especially in providing news about local politics and public affairs. So far, newspapers' lost revenues from print advertising have far surpassed the gains they've made in online advertising.[17]

The exception to this trend appears to be the *Washington Post*. In the three years after Bezos took over, from 2017 to 2020, the *Post* has experienced a boom in readership and revenues; it has hired 140 new reporters in three years, and it has become a potential model for how newspapers and traditional reporting can survive and succeed. Bezos offered the following advice to the industry based on his experience at Amazon and the *Post*: (1) "Focus on readers first, not advertisers"; (2) "You can't shrink yourself to relevance"; (3) "Don't look for a patron or charity"; (4) "Use technology, but don't be a slave to it"; and (5) "Advertising alone will not support investigative journalism." "When you are writing," Bezos concluded, "be riveting, be right, and ask people to pay. They will pay." If there is a lesson to be taken from the experience of the *Washington Post*, it might be that the newspaper industry lost sight of its central mission as it pursued the model of free content supported by lots of advertising, becoming more dependent on and driven by advertisers in the process. Whether Bezos's approach to running the *Post* can be replicated in other papers remains to be seen. However, the turnaround of the *Post* does reveal that the newspaper industry is not doomed, but it must adapt to survive.[18]

The possible demise of major city newspapers raises important concerns. Since the beginning of the Republic, newspapers have been ingrained in the

16 Michael Barthel, "Newspapers Fact Sheet," Pew Research Center, June 1, 2019, www.journalism.org/fact-sheet/newspapers (accessed 5/17/20).

17 24/7 Wall Street, "The 10 Most Endangered Newspapers in America," *Time*, March 9, 2009, http://content.time.com/time/business/article/0,8599,1883785,00.html (accessed 5/17/20). See also Barthel, "Newspapers Fact Sheet."

18 Matt Rosoff, "Jeff Bezos Has Advice for the News Business: 'Ask People to Pay. They Will Pay,'" CNBC, June 21, 2017, www.cnbc.com/video/2017/06/22/jeff-bezos-has-advice-for-the-news-business-ask-people-to-pay-they-will-pay.html (accessed 5/8/20).

way we think about political communication. The First Amendment specifically protects a "free press," and legal doctrines and laws in the United States have evolved around the idea that a robust press exists to serve every community. As cities now face the prospect of having no significant press in the conventional sense, laws governing many aspects of political communication in this country will likely be revisited—from campaign finance laws to obscenity standards to ownership guidelines. So far, the U.S. Supreme Court has not extended the same set of free press protections to broadcasters as it has to print journalists.[19] However, the tremendous changes in the media over the past decade may lead the Court to rethink the First Amendment protections afforded to providers of online content. The case of *Citizens United,* one of the most sensational campaign finance cases decided by the Supreme Court in recent years, turned on the fact that the lines between print and broadcast are blurred by online distribution of content. One can just as easily download a book online as view an advertisement, so one might argue that any restrictions on online advertisers would apply to book distributors as well.[20]

This transformation of print media may change the extent to which people are informed about politics. The media that replace newspapers may raise the public's overall level of information or may segment the audience further, reducing the number of people who are aware of public affairs.

Social science research suggests that the decline of newspapers is changing our news-gathering behavior. Rather than rely on a single source—the daily paper—Americans now sample many sources, a practice known as "grazing." It is common to read U.S. newspapers that contain relatively little reporting by the paper's own journalists on national politics; rather, newspaper content often consists of articles from the Associated Press, Reuters, the *New York Times,* and the *Washington Post* that have been printed under a licensing agreement.[21]

Broadcast Media. Television news reaches more Americans than any other news source. Tens of millions of individuals watch national and local news programs every day. In one recent survey, 41 percent of respondents reported that TV news was their most important source of news in 2019; 37 percent listed digital media (websites and social media), 13 percent said newspapers, and 8 percent said radio.[22] Even in the era of digital news, the most frequented sources of news online are the websites of ABC, CBS, NBC, CNN, and Fox News. Television news, however, covers relatively few topics and provides little

---

19 *Red Lion Broadcasting Company v. Federal Communications Commission,* 395 U.S. 367 (1969).

20 Michael W. McConnell, "Reconsidering *Citizens United* as a Press Clause Case," *Yale Law Journal* 123, no. 2 (2013): 412–458.

21 Pew Research Center, "Key News Audiences Now Blend Online and Traditional Sources," August 17, 2008, www.people-press.org/2008/08/17/key-news-audiences-now-blend-online-and-traditional-sources (accessed 5/17/20).

22 A.W. Geiger, "Key Findings About the Online News Landscape in America," Pew Research Center, September 11, 2019, www.pewresearch.org/fact-tank/2019/09/11/key-findings-about-the-online-news-landscape-in-america (accessed 5/17/20).

depth of coverage. More like a series of newspaper headlines connected to pictures, television news alerts viewers to issues and events but provides little else.

The 24-hour news stations such as CNN offer more detail and commentary than the networks' evening news shows. Cable news outlets grabbed some of their largest audiences ever with coverage of the invasions of Iraq in 1991 and 2003. At the start of these conflicts, CNN, Fox News, and MSNBC provided 24-hour coverage, including video of bombs targeting Iraqi government buildings and military installations, on-the-scene reporting by American journalists embedded in Iraq, expert commentary, and interviews with government officials. Normally, such networks offer a steady stream of headlines and commentary. But during wars, floods, earthquakes, and other disasters, the cable news networks are on the spot with continuous coverage.

Radio news is essentially a headline service without pictures. Usually devoting five minutes per hour to news, radio stations announce the day's major events with little detail. News stations such as WTOP (Washington, D.C.) and WCBS (New York City) generally repeat the same stories each hour to present them to new listeners. Recently, radio talk shows have become important sources of commentary and opinion. Numerous conservative radio hosts, such as Rush Limbaugh, have huge audiences and have helped mobilize support for conservative political causes and candidates. Liberals have had less success in talk radio and complain that biased radio coverage has hurt them in elections. Increasingly, people are accessing radio programs, including political news, in podcast form. From 2008 to 2016, the percentage of adults in the United States who said they had listened to a podcast in the past month grew from 8 percent to 22 percent.[23]

In recent years, much news content, especially local news, has shifted away from politics toward "soft news," focusing on celebrities, health tips, consumer advice, and other topics more likely to entertain than enlighten. Even a lot of political coverage is soft. For example, articles about the Obamas' new dog outnumbered stories about the Iraq War by three to two during April 2009.[24] Another category of programming, sometimes called *infotainment*, purports to combine information with entertainment. *The Daily Show with Trevor Noah* on Comedy Central calls itself America's "most trusted name in fake news," yet many people under age 35 consider it to be one of their main sources of political information and news. The news on *The Daily Show* offers a comedic twist on current events and on the media itself, especially CNN and Fox News.

Technology and the regulations applied to that technology have historically defined the organization and distribution of broadcast media. Originally, radio and television content was broadcast through radio wave signals projected from massive towers. The strength of a signal determined how far the broadcast would reach, and the frequency of the waves determined where on the radio or television dial the signal could be received. When radio broadcasts began in

23 Pew Research Center, "State of the News Media 2016," June 15, 2016, www.journalism .org/2016/06/15/state-of-the-news-media-2016 (accessed 5/17/20).

24 Tricia Sartor, "The Dog Days of Spring," Pew Research Center, April 22, 2009, www .journalism.org/numbers/thedogdaysofspring (accessed 5/17/20).

the 1920s, there was no regulation of signals, and it was chaos. Broadcasters would change their frequencies and increase their signal strength to drown out others. The federal government soon intervened. The spectrum of frequencies, the government determined, was a scarce commodity; there could not be an unlimited number of broadcasters and stations. The Communications Act of 1934 required every broadcast outlet to obtain a license establishing its right to broadcast at a given frequency and with a maximum strength.

This system defined broadcasting up until the emergence of digital transmission via the internet in the 1990s, which eliminated the spectrum scarcity that had limited the number of radio and television stations. Nonetheless, it has had a lasting effect on broadcast media. The Federal Communications Commission (FCC) restricted the number of television stations in every city. Most cities had only three television stations, though some had as many as seven, and those stations were the main vehicles through which people got their broadcast television news. The reach of these stations' signals defined each city's *media market*, or the cluster of counties in which a majority of households watched the city's TV stations. The map of the United States was divided into 200 or so such markets, from the largest in New York City and Los Angeles to the smallest in Glendive, Montana. These broadcasting areas also defined the audiences that advertisers could reach using radio and television. Typically, these markets were much larger than the populations that advertisers could reach through local newspapers. Radio advertising was made even more lucrative by the fact that, when radio emerged in the 1920s, the print media experienced a significant contraction in readership.

Broadcasting is further organized by networks of stations. ABC, CBS, NBC, and Fox are national organizations that provide branding, content, and advertising support to local stations in exchange for access to their media markets. An individual broadcaster will both hold a license for a station in a market and agree to belong to a national network. That individual broadcaster—the "local affiliate" of the network—carries the network's national news and other programming on its local station. Some stations operate as independent entities, but the television stations that most people watch are affiliated with networks. Networks have proven to be very successful, and they have defined the character and content of television in the United States.

Even though the networks have made broadcasting more resilient than newspapers to the changing media environment, they too are seeing declining audiences and advertising revenue as digital technology and media have grown.[25]

Digital Media. The digital media sector has exploded over the first two decades of the twenty-first century. In 2000, only a small percentage of people got their news online. Today, online sources rival TV broadcasts as the main way that Americans get their news.

The digital media sector centers around the internet, devices connected by the internet (such as smartphones), and media platforms made possible by the

---

25 Geiger, "Key Findings About the Online News Landscape in America."

internet (such as Facebook, YouTube, and other social media channels). The internet itself was initially conceived in the 1960s as a means of communication among scientists and researchers, but its commercial value wasn't realized until the mid-1990s. As computing power and data storage capacity improved, it became possible to share video and images online. The major computing firms in the world, working with academic institutions, organized an open system with a common set of standards for websites, such as protocols for website names. This organization was called the World Wide Web consortium, which is recognizable as the first three letters in the nomenclature of most websites today: *www*. This initial platform, the standards guiding it, and the creation of a licensing system for websites provided the foundation for the digital information revolution that we are living through today.

In many ways, the internet as a news medium parallels newspapers, television, radio, and magazines. As is the case with these other media, the pursuit of advertising revenue drives the business models of most digital media. Websites, however, can support many new, diverse types of advertising. On television, 30-second ad spots are a staple; classified ads were the bread and butter of newspapers. Advertisers who want to reach audiences though digital media, meanwhile, have a number of options: they can deploy video ads (which play before or while a user views a web page), display ads (such as banner ads, landing pages, and pop-up ads), search engine marketing and optimization (in which the advertiser pays to promote a website in search engine results), social media ads (including influencers), native advertising (ads that take the form of a web page's original content), pay-per-click advertising (in which the advertiser pays the website that hosts the ad any time the ad is clicked), remarketing (which uses cookies to show ads based on an internet user's previous online activity), and affiliated advertising (product placements on blogs and other sites). Like television and radio networks, search and social media platforms such as Google and Facebook present a large advertising marketplace. They enable users to search out and find the content they want, and in return they earn revenue on most transactions.

The political news and information on the internet parallels the content peddled by traditional media in important respects. Indeed, many of the main newspapers and television outlets—such as the *Wall Street Journal* and the *New York Times*, Reuters and the Associated Press, CNN and Fox News—are also mainstays of digital media. All of these platforms offer news and stories on their websites that duplicate or complement the content they provide via traditional media. Even so, the internet has revolutionized how content is provided and what content is accessible to audiences. Digital media combine the depth of newspaper reporting with the timeliness of television and radio, but they also allow for a breadth and diversity of coverage that traditional media simply can't match. Look at the website of any traditional media outlet, such as the *New York Times* or CNN. There you will see content reproduced from the print newspaper or TV headlines, but you'll also see streaming video that resembles television reporting, audio and podcasts similar to radio programs, animations like those that circulate on social media, and commentary from sources like those found in opinion or newsmagazines.

Unlike a newspaper, which is wholly new every day, a website can keep important stories up for many days. Most news websites contain easily searchable archives and also function as aggregators, accumulating news on a given topic from many different sources. Perhaps the most powerful aggregator is Google, whose news service accumulates information from organizations as different as the *Wall Street Journal* and Al Jazeera, Reuters and the Associated Press, and the Lebanese *Daily Star* and *Shanghai Daily*. In addition to traditional news sites, more specialized sites for online news have emerged, including BuzzFeed, Politico, and HuffPost. These frequently visited sites offer a wide range of content, including reporting, commentary, and analysis. Some sites are characterized by more focused content. *Slate*, for instance, specializes in commentary, and *Cook Political Report* offers analytics.

Social media have also transformed the ways in which people access, distribute, and even provide news online. Internet users frequently share information person to person via social media channels. Facebook is a good example of how social media are changing the distribution of information: half of all people who say that they receive news online report that they read news posted by others on Facebook.[26] Young people are more likely than older people to get news online and through social media. (Analyzing the Evidence on pp. 618–19 explores where Americans get news about politics.) Campaigns, public officials, and government agencies use Facebook, Twitter, and other outlets to communicate information to the public without relying on intermediaries such as newspapers, radio programs, or television programs. For example, social media have become a staple among police departments. A survey conducted by the International Association of Chiefs of Police found that 96 percent of law enforcement agencies in the United States use social media in some capacity, often for crime investigations (86 percent of departments) and to improve police-community relations (73 percent of departments).[27]

The internet differs from traditional outlets in another important way: it enables people to get involved and produce news directly. Twitter is a good example of how social media have altered how news information is generated and even the form and format of the news. On Twitter, those who are experiencing an event can provide their own reactions and reports in real time, without the editorial filters of television, radio, and newspapers. Individual citizens now can help create the news and interpret it. Most news sites allow readers to comment on stories and videos, and engaged users may offer their opinions or share links to their own photos, videos, blogs, and social media pages. Individuals at the scene of a natural disaster or key political event can provide coverage of a story more quickly (and sometimes even better) than reporters can.

---

26 Jeffrey Gottfried and Elisa Shearer, "News Use across Social Media Platforms 2016," Pew Research Center, May 26, 2016, http://assets.pewresearch.org/wp-content/uploads/sites/13/2016/05/PJ_2016.05.26_social-media-and-news_FINAL-1.pdf (accessed 5/17/20).

27 International Association of Chiefs of Police, "2013 Social Media Survey Results," www.berkeleyside.com/wp-content/uploads/2014/02/2013SurveyResults.pdf (accessed 5/8/20).

The ability to connect with others through the internet—whether through email, blogs, Facebook, Twitter, or other social media platforms—makes digital media a two-way street. Traditional media firms can distribute information, citizens can contribute to journalism, and people can also connect with one another directly. The power of these new media is not lost on political organizers and campaigns. Entrepreneurs within social movements and the political parties have organized online groups to raise money, communicate their positions through email and letter campaigns, and provide support for politicians who advocate for their views. Consider MoveOn.org, founded by two liberal Silicon Valley entrepreneurs. MoveOn builds electronic advocacy groups; members propose political issues and strategies, and then MoveOn facilitates action on behalf of petitions that appear to have the greatest member support. In 2016, the Republican Party began to build ActBlue, its response to MoveOn and other social networks on the left. In the run-up to the 2020 election, political activists on the left and the right universally agreed that the Republicans were far more sophisticated in their use of digital media and had developed a massive campaign advantage because of their mastery of new technologies and platforms.[28]

Why Digital Is Winning

Digital media are clearly winning the competition for audience attention. Americans increasingly rely on digital sources and devices to get their information, and over the past 10 years digital media have overtaken both print and broadcasting as the primary way that people get information. The shift is generational as well as temporal. As mentioned earlier, according to the Reuters Institute's Digital News Report, 57 percent of people under age 24 have their first contact with the news each day through social media, but people over age 35 first get their news directly from newspapers or broadcast media. That phenomenon is not limited to the United States; it is occurring throughout Europe as well.[29]

Digital media's potential scale and reach give them a significant advantage over print and broadcasting. To understand this advantage, consider a newspaper in a city of 100,000 people. It earns revenue by selling advertisements to local merchants, classified ads, and subscriptions. The scale of the newspaper is limited by the size of the city. It cannot reduce its costs of production substantially, because it needs a certain number of reporters covering a variety of stories in order to attract enough readers. Now suppose that a news website offers a classified ad service and sells banner ads to merchants, and this website

28 Thomas B. Edsall, "Trump's Digital Advantage is Freaking Out Democratic Strategists," *New York Times*, January 29, 2020, www.nytimes.com/2020/01/29/opinion/trump-digital-campaign-2020.html (5/17/20).

29 Antonis Kalogeropoulos, "How Younger Generations Consume News Differently," in Newman, Fletcher, Kalogeropoulos, and Nielsen, "Reuters Institute Digital News Report 2019," pp. 55-57.

Where Do Americans Get News about Politics?

Contributed by
Rasmus Kleis Nielsen
University of Oxford

Most of political life is distant from our own personal experience and social circles. Thus when we know something about a recent international summit, a deal made in Congress, or a war abroad, it is usually because someone covered it as news.

How people get news, however, is changing and varies across generations. Throughout the twentieth century, news media were Americans' number one source of information about politics. Traditionally, newspapers have produced the most detailed and extensive coverage, and television has reached the widest audiences and was for several decades the most important source of news for many.

The development and spread of digital media from the 1990s onward have changed the news media landscape. Newspapers have seen declining readership, make less money, and therefore invest less in news production. Television audiences have been more stable but are increasingly made up of older people. Younger people increasingly get news online.

By 2015, 85 percent of all Americans used the internet and 64 percent had a smartphone.[1] Among people who are online, digital media have now overtaken television as the most important sources of news. In 2015, 43 percent of American internet users named digital sources as their most important sources of news, compared to 40 percent who named television and 5 percent who named printed newspapers.

Main Source of News by Age

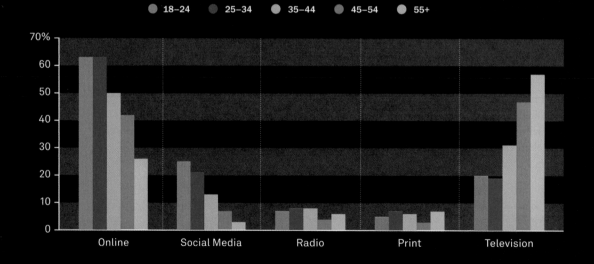

● 18–24   ● 25–34   ● 35–44   ● 45–54   ● 55+

1 Pew Research Center, www.pewinternet.org/2015/04/01/us-smartphone-use-in-2015 (accessed 7/12/20).

There are clear generational differences in how people get news. Older Americans rely far more on traditional media, such as television, than do younger people, who mostly get news online. For some people, getting news online is about going directly to the websites and apps of news organizations, whether newspapers like the *New York Times*, broadcasters like NBC, or digital-only news sites like HuffPost. But for many, online news is increasingly accessed via digital intermediaries like search engines, messaging apps, and social media. In 2015, 11 percent of American internet users named social media their main sources of news.

Relative Importance of News: Twitter and Facebook Compared

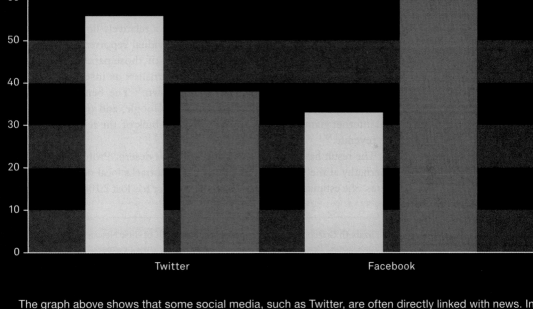

The graph above shows that some social media, such as Twitter, are often directly linked with news. In contrast, people mostly visit Facebook for other reasons but often stumble upon news when on the site. A changing media environment has sometimes been associated with the rise of selective exposure, where people seek out information that reflects their existing views. However, the rise of widely used social media like Facebook seems to be associated with a resurgence in incidental exposure, where people come across news unintentionally.

SOURCE: Nic Newman, Rasmus Kleis Nielsen, and David Levy, "Reuters Institute Digital News Report 2015," University of

can target not only people in the city but also residents of neighboring communities, even other nearby cities. The newspaper will lose advertisers because it cannot compete with the reach of the website. Social media firms are even more compelling because they can target very specific audiences, allowing merchants and other advertisers to reach their most likely customers. Newspapers simply cannot compete for advertising dollars against internet and social media firms. Since 2008, newsrooms have shed half of their employees.[30]

Broadcasters also struggle to earn sufficient advertising revenue to maintain their traditional levels of news production staff. The dynamic is the same. Media markets define the audiences of local TV and radio broadcasters and their stations and consequently limit the stations' advertising reach. The flexible scope of digital media give them marketing advantages over print and broadcast media: digital advertising can be broader because any one outlet has the potential to reach audiences far wider than a city or a cluster of counties (a broadcast media market), yet it can also be narrower in the sense that it can be more narrowly tailored to particular types of consumers.

New digital forms of advertising feed back into the organization and generation of the news. The compensation of journalists increasingly depends on advertising revenue generated by clicks on stories and ads.[31] This, of course, widens the advantage for news companies with large audiences and further weakens smaller papers and networks. A journalist working in a small or midsize city will almost always have a relatively limited online audience. As the revenue generated by any individual reporter in smaller news markets shrinks, so too does the profitability of those papers. Between 2008 and 2018, America lost a quarter of its journalists as insufficient advertising revenue forced small papers to shut down.[32] The beneficiaries of this shift to digital media have been Facebook, Google, and other social media and internet giants who appear to receive the bulk of the redirected advertising revenue.[33]

The result has been the emergence of news deserts. Professor Penny Muse Abernathy at the University of North Carolina tracks local news in the United States. She estimates that since 2004, the country has lost 2,100 newspapers, and

30 Elizabeth Grieco, "U.S. Newspapers Have Shed Half of their Newsroom Employees Since 2008," Pew Research Center, April 20, 2020, www.pewresearch.org/fact-tank/2020/04/20/u-s-newsroom-employment-has-dropped-by-a-quarter-since-2008 (accessed 5/17/20).

31 Jack Murtha, "What It's Like To Get Paid For Clicks," *Columbia Journalism Review,* July 13, 2015, www.cjr.org/analysis/the_mission_sounds_simple_pay.php (accessed 5/17/20).

32 Jonathan O'Connell, "Ghost Papers and News Deserts: Will America Ever Get its Local News Back?," *Washington Post,* December 26, 2019, www.washingtonpost.com/business/economy/ghost-papers-and-news-deserts-will-america-ever-get-its-local-news-back/2019/12/25/2f57c7d4-1ddd-11ea-9ddd-3e0321c180e7_story.html (accessed 5/17/20).

33 Alexis C. Madrigal, "The Huge Trend That Realigned the Media Industry Is Over," *Atlantic,* June 13, 2019, www.theatlantic.com/technology/archive/2019/06/massive-trend-drove-digital-media-over/591520 (accessed 5/17/20).

that another 1,000 newspapers are barely surviving.[34] News deserts are areas of the country in which no general news publications exist. There are 1,300 news deserts in the United States. Of the 3,143 U.S. counties, more than 2,000 no longer have a daily newspaper, and 171 counties, with 3.2 million residents, have no newspaper at all.[35] These counties tend to have higher poverty rates than the rest of the country, lower college graduation rates, lower median household incomes, and below-average rates of broadband internet access. They are rural counties and vote two to one for Republicans over Democrats.[36] Most of the 500 local or digital sites that have been established over the past decade are in metropolitan areas, and they do not serve the people in areas with few or no news outlets.[37]

Digital advertising is creating a second sort of problem: clickbait. Online media outlets often rely on outrageous and sensational content to attract readers' attention. The problem is that a lot of it isn't true or genuine journalism. Many posts look like real news stories but are in fact promotional videos for products or, worse, completely fictional stories. Conspiracy theories and other fake news have spread like viruses throughout the internet. And, like viruses, they are very difficult to prevent, contain, and cure.

While it is unknown how much fake news there is online, one study found that most of the "news" being shared on Twitter was probably fake. The Oxford Internet Institute identified all valid Twitter accounts belonging to individuals in the state of Michigan during the month leading up to the 2016 election. The number one source of all "news" stories that were retweeted was Russia Today, a Russian news outlet that is notorious for carrying fake or distorted stories. Russia Today stories, on the whole, were retweeted more times than stories from American news outlets such as Fox News, CBS, and the *New York Times*.[38] Efforts to drive traffic through fictitious or scandalous stories have proved very effective in terms of generating advertising revenue, but the prevalence of this content has had a very damaging effect on the public's trust in the news. Facebook, Google, and other digital media platforms have expressed concern about fake news, but they have done very little to regulate the truthfulness of their content.

34 O'Connell, "Ghost Papers and News Deserts."

35 Penelope Muse Abernathy, "Do You Live in a News Desert?," The Expanding News Desert, University of North Carolina Hussman School of Journalism and Media, www.usnewsdeserts.com (accessed 5/17/20).

36 The Editors, "Life In a News Desert," *Columbia Journalism Review*, Winter 2019, www.cjr.org/special_report/life-in-a-news-desert.php (accessed 5/17/20).

37 Penelope Muse Abernathy, "Who Is Trying to Fill the Void?," The Expanding News Desert, University of North Carolina Hussman School of Journalism and Media, www.usnewsdeserts.com/#1536249135878-b33b4a07-12c1 (accessed 5/17/20).

38 Greg Gordon and David Goldstein, "Twitter Study Shows Pro-Trump Tweets Swamped Clinton's in Michigan," McClatchy DC, March 26, 2017, www.mcclatchydc.com/news/nation-world/national/article140690083.html (accessed 5/27/20).

WHAT AFFECTS NEWS COVERAGE?

Because of the important role the media can play in national politics, it is essential to understand the factors that affect media coverage.[39] How do the media decide which issues and topics to cover? What explains the character of coverage? Why does a politician receive good or bad press? What factors affect how the media interpret, or spin, a particular story? Although many minor factors play a role, there are three major ones: (1) journalists and producers of the news, (2) politicians and other sources of the news, and (3) consumers.

Journalists

The people who produce the news shape its character. Although a strong norm of objectivity pervades the professional field of journalism, it is impossible to expect that reporters, editors, and media owners will always set aside their personal perspectives, interests, and biases. What motivates those who produce the news, and how do their beliefs and interests shape what we see and hear?

The marketplace of ideas sets out a single objective for owners of media organizations: making a profit. Owners seek to maintain a successful business, and if their personal political beliefs endanger that business, then they will be pushed aside by their newspaper or broadcasting station's internal organization. This has not always been the case. At one time, newspaper publishers exercised considerable influence over their papers' content. Publishers such as William Randolph Hearst and Joseph Pulitzer became political powers through their manipulation of news coverage. Hearst, for example, almost single-handedly pushed the United States into war with Spain in 1898 through his papers' relentless coverage of Spain's alleged brutality in its efforts to suppress a rebellion in Cuba, then a Spanish colony. The sinking of the American battleship *Maine* in Havana Harbor under mysterious circumstances gave Hearst the ammunition he needed to force a reluctant President William McKinley to lead the nation into war. Few publishers have that kind of power today, though some continue to impose their interests on the news. Overall, the business end dominates the papers' editorial content.

Today, individual reporters and editors have far more authority than publishers do over what is presented in the news. They also pursue their own interests and professional objectives, including considerations of ratings, career success, professional prestige, and political influence. These goals ultimately influence which stories and issues they deem newsworthy.

---

39 See the discussions in Michael Parenti, *Inventing Reality: The Politics of the Mass Media* (New York: St. Martin's Press, 1986); Herbert J. Gans, *Deciding What's News: A Study of* CBS Evening News, NBC Nightly News, Newsweek, *and* Time (New York: Random House, 1979); and W. Lance Bennett, *News: The Politics of Illusion*, 5th ed. (New York: Longman, 2002).

For all these reasons, journalists seek not only to report the news but also to interpret it. Those who cover the news for national media generally have considerable discretion to interject their own views when reporting stories. For example, some reporters' personal friendships with and respect for Franklin Delano Roosevelt and John F. Kennedy helped generate favorable news coverage for those presidents. In contrast, many journalists evinced their disdain for Ronald Reagan by reporting stories suggesting that he was often asleep or inattentive when important decisions were made.

Do Journalists Bias the News? From the perspective of the marketplace of ideas, perhaps most troubling is the possibility that journalism is biased heavily in favor of one party or one set of ideals. Surveys of major media outlets have repeatedly found that those who produce the news are overwhelmingly liberal and Democratic, and Democrats and liberals outnumber Republicans and conservatives by about two to one among journalists. One survey found that 28 percent of journalists (across all media) identify as Democrats, 7 percent identify as Republicans, and 50 percent say that they do not identify with any party. The remaining 15 percent identify with another party.[40]

Do journalists' political orientations color the news? A classic study by CBS and the *New York Times* in the 1980s suggested little evidence of political favoritism or bias.[41] Subsequent studies by the Pew Project for Excellence in Journalism echo that conclusion. Comparing press coverage of the first 100 days of the administrations of presidents Bill Clinton and George W. Bush, the Pew Project found nearly identical patterns of reporting: about half of printed stories were neutral toward the new presidents, a quarter were positive, and a quarter were negative. Barack Obama, however, received a much different welcome from the press. Using the same methodology, the Pew Project found that Obama's coverage was considerably more positive. He received positive coverage in 42 percent of stories, neutral coverage in 38 percent of stories, and negative coverage in 20 percent of stories.[42]

In the 2016 primary elections, many commentators pointed to the apparent biases in news coverage favoring Donald Trump over other candidates. One analysis found that Trump received considerably more coverage than other Republican candidates, while Democratic candidates Hillary Clinton and Bernie Sanders received roughly the same amount of coverage. Coverage of the initial Republican primary contests focused on Trump 37 percent of the time, compared with 28 percent for Ted Cruz and 25 percent for Marco Rubio,

40 Lars Willnat and David H. Weaver, "The American Journalist in the Digital Age: Key Findings," Indiana School of Journalism, 2014, https://archive.news.indiana.edu/releases/iu/2014/05/american-journalist-in-the-digital-age.shtml (accessed 5/17/20).

41 Michael J. Robinson and Margaret A. Sheehan, *Over the Wire and on TV: CBS and UPI in Campaign '80* (New York: Russell Sage Foundation, 1983).

42 Pew Research Center, "Obama's First 100 Days: How the President Fared in the Press vs. Clinton and Bush," April 28, 2009, www.journalism.org/2009/04/28/obamas-first-100-days (accessed 5/17/20).

and reporting on the subsequent contests shifted even more substantially toward Trump.[43]

Journalists may express more subtle biases through the language they use in their reporting. A 2005 study found that reporters use ideologically loaded terms when referring to some politicians but not others. Even when journalists mention both parties in an ostensibly balanced story, they do so with no small degree of editorializing, using words like *radical* or *extreme* to describe one politician or another. Analysis of such language revealed that most major media outlets slanted their reporting to the left, with three important exceptions. The *Wall Street Journal* and Fox News leaned to the right. Only PBS—the publicly owned and licensed network—presented balanced reporting of politics, government, and current events.[44]

Newspapers' editorial endorsements offer further evidence of news organizations' biases, albeit toward those in power rather than toward one party or another.[45] *Editor and Publisher*, a trade journal of the media business, tracks newspaper endorsements across the United States. Before the 1960s, newspaper editors' endorsements and political leanings were overwhelmingly Republican. Since the 1960s, however, newspaper endorsements for president, the U.S. Senate, the U.S. House, and statewide offices have generally balanced out between Democrats and Republicans. George W. Bush received a solid majority of endorsements in 2000, though John Kerry edged Bush out in 2004. In 2008, Barack Obama received nearly 70 percent of the endorsements over John McCain, and in 2012, Mitt Romney just edged out Obama (Figure 14.2). The figures for 2016 were most stunning. Hillary Clinton received 77 percent of major newspaper endorsements, and Donald Trump got just 2 percent, with the remainder going to other candidates.

Journalism, as a profession, has attempted to rise above personal motivations and biases. Most journalists adhere to strong norms of fairness and balance and attempt to report the perspectives of all sides in any given controversy. Even coverage of popular presidents still attempts to maintain balance. But the important ethos of objectivity and fairness appears to be changing.

Two shifts in journalism are eroding professional standards of objectivity. The first is the blurring of the line between editorializing and reporting in traditional media. For example, Fox News and MSNBC present ideological and partisan versions of the news, with Fox on the right and MSNBC on the left. Among professional journalists, much is made of the battle among cable

43 Thomas E. Patterson, "News Coverage of the 2016 Presidential Primaries: Horse Race Reporting Has Consequences," Shorenstein Center on Media, Politics, and Public Policy, Harvard Kennedy School, July 11, 2016, https://shorensteincenter.org/news-coverage-2016-presidential-primaries (accessed 5/9/20).

44 Tim Groseclose and Jeffrey Milyo, "A Measure of Media Bias," *Quarterly Journal of Economics* 120, no. 4 (2005): 1191–237. See also Tim Groseclose, *Left Turn: How Liberal Media Bias Distorts the American Mind* (New York: St. Martin's Press, 2011).

45 Stephen Ansolabehere, Rebecca Lessem, and James M. Snyder, Jr., "The Orientation of Newspaper Endorsements in U.S. Elections, 1940–2002," *Quarterly Journal of Political Science* 1, no. 4 (October 2006): 393–404.

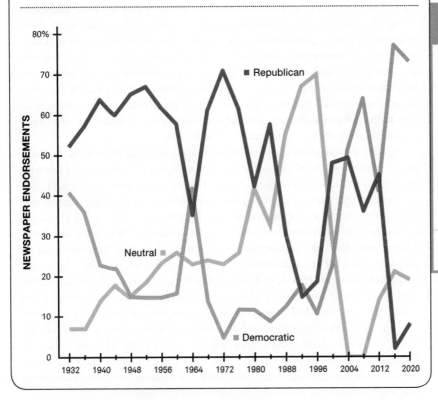

Figure 14.2
NEWSPAPER ENDORSEMENTS, 1932–2020

SOURCES: Harold W. Stanley and Richard G. Niemi, *Vital Statistics on American Politics, 2001–2002* (Washington, DC: CQ Press, 2001), pp. 194–5; 2004, 2008, 2012, and 2016 data from *Editor and Publisher*, www.editorandpublisher.com. 2020 data from "News Media Endorsements in the 2020 United States Presidential Election," compiled by Wikipedia, https://en.wikipedia.org/wiki/News_media_endorsements_in_the_2020_United_States_presidential_election (accessed 11/17/20).

ANALYZING THE EVIDENCE

What can the pattern of newspaper endorsements from 1932 through 2020 tell us regarding the biases of the print media? What other indicators might be used to evaluate media bias? What would an "unbiased" media look like?

networks to divide the audience along partisan lines. In a widely read opinion piece, Tom Edsall, a longtime journalist who has covered every level of American government, wrote that it was time for all journalists to throw off the norms of nonpartisanship and fairness.[46] Edsall, now a regular columnist for the *New York Times*, argues that Fox News and its large audience changed the old norms. The gloves are off, and at least from Edsall's corner, it is time for traditional journalists, most of whom have a liberal orientation, to take on the challenge from conservatives directly. Many traditional journalists have heeded Edsall's advice.

46 Thomas Edsall, "Journalism Should Own Its Liberalism: And Then Manage It, Challenge It, and Account for It," *Columbia Journalism Review*, October 8, 2009, https://archives.cjr.org/campaign_desk/journalism_should_own_its_libe.php (accessed 5/17/20)

Citizen Journalism. The second shift in journalism—the emergence of citizen journalism—is more profound and may be more far-reaching. Technologies such as smartphones, laptops, tablets, and the internet now make it possible for anyone to report on events. For example, CNN had a regular iReporter feature that published video sent by people at events such as natural disasters, political campaigns, and protests and rebellions. Needless to say, this is potentially a threat to traditional journalism, which relies on highly trained professionals. Newspapers and television stations no longer need to rely on large—and expensive—bureaus in order to get instant recordings of events. By the same token, these technologies have allowed journalism to flourish in countries with very little media or with tight government controls on television and the press, such as those in central Africa and the Middle East.

The revolutionary nature of citizen journalism lies in its reliance on the "subjective participant" in place of the "objective reporter." A traditional reporter from the *New York Times*, the Associated Press, or another agency will seek different perspectives on the same event and offer an investigative report that attempts to answer the key questions (also known as the 5 Ws and 1 H) taught on the first day of Journalism 101: what, who, when, where, why, and how? Citizen journalists, by contrast, become reporters of an event precisely because they are *in* the event. A protester who sends a video of a violent clash with police in Damascus, Tripoli, or London is in the event, as is a legislative staffer who tweets about a committee meeting or a campaign worker who posts about a rally. Citizens' text and video communications are raw and in the moment. Though this kind of reporting makes no attempt to rise above and answer the 5 Ws, it is some of the most compelling journalism today. This sea change in journalism will not replace the old style, which has survived many a technological revolution. Rather, citizen journalism will augment traditional journalism, and it gives traditional journalists license to be more subjective.

News Sources

Reporters. News is reported. And it is the reporter—the person who investigates an event and pieces together a story, or narrative—who is the source of the news that we read or hear. Professional reporters hired by newspapers, television stations, web outlets, and wire services usually have an education that emphasizes the skills necessary for the job, such as writing and investigative techniques. Journalism programs almost always emphasize professional ethics and norms alongside skills. In other words, journalism as a profession consists of people who are skilled at observing the world, understanding what events are important to society and of interest to the public, investigating those events, and presenting information.

Reporting is not just a matter of narrating events with factual accuracy. Journalists and editors must consider not only what seems like a good story to them but also what will interest potential readers or viewers. They ultimately provide the content that media outlets use to attract an audience. It is the ability both to investigate deeply and to present information in a compelling way that makes a good journalist.

Reporters always use their judgment about the importance of events, and those judgments affect what gets covered and how. And the news media themselves consume a steady stream of information from sources that present information to reporters in often sophisticated and strategic ways so as to get news coverage.

News Leaks. A news leak is the disclosure of confidential information to the news media. Leaks may emanate from a variety of sources, including "whistle-blowers": lower-level officials who hope to publicize what they view as their bosses' improper activities. In 1971, for example, a minor Defense Department staffer named Daniel Ellsberg sought to discredit official justifications for America's involvement in Vietnam by leaking top-secret documents to the press. The *New York Times* and the *Washington Post* published these classified documents, the so-called Pentagon Papers, after the U.S. Supreme Court ruled that the government could not block their release.

The social media era already has its own version of the Pentagon Papers and Daniel Ellsberg—WikiLeaks founder Julian Assange and contributor Edward Snowden. Over the years, WikiLeaks has released a number of high-profile, headline-grabbing confidential reports (usually from governments). In November 2010, WikiLeaks collaborated with the British newspaper the *Guardian*, the German newsmagazine *Der Spiegel*, and other global news organizations to release classified and highly sensitive U.S. State Department diplomatic cables and other documents related to the wars in Afghanistan and Iraq. In June 2013, WikiLeaks disclosed classified documents that were even more sensational; Edward Snowden, a computer programmer and analyst employed as a contractor for the National Security Agency (NSA), worked with several global news organizations, such as the *New York Times*, the *Guardian*, and *Der Spiegel*, to leak 9,000 to 10,000 NSA documents. The documents revealed that the agency was listening to the phone calls and harvesting the emails, texts, and additional communications of other governments and world leaders, even its allies. Thus Snowden exposed the extent of the United States' spying on foreign governments and its classified cyberwarfare program. Snowden fled the United States and eventually received asylum in Russia. More recently, during the 2016 presidential campaign, WikiLeaks released thousands of hacked emails from Democratic candidate Hillary Clinton's campaign.

Most leaks, though, originate with senior government officials and prominent politicians and activists. Such individuals often cultivate long-term relationships with journalists to whom they regularly leak confidential information, knowing that it will likely be published on a priority basis in a form acceptable to them. Their confidence is based on the fact that journalists generally regard high-level sources of confidential information as valuable assets whose favor must be retained. And the more that recipients of leaked information strive to keep their sources secret, the more difficulty other journalists will have in checking the information's validity.

Press Releases. The news also comes from thousands of press releases that are incorporated seamlessly into daily news reports. The press release is a story written by an advocate or publicist and distributed to the media in the hope that journalists will publish it under their own bylines with little or no revision. The inventor of the press release was a New York public-relations consultant named Ivy Lee. In 1906, a train operated by one of Lee's clients, the Pennsylvania Railroad, was involved in a serious wreck. Lee wrote a story about the accident presenting the railroad in a favorable light and distributed the account to reporters. Many papers published Lee's slanted story as their own objective account of events, and the railroad's reputation for safety remained intact.

Consistent with Lee's example, today's press releases present facts and perspectives that serve an advocate's interests, but the releases are written in a way that mimics the factual news style of the papers, periodicals, or television news programs to which they are sent. It is quite difficult for the audience to distinguish a well-designed press release from a news story. According to some experts, more than 50 percent of the articles in a newspaper on any given day are based on press releases. Indeed, more than 75 percent of journalists responding to a survey acknowledged using press releases for their stories.[47]

Journalists are certainly aware that the authors of press releases have their own agendas and are hardly unbiased reporters of the news. Nevertheless, the economics of publishing and broadcasting dictate that large numbers of stories will always be based on press releases. Newspapers and television stations are businesses, and for many the financial bottom line is more important than journalistic integrity.[48] The use of press releases allows a newspaper or a broadcast network to present more stories without paying more staff or incurring the other costs associated with investigating and writing news. As one newspaper executive said, the public-relations people who write news releases are our "unpaid reporters."[49]

Today, the printed press release has been joined by the video news release designed especially for television stations. The video release is a taped report, usually about 90 seconds long (the typical length of a television news story), designed to look and sound like any other broadcast news segment. In exchange for airing material that serves the interests of some advocate, the television station is relieved of the considerable expense and bother of identifying and filming its own news story. The audience is usually unaware that the "news" it is watching is someone's canned publicity footage.

Hiring Reporters. A number of cases have come to light in which governments or private entities have paid journalists to write favorable accounts of their activities. In 2005, for example, the U.S. military acknowledged that it had

47 Dennis L. Wilcox and Glen T. Cameron, *Public Relations: Strategies and Tactics*, 8th ed. (Boston: Allyn and Bacon, 2006), p. 357. See also Justin Grimmer, *Representational Style in Congress: What Legislators Say and Why It Matters* (New York: Cambridge University Press, 2013), chap. 8.

48 See, for example, Davis Merritt, *Knightfall: Knight Ridder and How the Erosion of Newspaper Journalism Is Putting Democracy at Risk* (New York: AMACOM, 2005).

49 Quoted in Wilcox and Cameron, *Public Relations*, p. 357.

hired the Washington-based Lincoln Group, a public-relations firm, to pay Iraqi newspapers to carry positive news about American efforts in the country. The firm ultimately placed more than 1,000 such news stories.[50] Iraqis reading the articles would have had no way of knowing that the material was produced at the behest of American authorities.

As local newspaper budgets have shrunk, some local governments have hired reporters or paid newspapers for reporters to cover local government. The regional government of Portland, Oregon, hires a local reporter to cover goings-on such as council meetings, events, and changes in policies and laws. The Los Angeles Kings hockey franchise, a Los Angeles County supervisor, and a California trial lawyers group all hire journalists to follow their activities. The list goes on.

The pharmaceutical industry is notorious for paying writers and reporters for favorable coverage. Indeed, articles written by pharma-bankrolled authors regularly appear in popular—and even scientific—journals; in other instances, the writer cited in the story's byline is not the actual author. Often, a ghostwriter employed by a drug company writes the story, while the nominal author is paid for the use of his name.[51]

All these practices—hiring reporters, press leaks, and planted news stories—offend our sensibilities about the news because we expect objectivity from reporters. Journalists are our main source of information, and fair and balanced reporting helps us sort out complex issues. The media also play an important watchdog role, making noise when something is amiss. This role becomes increasingly difficult to perform if the main revenues for the news come from the firm or government agency that the news covers. Of course, although politicians try to use the media to their advantage, reporters often have their own agendas. Often enough, hostile or merely determined journalists will break through the smoke screens thrown up by politicians and report the truth.

Consumers

The print, broadcast, and digital media are businesses that, in general, aim to turn a profit. Thus, like any other businesses, they must cater to the preferences of consumers. Doing so has important consequences for the content and character of the news media. The long-term success of the media as a political institution depends on their ability to find a sizable audience.

Catering to the Well-Educated Audience.
Especially in the political realm, the print, broadcast, and digital media as well as the publishing industry are particularly responsive to the interests of the better-educated and more affluent segments of their audience. The preferences of readers, viewers, and

50 Jeff Gerth, "Military's Information War Is Vast and Often Secretive," *New York Times*, December 11, 2005, p. 1.

51 Anna Wilde Mathews, "At Medical Journals, Writers Paid by Industry Play Big Role," *Wall Street Journal*, December 13, 2005, p. 1.

listeners have a profound effect on the content and orientation of the press, radio and television programming, and books, especially in areas of news and public affairs.[52]

Affluent and well-educated consumers are the core audience of newsmagazines, journals of opinion, books dealing with public affairs, newspapers such as the *New York Times* and the *Washington Post*, broadcast news, and evening and weekend public affairs programming. Of course, other segments of the public also read newspapers and watch television news. Overall, however, level of interest in "hard news" (world events, national political issues, and the like) is closely related to level of education (Table 14.1). As a result, well-educated Americans are overrepresented in the news and public affairs audience. The relative wealth of this audience makes news, politics, and public affairs very attractive topics to advertisers, publishers, radio broadcasters, and television executives.

As a result, entire categories of events and issues of interest to lower-, middle-, and working-class Americans receive scant attention from the national print and broadcast media. For example, no network or national periodical routinely covers labor organizations; trade union news and events are discussed only in the context of major strikes or revelations of corruption. Religious and church affairs likewise receive little coverage unless scandal is involved. The activities of veterans', fraternal, ethnic, and patriotic organizations are also generally ignored.

The rise of new media sources did not alter this picture. For example, a study by political scientist Markus Prior of the rise of cable television shows that the restructuring from three networks to a vast range of cable outlets during the 1980s and 1990s actually increased the knowledge gap among different groups in the electorate. Further, political scientist Gary Jacobson's research has found that viewers of different cable news channels (such as Fox News, MSNBC, and CNN) hold widely varying beliefs about basic facts concerning public affairs. Jacobson's research contrasts sharply with research from the 1970s on CBS, NBC, and ABC, which found that the three main networks—as well as print media—tended to present the same information from similar perspectives.[53]

The Media and Conflict. Although the media respond most directly to the more elite segments of their audience, groups that cannot afford media consultants and issues managers can publicize their interests through protest. Frequently, the media are accused of encouraging conflict for the benefit of

52 See Tom Burnes, "The Organization of Public Opinion," in *Mass Communication and Society*, ed. James Curran, Michael Gurevitch, and Janet Woollacott (Beverly Hills, CA: Sage, 1979), pp. 44–230. See also David L. Altheide, *Creating Reality: How TV News Distorts Events* (Beverly Hills, CA: Sage, 1976).

53 Markus Prior, *Post-Broadcast Democracy: How Media Choice Increases Inequality in Political Involvement and Polarizes Elections* (New York: Cambridge University Press, 2007); and Gary C. Jacobson, "How the Economy and Partisanship Shaped the 2012 Presidential and Congressional Elections," *Political Science Quarterly* 128, no. 1 (Spring 2013): 1–38. On TV and newspaper reporting in the 1970s, see Robinson and Sheehan, *Over the Wire and on TV.*

Table 14.1

EDUCATION AND ATTENTION TO THE NEWS

LEVEL OF EDUCATION	PERCENT WHO GOT NEWS ON A DAILY BASIS OR SEVERAL TIMES A WEEK	PERCENT WHO WATCHED, READ, OR HEARD IN-DEPTH STORIES IN PAST WEEK
College or graduate school	95	57
High school or some college	88	36
Not a high school graduate	83	20

SOURCE: American Press Institute, www.americanpressinstitute.org/publications/reports/survey-research/personal-news-cycle/single-page (accessed 5/20/20).

their audiences, who mostly watch news for the entertainment value that conflict can provide. Clearly, conflict can be an important vehicle for drawing media attention to groups that lack the financial or organizational resources to broadcast their views. However, conflict and protest ultimately do not allow groups low on the social ladder to compete effectively in the media landscape.

The chief problem with protest as a media technique is that, in general, the media have considerable discretion in reporting and interpreting the events they cover. For example, should the media focus on the conflict itself or on the issues that the conflict addresses? The answer is typically determined by the media, not by the protesters. Therefore, the media's interpretation of protest activities is more a reflection of the views of its core audience—usually segments of the upper-middle class—than it is a function of the wishes of the protesters themselves. It is worth noting that civil rights protesters in the 1960s received their most favorable media coverage when members of the White upper-middle class began to see Black people as potential political allies in the Democratic Party.

Social media magnifies this problem even further. For example, the organizers of a protest may intend to broadcast one message with their demonstration, but debate over social media can force the organizers to shift their message or may mire the protest in controversy. In the weeks following the election of President Donald Trump, two women, one in Hawaii and one in New York, independently proposed a women's protest. Working together over Facebook, they combined their activities and organized the 2017 Women's March on Washington. Then the disputes came: over message, over iconography, over location, even over the name of the march. This controversy played out not after the event in the traditional media, but before the event over Facebook, Twitter, and other social media. The normal back-and-forth required to organize any large event occurred very publicly, and the controversies about the meaning of the protest became a large part of the protest's story.[54]

REGULATING THE MEDIA

Each phase in the evolution of media in the United States—from the press to broadcasting to digital—raises profound questions about what sort of media our society needs to maintain its democratic culture and institutions. The American Founding saw the struggle between colonists and the British Crown over the right to publish and distribute pamphlets and weekly papers. Out of that struggle was born Americans' deep commitment to freedom of the press. That commitment is not always easy to maintain. What are the limits to a free press? Should a newspaper be free to publish instructions for building a nuclear bomb?

The emergence of broadcasting and the realization that access to the airwaves was limited by the spectrum of available frequencies created new problems. Even if there was little or no government censorship of the press, only those voices that owned broadcast licenses or had the money to advertise could be heard. How can we guarantee that there is robust discussion of issues and that all public officials can reach their audiences? Are the media universally accessible and fair?

Digital media have broken the technological limits of broadcasting, but new problems have arisen. How do we know that information in the news is authentic, especially if it has been curated by an algorithm or sent over social media? How do we ensure that the media environment can support coverage of local issues, especially in poorer regions of the United States where the advertising revenue is insufficient to support local newspapers?

These questions have long been debated in the courts and in Congress, and they will continue to be. Each phase in the evolution of American media has generated a different set of ideas, or models, about how our society should deal with these issues. The model that emerged from print media is the marketplace of ideas, or free press model, in which the press operates separately from the government and is protected from censorship and other forms of presidential or congressional interference. This model has been central to the way that the U.S. Supreme Court has ruled on cases concerning media regulation. The broadcast media generated a very different model of media regulation: the public utility model. Under this model, the media are a public institution and are charged with protecting the public good. They are granted monopoly powers through licenses and must act with the public's interest, rather than the private interest, in mind. The public utility model underlies

---

54 Jia Tolentino, "The Somehow Controversial Women's March on Washington," *New Yorker,* January 18, 2017, www.newyorker.com/culture/jia-tolentino/the-somehow-controversial-womens-march-on-washington (accessed 5/17/20).

many regulations on the ownership and operation of broadcast networks, and it has led to a separate set of ethical standards and responsibilities to which broadcasters must adhere. The digital age has yet to generate its own model, but these new media forms have already come into tension with the free press and public utility models.

For the past 100 years, these two models have operated side by side. The free press model is the more dominant strand of thinking, but the public utility model, with its emphasis on universal access to information and fair presentation of the news, has also shaped the evolution of the media. Problems of regulating content, of free speech and censorship, and of media ownership exhibit both the tension and the synergy between these two views. Americans' desires for free speech, a free press, and universal access to fair information define the role of the media in our society.

Content Regulation

In most countries, the government controls media content and owns the largest media outlets. In the United States, the government neither owns nor controls the communications networks, but it does regulate content and ownership of the broadcast media.

Print media in the United States are essentially free from government interference. Broadcast radio and television, in contrast, are regulated by the FCC, a federal independent agency. Radio and TV stations must renew their FCC licenses every five years. Licensing provides a mechanism for allocating radio and TV frequencies to prevent broadcasts from interfering with one another. License renewal requests are now filed online. The FCC also maintains regulations prohibiting radio and television stations from airing explicit sexual and excretory references between 6 a.m. and 10 p.m., the hours when children are most likely to be in the audience, though it has enforced these rules haphazardly.

For more than 60 years after the passage of the 1934 Communications Act, the FCC regulated and promoted competition in the broadcast industry. In 1996, Congress passed the Telecommunications Act, a broad effort to eliminate most of the 1934-era regulations. The act loosened restrictions on media ownership and allowed telephone companies, cable television providers, and broadcasters to compete for the provision of telecommunication services. Following the passage of the act, several mergers between telephone and cable companies and between other entertainment firms produced an even greater concentration of media ownership.

The Telecommunications Act of 1996 also attempted to regulate the content of material transmitted via the internet. The provision of the act known as the Communications Decency Act made it illegal to make "indecent" sexual material on the internet accessible to anyone under age 18. The act was immediately denounced by civil libertarians, and the U.S. Supreme Court ruled in 1997 that the act was an unconstitutional infringement of the First Amendment's guarantee of freedom of speech.

Although the government's ability to regulate the content of online media has been questioned, the federal government has used its licensing power to impose several regulations that can affect the political content of radio and TV broadcasts. The first is the **equal time rule**, under which broadcasters must provide candidates for the same political office equal opportunities to communicate their messages to the public. If, for example, a television station sells commercial time to a state's Republican gubernatorial candidate, it may not refuse to sell time to the Democratic candidate for the same position.

The second regulation affecting broadcast content is the **right of rebuttal**, which requires that individuals be allowed to respond to personal attacks. In the 1969 case of *Red Lion Broadcasting Company v. Federal Communications Commission*, for example, the U.S. Supreme Court upheld the FCC's determination that a radio station was required to provide a liberal author with an opportunity to respond to an attack that the station had aired by a conservative commentator.[55] Beyond these rules, applied at the time of licensing, the government does very little to regulate media in the United States. The right to free press is a fundamental one that has become a powerful norm in our society.

The emergence of the internet has presented two substantial regulatory challenges: (1) protecting intellectual property and (2) setting standards to create a rational system of domains and websites. The first issue concerns whether the internet can function as a profitable means of distributing content. In *A&M Records v. Napster*, the Ninth Circuit court sided with record companies against firms that offered free online distribution of copyrighted content.[56] Although this case involved the distribution of music, it has had far-reaching implications for all providers of content on the internet.

The second challenge is how to organize and govern the internet. In the 1990s, British computer scientist Tim Berners-Lee organized researchers, firms, and government agencies involved in the development of the internet in the international World Wide Web Consortium.[57] The consortium is a form of self-regulation by corporations and organizations, and it has developed concepts of intellectual property and communication that are wholly different from those of traditional print and broadcast media. The consortium's philosophy calls for much less government regulation, and it advocates a communal spirit that runs counter to the notion of competitive markets that underlies the United States' conception of print media. Reflecting this communal ethos, the World Wide Web Consortium alone does not run the internet; rather, the governance of the internet is distributed among a variety of organizations (see the Policy Principle box).

---

55 *Red Lion Broadcasting Company v. Federal Communications Commission* (1969).

56 *A&M Records v. Napster*, 239 F3d 1004 (Ninth Cir., 2001).

57 Tim Berners-Lee with Mark Fischetti, *Weaving the Web: The Original Design and Ultimate Destiny of the World Wide Web by Its Inventor* (New York: HarperCollins, 1999).

Who Runs the Internet?

As we saw in Chapter 1, individual self-interest can sometimes have damaging collective consequences for a community. This idea is known as the tragedy of the commons, which posits that unregulated use of a shared resource, such as land, inevitably results in negative consequences for the common good—leading, in the classic example, to overgrazing and the demise of everyone's cattle. The tragedy of the commons is often cited as a rationale for government action. In some realms, however, relatively unregulated private activity can produce positive results for everyone. One such realm is the internet. The internet is unlike traditional media such as television networks or newspapers. While television networks and newspapers are owned and run by corporations, no single company, organization, or government runs or owns the internet. Instead, the internet is a network of many independent networks throughout the world that are voluntarily linked together.

The U.S. government and European Commission created the networks that became the internet. Perhaps the most important part of these was the ARPANET, a system developed in 1960s that allowed researchers for the Defense Department to communicate remotely about collaborative research. Access to ARPANET was expanded to include other government agencies, and by the late 1980s, the commercial value of such networked communications had become increasingly obvious. At that time, Tim Berners-Lee, a researcher in the United Kingdom, developed protocols to link hypertexts, and the modern internet was born. Making the network function, however, requires a fair amount of coordination among those who develop the computer architecture for the various networks.

The governance of the internet is dispersed among many different voluntary organizations. The World Wide Web Consortium, for example, is a forum in which corporations and individuals discuss the issues facing the system and negotiate appropriate standards for web technologies. The Internet Society, whose mission is "to promote the open development, evolution, and use of the Internet for the benefit of all people throughout the world," is

Maintaining an open internet is increasingly difficult.

an international nonprofit organization with approximately 145 organizational and 65,000 individual members, half of whom are from the United States and half from other countries.[1]

These and similar organizations have shaped the way that the internet has developed. The members of these organizations negotiate the standards and other rules for the development of web technologies, including the configuration of software and hardware and website naming and numbering. These organizations also try to influence government policies that affect the internet, such as laws governing intellectual property and privacy.

Maintaining an open internet is extremely difficult in the face of both market and social pressures. One feature of the internet is that all traffic is treated equally—a principle called net neutrality. The FCC recently voted to allow internet providers to charge higher rates for some uses (for example, gaming) than other uses (such as telephone calls), scaling back net neutrality. Demands are growing for government regulation of the internet to protect users' privacy, to guard against cyberbullying, and to punish the authors of computer viruses and other malware. Despite these pressures, the internet remains organized around principles of openness and equality. And it has been a boon for businesses and individuals.

1 Internet Society, "Who We Are," www.internetsociety.org/who-we-are (accessed 5/20/20).

Censorship and Freedom of the Press

prior restraint

An effort by a government agency to block publication of material by a newspaper or magazine; censorship.

Unlike broadcast media, print media are not subject to federal regulation. Indeed, the great principle underlying the federal government's relationship with the press is the doctrine against **prior restraint**. Beginning with the landmark 1931 case of *Near v. Minnesota*, the U.S. Supreme Court has held that, except under the most extraordinary of circumstances, the First Amendment prohibits government agencies from preventing newspapers or magazines from publishing whatever they wish.[58] Indeed, in the 1971 case of *New York Times v. United States*, the so-called Pentagon Papers case, the Supreme Court ruled that the government could not even block the publication of secret Defense Department documents furnished to the *New York Times* by an opponent of the Vietnam War who had obtained the documents illegally.[59] In 1990, however, the Supreme Court upheld a lower-court order restraining CNN from broadcasting tapes of conversations between the former Panamanian leader Manuel Noriega and his lawyer, supposedly recorded by the U.S. government. The Court held that CNN could be restrained from broadcasting the tapes until the trial court in the Noriega case had heard them and decided whether their broadcast would violate Noriega's right to a fair trial. This case would seem to weaken the doctrine of prior restraint. But in later decisions, the Supreme Court ruled that cable television networks were entitled to essentially the same First Amendment protections as the print media.[60]

Even though newspapers may not be restrained from publishing whatever they want, they may be subject to sanctions after the fact. Historically, newspapers have been subject to libel laws, which stipulate that newspapers that print false and malicious stories can be compelled to pay damages to those they defame. Over time, however, American courts have greatly narrowed the meaning of libel and made it extremely difficult, particularly for public figures, to win a libel case against a newspaper. The most important case in this regard is *New York Times v. Sullivan* (1964), in which the Supreme Court held that to be deemed libelous, a story about a public official not only must be untrue but also must result from "actual malice" or "reckless disregard" for the truth.[61] In other words, the newspaper must deliberately print false and malicious material for it to count as libel. In practice, it is nearly impossible to prove this. Libel suits against CBS News by General William Westmoreland and against *Time* magazine by Ariel Sharon of Israel, both financed by conservative legal foundations that hoped to embarrass the media, were defeated because they failed to show evidence of actual malice. In the 1991 case of *Masson v. New Yorker Magazine*, this tradition was again affirmed by the Court's opinion that fabricated quotations

58 *Near v. Minnesota ex rel. Olson*, 283 U.S. 697 (1931).

59 *New York Times Company v. United States*, 403 U.S. 713 (1971).

60 *Cable News Network v. Noriega*, 498 U.S. 976 (1990); and *Turner Broadcasting System v. Federal Communications Commission*, 512 U.S. 622 (1994).

61 *New York Times Company v. Sullivan* (1964).

attributed to a public figure are libelous only if the fabricated account "materially change[s]" the meaning of what the person said.[62] Essentially, the print media can publish almost anything they want about a public figure. As a result, the media are given nearly total free rein in reporting on politics and public officials in the United States. This leverage allows the media to operate like a fourth branch of government through which our society deliberates issues publicly.

Organization and Ownership of the Media

The scope of the media industry in the United States is impressive: the country can count more than 2,000 television stations, approximately 1,400 daily newspapers, and more than 13,000 radio stations. There are 20 major television networks, as well as an extensive system of public television and radio stations.

The media environment since the 1980s has opened considerably, and wholly new networks devoted to news have emerged. CNN became a major news source in the late 1980s and gained a substantial market share during the first Gulf War in 1991, sometimes even providing live coverage of American bombing raids on Baghdad after the major networks' correspondents had fled to bomb shelters. In the 2000s, a competitor emerged: Fox News. By 2003, Fox had displaced CNN as the nation's primary cable news source, and by 2014 Fox News was the second-highest-rated weekday prime-time cable channel, trailing only ESPN.[63] Throughout 2019, Fox News averaged 2.57 million viewers nightly in prime time. By contrast, CNN had less than half that audience (1 million), and MSNBC had 1.8 million viewers.[64] The rise of Fox News has had important political implications because its coverage and commentators are considerably more conservative than CNN's. Fox News also demonstrates the importance of having more and varied news sources. When there are few sources, each is likely to appeal to the same broad national audience and to maintain a middle-of-the-road stance. When there are more sources, each is likely to position itself within an ideological or partisan niche, increasing the diversity of viewpoints presented.

News Concentration. Nonetheless, there is a real concern that these trends mask considerable concentration in the news media industry. The problem is most evident in the wire services, which provide a steady stream of stories and images. There is just one American wire service, the Associated Press. In Europe, Reuters has the dominant market position, and in 2009 CNN launched

62 *Masson v. New Yorker Magazine,* 501 U.S. 496 (1991).

63 Matt Wilstein, "2014 Cable News Ratings: CNN Beats MSNBC in Primetime Demo, Fox Still #1," Mediaite, December 30, 2014, www.mediaite.com/tv/2014-cable-news-ratings-cnn-beats-msnbc-in-primetime-demo-fox-still-1 (accessed 5/17/20).

64 Nellie Andreeva and Ted Johnson, "Cable Ratings 2019: Fox News Tops Total Viewers, ESPN WIns 18-19 Demo As Entertainment Networks Slide," Deadline, December 29, 2019, https://deadline.com/2019/12/cable-ratings-2019-list-fox-news-total-viewers-espn-18-49-demo-1202817561/ (accessed 7/12/20).

a wire service that licenses its stories to journalists.[65] There are only a handful of wire services and major newspapers with large reporting staffs, and other news outlets rely heavily on these sources.

Concentration of media ownership raises further concerns about the robustness of the marketplace of ideas. The 1996 Telecommunications Act opened the way for additional consolidation in the industry, and a wave of mergers and consolidations has further reduced the field of independent media nationwide. Among the major news networks, ABC was bought by the Walt Disney Company; CNN was bought by Time Warner; and NBC, which General Electric owned from 1986 until 2011, is now owned by Comcast. The Australian press baron Rupert Murdoch owns Fox plus a host of radio, television, and newspaper properties around the world. CBS remains a holding of the CBS Corporation but it merged with Viacom. As a result of these consolidations, a relatively small number of giant corporations now control a wide swath of media holdings, including television networks, movie studios, record labels, cable channels and local cable providers, book publishers, magazines, and newspapers. This development has prompted questions about whether enough competition exists among the media to produce a diverse set of views or whether the United States has become the prisoner of media monopolies (Figure 14.3).[66] Even though the internet has expanded the number of outlets for information distribution, there is concern that the news originates from a smaller and smaller set of organizations.

In 2003, the FCC announced new rules that seemed to pave the way for even more concentration in the media industry. The rules permitted the major networks to own television stations that collectively reached 45 percent of all viewers, up from 35 percent under the old rules. The new rules also permitted a single company to own both the leading newspaper and multiple television and radio outlets in a single market. Major media companies, which had long lobbied for the right to expand their activities, welcomed the new rules. Critics, however, expressed concern that the rules would result in a narrower range of views and issues being presented to the public. Following disagreement within Congress and a threatened presidential veto, a federal appeals court placed the new regulations on hold, and in 2007 the FCC debuted new rules to comply with the court's ruling. In 2012, a proposal to streamline the cross-ownership rules was introduced for the third time in a decade. The rules were ultimately eliminated in 2017 to allow for the diversification and expansion of entertainment, news, and media in the marketplace.

Distribution of news online bucks the trend of increased concentration of media ownership. From the audience's perspective, increased concentration will lead to less variety in the news and fewer voices heard. However, the internet has decreased people's dependence on a single local newspaper to

65 Helen Quinn, "CNN Offers On Demand Wire Service for News Organisations," Journalism.co.uk, September 15, 2009, www.journalism.co.uk/news/cnn-offers-on-demand- wire-service-for-news-organisations/s2/a535823 (accessed 5/17/20).

66 For a criticism of the increasing consolidation of the media, see the essays in Erik Barnouw et al., *Conglomerates and the Media* (New York: New Press, 1997).

Figure 14.3
NUMBER OF CORPORATIONS THAT CONTROL THE MAJORITY OF U.S. MEDIA, 1983–2019

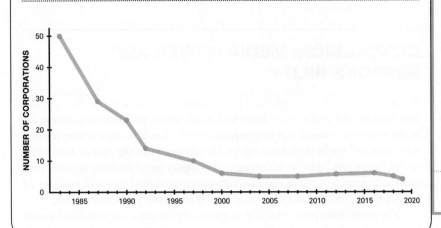

NOTE: Included are newspapers, magazines, TV and radio stations, books, music, movies, videos, wire services, and photo agencies.
SOURCES: Media Reform Information Center, www.corporations.org/media; *Business Insider*, www.businessinsider.com/these-6-corporations-control-90-of-the-media-in-america-2012-6; *New York Times*, www.nytimes.com/2014/07/26/business/a-21st-century-fox-time-warner-merger-would-narrow-already-dwindling-competition.html; and *Washington Post*, www.washingtonpost.com/news/business/wp/2017/12/14/disney-buys-much-of-fox-in-mega-merger-that-will-shake-world-of-entertainment-and-media/?utm_term=.5585b28e3c84 (accessed 5/20/20).

ANALYZING THE EVIDENCE

After several years of mergers and acquisitions, a small number of corporations has come to dominate the print, broadcast, cable, and internet industries. What factors precipitated this media consolidation? What effects, if any, does media consolidation have on news reporting?

get information. Using websites that aggregate news from many sources, consumers can readily get many views on the same event. And people can easily search official websites to find local information, such as meeting times of city councils and school committees.

One important question is whether internet news will follow the same consolidation trends that have befallen print and broadcast media. Google, the dominant search firm, has the power to block certain sites and thereby censor the news. This problem arose in 2015 in China, when the government forced Google China, a subsidiary of Google, to censor many websites, especially those of dissidents. To maintain access to the enormous Chinese market, Google complied, effectively blocking non-Chinese media from users within China and conversely blocking Chinese media websites from others, including users in the United States.[67] Eventually, Google directed traffic to the websites

---

67 One fascinating study of Chinese government censorship finds that the government censors various forms of collective action more often than it censors criticism of the government. See Gary King, Jennifer Pan, and Margaret E. Roberts, "How Censorship in China Allows Government Criticism but Silences Collective Expression," *American Political Science Review* 107, no. 2 (May 2013): 326–43.

in question through its Hong Kong subsidiary, and China responded by shutting down Gmail service in the country. The tense back-and-forth over access to the web and to the Chinese market continues between Google and the Chinese government.[68]

CONCLUSION: MEDIA POWER AND RESPONSIBILITY

The content and character of news and public affairs programming—what the media choose to present and how they present it—can have far-reaching political consequences. Media disclosures can greatly enhance or fatally damage the careers of public officials. Media coverage can rally support for or intensify opposition to national policies. The media choose what issues to cover and how and, as discussed in Chapter 10, set the national political agenda and frame political discourse.

The media have been central in shaping some of the most significant events in recent American political history, including the 2020 coronavirus pandemic mentioned at the beginning of this chapter. News media were critically important in the civil rights movement of the 1950s and 1960s, as television footage and photographs of marchers attacked by club-swinging police galvanized public support among northern White Americans and greatly increased pressure on Congress to end segregation.[69] The media were also central in the Watergate affair, which ultimately forced President Richard Nixon to resign in disgrace after investigations by the *Washington Post*, the *New York Times*, and the television networks disclosed abuses of power by those in the White House. Cable news gave us 24/7 coverage of events and live video from the battlefields of the first Iraq War.[70] Social media have made the news even more immediate; people can post videos of events directly on YouTube or Facebook and political leaders can communicate more directly with society through platforms such as Twitter.

Mass media have been central to every election of the past century. They cover the emergence and activities of the candidates, political debates and conventions, and election night returns. They are vehicles for political advertising. They even generate their own campaign news, especially by conducting public-opinion polls and reporting who is ahead and who is behind, who is gaining momentum and who is fading.

68 Aaron Mamiit, "Gmail Service Slowly Recovering in China: What Really Happened?," *Tech Times*, January 2, 2015, www.techtimes.com/articles/24108/20150102/gmail-service-slowly-recovering-in-china-what-really-happened.htm (accessed 5/17/20).

69 David J. Garrow, *Protest at Selma: Martin Luther King, Jr., and the Voting Rights Act of 1965* (New Haven, CT: Yale University Press, 1978).

70 Todd Gitlin, *The Whole World Is Watching: Mass Media in the Making and Unmaking of the New Left* (1980; repr. with a new preface, Berkeley: University of California Press, 2003).

And the media go to war along with the U.S. military. Since the time of the Civil War, news reporting and photography have brought wars home. Graphic depictions of atrocities in Vietnam and of American war dead and wounded helped turn popular sentiment against that war, which compelled the government to negotiate an end to the conflict.[71] Video of precision bombs destroying targets in Baghdad and of the rout of Saddam Hussein's army in 1991 lifted President George H. W. Bush's popularity and solidified his reputation as commander in chief.[72] News coverage of the Iraq War in 2003 portrayed the toppling of Hussein's statue in Baghdad, and President George W. Bush's announcement of "Mission Accomplished" at the end of combat in 2003 would later be used against him as the military struggled to restore stability in Iraq.

The tremendous power that reporters and editors sometimes wield emanates from the free hand the press enjoys in American politics. As long as they do not overstep the bounds of libel, journalists can criticize the government openly. Given the diversity of media outlets today, it is not uncommon to find defenders and critics of government or of particular political decisions, and often those on either side of the debate argue their positions side by side. Online media have brought more voices to the fore and have broadened the scope of the debate over public policy. Debate and criticism of public officials are essential, but they sometimes exact a social cost.

Free media are essential to democratic government. We depend on them to investigate wrongdoing, publicize and explain governmental actions, evaluate programs and politicians, and bring to light matters that might otherwise be known only to a handful of government insiders. In short, without free and active media, popular government would be virtually impossible. Citizens would have few means of knowing or assessing the government's actions other than the pronouncements of the government itself. Moreover, without active—indeed, aggressive—media, citizens would be hard-pressed to make informed choices among competing candidates at the polls. Often enough, the media reveal discrepancies between candidates' claims and their records and between the images that candidates project and the underlying realities.

At the same time, politicians increasingly rely on news coverage, especially favorable coverage. National political leaders and journalists have had symbiotic relationships, at least since Franklin Delano Roosevelt's presidency. Initially, politicians were the senior partners. Thus, for example, reporters did not publicize potentially embarrassing information, widely known in Washington, D.C., about the personal lives of such figures as Roosevelt and John F. Kennedy. Today, the balance has shifted. Often it seems that the journalists have the upper hand. Now that individual politicians depend so heavily on media to reach their constituents, journalists no longer need fear that their access to information can be

---

71 William M. Hammond, *Reporting Vietnam: Media and Military at War* (Lawrence: University of Kansas Press, 1998).

72 Jon A. Krosnick and Laura A. Brannon, "The Impact of the Gulf War on the Ingredients of Presidential Evaluations: Multidimensional Effects of Political Involvement," *American Political Science Review* 87, no. 4 (1993).

---

restricted in retaliation for negative coverage. It is not uncommon today to hear the White House press corps challenge the president's press liaison or even the president directly. The relationship between the Trump administration and the White House press corps has been antagonistic, with the president often attacking reporters personally. Attempts to confront the media, however, have often brought criticism of the president from other politicians, including those from his own party.[73]

Freedom gives the media enormous power. The media can make or break reputations, help launch or destroy political careers, and build support for or rally opposition against programs and institutions.[74] Wherever there is so much power, there exists at least the potential for its abuse. All things considered, free media are so critically important to the maintenance of a democratic society that we may be willing to take the risk that the media will occasionally abuse their power. The forms of government control that would prevent the media from misusing their power would also pose a serious risk to our freedom.

For Further Reading

Arnold, R. Douglas. *Congress, the Press, and Political Accountability*. Princeton, NJ: Princeton University Press, 2004.

Bagdikian, Ben H. *The New Media Monopoly*. Boston: Beacon Press, 2004.

Baum, Matthew A. *Soft News Goes to War: Public Opinion and American Foreign Policy in the New Media Age*. Princeton, NJ: Princeton University Press, 2003.

Cook, Timothy E. *Governing with the News: The News Media as a Political Institution*. Chicago: University of Chicago Press, 1998.

Groseclose, Tim, and Jeffrey Milyo. "A Measure of Media Bias." *Quarterly Journal of Economics* 120, no. 4 (2005): 1191–237.

Hamilton, James T. *All the News That's Fit to Sell: How the Market Transforms Information into News*. Princeton, NJ: Princeton University Press, 2004.

Iyengar, Shanto. *Media Politics: A Citizen's Guide*. 4th ed. New York: Norton, 2019.

Kellner, Douglas. *Media Spectacle and the Crisis of Democracy: Terrorism, War, and Election Battles*. Boulder, CO: Paradigm, 2005.

73 Eddie Scarry, "White House, Press Relations Collapse after Trump's Mika Brzezinski Face-Lift Tweet," *Washington Examiner*, June 29, 2017, www.washingtonexaminer.com/ white-house-press-relations-collapse-after-trumps-mika-brzezinski-face-lift-tweet (accessed 5/17/20).

74 Martin Linsky, *Impact: How the Press Affects Federal Policymaking* (New York: Norton, 1991).

Merritt, Davis. *Knightfall: Knight Ridder and How the Erosion of Newspaper Journalism Is Putting Democracy at Risk.* New York: AMACOM, 2005.

Norris, Pippa, Montague Kern, and Marion Just, eds. *Framing Terrorism: The News Media, the Government and the Public.* New York: Routledge, 2003.

Schudson, Michael. "The News Media as Political Institutions." *Annual Review of Political Science* 5 (June 2002): 249–69.

Starr, Paul. *The Creation of the Media: Political Origins of Modern Communications.* New York: Basic Books, 2004.

Appendix

The Declaration of Independence

In Congress, July 4, 1776

When in the course of human events, it becomes necessary for one people to dissolve the political bands which have connected them with another, and to assume among the Powers of the earth, the separate and equal station to which the Laws of Nature and of Nature's God entitle them, a decent respect to the opinions of mankind requires that they should declare the causes which impel them to the separation.

We hold these truths to be self-evident, that all men are created equal, that they are endowed by their Creator with certain unalienable rights, that among these are Life, Liberty, and the pursuit of Happiness. That to secure these rights, Governments are instituted among Men, deriving their just powers from the consent of the governed. That whenever any Form of Government becomes destructive of these ends, it is the Right of the People to alter or to abolish it, and to institute new Government, laying its foundation on such principles and organizing its powers in such form, as to them shall seem most likely to effect their Safety and Happiness. Prudence, indeed, will dictate that Governments long established should not be changed for light and transient causes; and accordingly all experience hath shown, that mankind are more disposed to suffer, while evils are sufferable, than to right themselves by abolishing the forms to which they are accustomed. But when a long train of abuses and usurpations, pursuing invariably the same Object evinces a design to reduce them under absolute Despotism, it is their right, it is their duty, to throw off such Government, and to provide new Guards for their future security.—Such has been the patient sufferance of these Colonies; and such is now the necessity which constrains them to alter their former Systems of Government. The history of the present King of Great Britain is a history of repeated injuries and usurpations, all having in direct object the establishment of an absolute Tyranny over these States. To prove this, let Facts be submitted to a candid world.

He has refused his Assent to Laws, the most wholesome and necessary for the public good.

He has forbidden his Governors to pass Laws of immediate and pressing importance, unless suspended in their operation till his Assent should be obtained; and when so suspended, he has utterly neglected to attend to them.

He has refused to pass other Laws for the accommodation of large districts of people, unless those people would relinquish the right of Representation in the Legislature, a right inestimable to them and formidable to tyrants only.

He has called together legislative bodies at places unusual, uncomfortable, and distant from the depository of their public Records, for the sole purpose of fatiguing them into compliance with his measures.

He has dissolved Representative Houses repeatedly, for opposing with manly firmness his invasions on the rights of the people.

He has refused for a long time, after such dissolutions, to cause others to be elected; whereby the Legislative powers, incapable of Annihilation, have returned to the People at large for their exercise; the State remaining in the mean time exposed to all dangers of invasion from without, and convulsions within.

He has endeavored to prevent the population of these States; for that purpose obstructing the Laws of Naturalization of Foreigners; refusing to pass others to encourage their migrations hither, and raising the conditions of new Appropriations of Lands.

He has obstructed the Administration of Justice, by refusing his Assent to Laws for establishing Judiciary powers.

He has made Judges dependent on his Will alone, for the tenure of their offices, and the amount and payment of their salaries.

He has erected a multitude of New Offices, and sent hither swarms of Officers to harass our People, and eat out their substance.

He has kept among us, in times of peace, Standing Armies without the Consent of our legislature.

He has affected to render the Military independent of and superior to the Civil Power.

He has combined with others to subject us to a jurisdiction foreign to our constitution, and unacknowledged by our laws; giving his Assent to their Acts of pretended Legislation:

For quartering large bodies of armed troops among us:

For protecting them, by a mock Trial, from Punishment for any Murders which they should commit on the Inhabitants of these States:

For cutting off our Trade with all parts of the world:

For imposing taxes on us without our Consent:

For depriving us in many cases, of the benefits of Trial by jury:

For transporting us beyond Seas to be tried for pretended offences:

For abolishing the free System of English Laws in a neighboring Province, establishing therein an Arbitrary government, and enlarging its Boundaries so as to render it at once an example and fit instrument for introducing the same absolute rule into these Colonies:

For taking away our Charters, abolishing our most valuable Laws, and altering fundamentally the Forms of our Governments:

For suspending our own Legislatures, and declaring themselves invested with Power to legislate for us in all cases whatsoever.

He has abdicated Government here, by declaring us out of his Protection and waging War against us.

He has plundered our seas, ravaged our Coasts, burnt our towns, and destroyed the lives of our people.

He is at this time transporting large armies of foreign mercenaries to compleat the works of death, desolation, and tyranny, already begun with circumstances of Cruelty & perfidy scarcely paralleled in the most barbarous ages, and totally unworthy the Head of a civilized nation.

He has constrained our fellow Citizens taken Captive on the high Seas to bear Arms against their Country, to become the executioners of their friends and Brethren, or to fall themselves by their Hands.

He has excited domestic insurrections amongst us, and has endeavored to bring on the inhabitants of our frontiers, the merciless Indian Savages, whose known rule of warfare, is an undistinguished destruction of all ages, sexes, and conditions.

In every stage of these Oppressions We have Petitioned for Redress in the most humble terms: Our repeated Petitions have been answered only by repeated injury. A Prince, whose character is thus marked by every act which may define a Tyrant, is unfit to be the ruler of a free people.

Nor have We been wanting in attention to our British brethren. We have warned them from time to time of attempts by their legislature to extend an unwarrantable jurisdiction over us. We have reminded them of the circumstances of our emigration and settlement here. We have appealed to their native justice and magnanimity, and we have conjured them by the ties of our common kindred to disavow these usurpations, which, would inevitably interrupt our connections and correspondence. They too must have been deaf to the voice of justice and of consanguinity. We must, therefore, acquiesce in the necessity, which denounces our Separation, and hold them, as we hold the rest of mankind, Enemies in War, in Peace Friends.

WE, THEREFORE, the Representatives of the UNITED STATES OF AMERICA, in General Congress, Assembled, appealing to the Supreme Judge of the world for the rectitude of our intentions, do, in the Name, and by Authority of the good People of these Colonies, solemnly publish and declare, That these United Colonies are, and of Right ought to be FREE AND INDEPENDENT STATES; that they are Absolved from all Allegiance to the British Crown, and that all political connection between them and the State of Great Britain, is and ought to be totally dissolved; and that as Free and Independent States, they have full Power to levy War, conclude Peace, contract Alliances, establish Commerce, and to do all other Acts and Things which Independent States may of right do. And for the support of this Declaration, with a firm reliance on the Protection of Divine Providence, we mutually pledge to each other our Lives, our Fortunes, and our sacred Honor.

The foregoing Declaration was, by order of Congress, engrossed, and signed by the following members:

John Hancock

NEW HAMPSHIRE	MASSACHUSETTS BAY	RHODE ISLAND
Josiah Bartlett	Samuel Adams	Stephen Hopkins
William Whipple	John Adams	William Ellery
Matthew Thornton	Robert Treat Paine	
	Elbridge Gerry	

CONNECTICUT
Roger Sherman
Samuel Huntington
William Williams
Oliver Wolcott

NEW YORK
William Floyd
Philip Livingston
Francis Lewis
Lewis Morris

NEW JERSEY
Richard Stockton
John Witherspoon
Francis Hopkinson
John Hart
Abraham Clark

PENNSYLVANIA
Robert Morris
Benjamin Rush
Benjamin Franklin
John Morton
George Clymer
James Smith
George Taylor
James Wilson
George Ross

DELAWARE
Caesar Rodney
George Read
Thomas M'Kean

MARYLAND
Samuel Chase
William Paca
Thomas Stone
Charles Carroll,
of Carrollton

VIRGINIA
George Wythe
Richard Henry Lee
Thomas Jefferson
Benjamin Harrison
Thomas Nelson, Jr.
Francis Lightfoot Lee
Carter Braxton

NORTH CAROLINA
William Hooper
Joseph Hewes
John Penn

SOUTH CAROLINA
Edward Rutledge
Thomas Heyward, Jr.
Thomas Lynch, Jr.
Arthur Middleton

GEORGIA
Button Gwinnett
Lyman Hall
George Walton

Resolved, That copies of the Declaration be sent to the several assemblies, conventions, and committees, or councils of safety, and to the several commanding officers of the continental troops; that it be proclaimed in each of the United States, at the head of the army.

The Articles of Confederation

Agreed to by Congress November 15, 1777;
ratified and in force March 1, 1781

To all whom these Presents shall come, we the undersigned Delegates of the States affixed to our Names send greeting. Whereas the Delegates of the United States of America in Congress assembled did on the fifteenth day of November in the Year of our Lord One Thousand Seven Hundred and Seventy seven, and in the Second Year of the Independence of America agree to certain articles of Confederation and perpetual Union between the States of Newhampshire, Massachusetts-bay, Rhodeisland and Providence Plantations, Connecticut, New-York, New-Jersey, Pennsylvania, Delaware, Maryland, Virginia, North-Carolina, South-Carolina and Georgia in the Words following, viz. "Articles of Confederation and perpetual Union between the states of Newhampshire, Massachusetts-bay, Rhodeisland and Providence Plantations, Connecticut, New-York, New-Jersey, Pennsylvania, Delaware, Maryland, Virginia, North-Carolina, South-Carolina and Georgia.

Art. I. The Stile of this confederacy shall be "The United States of America."

Art. II. Each state retains its sovereignty, freedom and independence, and every Power, Jurisdiction and right, which is not by this confederation expressly delegated to the United States, in Congress assembled.

Art. III. The said states hereby severally enter into a firm league of friendship with each other, for their common defence, the security of their Liberties, and their mutual and general welfare, binding themselves to assist each other, against all force offered to, or attacks made upon them, or any of them, on account of religion, sovereignty, trade, or any other pretence whatever.

Art. IV. The better to secure and perpetuate mutual friendship and intercourse among the people of the different states in this union, the free inhabitants of each of these states, paupers, vagabonds and fugitives from Justice excepted, shall be entitled to all privileges and immunities of free citizens in the several states; and the people of each state shall have free ingress and regress to and from any other state, and shall enjoy therein all the privileges of trade and commerce, subject to the same duties, impositions and restrictions as the inhabitants thereof respectively, provided that such restriction shall not extend so far as to prevent the removal of property imported into any state, to any other state of which the Owner is an inhabitant; provided also that no imposition, duties or restriction shall be laid by any state, on the property of the united states, or either of them.

If any Person guilty of, or charged with treason, felony, or other high misdemeanor in any state, shall flee from Justice, and be found in any of the united states, he shall upon demand of the Governor or executive power, of the state from which he fled, be delivered up and removed to the state having jurisdiction of his offence.

Full faith and credit shall be given in each of these states to the records, acts and judicial proceedings of the courts and magistrates of every other state.

Art. V. For the more convenient management of the general interests of the united states, delegates shall be annually appointed in such manner as the legislature of each state shall direct, to meet in Congress on the first Monday in November, in every year, with a power reserved to each state, to recall its delegates, or any of them, at any time within the year, and to send others in their stead, for the remainder of the Year.

No state shall be represented in Congress by less than two, nor by more than seven Members; and no person shall be capable of being a delegate for more than three years in any term of six years; nor shall any person, being a delegate, be capable of holding any office under the united states, for which he, or another for his benefit receives any salary, fees or emolument of any kind.

Each state shall maintain its own delegates in a meeting of the states, and while they act as members of the committee of the states.

In determining questions in the united states, in Congress assembled, each state shall have one vote.

Freedom of speech and debate in Congress shall not be impeached or questioned in any Court, or place out of Congress, and the members of congress shall be protected in their persons from arrests and imprisonments, during the time of their going to and from, and attendance on congress, except for treason, felony, or breach of the peace.

Art. VI. No state without the Consent of the united states in congress assembled, shall send any embassy to, or receive any embassy from, or enter into any conference, agreement, or alliance or treaty with any King, prince or state; nor shall any person holding any office or profit or trust under the united states, or any of them, accept of any present, emolument, office or title of any kind whatever from any king, prince or foreign state; nor shall the united states in congress assembled, or any of them, grant any title of nobility.

No two or more states shall enter into any treaty, confederation or alliance whatever between them, without the consent of the united states in congress assembled, specifying accurately the purposes for which the same is to be entered into, and how long it shall continue.

No state shall lay any imposts or duties, which may interfere with any stipulations in treaties, entered into by the united states in congress assembled, with any king, prince or state, in pursuance of any treaties already proposed by congress, to the courts of France and Spain.

No vessels of war shall be kept up in time of peace by any state, except such number only, as shall be deemed necessary by the united states in congress assembled, for the defence of such state, or its trade; nor shall any body of forces be kept up by any state, in time of peace, except such number only, as in the judgment of the united states, in congress assembled, shall be deemed requisite to garrison the forts necessary for the defence of such state; but every state shall always keep up a well regulated and disciplined militia, sufficiently armed and accoutred, and shall provide and constantly have ready for use, in public stores, a due number of field pieces and tents, and a proper quantity of arms, ammunition and camp equipage.

No state shall engage in any war without the consent of the united states in congress assembled, unless such state be actually invaded by enemies, or shall have received certain advice of a resolution being formed by some nation of Indians to invade such state, and the danger is so imminent as not to admit of a delay, till the united states in congress asssembled can be consulted; nor shall any state grant commissions to any ships or vessels of war, nor letters of marque or reprisal, except it be after a declaration of war by the united states in congress assembled, and then only against the kingdom or state and the subjects thereof, against which war has been so declared, and under such regulations as shall be established by the united states in congress assembled, unless such state be infested by pirates; in which case vessels of war may be fitted out for that occasion, and kept so long as the danger shall continue, or until the united states in congress assembled shall determine otherwise.

Art. VII. When land-forces are raised by any state for the common defence, all officers of or under the rank of colonel, shall be appointed by the legislature of each state respectively by whom such forces shall be raised, or in such manner as such state shall direct, and all vacancies shall be filled up by the state which first made the appointment.

Art. VIII. All charges of war, and all other expences that shall be incurred for the common defence or general welfare, and allowed by the united states in congress assembled, shall be defrayed out of a common treasury, which shall be supplied by the several states, in proportion to the value of all land within each state, granted to or surveyed for any Person, as such land and the buildings and improvements thereon shall be estimated according to such mode as the united states in congress assembled, shall from time to time direct and appoint. The taxes for paying that proportion shall be laid and levied by the authority and direction of the legislatures of the several states within the time agreed upon by the united states in congress assembled.

Art. IX. The united states in congress assembled, shall have the sole and exclusive right and power of determining on peace and war, except in the cases mentioned in the sixth article—of sending and receiving ambassadors—entering into treaties and alliances, provided that no treaty of commerce shall be made whereby the legislative power of the respective states shall be restrained from imposing such imposts and duties on foreigners, as their own people are subjected to, or from prohibiting the exportation of any species of goods or commodities whatsoever—of establishing rules for deciding in all cases, what captures on land or water shall be legal, and in what manner prizes taken by land or naval forces in the service of the united states shall be divided or appropriated—of granting letters of marque and reprisal in times of peace—appointing courts for the trial of piracies and felonies committed on the high seas and establishing courts for receiving and determining finally appeals in all cases of captures, provided that no member of congress shall be appointed a judge of any of the said courts.

The united states in congress assembled shall also be the last resort on appeal in all disputes and differences now subsisting or that hereafter may arise between two or more states concerning boundary, jurisdiction or any other cause whatever; which authority shall always be exercised in the manner following. Whenever the legislative or executive authority or lawful agent of any state in controversy with another shall present a petition to congress stating the matter in question and praying for a hearing, notice thereof shall be given by order of congress to the legislative or executive authority of the other state in controversy, and a day assigned for the appearance of the parties by their lawful agents, who shall then be directed to appoint by joint consent, commissioners or judges to constitute a court for hearing and determining the matter in question: but if they cannot agree, congress shall name three persons out of each of the united states, and from the list of such persons each party shall alternately strike out one, the petitioners beginning, until the number shall be reduced to thirteen; and from that number not less than seven, nor more than nine names as congress shall direct, shall in the presence of congress be drawn out by lot, and the persons whose names shall be so drawn or any five of them, shall be commissioners or judges, to hear and finally determine the controversy, so always as a major part of the judges who shall hear the cause shall agree in the determination: and if either party shall neglect to attend at the day appointed, without shewing reasons, which congress shall judge sufficient, or being present shall refuse to strike, the congress shall proceed to nominate three persons out of each state, and the secretary of congress shall strike in behalf of such party absent or refusing; and the judgment and sentence of the court to be appointed, in the manner before prescribed, shall be final and conclusive; and if any of the parties shall refuse to submit to the authority of such court, or to appear to defend their claim or cause, the court shall nevertheless proceed to pronounce sentence, or judgment, which shall in like manner be final and decisive, the judgment or sentence and other proceedings being in either case transmitted to congress, and lodged among the acts of congress for the security of the parties concerned: provided that every commissioner, before he sits in judgment, shall take an oath to be administered by one of the judges of the supreme or superior court of the state, where the cause shall be tried, "well and truly to hear and determine the matter in question, according to the best of his judgment, without favour, affection or hope of reward:" provided also that no state shall be deprived of territory for the benefit of the united states.

All controversies concerning the private right of soil claimed under different grants of two or more states, whose jurisdictions as they may respect such lands, and the states which passed such grants are adjusted, the said grants or either of them being at the same time claimed to have originated antecedent to such settlement of jurisdiction, shall on the petition of either party to the congress of the united states, be finally determined as near as may be in the same manner as is before prescribed for deciding disputes respecting territorial jurisdiction between different states.

The united states in congress assembled shall also have the sole and exclusive right and power of regulating the alloy and value of coin struck by their own authority, or by that of the respective states—fixing the standard of weights and measures throughout the united states—regulating the trade and managing all affairs with the Indians, not members of any of the states, provided that the legislative right of any state within its own limits be not infringed or violated—establishing and regulating post-offices from one state to another, throughout all the united states, and exacting such postage on the papers passing thro' the same as may be requisite to defray the expences of the said office—appointing all officers of the land forces, in the service of the united states, except regimental officers—appointing all the officers of the united states—making rules for the government and regulation of the said land and naval forces, and directing their operations.

The united states in congress assembled shall have the authority to appoint a committee, to sit in the recess of congress, to be denominated "A Committee of the States," and to consist of one delegate from each state; and to appoint such other committees and civil officers as may be necessary for managing the general affairs of the united states under their direction—to appoint one of their number to preside, provided that no person be allowed to serve in the office of president more than one year in any term of three years; to ascertain the necessary sums of Money to be raised for the service of the united states, and to appropriate and apply the same for defraying the public expences—to borrow money, or emit bills on the credit of the united states, transmitting every half year to the respective states an account of the sums of money so borrowed or emitted,—to build and equip a navy—to agree upon the number of land forces, and to make requisitions from each state for its quota, in proportion to the number of white inhabitants in such state; which requisition shall be binding, and thereupon the legislature of each state shall appoint the regimental officers, raise the men and cloath, arm and equip them in a soldier like manner, at the expence of the united states, and the officers and men so cloathed, armed and equipped shall march to the place appointed, and within the time agreed on by the united states in congress assembled: But if the united states in congress assembled shall, on consideration of circumstances judge proper that any state should not raise men, or should raise a smaller number than its quota, and that any other state should raise a greater number of men than the quota thereof, such extra number shall be raised, officered, cloathed, armed and equipped in the same manner as the quota of such state, unless the legislature of such state shall judge that such extra number cannot be safely spared out of the same, in which case they shall raise, officer, cloath, arm and equip as many of such extra number as they judge can be safely spared. And the officers and men so cloathed, armed and equipped, shall march to the place appointed, and within the time agreed on by the united states in congress assembled.

The united states in congress assembled shall never engage in a war, nor grant letters of marque and reprisal in time of peace, nor enter into any treaties or alliances, nor coin money, nor regulate the value thereof, nor ascertain the sums and expences necessary for the defence and welfare of the united states, or any of them, nor emit bills, nor borrow money on the credit of the united states, nor appropriate money, nor agree upon the number of vessels of war, to be built or purchased, or the number of land or sea forces to be raised, nor appoint a commander in chief of the army or navy, unless nine states assent to the same: nor shall a question on any other point, except for adjourning from day to day be determined, unless by the votes of a majority of the united states in congress assembled.

The congress of the united states shall have power to adjourn to any time within the year, and to any place within the united states, so that no period of adjournment be for a longer duration than the space of six Months, and shall publish the Journal of their proceedings monthly, except such parts thereof relating to treaties, alliances or military operations as in their judgment require secresy; and the yeas and nays of the delegates of each state on any question shall be entered on the Journal, when it is desired by any delegate; and the delegates of a state, or any of them, at his or their request shall be furnished with a transcript of the said Journal, except such parts as are above excepted to lay before the legislatures of the several states.

Art. X. The committee of the states, or any nine of them, shall be authorised to execute, in the recess of congress, such of the powers of congress as the united states in congress assembled, by the consent of nine states, shall from time to time think expedient to vest them with; provided that no power be delegated to the said committee, for the exercise of which, by the articles of confederation, the voice of nine states in the congress of the united states assembled is requisite.

Art. XI. Canada acceding to this confederation, and joining in the measures of the united states, shall be admitted into, and entitled to all the advantages of this union: but no other colony shall be admitted into the same, unless such admission be agreed to by nine states.

Art. XII. All bills of credit emitted, monies borrowed and debts contracted by, or under the authority of congress, before the assembling of the united states, in pursuance of the present confederation, shall be deemed and considered as a charge against the united states, for payment and satisfaction whereof the said united states and the public faith are hereby solemnly pledged.

Art. XIII. Every state shall abide by the determinations of the united states in congress assembled, on all questions which by this confederation are submitted to them. And the Articles of this confederation shall be inviolably observed by every state, and the union shall be perpetual; nor shall any alteration at any time hereafter be made in any of them; unless such alteration be agreed to in a congress of the united states, and be afterwards confirmed by the legislatures of every state.

AND WHEREAS it hath pleased the Great Governor of the World to incline the hearts of the legislatures we respectively represent in congress, to approve of, and to authorize us to ratify the said articles of confederation and perpetual union. KNOW YE that we the undersigned delegates, by virtue of the power and authority to us given for that purpose, do by these presents, in the name and in behalf of our respective constituents, fully and entirely ratify and confirm each and every of the said articles of confederation and perpetual union, and all and singular the matters and things therein contained: And we do further solemnly plight and engage the faith of our respective constituents, that they shall abide by the determination of the united states in congress assembled, on all questions, which by the said confederation are submitted to them. And that the articles thereof shall be inviolably observed by the states we respectively represent, and that the union shall be perpetual. In Witness whereof we have hereunto set our hands in Congress. Done at Philadelphia in the state of Pennsylvania the ninth Day of July in the Year of our Lord one Thousand seven Hundred and Seventy-eight and in the third year of the independence of America.

The Constitution of the
United States of America

Annotated with references to *Federalist Papers*

[PREAMBLE]

We the People of the United States, in Order to form a more perfect Union, establish Justice, insure domestic Tranquility, provide for the common defence, promote the general Welfare, and secure the Blessings of Liberty to ourselves and our Posterity, do ordain and establish this Constitution for the United States of America.

84 (Hamilton)

ARTICLE I

Section 1
[LEGISLATIVE POWERS]

All legislative Powers herein granted shall be vested in a Congress of the United States, which shall consist of a Senate and House of Representatives.

10, 45 (Madison)

Section 2
[HOUSE OF REPRESENTATIVES, HOW CONSTITUTED, POWER OF IMPEACHMENT]

The House of Representatives shall be composed of Members chosen every second Year by the People of the several States, and the Electors in each State shall have the Qualifications requisite for Electors of the most numerous Branch of the State Legislature.

39, 45, 52–53, 57 (Madison)

No Person shall be a Representative who shall not have attained to the Age of twenty-five Years, and been seven Years a Citizen of the United States, and who shall not, when elected, be an inhabitant of that State in which he shall be chosen.

52 (Madison)

60 (Hamilton)

Representatives and *direct Taxes*[1] shall be apportioned among the several States which may be included within this Union, according to their respective Numbers, *which shall be determined by adding to the whole Number of free Persons, including those bound to Service for a Term of Years,* and excluding Indians not taxed, *three-fifths of all other Persons.*[2] The actual Enumeration shall be made within three Years after the first Meeting of the Congress of the United States, and within every subsequent Term of ten Years, in such Manner as they shall by Law direct. The Number of Representatives shall not exceed one for every thirty Thousand, but each State shall have at Least one Representative; *and until such enumeration shall be made, the State of New*

54, 58 (Madison)

55–56 (Madison)

---

1   Modified by Sixteenth Amendment.

2   Modified by Fourteenth Amendment.

Hampshire shall be entitled to chuse three, Massachusetts eight, Rhode-Island and Providence Plantations one, Connecticut five, New-York six, New Jersey four, Pennsylvania eight, Delaware one, Maryland six, Virginia ten, North Carolina five, South Carolina five, and Georgia three.[3]

When vacancies happen in the Representation from any State, the Executive Authority thereof shall issue Writs of Election to fill such Vacancies.

79 (Hamilton)

The House of Representatives shall chuse their Speaker and other Officers; and shall have the sole Power of Impeachment.

Section 3
[THE SENATE, HOW CONSTITUTED, IMPEACHMENT TRIALS]

39, 45 (Madison)
60 (Hamilton)

The Senate of the United States shall be composed of two Senators from each State, *chosen by the Legislature thereof,*[4] for six Years; and each Senator shall have one Vote.

62–63 (Madison)
59, 68 (Hamilton)

Immediately after they shall be assembled in Consequence of the first Election, they shall be divided as equally as may be into three Classes. The Seats of the Senators of the first Class shall be vacated at the Expiration of the second Year, of the second Class at the Expiration of the fourth Year, and of the third Class at the Expiration of the sixth Year, so that one third may be chosen every second Year: *and if vacancies happen by Resignation, or otherwise, during the Recess of the Legislature of any State, the Executive thereof may make temporary Appointments until the next Meeting of the Legislature, which shall then fill such Vacancies.*[5]

62 (Madison)
64 (Jay)

No person shall be a Senator who shall not have attained to the Age of thirty Years, and been nine Years a Citizen of the United States, and who shall not, when elected, be an Inhabitant of that State for which he shall be chosen.

The Vice-President of the United States shall be President of the Senate, but shall have no Vote, unless they be equally divided.

The Senate shall chuse their other Officers, and also a President pro tempore, in the Absence of the Vice-President, or when he shall exercise the Office of President of the United States.

39 (Madison)
65–67, 79 (Hamilton)

The Senate shall have the sole Power to try all Impeachments. When sitting for that Purpose, they shall be on Oath or Affirmation. When the President of the United States is tried, the Chief Justice shall preside: And no Person shall be convicted without the Concurrence of two-thirds of the Members present.

84 (Hamilton)

Judgment in Cases of Impeachment shall not extend further than to removal from Office, and disqualification to hold and enjoy any Office of honor, Trust or Profit under the United States: but the Party convicted shall nevertheless be liable and subject to Indictment, Trial, Judgment and Punishment, according to Law.

Section 4
[ELECTION OF SENATORS AND REPRESENTATIVES]

59–61 (Hamilton)

The Times, Places and Manner of holding Elections for Senators and Representatives, shall be prescribed in each State by the Legislature thereof; but the

---

3 Temporary provision.

4 Modified by Seventeenth Amendment.

5 Modified by Seventeenth Amendment.

Congress may at any time by Law make or alter such Regulations, except as to the Places of chusing Senators.

The Congress shall assemble at least once in every Year, and such Meeting shall be on the first Monday in December, unless they shall by Law appoint a different Day.[6]

Section 5
[QUORUM, JOURNALS, MEETINGS, ADJOURNMENTS]

Each House shall be the Judge of the Elections, Returns and Qualifications of its own Members, and a Majority of each shall constitute a Quorum to do Business; but a smaller Number may adjourn from day to day, and may be authorized to compel the Attendance of absent Members, in such Manner, and under the Penalties as each House may provide.

Each House may determine the Rules of its Proceedings, punish its Members for disorderly Behavior, and, with the Concurrence of two-thirds, expel a Member.

Each House shall keep a Journal of its Proceedings, and from time to time publish the same, excepting such Parts as may in their Judgment require Secrecy; and the Yeas and Nays of the Members of either House on any questions shall, at the Desire of one-fifth of the present, be entered on the Journal.

Neither House, during the Session of Congress, shall, without the Consent of the other, adjourn for more than three days, nor to any other Place than that in which the two Houses shall be sitting.

Section 6
[COMPENSATION, PRIVILEGES, DISABILITIES]

The Senators and Representatives shall receive a Compensation for their Services, to be ascertained by Law, and paid out of the Treasury of the United States. They shall in all Cases, except Treason, Felony and Breach of the Peace, be privileged from Arrest during their Attendance at the Session of their respective Houses, and in going to and returning from the same; and for any Speech or Debate in either House, they shall not be questioned in any other Place.

No Senator or Representative shall, during the time for which he was elected, be appointed to any civil Office under the authority of the United States, which shall have been created, or the Emoluments whereof shall have been encreased during such time; and no Person holding any Office under the United States, shall be a Member of either House during his Continuance in Office.

55 (Madison)
76 (Hamilton)

Section 7
[PROCEDURE IN PASSING BILLS AND RESOLUTIONS]

All Bills for raising Revenue shall originate in the House of Representatives; but the Senate may propose or concur with Amendments as on other Bills.

66 (Hamilton)

Every Bill which shall have passed the House of Representatives and the Senate, shall, before it become a Law, be presented to the President of the United States; if he approve he shall sign it, but if not he shall return it, with his Objections to that House in which it shall have originated, who shall enter the Objections at large on their Journal, and proceed to reconsider it. If after such Reconsideration

69, 73 (Hamilton)

---

6 Modified by Twentieth Amendment.

two-thirds of that House shall agree to pass the Bill, it shall be sent, together with the Objections, to the other House, by which it shall likewise be reconsidered, and if approved by two-thirds of that House it shall become a Law. But in all such Cases the Votes of both Houses shall be determined by Yeas and Nays, and the Names of the Persons voting for and against the Bill shall be entered on the Journal of each House respectively. If any Bill shall not be returned by the President within ten Days (Sundays excepted) after it shall have been presented to him, the Same shall be a Law, in like Manner as if he had signed it, unless the Congress by their Adjournment prevent its Return, in which Case it shall not be a Law.

69, 73 (Hamilton)

Every Order, Resolution, or Vote to which the Concurrence of the Senate and House of Representatives may be necessary (except on a question of Adjournment) shall be presented to the President of the United States; and before the Same shall take Effect, shall be approved by him, or being disapproved by him, shall be repassed by two-thirds of the Senate and House of Representatives, according to the Rules and Limitations prescribed in the Case of a Bill.

Section 8
[POWERS OF CONGRESS]

The Congress shall have Power

30–36 (Hamilton)
41 (Madison)

To lay and collect Taxes, Duties, Imposts and Excises, to pay the Debts and provide for the common Defence and general Welfare of the United States; but all Duties, Imposts and excises shall be uniform throughout the United States;

To borrow Money on the Credit of the United States;

56 (Madison)
42, 45, 56
(Madison)

To regulate Commerce with foreign Nations, and among the several States, and with the Indian Tribes;

32 (Hamilton)

To establish an uniform Rule of Naturalization, and uniform Laws on the subject of Bankruptcies throughout the United States;

42 (Madison)

To coin Money, regulate the Value thereof, and of foreign Coin, and fix the Standard of Weights and Measures;

42 (Madison)

To provide for the Punishment of counterfeiting the Securities and current Coin of the United States;

To establish Post Offices and post Roads;

42 (Madison)

To promote the Progress of Science and useful Arts, by securing for limited Times to Authors and Inventors the exclusive Right to their respective Writings and Discoveries;

42, 43 (Madison)

81 (Hamilton)

To constitute Tribunals inferior to the supreme Court;

42 (Madison)

To define and Punish Piracies and Felonies committed on the high Seas, and Offences against the Law of Nations;

41 (Madison)

To declare War, grant Letters of Marque and Reprisal, and make Rules concerning Captures on Land and Water;

23, 24, 26 (Hamilton)

To raise and support Armies, but no Appropriation of Money to that Use shall be for a longer Term than two Years;

41 (Madison)

To provide and maintain a Navy;

To make Rules for the Government and Regulation of the land and naval forces;

29 (Hamilton)

To provide for calling for the Militia to execute the Laws of the Union, suppress Insurrections and repel Invasions;

To provide for organizing, arming, and disciplining, the Militia, and for governing such Part of them as may be employed in the Service of the United States, reserving to the States respectively, the Appointment of the Officers, and the Authority of training the Militia according to the discipline prescribed by Congress;

29 (Hamilton)
56 (Madison)

To exercise exclusive Legislation in all Cases whatsoever, over such District (not exceeding ten Miles square) as may, by Cession of particular States, and the Acceptance of Congress, become the Seat of the Government of the United States, and to exercise like Authority over all Places purchased by the Consent of the Legislature of the State in which the Same shall be, for the Erection of Forts, Magazines, Arsenals, dock-Yards, and other needful Buildings;—And

32 (Hamilton)
43 (Madison)

To make all Laws which shall be necessary and proper for carrying into Execution the foregoing Powers, and all other Powers vested by this Constitution in the Government of the United States, or in any Department or Officer thereof.

29, 33 (Hamilton)
44 (Madison)

Section 9
[SOME RESTRICTIONS ON FEDERAL POWER]

The Migration or Importation of such Persons as any of the States now existing shall think proper to admit, shall not be prohibited by the Congress prior to the Year one thousand eight hundred and eight, but a Tax or Duty may be imposed on such Importation, not exceeding ten dollars for each Person.[7]

42 (Madison)

The privilege of the Writ of *Habeas Corpus* shall not be suspended, unless when in Cases of Rebellion or Invasion the public Safety may require it.

83, 84 (Hamilton)

No Bill of Attainder or ex post facto Law shall be passed.

84 (Hamilton)

No Capitation, or other direct, Tax shall be laid, unless in Proportion to the Census or Enumeration herein before directed to be taken.[8]

No Tax or Duty shall be laid on Articles exported from any State.

No Preference shall be given by any Regulation of Commerce or Revenue to the Ports of one State over those of another; nor shall vessels bound to, or from, one State, be obliged to enter, clear, or pay Duties in another.

32 (Hamilton)

No Money shall be drawn from the Treasury, but in Consequence of Appropriations made by Law; and a regular Statement and Account of the Receipts and Expenditures of all public Money shall be published from time to time.

No Title of Nobility shall be granted by the United States: And no Person holding any Office of Profit or Trust under them, shall, without the Consent of the Congress, accept of any present, Emolument, Office or Title, of any kind whatever, from any King, Prince, or foreign State.

39 (Madison)
84 (Hamilton)

Section 10
[RESTRICTIONS UPON POWERS OF STATES]

No State shall enter into any Treaty, Alliance, or Confederation; grant Letters of Marque and Reprisal; coin Money; emit Bills of Credit; make any Thing but gold and silver Coin a Tender in Payment of Debts; pass any Bill of Attainder, ex post facto Law, or Law impairing the Obligation of Contracts, or grant any Title of Nobility.

33 (Hamilton)
44 (Madison)

---

7 Temporary provision.

8 Modified by Sixteenth Amendment.

No State shall, without the Consent of the Congress, lay any Imposts or Duties on Imports or Exports, except what may be absolutely necessary for executing its inspection Laws: and the net Produce of all Duties and Imposts, laid by any State on Imports or Exports, shall be for the Use of the Treasury of the United States; and all such Laws shall be subject to the Revision and Control of the Congress.

No State shall, without the Consent of Congress, lay any Duty of Tonnage, keep Troops, or Ships of War in time of Peace, enter into any Agreement or Compact with another State, or with a foreign Power, or engage in War, unless actually invaded, or in such imminent Danger as will not admit of Delay.

ARTICLE II

Section 1

[EXECUTIVE POWER, ELECTION, QUALIFICATIONS OF THE PRESIDENT]

The executive Power shall be vested in a President of the United States of America. *He shall hold his Office during the Term of four years and, together with the Vice-President, chosen for the same Term, be elected, as follows:*[9]

Each State shall appoint, in such Manner as the Legislature thereof may direct, a Number of Electors, equal to the whole Number of Senators and Representatives to which the State may be entitled in the Congress: but no Senator or Representative, or Person holding an Office of Trust or Profit under the United States, shall be appointed an Elector.

The electors shall meet in their respective States, and vote by ballot for two Persons, of whom one at least shall not be an Inhabitant of the same State with themselves. And they shall make a List of all the Persons voted for, and of the Number of Votes for each; which List they shall sign and certify, and transmit sealed to the Seat of the Government of the United States, directed to the President of the Senate. The President of the Senate shall, in the Presence of the Senate and House of Representatives, open all the Certificates, and the Votes shall then be counted. The Person having the greatest Number of Votes shall be the President, if such Number be a Majority of the whole Number of Electors appointed; and if there be more than one who have such Majority and have an equal Number of Votes, then the House of Representatives shall immediately chuse by Ballot one of them for President; and if no person have a Majority, then from the five highest on the List the said House shall in like Manner chuse the President. But in chusing the President, the Votes shall be taken by States, the Representation from each State having one Vote; A quorum for this Purpose shall consist of a Member or Members from two-thirds of the States, and a Majority of all the States shall be necessary to a Choice. In every Case, after the Choice of the President, the person having the greatest Number of Votes of the Electors shall be the Vice-President. But if there should remain two or more who have equal vote, the Senate shall chuse from them by Ballot the Vice-President.[10]

The Congress may determine the Time of chusing the Electors, and the Day on which they shall give their Votes; which Day shall be the same throughout the United States.

---

9 Number of terms limited to two by Twenty-Second Amendment.

10 Modified by Twelfth and Twentieth Amendments.

No Person except a natural born Citizen, or a Citizen of the United States, at the time of the Adoption of this Constitution, shall be eligible to the Office of President; neither shall any Person be eligible to that Office who shall not have attained to the Age of thirty-five Years, and been fourteen Years a Resident within the United States.

64 (Jay)

In Case of the Removal of the President from Office, or his Death, Resignation, or Inability to discharge the Powers and Duties of the said Office, the same shall devolve on the Vice-President, and the Congress may by Law provide for the Case of Removal, Death, Resignation, or Inability, both of the President and Vice-President, declaring what Officer shall then act as President, and such Officer shall act accordingly, until the Disability be removed, or a President shall be elected.

The President shall, at stated Times, receive for his Services, a Compensation, which shall neither be encreased nor diminished during the Period for which he shall have been elected, and he shall not receive within that Period any other Emolument from the United States, or any of them.

73, 79 (Hamilton)

Before he enter on the Execution of his Office, he shall take the following Oath or Affirmation:—"I do solemnly swear (or affirm) that I will faithfully execute the Office of President of the United States, and will to the best of my Ability, preserve, protect and defend the Constitution of the United States."

Section 2
[POWERS OF THE PRESIDENT]

The President shall be Commander in Chief of the Army and Navy of the United States, and of the Militia of the several States, when called into the actual Service of the United States; he may require the Opinion, in writing, of the principal Officer in each of the executive Departments, upon any Subject relating to the Duties of their respective Offices, and he shall have Power to grant Reprieves and Pardons for Offences against the United States, except in Cases of Impeachment.

69, 74 (Hamilton)

He shall have Power, by and with the Advice and Consent of the Senate, to make Treaties, provided two-thirds of the Senators present concur; and he shall nominate, and by and with the Advice and Consent of the Senate, shall appoint Ambassadors, other public Ministers and Consuls, Judges of the Supreme Court, and all other Officers of the United States, whose Appointments are not herein otherwise provided for, and which shall be established by Law: but the Congress may by Law vest the Appointment of such inferior Officers, as they think proper, in the President alone, in the Courts of Law, or in the Heads of Departments.

42 (Madison)
64 (Jay)
66, 69, 76, 77 (Hamilton)

The President shall have Power to fill up all Vacancies that may happen during the Recess of the Senate, by granting Commissions which shall expire at the End of their next Session.

67, 76 (Hamilton)

Section 3
[POWERS AND DUTIES OF THE PRESIDENT]

He shall from time to time give to the Congress Information of the State of the Union, and recommend to their Consideration such Measures as he shall judge necessary and expedient; he may, on extraordinary Occasions, convene both Houses, or either of them, and in Case of Disagreement between them, with Respect to the Time of Adjournment, he may adjourn them to such Time

69, 77, 78 (Hamilton)
42 (Madison)

as he shall think proper; he shall receive Ambassadors and other public Ministers; he shall take Care that the Laws be faithfully executed, and shall Commission all the Officers of the United States.

Section 4
[IMPEACHMENT]

39 (Madison)
69 (Hamilton)

The President, Vice-President and all civil Officers of the United States shall be removed from Office on Impeachment for, and Conviction of, Treason, Bribery, or other high Crimes and Misdemeanors.

ARTICLE III

Section 1
[JUDICIAL POWER, TENURE OF OFFICE]

65, 78, 79, 81, 82 (Hamilton)

The judicial Power of the United States, shall be vested in one supreme Court, and in such inferior Courts as the Congress may from time to time ordain and establish. The Judges, both of the supreme and inferior Courts, shall hold their Offices during good Behavior, and shall, at stated Times, receive for their Services, a Compensation, which shall not be diminished during their Continuance in Office.

Section 2
[JURISDICTION]

80 (Hamilton)

The judicial Power shall extend to all Cases, in Law and Equity, arising under this Constitution, the Laws of the United States, and Treaties made, or which shall be made, under their Authority;—to all Cases affecting Ambassadors, other public Ministers and Consuls;—to all Cases of admiralty and maritime Jurisdiction;—to Controversies to which the United States shall be a party;—to Controversies between two or more States;—*between a State and Citizens of another State;*—between Citizens of different States,—between Citizens of the same State claiming Lands under Grants of different States, *and between a State,* or the Citizens thereof, *and foreign States, Citizens or Subjects.*[11]

81 (Hamilton)

In all Cases affecting Ambassadors, other public Ministers and Consuls, and those in which a State shall be Party, the supreme Court shall have original Jurisdiction. In all the other Cases before mentioned, the supreme Court shall have appellate Jurisdiction, both as to Law and Fact, with such Exceptions, and under such Regulations as Congress shall make.

83, 84 (Hamilton)

The Trial of all Crimes, except in Cases of Impeachment, shall be by Jury; and such Trial shall be held in the State where the said Crimes shall have been committed; but when not committed within any State, the Trial shall be at such Place or Places as the Congress may by Law have directed.

---

11 Modified by Eleventh Amendment.

Section 3
[TREASON, PROOF, AND PUNISHMENT]

Treason against the United States, shall consist only in levying War against them, or in adhering to their Enemies, giving them Aid and Comfort. No Person shall be convicted of Treason unless on the Testimony of two Witnesses to the same overt Act, or on Confession in open Court.

43 (Madison)
84 (Hamilton)

The Congress shall have Power to declare the Punishment of Treason, but no Attainder of Treason shall work Corruption of Blood, or Forfeiture except during the Life of the Person attained.

43 (Madison)
84 (Hamilton)

ARTICLE IV

Section 1
[FAITH AND CREDIT AMONG STATES]

Full Faith and Credit shall be given in each State to the public Acts, Records, and judicial Proceedings of every other State. And the Congress may by general Laws prescribe the Manner in which such Acts, Records and Proceedings shall be proved, and the Effect thereof.

42 (Madison)

Section 2
[PRIVILEGES AND IMMUNITIES, FUGITIVES]

The Citizens of each State shall be entitled to all Privileges and Immunities of Citizens in the several States.

80 (Hamilton)

A person charged in any State with Treason, Felony or other Crime, who shall flee from Justice, and be found in another State, shall on Demand of the executive Authority of the State from which he fled, be delivered up to be removed to the State having Jurisdiction of the Crime.

No person held to Service or Labour in one State, under the Laws thereof, escaping into another, shall, in Consequence of any Law or Regulation therein, be discharged from such Service or Labour, but shall be delivered up on Claim of the Party to whom such Service or Labour may be due.[12]

Section 3
[ADMISSION OF NEW STATES]

New States may be admitted by the Congress into this Union; but no new State shall be formed or erected within the Jurisdiction of any other State; nor any State be formed by the Junction of two or more States, or Parts of States, without the Consent of the Legislatures of the States concerned as well as of the Congress.

43 (Madison)

The Congress shall have Power to dispose of and make all needful Rules and Regulations respecting the Territory or other Property belonging to the United States; and nothing in this Constitution shall be so construed as to Prejudice any Claims of the United States, or of any particular State.

43 (Madison)

---

12 Repealed by Thirteenth Amendment.

Section 4

[GUARANTEE OF REPUBLICAN GOVERNMENT]

39, 43
(Madison)

The United States shall guarantee to every State in this Union a Republican Form of Government, and shall protect each of them against Invasion; and on Application of the Legislature, or of the Executive (when the Legislature cannot be convened) against domestic Violence.

ARTICLE V

[AMENDMENT OF THE CONSTITUTION]

39, 43 (Madison)
85 (Hamilton)

The Congress, whenever two-thirds of both Houses shall deem it necessary, shall propose Amendments to this Constitution, or, on the Application of the Legislatures of two-thirds of the several States, shall call a Convention for proposing Amendments, which, in either Case, shall be valid to all Intents and Purposes, as Part of this Constitution, when ratified by the Legislatures of three-fourths of the several States, or by Conventions in three-fourths thereof, as the one or the other Mode of Ratification may be proposed by the Congress; *Provided that no Amendment which may be made prior to the Year One thousand eight hundred and eight shall in any Manner affect the first and fourth Clauses in the Ninth Section of the first Article;*[13] and that no State, without its Consent, shall be deprived of its equal Suffrage in the Senate.

ARTICLE VI

[DEBTS, SUPREMACY, OATH]

43 (Madison)

All Debts contracted and Engagements entered into, before the Adoption of this Constitution, shall be as valid against the United States under this Constitution, as under the Confederation.

27, 33 (Hamilton)
39, 44 (Madison)

This Constitution, and the Laws of the United States which shall be made in Pursuance thereof; and all Treaties made, or which shall be made, under the Authority of the United States, shall be the supreme Law of the Land; and the Judges in every State shall be bound thereby, any Thing in the Constitution or Laws of any State to the Contrary notwithstanding.

27 (Hamilton)
44 (Madison)

The Senators and Representatives before mentioned, and the Members of the several State Legislatures, and all executive and judicial Officers, both of the United States and of the several States, shall be bound by Oath or Affirmation, to support this Constitution; but no religious Test shall be required as a Qualification to any Office or public Trust under the United States.

ARTICLE VII

[RATIFICATION AND ESTABLISHMENT]

39, 40, 43
(Madison)

The Ratification of the Conventions of nine States, shall be sufficient for the Establishment of this Constitution between the States so ratifying the Same.[14]

---

13 Temporary provision.

14 The Constitution was submitted on September 17, 1787, by the Constitutional Convention, was ratified by the conventions of several states at various dates up to May 29, 1790, and became effective on March 4, 1789.

Done in Convention by the Unanimous Consent of the States present the Seventeenth Day of September in the Year of our Lord one thousand seven hundred and Eighty seven and of the Independence of the United States of America the Twelfth. *In Witness* whereof We have hereunto subscribed our Names,

G:^{0} WASHINGTON—
Presidt, and Deputy
from Virginia

NEW HAMPSHIRE
John Langdon
Nicholas Gilman

MASSACHUSETTS
Nathaniel Gorham
Rufus King

CONNECTICUT
Wm Saml Johnson
Roger Sherman

NEW YORK
Alexander Hamilton

NEW JERSEY
Wil: Livingston
David Brearley
Wm Paterson
Jona: Dayton

PENNSYLVANIA
B Franklin
Thomas Mifflin
Robt Morris
Geo. Clymer
Thos. FitzSimons
Jared Ingersoll
James Wilson
Gouv Morris

DELAWARE
Geo Read
Gunning Bedfor Jun
John Dickinson
Richard Bassett
Jaco: Broom

MARYLAND
James McHenry
Dan of St Thos Jenifer
Danl Carroll

VIRGINIA
John Blair—
James Madison Jr.

NORTH CAROLINA
Wm Blount
Richd Dobbs Spaight
Hu Williamson

SOUTH CAROLINA
J. Rutledge
Charles Cotesworth Pinckney
Charles Pinckney
Pierce Butler

GEORGIA
William Few
Abr Baldwin

Proposed by Congress and Ratified by the Legislatures of the Several States, Pursuant to Article V of the Original Constitution

Amendments I–X, known as the Bill of Rights, were proposed by Congress on September 25, 1789, and ratified on December 15, 1791. *The Federalist Papers* comments, mainly in opposition to a Bill of Rights, can be found in number 84 (Hamilton).

AMENDMENT I

[FREEDOM OF RELIGION, OF SPEECH, AND OF THE PRESS]

Congress shall make no law respecting an establishment of religion, or prohibiting the free exercise thereof; or abridging the freedom of speech, or of the press; or the right of the people peaceably to assemble, and to petition the Government for a redress of grievances.

AMENDMENT II

[RIGHT TO KEEP AND BEAR ARMS]

A well regulated Militia, being necessary to the security of a free State, the right of the people to keep and bear Arms, shall not be infringed.

AMENDMENT III

[QUARTERING OF SOLDIERS]

No Soldier shall, in time of peace be quartered in any house, without the consent of the Owner, nor in time of war, but in a manner to be prescribed by law.

AMENDMENT IV

[SECURITY FROM UNWARRANTABLE SEARCH AND SEIZURE]

The right of the people to be secure in their persons, houses, papers, and effects, against unreasonable searches and seizures, shall not be violated, and no Warrants shall issue, but upon probable cause, supported by Oath or affirmation, and particularly describing the place to be searched, and the persons or things to be seized.

AMENDMENT V

[RIGHTS OF ACCUSED PERSONS IN CRIMINAL PROCEEDINGS]

No person shall be held to answer for a capital, or otherwise infamous crime, unless on a presentment or indictment of a Grand Jury, except in cases arising in the land or naval forces, or in the Militia, when in actual service in time of

War or in public danger; nor shall any person be subject for the same offence to be twice put in jeopardy of life or limb; nor shall be compelled in any Criminal Case to be a witness against himself, nor be deprived of life, liberty, or property, without due process of law; nor shall private property be taken for public use, without just compensation.

AMENDMENT VI
[RIGHT TO SPEEDY TRIAL, WITNESSES, ETC.]

In all criminal prosecutions, the accused shall enjoy the right to a speedy and public trial, by an impartial jury of the State and district wherein the crime shall have been committed, which district shall have been previously ascertained by law, and to be informed of the nature and cause of the accusation; to be confronted with the witnesses against him; to have compulsory process for obtaining Witnesses in his favor, and to have the Assistance of Counsel for his defence.

AMENDMENT VII
[TRIAL BY JURY IN CIVIL CASES]

In suits at common law, where the value in controversy shall exceed twenty dollars, the right of trial by jury shall be preserved, and no fact tried by a jury shall be otherwise re-examined in any Court of the United States, than according to the rules of the common law.

AMENDMENT VIII
[BAILS, FINES, PUNISHMENTS]

Excessive bail shall not be required, nor excessive fines imposed, nor cruel and unusual punishments inflicted.

AMENDMENT IX
[RESERVATION OF RIGHTS OF PEOPLE]

The enumeration in the Constitution, of certain rights, shall not be construed to deny or disparage others retained by the people.

AMENDMENT X
[POWERS RESERVED TO STATES OR PEOPLE]

The powers not delegated to the United States by the Constitution, nor prohibited by it to the States, are reserved to the States respectively, or to the people.

AMENDMENT XI
[Proposed by Congress on March 4, 1794; declared ratified on January 8, 1798]
[RESTRICTION OF JUDICIAL POWER]

The Judicial power of the United States shall not be construed to extend to any suit in law or equity, commenced or prosecuted against one of the United States by Citizens of another State, or by Citizens or Subjects of any Foreign State.

AMENDMENT XII

[Proposed by Congress on December 9, 1803; declared ratified on September 25, 1804.]

[ELECTION OF PRESIDENT AND VICE-PRESIDENT]

The Electors shall meet in their respective states, and vote by ballot for President and Vice-President, one of whom, at least, shall not be an inhabitant of the same state with themselves; they shall name in their ballots the person voted for as President, and in distinct ballots the person voted for as Vice-President, and they shall make distinct lists of all persons voted for as President, and of all persons voted for as Vice-President, and of the number of votes for each, which lists they shall sign and certify, and transmit sealed to the seat of the government of the United States, directed to the President of the Senate;—The President of the Senate shall, in presence of the Senate and House of Representatives, open all the certificates and the votes shall then be counted;—The person having the greatest number of votes for President, shall be the President, if such number be a majority of the whole number of Electors appointed; and if no person have such majority, then from the persons having the highest numbers not exceeding three on the list of those voted for as President, the House of Representatives shall choose immediately, by ballot, the President. But in choosing the President, the votes shall be taken by states, the representation from each state having one vote; a quorum for this purpose shall consist of a member or members from two-thirds of the states, and a majority of all states shall be necessary to a choice. And if the House of Representatives shall not choose a President whenever the right of choice shall devolve upon them, before the fourth day of March next following, then the Vice-President, shall act as President, as in the case of the death or other constitutional disability of the President. The person having the greatest number of votes as Vice-President, shall be the Vice-President, if such a number be a majority of the whole number of Electors appointed, and if no person have a majority, then from the two highest numbers on the list, the Senate shall choose the Vice-President; a quorum for the purpose shall consist of two-thirds of the whole number of Senators, and a majority of the whole number shall be necessary to a choice. But no person constitutionally ineligible to the office of President shall be eligible to that of Vice-President of the United States.

AMENDMENT XIII

[Proposed by Congress on January 31, 1865; declared ratified on December 18, 1865]

Section 1

[ABOLITION OF SLAVERY]

Neither slavery nor involuntary servitude, except as a punishment for crime whereof the party shall have been duly convicted, shall exist within the United States, or any place subject to their jurisdiction.

Section 2

[POWER TO ENFORCE THIS ARTICLE]

Congress shall have power to enforce this article by appropriate legislation.

AMENDMENT XIV

[Proposed by Congress on June 13, 1866; declared ratified on July 28, 1868]

Section 1

[CITIZENSHIP RIGHTS NOT TO BE ABRIDGED BY STATES]

All persons born or naturalized in the United States, and subject to the jurisdiction thereof, are citizens of the United States and of the State wherein they reside. No state shall make or enforce any law which shall abridge the privileges or immunities of citizens of the United States; nor shall any State deprive any person of life, liberty, or property, without due process of law; nor deny to any person within its jurisdiction the equal protection of the laws.

Section 2

[APPORTIONMENT OF REPRESENTATIVES IN CONGRESS]

Representatives shall be apportioned among the several States according to their respective numbers, counting the whole number of persons in each State, excluding Indians not taxed. But when the right to vote at any election for the choice of electors for President and Vice-President of the United States, Representatives in Congress, the Executive and Judicial officers of a State, or the members of the Legislature thereof, is denied to any of the male inhabitants of such State, being twenty-one years of age, and citizens of the United States, or in any way abridged, except for participation in rebellion, or other crime, the basis of representation therein shall be reduced in the proportion which the number of such male citizens shall bear to the whole number of male citizens twenty-one years of age in such State.

Section 3

[PERSONS DISQUALIFIED FROM HOLDING OFFICE]

No person shall be a Senator or Representative in Congress, or elector of President and Vice-President, or hold any office, civil or military, under the United States, or under any State, who, having previously taken an oath, as a member of Congress, or as an officer of the United States, or as a member of any State legislature, or as an executive or judicial officer of any State, to support the Constitution of the United States, shall have engaged in insurrection or rebellion against the same, or given aid or comfort to the enemies thereof. But Congress may by a vote of two-thirds of each House, remove such disability.

Section 4

[WHAT PUBLIC DEBTS ARE VALID]

The validity of the public debt of the United States, authorized by law, including debts incurred for payment of pensions and bounties for services in suppressing insurrection or rebellion, shall not be questioned. But neither the United States nor any State shall assume or pay any debt or obligation incurred in aid of insurrection or rebellion against the United States, or any claim for the loss or emancipation of any slave; but all such debts, obligations and claims shall be held illegal and void.

Section 5
[POWER TO ENFORCE THIS ARTICLE]

The Congress shall have power to enforce, by appropriate legislation, the provisions of this article.

AMENDMENT XV
[Proposed by Congress on February 26, 1869; declared ratified on March 30, 1870]

Section 1
[NEGRO SUFFRAGE]

The right of citizens of the United States to vote shall not be denied or abridged by the United States or by any State on account of race, color, or previous condition of servitude.

Section 2
[POWER TO ENFORCE THIS ARTICLE]

The Congress shall have power to enforce this article by appropriate legislation.

AMENDMENT XVI
[Proposed by Congress on July 12, 1909; declared ratified on February 25, 1913]
[AUTHORIZING INCOME TAXES]

The Congress shall have power to lay and collect taxes on incomes, from whatever source derived, without apportionment among the several States, and without regard to any census or enumeration.

AMENDMENT XVII
[Proposed by Congress on May 13, 1912; declared ratified on May 31, 1913]
[POPULAR ELECTION OF SENATORS]

The Senate of the United States shall be composed of two Senators from each State, elected by the people thereof, for six years; and each Senator shall have one vote. The electors in each State shall have the qualifications requisite for electors of the most numerous branch of the State Legislature.

When vacancies happen in the representation of any State in the Senate, the executive authority of such State shall issue writs of election to fill such vacancies: Provided, That the Legislature of any State may empower the executive thereof to make temporary appointment until the people fill the vacancies by election as the Legislature may direct.

This amendment shall not be so construed as to affect the election or term of any Senator chosen before it becomes valid as part of the Constitution.

AMENDMENT XVIII

[Proposed by Congress December 18, 1917; declared ratified on January 29, 1919]

Section 1

[NATIONAL LIQUOR PROHIBITION]

After one year from the ratification of this article the manufacture, sale, or transportation of intoxicating liquors within, the importation thereof into, or the exportation thereof from the United States and all territory subject to the jurisdiction thereof for beverage purposes is hereby prohibited.

Section 2

[POWER TO ENFORCE THIS ARTICLE]

The Congress and the several states shall have concurrent power to enforce this article by appropriate legislation.

Section 3

[RATIFICATION WITHIN SEVEN YEARS]

This article shall be inoperative unless it shall have been ratified as an amendment to the Constitution by the legislatures of the several states, as provided in the Constitution, within seven years from the date of the submission hereof to the states by the Congress.[15]

AMENDMENT XIX

[Proposed by Congress on June 4, 1919; declared ratified on August 26, 1920]

[WOMAN SUFFRAGE]

The right of the citizens of the United States to vote shall not be denied or abridged by the United States or by any state on account of sex.

Congress shall have power to enforce this article by appropriate legislation.

AMENDMENT XX

[Proposed by Congress on March 2, 1932; declared ratified on February 6, 1933]

Section 1

[TERMS OF OFFICE]

The terms of the President and Vice-President shall end at noon on the 20th day of January, and the terms of the Senators and Representatives at noon on the 3rd day of January, of the years in which such terms would have ended if this article had not been ratified; and the terms of their successors shall then begin.

Section 2

[TIME OF CONVENING CONGRESS]

The Congress shall assemble at least once in every year, and such meeting shall begin at noon on the 3rd day of January, unless they shall by law appoint a different day.

---

15 Repealed by Twenty-First Amendment.

Section 3

[DEATH OF PRESIDENT-ELECT]

If, at the time fixed for the beginning of the term of the President, the President-elect shall have died, the Vice-President-elect shall become President. If a President shall not have been chosen before the time fixed for the beginning of his term, or if the President-elect shall have failed to qualify, then the Vice-President-elect shall act as President until a President shall have qualified; and the Congress may by law provide for the case wherein neither a President-elect nor a Vice-President-elect shall have qualified, declaring who shall then act as President, or the manner in which one who is to act shall be selected, and such person shall act accordingly until a President or Vice President shall have qualified.

Section 4

[ELECTION OF THE PRESIDENT]

The Congress may by law provide for the case of the death of any of the persons from whom the House of Representatives may choose a President whenever the right of choice shall have devolved upon them, and for the case of the death of any of the persons from whom the Senate may choose a Vice-President whenever the right of choice shall have devolved upon them.

Section 5

[AMENDMENT TAKES EFFECT]

Sections 1 and 2 shall take effect on the 15th day of October following ratification of this article.

Section 6

[RATIFICATION WITHIN SEVEN YEARS]

This article shall be inoperative unless it shall have been ratified as an amendment to the Constitution by the legislatures of three-fourths of the several States within seven years from the date of its submission.

AMENDMENT XXI

[Proposed by Congress on February 20, 1933; declared ratified on December 5, 1933]

Section 1

[NATIONAL LIQUOR PROHIBITION REPEALED]

The eighteenth article of amendment to the Constitution of the United States is hereby repealed.

Section 2

[TRANSPORTATION OF LIQUOR INTO "DRY" STATES]

The transportation or importation into any State, Territory, or Possession of the United States for delivery or use therein of intoxicating liquors, in violation of the laws thereof, is hereby prohibited.

Section 3
[RATIFICATION WITHIN SEVEN YEARS]

This article shall be inoperative unless it shall have been ratified as an amendment to the Constitution by conventions in the several States, as provided in the Constitution, within seven years from the date of the submission hereof to the States by the Congress.

AMENDMENT XXII

[Proposed by Congress on March 21, 1947; declared ratified on February 26, 1951]

Section 1
[TENURE OF PRESIDENT LIMITED]

No person shall be elected to the office of President more than twice, and no person who has held the office of President or acted as President for more than two years of a term to which some other person was elected President shall be elected to the Office of the President more than once. But this Article shall not apply to any person holding the office of President when this Article was proposed by the Congress, and shall not prevent any person who may be holding the office of President, or acting as President, during the term within which this Article becomes operative from holding the office of President or acting as President during the remainder of such term.

Section 2
[RATIFICATION WITHIN SEVEN YEARS]

This Article shall be inoperative unless it shall have been ratified as an amendment to the Constitution by the legislatures of three-fourths of the several states within seven years from the date of its submission to the States by the Congress.

AMENDMENT XXIII

[Proposed by Congress on June 21, 1960; declared ratified on March 29, 1961]

Section 1
[ELECTORAL COLLEGE VOTES FOR THE DISTRICT OF COLUMBIA]

The District constituting the seat of Government of the United States shall appoint in such manner as the Congress may direct:

A number of electors of President and Vice-President equal to the whole number of Senators and Representatives in Congress to which the District would be entitled if it were a State, but in no event more than the least populous State; they shall be in addition to those appointed by the States, but they shall be considered, for the purposes of the election of President and Vice-President, to be electors appointed by a State; and they shall meet in the District and perform such duties as provided by the twelfth article of amendment.

Section 2
[POWER TO ENFORCE THIS ARTICLE]

The Congress shall have power to enforce this article by appropriate legislation.

AMENDMENT XXIV

[Proposed by Congress on August 27, 1963; declared ratified on January 23, 1964]

Section 1

[ANTI-POLL TAX]

The right of citizens of the United States to vote in any primary or other election for President or Vice-President, for electors for President or Vice-President, or for Senator or Representative of Congress, shall not be denied or abridged by the United States or any State by reasons of failure to pay any poll tax or other tax.

Section 2

[POWER TO ENFORCE THIS ARTICLE]

The Congress shall have power to enforce this article by appropriate legislation.

AMENDMENT XXV

[Proposed by Congress on July 7, 1965; declared ratified on February 10, 1967]

Section 1

[VICE-PRESIDENT TO BECOME PRESIDENT]

In case of the removal of the President from office or his death or resignation, the Vice-President shall become President.

Section 2

[CHOICE OF A NEW VICE-PRESIDENT]

Whenever there is a vacancy in the office of the Vice-President, the President shall nominate a Vice-President who shall take the office upon confirmation by a majority vote of both houses of Congress.

Section 3

[PRESIDENT MAY DECLARE OWN DISABILITY]

Whenever the President transmits to the President pro tempore of the Senate and the Speaker of the House of Representatives his written declaration that he is unable to discharge the powers and duties of his office, and until he transmits to them a written declaration to the contrary, such powers and duties shall be discharged by the Vice-President as Acting President.

Section 4

[ALTERNATE PROCEDURES TO DECLARE AND TO END PRESIDENTIAL DISABILITY]

Whenever the Vice-President and a majority of either the principal officers of the executive departments, or of such other body as Congress may by law provide, transmit to the President pro tempore of the Senate and the Speaker of the House of Representatives their written declaration that the President is unable to discharge the powers and duties of his office, the Vice-President shall immediately assume the powers and duties of the office as Acting President.

Thereafter, when the President transmits to the President pro tempore of the Senate and the Speaker of the House of Representatives his written declaration that no inability exists, he shall resume the powers and duties of his office unless the Vice-President and a majority of either the principal officers of the executive departments, or of such other body as Congress may by law provide, transmit within four days to the President pro tempore of the Senate and the Speaker of the House of Representatives their written declaration that the President is unable to discharge the powers and duties of his office. Thereupon Congress shall decide the issue, assembling within 48 hours for that purpose if not in session. If the Congress, within 21 days after receipt of the latter written declaration, or, if Congress is not in session, within 21 days after Congress is required to assemble, determines by two-thirds vote of both houses that the President is unable to discharge the powers and duties of his office, the Vice-President shall continue to discharge the same as Acting President; otherwise, the President shall resume the powers and duties of his office.

AMENDMENT XXVI
[Proposed by Congress on March 23, 1971; declared ratified on June 30, 1971]

Section 1
[EIGHTEEN-YEAR-OLD VOTE]

The right of citizens of the United States, who are eighteen years of age or older, to vote shall not be denied or abridged by the United States or by any State on account of age.

Section 2
[POWER TO ENFORCE THIS ARTICLE]

The Congress shall have power to enforce this article by appropriate legislation.

AMENDMENT XXVII
[Proposed by Congress on September 25, 1789; ratified on May 7, 1992]

No law varying the compensation for the services of the Senators and Representatives shall take effect until an election of Representatives shall have intervened.

NO. 10: MADISON

Among the numerous advantages promised by a well-constructed Union, none deserves to be more accurately developed than its tendency to break and control the violence of faction. The friend of popular governments never finds himself so much alarmed for their character and fate as when he contemplates their propensity to this dangerous vice. He will not fail, therefore, to set a due value on any plan which, without violating the principles to which he is attached, provides a proper cure for it. The instability, injustice, and confusion introduced into the public councils have, in truth, been the mortal diseases under which popular governments have everywhere perished, as they continue to be the favorite and fruitful topics from which the adversaries to liberty derive their most specious declamations. The valuable improvements made by the American constitutions on the popular models, both ancient and modern, cannot certainly be too much admired; but it would be an unwarrantable partiality to contend that they have as effectually obviated the danger on this side, as was wished and expected. Complaints are everywhere heard from our most considerate and virtuous citizens, equally the friends of public and private faith and of public and personal liberty, that our governments are too unstable, that the public good is disregarded in the conflicts of rival parties, and that measures are too often decided, not according to the rules of justice and the rights of the minor party, but by the superior force of an interested and overbearing majority. However anxiously we may wish that these complaints had no foundation, the evidence of known facts will not permit us to deny that they are in some degree true. It will be found, indeed, on a candid review of our situation, that some of the distresses under which we labor have been erroneously charged on the operation of our governments; but it will be found, at the same time, that other causes will not alone account for many of our heaviest misfortunes; and, particularly, for that prevailing and increasing distrust of public engagements and alarm for private rights which are echoed from one end of the continent to the other. These must be chiefly, if not wholly, effects of the unsteadiness and injustice with which a factious spirit has tainted our public administration.

By a faction I understand a number of citizens, whether amounting to a majority or minority of the whole, who are united and actuated by some common impulse of passion, or of interest, adverse to the rights of other citizens, or to the permanent and aggregate interests of the community.

There are two methods of curing the mischiefs of faction: the one, by removing its causes; the other, by controlling its effects.

There are again two methods of removing the causes of faction: the one, by destroying the liberty which is essential to its existence; the other, by giving to every citizen the same opinions, the same passions, and the same interests.

It could never be more truly said than of the first remedy that it was worse than the disease. Liberty is to faction what air is to fire, an aliment without which it instantly expires. But it could not be a less folly to abolish liberty, which is essential to political life, because it nourishes faction than it would be to wish the annihilation of air, which is essential to animal life, because it imparts to fire its destructive agency.

The second expedient is as impracticable as the first would be unwise. As long as the reason of man continues fallible, and he is at liberty to exercise it, different opinions will be formed. As long as the connection subsists between his reason and his self-love, his opinions and his passions will have a reciprocal influence on each other; and the former will be objects to which the latter will attach themselves. The diversity in the faculties of men, from which the rights of property originate, is not less an insuperable obstacle to a uniformity of interests. The protection of these faculties is the first object of government. From the protection of different and unequal faculties of acquiring property, the possession of different degrees and kinds of property immediately results; and from the influence of these on the sentiments and views of the respective proprietors ensues a division of the society into different interests and parties.

The latent causes of faction are thus sown in the nature of man; and we see them everywhere brought into different degrees of activity, according to the different circumstances of civil society. A zeal for different opinions concerning religion, concerning government, and many other points, as well of speculation as of practice; an attachment to different leaders ambitiously contending for pre-eminence and power; or to persons of other descriptions whose fortunes have been interesting to the human passions, have, in turn, divided mankind into parties, inflamed them with mutual animosity, and rendered them much more disposed to vex and oppress each other than to co-operate for their common good. So strong is this propensity of mankind to fall into mutual animosities that where no substantial occasion presents itself the most frivolous and fanciful distinctions have been sufficient to kindle their unfriendly passions and excite their most violent conflicts. But the most common and durable source of factions has been the various and unequal distribution of property. Those who hold and those who are without property have ever formed distinct interests in society. Those who are creditors, and those who are debtors, fall under a like discrimination. A landed interest, a manufacturing interest, a mercantile interest, a moneyed interest, with many lesser interests, grow up of necessity in civilized nations, and divide them into different classes, actuated by different sentiments and views. The regulation of these various and interfering interests forms the principal task of modern legislation and involves the spirit of party and faction in the necessary and ordinary operations of government.

No man is allowed to be judge in his own cause, because his interest would certainly bias his judgment and, not improbably, corrupt his integrity. With equal, nay with greater reason, a body of men are unfit to be both judges and parties at the same time; yet what are many of the most important acts of legislation but so many judicial determinations, not indeed concerning the rights of single persons, but concerning the rights of large bodies of citizens? And what are the different classes of legislators but advocates and parties to the causes which they determine? Is a law proposed concerning private debts? It is a question to which the creditors are parties on one side and the debtors on the other. Justice ought to hold the balance between them. Yet the parties are, and must be, themselves the judges; and the most numerous party, or in other words, the most powerful faction must be expected to prevail. Shall domestic manufacturers be encouraged, and in what degree, by restrictions on foreign manufacturers? are questions which would be differently decided by the landed and the manufacturing classes, and probably by neither with a sole regard to justice and the public good. The apportionment of taxes on the various descriptions of property is an act which seems to require the most exact impartiality; yet there is, perhaps, no legislative act in which greater opportunity and temptation are given to a predominant party to trample on the rules of justice. Every shilling with which they overburden the inferior number is a shilling saved to their own pockets.

It is in vain to say that enlightened statesmen will be able to adjust these clashing interests and render them all subservient to the public good. Enlightened statesmen will not always be at the helm. Nor, in many cases, can such an adjustment be made at all without taking into view indirect and remote considerations, which will rarely prevail over the immediate interest which one party may find in disregarding the rights of another or the good of the whole.

The inference to which we are brought is that the *causes* of faction cannot be removed and that relief is only to be sought in the means of controlling its *effects*.

If a faction consists of less than a majority, relief is supplied by the republican principle, which enables the majority to defeat its sinister views by regular vote. It may clog the administration, it may convulse the society; but it will be unable to execute and mask its violence under the forms of the Constitution. When a majority is included in a faction, the form of popular government, on the other hand, enables it to sacrifice to its ruling passion or interest both the public good and the rights of other citizens. To secure the public good and private rights against the danger of such a faction, and at the same time to preserve the spirit and the form of popular government, is then the great object to which our inquiries are directed. Let me add that it is the great desideratum by which alone this form of government can be rescued from the opprobrium under which it has so long labored and be recommended to the esteem and adoption of mankind.

By what means is this object attainable? Evidently by one of two only. Either the existence of the same passion or interest in a majority at the same time must be prevented, or the majority, having such coexistent passion or interest, must be rendered, by their number and local situation, unable to concert and carry into effect schemes of oppression. If the impulse and the opportunity be suffered to coincide, we well know that neither moral nor religious motives can be relied on as an adequate control. They are not found to be such on the injustice and violence of individuals, and lose their efficacy in proportion to the number combined together, that is, in proportion as their efficacy becomes needful.

From this view of the subject it may be concluded that a pure democracy, by which I mean a society consisting of a small number of citizens, who assemble and administer the government in person, can admit of no cure for the mischiefs of faction. A common passion or interest will, in almost every case, be felt by a majority of the whole; a communication and concert results from the form of government itself; and there is nothing to check the inducements to sacrifice the weaker party or an obnoxious individual. Hence it is that such democracies have ever been spectacles of turbulence and contention; have ever been found incompatible with personal security or the rights of property; and have in general been as short in their lives as they have been violent in their deaths. Theoretic politicians, who have patronized this species of government, have erroneously supposed that by reducing mankind to a perfect equality in their political rights, they would at the same time be perfectly equalized and assimilated in their possessions, their opinions, and their passions.

A republic, by which I mean a government in which the scheme of representation takes place, opens a different prospect and promises the cure for which we are seeking. Let us examine the points in which it varies from pure democracy, and we shall comprehend both the nature of the cure and the efficacy which it must derive from the Union.

The two great points of difference between a democracy and a republic are: first, the delegation of the government, in the latter, to a small number of citizens elected by the rest; secondly, the greater number of citizens and greater sphere of country over which the latter may be extended.

The effect of the first difference is, on the one hand, to refine and enlarge the public views by passing them through the medium of a chosen body of citizens, whose wisdom may best discern the true interest of their country and whose patriotism and love of justice will be least likely to sacrifice it to temporary or partial considerations. Under such a regulation it may well happen that the public voice, pronounced by the representatives of the people, will be more consonant to the public good than if pronounced by the people themselves, convened for the purpose. On the other hand, the effect may be inverted. Men of factious tempers, of local prejudices, or of sinister designs, may, by intrigue, by corruption, or by other means, first obtain the suffrages, and then betray the interests of the people. The question resulting is, whether small or extensive republics are most favorable to the election of proper guardians of the public weal; and it is clearly decided in favor of the latter by two obvious considerations.

In the first place it is to be remarked that however small the republic may be the representatives must be raised to a certain number in order to guard against the cabals of a few; and that however large it may be they must be limited to a certain number in order to guard against the confusion of a multitude. Hence, the number of representatives in the two cases not being in proportion to that of the constituents, and being proportionally greatest in the small republic, it follows that if the proportion of fit characters be not less in the large than in the small republic, the former will present a greater option, and consequently a greater probability of a fit choice.

In the next place, as each representative will be chosen by a greater number of citizens in the large than in the small republic, it will be more difficult for unworthy candidates to practise with success the vicious arts by which elections are too often carried; and the suffrages of the people being more free, will be more likely to center on men who possess the most attractive merit and the most diffusive and established characters.

It must be confessed that in this, as in most other cases, there is a mean, on both sides of which inconveniencies will be found to lie. By enlarging too much the number of electors, you render the representative too little acquainted with all their local circumstances and lesser interests; as by reducing it too much, you render him unduly attached to these, and too little fit to comprehend and pursue great and national objects. The federal Constitution forms a happy combination in this respect; the great and aggregate interests being referred to the national, the local and particular to the State legislatures.

The other point of difference is the greater number of citizens and extent of territory which may be brought within the compass of republican than of democratic government; and it is this circumstance principally which renders factious combinations less to be dreaded in the former than in the latter. The smaller the society, the fewer probably will be the distinct parties and interests composing it; the fewer the distinct parties and interests, the more frequently will a majority be found of the same party; and the smaller the number of individuals composing a majority, and the smaller the compass within which they are placed, the more easily will they concert and execute their plans of oppression. Extend the sphere and you take in a greater variety of parties and interests; you make it less probable that a majority of the whole will have a common motive to invade the rights of other citizens; or if such a common motive exists, it will be more difficult for all who feel it to discover their own strength and to act in unison with each other. Besides other impediments, it may be remarked that, where there is a consciousness of unjust or dishonorable purposes, communication is always checked by distrust in proportion to the number whose concurrence is necessary.

Hence, it clearly appears that the same advantage which a republic has over a democracy in controlling the effects of faction is enjoyed by a large over a small republic—is enjoyed by the Union over the States composing it. Does this advantage consist in the substitution of representatives whose enlightened views and virtuous sentiments render them superior to local prejudices and to schemes of injustice? It will not be denied that the representation of the Union will be most likely to possess these requisite endowments. Does it consist in the greater security afforded by a greater variety of parties, against the event of any one party being able to outnumber and oppress the rest? In an equal degree does the increased variety of parties comprised within the Union increase this security? Does it, in fine, consist in the greater obstacles opposed to the concert and accomplishment of the secret wishes of an unjust and interested majority? Here again the extent of the Union gives it the most palpable advantage.

The influence of factious leaders may kindle a flame within their particular States but will be unable to spread a general conflagration through the other

States. A religious sect may degenerate into a political faction in a part of the Confederacy; but the variety of sects dispersed over the entire face of it must secure the national councils against any danger from that source. A rage for paper money, for an abolition of debts, for an equal division of property, or for any other improper or wicked project, will be less apt to pervade the whole body of the Union than a particular member of it, in the same proportion as such a malady is more likely to taint a particular county or district than an entire State.

In the extent and proper structure of the Union, therefore, we behold a republican remedy for the diseases most incident to republican government. And according to the degree of pleasure and pride we feel in being republicans ought to be our zeal in cherishing the spirit and supporting the character of federalist.

PUBLIUS

NO. 51: MADISON

To what expedient, then, shall we finally resort, for maintaining in practice the necessary partition of power among the several departments as laid down in the Constitution? The only answer that can be given is that as all these exterior provisions are found to be inadequate the defect must be supplied, by so contriving the interior structure of the government as that its several constituent parts may, by their mutual relations, be the means of keeping each other in their proper places. Without presuming to undertake a full development of this important idea I will hazard a few general observations which may perhaps place it in a clearer light, and enable us to form a more correct judgment of the principles and structure of the government planned by the convention.

In order to lay a due foundation for that separate and distinct exercise of the different powers of government, which to a certain extent is admitted on all hands to be essential to the preservation of liberty, it is evident that each department should have a will of its own; and consequently should be so constituted that the members of each should have as little agency as possible in the appointment of the members of the others. Were this principle rigorously adhered to, it would require that all the appointments for the supreme executive, legislative, and judiciary magistracies should be drawn from the same fountain of authority, the people, through channels having no communication whatever with one another. Perhaps such a plan of constructing the several departments would be less difficult in practice than it may in contemplation appear. Some difficulties, however, and some additional expense would attend the execution of it. Some deviations, therefore, from the principle must be admitted. In the constitution of the judiciary department in particular, it might be inexpedient to insist rigorously on the principle: first, because peculiar qualifications being essential in the members, the primary consideration ought to be to select that mode of choice which best secures these qualifications; second, because the permanent tenure by which the appointments are held in that department must soon destroy all sense of dependence on the authority conferring them.

It is equally evident that the members of each department should be as little dependent as possible on those of the others for the emoluments annexed to their offices. Were the executive magistrate, or the judges, not independent of the legislature in this particular, their independence in every other would be merely nominal.

But the great security against a gradual concentration of the several powers in the same department consists in giving to those who administer each department the necessary constitutional means and personal motives to resist encroachments of the others. The provision for defense must in this, as in all other cases, be made commensurate to the danger of attack. Ambition must be made to counteract ambition. The interest of the man must be connected with the constitutional rights of the place. It may be a reflection on human nature that such devices should be necessary to control the abuses of government. But what is government itself but the greatest of all reflections on human nature? If men were angels, no government would be necessary. If angels were to govern men, neither external nor internal controls on government would be necessary. In framing a government which is to be administered by men over men, the great difficulty lies in this: you must first enable the government to control the governed; and in the next place oblige it to control itself. A dependence on the people is, no doubt, the primary control on the government; but experience has taught mankind the necessity of auxiliary precautions.

This policy of supplying, by opposite and rival interests, the defect of better motives, might be traced through the whole system of human affairs, private as well as public. We see it particularly displayed in all the subordinate distributions of power, where the constant aim is to divide and arrange the several offices in such a manner as that each may be a check on the other—that the private interest of every individual may be a sentinel over the public rights. These inventions of prudence cannot be less requisite in the distribution of the supreme powers of the State.

But it is not possible to give to each department an equal power of self-defense. In republican government, the legislative authority necessarily predominates. The remedy for this inconveniency is to divide the legislature into different branches; and to render them, by different modes of election and different principles of action, as little connected with each other as the nature of their common functions and their common dependence on the society will admit. It may even be necessary to guard against dangerous encroachments by still further precautions. As the weight of the legislative authority requires that it should be thus divided, the weakness of the executive may require, on the other hand, that it should be fortified. An absolute negative on the legislature appears, at first view, to be the natural defense with which the executive magistrate should be armed. But perhaps it would be neither altogether safe nor alone sufficient. On ordinary occasions it might not be exerted with the requisite firmness, and on extraordinary occasions it might be perfidiously abused. May not this defect of an absolute negative be supplied by some qualified connection between this weaker branch of the stronger department, by which the latter may be led to support the constitutional rights of the former, without being too much detached from the rights of its own department?

If the principles on which these observations are founded be just, as I persuade myself they are, and they be applied as a criterion to the several State constitutions, and to the federal Constitution, it will be found that if the latter does not perfectly correspond with them, the former are infinitely less able to bear such a test.

There are, moreover, two considerations particularly applicable to the federal system of America, which place that system in a very interesting point of view.

First. In a single republic, all the power surrendered by the people is submitted to the administration of a single government; and the usurpations are guarded against by a division of the government into distinct and separate departments. In the compound republic of America, the power surrendered by the people is first divided between two distinct governments, and then the portion allotted to each subdivided among distinct and separate departments. Hence a double security arises to the rights of the people. The different governments will control each other, at the same time that each will be controlled by itself.

Second. It is of great importance in a republic not only to guard the society against the oppression of its rulers, but to guard one part of the society against the injustice of the other part. Different interests necessarily exist in different classes of citizens. If a majority be united by a common interest, the rights of the minority will be insecure. There are but two methods of providing against this evil: the one by creating a will in the community independent of the majority—that is, of the society itself; the other, by comprehending in the society so many separate descriptions of citizens as will render an unjust combination of a majority of the whole very improbable, if not impracticable. The first method prevails in all governments possessing an hereditary or self-appointed authority. This, at best, is but a precarious security; because a power independent of the society may as well espouse the unjust views of the major as the rightful interests of the minor party, and may possibly be turned against both parties. The second method will be exemplified in the federal republic of the United States. Whilst all authority in it will be derived from and dependent on the society, the society itself will be broken into so many parts, interests and classes of citizens, that the rights of individuals, or of the minority, will be in little danger from interested combinations of the majority. In a free government the security for civil rights must be the same as that for religious rights. It consists in the one case in the multiplicity of interests, and in the other in the multiplicity of sects. The degree of security in both cases will depend on the number of interests and sects; and this may be presumed to depend on the extent of country and number of people comprehended under the same government. This view of the subject must particularly recommend a proper federal system to all the sincere and considerate friends of republican government, since it shows that in exact proportion as the territory of the Union may be formed into more circumscribed Confederacies, or States, oppressive combinations of a majority will be facilitated; the best security, under the republican forms, for the rights of every class of citizen, will be diminished; and consequently the stability and independence of some member of the government, the only other security, must be proportionally increased. Justice is the end of government. It is the end of civil society. It ever has been and ever will be pursued until it be obtained, or until liberty be lost in the pursuit. In a society under the forms of which the stronger faction can readily unite and oppress the weaker, anarchy may as truly be said to reign as in a state of nature, where the weaker individual is not secured against the violence of the stronger; and as, in the latter state, even the stronger individuals are prompted, by the uncertainty of their condition, to submit to a government which may protect the weak as well as themselves; so, in the former state, will the more powerful factions or parties be gradually induced, by a like motive, to wish for a government which will protect all parties, the weaker as well as the more powerful. It can be little doubted that if the State of Rhode Island was separated from the Confederacy and left to itself, the insecurity of rights under the popular form of government within such narrow limits would be displayed by such reiterated oppressions of factious majorities that some power altogether independent of the people would soon be called for by the voice of the very factions whose misrule had proved the necessity of it. In the extended republic of the United States, and among the great variety of interests, parties, and sects which it embraces, a coalition of a majority of the whole society could seldom take place on any other principles than those of justice and the general good; whilst there being thus less danger to a minor from the will of a major party, there must be less pretext, also, to provide for the security of the former, by introducing into the government a will not dependent on the latter, or, in other words, a will independent of the society itself. It is no less certain than it is important, notwithstanding the contrary opinions which have been entertained, that the larger the society, provided it lie within a practicable sphere, the more duly capable it will be of self-government. And happily for the *republican cause,* the practicable sphere may be carried to a very great extent by a judicious modification and mixture of the *federal principle.*

PUBLIUS

Glossary

administrative adjudication The application of rules and precedents to specific cases to settle disputes with regulated parties.

administrative legislation Rules made by regulatory agencies that have the force of law.

adverse selection The problem of incomplete information—of choosing alternatives without fully knowing the details of available options.

affirmative action A policy or program designed to correct historical injustices committed against specific groups by making special efforts to provide members of these groups with access to educational and employment opportunities.

after-the-fact authority The authority to follow up on the fate of a proposal once it has been approved by the full chamber.

agency loss The difference between what a principal would like an agent to do and the agent's performance.

agency representation The type of representation in which representatives are held accountable to their constituents if they fail to represent them properly. That is, constituents have the power to hire and fire their representatives.

agenda power The control over what a group will consider for discussion.

agenda-setting effect The power of the media to focus public attention on particular issues.

amicus curiae "Friend of the court," an individual or group that is not a party to a lawsuit but has a strong interest in influencing the outcome.

amnesty A pardon extended to a group of persons.

appellate court See *court of appeals.*

appellate jurisdiction The class of cases provided in the Constitution and by legislation that may be appealed to a higher court from a lower court.

Articles of Confederation and Perpetual Union The United States' first written constitution. Adopted by the Continental Congress in 1777, the Articles were the formal basis for America's national government until 1789, when they were superseded by the Constitution.

Australian ballot An electoral format that presents the names of all the candidates for any given office on the same ballot.

authoritarian government A system of rule in which the government's power is not limited by law, though it may be restrained by other social institutions. Compare *constitutional government* and *totalitarian government.*

autocracy A form of government in which a single individual rules. Compare *democracy* and *oligarchy.*

bicameral legislature A legislative body composed of two chambers, or houses.

Bill of Rights The first 10 amendments to the U.S. Constitution, adopted in 1791. The Bill of Rights ensures certain rights and liberties to the people.

block grants Federal funds given to state governments to pay for goods, services, or programs, with relatively few restrictions on how the funds may be spent.

brief A written document in which an attorney explains—using case precedents—why a court should rule in favor of his or her client.

bureaucracy The complex structure of offices, tasks, rules, and principles of organization that large institutions use to coordinate the work of their personnel.

bureaucratic drift The tendency of bureaucracies to implement laws in ways that tilt toward the bureaucrats' policy preferences and possibly away from the intentions of the elected officials who created the laws.

Cabinet The heads of the major departments of the federal government.

casework Efforts by members of Congress to gain the trust and support of constituents by providing personal services. One important type of casework is helping constituents to obtain favorable treatment from the federal bureaucracy.

categorical grants-in-aid Funds given to state and local governments by Congress that are earmarked by law for specific policy categories, such as education or crime prevention.

caucus A meeting of a political or legislative group, normally closed to nonmembers, to select candidates, plan strategy, or make decisions about legislative matters.

checks and balances The ways in which each branch of government is able to influence the activities of the other branches.

chief justice The justice on the Supreme Court who presides over the Court's public sessions.

civil law Cases involving disputes among individuals or between the government and individuals that do not involve criminal penalties. Compare *criminal law* and *public law.*

civil liberties The protections of citizens from improper governmental action. Compare *civil rights.*

civil rights The rules that government must follow in regard to the treatment of individuals, especially concerning participation in political and social life. Compare *civil liberties.*

class-action suit A lawsuit in which a large number of persons with common interests join together under a representative party to bring or defend a lawsuit.

clear and present danger The criterion formerly used to determine whether speech is protected or unprotected, based on its capacity to present a clear and present danger to society.

clientele agency A department or bureau of government whose mission is to promote, serve, or represent a particular interest. Compare *regulatory agency.*

closed primary A primary election in which only those voters who have registered their affiliation with the party by a specified time before the election can participate. Compare *open primary.*

closed rule The provision by the House Rules Committee that restricts the introduction of amendments during debate. Compare *open rule.*

cloture A procedure by which three-fifths of the members of the Senate can set a time limit on debate over a given bill.

coalitional drift The prospect that enacted policy will change in the future because the composition of the enacting coalition is temporary and provisional.

collective action The pooling of resources and the coordination of effort and activity by a group of people (often a large one) to achieve common goals.

collective good See *public good.*

comity clause Article IV, Section 2 of the Constitution, which prohibits states from enacting laws that treat the citizens of other states in a discriminatory manner.

commander in chief The president's role as commander of the national military and of the state National Guard units (when they are called into service).

commerce clause The clause found in Article I, Section 8, of the Constitution that delegates to Congress the power "to regulate Commerce with foreign Nations, and among the several States, and with the Indian Tribes."

concurrence An opinion agreeing with the decision of the majority in a Supreme Court case but with a rationale different from the one provided in the majority opinion. Compare *dissenting opinion.*

concurrent powers Authority possessed by *both* state and national governments, such as the power to levy taxes.

conference committee A joint committee created to work out a compromise between House and Senate versions of a bill.

congressional caucus An association of members of Congress based on party, interest, or social characteristics such as gender or race.

Connecticut Compromise See *Great Compromise*.

conservative A person who generally believes that social institutions (such as churches and corporations) and the free market solve problems better than governments do, that a large and powerful government poses a threat to citizens' freedom, and that the appropriate role of government is to uphold traditional values. Compare *liberal*.

constituency The citizens who reside in the district from which an official is elected.

constitutional government A system of rule that establishes specific limits on the powers of the government. Compare *authoritarian government* and *totalitarian government*.

cooperative federalism The system of government that has prevailed in the United States since the New Deal era (beginning in the 1930s), in which grants-in-aid have been used strategically to encourage states and localities to pursue nationally defined goals. Compare *dual federalism*.

court of appeals A court that hears the appeals of lower-court decisions. Also called *appellate court*. Compare *trial court* and *supreme court*.

criminal law Cases arising out of actions that allegedly violate laws protecting the health, safety, morals, and welfare of the community. Compare *civil law* and *public law*.

de facto segregation Racial segregation that is not a direct result of law or governmental policy but a reflection of residential patterns, income distributions, or other social factors. Compare *de jure segregation*.

de jure segregation Racial segregation that is a direct result of law or official policy. Compare *de facto segregation*.

decisiveness rules A specification of when a vote may be taken, the sequence in which votes on amendments occur, and how many supporters determine whether a motion passes or fails.

delegated powers Constitutional powers that are assigned to one branch of the government but exercised by another branch with the permission of the first. Compare *expressed powers* and *inherent powers*.

delegates Legislators who vote according to the preferences of their constituents. Compare *trustees*.

delegation The transmission of authority to some other official or body (though often with the right of review and revision).

democracy A system of rule that permits citizens to play a significant part in government, usually through the selection of key public officials. Compare *autocracy* and *oligarchy*.

devolution The policy of delegating a program or passing it down from one level of government to a lower level, such as from the national government to state and local governments.

dissenting opinion A decision written by a justice who voted with the minority opinion in a particular case, in which the justice fully explains the reasoning behind his or her opinion. Compare *concurrence*.

distributive tendency The tendency of Congress to spread the benefits of a policy over a wide range of members' districts.

divided government The condition in American government in which one party controls the presidency, while the opposing party controls one or both houses of Congress.

double jeopardy The Fifth Amendment right providing that a person cannot be tried twice for the same crime.

dual federalism The system of government that prevailed in the United States from 1789 to 1937, in which fundamental governmental powers were shared between the federal and state governments, with the states exercising the most important powers. Compare *cooperative federalism*.

due process The requirement that citizens be treated according to

the law and be provided adequate protection for individual rights.

Duverger's Law Law of politics, formalized by Maurice Duverger, stating that plurality-rule electoral systems will tend to have two political parties.

elastic clause See *necessary and proper clause*.

Electoral College An institution established by the Constitution for the election of the president and vice president of the United States. Every four years, voters in each state and the District of Columbia elect electors who, in turn, cast votes for the president and vice president. The candidate receiving a majority of the electoral vote for president or vice president is elected.

eminent domain The right of the government to take private property for public use, with reasonable compensation awarded to the owner.

EOP See *Executive Office of the President*.

equal protection clause The provision of the Fourteenth Amendment guaranteeing citizens "the equal protection of the laws." This clause has been the basis for the civil rights of African Americans, women, and other groups.

equal time rule An FCC requirement that broadcasters provide candidates for the same political office an equal opportunity to communicate their messages to the public.

establishment clause The First Amendment clause that says,

"Congress shall make no law respecting an establishment of religion."

exclusionary rule The requirement that courts exclude evidence obtained in violation of the Fourth Amendment.

Executive Office of the President (EOP) The permanent agencies that perform defined management tasks for the president; created in 1939, it is made up of the Office of Management and Budget, the Council of Economic Advisers, the National Security Council, and other agencies.

executive order A rule or regulation issued by the president that has the effect of law.

executive privilege The claim that confidential communications between a president and close advisers should not be revealed without the president's consent.

expressed powers Powers that the Constitution explicitly grants to the federal government. Compare *delegated powers* and *inherent powers*.

Fed See *Federal Reserve System*.

Federal Reserve System (Fed) The system of 12 Federal Reserve banks that facilitates exchanges of cash, checks, and credit; regulates member banks; and uses monetary policy to fight inflation and deflation in the United States.

federalism The system of government in which a constitution divides power between a central government and regional governments.

filibuster A tactic in which members of the Senate prevent action on legislation they oppose by continuously holding the floor and speaking until the majority abandons the legislation. Once given the floor, senators have unlimited time to speak, and a cloture vote by three-fifths of the Senate is required to end a filibuster.

formula grants Grants-in-aid for which a formula is used to determine the amount of federal funds a state or local government will receive. Compare *project grants*.

framing The influence of the media over how events and issues are interpreted.

free exercise clause The First Amendment clause that protects the right of citizens to believe and practice whatever religion they choose.

free riding Enjoying the benefits of some good or action while letting others bear the costs.

full faith and credit clause The provision in Article IV, Section 1, of the Constitution requiring that each state normally honor the governmental actions and judicial decisions that take place in another state.

gatekeeping authority The right and power to decide if a change in policy will be considered.

GDP See *gross domestic product*.

gender gap A distinctive pattern of voting behavior reflecting the differences in views between women and men.

gerrymandering The drawing of electoral districts in such a way as to give advantage to one political party.

going public Trying to influence public opinion for or against some proposed action by the government.

government The institutions through which a land and its people are ruled.

grand jury A jury that determines whether sufficient evidence is available to justify a trial. Grand juries do not rule on the accused's guilt or innocence.

grants-in-aid Funds given by Congress to state and local governments on the condition that they be used for a specific purpose.

Great Compromise An agreement reached at the Constitutional Convention of 1787 that gave each state an equal number of senators regardless of the size of its population, but linked representation in the House of Representatives to population size. Also called the *Connecticut Compromise.*

home rule The power delegated by a state to a local unit of government to manage its own affairs.

impeachment The charging of a government official (president or other) with "Treason, Bribery, or other high Crimes and Misdemeanors" and bringing him or her before Congress to determine guilt.

implementation The development of rules, regulations, and bureaucratic procedures to translate laws into action.

implied powers Powers derived from the necessary and proper clause (Article I, Section 8) of the Constitution. Such powers are not specifically expressed in the Constitution but are implied through the interpretation of delegated powers.

incumbent A current officeholder.

inherent powers Powers claimed by a president that are not expressed in the Constitution but are said to stem from "the rights, duties, and obligations of the presidency." Compare *delegated powers* and *expressed powers.*

initiative A process by which citizens may petition to place a policy proposal on the ballot for public vote. Compare *referendum.*

institutions A set of formal rules and procedures, often administered by a bureaucracy, that shapes politics and governance.

instrumental Done with purpose, sometimes with forethought, and even with calculation.

interest group An organized group of people that attempts to influence governmental policies. Also called *lobby.*

intermediate scrutiny The test used by the Supreme Court in gender discrimination cases, which places the burden of justifying a law or policy's use mainly on the government. Compare *strict scrutiny.*

issue voting An individual's tendency to base the decision of which candidate or party to vote for on the extent to which he or she agrees with the candidate or party on specific issues.

judicial activism The judicial philosophy that the Court should see beyond the text of the Constitution or a statute to consider the broader societal implications of its decisions. Compare *judicial restraint*.

judicial restraint The judicial philosophy whose adherents refuse to go beyond the text of the Constitution in interpreting its meaning. Compare *judicial activism*.

judicial review The power of the courts to determine whether the actions of the president, the Congress, and the state legislatures are consistent with the Constitution.

jurisdiction The domain over which an institution or member of an institution has authority; the types of cases over which a court has authority.

legislative initiative The president's inherent power to bring a policy agenda before Congress.

legislative supremacy The preeminent position within the national government that the Constitution assigns to Congress.

Lemon test A rule, articulated in *Lemon v. Kurtzman*, that says governmental action with respect to religion is permissible if it is secular in purpose, does not lead to "excessive entanglement" of government with religion, and neither promotes nor inhibits the practice of religion. The *Lemon* test is generally used in relation to government aid to religious schools.

libel A written statement made in "reckless disregard of the truth" and considered damaging to a victim because it is "malicious, scandalous, and defamatory." Compare *slander*.

liberal A person who generally believes that the government should play an active role in supporting social and political change and generally supports a strong role for the government in the economy, the provision of social services, and the protection of civil rights. Compare *conservative*.

line-item veto The power of the president to veto specific provisions (lines) of a bill passed by the legislature (declared unconstitutional by the Supreme Court in 1998).

lobby See *interest group*.

lobbying An attempt by a group to influence the policy process through persuasion of government officials.

logrolling Agreements among members of Congress to vote for one another's bills.

majority leader The elected leader of the party holding a majority of the seats in the House of Representatives or in the Senate. In the House, the majority leader is subordinate in the party hierarchy to the Speaker. Compare *minority leader*.

majority party The party that holds the majority of seats in a legislative chamber, such as the U.S. House or Senate.

majority rule A type of electoral system in which, to win an office, a candidate must receive a majority (50 percent plus one) of all the votes cast in the relevant district. Compare *plurality rule*.

measurement error The failure to identify the true distribution of opinion within a population because of errors such as ambiguous or poorly worded questions.

median voter theorem A proposition predicting that, when policy options can be arrayed along a single dimension, majority rule will pick the policy most preferred by the voter whose ideal policy is to the left of half of the voters and to the right of exactly half of the voters (see Chapter 6 for further discussion).

minority leader The elected leader of the party holding less than a majority of the seats in the House or Senate. Compare *majority leader*.

Miranda rule The requirement derived from the Supreme Court's 1966 ruling in *Miranda v. Arizona* that persons under arrest must be informed of their legal rights, including the right to counsel, before undergoing police interrogation.

money bill A bill concerned solely with taxation or government spending.

moot No longer requiring resolution by the courts, typically because the facts of the case have changed or been resolved by other means.

moral hazard The problem of not knowing all aspects of the actions taken by an agent (nominally on behalf of the principal but potentially at the principal's expense).

National Security Council (NSC) A presidential foreign policy advisory council made up of the president, the vice president, the secretary of state, the secretary of defense, and other officials invited by the president.

necessary and proper clause The last paragraph of Article I, Section 8, which gives Congress the power to make all laws needed to exercise the powers listed in Section 8. Also called the *elastic clause*.

nomination The process by which political parties select their candidates for election to public office.

NSC See *National Security Council*.

oligarchy A form of government in which a small group of landowners, military officers, or wealthy merchants controls most of the governing decisions. Compare *autocracy* and *democracy*.

open primary A primary election in which voters can choose on the day of the primary which party's primary to vote in. Compare *closed primary*.

open rule The provision by the House Rules Committee that permits floor debate and the addition of amendments to a bill. Compare *closed rule*.

opinion The written explanation of the Supreme Court's decision in a particular case.

oral argument The stage in Supreme Court proceedings in which attorneys for both sides appear before the Court to present their positions and answer questions posed by the justices.

original jurisdiction The class of cases provided in the Constitution (Article III) that may be taken directly to a federal court.

oversight The effort by Congress, through hearings, investigations, and other techniques, to exercise control over the activities of executive agencies.

PAC See *political action committee*.

pardon Forgiveness of a crime and cancellation of relevant penalty.

party activist A partisan who contributes time and energy beyond voting to support a party and its candidates.

party caucus or party conference A nominally closed meeting to select candidates or leaders, plan strategy, or make decisions regarding legislative matters. Termed a *caucus* in the Democratic Party and a *conference* in the Republican Party.

party identification An individual's attachment to a particular political party, which may be based on issues, ideology, past experience, upbringing, or a mixture of these elements.

party machine In the late nineteenth and early twentieth centuries, the local party organization that controlled local politics through patronage and the nomination process.

party vote A roll-call vote in the House or Senate in which at least 50 percent of the members of one party take a particular position and

are opposed by at least 50 percent of the members of the other party.

path dependency The idea that certain possibilities are made more or less likely because of historical events and decisions—because of the historical path taken.

patronage Direct services and benefits that members of Congress provide to their constituents, especially making partisan appointments to offices and conferring grants, licenses, or special favors to supporters.

pluralism The theory that all interests are and should be free to compete for influence in the government.

plurality rule A type of electoral system in which victory goes to the individual who gets the most votes, but not necessarily a majority of the votes cast. Compare *majority rule*.

pocket veto A veto that occurs automatically when Congress adjourns during the 10 days a president has to approve a bill and the president has taken no action on it.

police power The power reserved to the state governments to regulate the health, safety, and morals of citizens.

political action committee (PAC) A private group that raises and distributes funds for use in election campaigns.

political party An organized group that attempts to control the government by electing its members to office.

politics Conflict and cooperation over the leadership, structure, and policies of government.

pork-barrel legislation Appropriations that members of Congress use to provide government funds for projects benefiting their home district or state.

precedents Past cases whose principles are used by judges as the bases for their decisions in present cases.

priming The use of media coverage to make the public take a particular view of an event or a public figure.

principal-agent relationship The relationship between a principal (such as a citizen) and an agent (such as an elected official), in which the agent is expected to act on the principal's behalf.

prior restraint An effort by a government agency to block publication of material by a newspaper or magazine; censorship.

privatization The act of moving all or part of a program from the public sector to the private sector.

probability sampling A method used by pollsters to select a representative sample in which every individual in the population has an equal probability of being selected as a respondent.

project grants Grants-in-aid for which state and local governments submit proposals to federal agencies, which provide funding for them on a competitive basis. Compare *formula grants*.

proportional representation A multimember district system that awards seats to political parties in proportion to the percentage of the vote each party won.

proposal power The capacity to bring a proposal before the full legislature.

prospective voting Voting based on the imagined future performance of a candidate. Compare *retrospective voting*.

public-assistance program See *noncontributory program*.

public law Cases involving the powers of government or rights of citizens. Compare *civil law* and *criminal law*.

public opinion Citizens' attitudes about political issues, personalities, institutions, and events.

public-opinion poll A scientific instrument for measuring public opinion.

random-digit dialing A method used by pollsters in which respondents are selected at random from a list of 10-digit telephone numbers, with every effort made to avoid bias in the construction of the sample.

recall The removal of a public official by popular vote.

referendum A direct vote by the electorate on a proposed law that has been passed by the legislature or on a specific governmental action. Compare *initiative*.

regulated federalism A form of federalism in which Congress imposes legislation on state and local governments that requires them to meet national standards.

regulatory agency A department, bureau, or independent agency whose primary mission is to make rules governing a particular type of activity. Compare *clientele agency*.

regulatory review The Office of Management and Budget's function of reviewing all agency regulations and other rule making before they become official policy.

reprieve Cancellation or postponement of a punishment.

reserved powers Powers that are not specifically delegated to the national government or denied to the states by the Constitution. Under the Tenth Amendment, these powers are reserved to the states.

retrospective voting Voting based on the past performance of a candidate or party. Compare *prospective voting*.

right of rebuttal An FCC requirement that broadcasters give individuals the opportunity to respond to the airing of personal attacks on them.

right to privacy The right to be left alone, which has been interpreted by the Supreme Court to entail individual access to birth control and abortions.

ripeness The requirement that a case must involve an actual controversy between two parties, not a hypothetical one.

roll-call votes Voting in which each legislator's yes or no vote is recorded.

rule making A quasi-legislative administrative process that produces regulations by government agencies.

rule of four The rule that *certiorari* will be granted for petitions to the Supreme Court only if at least four justices vote in favor of the petition.

sample A small group selected by researchers to represent the most important characteristics of an entire population.

sampling error A polling error that arises on account of the small size of the sample.

selection bias A polling error in which the sample is not representative of the population being studied, so that some opinions are over- or underrepresented.

selective benefits Benefits that do not go to everyone but, rather, are distributed selectively—to only those who contribute to the group enterprise.

senatorial courtesy The practice whereby the president, before formally nominating a person for a federal district judgeship, finds out whether the senators from the candidate's state support the nomination.

seniority The priority or status ranking given on the basis of how long an individual has served on a congressional committee.

"separate but equal" rule The legal principle that public accommodations could be segregated by race and still be equal.

separation of powers The division of governmental power among several institutions that must cooperate in decision making.

signing statement An announcement made by the president when signing a bill into law, sometimes presenting the president's interpretation of the law, as well as remarks predicting the benefits it will bring to the nation.

single-member district An electoral district that elects only one representative—the typical method of representation in the United States.

slander An oral statement made in "reckless disregard of the truth" and considered damaging to a victim because it is "malicious, scandalous, and defamatory." Compare *libel*.

socialization A process in which individuals take on their communities' perspectives and preferences through social interactions.

sovereignty Independent political authority.

spatial issue An issue for which a range of possible options or policies can be ordered, say, from liberal to conservative or from most expensive to least expensive.

Speaker of the House The chief presiding officer of the House of Representatives; elected at the beginning of every Congress on a straight party vote, he or she is the most important party and House leader.

speech plus Speech accompanied by activities such as sit-ins, picketing, and demonstrations.

staff agencies The agencies responsible for providing Congress with independent expertise, administration, and oversight capability.

standing The requirement that anyone initiating a court case must show a substantial stake in the outcome.

standing committee A permanent legislative committee that considers legislation within its designated subject area.

stare decisis Literally, "let the decision stand"; the doctrine whereby a previous decision by a court applies as a precedent in similar cases until that decision is overruled.

states' rights The principle that states should oppose the increasing authority of the national government. This view was most popular before the Civil War.

strict scrutiny The strictest standard of judicial review of a government's actions, in which the government must show that the law serves a "compelling state interest." Compare *intermediate scrutiny*.

supremacy clause A clause of Article VI of the Constitution stating that all laws and treaties approved by the national government are the supreme laws of the United States and superior to all laws adopted by any state or other subdivision.

supreme court The highest court in a particular state or in the country. Compare *trial court* and *court of appeals*.

third party A party that organizes to compete against the two major American political parties.

Three-Fifths Compromise An agreement reached at the Constitutional Convention of 1787, stating that for the purpose of distributing congressional seats on the basis of state populations, only three-fifths of enslaved people would be counted.

totalitarian government A system of rule in which the government's power is not limited by law and in which the government seeks to eliminate other social institutions that might challenge it. Compare *authoritarian government* and *constitutional government*.

tragedy of the commons The idea that a common resource, available to everyone, will more likely than not be abused or overused.

transaction costs The cost of clarifying each aspect of a principal-agent relationship and monitoring it to make sure both parties comply with all arrangements.

trial court The first court to hear a criminal or civil case. Compare *court of appeals* and *supreme court*.

trustees Legislators who vote according to what they think is best for their constituents. Compare *delegates*.

tyranny Oppressive government that employs the cruel and unjust use of power and authority.

unfunded mandates National standards or programs imposed on state and local governments by the federal government without accompanying funding or reimbursement.

valence issue An issue or aspect of a choice for which all voters prefer a higher value, in contrast to a spatial issue—for example, voters prefer their politicians to be honest, and honesty is a valence issue.

veto The president's constitutional power to reject acts of Congress.

veto power The ability to defeat something even if it has made it on to the agenda of an institution.

War Powers Resolution A 1973 resolution by Congress declaring that the president can send troops into action abroad only if Congress authorizes the action or if U.S. troops are already under attack or seriously threatened.

whip system A party communications network in each house of Congress. Whips poll their party's members to learn their intentions on specific bills and also convey the leadership's views and plans to members.

White House staff The analysts and advisers to the president, often given the title "special assistant."

writ of *certiorari* A formal request to have the Supreme Court review a decision of a lower court.

writ of *habeas corpus* A court order demanding that an individual in custody be brought into court and shown the cause for detention; *habeas corpus* is guaranteed by the Constitution and can be suspended only in cases of rebellion or invasion.

Credits

CHAPTER 2

Page 44 Table 2.1 reprinted by permission of The Green Papers.
Page 48 United States Senate

CHAPTER 3

Page 94 Joshua Rainey/Alamy Stock Photo

CHAPTER 4

Page 140 Brent Lewis/The Denver Post via Getty Images

CHAPTER 5

Page 179 ZUMA Press Inc./Alamy Stock Photo

CHAPTER 6

Page 214 Figure reprinted from "Legislative Staff and Representation in Congress," by Alexander Hertel-Fernandez, Matto Mildenberger, and Leah C. Stokes. *American Political Science Review* Vol. 113, No. 1, February 2019, pp. 1–18. Reprinted by permission of Cambridge University Press.
Page 241 AP Photo/Toby Talbot

CHAPTER 7

Page 271 Tribune Content Agency LLC/Alamy Stock Photo

CHAPTER 8

Page 327 Michael Williamson/The Washington Post via Getty Images

CHAPTER 9

Page 386 Alex Wong/Getty Images

CHAPTER 10

Page 429 Paul J. Richards/AFP via Getty Images

CHAPTER 11

Page 450 Tribune Content Agency LLC/Alamy Stock Photo

CHAPTER 12

Page 517 Nicholas Kamm/AFP via Getty Images

CHAPTER 13

Page 568 Jim R. Bounds/Bloomberg via Getty Images
Page 584 Table 13.3 from http://www.opensecrets.org/lobby/top.php?indexType=s. Reprinted with permission from the Center for Responsive Politics (opensecrets.org).

CHAPTER 14

Page 635 Mauricio Handler/National Geographic Creative

Index

freedom of the press and, 607
institutions in, 73
political parties and, 560
public opinion and, 393
representative, 11–12, 442
voting and, 454–55
Democratic Congressional
Campaign Committee
(DCCC), 488, 540, 541–42
Democratic National Committee
(DNC), 488, 539–40
Democratic Party, Democrats
1968 election and, 555–56
1988 national convention of, 470
2008 elections and, 486, 492
2012 elections and, 465
2016 elections and, 461, 540
2018 elections and, 103, 202,
225, 275, 465
2020 elections and, 497, 543
African Americans and, 21,
414, 478, 534
Americans identifying
themselves as, 528–29, *532*
antislavery, 548
Asian Americans and, 534
"blue states" and, 412–13
candidate recruitment, 518
Catholics and, 418, 535
Central Americans and, 415,
534
changes in presidential
nominating system, 555–56
changing character of, 544,
558–59
civil rights movement and, 552
Bill Clinton's impeachment
and, 202
divisions within, 552
factions in, 497
filibuster threat and, 288
formation of, 558
general philosophy, 522
Great Depression and, 551
group basis of, 533–37
history of, 547–56
importance of, 510–12
interest groups aligned with,
514–15, 533
Jackson's founding of, 547
Jewish Americans and, 21, 535

Latino support for, 415–16,
533, 534
legislative priorities of, 555
liberalism in, 552, 554–55
members of, *243*, 243–44, *245*
Mexican American and, 415,
534
New Deal and, 552
nominating processes, 461
partisanship and, 201–2,
220–21, 228–29, 236–37, *243,*
243–44, *245,* 246, 477, 560
platforms, 538
policies implemented by, 525
positioning of, 543
primary elections, 470, 471
Puerto Ricans and, 415, 534
reporters in, 623
Republicans' differences with,
32, 93, 476–79, 522–25, 543
shifting base, 512
South and, 544
Southern, 164, 220, 243, *245,*
397, 524, 548, 551, 552
Texas gerrymandering and, 211
two-party system and, 511–12
White southerners in, 548, 552
women and, 416–18, 478
Democratic-Republicans, 546,
561
Democratic Senatorial Campaign
Committee (DSCC), 488,
540, 541–42
Denmark, 52
Depression, Great, 278, 279, 280,
289n51, 321, 436, 550–51
deregulation, 338. *See also*
regulation
Derthick, Martha, 80n10
descriptive representation, 212,
412
desegregation, 163–66, 169–73,
172, 296, 357, 370, 377, 388,
389, 392, 397, 425, 544. *See
also* racial discrimination;
segregation
DeSilver, Drew, 452n4
devolution, 338–40
DeVos, Betsy, 131, 174, 398
Dewar, Helen, 457n12
Diermeier, Daniel, 428n62

Diet, Japanese, 194
digital media, 608–9, 614–17
advantages of, 617, 620–21
regulation and, 632–33
Digital News Report, 608
digital searches, 138, 140
Dilger, Robert Jay, 90n23
diplomacy, 319
ambassadors, 195, 250
diplomatic power of presidency,
262–63
direct democracy, 472–74
direct mail, 488
Disability Rights Education &
Defense Fund, 183
disabled people, rights of, 89,
154, 183–84
disaster response, 261, 310
discharge petition, 227, 231n38
discrimination. *See also specific types*
outgroups and, 419–20
Disney, 567, 585
"disparate impact," 175
dispersion of benefits, 73
dispute resolution, 360
dissenting opinions, 376–77
distributive tendency, 237–39,
320, 335, 341–42
District of Columbia, 134,
165n21, 352
voting procedures, 450, 451,
462, 475
District of Columbia circuit
court, 351
District of Columbia v. Heller, 134
divided government, 97–98, 510
division of labor, 311
divorce laws, 478
Dixiecrat Party, 397
DNA collection, routine, 148
DNC (Democratic National
Committee), 488, 539–40
Dodd, Lawrence C., 219n27,
220n28, 333n23
Dodd-Frank Wall Street Reform
and Consumer Protection
Act (2010), 317
Doherty, Carroll J., 251n61
DOMA (Defense of Marriage
Act; 1996), 184, 185, 375,
386, 425

political, 124–26
press freedom and, 128
speech plus action, 127
Supreme Court and, 114, 607
symbolic speech, 126–27
freedom of the press, *113,* 123,
127–30, 600–601, 610, 612,
632, 636, 637, 642
Supreme Court and, 114
free exercise clause, 122–23
free riding, 16–17, 302, 522,
574–75, 579n17, 600, 601
Free Soilers, 548
free trade, 528
French and Indian Wars, 33
Friends of the Earth, 430
Frisby, Michael K., 426n53
Frisch, Scott A., 205n13, 218n25,
526n17
Fritsch, Jane, 591n38
Frontiero v. Richardson, 176n42
FTC (Federal Trade
Commission), 83, 132, 320
Fuchs, Lawrence H., 178n48
fugitives, comity clause and, 77
full faith and credit clause, 77
Fulton, Sarah, 199n4
Furman v. Georgia, 143, 406

Gabbard, Tulsi, 543
Gabriele, Ashley, 610n15
Gailmard, Sean, 12n10
Gallup polls, 401, 434, 477
gambling, sports, 93, *101*
Gamm, Gerald, 221n29
Gans, Herbert, 622n39
GAO (Government
Accountability Office), 326
*Garcia v. San Antonio Metropolitan
Transit Authority,* 278n34
Garland, Merrick, 221, 358–59,
381
Garrow, David J., 640n69
Garzia, Alicia, 592
gatekeeping, 10, 223–24,
242, 328
Gates, Scott, 323n15
gay men and lesbians
adoption and, 77
civil rights of, 123, 154, 177,
184–86, 189, 389, 390

military service, 20
as "outgroup," 419
privacy rights, 147–48
same-sex marriage and, 120,
184, 185–86, 364, 385, 386,
406, 410, 425, 473, 535
GDP (gross domestic product),
405, 483, 486
Geiger, A. W., 612n22, 614n25
gender discrimination, 174,
176–78, 184–86, 189
equal pay and, 418
political engagement and,
530–31
Supreme Court and, 346, 378
gender gap
definition of, 417
in party identity, 416–18, 424,
478, 534–35, *537*
reasons for, 416–18
war and peace issues, *417*
gender inequities, 174
General Accounting Office, 182
General Electric, 600, 638
General Motors, 567
"general police power," 149
Genet, Edmond, 262
Geneva Conventions, 297n63,
366
geographical region, in party
identity, 412, 418–19, 536,
544, 552–53
geographic information systems
(GIS) software, 469
George III, King of England, 259
Georgia
assent to Bill of Rights,
108n3
majority rule in, 470
same-sex adoption and, 77
slavery in, 46
sodomy laws in, 147
Virginia Plan and, 46
Gerber, Alan, 411, 495, 597–98
German mercenaries
(Hessians), 36
Germany, elections in, 490
Germany, Nazi, 6
Gerry, Elbridge, *58,* 466
gerrymandering, 93, *101,* 211,
466, 468–69

Gerth, Jeff, 629n50
Gibbons, Thomas, 82
Gibbons v. Ogden, 82, *353*
Gideon, Clarence Earl, 142,
367
Gideon v. Wainwright, 113, 116,
142, 367
Gienapp, William E., 548n37
Gilens, Martin, 569n8
Gilmour, John B., 233n41
Ginsberg, Benjamin, 98n38,
99n39, 140n1, 142n95,
521n12
Ginsburg, Ruth Bader, 358, 359,
378, *382–83*
Gitlin, Todd, 640n70
Gitlow v. New York, 113, 114
Glaeser, Edward L., 35n5
going public strategy, 590–94
interest groups, 590
presidency and, 286, 288–90
protests and, 592–94
Goldberg, Arthur, 145–46
Goldstein, David, 621n38
Goldwater, Barry, 551
Gómez-Pérez v. Potter, 176
Gomillion v. Lightfoot, 162
Gonzales v. Carhart, 147
Gonzales v. Oregon, 92, *101,* 148
Google, 580–81, 615, 616, 620,
621, 639–40
Google China, 639
Google News, 431
Goostree, Robert E., 265n11
GOP. *See* Republican Party,
Republicans
Gordon, Greg, 621n38
Gore, Al, 559
Gorney, Cynthia, 428n61
Gorsuch, Neil, 202, 221, 237,
288, 357, 359, *382*
Gottfried, Jeffrey, 616n26
government
coalitions and, 440–41
definition of, 5
forms of, 5–6
public opinion and, 426–27,
440–42
regulation by, 405, 409, 570,
588, 595–96, 607, 632–40
representative, 393–94

health insurance, 590–91. *See also* Affordable Care Act (ACA, 2010)

Health Insurance Association of America, 590–91

Hearst, William Randolph, 622

Heberlig, Eric S., 219n26

Heinz, John P., 587n30

Heller, Dean, 525

Henry, Patrick, *58*

Heritage Foundation, 428

Herrera, Yoshiko M., 411n22

Herring, Pendleton, 590n36

Herrnson, Paul S., 519n9

Hersh, Eitan, 458n14

Herszenhorn, David M., 516n4

Hertel-Fernandez, Alexander, 214

Hetherington, Marc, 477n38

Hibbing, John R., 199n4

Hicklin v. Orbeck, 77

hidden information, 447

Hiebert, Ray Eldon, 606n5

Hill, The, 610

Hillygus, D. Sunshine, 487n52, 529n23

Hindus, 535

Hispanic Americans. *See* Latino Americans

Hispanic Caucus, 230

history principle, 7, 19–21, 22, 32
American Revolution and, 31
Bill of Rights and, 108–9
broadcast media and, 608
bureaucracy and, 312
civil liberties and, 149
civil rights and, 159, 179, 189
Confederate monuments and, 168
Constitution and, 40, 47
discrimination and, 154
elections and, 449
federalism and, 75
Federalists vs. Antifederalists, 61
judiciary and, 391
legal precedents and, 346
legislative committees and, 221
loyalties and alliances, 21
path dependency and, 20, 21, 67–68
political parties and, 524

pork-barrel legislation and, 206
presidency and, 303
public opinion and, 393
separation of powers and, 251–52
Supreme Court and, 107
voter turnout and, 455–56

Hitler, Adolf, 21

Hmong Americans, 534

Hobby Lobby, 123

Hojnacki, Marie, 585n26

Holder, Eric, 177

holds, 232, 249–50, 288

Hollingsworth et al. v. Perry et al., 185, 473

Holmes, Oliver Wendell, Jr., 51, 367

Holt v. Hobbs, 122

Homeland Security Department (DHS), U.S., 2
creation of, 262, 270, 306–7, 319
shape of, *308*
vacancies in, 331

home rule, 80

homosexuality, 116

Hoover, Herbert, 550
public appearances, *290*

Hoover Institution, 428

Horn, Murray J., 328n20

Horowitz, Donald L., 390n62

Horowitz, Juliana Menasce, 414n27

Horton v. California, 136

"hostile working environment," 131

House of Commons, British, 194

House of Representatives, U.S. *See also* Congress, U.S.; Speaker of the House
age restrictions, 519
Agriculture Committee, 218, 223, 225, 227–28, 328
Appropriations Committee, 237, 332, 599
Armed Services Committee, 223
bicameralism in, 200–202
bills per session of, 224
Budget Committee, 246n56
campaign committees, 540

campaign expenditures, *207*
Bill Clinton's impeachment and, 202
committee assignments, 205, 218, 246, 526
committee chair team limits, 225n35, 228
committee meetings, 332, 334
congressional districts, 209–12, *210*, 462–69
in Connecticut Compromise, 44, 48, 464
in Constitution, 47, 49, 157
constitutional amendments and, 62
debate in, 231–33
decision-making rules, 11
differences from Senate, *200*, 200–202
election of, 200, 440, 489
electoral system and, 202–12
Energy and Commerce Committee, 218, 223
flag-burning amendment and, 127
geographic population shifts and, *210*
Homeland Security Committee, 223
impeachment power of, 250–51
incumbency and, *204*, 204–6, 208–9
lawmaking ability of, 200–202
organization of, 217–30, *222*
oversight and, 334
partisanship in, 201–2, 231–32, *243, 245*
party leadership in, 200–202, 217–21
presidential elections and, 259
representation by state, *42–45*
representation in, 200–202
Rules Committee, 221, 223, 231, 237
seniority rule in, 225–26, 228, 526
standing committees in, *222*
subcommittees in, 225, 228, 231, 233, 237
tasks of, 49

House of Representatives *(continued)*
  terms of office, 47, 49, 201, 392
  Texas gerrymandering and, 211
  in Three-Fifths Compromise, 46
  Trump's impeachment and, 98, 103, 202, 251, 496, 497
  turnover in, *204,* 209
  vetos overridden by, 235, 265, 273
  Washington's refusal of request by, 264
  Ways and Means Committee, 218, 314
  whip system, 247
Housing and Urban Development Department (HUD), U.S., 318
Howell, William G., 250n60, 257n1, 261n5, 274n28, 276n29, 296nn60–61
Hoyer, Steny, 218
Huang, Jon, 533n24, 536n30
Huber, Gregory, 411
HuffPost, 616, 619
Hughes, Jonathan, 320n11
Hulse, Carl, 516n4
Human Rights Campaign, 184
Humphrey, Hubert, 397, 544
Humphrey, Hubert, III, 436
hurricanes, 261, 311
Hussein, Saddam, 238, 641

Idaho, electoral districts in, 462n17
identity, political. *See* party identity
identity politics, 410–20
  definition of, 410
  gender and, 417
  geography and, 418–19
  outgroups and, 419–20
  political, 410–12
  race or ethnicity and, 414–16
  religion and, 418
ideology. *See* political ideology
"I Have a Dream" speech, 166
Illinois, renewal portfolio standard, 79
immigrants, immigration, 422, 443, 507, 524

abortions for, 183
Arizona law, 93, 364
children's citizenship rights, 115, 181–82
Chinese denied, 181
civil rights and, 181–83, 189
by country of origin, *412–13*
deportation protection, 297, 366
effect of Connecticut Compromise on policy toward, 48
grants-in-aid and, 86
green cards and, 156–57
Latino Americans and, 414–15, 592
nativist rhetoric against, 550
Obama reform proposals, 286, 366
party identity and, 515, 534
quotas, 156, 181
residency requirements, 156
restrictions on, 473
rights protests, 592
right to work and, 157
sanctuaries for, 93, 182
Trump administration's policies on, 86, 91, 93, 97–98, 100, 102, 182, 261, 303, 331
undocumented, 93, 156–57, 181–83, 189, 294, 366, 456n10
Immigration and Nationality Services Act (1965), 181
Immigration and Naturalization Services v. Chadha, 100
Immigration Reform and Control Act (1986), 182
impeachment, 98, 103, 202, 250–51, 252, 265, 275, 299–300, 332, 401, 496, 497. *See also* Clinton, Bill, and administration; Johnson, Andrew; Trump, Donald, and administration
implementation, 312–13, 392
implied powers, 75
incitement, 125
income taxes. *See under* taxes
incorporation, 112–15, 139, 165n21

selective, 114–15, 139, 149
total, 114
incumbency, *204,* 204–6, *208,* 208–9, 433, 480
  advantages of, 461–62, 487, 489, 493–95
  economy and, 484–85
  fund-raising and, 206, *207,* 209, 493–95
Independent Community Bankers, 567
independent expenditures, 595–96, *598*
India, 52, 454n6
Indiana, 161
Indian Americans, 534
indirect election, 47, 49, 55, 60, 97, 200, 259, 463
informal bargaining, 13–14
in forma pauperis, 371
informational benefits, 577
informed electorate, media and, 607–8, 612, 614–17
infotainment, 613
inherent powers, 260, 273–76
initiatives. *See* ballot initiatives
In re Neagle, 260n2
In re Oliver, 116n13
In re Winship, 135
insider strategies, 582
institution principle, 6, 9–12, 21–22, 32
  agenda power and, 10–11
  bicameralism and, 200–201
  bureaucracy and, 307, 327, 334, 341
  civil rights and, 166–67
  collective action facilitated by, 14, 18, 72, 102–3, 106, 149, 189
  combating majoritarianism, 60, 103, 508
  committee system and, 228–29
  Congress and, 194, 217, 253
  congressional rules of procedure and, 235–37
  constitutional amendments and, 62–63
  Constitution and, 47, 55, 69
  decisiveness and, 11
  delegation and, 11–12

Karol, David, 533n25
Kasich, John, 427
Kastellec, Jonathan, 358n8
Katrina, Hurricane, 261, 310, 329
Katz, Harold A., 175n38
Katzenbach v. McClung, 175
Katz test, 136
Kaufman, Herbert, 80n9
Kavanaugh, Brett, 202, 221, 237, 288, 357, 359, *359*
Keeter, Scott, 477n37
Kellman, Ken, 238n44
Kelly, Alfred H., 123n37
Kelly, Sean Q, 205n13, 218n25, 526n17
Kelo v. City of New London, 142, *354*
Kennedy, Anthony, 375, 377–78, *382–83,* 386
Kennedy, Courtney, 477n37
Kennedy, John F., and administration
  Catholicism of, 121, 418
  election of, 284
  executive orders, 294
  New Frontier, 252
  personal life of, 641
  public appearances, *290*
  reporters and, 623, 641
Kennedy, Ted, 235–36
Kennedy v. Louisiana, 144
Kentucky, 161
Kernell, Samuel, 276n31, 286n46, 289n53
Kerry, John, 624
Kessel, John H., 280n37
Kettl, Donald F., 88n20
Key, V. O., 162n10
Khademian, Anne, 436n74
Kiewiet, D. Roderick, 196n2, 284n42
Killenbeck, Mark, 298n65
Kimball, David C., 585n26
Kinder, Donald, 432n70
King, Anthony, 520n10
King, David C., 223n30
King, Gary, 468n26, 639n67
King, Martin Luther, Jr., 166, 592
Kingdon, John W., 240n47, 306n1
King v. Burwell, 91, 285n44, 378

Kirkpatrick, David, 587n28
Kirschten, Dick, 182n54
Kissinger, Henry, 283
Klobuchar, Amy, 497, 543
Kluger, Richard, 165n20
Kmiec, Douglas W., 293n58
Knick v. Township of Scott, Pennsylvania, 142
Knight, Jack, 377n43
Know-Nothings, 548
Knox, Richard, 148n121
Kollman, Kenneth W., 590n36
Konvitz, Milton, 108n2
Korean Americans, 534
Korean War, 100, 252, 273, 297
Korematsu v. United States, 353
Krause, George, 282n39
Krehbiel, Keith, 218n24, 246n54, 288n47
Kriner, Douglas L., 302n78
Krosnik, Jon, 641n72
Ku Klux Klan, 124–25
Kumar, Martha Joynt, 276n31
Kurland, Philip B., 368n31
Kushner, Jared, 282
Kyllo v. United States, 137

Labor Department, U.S., 317–18, 320, 327
laborers, in colonial America, 32, 33–35
labor organizations, 567
labor unions, 7–8, 201, 428, 473, 527, 559, 578, 593, 597.
  See also unions
  Democratic Party and, 514, 533, 543, 551, 552
  media coverage and, 630
  strikes and, 593
Ladd, Everett Carl, 398n8
Lai, K. K. Rebecca, 533n24, 536n30
laissez-faire economics, 524
Lambda Legal Defense and Education Fund, 184
Landon, Alfred P., 436
Lane, Charles, 378n45
language minorities, civil rights of, 162, 181
La Raza Unida Party, 180
Larson, Ryan, 456n11

Lasswell, Harold, 6
Las Vegas, Nevada, 135
latent concern, 397
latent (interest) groups, 572
Latino Americans
  advocacy and representation for, 197, 412, 465–66
  civil rights of, 178, 180
  immigration and, 414–15, 592
  as judges, 356, *384*
  party identity of, 414–16, *416,* 478, 515, 533, 534
  proposed restrictions on, 182
  segregation of, 178, 180
  voter registration and, 180
  voting and, 162
  voting rights of, 211n20
Laumann, Edward O., 587n30
Lau v. Nichols, 181
law, statutory, 367
law clerks, 373–74
Lawless, Jennifer, 203n9
Lawrence and Garner v. Texas, 147–48, 185
Lawrence v. Texas, 386
lawsuits, 344, 370, 582
"layer cake federalism," 88
Lazarsfeld, Paul, 495
Lazarus, Edward, 374n38
League of United Latin American Citizens (LULAC), 178
League of Women Voters, 521
leaks, 128, 627
Leal, David, 438n75
Lear, Siegler v. Lehman, 298n70
Lebanon Daily Star, 616
Ledbetter Fair Pay Act (2009), 176, 275
Ledbetter v. Goodyear Tire and Rubber Co., 176
Lee, Ivy, 628
Lee, Jongho, 438n75
Lee, Richard Henry, 58
Lee, Robert E., 168
Lee, Taeku, 414n30
legal rights, 157
legislative branch, 194–253. *See also* Congress, U.S.
  from 1800–1933, 277
  character of, 49

Maine
  Election Day registration
    in, 476
  Electoral College
    representation, 462n18
  electoral districts, 462n18
  marijuana laws in, 94
Maine, 622
Maisel, L. Sandy, 199n4
Maitland, Ian, 585n25
majority, tyranny of the, 59–61,
  103
majority leader, 218, 252
  recognition power, 246–47
majority-minority districts, 197,
  211–12, 370, 465–66
majority party, 525
majority rule, 469, 508
  electoral districts and, 465–66
majority system, 471
MALDEF (Mexican American
  Legal Defense and
  Education Fund), 180, 182
Malik, Tashfeen, 138
Maltzman, Forrest, 199n5,
  373n36, 375n40
Mamiit, Aaron, 640n68
managerial presidency, 329, 332
mandates, 309
  unfunded, 90, *101*
mandatory sentences, 143
mandatory spending programs,
  240, 241
Manning, Chelsea (Bradley), 128
Manning, Jennifer E., 412n25
Mansbridge, Jane J., 176n41
Mansfield, Harvey C., Jr., 301n76
Mapp, Dollree, 136
Mapp v. Ohio, 113, 116, 136, *353*
"marble cake federalism," 88
Marbury, William, 362–63
Marbury v. Madison, 99, *353,*
  362–63
March on Washington, 166
marijuana laws, 93, 94
marital privacy, right of, 145–46
"marketplace of ideas," 607–8,
  622
marriage, same-sex, 184, 185–86,
  364, 385, 386, 406, 410, 425,
  473, 535. *See also* civil unions

Marshall, John, 356, 363, 385
  Bill of Rights and, 110
  on commerce clause, 82
  on implied powers, 81
  on judicial review, 99
Marshall, Thurgood, 356n7, 374
Martin, Andrew D., 378n46
Martin, Trayvon, 592
Martin v. Hunter's Lessee, 364n15
Martin v. Wilks, 187
Maryland, 81–82, 112
  bank tax and, 82
  electoral districts, 462n17
  gerrymandering in, *101*
  renewal portfolio standard, 79
  slavery in, 46
Maryland v. King, 148
Masket, Seth, 533n25
Mason, George, 46, *58*
Massachusetts
  assent to Bill of Rights, 108n3
  cigarette ads, 133
  Federalists in, 108
  gerrymandering in, 466
  marijuana laws in, 94
  same-sex marriage in, 185
  Virginia Plan and, 43, 48
massive resistance, 169
Masson v. New Yorker Magazine,
  636–37
mass shootings, 135
*Masterpiece Cakeshop v. Colorado
  Civil Rights Commission,* 123
material benefits, 577
Matthews, Anna Wilde, 629n51
Mayer, Kenneth R., 276n29,
  436n74, 476n33
Mayhew, David R., 8n4, 267n16,
  356n6
Mazmanian, Daniel A., 557n43
McCain, John, 485, 491–92, 624
McCain-Feingold Act. *See*
  Bipartisan Campaign
  Reform Act
McCarthy, Kevin, 218
McCarthy, Niall, 427n58
McCarty, Nolan, 269n21, 401n11,
  553n39
McClain, Paula D., 419n39
McClintock, Mary Ann, 161
McClure, Robert D., 203n9

McConnell, Grant, 302n79
McConnell, James, 386
McConnell, Michael W., 612n20
McConnell, Mitch, 201n6, 219,
  220–21, 237, 251, 267, 327
*McConnell v. Federal Election
  Commission,* 125, 493n59
McCreary County v. ACLU, 119
McCright, Aaron, 429
McCubbins, Mathew D., 196n2,
  218n24, 220n28, 247n57,
  284n42, 315n7, 326n18, 334,
  422n45, 514n3, 529n22,
  542n34, 553n39
McCulloch v. Maryland, 81–82, *353*
*McCutcheon v. Federal Election
  Commission,* 126
McDermott, Rose, 411n22
McDonald, Forrest, 74n3
McDonald, Michael P., 456n9
McDonald v. Chicago, 113, 135, 149
McGuire, Kevin, 373n36
McKinley, William, 550, 622
"means-tested" part of welfare
  state, 322
measurement error, 438
media, 572, 593, 604–42
  as advertising dependent, 607,
    610, 612
  bias in, 433, 613, 623–25
  broadcast, 608, 610, 612–14
  cable television, 613
  campaign coverage by, 451,
    489–90, 494, 495
  conflict and, 631–32
  consumers of, 629–32
  coverage of coronavirus
    pandemic, 604–5
  definition of, 605
  digital, 608–9, 614–17, 620–21
  education level and, 629–30, *631*
  endorsements by, 624, *625*
  factors affecting news
    coverage, 622–32
  First Amendment and, 607
  for-profit, 607, 622, 634
  as Fourth Estate, 606n5
  functions of, 606–8
  government's disputes
    with, 426
  grazing and, 612

media (continued)
  hard news and, 630
  informed electorate and, 607, 612, 614–17
  journalists and, 622–26
  leaks of information to, 627
  licensing of, 608, 614, 633–34
  as "marketplace of ideas," 607–8, 622
  news concentration in, 637–40
  news deserts, 620–21
  as news sources, *609,* 618–19, 626–29
  news websites, 609, 612, 615, 616, 619
  Obama and, 623, 624
  ownership of, 637–40, *639*
  as political institution, 608–21
  political struggles and, 3, 22
  politicians and, 623, 641–42
  politics and, 606–7, 613
  power and responsibility of, 640–42
  presidential press relations, 289, 432–33
  press releases and, 627–28
  print, 128, 608, 610–12, 617, *625,* 632
  public affairs content and, 606–7, 612, 613, 614–17, 629–30
  public opinion and, 426, 427, 430–33
  radio, 608, 612, 613–14
  regulation of, 607, 632–40
  reporters, 626–27
  social (*See* social media)
  soft news and, 613
  synergies among, 609
  technological changes, 292, 613–14
  types of, 608–17
media market, 614
median, 26
median-voter theorem, 226, *226, 482,* 482–83
Medicaid, 91, 92–93, 322, 338–39, 481
medical insurance. *See* health insurance
medical malpractice suits, 348
medical-service advertising, 133

Medicare, 405, 481, 536
  AARP and, 571
  Nebraska exemption and, 274
  opposition to cuts, 240
Medicare for All proposal, 497
Meese, Edwin, 298–99
membership associations, 569, 570
Mendez v. Westminster, 178
mental health, 340
mentally handicapped, rights of, 144
merchants, New England, 32, 33–35, 39, 68, 544, 546
  Constitution and, 41–48
  federalist ideas of, 57, *58*
Meritor Savings Bank v. Vinson, 131, 177
merit systems, 550
Merritt, Davis, 628n48
messaging apps, 609, 619
#MeToo movement, 177, 579
Mexican American Legal Defense and Education Fund (MALDEF), 180, 182
Mexican Americans, 178, 180
  party identity of, 414–15, *416,* 534
Mexico
  border wall and, 97–98, 268, 270, 271, 507, 516
  voting in, 453
Michigan, 161, 436
  lobbying in, 583
Michigan, University of, 187–88
  Law School, 187–88
Microsoft Corporation, 567, 585, 600
Middle East. *See also specific countries*
Miers, Harriet, 358
Mildenberger, Matto, 214
military
  under Articles of Confederation, 37–38
  in colonial America, 30–31, 33
  Congress's power over, 194, 195
  in Constitution, 40
  Defense Department and, 319–20

  desegregation of, 296
  LGBTQ issues in, 20, 178, 179, 184
  pork-barrel legislation and, 319–20, 335
  president's powers, 261–62, 283
  proposed base closings, 319, 337–38
  service, 157
  spending by, 268–69
Military Commissions Act (2006), 100
military tribunals, 297, 349–50, 366
militias, 133
Milkis, Sidney M., 288
Miller, Gary J., 324n16
Miller, Jonathan, 553n40
Miller, S. A., 91n26
Miller, Susan, 435n73
Miller, Warren, 411n23
Miller v. Alabama, 143
Miller v. California, 129
Miller v. Johnson, 370n35
Milligan, Susan, 427n55
Milliken v. Bradley, 171
Milyo, Tom, 624n44
Minersville School District v. Gobitus, 122n31
Minneapolis Star Tribune, 436
Minnesota, 386
  1998 gubernatorial election, 436
  caucuses in, 461
  Election Day registration in, 458, 476
minority leader, 218, 252
Minow, Martha, 110n4
Miranda, Ernesto, 139, 141
Miranda rights, 378
Miranda rule, 116, 141, 367–68
Miranda v. Arizona, 113, 116, 141, 367–68
"misplaced self-interest," 423
Mississippi, gerrymandering in, 469
Missouri, abortion laws in, 146n112
Missouri, University of, Law School, 164

Nelson, Robert L., 587n30
neo-Nazis and right-wing
    extremists, 132, 168
"netroots" campaign,
    489, 522
Neustadt, Richard E., 97n36,
    194, 263n9, 268n19,
    276n30, 392n1
Nevada
    caucuses in, 461, 521
    marijuana laws in, 94
New Deal, 83–85, 252, 294, 524,
    551, 559
    presidency and, 270, 278–79,
    280, 285
    Supreme Court and, 99–100,
    346, 356, 365
Newdow, Michael, 119
new federalism, 90–91, 102
New Frontier, 252
New Hampshire, 446n1
    electoral districts, 462n17
    Federalists in, 108
    public school expenditures
    in, 400
Newhauser, Daniel, 526n18
New Jersey
    electoral districts, 462n17
    Port Authority and, 80
    Virginia Plan and, 43
New Jersey Plan, 42–43
Newman, Nic, 608n11
New Mexico, 178n48
New Politics movement, 571–72,
    589–90
news. *See also* media
    concentration in, 637–40
    hard, 630
    interest in, 629–32
    leaks, 627
    sources of, 626–29
news apps, 609
news conferences, 289
news deserts, 620–21
newspapers, 618–19, 620,
    632–33. *See also* print media
    decline of, 621
    endorsements and, 624, *625*
    public opinion and, 430–33
New START treaty, 250
Newtown, Connecticut, 135

New York
    Federalists in, 108
    lobbying in, 583
    noncitizens denied voting
    rights in, 158–59
    Port Authority and, 80
    renewal portfolio standard, 78
    stop and frisk in, 138
    Tammany Hall in, 549
    under-representation of, 48
    Virginia Plan and, 48
    women's suffrage in, 161
New York Journal, 58
New York Times, 127, 610, 612,
    615, 621, 623, 625, 626, 627,
    630, 640
New York Times v. Sullivan, 128,
    492n57, 607n9, 636
New York Times v. United States,
    127, 636
NFIB (National Federation of
    Independent Business), 567
Nielsen, Rasmus Kleis, 608n11
Nineteenth Amendment, *65,* 161,
    174, *453*
Ninth Amendment, 64, *64,* 109,
    145–46, 148
Niskanen, William, 323–24
Nixon, Richard, and
    administration, 551–52
    approval rating, *291*
    attempted surveillance of
    Democratic campaign
    plans, 140
    in election of 1972, 483
    executive privilege claimed by,
    98, 100, 264, 366
    Ford's pardon of, 262
    judges appointed by, 356
    National Security Council
    and, 283
    public appearances, *290*
    public relations, 289n54
    regulated federalism under, 90
    resignation of, 251, 256, 264, 640
    southern strategy, 551–52
    vetos of, 273
NLRB (National Labor Relations
    Board), 83, 278, 314
Noel, Hans, 533n25
Noll, Roger G., 326n18

nomination
    by caucus, 521
    changes in, 555–56
    by convention, 519–20, 538–39
    definition of, 519
    by primary election, 520–21
    processes, *520*
nonpartisan voters, 522, 550. *See
    also* voters, independent
nonpreferentialist view, 117
nonprofit organizations, 405–6
nonvoters, 454–55, 475–76
Noriega, Manuel, 128, 636
normative questions, 4
North American Free Trade
    Agreement (NAFTA), 481
North Carolina, 497
    gender discrimination laws,
    178, 179
    gerrymandering in, *101*
    renewal portfolio standard, 78
    slavery in, 46
    Virginia Plan and, 43
North Dakota
    abortion laws in, 146
    disproportionate influence
    of, 48
    electoral districts, 462n17
Northern Marianas Islands, 351
North Korea, 6, 273, 496
"no taxation without
    representation" slogan, 32, 33
NOW (National Organization
    for Women), 176, 430, 515,
    570, 571, 590
NRA (National Rifle
    Association), 567, 597
NRCC (National Republican
    Campaign Committee), 540,
    541–42
NRSC (National Republican
    Senatorial Committee), 488,
    540, 541–42
NSA (National Security Agency),
    128, 138–39, 149, 261, 262,
    294, 627
NSC (National Security Council),
    261, 282, 283
nuclear disarmament, 571
"nuclear option" in Senate
    debate, 236, 237

Oregon
  assisted suicide and, 92, 148
  automatic voter registration
    in, 458
  marijuana laws in, 94
  renewal portfolio standard, 78
  voting by mail in, 451
original jurisdiction, 350–52, 369
Orlando, Florida, 135
Ortman, Jennifer, 404n13
OSHA (Occupational Safety
  and Health Administration),
  272, 320
Ostrom, Elinor, 17n14
Oswald, Kristine A., 606n5
outgroups, party identity and,
  419–20
outside strategies, 582
outsourcing, 340n29
overgrazing, 17
oversight, 224–25, 242, 315, 324,
  332–35
Oxford Internet Institute, 621

PACs. *See* political action
  committees
Page, Benjamin, 424
Page, Horace, 156
Page Act (1875), 156
Palko, Frank, 114
Palko v. Connecticut, 114–15,
  116, 139
Palmer, Kenneth T., 86nn17–18
Palmquist, Bradley, 527n21
Pan, Jennifer, 639n67
Panama Refining Company v. Ryan,
  99n41, 279n35
Paquette, Danielle, 478n41
Para Bellum Labs, 540
pardons, 259, 262
Parenti, Michael, 622n39
*Parents Involved in Community
  Schools v. Seattle School District
  No. 1,* 173
Paris, Treaty of (1783), 37
Paris Agreement on Climate
  Change (2016), 93, 296, 429
Parkland, Florida, 135
parliamentary government
  Cabinet in, 280
  electoral campaigns in, 490

executive control over, 194
judicial review and, 362
lack of presidency in, 52, 526
party system in, 512, 543
proportional representation
  in, 559
Parti, Tarini, 519n8
Partial Birth Abortion Ban Act
  (2003), 378, 428
parties, political. *See* political parties
party caucus, 218, 461, 538–41
party conference, 218
party discipline, 218, 228, 229,
  243–44, 246
  committee assignments and, 246
  floor access and, 246–47
  logrolling and, 247–48
  presidency and, 248, 288
  whip system and, 247
party identity, 400, 410–20, 476–79,
  527–29, *532,* 532–33
  age and, 536–37, *537*
  definition of, 412
  education and, *537*
  effect on vote for president,
    2020, *479*
  gender and, 412, 534–35, *537*
  geographic location and, 412,
    418–19
  as ideological affinity, 528–29
  income group and, 535–36, *537*
  of Jewish Americans, 21
  loyalties and alliances, 21, 474,
    476–79, 553–56
  outgroups and, 419–20
  as psychological attachment,
    527–28
  race or ethnicity and, 413–14,
    534, *537,* 552
  region and, 412, 418–19, 536,
    544, 552–53
  religion and, 412, 418, 535
  by social group, *537*
  stability of, 424–25
  as tally of experiences, 529,
    532–33
party labels. *See* branding
party leaders, 228, 229, 246, 518
  as constituents, 199n5
  in House of Representatives,
    217–21

in nineteenth century, 546–47
  public opinion and, 392
party machines, 541n32, 549
Party Politics (Duverger), 471
party rule, 511
party systems, 518–27, 542–60.
    See also political parties
  first, 544, 546
  second, 546–48
  third, 548–50
  fourth, 550
  fifth, 550–51
  sixth, 551–56
  balance of power in, 543
  changes in, 543–44
  definition of, 543
  evolution of, 544, *545,* 547–59
  function of, 511
  parliamentary governments
    and, 512, 543
  two-party, 20–21, 449, 471,
    508, 511–12, 542–44, 560
party vote, 243
patent law, 351, 354
Paterson, William, 42
path dependency, 20, 67–68
Patient Protection and
  Affordable Care Act. *See*
  Affordable Care Act
Patriot Act. *See* USA PATRIOT
  Act
patronage, 205–6, 549
Patterson, Thomas E., 624n43
Patty, John W., 12n10
Paulson, Henry, 323n15
PBS (Public Broadcasting
  System), 431, 624
Peace Corps, 296
Pearson, Kathryn, 219n27
Peffer, George Anthony, 156n4
Pelosi, Nancy, 103, 218, 228, 229,
  236, 251, 497
Pence, Mike, 284
Pennsylvania, 436
  Virginia Plan and, 43, 48
Pennsylvania Railroad, 628
Pentagon, 319. *See also*
  Defense Department,
  U.S.; September 11, 2001,
  terrorist attacks; terrorism
Pentagon Papers, 127, 627, 636

People for the American Way, 375

Peoples' Republic of China. *See* China

Pepper, Claude, 579

Perot, Ross, 465, 557–58

Perry, H. W., Jr., 374n37, 387n57

Persian Gulf War, 637, 640

Persily, Nathaniel, 460n15

petition, freedom of, 126–27

petroleum. *See* oil industry

Pevehouse, Jon C., 274n28

Pew Center on People and the Press, 410

Pew Project for Excellence in Journalism, 623

Pew Research Center, 433

Pfiffner, James P., 282n39

pharmaceutical industry, 583, 629

Phelps, Jordyn, 427n57

physician-assisted suicide, 92, *101*, 116, 148

Physicians for Social Responsibility, 430

Pianin, Eric, 202n7

pie chart, 27, *27*

Pierson, Paul, 423, 423n48

Piketty, Thomas, 423n46

Pildes, Richard, 441n78

piracy, 39

Piston, Spencer, 421n43

plaintiffs, 347, 348–49

Planned Parenthood, 145, 478

Planned Parenthood v. Casey, 146–47

planters, southern, 32, 33–35, 39, 68, 546

   Constitution and, 41–48

   federalist ideas of, 57, *58*

plea bargains, 349, *350*

Pledge of Allegiance, 119, 145

Plessy, Homer, 163

Plessy v. Ferguson, 163–64, *353*, 357

Plunkitt, George Washington, 12, 549

pluralism, 533, 564, 565–66, 572–74, 600

plurality system, 20–21, 469–72, 508, 559

pocket veto, 233, 265

podcasts, 613, 615

polarization, 244, *245*

   ideological, 401–4

   of political parties, 220–21, 429, 552

police misconduct, 154, 167–68, 189, 368, 377

police-patrol oversight, 334

police power, 76, 83, 346

police violence, fatal, 154, *167*, 397

policy entrepreneurs, 524

policy-making powers, 279

policy principle, 7, 18–19, 22, 32

   American Revolution and, 33

   bureaucracy and, 309, 335, 341

   climate and, 429

   Congress and the opioid epidemic, 241

   Constitution and policy outcomes, 48

   devolution and, 338–40

   election administration and automatic voter registration, 450

   elections and, 474

   federal vs. state marijuana laws, 94

   Fourth Amendment and government surveillance, 140

   gerrymandering and, 468

   internet ownership and, 635

   issue voting and, 479

   judiciary and, 389

   median-vote theorem and, *482*, 482–83

   mortgage interest tax deduction, 568

   parties and, 515, 517

   political knowledge and, 423–24

   pork-barrel legislation and, 19, 206, 238–39

   principal-agent relationships, 326, 327

   public opinion and, 440–42, 443

   separation of powers and, 102–3

   Supreme Court and, 368, 386

   transgender rights and policy, 179

   Trump's border wall, 271

   vetos and, 270, 271

political action committees (PACs), 125–26, 219, 242–43, 490–93, 577, 580–81, 594–95. *See also* Super PACs

political attentiveness, cost of, 422–23

political behavior, purpose of, 7–9

political caucus. *See* caucuses, caucus system

political entrepreneurs, 549, 578–79

political identity. *See* party identity

political ideology, 400–401, 408–10, 553–56

   as informational shortcut, 422–23, 522–23, 560

   Supreme Court and, 377–78, 379–80, 382–83

political knowledge

   preference stability and, 420–24

   public opinion and, 420–25

   trusted others and, 422–23

political parties, 217–21, 510–61. *See also* party identity; party systems

   activism and, 554–55, 596–98

   ambition controlled by, 514, 516

   as "big tents," 523

   branding and, 511, 514, 516, 522–23, 528

   campaign spending of, 125–26, 203

   candidate recruitment, 518–19

   cohesion of, 515

   collective action principle and, 512–15, 549

   Congress and, 510, 512, 525–27

   definition of, 508

   democracy and, 560

   electoral choice facilitated by, 522–23

   electoral vote share, 1789–2016, *554–57*

   in electorate, 527–37

   entrepreneurs of, 549

racism. *See* desegregation; racial
discrimination; segregation
radio, 288–89, 292, 430, 489, 608,
612, 613–14, 618–19
advertising on, 620
Radio Act (1927), 388
Rakove, Jack N., 35n6
Ramos v. Louisiana, 113
Randall, James G., 260n3
Randolph, Edmund, 41, 42
random digit dialing, 435–36
randomization, 435–36
Rapoport, Ronald B., 523n15
Rasul v. Bush, 100
rationality principle, 6, 7–9, 21
American Revolution and,
30–31, 34
bureaucracy and, 309, 311,
323, 324, 334, 341
checks and balances and,
98–99
Congress and, 253
Congress committee
assignments, 205
congressional rules of
procedure and, 236
elections and, 205, 449, 474
executive branch vs. legislative
branch, 272n26
free-ride incentive and, 576
incumbency and, 205
individual initiatives and, 18
judiciary and, 389
legislation and, 217
legislators and, 196
logrolling and, 247–48
motivations and, 8–9, 18–19
political knowledge and, 422
political parties and, 511, 512, 549
pork-barrel legislation and, 206
presidency and, 304
public opinion and, 393
suspending, 16
unitary decision making and, 301
U.S. Constitution and, 41
vetos and, 267–68, 269–70
Rational Public, The (Page and
Shapiro), 424
R.A.V. v. City of St. Paul, 131–32
Reagan, Ronald, and
administration, 98, 256, 528

approval rating, *291,* 292
coalition built by, 524, 525,
533, 552
in election of 1984, 483
gender gap in support of, 417
judges appointed by, 356, 358,
377, 390
partisanship under, 244
public appearances, *290*
public relations, 289n54
regulated federalism under, 90
regulatory review power, 257
reporters and, 623
signing statements, 298
tax cuts, 299
RealClearPolitics.com, 431
real estate. *See* property
reapportionment, 209–12
recall elections, 473
"reckless disregard," 128
recognition power, 246–47
reconciliation procedure, 236
Reconstruction, 251, 252, 288
African American voting
during, 161–62, 548
redistricting, 93, *101,* 159, 162,
197, 209–11, 346, 370,
463–64, 465–66, *467,*
468–69, 487, 497, 507
*Red Lion Broadcasting Company
v. Federal Communications
Commission,* 612n19, 634
Reed, Stanley F., 376
Reeves, Andrew, 302n78
referendums, 472–74
Reform Party, 465
*Regents of the University of California
v. Bakke,* 186–87, 188
registration. *See* voter registration
registration lists, 449, 458
regulated federalism, 88–90
regulation, 570, 588, 595–96
of media, 607, 632–40
self-interest and, 405
regulatory agencies, 277, 320
regulatory review, 257, 292–93,
299
"regulatory state," 84
Rehabilitation Act (1973), 183
Rehnquist, William H., 100, 141,
352, 358, 377–78, 380, 383

Reid, Harry, 201n6, 229, 237
religion
freedom of, *113,* 114,
117–23
party identity and, 418, 515,
524, 533, 535, 552
voting and, 121, 159, 535
religious discrimination, 121,
122–23, 155–56, 159,
164, 346
Religious Freedom Restoration
Act (RFRA), 123
Religious Right. *See* Christian
Right
Relyea, Harold C., 293n59
remarketing, 615
renewable energy, state policies
on, 78–79
renewable portfolio standard
(RPS), 78–79
Reno v. ACLU, 129
reparations, 154–55
reporters. *See* journalists
reprieves, 262
Republican National Committee
(RNC), 488, 540
Republican National Convention
of 1984, 126
Republican Party, Republicans
in 104th Congress, 228
2012 elections and, 465, 471–72
2016 elections and, 472, 540
2020 elections and, 497, 617
Americans identifying
themselves as, 528–29, *532*
anti-abortion position, 517
Asian Americans and, 534
"bridge to nowhere" and, 206
candidate recruitment, 518
Catholics and, 535
Bill Clinton's impeachment
and, 202
conservative base of, 552
Cuban Americans and, 415–16,
515, 533, 534
Democrats' differences with,
32, 93, 476–79, 522–25, 543
earmarks and, 206
factions, 497, 553–54
formation of, 548, 558
general philosophy, 522, 551

Republican Party *(continued)*
  group basis of, 533–37
  Growth and Opportunity
    Project, 540
  Hastert Rule of, 553–54
  history of, 548–56
  House committee system
    reformed by, 228–29, 526
  importance of, 510–12
  interest groups aligned with,
    514–15, 533
  Israel and, 21
  legislative priorities of, 556
  media use of, 617
  members of, *243,* 244, *245*
  men and, 416–18
  partisanship and, 201–2, 211n21,
    220–21, 228–29, 236–37, *243,*
    243–44, *245,* 246, 267, 275,
    286–88, 477, 560
  platforms, 517, 548
  policies implemented by, 525
  positioning of, 543
  Progressive faction, 515, 524
  Protestants and, 535
  redistricting and, 465
  "red states" and, 412–13
  religious conservatives in, 552
  reporters in, 623
  shifting base, 512
  social issues of, 524
  Texas redistricting by, 211
  two-party system and, 511–12
  Whites and, 414, 552
  White southerners in, 552
  women candidates, 518
reserved powers, 76
restrictive covenants, 164
"retail" politics, 8
retrospective voting, 480
Reuss, Carol, 606n5
Reuters, 612, 615, 616, 637
  Digital News Report, 608, 617
Reuters Institute for the Study of
  Journalists, 608
revenue agencies, 318
"reverse discrimination," 187
Reynolds v. United States, 122
Rhode Island
  Constitutional Convention
    and, 40, 55

liquor ads, 133
radical control of, 39
Ricci v. DeStefano, 188
Rice, Stuart, 553
Richey, Warren, 376n42
right of rebuttal, 634
right to bear arms. *See* arms,
  right to bear
right to counsel. *See* counsel,
  right to
right to die. *See* physician-assisted
  suicide
right to privacy. *See* privacy,
  right to
right to work, 157
Riker, William H., 57n21, 72n1,
  394n3
Riley v. California, 138
ripeness, 369
Rita, Hurricane, 261
RNC (Republican National
  Committee), 488, 539–40
Robert, Henry M., 11n9
Roberts, John, 124, 172–73, 358,
  359, 378, *382–83*
Roberts, Margaret, 639n67
Robinson, Michael J., 623n41,
  630n53
Robinson v. California, 113
Rocha, Rene R., 419n37
Rockman, Bert A., 280n37
Rocky Mountain News, 611
Rodden, Jonathan, 401n11,
  421nn42–43, 468n25,
  487n52
Roe v. Wade, 354, 389, 399,
  517, 589
  Blackmun's opinion on, 379
  mootness and, 370
  right to privacy and, 146, 379
Rogowski, Jon, 261n5
Rohde, David W., 199n3, 219n27,
  220, 236n43, 267n15,
  267n18, 378n49, 388n59,
  542n34, 553n39
Rojanasakul, Mira, 490n54
Roll Call, 610
roll-call votes, 243
Romer v. Evans, 184, 386
Romney, Mitt, 121, 251, 418,
  471–72, 511, 624

Roosevelt, Franklin D., and
  administration
  coalition built by, 524, 551
  Committee on Administrative
    Management of, 329
  in election of 1932, 551
  in election of 1936, 436
  executive orders, 181, 294
  fireside chats, 288–89
  Hundred Days, 278–79
  Jewish Americans under, 21
  New Deal program, 83, 84–88,
    99–100, 252, 278–79, 280,
    285, 294, 356, 365, 524, 551
  personal life of, 641
  public appearances, *290*
  reporters and, 623
  Supreme Court and, 99, 356,
    365
Roosevelt, Theodore, 288
Roper polls, 434
Roper v. Simmons, 354
Rosenberg, Gerald, 392n2
*Rosenberger v. Rector and Visitors of
  the University of Virginia,* 118
Rosenstone, Steven, 476n33
Rosenthal, Alan, 565n2
Rosenthal, Howard, 246n54,
  401n11, 553n39
Rosoff, Matt, 611n18
Rossiter, Clinton L., 49nn15–16,
  50n18, 60nn24–25, 61n30,
  72n2, 95nn34–35, 97n37,
  108n1, 108n3, 159n7,
  300n75, 322n13, 510n1,
  564n1, 565–66nn3–5
Roth v. United States, 129
royalists, 32, 33–35, 39
Rubio, Marco, 427, 623
Rucho v. Common Cause, 93, *101*
Rule 10, U.S. Supreme Court, 371
rule interpretation, courts and,
  361–62
rule making, 313–14, 441–42
rule of four, 371, 387
runoff elections, 470
Rusk, Jerold G., 461n16
Russia, 250, 627. *See also* Soviet
  Union
  alleged interference in 2016
    election, 264–65, 332, 496

as news source, 619, 620–21
  organized protests and, 592–93
  presidency and, 292
social networking, 289–90, 292
social regulation, 89
Social Security, 322, 405, 536,
    551, 571
  bureaucracy, 336–37, 341
Social Security Act (1935),
    83, 278
Social Security Administration
    (SSA), 322
"soft money," 125, 492, 541
"soft news," 613
solar power, state policies on,
    78–79
Soleimani, Qasem, *417*
Solicitor General, U.S., 373
solidary benefits, 578
Solove, Daniel J., 140n2
"sophomore surge," 208–9, 493
Sorkin, Ross, 323n15
Sotomayor, Sonia, 358, *359,*
    382–83
Souter, David, 358, 376, 378
South
  American Independent Party
    and, 559
  Deep, 169, 548
  desegregation in, 169–73, 357
  move to Republican camp by,
    524, 536, 551, 552
  Solid, 536
South Africa, 419n38
South Carolina, 174
  Constitution ratification, 62
  Federalists in, 108
  school segregation in, 164, 364
  slavery in, 46
South Dakota, 203
  electoral districts, 462n17
South Dakota v. Dole, 90
Southern Christian Leadership
    Conference (SCLC), 166
Southern Democrats, 164, 220,
    243, 244n53, *245,* 397, 524,
    550, 551, 552
"southern strategy," 544, 551–52
South Korea, 273
"sovereign immunity," *101*
sovereignty, 74, 141

Soviet Union, 5–6. *See also* Russia
Spaeth, Harold J., 380n53
Spain, 397
Spanish-American War, 622
spatial issues, 481–83
Speaker of the House, 218, 219,
    231, 252, 525
  recognition power, 246–47
special interests as constituents,
    199n5
specialization of labor, 11
"special master," 369, 468
speech, freedom of. *See* freedom
    of speech
speech plus, 127
speed limit, 86
Spence, David B., 203n8
Spicer, Sean, 427
Spiegel, Der, 627
Spitzer, Robert J., 265n12,
    277n32
split-ticket voting, 461–62, 550
Spriggs, James F., II, 375n39,
    375n40
SSA (Social Security
    Administration), 322
SSI (Supplemental Security
    Income), 322
staff agencies, 229–30
staff system, 229–30
stakeholders, 587
Stalin, Joseph, 5–6
Stamp Act (1765), 31, 33, 34
Stamp Act Congress, 31
standard of living, 157
standing, in court cases, 369,
    389–90
standing committees, 10, 221,
    222, 223, 332. *See also*
    committee system
Stanton, Elizabeth Cady, 161, 579
stare decisis, 348
State Department, U.S., 319
  diplomatic cables, 627
state legislatures, 37, 41, 47, 49,
    54, 55, 57
  apportionment in, 368, 389,
    390, 463–64
state/local spending, 1930–2012,
    84–85
State of the Union address, 265

state religion, nonestablishment
    of, *113,* 117–19
states, U.S.
  importance of, 75
  judicial review of actions, 364
  limitations on, 80, 110–11
  marijuana laws, 93, 94
  obligations to each other, 77
  powers of, 73, 76, 85, 391
  renewable energy policies,
    78–79
  sovereignty of, 74
  supreme courts of, 349
states' powers. *See* federalism
states' rights, 82–83, 91–93,
    110–11, 397
  under Articles of
    Confederation, 37–38
state supreme court, 349, *350*
*Statistical Abstract of the United
    States,* 404n14
statutory interpretation, 380
statutory law, 367
stays of execution, 354
Steel Caucus, 230
Steele, Andrea Dew, 518n6
steel seizure, 100, 297
Stein, Robert, 208n17
Steinberg, Brian, 605n4
Steiner, Gilbert Y., 176n41
Stenberg v. Carhart, 147
Stenglein, Christine, 456n10
Stephenson, Matthew, 346n3
Stevens, John Paul, 134, 378
Stewart, Charles H., III,
    487n51
Stewart, Potter, 129
Stimson, James, 424n50, 425,
    486n48, 544n35
stimulus bills, 248
stimulus packages, 229, 321
Stokes, Donald, 411n23
Stone, Harlan Fiske, 375
Stone, Walter J., 199n4, 487n50,
    523n15
"stop and frisk," 138
Storing, Herbert, 59nn22–23,
    61nn27–29, 62n31
straight party vote, 461
Strange, Marty, 593n41
Straus, Jacob, 587n29

"unalienable rights," 36
unanimous verdict, right to, *113*
undocumented workers, 183
"undue burden," 147
unemployment. *See* employment
unfunded mandates, 90, *101*
Unfunded Mandates Reform Act
  (UMRA; 1995), 90
unicameralism, 52
Uniform Code of Military
  Justice, 297n63, 349, 366
Uniform Congressional District
  Act (1967), 463
unilateral action, presidential
  power and, 263, 273–74,
  293–97, 299–30
Union of Concerned Scientists,
  567
unions, 7–8, 157, 201, 400, 419,
  428, 473, 527, 559, 578, 593,
  597. *See also* labor unions
  Democrats and, 514, 533, 543,
    551, 552
  media coverage and, 630
  privatization and, 340
  strikes and, 593
Unitarians, 535
unitary decision making, 256–58,
  263, 300–301, 304
United Auto Workers (UAW),
  597
United Kingdom
  American Revolution and,
    33–37, 632
  Cabinet in, 280
  changing relations with
    American colonies, 30–31
  elections in, 490
  House of Commons in, 194
  parliamentary system, 52
  plurality voting in, 470
  political parties in government,
    525, 526
  Scotland independence issue,
    397
  sovereignty of Parliament
    in, 362
  vote to leave EU, 75
  voting requirements, 160n8
United Mine Workers, 567
United Nations, 38, 409, 429

*United States v. American Library
  Association,* 130
United States v. Associated Press,
  607n10
United States v. Booker, 361–62
*United States v. Carolene Products
  Company,* 123
United States v. Eichman, 127
United States v. Jones, 138, 148
United States v. Lopez, 92, *101, 102*
United States v. Morrison, 101
United States v. Nixon, 100, 264, 366
United States v. O'Brien, 126
United States v. Pink, 250, 263n8
*United States v. Playboy
  Entertainment Group,* 130
United States v. Texas, 366
United States v. Virginia, 174
United States v. Williams, 130
United States v. Windsor, 185, 386
United States v. Wong Kim Ark, 181
*United Steelworkers of America v.
  Weber,* 187
universal suffrage, 449, 451–52,
  453, 476
Univision, 431
unprotected speech, 124, 128–30,
  132–33
urban development grants, 86
urban redevelopment, 405
U.S. Statutes at Large, 317n8
USA Freedom Act (2015), 262
USA PATRIOT Act (2001), 262
Utah, 161
  state conventions in, 520n11

valence issues, 481, 482, 486
values, 396, 397, 406–7
Van Buren, Martin, 547, 549
Van Drehle, David, 390n63
Van Orden v. Perry, 119
variables, 24–28, 399–400
Vavreck, Lynn, 486n49
Ventura, Jesse, 436
Verba, Sidney, 454n5, 476n34,
  569n8
Vermont, 446n1
  civil unions in, 185
  disproportionate influence
    of, 48
  Election Day registration in, 458

electoral districts, 462n17
renewal portfolio standard, 78
Vernonia School District v. Acton,
  137
Veterans' Affairs Department,
  U.S., 350
veto gates, 52–53
veto power, 10–11, 12, 72
  checks and balances and, 95,
    96
  legislative, 100, 107
  line-item, 100, 265–66
  overriding vetos, 50, 95, 235,
    265, 273
  pocket veto, 233, 265
  of president, 11, 50, 52–53,
    55, 60, 95, 100, 233, 235,
    265–70, *268–69,* 300
  of states, 86
  strategy of, 267–70
  veto process, *266*
vice presidency, 283–84
Vietnamese Americans, 534
Vietnam War, 21, 130, 252, 256,
  273, 335, 536, 551, 627,
  636, 641
  draft cards burned during, 126
  draft evaders, 262
  government efforts to shape
    opinion on, 426
  voting rights and, 156
*Violence against Women
  Act, 101*
Virginia
  Federalists in, 108
  gun laws, 134
  school segregation in, 164,
    364
  slavery in, 46
  Virginia Plan and, 43, 48
Virginia Military Institution, 174
Virginia Plan, 42–43
Virginia v. Black, 127
Virgin Islands, U.S., 351
V.L. v. E.L., 77
Vogel, David, 428n63, 430n64
Vogel, Kenneth P., 519n8
volunteer activists, 213,
  532–33
  political parties and, 512
voter ID laws, 460

military tribunals, 297, 349–50, 366

public opinion and, 409

War Powers Resolution (1973), 273

Warren, Earl, 139, 356, 388

Warren, Elizabeth, 497, 543

Warren, Kenneth F., 270n23

Warriner, Keith, 435n73

Washington

electoral districts, 462n17

marijuana laws in, 94

voting by mail in, 451

Washington, D.C. *See* District of Columbia

Washington, Ebonya, 418n35

Washington, George, 33n2, 39, *58*, 69, 108

disdain for political parties, 560

as Federalist, 561

Genet received by, 262

House request refused by, 264

political parties deplored by, 544

Washington Post, 610, 611, 627, 630, 640

Watergate scandal, 98, 125, 251, 256, 264, 640

Water Resources Development Act (2007), 235

Wattenberg, Benjamin, 396n6

Watts, Candis S., 419n39

WCBS (radio station), 613

weapons of mass destruction (WMDs), 282

Weaver, David H., 623n40

Weaver, Vesla, 421n43

Webster v. Reproductive Health Services, 146, 589

Weingast, Barry R., 35n6, 72n1, 224n32, 307n2, 326n18

welfare, 396, 438

agencies, 322

Congress and, *101*

"welfare state," 84

Westboro Baptist Church, 123–24

Westmoreland, William, 636

West Virginia

Election Day registration in, 458

electoral districts, 462n17

West Virginia State Board of Education v. Barnette, 122

Whig Party, 547–48, 558

whips, whip system, 218, 219, 233, 247

White House Communications Office, 289

White House Office of Management and Budget (OMB), 283, 322

White House press corps, 642

White House staff, *281*, 282

White primaries, 161–62, 164, 178, 375

Whites, 413–14

Democrats and, 536

disagreements with African Americans, *415*

Republicans and, 534, 552

"wholesale" politics, 8

Wickard v. Filburn, 83

Wiggins v. Smith, 143

WikiLeaks, 128, 627

Wilcox, Clyde, 565n2

Wilcox, Dennis L., 628n47, 628n49

Wildavsky, Aaron, 333n21

Wilkerson, John D., 203n8

Willbern, York Y., 80n10

Willnat, Lars, 623n40

Wilson, James, 43, 46

Wilson, Woodrow, 277, 288

management strategy, 329

Wilstein, Matt, 637n63

wind power, state policies on, 78–79

Winfrey, Oprah, 431

"winner takes all," 469–70

wiretapping, warrantless, 294

Wisconsin, 436

Election Day registration in, 458, 476

poll taxes in, 160

Wisconsin v. Mitchell, 132

WMDs (weapons of mass destruction), 282

Wolbrecht, Christina, 478n42, 531nn1–2

Wolf, Richard, 366n25

Wolfinger, Raymond, 476n33

Wolfram, Catherine D., 208n16, 425n52

Woll, Peter, 334n24

Wolton, Stephane, 257n1

women. *See also* gender discrimination; gender gap; League of Women Voters

advocacy and representation for, 197

affirmative action and, 190–91

athletics and, 174

as candidates, 518

in Congress, 209

discrimination against, 176–78, 189

economic rights for, 161

education rights and, 152, 173–74

as judges, 356–57, *384*

in military, 184

as "outgroup," 419

party identity of, 416–18, 478, 515, 534–35

as political candidates, 486

political engagement of young, 530–31

property rights and, 152, 160–61

sexual harassment issues, 131, 174, 176, 177

voting rights and, 152, 160–61, 189, 457, 515

Women's Caucus, 230

Women's Marches, 592, 631–32

women's movement, 176, 189

women's rights, 160–61, 378, 390, 416–18, 478, 570

Woollacott, Janet, 630n52

Works Progress Administration (WPA), 278

World Trade Center. *See* September 11, 2001, terrorist attacks; terrorism

World War I, 124, 252

as presidential war, 262

World War II, 21, 252, 280

grants-in-aid and, 86

internment of Japanese Americans during, 181, 294, 296

as presidential war, 262